MARLIN FIREARMS

*A History of the Guns
and the Company that Made Them*

Lt. Col. William S. Brophy, USAR, Ret.

Stackpole Books

Published by
STACKPOLE BOOKS
5067 Ritter Road
Mechanicsburg, PA 17055-6921
www.stackpolebooks.com

Printed in the United States of America

10 9

OTHER BOOKS BY THE AUTHOR
L.C. Smith Shotguns
The Krag Rifle
Specifications and Plans of the L.C. Smith Shotgun
Springfield Armory Annual Reports 1901–1948
The Springfield 1903 Rifles

Photographs in this book, unless otherwise noted, are by the author.

The Marlin Firearms Company, the writer, and the publisher
accept no responsibility for any injury or death as a result of the
use of any information in this book. All of the details furnished
here are for historical purposes and are not to be used for the purpose of handloading or manufacture of ammunition.

Library of Congress Cataloging-in-Publication Data

Brophy, William S.
    Marlin Firearms : a history of the guns and the company that made
them / William S. Brophy.
         p. cm.
    Bibliography: p.
    ISBN 0-8117-0877-2
    1. Marlin Firearms Company—History. 2. Firearms industry and
trade—Connecticut—History. I. Title.
    TS533.3.C8B76   1989
    338.7'6834'0097468—dc19   88-38768
                                                CIP
    ISBN 978-0-8117-0877-7

This book is dedicated to my wife, Gerry, without whose love and understanding this work would not have been possible.

Contents

The Marlin Firearms Co.

100 KENNA DRIVE
NORTH HAVEN, CONNECTICUT 06473

FRANK KENNA
PRESIDENT

This is the story of a distinctly American company. It began when a gunsmith named John Marlin hung a sign in front of his shop in New Haven, Connecticut one hundred and eighteen years ago.

His first products were tiny single-shot pistols for ladies to carry in their purses during the unsettled post-Civil War years. The company blossomed and strode into the twentieth century with an already famous line of sturdy lever action rifles that were proving themselves on the western frontier.

The company trudged along through war, changes of ownership, Depression, and war again, surviving by the wits of some very wise and talented men.

The diversity of products manufactured by the New Haven plant — in addition to guns — was extensive. Baby buggies, decoy anchors, button hooks, letter openers, kids' wagons, handcuffs, and razor blades (by the millions) all helped Marlin survive during this sometimes chaotic century.

Today, unlike some of the other great old names in the gun industry, Marlin is solid and thriving, in a modern plant manned by dedicated workers and a management committed to quality.

The author of this fascinating story began his research over fifteen years ago, and has gathered information from all over the country. The result is a book so detailed and accurate, that to call it the "definitive" work is almost an understatement.

All of us who are interested in the history of the American firearms industry owe a debt of gratitude to Bill Brophy for the perseverance and dedication that went into the creation of this historic book.

Frank Kenna

Preface

This book was written to try to collect and preserve for the Marlin collector, the potential collector, and the historian that information about The Marlin Firearms Company now in print, or known to exist, before it is gradually lost with time. Unfortunately, much of Marlin's history has already been lost, or has been incorrectly quoted. My effort, since joining Marlin in 1969, has been to try to rediscover some of the information that has been lost and to accurately describe the evolution of the present Marlin Firearms Company through its four previous owners.

Detailed information about the daily activities of the company and its leadership have been lost, or were never recorded during the J.M. Marlin Ballard rifle and handgun manufacturing period. Also there is little or no recorded data for the Marlin Fire Arms Company, Marlin Arms Corporation, Marlin-Rockwell Corporation, and Marlin Firearms Corporation periods of ownership, except for some catalogs and price sheets. The present company did not inherit (except for limited serial number records for lever action rifles and carbines for the period of 1883–1906) manufacturing records, blueprints, catalogs, or a collection of firearms manufactured by the previous four owners. Therefore the task of doing this book required years of preparation by locating printed material, catalogs, and representative models of each type of handgun, rifle, and shotgun produced, as well as the many diversified items the Marlin companies produced. The amount of labor involved in the actual writing of this book, and the taking, developing, and printing of the pictures, was not fully recognized in the beginning—and fortunately so, as otherwise the book would not have been started.

To dispel the rumor that I have done this book "on the job" while working for Marlin, I must state that the work was done, with few exceptions, as a personal effort at home. However, I would be remiss not to acknowledge the sincere support and personal interest Mr. Frank Kenna, president of Marlin, gave me during the years it has taken to complete this book. He opened all doors and channels available to him during my search and offered personal knowledge and background information, as best he knew it. In fact, frequently his was the only inside information about matters not recorded, or available through regular research channels. Without Mr. Kenna's help and understanding, this book would not have been completed. All readers are indebted to his leadership of the company and the support he has extended to the Marlin family of collectors.

It is my hope that this book will add to the already published information about Marlin firearms. It is also my desire that this book spur a new generation of collectors into recognizing that Marlin firearms have been successful in the field and are now desirable collector's items because of their place in American history, as well as their classic beauty and intrinsic value.

This book is the result of not only a personal search for data but of the collective interest and effort of many enthusiastic collectors, authors, historians, and museum personnel who supplied me with much valuable information. I want to express my appreciation to those individuals who have contributed to this book. Some offered their collections for study. Others provided special material not available from other sources and patiently answered my many questions, or offered valuable moral support.

First, I want to thank the many officers and employees of

Marlin who assisted me with research and encouragement. In particular I thank Anthony Aeschliman, George Allard, Robert Behn, my secretary, Marlene Colavolpe, Andrew Constant, Nicholas DeMusis, Ed Goldshinsky, Harold Finkle, Robert Flynn, William Johnson, Eli Kasimer, Gilbert Kenna, Nicholas Ketre, Jack Kelley, George Mendelsohn, John Miller, Stephen Morris, Robert Naylor, E. Ernest Oberst, William Osborne, Fred Prout, Wanda Pyrdol, Geraldine Roehl, Robert Rohr, Edward Stempeck, Virginia Sundius, and my outstanding typist, Mrs. Lynn Bibber, for her untiring efforts in deciphering my poor handwriting and the typing of a lengthy manuscript.

Next I extend special thanks to those who allowed me access to their fine collections for photo sessions or who furnished me photos that are included in this work, as follows: Joseph Baker, Don Carper, George Carr, Ev Cassagneres, John Dutcher, Charles Foster, Randy Gott, Robert Greenleaf, M.W. Grumbles, William "Pete" Harvey, Tom Johnson, Jim Lagiss, John Malloy, Jim Opp, Richard Paterson, Charles Petty, Rich Regnier, Robert Runge, Robert Selissen, Ed Stempeck, Dave Stewart, Sam Stilwell, and Bob Strauss, Circus Promotion Corporation.

Special thanks go to Millie Link, Curator of the Trapshooters Hall of Fame for the Mark Arie information; to W. Douglas Lindsay, Superintendent, and Joseph Polcetti, Small Arms Technician of Springfield Army National Park Service, for access to the Armory collection of military arms manufactured by the Marlin Arms Corporation and the Marlin–Rockwell Corporation; and to my daughter, Gail Brophy Barry, who spent countless hours reducing serial numbers to useful data.

Others who made material contributions and generously assisted me in response to my request to the Marlin Collectors Association for certain information were Dr. Charles Ross Adams, Lloyd A. Atwell, Ben Auslaender, Frank Beagan, Jerry Byrd, Allen Egbert, Ronald Ewald, Frank Gillespie, Danny Glenn, Lowell Green, Wayne Hogan, Lloyd A. Jones, Ralph W. Jones, B.F. Lester, Lyle A. Motzko, Dale Peterson, Rudi Prusok, Albert J. Reader, Richard Rohal, Frank F. Rosselot, Jim Schindler, Richard Schrock, and Jack Teraberry.

If, by chance, I have failed to properly recognize contributions made by others not named, it is because of an oversight on my part and was not intended. They, too, are thanked, along with all the others.

Unfortunately, the Marlin story is so complex and the firearms manufactured so diversified that the complete story can not be told in simple terms between the covers of one book. Therefore, it has been necessary to abbreviate some sections. For example, the Ballard rifle could warrant a book on that subject alone. A more complete coverage of many small details, or of manufacturing changes, could have been included; however, the book would then be impractical and beyond the reach of the average person having an interest in the overall history of Marlin and its products.

There is still much we do not know about the Marlin companies and the people who made them what they were, but a sincere effort has been made to present complete and accurate information. Your suggestions or criticism and additional new data will be appreciated and included in any future revisions.

Lt. Col. William S. Brophy,
USAR Ret.

Northford, Connecticut
August 15, 1988

Abbreviations

BAR	Browning Automatic Rifle	M-R	Marlin-Rockwell Corporation
C	Carbine	M1	U.S. Rifle, Caliber .30, M1 (Garand)
C	Cylinder Choke	NRA	The National Rifle Association
CB	Conical Ball	NSSF	National Shooting Sports Foundation
CL	Classic	Oct.	Octagon
Conn.	Connecticut	P.G.	Pistol Grip
CT	Connecticut	QD	Quick Detachable
DA	Double Action	RC	Regular Carbine
DC	Don Carper	RG	Randy Gott
DL	Deluxe	RP	Richard Paterson
DS	David Stewart	R-P	Remington-Peters
DT	Double Trigger	RS	Robert Selissen
EG	Ed Goldshinsky	R&D	Research and Development
ER	Extra Range	Rem.	Remington
F	Full Choke	SB	Smooth Bore
GA/Ga	Gauge/Gage	SC	Sporting Carbine
GC	George Carr	S, L & LR	Short, Long and Long Rifle
HC	High Capacity	SS	Sam Stilwell
HPS	High Power Special	ST	Single Trigger
HS	High Speed	S.T.	Set Trigger
H&A	Hopkins & Allen Arms Co.	S&W	Smith & Wesson
H&R	Harrington & Richardson	T	Texan
IC	Improved Cylinder Choke	TDS	Takedown with safety
JM	Marlin Proofmark	TJ	Tom Johnson
JO	James Opp	TM	Trademark
KO	Knock Out	UD	United Defense Corporation
LTS	Lightweight with cross bolt safety	U.S.	United States of America
M	Modified Choke	USMC	United States Marine Corps
M	Mountie	WCF	Winchester Center Fire
MFA Co.	The Marlin Fire Arms Company	WMRF	Winchester Magnum Rim Fire
MFC	The Marlin Firearms Co.	WW I	World War I
MF Corp.	The Marlin Firearms Corporation	WW II	World War II
MID	Marlin Industrial Division	Win.	Winchester
mm	Millimeter	ZG	Zane Grey

SECTION I

The History of Marlin
Firearms Companies

John Mahlon Marlin and The Marlin Fire Arms Company

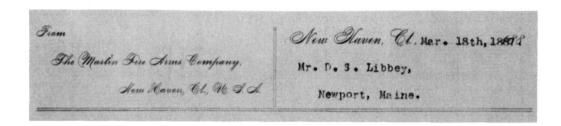

JOHN MARLIN'S BEGINNINGS

John Mahlon Marlin was born on May 6, 1836, in the vicinity of Boston Neck, near the town of Windsor Locks, Hartford County, Conn. At age 18 John Marlin became an apprentice machinist with the American Machine Works. The agreement that he signed was as follows:

A STATEMENT OF THE TERMS upon which John M. Marlin, son of James Doyle of Rainbow, Connecticut, is employed by the AMERICAN MACHINE WORKS, and agreed to by the parties hereunto.

John M. Marlin being eighteen years of age, on the sixth day of May One Thousand Eight Hundred and Fifty Four is to labor for the American Machine Works, under their direction, at the machinists trade, until such time as he shall have arrived at the full and entire age of twenty one years, for which service well and truly performed, the American Machine Works shall pay him, the said John M. Marlin the following sums, at such time and manner as they usually pay the workmen in their employ.

Viz: For the first six months they are to make no payment, and the said John M. Marlin is not to receive any compensation for services during that time. For the second six months they are to pay him one dollar and fifty cents per week. For the third six months he is to receive two dollars and fifty cents per week. For the fourth six months he is to receive three dollars per week. For the fifth six months he is to receive three dollars and fifty cents per week. For the sixth six months he is to receive four dollars per week, and so on, increasing in the same ratio, until his term of service shall have expired.

It is also expressly understood that in the computation of time, both for payment of service, and the change of rates for such service, no time shall be reckoned or counted that shall not have been spent in actual service for the said American Machine Works.

It is further expressly understood that the said John M. Marlin is to faithfully observe, and obey all the rules and regulations of the American Machine Works, and shall be liable to discharge at any time, without recourse or complaint, for any disobedience or insubordination.

In Witness Whereof the parties have hereunto set their hands and seals this fourteenth day of November A.D. 1853.

American Machine Works
by P.B. Tyler, Supt.
James Doyle

I the undersigned John M. Marlin consider myself in honor bound to fulfill all the conditions of the above contract.

John M. Marlin

Note that the statement John Marlin signed listed his father as James Doyle of Rainbow, Conn., who apparently was his stepfather.

It is not known exactly what employment John Marlin pursued between the age of 21 and when he first opened his pistol manufacturing business in New Haven. However, it has been written that he worked as a machinist and toolmaker at the Colt factory in Hartford until he moved to New Haven in 1863.

The New Haven city directories and voters registry record John Marlin's various addresses as follows:

1863 John M. Marlin—pistol maker, boarding at 130 James St.
1864 John M. Marlin—pistol maker, boarding at 241 State St. (Shop may have been 18 Williams St.)
1865 Listed as pistol maker; home, 142 Franklin St.
1866 Listed as pistol maker; home, 79 Bradley St.
1867–1869 No listing in either city directories or voters registry
1870 Listed as pistol maker; home on Mansfield St.
1871 Listed as manufacturer of firearms at State and Hamilton Sts; home at 22 Orange St. (voters registry lists home as 299 Central Ave.)
1872 Listed as manufacturer of firearms at State and Hamilton Sts; home at 59 Trumbull St.
1873 Listed as manufacturer of firearms at 599 State St. (probably this was the exact street address and at the corner of Hamilton St. The street number changed after 1874, and therefore cannot be verified)

John Mahlon Marlin, 1836–1901.

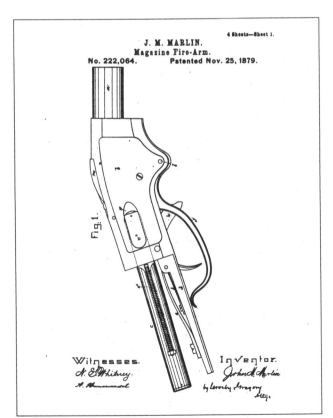

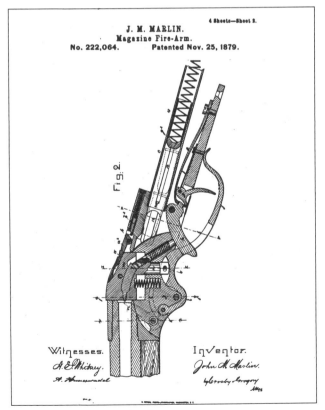

Patent drawings of J.M. Marlin's first repeating rifle with action closed.

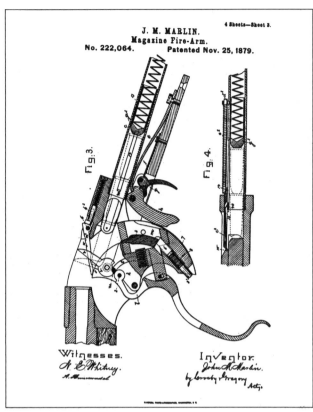

J. M. MARLIN.
Magazine Fire-Arm.
No. 222,064.   Patented Nov. 25, 1879.
4 Sheets—Sheet 3.

Fig.3.

Fig.4.

Witnesses.

Inventor.

Patent drawing showing action open.

1874 Same as 1873
1875 Listed as pistol manufacturer at State and Hamilton Sts.;
      home at 188 East Grand Ave.
1876 Same as 1875

Between 1867 and 1869, John Marlin was back in the Hartford area. His first two patents, dated February 8, 1870, and April 5, 1870, show him as being from Hartford, Conn. (The date of a patent is always a period of time after the patent application, so we can assume he was in Hartford at least into 1869 and then returned to New Haven to reestablish his pistol manufacturing business.)

We also know that John Marlin married Martha Susan Moore and they had four children: Mahlon Henry Marlin (July 23, 1864–September 14, 1949), Burton Louis Marlin (May 14, 1867–April 12, 1869), Jennette Bradford Marlin (March 18, 1871–September 4, 1883), and John Howard Marlin (September 21, 1876–February 5, 1959).

As a boss, John Marlin was stern and demanding, not accepting sloppy work or indifferent attitudes. Yet he was fair and treated his employees with consideration and understanding. Examples of his manufacturing skill and his employees' expertise are demonstrated by every Marlin firearm his organization manufactured. The fit and finish of parts, as well as their function and operation, attest to the excellence of all managers and workers in Mr. Marlin's factory. Even with today's high degree of technology in the firearms industry, it is nearly impossible to equal the fit, finish, and cosmetic appeal of early Marlin rifles. We recognize, of course, that the attention to detail and the handwork done by low-paid but skilled workers was much different then than it is now.

DEVELOPMENT AND EXPANSION OF THE FIREARMS INDUSTRY

John M. Marlin and The Marlin Fire Arms Company played an important role in developing and expanding an industry that has made significant contributions in the development of machinery and fabrication methods, interchangeability of parts, and testing and gauging techniques.

When America was first colonized, firearms were needed for obtaining food as well as for protection. The gunmakers and gunsmiths of the time were individuals who either apprenticed with a craftsman to learn a new skill or came to America already having knowledge in this field. Few of these men were capable, or equipped, to make the lock, stock, and barrel of a firearm; most of them used imported locks and barrels until their small businesses developed and expanded.

By the mid-1700s, production of hunting arms was adequate. The various parts were frequently made in cottage shops and then finished and assembled at the gunsmith's shop.

The eventual need for military arms resulted in the establishment of government installations, rather than the "gunsmith/gunshop" fabrication of firearms made on a custom basis.

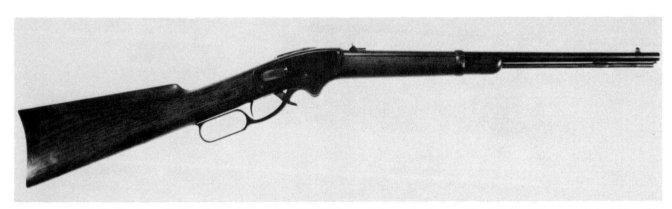

Prototype of J.M. Marlin's first rifle. Patented in 1879 (number 222,064), it was similar to the Spencer rifle. Note that it has an underhammer and a lever action with carbine dimensions. Underneath the barrel is a cleaning rod. The caliber was .44; the barrel is 20 inches long.

Side loading and top ejection are features of J.M. Marlin's first repeating rifle. Note that the hammer is in front of the trigger and protrudes through the trigger guard. It is shown in the cocked position. The magazine tube is in the buttstock.

Such places as Springfield Armory, Springfield, Mass., developed machines and methods of fabrication that were used for years.

Although the government was in the firearms business, other sources had to be found to meet the ever-expanding requirements for more arms. Many experienced gunsmiths were brought into the expanding industry, and manufacturers of other commodities envisioned an opportunity to do well in this new market. Names such as Eli Whitney, Simeon North, Spencer, Stone, Leonard, R. and J. Johnson, Nathan Starr, and others are found on contracts for stands of arms needed to supplement the government's manufacturing ability.

Eventually the manufacture of arms developed into an industry. In order to satisfy the need for increased production, many new methods of manufacture were developed. A good example is the Thomas Blanchard lathe for turning gunstocks. Developed in 1821, it revolutionized the manufacture of a gunstock that had previously been done mostly by hand.

The greatest changes occurred in the arms industry during the Civil War. Not only were demands made on the industry for large numbers of hand and shoulder arms, but dramatic changes in the types of ammunition used were taking place. Cap-and-ball muzzle-loaded ammunition was quickly being phased out by cartridges that could be loaded from the breech.

With the development of new cartridges, hundreds of mechanisms for handguns and rifles were invented. A number of them included a repeating capability: numerous cartridges were stored in the gun by many different systems. After all of

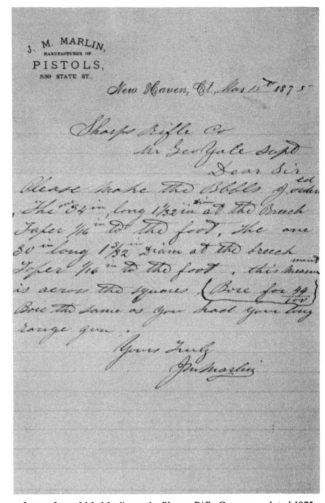

Letter from J.M. Marlin to the Sharps Rifle Company, dated 1875.

these many different cartridge and firearm systems were tested, under many different conditions, a few were found to be reliable and worthy of further development. The eventual result was two accepted types of cartridges—the rimfire and the center-fire—both of which are standard today. Breech-loading firearms were further developed once the type of ammunition was settled on. All Marlin firearms were manufactured for use with breech-loading metallic ammunition.

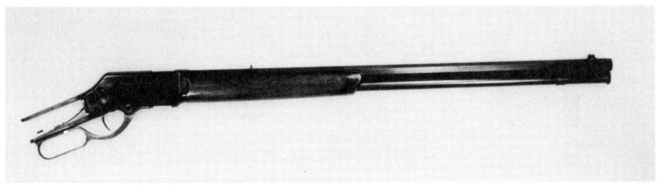

Remains of J.M. Marlin's experimental caliber .22 lever action repeating rifle.

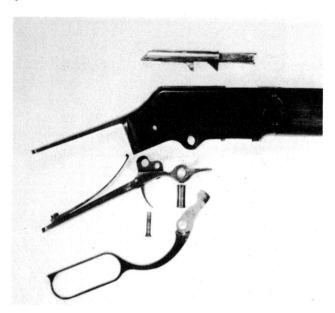

Remnant parts of experimental .22.

EARLY MARLIN PRODUCTS

With the manufacture of small single-shot derringer-type pistols, John Marlin entered into the firearms industry. The four variations produced from about 1863 until the 1880s included caliber .22, .30, .32, and .41 models. Typical of the small pistol manufacturer of the day, John Marlin himself named his first models. The names chosen were OK, Never Miss, and Victor. Approximately 16,000 of these small guns were manufactured.

Recognizing the limited potential for his petite single-shot derringers, John Marlin expanded his business to include single-action revolvers. Six models were produced between 1870 and 1887 — the OK and Little Joker pocket revolvers, and the larger XX, XXX, No. 32, and 38 Standard revolvers. In 1887 John Marlin introduced his Model 1887 double-action (DA) revolver. The last of his DA production was in 1899. Some of the Marlin pistols and revolvers were ornately engraved, were gold-, silver-, or nickel-plated, and had pearl, ivory, rosewood, or hard rubber grips. Seldom found in excellent condition today, these Marlin handguns are truly collector's items.

John Marlin's inventive skill developed as his business expanded. Among his 25 patents, 10 were related to handguns, as follows:

Patent Number	Date
99,690	Feb. 8, 1870
101,637	Apr. 5, 1870
140,516	July 1, 1873
222,066	Nov. 25, 1879
308,183	Nov. 18, 1884
367,535	Aug. 2, 1887
367,820	Aug. 9, 1887
367,821	Aug. 9, 1887
368,599	Aug. 23, 1887
371,608	Oct. 18, 1887
413,197	Oct. 22, 1889

The Ballard single-shot rifle was patented in 1861 by C.H. Ballard. This rifle was used during the Civil War by the state of Kentucky. It was manufactured by the Merrimack Arms Company, Newburyport, Mass., 1866–1869; by the Brown Manufacturing Company, Newburyport, Mass., 1869–1873; and then by John M. Marlin, 1875–ca. 1890. From available information, it appears that about 40,000 Ballards were manufactured by Marlin.

John Marlin obtained a patent for a reversible firing pin for the Ballard rifle. (It was number 159,592, dated February 9, 1875.)

John Marlin's first center-fire repeating rifle was a short-barreled, underhammer, lever action, tubular-magazine rifle with characteristics similar to the Spencer rifle. This new rifle was patented by John Marlin on November 25, 1879 (number 222,064). My examination of the prototype quickly revealed shortcomings in the feeding system and the breech-locking system. As designed, only short-length cartridges could be used in the gun and the strength of the receiver was questionable. Only a prototype rifle was manufactured, and fortunately, John Marlin did not proceed with production of this rifle. Instead, he looked elsewhere for a better repeating rifle.

The repeating rifle that was finally manufactured was identified as the Model 1881. Based on the patents of H.F. Wheeler, Andrew Burgess, E.A.F. Toepperwein, and John Marlin, this rifle gave John Marlin the start he needed to become successful in the firearms industry.

Patents awarded to John Marlin for the experimental rifle and the Model 1881 were as follows:

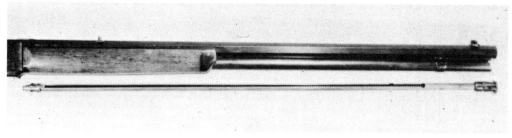

Inner magazine tube shown with barrel and outer magazine tube.

Patent Number	Date	Model
222,064	Nov. 25, 1879	Experimental lever action rifle
222,065	Nov. 25, 1879	Experimental lever action rifle
222,414	Dec. 9, 1879	Model 1881
234,309	Nov. 9, 1880	Model 1881
250,825	Dec. 13, 1881	Model 1881
271,091	Jan. 23, 1883	Model 1881
297,424	Apr. 22, 1884	Model 1881

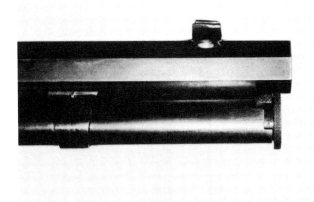

Front end of inner magazine tube locked in place.

JOHN MARLIN'S FIRST CALIBER .22 REPEATER

The first caliber .22 rifle that occupied the interest of J.M. Marlin was a lever action mechanism similar to the Winchester Model 1873 rifle. The experimental rifle had a tubular magazine and a vertical sliding carrier. The empties ejected out the top of the carrier opening in the receiver. The bolt, like the one in the Winchester 1873, was small in diameter and passed through the carrier in the process of chambering a cartridge. Having a fixed firing pin in its face, the bolt, when struck in the rear by the hammer, fired the rimfire cartridge.

Only part of what appears to be the prototype of this rifle remains today. The forearm, stock, carrier, hammer, trigger, and other small parts are missing. The workmanship is excellent and the polish and blue of the parts remaining are exceptionally fine.

Model 1881 roll-stamp on barrel of experimental .22 lever action rifle.

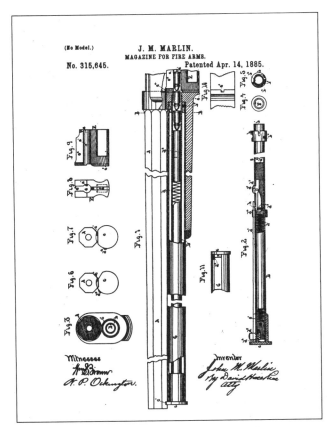

Patent number 315,645.

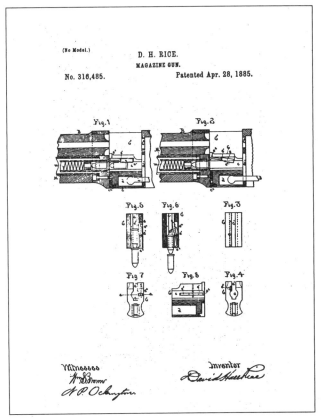

Patent number 316,485.

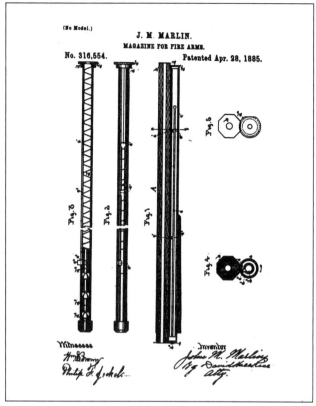

Patent number 316,554.

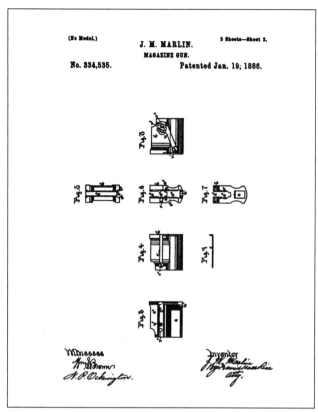

Patent number 334,535.

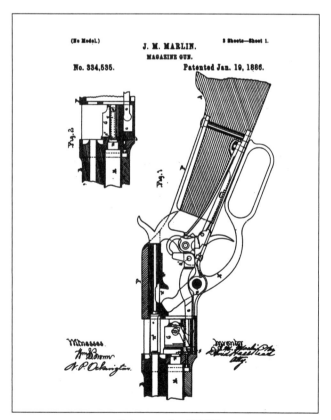

Patent number 334,535.

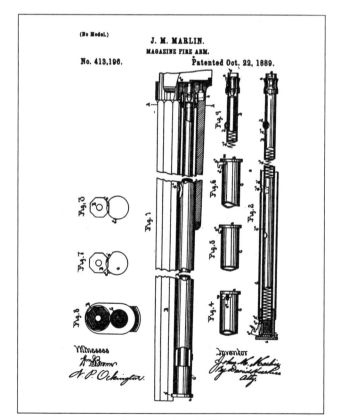

Patent number 413,196.

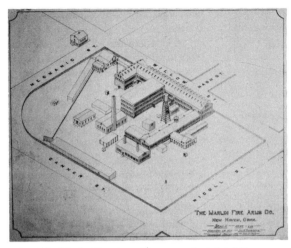

Sketch of The Marlin Fire Arms Company plant dated November 28, 1899.

Earliest known photo of Marlin factory (circa 1909).

There are five patents that apply to this first Marlin .22 rifle. To understand the development of the rifle, we cannot look at the patent dates and patent numbers sequentially. Instead, it is the date of the application for the patent that is important. Therefore, the patents are listed here in that order:

Application Date	*Patent*
Aug. 4, 1884	Application made by J.M. Marlin for a magazine for the caliber .22 lever action rifle. Patent number 316,554, dated April 28, 1885, awarded J.M. Marlin.

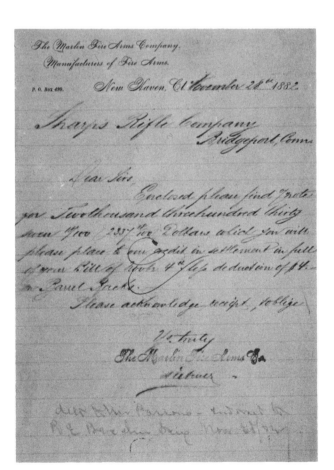

J.M. Marlin letterhead over stamped The Marlin Fire Arms Co. *and dated November 1882.*

The Marlin Fire Arms Company letter of November 28, 1882.

J.M. Marlin and family graves at the Evergreen Cemetery, New Haven, Conn.

Nov. 15, 1884	Application made by J.M. Marlin for a magazine gun similar to Winchester Model 1873 caliber .22 rifle. Patent number 334,535 awarded January 10, 1886, to J.M. Marlin.
Nov. 28, 1884	Application made by J.M. Marlin for a magazine tube mechanism similar to first type in patent number 316,554. Patent number 413,196, dated October 22, 1889 awarded to J.M. Marlin. This type
	of magazine is the one used in the prototype.
Dec. 6, 1884	Application made by J.M. Marlin for a tubular magazine for caliber .22 rifle. Patent number 315,645, awarded on April 14, 1885, to J.M. Marlin for this third type of magazine tube.
Feb. 24, 1885	Application for a magazine gun made by D.H. Rice, Lowell, Mass., which included an improvement of the carrier over J.M. Marlin's original mechanism in patent number 334,535. Patent number 316,485, awarded April 28, 1885 to Mr. Rice.

The magazine in this incomplete rifle is like the one in patent number 315,645: The carrier is missing, so the type of carrier used is unknown. The roll-stamp and patent dates marked on the barrel are the same as those on the Model 1881 rifle. For some unknown reason, the dates of the patents listed here are not marked on the gun.

Only one known example of this rifle exists. Like John Marlin's first repeating center-fire rifle, it was probably not considered worthy of production; however, that is only conjecture. It might not have been produced because of its similarity to the Winchester rifle, and because of problems with the tubular magazine, which apparently would be expensive to produce and fraught with functional problems. Fortunately for John Marlin, Lewis Hepburn was in the wings with his successful lever action rifle that has survived almost 100 years.

THE MARLIN FIREARMS CO.

MAKERS OF MARLIN REPEATING RIFLES, SHOTGUNS, ETC.
WILLOW, NICOLL, CANNER AND MECHANIC STREETS.
P. O. BOX V.

PACIFIC COAST BRANCH,
NO. 114 SECOND STREET,
SAN FRANCISCO, CAL.

NEW HAVEN, CONN., U. S. A.,

Mahlon H. and John H. Marlin

Upon the death of their father, John M. Marlin, president of The Marlin Fire Arms Company, in July 1901, Mahlon Henry Marlin, who had been vice president and secretary, became president and treasurer and his brother, John Howard Marlin, became vice president and secretary of the company. Without much change in either the product line or the method of marketing established by their father, the brothers maintained a "business as usual" air of confidence in the company and the fine guns they manufactured.

MAHLON HENRY MARLIN

Mahlon Henry Marlin, born in 1864 in Windsor Locks, Conn., near Hartford, had the same major interest as his father, which was running the plant. Prior to becoming an officer of the corporation, he had been in sales.

In his role as plant manager, Mahlon Marlin was responsible for the daily production of guns in the plant, as well as the development of new manufacturing techniques. He also directed the engineering department in the design of new models and changes in the old models. He thrived on work and had little time for social and recreational activities. He did find time, however, to be active in the New Haven Gun Club, with membership dating before 1898.

Mahlon H. Marlin died, at age 86, in 1949. He was interred in the Marlin family plot in the Evergreen Cemetery, New Haven, Conn.

JOHN HOWARD MARLIN

John Howard Marlin, born in 1876 in New Haven, was the salesman of the two brothers. He traveled far and wide, attending shooting events and calling on dealers. He had received his early education in Webster School and prepared for Yale at Williston Academy in Massachusetts. Upon graduation from Yale, he joined the Marlin Fire Arms business.

He was a director of The Interstate Association of Trapshooting along with such notables as W.F. Parker (Parker shotguns), T.H. Keller (Peters Cartridge Company), A.C. Barrel (U.M.C.), S.G. Lewis (Winchester), J.T. Skelly (E.I. DuPont), and A.H. Durston (Lefever Arms Company).

John H. (also known as J. Howard) Marlin was also a member of a number of clubs, including the New Haven Lawn Club, New Haven Country Club, Quinnipiack Club, Pine Orchard Club, and Westchester Biltmore Country Club. For 30 years he was a member of the New York Yacht Club. John H. Marlin was also a member of Hiram Lodge, AF&AM, and Pyramid Temple of the Shrine, in Bridgeport, Conn. In 1903, when Connecticut first required automobiles to be licensed, J. Howard Marlin's auto license for that year was number 424.

J. Howard Marlin died in 1959 at the age of 82 while visiting his son John B. Marlin in Glendora, Calif. At the time of his death he was president of the Driscoll Wire Company of Shelton, Conn. and of Perrigo, Inc. of New Haven, a wholesale plumbing firm.

Mahlon Henry Marlin, 1864-1949.

John Howard Marlin, 1876-1959.

In 1915, a syndicate that wanted to manufacture war items for England and Russia offered to purchase the company. Mahlon H. and John H. Marlin decided that to sell was the right move — the war in Europe would soon involve the U.S. and the manufacture and sales of sporting arms would be curtailed if the U.S. entered the war.

The New Haven city directories include the following data about John Marlin's two sons:

1898 Marlin, J. Howard with The Marlin Fire Arms, boards at 326 George St. Marlin, M. Harry, vice president and secretary, The Marlin Fire Arms Company; home, 382 Whitney Ave.
1899-1901 Same
1902 Marlin, J. Howard, vice president and secretary, The Marlin Fire Arms Company; home, 326 George St.
1903 Same
1904 Marlin, M. Harry, president and treasurer, The Marlin Fire Arms Company; home, 312 Temple St.
1905 Same
1906 Same
1907 Home, 911 Townsend Ave.
1908 Same
1909 Same
1910 Marlin, Mahlon H., president and treasurer, The Marlin Fire Arms Company; home, 911 Townsend Ave.

1911-1916 Same
1917 Marlin, J. Howard, Rem. to Pine Orchard; Marlin, Mahlon H.; home, 911 Townsend Avenue
1920 Marlin, J. Howard, treasurer, Perrigo, Inc., R.R. c New; home, at Branford
1923 Same
1926 Marlin, J. Howard, president, Perrigo, Inc., home, 45 Fair

During one period of time, Mahlon H. and J. Howard Marlin were president and treasurer and vice president and secretary, respectively, of the C.G. Clark Company, New Haven, manufacturer of Coe's Cough Balsam, Coe's Dyspepsia Cure, and Hegeman's Camphor Ice.

OTHER EARLY INVENTORS
Andrew Burgess

Andrew Burgess, born at Lake George, N.Y., on January 16, 1837, was an assistant to the famous Civil War photographer, Mathew B. Brady. During that war and in the early 1870s, Mr. Burgess bought out the Brady business. Although some of the famous pictures of Lincoln were taken by Andrew Burgess, his talent as a firearm inventor is of particular interest to the gun collector and Marlin historian.

The most complete biography of Andrew Burgess is found

Andrew Burgess, 1837–1908.

Lewis Lobdell Hepburn, 1832–1914.

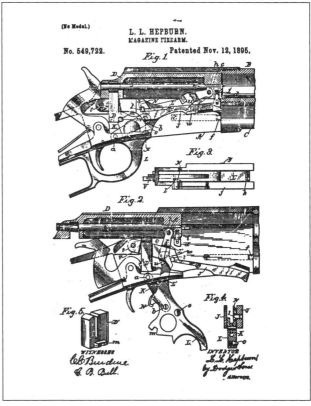

1895 LL. Hepburn patent drawing for a lever action shotgun.

in Sam Maxwell's excellent book, *Lever Action Magazine Rifles — Derived from the Patents of Andrew Burgess,* published by Sam Maxwell in 1976. This book is recommended reading for more complete information about this famous gun inventor who left his mark on Marlin, Colt, Winchester, Whitney, and his own Burgess gun company in Buffalo, N.Y.

Some of his patents that were used in the design of Marlin firearms are 134,589; 168,829; 168,966; 210,091; 210,181; 210,182; 210,294; 210,295; 213,869; 216,080; 250,825; and 250,880.

Although Andrew Burgess did not design or invent a specific model of Marlin rifle, fundamental features of some of his patents were incorporated into the design of the Model 1881 rifle. These included a side-loading, tubular-magazine, lever action rifle; a pivoted lever working on the bolt; a bolt locking on the end of the lever; the extractor; and raising the lever to prevent letting in two cartridges. Also, in conjunction with John Marlin, Andrew Burgess patented (250,825) the split carrier of the Model 1881.

As a result of Andrew Burgess's contributions to the Model 1881 rifle, John Marlin built a successful lever action rifle business. One can only wonder what would have happened if his genius had been incorporated into John Marlin's first successful repeating rifle when The Marlin Fire Arms Company had originally been organized.

A more in-depth discussion of the Model 1881 rifle, its variations, and its success is found in the rifle section of this book. When reviewing that section, the reader should keep in mind the name of Andrew Burgess. His contribution to the early success of the Marlin rifle will soon be recognized.

Andrew Burgess died on December 19, 1908, and he was interred at his home in Oswego, N.Y.

Prototype of lever action shotgun having a dummy pump handle that was patented by L.L. Hepburn.

Lewis Lobdell Hepburn

Lewis Lobdell Hepburn, born on March 2, 1832, in Colton, N.Y., first labored as an apprentice blacksmith. In 1855, he opened a gunsmith shop at his home in Colton.

Until the early 1870s, Mr. Hepburn made muzzle-loading rifles. In about 1871, he was hired by E. Remington & Sons in Ilion, N.Y., to supervise the manufacture of its sporting firearms.

In addition to his gunmaking skill, Lewis Hepburn was a champion long-range rifle marksman. This ability was recognized when he was selected to be a shooting member of the U.S. "Elcho Shield" Rifle Team. The Irish had challenged the U.S. shooters to a match to be fired at 800, 900, and 1,000 yards. Other famous shooters on the U.S. team included G.W.

Yale, T.S. Dakin, John Bodine, Henry Fulton, and H.A. Gildersleeve. In the match, held at Creedmore, Long Island, N.Y., in 1874, the U.S. team beat the Irish team by a score of 934 to 931.

Another demonstration of Lewis Hepburn's skill with the rifle at long ranges took place when he retired the Remington Diamond Badge after three wins. This match was also fired at Creedmore and at ranges of 500, 800, and 1,000 yards. His scores were September 19, 1874—78/100, June 19, 1875—98/100, and August 28, 1875—98/100.

In appreciation for the support his friends and fellow shooters had extended to him, Lewis Hepburn donated the Hepburn Trophy. He established a course of fire of 15 shots at 800, 900, and 1,000 yards, with no sighting shots or previous practice on the day of the match. The contest was open to any breech-loading rifle and was to be held at the Creedmore range.

Among the many inventions of Lewis Hepburn is the famous Remington–Hepburn No. 3 single-shot, breech-loading target and sporting rifle (patent number 220,285, October 7, 1879). The patent was assigned to the Remington Company, which produced various models from 1880 to 1907.

After trying to save the great Remington Armory and firearms business through a long, depressed period, Remington went into receivership. Due to this unfortunate situation, however, The Marlin Fire Arms Company was able to obtain the

1896 L.L. Hepburn patent drawing for shotgun takedown mechanism.

Close-up of lever action shotgun mechanism that has a takedown barrel as patented by L.L. Hepburn.

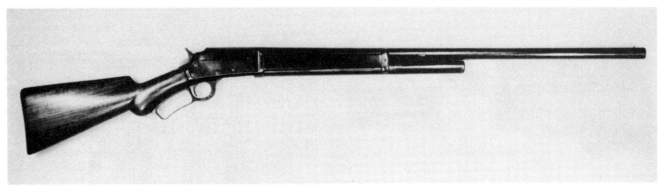

Fixed-barrel second variation of L.L. Hepburn's lever action shotgun.

services of Lewis Hepburn, one of the finest gun designers in the industry.

He can be credited with the success of Marlin lever action rifles and with making the name Marlin the leader that it is today in the lever action rifle field. Some of Lewis Hepburn's patents are Models 1888, 1889, 1891, 1892, 1893, 1894, 1895, and 1897. His other patents include takedown mechanisms, shotgun mechanisms, magazine tubes, lever action shotguns, pump action shotguns, shotgun safeties, sights, pump action .22 and center-fire rifles, semiautomatic rifles, and experimental lever action rifles.

In 1884, Lewis Hepburn patented (number 298,377, May 13, 1884) a lever action, center-fire rifle. He was residing in Ilion, N.Y., at that time. My guess is this patent eventually brought Lewis Hepburn and John Marlin together. Mr. Hepburn was available for such a collaboration because the Remington company had reduced its activities during its bankruptcy. John Marlin was committed to the lever action repeating rifle and Lewis Hepburn had a fairly good rifle design on hand, which was just what John Marlin needed. Both of them must have been astute enough to know that their relationship could be successful, and it was.

A pamphlet issued to honor Lewis Hepburn and his career was supposedly written by his nephew. Although the author-

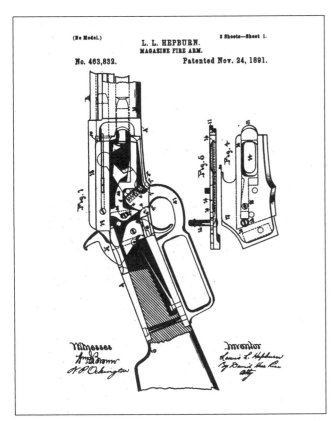

1891 patent drawing of L.L. Hepburn's unique lever action repeating center-fire rifle, which has a removable side plate similar to his Model 1891 side-loading .22 rifle.

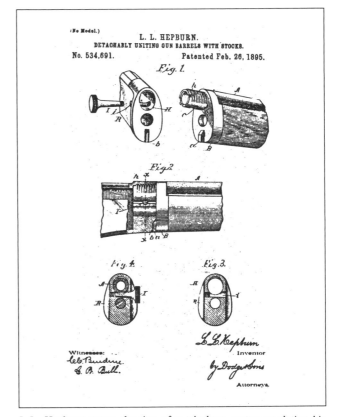

L.L. Hepburn patent drawing of a takedown system predating his Model 1897 takedown rifle.

Model 1892 rifle with an experimental takedown system.

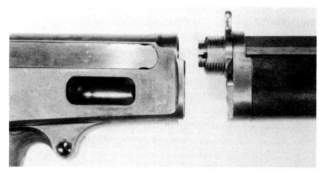

Barrel and receiver of prototype rifle's takedown.

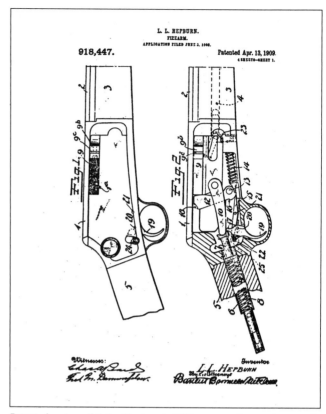

Patent drawing of L.L. Hepburn's 1909 patent of a semiautomatic rifle.

ship is uncertain and the date of publication is unknown, the written words exist, and the tribute to a loyal Marlin employee follows:

Lewis Lobdell Hepburn

Born: Colton, N.Y. March 2, 1832
Died: New Haven, Conn. Aug. 31, 1914

After the failure of E. Remington & Sons gun factory, Ilion, N.Y., Mr. Hepburn in 1886 accepted a situation with The Marlin Firearms Company, as inventor and mechanical expert, which position he held to the satisfaction of all concerned, as evidenced by the fact that the company is

running successfully and almost entirely on guns of his inventing and designing.

Generous to a fault, open-handed in charity, he must have made the world better for his having lived in it. He was not of a social turn, was hard to get acquainted with, never pushed himself or his ideas to the front, never went back on a friend, was modest and retiring except when aroused by some unworthy action or ignoble conduct, when his withering scorn was manifested in terms which, by some, might be called severe. No breath of scandal was ever uttered in connection with his name, and fraud and trickery never marred his most honorable career. He was a member of Ilion Lodge No. 591, F.&A.M., Iroquois Chapter, R.A.M., and

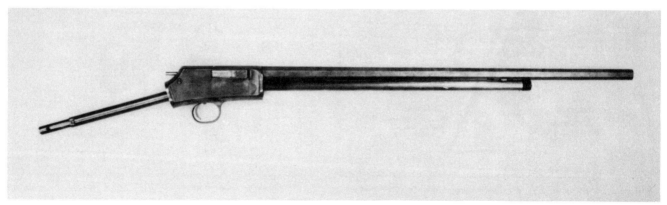

Unfinished prototype of L.L. Hepburn's semiautomatic tubular magazine rifle.

Internal mechanism of experimental semiautomatic rifle.

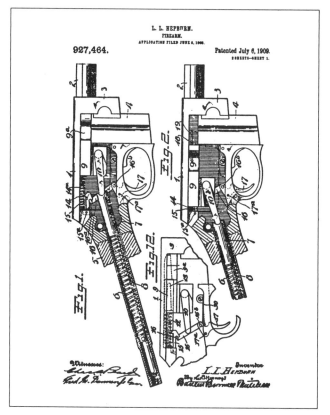

Patent drawing of L.L. Hepburn's clip magazine semiautomatic rifle.

Utica Commandery No. 3, Knights Templar. His word was his bond and his place is hard to fill.

Mr. Hepburn was thoroughly conversant with all the patents, designs, ideas and details of his profession, and was classed with John Browning as being one of the very best gun designers and inventors the world has ever known.

Considering the fact that nearly all other gun factories of note have made or are making guns under the patents of Mr. Browning and other outside inventors, it reflects especial credit on Mr. Hepburn that, during his many years of service, the Marlin Company never found it necessary to go outside their own factory for the ideas which have kept them in the very front rank of gun makers.

His work was his hobby, and he was never so happy as when working out the details of a new gun or an improvement in existing models.

Always at work, rain or shine (except when he left on the annual hunting trip which he enjoyed so much), it was his devotion to duty which indirectly led to his death. On the morning of January 6, 1910, following a cold, sleety rain, Mr. Hepburn ventured to walk the several blocks from his home to the Marlin factory, and when near his destination, slipped on the icy sidewalk and suffered a fracture of his hip.

Notwithstanding the best of medical treatment, the bones refused to knit, and in consequence he was confined to his bed until he passed away August 31, 1914. Through this four-and-a-half years of suffering he maintained the same cheerful, uncomplaining spirit, which characterized his entire life.

Anonymous.

The following patents were awarded to Lewis Hepburn during his 30-year career with Marlin:

Patent Number	Application Date	Item
354,059	Dec. 7, 1886	Model 1888 rifle
371,455	Oct. 11, 1887	Model 1889 rifle
400,679	Apr. 2, 1889	Model 1889 rifle
434,062	Aug. 12, 1890	Model 1891 rifle
463,832	Nov. 24, 1891	Experimental lever action rifle
502,489	Aug. 1, 1893	Model 1893 rifle
518,950	May 1, 1893	Rifle takedown

Patent Number	Application Date	Item
525,739	Sept. 11, 1894	Shotgun
528,905	Nov. 6, 1894	Shotgun
534,691	Feb. 25, 1895	Experimental takedown
549,722	Nov. 12, 1895	Lever action shotgun
560,032	May 12, 1896	Pump shotgun
561,226	June 2, 1896	Shotgun takedown

Internal parts of L.L. Hepburn's experimental semiautomatic rifle with clip magazine.

Patent Number	Application Date	Item
584,177	June 8, 1897	Model 1897 rifle
591,220	Oct. 5, 1897	Shotgun safety
662,427	Nov. 27, 1900	Shotgun safety
732,075	June 30, 1903	Sight
776,243	Nov. 29, 1904	Model 20 rifle
776,322	Nov. 29, 1904	Shotgun safety
882,562	Mar. 24, 1908	Shotgun takedown
882,563	Mar. 24, 1908	Model 20
883,020	Mar. 24, 1908	Model 20
12,823	July 7, 1908 (Reissue)	Model 20
918,447	Apr. 13, 1908	Semiautomatic rifle
927,464	July 6, 1909	Semiautomatic rifle
943,828	Dec. 21, 1909	Shotgun

Most of Lewis Hepburn's patents are included in the separate sections of this book that cover each of his models. Those listed above are patents that were awarded, but never put into production.

Melvin Hepburn, a son of Lewis, also obtained patents that were assigned to The Marlin Fire Arms Company. His patents were as follows:

Patent Number	Application Date	Item
755,660	Mar. 29, 1904	Takedown feature
888,329	May 19, 1908	Shotgun takedown

The Marlin Fire Arms Company's 1915 ad for the Ideal Hand Book.

Patent Number	Application Date	Item
997,642	July 11, 1911	Model 27 rifle (in conjunction with J.H. Wheeler and G.A. Beck)

IDEAL MANUFACTURING COMPANY
Establishment of the Company

On May 16, 1910, The Marlin Fire Arms Company took over the operation of the Ideal Manufacturing Company, New Haven, Conn. The company was formerly owned and managed by John H. Barlow. Born in England on April 26, 1846, Mr. Barlow came to this country at the age of two. He served in the American Civil War and was honorably discharged as a first sergeant while with the Army in Arizona among the Indians. He worked at the Parker shotgun factory in Meriden, Conn., during the early 1870s and at the Winchester Repeating Arms Company in New Haven as a contractor for twelve years. In 1884, John Barlow established the Ideal Manufacturing Company in New Haven, which designed and manufactured cartridge-reloading implements. His business was known throughout the world and his tools were in large demand among sportsmen.

John Barlow retired from the business world in order to travel. While visiting his daughter in Venice, Italy, he died of a heart attack on March 15, 1912.

Ideal from Marlin to Lyman

Until this time, The Marlin Fire Arms Company, under the guidance of Mahlon H. and J. Howard Marlin, continued the business with little or no change. Most of the reloading tools and other devices in the Ideal line were invented by John Bar-

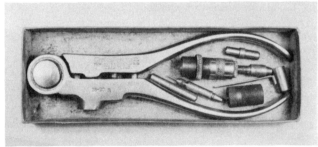

Top: *Box for Marlin-manufactured Ideal No. 3 tool.* Bottom: *Contents of box, including all the parts of the tool and a powder measure.*

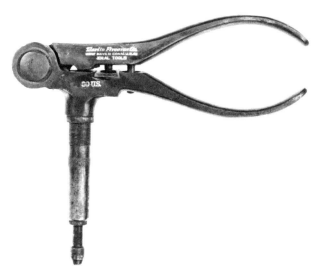

Ideal tool for loading the high-power .30 U.S. cartridge.

Marlin/Ideal broken-shell extractor.

low and had been used by sportsmen for years. The Marlin company found few reasons to make changes or to add to the line.

Although most of the tools were marked with the Ideal name, those that were manufactured after Marlin's purchase were stamped with the Marlin name. The printed matter furnished with tools, and the labels on boxes, were also changed to reflect the Marlin name.

The Ideal Hand Book, which contained "useful information for shooters," was the bible for handloaders, who made up their own ammunition for shotgun, rifle, or pistol. During the Marlin ownership, the manual continued in publication. Those books that relate to Marlin were numbers 20 through 26.

The Marlin Arms Corporation, which was formed in 1916, sold the Ideal business to Phineas M. Talcott of 103 Meadow St., New Haven. Mr. Talcott, like the Marlin brothers, operated the business without change, except for a thorough reorganization under his new management to improve quality and to make the business more profitable. In October 1925, he

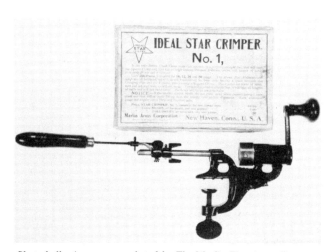

Shot shell crimper, as marketed by The Marlin Fire Arms Company, 1915–1916.

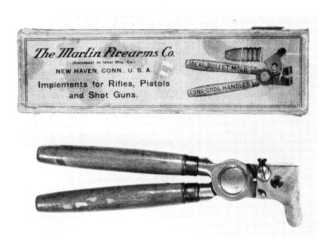

Ideal bullet mold and box, as made by Marlin.

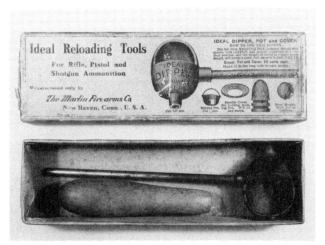

Ideal dipper, used to pour molten lead into a bullet mold.

sold the Ideal Manufacturing Company to the Lyman Gun Sight Corporation. To this day the Ideal name is still in use by Lyman.

New Haven city directories furnish the following information under the name Ideal Manufacturing Company.

1885 Ideal Manufacturing Company, manufactures cartridge-reloading implements, 187 St. John St. Barlow, John H., manager, Ideal Manufacturing Company, 187 St. John St.; home, 89 Bristol Street.

1886–1889 Same as above

1915 Marlin Fire Arms Company

1916 Marlin Arms Corporation

1917–1918 Ideal Manufacturing Company, Phineas M. Talcott, proprietor, 103 Meadow St.

1919–24 Same as 1917–1918 with added home, 1609 Chapel St.

1925 No Ideal nor Phineas Talcott listed

Only a few of the many Marlin Ideal items are illustrated here. A good collection of Marlin-marked Ideal tools can still be found. They make a fine display in themselves, or as added color to an arms display.

Marlin Arms Corporation/ The Marlin–Rockwell Corporation

FORMING THE MARLIN ARMS CORPORATION

As early as April 8, 1915, The Marlin Firearms Company was asked to bid on the manufacture of 100,000 7-mm Mauser rifles by the J.P. Morgan export department. In making Marlin's response to this request Mahlon H. Marlin said, "It is too large for our present equipment to be handled in a reasonable time, and we would not care to go into the work in the way of putting up new buildings and furnishing extra equipment and expanding our organization to an extent large enough to handle the quantities in time that would be satisfactory. . . ." The reply also went on to say that Marlin had an organization that was trained and experienced in making high-powered rifles and that its reputation was equal to the best in its class of work.

J.P. Morgan & Company was the sole purchaser of armament and war materials for England. Already involved in the war in Europe, England needed additional sources for arms until its home production could be increased to meet its needs. J.P. Morgan & Company tried in different ways to find sources for the necessary arms. When U.S. companies indicated a lack of interest, however, Morgan & Company encouraged investment companies to form syndicates in order to help meet those needs of the Crown and other European countries.

Albert F. Rockwell (1862–1925), president of the Marlin Arms Corporation and the Marlin–Rockwell Corporation from 1915 to 1920. (Peter M. Marron)

One such syndicate was formed by William P. Bonbright & Company, Incorporated and Kissell-Kinnicutte & Company, companies that were closely allied with J.P. Morgan & Company. This syndication resulted in the acquisition of The Marlin Fire Arms Company and the formation of the Marlin Arms Corporation on December 8, 1915.

This was an interesting change in direction and product line for a company that had been totally involved for 45 years in manufacturing sporting firearms. The switch to making tools of war is best shown in the early correspondence between the founders of the new syndicate.

April 8, 1915

MARLIN GUN CO.,
Meriden, Conn.
GENTLEMEN: Do you care to make us a bid on 100,000 Mauser rifles to take 7 m/m cartridges? If so, would you give us an idea of about what deliveries you could make. We understand specifications were mailed to us from England on April first and we can take up the matter of price with you after they are received.

We have a Mauser gun here in the office that you can examine if you so desire.

Awaiting your favors on this subject, we remain,
    Very truly yours,
                            EXPORT DEPT.,
                            By _____
WLC:Td

THE MARLIN FIREARMS COMPANY
New Haven, Conn., April 23, 1915

Messrs. J.P. MORGAN & CO.,
Export Dept., New York City
GENTLEMEN: We have your letter of April 17th, by Mr. Clark, and wish to apologize for not having replied to it sooner. We have been thinking the matter over and the writer has consulted with his associates, but it seems to us best not to undertake the work — it is too large for our present equipment to be handled in a reasonable time, and we would not care to go into the work in the way of putting up new buildings and furnishing extra equipment and expanding our organization to an extent large enough to handle the quantities in time that would be satisfactory to you.

We thank you for your expressed good opinion of the character of our work and we, ourselves, believe that we could make work that would be satisfactory and pass any fair inspection, as we have an organization trained and experienced in doing work on repeating arms for high-power smokeless ammunition, and our reputation is, we believe, equal to the best of this class of work.

Again thanking you for your offer and regretting that we are unable to do anything about it at this time, we beg to remain,
    Yours respectfully,
                            THE MARLIN FIREARMS CO.,
                            (Sgd.) M.H. MARLIN
MLP

WILLIAM P. BONBRIGHT, INCORPORATED,
14 Wall Street, New York,
November 12, 1915.

Colt machine guns.
E.R. Stettinius, Esq.
Export Department, Messrs. J.P. Morgan & Co.,
23 Wall Street, New York City.
DEAR SIR: I have entered into a contract for the purchase of the entire capital stock of the Marlin Fire Arms Co. of New Haven, Conn., and

I have made an arrangement for a new company which will purchase the Marlin plant to manufacture the Colt machine gun, enjoying the fullest cooperation of the Colt Company as to drawings, processes, and the personal attention of such of their heads of department, including that of Mr. Browning, as may be required, and

I have entered into a contract with A.F. Rockwell, of Bristol, Conn., under which he is now getting his organization together for the manufacture of the Colt machine gun in the Marlin plant, he agreeing to head the organization and personally direct the production.

The new company will be prepared to offer Colt machine guns for

A.F. Rockwell's estate, Brightwood Hall, in Bristol, Conn. (Peter M. Marron)

Pre-WW I photo of The Marlin Fire Arms Company.

delivery during the fifth month (say April) after taking charge of the plant, at the rate of 35 to 50 guns per day and running into a gradual increase of this production.

I am discussing the financing of this operation with Messrs. William P. Bonbright & Co., who wish to verify my promises of production, and as I desire to expedite so far as possible assurances to both you and them that the above quantities and deliveries may be had, I urge that you delegate a representative to whom I may prove the likelihood of realizing them.

Yours very truly,

(Signed) EDGAR PARK

WILLIAM P. BONBRIGHT & CO., INCORPORATED,
14 Wall Street, New York,
November 30, 1915

Messrs. J.P. MORGAN & CO.
23 Wall Street, New York City.
DEAR SIRS: The Marlin Arms Corporation, now being or about to be incorporated under the laws of the State of New York, will have an authorized capital of $3,500,000 7% cumulative preferred stock and 60,000 shares of non par value common stock. Subject to the Marlin Fire Arms Company receiving a contract through you for not less than 12,000 Colt machine guns, we have agreed to purchase the above preferred stock together with a certain amount of common stock at a price which will place the Marlin Fire Arms Corporation in funds to buy the present Marlin Fire Arms Company free and clear of all debt, and in addition to leave in the treasury of the company approximately $1,300,000 in cash.

The Marlin Arms Corporation will have assigned to it an exclusive working agreement with the Colt's Patent Fire Arms Manufacturing Company and will enjoy the co-operation of the latter in the manufacture of the Colt automatic machine gun.

Mr. A.F. Rockwell will accept the presidency of the Marlin Arms Corporation and, with an organization of his selection, personally supervise the production of the guns.

Among the provisions of the preferred stock is one by which the company agrees to retire at par one-third of the issue on December 1, 1916, one-third on March 1, 1917, and one-third on June 1, 1917. Both the common and the preferred stock will be placed in a voting trust of which a majority shall be of our selection. There is a further provision by which no dividends can be paid upon the common stock until the entire issue of preferred stock has been retired.

It is further agreed that the preferred stock — except with the consent

Colt Model 1914 machine gun mounted on Russian-type tripod.

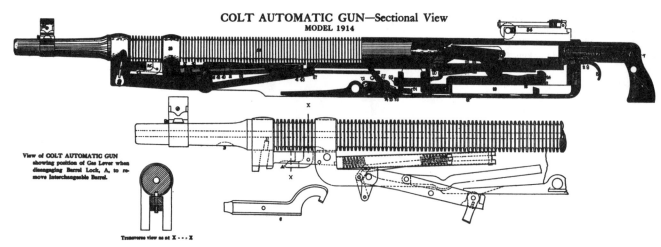

COLT AUTOMATIC GUN—Sectional View
MODEL 1914

View of COLT AUTOMATIC GUN showing position of Gas Lever when disengaging Barrel Lock, A, to remove Interchangeable Barrel.

Transverse view as at X - - - X

Sectional view of Colt Model 1914 machine gun manufactured by Marlin–Rockwell.

of J.P. Morgan & Co. – will not be retired prior to the dates specified unless the above referred to contract for 12,000 guns has been completed.

Yours very truly,

WILLIAM P. BONBRIGHT & CO.
By A. H. Lockin, Vice-Pres.
KISSELL—KINNICUTTE & CO.

GHK/JH/1

WILLIAM P. BONBRIGHT & CO.,
INCORPORATED,
14 Wall Street, New York,
December 10, 1915

Messrs. J.P. MORGAN & COMPANY,
Agent for His Britannic Majesty's Government,
23 Wall Street, New York City.

DEAR SIRS: In connection with the contract for 12,000 Colt automatic machine guns which, at our request, you are about to execute with the Marlin Arms Corporation, a New York State corporation, we respectfully advise you as follows:

1. The Marlin Arms Corporation was organized on December 9th, under the laws of the State of New York, with a capital stock of $3,500,000 par value of preferred stock and 60,000 shares of common stock having no par value. The incorporation is complete and the company is prepared for active business.

2. The Marlin Arms Corporation is purchasing today, and will demonstrate to you before asking you to deliver the contract for 12,000 Colt automatic machine guns that it has purchased and has in its possession free of all incumbrances all of the stock of the Marlin Fire Arms Company of Connecticut. This latter corporation owns, free and clear, the plant at New Haven, Connecticut, known as the Marlin plant. We have caused the title of this property to be examined, and we are advised that there are no mortgages, liens, or other incumbrances against either the real estate or machinery or equipment and that the business of the Marlin Fire Arms Company is taken over absolutely free of debt, except for petty items not exceeding $5,000 in amount.

3. Furthermore, we advise you that the Marlin Arms Corporation has made an agreement with the Colt's Patent Fire Arms Company of Connecticut, whereby the Colt's Company gives to the Marlin Company full right and authority to manufacture the Colt automatic machine gun, and agrees also to furnish drawings, advice, and such assistance as it may be able to, to the Marlin Company. This contract, duly executed by the two corporations, will be exhibited to you at the time that you deliver the contract for 12,000 Colt automatic guns.

4. The property of the Marlin Arms Corporation, besides the foregoing property, will include approximately the sum of $1,300,000 in cash. This money at the present writing has not been paid into the treasury of the new company, but the undersigned, as syndicate managers, have formed a syndicate which has been fully subscribed, and in fact over subscribed, which syndicate is bound and obligated to take over, not later than the 17th day of December 1915, a portion of the

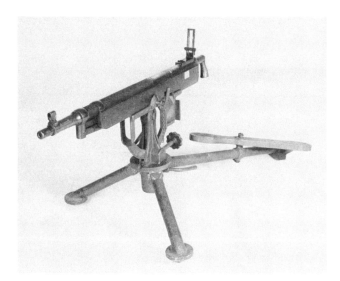

Marlin Arms Corporation-manufactured Colt Model 1914 machine gun in U.S.-type mount.

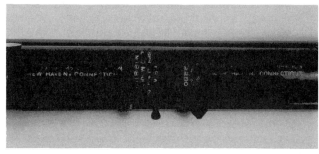

Second variation markings on Marlin/Colt machine gun.

stock of the Marlin Arms Corporation upon such terms that there will then remain in the treasury of that corporation as free working capital approximately the sum of $1,200,000. This syndicate is composed of a number of bankers and banking firms of the highest financial responsibility, and we are advised by our counsel, who have drawn the syndicate agreement, which they have executed that the obligations under it are fixed and determined and legally binding. Consequently, we can assure you that the company will receive not later than the 17th day of December, 1915 the said amount of approximately $1,300,000 of which $1,200,000 will be free working capital.

Very truly yours,

WILLIAM P. BONBRIGHT & CO.,
INCORPORATED,
By A.H. LOCKLIN, Vice-President.
KISSELL–KINNICUTTE & CO.

AHL-G-1

MARLIN ARMS CORPORATION PLAN AND SYNDICATE AGREEMENT, 1915

I

William P. Bonbright & Company, Incorporated, and Kissell-Kinnicutte & Company, hereafter called the managers, contemplate forming a new corporation under the name of Marlin Arms Corporation, or some similar title (herein referred to as the new company), which will have substantially the following capitalization:

(1) Preferred stock thirty five thousand shares of the par value of one hundred dollars each;

(2) Common stock sixty thousand shares having no par value.

The preferred stock will be preferred as to both earnings and assets, will bear dividends of, and limited to, seven per cent per annum cumulative from December 1, 1915, and no dividends shall be payable upon the common stock until all the preferred stock has been retired at one hundred (100) and accrued dividends. The preferred stock shall all be retired at one hundred (100) and accrued dividends in substantially equal installments on December 1, 1916, March 1, 1917, and June 1, 1917.

All the stock will be placed in a voting trust, approved by the managers, to extend for a period of two years or until the preferred stock has been retired and all bank loans paid.

II

The new company expects to acquire, either directly or through ownership of all the stock of the Marlin Fire Arms Company of Connecticut (herein called the old company), the following property and contracts as its principal assets:

(a) The present plant of the old company, located at New Haven, Connecticut, together with the machinery and equipment and other tangible assets of such company taken over as a going concern. The vendors with whom the managers are dealing will covenant that this property is free and clear of all mortgages, liens, debts, and obligations, and will include all of the assets of the present company, including the good will, excepting cash and securities on hand and the present company's receivables. A certain amount of cash will be available for the purposes of the new company.

(b) Orders on behalf of the British Government for twelve thousand (12,000) machine guns of the type known as the Colt automatic machine gun, at a minimum price of six hundred and fifty dollars ($650) per gun.

Left side of Navy gun.

Barrel and receiver markings on Navy-type Marlin machine gun. (Chicago Police Department Criminalistics Division)

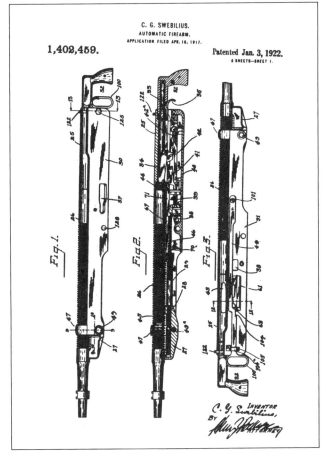

Drawing of patent number 1,402,459 of early Marlin machine gun.

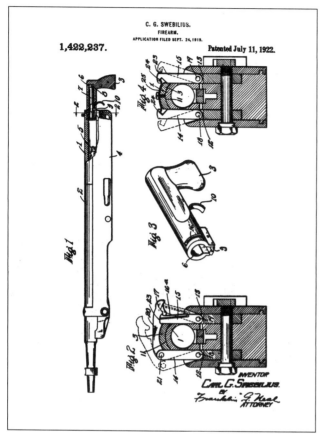

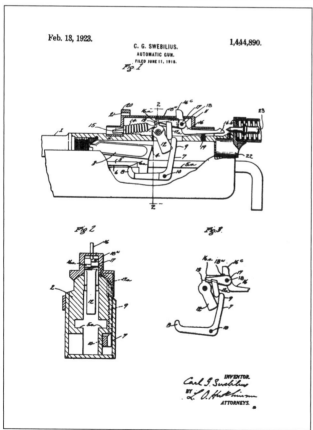

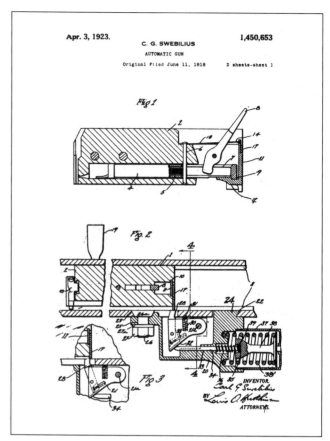

C.G. Swebilius patents that relate to Marlin–Rockwell Corporation machine gun development.

(c) A license or working agreement to be approved by the managers from the Colt's Patent Fire Arms Manufacturing Company under which such company will give the new corporation permission to manufacture such guns.

(d) A contract of employment with Mr. A.F. Rockwell of Bristol, Connecticut, whereby Mr. Rockwell will agree to devote his entire time and energy to the work of the new company for a period running from the incorporation of the new company to January 1st, 1917.

III

William P. Bonbright & Company, Incorporated, and Kissell-Kinnicutte & Company (acting individually and not as managers) are willing to sell to the syndicate to be formed under the attached agreement voting trust certificates representing thirty-five thousand shares of the preferred stock of the new company and seventeen thousand five hundred shares of the common stock of the new company for the total price of two million nine hundred and seventy-five thousand dollars in cash, and the syndicate is formed to make such purchase.

A corporation has been or is about to be formed known as the Marlin Arms Company (or some other appropriate name) with a capitalization of $3,500,000 7% preferred stock, divided into series, A, B, C of equal amounts, and 60,000 shares of common stock of no par value. Among the provisions of the preferred stock is one that the three series shall be retired at par and accrued dividends as follows:

Right side of Marlin-Rockwell improved Model 1917 machine gun; it has new type of pistol grip with a safety, lightened receiver and barrel, and new gas system. Serial number 17,882.

Series A. December 1, 1916.
      B. March 1, 1917.
      C. June 1, 1917.

There is a further provision that no dividends may be paid on the common stock until all the preferred is retired.

This corporation is to purchase for cash all the physical assets, buildings, plant, machinery, tools, inventory, etc. (excluding all bills and accounts payable or receivable), of the Marlin Fire Arms Co. of New Haven, Conn.

It is also to acquire an exclusive right from the Colt Fire Arms Co. of Hartford, Conn. to manufacture under a royalty of $100 per gun, the Colt machine gun. As a part of the agreement, the Colt Co. is to furnish to the Marlin Arms Co. all working drawings, patterns, analysis of raw material, etc., and such aid as may be necessary in the way of expert advice, including the services of Mr. Browning, the inventor of the gun.

The plant is under the management of Mr. Rockwell, now president of the Bristol Brass Co., who serves with a nominal salary, receiving as compensation part of the saving in cost of manufacture of the Colt gun below the figure of $300 per gun.

The company is to have assigned to it an order from the British Government placed through the export department of J.P. Morgan & Co. for a minimum of 12,000 Colt machine guns for delivery and at prices as follows:

1,250	April 1916	$750
1,500	May 1916	750
1,750	June 1916	750
2,500	July	650
2,500	August	650
2,500	September	650

Any deliveries made in March are at a price of $850, and in February of $950.

The contract is to have no cancellation clause nor any penalty clause. The only right of the British Government is the option to refuse to take delayed delivery on any guns not delivered of the amount specified for each month.

Payment is to be accrued by deposit of the British Government of 25% of the gross value of the contract with the right on the part of the Marlin Company to draw against the same after February 1st next for cost of labor and materials, such drawings to be secured by surety bonds.

Payment is to be made on delivery at the export point, 25% of each payment being drawn from the deposit and 75% in additional cash.

The order includes extra barrels at $25 each, and cartridge boxes at $4.00 each.

Before granting the license the Colt Company has satisfied itself as to the fitness of the Marlin plant and equipment to turn out the Colt machine gun, and also as to the qualifications of Mr. Rockwell to manage the operations.

Before placing the contract the same investigations were made by the export department of J.P. Morgan & Co.

It is estimated that there will be little capital outlay necessary to thoroughly equip and adjust the Marlin plant to the manufacture of Colt machine guns, the present machinery being for the most part suitable and adequate.

The ability of the plant under the above management to produce the required product at a cost not to exceed $300 per gun has been favorably passed upon by different independent authorities.

The money provided by the sale of the securities of the

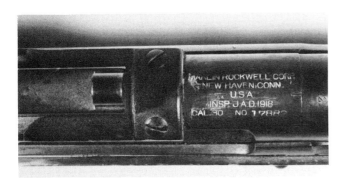

Receiver markings on Marlin-Rockwell Model 1917 machine gun.

Close-up of Krag Model 1896 rear sight used on improved Model 1917 machine gun.

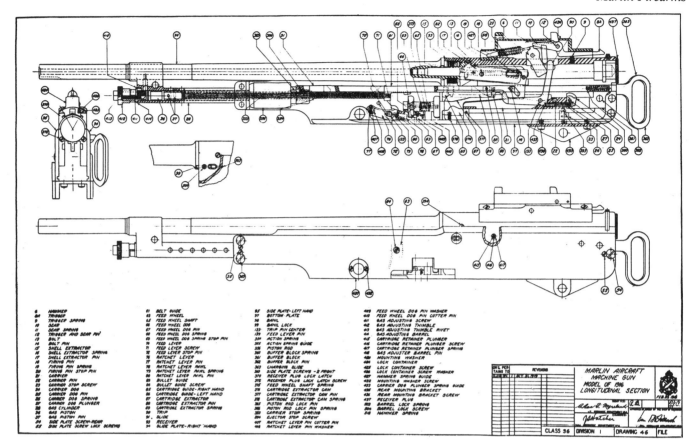

Sectional drawing of Marlin aircraft machine gun Model 1916.

company over and above the required for the purchase of the Marlin plant is estimated, after careful calculation, will be ample for working capital to fill the above order, in addition to which there will be right to draw on the cash deposit of the British Government for material and labor.

The question of raw material has been carefully investigated and the Colt Fire Arms Co. advise that this can be procured from their own sources of supply.

Eliminating all profits from accessories (extra barrels, ammunition boxes, etc.) all premium for advanced delivery, all savings in costs below $300 and all profits from any possible additional orders, the cash profit on the specific 12,000 guns delivered in the amounts and at the terms and prices specified would be approximately $3,500,000, equal to the face value of the entire preferred stock issue.

The common stock would then have as assets the entire plant and original working capital.

As a concern operating in normal times, the Marlin Fire Arms Co. has had a successful record covering a period of many years.

Mr. A. V. LOCKETT,
c/o Wm. P. Bonbright & Co., Inc.
14 Wall St., N.Y.
DEAR MR. LOCKETT: Referring to my correspondence with Mr. Davison in regard to the Colt machine gun proposition, quote as follows for your information:

"If Mr. Stettinius is willing to close the contract with the gun company to be organized, with the understanding that the Bankers Trust Company would advance up to say

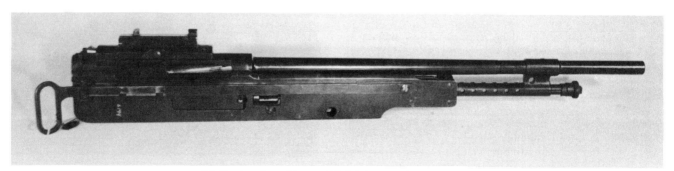

Marlin aircraft machine gun Model 1917, serial number 3326.

Marlin aircraft machine gun Model 1917 with mechanical trigger motor.

$1,000,000 of the 25% deposit, provided that the company's own money which had already been spent showed such satisfactory results that the Trust Company would be warranted in making the loan, it would seem to me that we would be justified, provided all the facts given as above prove to be correct, in agreeing to such an arrangement. Under no circumstances, however, do I believe that we should make any agreement that would necessitate putting out good money for the purpose of saving bad, provided the investment of the company's own money should prove that their ability to fulfill the contract was doubtful."

Very truly yours,

_____ , Vice-President.

FIK/MKS

A NEW NAME AND NEW PRODUCTS

During 1916, the new syndicate called the Marlin Arms Corporation was expanding its holdings and becoming more deeply entrenched in war work. When it appeared the U.S. would soon be involved in the war, A.F. Rockwell, president, introduced a reorganization that included a name change from Marlin Arms Corporation to Marlin–Rockwell Corporation. Both names will be found on military arms produced by these companies. But no sporting arms have been observed with the Marlin Arms Corporation name on them, although a Marlin handtrap (clay bird thrower) has been noted that had *Marlin Arms Corporation* clearly marked into the metal. Also, a net retail price list with prices of sporting arms, effective May 10, 1916, was printed under the Marlin Arms Corporation name and address. This was identical, except for price increases, to The Marlin Fire Arms Company's Nov. 1, 1915 price list.

The officers of the new Marlin–Rockwell Corporation until November 4, 1920 were A.F. Rockwell, president; Edgar Park, vice president; Louis E. Stoddard, vice president; Thomas W. Farnum, treasurer; Errol Kerr, secretary. In July 1919, John F. Moran became sales manager. He was formerly general manager of the Mayo Radiator Company.

Albert F. Rockwell

Albert F. Rockwell, although without a formal education beyond age 13, was an established and successful manufacturer and entrepreneur when he joined the Marlin Arms Corporation as its president.

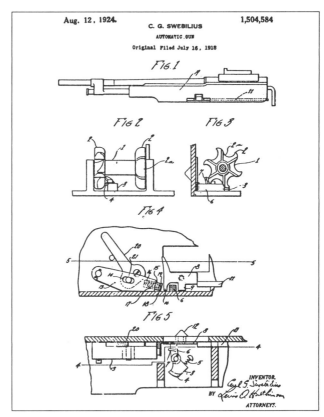

Patent drawing of jam prevention device for Marlin Model 1918 machine gun.

Receiver markings on Model 1918 machine gun.

Marlin-Rockwell aircraft machine gun equipped with hydraulic trigger motor mounted on top of the gun. Serial number 21,522.

Second variation Marlin-Rockwell receiver markings on Model 1918 aircraft machine gun.

Mr. Rockwell was born April 8, 1862, in Woodhull, N.Y. He spent his youth in Morris, Ill. His first job was in the Chicago dry goods store of Field, Leiter and Company. Later he went to Florida, where he managed a country store and a fruit business, and for four more years ran a hardware store. When he left Florida, he went to Bay City, Mich., and then on to Bristol, Conn. There he established, with his brother Edward D. Rockwell, the New Departure Bell Company, which manufactured bicycle bells, push and rotary doorbells, and fire bells. The brothers Rockwell eventually reached a production of about 15,000 bells a day. In 1893, Edward Rockwell formed the Bristol Spring Company as a separate company. Together, they also manufactured bicycle lamps that burned oil or acetylene gas. Another successful product of A.F. Rockwell was the

New Departure Automatic Coaster Hub, which was a bicycle coaster brake. In addition to the hub, A.F. Rockwell invented and manufactured double-row ball bearings that launched his New Departure Company into one of the largest bearing manufacturers in the world.

Now that A.F. Rockwell was well established in the automobile business by selling ball bearings, he plunged into making automobiles. In 1907 he formed the Bristol Engineering Company and designed the first cast en block motors in the U.S. The new engine, along with New Departure bearings, was used in a series of automobiles that he manufactured.

The New York Auto Show in 1908 launched the first Rockwell auto, called the Rockwell Public Service Cab. It was produced by the New Departure Company, which had taken over production of automobiles from Bristol Engineering. The Rockwell Service Cab became the Yellow Taxicab when Mrs. Rockwell selected that as her choice of color for the auto.

Albert F. Rockwell continually overextended himself; he got carried away with expectations for his businesses and spent little time on the money end of his enterprises. As a result, A.F. Rockwell closed the New Departure Automobile Manufacturing Company in 1911. This was the end of his automobile and taxicab businesses; however, the fine cars he manufactured will never be forgotten. Among them were the Rockwell Public Service Cab, the Houpt-Rockwell Close-Coupled Runabout, the Houpt-Rockwell Touring Car, the Allen-Kingston, the Houpt-Rockwell Landaulet, the Houpt-Rockwell Limousine, and the Houpt-Rockwell Raceabout.

Upon closing out the manufacture of automobiles by New

Experimental shoulder-fired Marlin aircraft machine gun with a wooden stock, pistol grip and trigger, and pivoting pintle attached. Missing are the sights that were attached to the aluminum bases affixed to the barrel. Serial number 10,590.

Right side view of Browning Model 1918 aircraft machine gun manufactured by Marlin-Rockwell Corporation. Serial number 60,471.

Left side of Browning Model 1918 aircraft gun, which has a trigger motor housing attached to the rear of the receiver. Serial number 59,745.

Departure, Albert F. Rockwell was ousted from the company by a proxy fight instituted by Charles T. Treadway. In 1913, A.F. Rockwell became president of Bristol Brass, which position he held into the 1920s. In 1915, the New Departure bearing business was acquired by General Motors.

Overlooked by historians is the great success of the Marlin Arms Corporation and the Marlin-Rockwell Corporation in manufacturing machine guns and automatic rifles during the 1915-to-1919 period of WW I. That success was a direct result of Albert F. Rockwell's ability to organize varied manufacturing operations at numerous sites in the eastern U.S. Most references include only information about his activities in Bristol, Conn., and overlook the great contributions of his mechanical genius and his leadership during his country's dire need for such abilities to bring products on line, in time, and economically.

A.F. Rockwell's son, Hugh, worked with his father at Marlin-Rockwell during the war. He obtained patents on some of his inventions and contributed to the daily operation of the corporation.

After the war's end, all of the holdings of the Marlin-Rockwell conglomerate were disposed of. However, the Plainville Division, Plainville, Conn., continued in business, making bearings, and became the Standard Bearing Company.

Albert F. Rockwell was a generous contributor to the Bristol community. He donated a park to the city and supported many other civic efforts with his money and time. He died on February 17, 1925, and was interred in Bristol's West Cemetery. Interestingly, the cemetery land was part of A.F. Rockwell's estate that he had donated to the city for a park.

More information about A.F. Rockwell and his automobiles can be found in the excellent book *The New Departure Clas-*

sics, by Chichester Percival Weldon, Phoenix Publishing, Canaan, N.H., 1986.

Developing Military Firearms

Before the outbreak of WW I, only Marlin-Rockwell and the Savage Arms Corporation were producing machine guns in any quantity in the U.S. Marlin by then had produced a large number of the old lever-type Colt guns for the Russian government. On June 2, 1917, the U.S. government placed an order with Marlin-Rockwell for 2,500 Colt guns, to be used in training machine gun crews. In September 1917, an order for 5,000 aircraft machine guns and 20,000 Browning automatic rifles was placed with Marlin-Rockwell. In December of 1917, an

Typical markings on Browning Model 1918 machine gun as manufactured by Marlin-Rockwell Corporation.

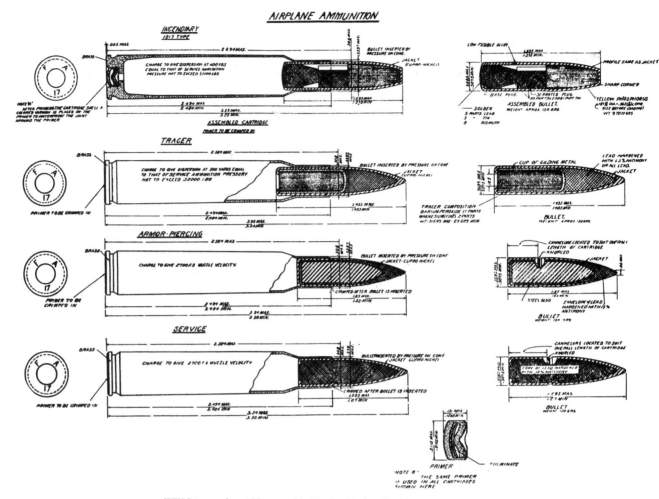

WW I types of cartridges used in Marlin–Rockwell caliber .30 machine guns.

Photograph of Marlin–Rockwell personnel testing Marlin aircraft machine gun on a mock-up airplane with a dummy propeller and disk, which allows study of bullet holes in relation to the propeller blades. Among the military and civilian observers is John Browning, who is shown on the extreme left.

order for 10,000 of a new Browning aircraft gun was placed with Marlin-Rockwell.

During this period the Hopkins & Allen Arms Company (H&A), Norwich, Conn., was working on a contract for military rifles for the Belgian government. Before it was completed, the Marlin-Rockwell Corporation took over the H&A plant and produced parts for the Browning Automatic Rifle (BAR) there. However, even the addition of these facilities did not quite do the job. To obtain additional manufacturing capability, Marlin also acquired the Mayo Radiator Company, 961 Dixwell Ave., New Haven, Conn. It was retooled for the making of BAR and machine gun parts, as well as radiators.

The first production Marlin-Rockwell BAR was delivered in June 1918. By the end of July, 5,650 had been produced. By November 11, 1918 (the end of the war), Marlin-Rockwell had built about 16,000 of these rifles.

During the period of manufacture of the Colt machine gun (John Browning's original invention), the Marlin engineers and inventors had been developing improvements to the gun. These made it lighter in construction and gave it a piston gas system rather than the original lever-type, "potato digger," system.

A synchronization mechanism was also developed, compati-

Carl Gustaf Swebilius, prolific inventor and patentee of most features of the Marlin aircraft machine gun, is seen here making adjustments to the mock-up synchronizing mechanism during test for U.S. and Allied officers.

Carl Swebilius making adjustments to the hydraulic synchronizer he invented for use with the Marlin machine gun.

Marlin Rockwell aircraft machine gun mounted to fire between the blades of the propeller.

ble with both hydraulic and mechanical systems, which allowed the gun to be fired while mounted behind the propeller of an airplane without the bullets striking the blades of the propeller. This mechanism was the first successful design that ensured safe firing of machine guns while in flight. As a result of these improvements, the Marlin–Rockwell Corporation, which was already tooled for large production of the Colt gun, was requested to turn out quantities of the newly designed Marlin Model 1917 gas-operated aircraft machine gun. In August 1917, the new guns were tested at the front in France. On February 28, 1918, General Pershing sent the following message with regard to the guns' performance: "Marlin aircraft guns have been fired successfully on four trips at 13,000 and 15,000 feet altitude, and at temperatures of minus 20 degrees F. On one trip guns were completely covered with ice. Both metallic links and fabric belts proved satisfactory."

By May 1918, Marlin–Rockwell had manufactured nearly 17,000 aircraft guns with synchronizing attachments. Thirty days later, the total had reached 23,000. On October 1, 1918, the entire order of 38,000 had been delivered.

On May 24, 1916, a verbal agreement between J.M. and M.S. Browning, the Colt Company, and the Marlin Arms Corporation was made that a royalty of one half — $3.75 — to the Brownings and one half — $3.75 — to the Colt Company would be paid for each machine-gun-belt-loading machine sold by the Marlin Arms Corporation. The ones sold to the Russians are marked *SHAW LOADING MACHINE for MARLIN BROWNING LINKS, Mfg. by Sargent and Company, New Haven, Connecticut, U.S.A., 8 m/m.*

On November 2, 1918, General Pershing cabled the following: "Marlin guns now rank as high as any with pilots and are entirely satisfactory."

Marlin airplane prepared for test of bomb release mechanism. Bombs can be seen hanging vertically on right-hand side just below rear cockpit (see arrow).

Army float plane marked Marlin Flying Corps *being launched for test of Marlin machine gun and Barlow bombs.*

Because of the success of the manufacture and performance of the Marlin Model 1917 aircraft machine gun, the government did not push production of the previously ordered Browning machine gun from Marlin-Rockwell. Only a few hundred of the new Browning machine gun were manufactured by Marlin-Rockwell before the end of the war.

MODIFYING MACHINE GUNS FOR TANKS

In the spring of 1918, the Ordnance Department recognized a demand for machine guns to be used in tanks. Many different makes of guns were considered. But since Marlin aircraft machine guns were available within the Air Service, the Ordnance Department decided to modify them by adding sights, hand grips, triggers, charging handles, and aluminum barrel

covers having fins to radiate the heat from firing the gun in an enclosed vehicle and gun mount.

On February 28, 1918, the Ordnance Department asked Marlin-Rockwell to assemble one Marlin machine gun modified for tank service. The gun was to have a heavy barrel (Navy type), old-type pistol grip, and a rate of fire as slow as was possible.

In April 1918, the development of the Marlin Model 1918 tank gun started. By October 23, 1918, only 171 had been shipped. On October 30, 150 more were to be ready for shipment. The problems of adapting an aircraft gun to a tank gun were numerous and were oversimplified by the Ordnance Department. The manufacturer also had problems with the many bureaucratic agencies that get involved with such a project. The record reflects that there was confusion, indecision, and

Marlin Rockwell Corporation Aviation Department planes and personnel.

Marlin Rockwell Corporation Aviation Department personnel outside shop building.

plain "dragging of heels" in this important project to equip U.S.-manufactured tanks with adequate U.S.-manufactured armaments. Marlin-Rockwell was not totally free from criticism. It appears that by the end of the war only about 1,470 Marlin Model 1917 aircraft machine guns were modified to the Model 1918 tank gun.

The total WW I Marlin Arms Corporation and Marlin-Rockwell Corporation production of guns for the U.S. government was as follows:

Colt Model 1914 Machine Guns	2,500
Marlin U.S. Navy Mark V Heavy Barrel Machine Gun	1,605
Marlin Model 1917 Aircraft Machine Guns	38,000
Marlin Model 1918 Tank Machine Guns	2,646
Browning Automatic Rifles	16,000
Total	60,751

It is interesting to note here that in February 1936, during hearings before the Seventy-Fourth Congress's special committee investigating the munitions industry, a letter dated December 16, 1933 by Albert Foster, Jr., sales manager of Colt's Patent Fire Arms Manufacturing Company, to the vice president of Colt was introduced. This letter stated the following about the disposition of the Marlin machine guns after the U.S. government had sold them as scrap: "He [Major McLaughlin] told me that the people who had quoted him on The Marlin gun were the H.H. Kiffie Company of 500 Broadway, N.Y.C., and it developed that it was just as expected, that these were the old guns which were sold by the U.S. Government after they were supposed to have made them useless for machine guns and that they had been worked over by Sedgley. . . ."

Interestingly, the R.F. Sedgley Company, Philadelphia, Pa., also made classic sporting rifles during the 1920s and 1930s using government surplus Model 1903 rifle parts and low-numbered (condemned) receivers.

EXPANSION AND DIVERSIFICATION

By December 1919, the Marlin-Rockwell empire had reached new heights in industrial conglomerate diversification. The executive offices were on Madison Avenue, New York City, and the following companies, or divisions, made up the corporation:

Standard Roller Bearings, Philadelphia, Pa.
Braeburn Steel Company, Pittsburgh, Pa.
Radiator Division (Mayo Company), New Haven, Conn.
Marlin-Rockwell Machine Shop, Tacony, Pa.
Plainville Division, Plainville, Conn.
Heany Laboratory, New Haven, Conn.
Insulated Wire Division, New Haven, Conn.
Marlin Arms Division, New Haven, Conn. (Marlin-Rockwell Corporation)
Marlin-Rockwell Loading Company, Wilmington, Del.
Norwich Division (H&A Company), Norwich, Conn.

The Norwich Division was the old Hopkins & Allen Arms Company converted over to war work, although during the war period any commercial gun parts still on hand were available and some gun repairs were done. At the end of the war, the machinery and fixtures were moved to the Marlin-Rockwell Arms Division in New Haven. The Norwich project was disposed of and the Norwich Division of Marlin-Rockwell no longer existed.

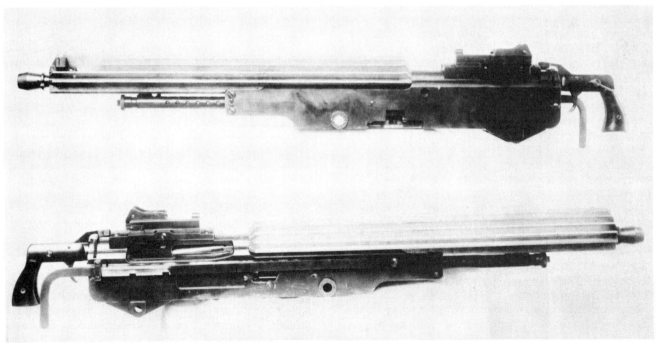

Marlin tank machine gun, Model 1918.

Marlin Model 1918 machine gun as installed in gun mount inside of WW I tank.

The Insulated Wire Division's asbestos wire was based on work originally done by the New Haven inventor J. Allen Heany of Heany Laboratory. Mr. Heany perfected a method of incorporating a core thread of cotton into a sheath of asbestos for strength. The Insulated Wire Division and the Heany Laboratory, which was located in one of the old Eli Whitney arms factory buildings, were combined and at the end of the war were moved into one of the arms division buildings. Early products were wires for electric stoves, heaters, flat irons, and other appliances where heat was a factor.

In 1920, Marlin-Rockwell decided to divest itself of all except its ball and roller bearing businesses. Arrangements were made to sell the Insulated Wire Division, along with Heany Laboratory and one of the large buildings built by Marlin-Rockwell during WW I to manufacture the Marlin machine gun, to a group headed by ex-governor Charles Haskell of Oklahoma. The new company was incorporated as the Rockbestos Products Corporation (the trade name of "Rockbestos" was a combination of "Rockwell" and "Asbestos"). The original building at Nicoll and Canner Streets had a total of 15,000 square feet.

Many aerial photographs of the former Marlin plant in New Haven included the part of the complex of buildings that was the Insulated Wire Division of Marlin-Rockwell Corporation (now Rockbestos Products Company). The photos did not identify which buildings belonged to which company, thereby making the Marlin Firearms Company plant appear much larger than it actually was.

The original Rockbestos plant in New Haven now has over 235,000 square feet of manufacturing floor space, and employs 500 people in New Haven and 800 people nationwide, with plants in three other locations. It continues to be in the forefront of its industry and produces a wide range of cable from .053-in. aircraft wire to 3.5-in. aluminum-sheathed power cable. Customers include electric utility companies, the aerospace industry, commercial and military aircraft manufacturers, transportation industries (locomotive, rapid transit, and railroad), mining machines, and electrical distributors. In fact, some Rockbestos products are now on the moon.

BOMB PRODUCTION

The Marlin-Rockwell Loading Company, Wilmington, Del., loaded bombs and high-explosive projectiles for the U.S. government. In conjunction with the Marlin-Rockwell Machine Shop, Tacony, Pa., and the Marlin Arms Division, Barlow aerial-drop bombs and bomb drop racks were manufactured. The best description of the Marlin-Rockwell bomb-making operation is Assistant Secretary of War Benedict Crowell's report in his book *American Munitions 1917-1918,* published by the Government Printing Office in 1919, as follows:

> The first contract let for drop bombs of any type was given to the Marlin-Rockwell Corporation of Philadelphia in June, 1917. This contract was for the construction of 5,000 heavy drop bombs of the design known as the Barlow, and also for 250 sets of release mechanisms for this bomb. We were able to go ahead with the production of this bomb at this early date since it was the only one of which we had completed designs and working drawings when we entered the war. In November, 1917, this order was increased to 13,000, and in April, 1918, to 28,000.
>
> The Barlow bomb, however, was destined never to cut a figure in our fighting in France. The production was slow, due to the necessity of constant experimentation to simplify a firing mechanism which was regarded as too complicated by the experts of the War Department.
>
> Finally, in June, 1918, when 9,000 of these bombs and 250 sets of release mechanisms had been produced, a cablegram came from the American Expeditionary Forces (AEF) cancelling the entire contract.
>
> In December, 1917, a contract for 70,000 of the size known as Mark II, weighing 25 pounds, was given to the Marlin-Rockwell Corporation. But in June the American Expeditionary Forces advised that this bomb would not be of value to the Air Service abroad because of its small explosive charge, and the contract was cut down to 40,000 bombs which number the Army could use in training its aviators. By the end of November, 1918 bomb bodies of the Mark II size to the number of 36,840 had been completed.

The Standard Roller Bearing Company, along with two added bearing companies, continued in business after the war as the Marlin-Rockwell Corporation. In fact, it was not until 1982 that the Marlin-Rockwell Corporation name was retired from corporate use when the conglomerate giant TRW acquired the company and its bearing companies. It was then known as the Bearing Division of TRW.

The Marlin-Rockwell aviation section, although not listed on its letterhead, did coordinate the fabrication and testing of Barlow bombs and bomb racks and the synchronization of machine guns that fired from aircraft. The division had two hangars, a seaplane, and a Jenny. The seaplane had a large circular logo painted on the side that read *MARLIN FLYING CORPS*.

An interview with Charles Tweed, a flying pioneer in the New Haven area, was conducted by Ev Cassagneres, on May 25, 1970, about early flying history in the New Haven area. The following questions and answers about Marlin-Rockwell explain firsthand the photographs of the aviation division personnel and airplanes:

Question: "What was the story about the airstrip behind your place at the New Haven Terminal?"

Answer: "Marlin-Rockwell had two hangars in there besides ours. The silk mill had been built."

Question: "So the Marlin outfit had the first airport in New Haven?"

Answer: "Certainly. They had the hangars and seaplane and Jenny for their own convenience. They did not operate a service like us. It was for testing bombs and

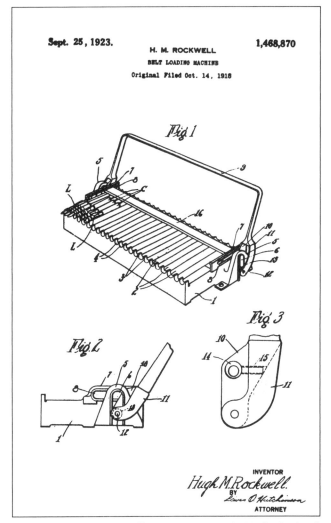

H.M. Rockwell & M. Kovaleff patents relating to the Marlin-Rockwell Corporation machine gun effort.

Frank Burton of the Winchester Repeating Arms Company, right, and John M. Browning, inventor of the Model 1918 machine gun, discussing the Browning Automatic Rifle Model of 1918, which was also manufactured by Marlin-Rockwell.

synchronizing machine guns shooting through the prop. Boy, there was plenty down there. Some wood too, where they missed and firing hit the props. Course they just used wooden clubs many times. A man by the name of Barlow was the bomb man at Marlin at that time. They dropped some in the mud down there."

During the WW I years of the Marlin-Rockwell Corporation's manufacture of automatic rifles and machine guns, numerous patents were applied for. Although issued in some cases many years later and assigned to the Marlin Firearms Corporation, which followed the Marlin-Rockwell Corporation, they are of interest to the collector. The following list, by inventor, includes those patents instrumental in the successful outcome of the war:

Inventor: Carl Gustaf Swebilius

Patent Number	Date Issued (Date Filed)	Remarks
1,402,459	Jan. 3, 1922 (Apr. 16, 1917)	Model 1917 Marlin machine gun
1,422,237	July 11, 1922 (Sept. 24, 1919)	Quick release grip for Model 1917 machine gun
1,422,238	July 11, 1922 (Sept. 24, 1919)	Trigger housing for Model 1917 machine gun
1,444,890	Feb. 13, 1923 (June 11, 1918)	Firing mechanism for Marlin machine gun when mounted on the aircraft
1,450,653	Apr. 3, 1923 (June 11, 1918)	Trigger mechanism for Browning machine gun
1,504,583	Aug. 12, 1924 (July 16, 1918)	Feed mechanism for Marlin aircraft machine gun
1,565,826	Dec. 15, 1925 (May 15, 1919)	Trigger mechanism for Browning Automatic Rifle (BAR)
1,571,975	Feb. 9, 1926 (May 29, 1920)	Extractor for BAR
1,601,514	Sept. 28, 1926 (May 20, 1920)	Sear mechanism for BAR

Inventor: Hugh M. Rockwell (son of A.F. Rockwell)

Patent Number	Date Issued (Date Filed)	Remarks
1,337,327	Apr. 20, 1920 (Sept. 14, 1918)	Gun mount that holds two BAR rifles together in a flexible aircraft mount
1,468,870	Sept. 25, 1923 (Oct. 14, 1918)	Machine-gun-belt-loading machine
1,483,987	Feb. 19, 1924 (Dec. 16, 1918)	Turret mount for automatic guns
1,496,324	June 3, 1924 (June 11, 1918)	Synchronizer for aircraft-mounted machine guns
1,558,566	Oct. 27, 1925 (Jan. 17, 1919)	Trigger mechanism for turret-mounted Browning machine gun

Patent Number	Date Issued (Date Filed)	Remarks
1,565,756	Dec. 15, 1925 (Jan. 17, 1919)	Reduced-length buffer for Browning machine guns

Inventor: Willard B. Darton

1,335,487	Mar. 30, 1920 (Nov. 1, 1918)	Device that prevents a cartridge jam in Colt and Marlin machine guns

Inventor: I. Michael Kovaleff

1,412,287	April 11, 1922 (Nov. 4, 1918)	Attachment for machine guns that held cartridge belt before and after firing

Some references state that the Marlin-Rockwell Corporation did not have any interest in the commercial sporting firearms business, and that when the contracts with the U.S. government for military arms were either completed or cancelled, it wanted to unload the gun division. This is not so, as there are examples of firearms marked Marlin-Rockwell. One example is the Model 27 rifle, which was marked *Marlin-Rockwell Corp., New Haven, CT, USA, PAT'D. NOV. 29, 1904, MAR. 24, 1908, JULY 11, 1911* on the barrel and *MARLIN MOD. 40* on the top tang.

Another indication that Marlin-Rockwell intended to continue in the sporting arms business is an insert it placed in the Marlin Fire Arms Company 1915 catalog (no new catalogs were printed from 1916 to 1919), which stated the following:

—— NOTICE ——

This Catalog is not up to date and most models cannot be furnished. Our entire plant has been given over to the service of the Government for the past two years.

Preparations are now being made for again taking up the manufacture of sporting firearms and we would suggest that you write us about May 1st for new catalog.

MARLIN-ROCKWELL CORP.

MARLIN-ROCKWELL MACHINE GUNS AND AUTOMATIC RIFLES

Marlin Model 1917

The Colt Model 1914 machine gun, as modified by Marlin-Rockwell for the caliber .30 Model 1906 cartridge and manufactured for the U.S. government (2,805), was designated the Model 1917 and was described as follows:

Air-cooled, gas-operated, full automatic, 250-round canvas ammunition belt, not suited for sustained fire or firing over a parapet on account of the interference of the lever action.

Weight of gun, 35 pounds
Weight of mount, 56.5 pounds
Weight of loaded belt, 15 pounds
Length of barrel, 28 inches
Rate of fire, 450–480 rounds/minute
Ammunition, caliber .30, 1906
Cost, $600 each

In September 1917, 50 Marlin-Rockwell Colt guns were shipped to each National Army cantonment, and in November 1917, 30 to each National Guard cantonment. The 305 guns purchased from Marlin-Rockwell in May 1918 were used on the Russian expedition of the American Forces.

Marlin Aircraft Gun, Model 1917

The design of this model is very similar to the Colt gun, except that it had a straight-line gas piston system. It was sometimes identified in government publications as the Aircraft Machine Gun No. 7.

Air-cooled, gas-operated
Weight: 23.50 pounds
Weight of loaded web belt: 15.25 pounds
Length of barrel: 24 inches
Caliber: .30, Model of 1906
Rate of fire: 680 rounds/minute (full automatic only)

This model of gun could be synchronized with the hydraulic or C.C. synchronizing gear, or with the Spad Type 2 of French design, and compared favorably with the Vickers. Marlin-Rockwell manufactured 38,000 of this model.

Marlin Aircraft Gun, Model 1918

This model is principally different from the Model 1917 in that its single-shot or automatic-fire mechanism, making a slower rate of fire possible, allowed for closer synchronization with four-bladed propellers and the Nelson mechanical gear. The gun had a larger gas piston and cylinder. In addition, the bolt was given a glass hard heat treatment, the bolt pin was changed to a chrome/nickel/steel alloy, the firing pin was redesigned to a longer taper, and the extractor shape was changed to prevent accidental firing. Other features included changing the receiver corner to eliminate twisting of the belt, the use of a key to fire the gun full automatic during testing, and the installation of a jam preventer. The trigger motor was placed at the forward end of the lock container, thus allowing the bolt to be removed without dismounting the trigger motor and carrier, as was the case with the previous Model 1917 gun.

Marlin Tank Gun, Model 1918

The Model 1918 tank gun was an altered Model 1918 aircraft machine gun with the following characteristics:

Air-cooled, gas-operated
Weight: 31 pounds
Length of barrel: 24 inches
Length of gun: 37.5 inches
Caliber: .30, Model 1906
Rate of fire: 600 to 700 rounds/minute
Continuous fire without injury: 75 rounds

The rear sight of this gun was the one used on the Browning Automatic Rifle. The front sight was attached to the aluminum barrel cooling jacket. Both were found to be inadequate and plans were made to change them to the British tube type. How-

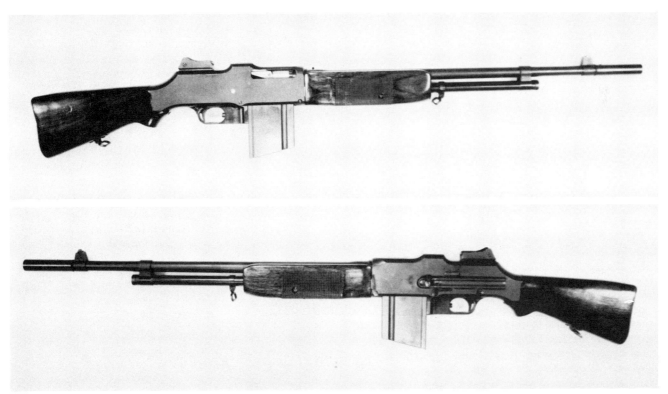

Top: *Right side of Browning Model 1918 Machine Rifle as manufactured by Marlin-Rockwell.* Bottom: *Left side of same.*

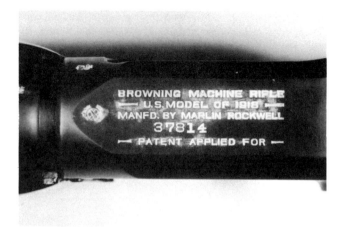

Typical markings on Marlin–Rockwell Browning Automatic Rifle Model 1918.

ever, the war ended and the Marlin tank guns were put into storage and reserved for emergency use.

Browning Automatic Rifle, Model 1918

The Browning Automatic Rifle Model 1918 (BAR) was manufactured during WW I by the Winchester Repeating Arms Company, the Colt Patent Fire Arms Company and the Marlin–Rockwell Corporation. Marlin–Rockwell did not reach its full potential in production of this rifle before the war ended. Of an original order for 131,174, only 16,000 were delivered before the contract was cancelled. This rifle had the following characteristics:

    Air-cooled, gas-operated
    Twenty-round box magazine
    Weight: 19 pounds
    Barrel length: 24^1/$_{16}$ inches
    Overall length: 47^{13}/$_{16}$ inches
    Caliber: .30 Model 1906
    Rate of fire: 500 to 600 rounds/minute
    Sustained fire: 40 to 60 rounds/minute
    Fired from an open bolt

This rifle was well-liked in France; France and other Allied nations wanted to purchase it from the U.S. However, the war ended and contracts were cancelled before full production was reached.

The BAR was manufactured by Fabrique Nationale in Belgium for the Swedish Army in 1921 and the Polish Army in 1928. The last version issued to the U.S. military had a flash hider, carrying handle, bipod, hinged butt plate, front sight cover, and a decelerating mechanism that allowed the gun to be fired at a slow or fast rate. When set on the slow rate, single fire could be accomplished by quickly releasing the trigger. A plastic stock was developed during WW II for the BAR and became standard equipment. A short-lived monopod was also developed for the BAR, and even after the monopod was declared obsolete, manufacture of stocks having a socket for the monopod continued.

ACQUISITION OF THE HOPKINS & ALLEN ARMS COMPANY

The Hopkins & Allen Arms Company (H&A) of Norwich, Conn., evolved from Merwin, Hulbert and Company, after that company discontinued manufacture of firearms in 1898. Previous acquisition by H&A had been made of both the W.H. Davenport Fire Arms Company of Norwich, Conn., and the Forehand and Wadsworth Company (Forehand Arms Company) Worcester, Mass.

Founded in 1867, the Hopkins & Allen Arms Company manufactured rifles, pistols, revolvers, and shotguns. Production reached hundreds of items a day before the company was acquired by the Marlin–Rockwell Corporation in 1917.

It appears that the failure to fulfill the contract to make army rifles for the Belgian government was the downfall of the Hopkins & Allen Arms Company.

With the war in full progress in Europe, it was necessary for the Allied countries to contract with U.S. firms for the production of their war needs. The Belgian government and the Hopkins & Allen Arms Company entered into such an agreement. The rifle manufactured was the Belgian Model 1889 Mauser.

The mechanics of how and when Marlin–Rockwell acquired the Hopkins & Allen Arms Company have never been fully explained. References reviewed are inconsistent and give varying dates and explanations concerning what happened.

The following copies of H&A letters with regard to loss of its plant to another company more closely represent the facts of the matter. They are reproduced here knowing the claims

Carl Gustaf "Gus" Swebilius, 1879–1948.

Takedown, pump action, center-fire rifle invented by C.G. Swebilius.

and statements are biased; however, they are probably more fact than fiction.

40 State Street,
Boston, Mass.
September 15, 1917

General William Crozier,
Bureau of Ordnance,
Army & Navy Building,
Washington, D.C.

My dear Sir:

We desire to bring to your attention the situation today of the Hopkins & Allen Arms Company.

In May of this year, at a meeting in your office at which I was present, Mr. Garcey, the representative of the Belgian Government, stated to you that owing to the promise of the Belgian Government given England, the Belgian Government would not apply to the United States Government for the necessary funds to complete the order for Mauser rifles that they had placed with our Company. Shortly after this, receivers for the Company were applied for, after which Mr. Garcey and others representing the Belgian Government did apply to the United States for a loan. They state that it was provisionally granted, on the condition that the contract for rifles be completed by the Marlin-Rockwell Corporation, and appended to their application, we are told, is a copy of a proposed contract between the Belgian Government and the Marlin-Rockwell Corporation. The Belgian Government would not offer us the same terms. In order to carry out this arrangement, the receivers applied to the Court for an order of sale.

At the hearing on Tuesday, a representative from the Ordnance Department stated that it was the purpose of the United States Government to utilize the plant of the Hopkins & Allen Arms Company at Norwich, Connecticut, for the manufacture of light machine guns and that they had selected their agent for this manufacture, who happened to be the same corporation with whom the Belgian Government had contracted to finish the contract for rifles. On Monday, September 17th, the Judge, I understand, will sign the order that a sale be held on October 17th.

Owing to these proceedings, there is no possible chance for the stockholders of the Hopkins & Allen Arms Company to recover their investment.

We stated to the Court that we should have no objection at all to the Government's taking over our plant and appointing anyone they chose as agents and then settling with the stockholders, but that we did object and did not think it fair for the Government to engineer the proposed deal by which the stockholders, who, by their investment,

have made it possible for the Government to obtain a very much needed plant, received nothing.

Should the stockholders or any concern make a bid at the sale, Marlin-Rockwell owing to the arrangement already made and to which the United States Government is a part, would have a preferential risk by $6,000,000. Even if this $6,000,000 were disregarded, a purchaser would not get the plant, as the Government is to give it to Marlin in any event. If the present scheme is carried out, there will certainly be united objection from the stockholders, and I do believe that before the present scheme of turning the plant over to Marlin is carried through, a reconsideration should be had.

We believe that as the United States is in any event furnishing the money to complete these rifles, the present Company should be kept in possession, with oversight, if the United States Government desires, of army officers or representatives. Whatever type of machine gun is desired could be built in the plant, either by the organization building the rifles or by the Government.

Yours truly,

(Signed) HOPKINS & ALLEN
(Signed) By George D. Haskell

COPY

WAR DEPARTMENT
Office of the Chief of Ordnance
WASHINGTON

In replying to No. 472.5/92

September 25, 1917

Mr. George D. Haskell
Hotel Lafayette,
Washington, D.C.

Dear Sir:

1. Confirming conversation recently had with you in my office, you are informed that it is the desire of the Ordnance Department of the Army to utilize the facilities of the Hopkins & Allen Arms plant at Norwich, Connecticut, for the execution of a considerable order for machine guns.

2. It is my understanding that this plant will be placed on sale in accordance with an order of the District Court on October 17th, next. I hope that there will be nothing in the circumstances or conditions of the sale, or the capacity of the purchasers, which will prevent the Department from placing an order for machine guns with any responsible party who may get control of the plant.

Respectfully,

(Signed) WILLIAM CROZIER,
Brig. Gen., Chief of Ordnance

The results of the October 17, 1917 court foreclosure and sale are unknown, but from the fact that Marlin-Rockwell did take control of the property and the H&A company, and did manufacture automatic guns in the plant, it can be assumed that what J.A. McGregor, George D. Haskell, and Brigadier General William Crozier claimed would happen, did happen.

During the war, Marlin-Rockwell continued to sell some maintenance parts to owners of H&A shotguns, rifles, and revolvers.

After the war ended, Marlin-Rockwell moved some of the H&A machines, tools, fixtures, and gauges to the New Haven plant. The buildings, real estate, and balance of the machines and equipment were eventually sold.

No H&A sales or serial number records survived the transition from H&A to Marlin-Rockwell, and then from Marlin-Rockwell to The Marlin Firearms Corporation, and in turn to the present Marlin Firearms Company. Therefore, Marlin cannot furnish any information about the H&A company and the firearms it manufactured.

Three H&A firearms were considered for reintroduction by The Marlin Firearms Corporation. They were a pistol, a revolver, and a single-barrel shotgun. Please see the chapter on The Marlin Firearms Corporation for details about these guns.

The manufacture of machine guns and war work was terminated in 1919. However, the Marlin-Rockwell Corporation continued a small organization into 1921 to make repairs to Marlin sporting arms, and to sell repair parts still on hand. In August 1921, the sporting arms business and plant was taken over by the newly formed Marlin Firearms Corporation with John Moran as its president.

CARL GUSTAF SWEBILIUS

Carl Gustaf Swebilius was born in Vingaker, Sweden, on April 19, 1879. He came to America when he was 17 and started work as a barrel driller for The Marlin Fire Arms Company. Early on his talents were recognized and he was given

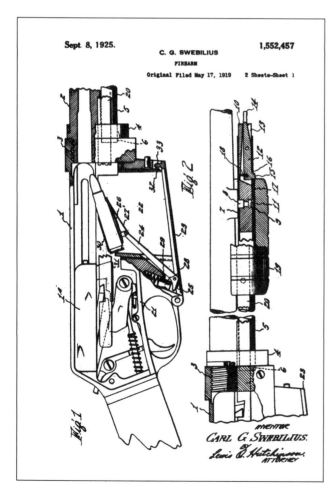
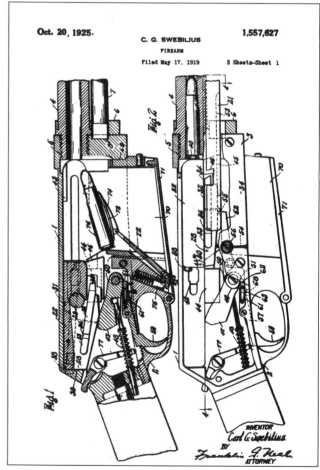

Patent drawings for Marlin experimental rifle.

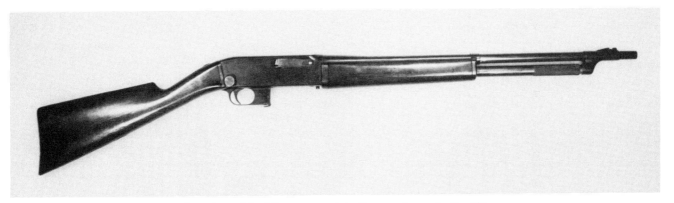

Experimental Swebilius gas-operated, clip magazine, center-fire rifle.

greater responsibilities. He became a toolmaker, design engineer, and finally one of America's leading gun inventors. His patents number over 60, at least 35 of which were assigned to Marlin.

From 1914 until into the late 1920s Carl "Gus" Swebilius was the master designer of Marlin shotguns, caliber .22 pump action rifles, gas and pump action center-fire rifles, and automatic firearms such as the WWI machine guns produced by the Marlin Arms Corporation and the Marlin–Rockwell Corporation.

After WW I, when the Marlin–Rockwell Corporation sold the gun division and the new Marlin Firearms Corporation was formed, Mr. Swebilius was chief engineer and gun designer. Upon failure of The Marlin Firearms Corporation, he was hired by the Winchester Repeating Arms Company to do design work. In 1926 he formed the High Standard Manufacturing Company. The main product of this company was deephole drills, which were used in the gun industry and in other industries that needed to drill holes deeper than standard-length shop drills would reach. In 1931 Carl Swebilius purchased the defunct Hartford Arms Company and entered into the pistol-manufacturing business. His High Standard pistols were used worldwide by competitive pistol shooters. (Major Bill McMillan, USMC Retired, using a High Standard pistol, won the rapid-fire pistol gold medal during the 1960 Olympics in Rome.)

No Marlin employees to whom I have talked were at Marlin during the time Carl Swebilius was with Marlin. However, a number of Marlin employees worked at High Standard during the WW II years and remember him with warm affection and great respect for his leadership, technical knowledge, and humanitarianism. All felt he was their friend, and that he could relate to their position in life and still retain the "boss" relationship that was required to obtain the results and keep the standards he demanded.

As chief designer and gun designer, Carl Swebilius, in addition to his contributions to the Marlin–Rockwell Corporation and design of machine guns during WW I, made major development contributions to The Marlin Firearms Corporation. The Model 37 and 38 rifles and Model 44 shotgun were mostly his inventions. He also made improvements to the Model 20 and 27 rifles and other pump shotguns. Unfortunately, they were not enough to help the company through serious postwar economic times and the added cost of reorganizing and restart-

ing a business that had been dormant for a number of years. However, his gun designs and inventions left a mark on the firearms industry.

Patents issued to Carl Swebilius span the years 1914 to 1945; however, the Marlin-assigned patents include only those up to 1929. His impressive list includes the following:

Patent Number	Date	Firearm
*1,083,708	Jan. 6, 1914	Pump action rifle
*1,090,351	Mar. 17, 1914	Experimental 22 rifle
*1,103,228	July 14, 1914	Pump action center-fire rifle
*1,105,467	July 28, 1914	Pump action shotgun
*1,110,837	Sept. 15, 1914	Model 38
*1,129,527	Feb. 23, 1915	Hammerless shotgun
*1,146,536	July 13, 1915	Model 38
*1,147,659	July 20, 1915	Model 38
*1,147,906	July 27, 1915	Pump action center-fire rifle
*1,149,795	Aug. 10, 1915	Pump action center-fire rifle
*1,150,791	Aug. 17, 1915	Sight
*1,176,873	Mar. 28, 1916	Gas operated center-fire rifle
1,401,568	Dec. 27, 1921	Pump action rifle
1,402,459	Jan. 3, 1922	Machine gun
1,412,298	Apr. 11, 1922	Model 38
1,422,237	July 11, 1922	Machine gun
1,422,238	July 11, 1922	Machine gun
1,444,890	Feb. 13, 1923	Machine gun
1,450,653	Apr. 3, 1923	Browning machine gun
1,504,584	Aug. 12, 1924	Machine gun
1,521,730	Jan. 6, 1925	Automatic rifle
1,550,757	Aug. 25, 1925	Shotgun
1,550,758	Aug. 25, 1925	Shotgun
1,550,759	Aug. 25, 1925	Automatic rifle
1,550,760	Aug. 25, 1925	Shotgun
1,552,457	Sept. 8, 1925	Pump action center-fire rifle

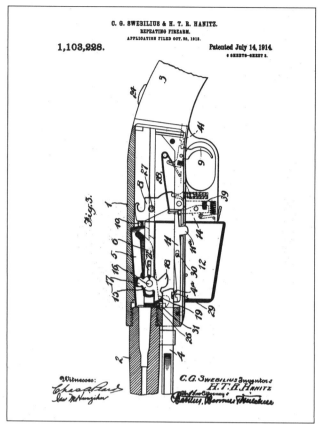

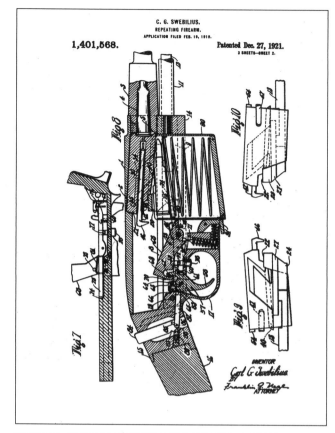

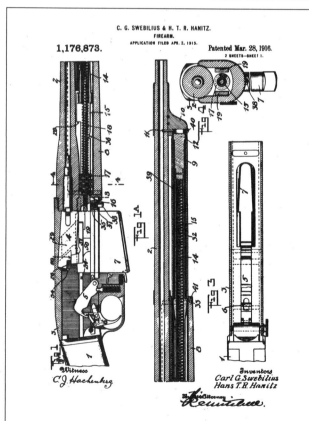

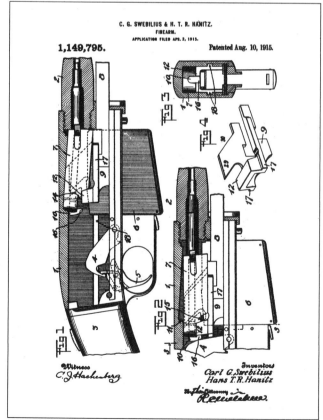

Patent drawings of experimental rifle.

Patent Number	Date	Firearm
1,557,627	Oct. 20, 1925	Pump action center-fire rifle
1,565,826	Dec. 15, 1925	Browning automatic rifle
1,571,975	Feb. 9, 1926	Browning automatic rifle
1,572,450	Feb. 9, 1926	Automatic rifle
1,575,018	Mar. 2, 1926	Model 36, single-shot
1,575,019	Mar. 2, 1926	Shotgun
1,578,777	Mar. 30, 1926	Model 39 ejector
1,587,049	June 1, 1926	Model 38
1,601,514	Sept. 28, 1926	Browning automatic rifle
1,702,063	Feb. 12, 1929	Model 38

*In conjunction with H.T.R. Hanitz, gun designer and engineer with Marlin-Rockwell Corporation and the first Marlin Fire Arms Company.

Carl "Gus" Swebilius died on October 18, 1948. His will reflected his great concern for man. After valuable trusts were established for members of his family, the balance of his great wealth was directed toward the betterment of man through medical research. Today a son and grandson operate a deep-hole-drilling company that continues the Swebilius tradition of excellence and quality.

Although no Carl Swebilius inventions or designs are still in production today, his contribution to the history of Marlin and the fine firearms it manufactured left a mark that has not been surpassed.

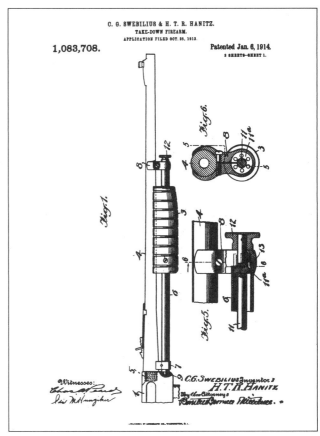

Patent for unknown Marlin experimental rifle.

The Marlin Firearms Corporation
FOUNDED 1870·RE·ORGANIZED 1921

CABLE ADDRESS
"MARLIN NEWHAVEN"

OFFICES & WORKS
NEW HAVEN, CONN.,U.S.A.

The Marlin Firearms Corporation

A NEW CORPORATION

At the end of WW I, the Marlin-Rockwell Corporation began divesting itself of all its holdings except the ball bearing companies. The process took place from 1919 to 1921. However, during this period, Marlin-Rockwell did try to take advantage of the prewar material, parts, and unfinished firearms still on hand from when it purchased the original Marlin Firearms Company in 1915, and made and sold a few sporting firearms with the Marlin-Rockwell name marked on them. Some noted have been the Model 97 (serial number 314,060); the Model 38; and the Model 36, a single-shot pump rifle (like the Model 18, except with a dummy magazine and single shot). There was also the Model 27S, but it is not marked *Model 27-S* on the top tang. Instead, it is roll-stamped on the barrel *Marlin-Rockwell Corp.* and *Model 40* on the top tang.

The last New Haven city directory listing of the Marlin--Rockwell Corporation was in 1920. Officers were listed as Albert F. Rockwell, president; Edgar Park, vice president; Louis Stoddard, vice president; Erroll Kerr, secretary; T.W. Farnum, treasurer; John E. Owsley, assistant treasurer; E.E. Neal, general manager.

The first listing in the city directory of The Marlin Firearms Corporation was in 1922. The officers listed were John F. Moran, president; Reuben Hill, vice president and secretary; Thomas M. Steele, vice president; and Robert C. Baird, treasurer.

This new corporation was incorporated in Delaware on July 23, 1921. (To more easily distinguish The Marlin Firearms Corporation from the other Marlin organizations, it is referred to here as the Corporation.)

A November 15, 1921, announcement in *Arms and the Man* magazine about the new corporation was as follows:

NEW ARMS CO. FORMED

A new company, known as the Marlin Firearms Corporation, has purchased the former Marlin Firearms plant in New Haven, and has acquired all of the machinery, tools, fixtures, gauges, patents, good-will, inventory, etc., of the Marlin firearms business, which has heretofore been conducted by the Marlin Firearms Company and the Marlin-Rockwell Corporation.

The business was originally established in New Haven by John M. Marlin, in 1870, and was carried on successfully by the Marlin family until 1916, at which time the plant was acquired by the Marlin-Rockwell Corporation and used principally for the manufacture of machine guns throughout the war. The Marlin plants were recognized as the largest producers of machine guns in the world.

The new corporation will manufacture the full Marlin line of repeating rifles and repeating shotguns, also single shot rifles, single guns, double guns and revolvers.

The work of reorganization is already under way and the company expects to progress rapidly, reestablishing the business so that within a short time the plant will be able to operate with a force of three hundred (300) or more men in regular production.

The Marlin Firearms Corporation was organized under the laws of Delaware and has an authorized capitalization of

14,000 shares of preferred stock (par value of $50.00 per share) and 27,500 shares of common stock.

The president of the new company, John F. Moran, is no newcomer in the firearms game, having been associated with the old Marlin company for many years.

The January 31, 1922 appraisal of the new corporation was as follows:

Extract from Appraisal of the Plant of
THE MARLIN FIREARMS CORPORATION
Prepared by Fletcher-Thompson, Inc.

	Replacement Value	Present Value
Land	18,000.00	18,000.00
Buildings & Building Equipment	420,645.00	354,260.75
Miscellaneous Construction	28,424.00	23,500.41
Underground Piping	15,000.00	11,250.00
Machinery	402,903.00	261,356.10
Machinery not in use	236,760.00	133,460.00
Furnaces & Forges	19,750.00	13,995.00
Power Transmission	19,561.00	16,317.60
Power Feed Wiring & Trans. Equip.	12,000.00	10,800.00
Special Tools	1,314,600.00	763,980.00
Small Tools	90,487.00	65,723.50
Automobile Trucks	1,650.00	1,650.00
Factory Furniture & Fixtures	34,305.00	28,687.00
Office Furniture & Fixtures	10,470.00	9,282.50
Oil Systems	6,375.00	6,000.00
Electro-Types, etc.	3,500.00	3,500.00
Drafting Room Equipment	1,645.00	1,480.50
Rifle Range Equipment	2,950.00	2,710.00
Pickle House	750.00	750.00
Magnetic Chuck System	2,000.00	1,800.00
Instruments, Clocks, etc.	1,750.00	1,575.00
Miscellaneous Effects	56,525.00	29,952.00
Total #1	2,700,050.00	1,760,030.36

	Replacement Value	Present Value
Materials on Hand		
Marlin Firearms Materials	375,000.00	375,000.00
H&A Materials	75,000.00	75,000.00
Total #2	450,000.00	450,000.00
Miscellaneous Assets		
Wood Patterns	50,000.00	25,000.00
Original drawings and tracings	100,000.00	75,000.00
Gun Stock Patterns	1,500.00	750.00
Model Guns & Pistols	78,000.00	78,000.00
Total #3	229,500.00	178,750.00
Grand Total (Totals #1–#2–#3)	3,379,550.00	2,388,780.36

John F. Moran, president of The Marlin Firearms Corporation.

	Replacement Value	Present Value
Assets Held in Abeyance		
Model #95 and H&A Tools	312,500.00	159,500.00
H&A Materials	75,000.00	75,000.00
Total Assets held in Abeyance	387,500.00	234,500.00
GRAND SOUND TOTAL	2,992,050.00	2,154,280.36
Deduct Non-Insurable Items		
Land		18,000.00
Excavations, Foundations, etc.		67,871.50
Underground Piping		11,250.00
Total		97,121.50
TOTAL NET INSURABLE VALUE January 31, 1922		2,057,158.86

The March 31, 1922 balance sheet of this new corporation was as follows:

Stock certificate of The Marlin Firearms Corporation.

BALANCE SHEET as of March 31st, 1922

ASSETS

CURRENT ASSETS:

Cash in bank and on hand ...$	20,192.02	
Accounts receivable — customers...............	23,093.95	
Notes receivable — due from Metropolitan Finance Corp. on stock purchase agreement	135,000.00	
Accrued interest receivable ...	3,812.51	
Total current assets...........		$182,098.48

INVENTORIES

Raw material, work in process, and finished products..$	541,237.46	
Supplies	10,302.95	
		551,540.41
Total current and working assets		$ 733,638.89

PLANT ASSETS

Land, buildings and building equipment ....$	375,917.79	
Dies, jigs, fixtures, special tools	766,632.92	
Machinery and equipment ...	419,721.94	
Miscellaneous construction...	36,550.41	
Models, patterns and drawings................	178,750.00	
Miscellaneous factory equipment	36,015.88	
Power transmission.........	16,494.60	
Transformer equipment and feed winding	11,135.84	
Small tools.................	67,852.38	
Electros	3,500.00	
Office and factory furniture and fixtures	41,798.26	
Total plant property.....	$1,954,370.02	
Less reserve, for depreciation .	17,229.06	
		$1,937,140.96

DEFERRED CHARGES:

Hopkins & Allen development expense................$	2,022.20	
Organization expenses.......	9,561.54	
Uncompleted development expenses................	20,223.18	
Prepaid interest............	553.84	
Unexpired insurance premiums...............	3,032.20	
Advanced traveling expenses..	660.67	
		36,053.63
		$2,706,833.48

LIABILITIES

CURRENT LIABILITIES:

Notes payable — bank........$	100,000.00	
Notes payable — other........	25,000.00	
Accounts payable — trade creditors and others	24,558.73	

Typical Corporation barrel marking on center-fire lever action rifle.

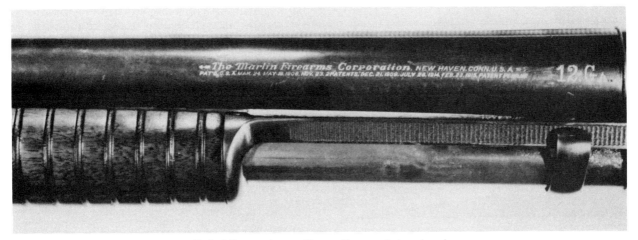

Typical Corporation marking on 12-gauge shotgun barrel.

Accrued accounts:
Excise taxes	1,359,07
Commission	315.41
Taxes (City)	2,137.15
Interest	1,819.01
Payroll	7,787.60
Compensation insurance	302.68

Total current liabilities........... $ 163,279.65

REAL ESTATE MORTGAGE (maturing
$75,000 in 1922 and $100,000 in 1923) ..... $ 175,000.00

CAPITAL STOCK AND SURPLUS:
Preferred capital stock—8%
cumulative (authorized,
14,000 shares of $50.00
each)...................
Outstanding 12,000 shares ...$ 600,000.00
Common capital stock
(authorized 27,500 shares,
no par value)............ Nil
Outstanding—26,500 shares
Capital Surplus............ 1,768,553.83

2,368,553.83

$2,706,833.48

I hereby certify that the foregoing statement of Assets and Liabilities of the Marlin Firearms Corporation is a true and correct statement thereof as shown by the books of said corporation at the close of business on March 31st, 1922.

ROBERT G. BAIRD,
Treasurer.

JOHN MORAN'S EFFORTS

John Moran was not new to the firearms industry. He joined the Marlin–Rockwell operation when it acquired the Mayo Radiator Company of New Haven. During the war, Mr. Moran held the position of ordnance manager in the Marlin–Rockwell operation, and he was well trained in marketing. The Marlin Firearms Corporation's sales philosophy and John Moran's sales policy are best illustrated by an article he wrote and had published in *The Sporting Goods Salesman* in September 1922. It read as follows:

MODERN IDEAS IN GUN SALES
The Sales Policy of Marlin Arms Begins With the
Design of Product
by John F. Moran, President,
The Marlin Firearms Corporation
If a man comes into your store tomorrow and says "Show me the instantaneous take-down feature of the Model 38 Marlin .22 Caliber repeater," the reason for this inquiry has a

Typical Corporation marking on Model 29N, 37, and 47 rifles.

Photo, circa 1920, of the Marlin Firearms Corporation building.

decided bearing upon the relations of the man behind the counter with the prospective gun purchaser.

The reason is partly because some of you salesmen behind the counter are not keeping up with the times and with your opportunities by having full information regarding the latest developments in firearms manufacture.

The average man buys only one or two guns in a lifetime — guns of the quality of Marlin arms will last throughout several generations, with reasonable care and ordinary use. It is therefore extremely important that, when a customer asks your advice in the selection of his gun, you should be able to place in his hands the gun that gives him the best possible investment in design, material, workmanship, equipment and accuracy within the limitations of his purse, taking into consideration the kind of game to be hunted, the territory over which he will hunt, and the limits of the open season.

While there are thousands of salesmen who are entirely familiar with the features of construction of all modern high-grade firearms, we find that there are other salesmen who are not so well informed and who depend entirely upon the customer to indicate his own preference in the purchase of a rifle, shotgun, revolver or pistol.

In many stores a purchaser who came in to purchase a .22 caliber repeating rifle would be shown whatever .22 repeaters the dealer had in stock, without comment or recommendation on the part of the salesman.

This is unfair to the customer, who very often depends upon the salesman's superior knowledge to help him select a gun which will last him throughout his lifetime.

The man behind the counter should accordingly be thoroughly familiar with the advantages of Marlin firearms. It is our purpose, through the personal demonstrations by our salesmen and through our contact with the dealers through trade publications and direct by mail, to inform every salesman of the many superior features in Marlin arms. If you will in turn discuss these Marlin features with your prospective customers, you can help them to make an intelligent choice and you can make them permanent, satisfied customers.

The sales policy of The Marlin Firearms Corporation takes into consideration the interests of the man behind the counter, as well as the best interests of the consumer. In all of our advertising and in our direct-by-mail contact with the ultimate consumer we discuss fully the importance of accuracy, of proper proportions in the gun, of the various types of

construction and the reasons why Marlin guns are made as they are. All Marlin guns are sold by the man behind the counter — we sell only through the legitimate trade — but we endeavor to save your time and help you in making sales by giving the consumer such information in advance of his visit as will enable him to intelligently understand the superior features of Marlin guns.

We are not satisfied merely to talk about "right goods at right prices." We do not depend upon the tradition behind our line of firearms to effect the sale. The shooter should not say "I know the Marlin is a good gun — it has 50 years of prestige as the most accurate of all American firearms — give me a Marlin," and it is not enough for the man behind the counter to say "Here is a Marlin rifle — the most accurate of all repeating rifles — you will surely be satisfied if you buy a Marlin, because of its 50 years of prestige." This would not justify the sale of a Marlin .22 hammerless rifle to a man who wanted a Marlin .22 repeater with a visible hammer. The man behind the counter should know whether this particular customer would best be served with a lever action or slide action rifle, or with a rifle having visible hammer or a hammerless rifle.

It is easy to say to your customer "Here are three or four leading makes of .22 caliber rifles — take your choice." This is putting the choice entirely up to the customer — it is not giving him the benefit of your own practical knowledge.

Our entire sales plan is based upon making guns that meet every possible requirement of the average shooter under normal conditions — making guns better in design, equipment, workmanship and of greater accuracy than competitive arms, yet selling them at fair prices, which are often lower than competitive prices.

Take our .22 caliber repeating rifle, for example. There are more .22's sold than any other type of repeating rifle — and our hammerless .22 repeater is the most modern and up-to-date gun of its kind. The hammerless type is the most popular because it is the most modern. In designing this gun we eliminated all unsightly screws and pins in the receiver, making a very symmetrical and pleasing appearance. We made this gun with a pistol grip — a full pistol grip that fits the shooter's hand perfectly. We put on a genuine hard rubber buttplate because it is better than composition buttplates. We raise the grain of the wood and give it an extra coat of varnish beyond competitive arms because we want our guns to show the superiority in workmanship as well as in design and equipment.

An essential in .22 caliber rifles is accuracy. All of our rifles have the famous Ballard rifling, making them the most accurate of all repeating arms in their respective types. The effect of the accuracy of a rifle is often lost by equipping the rifle with inferior sights; therefore, all Marlin .22 repeaters have Ivory bead front sights and Rocky Mountain or other rear sights of superior quality.

With a .22 caliber rifle your customer will want to shoot at small game and targets up to 50 yards with .22 short cartridges; and with the .22 long-rifle cartridges up to 200 yards, on account of the greater accuracy of this cartridge at the increased ranges. Therefore, we make all of our .22 repeater rifles to use, interchangeably, the .22 short, .22 long and .22 long-rifle cartridges. Any man or boy can shoot better with a gun having the standard (24 inches) length barrel and a full length buttstock — therefore, we use no short length barrels and no stubby buttstocks on any of our guns. The shooter is not handicapped in any way when he uses a Marlin gun.

Through our extensive advertising we are telling millions

of shooters of the superior features of Marlin guns. We are telling them to insist on seeing these features of Marlin guns. We have told them to put the Marlin gun alongside any competitive arm and compare the guns point by point, which comparison will invariably result in the selection of the Marlin gun. And finally, after making clear the general superiority of Marlin arms, we tell the prospective purchaser, in our advertisements, the retail price of Marlin guns at your store—because we have made the prices of Marlin guns sensible, satisfactory prices, which will be a further help to you in securing their orders.

Your time is worth money! By knowing your goods thoroughly you can explain to your customer convincingly, in the fewest possible words, the advantages of the gun which you know to be best for his purpose. In our advertising we have boiled down our sales points into the fewest possible words. By familiarizing yourself with these selling features of Marlin arms, you can close your sales quickly and save your valuable time and at the same time satisfy your customer.

The reason why we advertise to the consumer all of the points of contrast and superiority between our arms and others is partly because this is the best kind of sales talk—and partly because many men behind the counter are not as familiar with guns as they should be.

It is our custom to mail out to the salesmen behind the counter from time to time various "selling helps," for which we make no charge. This literature is proving of great assistance to the gun salesman, in that it goes a great way in assisting him to perfect himself in the handling and sale of firearms, assists the salesman in making gun sales, and aids him to become much more valuable to his firm or himself, should he be the proprietor. This material should be in the hands of everyone having to do with the sales of firearms. Boys—we want to work with you—we will be very glad to add your name to our list if you are selling guns.

John Moran announced in 1922 that he expected to build The Marlin Firearms Corporation into the leader of the commercial firearms business. To do this, he tried to use the Marlin-Rockwell Corporation's 1917 acquisition of the Hopkins & Allen Arms Company to promote an expanded line of firearms and an improved image of the Marlin company.

Included in a brochure distributed to dealers and jobbers of the period was a reprint of a July 1922 *Field and Stream* article by Edwin O. Perrin. Although I feel it is inaccurate, it included the following about the newly organized Marlin Firearms Corporation:

MARLIN HAS PURCHASED HOPKINS AND ALLEN FIREARMS BUSINESS

By its recent acquisition of the Hopkins & Allen Arms Company, The Marlin Firearms Corporation (which is 52 years young in its production of the famous Marlin firearms) has now taken its place as one of the oldest manufacturers of firearms in this country, for the Hopkins & Allen arms carry their tradition of gun manufacture back 100 years.

The Hopkins & Allen Arms Company was an industry located at Norwich, Connecticut since the early '40's. It was the successor of a number of firms, having at various times acquired other firearms industries through purchase and absorption. One of the best known of these firms was the W.H. Davenport Firearms Company, of Norwich, famous as manufacturers of single barrel shotguns, which they produced in great quantities. Another one of the large firms

1922 Marlin Firearms Corporation ad announcing the return to sporting arms manufacture.

which had been acquired by the Hopkins & Allen Arms Company was the Forehand Arms Company, established at North Grafton, Massachusetts, in 1832. This business in turn had been developed from the earlier gun plant of Ethan Allen, the Revolutionary War hero and one of the pioneers in the firearms industry in America, who, in his later years, was noted as the manufacturer of various rifled target pistols, the Lambert cane gun and also the famous "pepper-box," the first revolving arm made in America. From this arm evolved the modern revolver, in which the cylinder only revolves, discharging its load through a single barrel. Many of the readers of these pages will doubtless remember revolvers in common use years ago, bearing the imprint of "Forehand Arms Company" or "Forehand & Wadsworth."

A study of the many types of firearms that have been manufactured by the Hopkins & Allen Arms Company gives a comprehensive knowledge of the development of American firearms. It embraces the single-shot muzzle loading pistols widely used in the early '40's, and the famous "pepper box" revolver, a muzzle loading percussion cap revolver which even in those early days had the "double action" principle, which shows that this essential principle of the modern revolver is not a new one. It also included a repeating rifle with a revolving cylinder, also various light single-shot muzzle loading rifles and breech-loading military rifles, where the service

Letterhead of Hopkins & Allen Arms Company.

cartridge consisted of a bullet and a charge of powder contained in a paper envelope, the end of which had to be bitten off before the charge was placed in the gun, so the spark in the cap could reach the powder. A great many of these rifles were used in the Civil War.

Single action revolvers, adapted to the same form of ammunition, were succeeded by the "Derringer," which was made in 1870, used metallic cartridges and was very popular, especially throughout the South. Double action revolvers of the powder and ball type were later succeeded by single and double action revolvers of the present types for the greatly improved fixed ammunition. The Hopkins & Allen Arms Company brought out what was said to be the first breechloading double barrel gun manufactured in this Country—a well made, accurate and serviceable arm, adapted to special heavy metallic shells, as fixed ammunition for shotguns had not yet been perfected.

The Company was always progressive, and from time to time the older forms of firearms were dropped as the Company developed more up-to-date lines. The present types of firearms comprise single barrel shotguns, double barrel shotguns, single-shot rifles, revolvers and target pistols.

Specializing on moderate priced firearms the Hopkins & Allen Arms Company in recent pre-war years was probably the largest producer of sporting firearms in America, employing at times nearly a thousand men, which with the labor-saving machinery, permitted putting on the market a high grade line of firearms at a low cost.

The Hopkins & Allen plant and organization, greatly enlarged, was used by the Marlin organization during the War for the production of army rifles and machine guns for the United States and allied countries, and, in the recent reorganization of The Marlin Firearms Corporation, the entire Hopkins & Allen business has now been transferred to New Haven, where manufacture in the future will be carried on as part of the Marlin Firearms industries. The addition of this splendid line of single barrel guns, double barrel guns, single-shot rifles, revolvers, and target pistols, to the famous Marlin line of repeating rifles and shotguns, makes the combined Marlin lines the most complete line of practical firearms in the world.

PRODUCTS FROM H&A MATERIALS

The *Field and Stream* article is largely incorrect, since The Marlin Firearms Corporation did not acquire the Hopkins & Allen Company, and the entire Hopkins & Allen business was not transferred to New Haven. However, The Marlin Firearms Corporation did try to make use of some of the Hopkins &

Safety Police revolver marked The Marlin Firearms Corp. New Haven. Conn. U.S.A.

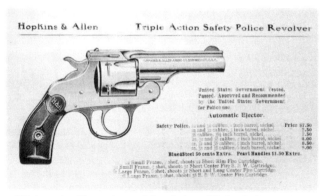

H&A catalog illustration and description of Safety Police revolver.

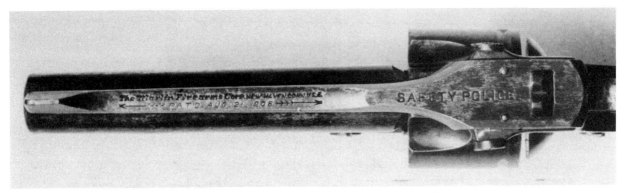

Roll-stamp markings on Marlin/H&A Safety Police revolver.

Allen parts and semifinished guns by finishing them and then adding them to its line of sporting arms. A few single-barrel shotguns, double-action revolvers, and single-shot target pistols, which had been manufactured by Hopkins and Allen prior to WW I, were produced in limited numbers and were marked with The Marlin Firearms Corporation name.

Safety Police Revolver

The Hopkins and Allen revolver assembled by Marlin, like the single-shot pistol and shotgun, grew out of parts on hand. The revolver was the Hopkins & Allen Safety Police double-action, top-break, caliber .38 revolver. Examples examined are identical to the Hopkins & Allen revolver, except for the roll-stamp on top of the barrel. The hard rubber grips have H&A embossed into them, and *Safety Police* is roll-stamped into the top of the barrel extension, above the cylinder. *The Marlin Firearms Corp. New Haven, Conn. U.S.A.* is roll-stamped into the top surface of the barrel rib. Stamped below the company name is ◄«*PAT'D AUG. 21. 1906*»►. The patent marking appears to have been done by an original Hopkins & Allen die,

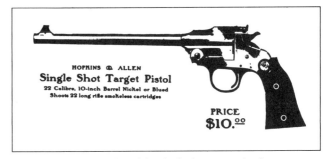

H&A catalog ad for single-shot target pistol.

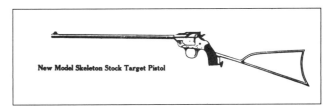

H&A catalog ad for skeleton stock target pistol.

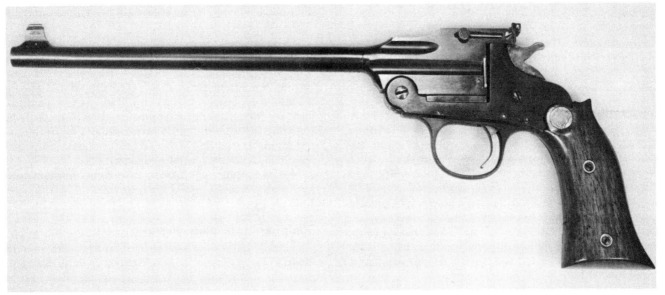

Marlin 10-in. barreled target pistol serial number 2326.

Marlin-marked H&A target pistol in what appears to be an original box.

Roll-stamp marking on top of Marlin target pistol, serial number 2455.

because it is not embossed as deeply into the metal as is the company name.

The patent date refers to patent number 829,082, which was awarded to J.J. Murphy. The main claim in this patent is for a "cam mounted hammer for safety."

There are no records available that can put light on the production of this revolver by The Marlin Firearms Corporation, but conversations with former employees, who could recall at least back to the 1930s, indicate that only about 100 of the Safety Police revolvers were assembled by Marlin. They are now rare collectors' items.

Target Pistol

In 1913, the Hopkins & Allen Arms Company advertised a combination target pistol and rifle. The pistol could be had with a 6-, 8-, or 10-in. barrel in a nickel or blued finish. When the pistol was used as a rifle, the skeleton stock was fitted to the back strap of the grip by a large-headed screw. The rifle stock could be used only with the rifle model, which had hard rubber grips and a back strap drilled and tapped for the stock. The target pistol model had wood grips. Both models had a rear sight adjustable for windage and elevation, and a Lyman bead front sight blade. In 1914, the Hopkins & Allen target pistol sold for $10.

In 1922, The Marlin Firearms Corporation completed some of the unfinished Hopkins & Allen single-shot, top-break, cali-

ber .22 target pistols. The Marlin pistol was identical to the Hopkins & Allen pistol. It had a 10-in. barrel, wooden grips, and single action. The pistol had a blued finish with a case-colored hammer and trigger. A brass insert with the Hopkins & Allen monogram was fitted into the top of each grip. The top-break mechanism and ejector system were identical to those of the Hopkins & Allen Safety Police revolver. The overall finish and workmanship were excellent.

The bottom of the barrel and bottom of the monoblock were serial-numbered. The pistol illustrated here is serial number 2326. This serial number is probably a Hopkins & Allen number that was already stamped onto the parts when Marlin assembled and roll-stamped the barrel. From those pistols examined, and from inquiries for information by pistol owners, one can assume that fewer than 50 were assembled by The Marlin Firearms Corporation. They are certainly rare, and most desirable items for the Marlin pistol collector.

Two examples examined are in a fitted cloth-lined maroon cardboard box that appears to be original.

Model 60 Single-Shot Shotgun

The only H&A model manufactured in any quantity was the Model 712 single barrel 12-gauge shotgun. After a redesign of the stock and forearm, the Model 712 was reintroduced as the Marlin Model 60. A Marlin flyer of 1923 described the gun as follows:

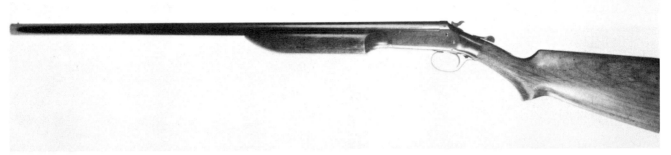

Marlin Model 60 single-barrel shotgun.

The New Marlin Model No. 60 Single-Shot Shotgun is an excellent all around gun which is meeting with the requirements and approval of gun lovers. The Pistol Grip stock is correctly proportioned. The large forend gives the gun an exceptional balance without adding materially to its weight, and is just the right size to permit of an easy and sure grip. This gun is made of the finest materials by expert workmen, and carries an excellent and lasting finish. The standard gun has a 12-gauge, 30-inch, full choke barrel. The barrel is made of Special Marlin Steel, matted on top its entire length—a high grade feature not found on other standard single-shot guns. A Take Down Gun—simply take off forend, swing aside top lever and remove barrel. Automatic Ejection—when gun is opened, the shell is automatically ejected; this method of ejection absolutely prevents shells from sticking in chamber. Handles perfectly all 2⅝ and 2¾-inch 12-gauge shells. Rebounding Hammer—the rebounding action of the hammer—a very desirable feature—provides a safeguard against accidental discharge. Has Compensating Locking Bolt; Coil Springs; Adjustable Main Spring; Patent Snap Forend and Rubber Buttplate. Buttstock and Forend are made of best American Black Walnut, and exceptionally well finished. Weight about 6¼ pounds. 30 or 32-inch Full Choke. Retail price . . . $15.00.

Serial numbers of 21 Model 60s examined have ranged from B138 to B2301, with good distribution through the range. It is speculated that not many more than 3,000 of this model were manufactured.

LOSING THE CORPORATION

In spite of the Herculean effort made by John Moran and his workers, The Marlin Firearms Corporation was headed for failure. Failure to meet payments due on mortgages and other liabilities ($162,279.65 in 1922) caused the mortgage holders to file with the court an action for foreclosure of mortgage against The Marlin Firearms Corporation for its money.

To best explain this never-told-before story, describing the following sequence of events is necessary:

1. Rockbestos Products Corporation (one of the Marlin-Rockwell conglomerate companies) conveys on August 21, 1921, to The Marlin Firearms Corporation, the land and property (less the Rockbestos building) bounded by Willow Street, Mechanic Street, Nicoll Street, and the Rockbestos building in exchange for a mortgage of $200,000.

2. Superior Court at New Haven renders a judgment in the action of *Lillian E. Haskell v. The Marlin Firearms Corporation,* wherein the real estate will be sold at public auction on February 4, 1924 at 11:00 a.m. to satisfy the mortgage she held.

3. On May 10, 1924, Charles N. and Lillian E. Haskell convey to Frank Kenna, for the sum of one dollar and other valuable considerations, the Marlin land and buildings. All unpaid taxes Frank Kenna assumes and agrees to pay.

4. In January 1925, Mr. Kenna conveys to The Marlin Firearms Company for one dollar and other valuable considerations, the property he received from the Haskells in May of 1924. (The premises were subject to taxes on the list of 1925, which the grantee assumed and agreed to pay, and a mortgage, originally amounting to $100,000 upon which $87,500 was due, which the grantee assumed and agreed to pay.)

The 1922 Corporation catalog listed these models: 20, 38, 39, 27, 93, 28, 31, and 42.

The January 1922 jobber's price list included the same models as the 1922 catalog.

A late 1922 sales brochure listed the models available as 20, 38, 39, 42A, 43A, and 44A. (No mention was made of 28, 31, or 42 shotguns.)

The February 1, 1923 dealer price list included the following list of models: 37, 38 (round barrel), 38 (octagonal barrel), 39, 27 (25 rimfire), 27 (25–20 and 32–20), 93 rifle (octagon barrel), 93 rifle (round barrel), 93 carbine, 42A shotgun, 43A shotgun, 44A shotgun, 43T trap-grade shotgun, 43TS Trap Special shotgun, and 44S Special shotgun.

1923 Marlin advertisement for Model 60 shotgun.

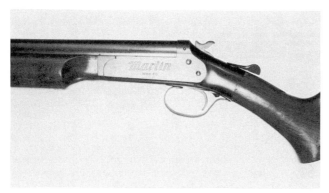

Left side view of Marlin Model 60 shotgun breech mechanism.

Markings on left side of Model 60 shotgun showing President J.F. Moran's approval of word Marlin.

Note that although the Model 39 was introduced during the Corporation period, all 39s, regardless of when made, have The Marlin Firearms Corporation's name on the barrel. (This does not include 39As and others made after 1940.)

John Moran and his staff, even with the genius of Carl "Gus" Swebilius, were not able to start from scratch and build the Corporation into a profitable gun company. The burdens of a large mortgage, back taxes, reorganizing costs, and the costs of restarting a dormant business were too heavy. In addition, the postwar economy left the average person without any funds for recreational purchases such as firearms. The fore-

closure was the final straw and the end of another chapter of Marlin history.

Firearms marked *The Marlin Firearms Corporation* are not uncommon. It appears to me that rather than make all new roll-stamps—which were expensive—the new Corporation used some of the old company's stamps. However, the Model 38 caliber .22 hammerless rifle and Model 44 hammerless shotgun were new guns first introduced by the Corporation. Also, the newly styled lever action Model 39 rifle, which was formerly the Model 97 rifle, was a Corporation introduction.

Plant and General Sales Offices:
79 WILLOW STREET, NEW HAVEN, CONN. 06502

Cable Address
"MARLIN NEW HAVEN"

The Marlin Firearms Co.
Makers of Fine Rifles and Shotguns Since 1870
NEW HAVEN, CONN.

The Marlin Firearms Company: 1924 to the Present

FRANK KENNA, SR., FOUNDER AND FIRST PRESIDENT

This new company was founded by Frank Kenna, Sr., who was born in New Haven, Conn., on June 22, 1874. His father, Thomas M. Kenna, was a Civil War sergeant who had been wounded at Fredericksburg. Thomas Kenna was a pattern and model maker who opened a small company at 22 Whitney Ave., New Haven, after the war. Later he was proprietor of the Seldon House at 440 State Street. Frank Kenna's mother was Ellen Leahy Kenna.

One of Frank Kenna's first jobs was in the advertising department of the newspaper *The Register*. He worked there for about seven years before deciding to enroll at Yale. He graduated from the Yale School of Law in 1905 with an LL.B. degree. After being admitted to the bar that same year, he opened a law practice that he continued until about 1939.

While attending Yale, Frank Kenna published the *Yale Law Journal,* conducted the Kenna Advertising Agency, and worked part-time at *The Register*. His classmates identified him as "the most energetic" member.

In 1912, Frank Kenna realized that current news pictures displayed in store windows would attract passersby to stop and look. The result of this idea was his founding of the Marlin Industrial Division's Illustrated Current News. His first news picture was of Judge McCall presenting a basket of American Beauty roses to Giants Manager John J. McGraw while opening the October 20, 1913 World Series game between the Philadelphia Athletics and the New York Giants. Pictures were changed three times a week. The first manager of the business was Milton Small, who had been with Marlin since he was a boy. Today's Marlin Industrial Division (MID) and Illustrated Current News activity is covered elsewhere.

While actively practicing law, Frank Kenna entered the real estate business. He purchased many pieces of property in the New Haven area as well as outside of the state. One parcel of 19 acres he developed into 70 homes. Others he improved and then sold at a profit. He often had to risk large sums of money, as was the case when he bought 198 houses in Newburg, N.Y.

During 1912 and 1913, Frank Kenna assisted in organizing the American Bank and Trust Company; was a member of the board of aldermen and the state legislature; and was president of the Associated Realty Company, M.J. Jordan Company, Connecticut Finance Company, Mortgage Loan Company, Groton Park Development, and the Illustrated Current News. He was listed in *Who's Who in America* and was a member of the American Bar Association, and the Connecticut and New Haven Bar Associations. With other prominent members of the New Haven community, he founded the Race Brook Country Club. In 1923, he purchased the property of the failed Shoninger Piano Company, at Chapel and Chestnut Streets in New Haven. He used $25,000 of his money and $10,000 credit from the receivers to make the purchase. In only a year and a half, the old piano property was rented to many tenants with small businesses.

Among Frank Kenna's recreational interests were skating and walking. He was active with the New Haven Skating Club and he was a champion walker, successfully competing in local races.

Post-WW II photograph of the Marlin factory buildings. The arrows indicate the building in which machine guns were manufactured during WW I by the Marlin–Rockwell Corporation. The building became the Rockbestos Insulated Wire Company after that war. (Fairchild Aerial Surveys, Inc.)

In 1924 Frank Kenna's real estate interest resulted in his reducing his successful legal practice and expanding his real estate interests. Although it was a legal notice that made the greatest change in the direction of his life, it was his keen sense of business and his ability to recognize opportunity, along with a dynamic personality and untiring energy, that caused him to respond to a foreclosure notice. The notice indicated that the recently closed Marlin Firearms Corporation property was to be auctioned on February 4, 1924 by the sheriff to satisfy the mortgage holders.

Frank Kenna attended the sheriff's sale. He opened and closed the bidding at $100 for the real estate—13 buildings with 140,000 square feet of space and the land on which they stood. The only catch was that there was a $100,000 mortgage on the property. Later Mr. Kenna purchased the firearms business and negotiated the mortgage down to $95,000.

On January 15, 1926, in Connecticut, Frank Kenna incorporated his new firearms company as The Marlin Firearms Company. The incorporators were Frank Kenna, Thomas W. Cahill, and Harold G. Wynne.

The following were named officers: Frank Kenna, president and treasurer; Edward J. Brennan, secretary and assistant treasurer. Members of the board were Frank Kenna, Edward J. Brennan, and Thomas W. Cahill.

The December 31, 1926 condensed statement of finance for The Marlin Firearms Company was as follows:

Assets

Current	$47,327.04
Inventories	137,362.04
Capital:	
Land and buildings, machinery and other fixed assets	389,355.33
Deferred	26,400.00
	$600,444.41

Liabilities

Current	$26,752.28
Capital:	
5-year mortgage bonds	150,000.00
Real estate mortgage	81,250.00
Capital and surplus	
Common stock and surplus (authorized and issued 3,000 shares of no par value)	342,442.13
	$600,444.41

Note: Upon the new issue of $100,000 of 8% preferred stock being sold, the proceeds will add $100,000 to assets and create an additional capital liability of $100,000.

Frank Kenna, in a 1926 stock offer, stated the following about the company:

Wherever men own and use rifles and shotguns, the Marlin name is known and respected, the hard-won result of fifty years and more of successful gun making. It was in 1870 that Marlin was organized, and since that time nearly a million guns have been produced. During these years full advantage has been taken of every improvement (many of them invented and controlled by Marlin), keeping Marlin guns at the forefront of the sporting field. To-day, the Marlin line might well be described by the slogan "a gun for every shooting need."

For forty years Marlin has specialized in repeating firearms, and for thirty years has made repeating rifles with the solid-top, side-ejecting construction (invented by Marlin and for many years controlled by Marlin under basic patents) and the deep, clean-cut Ballard rifling.

The Marlin solid-top construction gives the maximum safety and convenience to the shooter. The simple Marlin repeating mechanism, easy to operate and easy to clean, means real hunting satisfaction.

For twenty years and more Marlin has made high-grade shotguns with the solid-top construction and with shooting qualities that have enabled Marlin users to win national and international championships.

All Marlin firearms have extreme accuracy. The Marlin rifles, with their superior Ballard rifling, are known as the most accurate of repeating rifles, while Marlin shotguns are famous for their quick handling, perfect balance and fine shooting qualities.

Marlin guns are made in New Haven, Conn., in a factory

Marlin building showing the brick and concrete section built during WW I. Note that the water tank is still standing.

Picture of office section of Marlin plant (Willow Street entrance) in which The Marlin Firearms Corporation name has the word Corporation *retouched to read* Co.

which has thirteen buildings and 140,000 square feet of floor space. The great water tower, with the huge sign "MARLIN GUNS" is a familiar landmark to passengers traveling the main line of the New York, New Haven and Hartford Railroad. In this factory the equipment is modern and the machinery specially designed for fine gun production. To this factory come the raw materials that go into gun production. Here they go through more than two thousand operations, shaping, treating, testing and assembling, and here the famous Marlin guns come into being. Each gun is finished to the fraction of an inch, each is tested on the Marlin range, and each is inspected for flaws of material, workmanship and finish. When a Marlin gun leaves the factory, bearing the Marlin "star" stamped in the metal, it is as near perfection as the finest of materials, equipment and skill can make it.

Gun making, while utilizing the latest in machinery and equipment, is still largely a matter of craftsmanship. The secret of Marlin superiority lies back of the great factory with its splendid equipment, in the intangible something we call the human element. Some of the men who actually make the Marlin guns have been with the company more than thirty years. Each of them is a craftsman who knows guns and gun making from start to finish. Each of them is trained to strive for perfection down to the smallest and seemingly most insignificant detail. Each of them takes a personal pride in putting into every rifle or shotgun passing through his hands the finest his skill and experience make possible. Supervising their work is one of the world's best gun builders.

The result of this splendid craftsmanship is found in the popularity of Marlin guns among those who really appreciate honest workmanship and demand it in the articles they buy. Each gun is built conscientiously. One enthusiastic Marlin user aptly described the Marlin policy as "putting the New England conscience into every gun." Each gun that leaves the factory is the kind of firearm you can use with the assurance that you have the best in material, workmanship, accuracy and safety.

The key figures in the recovery of Marlin and restoration of its rightful place in the firearms industry were Frank Kenna, president and treasurer; T.W. Cahill, general manager; Charles F. Sharf, superintendent; and F.E. Bradley, sales manager.

The following is a 1928 letter sent out by Frank Kenna describing his effort to raise money by selling stock:

January 4, 1928

Dear Sir:

A little over three years ago, I became interested in MARLIN because I had faith in the immense popularity of its excellent product and the basic soundness of its well established business. I knew that it was good and that, under competent management, it would prove extremely profitable. Thanks to an expert organization in production and sales, composed of executives who have been identified with the concern for many years, MARLIN has fully justified that confidence.

As proof, I am proud to refer to an increase of more than $45,000.00 in sales for the first ten months of this year, contrasted to the same period of 1926, with a consequent increase in net profits of 80%.

I feel that we have just started. We are capable of doing more than twice as much—and it is going to be done. Plans for the ensuing year involve expansion to meet the increasing demand through more than 450 established Jobbers in 45 states, in Canada and abroad, created by the advertising of the well-known MARLIN guns in twenty-four recognized National mediums.

In order to facilitate this expansion, limited financing has been planned and I take this means of attracting your attention to an offer of definite dividends earned four times over and backed by tangible assets of four for one. Additionally, I invite your careful scrutiny of MARLIN common stock which I have brought up from "scratch," to a 10% basis, with never a deflection, but, on the contrary, a continuously increasing value which will be presently enhanced by the planned expansion referred to.

I offer you participation on an equitable basis that has paid me well—and will do the same for you. I would like to furnish you with a copy of the current balance sheet, the record of earnings, outline of personnel and policy, bank references and details of an offer which is fair and worthy of your careful consideration. If you can visualize the possibilities to-day, as I did three years ago, you will be repaid for mailing the enclosed card which will place all of the facts before you, without obligation.

Sincerely yours,
Frank Kenna, President

Frank Kenna, besides being a firm disciplinarian and one who expected excellence from his workers, was a fair-minded

The Marlin plant in the 1950s.

Frank Kenna, Sr., 1874–1947.

Frank Kenna, Sr., giving out free show tickets to parochial school children.

man who put a lot of faith in people. In so doing he looked at other fields and products to try to find ways to put more people to work and, of course, to make a profit. Some of his ventures were manufacture or sales of bicycles, baby carriages, brushes, razor blades, real estate, shaving cream, children's wagons, and the Marlin Industrial Division with its Illustrated News.

To bring in additional revenue, Frank Kenna leased office space or manufacturing space to a number of companies. Some of them were the following:

Accurate Insulated Wire Company
The Metal Craft Company (electrical fixtures)
D&I Shirt Company, Inc.,
Rollins-Zilsu Company, Inc. (furniture manufacturers)
Willow Shirt and Underwear Company
M.J. Jordan Corporation (real estate)
Cool-Rite Products Corporation (electrical equipment)
Illustrated Current News, Inc. (publishers)
Associated Realty Corporation
The New England Airship Company (inflatable boats)

A November 28, 1944 report by Frank Kenna to the stockholders summarizes his contributions to The Marlin Firearms Company since he first purchased the property and buildings at auction in 1924. The report read as follows:

> After practically fourteen years of constant sacrifice, toil and effort, primarily in behalf of the stockholders of the company, I feel that I have succeeded in preserving for the stockholders, a value for their shares much in excess of what the shares originally cost them, and further, established the company on a sound financial basis, capable of paying a fair dividend annually or semi-annually.
>
> Practically all of the stock now outstanding was issued during 1929 and 1930. Dividends to the extent of fourteen

($14.00) dollars were paid thereon. Then began the long period of depression which in 1933 almost wiped out the company. One of the largest gun companies in the country did go into receivership with the resulting loss of the stockholders' investment.

As a matter of fact, the investment of every stockholder in The Marlin Firearms Company, both the preferred and common, was entirely lost in 1933, but by using every possible means at my command, by personal endorsements, by hypothecation of my insurance policies, by personally borrowing from every source available, and by putting into the company every dollar I possessed, I managed to regain title to the company's real estate, machinery, equipment and business.

No appeal was made to any stockholder, for such an appeal, considering the time and conditions, was useless. The depression was at its depth, and what had to be done had to be done without delay.

Unable to pay real estate taxes due the City of New Haven, amounting to approximately $22,000.00, foreclosure proceedings were instituted by the City. At practically the same time, two other foreclosure actions were started, one by the first mortgage trustee, seeking payment of the sum of $41,875.00, the balance due on a first mortgage originally amounting to $100,000.00; and the second by the second mortgage trustee, seeking to foreclose a second mortgage of $150,000.00. Both of these mortgages encumbered the property when your stock was purchased.

All of these foreclosures, seeking approximately $193,000.00 were fought and defended for months in the courts, while every possible effort that I could make was exerted to find some way of saving the company, its real estate and equipment, and the investment of every stockholder. My own large investment, and the years of effort put into building up the company, were then a matter of secondary importance.

Although I had succeeded in raising funds sufficient to pay the taxes of approximately $22,000.00, these could not be paid in view of the pending mortgage foreclosures.

Again, months of effort were spent in trying to prevent the

complete loss of all of the properties, and these efforts were continued even after the courts had granted foreclosure judgements, and the first and second mortgage trustees had taken title to the property, both the real estate and all machinery and equipment. For more than eighty (80) days we were operating with a sheriff in legal possession of the plant. The real estate was in fact advertised for sale by the first mortgagee.

In the meantime, by means of a loan made to me for which I paid a large bonus, and for which I was personally responsible, by draining other companies which I owned personally, of every dollar they could spare, by pledging my insurance policies, by putting in all of the personal cash I could raise, and by personally guaranteeing repayment unconditionally, I managed to prevent the sale of the properties, by satisfying the mortgagees and the tax claims.

When title to the property, both real estate and machinery, was reconveyed by the mortgagees, although this title could have been retained by me and in fact was conveyed to me individually, it was arranged whereby title was conveyed by me, back to the company, and in fact back to the stockholders.

At no time during the long continuation of the court actions involved, and the efforts made to save the company, were the stockholders appealed to.

Subsequently, a Reconstruction Finance Corporation mortgage of $70,000.00 helped to tide over the difficult years that followed, and today the plant and equipment are entirely free and clear of any mortgage.

The foregoing tells only a part of the many difficult situations that the company has survived, but it may serve to make more clear just what I alone have done in carrying the company from foreclosure and bankruptcy to the present time when every preferred stockholder's original investment has been rebuilt, and the company established in a position where dividends may be resumed.

Each preferred stockholder who purchased four shares of stock paid $100.00. He received a $52.00 shotgun and $14.00 in dividends. His net investment on each $100.00 was $34.00. Today his stock is worth the full par value, on the basis of book value, although it might not sell for this amount in the open market.

We desire to establish the fair non-cumulative dividend rate of 4% per year, and to eliminate dividends unpaid during the several previous difficult years.

I feel that in asking the stockholders to consent to these provisions, considering what I have done to save their investment, is only requesting some small measure of recognition and appreciation for all that has been accomplished by my own unaided efforts.

Frank Kenna, President.

A March 17, 1945 *Collier's* magazine article by D.C. O'Flaherty accurately describes the "Frank Kenna Plan," which was given national recognition by *Collier's* when it printed this excellent article. Of course, Frank Kenna deserved the exposure. To do it justice, the following is quoted from D.C. O'Flaherty's postwar interview with Frank Kenna:

Kenna, whom the New Haven and Bridgeport papers are fond of referring to as the One Man Chamber of Commerce, first devised his plan for meeting unemployment in the thirties, when American business—including his own—was beginning to make hollow noises in its throat. Although he had

Frank Kenna discussing with WW II veterans the possibility of their starting up small businesses with his help. Left to right: *Al Wills, Ray Savaress, Jimmy Ionnuzzi, Chad Hannan, Mr. Kenna, and an unknown man.*

Roger T. Kenna, 1909–1959.

Theodore Lynch, 1903–1965. (Gilbert Kenna)

made a fortune in half a dozen different enterprises, Kenna himself was hard pressed on several fronts. And New Haven was a little bit worse off than many American cities because it had lost one of its largest industrial plants, that of the United States Rubber Company.

Kenna met New Haven's problem and his own by organizing the Associated Realty Company—in which he was associated chiefly with himself—and beginning to buy up all the vacant industrial space he could find, which was plenty. He advertised extensively for small businesses, for young men eager to work for themselves, and gradually he began to fill hundreds of thousands of square feet of floor space with tenants. . . .

Practically all of the concerns started with small capital, some with none. One concern did no more than repair broken peach baskets. Another enterprise was brand new—a diaper service. There were machine shops aplenty, all small, some paying as little as $15 a month rent. New Haven, with Kenna's help in diversifying its industry, licked the depression earlier than some, and those who remember it will admit that it was a right smart depression to lick.

Today, Kenna is owner of a group of thirty-nine loft buildings embracing 700,000 feet of light, well-ventilated floor space in New Haven, housing 110 small industries, most of which started with less than $2,000.00 capital.

In his quest for tenants, Kenna was a tireless advertiser and an omnivorous reader of trade papers. He still is. He went to near-by towns, investigated businesses which had failed—to see if they could be revived in the pure invigorating climate of

Photo of Marlin's assembly room, circa 1930.

Marlin's milling department, circa 1930.

New Haven. He once went to a foremen's association banquet and talked to the members like a Dutch uncle. A man smart enough to be a foreman ought to be smart enough to be an owner, he said. He talked a hand-picked few of them into going down to the bank and borrowing money to set up competing businesses of their own. Being a director and principal stockowner in said bank, Kenna had only to give the nod, and credit was extended.

The nod is all he gives. He doesn't lend money himself and he wouldn't endorse anybody's note. But he will set up bank credit for an individual whom he has spotted as a potential small capitalist and a worth-while citizen. He will do more than that. He will waive the rent, and has done so for as long as a year and as much as $2,000 when an infant business needed all of its cash.

It's obvious that only a shrewd judge of the human animal could pick business winners as Kenna did, but the fact that he did it is attested to by his rent records since he began his industrial center fifteen years ago. The rents total $2,500,750; of that sum he was gypped of $1,759, the record shows, or less than one tenth of one per cent.

There were many failures—due to the usual human reasons and occasional acts of God—but some of the failures paid their rent, or most of it. Sometimes Kenna fell heir to fifty dollars' worth of plumbing supplies, or a water tank, or a batch of ladies' hats. (He gave the hats to his women employees.) But a hundred and ten succeeded and stuck where thirty or forty failed or moved away. For the record, Kenna can rattle off successful case histories by the dozen. His files are full of them.

Kenna's postwar plan for veterans is essentially the same as the one which worked so well in bad times—with this dazzling difference: The returning veteran will probably have a fair amount of money—maybe as much as two thousand dollars—in his pocket plus the possibility of borrowing as much again at the bank, on his character. He will have it all over the guy who had to mend peach baskets twelve years ago. Kenna wants every man capable of doing so to use this money to become his own boss.

The Kenna Plan, if it can be called that, can best be described as a voluntary capitalist co-operative. It would have a group of hard-boiled rich men in every community get together and keep themselves and their communities prosperous by encouraging small, localized industry—varying the blue-print according to the region. . . .

To find likely candidates in New Haven, Kenna has asked the Yale University Rehabilitation Center to point out to him personally veterans most likely to succeed in an independent undertaking.

"Rehabilitation groups," says Kenna, "besides questioning

the veterans who come to them should study business and industrial opportunities in their communities and be in a position to make concrete recommendations. Above all, these groups should rid themselves of any notion that the day of small business is done in this country. They shouldn't simply administer the government nursing bottle to the returned veteran. They should help him to a new declaration of business independence."

It is Frank Kenna's idea that guaranteed jobs are not a good thing.

"I almost hate that word security," he says, although he is a life-long Democrat and argues stubbornly with his son Roger, vice-president and general manager of the Marlin Firearms Company, who thinks it would be more orthodox if Pop, who's president, would vote the Republican ticket.

As a banker, Kenna suggests that there are three vital questions to be asked of applicants for private financial backing beyond that obtainable under the GI Bill of Rights:

Has the applicant selected a business or industry on his own initiative?

Has he saved something in that field?

Has he saved something of his own to contribute, or is he simply willing to let the government set him up in business?

And Kenna would discourage the four men out of five whom he considers unable to meet this test, from investing slim capital in personal ventures. "They are the men who are better off with a weekly pay check," he says.

Kenna has been living his ideas of enterprise for more than half a century. It's a typical Horatio Alger story, except that instead of the typical stuffy, humorless Alger hero, Kenna is a jolly, ruddy Irishman who, at seventy, can still stay up until twelve or one o'clock dancing or ice skating.

Frank Kenna was a civic-minded man who contributed to his community by personal gifts as well as time and effort for a cause. His philanthropic interests were with the rehabilitation organizations and the Red Cross. He was also active with the New Haven Sporting Club, New Haven Skating Club, and the New Haven Country Club. On September 12, 1945, he received from The Advertising Club of New Haven its Golden Key award as the outstanding citizen of the year.

On December 26, 1947, Frank Kenna died. Fortunately, he left sons among his legacies, two of whom later on filled their father's shoes as president of Marlin.

ROGER KENNA'S TENURE

Upon the death of Frank Kenna, Sr., his eldest son, Roger T. Kenna, vice president of Marlin, assumed the leadership of the company.

Roger Kenna had definite ideas about how the company should be run. A born salesman, he concentrated on sales. His outgoing personality and friendly manner resulted in a flamboyant image, which he enjoyed.

Roger was born in New Haven on August 19, 1909. He attended Hillhouse High School, where he played football. After high school, he attended Lafayette College, Easton, Pa., and the Babson Business Institute in Boston. His first job with Marlin was as a razor blade salesman.

The board of directors appointed Roger Kenna to the office of president in 1948.

Roger was a member of the Uptown Club of New York City; Westchester Country Club, Rye, N.Y.; Union League, New Haven; Racebrook Country Club, New Haven; and the New York Sales Executive Club. He was one of the cofounders of one of the most exclusive clubs in the United States—the Young President's Organization. To qualify for membership in this club, one must be president of a corporation before reaching the age of 39, and the corporation must be doing at least $1,000,000 yearly in sales, or employ a minimum of 100 people. Roger Kenna was the treasurer of this 135-member club.

It was Roger's influence that moved the Marlin sales office in 1952 to 715 Fifth Ave., New York City. He felt he could better reach the buyers and distributors of Marlin firearms and razor blades by being closer to the center of the business world. It was he who introduced the Glenfield Products Division and the Glenfield Models for mass merchandisers. He expanded the Sears & Roebuck account and other large accounts with a 50% increase in orders, while other companies

Andrew Constantinople, now manager of Marlin's parts department, in 1969 when he handled all gun service shipments.

Marlin's gun service department in the turmoil of preparing to move to the new plant in 1969.

1969 photo of office entrance to Marlin factory building. The building's date, 1882, can be seen over the archway.

Photo taken of the Marlin plant on the last day of operation before moving to new quarters in North Haven, Conn., in 1969.

were still struggling to recover from WW II. In 1957, the offices moved to 17 East 42nd St., New York City, and then in June 1959 moved back to the New Haven plant.

Roger introduced successful spot radio and cartoon advertising of Marlin razor blades that kept the Marlin name in front of the public. He also marketed Marlin Shave Cream through the Kenro Capitol Corporation. (The name Kenro is taken from the names Roger and Kenna.)

Roger Kenna was an ardent baseball fan. He always had a Marlin box at Yankee Stadium and delighted in presenting Marlin firearms to the outstanding players. He once said, "I suppose you know that baseball stars are among our best customers. That's all right with me because I'm crazy about baseball. Tommy Henrich has a Marlin gun and so does Mickey Mantle. Former stars like Joe DiMaggio and Johnny Mize also use our guns. Ball players are generally good shots and, as most of them are from small towns, they know about guns and have been hunting since boyhood. Me? I like to shoot ducks and have gone after deer on occasion. I've never shot moose or elk or any of that big stuff."

When Marlin purchased the Hunter Arms Company at a court sale in 1945, Roger Kenna was appointed president of the L.C. Smith Gun Company, a solely owned subsidiary of Marlin. He took an active role in trying to save the L.C. Smith shotgun, and the plant in Fulton, N.Y.; however, a devastating flood partially destroyed the old building, which resulted in the demise of L.C. Smith shotgun production and the L.C. Smith Gun Company.

As Marlin's vice president and sales manager, Roger Kenna made a statement from his New York City office on September 28, 1945, that early development of postwar plans and speedy reconversion were being delayed because of a labor shortage. His explanation was as follows:

Official sources in New Haven advise thousands are unemployed, but we are finding it difficult to man our machines. Undoubtedly, the situation will change soon. Eventually we hope to double the number of our workers.

Meanwhile, every effort is being made to keep up with a huge backlog of orders and to meet the new market for sporting guns created by ex-soldiers, which has been strikingly indicated by advanced surveys.

During the war, two new buildings were added to the Marlin plant. New modern machinery has been installed. The works are geared to double pre-war capacity.

The Office of Price Administration has allowed manufacturers to increase prices to distributors 8 per cent over those of January 10, 1942, on rifles and 9 per cent on shot-guns. Distributors, however, may only increase prices 5.35 per cent on rifles and 6.54 per cent on shot-guns, while retailers may boost prices to the public 2.2 per cent on rifles and 3.7 per cent on shot-guns.

For the present hunting season amendments to the Restrictive Act L-286 as of Federal Register, September 1, provides "farmers, ranchers and other persons 150 rounds of .22 rim fire ammunition; 50 rounds of center fire ammunition; and 100 shot-gun shells in any gauge. Farmers and ranchers can get this supply in addition to their regular quarterly allotment."

Roger Kenna's pleasant personality, charm, and "uptown" manner brought him recognition that some might think chic. He was named the 17th "Man of Distinction" in national advertisements by the Calvert Distillers Corporation, makers of Lord Calvert whiskey. At the end of the statement in the ad, Roger admonished the reader that "Whiskey and guns do not mix. Drinking adds to gracious living when the hunting day is over."

Roger Kenna was the promoter of the Model 90 and L.C. Smith shotguns. He also used outside talent in his effort to expand the Marlin line of firearms. Gun designers such as W.H.B. Smith, John Pederson, Eugene G. Reising, Robert Jenkinson, E.A. Kiessling, and others were called on to submit ideas and gun designs for consideration. Some were rejected; however, the caliber .22 tubular bolt action rifle of today came from Mr. Reising and the original round bolt of the center-fire lever action rifle was submitted by Mr. Jenkinson.

Roger was considered a friendly person because he enjoyed life and people. He lived in the posh community of Harrison, N.Y., and commuted between the New York City office and the plant in New Haven. But Roger Kenna knew his business and dared to develop new and different marketing approaches to sell the items Marlin manufactured. Others might have done differently. Few would have done as well.

Roger Kenna died at his home on March 25, 1959, after a

short illness. He was 49 years old. He was survived by his second wife, Dorothy S., and his two sons, John Stephen and Roger Kenna, Jr.

FRANK KENNA, JR.: TO THE PRESENT DAY

Upon the death of his older brother, Roger, Frank Kenna, Jr., was elected by the board of directors to the presidency of the company. He had been on the board since February 8, 1951, assistant treasurer since February 18, 1954, and production manager since May 24, 1956. His brother-in-law, Theodore F. Lynch, became chairman of the board upon Frank's assuming the presidency.

Frank Kenna, Jr. — known as "Frank" by all his managerial staff and workers in the plant — was born at home December 27, 1923. He has a twin brother, Gilbert (a few minutes older than Frank). He was the fifth and last child of his parents, Frank and Vertie Kenna.

Frank attended New Haven public schools and Hopkins Grammar School. He also attended Choate School in Wallingford, Conn., where he completed high school in 1941. He entered Yale University (class of 1945W) but left to join the Marines in 1943. Frank served during WW II with the 5th Marine Amphibious Division in the Pacific Theater. He was honorably discharged in February 1946. He then continued his education at Clarkson College of Technology in Potsdam, N.Y., where he majored in mechanical engineering.

Frank began his career with Marlin as a toolmaker and progressed to assistant to the superintendent, superintendent, works manager, general manager, director, and finally, president.

Frank Kenna, Jr., and Joan Giese, of Hamden, Conn., were married in 1951. They are active in civic and charitable affairs. Interest in the welfare of the handicapped is reflected in their long volunteer affiliation with the New Haven Rehabilitation Center, where Frank is a director. He is chairman of the Center's Planning Committee for the $1,000,000 Building Fund Campaign. He is past chairman of the Building Fund for Hemlocks, and the Easter Seal Society for Crippled Children and Adults. In 1963, Frank was general chairman of the annual

Lobby entrance to The Marlin Firearms Company plant in North Haven, Conn.

United Fund–Red Cross Drive. He is past chairman of U.S. Savings Bonds in New Haven and Middlesex counties, and currently the volunteer Connecticut state chairman. He is Connecticut National Trustee of Ducks Unlimited, an organization dedicated to the preservation of breeding habitat wetlands of the Canadian provinces.

Frank is a past director of the United Illuminating Company, a member of the New Haven Chamber of Commerce, the American Management Association, the Manufacturers Association, the Newcomen Society in North America, the New Haven Colony Historical Society, the National Shooting Sports Foundation, the Hamden Fish and Game Association, the Hammonassett Fishing Association, and the National Rifle Association.

Frank Kenna, Jr., served on the examining committee of Northwestern Mutual Life Insurance Company in 1979 and then as chairman of the committee in 1980. He is a past director and chairman of the Yankee chapter of the Young Presidents' Organization. He is a past director of First Bank and the Second New Haven Bank and a former trustee of the Connecticut Savings Bank.

Frank also is a member of Mory's Association, Inc., the Yale Club of New Haven, the Quinnipiac Club, the New Haven Country Club, and the New Haven Lawn Club. He is a member of Assumption Church in Woodbridge, Conn.

Frank enjoys talking with aspiring young businessmen. He has lectured at the school of management of Boston University, and was for many years an annual speaker at the business school of the University of Massachusetts. In 1978, he was the executive-in-residence at Tulane University in New Orleans, La.

Frank Kenna, Jr., was awarded the Veritas Award in 1979 by the New Haven Club of Providence College. In 1983, he was the recipient of the Jimmie Fund Award. In 1984, he was inducted into the Free Enterprise Hall of Fame by Junior Achievement of South Central Connecticut, Inc., and in April 1986, was awarded the Knights of Columbus Marian Chair Award.

Frank and his wife Joan have six children — Margaret Alene, Cynthia Vertie, Frank III, Herman Robert, Matthew Gilbert, and Christine Joan.

During the 1968 Gun Control Act controversy, Frank Kenna, Jr., in conjunction with O.F. Mossberg & Sons (manufacturer of Mossberg rifles and shotguns) had published in the June 26, 1968 *New Haven Journal-Courier* their opposition to registration of sporting rifles and shotguns at the local, state, or national levels. Their statement read as follows:

> We, as manufacturers of sporting firearms, the primary purpose of which is recreational, are opposed to registration because:
> 1. Registration lists can be stolen or otherwise made available to unauthorized persons.
> 2. Registration information in the wrong hands can result in robbery of legitimate private collections of antique or modern arms.
> 3. The same data can pinpoint those homes without firearms protection, especially in rural or isolated areas far from municipal or state police surveillance.
> 4. Whereas confiscation of sporting arms may seem re-

mote, it is well to remember that dictatorship fears an armed citizenry. That was why the Second Amendment of the U.S. Constitution was written. The Connecticut Constitution, Article 1, Section 17 says: "Every citizen has a right to bear arms in defense of himself and the state."

5. Obviously no criminal will register a firearm.

6. COMPLETE ENFORCEMENT of a firearms registration law would require the wide-spread use of every law enforcement officer of this country plus the armed forces of the United States.

7. Such action as would be required for COMPLETE ENFORCEMENT of a firearms registration law may conflict with both the Fourth and Fifth Amendments to the U.S. Constitution.

8. The cost of registration of 100 million firearms would be astronomical.

Mr. Kenna and Mossberg did agree that the following proposals were worthy of consideration:

A. Three-day waiting periods for purchasing new firearms.
B. Prohibiting mail-order sales.
C. Sales by licensed dealers only.
D. Gun owner identification cards, issued in the same manner as hunting licenses.

On August 8, 1974, Frank Kenna, Jr., was the guest of honor and speaker at the National Luncheon of the Newcomen Society in North America held at Mystic, Conn.

His speech gave the listeners an excellent word picture of the man and his company. The text of his speech was as follows:

My fellow members of Newcomen: The company is honored. We have had a great success and people come up and say, "Now what's the reason for the success of The Marlin Firearms Company?" So I say, "It's very simple – it's astute management!"

The company has had a very strong and positive growth against the durable goods index in the United States and, of course, this is what I suppose we should all measure against. But there are intangibles about the sporting arms business which cannot be measured.

But that's the Marlin Firearms Company – you know, the tangible phase of it; manufacturing sporting rifles and shotguns. Then we have the intangible phase of it, communications. Steve Schramm is Vice President of our Marlin Industrial Division. I notice in your program it says that Newcomen is dedicated to insurance and communications in addition to business and finance. Well, The Marlin Firearms Company is one of the largest, if not the largest, seller of employee motivational communications in the United States. These are employee motivation communications from top management. Probably a lot of you have our bulletin boards in your plants and may not know it. You just pay that monthly bill. Thank you! But the bulletin board or news center, which you have, comes from The Marlin Firearms Company. There is a central picture of current news and the employee sees the management message on either side of it. The message concerns health, safety, welfare, productivity and so forth.

Here are two reasons for Marlin's success: There are today 15,000,000 deer in the United States – a lot of deer. There are 210,000,000 people. They're getting close! We also know that there are 40,000 industries employing over 100 people. So this

Frank Kenna, Jr., with his Marlin Model 1895 and fine Quebec/Labrador caribou taken at Ford Lake, Ungara region of Quebec, Canada. Left to right: Eskimo guides Johnny Sam and Willie Imudluk, Frank Kenna, Jr.

means that our Marlin Industrial Division – our communications motivational division – has a tremendous potential out there and is growing.

In 1870, John Marlin started it all. He was a businessman, an inventor, and they say he was a craftsman, not a genius, but he made up the difference in hard work. He was born in 1836. He was a toolmaker. He went to Colt's, worked for the American Machine Works, and in 1881 manufactured a lever action. Today Marlin has two famous guns – the 39A .22 lever action and the 336 lever-action 30/30, which are really the mainstay of our gun business. One of the first things John Marlin did was to bring out a pistol and he referred to this pistol as . . . the lady's companion, an improvement on the hatpin.

In 1875, he further developed the famous Ballard hunter's rifle. It was very popular. Then he incorporated in 1881 with $200,000 worth of capital stock.

In 1888, quality was the hallmark of the Marlin name and they won an award at the Centennial International Exhibition in Melbourne, Australia. In 1891, L.L. Hepburn invented a .22 lever action – a gun which we still make today and one of our most popular. In 1903, Marlin received the Highest Award of Merit from the Chicago World's Fair.

In 1901, John Marlin died and his sons Mahlon and Howard took over. Things went along for a few years when all of a sudden in 1913, a 1% Federal Graduated Income Tax took effect – temporarily. Well Mahlon and Howard were pretty smart fellows. They said, "This is not going to be temporary!" So they sold the company for one-and-a-half million dollars in 1915. They sold it to a group in New York who formed the Marlin Arms Corporation. At the same time, my father had a company called Illustrated Current News which sold a means of communication used in taverns, where he posted news pictures of ball games and ball scores and eventually this became our Marlin Industrial Division.

The synchronized machine gun was developed at Marlin. This machine gun is shot between the blades of an airplane propeller and is synchronized with it. They used to test these things at an airport in New Haven – and most of the time they worked! Well, Marlin made other materiel during WW I for example they made radiators. At that time they used the Guild System. Let's say you were a good polisher or a good heat treater. You would come and bring your own people into the plant and farm your time out to the company on the spot.

The company went bankrupt in 1923, and then my father bought it in 1924. At the sale the Sheriff said, "Frank, why don't you bid this in?" My father said, "Okay, I'll give you $100." "SOLD!" He bought The Marlin Firearms Corporation real estate and buildings for $100 and a $100,000 mortgage, and this is where leverage really started!

He believed the Edward Harriman rule. He said, "Borrow when money is tight, hoard when money is easy." I've been borrowing ever since! You know when we had recessions in '54, '58, '66, '70 and now '74, the GNP (Gross National Product) went down. But The Marlin Firearms Company has continued to grow. Gentlemen, in those years the prime rate was 7%. It's now only 12%. Not so bad, really, as long as we have a flow of funds. My father sold stock—common stock and preferred stock—to get money to operate the company, so technically Marlin is a public company. We have very, very little stock out—certainly way below the SEC amount that's needed for reporting, but technically we are public because some of this stock is still out.

During the '20s the whole company was sustained by a real estate venture. My father rented out the surplus factory space, helping young people with small businesses, in order to run the company. Of course, we talked about going public, but for some reason we've never done it. In 1932, during the depression, my father was working there with six employees and a lot of red ink. The prime rate then was 1½%. Now what's it going to be—1½% and no work or 12% and full employment? It's a tough situation.

In the early thirties we had two devaluations. One at $20 an ounce for gold and the other at $35 an ounce for gold. The official price is now at $42.22 an ounce, with the unofficial price now at approximately $150 an ounce. It didn't work then and it doesn't seem to be working now.

In 1937 Congress invoked an 11% federal excise tax on every gun made. These monies went into conservation and to this day these monies are going into conservation, because the people in the rifle and ammunition business were among the first to realize that you've got to have conservation in forests, rivers, and streams to ensure the propagation of game. It took them many years before they were successful in doing this, but the industry was one of the early pioneers in conservation. Those of you who are members of Ducks Unlimited know that in 1937 they raised $140,000, and this year $5,100,000 for the propagation of ducks and geese up in the north country. It's tremendously interesting.

Also in 1937, Marlin went into the razor blade business. We stayed in the razor blade business for many years because it was a strong consumer product—until 1968, when we got out of the business because all these young fellows were letting their beards grow long. If you subtract the square inches of shaving, and add a long-lasting stainless steel blade, there's no market.

Well, from 1941 to 1945 we did a lot of war work. We made parts for M1s, carbines, airplane fittings and a United Defense Supply Corporation submachine gun.

In 1945 our Marlin Industrial Division was started under a fellow by the name of Milton Small who is now gone. In 1947, my father died and my brother Roger became president, followed by my brother-in-law, Ted Lynch, as chairman of the board. That's also the year that I started as a toolmaker

and I was hooked. Some of those tools are still used in The Marlin Firearms Company today—just to show the president who he really is. But I enjoyed it. Nineteen-forty-five was also the year we started a very active credit union.

In 1951, I got married and I didn't care whether there was a recession or progression, and after that I had six children. We have three boys and three girls. You've got to say that is excellent planning!

In 1954, following a recession, we did our last war work. We haven't done any war work since then. We manufacture only sporting rifles and shotguns.

In 1955, Marlin really entered the finance business. We are really in the finance business, as all of us are. We had to go into dating, which means that we ship January, February, March, April, May and June, and collect our funds in the fall. We offer anticipatory dating, starting in April at 7%. So we are really financing our dealers and jobbers out in the field. Then, of course, we have to go back to the banks. But we had to do this to stay competitive with the likes of Remington and Winchester, who are great giants—Remington being owned by DuPont and Winchester by the Olin Corporation. That was the year I went to IBM school. That IBM school is really something! I went there—I saw the 1401, the 360 and the 360/22. We now have a System 3, Mod 15, with 96K, plus disks and teleprocessing. It's a great system, but when I get into trouble in the plant and something goes wrong, I bring my managers in and I say, "You forget about that computer. It will only do three things. It will add, it will subtract and it will compare. It will not manage. Get back to work."

In 1959, I became president when my brother died. Also, I got an IBM profile on 40,000 companies in the United States that year and this has been the source information for growth of our MID business and it has really been helpful to it. Then in 1962, there was another recession. Believe me, my whole residence with the company has been a series of recessions. Every four years we have a recession. You know what that fellow Harriman said, "Borrow when money is tight, hoard when money is easy." It has never been easy. So we just keep borrowing. We really have come very far since 1924 when my father bought the company for $100 and a $100,000 mortgage. Gentlemen, we haven't done very well. Our mortgage is much bigger today.

Then in 1963, the company got into short interval scheduling, which really is the constant management of men, machines, and materials. It is the most dynamic thing you could ever do within your company. If you haven't done it, I recommend it to you. Short interval schedules—it will drive you up a tree—it will cause walkouts—it will cause managers to quit, but those who are left, believe me, will be your best managers.

Then in 1966 there was another credit crunch. That's the year we decided to build a new plant. We bought the land and then in 1967 came the specter of gun control. Believe me, gun control polarized the citizenry like almost nothing else except the current proceedings against the President. People were for guns—they were against guns. Almost nobody was neutral, and I just hated to show up at a cocktail party. But it went on for two or three years and I'll tell you why. I have paraphrased this term. This is part of the Constitution. "A well regulated Militia, being necessary to the security of a free State, the right of the people to keep and bear Arms, shall not be infringed." There is no lawyer in the United States who can truly interpret what this means and the race goes on forever.

Well, we had a mail-order ban and I was in favor of the mail-order ban. As a matter of fact, I came out for it, in print. I felt we should have it so that the guns could be sold only over the counter and sold to people who had to sign a Form 4473. Lo and behold, this dignified the ownership of firearms. We started serializing them by a process on which we now have a patent and people said, "Well, my gun now has a serial number and this makes it a very valuable item." Guns have become more valuable over a period of time because they do truly represent an intrinsic value.

In 1969, we moved the plant. We moved in two weeks, believe it or not. Why? Because an informed source said there was going to be a riggers' strike at our move time. I said, "All right, we'll advance the schedule. What have we got to lose?" We closed the plant down, sent people off on their vacations, and got the riggers in earlier, and they worked night and day. They moved that place in two weeks and I never thought it was possible. It only shows you that Parkinson's Law applies: "A job takes as long as the time allocated to do it." The people came back from vacation and the machines started running. I won't tell you what happened after that! But it really did work and that was the same year we started renting space at the old plant. It was empty so, of course, we had to create a realty division. You know what happened the next year. Another recession. You know every four years they come along and the GNP goes down for a few quarters.

That was the year the Harvard Business School decided to study The Marlin Firearms Company. They did an in-depth study and they stopped the figures in June of 1970. This is used as a case study today because of the finance, because of the controversy, because we're an intangible company, because we're a tangible company. Because in June of 1970, after we moved into the plant and we had two fires and a couple of breakdowns, it looked like the company was going to go belly up. This was a tremendously difficult problem for the Harvard Business School students because they did not understand the concept of finance dating. In June our receivables are at the highest level and then they liquidate down very quickly and they go out completely in October. We stay out of the bank 60 days and return on an unsecured loan basis. The Harvard Business School study has been used all around the country.

1970 was also the year we made our commemorative issue. We made 1,000 pairs of engraved guns. They sold for $750 a pair and are now worth $1,500. Incidentally, Parke–Bernet has merged with Sotheby's and they frequently auction off guns. For the first time—the recognition of the intrinsic value of select guns.

1971 was the start of the next recession. This is the same year that 1,800,000 deer were taken in the United States and that's millions of pounds of meat for the table. So you can see why the gun business is a very viable, strong and necessary part of this country and our mode of life.

In 1973, Marlin pioneered the four-day work week. Actually the flexicore time of Germany. It works because the people have a choice. A lot of our people work four days (ten hours a day). Some of them work 4½ days and some of them work five days. They have a choice. It is very interesting. What happens? 99% of the people will make a definite choice for one of the three, but at least they had the choice, which was accomplished on a formal vote basis. They just think it's great because they had that choice. (The plant now works four ten hour days with any overtime on Fridays.)

Nineteen-seventy-three was also the year that we got into

1988 photograph of Frank Kenna, Jr., president of The Marlin Firearms Company, with his nephew Stephen Kenna, the new vice president of operations and manufacturing.

numerical tools. This has changed the complexion of manufacturing. It was also the year we took over the management of the A.C. Gilbert building to rent it out and we are the management contractors. It is also the year of our famous 45/70 rifle. It is one of our most popular guns today. People love to hand-load the 45/70 cartridge. '73 was the year that we faced another recession. In '74, the prime rate is 12%— the recession is here again, and what's new? This has been going on and on and we go on right through it. From 7% prime in 1923 to 1½% in 1932 and now 12%. So long as there's a flow of funds, gentlemen, in business and industry, we will get through regardless of auto, housing and the stock market. Our growth rate, from 1959 to 1974, has been 14.3% compounded. We are cognizant of the environment in which we operate. We have a Direct Line now in our MID division this year whereby we offer questionnaires to industry so that they can question their people and feed it back up. We have new models, we have old models, we have even thought of bicycles.

Well, you have seen where we have been. At present we are part of a big industry led by Remington and Winchester. Other arms manufacturers include Mossberg, which is still private; Ruger, which is public; Smith & Wesson, part of Bangor–Punter; Colt, part of Colt Industries; a little company called Charter Arms down in Bridgeport, Connecticut, and Browning—a public importer. We are vying with these people for the business that is out there and we are doing well. If I might say so, I'm proud of my people.

We will do about $28,000,000 worth of business this year and we will have a good cash flow (after tax net profit plus depreciation) in excess of $2,000,000 which I think is just great, and that's why the bankers like me. But it's going along very well. People say, well we've heard your story—we know where you are now—what are you going to do in the future? Well, I'll go back to Barney Baruch. When they said, "What's going to happen to the stock market?" He said, "Gentlemen, it will fluctuate." So now when people say, "What's going to happen to The Marlin Firearms Company?" I steal a little leaf out of his book and I say, "Gentlemen, it will fluctuate, but it will fluctuate upwards, and that is the story of Marlin." Thank you very much.

Robert W. Behn, vice president of marketing and new 1988 member of the board of directors.

Anthony L. Aeschliman, Marlin's director of advertising and public relations.

A FAMILY COMPANY

In the interest of offering employees additional fringe benefits, Frank Kenna started in 1980 a scholarship program for sons and daughters of employees who have been continuously employed by Marlin for a minimum of two years as of March 1 of each year.

Leaders in education and business are invited to participate as a three-person committee to make the final selection of winners after reviewing the applications of those being considered.

The scholarships have now reached $1,000 each to 12 scholars each year. Over 80 have been awarded thus far in this program.

Through the College Tuition Refund Plan, Frank Kenna also instituted a program that encourages employees to take courses of study related to their present employment. The company agrees to refund, upon satisfactory completion of such courses, 100% of all tuition fees, books, and so forth, provided that the employee maintains a B average.

Frank Kenna's move of the Marlin manufacturing facilities from New Haven to a new multimillion dollar plant in North Haven, Conn., was the salvation of the company. The New Haven plant was very old and tired. The complexity of moving material from one building to another, and from one level or floor to another, was costly and not conducive to good inventory control or economy of production. During periods of heavy snowfall (very likely in Connecticut), movement of parts from one building to another was sometimes impossible because the courtyard-type inside area between buildings was full of piled-up snow. Maintenance on the old buildings was expensive and frequently only a patch job. But most important of all, there was little or no room for expansion or introduction of new technology and methodology.

The new building, of 240,000 square feet under one roof, allowed for many improvements in working conditions for both plant and office workers, as well as better organization of machines, more efficient flow of parts, and introduction of new equipment.

To be profitable in today's market place, a company must make every effort to maintain quality while reducing scrap parts, rework of parts, downtime of machines, direct labor and absenteeism, while increasing productivity and maintaining flow of quality parts to meet the production schedule. It makes no sense to make models not scheduled for shipment and to warehouse them for long periods of time.

General instructions outlined by Frank Kenna, Jr., to his department heads were as follows:

> To be in a top competitive position we must run a "tight ship" with costs in line, quality high and the right merchandise when our customers want it.
>
> Items to watch for:
> 1. Absenteeism—check chronic offenders.
> 2. Daywork—Make sure all operations which should be piece work are on piece work basis.
> 3. Downtime—Determine why and what course of action to be taken.
> 4. Makeup—Determine why and wherefore.
> 5. Machine Tool Utilization—This is a very important area to manage. Remember—an idle machine is an unproductive machine which costs money just by existing.
> 6. Cleanliness—Cleanliness of areas and management efficiency go hand in hand.
> 7. Safety—A safe plant is a well managed plant.
> 8. Quality—Do not compromise.
> 9. Research your own departments for improvements: machinery, personnel, space, flow, quality, cost, lighting conditions, etc.
> 10. An orderly work flow is vitally important. Be sure each person contributes his fair share of the workload. A fair day's work for a fair day's pay is mandatory. Remember a poor worker puts an unfair burden upon the rest.

Marlin is a "heads up" organization with good merchandising, good sales and administrative policy, and an excellent product.

Frank Kenna, Jr.

It is under the leadership of Frank Kenna, Jr., that Marlin has reached a unique level in the firearms industry. For all intents and purposes the company is a family-owned company (none of the others can say this) and it now manufactures more shoulder-fired rifles than any other company in the U.S. It is also the largest manufacturer of caliber .22 rifles in the U.S.

Introduction of new models and new designs of firearms have been Frank's goal. Some of those he has introduced are the Model 444; the Model 1895 in .45–70; the Model 1894 in .357 magnum, .41 magnum, and .44 magnum; the Model 9 in 9mm; the Model 45 in .45ACP; the Midget Magnum bolt action .22, and the Papoose semiautomatic .22 takedown rifles; the 36-in. barrel Model 55 shotgun; and the present line of caliber .22 semiautomatic rifles.

Frank Kenna seldom displays anger and is always in control of the situation. He oversees all departments and contributes actively to all programs from research and development to engineering, production, assembly, testing, inspection, and packaging. Like his father, he is dedicated to the success of the company, even in a declining market and with great pressure from overseas competition.

In 1979 the late Roger Kenna's son, J. Stephen Kenna, joined The Marlin Firearms Company as a director. In 1986, he became a member of the executive committee and in 1987 assumed the additional responsibilities of secretary of the corporation and general counsel. On May 1, 1988, in addition to his other offices, Steve Kenna became the new vice president of operations and manufacturing.

Steve was born on October 21, 1945. He and his wife, Elizabeth, have two sons, Alex and Sam. He received a B.A. degree from Colgate University in 1967; a M.B.A. degree from The University of Pennsylvania (Wharton School of Finance and Commerce) in 1969; and a Degree in Jurisprudence from Syracuse University College of Law in 1975. He practiced law from 1975 to 1982 with the firms Day, Berry and Howard; and Murphy, Murphy and Kenna; both in Hartford, Conn. He has been co-owner of Olson Brothers Company, Plainville, Conn., since 1982; Chapman Machine Company, Terryville, Conn., since 1985; and Shaeffer Machine Company, Clinton, Conn., since 1986. Steve Kenna is also a general partner in New Cambridge Realty, A.D.K. Associates, and Litchfield Meadows Associates.

As vice president of operations, Steve is in charge of daily production, as well as engineering and maintenance operations. His keen interest in the company, outgoing personality, and experience and background in business management and manufacturing help him add a new dimension to the firearms industry, as have all the Kennas who preceded him.

Since Frank Kenna, Sr., acquired the remnants of a defunct company in 1924, the success of The Marlin Firearms Company can be attributed to one family. Frank Kenna, Sr., Roger Kenna, and Frank Kenna, Jr., deserve all the credit. Each in his way held the company together through tough times and enjoyed the challenge of a changing market and changing society. I predict the company will be around for a long time to come — or at least until they run out of Kennas.

World War II and the Korean War

WORLD WAR II PRODUCTION

In addition to manufacturing submachine guns during WW II, Marlin produced many other items for the war effort. Some were done on a direct contract with the government and others were as a subcontractor for a primary contractor.

One large job done by Marlin was government contract W19–059–ORD–2554, to set up and operate a production line for the manufacture of 20-mm links. The machinery was government-owned and was originally used by The Autotype Company. After hundreds of thousands of the 20-mm link had been made, the contract was terminated on August 9, 1945. Another smaller contract was W19–059–2570, to make parts for the M48 Fuze.

On April 5, 1943, Marlin received another large contract, for the manufacture of the barrel for the M1 carbine (W478–ORD–3362). The original contract was for 180,000, but on June 3, 1943, the quantity was reduced to 150,000. By September 1943, Marlin was delivering 500 a day and on September 23, 1943, the order was increased to 314,000 total. On November 26, 1943, 15,000 Marlin carbine barrels were shipped to Buffalo Arms and 2,300 more were shipped to Standard Products for its use. However, most of the Marlin production went into the spare parts system of the Ordnance Department. On April 8, 1944, Marlin production of the M1 carbine barrel was finished.

All Marlin-manufactured M1 carbine barrels are marked on the top of the barrel with the name *MARLIN*. The resident Ordnance inspector for the Ordnance contracts done by Marlin during the war was M.F. Powell.

Marlin also manufactured parts other than the barrel for the M1 carbine. For example, 32,000 triggers and 46,000 hammers were completed. The largest volume of production was in stocks and hand guards. By June 24, 1943, Marlin was producing 4,800 stocks each week. By September 23, 1943, production had increased to 7,200 a week. Production of the hand guard had reached 2,000 a day by August 12, 1943.

As of April 1, 1944, Marlin had received orders for the following gun- and non-gun-related government contracts, in addition to those already mentioned:

Part	Pieces
L-Wingfitting*	420
L-Wingfitting*	2,200
R-Wingfitting*	498
R-Wingfitting*	2,200
Housing**	2,222
Plate**	3,115
Cap**	3,653
Pawl*	10,935
Sliding cam***	20,262
Trigger cam***	20,262
Release pin***	277,902
Pawls*	152,250
Holders	202
Idler shaft	336
Idler shaft	2,522
Stocks	8,000
Foot pedal	2,838

Part	Pieces
Wood block	23,000
Down stop***	9,306
Flange	1,850
Buffing head	5,000
Tables****	2,000
Wood block	125,000

   * Bell Aircraft orders for P–63 plane
  ** Perkins
 *** Glenn Martin
**** Wallace Metals

The Marlin Firearms Company plant as it appeared in 1942. (Fairchild Aerial Surveys, Inc.)

UDM '42 SUBMACHINE GUN

One of the finest submachine guns manufactured during WW II was the Model UDM '42. It was designed by Carl G. Swebilius of the High Standard Manufacturing Company in October 1940, and the prototype caliber .45 guns were manufactured by that company. The production of the gun, however, was by The Marlin Firearms Company for the United Defense Supply Corporation. The production guns were in 9-mm Parabellum (9-mm Luger) instead of .45.

The High Standard caliber .45 gun, although tested by Ordnance, was not accepted for use by the military. The newly developed Thompson M1 submachine gun had been accepted as a substitute standard and the Thompson M1928A1 submachine gun was in production as the standard. Like the Thompson, the High Standard gun was expensive to make.

In November 1940, before the U.S. entered into WW II, the High Standard Manufacturing Company, under the leadership of C.G. Swebilius, took on the monumental task of manufacturing the caliber .50 machine gun for the British. Delivery of 12,000 guns was called for within 10 months. Almost overnight a plant was leased and a new building erected. The first gun was completed on April 19, 1941. Thereby, the commitment to manufacture the caliber .50 machine gun prevented High Standard from considering production of its own submachine gun for possible sale to other countries.

The United Defense Supply Corporation had no facilities, plant, machinery, engineers, or ability to manufacture any-thing. They did have, however, the U.S. government's cooperation and authority to have war material manufactured for friendly and Allied countries.

One of the items that needed to be manufactured in support of certain Allied operations was a submachine gun that would not detract from the supply of guns going to U.S. forces. The already designed and proven High Standard 1941 gun was therefore selected by the United Defense Supply Corporation. The Marlin Firearms Company, having the facilities and know-how to make firearms, was selected as the manufacturer.

The following notes and memoranda outline the problems encountered in Marlin's receiving a contract to manufacture the U.D. submachine gun:

March 3, 1942

MARLIN NOTES FOR CONFERENCE

Swebilius invented the 9MM and .45 calibre, had his inventions patented and assigned said inventions to the High Standard Manufacturing Company. High Standard's officers

Right side of the Marlin Firearms Company-manufactured submachine gun, caliber .45, M2, serial number 226.

Typical marking of WW II M2 submachine gun.

tried to sell both guns to no avail. High Standard hired Frank Sheridan Jonas as a commissioned agent on a 10% commission basis for one year on the sale of these guns to foreign governments (the year of Jonas' agreement has not passed). Jonas could not sell the gun to the Dutch or others in that no government or army officer of a government had approved the gun for military purposes. Jonas had been trying to interest the Netherlands Government in this gun.

With High Standard and Jonas unable to close the sale, Owsley of High Standard signed a letter of release of manufacturing rights to Pope and Jackson, then of the British Purchasing Commission, giving them entire manufacturing rights on this gun with the understanding that they take care of the previous obligation with Jonas. Pope and Jackson formed a corporation and took in Stewart Iglehart for obvious reasons. They then, through Jackson, secured a written report from Major General Henderson of the British Army that the gun was adaptable for military purposes. With this report in their hands, the Dutch gave them an order for 7,500 and a like number later on, making a total of 15,000. The order was given to Pope with the understanding that he take care of Jonas.

When the order was closed, High Standard tried to stop the U.D. from manufacturing the gun by delaying turn-over of a model and the manufacturing prints.

After months of non-cooperative conferences between High Standard and U.D., Pope received the 9MM gun and the rough prints. It was his intention to hand out these prints to various subcontractors and assemble the parts in a plant in Wallingford. Proceeding on this basis, Pope contacted John Lightfoot of Seymour Products. He intimated to Pope that it would be financial suicide for the U.D. to proceed on the subcontract and U.D. assembly plan. He then suggested Marlin as the manufacturer. Pope interviewed Lynch of Marlin and from that conference, Marlin was given the order to manufacture the gun and other subcontractors were called upon to manufacture the belt and strap and magazines.

This manufacture is now going on.

In the meantime the U.S. Ordnance Department heard of this gun and requested that models of the .45 calibre be submitted for government tests. It took High Standard approximately 6 months to make 5 models. They were submitted to the government to the best of my knowledge and have passed all government tests including mud tests, sand tests, water tests, etc.

About a month ago the U.S. Ordnance Department started negotiations for the purchase of this gun in .45 calibre. In the first conference in Colonel Studler's office, the latter raised a serious objection to the High Standard royalty (which incidentally is $7.50 per gun) and questioned the "Middle Man" feature of U.D. Messrs. Kenna and Lynch were in Washington, but not in that conference. At this time it was the Colonel's attitude that High Standard's royalty was exorbitant and that the Ordnance Department would handle that feature and that U.D. should work up its costs without royalty. Subsequent conferences revealed a different attitude by Colonel Studler. His attitude now changed to the fact that the "Middle Man" of U.D. should be eliminated from the negotiation. He said, in front of our Mr. Lynch, the only thing he was interested in was, not High Standard, not U.D., but Marlin as a facility. Thereupon the Ordnance Department wrote Pope requesting quotation on 94,000 guns at the delivery rate of 450 per day and 150,000 guns at the delivery rate of 1,000 per day, but subject to Pope releasing to the government the manufacturing right for further orders and Pope completing the above mentioned manufacture by December 31, 1942. A week ago Captain Costello and his Mr. Miller requested an answer to the letter calling for quotations. Messrs. Pope and Lynch worked on costs — Marlin's cost to U.D. being approxi-

Right side of UDM '42 caliber 9mm submachine gun manufactured by Marlin for the United Defense Supply Corporation. Serial number 2258.

mately $46.00 and U.D.'s cost to the government approximately $7.00 higher. In this quotation there was no time limit nor was there any release of manufacturing rights to the government beyond the aforementioned quantity. The only question brought up by Captain Costello was that no legal papers were submitted showing that the U.D. and Marlin were operating as one instead of what Studler has called the manufacturer and the "Middle Man."

Last night after 5:00 Mr. Miller received a call from Washington in which it was requested that Miller, Pope, Marlin's lawyer and High Standard's lawyer meet in Washington on Wednesday. That in brief is the history of this case to date.

SPECIAL NOTES FOR MARLIN CONFEREES

A. All Conferees
1. We should insist that the date set for Wednesday, the 4th, be kept and not postponed.
2. Marlin should not lease its facilities to U.D. Both lawyers should work out a Management Operating Plan on the U.D. gun for U.S. Government use. Said legal paper should be available for the conference in Washington.
B. For Mr. Kenna
1. That he should criticize Mr. Lynch for holding the facilities of the Marlin plant for such a long time with the expectation of this government order. In this he should bring out the recent curtailment of rifles and shotguns and the fact that we have other potential subcontractors who we are delaying because of Mr. Lynch's insistence that Marlin keep its facilities open for U.D. In this he should further state that certain parts of the plant are down due to the running out of the first operations on the 15,000 order causing a high overhead in the total overall picture.
C. For Attorney Brennan
1. That he should have a complete review of all negotiations between U.D. and the government and between U.D. and High Standard including the recent contract. Also review patent papers.
D. For Mr. Lynch
1. That the price as submitted to U.D. is based on the

Right side of UDM '42 receiver showing UD mark and fire controller.

present gun and present manufacturer and that if government tolerances are too stiff that he have the right to revise his price.
2. That the only justifiable reason to present to the War Department that the U.D. remain in the picture is that they are carrying on the sales negotiations of this gun, that, should Marlin submit a price without the U.D. then Marlin's price would have to stand the burden of hiring men for negotiation as well as technical experts on military points on which Marlin neither has the time nor ability at the present time. In brief, the U.D. is our Sales, Negotiation and Military Advice Department.
E. Special Note to all Conferees
There may be some criticism of the fact that we have not put out any U.D. 9MM Guns to date. All Conferees should know the basic reasons behind such a criticism.
1. Inspection
In our contract we were supposed to provide *a gun that shoots* and that is all. However, since that time

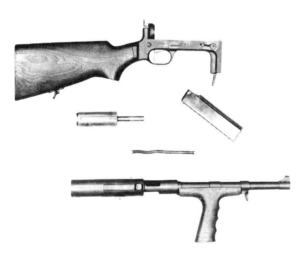

UDM '42 submachine gun disassembled for cleaning.

UDM '42 marking on left side of receiver. Although marked United Defense Supply Corporation, *these 9mm submachine guns were manufactured by The Marlin Firearms Company.*

Right side of High Standard Corporation caliber .45 UDM '42 sub-machine gun, serial number 3. Only prototype models were manufactured by this company.

we have had a cooperative Dutch inspector in the plant who has called for interchangeability and inspection of individual parts rather than the complete gun. This was not in the contract and such a change in inspection not only caused additional expense on Marlin's part, but a precision tool-up which took time. This may be a good fault in that with the receipt of a U.D. Government Order all the additional tool-up will be money well spent. Of course, it is to be understood that months ago the U.D. told us that a large government order was on its way to Marlin and hence such a tool-up was necessary.

2. Prints

No company could have made a completed gun on the prints submitted by High Standard. We have found that practically all prints had to be re-engineered by Mr. Scharf and Mr. Romberg with no aid from the engineers of High Standard. On two occasions the U.D. called upon High Standard to come over here, but the result was that their advice caused confusion and we had to revert back to Mr. Scharf's engineering of the subject under consultation. In fact, Mr. Scharf's ideas on this subject are now incorporated in the gun. Furthermore, these prints were not drawn up to manufacturing tolerances. On certain prints no tolerances were shown at all.

Furthermore, it is impossible to put the prints into production until the parts are re-dimensioned. Lastly,

it would have been financial suicide for Marlin and U.D. and High Standard's royalty if Mr. Scharf had attempted to make this gun from the prints. The mere fact that Mr. Scharf re-engineered this job saved Marlin, U.D. and High Standard's royalty as well as Jonas' commission.

3. Priorities

As we all know, an A1-I priority was assigned to this gun. Said priority has caused unfortunate delays in the receipt of base materials, considerable delays in Tool Room machinery. It was our understanding on the receipt of this order that the U.D. would better that priority. Requests have been made by Marlin for a better priority from the U.D. on various occasions on various items, but unfortunately the U.D. has been unable to obtain this better priority. A very good example of this is in the case of barrel steel. Under date of September 4th, 1941 an order was placed with the fastest supplier of this type of steel that we know of; namely, Wyckoff Drawn Steel Company. This company, through the friendship existing between Mr. Bialis and our Mr. Scharf, has given deliveries faster than could be obtained on a cold corporation to corporation order. Even with this cooperation this order which was placed on September 4, 1941 will not be shipped until the middle of April.

March 1942
MEMORANDUM

High Standard is the owner of the High Standard Sub-Machine Gun, having applied for a patent thereon, and has parted with the exclusive manufacturing and selling rights for the gun, to United Defense, in consideration for which United Defense has agreed to pay High Standard certain royalties. With respect to the United States Government, the royalty is 10%, or a minimum of $7.50 per gun.

After the gun was presented to the Ordnance Department for test and consideration, it was suggested, because the United States Government would not countenance the payment of royalties on possible orders placed by the Ordnance Department, that United Defense and High Standard get together to arrange for the elimination of this feature from their contract.

Several conferences were held and there was also an exchange of correspondence during which various proposals were made, in all of which it was stated and understood that the consideration to United Defense for relinquishing its rights to High Standard would be the placing of an order

M1 rifle (Garand) for which Marlin manufactured barrels during WW II and the Korean conflict.

M1 carbine for which Marlin manufactured barrels, stocks, and hand guards. Marlin also contracted to make many of the small parts of the carbine.

with United Defense by the Ordnance Department for guns. In fact, even after the last conference in Washington, in response to a War Department request on February 19, 1942 for an immediate price quotation on 96,000 and 150,000 guns, United Defense on February 24, 1942 made a quotation, United Defense having been furnished with the written United States regulations applying to the production of small arms.

On March 2, 1942 the War Department requested a meeting in Washington, as a result of which we are here today.

Today it was stated by Colonel Studler that the War Department wanted High Standard to be placed by United Defense in a position whereby the United States could deal directly with High Standard for the acquisition by the United States of the unrestricted right to make these guns for the United States wherever and by whom it wished; thus requiring United Defense to give up to High Standard all United Defense's rights in the gun, so far as United States orders are concerned. The War Department would make no commitments to United Defense for the placing of orders with it.

The position of United Defense is as follows:

1. High Standard has nothing to offer the United States except the bare legal ownership of the patent rights and the right to receive royalties.

2. United Defense has the exclusive manufacturing and selling rights for the gun, which the United States can readily acquire.

3. On the basis of the relinquishment by High Standard of its royalty rights, for one consideration or another, United Defense has been and is still ready to offer immediately to the United States the exclusive right to manufacture this gun for the United States and the only consideration which United Defense wants is that they be given an order by the Ordnance Department for guns, to the extent of their manufacturing facilities, at a price and upon terms to be mutually satisfactory, an order for which United Defense is now tooled up and ready to produce, being already in actual production of this gun for others.

United Defense rejects completely any suggestion that it is not a bona fide actual manufacturer of the High Standard Gun.

March 14th, 1942

Mr. Frank Kenna
P.O. Box 304
New Haven, Conn.

Dear Mr. Kenna:

There are two formal agreements outstanding between The High Standard Corporation and United Defense Supply Corporation, both executed December 12, 1941. At least, these were the only two agreements shown to me.

The primary agreement was one signed by High Standard, United Defense Supply Corporation, The Dixwell Corporation, and individually by Mr. Pope, Mr. Iglehart, Colonel Strode-Jackson.

This agreement grants to United Defense the sole and exclusive right, privilege and license to manufacture and sell submachine guns under patent application serial number 361208.

The agreement provides that a minimum royalty is to be paid in each year, the first year commencing May 22nd, 1941, of $13,125.00. This agreement provides for a royalty of 17½% of the selling price of all submachine guns, but in no event less than $13.50 or more than $20.00 per gun.

Note: This royalty arrangement was substantially changed in the second agreement executed the same day, December 12th, 1941, providing that on all guns ordered by the United States Government Lend-Lease or other governmental agencies, High Standard would receive a royalty of 10% of the selling price. In no event, however, was the royalty to be less than $7.50 per gun.

A further royalty of 10% is to be paid High Standard on all parts produced, excluding clips, magazines and slings, this royalty not to exceed one-half of the difference between United Defense manufacturing cost and its selling price. High Standard has agreed to make known to United Defense any and all improvements, but this paragraph is

M1 carbine barrel manufactured by Marlin for the government.

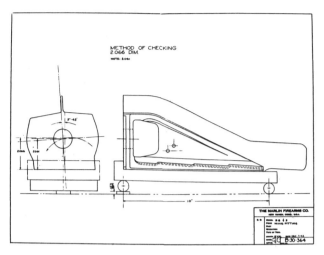

Wing fitting that Marlin manufactured for Bell Aircraft.

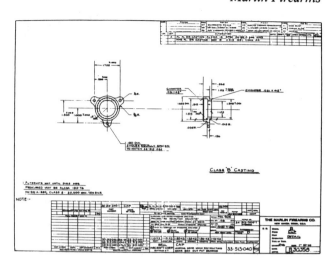

Cap that Marlin manufactured for Bell Aircraft.

not applicable to type development or improvements of magazines or clips.

The Dixwell Corporation, a party to the agreement, is to assist in the manufacturing and assembly at a cost of $1.00 per gun for the first 10,000 guns. The service of this corporation is to consist of consultation and engineering services. After the first 10,000 guns are produced, then a new arrangement is to be made between The Dixwell Corporation and United Defense.

High Standard is to have the right at all times to inspect the books and records of United Defense in connection with the royalties.

United Defense may not, without the written consent of High Standard, "assign or transfer, except by mortgage, the license herein granted, nor grant any sub-licenses thereunder." But this is not to prevent United Defense from having the guns or parts manufactured for it by others.

As to breach, in the event royalty is not paid within thirty days after becoming due, the agreement may be cancelled, and the royalties are to be paid before the tenth day of each month covering royalties which accrued upon guns or parts sold during the preceeding month. Likewise, if in any one year of the existence of the agreement, the agreement being for a term of five years, United Defense shall not make bona fide "sales" of at least 1,000 guns, the contract may be terminated.

As to prosecution of patents and infringements, High Standard agrees only to protect United Defense to a limited extent. In the event that United Defense is compelled to pay costs, expenses and damages, High Standard will pay a proportionate part thereof, based on the proportion of the royalties and selling price less the manufacturing cost to United Defense. In any event the same not to exceed $65,265.

In the agreement it is provided that a release from F.S. Jonas is to be obtained by United Defense and given to High Standard, and the further right is reserved by High Standard to utilize any improvements covered by the patent in guns other than sub-machine guns.

The second agreement, executed on the same day, between United Defense and The High Standard Manufacturing Corporation, covers the royalties on the Dutch order.

Under this agreement on the first 7,500 guns there is to be deducted from the selling price the sum of $10.00, to be paid to F.S. Jonas, and from the royalty due High Standard there is to be deducted one-half of the excess, if any, of the manufacturing cost to United Defense over $46.43 per gun, but in no event is the royalty to be paid to High Standard to be less than $7.50.

It should be noted that in arriving at any excess as covered by this agreement, the 17½% basis of royalty would have to be considered.

On the second 7,500 guns, High Standard's royalty is not to be less than $10.50 per gun.

This agreement also contains a paragraph already referred to covering guns ordered by the United States Government Lease-Lend, or other governmental organization, wherein it is provided that the High Standard royalty is to be 10% of the selling price, but in no event less than $7.50.

I am informed that the minimum payment required during the first year of the agreement, beginning May 22nd, 1942, has been paid, been received and delivered to High Standard. I am seeking to obtain a copy of this release.

Yours very truly,

EJB:nb
cc to T. F. Lynch, Works Manager

Improvements made to the gun after study of the Ordnance tests were to increase the magazine capacity from 25 cartridges to 40 cartridges and to slow the cyclic rate of fire from 880 rounds per minute to 750. It was also given the new designation of UDM '42.

UDM '42 Submachine Gun Specifications

Caliber: 9-mm Luger
Blowback operated
Fires from an open bolt
Semi- and full automatic
Cyclic rate of fire: 750 rounds/minute
Magazine capacity: 25 rounds
Rear peep sight adjustable for elevation and windage
Easy takedown
Walnut stock and grip
Sling swivels
Closed-in receiver with small ejection port
Steel butt plate
Trap in butt for oil can
Barrel length: 11 inches
Overall length: 32¼ inches
Takedown length: 19¾ inches
Weight: 9¼ pounds

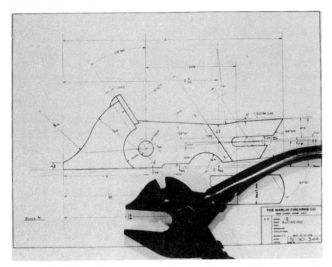

Cutter jaw for side-cutting pliers that Marlin manufactured by the thousands.

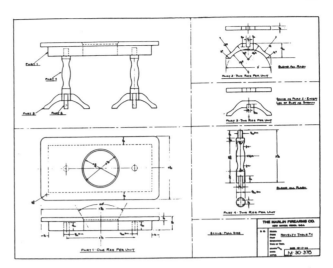

As the war effort contracts were nearing completion, Marlin manufactured some wooden furniture pieces for diversification. The table shown here was short lived and manufactured in very limited numbers.

Over 15,000 Model UDM '42 submachine guns were manufactured by Marlin. They were paid for by the Netherlands Commission, which then sold them to the U.S. government. A large number of them were used by the Office of Strategic Services (OSS). Reports indicate that most were dropped into France during 1944. The U.S. Navy moved some into China during October 1943. It was also reported by the Ordnance Office that others had been successfully used in Africa. On May 11, 1944, Colonel Studler of the Ordnance Office reported to Marlin that most of the UDM '42 guns had been captured in France by the Germans. Thus the possibility of a spare parts order was very unlikely.

The total production cost of the UDM '42 submachine gun was $400,000.

On March 18, 1948, The Marlin Firearms Company and the High Standard Manufacturing Corporation formally signed an agreement that Marlin had exclusive rights to manufacture the UDM '42 machine gun and could try to find a customer for whom Marlin might make the gun. Royalty payments were included in the agreement. The patents granted to Marlin were the following: 2,343,824, February 29, 1944; 2,345,077, March 28, 1944; 2,365,306, December 19, 1944; and 2,365,307, December 19, 1944. The inventor of all these patented items was Carl Swebilius.

Marlin was not successful in finding a customer worldwide for the submachine gun manufactured during WW II. Argentina and the Dutch showed some interest, but it soon waned and the project was dropped in 1952.

GUN, SUBMACHINE, CAL. .45, M2

George J. Hyde of Brooklyn, N.Y., designed and patented (2,049,776) a submachine gun in 1935. The M2 submachine gun was also designed by Mr. Hyde and had many of the features of his earlier patented model. The production version of his gun was developed by the Inland Division of General Motors. When introduced in April 1942 and submitted to Ordnance for testing, it was designated the Hyde-Inland 1.

The Hyde-Inland gun passed the Ordnance tests on April

27, 1943, and was found superior to the Thompson submachine gun, which was the standard submachine gun in the U.S. armed forces.

Wanting to improve the performance of his gun, George Hyde made modifications to the gun and resubmitted them as the Hyde-Inland 2.

The Hyde-Inland 2 gun with a 30-round magazine was classified as substitute standard in April 1942 and designated Gun, Submachine, Cal. .45, M2.

The Marlin Firearms Company was given the contract to manufacture the M2 gun. However, while Marlin was tooling for the new gun and preparing the many details for production, Colonel Rene Studler of the Ordnance Department had George Hyde and Frederick Sampson, chief engineer of Inland Division of General Motors, working on a new design of gun, made mostly of stamped parts. The new gun was submitted for

Marlin plant during WW II period.

tests and adopted in December 1942 as the M3 submachine gun (grease gun).

Marlin did not overcome the usually expected start-up problems and get production models of the M2 gun to Ordnance until May 1943.

The reduced cost of manufacture and potentially higher production of the M3 gun resulted in the order for M2 guns to be cancelled and production stopped. I was told by the late Armin Romberg, who was with Marlin prior to WW II and advanced to director of sales after the war, that only about 500 of the M2 submachine guns were produced before the contract was terminated on June 9, 1943. The highest serial number observed is 226.

Gun, Submachine, Cal. .45, M2
Specifications

Caliber: .45 Automatic Caliber Pistol
Blowback operated
Fires from open bolt
Semi- and full automatic
Cyclic rate of fire: 500 rounds/minute
Magazine capacity: 20 or 30 round Thompson magazine
Wood stock and grip
Sling swivels
Steel butt plate

Thomas R. Robinson, Jr.

Trap in butt for cleaning equipment and oiler
Barrel length: 12.1 inches
Overall length: 32.1 inches
Weight: 9.25 pounds
Sights: Fixed aperture rear with blade front between protective ears

It is frequently difficult to reconstruct precise data about certain periods of Marlin history. One such is the WW II period. However, small bits and pieces can sometimes be put together to confirm that something did happen, or get done, even if complete records no longer exist.

The production of barrels for the M1 rifle (Garand) during the Korean conflict is documented. But only a few references can be found that relate to the production of this barrel during WW II. One reference is the caption to a photograph in the June 1943 issue of Marlin's employee publication *The Marlin Gunzette.* The photo shows Charles H. Hildreth and his son Charles H. Hildreth, Jr., an MP at Camp Gordon, Ga. The caption states, "Charles H. Hildreth is operating a thread mill for Garand barrel productions in the barrel department. Son Charles is now in service."

Another reference to Garand barrel production is a short article about the Garand rifle that includes the following statement: "In the last issue of *The Gunzette* we discussed the M1 carbine. But over in the barrel department we have been turning out large quantities of Garand barrels for months. These barrels are being used for guns that have already seen heavy action."

Another reference is in a 1951 *Gunzette* where Theodore F. Lynch, vice president, states: "A military contract from the Springfield Ordnance District calling for the production of 50,000 M-1 (Garand) rifle barrel assemblies, valued at over $600,000, has been awarded to the Marlin Firearms Co." Mr. Lynch further stated that Marlin manufactured 25,000 M1 rifle barrels during WW II in 10 months, but that this new contract called for twice that number in half that time.

THOMAS ROBINSON, JR.

The late Thomas Robinson, Jr., known as "Tom" in the firearms industry, left his mark both on the industry and at Marlin.

Prior to his joining Marlin in November 1945, Mr. Robinson worked for Carl "Gus" Swebilius at High Standard. During WW II, he worked mainly on machine guns and received a number of patents for his inventions during the war period.

Tom Robinson joined Marlin as the director of research and development and worked tirelessly on new products and making improvements on the old ones. His efforts were directed toward the return of the company to the manufacture of sporting arms after four years of war work. Notable among Tom's efforts were the Model 88C and 89C semiautomatic .22 rifles; the Model 101 single-shot rifle; the Model 122 single-shot rifle; the Model 57, 57M, and 62 family of Levermatic rifles; the Model 59 shotgun; and the round bolt system in the center-fire lever actions.

Tom worked hard to overcome problems, develop new mate-

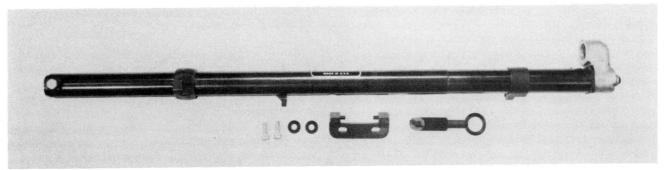

Walter Kidde & Company 20mm Orlikon gun charging mechanism for which Marlin made the main tube and some fittings.

rials, introduce new technology, and create modern and sound principles in firearms design and manufacture.

The patents issued to Tom Robinson while with Marlin were as follows:

Patent Number	Date Issued	Invention
2,454,885	Nov. 30, 1948	Operating handle and breech bolt
2,465,553	Mar. 29, 1949	Cartridge extractor
2,492,814	Dec. 22, 1949	Fire control mechanism
2,492,815	Dec. 27, 1949	Receiver closure
2,611,204	Sept. 23, 1952	Receiver and action
2,823,480	Feb. 18, 1956	Levermatic receiver
2,963,810	Dec. 13, 1960	Model 101 single-shot rifle
2,976,637	Mar. 28, 1961	Model 122 single-shot rifle
3,100,358	Aug. 13, 1963	Micro-Groove® rifling.

I first knew Tom Robinson in 1956. He impressed me as an intellectual who walked in the shadow of Charles Newton (inventor of the Newton rifle), and one who lived firearms to the point of eccentricity, yet many thought him a genius with the rare characteristic of enjoying people and life.

Many stories about Tom and his ways have been told. Two I remember are the one about his shooting blackbirds in the plant courtyard while testing an experimental 9-mm single-shot shotgun and the other about his testing .22 rifles by shooting into the large wood ceiling beams in the old plant. His casualness about such matters was legendary.

I considered Tom a friend. Although I only had a fringe social and business relationship with him, I'm sure glad I knew him. He was one of those demanding characters you could not help enjoying and from whom you learned something by having known him.

Thomas Robinson, Jr., died in 1968, after a short illness.

KOREAN WAR PERIOD

In support of the Korean War, Marlin manufactured for the Ordnance Department M1 rifle barrels, stock assemblies for the M1 carbine, barrels for the M3 submachine gun, and other items.

Making the carbine stock assembly was not a new experience for Marlin, as it had manufactured hundreds of thousands of them during WW II. The metal parts were all subcontracted out. They were the recoil plate screw escutcheon, A5196440;

recoil plate, C5557150; recoil plate screw, A5196442; front band locking spring, A5196484; butt plate, B200997; and butt plate screw, B146873. The exact number of carbine stock assemblies produced is not known. However, records do indicate that by Aug. 13, 1952, over 136,000 had been shipped to the National Export Company, 137 Hamilton St., New Haven, Conn. for government overseas packaging.

There were no markings placed on the Marlin-produced carbine stock or stock parts to identify them as being manufactured by Marlin. The WW II carbine barrels, however, were marked *MARLIN*.

The first barrel contract Marlin received was DA-19-059-ORD-430, for 18,000 M3 submachine gun (grease gun) barrels. By February 1951 the procedures of manufacture had been established and the 28 operation sheets finalized. The rifling of the first production of the M3 barrel was by the button process (see Micro-Groove section). In July 1952, use of either the button or broach system was authorized. Marlin borrowed from Harrington & Richardson two broaches, but after trial decided to stay with the button method. By September 1952, Marlin had done so well in producing this barrel on schedule and within the government standards that a third contract had been received.

This third contract authorized the use of seamless tubing, if the manufacturer wanted to use tubing instead of drilling a hole through bar stock. Marlin did purchase seamless tubing from Ellwood Iving Steel Tube Works, Inc., Philadelphia, Pa. Although the Iving Company could produce the tubing to the required dimensionial characteristics and Marlin could process the steel, a problem was experienced by both companies with regard to hardness, before and after heat treatment. The tubing method of the M3 barrel did not progress beyond a small pilot run. By August 1952, Marlin was delivering 500 M3 barrels per week. It is estimated that at least 25,000 M3 barrels were manufactured by Marlin. They can be identified by the assembly number 5653435 and by *Marlin* stamped on the inside of the collar. A *P* was also stamped on the inside, after proofing.

Marlin's gun-barrel-making expertise was put to good use in January 1951 on a subcontract for Walter Kidde and Company, Belleville, N.J., for 3,000 gun charging mechanisms that would hydraulically operate the action of the 20mm Orlikon automatic gun. This gun was sometimes mounted away from the gunner's reach (on the airplane wing, dual gun mount, and so on), requiring a strong mechanism to first charge the gun and also to operate it if the gun malfunctioned.

The fabrication of the tube included reaming, straightening, grinding, honing, copper brazing, and heat treating. About 1,600 of these tubes were completed by 1952. An interesting note: This job was the first engineering project on which Frank Kenna, Jr., worked.

All of the other work done by Marlin was done well and usually on time. The M1 rifle barrel contract, however, was another story, and only fragments of the problems Marlin encountered and the reasons for them can now be reconstructed.

A January 1951 news release announced that Marlin had received a fourth military contract. The story was as follows:

> A military contract from Springfield Ordnance District calling for the production of 50,000 M1 (Garand) rifle barrels, valued at over $600,000, has been awarded to the Marlin Firearms Company, it was announced by Theodore F. Lynch, vice president. Engineering and tooling have already started and special machinery for defense production used in World War II and rebuilt by Botwinik Brothers of Hamden is now in the process of delivery. Steel has been allocated in such a way as to give the company the promptest delivery from mill to manufacturer.
>
> Twenty-five percent of the plant's capacity will be placed on military production with the granting of this contract. The plant now employs 650 persons.
>
> Lynch said that Marlin manufactured 25,000 units of M1 (Garand) rifle barrel assemblies in 10 months during World War II, but that this new contract called for twice that number in half that time.
>
> This is the fourth military contract that Marlin has received. The company is now engaged in the manufacture of

aircraft and tank parts as well as 10,000 barrel assemblies for M3 caliber .45 sub-machine guns.

Marlin first bid on manufacturing M1 barrels on December 28, 1950. The price quoted was $10.95 each on 100,000 and $10.66 on 200,000. However, the final contract was negotiated at $11.20 each for 70,000. At a later date the total was reduced to 50,000 barrels.

Frequently in the fulfillment of a government contract, government-owned machinery, fixtures, and gauges are furnished by the contractor, in this case the Springfield Ordnance District and Springfield Armory.

Marlin did not need much help with machinery, except for a Magna-Flux® machine, which is used to check for cracks in a barrel. But there were 261 gauges used in the manufacture of the M1 barrel. Some would be required in duplicate or triplicate, depending on the number of machines being used to do the same operation, or on the number of inspectors needed to inspect the work properly. Springfield Armory furnished Marlin with all gauges used in the contract.

For some reason Marlin did not do a good job of gauge control, and frequent conflict existed between Marlin's production and inspection personnel and the government's resident Ordnance inspector. As is usual in such cases, the manufacturer can ask for a waiver if the out-of-gauge dimension is not critical to the function of the part. Also, some rework is allowed to correct differences found between the government and the manufacturer.

The gauge and manufacturing problems Marlin experienced in trying to complete the M1 rifle barrel contract caused delays. Additionally, some barrels cracked during production. Marlin felt this was related to the steel supplied by Republic Steel Company. About 10,000 barrels were rejected for cracks and Republic made good on only 2,500, pushing Marlin even further behind on deliveries.

In the interest of enlightening students and historians of

M3 submachine gun for which Marlin manufactured thousands of barrels.

Marlin-manufactured M3 barrel.

Markings inside of M3 barrel collar showing part number and Marlin name.

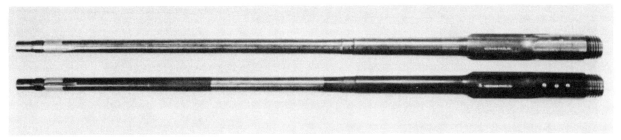

Top: *Marlin unfinished barrel for M1 (Garand) rifle.* Bottom: *Reworked M1 barrel.*

military rifles, and in particular the M1 rifle enthusiast who has heard an unfounded rumor that all Marlin M1 barrels were rejected and scrapped, the following Marlin production report is included here:

M1 BARREL CONTRACT

With the completion of the gage overhaul program and the subsequent submission of three lots, 500 each, of M1 barrels to Government inspection for processing, we are now able to predict with reasonable accuracy the outcome of the M1 contract, assuming we do no more than continue the salvage operations on the better material now on hand.

The Government has accepted to date 42,514 barrels. Our records show that we have been paid for 41,280 barrels, in addition to which 500 concentricity barrels are now at National Export and in addition to this, there are 699 barrels now in the Government crib, which have been passed.

It is our judgment that of the remaining material we have for submission to the Government, approximately 1000 may be acceptable on a waiver basis and approximately 1500 more will be acceptable as normal barrels after salvage operations have been carried out. This figure represents in our opinion the top or maximum possible production from material now on hand and will leave us with a minimum additional production requirement of 2,500 barrels in order to complete the minimum terms of our contract as to quantity. Stated differently, we do not see how it would be possible to complete a 50,000 piece order within the stated 5% tolerance without ordering stock for and machining at least 2,500 to 3,000 barrels, and preferably nearly twice that number.

It is Ralph's feeling, based upon experience he has had in the past in the Armory and with Ordnance Procurement in general, that we may very well run the risk of a Government wide blackball if we willfully sit down on the job before completing the minimum quantity requirement of this contract, especially in light of the fact that for the past six to

eight months Ordnance personnel inquiring about the status of our M1 barrel contract have been put off with rather liberal promises for future deliveries on a schedule which has been in the main highly unrealistic.

At the time of Colonel Ronan's visit to this plant from the Inspector General's office to investigate the reason for the extreme delinquency of the company in the matter of time of delivery, the Colonel clearly pointed out that it was always wise when unforseen difficulties occurred in production, to notify the Procurement Dept. to that effect and request a rescheduling based upon sound estimates of future production. Subsequent to Colonel Ronan's visit on July 17th, personnel from the production division of the Springfield Ordnance District have weekly checked with us on future deliveries, and have been put off by the writer with forecasts going no further ahead than two weeks at a time, due to our own uncertainty, until recently, as to just what we could do with the balance left in the plant. The most recent request coming from the production division of the Ordnance District is more pointed and explicit than earlier requests and commences with a letter from the district signed by W. Renton, dated 5th August, 1952, which requested explanation why our delinquent contract should not be cancelled for failure of performance. Following this letter, the production department of the district sent personnel to the plant to get not only running forecasts for future performances in our contract, but also a definite final statement in writing as to when all contracts, but particularly the M1, would be completed. We have not up to this time undertaken to give a final statement for the reason that we are not certain as to the course the company wishes to pursue in the matter.

It appears to the writer that we have three alternatives with reference to the M1 contract. One, simply to continue getting out as much waiver material and salvage material as possible with the sure knowledge that we will not complete the quantity requirement of the contract and, thereafter, simply give up, which in the writer's opinion would be a most fool-hardy

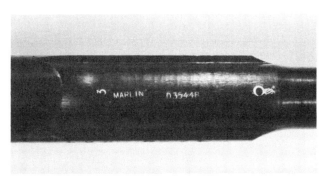

One of many variations of the markings on top of Marlin-manufactured M1 barrels.

Another variation of the Marlin- and Ordnance-marked M1 barrels.

Marlin display showing production steps of M1 rifle barrel.

course to adopt. The second alternative is to procure sufficient additional forgings or bar stock to round out the estimated three to four thousand barrels required, while at the same time ordering enough bar stock or forgings to take advantage of the 5% overage allowed and thus get a bigger or more economical run while staying within the 52,500 barrel limit. A third alternative, if the final tally on acceptable barrels comes close enough to 47,500, would be to negotiate with Harrington & Richardson for the procurement from them of sufficient barrels to make up the differential between what we have produced and the minimum required by the contract.

Meanwhile, it seems imperative that some final concrete action be taken particularly in the matter of the M1 contract, to acquaint the district with the present circumstances of the company, and it is the writer's belief that either procuring additional raw material to round out the contract, or obtaining finished barrels from Harrington & Richardson to fulfill our commitment are the only courses open to us. In the event that it is decided to go ahead with our own production, we should in advance go to the district with the complete story of our difficulties to the present and point out to them the impossibility, after the assessment we have recently made, of completing the contract in quantity without procuring and manufacturing additional barrels. We would, of course, point out that our revised production schedules based on obtaining additional forgings and machining them are factual and can be maintained, although not at the high volume previously estimated by the company. It should also be established in writing that the district will accept our revised schedule for completion of this contract to protect our investment in additional raw material and tools.

As to the possibility of manufacturing another small lot of M1 barrels at a profit, we feel that despite increases in labor costs, by utilizing the tool set-up already established and for the most part still intact, and the gaging which is moderately well under control and now amenable to control, and by operating at a realistic production rate of approximately 500 barrels per week rather than the attempted earlier rate of 500 barrels per day, we should be able to produce the balance of the order at a reasonable cost.

To continue with additional production of the M1 barrel, the company would have to plan on the purchase of several complete sets of thread gages, which we cannot make or adequately repair here at the plant, and which are now the gages giving us the most trouble in our salvage work. All other gages are amenable to tool room repair at modest cost. It is the writer's estimate that new gages and replacement tools where needed can be obtained for a little more than $5,000 to complete an 8,000 barrel run.

This activity if undertaken should tie in well with the expected decrease in high power and .22 commercial gun barrel activity in the next several months. Furthermore, we should have available a substantial labor pool from the carbine stock job which is approaching its conclusion.

Additional barrel material was purchased and the contract was completed on a reduced delivery schedule.

On June 7, 1952, an Ordnance display was conducted in Hartford, Conn., by the Ordnance District Office. Among other things, Marlin's display included some of the manufacturing steps in making the M1 barrel.

At least six different types of markings have been noted on Marlin-manufactured M1 barrels. All have the name *MARLIN* and the drawing number stamped into the top, or side of the large-diameter, at the rear of the barrel. Some have the date, for example, *3-53* or *5-53*. Also, a proofmark, *P*, is stamped into the barrel surface.

In spite of all the problems in completing the M1 barrel contract, Springfield Armory asked Marlin to discuss with representatives of the Armory various details in connection with Micro-Groove barrel development, and on April 29, 1954, they met to discuss a research and development contract to make, for test purposes, M1 (Garand) barrels with Micro-Groove rifling.

A number of barrels were made by using Springfield Armory partially finished barrels and then rifling them by the Marlin process. The result of the Armory test of these barrels is unknown. However, I think that the shallow and narrow lands of Micro-Groove rifling would not survive the Armory's endurance test.

Marlin also fabricated over 20 different hydromatic transmission parts for the Kopper Company, Baltimore, Md., between 1950 and 1952.

Other Marlin Enterprises

MARLIN INDUSTRIAL DIVISION

In 1913, Frank Kenna, Sr., had an idea that caught on nationally and is still in operation today. His idea was to distribute a current news picture to businesses for display in store windows as an "eye catcher." A potential customer would stop long enough to look at the picture and read the current news item, and then would inspect the displayed merchandise. The first picture distributed was a picture of Marconi.

This humble start of a communications medium expanded into what is now the Marlin Industrial Division (MID), with 8,000 customers in the Western Hemisphere, and 55 employees.

At first, the illustrated news feature was expanded into a business that supplied bulletin board material for industries to use to communicate with employees.

Dramatic news pictures were, and still are, used to catch a person's attention. Along with the "eye catcher" are messages from management to the work force.

Although the MID is directed by Frank Kenna, Jr., the day-to-day operation and development of the overall operation of MID was conducted by Stephen Schramm, vice president of MID, until his death.

Mr. Schramm's dynamic and aggressive leadership, along with an astute background in communications, has developed the bulletin board concept into a communications technique unequaled anywhere.

The old board concept is long gone. Marlin now furnishes with the service an attractively designed and illuminated message center. Across the top is a back-lighted "header" showing the name or logo of the company or organization using the service. The Illustrated Current News item is displayed in the top center panel. Below the news item and on both sides are additional glassed-in sections for display of either the Marlin-furnished messages, or for messages tailored to the customer's needs.

Locating the news centers in areas where employees may gather, such as cafeterias and drinking fountains, or in traffic areas, increases the likelihood that employees will read the messages. Managers consider the time it takes to read the material to be time well spent.

Besides the actual message center, the material Marlin furnishes includes news pictures, posters on quality standards, suggestions on waste and safety, letters from management, and many other subjects. MID's schedule of the service mailed to the customer reads as follows:

1. ENLARGED NEWS PICTURES (the Illustrated Current News). Supplied on an every-other-day schedule. These

Eli Kasimer, vice president of Marlin Industrial Division.

interesting photo features build regular and voluntary readership without controversy or irritation.

2. MOTIVATIONAL MESSAGES.
   Twelve brief and persuasive 10″ x 19″ printed panels promoting employee understanding and improved attitudes are supplied every four weeks. From these you select the four or five most suited to your needs. Each set includes a pre-printed panel for personalizing your own important messages to your employees.

3. BACKGROUNDS (17″ x 23″)
   Colorful, printed panels to spotlight your own lettersize communications. Four are supplied each four-week period.

4. POSTERS (17″ x 23″)
   These colorful, large pieces sell quick, visual impressions on safety, quality workmanship, waste prevention, and improved productivity. They include four color photographic reproductions, original art, and work by nationally known cartoonists. Four are furnished each four-week period.

5. PERSONALIZED COMMUNICATORS.
   These enable you to communicate specifically about your products, processes or personnel. They are produced on 10″ x 19″ stock from text that you furnish and are available at the rate of one every four weeks. (The message illustrated demonstrates the flexibility of these Communicators).

6. GIANT-SIZE "EXECUTIVE LETTER."
   Enlarged and reproduced from your letterhead and text, this 17″ x 23″ attention-getter is available, at your option, twelve times in a two-year period.

NEWS CENTER SPECIFICATIONS
Size Overall: 63″ x 31″
Material: Anodized aluminum with glass-enclosed panels under lock and key. Fluorescent-illuminated reflector of Plexiglas with die-cut plastic letters.

The Marlin program recognizes that an employee is a whole person who cannot be fragmented and tagged with separate job objectives. The employee who is encouraged to work productively is the same person who must produce a quality product or service and work safely. The slogan now used by MID is PRIDE®—Personal Responsibility In Daily Effort.

In addition to hospitals and manufacturing industries, service-oriented industries such as Federal Express, McDonald's, and the Connecticut Department of Transportation are also customers. The News Center is a one-direction communicator, from management down to the employee, whatever his or her job may be. Good communication goes in both directions—up and down. To complete the circle, the Marlin Industrial Divi-

Marlin News Picture Service eye-catching ad for Marlin 410 lever action shotgun.

Marlin News Picture Service news item with ad for Model 39 caliber .22 lever action rifle.

Marlin Industrial Division's Illustrated Current News photo of GIs during beach landing in Dutch New Guinea during WW II.

Steel used in making double-edge razor blades.

sion has developed a conduit for the employee to communicate with the employer. Called Direct Line®, it provides a method for the employee to express his feelings in a confidential manner and "straight to the boss."

Direct Line® includes a metal cabinet that has two sections. On one side are the forms and envelopes for the use of the employee. The other side is a slotted and locked box in which the communication can be placed. To customers subscribing to the Direct Line® service, Marlin sends every four weeks four motivating posters that are displayed on the cabinet.

The Marlin Industrial Division, Inc. was until recently a wholly owned subsidary of The Marlin Firearms Company. It has about 30 regional managers who contact all types of companies, hospitals, banks, agencies, and hotels to help them integrate the Marlin News Center plan into their internal communications system. For more information, write the Marlin Industrial Division, Inc., 100 Kenna Dr., North Haven, Conn., 06473.

On April 1, 1987, the Marlin Industrial Division was separated from The Marlin Firearms Company and is now owned by the Kenna family.

Upon the death of Stephen Schramm, Eli Kasimer assumed the vice presidency of MID.

Stamping machine that forms blades in steel strip.

RAZOR BLADE DIVISION

Frank Kenna, Sr., entered the razor blade business in November 1935. This was a personal business, financed by his personal funds, but he paid compensation to The Marlin Firearms Company for use of its name.

On January 9, 1939, Frank Kenna released his rights to any division of profit in connection with the razor blade business to Marlin; however, he would be paid a commission on all razor blades sold to the company for resale.

The registration of the name Marlin as a trademark in connection with the marketing of razor blades was awarded on April 27, 1939 (number 345,427); however, the original trademark of the name Marlin was registered with regard to firearms on August 7, 1906 (number 55,158). Between 1940 and 1948, the Marlin name was also registered with regard to razor

Machine that grinds and hones the blade edge.

Grinding and honing heads.

Machine that prints the Marlin name on the blades.

Machine that separates the finished individual blades from the steel strip.

blades in the following countries: Australia, Brazil, Chile, Cuba, Greece, Territory of Hawaii, Italy, Mexico, New Zealand, Peru, Portugal, Puerto Rico, Uruguay, and Venezuela. At first, The Marlin Firearms Company was in the razor blade business because it wanted diversified interests that would be profitable and an added source of income. But in due course, the Marlin Blade Division was a tool to keep the name Marlin visible to the men of America, especially during WW II, when millions of Marlin blades were sold to the government for issue to men of all services.

Most Marlin razor blades were manufactured by firms making blades for a number of customers similar to Marlin. Some of those companies were BlueStrike, GiltEdge, Club Razor, Pal, and Molkenthin Industries.

Between January 1945 and February 1953, Marlin manufactured blades in a plant located in New Jersey. When incorporated on January 23, 1945, the company was called Molkenthin Industries Incorporated. On January 14, 1949, the name of the corporation was changed to The Marlin Firearms Company Razor Blade Division, Inc. The plant and manufacturing facilities were located at 989 McCarther Highway, Newark, N.J. On February 17, 1953, all assets were transferred to The Marlin Firearms Company, and Marlin went back to the system of purchasing all razor blades. During WW II, Marlin sold about 3% of all blades manufactured and about 10% of the blades purchased by the government. At that time 90% of the Blue-Strike production was sold by Marlin. During 1945 Marlin sold its billionth blade.

After WW II, Marlin made a concerted effort to recapture a portion of the civilian market. Radio advertising and newspaper ads were used extensively; however, the government restrictions on available steel and the introduction of stainless steel into the razor blade business limited Marlin's sales. But even with a distressed postwar market, the name Marlin was still very evident in the homes of millions of men, in particular the service veterans who had used many millions of Marlin blades while overseas.

The Marlin razor blade business is best explained by the following chronological breakdown of events:

Grinding the ends of the blade after separation from the strip.

December 30, 1935—Frank Kenna, president of The Marlin Firearms Company, started a razor blade business with his own funds and resources.

January 9, 1939—Frank Kenna released his holdings in his blades business to The Marlin Firearms Company. A commission was to be paid him for the blades sold.

April 1, 1936—Razor Blade Department established at Marlin and 15,000,000 blades sold.

May 2, 1936—*Consumer research* magazine placed Marlin blades at head of recommended list, and ½ million sold in one week.

August 13, 1936—800,000 sold in one week.

November 12, 1937—Marlin bid on 200,000 blades for the government.

October 17, 1937—Razor Blade Department sales office moved to New York City with Gun Division sales office.

October 31, 1941—The Marlin Firearms Company Canada, Ltd. was established for the purpose of selling razor blades in Canada.

April 27, 1943—BlueStrike Company manufactured Marlin blades and bid on government contracts in the name of The Marlin Firearms Company.

May 13, 1943—Razor Blade Department name changed to Marlin Firearms Company Razor Blade Division.

June 10, 1943—Government cuts steel allocation by 30%. Blade operation moves into new Blades building.

July 1, 1943—Marlin sells 1,000,000 blades to U.S. government.

August 26, 1943—Marlin adds shaving cream to line. Sold exclusively by Kenro Products Corporation, New York,

Marlin's Molkenthin Industries plant in New Jersey, which Marlin operated from 1945 to 1953.

N.Y. Kenro also marketed a blade sharpener under the Marlin name that sold for 29¢.

September 23, 1943—Considered introduction of a razor to the product line. No actions taken because patent problems were anticipated.

December 7, 1943—Contract for 15,000,000 blades received from Armed Forces.

January 6, 1944—Blade industry limited to 168,000,000. Marlin authorized 8½% of total.

Picture of Brooklyn Dodger Pee Wee Reese taking the first pitch of the 1949 World Series at Yankee Stadium. The pitcher is Allie Reynolds, New York Yankees, and the catcher is Yogi Berra. The umpire is Cal Hubbard. Note the Marlin Blades sign on the building behind the outfield bleachers. (Acme)

"I won't take this mask off until he uses Marlin Blades!"

Typical Marlin cartoon ad for Marlin blades.

May 11, 1944—Shaving cream to be closed out.

July 20, 1944—Considered another razor for production. Dropped because of limitation on steel.

October 5, 1944—The name High Speed to be dropped.

October 26, 1944—Sales backlog for 875,000 tubes of shaving cream.

December 21, 1944—Cartoon advertising program was more successful and brought more business than previous techniques. Single-edge blade eliminated for the balance of war.

July 5, 1945—Marlin blades are 90% of BlueStrike Company production.

August 9, 1945—Introduced blade dispenser that can be hung up, making blades readily available.

October 11, 1945—Developing a package of 10 for 17¢.

October/November 1945—Red box, 12 for 25¢, single-edge, and bull's-eye High Speed show cards still in use.

November 30, 1946—Razor blade sales contest held for dealers and distributors. Marlin guns given as prizes.

1947—Radio ads with catchy songs and newspaper ads continue as main sales pitch.

1947/1948—60-blade pack introduced. Collar tie set of 60 Marlin blades, and gold-plated collar and tie pins offered.

January 15, 1948—Looking at both Ardell and Molkenthin razor plants.

1948—Red box, 2″ x 1″ x ¾″, introduced.

August 26, 1948—Purchased Barbasol machines. Being installed at Molkenthin plant.

April 1949—Marlin to contribute to the cancer fund the full retail price of blades sold when the purchaser returns the card attached to the package.

March 3, 1949—Manufacture of a razor blade trimming comb.

1949—Marlin has 3% of all razor blade sales. Savage Laboratories, La Mesa, Calif., proposes a feeding box for four-blade dispenser.

April 5, 1950—Set-up of magnetizing elements into Excell wrapping machine.

August 30, 1951—Magnetizing Schick-type blades introduced. Safti-Quik wrap added. Packages are 12 for 25¢, 27 for 50¢, 60 for $1.00. Counter and floor bulk display boxes introduced.

June 7, 1952—Utility Razor Blade Company machine purchased from Ohio Match Company.

November 15, 1952—Schick-type razor blade magazine in production.

1952—New items in 1952 are Christmas-wrapped blades, 1¢ sale, three 25¢ packs for 51¢, New Marlin ejector blade.

January 7, 1955—Received 510,000 blades from BlueStrike, New York.

January 11, 1955—Received 89,760 injector blade packages from GiltEdge, New Jersey. Also received blades from Club Razor Blade Company, New Jersey, and Perma Sharp Company, New York.

1967—Packaging now three-color. Sales directed toward industrial and hospital markets. Blades feature Teflon coatings and imported stainless steel.

April 24, 1967—Announced: Super Stainless Steel blister pack, Marlin Rifle Double Edge Super Blades, Lacquered Blue blades, Micro Edge blades, Marlin safety scraper, Marlin razor knife, and industrial package of 1,000 double-edge blades for $8.30.

May 1, 1967—Counter displays offered that hold 20 pounds of blades of various types and packages.

October 4, 1967—Super stainless, blister pack, Vydax®-coated edge now used. Vydax is a DuPont name for its fluoro-telomer coating.

September 25, 1968—Free color film given with purchase of Marlin Super Stainless Steel razor blades. Offer expires September 30, 1969.

Razor Blade Packaging

1939-1945. Double-edge blades were first packaged in a dark blue box. The box was the tray-and-sleeve type. A section in the box was for holding the used blades. Later during this period the color of the box was changed to a lighter blue. Single-edge blades were in red boxes of the double-edge type. Both types of blades were in envelopes, blue for double edge and red for single edge. Counter display boxes had a bull's-eye and blade printed on the stand-up top flap and were either 12

New Marlin Blades building, which was constructed during Marlin's WW II expansion. War work included packaging millions of razor blades for the military.

Typical countertop packaging of Marlin blades in 1946.

Window display material furnished dealers by Marlin during WW II. It highlights the letter from an Anzio Beachhead soldier who used a Marlin razor blade to make a workable "crystal" radio set.

boxes per carton at 12 for 25¢ or 6 boxes per carton at 27 for 50¢.

1946. Counter and hanging display cards were introduced that had 20 small boxes of blades attached in a manner for easy removal. The double edge were 5 for 10¢ and the single edge were 4 for 10¢. Brushless and lather shaving creams were 50¢ a tube.

1951. Safti-Quik box, white and blue panels now in use. The double-edge blade wrapper was made so that the blade could be hooked to the razor and the wrapper removed without the fingers touching the blade. Prices were 12 for 25¢, 27 for 50¢ or 60 for $1.00.

1952. Injector blade box of new design was introduced that was marked at 20 for 59¢. It was attached to a card that could be hung from a pegboard display. The metal blade container was not marked *Marlin*. At Christmas time a promotional package was also sold that had a "Merry Christmas" sleeve over the regular box. It was marked 60 for $1.00.

1966. A plastic dispenser of 40 blades, which were in a blister pack and card-mounted, was introduced. The dispenser was marked *ECONO—PAC, Micro-Edged, 40/98¢.*

1967. During this year a new package design was introduced. The image of a Marlin Model 336 rifle and *MARLIN RIFLE*

Shaving cream counter display.

Counter display of packages of Marlin double-edge blades.

Price	Razor Type	Year
5/10¢	DE	1946
4/10¢	SE	1946
12/25¢	DE	1946
12/25¢	SE	1946
25/50¢	DE	1947
60/$1.00	DE	1947–1948
20/59¢	Inj	1951
12/25¢	DE	1951
27/50¢	DE	1951
60/$1.00	DE	1951 Safti-Quik
10/$1.00	Inj.	1967
5/69¢	DE	1967 Super Stainless
8/35¢	SE	1967
40/98¢	DE	–
7/89¢	Inj.	1968

REAL ESTATE DIVISION

In 1969, the Marlin Gun Division and Industrial Division moved from New Haven to a new multimillion dollar plant and office facility in North Haven, Conn. Before finishing the new plant and making the move, Marlin considered the problem of what to do with the old location on Willow St. in New Haven—the home of the company since 1880. The company could sell the real estate and buildings, or rent the land and buildings to a single tenant. A third option was to revitalize the property by tearing down some of the obsolete buildings, refurbishing the remaining property by subdividing it into smaller sections, and renting to tenants desiring a small manufacturing facility or office space.

The choice decided upon was to form a subsidiary real estate division, and to refurbish and rent. As a result, this profit-making division of Marlin has taken old and obsolete factory space and revitalized it into modern offices, manufacturing facilities, and warehouse space that is usually 97% occupied and now has 36 tenants, among them about 19 architectural and graphic arts companies.

When George Allard, manager of the Marlin Realty Corporation, gave me a tour of the place (after 17 years of development), I was amazed and impressed with what had been done to the "old plant," where I first joined Marlin. New paint, elevator, partitions, heating, lighting, stairs, and modernization were well done and illustrate what can be done to tired and old real estate when the buildings are structurally sound.

Fortunately, the modernization of the old place did not alter the outward appearance. It still looks like it did when the 1882-dated keystone was placed into the top of the archway entrance into the inner parking area. Marlin collectors still get a nostalgic feeling when they visit the old Marlin factory buildings.

On April 1, 1987, Marlin Realty Corporation was separated from The Marlin Firearms Company and is now owned by the Kenna family.

BLADES were boldly printed on the top of the card. Double-edge packaging was gold, blue, and red in color. Single-edge blades were in a blue and red package. The double-edge blades were in a white plastic dispenser. The single-edge blades were in two four-blade tab boxes and then in a blister. The double-edge and single-edge cards were marked *Polymer coated.* The injector blade metal container had a red label pasted on the top side.

1968. The last package used highlighted a color film offer. The top of the card was to be returned to Marlin for a free roll of either 126, 127, or 620 film.

Prices for blades varied during the 30 years Marlin was in the razor blade business. Frequently, special promotional sales were conducted to increase sales, to move inventory, or to introduce a new feature to the retail consumer. Sometimes the price did not change but the number of blades did. Some of the variations in packaging and prices were as follows:

Price	Razor Type	Year
18/25¢	DE	Pre-1945
27/50¢	SE	Pre-1945

Incorporations

REVIEW OF MARLIN COMPANIES, 1881-1926

John Marlin manufactured pistols, revolvers, and the Ballard rifle as J.M. Marlin. In 1880, after John Marlin had expanded his operation and product line to include a repeating rifle, he needed additional capital and equipment to continue.

Charles Daly of Shoverling and Daly, New York City, had previously encouraged John Marlin to manufacture the Ballard rifle, for which Mr. Daly had acquired the manufacturing rights. Thus it was a natural thing to join Charles Daly's business ability and John Marlin's mechanical and manufacturing talents by forming a corporation. Charles Daly had the necessary capital and John Marlin had a business already well on the way. The incorporators and stockholders of this new company were John M. Marlin, Augustus Shoverling, Charles Daly, Joseph J. Sweeney, and Henry B. Moore. The officers of The Marlin Fire Arms Company, which was accepted as a corporation by the general assembly of Connecticut at its January 1881 session, were Charles Daly, president, and Joseph J. Sweeney, secretary. The amount of capital actually paid in and belonging to the corporation was $200,000.

The newly formed company purchased The Malleable Iron Foundry Company on Willow Street, constructed additional buildings, and moved Marlin's gun business from State and Hamilton Streets to the new location. Most of those first buildings still stand, including the one that was a foundry. The main building, parallel to Willow Street, is dated 1882.

Some years later, John Marlin purchased all of the outstanding shares of stock and from then until 1915 the corporation was solely owned by the Marlin family.

In 1915 the Marlin family sold The Marlin Fire Arms Company to a syndicate formed to manufacture military arms for England and Russia. The original Connecticut corporation was absolved and on February 4, 1916, a New York State corporation was formed. It was called the Marlin Arms Corporation. Later in 1916, the name only was changed to Marlin-Rockwell Corporation.

On February 8, 1918, the Marlin-Rockwell Corporation became an inactive New York corporation and Marlin-Rockwell proceeded to divest itself of all holdings.

On August 23, 1921, new owners of the sporting arms part of the Marlin-Rockwell Corporation incorporated in the state of Delaware as The Marlin Firearms Corporation.

Upon being foreclosed and sold at auction on May 10, 1924, The Marlin Firearms Corporation no longer existed.

On January 15, 1926, a new Connecticut corporation was formed by Frank Kenna, Sr. It was incorporated as The Marlin Firearms Company. This corporation exists to this date.

Other solely owned subsidiary corporations of the Marlin Firearms Company have been the following:

Illustrated Current News	January 13, 1914
Marlin Industrial Division	March 27, 1942
Photocraft	October 23, 1961
Marlin Realty Corporation	October 29, 1967
L.C. Smith Gun Corp. (Dissolved)	August 21, 1969
MAREX	May 26, 1983

The Marlin Industrial Division, Photocraft, Illustrated Current News, and the Marlin Realty Corporation, as of April 1, 1987, were no longer solely owned subsidiary corporations of The Marlin Firearms Company. They are now separate corporations, having their own officers and stockholders.

THE MARLIN FIREARMS COMPANY ACTIVITIES:

Extracts From Minutes of the Directors' Meetings, 1926–1966

January 19, 1926 — The Marlin Firearms Company is incorporated by Frank Kenna, Thomas W. Cahill, and Harold G. Wynne. Directors: Frank Kenna, Edward J. Brennan, and Thomas W. Cahill.

December 15, 1929 — Thomas W. Cahill, manager and director, resigns.

July 29, 1931 — Edward J. Brennan resigns; Roger Kenna and Milton Small become directors. Roger Kenna is named secretary.

December 1, 1935 — Corner lot sold to Atlantic Refining Company for $4,000.

December 30, 1935 — Razor blade business mentioned in a letter to stockholders.

1936 — Officers are Frank Kenna, president and treasurer; Roger Kenna, secretary; E.F. Liedke, assistant secretary; Milton Small, director; W. Herbert Frost, director.

February 4, 1936 — J.L. Galef Company has contract dated October 2, 1935 to purchase 5,000 Model 93 rifles and carbines. Reconstruction Finance Corporation makes $70,000 loan.

March 18, 1936 — Roger Kenna made vice president. Fifteen million blades to be made by April 1.

May 1, 1936 — Eight million blades sold. Possibility of a Marlin Carriage Company.

May 25, 1936 — Homer G. Sanborn, Jr., will manage carriage department.

May 28, 1936 — Half a million blades sold in one week. *Consumer research* magazine places Marlin blades at head of recommended list.

June 18, 1936 — Reconstruction Finance Corporation's $70,000 loan is payable in five years.

July 21, 1936 — Marlin makes telescope mounts for Sears. Carl Ekdahl (Tool maker during WW I and engineer and gun designer from 1928 to 1936) improves them with clicks, which are sold to Speigel and May Stern Company.

August 13, 1936 — Delivery of over-under shotgun: 1st week, 150; 2nd week, 100; 3rd week, 200; until total reaches 450 each week. 800,000 razor blades sold last week.

September 17, 1936 — Will have A.P. Curtis, formerly with Iver Johnson, for three months' trial.

October 22, 1936 — Theodore Lynch (son-in-law of Frank Kenna, Sr.) is to be employed in the carriage department. Matter of hiring women in plant being considered. 30,000 Model 100s to be manufactured. Thomas W. Cahill left company on October 17.

November 19, 1936 — Marlin paid Sears $1,000 for all rights, title, and interest in telescope mounts. Considering disposing of the carriage business. Mr. Rowe of Rowe Paints is interested in buying the business.

February 27, 1937 — Plans to make 90,000 guns in the year — 8,000 will be over-under shotguns.

March 24, 1937 — Workers voted to strike. Recognized CIO Union. 5% increase in pay. Expect to cease the carriage business, and keep only the carriage hardware business. Mr. Sanborn may carry on the bicycle business. Mr. Kenna is financing John Morrison in starting up the brush business. It will cost $1,500. Paid $2,100 to purchase from E.G. Reising a tubular magazine gun now called the Model 81.

June 24, 1937 — Mr. Herr, foreman of assembly department, died on June 15.

June 26, 1937 — Business for the year:

	$600,000
Shipments	146,000
To be shipped	454,000

As of May 31, 1937:

Firearms loss	$6,229.28
Blade profit	$1,605.12
Carriage loss	$2,945.38

Bikes purchased from Westfield Manufacturing Co. Sold 303 to date. Operation to cease end of June 1937. Attempting to sell carriage business for $16,000. Our coaches are styled for New York City use.

Inventory	$10,000
Machinery & Tools	6,000
	$16,000

Brush Department — all activities have been stopped. Mr. Johnson of Boston requested two models of his army rifle be made. Advance of $1,000 necessary to meet payroll.

July 15, 1937 — Through association of Johnson and North in lawsuit, Melvin Johnson engaged Marlin services in tool department to develop a military rifle for him. Direct labor plus 101% of overhead expenses required.

August 10, 1937 — W. Herbert Frost resigns as director because he and his New Haven bank do not agree on a plan to issue the company long-term notes without interest. The plan is to give the person lending the money a rifle free if he considers a no-interest loan.

August 10, 1937–October 10, 1937 — During this period, the company obtained numerous loans on finished inventory, which was held in escrow at the Durham Storage Company in New Haven. The loans were obtained from the New Haven Bank and were paid off before February 1938 by Sears and Galef & Son, at which time the firearms were delivered. Among the models involved were Model 100s, Model 90s and Model A1s.

November 12, 1937 — Bids for 200,000 razor blades for U.S. government filed.

November 22, 1937 — Owe Westfield Manufacturing Company of Westfield, Massachusetts $4,789.24 for bicycles. Turn over accounts receivable of $2,840.86 and pay all payments to Westfield; return 47 bicycles for $1,027.60 in credits and $813.79 in notes. End of bicycle business.

December 15, 1937 — Five-year note circulars violated a Missouri statute. Discounts of 8½%, 10½%, and ½% in addition to the regular 2% cash discount are given on any order for shipment. This will turn a part of large inventory into cash.

February 14, 1938 — $125,000 application made to Reconstruction Finance Corporation and New Haven Bank.

April 22, 1938 — Pennsylvania added to five-year loan restriction.

May 6, 1938 — Ohio added to objecting states on five-year loan proposal.

June 12, 1938 — CIO out; savings to $4,000.

July 21, 1938—Report by Ted Lynch of changes to be made and resultant savings. 1938 is an important year in Marlin progress.

October 17, 1938—Sales office and razor blade business to move to New York City for six months, effective November 1, 1938.

July 26, 1939—The officers are Frank Kenna, president; Roger Kenna, vice president; Frank Kenna, treasurer; R.C. Paine, assistant treasurer; Roger Kenna, secretary; R.C. Paine, assistant secretary; Sidney L. Carlson, manager of blades.

March 4, 1941—Marlin factory leased to United Defense Supply Corporation for purpose of government contract—85,000 guns to be manufactured.

May 19, 1941—Industrial Center incorporated; D&I Shirt Company a tenant.

July 3, 1941—Marlin will produce the 9-mm High Standard submachine gun for the United Defense Supply Corporation.

August 6, 1941—Government contract for 25 double-barrel shotguns received.

June 11, 1942—Agreement made with U.S. government for production of M2 submachine gun (W478-ORD-1925).

July 10, 1942—Roger Kenna named vice president and secretary.

April 5, 1943—Company receives carbine barrel contract. (W478-ORD-3362).

April 27, 1943—Blue Streak Razor Blade Company will bid on government orders for blades in the name of Marlin as its agent. Ordnance test of M2 gun is okay. Many changes to be made—powdered metal parts and redesign planned. 42,500 M2's to be produced on a reduced schedule—plus spare parts. It takes 38 minutes to rifle a barrel, whereas 32 barrels can be broached in one hour. Washington to permit Marlin to broach carbine barrels.

May 5, 1943—Contest for ideas for new and improved models—2,000 ideas so far.

May 13, 1943—Blades business now the Razor Blades Division of The Marlin Firearms Company.

June 3, 1943—Frank Kenna commended for wonderful ad that appeared in *New Haven Register*. Three modified and improved M2s being tested by Ordnance. Order for 180,000 rifle barrels for 1944 reduced to 150,000. 3,000 ideas submitted. Considering getting into the ammunition business after the war.

June 9, 1943—Mr. Scoville (Ordnance District) advised Frank Kenna that M2 contract was formally cancelled, and production was stopped.

June 10, 1943—32,000 triggers and 46,000 hammers on carbine job. Blade Division to move into new building on Friday. D&I Shirt Company using the third floor. Steel allocation to Blade Division cut by 30%.

June 24, 1943—Marlin bid of $7.70 per thousand blades accepted by government. Barrel broaching dropped. Producing 4,800 carbine stocks a week.

July 1, 1943—During July, August, and September, company is to make 50,000,000 blades, 1,000,000 to the Armed Forces. Marlin was paid by the Netherlands government for the United Defense gun, but the Netherlands through United Defense sold the guns to the U.S. Original contract was with the Netherlands, not United Defense Supply Corporation. Subcontracts with Shollhorn Company of New Haven (pliers) and Bell Aircraft (nine items, 84,000 units). Pope gun studied—36 parts—low priced. Shaving cream problems—must be kept in a cool place.

July 23, 1943—1,000 carbine barrels accepted to date.

July 29, 1943—1,500 carbine barrels passed inspection.

August 5, 1943—Three bolts being made for Bell. Preparing for wing strut contract.

August 12, 1943—Hand guard for carbine—2,000/day. Some question as to who owns Model 90—Sears or Marlin? First prize in idea contest was an interchangeable chamber.

August 26, 1943—Production cost of UDM '42 was $400,000. Profit on Garand barrel $22,000. M2 parts to be sold for scrap. Shaving cream to be purchased from Woodbury Company.

September 16, 1943—Jenkinson working on Model 36. He also designed unloading system for tubular magazine.

September 23, 1943—Carbine barrels at 55/day; 7,200 stocks a week. 200 stocks for Sprague & Carleton for their IBM contract. Strut job known as B4 to B9. M3 gun—2,900 produced. Pal furnishes 100,000 blades a month. Frank Kenna looking into production of a bicycle. Razor at 18¢ each—should Marlin make or have made? Government contract received for 12,000,000 blades for next quarter. Subcontract carbine stocks for Underwood, Elliot and Underwood. 15,000 in September. Marlin only contractor to make carbine barrel quota. M2 parts sold for $15.40 a ton. Schollhorn contract to be completed by April 1944. Discussed the new Reising caliber .30 gun and that H&R claimed it basically their design with gas system added. Want H&R, Reising, and Marlin to set up a meeting to agree on paying Reising a royalty to be shared with H&R so they can proceed with making the gun. Discussed with Washington the possibility of making the '03 or Enfield for Ecuadorian government.

October 23, 1943—Carbine barrel contract extended to 314,000 total.

November 4, 1943—Unofficial report that the United Defense gun being used successfully in Africa. Looking into Pope/High Standard/United Defense agreement. Carbine guard production off.

November 26, 1943—Bob Jenkinson, Teaneck, N.J., designer for the company, explained details of improvements for Models 36 and 39. 15,000 carbine barrels shipped to Buffalo Arms. Standard Products complained that 2,300 barrels sent them are not straight.

December 7, 1943—F. Powell resident Ordnance inspector at Marlin. Marlin carbine barrels sand-blasted and Dulited. Blades contract for 15,000,000 blades.

December 30, 1943—Bell Aircraft contract is $501,244.16. Industrial Division is $866,800. Looking into cost of making hair brushes.

January 6, 1944—Blades—$1,105,000; Gun—$3,145,000. Blades limited to 168,000,000 blades. Looking into making fishing lures. Blades Division has 8½% of business. Commercial gun restart will require study of steel allocations, carton material, increased wages, War Production Board. Only barrels on hand.

February 10, 1944 — Postwar ammunition business discussed. Also discussed are toy guns, hobby horses, furniture, subcontracting some parts, and machine operation during restart.

March 16, 1944 — Four wood tables of different sizes manufactured. Sell for $5.50 with retail at $6.95. Barrel job to stop on April 1, 1944. Stock job to run to April 8. Number of employees — 160.

April 27, 1944 — Looking into razor blade sharpener.

May 11, 1944 — Shaving cream to be closed out. Mr. Studler informed Marlin that the United Defense guns have been captured by the Germans and the possibility of any spare parts order was very unlikely.

June 1, 1944 — Contract for 3rd quarter of 20 million blades received. Considering the purchase of the Sedgley Company of Philadelphia. Sears considers it important to get back into the gun business. Discussed Reising gun.

June 15, 1944 — Expect to make 15,000 toy guns. Macy's ordered 720. May Company ordered 600 and Spiegel wants 12,000.

June 29, 1944 — Discussed the Reising improvement on the .45 automatic. Adopting the Reising improvements on the .22. Now classified as an aircraft plant rather than an Ordnance plant. Savage 300 only new model now in plant. War Manpower Commission set ceiling at 159 male workers. Only 7% of the employees have been with the company over three to four years.

July 15, 1944 — Shipped 1,071 tables; 300 in process. Will stop production at 2,000.

July 20, 1944 — It was suggested that Marlin manufacture razor blades rather than purchase them from other companies.

August 17, 1944 — Toy gun business being liquidated — cannot get substantial numbers of defective stocks.

September 28, 1944 — Birch wood stocks for Canada. (100,000)

October 5, 1944 — Drop High Speed from razor blades.

October 12, 1944 — Bob Jenkinson working on automatic .22.

October 26, 1944 — Signs on ends and front of building to be installed. Single-barrel shotgun (Model 45) inspected. Mr. Kenna was surprised to learn that one had previously been manufactured. Purchasing reject walnut M1 rifle stock blanks. Designing toy gun (Marlin Junior). Backlog of 875,000 tubes of shaving cream of both types.

November 16, 1944 — Henry and Leo Molkenthin hired by Marlin — Henry was formerly president of the American Razor Blade Company. Marlin to form a subsidiary company.

December 21, 1944 — Cartoon advertising was successful and better than other forms. Single-edge business eliminated during war.

January 4, 1945 — Can have ready for delivery by March 15 3,000 Model 100s, 1,000 Model 80s, and 1,000 Model 81s.

January 25, 1945 — Pope gun has interchangeable .45 and 9-mm barrels.

February 8, 1945 — Have enough material on hand for 4,700 Junior toy guns.

February 28, 1945 — The following pieces are being manufactured on subcontracts:

Bell Aircraft	Perkins	Glen Martin	Wallace Metals
Wing Fittings	Housing	Sliding cam	Tables
Pawls	Plate	Trigger cam	Link
Brackets	Cap	Turntable	Fuze

March 8, 1945 — Frank Kenna, Jr., present for meeting.

March 9, 1945 — Article about Frank Kenna in *Colliers* magazine. 3,000 Trainer guns shipped to date.

March 22, 1945 — Two types of 100s (large and small stocks). Want to move the Model T's (small stock) now.

March 24, 1945 — Contracts received for 20-mm Link (W19-059-ORD-2254), and M48Fuze (W19-059-ORD-2570).

March 29, 1945 — Company is purchasing all the scrap stocks it can find.

April 5, 1945 — Mr. Kenna stated that no further effort will be made to sell the trainer gun. In 1940, Marlin sold 70 million razor blades.

April 19, 1945 — $16,000 was expended on development of Reising gun, which was actually produced here. 16,588 Junior guns shipped up to April 15. 52 people working on Junior gun.

May 10, 1945 — No men in polishing department — all women. Mr. Kenna wants to maintain aggressive advertising in connection with Blades, in that he feels he would rather have advertising than cash. No mortgage, no bonds, or any bank loans. Advertising will help to make *Marlin* a household name so that people will automatically go to Marlin products.

May 31, 1945 — Wing fitting job cancelled by Bell. Model 90 tools belong to Marlin. 147 people employed; 40% on government work.

June 28, 1945 — Company to start shipping guns. Marlin uses 90% of BlueStrike production of blades. Royalty proposal made to Mr. Swebilius at High Standard.

July 12, 1945 — Company has never made more than 5,000 Model 39s in one year before.

July 19, 1945 — Looking into L.C. Smith shotgun and Hunter Arms Company — worth buying at $100,000. 214 employees. Model 39 being drilled for Lyman sight.

August 9, 1945 — 221 employees. Dispenser for blades to be hung up, making blades readily available. 20-mm link contract made with Auto Type Company. Sears wants Marlin name on Model 90.

September 6, 1945 — Frank Kenna selected by the Advertising Club of New Haven as its outstanding citizen of the year. He will speak on the matter of providing opportunities for returning veterans (September 12, 1945).

September 27, 1945 — Toy gun business dried up. Tom Robinson coming in for interview.

October 4, 1945 — Robinson and Johnson to start work.

October 11, 1945 — Model 36 will be heat treated and blued. Model 39A will be case hardened and blued. L.C. Smith Gun Company formed, a solely owned subsidiary. 332 on payroll. Blades developed package of ten for 17¢.

October 25, 1945 — 46 on L.C. Smith payroll. 383 on Marlin payroll. Hiring a blind veteran.

November 21, 1945 — 402 employees ($19,000 payroll). Acquired Hunter Arms Company on November 20, 1945. Roger Kenna elected president of L.C. Smith Company.

December 13, 1945 — 486 employees. Model 39s now in production.

January 15, 1948 — Visited Ardell and Molkenthin blade plants in Newark, N.J.

January 20, 1948 — First Model 88 off the line.

January 26, 1948 — Roger Kenna, now president; Vertie M

Kenna, director *ex officio.*

February 5, 1948 – First round bolt inspected.

February 15, 1948 – Round bolt tested.

March 15, 1948 – New Haven has shipped 6118 turned L.C. Smith stocks to Fulton, N.Y.

April 7, 1948 – Caliber .35 barrel received from Remington for fitting to new round bolt receiver, with plan to add this caliber to line.

April 22, 1948 – Caliber .35 rifle made up.

May 6, 1948 – Round bolt caliber .32 Special made.

May 27, 1948 – Discussed with Springfield Armory the possibility of furnishing 3½- and 4½-pound over-under survival guns. Investigated the porting of the left side of the receiver of the 39A to reduce back blast of gas.

May 28, 1948 – Meeting with W.H.B. Smith on making stocks for Model 1898 Mauser rifle for Firearms International.

June 24, 1948 – Investigating the three types of single triggers for the Model 90. The Crowe and Lard are selective and the Romberg was nonselective. First production of 336 tested.

August 26, 1948 – Redesign of the 39 locking shoulder is started, moving the finger lever from the tang side to the left side. Plan to check Barbasol machines at Molkenthin plant.

October 7, 1948 – All Barbasol equipment located within plant.

January 25, 1949 – Industrial Center incorporated. Rents Molkenthin building to Blades Division. Nick DeMusis joins company.

February 8, 1949 – Medallion grip cap design submitted. Investigation of manufacture of Bendix outboard motor begins. Mr. Townsend submits caliber .35 Remington tubular magazine rifle.

February 17, 1949 – Model 88 rifle in production.

March 3, 1949 – Razor blade trimming comb suggested by Mr. Small.

March 31, 1949 – Mr. Townsend submits 219 Zipper 336. Patent on new extractor for Models 80, 81 and 336 issued on March 29, 1949.

June 22, 1949 – Tools and drawings for the 16- and 20-gauge Model 90 are being made. Prototype of new left side of the Model 39A receiver is made up. Also angular vent cut in barrel butt and gas port demonstrated.

August 4, 1949 – Designing flat spring extractor for Model 39A.

August 11, 1949 – John Gregoire presented a design of a hammerless Ballard-type rifle. In 1950, plan for 60,000 Model 336s and 15,000 Model 39As of the improved type.

August 14, 1949 – Investment cast 39A bolts received. 6,000 not up to specs will be used by repair department.

August 18, 1949 – 1,750 Model 336s a week. Rights for the H&R clip magazine may be required. Pilot lot of 16- and 20-gauge Model 90s going through the plant.

August 25, 1949 – Three self-cocking W.H.B. Smith single-shots were evaluated.

September 15, 1949 – Death of Mahlon H. Marlin announced. Model 336s oversold by 19,000 guns.

September 22, 1949 – 60,000 deer rifles to be made.

September 29, 1949 – Associated Realty's first six month profit is $19,393. Industrial Center profit – $3,500.

October 30, 1949 – Model 88 sales planned for 50,000, but actual sales only 19,282.

November 3, 1949 – Jenkinson, Crowe, and Curtis selective single triggers and Petersen and Romberg nonselective triggers tested for Model 90. Also Crowe ejector model with ventilated rib and Curtis model with solid rib available for testing. Romberg nonselective to be used. The Capra Stilson wrench is formed chiefly from tubing and blanked stock. A sample was made up and submitted for consideration.

April 5, 1950 – Eugene Reising trombone action high power rifle is examined. Safety sear – along the lines of the Model 1891 – is being fitted to the Model 336. Magnetizing elements will be set up in the Excell razor blade wrapping machines.

June 21, 1950 – W.H.B. Smith Pump action rifle has some fatal weaknesses. No further consideration will be given his design.

September 20, 1950 – Will modify a Model 88 for submachine gun use.

October 19, 1950 – Remington and Winchester will correct their differences in caliber .35 ammunition.

December 28, 1950 – Remington button-rifled barrel tested.

February 8, 1951 – The Marlin Firearms Company to lease the L.C. Smith Gun Company equipment and machinery, paying rent there. Kenro Products, Inc. to be changed to the Marlin Sales Agency Inc., Frank Kenna, Jr., elected to directorship in the company.

February 15, 1951 – Company to pay $2,000 a month rental for L.C. Smith equipment and machinery. David Mathewson retained as developer of high-power rifle.

March 29, 1951 – Contract obtained for $900,000 for the manufacture of carbine stocks. Marlin already has two barrel contracts (52,500 M1 barrels).

June 7, 1951 – Walter Howe joins research and development. 10¢-a-gun royalty to Winchester on takedown safety feature.

June 11, 1951 – 1,000 M1 barrels in process. 2,000 move up to rifling. 30,000 pounds of crucible steel for M1 barrels.

June 20, 1951 – Harold Romberg authorized to subcontract on M1 and M3 barrels.

August 30, 1951 – Walter Howe proposed bolt hold-open feature for the Model 88. Side loading port proposed for Model 88. Magazine plate suggested by Walter Howe for 89C. Peep sight for 88 planned (88C).

October 25, 1951 – Tom Robinson proposed to stop paying Winchester 10¢ royalty a gun to takedown button cut that prevents gun from being disassembled when cocked. He has fix for the problem.

February 10, 1952 – 48,700 M1 barrels manufactured.

July 31, 1952 – 14 new operations on M1 barrel – button or broach can be used on M3 barrel.

September 10, 1952 – 2,500 M1 barrel blanks replaced by Republic Steel Company.

September 23, 1952 – Third M3 barrel order. Will try seamless tubing. 500 a week to be shipped to Export. P. Melchionda resident Ordnance inspector.

October 17, 1952 – Tested Sunamatic pistol. Not recommended.

November 6, 1952 – Button rifling on the 39A looks good.

December 18, 1952 — Republic Lens Company and Dr. Polack-off designing a telescope for Marlin (caliber .22).

February 12, 1953 — The Glenfield Products Company handles sale of only brand name guns.

December 17, 1953 — Brank-Neal family of guns discussed. Tom Robinson proposes to drop project, since nothing of worth has been produced by them. Receiving complaints that 322 rifles keyhole.

February 18, 1954 — Frank Kenna, Jr., named assistant treasurer.

April 5, 1954 — All bolt action and semiautomatic rifles will have the receivers dovetailed for telescopes.

April 10, 1954 — Of the 150 Model 322s planned for production, 93 have been sold (as of April 12, 108 had been sold). 1,000 more receivers should be ordered from Jan Winters of Firearms International.

May 5, 1954 — About this date all 39As for Sears will have barrels drilled and tapped for Weaver N-type telescope mounts.

May 17, 1954 — Model 39s drilled and tapped for receiver sight.

July 13, 1954 — Katz 80Cs were shipped with plastic gun case and a compass.

August 2, 1954 — Model 55 will be drilled and tapped for Lyman Model 40-SM receiver sight.

August 5, 1954 — 1,800 cleaning kits on hand. Idea of Marlin putting together own cleaning kit dropped.

September 8, 1954 — Production of 90DT stopped — have sold 1,700 pieces to date — 3,400 in inventory. 700 Model 322s sold to date; 1,350 in production.

October 5, 1954 — Model 336 in 1955 will have Micro-Groove barrel. A telescope may also be available.

July 12, 1955 — Cobra Choke to be used on Model 55. First run will be for Coast to Coast. Multi-Choke delivery in November. Model 455 available in September or October. Will order Bishop stocks. With regard to the Sears private brand 90DT, must make 12,000 pieces to get a $48.12 cost. Model 336s with engraved receivers should be ready within two weeks.

October 25, 1955 — Sears wants 3,000 Model 90s during the next three years; Sears to take 2,000, Marlin 1,000. Adapter base for 39A and 56 now being made.

January 5, 1956 — Levermatic 12-gauge shotgun in process. Center-fire Levermatic on the drawing board.

January 24, 1956 — For 1956, Sears wants 275 of 20/28, 500 of 16/28, 725 of 12/28. 219 Zipper available in March or April of 1956.

March 27, 1956 — Prototype lever action shotgun was shown first in 12-gauge; idea dropped. *Outdoor Life* magazine ad for catalog and sighting-in guide for $1.00.

May 24, 1956 — Frank Kenna, Jr., named assistant treasurer and production manager.

October 23, 1956 — Model 39As to have gold trigger, fixed swivels, grip cap, and walnut filled stock. Tip-off mount base standard equipment. Model 39A to have bright crowned muzzle. 800–900 caliber .22 cleaning kits still on hand. New Model 98 prototype shown. New bead front sight to be standard. Model 336 in next run will have pistol grip cap and white line spacer. Model 336A to have Lyman 16B folding leaf sight, Monte Carlo stock, and fixed swivel. All will have new stock finish.

November 13, 1956 — Offset hammer spur for 39A will be made at slight additional cost. Later on will be standard equipment. Marlin Super 98 Automatic will be available about January 30, 1957. New stainless bead sight to be available January 1957. New oil stock finish to be ready the first of 1957. Cheekpiece stock for 336 additional.

December 4, 1956 — Advertising for Golden 39A scheduled for April 1957 issues of selected magazines. Paper targets for 80 and 81. Military training rifle delivered to Marine Corps.

April 9, 1957 — Model 322 inventory sold. 1,000 Sako actions on hand. New name *Varmint King* to be used. Will have lightweight barrel and a Bishop cheekpiece stock. Weight will be six pounds with a 3-shot caliber .222 magazine.

June 4, 1957 — To run ad that Model 90DT can be converted to single trigger for $25.00.

April 29, 1965 — Reconsidering dropping Model 122. T-knob on 101 instead of ring. Forget 80 and 81 DLs.

May 6, 1965 — Pilot run of 444s next week. 7,500 for next year. Model 122 will not be in 1966 catalog. Engraved Model 39A sent to *Gun Digest*.

May 13, 1965 — New L.C. Smith will have ventilated rib installed with epoxy. Model 99 with brass frame and aluminum barrel to be made. Model 62 will be chambered for .30 caliber carbine cartridge. 22 Jet is deferred.

June 10, 1965 — T-handle for Model 101 approved. Brass frame 99 dropped. The following models to be dropped in 1966: 57, 57WA, 57MWA, 59, 59WA, 55-16-gauge, Swamp gun, 989G, 989, 122, 980 Sears, 81G, 80DL, 81DL.

August 5, 1965 — Model 99 to start with number AA1000.

August 26, 1965 — Caliber .256 to be dropped in 1966 catalog. Carbine version of 99G to be added to 1966 catalog.

October 14, 1965 — 4140 steel approved for 444 barrel. Model 99WA (#120) to be serial-numbered.

January 20, 1966 — Possible ideas for 1970 commemorative: special 39C, commemorative medallion, special new 1894, gifts to land grant colleges, engraved 336.

March 10, 1966 — For 1970 Centennial, 39AW with octagon barrel. New Model 49 (99 with two-piece stock).

March 17, 1966 — Model 336/44 to stay in line one more year.

August 4, 1966 — Bolt hold-open to be phased in in 1967. L.C. Smith to be in 1967 catalog.

October 20, 1966 — Squirrel and deer head engraved in stocks.

December 15, 1966 — 39A with 24-in. octagon barrel due February 1, 1967.

April 13, 1967 — Recommended gunsmiths are to be set up across the country.

April 27, 1967 — Model 1894 in .44 magnum for 1969. Centennial model to be 39 with full octagon barrel.

May 11, 1967 — Model 49 will first be for Western Auto. Model 1894 will start June 1 for 1969 catalog. Goose gun should be stamped *Original Goose Gun*.

August 3, 1967 — Model 49 will be in 1968 catalog. Robert Kain quoted $44 each for 336s and $36 each for engraving 39s. Production will be 15 a week.

November 3, 1967 — Retain 336/44 in 1968 catalog; 336T/44 not to be in retail catalog.

November 29, 1967 — Model 60 to have impressed checkering.

SECTION II

Descriptions of
Marlin Firearms

Handguns

John M. Marlin's introduction into the firearms business was a small, single-shot pistol that could easily be hidden in the palm of one's hand. It challenges the imagination to visualize that from such a simple start, the subsequent Marlin-named companies developed into today's multimillion dollar facility, which makes hundreds of thousands of firearms each year.

At the time John Marlin started production of his first pistol, there were a number of similar pistols that had been produced, some of which were still in production. Also, there were a few patents on pistol mechanisms very much like those of the Marlin pistol. Those that had the common feature of the barrel moving laterally on a vertical pin were the following:

Patent Number	Inventor	Date
35,941	J. Lee	June 22, 1862
43,259	S.M. Perry	June 21, 1864
43,260	S.M. Perry	June 21, 1864
46,617	E. Allen	Mar. 7, 1865
47,396	J.W. Cochran	Apr. 25, 1865
52,959	F.D. Newbury	Jan. 9, 1866
63,605	C.H. Ballard	Apr. 9, 1867
100,227	R. White	Feb. 22, 1870
101,637	J.M. Marlin	Apr. 5, 1870

The first Marlin pistol is identified here, and by most collectors, as the Marlin 1st Model. Some references identify it in-correctly as the Marlin Pocket Derringer. But because there were five different small pistols manufactured by John Marlin that could be so identified, the first one should be given the distinction of being first.

Of the five small single-shot pistols made by John Marlin, the 1st Model is the only one not identified by having a proper name marked on the gun. The others are identified and marked *OK, Victor, Never Miss* or *Stonewall.*

The word *derringer* is identified by Webster as a small pistol. Henry Deringer, Philadelphia, Pa., made small percussion and cartridge pistols during the 19th century. His name became synonymous with small pistols and is now used as a generic term to describe them. Unfortunately, at some point in time, the Deringer name was corrupted and is now generally found with two r's instead of one.

An interesting feature of all of the Marlin derringer-type pistols is the use of the latch (barrel lock) feature of the Ballard patent of 1867. It is my guess that some arrangement was made with Mr. Ballard to adopt this feature. It is an identifying feature of all of Marlin's small single-shot pistols. Those similar pistols without the small lock button between the trigger and hinge screw were not manufactured by Marlin. However, some other makes of derringer-type pistols have the same latch button; two examples are the one marked *GEM,* which was manufactured by J. Stevens and Company, Chicopee Falls, Mass., and the *XL DERRINGER*-marked pistol manufactured by Hopkins & Allen under the Marlin patent of April 5, 1870.

John Marlin's 1870 patent was for an ejector system, which

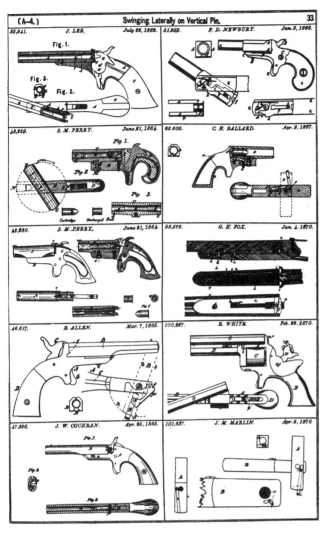

Patent drawings of patents similar to J.M. Marlin's 1st Model.

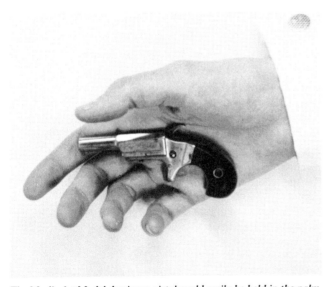

The Marlin 1st Model derringer pistol could easily be held in the palm of the hand, as shown here.

The 1st Model is not identified by a model designation. Shown is the typical marking on top of the barrel of this model.

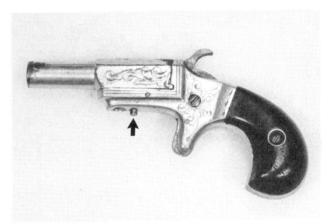

Typical nickel-plated and engraved 1st Model derringer-type pistol. The arrow points to the C.H. Ballard-patented barrel latch.

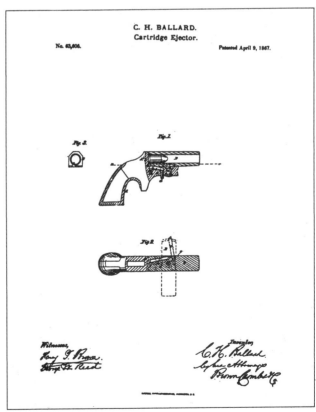

C.H. Ballard patent illustration of barrel latch mechanism used by J.M. Marlin, and others, to lock the barrel in the closed position. The ejector part of the patent was not used by Marlin.

Top: *Engraved 1st Model, which has a silver-plated frame, blued barrel, and rosewood grips.* Bottom: *Nickel-plated standard 1st Model pistol.*

Top: *Right side of caliber .22 OK derringer with a silver-plated (nearly gone) brass frame and blued steel barrel. Note the front sight, which all except the 1st Model derringers have.* Bottom: *Left side of OK derringer.*

Bottom view of 1st Model barrel showing the serial number 14105 and the narrow notch in which the barrel latch engages to hold the barrel closed.

Top of barrel showing OK model designation.

was used on only the Victor, Never Miss, and Stonewall models. It was not used on the 1st Model or OK derringers.

The 1867 Ballard patent for the barrel lock system included an ejector mechanism. However, the Ballard ejector worked when the barrel was rotated to the left. The barrel of all Marlin derringer pistols rotated to the right for loading and ejecting.

Characteristics of the Marlin derringer-type pistols, and serial numbers of those examined, are as follows:

1st Model
Made: 1863–1867
Quantity: Unknown
Serial Number: 43–10,430; bottom of barrel
Caliber: .22
Barrel: 2¹⁄₁₆ inches, blued or nickel, flat sides, no front sight
Frame: Brass, nickel-plated, fluted sides

Weight: 3.1 ounces
Grips: Rosewood
Markings: On top of barrel: *J.M. Marlin/New Haven, Ct.*

OK Model
Made: 1863–1870
Quantity: Unknown
Serial Number: 28–16,664; bottom of barrel
Caliber: .22, .30, .32 short, rimfire
Barrel: Part round, part octagon, flat sides, front sight, 2⅛ inches to 3⅛ inches
Frame: Brass, nickel-plated
Weight: 6.4 ounces
Grips: Rosewood
Markings: Right side of barrel: *J.M. Marlin/New Haven, Ct.*
Top of barrel: *OK*

Serial numbers were marked on the frame, grip, and barrel of the OK derringer.

Right side view of short-barrel Marlin Victor model derringer.

Parts of the OK derringer pistol.

Caliber .22 Never Miss derringer.

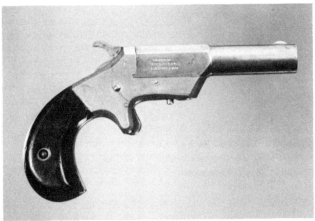

Right side view of caliber .32 Victor model derringer. Note that this model has the three-line roll-stamp that includes the J.M. Marlin ejector patent date, and flat sides to the barrel and frame.

Caliber .32 Never Miss derringer.

Caliber .41 Never Miss derringer.

Caliber .41 Never Miss derringer with ivory grips.

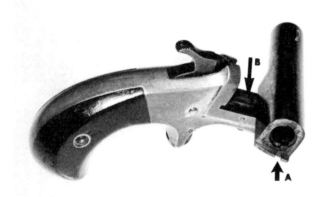

Never Miss derringer with the barrel rotated for loading. Arrow A indicates the ejector. This type of ejector was used on only the Never Miss and Victor models of Marlin derringers. The Ballard-patented barrel latch can be seen at arrow B.

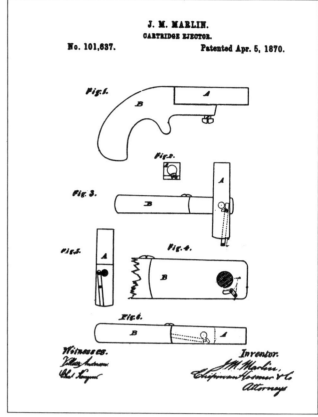

Patent drawing of J.M. Marlin patent number 101,637, dated April 5, 1870, which was used in the Never Miss and Little Joker derringer pistols.

Victor Model
Made: 1875–1881
Quantity: Unknown
Serial Number: 183–13,954; ejector bar, frame, barrel, grip
Caliber: .38 short, rimfire
Barrel: 2¹¹⁄₁₆ inches, flat sides, with ejector, front sight, part round, part octagon, six grooves, right-hand twist
Frame: Nickel- or silver-plated brass, with flat sides
Weight: 10 ounces
Grips: Rosewood
Markings: Right side of barrel: *J.M. Marlin/New Haven, Ct/ PAT. APRIL 5, 1870.* Top of barrel: *VICTOR.*

Never Miss Model
Made: 1870–1881
Quantity: Unknown
Serial Number: 68–11,193; barrel, ejector bar, frame, grip
Caliber: .22, .32 short, .41 rimfire.
Barrel: 2½ inches, round with front sight and ejector
Frame: Nickel- or silver-plated brass, fluted sides
Weight: 7½ to 10 ounces
Grips: Rosewood
Markings: Right side of barrel: *J.M. Marlin/New Haven, Ct/ PAT. APRIL 5, 1870.* Top of barrel: *NEVER MISS.*

Stonewall Model
Same as *Never Miss* in .41 caliber. Very rare.

Right side view of Stonewall derringer pistol.

Stonewall *marking on Marlin derringer.*

J.M. MARLIN STANDARD POCKET REVOLVERS

The Manhattan Firearms Company, New York, was incorporated in 1855. It manufactured percussion revolvers in .31 and .36 caliber, which outwardly looked very much like the Colt percussion revolvers of the period.

In anticipation of the Rollin White 1855-dated patent number 12,648 ("... chamber of the rotating cylinder right through the rear of the cylinder, for the purpose of enabling the said chambers to be charged at the rear either by hand or by a self-acting charger . . .") expiring in 1869, the Manhattan Firearms Company manufactured a near copy of the Smith & Wesson Model 1 caliber .22 cartridge revolver. This first 1861 variation of the Manhattan revolver was marked with a New York address. After September 15, 1863, when the Manhattan Company relocated and incorporated in New Jersey, the revolvers were marked differently.

On November 23, 1868, the Manhattan Company closed out its business, and a new company called the American Standard Tool Company was incorporated. This new company continued production of Manhattan-type caliber .22 revolvers until the stockholders voted to consent to dissolution of the corporation on February 20, 1873.

Although not found in writing, it appears that the American Standard Tool Company spur-trigger, tip-up barrel revolvers are the forerunners of the J.M. Marlin Standard revolvers. By comparing the Manhattan revolvers with the American Standard Tool Company revolvers, and in turn with the J.M. Marlin XXX and XX Standard spur-trigger, tip-up barrel revolvers of the first variations, it is evident that a connection existed. In 1872, John Marlin most likely had made an agreement with the

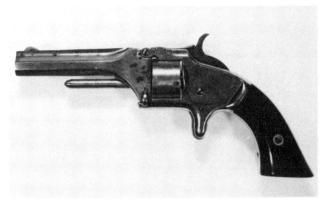

Smith & Wesson first-model, second-variation revolver, which was copied by the American Standard Tool Company.

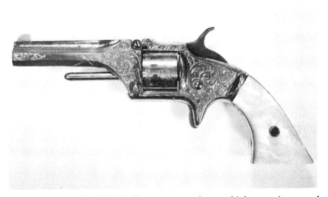

American Standard Tool Company revolver, which was improved upon and then manufactured by John Marlin.

Caliber .22 revolver marked AETNA ARMS CO. NEW YORK.

American Standard Tool Company to purchase the rights and the tools to manufacture its copy of the S&W revolver, which was no longer under the protection of the Rollin White patent.

The major differences between John Marlin's revolvers and the American Standard Tool Company's guns are that John Marlin's had a bird's-head (rounded) butt, a contoured curved abutment between frame and grip, a narrower barrel latch, and a patented pawl-spring mechanism. The Marlin revolvers also

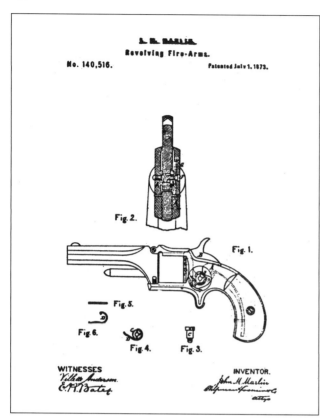

J. M. Marlin patent number 140,516, dated July 1, 1873, which was used in all Marlin Standard model pistols.

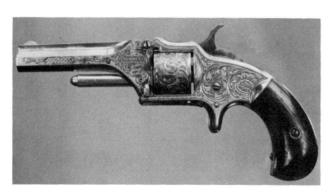

Engraved first variation of XXX Standard 1872 revolver, which has a flat-sided barrel with nonfluted cylinder.

J.M. Marlin marking on first-variation model XXX Standard 1872 revolver.

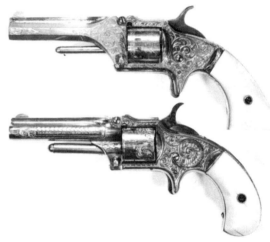

Top: *American Standard Tool Company revolver.* Bottom: *Second-variation XXX Standard revolver.*

Typical top-of-the-barrel roll-stamp for the round-barrel XXX model.

Typical roll-stamp on left side of round-barrel XXX revolvers.

Roll-stamp on barrel of special-order, short-barrel XXX revolver.

Third-variation XXX Standard 1872 caliber .32 short revolver, serial number 1.

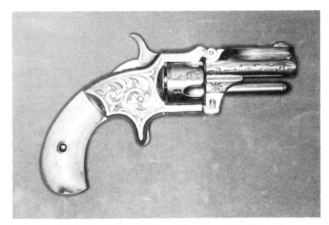

Special-order caliber .32 short, short barrel XXX revolver.

did not have extra cylinder stop notches between chambers, as did the American Standard Tool Company revolvers.

It appears that the chronological order of events in the development of J.M. Marlin Standard models of pocket revolvers was as follows:

1. Manhattan Firearms Company incorporated in New York — 1855
2. Manhattan Firearms Company introduced S&W copy — 1861
3. Manhattan Firearms Company relocated to New Jersey — 1863
4. Manhattan Firearms Company closed business — November 23, 1868
5. American Standard Tool Company formed in New Jersey — November 23, 1868
6. American Standard Tool Company closed — February 20, 1873
7. J.M. Marlin introduces Standard revolvers — 1872–1878

The Marlin Standard pocket revolvers include the following variations:

XXX Standard 1872 (first variation — octagon barrel)
Made: 1872–1873
Quantity: Approximately 500
Serial Number: On frame, barrel, cylinder, and barrel latch
Caliber: .30 short, rimfire

Box cover of caliber .30 cartridges manufactured by Union Metallic Cartridge Company, suited for XXX Standard revolvers.

Barrel: 3⅛ inches flat sides with rib (octagon)
Cylinder: nonfluted, with cylinder stop notches forward, 5-shot
Frame: Core-cast brass
Weight: 11½ ounces
Grip: Rosewood, pearl, and ivory
Markings: Top of barrel: *XXXStandard 1872;* Left side of barrel: *J.M. Marlin — New Haven, Connecticut.*

XXX Standard 1872 (second variation — round barrel, nonfluted cylinder)
Made: 1873
Quantity: Approximately 500
Serial Number: On frame, barrel, cylinder, and barrel latch
Caliber: *.30 short,* rimfire
Barrel: 3 inches, round with rib

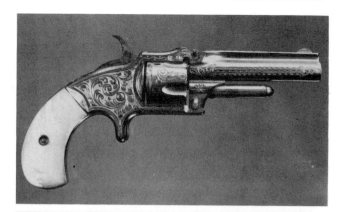

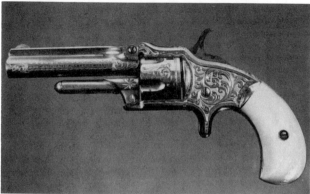

These five XXX revolvers typify the similar yet different New York-style engraving found on Marlin Standard revolvers. All five are chambered for the .30 short rimfire cartridge and have pearl or ivory grips.

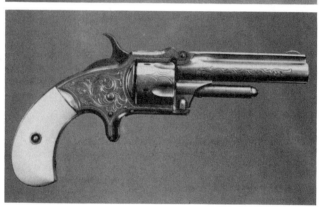

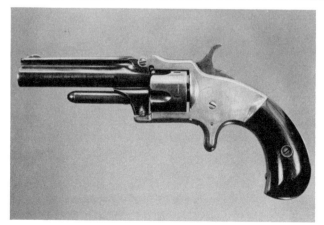

Marlin Standard revolver in frequently found finish of nickel frame with blued barrel and cylinder.

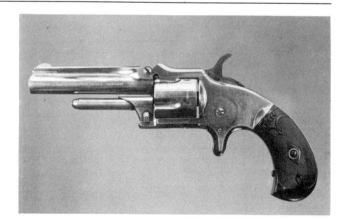

Nickel plated, and with MFA Co. hard rubber grips, this XXX Standard caliber .30 long rimfire revolver is typical of the fourth variation of the XXX Standard revolver.

Left side of silver-plated caliber .30 long rimfire XXX Standard revolver. Grips are ivory.

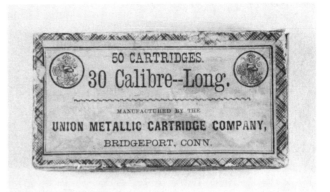

Cover of box for caliber .30 long, rimfire cartridges, which were used in fourth-variation XXX Standard revolvers.

Nickel-plated caliber .30 long XXX Standard revolver, which has the hard rubber "star" grips.

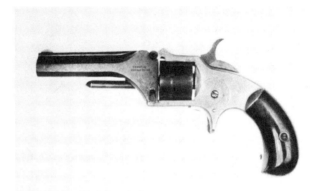

First variation of the XX Standard 1873, which had flat sides to the barrel, and cylinder stop notches toward the front of the cylinder (G.C.)

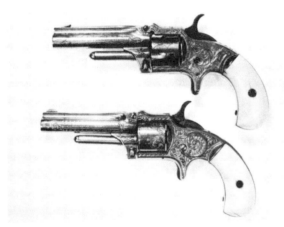

Top: *Third-variation XXX Standard revolver.* Bottom: *Second-variation XXX Standard revolver.*

Right side of first variation of the XX Standard revolver. (G.C.)

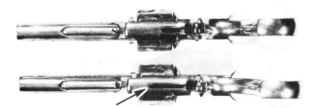

Bottom view of XXX Standard revolvers of second variation (bottom) and third variation (top). Note the arrow, which indicates the long front type of cylinder catch of the first and second types.

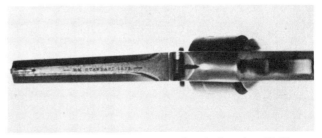

Top of barrel and roll-stamp of the XX Standard revolver. (G.C.)

J.M. Marlin mark on left side of first-model XX Standard, which had a flat-sided barrel. (G.C.)

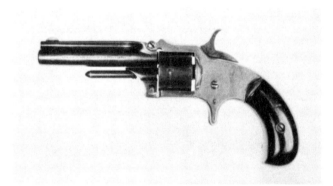

Second variation of XX Standard revolver, which has a round barrel and nonfluted cylinder. (G.C.)

Right side of second-variation XX Standard. (G.C.)

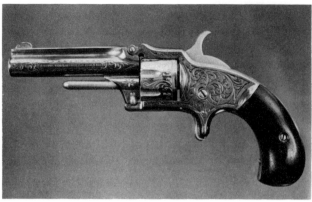

Engraved XX Standard 1873, caliber .22 long, rimfire revolver having rosewood grips. (RS)

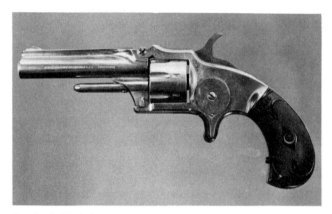

Standard nickel-plated XX Standard revolver with MFA Co. hard rubber grips. (RS)

Cylinder: Nonfluted with cylinder stop notches forward, 5-shot
Frame: Core-cast brass
Weight: 11 ounces
Grips: Rosewood, pearl, and ivory
Markings: Top of barrel: *XXX Standard 1872;* Left side of barrel in one line: *J.M. Marlin, New Haven, Connecticut, U.S.A. Patent July 1, 1873.*

XXX Standard 1872 (third variation—round barrel, short-fluted cylinder)
Made: 1873–1876
Quantity: Approximately 10,000
Serial Number: On frame, barrel, cylinder, and barrel latch
Caliber: .30 short, rimfire
Barrel: 3 inches, round with rib
Cylinder: Short flutes, 5-shot with stop notches toward rear
Frame: Core-cast brass
Weight: 11 ounces
Grips: Rosewood, pearl, ivory, and hard rubber
Markings: Same as second variation

XXX Standard 1872 (fourth variation—round barrel, long-fluted cylinder)
Made: 1873–1876
Quantity: Approximately 15,000

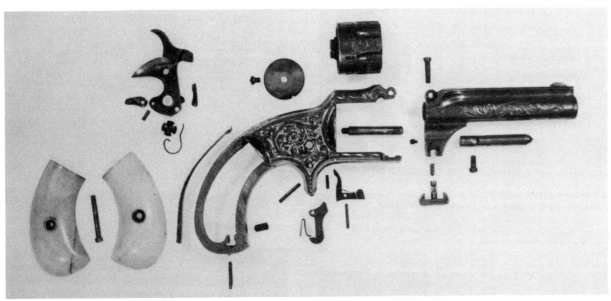

Parts of Marlin Standard revolver shown in positions relative to each other. Pistol shown is a XX Standard; however, it is representative of all the Marlin XX and XXX Standard models.

Serial Number: On frame, barrel, cylinder, and barrel latch
Caliber: .30 long rimfire
Barrel: 3 inches, round with rib
Cylinder: Long flutes, 5-shot with stop notches toward rear
Frame: Core-cast brass
Weight: 12 ounces
Grips: Rosewood, pearl, ivory, and hard rubber
Markings: Same as second variation

XX Standard 1873 (first variation—octagon barrel)
Made: 1873
Quantity: Approximately 500
Serial Number: On frame, barrel, cylinder, and barrel latch
Caliber: .22 long rimfire
Barrel: 3⅛ inches, flat sides with rib (octagon)
Cylinder: Nonfluted with cylinder stops toward front, 7-shot
Frame: Core-cast brass
Weight: 11½ ounces
Grips: Rosewood, pearl, ivory, and hard rubber
Markings: Top of barrel: *XX STANDARD 1873;* Left side of
barrel: *J.M. Marlin—New Haven, Connecticut.*

*XX Standard 1873 (second variation—round barrel, nonfluted
cylinder)*
Made: 1874
Quantity: Approximately 500
Serial Number: On frame, barrel, cylinder, and barrel latch
Caliber: .22 long rimfire
Barrel: 3 inches, round with rib
Cylinder: Nonfluted, 7-shot, with stop notches toward front
Frame: Core-cast brass
Weight: 11½ ounces
Grips: Rosewood, pearl, ivory, and hard rubber
Markings: Top: Same as first variation; Left side: *J.M. Marlin
New Haven, Ct. U.S.A. Pat. July 1, 1873.*

Roll-stamp on top of XX Standard 1873 barrel.

Roll-stamp on left side of XX Standard 1873 barrel.

No. 32 Standard 1875, caliber .32 short, rimfire revolver, which has MFA Co. hard rubber grips. (RS)

No. 32 Standard 1875, caliber .32 short and long, rimfire revolver, serial number 3383, which has ivory grips. (RS)

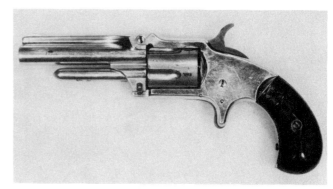

No. 32 Standard 1875 revolver with hard rubber "star" grips.

Roll-stamp on top of No. 32 Standard revolver.

Roll-stamp on left side of No. 32 Standard revolver.

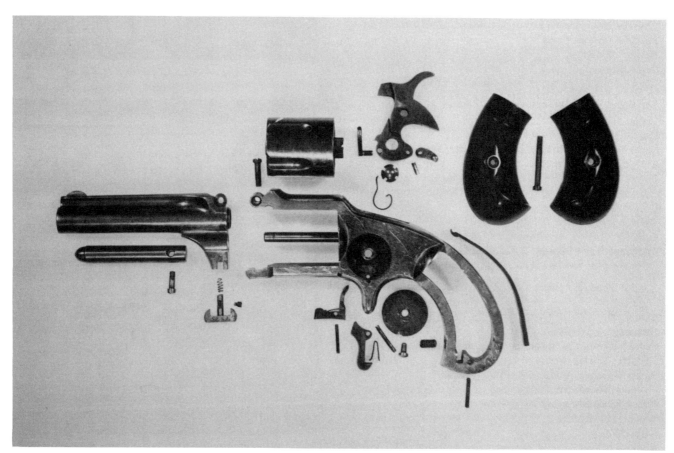

Individual parts of No. 32 Standard 1875 revolver.

XX Standard 1873 (third variation—round barrel, fluted cylinder)
Made: 1875–1887
Quantity: Approximately 9,000
Serial Number: On frame, barrel, cylinder and barrel latch
Caliber: .22 long rimfire
Barrel: 3 inches, round with rib
Cylinder: Short, fluted with cylinder stops toward rear, 7-shot
Frame: Core-cast brass
Weight: 11½ ounces
Grips: Rosewood, pearl, and ivory
Markings: Same as second variation

Original end label on 38 Standard cardboard box.

38 Standard 1878 steel-framed, caliber .38, center-fire revolver, which has the early MFA Co. hard rubber monogram grips. (RS)

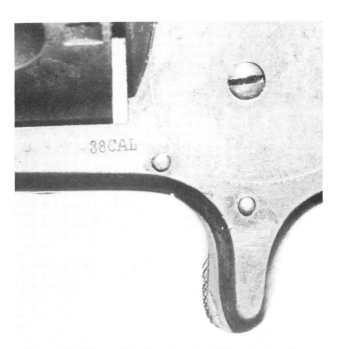

Unusual 38 CAL marking found on a few 38 Standard revolvers.

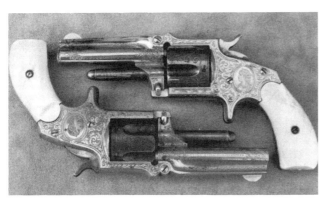

Pair of 38 Standard revolvers, consecutively serial-numbered 2005 and 2006. (R.R.) (George Carr)

Roll-stamp on top of the barrel of 38 Standard 1878 revolver.

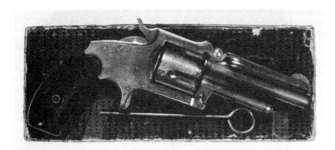

38 Standard revolver with original cardboard box and cleaning rod. (RP)

Roll-stamp on top of the barrel of 38 Standard 1878 revolver.

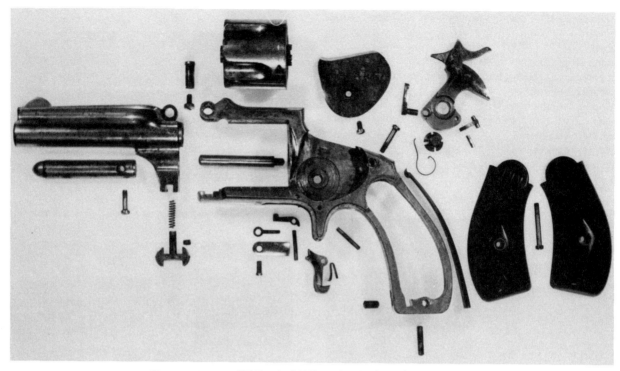

Component parts of 38 Standard 1878 revolver in their relative positions.

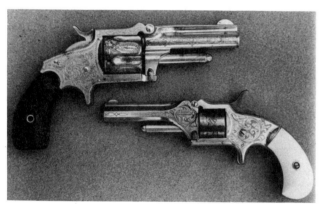

Top: *Engraved 38 Standard 1878 revolver, last of the Marlin Standard model revolvers.* (RG) Bottom: *Engraved XXX Standard 1872 revolver, first of the Marlin Standard model revolvers.* (RG)

This dug-up 38 Standard represents what happened to many firearms when lost.

No. 32 Standard 1875 (first variation)
Made: 1875
Quantity: Approximately 15,000
Serial Number: On frame, barrel, cylinder, and barrel latch
Caliber: .32 short rimfire
Barrel: 3¼ inches, round with rib
Cylinder: Fluted, 5-shot, long
Frame: Core-cast brass
Weight: 12 ounces
Grips: Rosewood, walnut, hard rubber, pearl, ivory, and imitation ivory (plastic)
Markings: Top of barrel: *No. 32 Standard 1875;* Left side of barrel: *J.M. Marlin, New Haven, Ct. U.S.A. Pat. July 1, 1873.*

No. 32 Standard 1875 (second variation)
Made: 1876–1887
Quantity: Approximately 18,000
Serial Number: On frame, barrel, cylinder, and barrel latch
Caliber: .32 short or long rimfire
Barrel: 3¼ inches, round with rib
Cylinder: Fluted, 5-shot, long
Frame: Core-cast brass
Weight: 12½ ounces
Grips: Rosewood, walnut, hard rubber, pearl, ivory, and imitation ivory (plastic)
Markings: Same as first variation

38 Standard 1878
Made: 1878–1887
Quantity: Approximately 12,000
Serial Number: On frame, cylinder, barrel, and barrel latch
Caliber: .38 center-fire

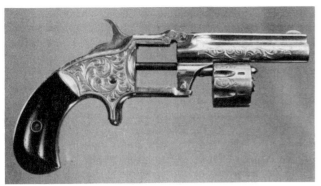

XX Standard revolver with the cylinder shown in position for ejecting fired cartridge cases.

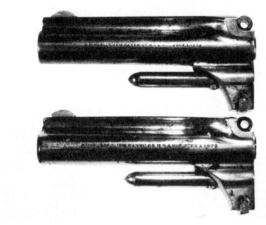

Top: *Short patent date roll-stamp, 1.620 inches in length.* Bottom: *Long patent date roll-stamp, 1.880 inches in length.*

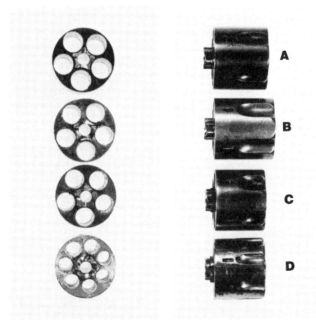

A. No. 32 Standard caliber .32 short, rimfire cylinder. B. XXX Standard caliber .30 long, rimfire cylinder. C. XXX Standard caliber .30 short, rimfire cylinder. D. XX Standard caliber .22 long, rimfire cylinder.

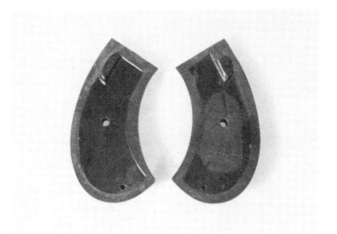

Hard rubber Standard model grips, which have a raised lug that rests against the inside of the frame to prevent the grips from moving once in place.

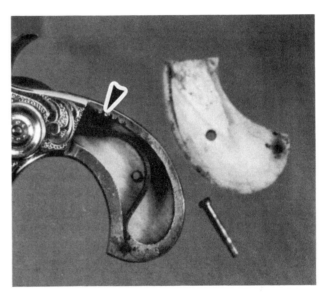

Arrow indicates the raised notches on the inside of the frame, which engage grooves cut into ivory and pearl grips to prevent them from moving during use.

Inside of imitation ivory grips, which are made from an early type of plastic and have a metal insert for strength.

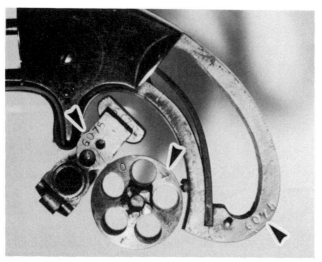

Arrows indicate serial numbers marked on frame, cylinder, barrel, and barrel catch of Standard revolvers.

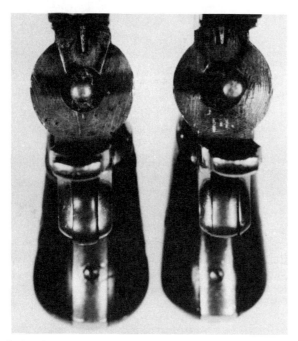

Left: *XX Standard breech face and firing pin.* Right: *XXX Standard breech face and firing pin.*

Barrel: 3¼ inches, round with rib
Cylinder: Fluted, 5-shot
Frame: Machined steel
Weight: 17½ ounces
Grips: Black plastic marked *JMM* or *MFA Co.,* ivory and pearl
Markings: Top of barrel: *38 Standard 1878;* Left side of barrel: *J.M. Marlin, New Haven, Ct., U.S.A., Pat. July 1, 1873.*

All of the Marlin Standard pocket revolvers, regardless of the model or model variation, are made according to the principle of J.M. Marlin's patent number 140,516, which was awarded to Mr. Marlin on July 1, 1873. The main features of this patent are the headed arbor, which holds the hammer and pawl-spring in place within the frame, and the pawl-spring, which works without friction against the cylinder pawl.

It should be noted that the Marlin patent is dated July 1, 1873, and that application was made for the patent on May 10, 1873. However, John Marlin gave his XXX Standard and XX Standard pocket revolvers an 1872 date. It is also interesting to note that, except for the bird's-head grip, the patent illustration has the American Standard Tool Company profile and distinct flat-sided barrel.

The similarity between the American Standard Tool Company and Marlin Standard revolvers is confirmed when random exchanges of barrels, cylinders, and frames are tried. They do not easily interchange; however, the closeness is more than by chance. First-variation XXX and XX Standard parts are dimensionally close, and except for the narrower bottom front end of the XXX and XX Standard frames, some American Standard parts could also be fitted-to the Marlin parts.

Except for the flat-sided barrels, the XXX, XX, and No. 32 Standard barrels were made on the same machines. The only differences in the standard lengths are in the bore size and ejector rod size. Some shorter-length barrels were made to special order. Extra-length barrels have never been noted. Except for the length of the front part of the frame that accepts the cylinder, the XXX, XX, and No. 32 Standard frames are alike and most parts are interchangeable with hand fitting.

All of the Marlin Standard pocket revolvers had numerous hand operations done to the various parts. Hand filing, deburring, and fitting were the rule and the main reason that serial numbers were applied to the frame, cylinder, barrel, and barrel latch. After fitting the parts to each other, and then polishing, engraving, and plating the parts, final reassembly was simplified by having the parts serial-numbered.

Grips of various materials are not uncommon on Marlin Standard revolvers. Rosewood was usually standard for the XXX and XX Standard models, and hard rubber was usually standard for the No. 32 and 38 Standard revolvers. However, pearl and ivory are not uncommon, and an imitation ivory grip made of an early plastic, which had a metal plate molded into the grip for strength, is frequently found on the XXX and XX models.

I have been told there are imitation pearl grips; however, I have never inspected any that I thought to be so. (An old test to tell if the pearl is real or not is to rub the pearl across the front surface of your teeth. If it's real pearl, it should feel dry and have a resistant drag to the movement. If it's not genuine, it will slide easily. I do not know if there is any scientific fact to this test—just thought it was interesting to pass along, as I've heard it to be true for years!)

The 1882 Marlin catalog prices of XX, XXX, and No. 32 Standard revolvers were as follows:

	XX Standard .22 Caliber	XXX Standard .30 Caliber	No. 32 Standard .32 Caliber
Rubber stocks	$4.66	$5.33	$6.00
Ivory stocks	5.80	6.46	7.13
Pearl stocks	7.00	7.66	8.33

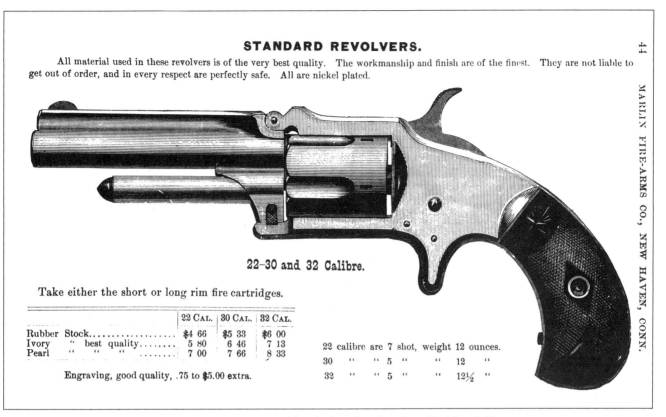

STANDARD REVOLVERS.

All material used in these revolvers is of the very best quality. The workmanship and finish are of the finest. They are not liable to get out of order, and in every respect are perfectly safe. All are nickel plated.

22-30 and 32 Calibre.

Take either the short or long rim fire cartridges.

	22 CAL.	30 CAL.	32 CAL.
Rubber Stock	$4 66	$5 33	$6 00
Ivory " best quality	5 80	6 46	7 13
Pearl " " "	7 00	7 66	8 33

Engraving, good quality, .75 to $5.00 extra.

22 calibre are 7 shot, weight 12 ounces.
30 " " 5 " " 12 "
32 " " 5 " " 12½ "

Marlin catalog illustration of Standard revolvers in caliber .22, .30, and .32.

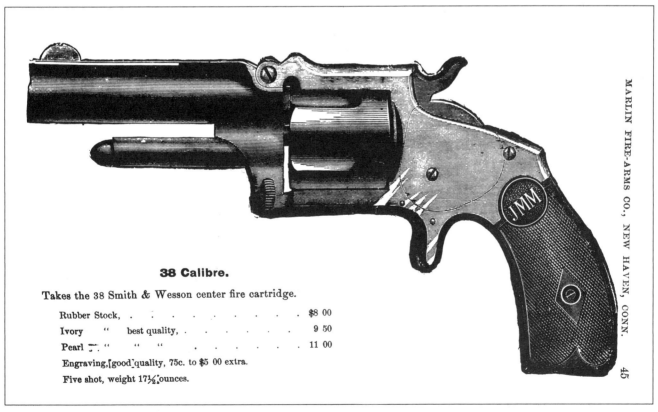

38 Calibre.

Takes the 38 Smith & Wesson center fire cartridge.

Rubber Stock, ... $8 00
Ivory " best quality, ... 9 50
Pearl " " " 11 00
Engraving, good quality, 75c. to $5 00 extra.
Five shot, weight 17½ ounces.

Marlin catalog illustration of 38 Standard revolver.

Engraving of good quality was available for $.75 to $5.00 extra. The type of engraving used by Marlin is of the New York style and at best is mediocre in artistic rendition. The patterns used were stylized and usually included a scroll pattern with a stippled background. Variations are found in the pattern on the cylinders, hinge, top, back strap, and sides and top of the barrels. But the general likeness among guns engraved in the New York style can be studied in the photographs included throughout this handgun section. However, the simplest of engraving does add to the value of Marlin handguns, although they are not rare or uncommon. Engraved pieces in excellent condition are the most desired by collectors and are hard to find. It appears that Marlin handguns were tools of the working man and saw a lot of use and little care.

Nickel plate was the standard finish of the Standard pocket revolvers; however, a nickel-plated frame with a blued barrel and cylinder is quite common. Combinations of gold and silver plating, although rare, are also found.

The .38 Standard pocket revolver was introduced in 1878 after a number of years' production of the XXX, XX, and No. 32 Standard models. It is a larger gun with a machined steel frame, instead of the brass type of the earlier Standard revolvers; it is also center-fire, rather than rimfire of the earlier type.

The cartridge used with this model was the .38 S&W center-fire cartridge, which S&W introduced with its model No. 2 single-action spur-trigger revolver in 1876. The S&W was a top-break model, whereas John Marlin stayed with the tip-up barrel system of all of his previous Standard revolvers.

Two types of hard rubber grips are noted on this model. The first type has *JMM* embossed into the circular top of the grip. After 1881 and the formation of The Marlin Fire Arms Company, the *MFACo.* monogram was used in a similar position. The side plate of this model is larger than on earlier models and is held in place by two screws. Like the previous models, it has a tip-up barrel and spur trigger.

The roll-stamp on the left side of the barrel on Marlin Standard revolvers is found in two different lengths. It appears that there was no order of use of the two roll-stamps and that they were used interchangeably. The short roll-stamp is 1.630 inches

in length with a vertical bar at each end, and the long roll-stamp is 1.880 inches in length. It is also noted that the date 1873 appears to be 1878 on some revolvers; however, by close examination, the date can be identified as 1873, which is the only patent date marked on any of the Standard revolvers.

Other variations of roll-stamps are a broken *N* in New Haven, a broken *U* in July, the *AT* broken away in *PAT,* and *New Haven* with and without a dash between the words *New* and *Haven;* i.e., *New-Haven* and *New Haven.*

MARLIN SOLID-FRAME SINGLE-ACTION REVOLVERS

Recognizing that there was a limited market for single-shot pistols, most manufacturers of derringer-type pistols soon added small repeating revolvers to their product lines. John Marlin was one of the manufacturers who did just that. He manufactured a small, 7-shot, solid-frame caliber .22 short, rimfire, single-action handgun that was not much larger than his .22 derringers. However, it had the advantage of being a repeater. His first model he called the OK, as he had called one of his derringers. A second variation was the same as the OK except that it had a different system of locking the cylinder pin in place; it was called the Little Joker.

The characteristics of these two spur-trigger, solid-frame revolvers were as follows:

OK

Made:	1870–1875
Quantity:	2,000
Serial Number:	28–8265; on frame and inside of grip
Caliber:	.22 short, rimfire
Barrel:	2¼ inches, round
Cylinder:	Unfluted, 7-shot
Frame:	Brass
Weight:	6¼ ounces
Grips:	Rosewood
Markings:	Top of barrel: *OK.* Side of barrel: *J.M. Marlin. New Haven. Conn. U.S.A.*

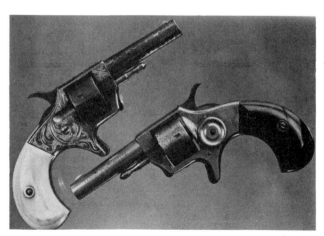

Left: *OK serial number 28 with full engraving, ivory grips, and nickel plating.* Right: *Full nickel-plated OK, serial number 6567.*

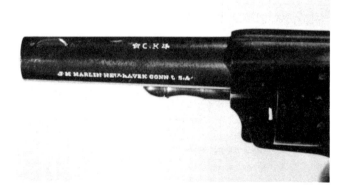

OK *marking on top of barrel (broken O) and* J.M. Marlin *marking on left side of OK barrel.*

Little Joker

Made:	1871–1873
Quantity:	1,100
Serial Number:	5–5144; on frame and on inside of grip
Caliber:	.22 short, rimfire
Barrel:	2¼ inches, round with flat sides
Cylinder:	Unfluted, 7-shot
Frame:	Brass
Weight:	5¾ ounces
Grips:	Rosewood
Markings:	Top of barrel: *Little Joker.* Side of barrel: *J.M. Marlin. New Haven. Conn. U.S.A.*

The OK revolver had a blade latch that, when pushed in from the front end of the frame, allowed the cylinder pin to be withdrawn and the cylinder removed for extraction of the fired cartridge cases and for reloading. The cylinder pin was used to push the empties out of the cylinder.

The Little Joker revolver was quite similar. The major differences were in the flat sides on the round barrel and the push-button latch that locked the cylinder pin in place.

Lacking accurate records for reference, it is conjecture on my part that the OK was probably the first variation, and the Little Joker the second. It just doesn't make sense to have both types available at the same time when there is so little difference between the two. The button-type latch also appears to be an improvement over the blade type, and seems to be a logical second variation to better lock the cylinder pin in place and to make it easier to remove.

The standard finish for both the OK and Little Joker revolvers was nickel plate. Engraved examples are scarce, and worth a premium to the collector. Ivory and pearl grips are also desirable features, but are rarely encountered.

MARLIN DOUBLE-ACTION REVOLVER

The Marlin Fire Arms Company introduced in its 1887 catalog a new double-action revolver in caliber .38, center-fire. This new revolver was made of steel and was of the top-break type, and similar to the Smith & Wesson top-break revolver. However, three patents by John Marlin were incorporated in the first model, the Marlin Double-Action revolver, which precluded infringement on the S&W revolver. The patent numbers and dates were 367,535, August 2, 1887 (cylinder-locking mechanism); 367,820, August 9, 1887 (cylinder-retaining catch); and 367,821, August 9, 1887 (extractor mechanism).

The second variation of the Marlin Double-Action revolver had an extractor mechanism invented by D.H. Rice, which replaced the John Marlin-patented extractor mechanism. Rice's patent number 385,009, dated June 26, 1888, was assigned to The Marlin Fire Arms Company. Revolvers with Rice's invention can be identified by the added small screw directly over the barrel hinge screw. In the 1887 catalog, Marlin stated the following about this new double-action revolver:

> We desire to call to the attention of the public, our new Double-Action revolver illustrated on the opposite page. No expense or care has been spared to make this arm as near

Markings on Little Joker revolver.

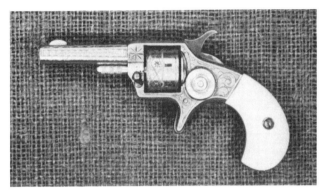
Left side of engraved Little Joker revolver.

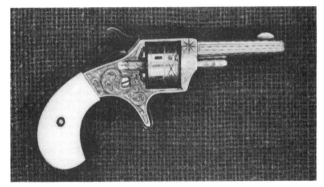
Right side of engraved Little Joker revolver.

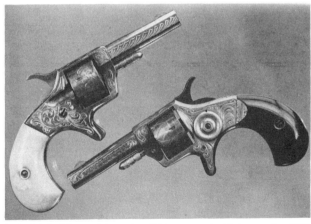
Left: *Little Joker serial number 5144, engraved with ivory grips.* (RS) Right: *Little Joker serial number 3257, nickel-plated, engraved, and with rosewood grips.* (RS)

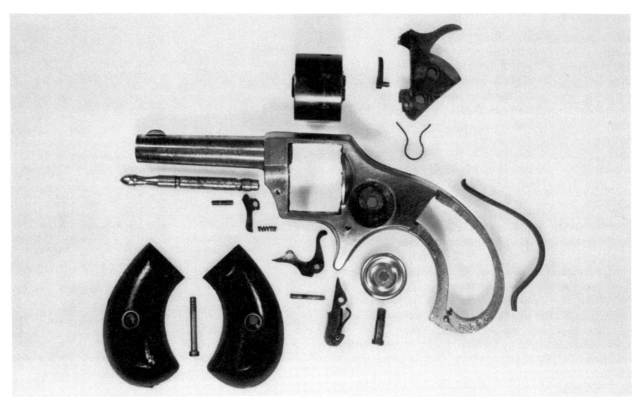

Parts of OK revolver.

Marlin catalog illustration of first variation of the Marlin Double-Action revolver. The lack of a cylinder hook and the medallion-type hard rubber grips should be noted.

Catalog illustration of first-variation Double-Action revolver with cylinder hook showing.

First variation of Marlin Double-Action revolver, which is marked on left side of the barrel PAT. APPLIED FOR.

Close-up of first-variation Double-Action patent marking on left side of barrel.

Roll-stamp on top of first-variation Double-Action revolver. Note that there are no patent dates.

Marlin Double-Action revolver with special-order features of engraving, gold screws, and pearl grips.

perfection as it is possible to get. The style is identical with the Smith & Wesson revolver, and in no respect whatever is it inferior. Our rifles have enjoyed the reputation of being superior in workmanship, finish and accuracy of shooting to any others in the world; this position we mean to hold, and the Marlin revolvers will be found to be in these points, so essential to a high class arm, equal to anything we have heretofore made. Realizing the immense hold that S&W revolvers have on the markets of the world, by having for a long series of years stood alone as perfectly made weapons, we have made our price sufficiently low to attract the notice of the trade and of the public, feeling confident that as soon as they are sufficiently known, they will be only appreciated and will command as high an estimation as any other goods the world over.

Left and right views of another engraved special-order Double-Action revolver, which is nickel-plated with case-colored hammer and trigger, and with blued trigger guard and pearl grips.

Roll-stamp marking on top of second-variation Double-Action revolver.

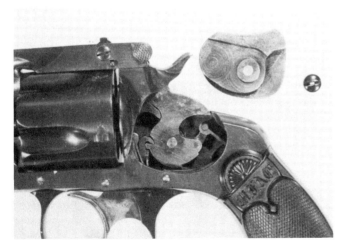

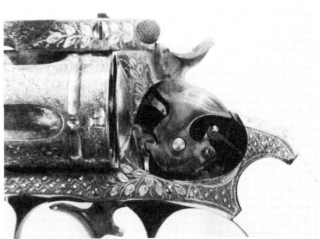

Left: *Inside parts of Marlin Double-Action revolver. Note MFA Co. hard rubber grip.* Right: *Inside parts of S&W revolver. Note the similarity of the Marlin Double-Action revolver to this earlier-designed S&W revolver.*

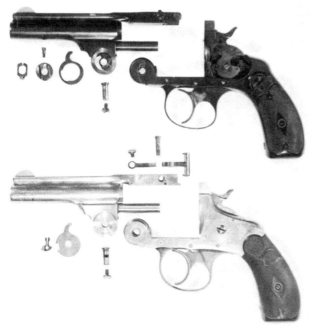

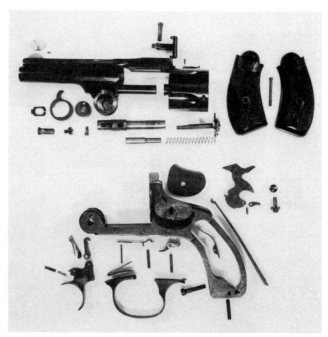

Top: *Blued Marlin Double-Action revolver with second variation of extractor cam mechanism (Rice patent). Bottom: Nickel-plated Marlin Double-Action revolver with first variation of extractor cam mechanism (Marlin patent), equipped with monogram hard rubber grips.*

Parts of Marlin Double-Action revolver in their positions relative to each other.

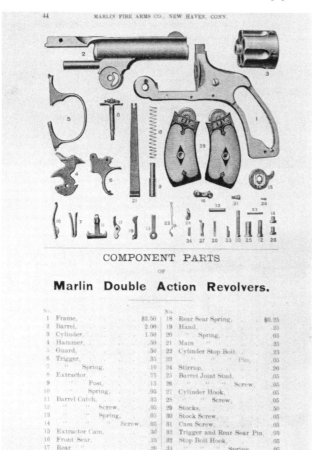

Page from Marlin 1888 catalog, which lists all the parts of the Marlin Double-Action revolver.

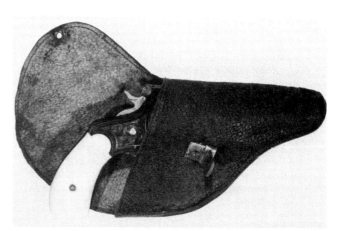

Deluxe Marlin Double-Action revolver that has a blued finish with gold-plated screws and pearl grips in original holster, which was commercially available for this revolver.

The very earliest of Marlin's Double-Action revolvers have *PAT. APPLIED FOR* stamped into the left side of the barrel above the barrel hinge. The roll-stamp on top of the barrel of this model does not include patent dates. The second-variation revolver has both the August 2 and August 9 dates added to the roll-stamp.

The barrel is ribbed and 3¼ inches long. The 1897 catalog advised that longer or shorter barrels could not be furnished. The .38 caliber revolver is 5-shot and the .32 caliber revolver, which was introduced in 1888, is 6-shot. Either full nickel or full blue was available when introduced. The trigger guard, barrel catch, and extractor cam were blued, and the hammer and trigger were case-colored. It was not until the 1897 catalog that special plating was offered.

Two styles of hard rubber grips are found. The 1888 catalog

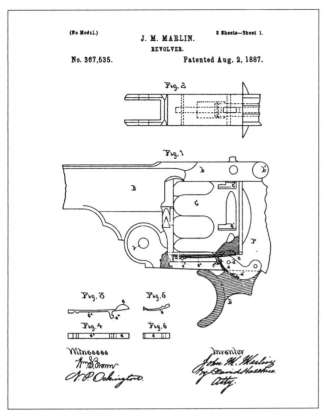

J.M. Marlin's patent of a cylinder latch system.

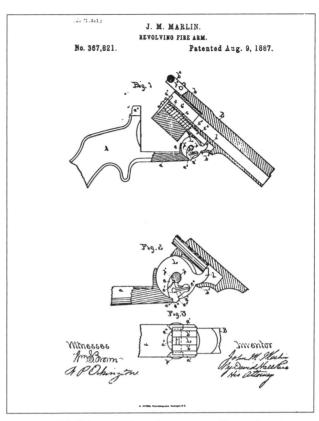

J.M. Marlin's patented revolver extractor (first variation).

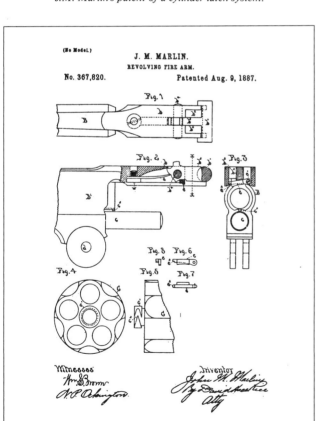

J.M. Marlin's patent of a cylinder lock system.

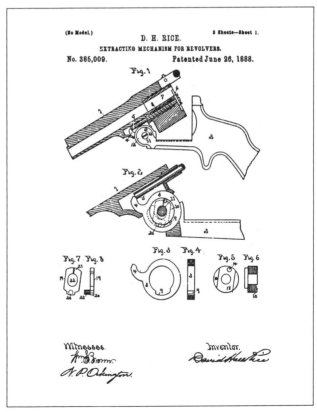

D.H. Rice's patent of an extractor mechanism (second variation).

illustration shows grips with *MFA Co.* embossed at the top. Later illustrations show the Marlin monogram in a circle at the top. Oddly, Marlin used one illustration for many years that did not show the second type of extractor cam or the barrel catch. In fact, two conflicting illustrations were used in catalogs during most of the years the revolver was manufactured. This sort of confusion is common, and surely does not help the collector of today.

Winchester revolver that has an experimental swing-out cylinder and ejector mechanism and a barrel marked J.M. Marlin. New Haven, Conn. U.S.A.

Winchester revolver shown with the cylinder in the open position.

Close-up of the cylinder and ejector mechanism believed to be the design of S.W. Wood, a gun designer for Winchester during the 1870s.

Patents issued to John Marlin that relate to double-action revolvers, but were not used in the Marlin Double-Action revolver, or any other known revolver, were the following: 308,183, November 8, 1884; 368,599, August 23, 1887; 371,608, October 18, 1887; and 413,197, October 22, 1889.

The Marlin Double-Action revolver is serial-numbered on the bottom of the butt, the barrel catch, and hinge part of the barrel. Serial numbers from 27 to 11,845 have been observed.

The catalog prices of the Double-Action revolvers, and extra features available, were as follows:

	1887	1888-1894	1896-1899
Rubber stock, nickel-plated or blued	$11.00	$10.00	$ 7.50
Ivory stock, nickel-plated or blued	12.50	11.50	9.00
Pearl stock, nickel-plated or blued	13.50	12.50	10.00
Engraving extra $1.50 and upwards.			
Morocco case, lined with satin	3.75	3.50	
Cartridges, .32 S&W, per 1000		11.00	
Cartridges, .38 S&W, per 1000	13.50	13.50	

	1897-1899
Full silver plating, extra	$ 2.75
Gold trimmings, extra	2.75

WINCHESTER REVOLVER

A very unusual double-action, caliber .44 Russian revolver exists that is roll-stamped on top of the barrel *J.M. Marlin. New Haven, Conn. U.S.A.* It is marked *2* on the frame.

Although the revolver has the J.M. Marlin name on the barrel, there is nothing about the gun that looks like a Marlin. Also, it has no Marlin features or patents incorporated into it. The workmanship in this pistol is excellent. The inside and outside finishes are equal to the best produced in the U.S. handgun industry. The butt, frame, grips, hammer, and trigger have a European look to them and are not like those of any U.S. revolver of the 1870-to-1900 period. The unique feature of this gun is that the cylinder swings to the right, whereas most other cylinders swing out of the frame to the left.

The Winchester Repeating Arms Company embarked on an experimental pistol program in 1876. The first model was designed by Stephen W. Wood. It had an ejector system that Mr. Wood patented. The pistol was called the 1876 Centennial Model, since it was displayed during the Philadelphia Centennial Exposition.

Another second model by Stephen W. Wood had a slightly different extractor system. A third model pistol, using the Stephen Wood-patented swing-out cylinder mechanism (number 186,445, dated January 23, 1877), was also manufactured by Winchester. All three of these experimental pistols were toolroom prototypes made by hand and not produced in large

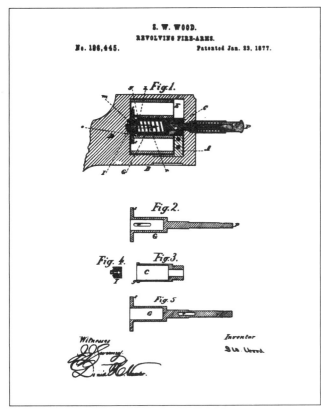

S.W. Wood patent for revolver ejector mechanism.

Internal parts of Winchester revolver. Note the number 2 stamped into the frame.

numbers by production methods. They also have the same characteristic European butt and grip of the J.M. Marlin-marked pistol.

Herbert Houze, curator of the Winchester Museum, Buffalo Bill Historical Center, Cody, Wyo., was generous enough to allow me to photograph the unfinished parts of a revolver that is in the Winchester collection. By comparing various parts (the hammer, trigger, sear, hand, trigger guard, and frame), internal machine cuts, and arrangements of parts of this "in-the-white" unfinished pistol with the J.M. Marlin pistol, it is evident that they are more than accidentally alike.

I studied the Winchester collection of pistols, the unfinished

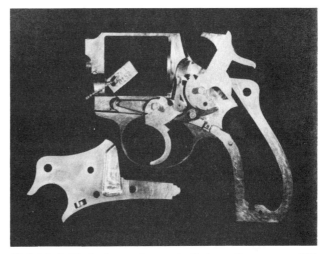

Unfinished Winchester revolver parts that are the same as J.M. Marlin-marked revolver's. (Courtesy of Winchester Museum, Cody, Wyo. Herbert Houze, curator.)

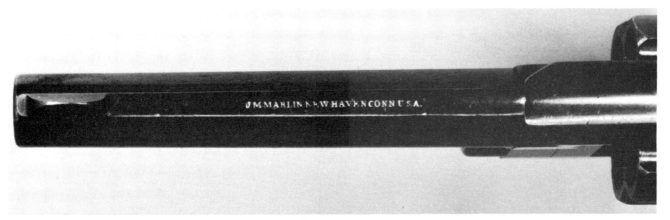

Marking on top of unusual swing-out cylinder revolver that is marked with the number 2.

Illustration of Winchester experimental revolver.

parts of a Winchester pistol, and the excellent photographs of the J.M. Marlin pistol; I also examined the gun when it was in the collection of my friend, the late Archer Jackson. Based on my examinations, I conclude that the J.M. Marlin revolver was made by Winchester. The similarity of the swing-out cylinder

mechanism of the J.M. Marlin pistol with the S.W. Wood patent and prototypes makes me feel that that system was also from the mind of Stephen Wood.

One of the third-model Winchester pistols was submitted to the U.S. Navy for testing. The instructions for opening this pistol were quite similar to those for the Marlin pistol, i.e.,

> Take the pistol in the left hand, draw the rod on the underside toward the muzzle with the right hand and press it toward you. The revolving chamber opens toward you. The extractor is pressing down on the end of the rod, and it closes with a twist of the left wrist.

In spite of my research and reasonable proof that the pistol was made by Winchester, and has an S.W. Wood-invented cylinder and ejector mechanism, it still has a J.M. Marlin-marked barrel. For now, that cannot be explained. I hope that some day it will.

Ballard Rifles

John M. Marlin started manufacturing the Ballard rifle in 1875. It remained in production until about 1890. During these years, the Ballard reached a popularity shared with only the finest of single-shot target and hunting rifles.

The Ballard was designed and patented by C.H. Ballard. His patent number 33,631, dated November 5, 1861, states as his invention the following:

What I claim as my invention, and desire to secure by Letters Patent is:

1. The breech B, composed of a long block with shoulders a b, fitted to corresponding shoulders, e f, within the breachsupporter A, and arranged, in combination with a lever, D, to move upward and downward, as well as longitudinally, within a parallel-sided cavity in the said supporter, under control of guides d d above and below its rear portion, all substantially as herein specified.

2. The arrangement of all the parts of the lock of breech-loading rifle on other small-arm within a slot in the moveable breech, substantially as herein specified.

3. The link E, having a protuberance, e, applied in combination with the lever D, the breech, and the hammer, for the purpose of bringing the hammer to half-cock by the act of opening the breech, substantially as herein specified.

4. Combining the lever F with the hammer H by means of a horn, n or its equivalent, substantially a b, and for the purpose herein specified.

C.H. Ballard

Witnesses:
Hartley Williams,
R. Ball

Until it was manufactured by J.M Marlin, the Ballard rifle traveled a rocky road. The following companies manufactured and marketed the Ballard prior to J.M. Marlin:

1. Ball & Williams, Worcester, Mass.	1861–1864
2. Dwight, Chapin & Company, Bridgeport, Conn. (Made Ballard Rifles under contract for Merwin & Bray)	1862–1864
3. R. Ball & Company, Worcester, Mass. (Succeeded Ball & Williams)	1864–1866
4. Merrimack Arms & Manufacturing Company Newburyport, Mass.	1867–1869
5. Brown Manufacturing Company, Newburyport, Mass.	1869–1873

During the Civil War, the U.S. purchased over 1,000 Ballard carbines. Government tests in 1866 indicated the Ballard could be fired at the rate of 18 times a minute.

An 1865 ad about the Ballard rifle in *Harper's Weekly* stated: ". . . The General Government of the State of Kentucky have about twenty thousand now in active field service, of which the highest testimonials are received."

In 1864, patent number 41,166 was awarded to Joseph Merwin and Edward P. Bray for a percussion device that provided for loading a Ballard rifle with either fixed cartridges or with loose powder and ball. The claim in the patent stated:

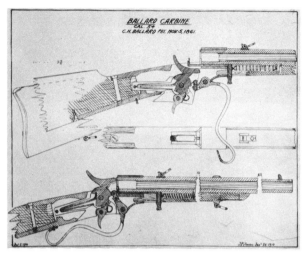

Drawing of pre-Marlin Ballard carbine.

Pictures of two Civil War soldiers with Ballard carbines. (Herb Pack, Jr.)

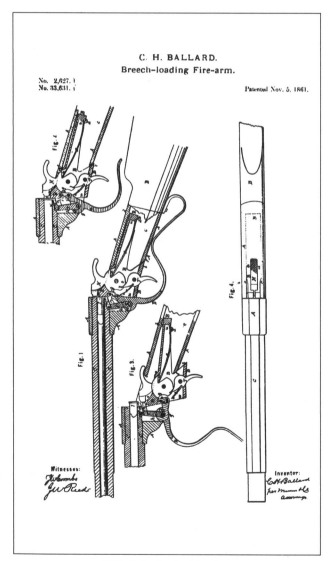

C.H. Ballard patent drawing.

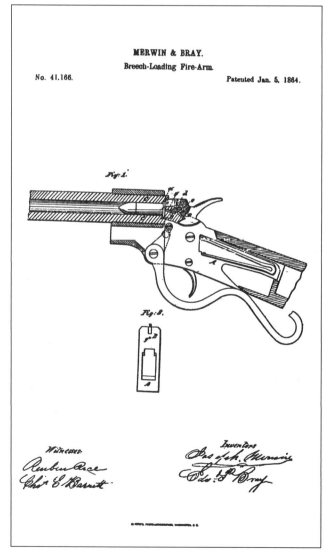

Merwin and Bray patent drawing.

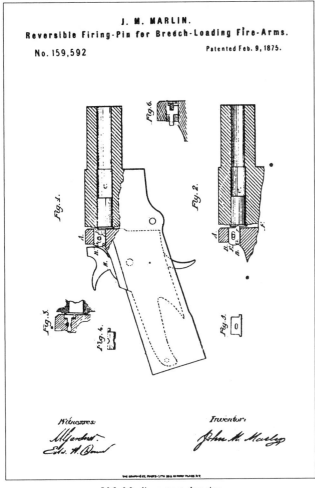

J.M. Marlin patent drawing.

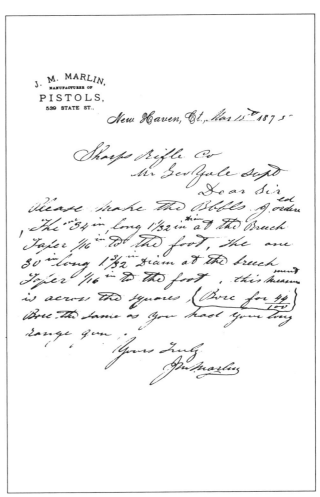

J.M. Marlin letter to Sharps Rifle Company.

The arrangement of the vent and nipple in a breech-piece in combination with the hammer, the recess, nose, chamber and shell as herein shown and described, so that without removal and alteration of the breech-piece either fixed or loose ammunition may be employed, as set forth.

John Marlin did not use this Merwin and Bray patent in the production of his Ballards.

The Brown Manufacturing Company had reached a point where it needed new machinery and equipment to manufacture a breech-loading bolt action rifle and was struggling to keep afloat by producing the *Southerner* derringer pistol and the Ballard rifle. However, before Brown could raise the capital needed to survive, the following mortgage sale was published:

On Wednesday July 23, 1873 there will be a mortgage sale of the entire property owned and operated by the "Brown Mfg. Co." for the manufacture of arms, consisting of a large brick factory building, with engine, boilers, shafting, and machinery, and machinists tools now therein; with the land under the same, and the yard and warf, there with connected.

All the details of the Brown sale are not known, but the firm of Schoverling and Daly acquired the patent and manufactur-

ing rights to the Ballard rifle. Schoverling and Daly then requested J.M. Marlin to make improvements to those made by the Brown Manufacturing Company, and to manufacture the rifle in variations that would have greater appeal to outdoor sportsmen, hunters, and marksmen. Schoverling and Daly were sole agents for the Marlin Ballards for some years.

Unfortunately, the details of the relationship between Marlin and Schoverling and Daly have not been preserved. In fact,

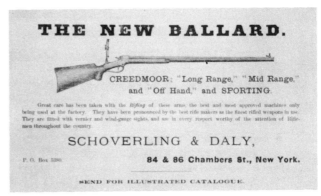

Illustrated ad in early score book for the Ballard rifle.

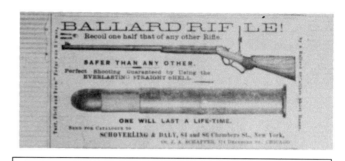

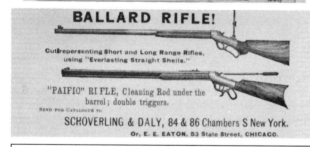

Early Ballard ads.

no records, drawings, serial number information, or production data are known to exist anyplace. The present Marlin company has only a limited representation of catalogs (all of which are post-1882) and no gun collection representative of the various models produced.

There are indications that, like today, Marlin did not always make all the parts and pieces of a gun. An early example is a March 15, 1875 letter by J.M. Marlin to the Sharps Rifle Company requesting it manufacture "one barrel 34 in long, 1¹/₃₂ inch. diameter at the breech. Taper ¹/₁₆ in to the foot. This measurement is across the squares. Bore for ⁴⁴/₁₀₀ for the same as you had your long range gun."

The above barrel was probably to be used by J.M. Marlin before he had his barrel-making operation set up.

Another reference to an outside source for pieces is found in A.C. Gould's 1892 book *Modern American Rifles,* in which he reproduced the following communication from the Billings & Spencer Company:

Dear Sir . . . we make drop forgings for rifle parts as follows:
For the Marlin Fire Arms Co. of New Haven, Conn.: Barrel catches, wind gauges, Ballard lock-plates, Ballard hammers, Ballard levers, Ballard links, Ballard front-sight slides, Ballard Creedmoor-sight slides, Ballard back-sight slides, buck-horn sights, Ballard receivers, knife-blade sights, Ballard extractors, frames, side plates, hammers, triggers, stirrups, stop bolts, pawls, breech bolts, main springs, small-sight levers.

The Billings & Spencer Co.,
H.E. Billings

It is known that John Marlin used many of the Brown Manufacturing Company parts and pieces to assemble his No. 1 Hunting Rifle. We also know that John Marlin patented (patent number 159,592, dated February 9, 1875) a reversible firing pin that allowed the user to easily change the firing pin for use with either rimfire or center-fire cartridges. (All Ballards

Hunter with his Ballard rifle. I wonder why the open knife is hanging as it does by a very fine thread. (Herb Peck, Jr.)

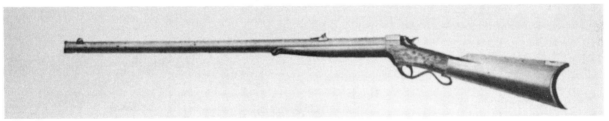

No 1½ Hunters Rifle.

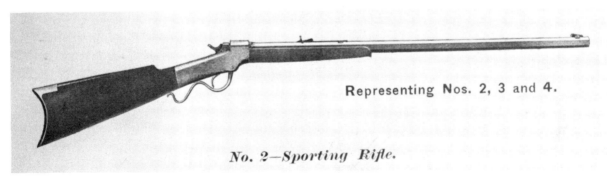

Representing Nos. 2, 3 and 4.

No. 2—Sporting Rifle.

No. 2 Sporting; No. 3 Gallery; No. 4 Perfection Rifle.

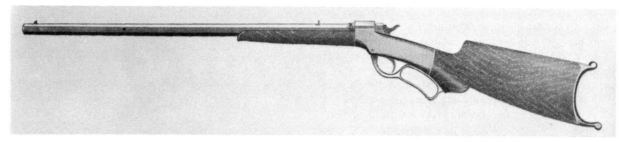

No. 3 F Fine Gallery Rifle.

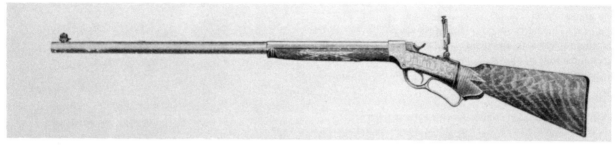

No 4½ A-1 Mid-Range Rifle.

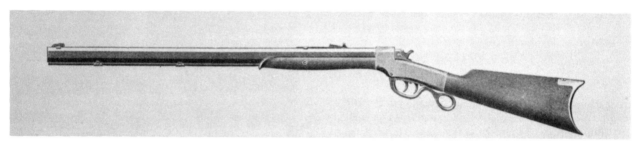

No. 5 Pacific Rifle, 5½ Montana Rifle.

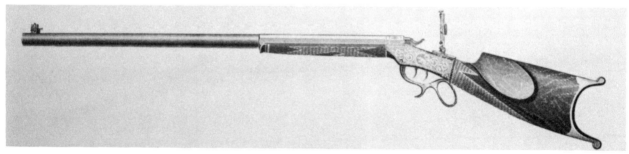

No. 6 Schuetzen Rifle.

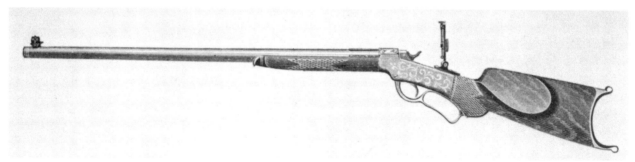

No. 6½ Off-Hand Rifle.

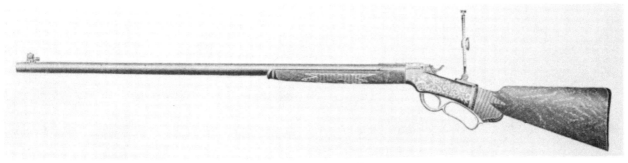

No. 7 Long Range Rifle.

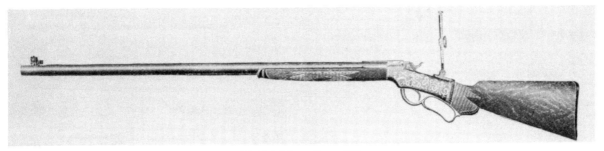

No. 7 A-1 Long Range Rifle.

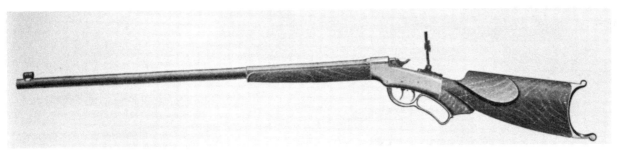

No. 8 Union Hill Rifle, No. 9 Union Hill Rifle, and No. 10 Schuetzen are "Junior" rifles.

prior to Marlin's production were for use only with rimfire ammunition.)

In using the leftover Brown parts (including the outside hand ejector) and his new reversible firing pin, John Marlin was able to assemble and ship complete No. 1 rifles without having his production in full swing. This gave him time to make the changes in design and production necessary to make an improved Ballard.

Early J.M. Marlin-manufactured Ballards are marked with the original C.H. Ballard patent date on the left side of the receiver in this way:

J.M. MARLIN. NEW-HAVEN. CONN. U.S.A.
BALLARD'S PATENT. NOV. 5. 1861.

Later J.M. Marlin Ballards were marked in three lines; added was the Marlin patent date of February 9, 1875.

After the incorporation of The Marlin Fire Arms Company in 1881, the marking on the left side of the receiver was changed from *J.M. Marlin* to *Marlin Fire Arms. Co.* with no change to the address or the Ballard patent date. Later, Marlin Fire Arms Company Ballards had both the Ballard patent date

and the J.M. Marlin patent date, like the second type of J.M. Marlin marking.

Marlin-manufactured Ballards had both numerical and noun designations. The numbers used were from 1 to 10, with fractions, such as 1½, to identify some variations.

Unfortunately, the Ballard story from here on would require a book in itself. Naturally, that cannot be done here. However, if the reader is interested in more detail than what I have provided, he may study the following references:

Autry, Peyton. "Collecting The Ballard—A Great American Rifle." *Guns/Game,* 1964.

Cary, Lucian. "The Ballard of J.M. Marlin." *True Magazine,* April 1949.

Dutcher, John. "The Marlin Ballard No. 1 Hunting Rifle." *American Single Shot Rifle News,* May/June 1985.

Grant, James J. *Single Shot Rifles.* New York: William Marrow & Company, 1947.

———. *More Single Shot Rifles.* New York: William Marrow & Company, 1959.

———. *Boys' Single Shot Rifles.* New York: William Marrow & Company, 1967.

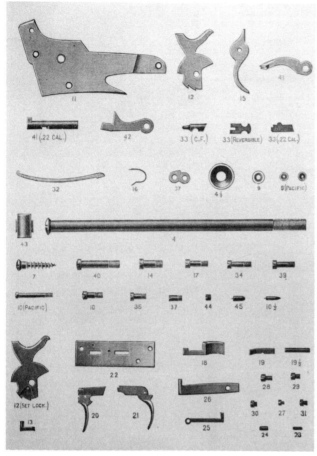

Component parts of the Ballard rifle.

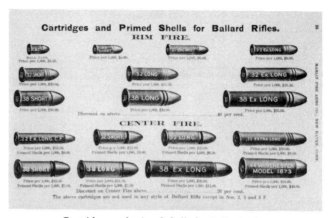

Cartridges and primed shells for Ballard rifles.

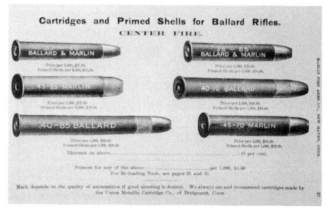

Cartridges and primed shells for Ballard rifles.

Ballard reloading tools.

Everlasting center-fire shells for Ballard rifles.

Bullets for use with Everlasting shells.

——. *Still More Single Shot Rifles.* Union City: Pioneer Press, 1979.

Serven, James E. "Marlin Ballard Single-Shot: 19th Century Match winner." *The American Rifleman,* Washington, D.C., 1970.

Sharpe, Philip B. *The Rifle in America.* New York: Funk and Wagnalls, 1938.

Wolff, Eldon G. "Ballard Rifles in the Henry J. Nunnemacher Collection." *Bulletin of the Public Museum of the City of Milwaukee,* December 1945.

The above-listed references describe and illustrate various Ballard rifles. To confuse the issue, some writers make separate listings for J.M. Marlin and Marlin Fire Arms Company models. However, dealer and company catalogs do not show any important differences between models marked with the two different names, although some early J.M. Marlin features are not found in Marlin Fire Arms Company models.

It appears that not long after John Marlin got into full production of the Ballard, different combinations of the available features could be specially ordered. As a result, there are many fine Ballards that do not fit a category, ad description, or model number precisely. To add to the confusion, the Ballard was a favoritie of custom-stock, accessory, and barrel manufacturers; this resulted in many changes being made to the original factory product at the request of the owner. Therefore, many special-order Ballards were produced by both Marlin and custom gunsmiths.

Boxes of Everlasting shells and bullets for the Ballard rifle manufactured by Marlin and Winchester.

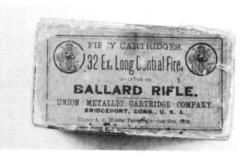

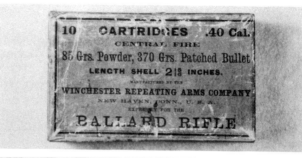

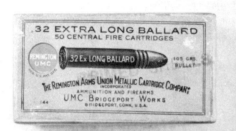

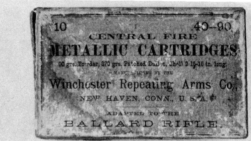

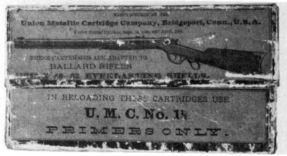

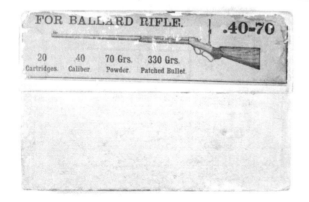

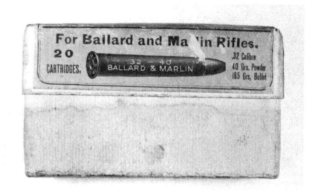

Ammunition boxes for Ballard rifle cartridges.

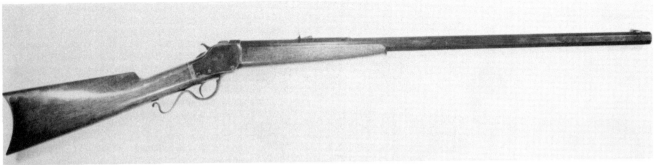

Single-shot rifle believed to be a Marlin prototype to replace the Ballard.

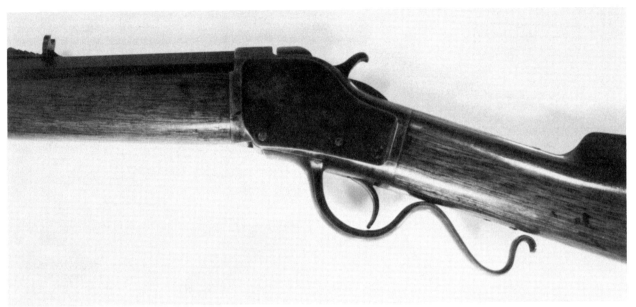

Close-up of prototype rifle action.

Among the various standard models can be found at least four types of barrels, three types of receivers, three different types of extractors, eight different levers, three different triggers, two types of hammers, four different-shaped butt plates, four variations of buttstocks, three types of breech blocks, and numerous types of front and rear sights. The forestocks made by J.M. Marlin and The Marlin Fire Arms Company had a schnabel front end and were of at least three different shapes; some had a tip of horn.

In all, there were 20 cataloged and identified models of Ballard rifles manufactured by J.M. Marlin and The Marlin Fire Arms Company. Without trying to distinguish the J.M. Marlin from Marlin Fire Arms Company variations, or to include those known rifles that don't clearly fall into one of the cataloged models, the catalog descriptions were as follows:

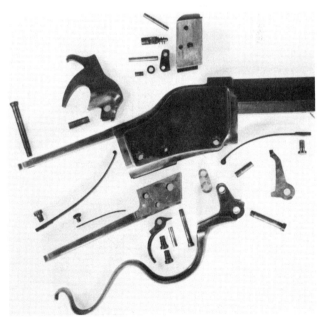

Parts of unknown prototype rifle.

Model	Description
No. 1	*Hunting Rifle,* round barrel, Marlin's patent reversible firing pin, using 44 Ballard rim and centerfire cartridge 8 to 9½ lbs. Using 45 Govt. cartridge 9 to 10½ lbs. 26, 28 and 30 inch barrels. Dependent on barrel $25 to $27.00.

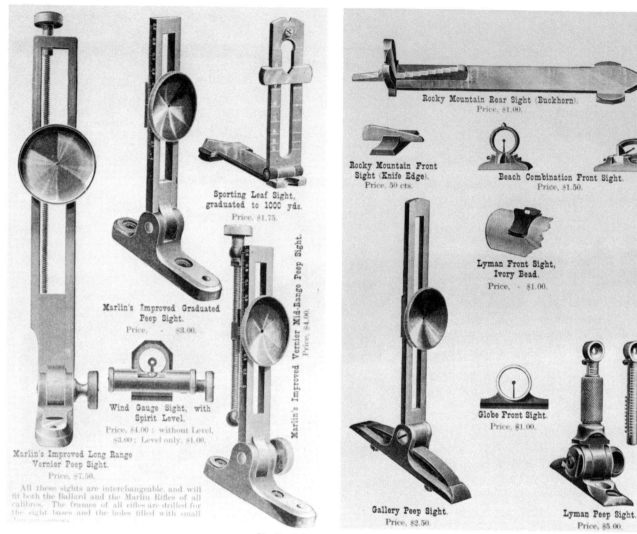

Marlin sights used on Bullard rifle.

Classic engraving on Ballard A-1 Rifle.

Style of engraving found on many of the better-grade Ballard rifles.

Lyman No. 15 sight for Ballard caliber .22 rifle.

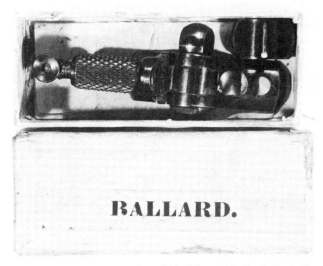

Lyman combination rear sight and No. 3 front sight for Ballard rifle.

Case for Ballard sights.

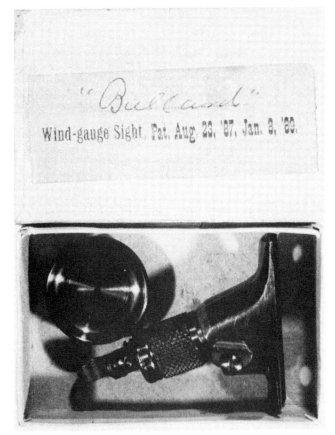

Lyman No. 15 sight in original box.

Cased set of Ballard front and rear sights.

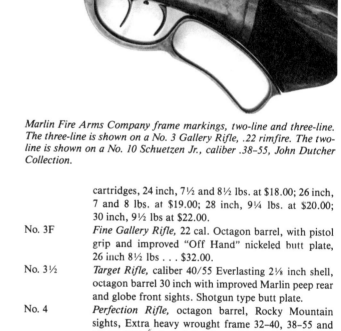

J.M. Marlin frame markings. The top is a plain No. 7 Long Range Rifle, caliber .44–100, 1¹³/₁₆-in. Everlasting, serial number 568. The bottom rifle is an early No. 1 Hunter's rifle, serial number 376, caliber .44, made from Brown parts, Art Jaeger Collection.

Marlin Fire Arms Company frame markings, two-line and three-line. The three-line is shown on a No. 3 Gallery Rifle, .22 rimfire. The two-line is shown on a No. 10 Schuetzen Jr., caliber .38–55, John Dutcher Collection.

No. 1½   *Hunter's Rifle,* round barrel, extra heavy wrought frame. Rocky Mountain rear and knife-edge front sights, using 45 Govt. cartridges and 40–63 Everlasting Shells – 30 inch, 9½ lbs. —–$22.50
　　　　　　　　32 inch, 10 lbs. —–$24.50

No. 1¾   *Far West Rifle,* same as No. 1½ but with double set triggers in 40–65 Everlasting 2⅛" and 45 Govt.

No. 2   *Sporting Rifle,* octagon barrel, reversible firing pin, using rim and center fire cartridges, 32 long and 38 long and 44 Colt and Winchester center fire. 32 Cal. are made in 28 in., 8¼ lbs; 38 cal. are made in 30 in. 8¾ lbs; 44 cal. are made in 30 in. 9 lbs. . . . $22

No. 3   *Gallery Rifle,* octagon barrel, caliber .22 long or short

cartridges, 24 inch, 7½ and 8½ lbs. at $18.00; 26 inch, 7 and 8 lbs. at $19.00; 28 inch, 9¼ lbs. at $20.00; 30 inch, 9½ lbs at $22.00.

No. 3F   *Fine Gallery Rifle,* 22 cal. Octagon barrel, with pistol grip and improved "Off Hand" nickeled butt plate, 26 inch 8½ lbs . . . $32.00.

No. 3½   *Target Rifle,* caliber 40/55 Everlasting 2⅛ inch shell, octagon barrel 30 inch with improved Marlin peep rear and globe front sights. Shotgun type butt plate.

No. 4   *Perfection Rifle,* octagon barrel, Rocky Mountain sights, Extra heavy wrought frame 32–40, 38–55 and 40–63, 30 inch barrel, 9½ lbs . . . $25.00

No. 4½   *Mid Range Rifle* checkered forearm and pistol grip

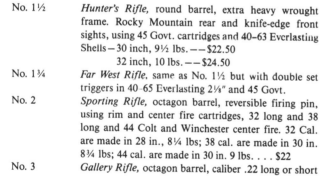

A plain No. 2 Ballard in .32 long caliber with reversible firing pin using both rimfire and center-fire ammunition. Note special-order shotgun butt plate and folding rear barrel sight, and plain adjustment sliding tang sight and Beach combination front sight. Marlin Fire Arms Company, John Dutcher Collection.

butt stock, 40-65 Everlasting 2⅛ inch shell, 30 inch half or full octagon barrel, Marlin improved peep and globe sights.

No. 4½ A-1   *Mid-Range Rifle,* same as No. 4½ except with fine English walnut pistol grip stock and either shotgun or rifle butt plate. Engraved "Mid-Range A-1" on side of receiver. 30-inch barrel chambered for 40-65 Everlasting shells, 38-50 Ideal Everlasting shell, and 40-63, 30 inch, 10 lbs. . . . $65.00.

No. 5   *Pacific Rifle,* octagon barrel, double set triggers, extra

heavy wrought frame, cleaning rod under barrel, Rocky Mountain sights.

38-55 — 30 inch, 10 lbs.; 32 inch, 11 lbs.
40-63 — 30 inch, 10 lbs.; 32 inch, 11 lbs.
40-85 — 30 inch, 10½ lbs.; 32 inch 11½ lbs.
44 W.C.F. are made 30 inch, 10 lbs.
45-70 are made 30 inch, 10½ lbs., 32 inch, 11½ lbs.
45-100 are made 30 inch, 11 lbs; 32 inch, 12 lbs.
   30 inch : . . $30.00 — 32 inch . . . $32.00

No. 5½   *Montana Rifle,* same as No. 5, but extra heavy for

Early Pacific model Ballard rifle, caliber .44–77 Sharps. This is a J.M. Marlin and is typical of the early pieces. Original. John Dutcher Collection.

Many customized Ballard rifles were made up into fine target rifles. Here is an old No. 5½ Montana action reworked by the highly regarded George C. Schoyen, Denver, Colo. The story of Ballard rifles would be incomplete without mention that many were altered to Schuetzen rifles such as this one. Schoyen made the barrel, buttstock and plate, forearm, perhaps the lever, which is custom, and altered the action to take down by means of a taper pin fitted through it just under the barrel shank. Note the cutaway frame, making a closer pistol grip. John Dutcher Collection.

Ballard No. 6 Schuetzen rifle, caliber .38–55. Made with both part-octagon and full-octagon barrels. Some of the early pieces weren't engraved. John Dutcher Collection.

A richly engraved and very early No. 6½ Ballard Rigby rifle, caliber .40–65 Everlasting. Perhaps this elegantly engraved rifle is the work of Nimschke. J.M. Marlin. John Dutcher Collection.

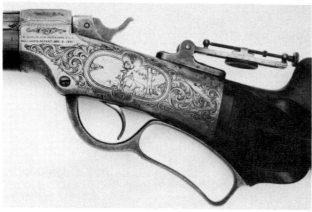

An unusual engraved No. 6½ Ballard Rigby rifle in a scarce, for this model, caliber .40–63. Handsome, indeed. J.M. Marlin. John Dutcher Collection.

This Ballard Rigby No. 6½ was originally owned by N.C. Nash, once president of the famous Walnut Hill rifle range near Boston. Note the very handsome engraving and small early hammer. .38–50 Everlasting caliber. J.M. Marlin. John Dutcher Collection.

hunting the largest game. Sharps 45–2⅞ inch cartridge.

30 inch 14 lbs – rifle or shotgun butt . . . $32.00
32 inch 14 lbs – rifle or shotgun butt . . . $34.00

No. 6 — *Schuetzen Rifle,* half octagon barrel, double set triggers, Marlin's vernier mid-range peep and wind gauge sights, hand made polished selected stock with check piece, Swiss pattern, nickel butt plate full checkered, finely engraved frame. 32–40 & 38–55, 32 inch, 13 & 15 lbs . . . $70.00

No. 6½ — *P.G. – Off Hand Rifle,* Rigby barrel, mid-range Vernier peep and Windgauge sights, fine English walnut stock, modified Swiss pattern, pistol grip, full checkered, improved "Off Hand" nickeled butt plate exactly fitting the arm, finely engraved and every part highly finished. 32–40 & 38–55, 28 and 30 inch, 10 lbs. . . . $70.00

No. 7 — *Long Range Rifle,* half octagon, 34 inches, Marlins improved Vernier peepsight, graduated to 1,300 yards, wind gauge sight with spirit level, bead and aperture discs, Morroco sight case, hand made pistol-grip stock, regulation weight and pull, using Everlasting Shells, 45–100, 34 inch, 10 lbs. . . . $75.00

No. 7 A-1 — *Long Range Rifle,* Rigby barrel, extra handsome English walnut stock, pistol grip, full checkered, finely engraved, rubber butt plate, long range vernier peep and wind gauge sights, with spirit level and three discs, Morroco sight case, every part finished in the very best style and with the greatest care. 45–100 – 34 inch – 10 lbs. . . . $90.00

No. 7 A-1 Extra — Same as No. 7 A-1 with extra quality wood and engraving.

No. 8 — *Union Hill Rifle,* half octagon barrel, pistol grip stock, with check piece, "Off Hand" nickeled butt plate, double set triggers, graduated peep and globe sights 32–40 and 38–55, 29 and 30 inch, 9¼ lbs. . . . $37.50

No. 9 — *Union Hill Rifle,* same as No. 8, but having single trigger, 32–40 and 38–55, 28 and 30 inch, 9¼ lbs. . . . $33.00

No. 10 — *Schuetzen "Junior" Rifle,* same as No. 8, but having 32 inch barrel, weight 12 lbs, vernier mid-range and wind gauge sights. 32–40 and 38–55, 32 inch, 12 lbs. . . . $50.00

Interspersed among the Marlin Model 1881 Repeating Rifle serial number records are a few Ballard serial numbers. The following list is all of the surviving factory records:

Ballard Model	Serial Number	Shipped
	4779	5-20-1900 (frame only)
	5013	11-29-1905 (28″ oct.; 22 cal.)
5	19534	5-20-1885
6 S.T.	10535	5-20-1885
5 S.T.	10546	6-16-1885
6 S.T.	10547	8-11-1885
5 S.T.	10548	6-9-1885
6 S.T.	10549	6-16-1885
5	10551	7-9-1885
6 S.T.	10552	8-11-1885
5 S.T.	10556	7-7-1885
5	10557	7-9-1885
5½	10561	6-22-1885

Very rare No. 7–A EXTRA GRADE Long Range rifle, caliber .45–100 Ballard Everlasting using a 2⁹/₁₆-in. Everlasting case, which is quite rare itself. These were deluxe rifles with Rigby flats on the barrel and highly engraved frames. Note the heel position sight, 34-in. barrel. J.M. Marlin. John Dutcher Collection.

Ballard Model	Serial Number	Shipped
6 S.T.	10563	8-15-1885
6	10607	6-3-1885
5	10608	6-3-1885
5	10609	6-9-1885
6	10612	6-3-1885
6	10614	6-9-1885
6	10632	6-9-1885
5	10636	6-9-1885
6	10639	6-5-1885
6	10642	6-16-1885
6	10644	8-11-1885
6	10646	6-9-1885
5½	10648	6-20-1885
6	10650	6-8-1885
6	10652	6-9-1885
Not marked	12983	9-3-1886
Not marked	23777	5-23-1904
32 long	28037	8-6-1903

Note: S.T. = Set Trigger

J.M. Marlin No. 7–A EXTRA GRADE Long Range Rifle. Note the very unusual geometric pattern engraving, the beveled, faceted, and rebated frame. This was a made-to-order rifle. John Dutcher Collection.

Among writers and students of the Ballard, it is generally agreed that production and sale of Ballard rifles by The Marlin Fire Arms Company terminated between 1889 and 1890. Although some dealer catalogs illustrated and described some models as late as 1890, Marlin discontinued listing the Ballard in 1888.

An interesting conclusion to The Marlin Fire Arms Company's manufacturing single-shot rifles for sporting and target use is the comment made by E. Hough in a report he did about the Marlin exhibit at the 1893 Chicago World's Fair. After

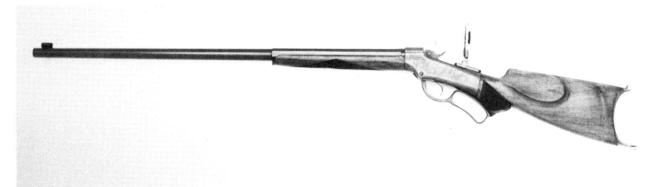

The popular Union Hill No. 9 Ballard rifle. All Union Hill models were made by The Marlin Fire Arms Company. This one is in .32–40 caliber with 30-in. barrel. Note the rare after market Farrow tang sight with windgauge.

glowing remarks about the many fine Marlin rifles, their beauty, and excellence in engraving and wood, Mr. Hough stated: "The Marlins show a single-shot which they think will be better than the old Ballard."

Illustrations shown here are of a single-shot rifle believed to be the rifle to which E. Hough refers. It has the outward appearance of a Winchester high-wall rifle, but is quite different on the inside. There are no markings to indicate the maker and there are no numbers on parts or pieces. The workmanship is superb and has the character of inventor L.L. Hepburn's work.

BALLARD MODELS PRODUCED BY YEARS

	1876	1877	1878	1879	1880	1881	1882	1883	1884	1885	1886	1887	1888
No. 1 Hunters	x	x	x	x	x								
No. 1½ Hunters					x	x	x	x	x				
No. 1¾ Far West				x	x	x	x						
No. 2 Sporting	x	x	x	x	x	x	x	x	x	x	x	x	x
No. 3 Gallery	x	x	x	x	x	x	x	x	x	x	x	x	x
No. 3F Gallery							x	x	x	x	x	x	
No. 3½ Target						x	x						
No. 4 Perfection	x	x	x	x	x	x	x	x	x	x	x	x	x
No. 4½ Mid Range				x	x	x	x						
No. 4½ A-1					x	x	x	x	x				
No. 5 Pacific	x	x	x	x	x	x	x	x	x	x	x	x	x
No. 5½ Montana						x	x						
No. 6 Schuetzen	x	x	x	x	x	x	x	x	x	x	x	x	x
No. 6½ Rigby O.H.	x	x	x	x	x	x	x	x	x	x	x	x	x
No. 7 Long Range		x	x	x	x	x					x	x	
No. 7 A1 Long Range		x	x	x	x								
No. 7 A1 Extra	x	x	x										
No. 8 Union Hill									x	x	x	x	x
No. 9 Union Hill									x	x	x	x	x
No. 10 Junior Sch.									x	x	x	x	x

Sources: Unknown dealer lists; E.C. Meacham Arms Company Catalogs; Chas. J. Godfrey, N.Y., catalogs; Marlin Fire Arms Company catalogs 1882-1888; James J. Grant's books; Schoverling & Gales catalogs; Great Western Gun Works catalogs; Homer Fisher's catalogs.

CARTRIDGES FOR WHICH BALLARD RIFLES WERE CHAMBERED

No. 1	.44 long rimfire or center-fire
No. 1½	.40-65 Everlasting 2⅜", .45-70 Govt., .40-63
No. 1¾	Same as No. 1½ Rifle
No. 2	.32 & .38 long rimfire or center-fire, .41 long Ballard, .44 extra long Ballard center-fire, .44-40 Winchester
No. 3	.22 short and long rimfire, .22 extra long, .22 WCF
No. 3 F	.22 long rimfire
No. 3½	.40-65 Everlasting, 2⅜"
No. 4	.40-70, .44-77 Sharps, .50-70 Govt., .38-50 Ballard Everlasting 1¹⁵⁄₁₆", .40-65 Ballard, .40-63 Everlasting, .38-55 Everlasting, .40-70 Ballard Everlasting 2⅜", .44-75 Ballard Everlasting 2¼", .32-40
No. 4¼	.40-70 Sharps, .40-90 Sharps, .38-50 Ballard Everlasting, .44-77 Sharps, .44-90 Sharps 2⅞" & 2⅝", .44-90 Sharps 2⅞" & 2⅝", .40-90 Ballard, .44-75 Everlasting 2½", .44-100 Ballard Everlasting 2¹³⁄₁₆", .45-70 Govt., .50-70 Govt.
No. 4½ A-1	.38-50 Ballard Everlasting 1¹⁵⁄₁₆", .40-65
No. 5	.40-70 Sharps, .44-77 Sharps, .50-70 Govt., .38-50 Everlasting 1¹⁵⁄₁₆", .40-65 Everlasting 2⅜", .40-90 Everlasting 2¹⁵⁄₁₆", .44-75 Everlasting 2¼", .45-70 Govt. 2¹⁄₁₀", .44-100 Ballard Everlasting 2¹³⁄₁₆", .38-55 Everlasting, .44-63 Everlasting, .40-85 Everlasting, .45-100 Everlasting, .44-40 Winchester
No. 5½	.45 Sharps 2⅞"
No. 6	.40-65 Everlasting 2⅜", .44-75 Everlasting, .38-50 1¹⁵⁄₁₆", .32-40 & .38-55 Ballard.
No. 6½	.38-50 Everlasting, .40-65 Everlasting, .38-55 Ballard, .32-40 Ballard
No. 7	.44-100 Ballard Everlasting 2¹³⁄₁₆" & 2⅝"
No. 7 A-1	.44-100 Ballard Everlasting 2¹³⁄₁₆" & 2⅝", .45-100 2¹⁵⁄₁₆"
No. 8	.32-40 Ballard, .38-55 Ballard
No. 9	Same as No. 8
No. 10	.32-40 Ballard, .38-55 Ballard

Lever Action Rifles

MODEL 1881

Even though John Marlin established his reputation as a Yankee craftsman and gun manufacturer as early as 1870, his first production repeating rifle did not appear until 1881. Over one hundred years later, we can look closely at this lever action rifle and recognize the contribution John Marlin made to the sporting arms industry.

Andrew Burgess had already developed and patented lever action rifles with tubular magazines underneath the barrel. It was inevitable that John Marlin's search for a repeating rifle to manufacture—in addition to the Ballard rifles and handguns he had been manufacturing so successfully—would bring the two men together. In due course, a rifle was designed that incorporated patents of a number of inventors. The rights to use early H.F. Wheeler, Andrew Burgess, and E.A.F. Toepperwein patents were obtained, in addition to new patents of Andrew Burgess and John Marlin.

Not identified as Model 1881 until the year 1888, the new Marlin repeater was a side-loading, top-ejection, lever action rifle of the bolt class. When first introduced it was available in either caliber .45 Govt. (.45-70) or .40 (.40-60). The octagon barrel was 28 inches long and the rifle held 10 cartridges. It was priced at $32. (At this time, it was one of the most expensive lever action repeaters available.) Charts in this section show price changes, barrel lengths, and set-trigger models as shown in catalogs from 1882 through 1889.

The catalog description of the operative parts identified in the 1882 catalog is as follows:

Figure 2 shows the Rifle with all the operative parts in open position.

Throwing forward the Lever A withdraws the Firing Pin I, unlocks the Bolt B, and causes it to recede, carrying with it the Extractor C, which extracts the shell of the cartridge just fired, while the Ejector E, attached to the lower section of the bolt, ejects the same from the receiver. By the same motion, the Carrier Block D is raised from its natural position, as in Figure No. 1, brings the cartridge with it, and places the same in line with the chamber of the barrel, while the spring F firmly holds the cartridge in place.

The hammer G is brought to full cock by the same motion, and held there by the action of the Trigger H, entering its full cock notch.

Bringing the Lever back to its natural position causes the bolt to move forward, pushes the cartridges into the chamber, lowers the carrier block to recieve a fresh cartridge, securely locks the breech mechanism, and leaves the arm ready to fire.

The magazine is loaded through an opening in the side of the receiver, which opening is closed by a cover. . . . When loading, the rifle may be *either open or closed.*

Directions for taking the action apart are as follows:

"FIRST—Take out the lever pin screw, and drive out the lever pin, which allows the lever to be removed.

SECOND— Take out the tang screw (this allows the stock to be removed), hammer screw, and front pin that goes through

Marlin catalog page illustrating Marlin's new repeating rifle.

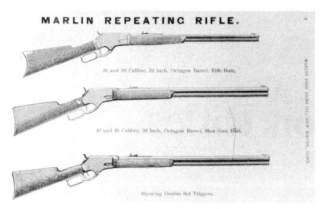

Marlin catalog page showing checkering, pistol grip, and engraving, which could be ordered as an extra.

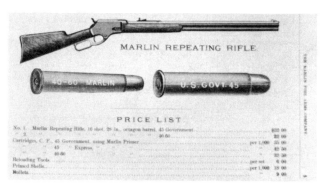

Prices for the new repeating rifle.

Catalog page now listing the Marlin repeating rifle as the Model 1881.

Illustration from 1885 book Trajectories of American Hunting Rifles, *which included tests of the Marlin Model 1881 rifle.*

Shoverling, Daly and Gales (sole agents for Marlin firearms) circular about the new Marlin repeating rifle.

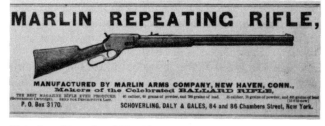

Note that this early ad identifies Marlin as Marlin Arms Company rather than The Marlin Fire Arms Company.

the trigger strap; now remove the trigger strap with the lock work attached.

THIRD—The bolt can then be slipped out. To assemble the action, put the parts into the receiver in reverse order from that in which they were taken out.

There are three different barrel markings found on the Model 1881. The first is in one line and lists patents dated from 1865 to 1880. Probably fewer than 65 rifles were marked with this one-line roll-stamp. The second type of marking is in two lines. It includes the same patent dates as the first type and was in use until the company name changed from J.M. Marlin to The Marlin Fire Arms Company in 1881. The third type of marking is *Marlin Fire-Arms Co.* The abbreviation for Connecticut is now CT, rather than *CONN* of the second type, and the word *reissue* is now hyphenated thus: *RE-ISSUE*.

Roll-stamps usually have a decorative cartouche at both ends of the stamping. In addition to being a decoration, the fancy ends act as a lead-in buffer to the steel roller, taking the

initial pressure of contact and causing the roll-stamp to rotate down the barrel.

It is interesting to note that patents, other than those originally marked on the barrel, were also used in the Model 1881, yet the barrel markings were never updated. This could have been to save money, because the hand-engraved dies were very expensive.

When introduced, the Model 1881 rifle was designed for the large .45 and .40 caliber cartridges. Necessarily, the whole rifle was rather massive. The barrels were long (28 inches and 30 inches) and octagon. Holding 10 cartridges, they were heavy. Thus, the receivers were also massive. In due course, to make a lighter rifle, shorter (24-in.) barrels were made available and the receivers were lightened. The changes in the receivers were as follows:

Heavy Receiver (first variation): Front bottom of receiver stepped (rebated). Top tang has square corner where it meets the receiver. Weight—9-11 pounds. Wide front and rear flanges to receiver.

Ad for Marlin repeating rifle (Model 1881), which claims that Dr. Carver and Buffalo Bill use Marlin rifles during their exhibitions.

Picture of three "men of the West" in their typical apparel and with their rifles. The man on the left is leaning on his Marlin Model 1881. The man in the middle appears to have a Winchester. The rifle on the right cannot be identified.

Marlin 1885 catalog page that shows the cartridges for which the Model 1881 rifles were chambered.

Studio photo of hunter and his Model 1881 rifle (Herb Peck, Jr.)

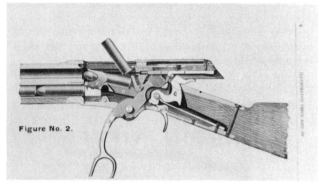

The Model 1881 rifle included the genius of both A. Burgess and J.M. Marlin. Catalog illustrations in the 1882 catalog illustrate the simple lever action system of the Model 1881.

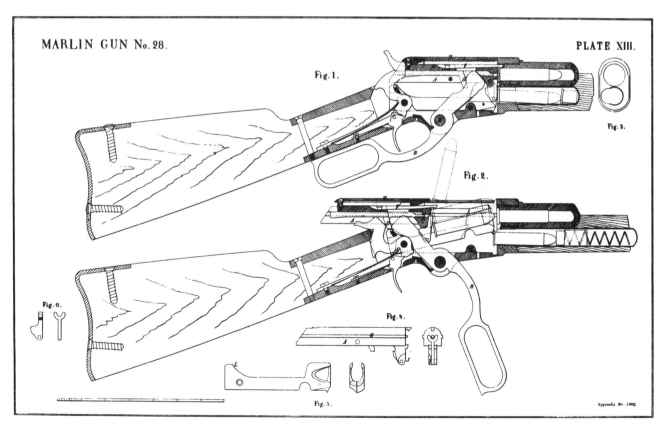

1882 Chief of Ordnance Report drawing of Marlin Repeating Rifle tested for possible military use.

Heavy Receiver (second variation): No step in bottom of receiver and now has radius at junction of top tangs and receiver. Weight — 9–11 pounds. Wide front and rear flanges to receiver.

Light Receiver: Introduced in the 1885 catalog, the .45–70 Light and .40–60 Light were listed as a ". . . lighter model especially adapted to export trade . . ." This rifle weighed one to two pounds less (8¼ to 8¾ pounds) than the heavy rifle. The original offering had barrels of 24- or 28-in. length. Front receiver flange wide, rear flange narrow.

Small receiver: Thinner and smaller, this Model 1881 was available only in calibers .32–40 and .38–55. Weight — 7¼ to 7½ pounds. Both front and rear flanges narrow.

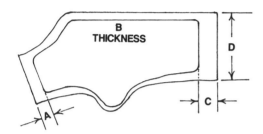

DIMENSIONS OF RECEIVER

	A	B	C	D
Heavy Receiver 1st Variation	.375″	1.140″	.625″	2.160″
Heavy Receiver 2nd Variation	.375	1.140	.625	2.260
Light Receiver	.145	1.025	.450	2.240
Small Receiver	.145	.950	.270	2.250

Figures shown are an average of 10 receivers measured, except for the light receiver, which is an average of five measured.

In comparison with some of the lever action rifles introduced by Marlin and other manufacturers after the Model 1881 was placed on the market, the 1881 did not enjoy a great deal of popularity. Yet, compared with its predecessors, it was well received and widely used for hunting large game. It was the first successful large-caliber lever action repeating rifle.

There were two basic weaknesses to the Model 1881. Neither related to strength, but rather to mechanical operation. The first was the top-ejection system that John Marlin did away with in his subsequent Models 1889, 1893, and 1894. In fact, much of the great success of today's Marlin center-fire lever action rifles can be traced to John Marlin's change from the Model 1881 top-ejection to his improved side-ejection models.

The second weakness was the continual problem of getting cartridges from the magazine tube onto the carrier without jamming the mechanism. A number of patents were issued that were intended to eliminate the problem. Wedges, and a split carrier with fingers added were two approaches incorporated some time after 1884. Photos here illustrate these features. They are easily identified. The split carrier and wedge were used in all caliber .32–40 and .38–55 small-receiver 1881s. The two added fingers in the carrier are features of heavy- and light-receiver rifles. Carriers with these features are stamped on the left side *PAT. APRIL 22, 1884.*

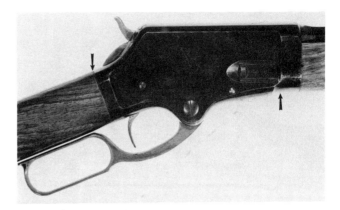

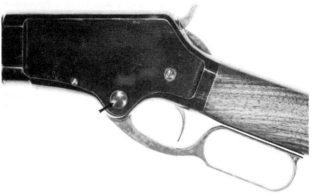

Top: *Right side of heavy receiver, Model 1881 rifle. (Arrows indicate square corner junction of the top tang and the stepped receiver of the first variation of the heavy receiver Model 1881.)* Bottom: *Left side of Model 1881 rifle. (Note that the unslotted solid head of the lever pin belongs on the left side of the receiver; see arrow.)*

The second variation of the heavy receiver — in addition to not having the step in the bottom front of the receiver, this variation had a rounded corner at the junction of the top tang and the receiver (see arrow). Also shown here is the bolt in the open position and with a fired cartridge case ready to be ejected.

Unfortunately for the collector and historian who likes everything black and white, the Model 1881 serial number records are not complete and frequently not all-revealing. Although the ledgers start with serial number 4,000, the first entry is for number 4,096, and up to about number 4,600 very few have data posted. The first entries start in May 1883. Also, there are numerous blank entries for which I know rifles do

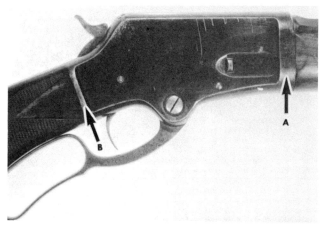

Model 1881 light receiver advertised as for the export trade. Note that the front forearm flange is narrower on the light receiver than that of the heavy receiver (arrow A). The rear stock flange is the same width as that of the small receiver (arrow B).

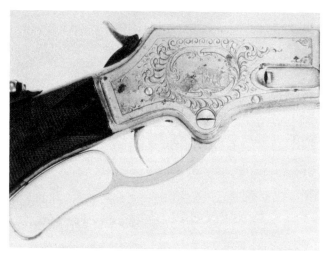

Rare nickel-plated and engraved small-receiver Model 1881. The tangs of all small receivers were drilled and tapped for tang sights.

Typical high-grade, special-order, small-receiver rifle. The small receiver was only manufactured in .32–40 and .38–55. This one has set triggers.

exist, having inspected many of them. In addition to this confusion, there are numerous entries indicating that rifles with duplicate and, in one case, triplicate numbers exist. I have inspected only one pair of duplicate numbers, and the features of both rifles agreed with the entries. For example, up to serial number 10,700, there were 117 entries showing duplicate numbers, one entry showing three guns made with the same number, and 224 entries that had no information listed at all. The recapitulation of data in the records includes duplicate entries; however, entries that were blank were not counted as having been manufactured, although we know that some are extant. Few entries show extra features, except for pistol grip, set-triggers and special-order barrel lengths. Also, the light-receiver guns can only be identified by the caliber. The records are very complete with regard to caliber and barrel length.

A change in the characteristics of the Model 1881 rifle cannot be tied down to specific serial numbers. As even in today's operation, Marlin receivers were serial-numbered during manufacture and before being completely finished, polished, and blued. As a result, receivers with low numbers frequently have a characteristic of a late gun, one that shows up in the records as having been completed and shipped much later than the group of numbers it belongs to. For example, one can find

Hand-engraved barrel markings on Model 1881 rifle, serial number 1. The first production roll-stamped markings were similar, except for the added patent dates reading February 7, '65 *and* Nov. 9, '80, *and* REISSUE Nov. 9, '80.

Second-type roll-stamped barrel markings found on Model 1881 rifles manufactured before the new Marlin Firearms Company name was used.

Third variation of the Model 1881 barrel markings, which now include the name of the new company.

The arrow indicates the stepped (rebated) bottom front of the first-type receiver.

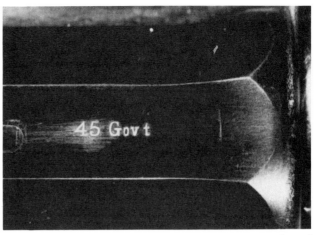

The caliber of 1881s was usually stamped into the top rear surface of the barrel.

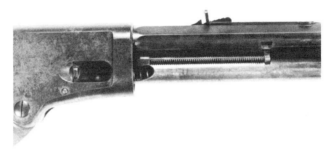

Patent number 222,414, dated December 9, 1879, covered the spring-activated loading gate cover.

Typical hand-stamped serial number on bottom front of 1881s.

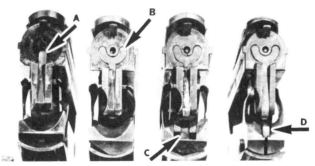

Left: *First variation of bolt face and ejector covered by patent number 222,414, dated December 9, 1879. Rifles of this variation are very rare and probably don't number over 65 (arrow A).* Left of center: *Second variation of bolt face and ejector included in patent number 271,091, dated January 23, 1883. All Model 1881 rifles except for the few of the first variation have this type of ejector (arrow B).* Right of center: *Patents number 271,091 (January 23, 1883) and number 297,424 (April 22, 1884) were for improvements made to the cartridge carrier of the Model 1881 rifle. The arrow C indicates the two fingers added to the second variation of carrier that were to improve feeding of cartridges from the magazine tube onto the carrier.* Right: *The caliber .32–40 and .38–55 rifles used the split carrier and wedge improvement of patent number 297, 424 of April 22, 1884. Arrow D indicates the wedge that was depressed by the lower end of the ejector that in turn expanded this third variation of carrier allowing a cartridge to feed from the magazine tube. Used in only the small-receiver rifle.*

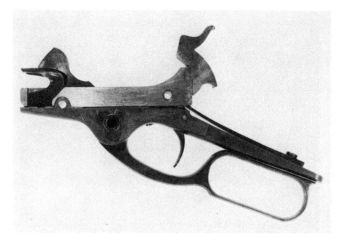
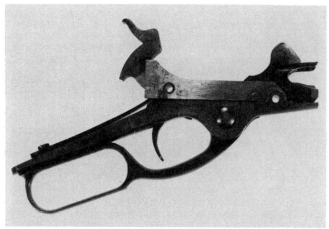

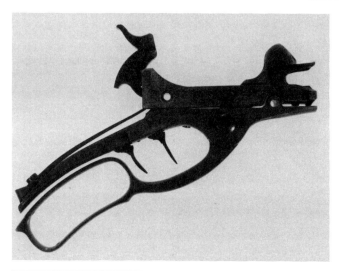
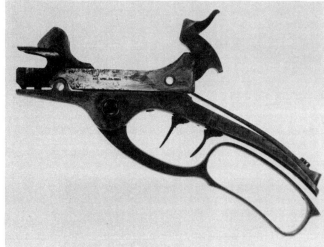

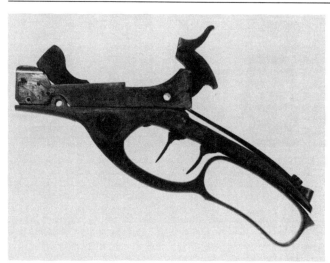
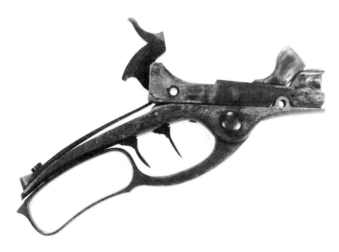

Top: *Left and right sides of first-variation Model 1881 trigger strap, carrier block, lever, and hammer. The end of the lever opens the spring fingers to allow a cartridge to enter the carrier.* Middle: *Second variation of carrier system covered in patent number 297,424, with two fingers in front end of carrier. Note that the 1884 patent date is stamped on left side of the carrier block. Set trigger; pistol grip trigger strap is shown.* Bottom: *Third variation of carrier system used in caliber .32–40 and .38–55 small-receiver Model 1881 rifles. The lever depressed a wedge that expanded the carrier block, allowing a cartridge to feed onto the carrier.*

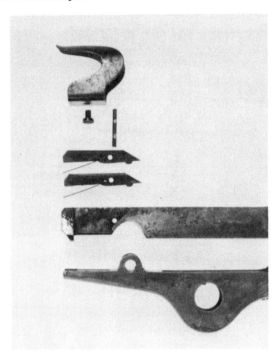

Illustrated are the parts of the front end of the cartridge carrier covered by patent number 297,424 and used in late caliber .40 and .45 Model 1881 rifles.

J.M. Marlin patent number 234,309, dated November 9, 1880, covered the screw with dovetailed stud system of fixing the magazine tube to the barrel. This photo illustrates the protruding end of the screw and its matting recess in the barrel.

1881s that have carriers stamped 1884. The only explanation is that receivers were not put through production in sequential order, and many were at the bottom of the pile for quite a while before surfacing and being completed. To complicate matters, after the Models 1888 and 1889 were added to John Marlin's family of models, serial numbers continued in sequence, and included all three models.

The early Marlin catalogs included many extra features that could be special-ordered. In addition to the regular catalog extras, rifle butt plates could be ordered in place of the standard shotgun type on heavy rifles. Extra-heavy, half-octagon, and different-length barrels could also be ordered.

A Browning-patented loading tool for the Model 1881 was introduced by Marlin in 1883. It eventually was available for calibers other than for the Model 1881. Today, it is a choice collector's item and adds to the story of the Model 1881.

The top tang of late Model 1881s is drilled and tapped for tang sights. The hole spacing is 1⅛ inches on centers. Many rifles are observed with three or more sight holes in the top tang. The factory only drilled two; any others were done after the gun left the Marlin plant.

Many of the parts of the Model 1881 are serial-numbered, along with the receiver. It is common to find bolts, barrels, buttstocks, butt plates, mortise covers, extractors, firing pins, forearms, and receivers marked with the serial number.

John Marlin submitted his Model 1881 rifle in caliber .45 Govt. (.45–70) to the 1881–1882 "U.S. Military Trials to Select a Magazine Gun." The rifle submitted had a split carrier system that was quite different from the carriers in production guns. The lever expanded the split carrier to allow a cartridge

to feed from the magazine. Production heavy-receiver guns had expanding spring steel fingers. The gun failed in the trials because of explosions in the magazine tube and was eliminated from further testing. The findings reported in the "Report of the Chief of Ordnance" for the fiscal year 1882 were as follows:

New York City, April 3, 1882.

Board met pursuant to adjournment.

Present, Captains Benteen, Shorkley, Litchfield, and Greer, and the recorder.

Absent, Colonel Brooke

The Board continued the tests of the Boch gun No. 26, and Marlin gun, No. 28, with results as stated in the synopsis, after which it adjourned to meet to-morrow at 10 o'clock a.m.

MARLIN MAGAZINE GUN, NO. 16
Description

This gun, being the same in all respects as No. 28, is shown in section with breach opened and closed in Plate XIII.

The breech-block A, Figs. 1,2, and 4 is operated by the lever, B, the upper end of which lies between the front shoulder, C, of the block, and an arm, D, of the firing-pin. When the lever is thrown to the front its upper extremity bears on the arm of the pin and causes the breech-block to move to the rear.

When the lever is carried to the rear the block is closed and supported against the pressure of the gas by the end of the lever bearing against the shoulder C, as seen in Fig. 1. The lever is itself supported by a strong pivot, E.

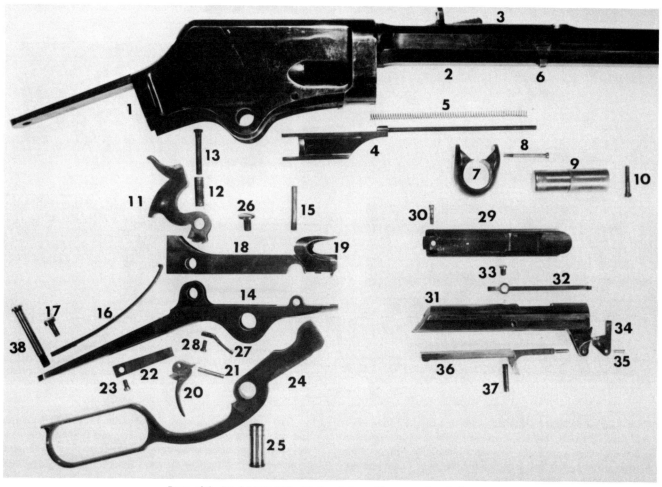

Parts of the Model 1881 Rifle (First variation of heavy receiver is shown)

1. Receiver
2. Barrel
3. Rear sight
4. Slide cover
5. Slide cover spring
6. Slide cover stud
7. Forearm tip
8. Forearm tip screw
9. Magazine follower
10. Magazine tube screw
11. Hammer
12. Hammer bushing
13. Hammer screw
14. Trigger strap
15. Trigger strap pin
16. Mainspring
17. Mainspring screw
18. Carrier block
19. Carrier block spring
20. Trigger
21. Trigger pin
22. Trigger spring
23. Trigger spring crew
24. Lever
25. Lever pin
26. Lever pin screw
27. Lever spring
28. Lever spring screw
29. Mortise cover
30. Mortise cover screw
31. Bolt
32. Extractor
33. Extractor screw
34. Ejector
35. Ejector pin
36. Firing pin
37. Firing pin pin
38. Tang screw

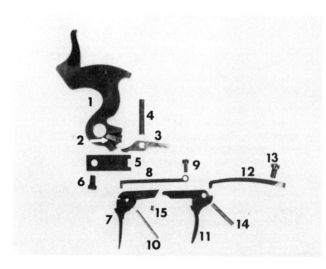

Set Trigger Parts

1. Hammer
2. Hammer fly
3. Sear
4. Sear pin
5. Sear spring
6. Sear spring screw
7. Front set trigger
8. Front set trigger spring
9. Front set trigger spring screw
10. Front set trigger pin
11. Rear set trigger
12. Rear set trigger spring
13. Rear set trigger spring screw
14. Rear set trigger pin
15. Trigger set screw

Heavy receiver serial number 1, blued, straight stock, shotgun butt, 28-in. octagon barrel, caliber .45 Govt.

The extractor is simply a spring-hook, F, Figs. 1 and 2, on top of the barrel-block. On the sides of the block are two ribs, G, Fig. 4, which running in grooves on the inner sides of the receiver, guide the block when it is opened and closed.

A cover, H, Figs. 1 and 2, attached to the breech-block at its rear by a small screw, N, slides in grooves in the receiver in the same manner.

The magazine is in the tip-stock and consists of the usual metallic tube, spiral spring, and cartridge follower. The cartridges are loaded in the magazine through a side gate in the receiver. They are prevented from escaping by the projecting arm J, Fig. 4, of the breech-block. When the block is opened the first cartridge, under pressure of the magazine spring,

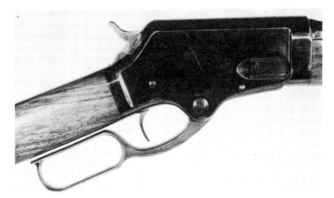

Receiver of Marlin Repeating Rifle, serial number 1 (first variation).

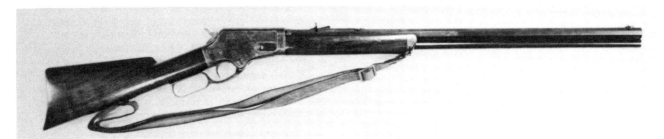

Heavy-receiver rifle serial number 68 (first variation). Case-colored receiver, straight stock with shotgun butt and caliber .45 Govt. 28-in. barrel. Note the original sling and sling loops.

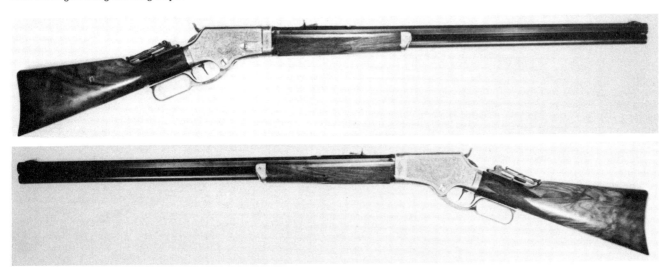

Top & Bottom: *Model 1881 serial number 2041, which is in .40 caliber and has a 28-in. octagon barrel and set triggers. It is also engraved and has nickle-plated receiver and forearm cap. A true deluxe gun with extra fancy wood and checkering.* (DS)

Close-up 1881 serial number 2041 showing typical Model 1881 engraving and NRA medallion awarded this rifle as one of the 10 best guns displayed at the 1981 NRA show. (DS)

backs into the carrier, Fig. 5, the operation being a gradual one, thus avoiding shocks.

The carrier is rotated about its axis, K, Figs. 1 and 2, by the upper arm of the lever striking on its curved surface, L, thus bringing the point of the cartridge opposite the chamber. Closing of the lever and block forces the cartridge into the chamber and also depresses the carrier to the bottom of the receiver in position to receive another cartridge when the block is opened.

The piece is fired by a center lock of the usual form.

This gun carries 9 shots in the magazine and 1 in the chamber.

SYNOPSIS OF TESTS.
This gun was presented and handled in the safety test by Mr. J.J. Sweeney, who fired the 10 shots in 7 seconds.

Regular tests
I. — *Rapidity with accuracy.*
Thirty-two shots were fired, making 18 hits and leaving 2 in the magazine. One shot was fired before bringing the piece to the shoulder.

As a single shooter.
Twenty-seven shots were fired, making 22 hits.
II. — *Rapidity at will.*
Twenty-three shots were fired, leaving 4 in the magazine.

As a single shooter.
Twenty shots were fired.
III. — *Endurance*
On firing the 48th shot a cartridge exploded in the magazine.

On examination it was found that this was the first cartridge put in at the last filling of the magazine, and at the time it exploded had one cartridge behind it. The cartridge behind it was found to be much compressed and shortened, and somewhat disturbed in shape, the bullet being driven back nearly into the shell, but this cartridge had not exploded.

The Board was of the opinion that the explosion was due to the jolting encountered in feeding down through the magazine, and the repeated blow on the base of the cartridge from the column behind it, caused by the recoil of the piece at each shot and possibly combined with an oversensitive cartridge, due to imperfect manufacture or deterioration.

The result of the explosion was the compression and carrying away of the spiral magazine spring, and also the tip piece of the stock, to the front, against the target butt, in which the bullet was found partially imbedded. The stock in front of the middle band was split; the magazine tube, of brass, slightly bulged at the point where the explosion took place; the shell was bursted and the magazine closer was bent outward by the escape of gas to the rear. No injury resulted to the shooter.

The gun was withdrawn for repairs.

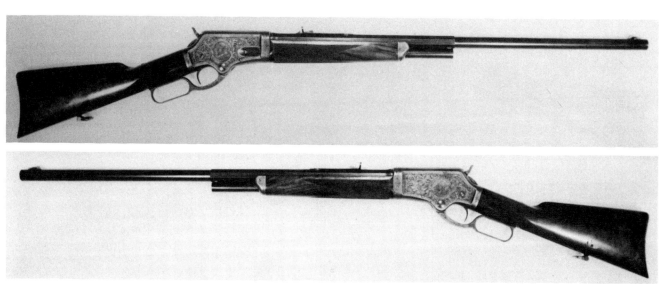

Top and bottom: *Model 1881, serial number 10,350, with caliber .40, half-octagon barrel, half magazine, deluxe wood, engraved receiver, and sling loop. (DS)*

Right side of 1881 serial number 10,350. (DS)

Left side of 1881 serial number 10,350. (DS)

MARLIN GUN, NO. 28.
(Plate XIII)
Description.
This was the same gun described and tested as No. 16, it having been withdrawn for repairs.

SYNOPSIS OF TESTS.
The gun was handled in the safety test by Mr. J.J. Sweeney (representing the Marlin Fire-Arms Company, of New Haven, Conn.), who fired the ten shots in 8 seconds.

Regular tests.
I. — *Rapidity with accuracy.*
Thirty-six shots were fired, leaving 8 in the magazine, making 25 hits.

Same as a single shooter.
Thirty-six shots were fired, making 21 hits.

At the thirty-fourth shot the stock-tip broke off, caused by jarring forward of the forestock and magazine, the stud securing it to the barrel in front becoming unsoldered. And at this point the tests were suspended for repairs.

Top of rifle serial number 10,350. Note the delicate engraving and use of fine-line borders to accentuate the lines of the receiver. (DS)

II. — *Rapidity at will.*
Twenty-five shots were fired.
Same as a single shooter.
Twenty-three shots were fired, the gun working well.

III. — *Endurance.*
Five hundred shots were fired, gun working well through the test.

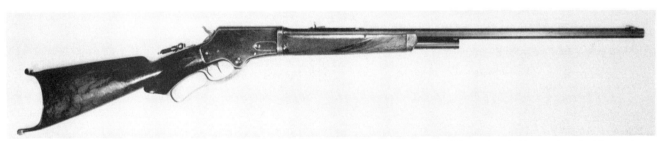

Model 1881, serial number 13,358, with 28-in. caliber .40 barrel, deluxe checkered pistol grip stock, light receiver, half magazine, double set triggers and rare Swiss-type butt plate. (DS)

Left side of 1881 serial number 13,358.

Model 1881 light receiver.

IV. — *Defective Cartridges*

No. 1. Very slight escape of gas above and below.
No. 2. Same as No. 1.
No. 3. No escape perceptible.

V. — *Dust.*

Dust seemed to have little or no effect on the gun, which worked as easily at the close as before being subjected to the foregoing tests.

VI. — *Rust*

Gun very thoroughly rusted, and opened with some difficulty.

VII. — *Excessive Charges.*

Eighty-five grains powder and 1 bullet. Failed to extract the shell, which was driven out from the muzzle.

Ninety grains powder and 1 bullet. Opened hard.

Ninety grains powder and 2 bullets. Opened with great difficulty; finally effected after long continued effort, and with use of leaden mallet, when it was found the head was off the shell.

SUPPLEMENTARY TESTS

I. — Defective Cartridges.

No. 1. Large escape of gas, blowing open the magazine feed-gate.
No. 2. About the same escape of gas.

First dusting

Gun worked all right.

Second dusting.
Failed to extract twice, and failed to eject twice.

II. — Excessive Charges.

First. Head of shell blown off and piece of shell lodged under the extractor; opened hard.

Second, third, fourth, and fifth. Heads of shells blown off, and opened about the same.

Cartridges in the magazine found to be discolored and the bullets of those nearest the receiver flattened and bruised at the points.

III.

The usual motions for working a lever gun. Sometimes working a little hard with the folded-head cartridges.

IV.

It being impracticable to work this gun to advantage in the fixed rest, the test, A, was omitted.

Frankford ammunition

B. — One hundred shots (magazine partly filled, &c). Cartridges nearest the chamber showed some discoloration from escape of gas; bullets somewhat flattened at the points, while all were heated and lubricants melted.

C. — One hundred shots (magazine entirely filled, &c). Same effects produced as in B, but more marked; one failure to extract shell.

U.M.C. ammunition

B. — One hundred shots fired. Same remarks. Three misfires and one failure to extract the shell.
C. — One hundred shots fired. Same remarks. Two misfires and one failure to extract the shell.

Winchester ammunition

B. — One hundred shots fired. About the same as before. Two misfires and one failure to extract the shell.
C. — One hundred shots fired. Same remarks. Two misfires.

Lowell ammunition

B. — One hundred shots fired. Same as before.
C. — Fifty-two shots fired. First 50 shots, six failures to extract shell. Extractor-screw found to have worked loose, and was screwed up.

Second 50. At the second shot, after renewing the cartridges in the magazine, the third cartridge from the chamber exploded in the magazine. Doubtless due to the effects of the recoil on an over-sensitive cartridge.

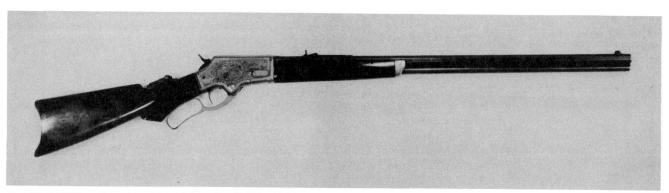

Rare Model 1881 small-receiver rifle, serial number 15,592, which is engraved with nickel-plated receiver and forearm cap. The 28-in. octagon barrel is in caliber .38–55. The butt plate is of the Swiss type but with the two prongs removed.

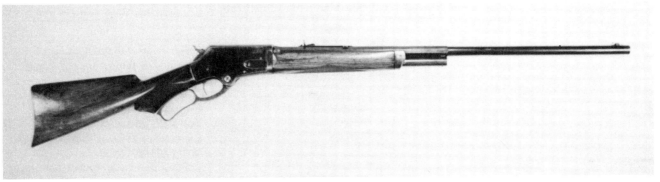

Caliber .45 Govt. Model 1881, serial number 18,380, of the light-receiver type with a blued receiver, 28-in. half-octagon barrel, half magazine, and checkered pistol grip stock with a shotgun butt plate.

A favorite of Dr. Carver, Buffalo Bill, and sportsmen everywhere, the Model 1881 saw varied service and received much praise, but it was destined to be replaced by other, improved mechanisms and more reliable rifles.

Of the serial numbers recorded in the old Marlin records that list the features of the gun, the following is a recapitulation of the recorded data:

Totals by Length of Barrel		Totals by Caliber	
20"	4	.32	1,785
21½"	1	.38	3,563
22"	2	.40	6,261
24"	2,788	.45	4,769
26"	277	Recorded Total	16,378
28"	12,482	Also recorded were special	
30"	780	features as follows:	
32"	42	Set trigger	2,929
34"	3	Half magazine	194
Recorded Total:	16,379	Pistol grip	1,303

Model 1881 rifles having smooth bores for use with shot cartridges were not mentioned in Marlin catalogs. However, a few Marlin advertisements did indicate that smooth-bore guns could be special-ordered.

The old records list only 11 as "shotgun" and two as "not rifled." The two not rifled were .38–55. One of the shotguns is listed as .45–70, and no caliber is indicated for the others. The serial numbers of the 11 listed as "shotgun" are between 8,199 and 8,220.

Model 1881 Production By Years

Existing serial number records start at 4,000, and the first annotated records are for 1883. Therefore, it is assumed that the first 4,000 Model 1881s were manufactured during 1881 and 1882.

Year	Total	Low Number	High Number
1883	2,207	4,096	17,425
1884	2,214	4,206	9,554
1885	2,401	5,424	18,330
1886	3,524	4,918	15,981
1887	2,315	7,643	18,316
1888	1,660	7,292	22,063
1889	1,036	13,063	29,474
1890	543	14,651	45,211
1891	469	14,218	51,233
1892–1903	16*		

Recorded Total: 1883–1891 – 16,385
Estimated Grand Total: 1881–1903 – 20,535

*Between 1892 and 1903, the records list 16 Model 1881s as being shipped. The serial numbers range from 11,432 to 37,706. It is therefore assumed that these guns were either complete and on hand or assembled from receivers previously serial-numbered and on hand.

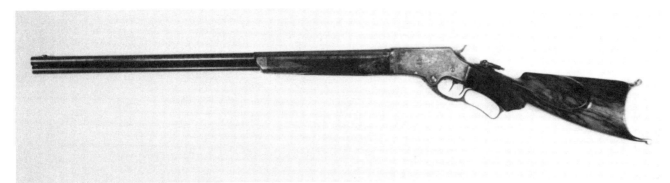

Serial number 18,380 Model 1881 with a blued light receiver, pistol grip stock with cheek piece and Swiss butt plate, and 28-in. caliber .45, half-octagon barrel with a half magazine.

Patents Used in the Marlin Model 1881 Rifle

Number	Date	Name	Claim
46,286	Feb. 7, 1865	H.F. Wheeler	Lever action with tubular magazine
134,589	Jan. 7, 1873	A. Burgess	Side-loading tubular magazine and lever action
167,712	Sept. 14, 1875	E.A.F. Toepperwein	Tipping carrier
210,091	Nov. 19, 1878	A. Burgess	Pivoted lever working bolt
210,181	Nov. 26, 1878	A. Burgess	Bolt locks on end of lever
216,080	June 3, 1879	A. Burgess	Extractor and raising lever to prevent letting in two cartridges
222,444	Dec. 9, 1879	J.M. Marlin	Loading port cover, ejector, and spring fingers on carrier
234,309	Nov. 9, 1880	J.M. Marlin	Magazine tube stud and screw
250,825	Dec. 13, 1881	J.M. Marlin / A. Burgess	Split carrier
271,091	Jan. 23, 1883	J.M. Marlin	Extractor, ejector, and split carrier
297,424	Apr. 22, 1884	J.M. Marlin	Split carrier

Catalog Prices of Standard Trigger and Set-trigger Rifles by Barrel Length and Year

		Heavy Frame		Light Frame****		Small Frame	
Year	Barrel	Standard Trigger	Set Trigger	Standard Trigger	Set Trigger	Standard Trigger	Set Trigger
1882*	28″	$32.00					
"	30″	32.00					
1883**	24″	$30.00	$35.00				
"	28″	32.00	37.00				
"	30″	35.00	40.00				
1885	24″	$23.00	$28.00	$23.00	$28.00	$22.00	$27.00
"	28″	25.00	30.00	25.00	28.00	24.00	29.00
"	30″	27.50	32.50				
1886	24″	$21.00	$25.00	$21.00	$25.00	$20.00	$24.00
"	28″	22.50	26.50	22.50	26.50	21.50	25.50
"	30″	25.00	29.00				
1887	24″	$21.00	$25.00	$21.00	$25.00	$20.00	$24.00
"	28″	22.50	26.50	22.50	26.50	21.50	25.00
"	30″***	25.00	29.00			25.00	29.00
1888	24″	$21.00	$25.00	$21.00	$25.00	$20.00	$24.00
"	28″	22.50	26.50	22.50	26.50	21.50	25.50
"	30″	25.00	29.00				
1889	24″	$20.00	$24.00			$20.00	$24.00
"	28″	21.50	25.50			21.50	25.50
"	30″	24.00	28.00				

*In 1882 the set trigger was not an option. The 1883 catalog stated: "The Set Trigger Marlin is now offered to the public for the first time. . . ."
**The 24″ barrel was an added listing in the 1883 catalog.
***The 30″ barrel was listed for the small-frame gun in 1887 only.
****The light-frame gun was listed only from 1885 to 1888.

Availability and Price of Extras as Listed in Catalogs from 1882 to 1888

			YEAR			
Extra	*1882*	*1883*	*1885*	*1886*	*1887*	*1888*
Engraving	$5.00 & up	$5.00 & up	$5.00 & up	$5.00 & up	$5.00 & up	$5.00 & up
Gold plating	10.00	10.00	10.00	10.00	8.00	8.00
Silver plating		5.00				
Full nickel plating	5.00	5.00	5.00	5.00	4.00	4.00
Nickel-plated trimmings	3.00	3.00	3.00	3.00	2.50	2.50
Fancy walnut stock	5.00	5.00	5.00	8.00	8.00	8.00
Checkering buttstock & forearm	5.00	5.00	5.00			
Double set trigger		5.00	5.00	4.00	4.00	4.00
Case hardening	1.50	1.00	1.00	1.00	1.00	1.00
Swivels and sling	1.50	1.50	1.50	1.50	1.50	1.50
Pistol grip, plain wood			5.00			
Pistol grip, selected and checkered			15.00	12.00	12.00	12.00
Shorten or lengthen butt					3.00	3.00
Leaving off rear sight slot					2.00	2.00
Changing position of rear sight slot					2.00	2.00
Blank piece to fill rear sight slot					.25	.25
Lyman rear sight						3.00
Lyman front sight						.50
Lyman front ivory bead						1.00

Weight and Number of Cartridges by Barrel Length

Frame	*Caliber*	*Barrel Number*	*Barrel Length*	*Number of Cartridges*	*Weight in Pounds*
Heavy (1882–1889)	.40	2½	24″	8	9
″	.40	2	28″	10	9
″	.40	4	30″	10	11
″	.45	1½	24″	8	9
″	.45	1	28″	10	9½
″	.45	3	30″	10	11
Light (1885–1889)	.40		24″	8	8¼
″	.40		28″	10	8¾
″	.45		24″	8	8¼
″	.45		28″	10	8¾
Small (1885–1889)*	.32		24″	8	7¼
″	.32		28″	10	7½
″	.32		30″ (1887)**	10	8½
″	.38		24″	8	7¼
″	.38		28″	10	7½
″	.38		30″ (1887)**	10	8½

*Starting in 1886, the small-frame gun in calibers .32 and .38 could be special-ordered with an extra heavy barrel 1 pound more in weight for $1.00 extra.

**A 30″ barrel was announced as available in the small-frame rifle in the 1887 catalog.

The remnants of a dug-up Model 1881 that had been lost. The end of a fine rifle.

MODEL 1888

Early Marlin catalogs that first listed the Model 1881 rifle touted that their large caliber rifles were far superior to those of other makes, which were made to handle only the less powerful pistol length cartridges, such as the .32–20, .38–40, and .44–40. However, in due course the popularity of these cartridges resulted in successful production and sale of a new

generation of lever action rifles by the Marlin company. The new rifles were chambered for these same short cartridges that Marlin condemned.

The first in the series was a tubular-magazine, lever action rifle called the Model 1888, which was invented by L.L. Hepburn. Hepburn's patent number 371,455, dated October 21, 1888, covers this model; however, his earlier patents, number

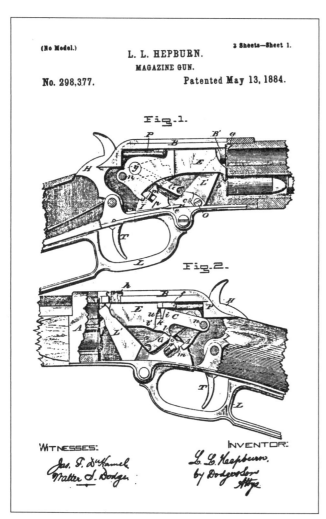

L.L. Hepburn patent number 298,377, dated May 13, 1884, showing action closed.

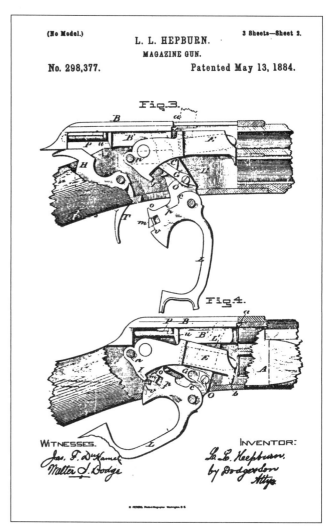

Illustration in patent number 298,377, showing action open.

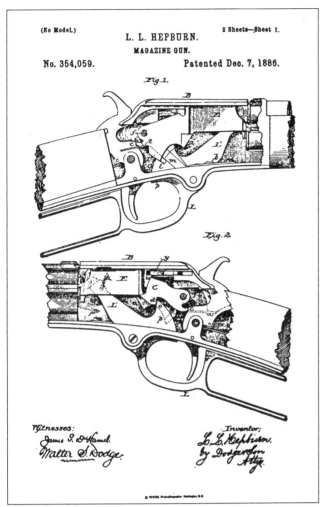

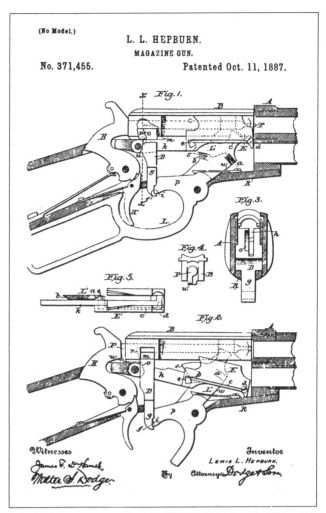

L.L. Hepburn patent number 354,059, dated December 7, 1886; predecessor of Model 1888 rifle.

L.L. Hepburn patent number 371,455, dated October 11, 1887, which is for the Marlin Model 1888 rifle.

298,377 of May 13, 1884, and number 354,059, dated December 7, 1886, are referred to in the 1887 patent as being of the "same general characteristics."

All three of these patented mechanisms are for side-loading, tubular-magazine, top-ejection rifles designed for pistol length cartridges.

Marlin's first ads for the Model 1888 described the rifle as

selling in preference to all others. The following description of the "New Model 1888" is from a circular sent by Marlin to dealers and distributors.

. . . because it combines the simplest and strongest possible locking mechanism with the greatest accuracy and beauty of outline. It is light in weight with a very strong action which is

L.L. Hepburn-marked prototype rifle of patent number 354,059, which is also the prototype rifle for the Model 1888. (C.F.)

Top view of Model 1888 prototype rifle showing top ejection bolt and L.L. Hepburn marking. (C.F.)

Prototype Model 1888 rifle with the action open. (C.F.)

Charles J. Godfrey, New York, ad for Marlin Repeating Rifles. The Model 1888 is listed as available with 24-in. barrels, either octagon or round, in calibers .32, .38, and .44.

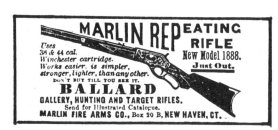

Early Marlin Fire Arms Company ad for Model 1888 rifles in calibers .38 and .44 WCF.

Marlin Fire Arms Company ad for the "Now Ready" Model 1888.

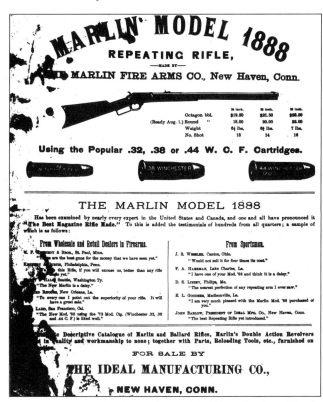

Descriptive circular for the Marlin Model 1888 as distributed by the Ideal Manufacturing Company, New Haven, Conn.

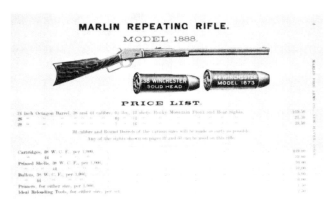

Page from Marlin catalog showing the Model 1888 rifle.

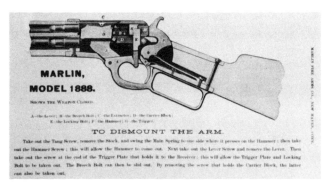

Sectionalized Model 1888 showing the internal parts with the breech closed.

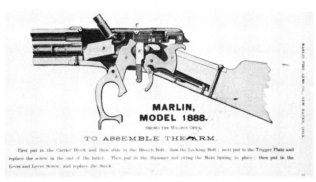

Model 1888 with breech open.

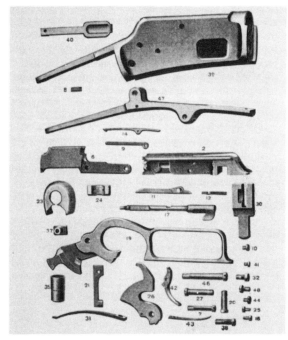

Catalog illustration of Model 1888 parts.

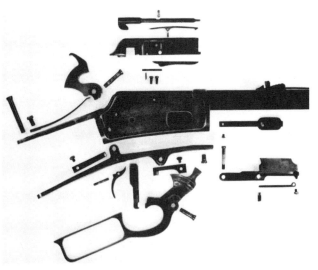

Parts of the Model 1888 rifle.

Rare Model 1888 with a half magazine and 28-in. barrel.

absolutely safe, having been severely tested in order to discover if there were any weak points in it. The lock mechanism is simple, having but very few pieces, and those so constructed as not to be liable to get out of order. The breech bolt, which is of steel, comes up solidly against the end of the barrel, and is locked in its place by a square locking bolt of tempered steel which slides up and down in grooves in the frame, on the same plain as the breech block in the well known Sharps rifle, and has also as a backing, the solid part of the frame. This arrangement does away with all weak devices which are liable to break or get out of order. This locking bolt is operated directly by the lever, without the aid of any links or other pieces. The firing pin is drawn back by the locking bolt, and is held by it until the cartridge is placed in the chamber of the barrel and the bolt firmly locked in its place, by this means making the premature explosion of a cartridge impossible.

The gun is so constructed that in operating it the cartridges do not jump back into the carrier block, as in many rifles of this kind, but slide back with the opening of the bolt, thus avoiding the danger of having a cartridge explode in the magazine tube by the sudden jumping of the whole column

of cartridges in the tube. This manipulation is exceedingly easy and almost noiseless.

By pressing in a very little on the loading cover and holding it there the supply of cartridges in the magazine is cut off and none can enter the carrier, but the rifle can be operated as usual thus making a single-shot of it while the supply in the magazine is held in reserve. This is of great convenience in throwing out the empty shell after firing when it is desired not to leave the arm loaded.

This action, because of its great simplicity, admits of being made in a much more compact and very much lighter model than any of the antiquated arms for which the same money is asked as for the NEW MODEL 1888.

The Marlin Fire Arms Company's first 1888 ads listed this model available for .38 and .44 Winchester cartridges. Ads later in 1888 added the .32 cartridge. The model was available with barrel lengths of 24, 26, and 28 inches. The rifle with a 24-in. octagon barrel was priced at $19.50. When it became available after August 1, the round-barrel model was priced at $18.00. Extra-length barrels were available at $2.00 for every

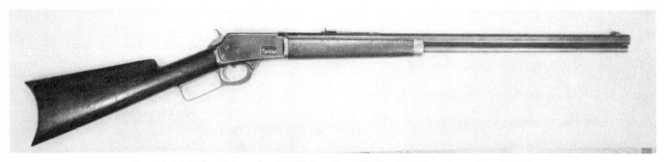

Rare Model 1888, serial number 22,796, in caliber .32–20 with 24-in. octagon barrel. (C.F.)

Rare Model 1888, serial number 24,530, in caliber .44–40 with a 24-in. octagon barrel and deluxe checkered wood. (RG)

Left side of standard Model 1888 rifle. (DS)

2 inches. The weight of the Model 1888 with 24-in. barrel was listed as only 6½ pounds. A 28-in. model weighed 7 pounds. The standard finish was blued with case-hardened lever, hammer, and butt plate.

Magazine capacity depended upon barrel length. The 24-in. barrel gun held 16 shots, the 26-in. model held 14 shots, and the 28-in. rifle held 16 shots.

Half-octagon and round-barrel Model 1888 are rare, as the records reflect that only 23 and 266, respectively, were made. A total of only 4,814 of this model were produced. The lowest serial number is 19,559 and the highest is 25,820. The lowest in caliber .32 is 22,341, the lowest in caliber .38 is 19,599, and the lowest in caliber .44 is 19,559. Other data are shown on the following chart:

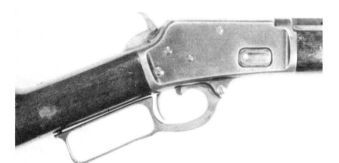

Right side of Model 1888 receiver. (DS)

MODEL 1888

Caliber	Barrel Length		Year Made		Serial Numbers Lowest–Highest
.32/40 – 1,298	16″ –	1	1888 – 1,568		19,559–22,340
.38/40 – 1,776	20″ –	25	1889 – 3,242		20,389–27,854
.44/40 – 1,727	22″ –	1	1890 –	2	22,133–25,820
	24″ – 4,312		1892 –	1	20,528
	26″ –	264	1892 –	1	24,667
	28″ –	198			
	30″ –	1			
	44″ –	1			
4,801	4,803		4,814		

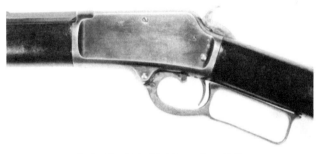

Left side of Model 1888 receiver. (DS)

Pistol Grip –	2
Set Trigger –	4
Half Magazine –	78
Half Octagon –	23
Round –	266
Octagon –	4,548
	4,637

The factory description of disassembling the Model 1888 read like this:

Take out the tang screw, remove the stock, and swing the Main Spring to one side where it presses on the hammer; then take out the Hammer Screw; this will allow the Hammer to come out. Next take out the Lever Screw and remove the Lever. Then take out the screw at the end of the Trigger Plate that holds it to the receiver; this will allow the Trigger Plate and Locking Bolt to be taken out; the Breech Bolt can then

Model 1888 rifle with action open. (DS)

Top of Model 1888 rifle. (DS)

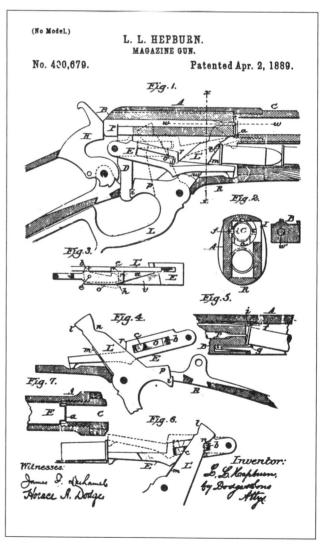

be slid out. By removing the screw that holds the Carrier Block, the latter can also be taken out.

To reassemble the gun, the parts are replaced in reverse order.

The top of the barrel of the Model 1888 is marked *Marlin Fire Arms Co., New Haven, Ct. USA. Pat'd October 11, 1887.* The caliber is usually marked on the top of the barrel just forward of the receiver. The serial number is stamped into the metal on the bottom front end of the receiver. The model designation is *not* marked on the top tang of the receiver. Top tangs are drilled and tapped for tang sights. Most stocks of the Model 1888 are straight; only two were manufactured with a pistol grip. Butt plates were of the steel rifle type.

MODEL 1889

John Marlin and The Marlin Fire Arms Company's first two repeating lever action rifles, the Models 1881 and 1888, were top-ejection rifles. The top-ejection feature was considered

L.L. Hepburn patent drawing for early 1884 lever action rifle.

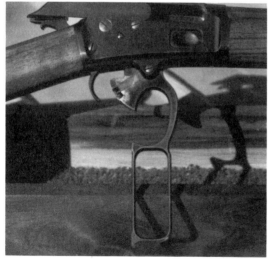

Prototype rifle by L.L. Hepburn with features of his patent number 298,377; however, with side ejection system. (C.F.)

L.L. Hepburn patent drawing for the Model 1889 rifle as manufactured by Marlin.

objectionable and not any different from the rifles of their competition. Therefore, L.L. Hepburn produced another mechanism that revolutionized Marlin lever action rifles; it evolved into one that is still in production at this writing. The main features of the new mechanism, called the Model 1889, were the solid-top receiver and ejection of fired, or live, cartridges out the right-hand side of the receiver.

As mentioned in the Model 1888 section, the L.L. Hepburn patent number 298,377 was for a side-loading, top-ejection mechanism. The locking of the bolt, however, was inferior to the Model 1888 system covered by L.L. Hepburn's patent number 371,455, dated October 11, 1887. Yet when Mr. Hepburn made his first prototype of a side-ejecting system, he used the earlier mechanism modified to side ejection. A photograph of this prototype rifle is shown here to illustrate one of the many steps it sometimes takes to develop a product into its final form.

L.L. Hepburn was awarded letter patent number 400,679 dated April 2, 1889 for the new Model 1889 rifle. The bolt, carrier, and right-hand ejection system were the main differences between this model and the earlier Model 1888. Barrels of the Model 1889 are marked *MARLIN FIRE ARMS CO., NEW-HAVEN, CT. U.S.A. Pat'd Oct. 11, 1887, April 2, 1889.* The top of the receiver is marked *MARLIN SAFETY;* this practice continued until the 1940s.

When introduced in September 1889, the Model 1889 was chambered for the caliber .32, .38, and .44 cartridges. The top of the barrel, just in front of the receiver, was usually marked either *32W* or *44W.* The *W* stood for *Winchester.* It was part of the industry name for these cartridges at that time, because Winchester was the first company to introduce them. Later the

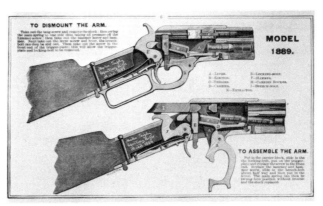

Illustration of internal mechanism of Model 1889.

Standard models of the Model 1889 illustrated in catalog.

Marlin ad for the new Model 1889.

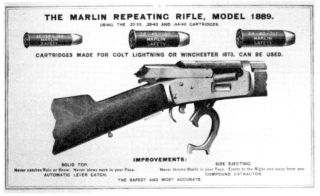

Catalog page illustrating the Model 1889.

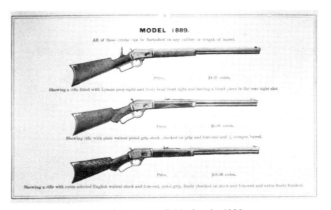

Extra features available for the 1889.

Model 1889 Musket.

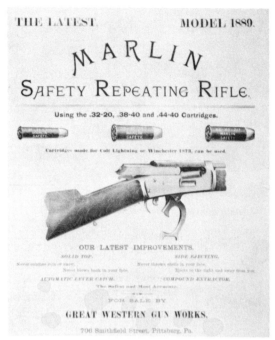

Marlin Safety Repeating Rifle ad for the latest Model 1889.

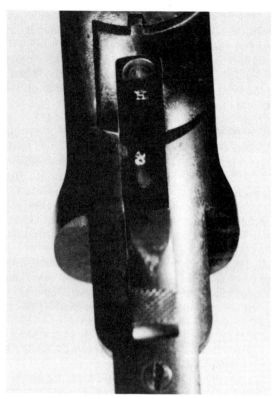

Assembler's marks found on frames and bolts of Marlin rifles.

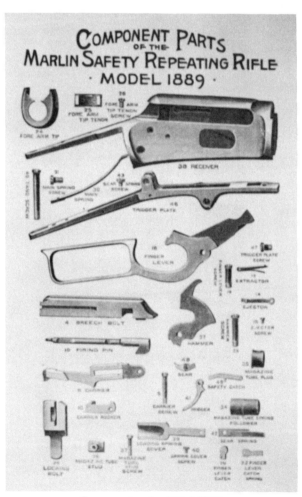

Component parts of Model 1889.

Right side of cut-down salesman's sample Model 1889 rifle. (MFC)

Left side of sectionalized salesman's sample rifle, serial number 50. (MFC)

Barrel of salesman's sample gun showing location of roll-stamp.

End of Model 1889 stock showing serial number. (Most Marlin stocks were serial-numbered to the receiver.)

identifying name for these three cartridges had *WCF* added after the bore size. The *WCF* indicated *Winchester Center Fire.* There are three identifications for these cartridges that can be used interchangeably, for example, .32W, .32–20, and .32WCF. They are all the same cartridges. See the section on ammunition for more details.

Marlin described the new rifle as the "New Safety Repeating Rifle." The company advertised it as follows:

> This gun is so arranged that there is no danger of the action being clogged or prevented from working by getting a short cartridge in the magazine, as by the action of the lever and carrier the end of the carrier is raised automatically to close the end of the magazine sufficiently (after the head of the cartridge has passed into the carrier), to prevent the next cartridge from entering the carrier. This is done without the aid of springs or other parts, simply by the lever and carrier. The top of the action being closed solid and open on the side, no rain, snow or ice can get in to interfere with the parts as in other magazine guns open on top.
>
> In case of a defective cartridge giving out around the head as it very often does from reloading or from poor metal, no injury can come to the person using the arm by having powder blown in his face and eyes, as the solid top forms a perfect shield to protect him. We have thoroughly tested this by using .45 caliber Government cartridges, and firing them in one of our Safety Rifles with the heads cut open in various ways (as required in Government tests of rifles), holding the rifle the same as if loaded with perfect shells. This we have done repeatedly with no injury to the gun or the person using it.
>
> We have also placed on this arm an additional safety device for preventing the firing of the arm until it is completely locked by closing the lever. This is in addition to the firing pin

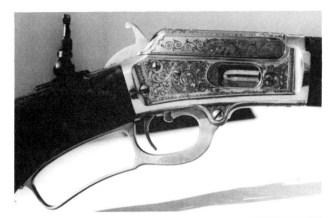

Top: *Right side of engraved and gold-washed Model 1889, serial number 85,491.* (H.D.C.) Bottom: *Left side of beautiful and rare Model 1889 rifle.* (H.D.C.)

Model 1889 rifle, serial number 98,560, which was presented by Marlin to Annie Oakley.

Case-colored Model 1889, serial number 64,518, with half-octagon 26-in. barrel, half magazine, deluxe wood, No. A checked, rifle butt plate, Freund sights, and matted barrel. (RG)

Model 1889, serial number 64,523, with a case-colored engraved receiver, 24-in. octagon barrel, pistol grip rifle butt with No. B checking, and two-thirds magazine. (RG)

Model 1889, serial number 40,601, with rare 30-in. octagon barrel and 28-in. magazine. (DS)

Model 1889 short rifle, serial number 100,174, with half-octagon 20-in. barrel, half magazine, No. B checking, straight stock with 1881 butt plate. (RG)

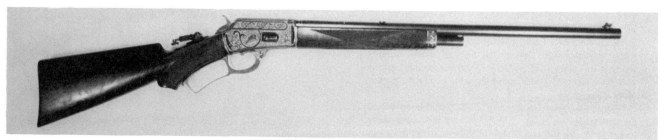

Right side of Model 1889 Deluxe rifle, serial number 87,983, with caliber .38 22-in. round barrel, short magazine, pistol grip stock with No. B checking, No. 10 engraving, gold-wash receiver and forearm cap, inlaid plated hammer and lever, rubber butt plate, and gold Beach front sight. (DS)

Left side of rifle, serial number 87,893. (DS)

being so constructed that it cannot be pressed down on the primer until the locking-bolt is in its place as the firing pin is held back by this bolt until the arm is completely locked; the end of the breech-bolt is made so as to enter a portion of the barrel, and thus giving additional support to the breech-bolt.

The locking parts are the same as in the 1888 Model, and consist of a square steel locking-bolt, which slides up in the grooves cut in the sides of the frame, and is also backed up by the back part of the frame. This bolt is operated by the lever without the aid of links or other parts, and is forced up into a square slot on the under side of the breech-bolt, thus making

a solid lock and doing away with all links or other weak devices that are liable to break or get out of order.

Another good feature of this gun is that very often, the .38 and .44 cartridges get mixed, they being so near alike. We have sometimes found .44 cartridges in among the .38, having become mixed in putting them up. A person using a .38 gun getting a .44 cartridge into it is almost always in trouble, and has hard work in getting them out; whereas with our New Model, if a .44 cartridge gets into a .38 gun, all you have to do when you find your lever will not close with a cartridge in the chamber is to throw it out by operating your lever the same as if it was an empty shell. It is unnecessary to mention that the shells are never thrown in your face with this gun, being thrown out of the side and away from you.

When first introduced, Model 1889 rifles were available with round or octagon barrels. Carbines had 20-in. round barrels. Later, 15-in. carbine barrels were added. A limited number of 30-in. barreled muskets were also available. Here is some catalog information.

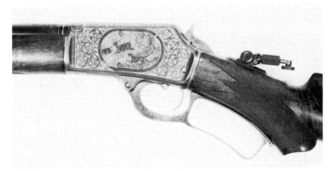
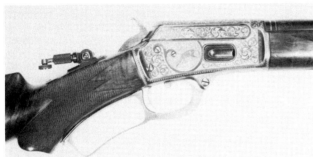

Top: *Close-up of left side of Deluxe Model 1889 rifle, serial number 87,983.* (DS) Bottom: *Right side of same rifle.*

Top of Deluxe rifle, serial number 87,983. (DS)

Top: *Right side of Deluxe Model 1889 rifle, serial number 36,400.* (RG) Bottom: *Left side of same rifle.* (RG)

Deluxe caliber .38 Model 1889 rifle, serial number 36,400, with a 26-in. full octagon barrel, short magazine, rare blued frame engraved No. 1, pistol grip deluxe wood stock checked No. B, and tang rear sight and Beach folding front sight. (RG)

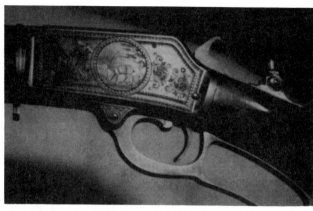

Rare takedown Model 1889 rifle. Only 28 of this model are recorded as having the takedown feature. (CF)

Rifle	24 inch	26 inch	28 inch
Octagon barrel	$19.50	$21.50	$23.50
Round barrel	18.00	20.00	22.00
Weight	6¾ lbs	7 lbs	7¼ lbs
Number of shots	14	15	16
Calibers	32	38	44

Pistol grip with checking—on any size—$4.00 extra.

Carbine	20 inch
Round barrel	$17.50
Weight	6 lbs
Number of shots	12
Calibers	32, 38, 44

Extras

Selected walnut stock and forearm . . . .$ 6.00
Pistol grip stock, selected and finely checked 12.00

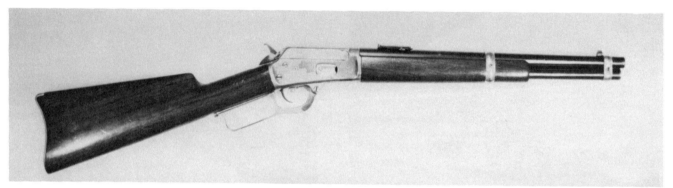

Short carbine Model 1889, serial number 73,842, with 15-in. barrel, nickel frame and trimmings, and staple for saddle ring. (RG)

Blued Model 1889 carbine, serial number 28,505, with English proofmarks, 20-in. round barrel, carbine front and rear sights, carbine butt plate, and saddle ring. (DS)

Left side of Deluxe Model 1889 carbine, serial number 51,950, which is silver- and gold-plated and has deluxe wood and a 20-in. caliber .38 carbine barrel with carbine sights. (JO)

Extra length barrels over 24 inches, every 2 inches 2.00
Swivel and sling strap 1.50
Rifle or shotgun butt, same price . . . . —

Like the Model 1888, the Model 1889 was blued, with a case-colored hammer, lever, and butt plate. The serial number, likewise, was stamped into the metal at the bottom front end of the receiver and trigger plate. Wood parts were made from American walnut.

Rifle magazines could be special-ordered in half-magazine or short-magazine lengths, but full-length magazines were standard. Rare exceptions to this rule are Model 1889 carbines serial numbered 106,475 and 106,476, which are listed in the records as having half magazines. For more information about magazines, please refer to that section in the Expanded Glossary.

The sights standard to the Model 1889 are the typical buckhorn rear that has an adjusting plate, as well as a stepped elevator for vertical adjustment and a German silver blade-type front sight. The rear tang was drilled and tapped for installation of a tang sight.

Besides the short receiver and the capacity for pistol-length cartridges, the feature that makes the Model 1889 different from any other Marlin lever action rifle is the finger lever catch at the rear of the lever. This keeps the lever from dropping when it is in the closed position. The feature was eliminated in Marlin's subsequent Models, 1893, 1894, and 1895.

A total of 55,119 Model 1889 rifles were manufactured. The scarcest variations are those having some of the following features: case-colored, engraved, takedown, musket, 15-in. barrel carbines, and short rifles with 20-in. round or octagon barrels, caliber .25-20, and half-octagon barrels. The majority had octagon barrels. Caliber .44 was the most popular caliber, and the most popular barrel was 24-in. octagon.

The Model 1889 carbine was Marlin's first carbine. It was furnished with saddle rings and carbine-type rear sights. About 10,000 were manufactured, of which only 367 had 15-in. barrels. The balance had 20-in. barrels.

A breakdown of the old Marlin records furnishes the following data about features and numbers of the Model 1889.

Top: *Right side of engraved Model 1889, serial number 51,950.* (JO)
Bottom: *Left side of same carbine.*

Uniquely engraved Model 1889 rifle that appears to have been done by the hand of L.D. Nimschke.

Year	Total	Low Serial Number	High Serial Number
1889	3,629	20,845	30,793
1890	13,122	22,133	46,469
1891	13,568	26,577	75,667
1892	12,629	26,707	89,257
1893	7,171	30,192	101,408
1894	4,498	29,023	116,008
1895	319		121,589
1896	37*	40,125	109,547
1897	26*		109,578
1898	25*	31,374	109,546
1899	55*		109,579
1900	1*	40,149	40,149
1903	39*		87,986
Total	55,119		

*Assembled from parts on hand.

Model 1889 Features

Caliber		Barrel Lengths		Special Features	
.25—	34	15"	367	Short Magazine	207
.32—	15,440	20" Round	9,030	Half Magazine	854
.38—	18,641	20" Octagon	97	Pistol Grip	2,296
.44—	20,984	22"	10	Takedown	28
		24"	39,363	Muskets .44	64
		26"	3,729	Muskets .38	3
		28"	2,268	Half Octagon	508
		30"	164	Round Barrel	8,848
		32"	99	Octagon Barrel	45,775
		40"	3		
		54"	1		

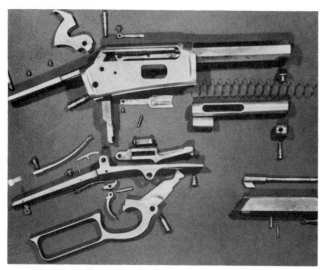

Parts of Model 1889 shown in their positions relative to each other. (Salesman's sectionalized rifle used.)

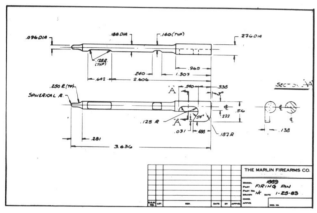

Model 1889 firing pin (average of 5).

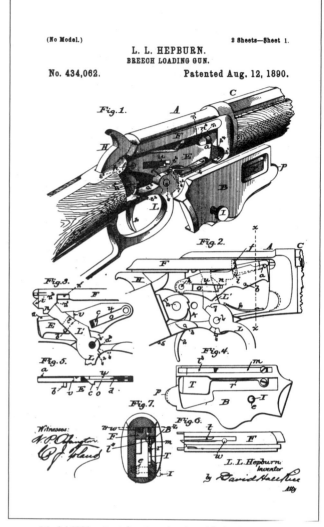

Model 1891 patent drawing showing side-loading feature.

MARLIN SAFETY REPEATING RIFLE, MODEL 1891

The combination of increased interest in lever action rifles and the popularity of the caliber .22 rimfire cartridge resulted in John Marlin introducing in 1891 a lever action .22 rifle that had been invented by L.L. Hepburn and patented in 1890. The new rifle had a locked breech similar to that of the earlier center-fire Model 1888 rifle, which utilized the end of the lever to reciprocate the bolt, as well as to lock it in the closed position. Like the Model 1889, the rifle had a solid top and was side-loading.

There are four variations of the Model 1891 rifle. They are as follows:

1. Caliber .22, side-loading, without model designation on top tang.
2. Caliber .22, tube-loading, without model designation on top tang.
3. Caliber .22, tube-loading, with model designation on top tang.

4. Caliber .32, tube-loading, center-fire or rimfire by changing the firing pin.

The following are the patents that covered the side-loading model and the tube-loading model:

Number	Date	Inventor	Invention
210,091	Nov. 19, 1878	A. Burgess	Firearm
400,679	Apr. 2, 1889	L.L. Hepburn	Firearm
434,062	Aug. 12, 1890	L.L. Hepburn	Breech-loading rifle
469,819	Mar. 1, 1892	J.M. Marlin	Magazine

The Marlin 1891 catalog described the new caliber .22 lever action Model 1891 rifle as follows:

The Marlin safety repeating rifle, Model 1891: The public has for a long time been making a strong demand for, and manufacturers have often tried to furnish a repeating rifle to use the cheap rim-fire 22 caliber ammunition. We believe that

L.L. Hepburn patent drawing showing trigger block safety.

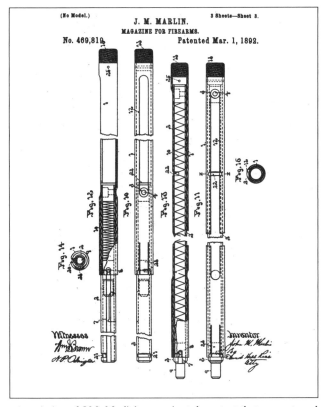

A variation of J.M. Marlin's magazine tube patent that was not used.

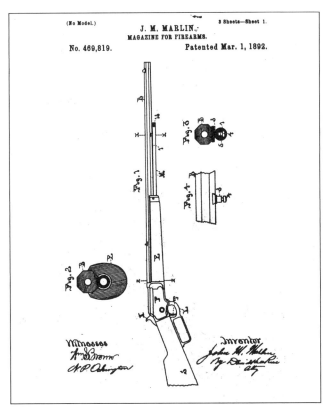

J.M. Marlin patent drawing of the second-variation Model 1891 magazine tube.

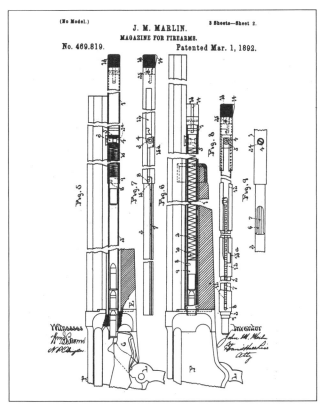

Latch-type magazine tube patented by J.M. Marlin that was used from 1892 to 1915 on many Marlin tube-loading .22 rifles.

December 1892 ad in Sports Afield *magazine for the Model 1891 rifle.*

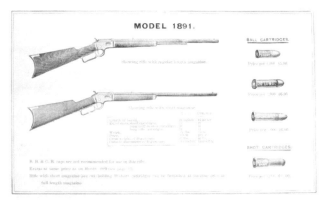

1891 catalog page showing internal parts of Model 1891 rifle.

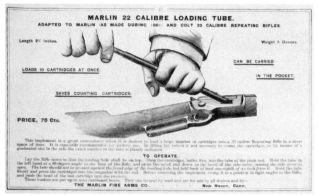

Catalog page from 1891 catalog that illustrates side-loading Model 1891 rifles.

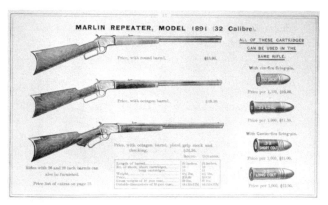

Page from 1892 catalog illustrating the caliber .22 Model 1891 rifles.

Catalog page illustrating and describing the use of the Marlin loading tube for the Model 1891 rifle.

Ace of hearts playing card with shot group fired by Miss Annie Oakley in 1893 with a Model 1891 rifle.

Photo of Annie Oakley with some of her many awards for excellence in marksmanship.

the Marlin Safety Rifle, Model of 1891, is the first to fully meet the popular want.

This arm is designed for short range target work, both as a source of recreation and as a means of perfecting one's skill; also for snap shooting on the wing, and for hunting small game. We also recommend it for ladies' use. With the magazine extending to the end of the forearm, and holding 10 short cartridges it will be found just the thing for a gallery gun.

IN ONE AND THE SAME RIFLE, WITHOUT ANY ADJUSTMENT, MAY BE USED ANY OR ALL OF THE FOLLOWING WELL-KNOWN RIM-FIRE CARTRIDGES: 22 SHORT, 22 LONG, 22 LONG RIFLE AND 22–50 SHOT. Of these cartridges the 22 short gives good results at distances less than 125 feet. The 22 long gives fair results at distances less than 150 feet. The 22 long rifle gives excellent results up to 200 yards. The 22–50 shot is of the same length as the 22 long and is loaded with dust shot. It gives a good target at 30 feet. All of these cartridges are cheap and can be obtained everywhere. C.B.C.'s and B.B.C.'s are loaded with fulminate, which contains glass, and they will ruin a rifle barrel in a short time.

This rifle is operated by a finger lever and any one using this system for home practice will find such practice to be a great help instead of a positive detriment, when he goes into the woods with his larger caliber and finds himself in the presence of game or danger. The throw of the lever is very short and the manipulation remarkably easy. The solid top and side ejecting principle, so successfully introduced in our Model of 1889, is retained in this arm and is of very great importance because rim-fire cartridges are very often prema-

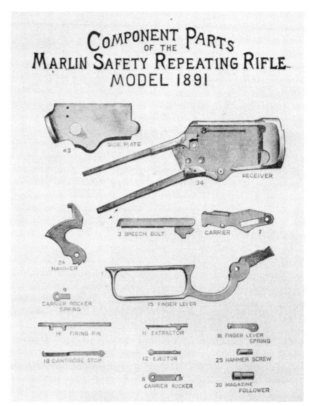

Catalog illustration of second-variation Model 1891 parts.

Model 1891 rifle, serial number 55,704, with a full octagon barrel, pistol grip and checked deluxe stock, standard magazine, steel rifle butt plate, special order engraving, and No. B checking. (RP)

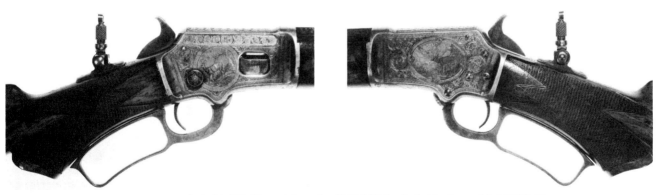

Left: *Right side of Model 1891 rifle, serial number 55,704.* Right: *Left side of same Model 1891 rifle.*

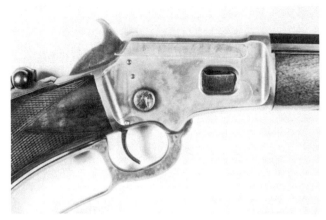

Typical case-colored Model 1891 rifle receiver, serial number 58,516. (RP)

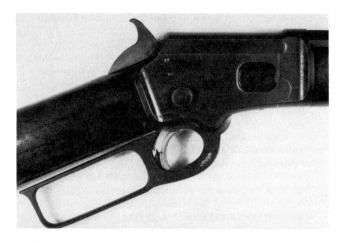

Model 1891 side-loading rifle with the side plate removed.

Top: *Inventor's model of two-piece trigger mechanism fitted to Model 1891 rifle, serial number 47,889.* (RP) Bottom: *Internal parts of same rifle.*

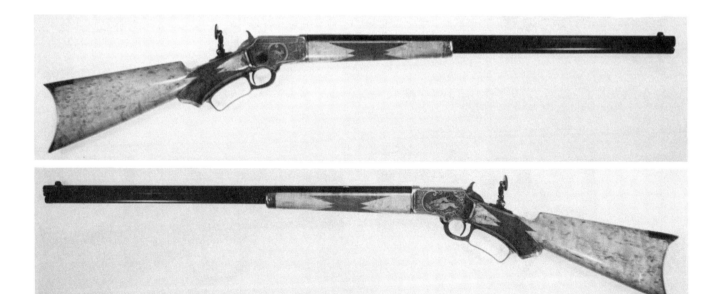

Top: *Model 1891, serial number 87,936, of the second variation (tube loading without model designation on top tang), which has a 24-in. full octagon barrel, full-length magazine, special-order engraving, nickel-plated trimmings, pistol grip bird's-eye maple buttstock with rifle butt plate and No. B checking.* (RP) Bottom: *Left side of same rifle.*

turely discharged. A slight squeezing of any part of the rim is all that is necessary to explode them. Such explosions are neither dangerous or disagreeable on a Solid Top gun.

Our loading device consists of only one piece, a spring cover. It will not get out of order and is not a dirt trap. It is the easiest gun to load we have ever seen.

The two greatest difficulties in the way of making a 22 caliber Magazine Rifle are brought about because the ammunition is lubricated on the outside of the bullets and because the shells are not firmly crimped onto the bullets. Lubricating on the inside makes the ammunition expensive. Crimping the shell makes it less accurate. From the first condition it results that when the arm is heated the lubricant melts and unites with the burnt powder and penetrates every recess of the action, hardening as the arm cools. After using a few days, "The gun works hard"; the action must be cleaned. From the second condition it sometimes results that the cartridge breaks in two in the action and the shell and bullet are jammed in all manner of ways, completely locking the arm. In order to counteract as much as possible these objectionable features we introduce our greatest improvement, a removable side; an entirely new feature and one which will be of great practical value.

The unscrewing of the thumb screw on the right hand side of the action allows the entire side of the receiver to be removed and also in turn the carrier block, finger lever and breech bolt. From the breech bolt may be taken the firing-pin and extractor; all this without any tools whatever and with the lever in any position. This allows the action to be thoroughly cleaned without trouble or tools and allows the barrel

Top: *Left side of Model 1891 rifle, serial number 87,936.* Bottom: *Right side of same rifle.*

Model 1891, serial number 117,446, of the third variation that has the model designation on the top tang. It has a 24-in. full octagon barrel, full-length magazine, special-order engraving, pistol grip, No. B-checked extra select walnut stock. (RP)

Right side of third-variation Model 1891 rifle.

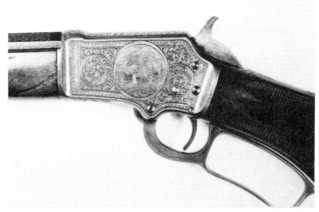

Left side of special-order Model 1891 tube-loading rifle.

Tube-loading Model 1891 with side plate removed.

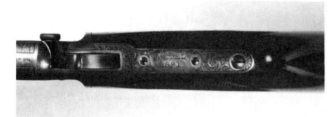

Top tang marking of Model designation of third-variation Model 1891 rifle, serial number 117,446.

to be wiped out from the breech, which is very desirable in a small bore gun, and if the action becomes clogged, one minute is time sufficient to open the gun and remove the obstruction.

The Marlin 1892 catalog repeated the information in the 1891 catalog, except that it eliminated the side-loading information and added the following information about the new magazine:

TO FILL THE MAGAZINE: Take hold of the magazine tube and draw it straight out until the loading hole is open. Drop in the cartridges and close down the tube. The cartridges are loaded directly into the inside tube, and there is no jamming when the outside tube is pushed down after filling the magazine. The outside tube is automatically held in position both when open and closed. When the arm is in use the loading hole is covered.

The caliber .32 Model 1891 rifle was announced in the 1892 catalog with the following comments:

MARLIN REPEATER, MODEL 1891 (32 CALIBER): This rifle is the same system as the 22 caliber, previously described, and what has been said of that applies equally to this size. It is made so that *IN THE SAME RIFLE MAY BE USED 32 SHORT RIM-FIRE AND 32 LONG RIM-FIRE CARTRIDGES, AND BY CHANGING THE FIRING PIN*

32 SHORT CENTER-FIRE AND 32 LONG CENTER-FIRE CARTRIDGES. The rifle as sent out from the factory is adapted to use rim-fire ammunition, but a center-fire firing pin is attached in an envelope to the finger lever. The firing pins can be interchanged by any one without use of tools.

This rifle is loaded by drawing out the outside magazine tube in the same way as in the 22 caliber. The magazine will hold 18 short rim-fire, 17 short center-fire, or 15 long either rim- or center-fire cartridges. One additional cartridge can be carried in the chamber if desired.

THIS AMMUNITION IS CHEAP, and as compared with repeaters using the 32-20 or 32 W.C.F. cartridges, *WILL SAVE THE ENTIRE COST OF THE RIFLE ON THE FIRST TWO OR THREE THOUSAND CARTRIDGES. THE AMMUNITION IS WHAT COSTS IN THE LONG RUN. GET THE BEST RIFLE MADE TO SHOOT CHEAP CARTRIDGES.*

We particularly recommend this repeater to the farmer as an all round rifle, combining the many good points of the old muzzleloading squirrel rifle with the convenience, cheapness, rapid fire, etc., of the most improved system of repeaters. The short cartridges are just the thing for small game, and the long ones will kill hogs or beef very handily. It can be used with short cartridges where a 32–20 would be dangerous. If you throw your shells away use rim-fire cartridges, they are just as good and cheaper. If you wish to reload your shells use center-fire cartridges.

This rifle can be used as a single shot with the greatest facility. It is only necessary to drop the cartridge into the receiver when the action is open, and close with the lever. The barrels used are exactly the same as used by us for years in the Ballard rifles. They are rifled deep, and will not foul as quickly as barrels not rifled as deep. This also adds to the life of the barrel, as they will not become shot out as quickly. *THE ACCURACY OF OUR BARRELS HAS BEEN A STANDARD OF EXCELLENCY FOR YEARS.*

The model and style of these rifles is elegant, the fit perfect, and the finish unsurpassed. The breech mechanism is very simple and will stand any strain that can be put upon it.

When introduced, the Model 1891 caliber .22 rifle was available with either a 24-in. round or octagon barrel, either a short magazine or a regular-length magazine, and a straight stock. The short magazine was flush with the forearm tip. The regular length was about two-thirds the length of the barrel (one-half the distance from the forearm tip to the muzzle). The characteristics of this model were as follows:

Model 1891, side-loading	Round	Octagon
Length of barrel	24 inches	24 inches
No. of shots, short cartridge	19	19
No. of shots, long or short	16	16
No. of shots, long rifle	14	14
Weight	6¼ lbs.	6 lbs.
Price	$18.00	$19.50

A rifle with a short magazine holding 10 short cartridges was available at the same price.

When the second variation was introduced in the 1892 catalog, the new Model 1891 with a tube-loading magazine was listed as follows:

Model 1891, tube loading	Round	Octagon
Length of barrel	24 inches	24 inches
No. of shots, short cartridge	25	25
No. of shots, long or short	20	20
No. of shots, long rifle	18	18
Weight	6¼ lbs.	6 lbs.
Price	$18.00	$19.50

Rifles with 26- and 28-in. barrels can also be furnished.
Price with octagon barrel, pistol grip stock, and checking, $24.50.

The Model 1891 rifle in caliber .32 was listed in the 1892 catalog as having the following characteristics:

Model 1891, caliber .32	Round	Octagon
Length of barrel	24 inches	24 inches
No. of shots, short rimfire cartridges	18	18
No. of shots, short center-fire cartridges	17	17
No. of shots, long cartridges	15	15
Weight	6½ lbs.	6¼ lbs.
Price	$18.00	$19.50
Price with octagon barrel, pistol grip stock, and checking		$24.50

Rifles with 26- and 28-in. barrels can also be furnished.

In the caliber .22 Model 1891, caliber .22 short, .22 long, .22 long rifle, and .22 shot cartridges could be used interchangeably. The caliber .32 Model 1891 rifle was designed for use with either rimfire or center-fire cartridges, depending on the firing pin being used. Short and long cartridges of both types could be used. The catalog listed the rimfires as .32 short and .32 long. The center-fire cartridges were listed as .32 short Colt and .32 long Colt.

To help in the loading of the side-loading .22 rifle, Marlin sold a loading tube device. Marlin said that by preloading the tube, the cartridges could then be pushed into the side of the receiver in a "short space of time." The tube was also recommended for use with the Colt .22 caliber repeating rifle.

Extra features available for the Model 1891 were listed in catalogs as follows:

Top: *Late .22 rimfire firing pin.* Bottom: *Early Model 1891 center-fire firing pin.*

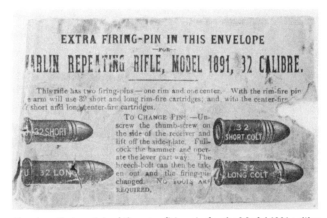

Envelope that contained the extra firing pin for the Model 1891 caliber .32 rifle. The envelope was attached to the trigger guard when the rifle left the factory.

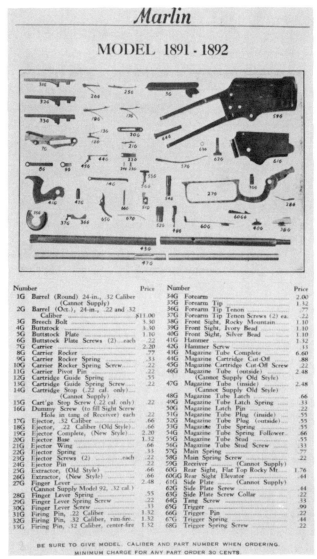

1891/1892 parts list included in 1930s Marlin parts catalogs.

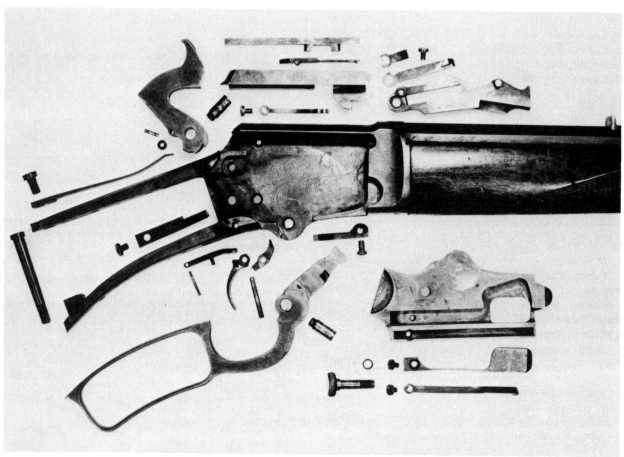

Parts of side-loading Model 1891 rifle receiver, in positions relative to each other.

Feature	1891	1892–1894
Selected walnut stock and fore-end	$ 6.00	$ 6.00
Selected walnut stock and fore-end, finely checked	10.00	10.00
Selected pistol grip stock and fore-end	–	10.00
Selected pistol grip stock and fore-end, finely checked	–	15.00
Extra selected English walnut stock and fore-end, pistol grip, finely checked and extra finely finished	–	18.00
Pistol grip plain walnut stock and fore-end; checked	–	5.00
Shortening or lengthening buttstock or changing drop	10.00	10.00
Swivel and sling straps (leather)	–	1.50
Case hardening receiver	1.00	1.00
Nickel plating trimming	2.50	2.50
Full nickel plating	4.00	4.00
Silver plated trimmings	4.00	4.00
Full silver plating	9.00	9.00
Gold plated trimmings	10.00	10.00
Full gold plating	20.00	20.00

Feature	1891	1892–1894
Leaving off rear sight slot or changing its position	1.00	1.00
Matted barrels	5.00	5.00
Rubber buttplates on shotgun butts	2.00	2.00
Engraving from $5.00 up		
Barrels cannot be furnished longer than 32 inches.		
Shotgun butts same price as rifle butts.		
Half octagon barrels same price as full octagon.		

Two features were unique to the Model 1891 rifle, and were not used in Marlin's subsequent .22 lever action rifle. They were the side-loading feature and the lever-operated safety catch that prevented the trigger and sear from functioning until the lever was completely closed. The safety system was possible only because the Model 1891 had a separate sear and trigger, whereas later models had a one-piece trigger and sear.

The Model 1891 side-loading system was eliminated and a

second variation, having a new magazine tube-loading system, was incorporated into the Model 1891 before the Model 1892 was introduced. The caliber .32 Model 1891 was never produced as a side loader; it was tube-loaded from its introduction.

The standard finish of the Model 1891 was blued. Case-colored receivers could be special-ordered. Levers, hammers, and steel butt plates were case-hardened. Stocks were varnished walnut with a straight grip. Pistol grip stocks could be special-ordered. Serial numbers were stamped into the bottom front end of the receiver. Receivers were round on top and were marked *MARLIN SAFETY*. The barrels of Model 1891 side loaders were roll-stamped in two lines, *MARLIN FIRE-ARMS CO., NEW HAVEN CT. U.S.A. PAT'D NOV. 19, 1878. APRIL 2, 1889, AUG. 12. 1890.*

When the new magazine tube-loading system was introduced, the 1892 patent date for John Marlin's magazine tube patent was added to the roll-stamp as follows: *PAT'D NOV. 19, 1878, APRIL 2, 1889, AUG. 12, 1890, MARCH 1, 1892.*

The original side-loading Model 1891 had a rear sight that was unique to this model. The sight was fixed for elevation, but could be moved sideways in its dovetail for lateral adjustment. With the introduction of the tube-loading Model 1891, and for the caliber .32 Model 1891, a regular Marlin buckhorn open sight having a stepped wedge for elevation correction was standard.

Serial numbers of side-loading Model 1891 rifles, reported or observed, have been between the low of 47,889 and the high of 77,943. The exact number of this variation manufactured cannot be determined, because Marlin mixed models and did not have a separate series, or block of serial numbers, for models or variations of models. However, it appears that about 5,000 must have been manufactured.

The following data are the result of careful review of the old Marlin records. However, there may be errors and omissions, due to the difficulty in interpreting old handwritten ledgers.

MODEL 1891

Caliber	Barrel Length	Total per Year	Serial Number Range	
			Lowest	Highest
.22 — 12,372	20″ — 2	1891 — 4,846	46,799	74,792
.25 — 1	21″ — 1	1892 — 5,158	37,492	87,030
.32 — 6,269	22″ — 1	1893 — 3,143	58,488	98,646
.38 — 1	24″ — 18,090	1894 — 3,001	52,494	117,249
	25″ — 1	1895 — 2,315	48,847	124,162
	26″ — 283	1896 — 141	55,069	116,569
	27″ — 2	1897 — 14	73,375	102,771
	28″ — 259	1898 — 1	68,773	
	30″ — 4	1899 — 1	102,889	
	32″ — 1	1900 — 2	48,267	61,590
	40″ — 1	1901 — 2	74,324	74,547
		1902 — 1	58,511	
		1903 — 16	56,388	81,331
		1904 — 1	117,411	
		1905 — 1	77,605	
Totals 18,643	18,645	18,643		

Half Octagon	233		Short Magazine	22
Half Magazine	4		Checkered	1
Round	3,435		O.S.	30
Pistol Grip	1,068		Double Magazine	1

(1) S/N 48,966 shows to be an 1891 with a 40-in. barrel.
(2) S/N 56,311 shows Model 1891 as being .38 caliber with a 26-in. barrel. However, this is felt to be in error, as it is the only 1891 listed among a large number of 1889s in .38 caliber.
(3) S/N 56,388 lists a Model 1891 with double magazine.
(4) S/N 84,438 shows Model 1891 as in .25–36 caliber with a 26″ barrel.
(5) S/N 116,935 shows Model 1891 as being caliber .22 with a 28-in. octagon barrel with checkering.

MARLIN REPEATER, MODEL 1892

The Model 1892 lever action rifle was the 1896 successor to the tube-loading Model 1891 rifle. Like the Model 1891, it was also available in both caliber .22 and caliber .32.

Marlin stated in 1896 that the Model 1892 was the only repeater available for the .22 long rifle cartridge and recommended that BB caps and CB caps not be used in this rifle. The caliber .32 model could be used with both rimfire and centerfire by changing the firing pin.

Marlin stated in its catalog these details about the Marlin Repeating Model 1892 rifle:

> In the Marlin Repeater the unscrewing of the thumb screw on the right hand side of the action allows the entire side of the receiver to be removed and also in turn the carrier block, finger lever and breech bolt. From the breech bolt may be taken the firing-pin and extractor; all this without any tools whatever. This allows the action to be thoroughly cleaned without trouble or tools, and allows the barrel to be wiped out from the breech, which is very desirable in a small bore gun. If the action becomes clogged, one minute is sufficient time to open the gun and remove the obstruction.
>
> To fill the magazine, take hold of the magazine tube and draw it straight out until the loading hole is open. Drop in the cartridges and close down the tube. The cartridges are loaded directly into the inside tube, and there is no jamming when the outside tube is pushed down after filling the magazine. The outside tube is automatically held in position both when open and closed. When the arm is in use the loading hole is covered.

This rifle is operated by a finger lever, and any one using this system for home practice will find such practice to be a great help instead of any disadvantage, when he goes into the woods with his larger caliber and finds himself in the presence of game or danger. The throw of the lever is very short, and the manipulation remarkably easy. The solid top and side ejecting principle, so successfully introduced in our other models, is retained in this arm.

To clean the action, unscrew the thumb-screw on the right hand side of the receiver, and lift off the side plate. The carrier, breech-bolt and lever can then be taken out. The firing pin and extractor may be removed from the breech-bolt.

To take off the magazine, draw out the outside tube to the position in which the magazine is filled. Take out the magazine tube-stud screw. Take out the forearm tip screws. The entire magazine and forearm can then be removed.

The caliber .32 Model 1892 rifle is so made that in the same rifle may be used .32 short rim-fire and .32 long rimfire cartridges, and by changing the firing pin, .32 short center-fire and .32 long rifle center-fire cartridges. The rifle as sent out from the factory is adapted to use rim-fire ammunition, but a center-fire firing pin is furnished with rifle without extra charge. This is usually placed in an envelope attached to the finger lever. The firing pins can be interchanged by any one without using tools. (In ordering the long center-fire cartridges, if of Winchester make, always specify Colt. What they call 32 long center-fire is not the original but a special longer cartridge and is not suited to this rifle.) U.M.C. Co.'s cartridges are now inside lubricated.

This ammunition is cheap, and as compared with repeaters

Caliber .22 Model 1892 rifle, serial number 140,491, which has a 26-in. half-octagon barrel, full magazine, extra selected pistol grip stock with a special-order cheek piece and No. B checking. The engraving is also special-order. The receiver is of the early round-top type. (RP)

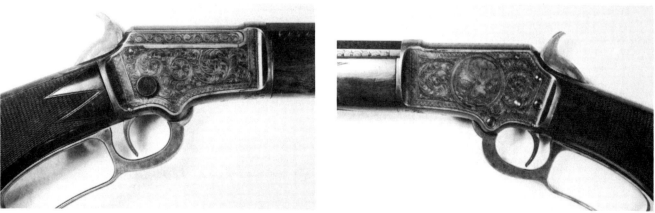

Left: *Right side of special-order Model 1892 rifle, serial number 140,491.* Right: *Left side of same rifle.*

Caliber .32 Model '92 rifle, serial number 428,480, which has a 32-in. round barrel and straight stock. The butt plate in S-shaped steel. Note the swivels. (W.J.)

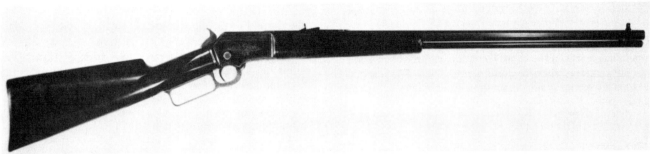

Caliber .22 Model '92 rifle, serial number 424,501, with an octagon barrel and straight stock with "B" checking and hard rubber butt plate. The front sight is of the Beach type and the engraving is No. 1. (RP)

using the 32–20 or 32 W.C.F. cartridges, will save the entire cost of the rifle on the first two thousand cartridges. The ammunition is what costs in the long run. Get the best rifle made to shoot cheap cartridges.

We particularly recommend this repeater to the farmer as an all-round rifle, combining the many good points of the old muzzle-loading squirrel rifle with the convenience, cheapness, rapid fire, etc., of the most improved system of repeaters. The short cartridges are just the thing for small game, and the long ones will kill hogs or beef very handily. It can be used with short cartridges where a 32–20 would be dangerous. If you throw your shells away use rim-fire cartridges, they are just as good and cheaper. If you wish to reload your shells, use center-fire cartridges.

This rifle can be used as a single shot with the greatest facility. It is only necessary to drop the cartridge into the receiver when the action is open, and close with the lever. The barrels used are exactly the same as used by us for years in the Ballard rifles. They are rifled deep, and will not foul as quickly as barrels with shallow rifling. This also adds to the life of the barrel, since they will not become shot out so quickly.

The main difference between the earlier Model 1891 and the new Model 1892 was the elimination of the lever-operated trigger safety device. The Model 1892 had a one-piece trigger and sear that eliminated the objectionable play of the Model 1891 trigger, yet the rifle could not be fired until the bolt was fully locked. To ensure that the rifle could not accidentally fire until the bolt was fully closed and locked, a tang was added to the lower part of the firing pin. By so doing, forward movement of the tang was prevented and the firing pin was blocked by the

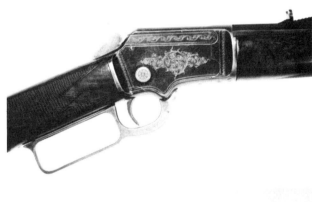

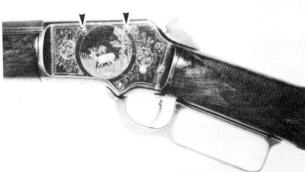

Top: *Right side of Model '92 rifle. Note that the finish of the frame is blue (standard for this model) and the lever and hammer are case-hardened.* Bottom: *Left side of same No. 1-engraved Model '92 rifle. Arrows indicate the two ejector plate screws introduced in this model about 1908.*

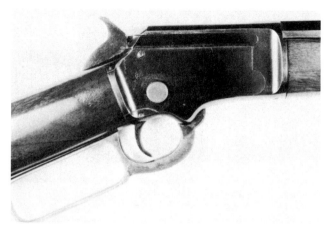

Typical blued caliber .22 Model '92 rifle, serial number A1265. Note the small-diameter thumbscrew that is standard for this model.

until 1915. The 1896 catalog listed them as available in the same configurations as the Model 1891. Twenty-four-inch octagon and round barrels and straight stocks were standard. But available on order were octagon and round 26- and 28-in. barrels, as well as 24-, 26- and 28-in. half-octagon barrels. The only magazine available from 1896 to 1898 was 24 inches long.

When introduced, the Model 1892 had an ejector like the Model 1891 that was held in place by a screw. The 1897 catalog illustrated a new type of ejector for the Model 1892 that was not held in place by a screw, but had a spring. The catalog parts list footnoted the ejector as "a double spring ejector that fits in without a screw and that is correct for any model 22 repeater, whether made for a screw or not."

Another change to the Model 1892 was the addition of a magazine cartridge cutoff. The 1897 parts list did not include this part. It first appeared in the 1899 parts list for the Model 1892, as well as for the new Model 1897. The purpose of the new cutoff was to allow only one cartridge, whether it was a short, long, or long rifle, to enter the receiver at a time. This allowed the three different-length cartridges to be mixed in the magazine tube. A screw on the outside of the left side of the receiver held the cutoff in place.

In 1904, the Models 1892 and 1897 also had a cartridge guide. The guide was installed inside the top of the receiver,

upper rear surface of the lever. Therefore, until the breech bolt was fully locked, the rifle could not be fired. This feature, along with other design improvements, remains in today's Model 39s.

Production of the Model 1892 started in 1895 and continued

Sectional View of Action Closed

MARLIN SAFETY REPEATING RIFLE MODEL 1892

Note the strength and simplicity of the construction, which allows easy cleaning and insures smooth operation, better care and a longer life for the rifle.

TO CLEAN THE ACTION

Unscrew the thumbscrew on the right hand side of the receiver, and lift off the side plate. The carrier, breech bolt and lever also, if desired, can then be taken out. The firing pin and extractor may be removed from the breech bolt, *all without tools.* When replacing the ejector in .32 caliber rifle, be sure you place the flat spring side down in the slot.

RIFLE WITH SIDE PLATE REMOVED—Action Open

MARLIN SAFETY REPEATING RIFLE MODEL 1892

A—Carrier.   B—Hammer.   C—Breech Bolt.   D—Finger Lever.
E—Carrier Rocker   H—Ejector.   I—Lever Spring.

Catalog page that illustrates and describes the internal parts of the Model 1892 rifle.

Model 1892 rifle shown with the side plate removed.

Typical Marlin Safety *roll-stamp on round top of pre-1903 frame.*

Typical barrel marking on Model 1892 round barrel.

and guided the cartridge into the chamber. A screw in the top front of the receiver held the guide in place. The 1906 catalog listed the cartridge guide as only for the caliber .22 Model 1892 rifle.

During 1907, the caliber .22 Model 1892 ejector was changed from the double spring type that did not have a screw holding it in place to one that had an ejector base, ejector wing (ejector), ejector spring, ejector pin, and two assembly screws. The two screws that held the ejector parts into their recess in the left half of the frame were installed from the outside and identify the last variation of the Model 1892/92 rifle. The 1908 catalog first identified this improved ejector. It remained unchanged for the life of the model.

The caliber .32 rifles retained the earlier double spring type of ejector that could easily be removed after the bolt was removed during disassembly.

Other features of the Model 1892 were as follows:

Caliber .22 Model 1892

Barrels: 24-in. standard and 26- and 28-in. round, octagon, and half octagon on special order. Half octagon same price as octagon. In 1903, a 16-in. barrel was added to the catalog information.

Butt plate: Hard rubber standard. Rifle butt plate could be furnished at same price.

Receiver: Blued standard, case-colored on order for extra price.

Sights: From 1896 to 1906, the Model 1892 in caliber .22 had the Model 1891 rear sight and bead front sight. From 1907 to 1915, Rocky Mountain front and rear sights were standard.

Stocks: Straight stock standard. Pistol grip and checking available on special order for additional cost. With rifle butt plate, the stock was 13 inches in length with 2⅞-in. drop. With rubber butt plate, the length was 13⅛ inches and the

First-type Model 1892 marking on top tang of Model 1892 caliber .22 and .32 rifles.

Second type of model designation marked on Model 1892 rifles after 1905.

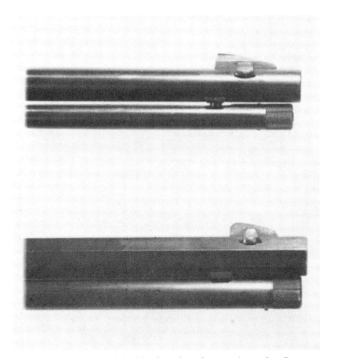

Top: *Caliber .22 Model 1892 barrel and magazine tube.* Bottom: *Caliber .32 Model 1892 barrel and magazine tube.*

190

Marlin Firearms

drop was 2⅞ inches. The rubber butt plate was 4½ inches, tip to tip.

Magazine capacity: Round or octagon barrels with 24-in. magazine held 25 short, 20 long, or 18 long rifle cartridges. The 16-in. magazine held 16 short, 12 long, and 10 long rifle cartridges.

Length overall: With 24-in. barrel, 41 inches; with stock removed, 31 inches.

The caliber .32 Model 1892 rifle was not greatly different from the caliber .22 rifle of this same model designation. However, the following differences are noted in catalogs:

Barrels: Barrel lengths for both caliber rifles were the same and the options of type were the same. But weights of barrels varied because of the larger bore and a larger-diameter magazine tube of the caliber .32 rifle.

Top: *Right side of sectionalized Model 1892 receiver.* Bottom: *Left side of same receiver.*

Butt plate: The caliber .32 rifle had a steel butt plate as standard. The first type was identified as a rifle butt plate. However, the configuration of the butt plate changed in 1908 to an S-shaped steel plate that had both mounting screws into the butt end of the stock. The hard rubber butt plate was available at no extra charge. The rubber butt plate weighed ⅛ pound less than the S-type and ¼ pound less than the early rifle type.

Sights: The caliber .32 rifle had Rocky Mountain front and rear sights during its total production span, whereas the caliber .22 rifle did not have them until 1907.

Magazine: The caliber .32 rifle had only one magazine listed as standard. It was full length and held 18 long or 15 short cartridges of both rimfire and center-fire types.

In 1915, the catalog listed the standard caliber .22 and .32 Model 1892 rifles as having 24-in. octagon barrels and full-length magazines. Prices for other lengths or types were not listed.

Upon introduction of the L.L. Hepburn receiver sight in 1903, the round top receiver was changed to one having a flat top so that the new flat-bottomed sight could be attached. At this same time, two holes were drilled and tapped into the flat top for the sight. Dummy screws were placed in these holes when rifles were shipped. The *Marlin Safety* marking on top of the receiver was eliminated, since the screw holes would damage the wording and, when installed, the sight would cover most of the wording.

The tangs of all Model 1892 rifles were drilled and tapped for installation of tang-mounted rear sights. Dummy screws were also placed in these holes when the rifle left the factory.

During 1905, the model designation on the top tang of the frame was changed from *MODEL 1892* to *MODEL '92*. However, catalogs and price lists continued to identify the model as the Model 1892 until the end of production in 1915.

The price of the Model 1892 in caliber .22 and in caliber .32 was the same. The following list of retail prices was compiled from catalogs and price lists:

Year	Barrel Length In Inches	Retail Price Round	Octagon
1896	24	$18.00	$19.50
1897–1902	24	13.25	14.35
	26	14.75	15.85
	28	16.25	17.35
1902–1910	24	13.75	14.75
	26	15.25	16.25
	28	16.75	17.75
1911–1914	24	12.15	13.15
	26	13.65	14.65
	28	15.15	16.15
1915	24	13.50	14.60
	26	15.00	16.10
	28	16.50	19.60
1916	24	15.30	16.60
	26	16.80	18.10
	28	18.30	19.60

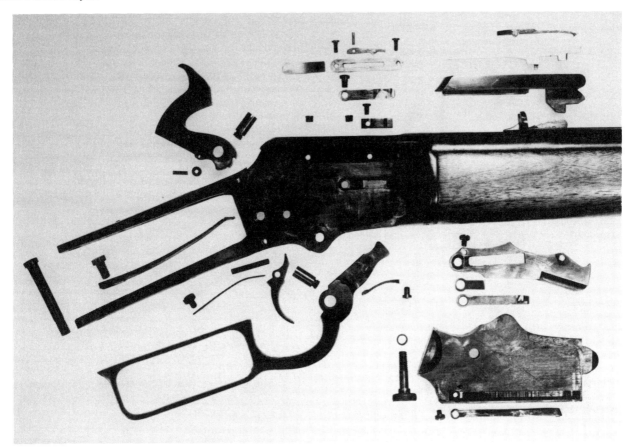

Parts of Model 1892 receiver in their positions relative to each other.

The weight in pounds of the Model 1892 rifle as listed in catalogs was as follows:

Year	Barrel Length In Inches	Weight in Pounds Caliber .22 Round	Octagonal	Weight In Pounds Caliber .32 Round	Octagonal
1896	24	6¼	6	6½	6¼
1897–1910	24	6	5¾	6¼	6
	26	6⅛	5⅞	6½	6¼
	28	6¼	6	6¾	6½
1911–1915	24	5⅝	5⅜	6¼	6
	26	5⅞	5⅝	6½	6¼
	28	6⅛	5⅞	6¾	6½

The caliber .22 rifle with rifle butt weighed ¼ lb more.
The caliber .32 rifle with rubber butt weighed ¼ lb less.

The following are the low and high serial numbers reported or observed for the Model 1892 rifle.

Model	Low	High
1892	A1,823	A8,475
	123,075	436,495

Production of the Model 1892 from 1895 to 1906, as listed in the old Marlin records, was as follows:

	Caliber .22	Caliber .32
Model 1892/92	30,706	10,327
Earliest date recorded	123,198	July 8, 1895
Lowest caliber .22 serial number	123,075	August 31, 1895
Lowest caliber .32 serial number	124,378	July 29, 1895

Exceptions: Rifles serial-numbered 104,732 (May 14, 1896), 121,621 (January 16, 1906), and 123,075 (August 21, 1895) have lower serial numbers than those listed above. However, they are exceptions to the rule and are out of sequence with the production run of this model that started with serial number 123,194 on August 23, 1895.

MODEL 1893

Improvements were made by L.L. Hepburn to his Model 1889 rifle that resulted in his being awarded patent number 502, 489, dated August 1, 1893. This new patent incorporated a new locking bolt system and a two-piece firing pin that were markedly different from those in his Model 1889 rifle.

The new mechanism designed by Mr. Hepburn was incorporated into all of Marlin's subsequent center-fire lever action rifles of the Model 1889 type. The first was the Model 1893.

The Model 1893 was a radical departure from the Models 1888 and 1889 because it was designed to handle longer cartridges than were the previous two models. When introduced

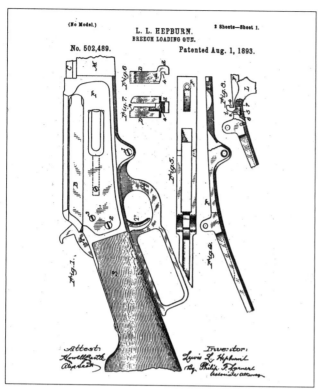

Patent drawing of L.L. Hepburn's patent number 502,489, dated August 1, 1893, that was the foundation for the Marlin Model 1893, 1894, and 1895 rifles.

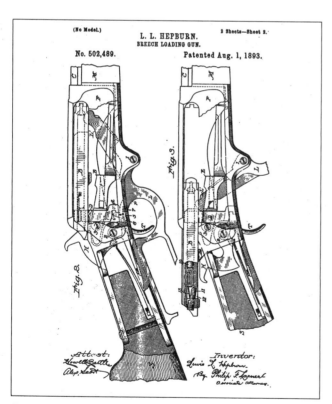

Patent drawing showing the internal parts of Marlin Model 1893, 1894, and 1895 rifles. It should be noted that L.L. Hepburn's patented design is, without much change, still in use today.

in 1893, it was chambered for the caliber .32–40–165 and .38–55–255 cartridges. Marlin stated the following about the new model:

The Model 1893 is the same system as the Model 1894, but made larger and stronger for the larger cartridges. The dif-

Page from Marlin's 1893 catalog illustrating and describing the Model 1893 carbine and rifle.

1896 Marlin ad for the Model 1893.

ference between the Models 1893, 1894 and 1895, is a difference of size only.

The Marlin Model 1889, with its solid top and side ejection, was a distinct advance in the manufacture of repeating arms. This was the first of our repeaters with solid top and side ejection. So apparent was the value of these radical improvements that we discarded our top ejecting rifles and commenced to develop a full line along our new system, determined to manufacture no repeater which did not possess these features so important to the shooter from the standpoint of safety and convenience.

In constructing our Model 1893 to use the .32–40 and .38–55 cartridges, improvements were devised simplifying the action and rendering it much safer, in that with these changes it is impossible to shoot a cartridge unless all the parts are in place and the action completely locked. No person can by any accident leave out one or more of the parts of his rifle and then discharge a cartridge with the action in an incomplete state.

Action—The breech mechanism consists of but three pieces, viz., the breech bolt, locking bolt and finger lever.

The breech bolt is a straight bolt which slides horizontally backward and forward, the sides and top of receiver forming a path for the same, insuring correct motion. The breech bolt is further laterally guided by a rib on the top which fits in a corresponding groove in the top of the receiver. As the barrel is chambered to admit the head of the cartridge and also the

1908-dated ad for the Model 1893.

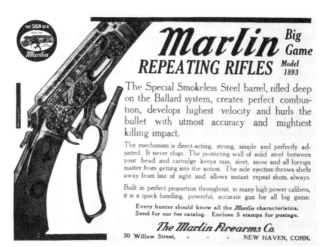

1910-dated ad for the Model 1893.

Early photograph of two proud Model 1893 Marlin rifle owners.

Photo of hunter showing off his two whitetail bucks taken with his Marlin Model 1893 rifle. (Herb Peck, Jr.)

Model 1893 rifle, serial number 111,261, with a 32-in. caliber .38–55 full octagon barrel, No. A-checked pistol grip stock with rifle butt plate, full-length magazine, and case-colored receiver. (DS)

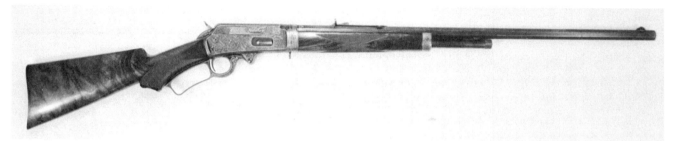

Model 1893 rifle, serial number 119,317, which has No. 15 engraving, No. B-checked pistol grip stock with rubber butt plate, 26-in. caliber .32–40 octagon barrel, half magazine, gold-inlaid hammer, lever, the name Carl E. Akeley *on the bolt, and gold and platinum bands on the barrel muzzle and breech. (JO)*

Receiver of No. 5–4-engraved Model 1893, serial number 119,317. (JO)

Left side of Carl E. Akeley's Model 1893 rifle. (JO)

Telescope-mounted Model 1893 rifle, serial number 125,350, which has unusual mixed Nos. 5, 10, and 15 engraving, No. C-checked pistol grip stock that has a rubber butt plate, case-colored receiver, full-length magazine, and 26-in. caliber .32–40 full octagon barrel. (DS)

Model 1893 rifle, serial number 125,350, which has a telescope fitted to the barrel and receiver. (DS)

front end of the breech bolt, the bolt coming up solidly, not only covers the cartridge completely, but is itself supported by the barrel. The locking bolt sliding in vertical grooves cut in the sides of the receiver, fits squarely up into the breech bolt. A section of the receiver is directly behind the locking bolt, supporting it solidly.

Not only is the breech bolt of this rifle securely locked, but further its position is correct and exact. As the finger lever operates both the breech bolt and locking bolt directly, all connecting links and other weak pieces liable to be broken are thus avoided and there is no lost motion and waste of power. The throw of the lever is short and easy.

The carrier in this arm is to be noted for its simplicity and positive action. As may be seen from the illustrations, there is a projection on the lower side of the carrier, which is acted against by the cam on the lever, in such a manner that as the lever is thrown down and a cartridge enters the carrier, the carrier is slightly raised and partially closes the entrance from the magazine.

No matter how short the first cartridge may be, the head of the following one will strike against the front of the carrier and can not enter the action until the lever is again closed. In consequence, the action will pass cartridges varying in length from the empty shell as a minimum up to the full size cartridge as a maximum. Cartridges are sometimes found in which by some accident, the bullets have been seated too far in the shell or have been driven down to this position during transportation. Such ammunition causes no difficulty in a Marlin repeater.

The carrier is raised and lowered by the action of the finger lever against an automatic rocker pivoted near its rear end.

Safety—The safety on this rifle is very simple in its construction. The firing pin, a cylindrical piece of steel, is cut completely in two. When the action is closed and locked, these two pieces are brought up by the locking bolt into a

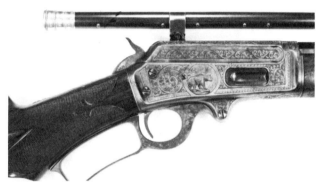

Right side of Model 1893 rifle, serial number 125,350, which shows many special features that could be special-ordered from the factory. (DS)

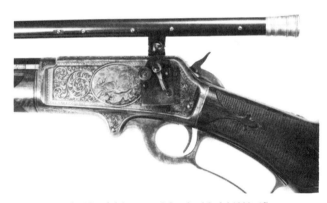

Left side of deluxe special-order Model 1893 rifle.

Model 1893 rifle, serial number 136,243, which has special-order engraving and checking of patterns that do not fit any catalog description or style. The rifle is caliber .38–55 and has a 26-in., half-octagon, matted, takedown barrel, full-length magazine, pistol grip stock with rubber butt plate, matted case-colored receiver, jeweled hammer and bolt and M.S.H. monogram engraved on right side of receiver. (JO)

Right side of special-order Deluxe Model 1893 rifle, serial number 136,243.

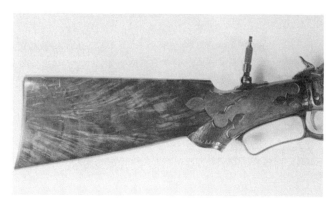

Fancy buttstock and deluxe checking of special-order Marlin Model 1893 rifle. (JO)

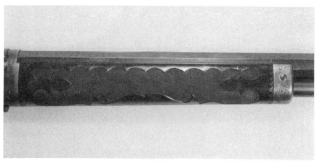

Special checking pattern of Deluxe Model 1893. (JO)

direct line and practically form one piece. But the slightest motion of the finger lever draws back the firing pin, the locking bolt is lowered and the front end of the rear piece of the firing pin drops down into the slot in the breech bolt, where the locking bolt operates. With the firing pin in this position, it is held back positively and it is impossible to drive it forward until the breech bolt is closed and firmly locked by the locking bolt, when the firing pin is again connected with the locking bolt. This can happen only when the whole action is fully locked. If, in taking apart and assembling the rifle, the locking bolt should be accidentally left out, the rifle cannot be fired, thus effectually preventing any accidents of this character arising from carelessness or ignorance.

The lever is held in position by an automatic lever catch placed near the front end of the lever, thus avoiding a projecting safety catch.

The locking bolt does not project, being entirely within the receiver, whether the action is open or closed. The rifle is not only improved in appearance, owing to the fact of its being smooth and free from projections, but further, there are no links or bolts to interfere with the hand or catch the clothes, and no parts of the action are exposed to catch twigs, dirt, etc.

The trigger is in one piece, instead of being divided into a trigger and sear as in the Model 1889 rifle. This improvement does away with all play about the trigger and simplifies the action, by reducing the number of parts. The trigger engaging directly with the hammer allows of the finest adjustment and gives the quickest lock made. Marlin locks are always smooth, free from creep and quick.

The ease with which this arm can be dismounted and assembled is an important consideration. Any person of ordinary intelligence can do this without previous experience. To take the action apart, but one screwdriver is necessary, inasmuch as the essential screws are made with practically the same head and slot.

We believe that this action is unequalled in strength, simplicity, convenience and easy working.

This model was originally made to take the well-known and popular cartridges, .32–40–165 and .38–55–255. These cartridges as regards accuracy occupy a commanding position. They are probably the best all-round cartridges for hunting and target purposes. The Marlin Fire Arms Company originated these two cartridges, and our experience in making fine Ballard Target Rifles for these cartridges justifies us in claiming that this repeater is unsurpassed in accuracy by any repeating arm made. The barrels are exactly the same as those used by us in our finest Ballard Target Rifles.

This rifle is also adapted to take the .25–36 high power smokeless, the .30–30 high power smokeless and the .32 spe-

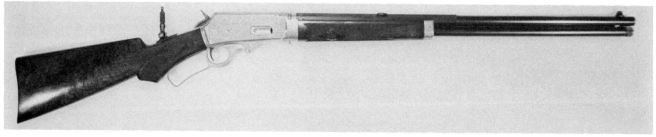

Deluxe, No. 10-engraved Model 1893 rifle, serial number 190,191, which has a 24-in. half octagon takedown barrel in caliber .30–30, full-length magazine, pistol grip No. D-checked stock with rubber butt, gold and platinum bands on the barrel, platinum inlay on the hammer, gold-plated receiver and forearm tip, and monogram ABP engraved on right side. (JO)

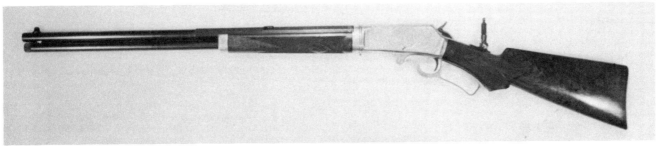

Left side of Deluxe Model 1893 rifle. (JO)

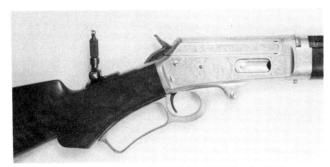

Right side view of gold-plated Model 1893 rifle. (JO)

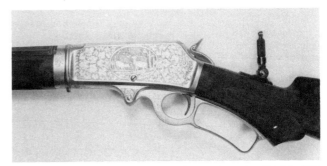

Left side of gold-plated Model 1893 rifle, serial number 190,191. (JO)

Standard takedown Model 1893 that has a 26-in. caliber .30–30 full octagon barrel and full-length magazine, a straight stock with rifle butt plate, and case-colored receiver. (DS)

Left side of Model 1893, serial number 281,661. (DS)

Gold-plated Model 1893 rifle, serial number 288,311, which has a 26-in. takedown, half-octagon, caliber .32–40 barrel, full magazine, No. B-checked deluxe buttstock with a rifle butt plate, and engraved No. 2 gold-plated receiver. Uniquely, the name Thos. S. Jones *is engraved on the trigger plate, by the serial number. (JO)*

Engraved name on the bottom of Model 1893 rifle, serial number 288,311. (JO)

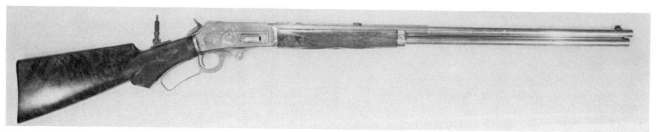

Full-nickel-plated engraved No. 2 Model 1893 rifle, serial number 373,423, which has a 26-in. half-octagon barrel, No. D-checked pistol grip stock with rubber butt plate, and the name Sam Rosenan *engraved on the left side. The tang sight is by Lyman. (JO)*

Right side of Model 1893 rifle, serial number 373,423, which shows the No. 2 engraving and style No. D checking. (JO)

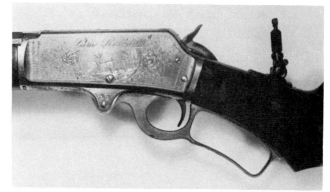

No. 2-engraved, full-nickel-plated Model 1893 rifle, serial number 373,423.

Unique special order Deluxe Model 1893 rifle, serial number 377,022, which has a 26-in. caliber .30–30 half-octagon takedown barrel, half magazine, No. E-checked deluxe pistol grip stock with rubber butt plate, sling swivels, No. 5-4 engraving, and two special sights. The rear sight is a Marlin receiver sight, but the one fitted to the normal rear sight dovetail is a Winchester sight. (DS)

cial high power smokeless, as well as the .32–40–165 and
.38–55–255 high power smokeless cartridges, which have recently been brought out and are extremely popular, as well as
valuable cartridges for hunting purposes.

This model without doubt furnishes the finest repeating
rifle on the market, of medium weight, using accurate and
powerful cartridges. The action is simple and compact; there
are no projecting notches, no loose parts to catch any obstructions, neither is the gun in any way open so as to catch
rain, dirt, twigs, etc. The balance of this rifle is perfect; in
finish it is excelled by no rifle on the market, of any type
whatsoever.

This rifle, like those of all our other models, can be used as
a single breech loader with the greatest facility. In so using it,
the cartridge is dropped into the receiver, ahead of the breech
bolt when the action is open, and then, when the breech bolt
is closed, the gun is loaded and ready for firing. It can be so
used with great rapidity. In case it is desired to hold the
magazine in reserve, while constantly shooting, it is merely
necessary to load cartridges into the magazine through the
side loading spring cover, as fast as one is chambered.

Since the action is the same for all five of these cartridges
(the barrel alone being different), a Take-Down rifle can be
obtained, and with extra barrel parts there will be five rifles
using cartridges varying from .25 to .38 caliber. In the case of
a rigid repeater, any one of these barrels can be fitted if a
change is desired.

Special Steel—In the barrel and action of these rifles we
use our special smokeless steel, guaranteed to the regulation
specifications of the United States Government, for steel
used in the manufacture of the same parts of the Government
rifle using the .30 caliber United States Government cartridge. In consequence, these rifles are perfectly adapted to
the cartridges hereafter described as suitable for these rifles.

To dismount the arm—Take out the tang screw and remove

*No. 5–4 engraving and No. E checking of Model 1893 rifle, serial
number 377,022. (DS)*

*Left side of No. 5-4-engraved Model 1893 rifle showing majestic
"Monarch of the Dell" stag typical of Marlin's best work. (DS)*

*Model 1893 rifle, serial number 437,078, which has a 32-in. takedown full octagon barrel, full-length magazine, No. A-checked pistol grip stock that
has a carbine-type butt plate, and exceptionally beautiful case-colored receiver. (J.B.)*

Typical straight-stock lightweight Model 1893 rifle. (J.B.)

Typical lightweight Model 1893 having a pistol grip stock and extra barrel assembly. (J.B.)

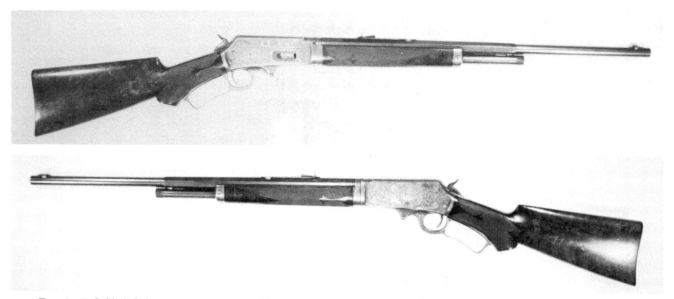

Top: *Annie Oakley's Deluxe engraved and gold-inlaid Model 1893 rifle, serial number 419,119.* Bottom: *Left side of Annie Oakley rifle.*

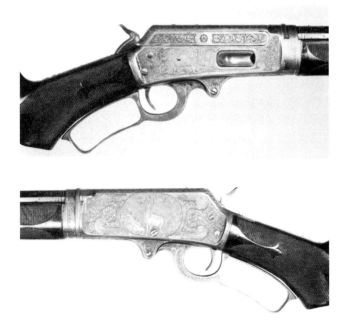

Top: *Right side of Annie Oakley Model 1893 rifle.* Bottom: *Left side of same rifle.*

the buttstock. Swing the main spring to one side, thus removing all pressure from the hammer screw; take out the hammer screw and remove the hammer. Remove the lever screw and lever; the breech bolt can then be drawn out. Take out the trigger plate screw at the front end of the trigger plate and the screw on left side of receiver, when the trigger plate and locking bolt may be removed. As all of these screws have practically the same size head, it will be observed that a single screwdriver is the only tool necessary to dismount the rifle conveniently. If desired, the carrier and likewise the loading spring cover may be removed, as the screws holding these are on the right side of the action.

To take apart the breech bolt — Drive out the extractor pin: the extractor can then be removed. Drive out the pin holding the rear part of the firing pin, which can then be removed; also drive out the front firing-pin pin; this part of the firing pin and the firing-pin spring can then be removed. In driving out these pins, drive from the bottom of the breech bolt. In driving in, drive from the top.

To assemble the arm — If the loading spring cover and carrier block are out, put these in first. Slide in the locking bolt, put on the trigger plate and screw in the trigger plate screw. Replace the hammer and screw in the hammer screw. Place ejector in its slot, being sure that the flat spring side is down in the slot (some shooters place it up-side down). Slide in the breech bolt about two-thirds of the way and put in the lever

Top: *Right side of Deluxe Model 1893 rifle with special engraving, checking, wood, gold, and platinum inlays. One of a few extra-special special-order rifles beyond description.* (W.E.) Bottom: *Left side of same rifle.*

being careful to see that it fits up into the breech bolt. Screw in the lever screw. Swing the main spring into position and replace the buttstock.

To remove the magazine—It is necessary merely to take out the magazine tube stud screw and the two forearm tip screws. The entire magazine forearm tip and forearm can then be removed.

For illustration, see the Model 1894 section.

The Model 1893 was manufactured in rifle, carbine, musket, and special lightweight models. Both pistol grip and straight stocks were available, as well as octagon, round and half octagon barrels. Takedown models were also available, except in the carbine and musket models.

When introduced, the Model 1893 rifle was available with either octagon or round barrels 20, 24, 26, 28, 30, or 32 inches long. The standard rifle had a 26-in. barrel and full-length magazine.

The standard carbine had either a 15- or 20-in. round barrel, carbine butt plate, straight stock, carbine sights, and a saddle ring. If special-ordered, the carbine would be supplied without the saddle ring or with sling swivels.

The special lightweight model had lightweight 18- or 20-in. barrel, short forearm, and short magazine. (For additional information, see the section on carbines and lightweights.)

The longest-length magazine available for the Model 1893 was 30 inches. Therefore, those rifles having a 32-in. barrel would have a full-length magazine the same length as a 30-in. barrel full-length magazine.

In 1905, Marlin introduced a Grade B model that had a barrel made for use only with black powder cartridges. Grade B rifles were marked on the barrel *For Black Powder.* Regular Model 1893 rifles were marked on the barrel *Special Smokeless*

Right side of ornately engraved and gold-inlaid Model 1893 rifle that is one of the two finest Marlin Model 1893 rifles extant. (W.E.)

Close-up view of the left side of one of the finest examples of a Marlin Model 1893 rifle. (W.E.)

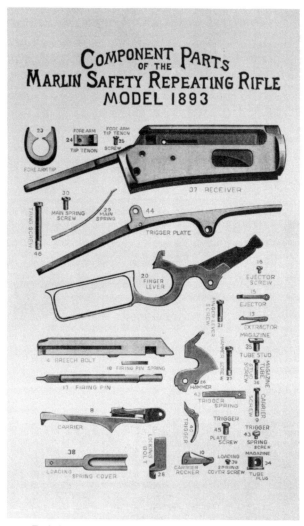

Early Marlin catalog parts list for the Model 1893 rifle.

MODEL 1893 - 1894 - 1895 - 1889 - 410

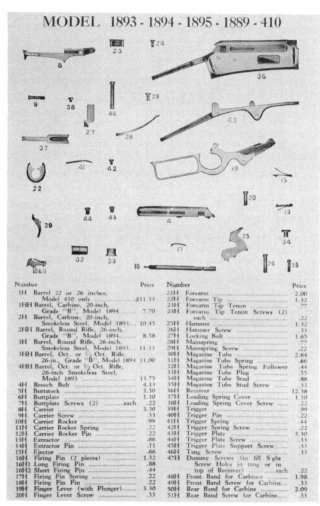

Number	Price	Number	Price
1H Barrel 22 or 26 inches, Model 410 only	$11.33	21H Forearm	2.00
1HH Barrel, Carbine, 20-inch, Grade "B", Model 1894	7.70	22H Forearm Tip	1.32
2H Barrel, Carbine, 20-inch, Smokeless Steel, Model 1893	10.45	23H Forearm Tip Tenon	.77
		24H Forearm Tip Tenon Screws (2) each	.22
2HH Barrel, Round Rifle, 26-inch, Grade "B", Model 1894	8.58	25H Hammer	1.32
3H Barrel, Round Rifle, 26-inch, Smokeless Steel, Model 1893	11.33	26H Hammer Screw	.33
3HH Barrel, Oct. or ½ Oct. Rifle, 26-in. Grade "B", Model 1894	11.00	27H Locking Bolt	1.65
		28H Mainspring	.77
		29H Mainspring Screw	.22
4HH Barrel, Oct. or ½ Oct. Rifle, 26-inch Smokeless Steel, Model 1893	13.75	30H Magazine Tube	2.64
4H Breech Bolt	4.13	31H Magazine Tube Spring	.66
5H Buttstock	3.30	32H Magazine Tube Spring Follower	.44
6H Buttplate	1.10	33H Magazine Tube Plug	.55
7H Buttplate Screws (2) each	.22	34H Magazine Tube Stud	.88
8H Carrier	3.30	35H Magazine Tube Stud Screw	.33
9H Carrier Screw	.33	36H Receiver	12.38
10H Carrier Rocker	.99	37H Loading Spring Cover	1.10
11H Carrier Rocker Spring	.22	38H Loading Spring Cover Screw	.22
12H Carrier Rocker Pin	.22	39H Trigger	.99
13H Extractor	.66	40H Trigger Pin	.22
14H Extractor Pin	.11	41H Trigger Spring	.44
15H Ejector	.66	42H Trigger Spring Screw	.22
16H Firing Pin (2 pieces)	1.32	43H Trigger Plate	3.30
16H1 Long Firing Pin	.88	44H Trigger Plate Screw	.33
16H2 Short Firing Pin	.44	45H Trigger Plate Support Screw	.33
17H Firing Pin Spring	.22	46H Tang Screw	.33
18H Firing Pin Pin	.22	47H Dummy Screws (to fill Sight Screw Holes in tang or in top of Receiver) each	.22
19H Finger Lever (with Plunger)	3.30	48H Front Band for Carbines	1.98
20H Finger Lever Screw	.33	49H Front Band Screw for Carbine	.33
		50H Rear Band for Carbine	2.09
		51H Rear Band Screw for Carbine	.33

Marlin catalog parts list that includes all of the models with similar parts, including the Model 1893.

Typical hard rubber butt plate used on Model 1893 rifles.

Tang marking on early Model 1893s.

Model mark on tang of late 1893s. The one shown is on an engraved gun.

Steel. Grade B rifles were made in .32–40 and .38–55 only. They are identical to the standard rifles except that the barrels were made of a high grade of soft gun-barrel steel instead of the "Special Smokeless Steel" of the regular model. Frames of these B guns were blued instead of case-hardened. They were not recommended for use with High Power Smokeless ammunition.

Rifles and carbines were available in Grade B. The carbines had 15- or 20-in. barrels, and rifles having either octagon or round barrels in lengths of 26, 28, 30 or 32 inches could be purchased. The prices listed for Grade B and Special Smokeless Steel guns from 1905 to 1917 were as follows:

Year	Barrel	Grade B Round	Grade B Octagon	Special Smokeless Steel Round	Special Smokeless Steel Octagon
1905	20"			16.50	17.00
	24"			16.50	17.00
	26"	13.35	14.40	16.50	17.00
	28"	14.85	16.00	18.00	18.50
	30"	16.35	17.60	19.50	20.00
	32"	17.65	19.20	21.00	21.50
	Carbine	12.95		15.50	
	Musket			17.00	
1906	Same as 1905				
1907	26"	12.15	13.16	15.00	15.53
	28"	13.50	14.56	16.40	16.88
	30"	14.85	15.87	17.80	18.23
	32"	16.20	17.22	19.20	19.58
	Carbine	11.82		14.18	
	Musket			15.00	
1908	20"			16.25	17.50
	26"	13.35	14.40	16.25	17.50
	28"	14.85	16.00	17.90	19.10
	30"	16.35	17.60	19.60	20.70
	32"	17.85	19.20	21.30	22.30
	Carbine	12.95		15.50	
	Musket			17.00	
1909	26"	12.15	13.15	15.00	16.00
	28"	13.65	14.65	16.50	17.50
	30"	15.15	16.15	18.00	19.00
	32"	16.65	17.65	19.50	20.50
	Carbine	12.00			
	Musket			15.25	
1911	Same as 1909				
1913	Same as 1909				
1914	Same as 1909				
1915	26"	13.50	14.60	17.25	18.35
	28"	15.00	16.10	18.75	19.85
	30"	16.50	17.60	20.25	21.35
	32"	18.00	19.10	21.75	22.85
	Carbine	13.10		15.75	
1916	26"	15.30	16.60	19.55	20.85
	28"	16.80	18.10	21.05	22.35
	30"	18.30	19.60	22.55	23.85
	32"	19.80	21.10	24.05	25.35
	Carbine	14.90		17.85	
1917	26"	18.35	19.90	23.45	25.00
	28"	20.15	21.70	25.25	26.80
	30"	21.95	23.50	27.05	28.60
	32"	23.75	25.30	28.85	30.40
	Carbine	17.90			

Barrel marking on early Model 1893 rifle.

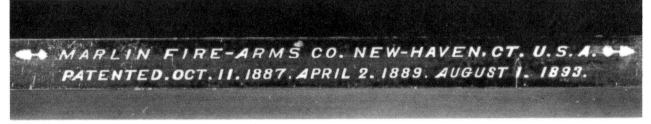

Barrel marking on Model 1893 rifle. Note that Fire-Arms *is hyphenated.*

Barrel marking that had Firearms *as a single word.*

Typical Marlin Safety *marking on top of Model 1893 receiver. This slogan was used from the Model 1889 up until the end of Model 36 production.*

Typical Special Smokeless Steel *marking on Model 1893 rifles.*

Typical For Black Powder *barrel marking used on Model 1893 rifles and carbines suited for use only with black powder cartridges.*

A review of the old serial number records uncovered a few interesting facts. However, because the records that have survived time—and the three previous companies—are incomplete, and only cover the Model 1893 to the 1905–1906 period, no total production numbers can be developed. Also, because The Marlin Fire Arms Company during the period of 1883 to 1906 had only one series of numbers for all of its lever action repeating rifles, serial numbers on Model 1893s do not reflect the place in production, or sequence number, of a gun in the Model 1893 family of guns.

For example: There is listed in the records a Model 1893 with serial number 81,393 that is caliber .32–40 and has a 28-in. octagon barrel. The date shown for this gun is January 13, 1893. However, the earliest date is January 12, 1893 for the same rifle. This is the lowest number in the records for a Model 1893 *except* for number 20,469. The entry for this number shows a .30–30 Model 1893 that has a 26-in. octagon barrel and a date of January 18, 1901. Either the gun was incorrectly numbered or the posting of the information was incorrect, as there is no reason for this gun to be listed along with a Model 1888 having the same serial number and dated October 19, 1888.

At the risk of possibly being proven wrong, I offer the following trivia about the Model 1893, gathered from the old, and sometimes misleading, records:

Takedown

Lowest	111,002	Aug. 30, 1894
Earliest	111,003	Aug. 27, 1894

Carbine

Lowest	89,392	Aug. 16, 1894
Earliest	91,386	June 28, 1893

Caliber .25–36

Lowest	115,038	July 8, 1896
Earliest	122,813	June 7, 1895

Model 1893 serial numbers are stamped into the bottom front end of the trigger plate. The highest reported to date is 448,355.

A total of 69,100 Model 1893 rifles and 4,086 carbines were produced from 1893 to 1906 for a grand total of 73,186 Model 1893s made.

There was a new series started without a prefix, and there were some rifles with an alphabetical prefixed number that were also marked on the trigger plate. To add to the number-game confusion, the model designation was changed from Model 1893 to Model '93. Some of the '93 serial numbers included B, C, and D prefixes that are found on either the trigger plate or the lower tang.

For information about muskets, carbines, the takedown feature, stocks, magazines, butt plates, and ammunition, please see their respective sections in this book. Otherwise, I would be required to repeat each feature for each model produced by Marlin.

The weights and measurements of the Model 1893 were as follows:

Carbine Length in Inches	Number of Shots	Weight in Pounds	
15	5	6⅝	
20	7	6¾	

Rifle Length in Inches		Round	Octagon
20	7	7½	7¼
24	9	8	7⅝
26	10	8¼	7¾
28	11	8½	8
30	11	8⅝	8⅛
32	11	8¾	8¼

At a point between serial numbers 137,412 and 190,191, an additional screw was added to the left side of the Model 1893 receiver. The purpose of the screw was to give added support to the trigger plate. (This screw is still part of the Model 336 rifle as manufactured today.)

Shown for comparison are the early and late types of Model 1893 trigger plates. The arrow indicates the added support boss of the late type.

Typical caliber marking on Model 1893 barrel. The arrow indicates the hand stamp that was used to mark this barrel.

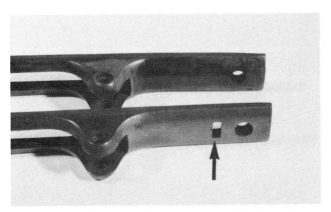

When the cartridge stop on the carrier was lengthened, a hole was added to the front end of the Model 1893 trigger plate. The hole would allow checking the carrier for proper function.

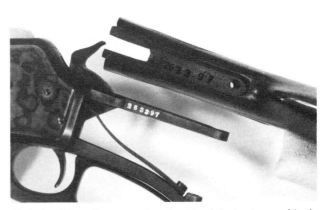

Typical serial number stamped on the side of the top tang and in the tang recess cut in the top of the stock.

𝕸𝖆𝖗𝖑𝖎𝖓
LEVER ACTION HIGH POWER BIG GAME RIFLES

Powerful, accurate, strongly built throughout, with the simplest and most durable
mechanism used in any high power repeater.

Shoots all New HIGH SPEED, HIGH VELOCITY Smokeless & Low Power Loads

SOLID TOP RECEIVER — CLOSED IN FRAME — SIDE EJECTION

𝕸𝖆𝖗𝖑𝖎𝖓 LEVER ACTION CARBINE

**MODEL
93
CARBINE**

The Marlin Model No. 93 Carbine is built on Carbine lines
throughout and is a thoroughly accurate, quick handling and effective
arm for hunting big game. From buttplate to muzzle it is built
for hard service. It is a very powerful gun and its use has met
with success for many years. This arm is made of the very best
of materials, the workmanship is of the highest character, and the
gun carries a finish far superior to other makes.

Full Magazine — 7 Shots   30-30 and 32 SPECIAL CALIBERS

SPECIFICATIONS—Solid Frame, 20 inch Round Tapered Special Smokeless Steel Barrel, Proof Tested, Crown
Muzzle, **Famous Ballard Type Rifling.** Visible Hammer, Case Hardened Receiver. **Genuine American Black
Walnut** Buttstock and Forearm. Steel Butt Plate. Length of Buttstock 13⅛ inches, Drop at Comb 1¾ inches,
Drop at Heel 3 inches. Silver Bead Front Sight and Flat Top Rocky Mountain Rear Sight, especially adapt-
ed to quick, accurate shooting. Length over all 38 inches. Weight about 6½ pounds.

𝕸𝖆𝖗𝖑𝖎𝖓 LEVER ACTION SPORTING CARBINE

**MODEL
93
SPORTING
CARBINE**

The Model 93 "Sporting" Carbine is made for big game hunting.
A special light weight, accurate, quick handling, finely made gun,
handling cartridges sufficiently powerful to bring down all North
American big game.

2/3 Magazine — 5 Shots   30-30 and 32 SPECIAL CALIBERS

SPECIFICATIONS—Solid Frame, 20 inch Round Tapered Special Smokeless Steel Barrel, Proof Tested, Crown
Muzzle, **Famous Ballard Type Rifling.** Visible Hammer, Case Hardened Receiver. **Genuine American Black
Walnut** Buttstock and Forearm. Steel Butt Plate. Length of Buttstock 13⅛ inches, Drop at Comb 1¾ inches,
Drop at Heel 3 inches. Silver Bead Front Sight and Flat Top Rocky Mountain Rear Sight, especially adapt-
ed to quick, accurate shooting. Length over all 38 inches. Weight about 6½ pounds.

𝕸𝖆𝖗𝖑𝖎𝖓 LEVER ACTION RIFLE

**MODEL
93
RIFLE**

The Marlin Model 93 Rifle is the ideal rifle for hunting all species
of big game found on the North American Continent. The barrel
is made of Special Smokeless Steel, which permits of the continued
use of high power smokeless loads with metal jacketed bullets.
Because of its simple, quick-working mechanism, its solid-top and
side-ejection construction, it is the ideal rifle for the big game
hunter.

Full Magazine — 9 Shots   30-30 and 32 SPECIAL CALIBERS

SPECIFICATIONS—Solid Frame, 24 inch Round Tapered Special Smokeless Steel Barrel, Proof Tested, Crown
Muzzle, **Famous Ballard Type Rifling.** Visible Hammer, Case Hardened Receiver. **Genuine American Black
Walnut** Buttstock and Forearm. Steel Butt Plate. Length of Buttstock 13⅛ inches, Drop at Comb, 1¾ inches,
Drop at Heel 3 inches. Rocky Mountain Front and Flat Top Rocky Mountain Rear Sight. Length over all
42 inches. Weight about 6¾ pounds.

Marlin flyer describing and illustrating the Model 93s.

The trigger plate had a hole added at the front end that allowed the lengthened bottom front end of the carrier to be checked for proper fit. Thus, with the first type, and the ones described here and above, there are three different trigger plates. The trigger plate has always been fitted to the receiver to ensure a smooth junction between the trigger plate and the receiver. If found to be otherwise, it would indicate the two were not original to each other.

MODEL '93

The *Model 1893* marking on the tang of Model 1893s was changed in 1905 to *Model '93*. However, this change in designation marked on the gun did not result in any change in the characteristics of the gun, or in the models and variations available, until 1922, when the new Marlin Firearms Corporation resumed production of sporting arms after WW I. The new postwar Model '93 was an extension of the prewar model, except that some of the options, such as half-octagon and takedown barrels, and most extra features, were no longer available.

The rifle variation had either a round or octagon barrel in .30–30, .32 Special, .32–40, or .38–55. The carbine model was made in either .30–30 or .32 Special. The 1922 catalog description of the two variations was as follows:

Model No. 93 Rifle, .30–30, .32 Special, .32–40, .38–55 Calibers, Center-Fire, solid frame, 26-inch round or octagon Special Smokeless Steel barrel, full magazine, 10 shots, weight about 7¼ pounds.

This rifle has lever action; visible hammer; side ejection; solid-top, closed-in frame; Rocky Mountain front and rear sights, the ideal combination of sights for big game hunting; case hardened receiver; blued steel buttplate; length over all,

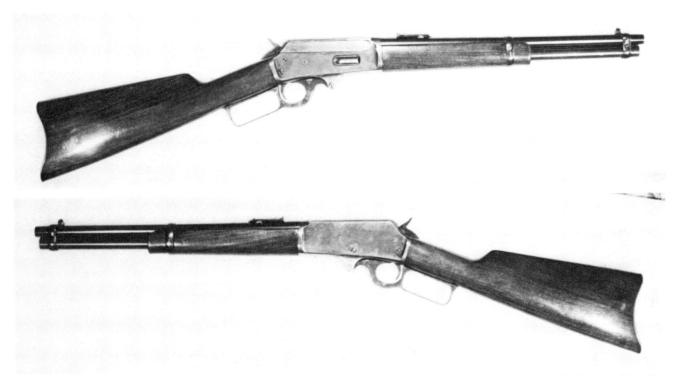

Top: *Model '93 carbine, serial number 2180 (on lower tang), which has a 15-in. caliber .32 HPS barrel.* (DS) Bottom: *Left side of same carbine. Note that this carbine was ordered without the saddle ring.*

Sporting Carbine Model '93 carbine that has a 20-in. .32 HPS round barrel, half magazine, straight stock with rubber butt plate and bull's-eye (Marlin Firearms Corporation), and case-colored receiver. The serial number, 6219, is stamped into the lower tang, under the lever. (DS)

Top: *Model '93 saddle ring carbine, serial number 8978 (on lower tang), which has a .32 HPS 20-in. round barrel, carbine buttstock (with bull's-eye), and case-colored receiver.* (DS) Bottom: *Left side of same carbine, showing carbine sights and saddle ring.*

Typical case-colored receiver of late Model '93 carbine.

1928 Marlin Firearms Company ad that illustrated and described the Model 93CS Sporting Carbine.

44⅞ inches drop at comb, 1¾ inches; drop at heel, 3 inches; buttstock and forearm made of best American Black Walnut.

The Marlin Model No. 93 Rifle is the ideal rifle for hunting all species of big game found on the North American continent. This is a quick handling, powerful, accurate arm, strongly built throughout, with the simplest and most durable mechanism used in any high power repeater. The barrels are made of Special Smokeless Steel which permits of the continued use of high power smokeless loads with metal jacketed bullets, and also black powder ammunition and equivalent loads such as low power smokeless. Because of its simple, quick-working mechanism, its solid-top and side ejecting construction, it is the best all-around rifle for the big game hunter. This ammunition is obtainable everywhere.

To Clean the Rifle: By removing the breechbolt, the barrel may be cleaned by inserting cleaning rod and rag in the breech and drawing through the barrel.

To Remove Breechbolt: With action open, remove the finger lever screw; draw finger lever away from the bottom of receiver; the breechbolt can then be withdrawn from the rear of the receiver and the ejector removed from its slot.

Model No. 93 Carbine, .30–30 or .32 Special caliber, center-fire, solid frame, 20-inch round Special Smokeless Steel barrel, full magazine, 7 shots, weight about 6¾ pounds.

Has lever action; visible hammer; side ejection; solid-top, closed-in frame; carbine front and rear sights, the finest set of carbine sights obtainable; case-hardened receiver; blued steel buttplate; length over all, 38 inches; drop at comb, 1¾ inches; drop at heel, 3 inches; American Black Walnut buttstock and forearm. Adapted to use high power smokeless cartridges.

The Marlin Model No. 93 Carbine is built on carbine lines throughout and is a thoroughly accurate, quick handling and effective arm for hunting big game. From buttplate to muzzle it is built for hard service. It is a very powerful gun and its use has met with success for many years. This arm is made of the very best of materials, the workmanship is of the highest character, and the gun carries a finish far superior to other makes. This arm handles high power smokeless loads as well as low power smokeless. A sling ring is attached to left side of receiver for convenient carrying on horseback.

In 1923 a Model 93CS "Sporting Carbine" was added to the line. This new model had a hard rubber butt plate, ivory bead front sight, and a two-thirds magazine; otherwise it was like the carbine. The 1923 catalog described it this way:

Model No. 93CS "Sporting" Carbine, .30–30 or .32 special caliber, center-fire, solid frame, 20-inch round Special Smokeless Steel barrel, two-thirds magazine, 5 shots, weight about 6½ pounds.

Has lever action; visible hammer; side ejection; solid-top, closed in frame; ivory bead front and Rocky Mountain rear sights, a set of sights especially adapted to quick, accurate shooting; case-hardened receiver; hard rubber buttplate; length over all, 38 inches; drop at comb, 1¾ inches; drop at heel, 3 inches; American Black Walnut buttstock and forearm.

The new Model 93CS "Sporting" Carbine is made for big game hunting. A special light weight, accurate, quick handling, finely made gun, handling cartridges sufficiently powerful to bring down all North American big game. All Model 93 .30–30 Rifles and Carbines are perfectly suited to the new High Velocity smokeless loads that have added so tremendously to the range and power and accuracy of the famous .30–30 cartridge.

The February 1923 dealers' price list indicated the Model 93 carbine was available with a sling ring if so ordered.

The 1935 catalog illustrated all of the Model 93s as having a steel butt plate of the "S" carbine type. Earlier catalogs showed the rifle with a "crescent" butt plate, the carbine with an "S" butt plate, and the Sporting Carbine (SC) with a hard rubber butt plate.

Also in 1935, the carbine and Sporting Carbine were listed as having a silver bead front sight, and the rifle as still equipped with Rocky Mountain front and rear sights.

Additional changes made in 1935 were the elimination of the

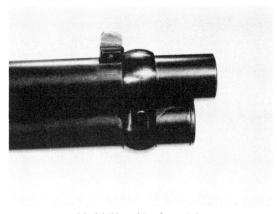

Model '93 carbine front sight.

Typical Marlin Firearms Corporation *marking on Model '93 carbine.*

Model '93 carbine rear sight.

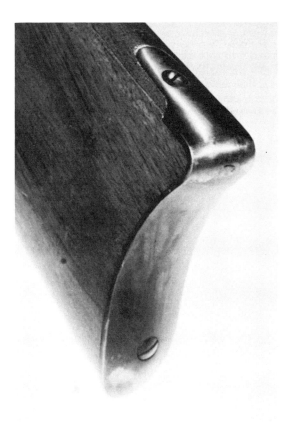

Model '93 carbine butt plate.

Typical tang marking on Model '93s.

Typical serial number marking on bottom tang of Model '93 rifle.

calibers .32–40 and .38–55 and discontinuance of the octagon-barrel model.

Barrel markings on the Model 93s, like some other models, are found with both The Marlin Firearms Corporation (1922–1924) and The Marlin Firearms Company (1926–1935) name. It appears that during the 1926–1935 period, the new company assembled many guns with the predecessor company's name on them. Also, serial numbers are mixed between the two companies.

The last of the Model 93 rifles and carbines were sold on an October 2, 1935 contract, for delivery in 1936, to the J.F. Galef Company, New York.

The prices of the Model 93 from 1922 to 1936 were as follows:

| | 93 Rifle | | | 93 Sporting |
Year	Octagon	Round	93 Carbine	Carbine
1922	$34.00	32.50		
1925	34.00	32.50	32.50	35.80
1926	35.25	33.80	32.20	37.25
1932	30.10	28.40	28.40	30.10
1932	36.00	34.65	34.20	37.10
1933	30.10	28.40	28.40	30.10

1936 Model 93 Rifles, Carbines and Sporting Carbines, $25.00 each.

The Model 93 was replaced by the short-lived Model 1936, which, in turn, was replaced by the Model 36 series of center-fire lever actions.

MODEL 1894
"New Marlin Repeater Model 1894"

Improvements in the Model 1889 rifle were patented by L.L. Hepburn in his patent number 502,489, dated August 1, 1893. The improvements included a new locking bolt and two-piece firing pin. First used in the new Model 1893 rifle, which was designed for use with cartridges longer than those used in the earlier Models 1888 and 1889, this 1893 patent was also used for the new Model 1894. The 1894 had a short receiver and was designed for use with the same cartridges as those used in the 1888 and 1889 models.

When Marlin introduced the "NEW MARLIN REPEATER MODEL 1894," it was described as follows:

Rifles can be furnished with all lengths of barrels up to 32 inches at an extra cost of $1.00 per inch, round, octagon or half octagon. The rifles will be furnished with case-hardened receiver, carbines with blued receivers. At present, we are prepared to furnish this Model in .38–40 and .44–40 calibers only, straight grip rifles, .32–20 rifles and rifles with pistol grip stocks will for the present be supplied in 1889 Model. The .32–20 in the Model 1894 will be ready shortly.

The Model 1894 is the latest and most improved repeating rifle to use the popular .32–20, .38–40, and .44–40 cartridges, and is the successor to our well known Model 1889. In the Model 1894 rifle, every desirable feature of the 1889 is retained and the improvements suggested by five more years of experience and experiment are added. This rifle is practically the Model 1893 rifle adapted to the shorter cartridges. Improvements which have been tried and shown to be an advance are now embodied in our rifle to use the Model 1889 cartridges.

Marlin's announcement about the new Model 1894 Repeater.

The improvements are as follows:

SAFETY—The firing pin is cut completely in two. When the action is closed and locked these two pieces are in direct line. But the slightest motion of the finger lever draws back the firing pin and the front end of the rear piece drops down into the slot in the breech-bolt where the locking-bolt operates. With the firing pin in this position, it is held back positively and it is impossible to drive it forward until the breech-bolt is closed and firmly locked by the locking-bolt. This only can happen when the whole action is fully locked.

If in assembling the rifle the locking-bolt should be accidentally left out, the rifle cannot be fired, thus effectually preventing any accidents of this character arising from carelessness or ignorance.

THE AUTOMATIC LEVER CATCH has been placed near the front of the lever, thus avoiding the projecting safety catch.

THE LOCKING-BOLT in this model does not project at all, being within the receiver at all times, which makes this rifle neat and clean at all times, as there are no projecting catches, links or bolts to interfere with the hand.

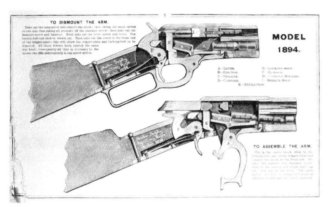

Page from Marlin 1894 catalog that shows internal parts of Model 1894 mechanism.

Catalog illustration of Model 1894 carbine and rifle.

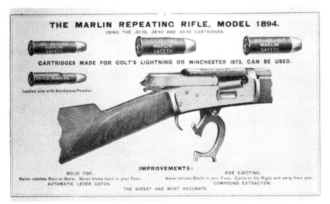

Catalog illustration of Model 1894.

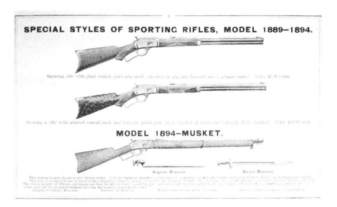

Catalog illustration of Model 1894 special styles and musket.

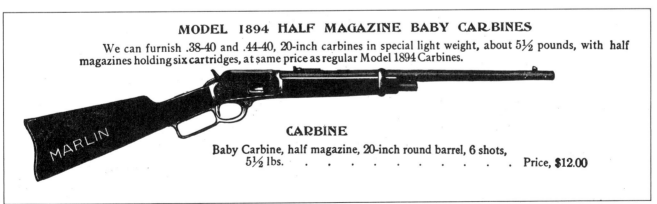

Catalog illustration of Model 1894 half magazine baby carbine.

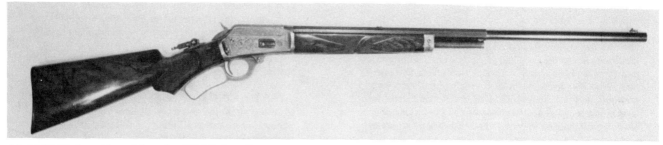

Model 1894 Deluxe rifle, serial number 132,945, in caliber .25–20 with a 24-in. half-octagon barrel, deluxe wood, No. G checking, and case-colored No. 3-engraved receiver with pistol grip stock and half magazine. (RG)

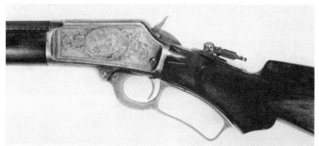

Top: *Right side of rifle serial number 132,945.* (RG) Bottom: *Left side of same rifle.*

Bottom of Model 1894 rifle serial number 132,945 showing the usual location of serial numbers on early Marlin lever actions. The engraved animal on the trigger plate is seldom encountered. (RG)

THE TRIGGER is in one piece instead of being divided into a trigger and sear as in the 1889 rifle. This improvement does away with all "play" about the trigger.

It is interesting to note that when the first announcements about the new Model 1894 were made by Marlin, they also indicated that the Model 1889 was available as a takedown rifle in .32–20, .38–40, and .44–40 calibers (no mention of .25–20), and that any length or style of barrel, any style of magazine, straight or pistol grip, and plain or fancy wood could be ordered.

A newspaper article dated November 17, 1894 stated that The Marlin Fire Arms Company had just brought out a .25–20 in the Model 1894 repeater. The article also mentioned that in the case of pistol grip rifles, the Model 1889 would be furnished with them for the present. The article also went on to say that the Marlin rifle was the only .25 caliber repeater on the market.

A review of the Marlin serial number records reveals interesting data about the Model 1894. A few important to the collector follow:

First Model 1894	107,678	7/9/1894
First in caliber .38	107,678	7/9/1894
Lowest in caliber .38	107,678	7/9/1894
First in caliber .44	107,689	7/9/1894
Lowest in caliber .44	107,679	9/13/1894
First in caliber .32	108,028	12/10/1894
Lowest in caliber .32	107,976	6/21/1895
First in caliber .25	107,987	11/8/1894
Lowest in caliber .25	107,978	12/12/1894
First pistol grip	109,002	6/14/1894
Lowest pistol grip	107,989	12/12/1894
First takedown	107,989	12/12/1894

Rare No. 3-engraved Model 1894 serial number 128,398 that has No. B-checked deluxe pistol grip wood, caliber .38–40 half octagon 24-in. barrel, and half magazine. It is full-silver-plated. (DS)

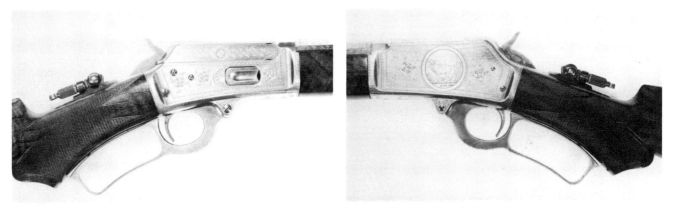

Left: *Right side of silver-plated Model 1894, serial number 128,398.* Right: *Left side of same rifle.*

Caliber .32–20 Model 1894 rifle, serial number 137,123, with a 30-in. round barrel and 28-in. magazine. This rifle's barrel has the earlier Model 1889 markings. (DS)

Model 1894 Musket that has a carbine-type stock, 30-in. round barrel, and full-length forearm and cleaning rod beside barrel.

Case-colored receiver of late-type 1894 rifle that has blued bolt. (DS)

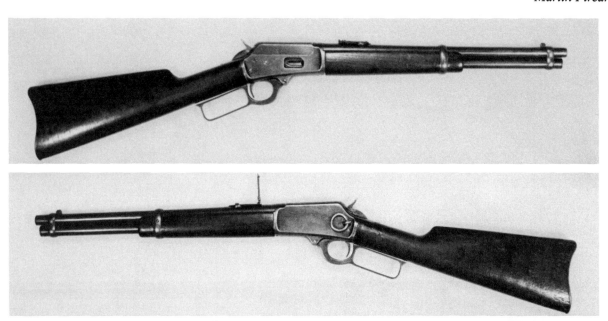

Top: *Caliber .44–40 Model 1894 saddle ring carbine with 15-in. barrel. Serial number 375,780.* (DS) Bottom: *Left side of same carbine.*

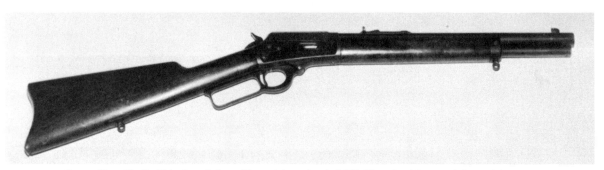

Rare caliber .38–40, 14-in. barrel short rifle, serial number 326,718. Note the rifle-type sights and forearm.

Lowest takedown	107,977	6/21/1895
First carbine	109,584	7/3/1894
Lowest carbine	109,582	8/16/1894
First half magazine	107,701	9/3/1895
First round barrel	107,698	8/8/1894

The roll-stamp used on the Model 1894 is the same as that used on the Model 1893. It includes the earlier L.L. Hepburn patents and has his 1893 patent added as follows:

MARLIN FIRE ARMS CO., NEW HAVEN, CT. USA PAT-ENTED OCT. 11, 1887.
APRIL 2, 1889. AUGUST 1, 1893.

Because a supply of 1889 barrels was still on hand, collectors will find a few Model 1894 rifles that have the earlier Model 1889 roll-stamp on the barrel. Examples noted do not indicate that these 1889 barrels were necessarily used first; for example, rifle serial number 137,123 (April 21, 1896) has a 30-in. round barrel marked this way.

The 1894 model designation was marked on the top tang, just behind the hammer. However, a few unmarked receivers have been noted that may have been Model 1889 receivers finished in the Model 1894 fashion. The usual marking was *MODEL 1894*. After about 1905, the tang marking was changed to read *MARLIN MODEL '94* in two lines.

Starting with the Model 1889 and solid-top receiver, the receivers were stamped *MARLIN SAFETY*. The Model 1894 was no exception. However, in 1903, when the L.L. Hepburn-patented receiver rear sight holes were placed into the top of 1894 receivers, there was no longer room on the short receiver for both the *MARLIN SAFETY* marking and the screw holes. Thereafter, the roll-stamp was discontinued on those receivers that were so drilled and tapped. (The Model 1893 and 1895 receivers had enough room on top so that the *MARLIN SAFETY* marking could be moved forward out of conflict with the holes or the sight.)

The Model 1894 was available in rifle, carbine, and musket configurations. The standard rifle had a 24-in. octagon or round barrel in calibers .25, .32, .38, or .44 with full-length magazines. The receiver, hammer, butt plate, and forearm cap were case-colored. Barrels and magazines were blued. Carbines and muskets had blued receivers. The standard carbine barrel length was 20 inches and musket barrels were 30 inches long.

From 1894 to 1917, the Model 1894 suggested retail prices were as follows:

Year	20-in.		24-in.	26-in.	28-in.	30-in.	32-in.	15/20 in. Carbine	Musket
1894–1896	Oct.	$19.50	$19.50	$21.50	$23.50	$25.50	$27.50		
	Rnd.	18.00	18.00	20.00	22.00	24.00	26.00	$17.50	
1897–1899	Oct.	14.40	14.40	15.90	17.40	18.90	20.40		
	Rnd.	13.35	13.35	14.88	16.35	17.85	19.35	12.95	$14.25
1901	Oct.-½ Oct.	11.25	12.40	13.60	14.75	15.90			
	Rnd.	10.40	11.55	12.75	13.90	15.05		10.00	10.95
1902–1904	Oct.-½ Oct.	11.85	13.50	14.45	15.75	17.06			
	Rnd.	10.95	12.20	13.45	14.70	15.95		10.63	11.75
1907	Oct.-½ Oct.	13.16	14.52	15.87	17.22	18.57			
	Rnd.	12.15	13.50	14.85	16.20	17.55		11.82	12.83
1908	Oct.	15.00							
	Rnd.	13.85						13.46	
1909–1914	Oct.	13.15	14.65	16.15	17.65	19.15			
	Rnd.	12.15	13.65	15.15	16.65	18.15			
1915	Oct.	14.60	16.10	17.60	19.10	20.60			
	Rnd.	13.50	15.00	16.50	18.00	19.50			
1916	Oct.	16.60	18.10	19.60	21.10	22.60			
	Rnd.	15.30	16.80	18.30	19.80	21.30			
1917	Oct.	19.90	21.70	23.50	25.30	27.10			
	Rnd.	18.35	20.15	21.95	23.70	25.55			

Full-nickel-plated Model 1894 caliber .44–40, 20-in. barrel carbine, serial number 185,126. (JO)

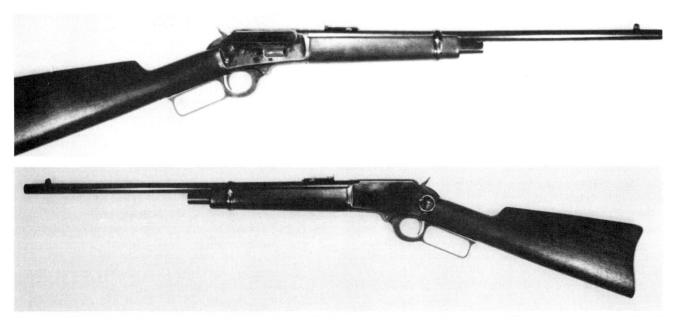

Top: *Model 1894 Baby Carbine, serial number 332,947, with rare .44–40 smooth-bore 20-in. carbine barrel, saddle ring, and blued receiver, barrel, and magazine.* (DS) Bottom: *Left side of same.*

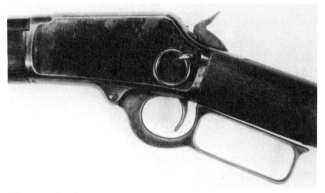

Photograph of typical saddle ring Model 1894 carbine receiver. Hammer and lever are case-colored. (DS)

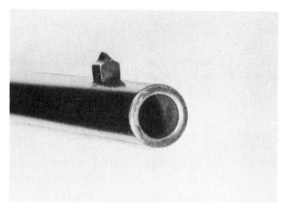

Muzzle end of smooth bore carbine barrel serial number 332,947.

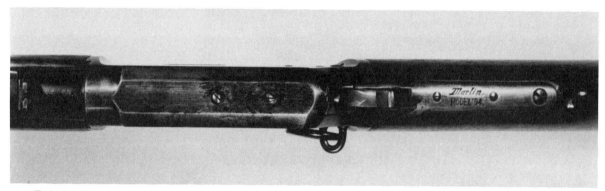

Typical tang marking of late-type Model '94 carbine. Note screw holes for L.L. Hepburn receiver sight and tang sight. (DS)

Many special options were available to the Model 1894 purchaser. For example, longer barrels could be ordered at $1.00 per inch extra. Magazines were available in short, half, and full length. Takedown and extra barrels were also available, as were special plating, engraving, checkering, and special deluxe wood. Lightweight rifles and baby carbines were also made by Marlin for the sportsman desiring those features.

Carbines with blued receivers had either 15-in. or 20-in., .25, .32, .38, or .44 caliber barrels. The 15-in. model held 9 shots and weighed 5¾ pounds. The 20-in. carbine held 12 shots and weighed 6 pounds. A baby carbine in .38–40 or .44–40 that weighed about 5½ pounds could be had. It had a half magazine and held only 6 shots. The barrel was 20 inches long.

A total of 10,738 Model 1894 carbines and 35,948 rifles were manufactured from 1894 to 1906. Carbines with 15-in. barrels have been examined that were manufactured after 1905; they are factory originals.

From 1929 to 1933, the Model 94 was listed in price lists. It was not listed in ads or catalogs as being available. From this, we can assume that the balance of parts and pieces were carried over from before WW I, and, with some new manufacturing, Marlin did finish and sell some Model 94s.

The post-WW I price lists indicate that the Model 94 was available in caliber .25–20 or .32–20, and only with a 24-in. octagon or 24-in. round barrel. Carbines and other barrel lengths were not mentioned as available.

Some of these "tail end" Model 94s have been observed that have the Marlin Firearms *Corporation* name on them. It is possible that The Marlin Firearms Corporation had planned to reintroduce the Model 94 before it went bankrupt in 1924. The new Marlin Firearms Company was not able to restart the task until 1929. Its prices were listed as follows:

Year	24-in. Octagon	24-in. Round
1929–1932	$28.90	$27.75
June 1932	31.65	30.20
1933	30.10	28.40
1934–1935	No information available.	

New Model 1894 (1969 to present)

After a few difficult years of manufacturing the Model 336 in caliber .44 magnum, Marlin decided to eliminate the frustration of trying to get a rifle designed for long rifle length cartridges to function correctly with a short pistol length cartridge. It discontinued the 336/.44 magnum.

Knowing that there was still a market for a shoulder-fired .44 magnum, Marlin reintroduced, in 1969, the old Marlin Model 1894. (It was originally designed in 1894 by Marlin's L.L. Hepburn for the .25–20, .32–20, .38–40, and .44–40 cartridges.)

The Model 1894 was an ideal mechanism for the .44 mag-

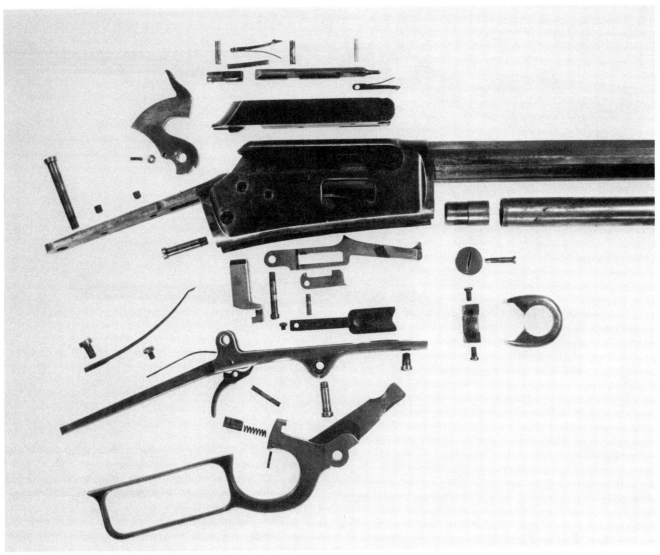

Model 1894 parts in their positions relative to each other.

num and other short cartridges, and soon became popular among recreational shooters and sportsmen.

The variations of the New Model 1894 that have been manufactured were as follows:

1969–1984	Model 1894	(caliber .44 Rem. magnum)
1973	Model 1894 Octagon	(caliber .44 magnum)
1973	Model 1894 Sporter	(caliber .44 magnum)
1979–1984	Model 1894C	(caliber .357 magnum)
1982–1986	Model 1894M	(caliber .22 WMRF)
1984 to date	Model 1894S	(caliber .44 magnum)
1985–1988	Model 1894S	(caliber .41 magnum)
1985 to date	Model 1894CS	(caliber .357 magnum)
1989 to date	Model 1894S	(caliber .45 Colt)
1988 to date	Model 1894CL	(caliber .25–20 and .32–20)

The following is a resumé of the above variations of the basic New Model 1894 carbine as introduced in 1969.

Model 1894, Lever Action, Caliber .44 Magnum, Carbine (1969–1984). The 1969 Marlin catalog announced to the public that this new model would be available September 1, 1969. It also described the model as follows:

. . . The fastest-handling .44 brush-buster going. Marlin is proud to offer this re-creation of the highly-prized, original Model 1894 carbine introduced way back in 1894. All of the quality features and traditional craftsmanship that made the original Marlin 1894 a favorite sporting arm have been retained—solid top receiver, side ejection, stocks and actions hand-fitted. Even the square bolt of the old Model 1894 has been retained.

Chambered for the potent .44 Magnum, the new straight grip 1894 carbine combines Micro-Groove accuracy with ter-

Marlin 1894 lever action rifle, cal 44 Magnum

New Model 1894.

MARLIN Model 1894

Second variation of Model 1894.

rific knockdown power. This big bore brush-buster is ideal for hunting deer or black bear in thick cover because it goes into action pronto! You get 10 fast, power-packed shots.

The specifications for the Model 1894 included the following:

Cal. .44 Magnum; 10-shot repeater. Approx. 6#, straight-grip selected walnut stock; 20″ Micro-Groove barrel; 37½″ o.a. length; adjustable open rear, ramp front sight; 24K gold-plated trigger; tapped for receiver sights and scope mounts; free offset hammer spur for scope use—works left or right; deeply blued metal surfaces; receiver top sand blasted to prevent glare.

From 1969 to 1971, the Model 1894 was fitted with a brass saddle ring. The practice was discontinued after it was realized that the ring had no practical purpose and was frequently removed to eliminate the rattle of the ring against the side of the receiver.

In 1970, the Model 1894 had a 100th anniversary commemorative medallion embedded into the stock.

The 1973 catalog stated that a new carrier design allowed a cartridge up to 1.710 inches to function in the gun.

In 1974, the ramp front sight was changed to a new Wide-Scan hooded type. The forearm and barrel bands were eliminated in favor of a forearm tip in 1975. In 1977, Marlin listed the receiver, trigger plate, hammer, locking bolt, and lever as forgings. Marlin added the carrier to the list of forgings in 1978.

Up to 1979, the Model 1894 had a gold-plated steel trigger. From 1980 on, the trigger was blued steel.

In 1982, Marlin included the .44 S&W Special cartridge as also usable in the caliber .44 Magnum Model 1894, without change or adjustment.

In 1984 Marlin added a cross-bolt safety to the Model 1894. In so doing, the model designation was changed to Model 1894S.

Model 1894 Octagon, Lever Action, Caliber .44 Magnum Rifle (1973). The Model 1894 Octagon was introduced in 1973 at the same time that Marlin produced some other octagon-barreled lever actions. The catalog description was as follows:

This famous brushbuster is now offered in a new style with octagon barrel. This barrel provides a traditional classic look that has been preferred by shooters for generations. Marlin's new octagon models, like this Model 1894, provide a nostalgic link with the past.

Today's 1894 is a faithful copy of the original Marlin 1894. Lighter and smaller than the Marlin 336, it's made the same way except that it retains the original squared bolt to maintain the traditional look of an old favorite. Ten fast shots make this light, easy-handling lever action ideal for thick-cover deer and bear hunting.

Chambered for the potent .44 Rem. Magnum, this rifle drives a big, heavy bullet with terrific knock-down power.

Handloaders will be pleased to hear that the 1894 is now capable of handling cartridges up to 1.710″ in length, giving you additional load options.

The Model 1894 Octagon specifications were listed as follows:

Caliber: .44 Rem. Magnum
Capacity: 10-shot full-length tubular magazine
Action: Lever action with traditional squared finger lever; solid-top receiver; side ejection; blued steel trigger; deeply blued metal surfaces; receiver top sandblasted to prevent glare
Stock: Two-piece straight-grip American walnut; traditional hard rubber butt plate; blued steel forend cap; tough Mar-Shield™ finish.
Barrel: 20-in. octagon with Micro-Groove® rifling.
Sights: Adjustable semibuckhorn folding rear, bead front sights; solid-top receiver tapped for scope mount; receiver tapped for receiver sight; offset hammer spur for scope use—works left or right.
Overall length: 37½ inches.
Weight: About 6 pounds.

The suggested retail price of the Model 1894 Octagon was $135.00. A total of 2,957 of the model were manufactured. It was manufactured for only one year, 1973.

Model 1894 Sporter, Lever Action, Caliber .44 Magnum Rifle (1973). Like the Model 1894 Octagon, the Model 1894 Sporter was produced for only one year. It was another attempt by Marlin to test the waters and see if any variations of the Model 1894 might catch on. Unfortunately, this neat little rifle did not survive the test.

The Model 1894 Sporter was the same as the Model 1894 Octagon, only with a half magazine and a "classic" hard rubber butt plate. The specifications were the same as for the 1894 Octagon, except for the 6-shot magazine and traditional butt plate. The butt plate was the same as the one used on the Model 1895 .45–70 rifle when it was introduced.

The suggested retail price of the Model 1894 Sporter was $115.00. Only 1,398 of this model were manufactured.

Model 1894C, Lever Action, Caliber .357 Magnum/.38 Special Carbine (1979–1984). The Model 1894C was introduced as a new model, although it is very much like the Model 1894. Instead of being chambered for the caliber .44 magnum cartridge, the 1894C is chambered for the exceptionally popular .357 magnum pistol cartridge. It was an immediate success and took off like a rabbit. It is still popular, especially to the person owning a .357 Magnum pistol. It's easier to shoot than a handgun and uses the same kind of ammunition so popular with hand-gunners, as well as .38 Special cartridges. The 1894C fills many needs.

The Model 1894C will handle all .357 magnum factory-loaded cartridges, except shotshells and wadcutters. Its classic

Model 1894 Octagon.

Model 1894 Sporter.

Model 1894C.

Model 1894M.

Model 1894S.

Model 1894CS.

Model 1894CL.

looks are because of the 18½-in. barrel and the barrel and forearm bands. It has the squared lever and other features of the Model 1894. The magazine holds 9 shots. The front sight is a brass bead dovetail sight without a ramp or a hood. The overall length is 36 inches and the gun weighs 6 pounds.

In 1982, the trigger was changed from gold-plated steel to blued steel.

In 1984, when the cross-bolt safety was added to the Model 1894C, the designation was changed to Model 1894CS.

The suggested retail prices of the Model 1894C were listed as follows:

Year	Model 1894C
1979	$162.95
1980	193.95
1981	232.95
1982	259.95
1983	262.95
1984	272.95

A total of 90,414 Model 1894C carbines were manufactured from 1979 to 1984.

Model 1894M, Lever Action, Caliber .22 WMRF Rifle (1983–1986). The Model 1894M had the classic look of the Model 1894. It was well-balanced and perfect for informal target shooting and small game. The Model 1894M was similar to its big brother except that it had an outside tube-loading magazine and was chambered for the caliber .22 Winchester Magnum Rim Fire (.22 WMRF) cartridge. The magazine held 11 cartridges. The barrel was 20 inches in length and the overall length was 37½ inches. It weighed 6¼ pounds.

No cartridge other than the .22 WMRF can be used in this rifle, and experimenting with other types should be discouraged, as injury may result.

All Model 1894M rifles have the cross-bolt safety that was introduced by Marlin in some models in 1983.

The suggested retail prices of the Model 1894M were as follows:

Year	Model 1894M
1983	$269.95
1984	280.95
1985	300.95

Year	Model 1894M
1986	315.95
1987	340.95
1988	357.95

A total of 12,088 Model 1894M rifles were manufactured.

Model 1894S, Lever Action, Caliber .44 and .41 Magnum Carbine (1984 to date); and Model 1894S, Lever Action, Caliber .45 Colt Carbine (1988 to date). The Model 1894S carbine is the same gun as the Model 1894. The addition of a cross-bolt safety changed the designation from 1894 to 1894S. Simple, but sometimes confusing!

As previously mentioned, the Model 1894 handled the .44 magnum and .44 S&W Special cartridges interchangeably. Additionally, in 1985 a short run of the new 1894S was manufactured in the popular .41 magnum pistol cartridge.

The first run in 1984 of the .41 magnum was for only 1,040 units. A second run is scheduled for 1988 of 2,500 more.

It is a fact that the sportsmen purchasing the .41 magnum carbine are owners of handguns chambered for the .41 magnum cartridge. The same is true of the .44 magnum and .357 magnum carbines. Therefore, it is obvious that Marlin has capitalized on the popularity of handguns and the handgun market by manufacturing companion carbines that would be popular to the handgun owner.

The 10 quick shots with terrific knockdown power and the nostalgic lever action image of the Model 1894S also make it popular to the recreational shooter, hunter, or law enforcement person who wants a lightweight, handy firearm.

In 1988, the Model 1894S butt plate was changed to a rubber rifle pad. Marlin announced for 1988 the addition of the .45 Colt cartridge to the Model 1894S. The 1894S will then be chambered for the .44 magnum/44 S&W Special, .41 magnum, and .45 Colt.

The suggested retail prices of the Model 1894S were as follows:

Year	Price
1984	$280.95
1985	300.95
1986	325.95
1987	340.95
1988	357.95

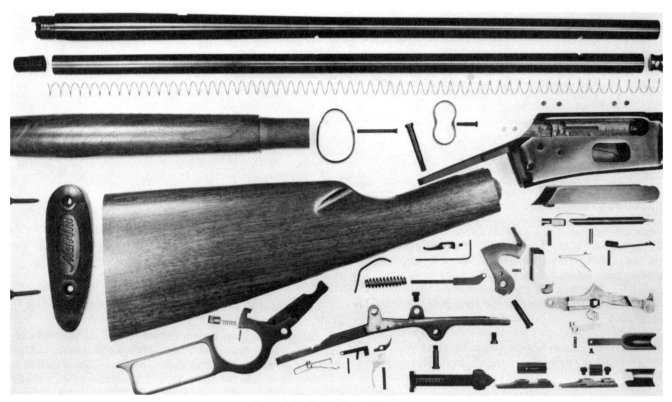

Parts of the first-variation Model 1894.

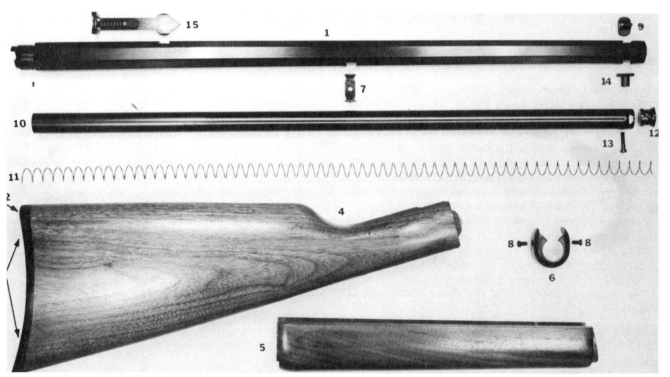

Parts peculiar to the Model 1894 Octagon.

Model 1894CS, Lever Action, Caliber .357 Magnum Carbine (1985 to date). The Model 1894SC is the Model 1894C with the cross-bolt safety added. Otherwise there were no changes in design or construction. See the Model 1894C above for details.

Model 1894CL "Classic," Lever Action, Caliber .25–20 and .32–20 Carbine (1988 to date). Marlin announced the return of the .25–20 and .32–20 cartridges to the Model 1894 in 1988. The new model is called the Model 1894CL ("Classic"); it has a 22-in. barrel, a half magazine that holds 6 cartridges, and a straight-grip walnut stock that has a black butt plate and no white line spacer. The front sight is a beaded drive-in dovetail sight and the rear sight is Marlin's patented folding, adjustable semibuckhorn open sight. The receiver is drilled and tapped for telescope mounting and receiver sight. The Model 1894CL is 38½ inches long and weighs 6¼ pounds. Its suggested retail price for 1988 was listed as $383.95.

MODEL 1895

Earlier Model 1895 Rifles

The Model 1895 rifle system is identical to the Model 1893 rifle invented by L.L. Hepburn, except that it is made larger in the receiver, barrel, and magazine to accommodate the larger cartridges for which it was designed. It was available as a carbine, round barrel rifle, half-octagon or full-octagon rifle, and a lightweight rifle. The rifles were available in straight-grip or pistol grip and takedown styles. It was first listed in the 1896 catalog.

1896 ad for the new Model 1895.

When introduced, the Model 1895 was chambered for the .38-56; .40-65, the same as the old .40-60 Marlin; .40-82; .45-70 (taking the various cartridges to include the .45-70-405 and .45-70-500 U.S. Government); and the .45-90, and its various loads.

In 1897 the .40-70 WCF cartridge and in 1912 the .33 WCF cartridge were added to the Model 1895 list of calibers.

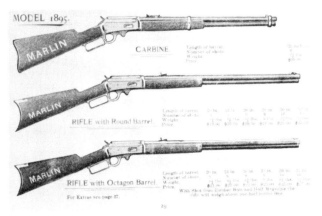

1896 catalog page for the Model 1895.

Catalog page showing cartridges used in the Model 1895 rifle.

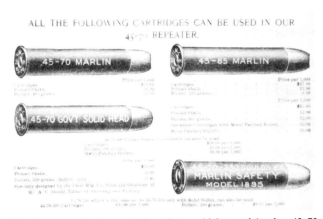

Catalog page showing cartridges that could be used in the .45–70 Model 1895.

COMPONENT PARTS
OF THE
MARLIN SAFETY REPEATING RIFLE,
MODEL 1895.

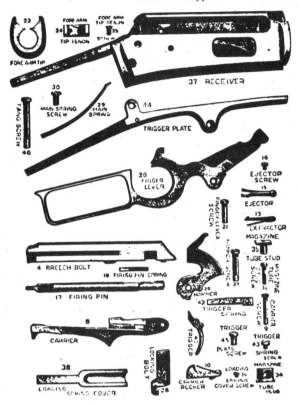

Catalog page showing the parts of the Model 1895 rifle.

Insert page for the 1911 catalog that announces the new caliber .33 rifle.

"Man of the West" armed with a straight-stocked, round-barreled Model 1895 rifle.

The Marlin 1896 catalog listed the following interchangeability of cartridges for the Model 1895:

Used in .40–82	.40–82, same as .40–82 WCF
	.40–70–330
Used in .40–65	.40–65, same as .40–65 WCF
	.40–60 Marlin
Used in .45–70	.45–70 Marlin
	.45–70–405 U.S. Government
	.45–70–500 U.S. Government
	.45–70–330 Gould's Express
	.45–70–350
	.45–85–285
Used in .45–90	.45–90, same as .45–90 WCF
	.45–85–350
	.45–82–405
	.45–85–300 Express

The standard Model 1895 rifle was fitted with a rifle butt plate. A rubber butt plate would be furnished at the same price as the steel type. With a rubber butt plate, the rifle weighed one-eighth pound less.

The standard receiver finish of Model 1895 carbines and rifles was case-hardened. If special-ordered, the receiver would be furnished with a blued finish at no additional cost. Hammers, levers, steel butt plates, and forearm tips were normally case-hardened and not blued. Barrels and magazines were blued.

The standard rifle buttstock length was 13 inches; the drop was 3¼ inches at the heel. With the rubber butt plate, the length of the stock was 13⅛ inches.

The overall length of the 1895, with a 26-in. barrel, is 35½ inches. When taken down, the rifle could be packed in the length of the barrel.

When introduced, the Model 1895 carbine was furnished with a 22-in. round barrel. In 1897, a 15-in. barrel was added at the same price as the 22-in. model.

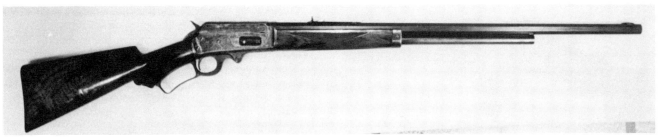

Caliber .45–70 Model 1895, serial number 148,435, with a 28-in. octagon barrel, pistol grip stock that is No. B checked, half magazine, Ballard-type rubber butt plate, and case-colored engraved No. 3 receiver. (DS)

No. 3-engraved Model 1895 rifle, serial number 148,435. (DS)

Left side of No. 3-engraved Model 1895 serial number 148,435. (DS)

Caliber .40–82 Model 1895 rifle, serial number 146,516, which has a 26-in. round barrel, rubber butt plate, No. B checking, pistol grip stock, and No. 1-engraved case-colored receiver. (DS)

No. 1-engraved Model 1895 receiver, serial number 146,516. (DS)

Rare variation of No. 1 engraving pattern that includes the figure of a moose. (DS)

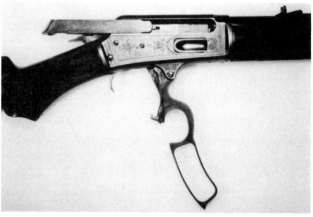

Model 1895 rifle shown with the lever and bolt in the open position.

The standard carbine had a sling ring on the left side of the receiver. The ring would be eliminated on special order. Also, if sling swivels were ordered, the ring would be omitted unless ordered to be retained.

Some very early Model 1895s were not stamped *Marlin Safety*. They are scarce, however. Soon after production started, the tops of receivers were stamped *Marlin Safety*.

Starting in 1903, two holes for the Hepburn receiver sight were drilled and tapped into the top of the receiver. At this same time, the *Marlin Safety* marking was moved forward so that the sight would not cover it when the sight was fitted to the rifle.

The top tang of the Model 1895 was drilled and tapped for a tang sight.

In August 1912, Marlin introduced a new variation of the Model 1895 rifle. It was of the lightweight style and was cham-

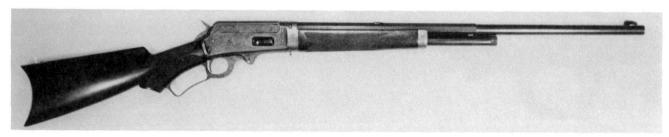

Model 1895 rifle, serial number 140,994, with a 26-in. caliber .40–65 half-octagon takedown barrel, half magazine, rifle butt plate, No. C-checked pistol grip stock, and case-colored engraved No. 3 receiver. (DS)

No. 3-engraved Model 1895 rifle, serial number 140,994. (DS)

Left side of No. 3-engraved Model 1895 rifle. (DS)

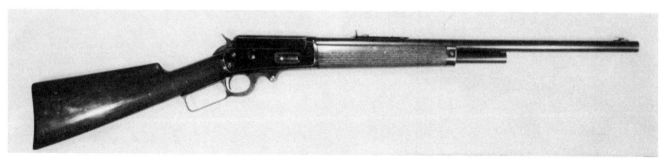

Special Light Weight Model 1895 .45–70 rifle, serial number 406,185, which has a 22-in. round barrel, half magazine, straight stock, rubber butt plate, and blued receiver. (DS)

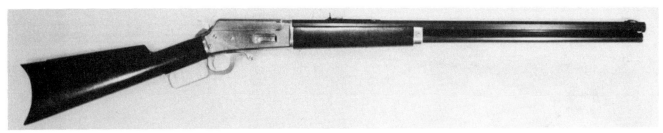

Nickel-plated and sectionalized .45–70 Model 1895, serial number 135,469, which has a 26-in. octagon barrel, full-length magazine, and straight stock with rubber butt plate. (DS)

Left side of sectionalized Model 1895 rifle, serial number 135,469. (DS)

Standard Model 1895 rifle, serial number 144,371, with a 26-in. caliber .40–65 full octagon barrel, full-length magazine, and rifle-type butt plate. (DS)

Model 1895 rifle, serial number 242,054, with a rare 24-in. caliber .40–82 takedown octagon barrel, pistol grip No. A-checked stock, full magazine, rifle butt, and case-colored receiver. (DS)

Model 1895 short rifle, serial number 338,278, with a 20-in. caliber .38–56 takedown round barrel, modified carbine buttstock, and case-colored receiver. (DS)

Model 1895 rifle, serial number 141,282, with a 28-in. half-octagon .40–65 barrel, short magazine, straight stock with rifle butt, and case-colored receiver. (DS)

Model 1895 rifle, serial number 137,976, which has a 28-in. .45–90 half octagon barrel, full-length magazine, pistol grip stock with rubber butt plate, and case-colored receiver. (Nonchecked pistol grip stocks are scarce.) (DS)

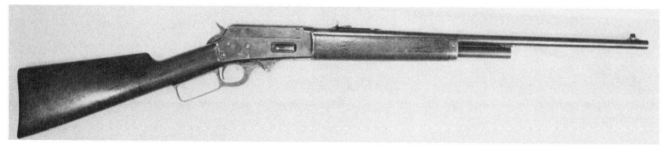

Special Light Weight Model 1895 rifle, serial number 439,199, which has a 22-in. caliber .33 lightweight barrel, short magazine tube, straight stock with rubber butt plate, and case-colored receiver. (DS)

Top: *Standard Model 1895 receiver.* Bottom: *Arrows indicate rebated receiver and lever of some Model 1895 lightweights. (DS)*

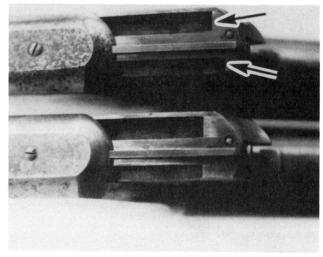

Top: *Bolt of lightweight Model 1895 rifle. Arrows indicate where metal has been removed to lighten the bolt.* Bottom: *Standard Model 1895 bolt.*

The arrow indicates the thinned and rebated lever of some lightweight Model 1895 rifles.

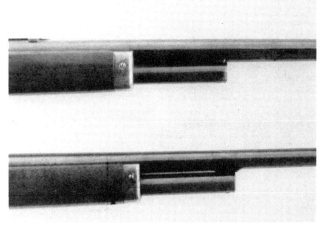

Top: *Standard short magazine of Model 1895 rifles.* Bottom: *Magazine end of Model 1895 lightweight magazine and barrel.*

bered for the new caliber .33 high-power smokeless cartridge. The rifle had a 24-in. Special Smokeless Steel round barrel, half magazine, shotgun rubber butt plate, 5-shot capacity, and 7¾-pound weight. It was priced at $18.50 for the solid-frame model and $22.00 for the takedown model.

Marlin stated the following about this new cartridge:

> The .33 caliber cartridge is one of the most powerful of all modern high power cartridges, throwing a heavy bullet with extremely high velocity (over 2,050 feet per second), very flat trajectory, deep penetration and tremendous shocking and killing power. It quickly brings down moose, bear, deer and all other big game.

Between serial numbers 148,435 and 167,166, an extra screw was added to the left side of the Model 1895 receiver to give additional support to the trigger plate.

The sights fitted to the rifle were the Rocky Mountain rear and German silver blade-type front sight. Later, the front sight had a bead instead of the usual blade. Carbine sights were the same as for the Model 1893 — a leaf rear sight and stud-type front.

All barrels for the Model 1895 were made of Special Smokeless Steel, and were so marked on the left side.

Buttstocks were made of walnut and had a varnish finish. Both straight- and pistol grip were available. Two types of steel

Top: *Front sight of standard Model 1895 rifles.* Bottom: *Front sight ramp of some Model 1895 lightweight barrels.*

Model 1895 carbine, serial number 148,384, which has a 22-in. caliber .38–56 round barrel, full-length magazine, straight stock, carbine butt, carbine sights, carbine bands, and sling loops. (DS)

Bottom view of carbine barrel band and sling loop.

Bottom view of typical buttstock sling loop.

rifle butt plates were used. The first was crescent-shaped, and the later plate was the S-type. This second type did not have the top screw into the top of the stock, but rather into the end grain of the wood. Likewise, the early carbine butt plate had its top screw into the top of the heel of the stock, whereas the late-type carbine butt plate had both screws into the end grain of the wood. The hard rubber butt plate was only available by special order and only for rifle stocks.

The Model 1895 was available in takedown and with many other extras. Please see the Extras section of this book for more information about the options available.

Standard barrel lengths, cartridge capacities, and weights were as follows:

	Barrel Length in Inches	Number of Shots— Full-Length Magazine	Weight in Pounds
Carbines	15	5	7
	22	6	7¾
Rifles			
Round	20	6	8¼
	24*	8	8½
	26	9	8¾
	28	9	9
	30	10	9⅜
	32	10	9¼
Octagon	20	6	8¼
	24	8	8½
	26	9	8¾
	28	9	9
	30	10	9⅛
	32	10	9¼

*24-in. barrel available from 1896 to 1898 and again from 1912 to 1915.

With the shotgun rubber butt and half magazine the rifle weighs about one-half pound less. Short or half-length maga-

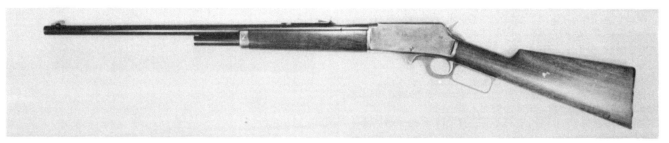

Model 1895 lightweight rifle, serial number 438,212, which has a 24-in. round caliber .33 barrel, straight stock, short magazine, rubber butt plate, and case-colored receiver. (DS)

Model 1895 rifle, serial number 436,381, which has a 28-in. round caliber .45–90 barrel, case-colored receiver, full-length magazine, and carbine buttstock. (DS)

Top: *Right side of rare bird's-eye maple-stocked Model 1895 rifle.* Bottom: *Left side of same rifle.*

zines were available at the same price as the full-length magazine. The half magazine will hold 5 of the .38–56, .40–65, and .45–70 cartridges or 4 of the .40–82 and .45–90 cartridges. The short magazine will hold 3 cartridges. Barrels over standard lengths listed above were $1.00 per inch extra. For extras, please see the Extras section of this book.

Model 1895 Trivia

Lowest rifle serial number	131,180	Nov. 27, 1895
Earliest date	131,180	Nov. 27, 1895
Lowest carbine serial number	136,003	Aug. 22, 1896
Earliest carbine date	138,488	Aug. 13, 1896
First takedown	131,303	Dec. 6, 1895
First round barrel	132,610	Dec. 17, 1895
First 24-in. barrel	132,572	Dec. 16, 1895

A total of 5,304 Model 1895s, of which only 205 were carbines, were manufactured from 1895 to 1906.

Full-length, half, and short magazines were available. Full-length was standard. Rifle barrels were 20, 24, 26, 28, 30, and 32 inches long and were available in round, octagon and half-octagon shape. The standard models were either full octagon or round. The lightweight, when introduced in 1912, was listed as having a 24-in. barrel. But 1913, 1914, and 1915 catalogs list this variation of the Model 1895 as having a 22-in. barrel.

The 1913 catalog listed the regular carbine and rifle variations of the Model 1895, but the 1915 catalog, and the 1916 Marlin Arms Corporation and 1917 Marlin-Rockwell Corporation price lists, no longer listed any Model 1895 except the special lightweight model in calibers .33 and .45–70. This variation of the Model 1895 had barrels 22 inches long, half magazines, straight stocks, shotgun hard rubber butt plates, and weight of about 7¾ pounds. It was the last of the 1895s.

Examination of Model 1895 rifles that fall into the special lightweight category reveals an inconsistency among them that cannot be explained. One may speculate that during the 1912–1915 period the Marlin company was searching for ways to keep the weight of the rifle down and within its advertised

Top tang of Model 1895 rifle showing typical model marking and tang sight screw holes.

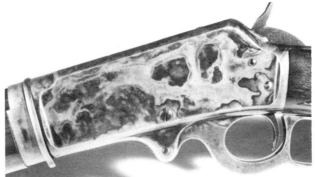

Top: *Right side of Model 1895 rifle showing ornate pattern of Marlin's case-color finish.* Bottom: *Left side of same rifle.*

Model 1895 saddle ring carbine, serial number 141,940, which has a rare 15-in. round barrel. This carbine is owned by an advanced Marlin collector in New Zealand. (K.A.)

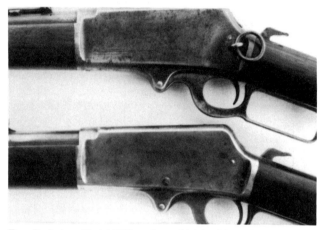

Top: *Early-type Model 1895 receiver, which is without the trigger plate support screw. Note the saddle ring.* Bottom: *Late-type Model 1895 receiver, which has the side support screw.* (DS)

specifications. Variations found that contradict the catalog description are as follows:

Serial Number	Description
406,185	.45–70 with 22-in. barrel and all standard Model 1895 parts.
437,817	.33 caliber with 24-in. heavy barrel and rebated lever and bolt.
438,212	.33 caliber with 24-in. barrel and all standard parts.
439,199	.33 caliber with 22-in. light barrel, small frame, lightened bolt, and rebated lever.

The Model 1895 barrel was stamped *MARLIN FIRE-ARMS CO. NEW HAVEN. CT. U.S.A. PAT'D Oct. 11, 1887, April 2, 1889, Aug. 1, 1893.*

Model 1895 rifle, serial number 137,412, with a 26-in. caliber .45–70 octagon barrel, full magazine, No. G-checked pistol grip stock with rubber butt plate, gold-plated lever, silver presentation plate in the stock engraved George H. Rimbach—1896, *and a No. 5–1-engraved case-colored receiver.* (JO)

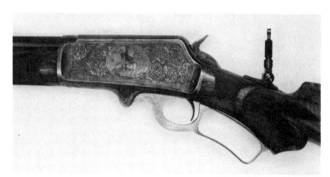

Left side of Model 1895 presentation rifle. (JO)

Silver plate inlaid into the stock of presentation Model 1895 rifle, serial number 137,412. (JO)

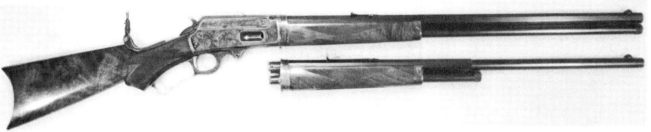

Model 1895 rifle, serial number 211,906, which has a No. 5-4-engraved and case-colored receiver, No. B-checked pistol grip stock with rubber butt plate, and set of two barrels. One barrel is full octagon with a full-length magazine tube in caliber .38-56, and the other barrel is .45-70 in half octagon with a short magazine. The barrels are matted and 26 inches long. (JO)

The top tang was stamped *MODEL 1895* and the caliber was stamped on the barrel just forward of the receiver. Serial numbers were stamped into the bottom front end of the trigger plate.

The spread of retail prices for the Model 1895 was as follows:

Barrel Length In Inches		1896	1903	1911	1913
Round:	20	$19.50	$16.25	$15.50	$15.50
	24	19.50			
	26	19.50	16.25	15.50	15.50
	28	21.50	17.90	17.00	17.00
	30	23.50	19.60	18.50	18.50
	32	25.50	21.30	20.00	20.00
Octagon:	20	21.00	17.50	16.75	16.75
	24	21.00			
	26	21.00	17.50	16.75	16.75
	28	23.00	19.10	18.25	18.25
	30	25.00	20.70	19.75	19.75
	32	27.00	22.30	21.25	21.25

		1896	1897	1903	1911	1913
Carbine:	15		$16.50	$15.60	$15.00	$15.00
	22	$19.00	16.50	15.60	15.00	15.00

		1912	1913	1917
Light-weight:	22		$18.50	$27.00
	24	$18.50		

New Model 1895, Lever Action, Caliber .45-70 Rifle (1972-1979); New Model 1895S, Lever Action, Caliber .45-70 Sporter (1980-1983); and New Model 1895SS, Lever Action, Caliber .45-70 Sporter (1984 to date)

The New Model 1895 rifle was introduced in limited numbers in 1972. It was built upon the famous Model 336 receiver and lever action system in response to reports from the field that sportsmen wanted manufacturers to reintroduce some of the old classic cartridges. The .45-70 was a famous cartridge that played a part in frontier history and was a logical choice for Marlin to add to its popular lever action line. It was introduced as follows:

Way back in 1895 Marlin introduced a powerful big bore game rifle chambered for the framed .45/70. This mighty old classic has been a favorite for decades.

The U.S. Army adopted the .45/70 cartridge in 1873 and it remained the standard issue until 1898 when the .30/40 Krag was adopted. In the years following, acceptance of the .45/70 grew steadily while many higher velocity cartridges were introduced, only to fail soon after. Shooters and hunters never forgot their old favorite—the .45/70. It has now begun a dramatic comeback. Small wonder! Anything it hits stays down for keeps.

A 5-shot repeater featuring the famous solid top receiver, the big bore gun was in great demand by Western hunters where the game was tough and dangerous.

Big game hunters will welcome the return of this old friend. For hunting large North American game it has no peer, especially in the deep woods. And deer hunters will find the .45/70 more than adequate in the swamps and thickets of whitetail country.

New Model 1895 rifle.

Model 1895S Sporter rifle.

Model 1895-SS Sporter rifle.

Model 1895 rifle of 1988.

Marlin's new Model 1895 has been built upon a solid foundation of experience gained through years of Model 336 production. The use of modern alloy steels, forged, machined and heat-treated to increase strength, makes this modern version a stronger, lighter and more reliable rifle afield.

Originally a black powder government cartridge with 500-grain lead bullet, it was cataloged under the old black powder system where the first number indicated caliber (.45-inch), the second represented the powder charge (70-grains of black powder). Today's factory loaded .45/70 features a 405-grained jacketed bullet and smokeless powder.

Note: The Marlin Model 1895 is designed to use modern, factory loaded cartridges using 405-grain jacketed bullets only. Handloads equivalent to factory load specifications can be used provided loaded cartridge length does not exceed 2.550″.

When introduced in 1972, the New Model 1895 was styled very much like the first model when it was discontinued in 1915. The new model had a straight walnut stock. The butt plate was a copy of the earlier curved hard rubber butt plate. The lever was square and the 4-shot magazine was of the short half-magazine type. The front sight was a gold-bead drive-in dovetail type. The rear sight was the Marlin folding Rocky Mountain type. The receiver was tapped for both receiver sight and telescope mount and was sandblasted to prevent glare. The barrel was 22 inches long. The overall length was 40½ inches, and the rifle weighed about 7 pounds.

Some of the first year's production of the new Model 1895 had 8-groove rifling. Later production had 12 grooves.

It took a few years to fulfill the demand of sportsmen for a classic lever action in .45–70. Then, after that first demand for a classic model was filled, the sale of the .45–70 dropped off. Surveys and comments from the field indicated that there was an additional requirement for a sporting version of the .45–70. As a result, Marlin introduced in 1980 a pistol grip model that was similar to the Model 444S Sporter.

Now identified as the Model 1895S, the new configuration included a pistol grip stock that had a hard rubber *Marlin*-marked butt plate, and a pistol grip cap, both with white line spacers. The lever was changed to the round type and the front sight was changed to the ramp type with Wide-Scan hood. Quick detachable (QD) sling swivels and a sling were added. All other features remained the same.

The 1895 Sporter increased sales, and there were no loud comments from the field that the "classic" configuration should have been retained. With an ongoing trend for the big cartridges, it is now more popular than ever before.

In 1984, Marlin introduced a cross-bolt safety in the center-fire lever action models. When it was added to the Model 1895S, the model designation was changed from Model 1895S to Model 1895SS. All other features remained the same.

In 1988, the QD swivels and sling were dropped in favor of sling studs.

The suggested retail price of the Model 1895s has been as follows:

Year	Model 1895	Model 1895S	Model 1895SS
1972–1975	$185.00		
1976	195.95		
1977	209.95		
1978	215.95		
1979	234.95		

Year	Model 1895	Model 1895S	Model 1895SS
1980	266.95		
1981		$309.95	
1982		346.95	
1983		349.95	$357.95
1984		294.95	302.95
1985			323.95
1986			339.95
1987			367.95
1988			385.95

When introduced, the new Model 1895 had the letter *B* as a prefix to the serial number. In 1980, the number was changed to one having eight digits without an alphabetical prefix.

MARLIN REPEATER, MODEL 1897

The success of the Model 1891 and Model 1892 caliber .22 rifles, and the popularity of the takedown system of Marlin's center-fire lever action rifles, prompted John Marlin to develop a takedown .22 lever action rifle. The result was the Model 1897, introduced in 1897.

Patent number 584,177, dated June 8, 1897, was awarded to L.L. Hepburn for the Model 1897 rifle and its takedown system. An interesting note to firearm students of today: The system is still in use by Marlin in the Model 39 series of rifles.

The following description of the Model 1897 is extracted from the Marlin 1897 catalog:

This is a Take-Down Repeater in 22 caliber, adapted to use in one rifle without any change in adjustment, the 22 short 22 long and 22 long rifle cartridges, including, of course, the

Parts of New Model 1895 rifle.

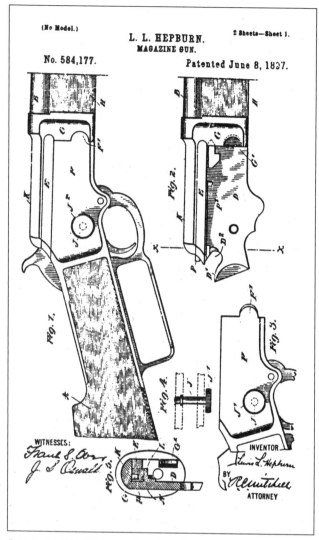

Patent No. 584,177 illustration from L.L. Hepburn's patent dated June 8, 1897 for the takedown feature of Marlin's Model 1897 rifle.

1900 ad suggesting the Model 1897 as a woods companion.

1900 ad for the Model 1897 takedown rifle.

1907-dated photo of Freda O'Connell, Quebec, Canada. She stated, "My papa told me that this gun was the first one sent to Quebec. It is now mine."

smokeless cartridges in these sizes, as well as the special cartridges with mushroom bullet, blank and shot cartridges.

This is just the gun to take on a summer vacation, or to the woods; it will come in handy for birds, snap shooting, killing time on rainy days, etc.; it takes no room; it weighs next to nothing and can be put together and taken apart in less time than it takes to describe it. Just the thing to take on a bicycle trip through the woods and country. With the short barrel it can be carried handily in a diamond frame.

As will be observed, it is our Model 1892 in Take-Down form; with many other improvements, here described:

IN EXTERNAL APPEARANCE the following differences may be noted: the larger thumb-screw; the finely tapered barrel, which with the neat rubber plate gives the arm a light and graceful appearance; the case-hardened receiver; the Rocky Mountain rear and front sights. The standard rifle will have a shot gun butt stock with rubber buttplate, but if desired, our rifle butt will be fitted without extra charge.

ACTION, as will be noted, the action is that of the Model 1892 with, of course, the addition of the Take-Down principle and consequent improvements. We would also note the following:

THE RECEIVER is made of the special steel used in our high power smokeless rifles, which insures a solid rifle, and is finely case hardened, adding greatly to the appearance and durability of the same.

INSIDE FINISH. This rifle has the inside of receiver and all the inner parts finely finished, not only giving a pleasing effect when the rifle is apart, but further improving the action and rendering it especially easy to work.

1914 ad for the Model 1897 rifle as the best-made .22 rifle in the world.

Early Model 1897, with a round top to the receiver. Note that the early 1897s did not have either the cartridge guide or the magazine cutoff.

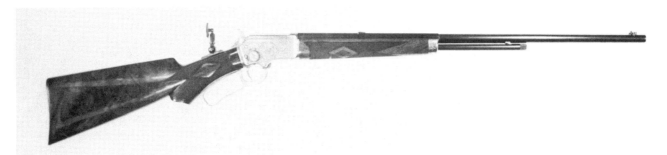

Model 1897 rifle, serial number 194,694, which has a 24-in. half-octagon barrel, round-top No. 5-engraved and gold-plated frame, half magazine, select walnut pistol grip and No. D-checked stock, and a Lyman tang rear sight. (RP)

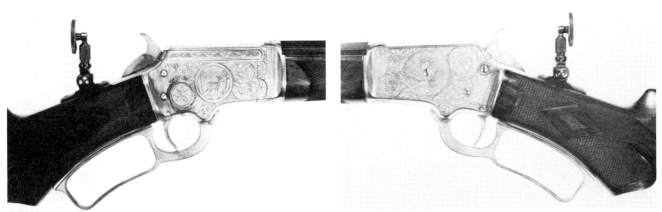

Left: *Right side of No. 2-engraved Model 1897 rifle, serial number 194,694. (RP)* Right: *Left side of same rifle.*

Model '97 rifle serial number 310,444, with a No. 2-engraved 24-inch round barrel, half magazine, straight stock, and No. B checking. (RP)

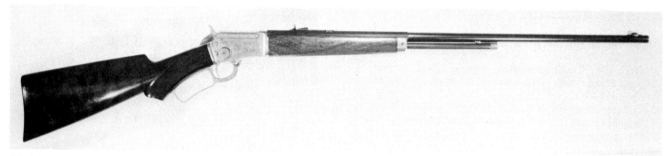

Model 1897 rifle, serial number 246,627, with a 26-in. half-octagon barrel, half magazine, No. 1-engraved round-top frame, nickel-plated trimmings, select walnut pistol grip stock checked No. A, and Rocky Mountain sights. (RP)

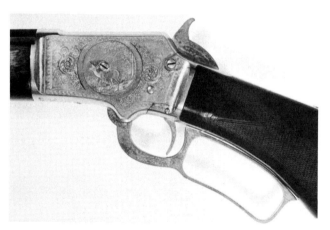

Left side of Model 1897 rifle, serial number 246,627.

THE WORKING PARTS, viz.: — the carrier, breech bolt, etc., are made of tool steel carefully hardened, which insures freedom from wear and in consequence a permanent adjustment. We can guarantee this rifle to give satisfaction and to stand the continued use to which a 22 caliber is subjected, without losing its adjustment.

It will be observed that the breech bolt is secure, so there is a groove on the under side of the breech bolt in which a projecting lip on the support at the rear end of the receiver fits. Consequently, to remove the bolt it must be pushed back to the limit of its path, when it is free. Except in this position the bolt cannot be removed.

All parts are securely fastened in the rifle, making it impossible to lose any when the rifle is apart, while at the same time they can be easily removed, if desired, although the rifle can be thoroughly and conveniently cleaned without taking out a single part of the action.

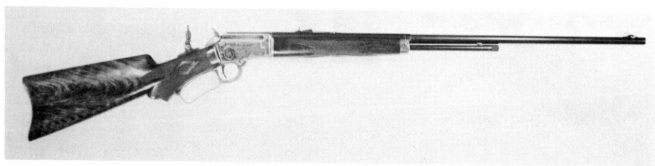

Flat-top Model '97 rifle, serial number 354,062, with a half-octagon barrel, half magazine, select pistol grip walnut stock with steel S-type butt plate, No. F checking, and No. 3 engraving. (RP)

EASY TO CLEAN. — Every 22 caliber rifle should be frequently and carefully cleaned. We here furnish one in which not only the action, but also the barrel can be readily cleaned. In this rifle the breech bolt can be removed and likewise the ejector, as it is our new type of ejector. The barrel is then just as free and clear as a single barrel apart from any action, and can be cleaned by inserting the rod at either end and drawing the cloth through the barrel, which is the only way to clean a 22 caliber barrel thoroughly. In these respects it is superior to any rifle made, even excelling our Model 1892.

When the breech bolt is removed the magazine may readily be cleaned, as the wiping rod and cloth can be pushed right up into the inside tube. In this way the grease and dirt from the lubricant is removed, and the spring and follower will naturally work more easily.

TO TAKE RIFLE APART — It is necessary merely to cock the hammer, and unscrew the thumb-screw. Then take apart, which will be done very naturally by lifting the buttstock part, while holding the barrel.

TO PUT RIFLE TOGETHER. — Cock the hammer; then place the right side of receiver on the left side so that the lip fits in the recess being provided to receive it. Then as the right side of the receiver is pressed on the left side, the beveled shoulders fit in the corresponding curves; screw in thumb-screw.

SPECIAL STYLE BICYCLE RIFLE. We are prepared to furnish this rifle with 16 inch barrel and full magazine. It is

Left side of Model '97 rifle, serial number 345,062.

Left side of Model '97 rifle, serial number 417,498, which is No. 3 engraved and No. F checked. Arrows indicate the two screws that hold the second-variation ejector in place.

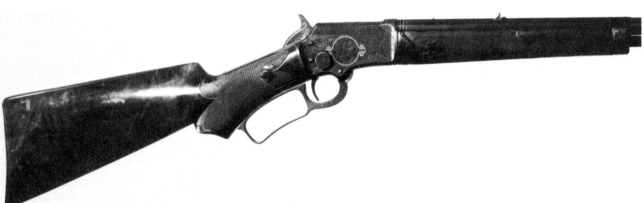

One of very few known gold-inlaid Model 1897 rifles. There are gold and platinum bands around the barrel and gold lines inlaid into the hammer. The engraving and checking are of the No. 10 style.

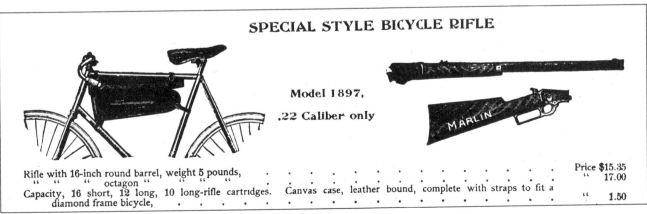

Catalog illustration of 16-in.-barreled Model 1897 Bicycle Rifle.

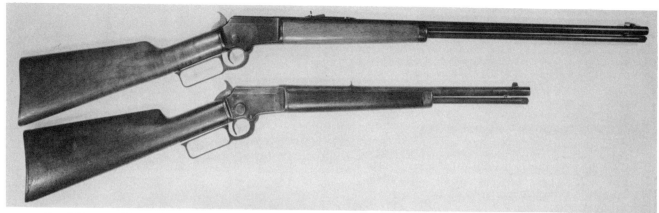

Top: *24-in. round-barreled Model 1892 rifle.* Bottom: *16-in.-barreled Bicycle Rifle, serial number 157,639, shown for comparison.*

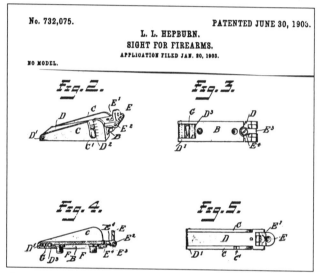

Patent number 732,075, dated June 30, 1903, was issued to L.L. Hepburn for his adjustable rear sight that mounted on the top of Marlin's solid-top receivers.

Model '97 rifle, serial number 354,151, with the L.L. Hepburn combination receiver sight fitted to the flat top of the receiver. The sight part could be moved in elevation and either a peep or an open notch could be used. However, the open notch was too close to the eye to be practical.

Second-variation receiver had a flat top and was drilled and tapped for the L.L. Hepburn receiver sight. The front screw held the cartridge guide in place, and the rear two dummy screws were removed when the sight was to be installed.

of convenient length to strap within a diamond frame. Capacity, 16 short, 12 long, 10 long rifle cartridges.

We can furnish canvas case, leather bound, complete with straps, of proper form to fit securely within a diamond frame. Price—$1.75.

The Standard Model 1897 had a 24-in. round or octagon barrel, and straight stock. It was fitted with a rubber butt plate, but would be furnished with the rifle butt plate at no extra charge.

Other features of the Model 1897 were the following:

Barrels: 24-in. standard and 26- and 28-in. round, octagon, and half octagon on special order. Half octagon were the same price as octagon. Magazines for all these barrels were 24 inches in length. The Bicycle Rifle had a 16-in. barrel and 16-in. magazine.

Butt Plate: Hard rubber standard. Rifle butt plate could be furnished at same price.

Receiver: Case-colored was standard.

Sights: Rocky Mountain front and rear sights were standard until 1907, when an ivory bead front sight was introduced.

Stocks: Straight stock was standard. Pistol grip and checking were available on special order for an additional cost. Also, select and extra select wood could be ordered.

Magazine: The magazine of the Model 1897 rifle was of the latch type, the same as the Model 1892. Originally, the longest furnished was 24 inches long. However, in 1899 a 16-in. magazine (half magazine) was listed as available in

Model '97 rifle, serial number A7376, having a 24-in. round barrel, straight stock, and half magazine.

Typical roll-stamp on Model 1897 barrel. Note that the patent dates are the same as those marked on Model 1892/92 barrels.

Model marking on top tang of Model 1897 rifles.

addition to the standard 24-in. magazine. This magazine held 16 short, 12 long, or 10 long rifle cartridges.

Early round-top Model 1897 rifles were marked *Marlin Safety* on top of the frame. But when the two receiver sight holes were added to the top of the frame, the slogan was no longer used.

A magazine cartridge cutoff was added to the internal mechanism of the Model 1897 in 1899. The purpose of the new cutoff was to better allow only one cartridge, whether it was a short, long, or long rifle, to enter the receiver at a time. This allowed the three different-length cartridges to be mixed in the magazine tube. A screw on the outside of the left side of the receiver held the cutoff in place.

In 1904 the Model 1897 also had added to it a cartridge guide that was located on the inside top front of the receiver and just to the rear of the butt end of the barrel. A screw in the top of the receiver held the guide in place. The purpose of the guide was to ensure that cartridges would be guided into the chamber, without stubbing on the end of the barrel.

During 1905, the model designation on the top tang of the frame was changed from *MODEL 1897,* in two lines, to *Marlin* (in script) above *MODEL '97.* However, catalogs and price lists continued to identify this model as the Model 1897.

During 1907, the ejector of the Model 1897 was changed to a new type. The new type (first illustrated in the 1908 catalog) had an ejector base, ejector wing (ejector), ejector spring, ejector pin, and two assembly screws that held the assembly into a recess in the left half of the frame. The two screws were installed into the outside of the frame and identify this last variation of the Model 1897/97 rifle.

All Model 1897 frames were drilled and tapped for tang

Model marking on top tang of Model '97 rifles.

The L.L. Hepburn takedown Model 1897 patent date of June 8, 1897 is stamped into the inside of the frame. See arrow.

The serial number of Model 1897/97 rifles is stamped into the bottom front of the frame, as shown here.

Hard rubber butt plate used on the Model 1897/97 rifles.

sights. The hole spacing is 1⅛ inches between the centers of the two holes. The front hole is about ½ inch in back of the slot for the hammer in the frame.

The patent dates and company name marked on the top of Model 1897 barrels were the same as on the late Model 1892 rifle. They were roll-stamped *MARLIN FIRE-ARMS CO. NEW-HAVEN. CT. U.S.A.* on the top line and *PAT'D NOV. 19. 1878. APRIL 9. 1889. AUG. 12. 1890. MARCH 1. 1892* on a line below. Various arrows and decorative designs were at both ends of the roll-stamp.

The L.L. Hepburn patent date for the takedown system of June 8, 1897 was stamped into the inside of the left half of the receiver. This marking is visible when the rifle is taken down and the carrier is removed.

As previously mentioned, the Model 1897 Bicycle Rifle was listed in the September 1899 and later catalogs as having a 16-in. barrel. Although the 1897 and February 1899 catalogs imply that other barrel lengths were also available for this model, it is my opinion that, because of the change in the text of the September 1899 and later catalogs, and because it is stated elsewhere that a 16-in. (half) magazine could be furnished with any barrel length, the Bicycle Rifles had only a 16-in. barrel. This opinion is reinforced by Marlin's statement: "With the short barrel it can be carried handily in a diamond frame."

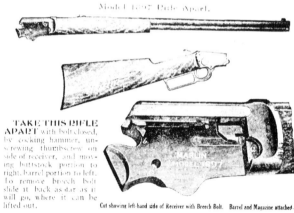

Model 1897 Rifle Apart.

TAKE THIS RIFLE APART with bolt closed, by cocking hammer, unscrewing thumbscrew on side of receiver, and moving buttstock portion to right, barrel portion to left. To remove breech bolt slide it back as far as it will go, where it can be lifted out.

Cut showing left-hand side of Receiver with Breech Bolt, Barrel and Magazine attached.

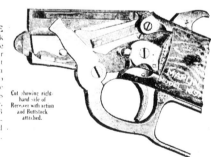

TO PUT RIFLE TOGETHER. Cock the hammer; then place the right side of receiver on the left side so that the lip "A" fits in *a*, a recess being provided to receive A. Then as the right side of receiver is pressed on the left side, the beveled shoulders B and C fit in the corresponding curves *b* and *c*; screw in thumbscrew.

Cut showing right-hand side of Receiver with action and Buttstock attached.

It will be observed that the breech bolt is secure, so there is no danger of its dropping out and being lost, and there is a groove on the under side of the breech bolt in which a projecting lip on the support at the rear end of the receiver fits. Consequently, to remove the bolt it must be pushed back to the limit of its path, when it is free. Except in this position the bolt cannot be removed.

All parts are securely fastened in the rifle, making it impossible to lose any when the rifle is apart, while at the same time they can be easily removed, if desired, although the rifle can be thoroughly and conveniently cleaned without taking out a single part of the action.

Catalog page showing inside of Model 1897 rifle and instructions for cleaning.

The records reflect that a total of only 216 Model 1897 rifles with 16-in. barrels were manufactured. They were as follows:

Barrel Type	Number Made
½ Oct.	5
Octagon	114
Round	97
Total	216

The retail prices of the Model 1897 as listed in catalogs and price lists were as follows:

Year	Barrel Length In Inches	Retail Price Round	Octagon
1897	24	$15.35	$16.80
	26	16.85	18.30
	28	18.35	19.80
Bicycle Rifle	16	15.35	16.80

Bicycle Rifle leather bound canvas case—$1.75

1899–1902	Same as 1897 except ½ magazine added that held 16 short, 12 long and 10 long rifle cartridges. Bicycle rifle case—$1.40.

		Octagon & ½ Octagon
1903–1908	16	$17.00
	24	17.00
	26	18.00
	28	20.20

		Round	Octagon
1909–July 1915	16	$14.50	$16.00
	24	14.50	16.00
	26	16.00	17.50
	28	17.50	19.00
Bicycle Rifle	16	14.50	16.00

Bicycle case—$1.50

Nov. 1915	Same as 1909–July 1915, except that no 26-in. barrel or Bicycle Rifle was listed in price list.

May 1916	24	17.20	18.80
	26	18.70	20.30
	28	20.20	21.80

October 1917	24	20.65	22.55
	26	22.45	24.35
	28	24.25	26.15

The weight of the Model 1897 rifle was listed in catalogs as follows:

Catalog	Barrel Length In Inches	Weight In Pounds Round	Octagon or ½ Octagon
1897	24	5½	5½
	26	5¾	5¾
	28	6	6
1900–1906	16	5	5

Catalog	Barrel Length In Inches	Weight In Pounds Round	Octagon or ½ Octagon
1907–1915	16	5	5
	24	5⅜	5⅝
	26	5⅝	5⅞
	28	5⅞	6⅛

The 24-in. magazine length could accommodate 25 short, 20 long, or 18 long rifle cartridges; the 16-in. length, 16 short, 12 long, or 10 long rifle cartridges.

The stock with rubber butt plate was 13⅛ inches in length and had a 2⅞-in. drop. The stock with a steel rifle butt plate was 13 inches in length and had a 2⅞-in. drop. The rubber butt plate was 4½ inches from tip to tip.

Frames of the Model 1897 rifle were manufactured from Special Smokeless Steel, and working parts were made from tool steel.

Hammers, levers, forearm tips, and frames (receivers) were case-hardened for color. After case hardening, the surface of the frames was lightly lacquered to protect the surface and to enhance the color.

The low and high serial numbers reported or observed have been as follows:

Model	Low	High
Model 1897	150,021	?
Model 97	293,615	450,036
	A441	A7938

From its introduction in 1897 until the end of existing records in 1905, 38,490 Model 1897 rifles are listed as being manufactured, for an average of 4,284 per year.

By projecting the above yearly average for 10 more years of production—until 1916—it is speculated that over 81,000 Model 1897 rifles were manufactured.

MODEL 1936

Marlin's basic center-fire lever action rifle chambered for the .30–30 and similar cartridges has had its model designation changed five times. The model names have been Model 1893, Model 93, Model 1936, Model 36, and Model 336. Except for the Model 336, few changes were made to the basic Model 1893 during the production life of these models. For example, the Model 93 was discontinued in name only when the new identifier of Model 1936 was given this classic center-fire lever action rifle. Intended to be used the same way as were the earlier model designations such as Model 1893 and Model 93, the new Model 1936 was an attempt to put new life into the prior variation called the Model 93, which had changed only slightly since 1922. By changing the stock, forearm, and sights of the Model 1936, it was hoped that sales would increase and that the new model would better compete with the new look of the Winchester lever action rifle that was appearing at the same time.

The new stock design shown in catalogs included fluted combs and pistol grips for the carbine, rifle, and sporting carbine models. The new forearm shape, instead of being straight,

Marlin

A New Gun Made Especially for American Big Game

"Sure Grip" Semi-Beaver Tail Forearm—Shotgun Style Buttstock.

SOLID TOP RECEIVER—CLOSED IN FRAME—SIDE EJECTION

MARLIN MODEL 1936 CARBINE

Full Magazine—7 Shots

30-30 and 32 SPECIAL CALIBRES

SPECIFICATIONS—Solid Frame, 20 inch Round Tapered Special Smokeless Steel Barrel, Proof Tested, Crown Muzzle, **Famous Ballard Type Rifling.** Visible Hammer, Case Hardened Receiver. Steel Butt Plate. New Design Full Pistol Grip Buttstock of Genuine American Black Walnut. Length 13¼ inches, Drop at Comb 1⅞ inches, Drop at Heel 2⅞ inches. New "SUREGRIP" Semi-Beaver Tail Forearm, rounded and nicely shaped. Silver Bead Front Sight and Flat Top Rocky Mountain Rear Sight, especially adapted to quick accurate shooting. Length over all 38 inches. Weight about 6½ pounds.

PACKED 10 IN CASE—WEIGHT ABOUT 90 POUNDS

MARLIN MODEL 1936 SPORTING CARBINE

2/3 Magazine—6 Shots

30-30 and 32 SPECIAL CALIBRES

SPECIFICATIONS—Solid Frame, 20 inch Round Tapered Special Smokeless Steel Barrel, Proof Tested, Crown Muzzle, **Famous Ballard Type Rifling.** Visible Hammer, Case Hardened Receiver. Steel Butt Plate. New Design Full Pistol Grip Buttstock of Genuine American Black Walnut. Length 13¼ inches, Drop at Comb 1⅞ inches, Drop at Heel 2⅞ inches. New "SUREGRIP" Semi-Beaver Tail Forearm, rounded and nicely shaped. Steel Forearm Tip. New "HUNTSMAN" Non-Glare Ramp Front Sight with Silver Bead and Quick detachable Hood. Flat Top Adjustable Rocky Mountain Rear Sight. Length over all 38 inches. Weight about 6½ pounds.

PACKED 10 IN CASE—WEIGHT ABOUT 90 POUNDS

MARLIN MODEL 1936 RIFLE

2/3 Magazine—6 Shots

30-30 and 32 SPECIAL CALIBRES

SPECIFICATIONS—Solid Frame, 24 inch Round Tapered Special Smokeless Steel Barrel, Proof Tested, Crown Muzzle, **Famous Ballard Type Rifling.** Visible Hammer, Case Hardened Receiver. Steel Butt Plate. New Design Full Pistol Grip Buttstock of Genuine American Black Walnut. Length 13¼ inches, Drop at Comb 1⅞ inches, Drop at Heel 2⅞ inches. New "SUREGRIP" Semi-Beaver Tail Forearm, rounded and nicely shaped. Steel Forearm Tip. New "HUNTSMAN" Non-Glare Ramp Front Sight with Silver Bead and Quick detachable hood. Flat Top Adjustable Rocky Mountain Rear Sight. Length over all 42 inches. Weight about 6¾ pounds.

PACKED 10 IN CASE—WEIGHT ABOUT 102 POUNDS

Catalog page showing types of the Model 1936.

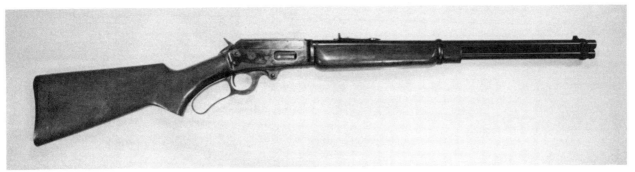

Second variation of the Model 1936.

had a slight fish-belly shape that Marlin called "a 'Sure-grip' semi-beavertail forearm." The new front sight of the sporting carbine and rifle variations was a hooded ramp that attached to the barrel by means of a dovetail. The front sight insert had a silver bead. This new nonglare front ramp sight was identified as the Huntsman sight.

The Marlin 1936 price list included the Model 93 in rifle, carbine, and sporting carbine variations at $25.00 each. The 1937 Marlin price list included the new Model 1936 rifle, carbine, and sporting carbine as replacements for the Model 93.

There were two variations of the Model 1936. The first had a long top tang and flat hammer spring, like the Model 93, and no prefix to the serial number stamped on the lower tang, whereas the second variation had a short top tang, a coil-type hammer spring and a *B* prefix to the serial number, also marked on the lower tang.

The Model 1936 was made in rifle, carbine, and sporting carbine types, as was the Model 93.

The catalog identified this model as "a new gun especially for American big game" that had a Sure-Grip semibeavertail forearm, shotgun-style buttstock, solid-top receiver, closed-in frame, and side ejection. The catalog information also included the following about the carbine:

Marlin Model 1936 Carbine: Solid frame, 20-inch round tapered special smokeless barrel, proof-tested, crown muzzle, Ballard-type rifling, visible hammer, case-hardened receiver, steel butt plate. New design full pistol grip buttstock of genuine American black walnut. Length 13¼ inches, drop at comb, 1⅞ inches, drop at heel, 2⅞ inches. New "Sure-Grip" semi-beavertail forearm, rounded and nicely shaped. Silver bead front sight dovetailed to the barrel and flat top Rocky Mountain rear sight, especially adapted to quick accurate shooting. Length overall 38 inches. Weight about 6½ pounds. Full magazine. Seven shots and in caliber .30–30 or .32 Special.

The Model 1936 Sporting Carbine (CS) was described in the catalog the same as was the carbine model, except that the CS had a steel forearm tip instead of the carbine-type forearm band, a two-thirds magazine of 6 shots, and a Huntsman nonglare ramp front sight dovetailed to the barrel that had a silver bead and quick detachable hood.

The Model 1936 Rifle was described the same as the Sporting Carbine, except that it had a 24-in. barrel and an overall length of 42 inches. It weighed about 6¾ pounds.

All Model 1936s are marked *Marlin Safety* on the top of the receiver. The top tang is marked *Marlin/Model 1936*. Receivers were case-hardened in color. Barrels were marked *The Marlin Firearms Corporation/New Haven Conn. U.S.A.-Patented,* or *Marlin Firearms Co.—New Haven Conn. U.S.A./(Caliber .[x])—Special Smokeless Steel.* Caliber .30–30 and .32 Special were marked separately on the barrel of the first variation and along with the company name on the second variation.

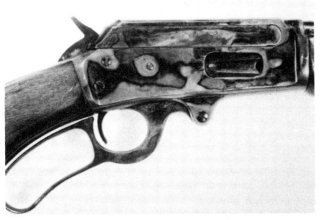

Case-colored receiver of Model 1936 Carbine.

Barrel marking on Model 1936.

Typical Model marking on top tang of the Model 1936. Note that the tang is drilled and tapped for the installation of a tang sight.

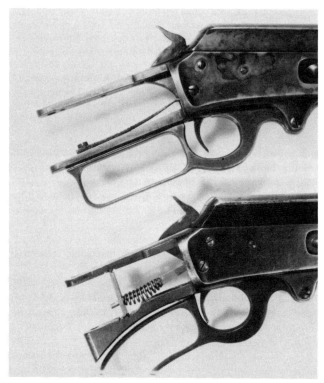

Top: *Flat mainspring of the Models 1893/93/1936.* Bottom: *Coil mainspring introduced in the Model 1936.*

Model 36 Carbine
Especially Built for American Big Game
Calibers, .30-30 and .32 Special

Full magazine. 7 Shots

SPECIFICATIONS:—Lever action repeater with solid frame. Barrel, 20 inch, round tapered and crown muzzle. Steel, special smokeless, proof tested. Famous Ballard type of rifling. Receiver case hardened. Visible hammer. Checkered butt plate, unbreakable. Full pistol grip butt stock, shot gun style. Genuine American black walnut. Length, 13¼ in., drop at comb. 1⅛ in.. drop at heel, 2⅞ in. "Sure grip" semi beaver tail forearm. Sights, silver bead front and flat top Rocky Mountain rear, excellent for quick, accurate shooting. Length over-all, 38 inches. Weight, about 6½ lbs.

Model 36 Sporting Carbine

2/3 Magazine. 6 Shots

Same general specifications as the 1936 carbine. Steel forearm tip. New "Huntsman" non-glare ramp front sight with silver bead and quick detachable hood.

Model 36 Rifle

2/3 Magazine. 6 Shots

Same general specifications as the 1936 Carbine. 24 inch barrel. Steel forearm tip. New "Huntsman" non-glare, ramp front sight with silver bead. Quick detachable hood. Rocky Mountain rear sight. Length overall, 42 inches. Weight about 6¼ lbs.

Catalog illustration of Model 36 Carbine, sporting carbine, and Model 36 Rifle.

Catalog illustrations and known examples show the rear sight of the Model 1936 rifle (and Model 36 rifle) as being located farther forward on the barrel than are the rear sights for the Model 1936 Carbine and Sporting Carbine.

Although Marlin was trying to make a new image for the center-fire lever action rifle by giving it a new model designation, it was also necessary to make a few shortcuts. One was to temporarily discontinue the use of the bull's-eye trademark embedded into the bottom edge of the buttstock and another was to use a less expensive butt plate. Although the catalog listed a steel butt plate for the Model 1936s, only hard rubber ones have been noted. The first-variation 1936 had predominately flat butt plates and the second variation had both flat and curved types.

The first-variation Model 1936s had fluted combs to the stock and a swelled forearm shape that was slightly larger in the middle than was the old Model 93 forearm. The second variation of the Model 1936s had enlarged semibeavertail forearms and no flute to the comb of the stock. Both of the new forearms were advertised as Sure-Grip semibeavertail. The catalog illustrations continued to show a fluted comb to the stock, even after the flute was no longer used. The Model 1936 ads and catalog illustrations indicated steel butt plates when, in fact, they were not steel, but hard rubber.

In addition to the change in designation and minor changes to the types manufactured, the Model 1936 carbine's pistol grip stock and the attachment of the front sight by means of dovetail (rather than the traditional straight stock and fixed base front sight) were departures from all previous Marlin carbines. Whether for better or worse, the sportsman would have to judge, but for the manufacturer they must have been cost-effective. The expensive fitting and soldering of the Model 93 Carbine front sight stud was eliminated by dovetailing the barrel for the new front sight, and the now-interchangeable pistol grip stock, among the three types, reduced tooling, fixturing, and inventory of noninterchangeable parts to a minimum.

In the 1937 price list, the Model 1936 Rifle, Carbine, and Sporting Carbine were all priced at $32.00 each.

MODEL 36

Production of the Model 1936 rifle was started late in 1936 for the 1937 market. The 1936 model designation was used into 1937, when it was changed to Model 36. By this time all Model 93s had been sold from an inventory that carried over along with the Model 1936. At this same time, changes were being made to improve the styling of the Model 1936 and first variations of the Model 36.

All Model 1936 and 36 carbines, sporting carbines, and rifles had pistol grip stocks, whereas the 1922–1937 Model 93s were standard with straight stocks. Also, Model 93 carbines and sporting carbines had forearm bands; only the rifle had a forearm tip. The Model 1936 and 36 sporting carbines both had forearm tips, as did the 93 rifle. The 93s had steel butt plates and the Model 1936 and 36s all had hard rubber plates. The Model 93s had square levers of the straight-stock type and

1936s and 36s had a new rounded-type lever to go with the pistol grip stocks.

The variations of the Model 36 are easily identified as follows:

First Variation: *C* prefix to serial number, case-colored receiver, beavertail forearm. Drilled and tapped for tang sight but not drilled and tapped for receiver sight.
Second Variation: *C* prefix to serial number, case-colored, drilled and tapped for receiver sight and tang sight.
Third Variation: *D* prefix, blued receiver that is sandblasted on top.

All variations were made in carbine, sporting carbine, and rifle styles from 1938 to 1947. In November 1940, a Model 36ADL was added to the line. This new rifle was a Deluxe

Model 36 Carbine (case-colored).

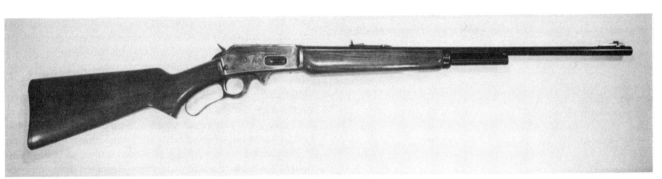

Model 36A Rifle (case-colored).

Model 36SC Sporting Carbine (blued receiver).

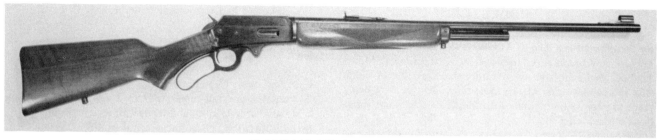

Model 36ADL Rifle (blued receiver).

Blued receiver of Model 36SC Sporting Carbine.

Roll-stamp on barrel of 36ADL rifle, which is also found marked on many Model 36A rifles. Whether this is by error or intentional is unknown. The reason for the A at the right-hand end of the roll-stamp is also unknown.

version of the Model 36A. The ADL was checked and equipped with detachable sling swivels and a leather sling strap.

The 1937 catalog descriptions of the Model 36s were as follows:

> *Model 36 Carbine:* Lever action repeater with solid frame. Barrel 20 inches, round tapered and crown muzzle. Steel, special smokeless, proof tested. Famous Ballard type of rifling. Receiver case hardened. Visible hammer. Checkered buttplate, unbreakable. Full pistol grip buttstock, shotgun style. Genuine American black walnut. Length, 13¼ inch; drop at comb, 1⅛ inch; drop at heel, 2⅞ inch. "Sure Grip" semi-beavertail forearm. Sights, silver bead front and flat top Rocky Mountain rear, excellent for quick, accurate shooting. Length overall, 38 inches. Weight, about 6½ pounds. Full magazine. 7 shots.
>
> *Model 36 Sporting Carbine:* Same general specification as the 1936 carbine. Steel forearm tip. New "Huntsman" nonglare ramp front sight with silver bead and quick detachable hood. ⅔ magazine. 6 shots.
>
> *Model 36 Rifle:* Same general specifications as the 1936

carbine. 24 inch barrel. Steel forearm tip. New "Huntsman" nonglare, ramp front sight with silver bead. Quick detachable hood. Rocky Mountain rear sight. Length overall, 42 inches. Weight, about 6¼ pounds. ⅔ magazine, 6 shots.

The 1941 description of the Model 36ADL indicated that this model had the same general specifications as the Model 36A rifle, but had special hand checkering on grip and forearm, a pistol grip cap, detachable swivels, and a 1-in. sling.

The 36ADL was illustrated and described from 1940 to 1947 as having a pistol grip cap. However, all the ADLs I have inspected have pistol grip stocks, but none have been noted as being originally manufactured with a grip cap. This, of course, may be another case wherein Marlin cataloged and described a planned change that did not happen; or perhaps I have not examined enough 36ADLs to find one with a pistol grip cap. It is most likely that none were produced with a grip cap, because the Model 336ADL, which replaced the Model 36ADL, was also lacking this feature.

One catalog discrepancy uncovered is the use of early Model 36 illustrations in catalogs and price lists after changes had taken place. An example is the use of Model 36 illustrations showing fluted stocks and small forearms after these features had been discontinued. Another error was an illustration in a catalog of case-colored receivers, where the text described the receiver and lever as being blued—which they were.

The Model 36 butt plates varied between periods of time. Also, two types of screws were used to attach the plate. Some variations had regular screwdriver-slotted heads, and others were mostly the Phillips cross-slot type. However, all types of butt plates and screws were mixed, as the supply of one was being phased out when another type was introduced.

The hammer of the Model 36 was described as either "new designed visible hammer" or "low hammer spur for low mounting of telescope." Serrations on the Model 36 hammer spur that were cross-hatched and embossed into the metal (as in the Model 93), as well as milled serrations across the spur, have been noted. The milled serrations were of two basic types. The first had a convex top to the hammer, in front of the serrations, and the latter type was flat at this point. These, too, are mixed among variations.

The forearm used on the Model 36s was a fat, bulbous thing that did not have the sleek and graceful lines of its predecessors, the Models 1936 and 93. Advertised as "Semi-beavertail forearm, designed to prevent canting," it is still standard on the Model 336 of today. Like white line spacers, it gives identity to the Marlin lever action center-fire rifles. But that is all!

The features of the Model 36 in comparison with the Model 1936 were as follows:

	MODEL 1936		MODEL 36		
	1st Var.	*2nd Var.*	*1st Var.*	*2nd Var.*	*3rd Var.*
Case Colored	Yes	Yes	Yes	No	No
Blued	No	No	No	Yes	Yes
Sandblasted	No	No	No	No	Yes
Cal. .30-30	Yes	Yes	Yes	Yes	Yes
Cal. .32 Spec.	Yes	Yes	Yes	Yes	Yes
20-in. Barrel	C & SC	C & SC	C & SC	C & SC	C & SC
24-in. Barrel	Rifle	Rifle	36A & DL	36A & DL	36A & DL
Full-length Magazine	C	C	C	C	C
²/₃ Magazine	R & SC	R & SC	36A & SC	A, ADL & SC	A, ADL & SC
Tang	Long	Short	Short	Short	Short
Prefix	None	"B"	"C"	"C"	"D"
Pistol Grip	Yes	Yes	Yes	Yes	Yes
Fluted Comb	Yes	No	No	No	No
Butt Plate	H.R.	H.R.	H.R.	H.R.	H.R.
Bull's-Eye	No	Yes	No	No	No
Checking	No	No	No	ADL	ADL
Swivels	No	No	No	ADL	ADL
Sling	No	No	No	ADL	ADL
D&T for Tang Sgt.	Yes	Yes	Yes	Yes	Yes
D&T for Rec. Sgt.	No	No	No	Yes	Yes
Forearm Tip	R & SC	R & SC	R & SC	A, ADL & SC	A, ADL & SC
Forearm Band	C	C	C	C	C
Mainspring	Flat	Coil	Lg Coil	Lg Coil	Lg Coil
Ramp Front Sight	R & SC	R & SC	R & SC	A, ADL & SC	A, ADL & SC
Dovetail Front	C	C	C	C	C
R.M. Rear	Yes	Yes	Yes	Yes	Yes
Forearm	Small	Large	Large	Large	Large

Code:
C—carbine; SC—sporting carbine; A—rifle; R—rifle; ADL—deluxe; H.R.—hard rubber; B—serial number prefix B; C—serial number prefix small c; D—serial number prefix D.

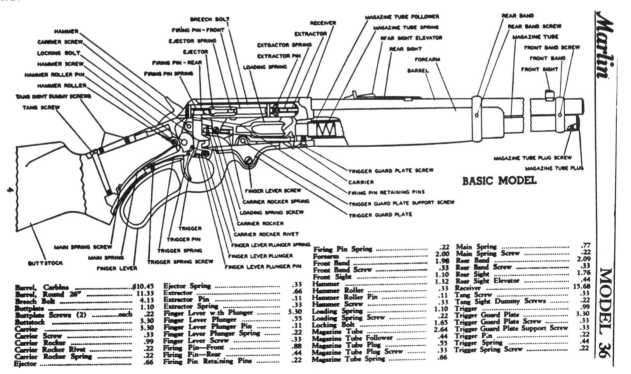

Barrel, Carbine	$10.45
Barrel, Round 26″	11.33
Breech Bolt	4.13
Buttplate	1.10
Buttplate Screws (2) each	.22
Buttstock	3.30
Carrier	3.30
Carrier Screw	.33
Carrier Rocker	.99
Carrier Rocker Rivet	.22
Carrier Rocker Spring	.22
Ejector	.66
Ejector Spring	.33
Extractor	.66
Extractor Pin	.11
Extractor Spring	.33
Finger Lever w.th Plunger	3.30
Finger Lever Plunger	.55
Finger Lever Plunger Pin	.11
Finger Lever Plunger Spring	.22
Finger Lever Screw	.33
Firing Pin—Front	.88
Firing Pin—Rear	.44
Firing Pin Retaining Pins	.22
Firing Pin Spring	.22
Forearm	2.00
Front Band	1.98
Front Band Screw	.33
Front Sight	1.10
Hammer	1.32
Hammer Roller	.33
Hammer Roller Pin	.11
Hammer Screw	.33
Loading Spring	1.10
Loading Spring Screw	.22
Locking Bolt	1.65
Magazine Tube	2.64
Magazine Tube Follower	.44
Magazine Tube Plug	.55
Magazine Tube Plug Screw	.33
Magazine Tube Spring	.66
Main Spring	.77
Main Spring Screw	.22
Rear Band	2.09
Rear Band Screw	.33
Rear Sight	1.76
Rear Sight Elevator	.44
Receiver	15.68
Tang Screw	.33
Tang Sight Dummy Screws	.22
Trigger	.99
Trigger Guard Plate	3.30
Trigger Guard Plate Screw	.33
Trigger Guard Plate Support Screw	.33
Trigger Pin	.22
Trigger Spring	.44
Trigger Spring Screw	.22

Model 36 parts listed in Marlin parts catalog.

The retail prices of the Model 36 were as follows:

Date	Carbine	Sporting Carbine	Rifle	A–DL
1937	$32.00	$32.00	$32.00	
1938	32.00	32.00	32.00	
Jan. 20, 1939	32.00	32.00	32.00	
Jan. 1, 1940	32.00	32.00	32.00	
July 1, 1940	28.76	28.76	31.29	
Nov. 30, 1940	32.00	32.00	34.85	44.68
May 26, 1941	33.00	33.00	36.00	45.85
Nov. 24, 1941	37.95	37.95	41.40	52.75
1942–1944	WW II—No sporting arms available.			
Jan. 22, 1945	38.50	38.50	42.00	53.50
Sept. 22, 1946	56.00	56.00	65.95	80.70
1948	61.45	61.45	72.55	87.50

MODEL 336

Included in this section are those lever action rifles in the Model 336 family that were manufactured under the original L.L. Hepburn design from 1949 to the present. The feature common to all the 336 variations included here is the round bolt, which was introduced in the Model 336 to replace the square one of the original design.

From the numerous variations of the Model 336 that have been manufactured, it would appear that every different style

Red-hot receiver during the forging process.

or type of lever action has been produced to satisfy the needs of all sportsmen. Not so! The quest goes on.

The only feature not available in Marlin lever action rifles is a rifle chambered for a cartridge effective out to 300 yards. However, Marlin lever action rifles are now the most popular lever gun used by sportsmen, and many are very capable to ranges of 200 yards. Of course, it is frequently a combination of the hunter's ability and the cooperation of the game that results in taking a trophy. The gun and ammunition are only two members of a four-element team; no matter how good they are, if the shot is not well placed by the hunter, he will not be successful. Frequently the gun and ammunition are blamed for poor performances. Taking a shot beyond the capability of the hunter, or cartridge, is difficult for most of us to admit. Knowing your equipment, knowing the capabilities of your cartridge, being sighted-in correctly, knowing the habits of the game, and knowing your skill level and limitations are the ingredients to success. Your Marlin lever action will do the job if given a fair chance!

Please note that the New Model 1894 models are included in the Model 1894 section, and the New Model 1895 rifles are in the Model 1895 section. All other round-bolt lever action center-fire models are discussed here.

A list of variations of the Model 336 is as follows:

Dates	Model Number	Type
1948–1983	Model 336C	Carbine
1948–1962	Model 336A	Rifle (first issue)
1948–1962	Model 336A	Deluxe Rifle
1948–1963	Model 336SC	Sporting Carbine
1954–1983	Model 336T	Texan
1954–1962	Model 336SD	Deluxe Sporting Carbine
1955–1960	Model 336SC	.219 Zipper
1962–1963	Model 336TDL	Deluxe Texan
1963–1964	Model 336 Marauder	16¼ inch barrel
1963–1964	Model 336 Magnum	Caliber .44 magnum
1970	Model 336	100th Anniversary Commemorative
1972	Model 336	Zane Grey Century
1973–1980	Model 336A	Rifle (second issue)
1973	Model 336 Octagon	
1983–1986	Model 336ER	Extra Range, caliber .356

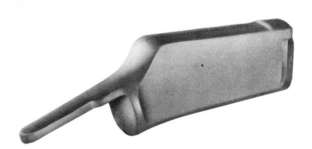

Forged receiver before any machining was done.

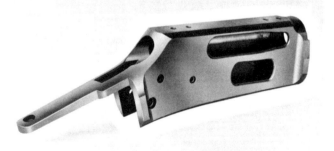

Partially finished Model 336 receiver.

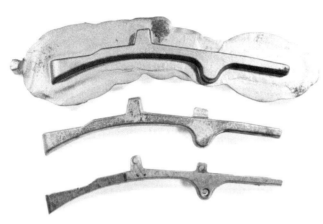

Top: *Trigger plate as forged.* Middle: *Trigger plate after flashing was removed and the piece was coined (straightened).* Bottom: *Trigger plate as machined and ready to be fitted to the receiver.*

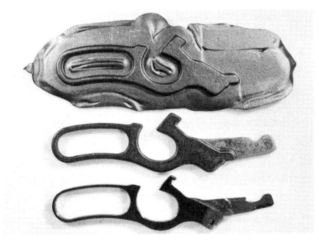

The three major steps in the fabrication of the 336 finger lever.

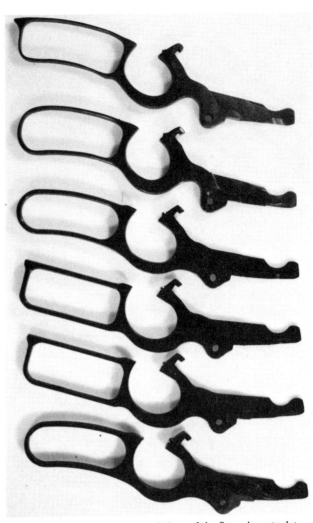

From top to bottom are the variations of the finger lever to date.

Dates	Model Number	Type
1984 to date	Model 336CS	
1984–1987	Model 336TS	
1988 to date	Model 336LTS	Lightweight
1980–1983	Model 375	Rifle
1965–1971	Model 444	Rifle
1971–1983	Model 444S	Rifle
1984 to date	Model 444SS	Rifle
1964–1983	Glenfield Models	
1984 to date	Promotion Model 30AS	

MODEL 336 CARBINE, LEVER ACTION, CALIBER .30–30 AND .32 SPECIAL CARBINE (1948–1950); MODEL 336C, LEVER ACTION, CALIBER .30–30 AND .32 SPECIAL (CALIBER .35 REM ADDED IN 1953) (1951–1983); AND MODEL 336CS, LEVER ACTION CARBINE (1984 TO DATE)

When introduced, the Model 336 had the word *carbine* as part of the model designation. Later it was changed to 336C.

With the introduction in 1948 of the Model 336, replacing the Model 36, Marlin incorporated a newly designed round-bolt mechanism that is still in production. The catalog information about the new gun read as follows:

ALL MARLIN 336 HIGH-POWER LEVER ACTION REPEATERS BUILT WITH NEW, RUGGED LOCKING MECHANISM.

All Marlin 336 Rifles and Carbines are built with a new, rugged locking system that assures smooth functioning. In this sturdy locking mechanism the round breech bolt is completely encased in the area of the locking bolt by a solid bridge of steel in the receiver. Round type breech bolt is made of alloy steel and is chrome-plated.

This massive locking bolt is firmly supported in the receiver and engages in the broad, deep locking surface of the breech bolt, furnishing a strong, safe breech for the .35 caliber cartridge and other cartridges for which the Marlin 336 rifles and carbines are made.

The round breech bolt was first used by the Marlin Firearms Co. in 1948 to replace the rectangular type bolt used in the Model 36 line of high-power repeaters. New refinements, the new round type breech bolt and the recent addition of the

Catalog illustration of the Model 336 parts in the fired position.

Catalog illustration of the Model 336 parts during extraction and cocking.

Catalog illustration of the 336 during loading.

Representative of the many changes made to parts of the Model 336 during 40 years of production are the two triggers and sears shown here. The left pair are the latest type. The right pair are of an earlier period.

new Micro-Groove barrel characterize Marlin's new group of 336's.

Equipped with the new type round breech bolt Marlin 336's assure cartridge feeding that is virtually jam-proof. And, with a newly designed extractor, these high-power repeaters function smoothly with the new bolt. Marlin's use of the round type breech bolt provides a refined and modern action, greater strength and a stream-line appearance due to smoothness of the new bolt's construction and its perfect fit to the action.

The time proven Marlin Safety firing pin operation is so engineered that at any time when the locking bolt is not in full engagement with the breech bolt — due to a partially open lever position — the rear and front firing pins are not in alignment and thus the gun cannot fire.

The Model 336 Carbine was described as follows:

The Marlin Model 336 Lever Action Carbine is a 7-shot carbine with full magazine. New type round breech bolt of alloy steel. Bolt chrome-plated and easily removed for cleaning and oiling. Redesigned carrier for positive feeding. New and more durable extractor. New matted receiver surface gives non-reflecting sighting plane. Solid top receiver, side ejection. 20″ round-tapered barrel of special smokeless steel. Crowned muzzle. Ballard type rifling. Full pistol grip buttstock, semi-beavertail forearm of American black walnut. New unbreakable coil main and trigger springs. Rocky Mountain rear sight for quick, accurate shooting. Bead front sight. Drilled and tapped for Lyman and other standard receiver sights. Low hammer spur for low mounting of telescope. All exposed metal parts blued. Overall length 38″; weight about 6½ pounds.

In 1951, the 336 Carbine was changed to the Model 336C Carbine.

The 1951 and 1952 catalogs illustrated the Model 336 Carbine as having a pistol grip stock with a grip cap and white line spacer. The cap was made so that the owner's initials could be engraved into an insert.

In 1953, the caliber .35 Remington cartridge was added to the Model 336C. The grip cap was no longer shown.

In 1956, Marlin stated that the 336C was drilled and tapped for telescope mounts, and Micro-Groove rifling was added in place of Ballard-type rifling in the center-fire lever actions.

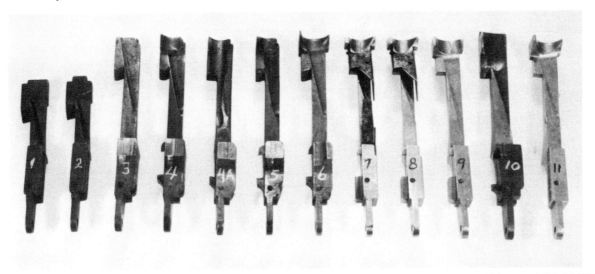

The various carriers used in Marlin center-fire lever action rifles were as follows: 1. Model 1889, 2. Model 1894, 3. Unknown, 4. Model 1893, 4A. Model 410, 5. Model 36, 6. Model 336 (first type), 7. Model 336 .44 magnum, 8. Model 444, 9. New Model 1895, 10. Old Model 1895, 11. Model 336.

The 1957 catalog illustrates the Model 336C with a pistol grip stock having a pistol grip cap and white line spacer. A hooded ramp front sight was also illustrated.

In 1959, gold-plated triggers were added; in 1960, the top and bottom of receivers were now sandblasted to reduce glare.

In 1962 the .32 Special cartridge was available in only the 336C, and the .32 Special cartridge was dropped from the Model 336 line in 1964.

In 1970, each Model 336C manufactured had a 100th-anniversary medallion embedded into the right side of the stock.

The hooded ramp front sight was dropped in 1971 in favor of a ramp sight without a hood. The Marlin/Osborne folding leaf rear sight became standard in 1971. In 1973, a new Wide-Scan front sight hood was added to a new ramp.

Marlin introduced a new method of fitting stocks to receivers in 1974. By burning the end of the stock by induction-heating the rear of the receiver and pressing the receiver and stock together, a close fit was achieved.

In 1982, gold-plated triggers were changed to blue.

In 1984, the new Marlin cross-bolt safety was added to the Model 336C and the model designation was changed to Model 336CS. Otherwise there were no changes to the 336C. Also in

1984, the caliber .375 Win. was added to the Model 336CS carbine, and a new type of hammer spur (Uncle Mike's) was introduced with all models having the new cross-bolt safety.

In 1987 the .375 Win. cartridge was dropped from the 336CS.

Model 336 receivers, trigger plates, hammers, levers, carriers, and locking bolts are all made from steel forgings, and over the years minor changes were made in them. For example, the trigger plate was changed at least four times. The first type did not have the trigger block mechanism of the next three variations. The first two having the trigger block device were either with or without a bridge of metal in front of the trigger. The third type that had the trigger block had a cross pin, instead of a bridge of metal, upon which the lever plunger operated. Changes in the method of making parts resulted in changes to some parts; some were interchangeable and others were not. The total variations of all the parts are too numerous to list here. Different variations and types of sights, however, are covered in the sight section. Included are variations of open buckhorn rear sights and hooded and nonhooded short ramps, long ramps, and dovetail drive-in beaded front sights that were used on the Model 336 rifle.

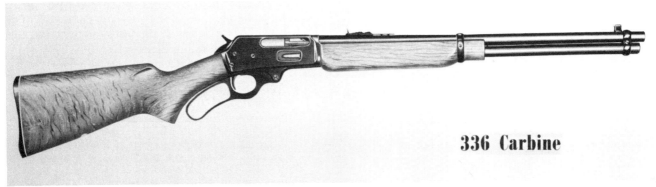

336 Carbine

Model 336 Carbine.

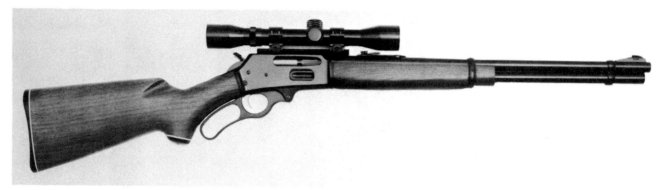

Model 336C (first variation).

MARLIN Model 336C

Model 336C (second variation).

The suggested retail prices of the Model 336C variations were as follows:

Year	Model 336C (Carbine)	Model 336CS
1949	$ 61.45	
1950–1952	68.30	
1953–1954	68.95 (.30–30)	
	78.95 (.35 Rem.)	
1955–1956	73.70	
1957–1958	76.95	
1959	80.75	
1960	82.00	
1961	84.95	
1962–1964	86.95	
1965–1967	89.95	
1968	94.95	
1969	99.95	
1970	105.00	
1971–1973	115.00	
1974	116.95	
1975	126.95	
1976	134.95	
1977	144.95	
1978	149.95	
1979	162.95	
1980	187.95	
1981	220.95	
1982	246.95	

Year	Model 336C (Carbine)	Model 336CS
1983	249.95	$256.95
1984		268.95
1985		281.95
1986		295.95
1987		313.95
1988		325.95

MODEL 336A, LEVER ACTION RIFLE (1ST ISSUE) (1948–1962); MODEL 336A, LEVER ACTION RIFLE (2ND ISSUE) (1973–1980); AND MODEL 336A-DELUXE (336ADL), LEVER ACTION RIFLE (1948–1962)

The first-issue Model 336A was like the Model 336 Carbine, except it had a 24-in. barrel and a forearm tip, instead of the barrel bands of the carbine. It also had a two-thirds magazine that held six cartridges.

The 1959 catalog listed the Model 336A as follows:

Lever action ⅔ tubular magazine repeating rifle. Available in calibers .30–30, .32 Special and .35. 24-inch round tapered blued steel barrel, crowned muzzle. Bishop style Monte Carlo stock. Pistol grip with grip cap. Finest quality walnut throughout. 6-shot capacity. Lyman 16 B folding leaf rear sight, ramp front sight with detachable hood. Semi-beaver-tail forend. Drilled and tapped for standard receiver sights and for Weaver and other top mount bases. All exposed metal parts blued. Matted receiver surface for non-glare

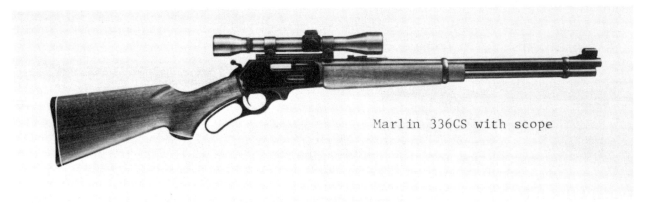

Model 336CS Carbine.

Model 336A Rifle (first variation).

sighting plane. Automatic side ejection, solid top receiver and low hammer spur permit lowest possible mounting of scopes. Overall length 42"; weight about 7 pounds depending on density of wood.

The second issue of the Model 336A was available from 1973 to 1980. It was described as follows:

> Marlin 336A Specifications: Same action as 336C, with 24" barrel, ½ magazine tube with 5-shot capacity, blued steel fore-end cap and sling swivels. Approx. 7 lbs. Available in either .30/30 Win. or .35 Rem. caliber.

The Model 336A was equipped with a hooded ramp front sight and a Marlin open buckhorn rear. In 1951, the .35 Rem. cartridge was added to the Model 336A and 336ADL. Sling swivels and a Monte Carlo stock were added in 1957. The stock was listed as a Bishop type. For other changes, see the Model 336C section above.

The Model 336A Deluxe rifle was listed as 336A Deluxe, 336A-DL, or 336ADL. These models are the same rifle and only differ from the Model 336A rifle by having a checked pistol grip and forearm, swivels, and a sling. The Model 336A Deluxe was available in .30–30 and .32 Special. The .35 Rem. cartridge was added to this model in 1951.

This model was described in 1949 as follows:

The Marlin Model 336A-DL is a 6-shot lever action repeater with ⅔ magazine. New type round breech bolt of alloy steel. Bolt chrome-plated and easily removed for cleaning barrel from breech. Re-designed carrier for positive feeding. New matted receiver surface gives non-reflecting sighting plane. Solid top receiver, side ejection. 24" round-tapered barrel of special smokeless steel. Crowned muzzle. "Huntsman" non-glare ramp front sight with bead, quick detachable hood. Ballard type rifling. Full pistol grip butt-stock, semi-beavertail forearm of American black walnut. New unbreakable coil main and trigger springs. Rocky Mountain rear sight. Drilled and tapped for Lyman and other standard receiver sights. Low hammer spur for low mounting of telescope. All exposed metal parts blued. Beautifully hand-checkered on grip and forearm. Detachable swivels and 1" high-grade leather sling strap. Length overall 42"; weight 6½ pounds.

In 1957, the Model 336ADL had a new stock designed by Bishop. It was different from the 336A stock of this period because it had a cheek piece. The rear sight was changed to a Lyman 16B folding leaf sight.

The suggested retail prices of the Model 336A and 336ADL were as follows:

Year	(1st Issue)	Model 336A	Model 336ADL
1949		$ 72.55	$ 87.50
1950	.30–30 – .32 Special	80.75	97.10
	.35 Rem.	90.75	

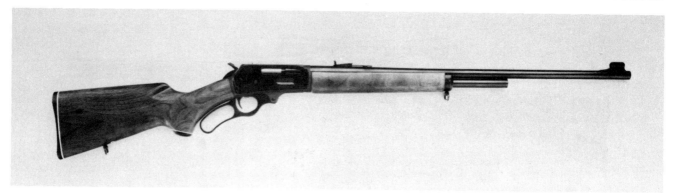

Model 336A Rifle (second variation).

Model 336A Rifle (third variation).

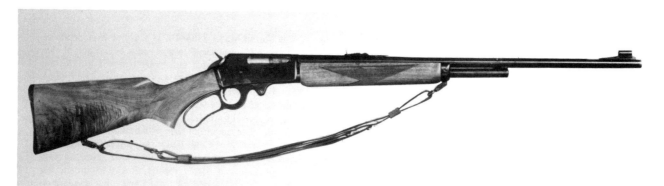

Model 336ADL, Deluxe Rifle.

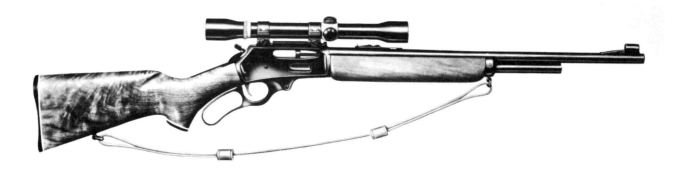

Model 336SC Sporting Carbine.

Year	(1st Issue)	Model 336A	Model 336ADL
1953	.30–30 – .32 Special	83.95	99.95
	.35 Rem.	89.95	109.95
1955–1956		84.75	100.80
1957–1958		89.95	99.95
1959–1960		90.75	100.80
1961		94.95	105.00
1962		96.95	107.00
	(2nd Issue)		
1973		119.95	
1974		121.95	
1975		132.95	
1976		141.95	
1977		151.95	
1978		156.95	
1979		170.95	
1980		195.95	

A total of 39,290 Model 336A rifles were manufactured between 1952 and 1980, and 5,217 Model 336ADLs were produced between 1952 and 1962. Production statistics for the years 1949 to 1951 are not available.

MODEL 336SC (SPORTING CARBINE) LEVER ACTION RIFLE (1949–1963) AND MODEL 336SD (DELUXE SPORTING CARBINE) LEVER ACTION RIFLE (1954–1962)

The Model 336C was considered the "regular carbine" and was marked *RC* on the barrel. The Sporting Carbine was marked *SC*.

The Model 336SC was similar to the Model 336A, except that it had a 20-in. instead of a 24-in. barrel. All changes made to the Model 336C and 336A were done to the Model 336SC at the same time.

The 1949 catalog listed the following information about the new 336SC:

The Marlin Model 336 Sporting Carbine is a 6-shot lever action carbine with ²/₃ magazine. This model has all the fine features of the 336 Carbine. It is equipped with new "Hunts-man" non-glare ramp front sight with bead and a quick detachable hood. 20″ round-tapered barrel of special smokeless steel. Overall length 38″; weight about 6¼ pounds.

The 1957 catalog added the following details for the Model 336SC:

Lever action ²/₃ tubular magazine repeater. 6-shot capacity. Available in calibers .30–30, .32 Special and .35. 20-inch round tapered blued steel barrel, crowned muzzle. Pistol grip with grip cap. New type breech bolt for greater strength. Automatic side ejection, solid top receiver and low hammer spur permit low scope mounting. Semi-beavertail forearm. Finest quality walnut throughout. Drilled and tapped for standard receiver sights and for Weaver and other top mount bases. Open rear sight, ramp front sight with detachable hood. All exposed metal parts blued. Matted receiver surface for non-glare sighting plane. Overall length 38½″; weight about 7 pounds depending on density of wood.

The Model 336SD was the "deluxe" version of the Model 336 sporting carbine. It had a Bishop-style Monte Carlo stock with checkering, and swivels and a sling added. Otherwise it was the same as the Model 336SC. It was described in the 1957 catalog as follows:

Deluxe Lever Action ²/₃ tubular magazine repeater. 7-shot capacity. Available in caliber .30–30, .32 Special and .35. Bishop style Monte Carlo stock. Expertly hand-checkered at grip and forend. Finest quality walnut throughout. Detachable swivels and 1″ high-grade leather sling strap. 20-inch round tapered blued steel barrel, crowned muzzle. Pistol grip with grip cap. New type breech bolt for greater strength. Automatic side ejection, solid top receiver and low hammer spur permit low scope mounting. Open rear sight, ramp front sight with detachable hood. Drilled and tapped for standard receiver sights and for Weaver and other top mount bases. All exposed metal parts blued. Matted receiver surface for non-glare sighting plane. Overall length 38½″; weight about 7½ pounds depending on density of wood.

Changes to the Model 336SC and 336SD were the same as those made to the other models in the 336 family. Please see descriptions of the previous models for more details.

Model 336T Texan Carbine (first variation).

Model 336T Texan Carbine (second variation).

Marlin 336TS

Model 336TS Carbine.

The suggested retail prices of the Model 336SC and 336SD were as follows:

Year		Model 336SC	Model 336SD
1949		$61.45	
1950	.30–30 – .32 Special	68.30	
	.35 Rem.	77.70	
1953	.30–30 – .32 Special	68.95	
	.35 Rem.	78.95	
1955–1956		73.70	$ 90.75
1957–1958		76.95	89.95
1959		80.75	90.75
1960		82.00	94.95
1961		84.95	99.95
1962		86.95	102.95
1963		86.95	

Brass saddle ring fitted to some Model 336s.

Between 1952 and 1963, 74,215 Model 336SC carbines were manufactured; from 1955 to 1962, 4,392 Model 336SD (deluxe) carbines were manufactured.

MODEL 336 MICRO-GROOVE ZIPPER, SPORTING CARBINE (1955–1959)

The Model 336 Zipper was chambered for the .219 Zipper cartridge. It was introduced as a lightweight lever action varmint rifle, and was described in 1955 as follows:

> This fast-handling, light weight lever action chambered for the hard-hitting .219 Zipper cartridge is made expressly for farmers and ranchers who are faced with a pest control problem, as well as for the shooter who enjoys all types of varmint hunting. It is the only rifle available today for the .219 cartridge, a cartridge specially suitable for doing away with larger types of pests.
>
> It has the same fine design and engineering features as the popular Model 336 Sporting Carbine, except for the chambering and that it comes with Micro-Groove rifling. Overall 38 inches; weight about 6¾ pounds depending on density of wood.

It should be noted here that the weight listed above is 6¾ pounds. The 1956 and later catalogs list the weight as 7¾ pounds. This weight difference is because when first manufactured, the barrel's outside dimensions were the same as for the caliber .30–30 Model 336SC. In 1956, because of marginal accuracy results, the barrel diameter was increased by about 1/10 inch at the muzzle. This change resulted in about one pound more weight in the second variation without any marked improvement in accuracy.

The 1957 description of the second-variation 336 Zipper was as follows:

> Lever action ⅔ tubular magazine repeater in caliber .219 Zipper. 6-shot capacity. 20-inch round tapered blued steel barrel, crowned muzzle. Pistol grip with grip cap. New type breech bolt for greater strength. Automatic side ejection, solid top receiver, low hammer spur permit lowest possible scope mounting. Semi-beavertail forearm. Finest quality walnut throughout. Open rear sight, ramp front sight with detachable hood. Drilled and tapped for standard receiver sights and for Weaver and other top mount bases. All exposed metal parts blued. Matted receiver surface for non-glare sighting plane. Overall length 38½ inches; weight about 7¾ pounds depending on density of wood.

The Model 336 Zipper failed in the marketplace because of poor accuracy and a short barrel life. If conventional rifling had been used, probably both would have been improved. Also, the varmint hunter frame of reference for accuracy was 1-inch, or better, 10-shot groups at 100 yards, which could be obtained from bolt action or custom single-shot varmint rifles. The fact that a lever action rifle having a tubular magazine will generally not shoot as accurately as some other types of more expensive rifles has always been a hurdle the lever action manufacturer has been faced with. Most experienced custom rifle builders and dedicated varmint hunters could have predicted that the .219 Zipper cartridge, a lever action rifle, and Micro-Groove rifling would not pass the test of excellence needed in a varmint rifle.

The Model 336 Zipper Sporting Carbine suggested retail prices were as follows:

Year	Model 336 Zipper
1955–1956	$73.70
1957–1958	76.95
1959	80.79

A total of 3,230 Model 336 .219 Zipper Sporting Carbines were manufactured. About 10 of this number were Deluxe Sporting Carbines (336SD Zipper).

The caliber .219 Zipper cartridge is no longer in commercial production, and Marlin can no longer furnish barrels for this model.

MODEL 336T (TEXAN), LEVER ACTION, CENTER-FIRE CARBINE (1954–1983); MODEL 336TDL (DELUXE TEXAN), LEVER ACTION, CENTER-FIRE CARBINE (1962–1963); MODEL 336 MARAUDER, 16¼-INCH BARREL CARBINE (1963–1964); MODEL 336, .44 MAGNUM, 20-INCH BARREL CARBINE (1963–1964); AND MODEL 336TS "TEXAN," LEVER ACTION CARBINE (1984–1987)

The 1957 catalog described the straight-stocked Model 336T (Texan) as follows:

> Model 336T: Lever action full tubular magazine repeater. 7-shot capacity. Straight grip for scabbard carrying. 20-inch round tapered blued steel barrel, crowned muzzle. Available in calibers .30–30 and .35. New type breech bolt for greater strength. Automatic side ejection, solid top receiver and low hammer spur permit low scope mounting. Semi-beavertail forearm. Finest walnut throughout. Drilled and tapped for standard receiver sights and for Weaver and other top mount bases. Open rear sight, ramp front sight with detachable hood. All exposed metal parts blued. Matted receiver surface for non-glare sighting plane. Overall length 38½"; weight about 6¾ pounds depending on density of wood.

About 1959, a ramp front sight with a detachable hood was introduced to this model. Like the Model 336C, the Texan had barrel bands, but the forearm was not as large. It was slimmer and more like the pre-WW I forearms.

In 1963, the caliber .44 magnum cartridge was added to the Model 336T, and was then dropped in 1964. A brass saddle ring was added to the left side of the Model 336T in 1965, and the .35 Rem. cartridge was dropped from the Model 336T this same year. In 1967, the .44 magnum cartridge was dropped.

A 100th-year commemorative medallion was embedded into each buttstock manufactured in 1970.

In 1971, the 336T lever was changed to the square type that was used on the octagon-barrel models. Also in 1971, a ramp front sight without a hood was also introduced, the saddle ring was eliminated, and a new folding semibuckhorn rear sight was introduced.

In 1972 the Marlin Wide-Scan front sight with hood was introduced. Stock flutes in the comb of the Model 336T were eliminated in 1976.

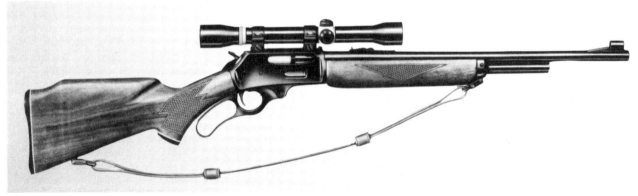

Model 336SD Deluxe Sporting Carbine.

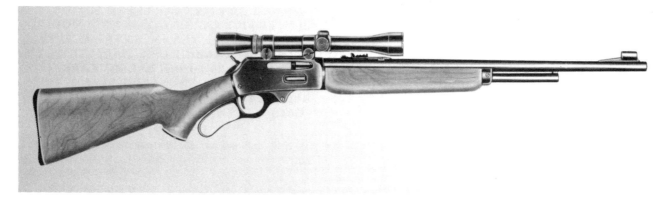

Model 336SC Zipper.

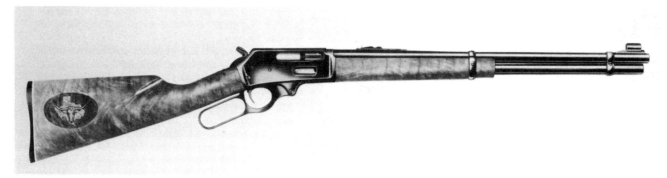

Model 336 Deluxe Texan.

In 1982, the gold-plated steel triggers were changed to blued steel triggers. The barrel length of the Model 336T was changed from 20 inches to 18½ inches in 1983. The capacity of the magazine remained at 6 cartridges.

In 1984, a cross-bolt safety was added to the Model 336T and at that time the designation was changed to 336TS. All other features remained the same except that a new type of offset hammer spur (Uncle Mike's) was now furnished.

In 1988, the Model 336TS was replaced by the new Model 336LTS, which has a 16¼-in. round barrel, straight stock, square lever, carbine-type front sight, and a 5-shot full-length magazine.

Marlin had introduced a Model 336 chambered for the .44 magnum cartridge in 1963. It was described as the same as the 336 Marauder, except it had a 20-in. barrel. It was first called the Model 336 .44 Magnum. Then in 1964 it was shown as just another cartridge choice in the Model 336T. The last year the caliber .44 magnum was available in the Model 336T was 1967.

The 1963 Model 336 Marauder was described as follows:

"NEW! MARLIN 336 MARAUDER CARBINE—You can get this compact new carbine into action fast! Straight grip, slim forend, tapered 16¼″ Micro-Groove barrel. Choice of popular .30/30 or brush-busting .35 caliber. Solid top receiver and side ejection give you low, centered scope mounting! Specifications: 6 quick shots; approx. wt 6¼ lbs., 34¾ inc. overall lgth; American black walnut stocks; precision open rear, bead front sights; gold-plated trigger; drilled and tapped for receiver sights, scope mounts; free offset hammer spur for use with scope—works right or left side.

The Model 336 .44 magnum carbine was listed as follows in 1963:

NEW! MARLIN .44 MAGNUM—Hard-hitting new carbine combines smashing .44 Magnum power with "dead center" Micro-Groove accuracy! Tops for heavy-timber deer and bear hunting. Big capacity. Solid top receiver and side ejection for low, centered scope mounting. Light and fast, powerful and sure! Available June 1, 1963. $86.95.

Specifications: Same as Marauder, but 20-inch Micro-Groove barrel; 38½ inches overall length; approximately 7 pounds; 10 power-packed shots.

MODEL 336 ZANE GREY CENTURY (1972)

In 1972, when Marlin still had the capability to make octagon barrels, a special 336 was produced to commemorate the 100th anniversary of the birth of Zane Grey, the famous writer of Western stories, and world-record fisherman. Marlin's news release about this commemorative rifle was as follows:

Marlin celebrates the 100th anniversary of the birth of the Giant of Western Writers with the limited edition Zane Grey Century rifle. Zane Grey breathed the spirit of the West into two generations of Americans with his classic yarns, "Riders of the Purple Sage," "The Heritage of the Desert," "Nevada," and over 50 others. More than 60 million volumes have been sold. And legions of readers are still riding the range with Zane Grey's straight-shooting, hell-for-leather heroes.

Because Zane Grey favored the lever action rifle, we have

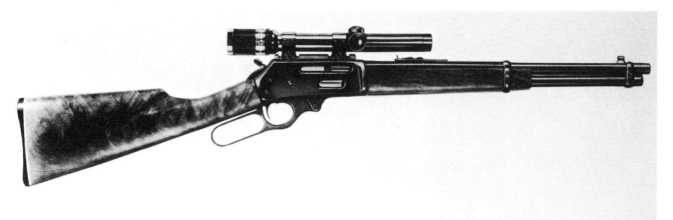

Model 336 Marauder Carbine.

Model 336 Magnum (caliber .44 magnum).

Model 336 100th-Year Commemorative.

Model 336 Zane Grey Century.

made this handsome new Marlin a rifle he'd be proud to see bear his brand. A special version of the famed Marlin 336 .30/30 cal. deer gun, the Zane Grey Century features a traditional 22″ fully tapered octagon barrel, cartridge brass buttplate and fore-end cap, and select American walnut stock with classic pistol grip. Inlaid in the receiver is a portrait medallion in gleaming cartridge brass inscribed "Zane Grey 1872-1972."

Only 10,000 Zane Grey Century rifles will be manufactured, consecutively numbered from 1 to 10,000. Suggested retail price is only $150.00.

The Zane Grey Century is sure to go over big with collectors and Zane Grey devotees. And for hunters who seek more than just a superb lever action, the Zane Grey Century combines classic frontier styling with the solid strength and functional dependability of our most famous deer rifle.

The 1972 catalog promoted along with the rifle an exclusive introductory offer to acquire the Zane Grey Library. By sending $1.00 to the Zane Grey Library in Roslyn, N.Y., the sender would receive three books on a trial offer. Thereafter, other volumes would be sent for $3.39 each. As is usual, the reservation for additional books could be cancelled at any time.

The suggested retail price of the Zane Grey Century was $150.00.

Although advertised that the Zane Grey Century would be limited to 10,000 units, the total manufactured was only 7,871.

MODEL 336 OCTAGON, LEVER ACTION, CALIBER .30/30 RIFLE (1973)

In 1973, Marlin introduced a limited run of octagon-barreled rifles. By so doing, it made use of the special octagon-barrel-making machinery still on hand from making the 1970 100th year commemorative models.

The Model 336 Octagon was described as having the same action as the Model 336T with a classic fully tapered 22-in. octagon barrel, traditional hard-rubber rifle butt plate, and an American walnut straight stock. The forearm was of the rifle type with a forearm tip. The lever was the new square type and the front sight was a dovetail type with a gold bead. The trigger was blued steel and the full-length magazine held 6 shots. The rifle weighed 7 pounds. It was made in caliber .30–30 only.

The Model 336 Octagon's suggested retail price was $135.00. Only 2,414 Model 336 Octagon rifles were manufactured.

MODEL 336, LEVER ACTION, CALIBER .30–30, CARBINE, SERIAL NUMBER 3,000,000

In 1979, Marlin reached a milestone in its production of center-fire lever action rifles. The three-millionth Model 336 came off the production line that year. To commemorate the occasion, Marlin had the carbine engraved, gold inlaid, and beautifully stocked, and then gave it to the NRA for display in the NRA Museum.

The delicate engraving and gold inlay work on the 3,000,000th Marlin 336 was done by Dan Goodwin in his classic style, and the handmade stock and forearm of AAA Fancy American walnut was done by Fred Weinig of the Reinhart Fajen Company of Warsaw, Mo.

The right side of the receiver has the Marlin horse and rider inlaid in gold with the detail of the design engraved into the gold. The left side has the classic Marlin name inlaid in gold, and the serial number 3,000,000 is inlaid in gold on the top tang. A gold band around the barrel, just in front of the receiver, adds a touch of class only found on engraved high-art Marlins of old. The gold-plated bolt and trigger add to the symmetry of the gold and blue colors of the other parts.

The stock and forearm are flawless, with the fit of metal to wood like they grew together. The checkering is of a classic style similar to that done by Marlin craftsmen over 80 years ago. The Niedner-style steel butt plate adds quality and beauty to an already super example of a firearm artificer's work.

One of the finest examples of a modern Marlin Model 336, this one will always be available to view through the courtesy of the National Rifle Association and the National Firearms Museum.

MODEL 336ER (EXTRA RANGE), LEVER ACTION, CALIBER .356 WIN. RIFLE (1983–1986)

The Model 336ER was introduced in 1983. It was first advertised as being chambered for both the .307 Win. and .356 Win. cartridges. But Marlin never put the .307 model into production.

The .356 cartridge had only limited interest among sportsmen, even though Marlin described the rifle as having new and interesting characteristics, as follows:

The Marlin Firearms Company announces a new lever-action rifle chambered for the powerful 356 Win. cartridge.

Model 336 Octagon.

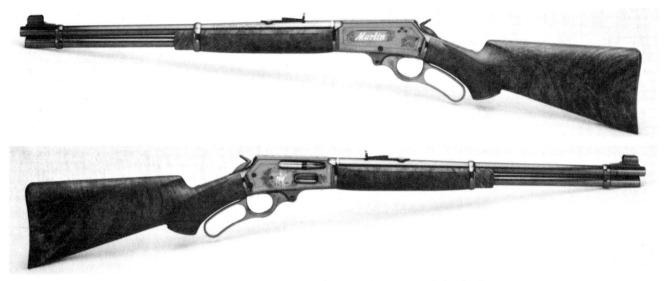

Top: *Marlin Model 336, serial number 3,000,000.* Bottom: *Left side of same.*

Marlin 336ER

Model 336ER (Extra Range).

Ballistics figures for this cartridge are quite impressive, and result in rifles with excellent performance at ranges well beyond 200 yards. The new Marlin Extra-Range (Model 336ER) joins the popular line of Marlin lever action center fire rifles, which includes Models 336C, 336T, 1894, 1894C, 375, 1895S and 444S.

The Extra-Range has Marlin's classic lever action styling and quality. Its action is machined from six solid steel forgings that are heat treated to provide even greater strength and durability. It features a solid top receiver with true side ejection, allowing low centered scope mounting. It also has quick detachable sling swivels, leather carrying strap, and a rubber butt pad.

The pistol grip stock is made from genuine American black walnut with a fluted comb. In addition, the Model 336ER features a new hammer block safety.

The new 336ER is 38½ inches long, weighs 6¾ pounds, and has a five-shot tubular magazine and 20 inch barrel. The new rifles will be available in June 1983.

The suggested retail prices of the Model 336ER were as follows:

Year	Model 336ER
1983	$283.95
1984	302.95
1985–1986	323.95

A total of 2,441 of the Model 336ER were manufactured.

MODEL 336LTS, LEVER ACTION, CALIBER .30/30 CARBINE (1988 TO DATE)

In 1988 Marlin, in deference to the wishes of the lever action fans and sportsmen of America, introduced a new short-barreled, straight-stocked carbine similar to the Marauder of the 1963–1964 period. Feeling the name "Marauder" inappropriate for a sporting firearm in today's society, Marlin felt that "Lightweight" would be a more descriptive designation for the new model. Therefore, the old Texan (originally with a 20-in. barrel and later with an 18½-in. barrel) and the old Marauder models are now the Model 336LTS. The *S* indicates it has the new cross-bolt safety. The Model 336TS has now been discontinued.

The 1988 catalog stated the following about the Model 336LTS:

> Here's a new version of the famous 336 that's built for lightning fast handling. Thanks to its short 16½ inch barrel and scaled down forearm, the 336LTS weighs in at 6½ pounds. An ideal scabbard gun, this little .30/30 features an American black walnut stock, a rubber rifle butt pad, and super-accurate Micro-Groove® rifling.

> The Model 336LTS is in caliber .30–30 only. It has a 5-shot full length magazine tube. The buttstock has a straight grip and the lever is the "classic" square type. The rear sight is the Marlin folding buckhorn type and the front sight is a drive-in dovetail carbine sight with a head. The overall length is 34⅜ inches and it weighs 6½ pounds.

The 1988 suggested retail price of the Model 336LTS was $325.95.

MODEL 375, LEVER ACTION, CALIBER .375 RIFLE (1980–1983)

The Model 375 was introduced in 1980 in the new Winchester .375 cartridge, and was styled much like the Models 444 and 1895. It was described as follows:

> The latest addition to our line of big-caliber woods rifles. A classic Marlin lever action, chambered for the potent new 375 Win. cartridge.

Like all Marlin lever guns, the 375's action is machined from six steel forgings, and its solid top, side-ejecting receiver allows low, centered scope mounting. It features a 20″ Micro-Groove® barrel, 5-shot tubular magazine, folding semi-buckhorn rear sight, and a ramp front sight with Wide-Scan™ hood. The stock is genuine American black walnut, with fluted comb, full pistol grip, and a new rubber rifle butt pad. Overall length 38½ inches. Weight about 6¾ pounds.

The .375 cartridge was developed by Winchester for its Model 94 rifle. It is a takeoff on the old .38–55 cartridge, but is a lot more powerful. It must not be used in guns chambered for the .38–55. Damage or injury could result.

The .375 was a good cartridge that had promise for lever action-type rifles used in hunting at short ranges. Its downfall was the nonavailability of the ammunition in the marketplace, and the fact that only two companies were manufacturing rifles chambered for it.

Short-lived and now a Marlin collectible, the Model 375 was a fine rifle that was not totally accepted by sportsmen.

The suggested retail prices of the Model were as follows:

Year	Model 375
1980	$210.95
1981	250.95
1982	280.95
1983	283.95

A total of 16,315 Model 375 rifles were manufactured.

Model 336LTS (Lightweight).

Model 375 Rifle.

MODEL 444, LEVER ACTION, CALIBER .444 MARLIN RIFLE (1965-1971); MODEL 444S, LEVER ACTION, CALIBER .444 MARLIN RIFLE (1971-1983); MODEL 444SS, LEVER ACTION, CALIBER .444 MARLIN RIFLE (1984 TO DATE)

The Model 444 rifle was introduced in 1965 having a 24-in. barrel, and was the most powerful lever action rifle on the market, with more than 1½ tons of energy at the muzzle. It was designed for hunting any North American game.

The Model 444 has the same basic lever action mechanism as the Model 336 that was modified to handle the potent .444 cartridge. The cartridge was the brainchild of Thomas Robinson and Arthur Burns, Marlin's director of research and development and metallurgist, respectively. The .444 cartridge case was developed from an unfinished caliber .30-06 case that was drawn straight, but without the head finished, so that it could be turned with an extractor rim, rather than a rimless cannelure. Mr. Burns made the presentation to Remington, presenting also the prototype rifle and a pressure gauge, seeking Remington's interest in producing the new cartridge. Earl Larson of Remington carried the project through the usual committee presentations and succeeded in getting this new Marlin cartridge into Remington's production. It was first loaded with the 240-grain .44 magnum pistol bullet. In 1980, again with Mr. Larson's help, Remington added a 265-grain loading that improved the performance of the Model 444 greatly.

Early .444 experimental cartridges were head-stamped *R-P 30-06 SPRG*. Later ones were head-stamped *R-P-4-Mag*. When finally adopted for production, the head stamp became *R-P 444 MARLIN*. Remington has been the only commerical manufacturer of the .444 Marlin cartridge. However, Hornady's 265-grain bullet for the 444 has been available for the handloader since 1961. The 444 delivered 3,070 foot-pounds of energy at 2,400 feet per second.

The Model 444 held 4 cartridges in the magazine and one in the chamber, for 5 shots. It had a 24-in. Micro-Groove barrel until reduced to 22 inches in 1971. It weighed 7½ pounds and was 42½ inches overall in length. The straight stock was walnut with a Monte Carlo comb when introduced. Also, in 1971 the stock was changed to a pistol grip sporter type. The model designation was also changed at that time to the Model 444S (Sporter). The rifle now weighed 7½ pounds and was 40½ inches long. A recoil pad butt plate was standard for the Model 444 and was needed to soften the substantial recoil of this model. The rear sight was the Lyman 16B adjustable folding leaf sight until 1974, when it was changed to the Marlin/Osborne folding open sight and a hooded ramp front sight was added. In 1976, the two barrel bands were eliminated in favor of the forearm tip system of retaining the forearm. This gave the Model 1895 a true "Sporter" look. Quick detachable (QD) swivels and a sling were standard for the Model 444 until 1988, when only swivel studs were furnished.

In 1984, Marlin added a new cross-bolt safety to the

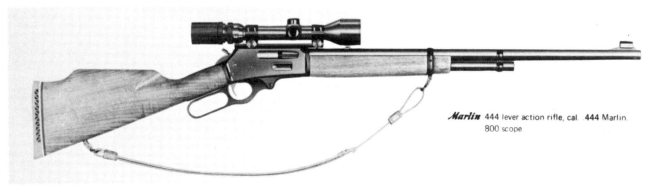

Marlin 444 lever action rifle, cal. 444 Marlin. 800 scope

Model 444 Rifle (first variation).

Model 444 Rifle (second variation).

Model 444S Rifle.

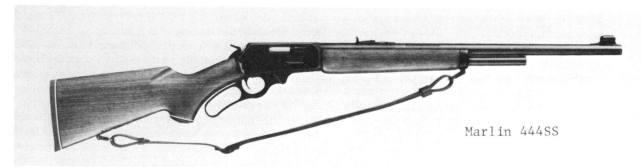

Model 444SS Rifle (first variation).

Model 444SS Rifle (second variation).

Model 444. At that time the model designation was again changed. The new model is now the Model 444SS.

The 1965 catalog included information about "Knock-Out values." Knock-Out value was described for the 444 as follows:

Although muzzle velocity and energy are commonly used as comparative figures to weigh one cartridge against another, they lack certain elements which bear a direct relationship to shocking power. These factors include bullet diameter, shape and construction features—all of which are vitally important in translating sheer energy—produced by velocity and bullet weight—into shocking power. Shocking power may be defined as the transmission of the energy to massive bone and muscle in dangerous animals.

Certain formulas have been used over the years to incorporate all the factors involved in shocking power.

One formula was worked out by the American expert, Elmer Keith; another by African expert, John Taylor. Working with these formulas, Marlin's Research & Development Department had up-dated them and applied the factors to several modern loads for comparison.

The mighty Marlin .444 has a higher Knock-Out value than even the .338 Winchester Magnum at ranges beyond 100 yards! At 150 yards, its K-O score dwarfs even the .300 H&H Magnum and .30–06. Yet the .444's recoil is approximately the same as the .30–06 and far less than the .338. And, the smooth Marlin lever action gives you much faster repeat shots than any bolt action. This tremendous shocking power, plus the fast-handling of the popular Marlin lever action, provides you with the greatest power package available for the largest North American game.

The suggested retail prices of the Model 444 were as follows:

Year	Model 444	Model 444S	Model 444SS
1965–1968	$124.95		
1969	129.95		
1970	135.00		
1971	145.00	$145.00	
1972–1975		145.00	
1976		152.95	

Year	Model 444	Model 444S	Model 444SS
1977		163.95	
1978		167.95	
1979		182.95	
1980		210.95	
1981		250.95	
1982		280.95	
1983		283.95	
1984			$302.95
1985			323.95
1986			339.95
1987			367.95
1988			385.95

GLENFIELD LEVER ACTION CENTER-FIRE RIFLES

The original purpose of the use of the name Glenfield goes back to when mass-merchandisers and chain outlets wanted brand names that would be identified with their businesses. There was also a need for manufacturers to protect their first-line models from being "footballed" around by price cutters. That's how the name Glenfield came into being. By having a separate series of models with a less expensive cosmetic appearance but with no less quality in material or workmanship for the big dealers, Marlin protected the small shops and stores handling the Marlin line.

In recent years, the mass-merchandisers no longer prefer the brand names of old. They now want the top-of-the-line items. To meet the demand, Marlin has dropped the use of the name Glenfield. Some of the later Glenfield models are now sold under a new model number and under the Marlin name, without material change to the Glenfield configuration.

Marlin marketed the following lever action center-fire rifles under the Glenfield name:

Dates	Model
1964–1965	Model 36G
1966–1972	Model 30
1973–1983	Model 30A
1979–1980	Model 30GT
1983	Model 30AS

The Model 36G was a no-frills variation of the regular Model 336. It was available only in caliber .30–30. It had a hardwood (birch) pistol grip stock, 4 shots, half magazine, 20-in. barrel, hard-rubber butt plate without a white line spacer, and a beaded dovetail front sight. It was drilled and tapped for scope and receiver sights. The Model 36G was a great woods gun at low cost. It was replaced by the Model 30 in 1966.

The suggested retail prices of the Model 36G were as follows:

Year	Model 36G
1964	$83.95
1965	84.95

A total of 5,930 Model 36G carbines were manufactured.

Glenfield 30 lever action rifle, cal. 30-30.
Glenfield 400 scope.

Glenfield Model 30 (first variation).

Glenfield Model 30 lever action rifle, cal. 30-30
Glenfield Scope 400

Glenfield Model 30 (second variation).

Glenfield Model 30A (first variation).

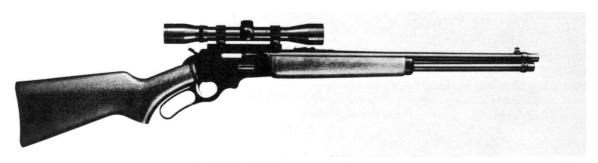

Glenfield Model 30A (second variation).

Glenfield Model 30GT.

The Model 36G was changed to the Model 30 in 1966; however, no other change was made at that time. In 1969, the Model 30 Glenfield had impressed checking added to the pistol grip and the forearm.

A total of 77,603 Model 30 Glenfield carbines were manufactured.

In 1971, the Model 30 was changed to the Model 30A when the half magazine was changed to a full-length magazine. The magazine capacity is now 6 shots, making the 30A a 7-shot carbine.

A total of 268,905 Model 30As were manufactured.

In 1979, Marlin introduced a Model 30GT (Texan), .30–30, straight-stocked model that was the same as the Model 30A, except for an 18½-in. barrel and the straight stock. The lever was square instead of round and the magazine tube was full length. It held 6 cartridges, as did the 30A magazine.

The Model 30GT remained in the Marlin line for only 1979 and 1980 and proves the popularity of the pistol grip stock over the straight grip stock. Pistol grip stocks are in demand 10 to 1 over the straight-grip stock.

The suggested retail prices of the Glenfield Model 30GT were as follows:

Year	Price
1979	$158.95
1980	174.95

A total of 7,737 of the Model 30GT were manufactured.

In 1982, the impressed checking was discontinued. In 1983, Marlin introduced a cross-bolt safety to the Model 30A. It then became the Model 30AS. Otherwise, it was the same as the Model 30A. Also in 1983, the name *Glenfield* was discontinued, which resulted in the Glenfield Model 30AS becoming the Marlin Model 30AS.

The suggested retail prices of the Glenfield Models 30, 30A, and 30AS were as follows:

Year	Model 30	Model 30A	Model 30AS
1966–1967	$ 86.95		
1968	89.95		
1969	94.95		
1970	99.95		
1971–1972	105.00		
1973		$105.00	
1974		109.95	
1975		118.95	
1976		124.95	
1977		136.95	
1978		140.95	
1979		158.95	
1980		174.95	
1981		205.95	
1982		230.95	
1983		232.95	$239.95

Production of the Glenfield Model 30 and 30A was as follows:

Model	Total
30	79,815
30A	336,113

PROMOTION MODEL 30AS (1984 TO DATE)

When Marlin discontinued the use of the Glenfield line of economy models, the Glenfield Model 30AS remained in production as the Marlin Model 30AS.

The Marlin 30AS was identical to the Glenfield Model 30AS and had many of the Model 336 features, but at an attractive price. The Model 30AS is considered by many sportsmen as the best buy of all Marlin .30–30s.

The suggested retail prices of the Promotion Model 30AS were as follows:

Year	Model 30AS
1984	$249.95
1985	253.95
1986	244.95
1987	261.95
1988	277.95

MODEL 39

The Marlin lever action caliber .22 rifle was invented by L.L. Hepburn and first introduced as the Model 1891. The Model 1891 developed into the Model 1892. When made into a takedown variation by Mr. Hepburn, it was identified as the Model 1897. The Models 1897 and 1892 continued in production until 1915, when Marlin was acquired by a syndicate interested in making machiné guns. After WW I, the old sporting arms business was acquired by John Moran, who formed The Marlin Firearms Corporation. The first catalog of this new company was issued in 1922. Included in this catalog were those models the new corporation was going to manufacture and sell. Among them was a lever action caliber .22 rifle called the Model 39. The prewar Model '92 and Model '97 were not listed.

The Model 39 rifle was originally designed by the Marlin-Rockwell Corporation before the decision to sell the sporting arms business had been made. Examples of Model 39s marked *Marlin–Rockwell* are very rarely encountered and bring a premium among collectors.

The only factory record about the Marlin–Rockwell Model 39, except for rifles so marked, is a drawing dated May 16, 1919 that has the Marlin-Rockwell Corporation name and address and the usual drawing information in the lower right-hand corner.

The new Model 39 was identical to the pistol grip-stocked, octagon-barreled Model 1897/97. It was manufactured from 1922 until 1936, when it was replaced by the Model 39A.

The Model 39 was described in the 1922 catalog as follows:

Model No. 39 Rifle: .22 caliber, rim fire, take-down, pistol grip, 24 inch octagon barrel, full magazine. 25 shots, weight about 5¾ pounds. It has lever action, side ejection, solid top, closed in frame; genuine ivory bead front and flat top Rocky Mountain rear sights; a wonderful combination of sights for a .22 rifle; blued barrel and case-hardened receiver; hard rubber buttplate; length over all 41 inches; length taken down, 27½ inches; length of buttstock, 13⅛ inches; drop at comb, 1¾ inches; drop at heel, 2⅞ inches; pistol grip stock and forearm of black walnut; rifle handles at one loading: 25 short, 20 long or 18 long rifle cartridges.

Handles without change or adjustment all .22 short, long and long-rifle cartridges. The only .22 caliber repeater with lever action.

The Marlin Model No. 39 lever action rifle is the most accurate .22 repeating rifle in the world, and is the choice of expert shooters for hunting small game such as rabbits,

Marlin 30AS with scope

Marlin Model 30AS.

How will you buy your rifle? On tradition? Will you take whatever the dealer offers?—Or, will you carefully select the one best rifle for you—and **insist on getting the rifle you want?**

Marlin
.22 Repeating Rifles

There are 50 years of tradition behind these Marlin rifles—50 years' experience in making the best in sporting firearms. 50 years of development—consequently there is not an old-style gun in the entire Marlin line. **Marlin invented side ejection in firearms**—Marlin discarded all old-style top-ejecting guns 30 years ago.

The fundamental requirements in a .22 repeater are: **Accuracy**—the Ballard rifling has made Marlin accuracy famous; **good sights**, to get full benefit of accuracy—Marlin .22's are the only repeaters regularly furnished with the superior Ivory Bead sights; **side ejection**, the modern construction—all Marlin rifles and shotguns have side ejection; **standard 24-inch barrels**—we make no guns with stubby, sawed-off barrels.

You need **standard length buttstocks**—no short length, cheap-looking buttstocks are used on any Marlin guns; the rifle must be a take-down, for convenience in carrying and cleaning—these Marlin repeaters have the quickest take-down constructions, action parts remove instantly without using tools, the barrels can be cleaned from both ends.

You will want to use .22 short cartridges up to 50 yards; .22 long-rifle up to 200 yards—all Marlin .22 repeaters use, interchangeably, .22 short, long and long-rifle cartridges.

Model No. 20—a man's size repeating rifle with full 24-inch octagon barrel, full length buttstock, Ivory Bead Sight. 25 shots. Slide action and visible hammer. Retails at $19.50.

Model No. 38—The wonderful new slide action repeater; Hammerless; Instantaneous Take-Down, Ivory Bead Sight, Full Pistol Grip Buttstock. Perfect build and balance. Retails. Round Barrel, $21.50. Octagon barrel, $23.50.

Model No. 39—The only 22 Caliber Lever Action Repeater made. The choice of expert and professional shooters. The best .22 Rifle in the world. Retails at $26.50.

Any dealer can supply you—give us your dealer's name. Send now for new illustrated catalogue of all Marlin repeating rifles and shot guns—free.

Model 20 Retails $19.50
Model 38 Round Bbl. $21.50 Octagon Bbl. $23.50
Model 39 Retails $26.50

Address Dept. S-55

The Marlin Firearms Corporation
New Haven, Connecticut

Marlin Firearms Corporation ad for Model 20, 38, and 39 rifles.

Shoots short, long and long rifle cartridges interchangeably.

Get this right: The world's best .22 repeater—bar none!—is the Marlin Model 39.

Fifty years of leadership in barrel boring make Marlin Rifles and Shotguns the wonder guns the whole world over.

Buy a better shooter—get a Marlin. Ask your dealer.

Write for latest Pocket Catalog.

THE MARLIN FIREARMS CO., 65 Willow St., New Haven, Conn.

1924 Marlin Firearms Company ad for the Model 39 rifle.

Each Shot gets away faster from this .22 cal.
Lever Action Takedown

YOU can pull the lever with split-second speed without once taking your eye off the mark as the stock sets snugly against your cheek and shoulder.

Never has a gun so thoroughly proved itself as the Marlin 39, the only .22 lever action made and the sweetest handling rifle that ever roamed the fields. She has the celebrated solid top and side ejection action originated by Marlin, and one of the famous Marlin barrels with its special costly rifling. The few simple parts are easily removed and cleaned.

From an illustrious family, Marlin 39, her friends are legion. She is a trustworthy lifetime companion.

Send for catalog containing complete description of this and other famous Marlin guns. THE MARLIN FIREARMS CO., 99 Willow St., New Haven, Conn.

Free

Please send catalog
Name....................
Address..................
Dealer...................

Expert Repair Service

Marlin

1928 Marlin Firearms Company ad for the Model 39 rifle.

squirrels, crows, foxes, etc., and for target shooting up to 200 yards.

Easy to clean: In this rifle not only the action, but also the barrel can be readily cleaned. The breech bolt is easily removed with your fingers. The barrel is then just as free and clear as a barrel apart from the action, and can be cleaned by inserting the rod at breech end and drawing the rod and cloth through the barrel.

To take rifle apart: Cock the hammer, unscrew the thumb-screw on side of receiver, move buttstock portion to the right and the barrel portion to the left. To remove breech bolt, slide it back as far as it will go, when it can be lifted out.

A great many big game hunters prefer this lever action rifle, as it has the "feel" of a big-game rifle and permits them to keep in practice at small expense.

Importance of having a rifle that will shoot .22 short, long

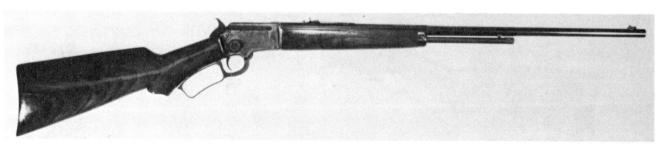

Rare Model 39 rifle, serial number 12,959, with a half-octagon barrel and half magazine. The top tang is marked with a star and the barrel is marked The Marlin Firearms Corporation.

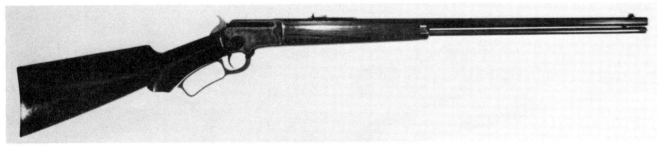

Right side of Model 39 rifle.

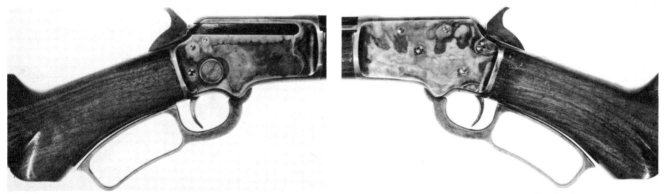

Left: *Right side of case-hardened Model 39 rifle showing typical pistol grip and squared lever.* Right: *Left side of same.*

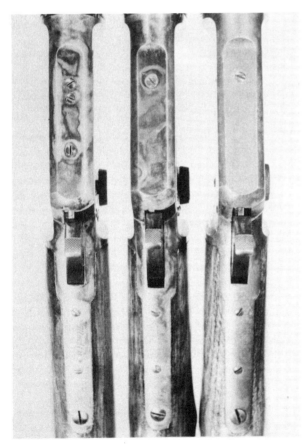

From left to right are shown the tops of the Model 97, Model 39, and Model 39A receivers. Note that the Model 39 and 39A are identical, except for the finish.

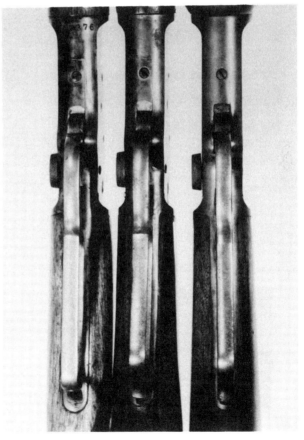

Left: *Bottom of Model '97 receiver.* Center: *Bottom of Model 39 receiver.* Right: *Bottom of Model 39A receiver.*

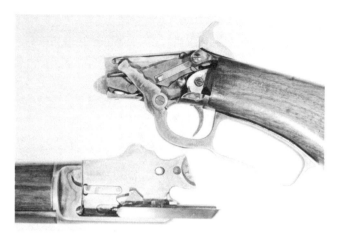

Internal parts of Model 39 rifle.

Top: *Model 1897/97 magazine tube latch.* Bottom: *Model 39 button-type magazine tube lock.*

Ivory bead front sight of Model 39 rifle.

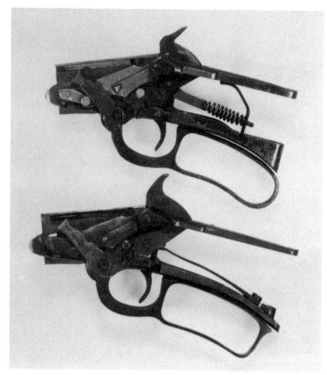

Top: *Model 39A receiver with a coil hammer spring.* Bottom: *Model 39 receiver with a flat hammer spring.*

and long rifle cartridges in the same rifle: A rifle that uses .22 short cartridges only is limited in its accurate range to about 59 yards because that is the limit of dependability of the .22 short cartridge. For ranges from 50 to 200 yards, the .22 long rifle cartridge in Marlin rifles has remarkable accuracy and power and is ideal for all small game requirements.

C. G. "Gus" Swebilius invented a new ejector that was used in the Models 38 and 39. The patent covering this new device is number 1,578,777, dated March 30, 1926. The patent was filed July 18, 1923; however, it is not recorded exactly when the new idea went into production. Gus Swebilius's invention solved the problem of the spring-loaded ejector being in the way of a cleaning rod during barrel cleaning. By pushing the ejector into the ejector base, and turning the slotted rivet, the ejector would be held out of the way. One had to remember, however, to release the ejector after cleaning; otherwise, the rifle would not function correctly.

The pistol grip of the Model 39 has the same S-shape at its bottom as the previous Model 1897/97 models had. The only barrel available for the model was 24-in. octagon. According to catalogs, round and half-octagon barrels were no longer available on special order. However, one exception has been examined; it had a half-octagon barrel that was correctly marked with the Marlin Firearms *Corporation* name on the barrel.

It should be noted here that all Model 39s made after the few Marlin–Rockwell 39s were manufactured were marked with the Marlin Firearms Corporation name on the barrel. This must have been a cost-saving measure of the 1926 Marlin Firearms *Company* to continue using the roll-stamp and barrel inven-

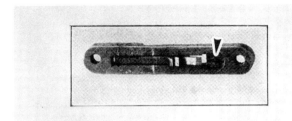

New Ejector for Marlin Model 39 Rifles

Marlin ad for the new ejector mechanism. The arrow indicates the hold-down rivet.

tory of the prior company, rather than to make new roll-stamps or to scrap barrels on hand.

All Model 39 top tangs were drilled and tapped for tang sights. The top tangs were also stamped *Marlin/MOD .39.* Some top tangs were also stamped with a six-pointed star. This star mark was the final inspector's mark to certify that "the gun was as near perfection as the finest of materials, equipment and skill can make it."

The first type of Model 39 butt plate was a curved hard rubber plate that had the name *Marlin* in an oval, oriented vertically. There were two variations of this type. The first was the short-lived Model '97 type; it had a lump on the top front that required the stock to be inletted for it. To save the cost of fitting each butt plate to each stock, this type of butt plate was soon made without the lump on the top. Around the outside of the oval, except for borders around the outside edge, and around the screw holes and the name *Marlin*, the plate was attractively checked.

Late Model 39s had a flat unbreakable butt plate that appears to be made of a fiber material, instead of the usual hard rubber. This plate had seven groups of four horizontal serrations.

If high-speed (HS) caliber .22 ammunition was used, the bolt of the Model 39 would crack. A large horizontal cut across the bolt, just behind the locking lug on the bottom of the bolt, created a weak condition. After changing the machining operation at this point, the bolt no longer failed. All Model 39s that have either no prefix to the serial number or an *S* prefix should not be used with high-speed cartridges. Rifles with the improved bolt have *HS* as a prefix to the serial number, indicating that the bolt was of the improved type. This change came about in 1932.

An NRA statement in the *American Rifleman* magazine for May 1932 about the Model 39 read as follows:

THE MARLIN MODEL 39 IMPROVED

The lever action Marlin rifle in .22 rim-fire caliber has recently been improved for use with high-velocity rim-fire ammunition. The breech bolt has been strengthened by omitting a clearance cut in its bottom surface near the front end where the arm of the working lever engages it. The bearing surface between the lug on the breech bolt and the locking arm of the lever has been increased for greater resistance

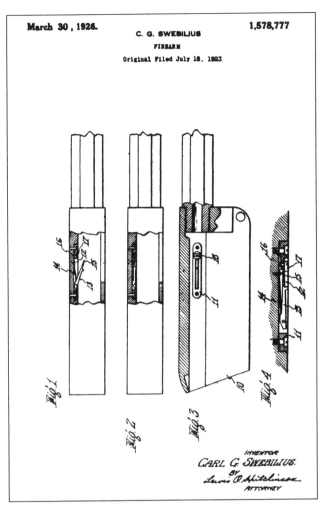

Patent drawing of new type of ejector base.

Top: *Model 39 marking on top tang. Note that the tang is drilled and tapped for a tang sight and the tang is stamped with the inspector's star mark.* Bottom: *Top tang is not marked with a star.*

Typical barrel marking found on all Model 39 rifles.

Typical caliber marking on Model 39 rifle.

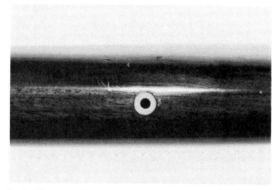

Marlin bull's-eye trademark (registered in 1922 by The Marlin Firearms Corporation) that was embedded into the bottom edge of some Model 39 rifle stocks.

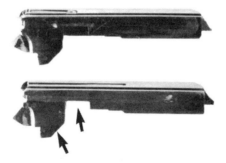

Top: *This bolt illustrates the modification of 1932 when more metal was left on the locking lug and bottom of bolt.* Bottom: *This bolt represents those bolts that cracked when used with high-speed (HS) cartridges. The arrows indicate the two weak areas.*

to the back thrust of the discharge. The result is a tighter breeching up and a stronger locking of the parts against any tendency of the breech bolt to yield and allow an increase in headspace.

There is no swelling of the cases near the head when fired in this rifle. Three standard makes of modern high-velocity ammunition were tried, with perfect functioning.

This Marlin 39 is an important rifle, because it is the only small-bore lever-action arm available for cheap practice for those shooters who habitually use a lever-action hunting rifle. Rapid-fire practice is an essential part of a hunter-rifleman's training, and that training may be had very economically with this Marlin 39. It is the only light-weight repeater or manually operated "plinking" rifle with a solid forestock, and it leads all other rifles in this "tin-can" class because of this feature. It has an unusually tight, strong and durable take down design. Taken down, both the bore and the magazine may be cleaned from the breech. The ejector in the left side of the receiver is provided with a locking screw to hold it out of the way during cleaning.

Like other rifles in this class, it is effective on small game up to 75 yards when equipped with a peep rear sight on the tang or on the receiver. The stock is well adapted for fast aiming in the standing position or sitting position. The gun can also be used in the high or hunting style prone position, but not in the low prone position used by target shooters. It is not designed for N.R.A. match shooting or training. All plinking rifles, without exception, lack proper stock dimensions, sling equipment and the very fine accuracy needed in match work.

This Marlin was originally issued in 1891 with receiver loading port and in solid frame. The present type of magazine and the removable side plate came out in the Model 1892. The take-down feature and the "smokeless-steel" receiver was introduced in the Model 1897. The Marlin 39 version with pistol grip was brought out in 1921, making the 24 inch octagon barrel and full-length magazine standard. Since that time the ejector lock and a stronger magazine design preceded the minor changes made this year in the action.

The magazine tube used with the Model 39 should be the button type, rather than the Model '97 latch type. However, some early Model 39s do have the earlier magazine tube. Again, this was probably a matter of using up inventories of the earlier parts while phasing in the new magazine. Additionally, the bayonet-type magazine tube of the Model 39A was listed for the Model 39 in parts catalogs; however, I have not inspected one with that type of magazine tube.

All Model 39s had 24-in. octagon barrels, case-hardened receivers, levers, and pistol grip stocks. This model was the start of a trend by Marlin to eliminate options, variations, and extra features. This policy continues to this day.

The retail prices of the Model 39 were listed in price lists as follows:

Date	Price
January 1922	$28.40
June 1922	26.50
February 1923	28.35
March 1926	28.00
April 1932	25.00
June 1932	30.80

Flat unbreakable butt plate used on some late Model 39s and early Model 39As.

Date	Price
March 1933	25.00
August 1936	25.00
January 1938	25.00
April 1939 (39A)	29.75

The front sight bead was made of ivory from 1922 to 1934. From 1935 to 1938, the bead was silver-colored metal.

The high and low serial numbers recorded or reported were the following:

	Low	High
No prefix	1002	12,959
S prefix	S696	S16,135
HS prefix	HS456	HS18,784

MODEL 39A

The progenitor of the Model 39A was the Model 1891 side-loading, lever action, caliber .22 rifle that was invented by L.L. Hepburn. Between 1939 and 1988, this rifle went through numerous changes, some mechanical and some cosmetic. The following models are covered in their order of introduction by Marlin:

Page from Marlin parts catalog that shows parts for both the 39 and 1897/97 models.

Model 39A
Model 39A–Mountie (39M)
Model 39A–Presentation (90th Anniversary) (1960)
Model 39A Mountie Presentation (90th Anniversary) (1960)
Model 39A–DL (Deluxe) (1961–1963)
Model 39 Carbine (1963–1968)
Model 39 Presentation (Centennial Matched Pair) (1970)
Model 39 Century Limited (1970)
Model 39A Article II (1971–1972)
Model 39M Article II (1971–1972)
Model 39D (1971) (1973)
Model 39A Octagon (1973)
Model 39M Octagon (1973)
Model 39 Serial Number 2,000,000 (1983)
Model 39AS (1988)
Model 39MS (1988)
Model 39TDS (1988)

Hudson Sporting Goods Company, New York City, ad for the first variation Model 39A rifle. Note that it was priced at only $26.95.

Marlin flyer of 1939 advertising the "World's Best All Around Rifle," the Model 39A.

Barrel marking on Model 39A rifle.

Except for two short breaks during WW I and WW II, the Marlin lever action .22 rifle has been in continuous production since it was first introduced in 1891. It is the longest-lived rifle still in production in the world today.

Please note that the Marlin Models 56, 57M, and 1894M are also caliber .22 lever action rifles. The Models 57 and 57M are covered in the Levermatic section along with the Model 62. The Model 1894 is covered in the late Model 1894 section.

Model 39A

When first introduced in 1939, the Model 39A was an improved version of the Model 39. A new long beavertail forearm and round barrel were the most important changes from the older model.

All Model 39A rifles have pistol grip buttstocks. However, there are a number of straight stocked variations that will also be covered in order.

The 1939 Marlin catalog introduced the new Model 39A with the following:

World's Best All Around .22 Caliber Repeating Rifle

Noted for its unique construction, reliability and accuracy since 1891, Model 39A is greatly improved this year. It is the only lever action .22 repeater made, the only take-down rifle exposing all working parts for cleaning and oiling by the turning of a single hand-operated screw. Unsurpassed for rabbits, foxes, squirrels, chucks, crows, plinking—and a great arm for targets up to 200 yards. Looks and handles like a custom job!

New semi-heavy round tapered blue-steel barrel, crowned muzzle, deep-cut Ballard type rifling, Safe side ejection, solid top case-hardened receiver, low sighting plane for telescope-mounting. Rocky Mountain rear sight, silver bead front sight, drilled and tapped for tang peep sight. Magazine holds 25 short, 20 long, 18 long rifle caliber .22 cartridges. Shoots regular and high speed loads without adjustment. NEW long semi-beaver tail forearm; NEW beautifully designed pistol grip buttstock; both American black walnut, hand-rubbed, oil finish. NEW large corrugated buttplate of light, unbreakable material. (Seven sets of four serrations.) Overall length 41 inches; approximate weight 6½ pounds. Retail price—$29.75.

Features peculiar to this first variation of the Model 39A are the flat butt plate and the classic S-shaped pistol grip, along with the 24-in. round barrel, beavertail forearm, and squared

First-variation Model 39A as styled when introduced in 1939.

Second-variation Model 39A with rounded lever, curved rubber butt plate, and semibeavertail forearm.

Third variation of Model 39A having fluted comb, white line spacer with butt plate, large forearm, and hooded ramp front sight.

First variation of the Model 39A–Mountie, which had a 24-in. barrel and small forearm.

Second variation of Model 39A–Mountie, which had a large forearm.

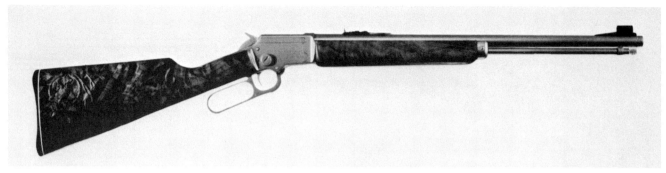

Model 39A–Mountie presented to Gail Davis, who played Annie Oakley on Broadway in 1958 and used the rifle in the show.

lever. There was no prefix to the first-variation serial number. The number was stamped under the lever on the outside of the bottom tang.

The 1940 catalog parroted the 1939 catalog and added:

> New design, full pistol grip buttstock of Genuine American walnut; New design visible hammer; New "non-slip" unbreakable flexible rubber buttplate; New hand-filling, semi-beavertail forearm, designed to prevent cant; New unbreakable coiled main and trigger springs; New—all rifle bores are treated with a new process to discourage rust or corrosion.

The new stock illustrated in the 1940 catalog of this second variation of the Model 39A had a full, flat-bottomed pistol grip, and the butt plate had a curved back surface. The S-shaped pistol grip of the first-variation Model 39A, which was used by Marlin since the Model 1891 pistol grip stock was introduced, was now discontinued. The full semibeavertail forearm of the 1940 model is still in use on the Model 39A.

The 1939–1941 case-hardened Model 39As were serial-numbered either without an alphabetical prefix to the number or with a *B* prefix.

No Model 39As were manufactured during the WW II period of 1942–1944.

The 1945 catalog described the third variation of the Model 39A the same as in the 1940 catalog, except that the solid top receiver was listed as blued instead of case-hardened, and the receiver was listed as now being drilled and tapped for receiver sights. A new ramp front sight was also listed; however, the illustration showed a drive-in dovetail sight without a ramp.

Deluxe wood stock with hand-carved design of a cowgirl on her horse, rope lasso, and sixguns on "Annie Oakley" Gail Davis special presentation rifle.

The magazine tube of the Model 39A and its variations was of the bayonet catch type that was introduced with the production of this model.

The finger lever of the first variation of the Model 39A (1939) was the same as that used on the Model 39. It had a square shape and a small projection at its top rear end. The finger lever of the second variation of the Model 39A had a rounded rear end.

Front sights of the 1939–1941 period were dovetailed to the barrel. In 1945, a new ramp front sight base with a protective hood was introduced. A sight insert was dovetailed into the ramp and the ramp was held to the barrel by a dovetail. The ramp was flat-bottomed, to match a flat place machined on the top of the barrel.

Model 39A–Mountie

The 1953 catalog introduced the Model 39A–Mountie as follows:

> Feather light, fast handling, .22 caliber repeater with straight grip. The Marlin 39A Mountie is the trimmest looking, fastest shooting Western style .22 caliber lever action repeater with straight grip you'll see anywhere today. In straight grip, with slim forend and weighing only 6 pounds, the 39A–Mountie is an ideal repeater for saddle-shooters. 20″ tapered blued steel barrel. Marlin rifling for greater accuracy. Solid top receiver, automatic side ejection which permits lowest possible central telescope mounting. Easy take-down. Turning of a single hand-screw exposes all working parts for cleaning and oiling. Magazine holds 20 short, 15 long or 14 long rifle cartridges. Shoots regular or high velocity loads without adjustment. Straight grip for scabbard carrying. Visible hammer for safety. Overall length—36½ inches.

Model 39A and Model 39M–Mountie, 1960 Presentation Models

In 1960, to commemorate the 90th anniversary of the name *Marlin* in the firearms business, Marlin produced a special pair of .22 rifles. The catalog description of them was as follows:

> These commemorative Model 39A's and 39A–Mounties are being made available in 1960. They will bear the serial numbers of 1 through 500. These presentation models will have all of the same fine features that the standard Golden 39A and 39A–Mountie have, plus these special design and equipment features: Specially matched first quality seasoned

Fourth variation of Model 39A, which had a pistol grip cap with white line spacer and sling swivels added (1957).

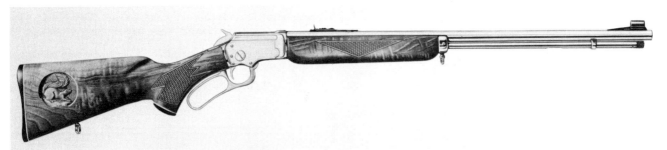

90th-Anniversary Model 39A (1960).

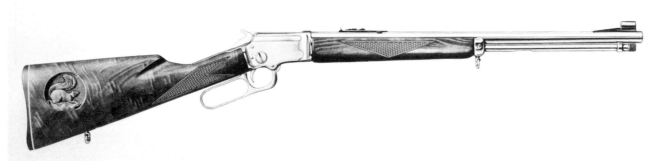

90th-Anniversary Model 39A-Mountie (1960).

walnut stocks. Stock hand engraved with the figure of a gray squirrel. All metal parts with the exception of the sights are chrome plated for smart appearance and extreme durability. Foreend and stock of the 39–A Presentation Model are fine-line hand checkered. The foreend and the straight grip of the 39A "Mountie" Presentation Model are also fine-line hand checkered for comfortable grip and rich appearance. Both models handle .22 caliber cartridges, regular or high-velocity loads, without adjustment. 39A Presentation has full tubular magazine taking 25 short, 20 long or 18 long rifle cartridges. The 39A "Mountie" Presentation model has full length tubular magazine and will handle 20 short, 15 long or 14 long rifle cartridges. Overall length of the 39A Presentation model is 40½ inches, weight about 6¾ pounds depending on density of wood. Overall length of the 39A "Mountie" Presentation model is 36¾ inches. Weight about 6 pounds, depending on density of wood. Price – $100.00.

These presentation rifles are much-sought-after collector's firearms. Unfortunately, when Marlin sold and shipped them, they did not ship them in pairs. There are very few pairs with matched Presentation series serial numbers in collections. In addition to the special 1-to-500 serial numbers, they are stamped with a regular Marlin serial number.

From inspection of the carving of the squirrel in the buttstock, and from information from employees involved, I conclude that the carving was done on a pantograph machine and that the only hands on the job were those of the person operating the machine. However, the master pattern used in the pantograph machine was carved by hand.

	Serial Numbers
1960 39A Presentation rifle	1 to 500
1960 39A–Mountie Presentation rifle	1 to 500

Model 39A-DL

In 1961, Marlin introduced a deluxe model of the 39A. It was like the 1960 90th-anniversary rifle, except that it was not chrome-plated. It was described as follows:

It has all the features that have made the 39A so popular, plus these exclusive extras: fine-line hand checkering on grip and on forend; buttstock hand carved with grey squirrel; genuine leather sling strap. Price – $100.00.

A total of 3,306 Model 39A-DLs were manufactured from 1961 to 1963, when the model was discontinued.

Model 39 Carbine

In 1963, Marlin introduced a new straight stock carbine, about which the catalog stated:

> You can get the jump on rabbits, squirrels, other small game with this new slim, trim Marlin .22 repeater! Compact, 20 inch tapered Micro-Groove barrel helps you shoot fast and sure! Straight grip and *slim forend* give you an extra-high speed handling; shoots 18 shorts, 14 longs or 12 long rifle cartridges approximately 5¼ pounds. Slimmer, lighter version of Model 39A-Mountie, 36″ overall, short magazine, dovetail front sight without ramp or hood.

A total of 12,140 Model 39 carbines were manufactured from 1963 to 1967, when the model was discontinued.

Marlin 1970 Centennial Matched Pair (Model 39)

To commemorate the 100th year of the name *Marlin* in the gunmaking business, Marlin introduced the Centennial Matched Pair Presentation rifles. The set consisted of a custom-engraved Model 336 and Model 39. (The Model 336 Presentation rifle is covered in that section of this book.) The catalog information about these very special rifles was as follows:

Model 39ADL (1963).

Model 39 Carbine (1963–1971).

Model 39 Presentation rifle that, with a Model 336 Presentation rifle, made up the 1970 Centennial Matched Pair.

Robert Kain hand-engraved prototype Model 39 Presentation that was a Model 1897 rifle. The stock and forearm are of rosewood.

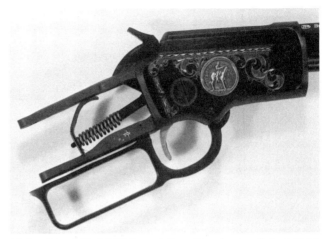

Right side of Model 39 Presentation rifle, showing Robert Kain's engraver's mark on bottom tang.

Top tang of Model 39 Presentation with hand-engraved and -stamped serial numbers.

Model 39 Presentation barrel marks.

Roll-stamp on top of Model 39 Presentation octagon barrel.

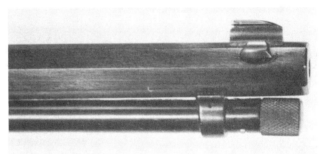

Marble's front sight of Model 39 Presentation.

Both guns feature: a beautifully hand engraved receiver with an inlaid mint-struck Centennial medallion of cartridge brass; 20 inch classic tapered octagon barrel with Micro-Groove® rifling; curved buttplate and fore end cap of cartridge brass; and identical set numbers for both. The classic squared finger lever and selected fancy American walnut straight grip stock highlight the traditional styling of both rifles. Each set has a lifetime guarantee and original owner's certificate personally signed by Marlin president, Frank Kenna.

Matched pair rifles are nestled in a rugged, handsome luggage case featuring polished brass locks with keys and polished brass corners. The box is tongue and groove construction, covered with rich, buffalo grain vinyl. A full length piano hinge and saddle stitched handle complement the richness of these rifles.

Only 1,000 Centennial Matched Pairs will be produced. They're bound to be a valuable collector's item. Reflecting Marlin's way with walnut, steel and brass, these commemorative models are the epitome of traditional Marlin craftsmanship and quality.

The specifications of the Presentation 39 were described as follows:

.22 caliber Western style lever action carbine; tubular magazine capacity—21 short, 16 long or 15 long rifle; 20″ tapered octagon Micro-Groove® barrel; 36 inches overall length; approximately 6 pounds; straight-grip selected fancy American walnut stock and fore-end with tough outdoor finish; hand engraved receiver with inlaid Centennial medallion

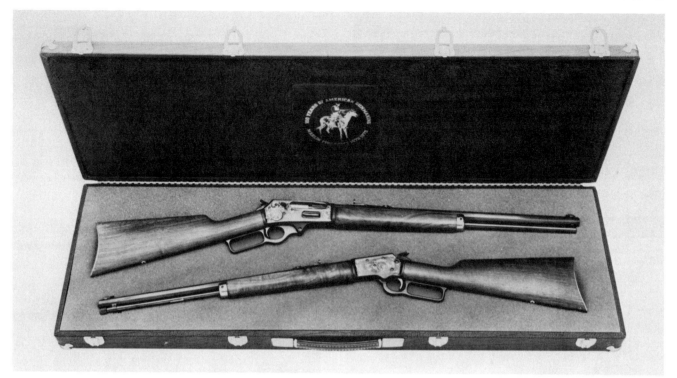

Marlin 1970 Centennial Matched Pair.

of cartridge brass; curved buttplate and fore-end cap of cartridge brass; adjustable open rear sight; ramp front sight with brass bead; 24 carat gold plated trigger; tapped for receiver sight scope mounts; square lever; deeply blued metal surfaces.

The front and rear sights of this model were manufactured by Marble. The front was not a ramp as described in the catalog. It was the Marble Contour No. 37W with a ¹/₁₆-in. gold bead. The rear was the Marble short-blade semibuckhorn No. 67.

Only 1,000 Centennial Matched Pair commemoratives were manufactured. They were engraved by master engravers Robert Kain and Winston Churchill. Mr. Kain's mark is an *R* with a cane superimposed upon it—. Winston Churchill's mark is a *W* superimposed upon a *C—W.* The serial number is hand-engraved on the top tang, as well as stamped into the side of the top tang.

Model 39 Century Limited (39CL)

To commemorate Marlin's 100th anniversary, a special rifle was introduced. The catalog copy reads as follows:

> Western style lever action carbine; .22 caliber tubular magazine capacity—21 short, 16 long or 15 long rifle; 20 inch tapered octagon Micro-Groove® barrel; 36 inches overall length; approximately 6 pounds, straight grip selected fancy American walnut stock and fore-end with tough outdoor finish; buttplate, fore-end cap and engraved name plate of cartridge brass. Adjustable semi-buckhorn rear sight; brass bead front sight; tapped for receiver sights and scope

mounts; 24K gold plated trigger; comes with scope adapter base and offset hammer spur. Price—$125.00.

A centennial medallion, mint-struck from cartridge brass, was inlaid in the right-hand side of the receiver. The medallion is embossed with Marlin's horse and rider logo. Circled around the logo are *Marlin* and *1870.* At the bottom of the medallion is the year 1970. This same medallion was also embedded into the right-hand side of each Marlin rifle manufactured during 1970. (This did not include the Glenfield-brand firearms.)

In addition to the medallion on the receiver, the Model 39CL had an oval brass plate attached to the right-hand side of the stock. The plate was attached by two brass round-headed nails. Across the top of the football-shaped plate was *39 CENTURY LTD.* The bottom edge was stamped *100 Marlin YEARS* with the word *Marlin* in the usual Marlin style.

The rear sight used on the 39CL was manufactured by Marble. The front sight was also a Marble blade-type sight with a brass bead.

There were 34,197 Model 39 Century Limited rifles manufactured during 1970.

Model 39 Article II

The Marlin Model 39A and 39M Article II rifles were a salute to the National Rifle Association of America (NRA) for its 100 years of dedication to its original objective of promoting the safe, proper, and efficient use of firearms, as well as the legal ownership of firearms and the right to "keep and bear arms." (Marlin suggests that every hunter, shooter, or anyone who believes in the right of law-abiding Americans to keep and bear arms should be a member of the National Rifle Association of America. Write the NRA, 1600 Rhode Island Avenue, NW, Washington, D.C. 20036 for details.)

These commemorative rifles were produced only in 1971.

Catalog copy for the Model 39A Article II Rifle reads as follows:

> Western style lever action carbine; .22 caliber tubular magazine capacity — 26 short, 21 long or 19 long rifle cartridges; 24 inch fully tapered octagon Micro-Groove® barrel; 40 inches overall length; approximately 6¾ pounds; pistol grip, selected American walnut stock and fore-end with tough Mar-Shield™ finish; buttplate, fore-end cap of cartridge brass. Adjustable semi-buckhorn rear sight; brass bead front sight; tapped for receiver sights and scope mounts; scope adaptor base and offset hammer spur for use with telescope included.

Mounted on the right side of the receiver is an inset medallion commemorating the Second Amendment to the Constitution, which guarantees the right to bear arms, and the 1871-1971 dates of the NRA dedication to that constitutional right. The medallion is brass, with a blue band around a red center, upon which is embossed an eagle with outspread wings clutching crossed rifles.

The Article II rifles had Marble rear sights and Marble front blade-type sights with a brass bead.

The 39M Article II Carbine was identical to the rifle model except that it had straight-grip selected American walnut stock; squared Western style finger lever; 20-in. fully tapered octagon barrel; weight of approximately 6 pounds; magazine capacity of 21 short, 16 long, or 15 long rifle cartridges.

A total of 6,265 Model 39A Article II rifles and 3,824 Model 39M Article II carbines were manufactured in 1971.

Marlin 1970 Model 39 Century Limited (1970).

Model 39A Article II (1971-1972).

Model 39M Article II (1971-1972).

Model 39D

Introduced in 1971, the Model 39D was described as follows:

> Caliber .22 lever action carbine. Tubular magazine capacity 21 short, 16 long or 15 long rifle; 20½ inch round Micro-Groove® barrel; 36½ inches overall length; approximately 5¼ pounds; select American walnut stock with fluted comb, full pistol grip, grip cap, white buttplate and pistol grip spacers and tough Mar-Shield™ finish. Adjustable rear, target front sight tapped for receiver sights and scope mounts; scope adapter base with right or left-hand offset hammer spur for scope use included.

In 1972 the Model 39D was not in the catalog, but in 1973 it was reintroduced with some changes. The 1973 model had a pistol grip stock that did not have a grip cap or white line spacer at the butt plate. Otherwise both guns were the same. Both had drive-in dovetail front sights and nonfolding sheet metal rear sights, with an elevator.

Of the first variation, 15,657 were manufactured during 1971 and 1972. An additional 7,891 of the second variation were produced, for a total of 23,548 Model 39D rifles manufactured.

Model 39A Octagon and Model 39M Octagon

In 1972, Marlin introduced Model 39A Octagon and Model 39M Octagon models along with the reintroduced Model 39A and 39M rifles.

The machinery and equipment, as well as the know-how, for making the 39CL and Article II barrels were on hand, along with a short overrun of unfinished octagon barrels. So it was smart for Marlin to explore making a noncommemorative octagon-barreled rifle in the hope it would do well in the marketplace. The result was not a disaster; however, the poor sales of the 1972 Models 39A Octagon and 39M Octagon were disappointing.

The catalog described these two limited production rifles as follows:

> *Model 39A Octagon:* Now you can own a 39 with the classic style and heft only an octagon can provide. The Model 39 Octagon is the same as the Golden 39A with a fully tapered 24-inch octagon barrel, blued steel trigger, traditional hard rubber rifle buttplate, blued steel fore-end cap adjustable folding semi-buckhorn rear, bead front sight and pistol grip stock of American walnut.
>
> *Model 39M Octagon:* This is not a "replica" meant to be put on the wall—it's a Marlin 39, made exactly like the round barreled models, made for hunting, plinking or informal target shooting. The Model 39M Octagon has the same action as the Marlin Model 39M with a fully tapered 20 inch octagon barrel, blued steel trigger, traditional hard rubber rifle buttplate, blued steel fore-end cap, bead front and adjustable folding semi-buckhorn rear sight.

The front sight used on the octagon models was a Marble sight with a brass bead, the same as the one used on the Article II and CL rifles. The rear sight was the new Osborne folding buckhorn type introduced in 1972.

The butt plate of the octagon models was the same butt

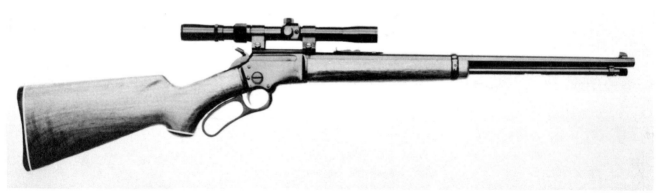

First-variation Model 39D (1971).

Second variation of Model 39D (1973).

Model 39A Octagon (1973).

Model 39M Octagon (1973).

Model 39M with square lever, Wide-Scan front sight hood, and no stock flutes (1974).

plate used on the Model 1895 rifle introduced this same year. It was curved hard rubber and had a Marlin logo embossed in a circle on the checked back surface.

There were 2,551 Model 39A Octagon rifles and 2,140 Model 39M Octagon carbines manufactured in 1973.

Model 39 Serial Number 2,000,000

The Marlin Firearms Company produced its two-millionth Model 39 in 1983. To commemorate the occasion, Marlin commissioned artisans recognized worldwide for their skill in metal and wood to decorate and stock the rifle that would bear the serial number 2,000,000. Upon completion, Marlin donated the rifle to the National Shooting Sports Foundation (NSSF), to be auctioned off by sealed bids at the 1984 SHOT Show in Dallas, Tex. The monies raised by this auction would be used by NSSF to finance the expansion of its shooting

education programs in the nation's schools. It was estimated that the proceeds from the auction of this Model 39 would allow NSSF to expand its educational efforts to as many as 5,000 additional schools.

The NSSF's promotional brochure about this rifle included the following description:

ENGRAVING: All engraving is by master American engraver Alvin A. White, who has signed his work on the lower tang. The detailed description that follows supplements the photographs shown.

RECEIVER/RIGHT SIDE: The right side of the receiver features the famous Marlin "Horse and Rider" sculptured in intricate detail in 18 carat gold. This figure is not only inlaid into the receiver but also extends above the surface to provide extraordinary detail and dimension to the design. Four inlaid gold leaf designs also decorate this side of the receiver along with the bold inscription "No. 2,000,000." Large areas are

Model 39A with short ramp front sight and Wide-Scan front sight hood and no swivels (1983).

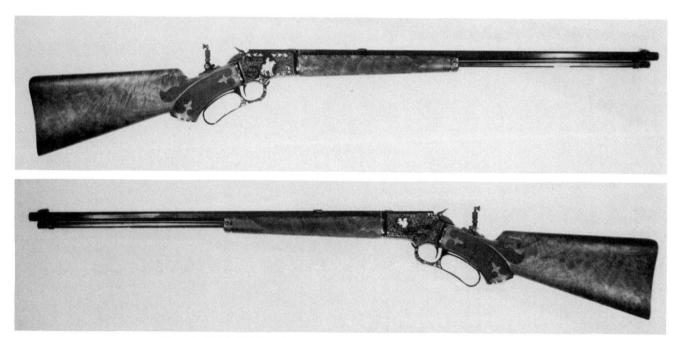

Top: *Marlin Model 39 serial number 2,000,000 (1983).* Bottom: *Left side of same.*

Right-hand side of Model 39 serial number 2,000,000.

Left-hand side of Model 39 serial number 2,000,000.

decorated with "Ulrich Style" scroll engraving. The head of the take-down screw is fully engraved.

TOP OF RECEIVER: The top of the receiver is fully engraved in a handsome scroll pattern. The scroll engraving is bordered by an ornate band of 24 carat gold.

RECEIVER/LEFT SIDE: The left side of the receiver features a gold sculptured squirrel in intricate detail above the inscription "Marlin Golden 39A No. 2,000,000." Below the inscription is a running rabbit engraved in perfect detail. The squirrel and rabbit symbolize the stature of the Marlin Model 39 as one of the world's most popular small game rifles. Both sides of the receiver are highlighted with inlaid lines of 24 carat gold.

HAMMER AND TANG: Each side of the hammer features scroll engraving surrounding a 24 carat inlaid "Arrow Design." The hammer spur is completely covered by fine line metal checkering. The same style of scroll engraving which decorates the hammer is featured on upper and lower tang. A thin line of 24 carat gold borders the top of the tang, extends down the rear of the receiver, around the lower tang and continues up the other side of the receiver. The detailing of this fine gold border is exemplary of the creativity and workmanship invested in this extraordinary rifle.

TRIGGER AND LEVER: The trigger face and bottom surface of the lever also incorporate precise metal checkering. Each side of the lever features scroll engraving high lighted by 24 carat gold leaf designs corresponding to the designs used on each side of the receiver. Scroll engraving also surrounds the checkered area of the bottom surface of the lever.

BARREL: The 24″ tapered octagon barrel features several inches of scroll engraving at the receiver end of the barrel. Scroll engraving also decorates the area of the rear sight and surrounds the muzzle. Bands of 24 carat inlaid gold also adorn the rear of the barrel and the muzzle. The inscription, "The Marlin Firearms Co., North Haven, Conn., U.S.A.," is inlaid in 24 carat gold along the top of the barrel. The rifle is chambered in .22 caliber rimfire.

SIGHTS: In keeping with the historic significance of this firearm, all sights are authentic design, as advertised in Marlin catalogs of the early 1900's. The front sight is an original Marlin "Rocky Mountain" bead type sight with an 18 carat gold blade. The open rear sight is an original Lyman fold-down, two-leaf sight. The rifle is also equipped with a Lyman No. 2A fold-down tang peep sight.

GRIP CAP: One of the most striking elements of this rifle is a superb likeness of John Marlin sculpted in 18 carat gold in the center of an H.L. Grisel skeletonized grip cap. A thin line of 24 carat gold is inlaid around the circumference of the grip cap, framing the sculptured gold portrait.

STOCK: The stock is hand-fitted from "AAA Fancy" American walnut by The Reinhart Fajen Company under the direction of Fred Wenig. The feathered crotch grain pattern of this eye-catching stock is one of the more striking ingredients of this extraordinary rifle. The buttstock features a fluted comb, superb 24-line checkering on the pistol grip and is capped with a Neidner recurved and checkered steel buttplate. The forearm also features a 24-line hand checkering along its full length. The checkering pattern is faithful to an authentic Marlin pattern. The stock has a classic hand-rubbed oil finish.

PRESENTATION CASE: A handsome American walnut presentation case has been custom made to display the historic TWO MILLIONTH Model 39. Handcrafted by the Rosborg Company of Newtown, Ct., the locking case features red velvet, French fit lining, brass locks and accessories

Gold bust of John Marlin inlaid into pistol grip of the 2,000,000th Marlin Model 39.

Gold-inlaid Marlin name and engraved rear sight of 2,000,000th Model 39.

and a unique take-down pedestal designed to display the rifle so its intricate engraving and superb workmanship can be fully appreciated.

Models 39AS and 39TDS

Model 39AS. In 1988, Marlin offered the sportsmen of the world an improved Golden 39A, called the Model 39AS. The 39M was now the 39MS. The added *S* indicated the addition of a hammer block safety and rebounding hammer. The Model 39AS also had swivel studs added to the buttstock and forearm tip. The studs were of a standard type that would accept "Uncle Mike's" and other QD swivels.

The changes made to the Model 39A in 1988 made the most popular .22 in America even better. The action was still machined from six steel forgings that are heat treated after being machined to give greater strength and wearability. No changes were made to the barrel, wood, finish, and fit of parts, or to the quality of workmanship.

Model 39TDS. In addition to the Model 39AS, Marlin introduced in 1988 the new and innovative Model 39TDS that replaced the Model 39M. The catalog described it as follows:

This new mini-version of the famous Model 39 is designed to travel. It comes apart in seconds without tools (as does the

Model 39AS (1988).

Model 39TDS (1988).

39A) and goes back together just as easily. It zips into its own padded floatable Cordura® carrying case, which even has enough room to accommodate the gun with a scope mounted. The new 39TDS is ideal for campers, backpackers, RV enthusiasts and boaters.

The Micro-Groove barrel of the Model 39TDS is 16½ inches long. The tubular magazine holds 16 short, 12 long, or 10 long rifle cartridges.

The sights are the usual Model 39 type of an adjustable semibuckhorn rear and ramp front with a brass bead and Wide-Scan hood. The solid top receiver is tapped for telescope mount and receiver sight.

Both the Models 39AS and 39TDS have a gas escape hole in the top left-hand side of the receiver. Also in the left side of the receiver is an inspection hole that allows the user to ensure that

a cartridge does not remain inside the magazine tube during unloading.

The Model 39TDS has a straight-grip stock, square lever, gold trigger, and a hard rubber butt plate that does not have a white line spacer. The forearm is scaled down to be compatible with the short 16½-in. barrel.

In short, the Model 39TDS is a first cousin to the old Model 1897 bicycle rifle.

CHRONOLOGY OF THE 39A

The chronological order of some of the addition, deletions, and modifications of the Model 39A and Model 39A–Mountie, from 1939 to 1988, were as follows:

1939	39A has a 24-in. round barrel, beavertail forearm, lightweight unbreakable butt plate drilled and tapped for tang sight, S-shaped pistol grip, case-colored receiver.
1940	39A now has a flat-bottomed pistol grip, rubber butt plate, coiled main and trigger springs, round lever.
1942–1944	No production (WW II).
1945	Receivers are now blued. Ramp front sight. Tapped and drilled for receiver sight.
1946–1950	No changes.
1951	White line spacer added to butt plate. Pistol grip cap with insert for initials, fluted comb.
1953	Model 39A–Mountie with 24-in. barrel and straight stock introduced. (1953 catalog illustrated the Model 39A–Mountie with a 24-in. barrel, but the text stated this new model had a 20-in. barrel.)
1954	The Model 39A–Mountie barrel now shown as 20 inch. Micro-Groove rifling added in place of Ballard type. Sears guns to have four telescope mounting holes in the barrel.
1956	Drilled and tapped for telescope mounting adapter base, oil-finished wood. 39A–Mountie now has semibeavertail forearm. Low hammer spur is new.
1957	Adapter base now packaged with rifle, pistol grip cap with white line space added, sling swivels and gold-plated trigger added. Bishop-style stock. Now called "Golden" 39A and "Golden" 39A–Mountie. Bright crowned muzzle and walnut-filled stock.
1958	Hammer modified for new offset hammer spur (extension).
1960	90th-anniversary Model 39A and Model 39A–Mountie introduced. Chrome-plated and checkered, with squirrel carving on buttstock.
1961	Model 39A–DL introduced—like 90th-anniversary model except that it isn't chrome-plated.
1963	Model 39 carbine (5¼ pounds), with lightweight barrel and ⅔ magazine, introduced.
1964	Use of the name "Golden" dropped from catalog.
1968	Model 39 carbine discontinued.
1970	Model 39 Presentation and Model 39 Century Limited introduced. No Model 39A or Model 39A–Mountie listed in catalog or produced.
1971	Model 39A Article II, Model 39M Article II, and Model 39D introduced.
1972	Model 39A–Mountie designation changed to Model 39M. "Golden" reinstated. Folding buckhorn rear sight now standard. Article II and 39CL rifles also listed in catalog.
1973	Model 39D reintroduced without white line

Serial number marked on the bottom tang of the first variation of the Model 39A.

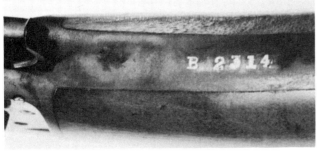

Serial number of the second variation of the Model 39A, as marked on the bottom tang.

Top tang of Model 39A showing dummy screws in the holes for tang rear sights.

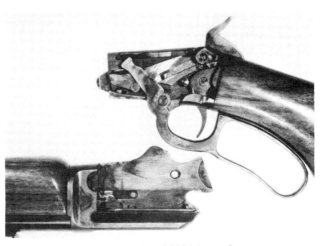

Early case-colored Model 39A internal parts.

Top: *Early flat-spring, first-variation Model 39A. The arrow indicates the lug that later was moved to the left side of the receiver.* Bottom: *Late Model 39A with the large coil spring and no lug.*

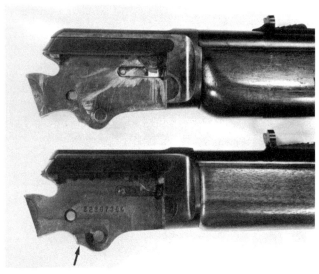

Top: *Second-variation Model 39A.* Bottom: *Late Model 39A that has the lever support lug on the left half of the receiver. See arrow.*

Telescope mounting holes placed in 39A barrels for Sears, Roebuck.

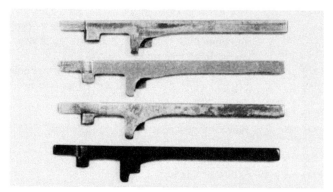

Four variations of firing pins that have been used in Model 39A and 39M rifles.

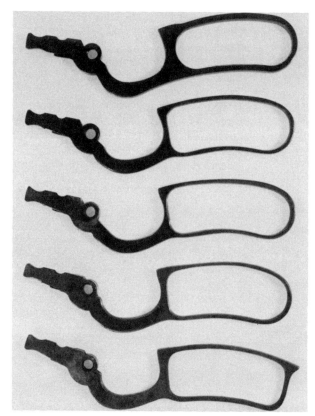

Various levers used in the Model 39A pistol grip rifles. The first variation is at the bottom and the latest type is at the top.

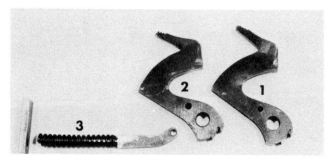

1. High hammer used on early Model 39As. 2. Low hammer used on later Model 39As. 3. First-variation mainspring.

	spacers or pistol grip cap. Model 39A Octagon and Model 39M Octagon models introduced.
1974	Square lever added to Model 39M.
1975	New tapered Model 39M barrel introduced. New patented magazine closure and new design scope adapter base with double grooves for ¾-in., ⅞-in., and 1-in. rings introduced.
1976	Stock flutes eliminated in Model 39M.
1978	New lightweight barrel for Model 39M introduced. Similar to old Model 39 carbine barrel.
1979	Gas escape hole installed in top left side of receiver.
1980	Warning to read and follow the owner's manual added to barrel markings.
1982	Gold-plated triggers discontinued. Model 39A and 39M triggers now blued.
1983	Sling swivels discontinued on Models 39A and 39M.
1984	2,000,000th Model 39 manufactured.
1985	Gold triggers reinstated.
1987	Inspection hole in left side of receiver allows user to ensure that a cartridge does not remain inside the magazine during unloading.
1988	Model 39TDS introduced. Model designation of 39A and 39M changed to 39AS and 39MS with addition of cross-bolt safety and rebounding hammer. Model 39AS now has sling swivel studs.

During the life span of the Model 39A and 39M rifles, they underwent many cosmetic and production changes. The cosmetic ones are covered in the discussions about the various models. The mechanical and production changes however, cannot easily be covered in a work of this type. Therefore, only some of the more obvious ones are listed here.

Mainsprings	Both flat and coil types used.
Receivers	Drilled and tapped for tang sight.
	Drilled and tapped for tang and receiver sights.
	Drilled and tapped for receiver sights only.
	Drilled and tapped for telescope adapter base and receiver sights.
	Case-colored and blued receivers.
	Blued and sandblasted receivers.
	Long, short, and no-lug receivers were used, as well as two types of lever support lugs.
Levers	Rounded and square types for straight stocks.
	Case-colored, blued, and sandblasted.
	Round and squared for pistol grip stocks.
Barrels	Made for drive-in dovetail sights.
	Made for drive-in rear and drive-in ramp front.
	Made for dovetail rear and screw-on ramp front sight.
	Octagon 24-in. and 20-in.
	Round 24-in., 20-in., and 16½-in.
	Drilled and tapped for Weaver *N* telescope mount.
Magazine inner tubes	Brass except for one period of aluminum inner tubes.
Cartridge stop	Early type, machined steel. Later type, stamped steel.
Cartridge guide spring	Early type, machined steel. Later type, stamped steel.
Ejector plate	Early type, steel; later type, brass.
Cartridge stop	Early type, stamped metal; later type, solid powdered metal. Very late models do not have a cartridge stop.
Bolts	About 500 powdered metal bolts were made for experimental purposes. Although not used in production, they were used in the repair department.
Trigger	Both blued and gold-plated steel triggers have been used.

In summary, the Marlin .22 is best described by the following poem.

My Old Marlin 22
by Sandy Carroll

Some childhood memories swell the heart,
But one stands by itself,
For it's still around to accompany me,
Above the fireplace on a shelf.

Raised on a farm when times were hard,
Meant you never got anything new,
But somehow my Dad scraped enough,
For my Marlin 22.

This Marlin was my constant friend,
As I roamed the hills 'round home,
With it in my youthful grip,
I never was alone.

The years have passed, I'm forty-one,
Been to Vietnam and back,
Got a good home and a family now,
There's nothing that I lack.

I'm proud of everything I have,
Of traditions old and new,
And the memory of my father's gift,
My own Marlin 22.

(Reproduced with the permission of Sandy Carroll.)

The suggested retail prices of the various models of the 39 were as follows:

	39A	39A–Mountie	39A–DL	39 Carbine
1939	$29.75			
July 1940	29.77			
November 1940	30.65			
May 1941	31.55			
November 1941	35.95			
1942–1944	WW II – No Production			
1945	36.45			
1946	50.85			
1947	50.85			
1948	50.45			
1949	52.30			
September 1950	57.95			
December 1950	61.95			
1953	60.85	$60.85		
1954	60.85	60.85		
November 1955	65.95	65.95		
1956	65.95	65.95		
1957	72.95	72.95		
1958	74.95	74.95		
1959	78.50	78.50		
1960	79.95	79.95		
1960 Presentation	100.00	100.00		
1961	79.95	79.95	$100.00	
1962	79.95	79.95	100.00	

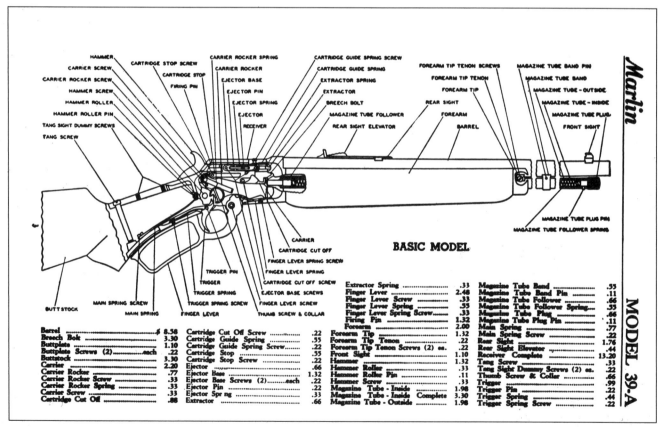

Marlin parts catalog page showing parts for the second variation of the Model 39A.

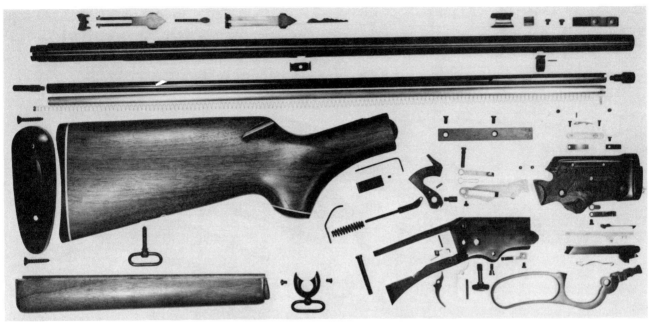

Pre-1988 parts of the Model 39A in their positions relative to each other.

	39A	39A-Mountie	39A-DL	39 Carbine
1963	79.95	79.95	100.00	$79.95
1964	79.95	79.95		79.95
1965	79.95	79.95		79.95
1966	84.95	84.95		84.95
1967	89.95	89.95		89.95
1968	89.95	89.95		
1969	94.95	94.95		

	39A	39M	39CL	Art. IIA	Art. IIM	39D
1970			$125.00			
1971			125.00	$135.00	$135.00	$99.95
1972	$109.95	$109.95	125.00	135.00		99.95
				39A Oct.	*39M Oct.*	
1973	109.95	109.95	125.00	125.00	125.00	99.95
1974	111.95	111.95		125.00	125.00	
1975	122.95	122.95				
1976	127.95	127.95				
1977	134.95	134.95				
1978	139.95	139.95				
1979	151.95	151.95				
1979	157.95	157.95 (June Rev.)				
1980	181.95	181.95				
1981	214.95	214.95				
1982	240.95	240.95				
1983	242.95	242.95				
1984	252.95	252.95				
1985	267.95	267.95				
1986	281.95	281.95				
1987	303.95	303.95		*39AS*	*39TDS*	
1988				318.95	355.95	

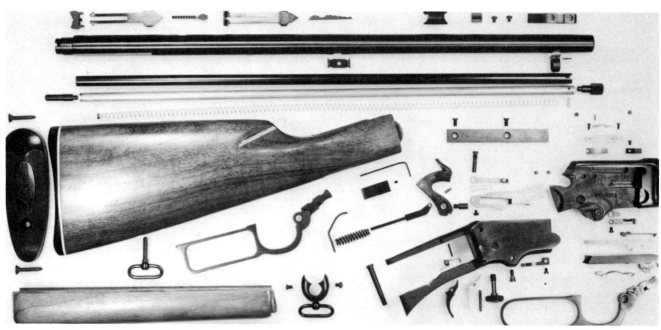

Pre-1988 parts of the Model 39M in their positions relative to each other.

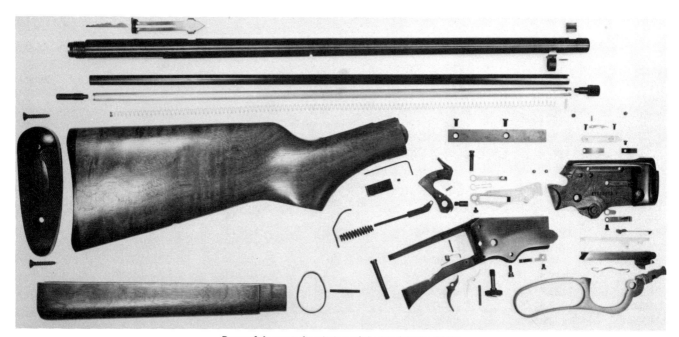

Parts of the second variation of the Model 39D (1973).

LEVERMATIC LEVER ACTION RIFLES

On May 6, 1955, Marlin announced a new lever action caliber .22 repeating rifle. The rifle had a number of unique features. They were a one-piece stock with the rigidity of a bolt action stock, a removable clip magazine, and a lightning-fast short-stroke lever action. This rifle and its variations became known as the Levermatic series.

The action of the Levermatic series of rifles was invented by Bandell and Neal, Chicago, Ill. It was developed by Ewald Nichol and Tom Robinson of Marlin's research and development department.

The lever mechanism of the Levermatics had a short smooth action achieved by use of a cam and roller accelerator system. This system operated the bolt through its full stroke during ejection, feeding, and loading by only a 2-in. flick of the fingers in the loop of the lever. Other Marlin systems required six or more inches of movement. Another advantage of this system was the fact that the lever could be operated without the hand leaving the pistol grip of the stock.

There were five variations of the Levermatic system, as follows:

Model	Caliber	Magazine Type
Model 56	caliber .22	clip magazine (1955–1964)
Model 57	caliber .22	tubular magazine (1957–1965)
Model 56DL "Clipper King"	caliber .22	clip magazine (1958)
Model 57M	caliber .22 Win. magnum	tubular magazine (1961–1969)
Model 62	caliber .256 and .30 carbine center-fire	clip magazine (1964–1969)

Model 56

The 1960 catalog described the Model 56 this way:

The 56-Levermatic offers some of the most striking improvements made in a .22 repeater in many years. Its lightning-fast action requires less than a 25 degree stroke of the lever to open breech, eject shell and close breech on a new cartridge.

Specifications: Type of action: Extremely fast short-throw lever action. Action securely bedded in one-piece stock assures accuracy—performance equal to that of a high-power bolt action rifle. 7 shot clip magazine handles .22 caliber short, long or long rifle cartridges, greased or waxed, regular

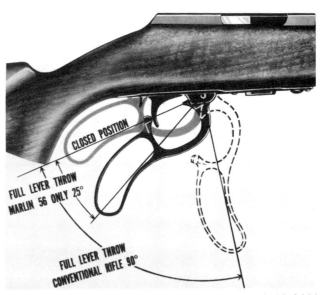

Illustration of the short throw of the levermatic lever on the Model 56 Levermatic rifle.

or high-velocity loads, without adjustment. (10- or 12-shot clips available on special order.) Finger safety on trigger guard plate. Flush magazine catch in floor plate. Barrel: 22″ round tapered blued steel barrel of Special Analysis Ordnance Steel. Special Features: Automatic side ejection, receiver solid at rear. Easy to take-down by removing front and rear receiver screws. Drilled and tapped for standard receiver peep sights. Top of receiver drilled and tapped for adapter

First variation of Model 56 rifle.

Model 56DL "Clipper King" rifle.

base for replacement of Tip-Off and Top Mounts. Adapter base packed with rifle at no additional cost. Open rear sight, ramp front sight with detachable hood. Gold plated trigger. Stock: One-piece Bishop-style stock of finest quality walnut with Monte Carlo comb with special finish to withstand all kinds of weather and hard usage. Pistol grip with grip cap. Custom-style hard rubber buttplate with white liner-cushion. Fluted comb. Exclusive feature: Supplied with Micro-Groove barrel for extreme accuracy-performance. Length and Weight: Overall length 41″; weight about 6¼ pounds.

When introduced in 1955, the receiver of the Model 56 was steel with a squared-off rear end. In 1956, the receiver was changed to one of aluminum that curved at the rear. At this same time, the stock was changed from one with a straight comb to one having a Monte Carlo comb.

The Model 56 rifle was serial-numbered when introduced. However, after evaluating the cost of doing the work and keeping the records of the serial numbers (federal law at that time required that records be kept on all serial numbers given to firearms), the practice was discontinued. The practice was rein-

stated for all firearms in 1968 upon passing of another federal law.

Production of the Model 56 was as follows:

Model	Total
56	31,116
56 — Sears	118
56 — Royal Canadian	289
Total	31,523

The suggested retail prices of the Model 56 were as follows:

Year	Price
1955–1958	$49.50
1957–1960	44.95
1961	46.95
1962	48.95
1963	49.95
1964	49.95

Model 56DL "Clipper King" Levermatic Rifle

The Clipper King was a 1959 offering of a Model 56 rifle specially packaged in a gun-case-shaped cardboard box, along with a tube of Marlin Rustopper, a game and target record book, Marlin's "Sighting In Guide and Manual," a game map, and 50 assorted targets. The magazine furnished with this rifle was the 12-shot clip type, which was also available for other models on special order. An added feature of the Model 56DL was the 4-power Micro-Vue telescope that was mounted and zeroed-in at the factory. The butt plate of the Model 56DL was red-colored hard rubber, instead of the usual black. The name *Marlin* was filled in with gold paint. The front sight of the Clipper King was a dovetail drive-in type instead of the hooded ramp type used on all other Levermatics.

The barrel of the Clipper King was specially stamped with the name *Marlin Clipper King* and a crown-shaped logo. A total of 152 were manufactured. It was listed at $60.75, with a retail value of $70.80.

Model 57

The Model 57 Levermatic caliber .22 tubular-magazine rifle was introduced in 1959. It had the curved second-type aluminum Model 56 receiver and a tubular magazine, instead of the

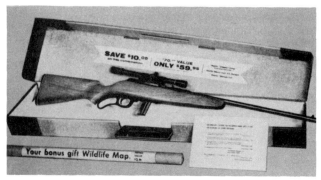

Clipper King rifle and bonus items of wildlife map, telescope, game record book, and Rustopper.

Barrel roll-stamp on Model 56DL "Clipper King" rifles.

Second variation of Model 56 rifle.

First variation of Model 57 rifle.

Second variation of Model 57 rifle.

clip magazine of the Model 56. It was described by Marlin as follows:

> For those who prefer a fast operating lever action with tubular magazine this is exactly the fast handling rifle they want. Specifications: Type of action: Fast, short-throw lever action repeater. Full tubular magazine. Handles 25 short, 20 long or 18 long rifle .22 caliber cartridges, regular or high-velocity loads, greased or waxed, without adjustment. Finger safety on trigger guard plate, flush magazine catch in floor plate. Easy to take-down by removing front and rear receiver screws. Barrel: 22″ round tapered blued steel barrel of special analysis ordnance steel. Special Features: Automatic side ejection, receiver solid at rear. Drilled and tapped for standard receiver peep sights. Top of receiver drilled and tapped for adapter base for placement of tip-off and top mounts. Adapter base packed with rifle at no additional cost, Open rear sight, ramp front sight with detachable hood. Gold-plated trigger. Stock: One piece Bishop-style stock of finest quality walnut with Monte Carlo comb with special finish to withstand all kinds of weather and hard usage. Pistol grip with grip cap. Custom-type hard rubber buttplate with white liner-cushion. Fluted comb. Exclusive Feature: Supplied with Micro-Groove® barrel for extreme accuracy-performance. Length and weight: Overall length 41″; weight about 6½ pounds depending on density of wood.

When introduced in the 1959 catalog, the Model 57 was illustrated with an aluminum receiver. In the 1960 catalog, a new steel receiver with a squared-off back end was illustrated. The stock was also shown for all years with a Monte Carlo comb. In 1966, a new rearward-sloping forend tip was illustrated that was identified as a "new design hand fitting fore-end shape."

The production of the Model 57 was as follows:

Model	Total
57	23,666
57 — Royal Canadian	440
57 — Western Auto	10,522
Total	34,628

The suggested retail prices of the Model 57 were the following:

Year	Price
1957–1961	$49.95
1962	52.95
1963	54.95
1964	56.95
1965	56.95

Model 57M

The Model 57M was introduced in 1959. It added the popular .22 Winchester magnum rimfire (WMRF) cartridge to the Levermatic family. The catalog for 1961 described the new addition as follows:

> The Model 57M was the first lever action repeater chambered for the high-velocity rimfire .22 Magnum cartridge. The combination of the 57M with Micro-Groove® rifling and the new ,22 Magnum cartridge provides the shooter with power, speed and accuracy never before available in a .22 caliber rifle chambered for a .22 caliber rimfire load. The 57M in combination with the powerful .22 Magnum cartridge with a muzzle velocity of 2,000 ft. per second and muzzle energy of 355 ft. pounds, fills a much needed place in the sporting rifle field between the .22 caliber high-speed

long rifle cartridge performance of about 1,335 ft. per second muzzle velocity and 158 ft. pounds muzzle energy and, the 2,690 ft. per second muzzle velocity and the 740 ft. pounds muzzle energy of the more expensive .22 Hornet center-fire cartridge. The 57M in .22 Magnum caliber offers varmint shooting for less than 6 cents a round . . . an important factor to most varmint shooters.

When introduced in 1959, the Model 57M was illustrated with a curved rear-end aluminum receiver. However, in 1960, the receiver was changed to the square steel type. In 1966, the forearm shape was changed to a new "hand fitting forend shape."

The production of the Model 57M from 1959 to 1969 was as follows:

Model	Total
57M	64,301
57M – Sears	1,200
57M – Western Auto	1,388
Total	66,889

The suggested retail prices of the Model 57M were the following:

Year	Price
1959	$49.95
1960–1961	54.95
1962	56.95
1963	58.95
1964	59.95
1965–1966	64.95
1967–1968	65.95
1969	72.95

Model 62

The Model 62 rifle was introduced in 1963. It was unique to the Levermatic family because it was a center-fire rifle. When first cataloged, it was listed as becoming available for the .357 magnum, .256 magnum, and .22 Jet cartridges. However, the Model 62 was chambered for only the .256 cartridge from 1963 until 1965. In 1966, the .30 carbine cartridge, of military fame, was added.

First variation of Model 57M.

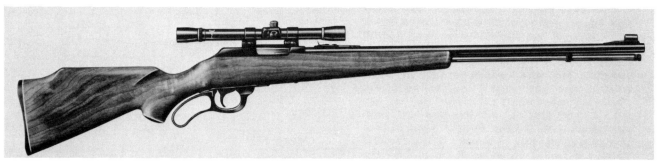

Second variation of Model 57M.

Marlin 57 M Levermatic rifle, cal .22 Magnum rimfire.

Third variation of Model 57M, which has new shape to forearm.

First variation of Model 62 center-fire rifle, which was without swivels.

Second variation of Model 62, which was equipped with swivels and a sling.

The 1964 catalog described the Model 62 as follows:

Marlin Levermatics, with a shorter lever stroke than any other lever action rifle, can be fired as fast as you can open and close your hand. You don't even have to change your grip—just flex your fingers down and up and you're ready for a quick repeat shot. The Marlin Levermatic was the first short-stroke action, it's been imitated but no other rifles match the short, 23-degree stroke of a Marlin.

Now available in powerful medium-range calibers, Levermatics are suitable for a wide range of game such as coyotes, wolves, cougar, bobcats and chucks.

NEW MARLIN 62 LEVERMATIC—First rifle ever made to shoot the .22 Jet and .256 Magnum—two fine cartridges just introduced.

Coupled with the superior accuracy and rapid fire capabilities of the Marlin Levermatic, both cartridges are spectacular performers. And Marlin side ejection lets you mount the great new Marlin 3X–9X Variable low—making an unmatchable combination in either caliber!

Specifications: Calibers .22 Jet, (available Feb., 1964) .256 Magnum. 4-shot repeater; approx. wt. 7 lbs; 23-in. Micro-Groove® barrel; 42-in. o.a. lgth.; adjustable rear, ramp front sight with protective hood; positive handy safety (locks lever and trigger); drilled and tapped for receiver sights, scope mounts; genuine American walnut stock with rugged outdoor finish; engine-turned bolt; extra-wide trigger; white line spacers; deluxe pistol grip cap; clip magazine; leather carrying strap and swivels.

Although it was stated in the catalog that the .22 Jet cartridge would be available in February 1964, the Model 62 was never chambered for the .22 Jet. However, a sling and swivels were added in 1964.

The 1966 catalog added the .30 carbine cartridge to the Model 62. It stated:

The .30 U.S. Carbine cartridge was tested on battlefields in World War II and Korea. It's proved very popular with small and medium game hunters and target shooters. Commercial hunting type ammunition is available in popular brands.

When first manufactured, the Model 62 was not serial-numbered. This was, of course, in violation of the federal law that stated that all center-fire firearms would be serial-numbered and that records would be maintained showing date of manufacture and to whom shipped. About 4,000 Model 62s were shipped without numbers. Marlin conducted a recall program by contacting distributors to have the guns returned for numbering. Owners of Model 62 rifles that do not have serial numbers can still return them for numbering.

Production of the Model 62 was as follows:

Model	Total
62 (.256)	5,960
62 (Western Auto .256)	1,758
62 .30 Carbine	7,996
Total	15,714

The suggested retail prices of the Model 62 were as follows:

Year	Price
1963–1967	$69.95
1968	72.95
1969	74.95

Semiautomatic Rifles

DESCRIPTIVE SUMMARIES

Caliber .22

A few years after Frank Kenna, Sr., acquired The Marlin Firearms Company, he introduced a new type of mechanism that the company had not yet manufactured in a sporting firearm. Remington, Winchester, and others had marketed blowback, semiautomatic (autoloading) rifles for many years. Up to 1930, Marlin had only made prototypes of autoloaders similar to the ones others already had on the market. In 1931, Marlin did introduce a new caliber .22 semiautomatic that had a clip magazine. Called the Model 50, the new rifle was the first in a long line of semiautomatic .22s that became the most popular .22s in the world. The sequence of the models and variations of each model produced by Marlin from 1931 to 1988 has been as follows:

Dates	Model	Type
1931–1935	Model 50	clip magazine
1936–1940	Model A1	clip magazine
1941–1946	Model A1C	clip magazine
1941–1946	Model A1DL	clip magazine
1948–1961	Model 89C	clip magazine
1948–1956	Model 88C	tubular magazine in butt
1953–1956	Model 88DL	tubular magazine in butt
1957–1959	Model 98	tubular magazine in butt
1959–1960	Model 99	tubular magazine
1960–1964	Model 99DL	tubular magazine
1961–1978	Model 99C	tubular magazine
1962–1965	Model 989	clip magazine

Dates	Model	Type
1964–1978	Model 99M1	tubular magazine
1965–1978	Model 989M2	clip magazine
1968–1970	Model 49	tubular magazine
1975–1978	Model 49DL	tubular magazine
1979	Model 40	tubular magazine
1960–1982	Model 60G and Model 60 Glenfield	tubular magazine
1983 to date	Model 60 Marlin	tubular magazine
1968	Model 65 Glenfield	tubular magazine
1967 to date	Model 70 Glenfield	clip magazine
1967 to date	Model 75 Glenfield	tubular magazine
1983 to date	Model 70 Marlin	clip magazine
1979 to date	Model 990	tubular magazine
1979 to date	Model 995	clip magazine
1986 to date	Model 70P	"Papoose" clip magazine
1986 to date	Model 70HC	25-shot clip magazine

Model 50, Caliber .22, Autoloading Rifle (1931–1935). The Model 50 rifle was described by Marlin as follows:

> There is something fascinating about shooting an autoloading rifle that grows on you the more the gun is used. No pump handle to operate but simply hold your aim with rifle to shoulder and pull the trigger.

Model 50 autoloading .22 rifle.

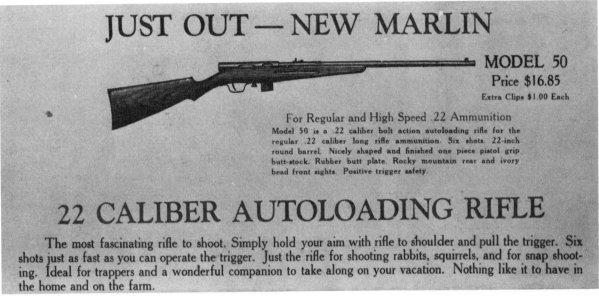

Marlin 1932 ad for the Model 50 rifle.

Simple Construction — This rifle is so constructed that it can be used continuously without cleaning the action, but if it becomes necessary to do this the action being so simple in construction can be taken apart in a few moments with the aid of only a screwdriver. There is no separate hammer, firing pin or carrier in this rifle as these parts are built into a one piece action block. Practically nothing to get out of order or break — all parts are made of Special Steel, guaranteeing long life.

Barrel — Bored and rifled to give the same accuracy for which Marlin Rifles have long been famous.

This latest addition to the Marlin line is a worthy achievement and a gun anyone would always feel proud to own.

The catalog's specifications for the new rifle were as follows:

A .22 caliber bolt action autoloading rifle; for regular long rifle and new high speed loads; 6 shots, 22-inch round barrel; weight about 5 pounds; nicely shaped and finished one piece pistol grip butt-stock; rubber buttplate, Rocky Mountain rear and ivory bead front sights. Positive trigger safety.

For regular .22 caliber long rifle cartridges and adjustable for the new high speed loads by fitting a simple balancing block that is furnished with each rifle which can be put in by anyone outside of the factory in a few moments with the use of only a screwdriver.

The lowest priced .22 caliber autoloading rifle and the best value ever offered. A real Marlin barrel and a rifle built throughout with real Marlin quality and workmanship at an unusually low price.

When equipped with the Marlin No. 22 rear peep sight, the Model 50 was identified as the Model 50E. Otherwise there was no difference between the two.

The unique feature of this blow-back-operated autoloader

Model and caliber markings on Model 50 rifle.

Marlin
MODEL 50 · 50E

Number		Price	Number		Price
1D	Barrel	$ 5.50	21D	Receiver Bumper Plug Retaining Screw	.11
2D	Balancing Block, small	.33	22D	Recoil Spring	.44
3D	Balancing Block, large	.33	23D	Sear	.33
4D	Breech Bolt	1.98	24D	Sear Spring	.11
5D	Breech Bolt Cocking Handle	.33	25D	Sear Trip	.22
6D	Buttstock, with Plate	3.85	26D	Sear Trip Pin	.11
7D	Buttplate, rubber	1.10	27D	Sear Trip Spring	.11
8D	Buttplate, steel	.66	28D	Sear Block Pin	.11
9D	Buttplate Screws (2) each	.11	29D	Take Down Screw	.44
10D	Ejector (pin)	.11	30D	Take Down Screw Stud	.33
11D	Extractor (old model)	.66	31D	Trigger	.66
12D	Magazine Complete	1.10	32D	Trigger Block	.88
13D	Magazine Follower with Pin	.22	33D	Trigger Pin	.11
14D	Magazine Spring	.22	34D	Trigger Spring	.11
15D	Magazine Bottom Plate	.22	35D	Trigger Safety	.55
16D	Magazine Catch	.22	36D	Trigger Safety Washer	.11
17D	Magazine Catch Pin	.11	37D	Trigger Guard	.44
18D	Magazine Catch Spring	.11	38D	Trigger Guard Screws (2) each	.11
19D	Receiver	2.20			
20D	Receiver Bumper Plug Screw	.44			

SIGHTS

39D	Front Sight, Ivory Bead	$ 1.10	44D	Rear Sight Elevator, Sporting	.44
40D	Front Sight, Silver Bead	1.10	45D	Receiver Peep Sight, Marlin No. 22	2.50
41D	Front Sight, Silver Bead with Hood	1.32	46D	Receiver Peep Sight Screws (2) each	.11
42D	Front Sight Hood	.33	47D	Slot Blank	.33
43D	Rear Sight Complete, Sporting	.88			

Parts catalog list of component parts of the Model 50 rifle.

was the fact that the Model 50 fired from an open bolt. When the rifle was cocked, the bolt was held open. Upon pulling the trigger, the bolt slammed forward, stripping a cartridge from the magazine, loading it into the chamber, and firing it. In the face of the bolt was a fixed firing pin that fired the cartridge

when the bolt closed. As can be imagined, the bolt slamming home would disturb the aim, and as a result, the system did not get any raves from the sportswriters or sportsmen comparing the Model 50 with other companies' semiautomatic .22s that fired from a closed bolt.

When a misfire was experienced, or if the fired case did not blow out of the chamber, the bolt stayed closed. It was then necessary to operate by hand an extractor that was fitted into the right side of the barrel, just forward of the receiver. A later variation did not require the manual extractor.

The total production of the Model 50 is not known. It is speculated that no more than 5,000 were manufactured.

The prices of the Model 50 were as follows:

Year	Model 50	Model 50E
Apr. 1932	$14.30	
Nov. 1932	16.85	
1933	16.85	
1934	16.85	
1935	16.85	$19.85

Model A1 and Model A1E, Caliber .22, Autoloading Rifles (1936–1940). The next autoloading rifle manufactured by Marlin was made in four variations. They were:

1. Model A1, safety at rear of receiver and stamped metal trigger guard.
2. Model A1, safety on right side of receiver and plastic trigger guard.
3. Model A1E, like first variation except with target sights.
4. Model A1E, like second variation except with target sights.

The Model A1 rifle was similar to the previous Model 50 except that it fired from a closed action. Also, the rifle was designed to function with either regular or high-speed cartridges without adjustment. Marlin stated that the Model A1 was:

> . . . the very last word in gun design. Item braces new mechanical features ingeniously contrived and developed by Marlin expert engineers. Everything essential to an automatic is built into this rifle. Never before in the history of gun making has so much gun been offered for the money.

Model A1

First variation of the Model A1 rifle.

First variation of the Model A1E rifle.

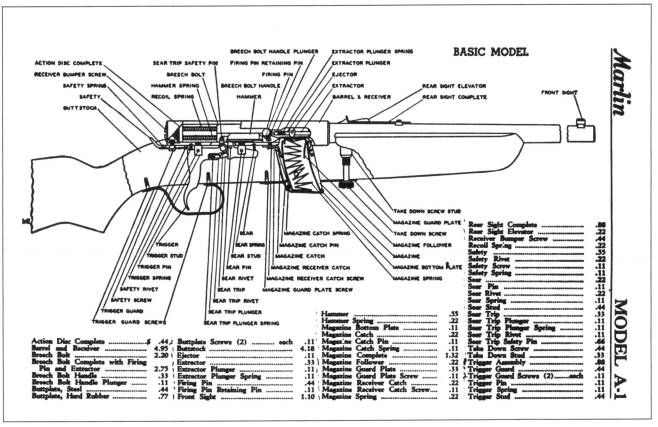

Model A1 parts list from Marlin catalog.

The rifle had a 6-shot clip magazine, 24-in. round tapered barrel, Ballard rifling, positive safety, crowned muzzle, American black walnut pistol grip stock, unbreakable butt plate, silver bead front sight, and adjustable sporting rear sight. The length was 41 inches and the rifle weighed 6 pounds.

No model designation is marked on the Model A1 and Model A1E, or on the later Model A1C and Model A1DL. However, they can be identified by the *22 Long Rifle Only—Smokeless Greased* roll-stamp on the barrel, as no other Marlin has this information on the barrel.

The first variation of the Models A1 and A1E had a flat hard fiber butt plate that had seven sets of four serrations, as did other models of this period. The second variation had a hard rubber plate.

The Model A1 rifle, when equipped with the Marlin rear peep sight and a hooded front sight, was identified as the Model A1E. Except for the sights, the rifles were identical.

The 1936 Marlin catalog illustration shows what appears to be checkering on the grip. A Model A1 or A1E having such checkering has not been observed. The 1937 catalog illustra-

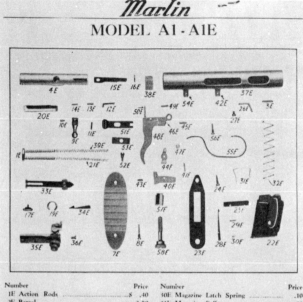

Marlin
MODEL A1 · A1E

Number	Price		Number	Price
1E Action Rods	$ .40		30E Magazine Latch Spring	.10
2E Barrel	3.50		31E Magazine Follower	.20
3E Barrel Pin	.10		32E Magazine Follower Spring	.20
4E Breech Bolt Only	2.00		33E Rear Sight	.80
5E Breech Bolt Complete with Firing			34E Rear Sight Elevator	.20
Pin and Extractor	2.50		35E Receiver Peep Sight Complete	2.00
6E Buttstock Complete	3.80		36E Receiver Peep Sight Screws (2) each	.10
7E Buttplate	.40		37E Receiver	2.00
8E Buttplate Screws (2) each	.10		38E Receiver Bumper Screw	.40
9E Cocking Handle	.30		39E Recoil Spring	.20
10E Cocking Handle Plunger	.10		40F Sear	.20
11E Ejector	.10		41E Sear Spring	.10
12E Extractor	.30		42E Sear Stud	.40
13E Extractor Plunger	.10		43E Sear Stud Pin	.10
14E Extractor Spring	.10		44E Sear Trip	.30
15E Firing Pin	.40		45E Sear Trip Plunger	.10
16E Firing Pin Pin	.10		46E Sear Trip Plunger Spring	.10
17E Front Sight Silver Bead	1.00		47E Sear Trip Rivet	.10
18E Front Sight Silver Bead with Hood	1.20		48E Trigger	.60
19E Front Sight Hood	.20		49E Trigger Pin	.10
20E Hammer	.50		50E Trigger Spring	.10
21E Hammer Spring	.20		51E Trigger Safety	.50
22E Magazine Complete	1.00		52E Trigger Safety Screw	.10
23E Magazine Stock Plate	.30		53E Trigger Safety Spring	.10
24E Magazine Stock Plate Screw	.10		54E Trigger Stud	.40
25E Magazine Bottom Plate	.10		55E Trigger Guard	.40
26E Magazine Catch	.20		56E Trigger Guard Screws (2) each	.10
27E Magazine Catch Screw	.10		57E Take Down Stud	.30
28E Magazine Latch	.20		58E Take Down Stud Screw	.40
29E Magazine Latch Pin	.10			

Marlin A1E parts list from Marlin catalog. Note the butt plate.

tions appear to have been "doctored" so that the checkering on the grip does not show. The 1939 catalog has new illustrations that do not show checkering.

The retail prices of the Model A1 and A1E rifles were the following:

Year	A1	A1E
1936	$12.95	$14.25
1937	13.95	14.95
1939–1940	12.60	13.30

Models A1C and A1DL, Caliber .22, Autoloading Rifles (1941–1946). The Models A1C and A1DL were an improvement over the earlier A1 and A1E models. The 1945 catalog described the A1C as follows:

> Redesigned and improved; shoots as fast as the trigger can be pulled. New military type one-piece buttstock with fluted comb and semi-beavertail forearm, equipped with Rocky Mountain type rear sight, bead front sight, 24 inch round tapered blued steel barrel, crowned muzzle, Ballard type rifling. For regular or high speed .22 long rifle greased cartridges only. Automatic side ejector, new OFF and ON safety, flush take-down screw. Overall length 42½ inches; weight about 6 pounds.

The stock of this new variation of the earlier Model A1 and A1E was the basic difference between them. The new stock had an enlarged forearm that resulted in a very pronounced step on each side at about the ejection port of the receiver. Also added was a fluted comb.

The Model A1DL was identical to the A1C except for the addition of target sights and sling swivels. The new front target sight now had a ramp and a hood.

The retail prices of the Models A1C and A1DL were as follows:

Year	Model A1C	Model A1DL
1941	$16.80	$18.20
1942–1944	WW II – No production	
1945	17.00	18.45
1946	22.85	24.70

Model 88C and Model 88DL, Caliber .22, Semiautomatic Rifles (1948–1956). The previous autoloading (semiautomatic) rifles were all of the clip magazine type. The Model 88C was the first that had a tubular magazine. The Marlin catalog identified it this way:

> Completely new and modern the Marlin Model 88C is outstanding in the semi-automatic caliber .22 field, because

Second variation of the Model A1 rifle.

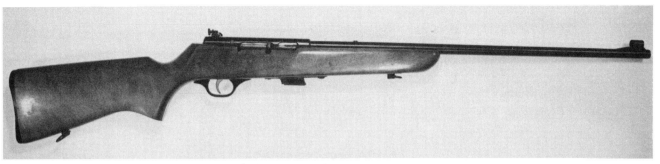

Model A1E rifle that is equipped with target sights and sling swivels.

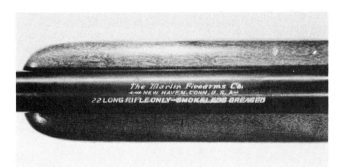

Barrel marking found on Model A1, A1E, A1C, and A1DL autoloading caliber .22 rifles.

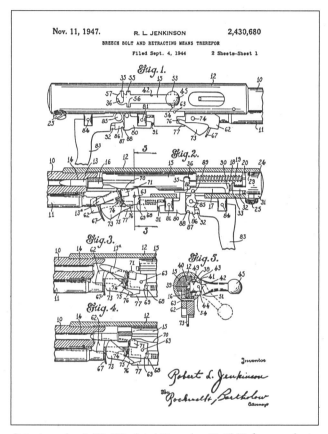

Patent number 2,430,680, dated November 11, 1947, for a semiautomatic rifle mechanism that could be fired as a single shot or as an autoloader.

of its many improvements in action and its smart streamlined appearance.

In the field of new guns, Marlin has developed two completely new, modern caliber .22 semi-automatic rifles. One is the Marlin Model 88–C, a tubular magazine auto-loader; the other the Marlin Model 89–C, a clip magazine fed semi-automatic. Both of these new models have the same operating mechanism for receiver, barrel, safety and internal action.

The Marlin Model 88–C is a 15-shot semi-automatic caliber .22 rifle with tubular feed. Magazine is located in the buttstock with a funnel loading feature. This new model shoots all forms of standard long rifle .22 caliber ammunition, greased or waxed, regular and high speed velocity. 24″ round-tapered blued steel barrel with crowned muzzle. Overall length 45″; weight about 6¾ pounds.

The one single feature of the Model 88 rifles that hindered their popularity was the problem of loading the magazine. The tubular magazine was located in the buttstock. When loading the rifle, it was necessary to remove the inner magazine tube and drop the cartridges into the hole in the steel butt plate. Called "funnel" loading by Marlin, it was not easy! The inner magazine tube, rifle, and cartridges all had to be held, and only two hands were available. Therefore, it was necessary either to hold the inner tube under the arm or to lay it down. Neither was a good choice.

The operation and appearance of the Model 88C and 88DL were very much like the earlier Model A1 and A1DL, except, of course, that these new models had tubular magazines.

The Model 88DL had the same features as the Model 88C except for a new design of peep sight that was mounted on the

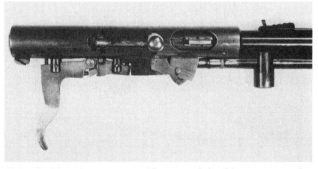

R.L. Jenkinson's prototype rifle covered by his patent number 2,430,680.

Model 88C tubular-magazine rifle.

Model 88DL rifle.

rear end plug. It also had sling swivels. The pistol grip and forend were expertly checked.

The prices of the Models 88C and 88DL were as follows:

Year	Model 88C	Model 88DL
1948	$30.50	
1949	32.50	
1950–1952	33.30	
1953–1954	33.95	$39.95
1955	34.70	40.70
1956	39.70	45.70

Model 89C, Caliber .22, Semiautomatic Rifle (1948–1961). The Model 89C was a clip-magazine version of the Model 88C. The 1948 catalog made the following comparison:

> The Marlin Model 89C is a 7-shot clip magazine caliber .22 semi-automatic rifle. It has a concealed magazine catch which prevents accidental release. The protected magazine catch is easy to release when reloading. Shoots all forms of standard long rifle .22 caliber ammunition, greased or

Butt end of Model 88 rifle with its magazine tube.

waxed, regular and high velocity. 24″ round-tapered blued steel barrel with crowned muzzle. Overall length 45″; weight about 6¾ pounds.

Both the Marlin Models 88–C and 89–C have a new type of bolt support which reduces to a minimum the effect of powder fouling in the action of the rifles. Each model has only one horizontal opening between the mechanism and the exterior — and that is the side ejection port.

Cocking handle on both models is on the bolt in the side ejection space well forward of the shooter's hand. Take-down feature is quick and simple for oiling and cleaning. All light parts of these new rifles are made of finest drawn steel for greater durability and reliability. Action is fast and fool-proof. Positive sear lock safety. Solid top blued steel receiver. Side ejection. Low sighting plane for low telescope mounting.

Full pistol grip buttstock. Stock and forearm made of American black walnut. Safety button conveniently placed on right hand side of receiver, directly above trigger. Both models function with remarkable smoothness and with minimum of blast and smoke-escape at the breech. Ramp front sight with Bead; Rocky Mountain type rear sight.

Note that the magazine is listed above as 7-shot.
The 1953 catalog added the following comments:

> The new model 89–C is a clip magazine version of the popular 88–C and 88–DL. It comes equipped with Marlin's new, revolutionary Micro-Groove barrel that increases accuracy-performance by about 20%. The new Micro-Groove barrel has many more rifling lands than conventional barrels have, resulting in engravings on the bullet, made gently but firmly, giving a secure spinning grip for stabilization. Gas leakage between bullet and bore is practically eliminated due to the use of a special land design in the new type barrel. Leading and other types of bore fouling are greatly reduced by shape and surface condition of the bore.
>
> Model 89–C handles .22 caliber Long Rifle cartridges only. Each 89–C is packed with two clip magazines each holding

five shots. Automatic side ejection, positive sear lock safety, easy to take-down for cleaning and oiling, red and green safety dots tell shooter fire and safe position of safety button. Low sighting plane for 'scope mounting, chrome-plated cocking handle spur, stock and forearm of seasoned walnut, 24″ round tapered blued-steel barrel, hooded ramp front sight with bead and Rocky Mountain type rear sight, overall length 45 inches; weight about 6¾ pounds.

Note that now the magazine is listed as 5-shot, two magazines are furnished with each rifle, and the barrel is 24 inches long.

The 1957 catalog describes the Model 89C as having a 12-shot magazine, a 22-in. barrel and a Bishop-style stock. The text was as follows:

> Auto-loading 12-shot clip magazine .22 caliber long rifle automatic. 22 inch round tapered blued steel barrel, crowned muzzle. Open rear sight, ramp front sight with detachable hood. Bishop style stock. Finest quality walnut. Shoots all forms of standard .22 caliber long rifle ammunition, greased

or waxed, regular or high velocity, without adjustment. Easy to take-down for cleaning and oiling. Positive sear lock safety. Red and green safety dots tell fire position of rifle. Solid top receiver, automatic side ejection. Special new finish on receiver. Pistol grip. Receiver dovetail grooved for tip-off mounts and top-mounts. Overall length 42″; weight about 6 pounds depending on density of wood.

The prices of the Model 89C were as follows:

Year	Price
1953–1954	$27.95
1955	30.70
1956	34.70
1957–1959	37.95
1960–1961	39.95

Model 98, Caliber .22, Semiautomatic Rifle (1957–1959). The Model 98 was an attempt to put new life in the Model 88 rifle by changing the tubular magazine in the buttstock to one that

Model 89C rifle with 7-shot magazine.

Model 89C rifle with 12-shot magazine.

Model 89C rifle with 12-shot magazine and Bishop-style stock.

Model 98 rifle with open sights.

Model 98 rifle with peep rear sight.

Left side of Model 98 rifle showing Bishop-style cheek piece stock.

loaded through the side of the stock instead of through the butt plate. The capacity of the magazine was not reduced, but the loading system was greatly improved. The 1957 catalog had the following description of the Model 98:

> Model Super-automatic 98: Autoloading 15-shot tubular magazine, .22 caliber long rifle automatic, 22-inch round tapered blued steel barrel, crowned muzzle. Receiver peep sight with windage and elevation settings. Ramp front sight with detachable hood. Bishop style Monte Carlo stock with cheekpiece. Finest quality walnut. Loading port on right side of buttstock. Shoots all forms of standard .22 caliber long rifle ammunition, greased or waxed, regular or high velocity loads, without adjustment. Easy to take-down for cleaning and oiling. Magazine located in stock. Special new finish on receiver. Positive sear lock safety. Solid top receiver, automatic side ejection. Pistol grip. Dovetail grooved on receiver for tip-off mounts and top-mounts. Overall length 42″; weight about 6½ pounds depending on density of wood.

The suggested retail price of the Model 98 was as follows:

Year	Price
1957–1959	$43.95

A total of 9,061 Model 98 rifles were manufactured.

Model 99, Caliber .22, Automatic Rifle (1959–1961). Even though refinements and improvements had been made to the autoloaders from 1936 to 1957, the success of each variation did not reach the potential expected. As a result, Marlin had been working on a totally new design of autoloader that replaced the Model 98. In 1959 a new rifle, designed by Marlin's design engineer, the late Ewald Nichol, was introduced as the Model 99. The 1959 catalog included the following details about the new rifle:

> The Marlin Model 99 Automatic is a new sleek .22 caliber automatic for all-round shooting and hunting purposes. Micro-Groove rifling for extreme accuracy—18-shot capacity—Handles .22 caliber long rifle cartridges, regular or high velocity loads without adjustment—solid top receiver for low scope mounting—automatic side ejection drilled and tapped

on left side of receiver for standard receiver peep sights — top of receiver drilled and tapped for adapter base for telescope top mount — packed with adapter base — easy to take-down — pistol grip — cross bolt safety — streamlined receiver — 22″ blued round tapered barrel of Special Analysis Ordnance steel — New design one piece stock of finest walnut — overall length 42″; weight about 5½ pounds depending on density of wood.

A complete success from the beginning, the Model 99 mechanism and styling developed into a number of variations to include private brand models, as well as clip magazine models. The suggested retail prices of the Model 99 were:

Year	Price
1959	$39.95
1960	42.95
1961	43.95

A total of 116,239 Model 99s and brand-name variations were manufactured.

Model 99DL, Caliber .22, Automatic Rifle (1960–1964). The Model 99DL was a Model 99 rifle with minor changes to make it a fancier rifle. The operation of the rifle and its mechanism were identical to those of the Model 99.

The 1960 catalog added to the Model 99 information the following about the Model 99DL:

Gold plated trigger, new gold finished trigger guard, swivels for leather sling strap, new style one-piece stock with fluted comb and Monte Carlo made of finest quality seasoned walnut and specially finished to withstand all kinds of weather and usage, pistol grip and grip cap and white line spacer, custom type hard rubber buttplate with white liner-cushion.

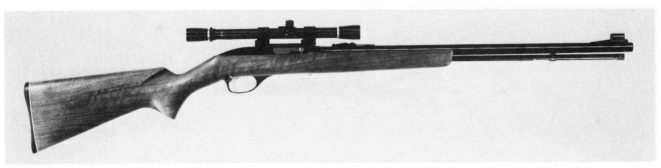

Model 99 rifle.

Model 99DL rifle (scope was not included in price of gun).

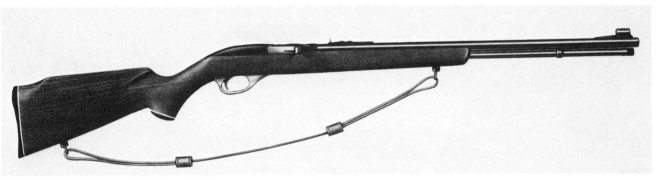

Made in 1962 and after, this Model 99DL came fitted with a sling.

In 1962, a leather sling was added to the Model 99DL.

The Model 99DL was available from 1960 to 1964 at following prices:

Year	Price
1960	$48.95
1961–1962	49.95
1963	53.95
1964	54.95

A total of 5,279 Model 99DLs were manufactured.

Model 99C, Caliber .22, Automatic Rifle (1961–1978). The Model 99C was almost the same as the Model 99 rifle. Only minor differences existed between the two. For example, the 99C had a Micro-Groove rifled barrel, and the trigger was gold-plated.

In 1963, a Monte Carlo stock was featured and the bolt was illustrated as being damascened. Recievers were grooved for tip-off scope mounts in 1964. In 1969, the ramp front sight was changed to a one-piece band type that included the band for the magazine tube.

In 1970, all Model 99C rifles manufactured that year had a 100th-year commemorative medallion embedded into the right side of the buttstock. In 1971, impressed checkering was added to the pistol grip and forearm of the Model 99C. The pattern of the checkering changed slightly in 1975.

The band-type front sight was eliminated in 1976. A ramp front sight with bead was now standard. In 1977, the checkering was again changed. It now had a more decorative pattern with a diamond and carved-leaf motif.

The suggested retail prices of the Model 99C were listed as follows:

Year	Price
1961	$42.95
1962	44.95

1963 Model 99C rifle.

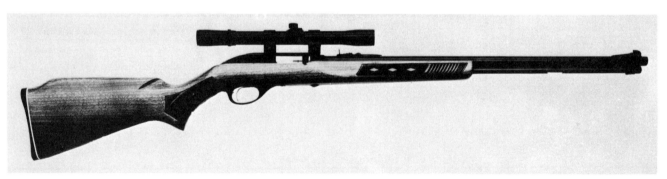

1971 Model 99C rifle.

MARLIN Model 99C

1976 Model 99C rifle.

Year	Price
1963–1965	47.95
1966	48.95
1967–1969	49.95
1970	59.95
1971	52.95
1972	54.95
1973	57.95
1974	58.95
1975	62.95
1976	66.95
1977	69.95
1978	73.95

Over 100,000 of the Model 99C were manufactured.

Model 989, Caliber .22, Semiautomatic Rifle (1962–1965). The Model 989 was the first clip magazine semiautomatic rifle of the new breed of autoloaders started in 1959. It was described by Marlin as:

> A clip loading version of the Model 99C, having the same popular features, high grade workmanship, fast accurate shooting. 8 sure shots, walnut stock, solid top non-rusting receiver and side ejection give you low, centered scope mounting.

When introduced in 1962, the Model 989 had a straight-comb stock. In 1963, the stock was changed to one having a Monte Carlo comb.

Although short-lived, the Model 989 was the first of the clip loaders that soon became part of a family of autoloaders manufactured and distributed throughout the world. In fact, Marlin's .22 autoloaders, both clip and tubular models, became the most popular .22s in the world.

The suggested retail prices of the Model 989 were as follows:

Year	Price
1962	$39.95
1963	42.95
1964	43.95
1965	44.95

A total of 24,843 Model 989 rifles were manufactured.

Model 99M1, Caliber .22, Autoloading Carbine, (1964–1978). The new Marlin Model 99M1 was a short carbine with the same tubular magazine action as the Models 989 and 99C. It was different in that it had a hand guard and an 18-inch barrel. It was described in 1964 as follows:

> New Marlin 99M1 Carbine: Short, rapid firing carbine, genuine American walnut handguard to match stock. Rear sight is adjustable and quickly removable for scope use. Tubular magazine; 18-inch Micro-Groove barrel; 37-inch overall length; approximately 4¾ pounds; capacity 10 shots; ramp front, adjustable and removable rear sight; drilled and tapped for receiver sights; grooved for tip-off scope mounts; 24K gold-plated trigger; white line spacer; leather strap and swivels.

The Model 99M1 carbine's rear sight was adjustable for windage and elevation. It attached to the telescope mounting dovetail on the top of the receiver. The front sight was a band

First variation of Model 989 rifle, with a straight comb to the stock. A second variation had a Monte Carlo comb.

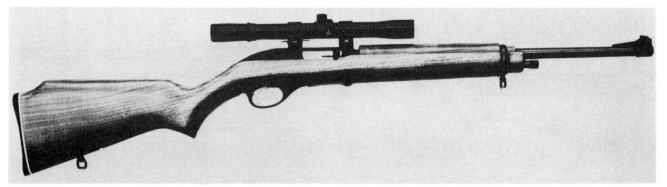

Model 99M1 carbine shown with telescope attached.

Marlin 99M1 matched with Marlin 300 scope

Model 99M1 carbine of the 1970 production, with the 100th-anniversary commemorative medallion in the stock.

type of sight held to the barrel by a set screw. The carbine was equipped with sling swivels.

In 1969, a new bolt hold-open feature was added. By pulling the charging handle to the rear and pushing it in, the bolt could be locked open for inspection of the chamber and feed throat during unloading.

In 1970, a 100th-anniversary medallion was embedded into the right side of the buttstock.

If there were shortcomings in the Model 99M1 carbine, they were the open rear sight that was too close to the eye, and the fact that to load the magazine it was necessary, as it was with the Model 88 rifle, to remove the inner magazine tube and hold it while loading.

The marketing thought behind the Model 99M1 semiautomatic carbine was to capitalize on its hand guard, short barrel, and M1 suffix to the model number as it was felt that the casual similarity to the Cal. 30 U.S., Carbine, M1 would appeal to the thousands of WW II veterans who had trained and carried into combat the larger caliber M1 carbine. It must have worked, because over 160,000 of this model were manufactured.

The suggested retail prices of the Model 99M1 were as follows:

Year	Price
1964–1970	$49.95
1971	52.95
1972	54.95
1973	57.95

Year	Price
1974	58.95
1975	62.95
1976	66.95
1977	69.95
1978	73.95

Model 989M2, Caliber .22, Automatic Carbine (1965–1978). The Model 989M2 had all the same pluses and minuses that the Model 99M1 had, except that the tube-loading problem of the 99M1 was eliminated by giving this carbine a clip magazine.

Many sportsmen (I'm one of them) prefer the clip magazine over a tubular magazine. Extra magazines can always be preloaded and carried in a pocket. Unloading is also much more convenient with clip magazine guns. (However, it is fun to shoot a string of caliber .22 rapid-fire from a large-capacity tubular magazine gun.) Two 7-shot magazines were furnished with the Model 989M2 through 1969. In 1970, the practice was discontinued.

In 1979, the Model 989M2 was replaced by the Model 995.

The suggested retail prices of the Model 989M2 were as follows:

Year	Price
1965–1970	$49.95
1971	52.95
1972	54.95
1973	57.95

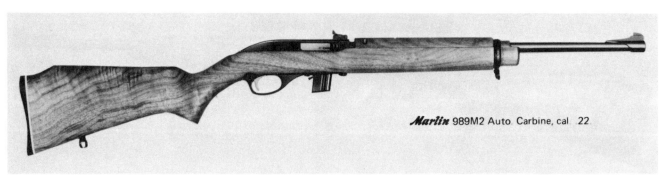

Marlin 989M2 Auto. Carbine, cal. 22

Model 989M2 carbine.

Year	Price
1974	58.95
1975	62.95
1976	66.95
1977	69.95
1978	73.95

More than 110,000 of the Model 989M2 were manufactured.

Models 49 and 49DL, Caliber .22, Autoloading Rifles (1968–1978). The Model 49 was first developed for a mass-merchandiser that wanted a model unique to it. After about 65,000 were supplied to that outlet, Marlin started to market them through the Marlin product catalog and no longer supplied them exclusively to a mass-merchandiser.

Unique among the Marlin autoloaders, because of a two-piece stock, the Model 49 was described in this way:

> Here's a brand new personal gun for those who want the best. The Marlin 49 features a 2-piece selected American walnut stock. It fires 19 Long Rifles as fast as you pull the trigger. Its solid top receiver is rust proof and the dependable action assures reliable service.
>
> The new Model 49 is typical Marlin personal gun quality—made the old-fashioned way and hand finished by engine turned damascening, adding a custom feature found only on the best guns.
>
> Model 49 features a new bolt hold-open—an added safety feature that lets you see inside the action at a glance and provides easy cleaning.
>
> Specifications: Cal. .22 Long Rifle only, high speed or regular, 22″ Micro-Groove barrel; 40½″ overall; approximately 5½ pounds; adjustable open rear sight, ramp front

sight, grooved for tip-off scope mounts and receiver sights; 24K gold-plated trigger; white spacers; Monte Carlo American walnut stock with full pistol grip, slim forend. Manual bolt hold-open holds bolt back with action open.

Impressed checkering was added to the pistol grip and forearm in 1970. In 1971, handsome scrollwork was embossed into the sides of the receiver, and the model was changed from Model 49 to Model 49 Deluxe (49DL). The plain Model 49 was dropped.

In 1976, the combination front sight band and magazine tube band was changed to a screw-on ramp front sight and a separate band for the magazine tube. The Model 49DL was dropped from the line in 1979.

The suggested retail prices of the Model 49 and 49DL were as follows:

Year	Model 49
1968–1970	$59.95
	Model 49DL
1971	$59.95
1972	61.95
1973	64.95
1974	65.95
1975	69.95
1976	75.95
1977	79.95
1978	82.95

The total production of the Model 49 and 49DL was as follows:

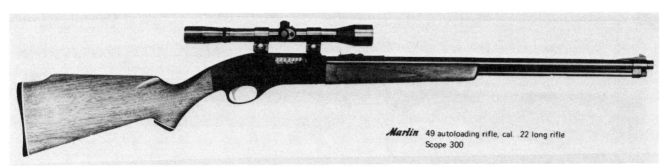

Model 49 rifle.

Model 49DL rifle.

Model	Total
Model 49	79,458
Model 49DL	30,964
Grand Total	110,422

Model 40, Glenfield, Caliber .22, Autoloader (1979). The Model 40 rifle was a limited-production Glenfield rifle, which was the same as the Marlin Model 49DL rifle that was discontinued in 1978.

When the 49DL was made into the Model 40, the stock and forearm were changed from walnut to birch wood; the butt plate spacer and damascening of the bolt were eliminated, and the trigger was chrome-plated instead of gold-plated. Otherwise it was identical to the Model 49.

The suggested retail price of the Model 40 was $84.00.

Model 990, Caliber .22, Semiautomatic Rifle (1979–1987). The Model 990 rifle was the old Model 99C rifle with refinements. It was caliber .22 long rifle only. It had an 18-shot tubular magazine with the new Osborne patented closure system, a side ejection bolt hold-open device, and the new type of receiver top that was serrated for nonglare. The stock finish was now the new tough Mar-Shield type that was electrostatically applied. The barrel was 22 inches long with Micro-Groove rifling (16 grooves). The new ramp front sight had a brass bead and a Wide-Scan front sight hood. The rear sight was a new folding leaf type. The impressed checkering was that of the Model 99C, second type. The stock was of American walnut, the classic stock material. The overall length was 40¾ inches, and the rifle weighed 5½ pounds.

In 1985, a last-shot bolt hold-open feature was added to the Model 990 rifle. The Model 990 was not listed in the catalog in 1988.

The suggested retail prices of the Model 990 were as follows:

Year	Price
1979	$ 81.00
1980	93.95
1981	110.95
1982	124.95
1983	125.95
1984	130.95
1985	140.95
1986	147.95
1987	148.95
1988	156.95

Model 995, Caliber .22, Autoloader Carbine (1979 to date). The Model 995 was introduced in 1979 at the same time as the Model 990. It, too, was a new model designation for the earlier Model 989M2 carbine, rather than a new carbine. However, the necessary changes were made, and the carbine is a real dandy with its new look.

The hand guard and band-type front sight of the Model 989M2 were eliminated, and the open rear sight was placed on the barrel, where it belonged. The front sight was the new screw-on ramp with brass bead and Wide-Scan hood. The magazine was Marlin's standard 7-shot, which has been in use since introduction of the Model 989 in 1962. Like the Model 989M2, the Model 995 was equipped with a barrel band and sling swivels.

Over the years, the suggested retail price of the Model 995 has been as follows:

Year	Price
1979	$ 75.95
1980	87.95

Model 990 rifle.

Model 995 rifle.

Year	Price
1981	103.95
1982	115.95
1983	117.95
1984	122.95
1985	131.95
1986	137.95
1987	148.95
1988	156.95

Model 60G (1960–1965) and Model 60, Glenfield, Caliber .22, Autoloading Rifle (1966–1982). The Glenfield line of rifles and shotguns were mostly sold to chain outlets and mass-merchandisers. This Glenfield Model 60 rifle was the most popular by far of all autoloaders, regardless of make or model. The rifle had the same rifle mechanism as the Model 99C and the later Model 990, except that the stock was made of birch wood, rather than walnut, and it had a less expensive rear sight. When introduced, it had a combination front sight and magazine tube band. Later ones had a screwed-on ramp front sight.

Model 60, Marlin, Caliber .22, Autoloading Rifle (1983 to date). Since 1983, Marlin has dropped the use of the name Glenfield, and the Model 60 became a Marlin having a ramp sight with Wide-Scan hood and folding leaf rear sight. The Marlin Model 60 does not have impressed checkering; however, the stock is birch wood. Being birch wood, it does not have the typical Marlin bull's-eye embedded into the bottom edge of the stock.

In 1985, the Model 60 had a new last-shot bolt hold-open feature added. All Marlin tubular magazine repeating semiautomatic rifles and carbines made thereafter have the same feature.

From 1983 to 1988, the suggested retail prices of the Model 60 Marlin have been as follows:

Year	Price
1983	$104.95
1984	93.95
1985	98.95
1986	109.95

Glenfield Model 60 autoloading rifle, cal. 22 Long Rifle
Glenfield Scope 200

Model 60 Glenfield, first variation.

GLENFIELD Model 60

Model 60 Glenfield, second variation.

Marlin 60

Model 60 Marlin rifle.

Year	Price
1987	111.95
1988	116.95

Model 65, Glenfield, Caliber .22, Autoloading Rifle (1968).
The Model 65 Glenfield rifle was identical to the first-variation
Model 60 Glenfield, except that it had a solid brass outer
magazine tube. It was sold to Oklahoma Tire & Supply Company as a promotion item. It was not a regular catalog item. A
total of 44,369 of this model were manufactured.

**Model 70, Glenfield, Caliber .22, Autoloading Carbine (1967
to date).** The Model 70 Glenfield was the economy version of
the Model 989M2 carbine. It was a clip magazine model with
an 18-in. barrel. It had a barrel band and sling swivels. The
front sight was the band type.

**Model 75, Glenfield, Caliber .22, Autoloading Carbine (1967
to date).** The Glenfield Model 75 was the tube magazine version of the Marlin Model (formerly Glenfield Model) 70. Like
the Model 70, the 75 had a barrel band and swivels. It also had
the short 9-shot tubular magazine of the Model 99M1, but did
not have the hand guard of the 99M1. Like all the Marlin semi-
automatics, it was made for use with only the caliber .22 long
rifle cartridge. The barrel was 18 inches long. The stock was
walnut-finished hardwood with a pistol grip and Monte Carlo
comb. It was also equipped with a barrel band and sling
swivels. The overall length was 37 inches and it weighed
4½ pounds.

The Model 75 was not a standard Glenfield cataloged item.
It was sold as a promotional item only, and was packaged with
a Marlin Model 200 telescope in the box.

**Model 70, Marlin, Caliber .22, Autoloading Carbine (1983 to
date).** In 1983, the Glenfield name was dropped by Marlin, and
the Glenfield Model 70 became the Marlin Model 70. When
the change in name took place, the impressed checkering on
the stock, the barrel band, and the swivels were eliminated.

Model 65 Glenfield, which has a brass outer magazine tube.

Glenfield Model 70 autoloading rifle, cal. .22 Long Rifle
Glenfield Scope 200

Model 70 Glenfield carbine.

Model 75 Glenfield carbine.

Model 70 Marlin carbine.

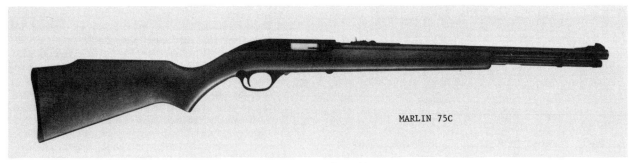

Model 75C Marlin carbine.

Model 70P "Papoose" takedown carbine.

The front sight was also changed from a band type to a screwed-on ramp. The new image was neat, streamlined, and functional. The suggested retail prices were as follows:

Year	Price
1983	$104.95
1984	93.95
1985	98.95
1986	109.95
1987	111.95

Model 70P, "Papoose," Caliber .22, Semiautomatic Carbine (1986 to date). The Marlin Model 70P is probably the most innovative new item Marlin has produced in some time. Its takedown feature and packaging concept are totally new for the company. It is quickly taken down and easily transported in its own padded case that will float. Colored bright red, the case and rifle can be easily identified when in the camp, boat, truck, or snowmobile.

The Model 70P has all the semiautomatic mechanical features of the Model 70 clip magazine autoloader, plus the simple takedown barrel. The barrel is 16¼ inches long, and assembled, the rifle is 35¼ inches long. It weighs only 3¾ pounds. It has a 7-shot clip magazine, manual bolt hold-open, cross-bolt safety, and a disconnect mechanism that prevents the gun from being fired if the barrel is removed. It comes packaged with a 4X telescope that can be left mounted to the receiver when packed in the carrying case. An adjustable rear and a ramp front sight are standard. The receiver is grooved to accept the telescope. The stock is walnut-finished hardwood (birch) with a pistol grip and hard rubber butt plate. The 70P is truly a fun gun from the company that makes more .22 rifles than any other manufacturer in the world.

The suggested retail prices of the Model 70P "Papoose" rifle have been the following:

Year	Price
1986	$135.95

Model 70P "Papoose" as stowed in its carrying case.

Year	Price
1987	144.95
1988	153.95

Model 70HC, Caliber .22, Semiautomatic Carbine (1988 to date). The Model 70HC is the Marlin Model 70 with a high capacity (HC) clip magazine that holds 25 caliber .22 long rifle cartridges. The Monte Carlo stock is walnut finished hardwood (birch) that has a full pistol grip, Mar-Shield finish, and a hard rubber butt plate. The 18-in. barrel has Micro-Groove rifling (16 grooves). The sights are the usual adjustable open rear and ramp front. The receiver is grooved for tip-off telescope mounts. The overall length is 36½ inches, and the 70HC weighs 5 pounds empty. The magazine will fit other Marlin and Glenfield clip magazine semiautomatic rifles.

The 1988 suggested retail price of the Model 70HC was $130.95.

Center-Fire Semiautomatics

Model 9 Camp Carbine, 9mm Semiautomatic (1985 to date). In 1985, Marlin took a giant step away from its usual conservative product line and introduced a caliber 9mm semiautomatic carbine that is best described by the following catalog information:

> If there's one caliber that's really catching on in this country, it's the 9mm. It's been a favorite with handgunners for years.
>
> The number one European military and police caliber for decades, the 9mm may soon replace the 45 as the official handgun cartridge of the United States Armed Forces. Also, many American police departments have already switched to 9mm.
>
> And now Marlin is bringing this increasingly popular cartridge to one of the most innovative semiautomatic carbines ever offered. The Model 9 Camp Carbine.
>
> The Model 9 has classic, sporting lines. A machined steel receiver. A standard 12-shot magazine. And a one-piece magazine housing/trigger guard.
>
> The Model 9 is an ideal small game and home defense gun, with an impressive improvement over handgun ballistics out of its 16½" barrel (over 22% improvement in muzzle velocity and 50% increase in energy over a 4-inch barreled 9mm handgun).
>
> As for safety features, the Model 9 is full of them, with things like a magazine disconnect to prevent firing once the clip is removed, a Garand type safety, and a loaded chamber indicator. It also has both a manual bolt hold-open and a "last-shot" automatic bolt hold-open.

Marlin 70HC
Cal. 22 L.R.

Model 70HC rifle.

Model 9 Camp Carbine.

Model 45 carbine.

But best of all, the Model 9 has a price you're just going to have to see to believe.

Solid-top, machined steel receiver. Sandblasted to prevent glare, and is drilled and tapped for scope mounting.

The Model 9 is loaded with important safety features. Like a "last-shot" automatic bolt hold-open to clearly indicate chamber is empty.

The Model 9 is shipped with a 12-shot magazine; however, a 20-shot magazine is available. The semiautomatic system is of the blow-back type. It was designed by the Marlin Research and Development Department headed by Mr. William Osborne. (The hole spacing is the same as for the Model 336 carbine and will accept telescope mounts designed for the Model 336.)

The stock is walnut-finished hardwood with a pistol grip, tough Mar-Shield™ finish, and a rubber rifle pad. The barrel is 16½ inches long and has Micro-Groove® rifling. The sights are an adjustable open rear and a ramp front sight with brass bead and Wide-Scan™ hood. The magazine is a copy of the S&W 9mm pistol magazine.

The overall length of the Model 9 is 35½ inches, and the weight is about 6¾ pounds.

The suggested retail prices of the Model 9 Camp Carbine have been as follows:

Year	Price
1985	$247.00
1986	259.95

Year	Price
1987	280.95
1988	294.95

Model 45, Caliber .45 ACP, Semiautomatic Carbine (1986 to date). In 1986, Marlin added a new caliber .45 automatic pistol cartridge (ACP) model of the Model 9. Called the Model 45, it had many similarities to the Model 9 (Camp Carbine name was now dropped from the 9mm model).

The major differences in the Model 45 from the Model 9 were, of course, the caliber and the magazine. The versatility of the .45 ACP is appreciated by many, and hand-gunners enjoy the interchangeability of ammunition between their handgun and a shoulder-fired carbine. The magazine of the Model 45 is a copy of the Colt Model 1911 pistol magazine, and in some cases will interchange between the two.

The safety features and specifications of the Model 45 and Model 9 are the same, except that the Model 45 has a 7-shot magazine, whereas the Model 9 has both 12-shot and 20-shot available.

The suggested retail prices of the Model 45 have been as follows:

Year	Price
1986	$259.95
1987	280.95
1988	294.95

Bolt Action Rifles

DESCRIPTIVE SUMMARIES

Brief History of Caliber .22 Bolt Action Rifles

The year 1935 was the big year for Marlin caliber .22 bolt action rifles. Three single-shot and two repeaters were introduced that year and, ever since, Marlin has had those three, or more, in its product line.

Easy and more economical to manufacture than the more complex pump actions Marlin was noted for, the .22 bolt action rifle has always been popular among first gun owners because of its ease of operation, lower cost, and similarity to high-power bolt action rifles, which are the most popular sporting rifle of them all.

Marlin's bolt action .22s went through a number of changes in both their mechanism and cosmetic design. Many of the early models had both a "plain Jane" model with open sights and a Deluxe (DL) version that had an aperture rear sight and a hooded target-type front sight—and, in some cases, sling swivels.

The impressive list of bolt action .22s Marlin has manufactured were as follows:

Years Manufactured	Model	Type
1935–1937	Model 65	Single-shot rifle
1935–1937	Model 65E	Single-shot rifle
1935–1959	Model 100	Single-shot rifle
1935–1959	Model 80	Clip magazine rifle
1935–1939	Model 80E	Clip magazine rifle
1937–1938	Model 100S "Tom Mix Special"	Single-shot rifle
1939	Model 81	Tubular magazine rifle
1939	Model 81E	Tubular magazine rifle
1940	Model 80B	Tubular magazine rifle
1940	Model 80BE	Tubular magazine rifle
1940	Model 81B	Tubular magazine rifle
1940	Model 81BE	Tubular magazine rifle
1941–1977	Model 101	Single-shot rifle
1941–1945	Model 101DL	Single-shot rifle
1941–1971	Model 80C	Clip magazine rifle
1941–1964	Model 80DL	Clip magazine rifle
1941–1971	Model 81C	Tubular magazine rifle
1941–1964	Model 81DL	Tubular magazine rifle
1941	Model 80CSB	Smooth-bore repeater
1941	Model 100SB	Smooth-bore single-shot rifle
1959	Model 101 "Crown Prince"	Single-shot rifle
1962–1965	Model 122	Single-shot rifle
1966–1971	Model 980	Clip magazine magnum rifle
1971–1988	Model 780	Clip magazine rifle

Years Manufactured	*Model*	*Type*
1971–1988	Model 781	Tubular magazine rifle
1971–1988	Model 782	Clip magazine magnum rifle
1971–1988	Model 783	Tubular magazine magnum rifle
1988 to date	Model 880	Clip magazine rifle
1988 to date	Model 881	Tubular magazine rifle
1988 to date	Model 882	Clip magazine magnum rifle
1988 to date	Model 883	Tubular magazine magnum rifle

From 1952 onward, many additions, deletions, and changes took place in the various bolt action .22 rifles. Rather than list every change to each model, I have summarized the major changes, by period of time, in the following discussion.

1952 New patented extractor introduced in Models 80 and 81.

1960 Stocks have fluted and Monte Carlo combs and pistol grip caps. Receivers are now grooved for tip-off telescope mounts. Models 80 DL and 81DL now have swivels. New streamlined plastic trigger guard now standard. White line spacer now at butt plate and grip cap.

1961 Ramp front sight added.

1962 Model 122 Junior Target single-shot rifle, which has a grip cap, swivels and a sling, introduced. New feed throat, patent number 2,963,810, introduced in single-shot rifles. Deluxe models now have sling. Gold-plated triggers standard. Model 980, .22 magnum added—without swivels or sling. Model 980 receiver top now serrated.

1963 980 now has swivels and sling and hooded front sight. Models 80DL and 81DL shown with sling and ramp front sights. Models 80C and 81C are shown with standard dovetail front sights.

1964 Gold-plated triggers added to Models 80, 81, and 980. Models 80 and 80DL now with hooded ramp front sight.

1965 980, 80C, and 81C shown without ramp-type front sight. Models 80DL and 81DL now discontinued.

1966 Ramps back. Model 122 discontinued.

1969 Band-type front sights in use, except for 101.

1970 100th-anniversary medallion embedded in all stocks manufactured in 1970. Model 101 now has band-type front sight.

1971 Models 80 and 81 replaced by Models 780 and 781. Impressed checking and new-shaped trigger guard added. Pistol grip caps dropped. Model 782 replaces Model 980. Black triggers.

1972 New tubular magazine magnum Model 783 added to line. Magnum bolts chrome-plated. Standard Models 780 and 781 have blued bolts.

1973 New Wide-Scan hood added to the front sight. Models 782 and 783 have new type of ramp front sight. Band sights still on 780, 781 and 101. Folding rear sight now on 782 and 783. New type of sling shown on 782.

1974 Wide-Scan hood now on all models. Folding rear sight now on all models.

1977 New magazine closure system now on all tubular magazines. Model 101 discontinued.

1978 Model 101 not listed.

1980 New sling now on 782 and 783. New checkering design includes both sides of forearm. Gas escape hole added to left side of receiver.

1982 Bolt action rifles now have new hooded ramp front sight added to Models 80DL, 81DL, 80C, and 980. Model 81C shown with dovetail front sight.

1983 Models 15, 25, and 25M introduced.

1984 Model 15Y introduced.

1985 New shape to bolt sleeve. Model 15 discontinued.

1986 Model 25MB introduced.

1987 Slings not included with rifles. Model 25M has swivels. New Model 25MB added to line.

1988 Models 780, 781, 782, and 783 to be 880, 881, 882, and 883.

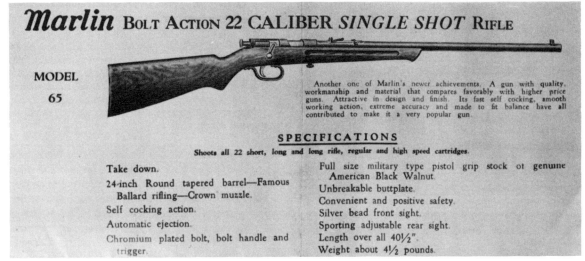

1936 illustration of the Model 65 single-shot rifle.

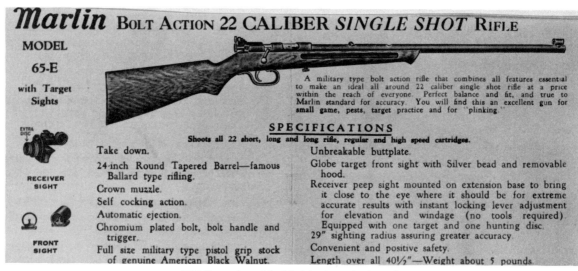

1936 illustration of the Model 65E single-shot rifle.

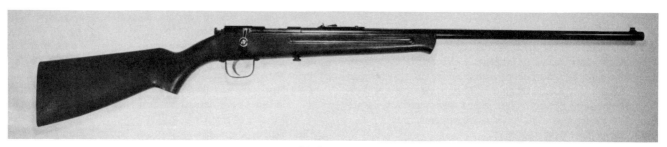

Model 65 rifle.

Patents that were used in the bolt action .22 rifles were as follows:

Number	Date	Inventor	Invention
2,465,553	Mar. 29, 1949	T.R. Robinson	Extractor mechanism
2,963,810	Dec. 13, 1960	T.R. Robinson	Feed throat (Model 101/122)
2,976,637	Mar. 28, 1961	T.R. Robinson	Trigger and safety
3,100,358	Aug. 13, 1963	T.R. Robinson	Micro-Groove rifling
3,755,912	Sept. 4, 1973	W.E. Osborne	Open rear sight
3,883,976	May 20, 1975	W.E. Osborne/ Gerald Norman	Magazine tube catch

Models 65 and 65E, Single-Shot, Bolt Action, Calibber .22 Rifles (1935–1937). The Model 65 was a simple, yet attractive and handy, little .22 rifle. It was described by Marlin as:

Another one of Marlin's newer achievements. A gun with quality, workmanship and material that compares favorably with higher price guns. Attractive in design and finish. Its fast self-cocking, smooth-working action, extreme accuracy and made-to-fit balance have all contributed to make it a very popular gun.

The specifications listed for the Model 65 were:

Shoots all .22 short, long and long rifle, regular and high speed cartridges, take-down, 24-inch round tapered barrel, Ballard rifling, crowned muzzle, self cocking action, automatic ejection, chrome plated bolt, bolt handle and trigger, full size military type pistol grip stock of genuine American black walnut, unbreakable buttplate, convenient and positive safety, silver bead front sight, sporting adjustable rear sight, overall length 40½ inches, weight about 4½ pounds.

The Model 65E was identical to the Model 65, except for the sights. The catalog description of the sights was as follows:

Globe target front sight with silver bead and removable hood. Receiver peep sight mounted on extension base to bring it close to the eye where it should be for extreme accurate results with instant locking lever adjustment for elevation and windage (no tools required). Equipped with one target and one hunting disk. 29 inch sighting radius assures greater accuracy.

The stock of the Models 65 and 65E had finger grooves and a schnabel (bulge) at the end of the forearm. The trigger guard was a simple steel stamping. The takedown feature was a large-headed stock screw, which held the stock and barrel and receiver together. The large head was knurled so that the screw could be turned with the fingers to take the gun down.

The Model 65 (and 65E) can be distinguished from other Marlin single-shot rifles by the location of the bolt handle on the bolt. In this model, the bolt handle locks into the receiver in its own locking recess, and the loading port is a separate opening in the receiver. Also, to put this model on safe, the cocking knob is pulled back and rotated 90°.

The retail prices of the Models 65 and 65E were as follows:

Year	Model 65	Model 65E
1935	Unknown	Unknown
1936	$5.75	$6.75
1937	5.65	6.40

Model 100, Single-Shot, Bolt Action, Caliber .22 Rifle (1935–1959). The Model 100 bolt action was different from the Model 65 in that the bolt handle and loading port were in the same receiver opening. Also, this model did not have a safety mechanism *per se* and was not self-cocking. The cocking knob had to be pulled to cock the rifle. Early Model 100s had a stamped steel trigger guard; later ones had a plastic trigger guard.

The Model 100 would handle .22 short, long, and long rifle cartridges of either the regular or the high-speed type. It had a 24-in. barrel, Ballard rifling, a crowned muzzle, automatic ejection, rebounding hammer for safety, unbreakable butt plate, pistol grip stock (not walnut until 1956), silver bead front sight, and sporting adjustable open rear sight. The length was 40½ inches overall and the weight about 4½ pounds.

Although not available from 1951 through 1953, the Model 100 was illustrated in some catalogs. In the 1947 catalog, the Model 100 was illustrated with a plastic trigger guard, and in 1948 the text indicated the stock was walnut. In 1957, the stock was again listed as walnut; however, prior to that year it was birch.

In 1954, Micro-Groove rifling was introduced into the Model 100. The last year the Model 100 was cataloged was 1959. By year, the retail prices of this model were the following:

Year	Price
1935	Unknown

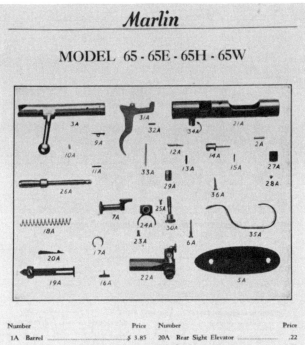

Marlin

MODEL 65 · 65E · 65H · 65W

Number		Price	Number		Price
1A	Barrel	$ 3.85	20A	Rear Sight Elevator	.22
2A	Barrel Pin	.11	21A	Receiver	1.65
3A	Breech Bolt	1.76	22A	Receiver Sight Complete	2.50
4A	Buttstock with Plate	3.85	23A	Receiver Sight Screws (2)....each	.11
5A	Buttplate	.44	24A	Receiver Sight Complete	
6A	Buttplate Screws (2)....each	.11		model 65-W) Cannot Supply	
7A	Cocking Knob	.44	25A	Receiver Sight Screws (2)....each	.11
8A	Cocking Knob Pin	.11	26A	Striker	.55
9A	Extractor	.44	27A	Striker Sleeve	.22
10A	Extractor Spring	.11	28A	Striker Sleeve Screw	.11
11A	Extractor Pin	.11	29A	Take Down Stud	.33
12A	Ejector	.11	30A	Take Down Screw	.44
13A	Ejector Pin	.11	31A	Trigger	.66
14A	Firing Pin	.44	32A	Trigger Pin	.11
15A	Firing Pin Pin	.11	33A	Trigger Spring	.11
16A	Front Sight Silver Bead	1.10	34A	Trigger Stud	.44
17A	Front Sight Hood	.22	35A	Trigger Guard	.44
18A	Mainspring	.33	36A	Trigger Guard Screws (2)....each	.11
19A	Rear Sight	.88			

Parts catalog list of Model 65 parts.

Marlin BOLT ACTION 22 CALIBER *SINGLE SHOT* RIFLE

MODEL
100

Here's the most outstanding value in the whole rifle field.

Built by *Marlin* experts with over 65 years of gun making experience.

This model 100 tops the list of values. A light weight but man's size arm embracing Marlin quality workmanship and super accurate shooting qualities.

SPECIFICATIONS

Adapted to all 22 short, long and long rifle regular and high speed cartridges. 24-inch Round tapered barrel, famous Ballard type rifling, Crown muzzle. Automatic ejection. Chromium plated Bolt, Bolt Handle and Trigger. Walnut finish military type pistol grip stock. Unbreakable butt plate. Silver bead front sight. Sporting adjustable rear sight. Length overall 40½"—Weight about 4½ pounds.

Marlin catalog information about the Model 100 single-shot rifle.

Bolt and receiver of the Model 100 rifle.

Model 65 barrel roll-stamp of The Marlin Firearms Corporation found on many early Marlin Firearms Company firearms.

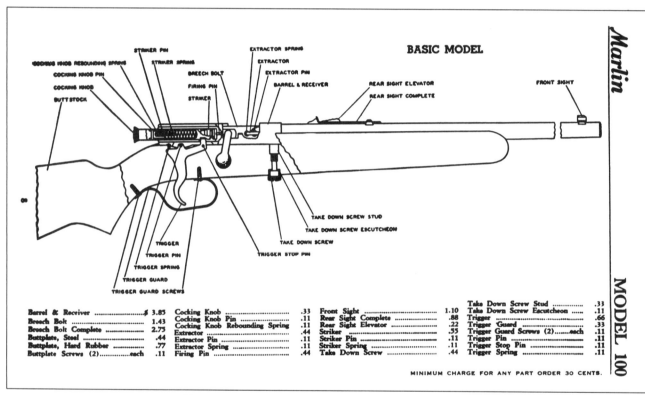

Marlin parts catalog information for the Model 100 single-shot rifle.

Model 100 rifle equipped with target sights.

Model 101 rifle with experimental rear sight.

Second variation of Model 100 rifle.

Third variation of Model 100 rifle equipped with target sights.

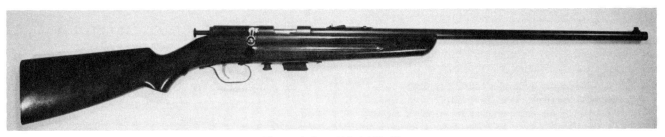

First variation of Model 80 rifle.

Year	Price
1936	$ 4.80
1937–1939	5.25
1940	5.35
1941	6.15
1945	7.05
1955	15.60
1956	16.40
1957–1959	16.95

Models 80, 80E, 80B, and 80BE, Clip Magazine, Bolt Action, Caliber .22 Rifles (80 and 80E, 1935–1939; 80B and 80BE, 1940). When introduced, the Model 80 and Model 80E both had finger groove stocks, metal trigger guards, and a bolt mechanism and receiver very much like the previously described Model 100 rifle. The major difference was the 8-shot clip magazine of the 80 and 80E. Marlin described the model as follows:

Here is a sporting rifle that has won its way to the front in remarkable and astonishing short time. A recent Marlin development but already it has made gun history — already a leader acclaimed by thousands and generally conceded the very best rifle of its class. In every point from butt to muzzle it is outstanding. You have to see and handle this already famous rifle to get a real appreciation of its worth. It is a gun once you get your hands on that you can not resist actually

Model 80

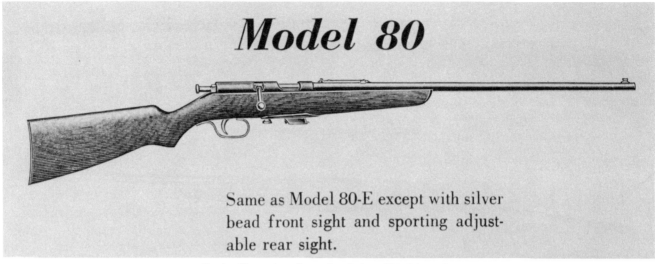

Same as Model 80-E except with silver bead front sight and sporting adjustable rear sight.

Catalog illustration of second variation of Model 80 rifle.

Model 80E

8 Shot Bolt Action .22 Caliber Rifle

Shots: .22 Short, Long, and Long Rifle Regular or High Speed without adjustment.

Catalog illustration of second variation of the Model 80E rifle.

possessing. Its graceful design, beautiful finish, smooth and easy working action and genuine Marlin high quality material and workmanship are all so pronounced that your appreciation of a real gun and real gun value act like a magnet which draws this rifle closer and closer to you the more you see and handle it. Yet, all this is but one side of the picture of its success, for the true value of any arm is in its ability to shoot true.

Marlin's reasons why the Model 80 is better were the following:

1. Shoots all .22 short, long and long rifle regular and high speed cartridges.
2. 8-shot detachable clip magazine.
3. Convenient quick take down.
4. 24-inch Round tapered barrel.
5. Famous Ballard type rifling.
6. Crown muzzle.
7. Genuine American black walnut full size military type stock.
8. Pistol grip.
9. Unbreakable butt plate.
10. Self cocking fast smooth action.
11. Automatic ejection.
12. Positive and convenient safety.
13. Chromium plated bolt, bolt handle and trigger.
14. Bolt instantly removed by holding back on trigger.
15. Double extractors assuring positive extraction.
16. Nicely shaped cocking handle.
17. Large strong locking lug.
18. Short hammer fall.
19. Globe target front sight with silver bead and removable hood (Model 80E).
20. Receiver peep sight mounted on extension base to bring it close to the eye where it should be for extremely accurate results. Instant locking lever adjustment for elevation and windage (no tools required). Equipped with 1 target and 1 hunting disc (Model 80E).
21. 31″ sighting radius assuring greater accuracy.
22. Rear sight slot blank (Model 80E).

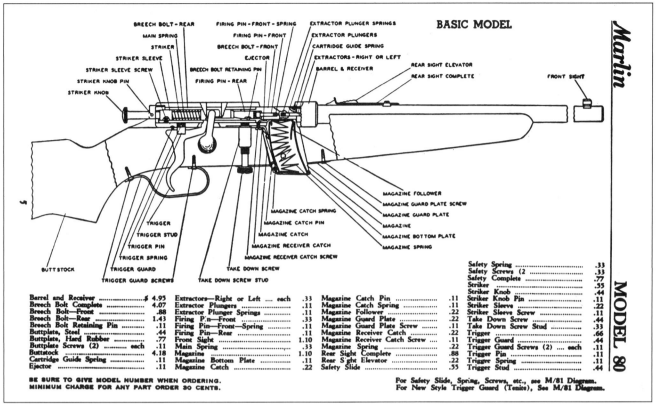

Parts of Model 80 rifle.

23. Especially adapted to telescope sight.
24. Length overall 42½".
25. Weight about 5¾ pounds.

In 1937, the Models 80 and 80E no longer had finger groove stocks; in 1939, the trigger guards were listed as being of "modern plastic." The stock was also now listed as walnut wood. The takedown screw was also changed to a flush type, and a new safety was now located on the right rear of the receiver.

As in the Models 65 and 65E, the only difference between the Model 80 and the Model 80E was that the Model 80E came equipped with a peep rear sight and a removable hooded front sight. Otherwise, the two were identical.

The Models 80B and 80BE were identical to the 80 and 80E. They were models cataloged only during 1940. Both had plastic trigger guards, and the wood was listed as walnut finish.

The safety was of the second type. The only difference between the 80B and 80BE was the target sights on the Model 80BE.

The retail prices of the Models 80, 80E, 80B, and 80BE were as follows:

Year	80	80E	80B	80BE
1935	Unknown	Unknown		
1936	$8.95	$ 9.50		
1937–1938	9.95	10.95		
1939	9.40	10.10		
1940			$9.45	$10.19

Model 100S, "Tom Mix Special," Single-Shot, Caliber .22 Rifle (1937). In 1937, Marlin introduced the Model 100S "Tom Mix Special" rifle, which was the basic Model 100 rifle with the added features of target sights, drilling for telescope blocks,

Model 100S "Tom Mix Special."

Tom Mix, 1880–1940.

swivels, and a sling. The Marlin catalog described it in this way:

The most remarkable value in the whole rifle field. Chambered for all .22 short, long or long rifle cartridges in regular or high speed. Just pick up this beauty. Feel its perfect balance. Nestle it into your shoulder and watch how easily the sights line up. It's a man sized gun yet not too heavy. You'll get many a thrill from a pin wheel shot on game or target. No gun offers so much in real quality in this popular price. Like its big brother the Tom Mix Special has a Walnut finish butt stock of real military type, ample in size and with a well designed pistol grip, so that the gun aims quickly and fits comfortably. The 24 inch round tapered barrel with crown muzzle has the famous Ballard type of rifling which insures accurate shooting. The take-down feature is provided for convenient packing. Ejector is automatic. Bolt and trigger are chromium plate which adds to attractive appearance of this Tom Mix Special. Special target sights are furnished as standard equipment. The rear peep sight is mounted as close to the eye as possible to give a long sighting radius, and carries sighting disk. Adjustments can be made for both elevation and windage. The front sight is of globe type, silverbead, with quick detachable hood, length overall, 40½ inches. Weight 4¾ lbs. This rifle is drilled and tapped ready to mount either the No. 1 or No. 2 Marlin 4-Power Telescope Sights.

Marlin flyer about the Tom Mix Special.

Marlin ad for Capt. E.C. Crossman's articles, Marlin military-type ring, Marlin's "Bicycle Handbook" about how to make money to buy a Marlin bicycle, and "Open Road for Boys" rifle match.

Model 100 single-shot rifle.

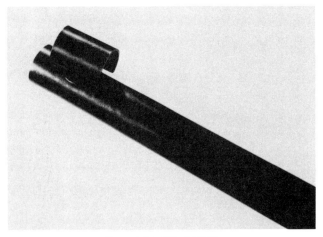

Front sight of Model 100S.

Tom Mix, the "King of the Cowboys," was born in 1880 and died in 1940. He is still recognized as one of the leading cowboy movie actors of all time. During the 1930s, it was every boy's desire to see the Saturday matinee with Tom Mix and his wonder horse Tony at the local movie house. He also sponsored the "Ralston Square Shooters" of breakfast food fame.

Adding the Tom Mix name to a product generally ensured success. However, in the case of the Tom Mix Special, success was limited because of Tom Mix's untimely death in an automobile accident while driving his Cord sports car in Arizona.

The limited period the Tom Mix Special was available, and the introduction by Marlin of the improved Model 101 single-shot rifle, have resulted in the Model 100S rifle being very scarce in its original condition. The unique features that help identify this model are that it is drilled and tapped for the telescope blocks, which were used with the Marlin No. 1 or No. 2 telescopes, and the sling swivels and target sights.

In appreciation of his allowing Marlin to use his name, Marlin presented Tom Mix with an engraved and gold-inlaid

Model 90 shotgun. Please see the Model 90 section for more information about that gun.

Models 81, 81E, 81B, and 81BE, Tubular Magazine, Bolt Action, Caliber .22 Rifles (81 and 81E, 1937–1939; 81B and 81BE, 1940). These tubular magazine versions of the Model 80 rifles were not introduced until 1937. Like the Model 80E, the 81E and 81BE had target sights. When introduced in 1937, the Model 81 was described as follows:

> A new patented tubular magazine repeater with feeding mechanism that is unique, simple and positive. Holds 25 short, 20 long, or 17 long rifle cartridges. Take down. 24 inch round tappered barrel, crown muzzle, Ballard type rifling. Automatic ejection. Positive, convenient safety. Self cocking action. Genuine American black walnut stock, military type. Unbreakable butt plate. Chromium plated bolt, bolt handle and trigger. Sporting adjustable rear sight and silver bead front sight. Length 42½ inches. Weight about 6¼ pounds.

Second variation of Model 81 rifle.

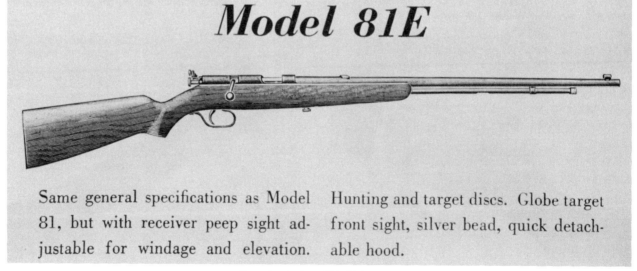

Same general specifications as Model 81, but with receiver peep sight adjustable for windage and elevation. Hunting and target discs. Globe target front sight, silver bead, quick detachable hood.

Second variation of Model 81E rifle.

Model 81B rifle.

Model 81BE rifle.

As previously mentioned, the Model 81E had the same general specifications as the Model 81 with the addition of the target sights. However, the Models 81B and 81BE had a new flush takedown screw; new positive thumb-controlled safety; new nonslip shaped rubber butt plate; new modern plastic trigger guard; new quick release trigger; and man-sized, walnut finish, military-type, full pistol grip stock with a hand rubbed oil finish.

The prices of the Models 81, 81E, 81B, and 81BE were as follows:

Year	81	81E	81B	81BE
1937	Unknown	Unknown		
1938	Unknown	Unknown		
1939	$11.60	$12.30		
1940			$12.07	$12.77

Models 101 and 101DL, Single-Shot, Bolt Action, Caliber .22 Rifles (1941–1977). The Model 101 rifles were listed as:

Fine sturdy, safe single shot .22 caliber rifles ideal for youngsters and those just beginning to learn and enjoy the excitement and pleasures of rifle shooting. It is light weight and easy to handle.

When introduced in 1941, the Model 101 had a side thumb-operated safety, flush takedown screw, and a step-sided stock that had an enlarged forearm section. Like the 80E, 80BE, 81E, and 81BE, the Model 101DL had the target peep rear sight and a new hooded ramp front sight. The trigger guard of the Model 101 and Model 101DL was modern plastic.

In 1959, a new Model 101 bolt action system was introduced. It was described as a nonjamming loading throat. To load the rifle, it was necessary only to drop the cartridge into the open feed throat, and then push the bolt forward to load the cartridge into the chamber. The feed throat was originally plastic. Later, it was changed to a die-casting. To fire the rifle, it was then necessary to pull the cocking knob back to the cocked position manually. In 1960, the knob was changed to a ring. In 1966, it was changed to a T-shaped knob.

The 1960 specifications for the Model 101 were as follows:

Marlin ad for the 1939 Model 81 rifle.

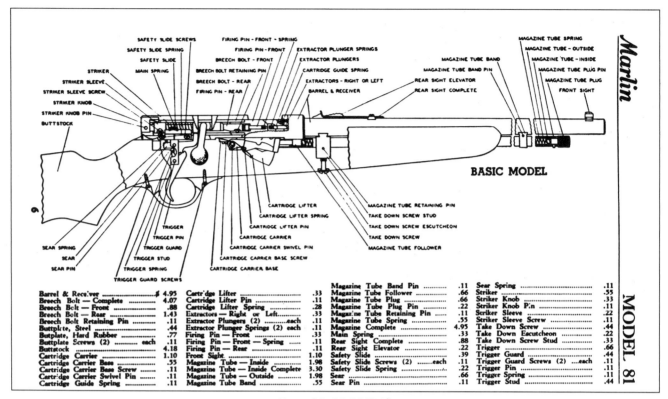

Parts of the Model 81 rifle.

First variation of the Model 101 rifle.

Single-shot bolt action. Handles .22 caliber short, long and long rifle cartridges, regular or high-velocity loads, waxed or greased, without adjustment. Positive safety. Easy to take-down for cleaning and oiling. Barrel: 22″ round tapered blued steel barrel of Special Analysis Ordnance Steel. Special features: Receiver dovetail grooved for tip-off style telescope mounts. Automatic side ejection. Removable bolt for easy cleaning. Flush take-down screw. Bead front sight and adjustable open rear sight. Gold-plated trigger and new style streamlined black trigger guard. Flat bolt handle. New military type ring striker knob. Stock: One piece Bishop-style stock with Monte Carlo comb of finest quality walnut with special finish to withstand all kinds of weather and hard usage. Pistol grip with grip cap. Custom-type hard rubber buttplate with white liner-cushion. Fluted comb. Exclusive features: Equipped with Marlin's new Micro-Groove® rifling for extreme accuracy-performance. Non-jamming loading throat for positive feeding. Length and weight: Overall length 39″; Weight about 5 pounds depending on density of wood.

The Model 101DL was discontinued in 1945. The Model 101 was discontinued in 1977.

The retail prices of the Models 101 and 101DL, except for the period of 1946 to 1958 when they were not available, were as follows:

Year	101	101DL
1941	$ 6.50	$7.80
1942–1944	WW II — No production	
1945	7.45	8.95
1946–1958	Not available	
1959	19.95	
1960	20.60	
1961–1962	19.95	
1963	16.00	
1964	19.95	
1965	22.95	

Second variation of the Model 101 rifle.

1970 third variation of the Model 101 rifle.

Fourth variation of the Model 101 rifle.

Fifth variation of Model 101 rifle.

First variation of Model 80C rifle.

Year	101	101DL
1966–1967	23.95	
1968	24.95	
1969	28.95	
1970–1971	29.95	
1972	36.95	
1973	37.95	
1974	38.95	
1975	42.95	
1976	44.95	
1977	47.95	

Models 80C and 80DL, Clip Magazine, Caliber .22 Rifles (80C, 1941-1971; 80DL, 1941-1964). The Models 80C and 80DL were an extension of the Models 80, 80E, 80B, and 80BE, which were all caliber .22 clip magazine rifles.

When introduced, the Models 80C and 80DL had walnut-finished buttstocks. By 1957, the stocks were walnut. The 1957 catalog described the model as follows:

> Bolt action 8-shot clip magazine .22 caliber repeating rifle. 22-inch round tapered blued steel barrel, crowned muzzle. Special new finish on bolt and receiver. Bishop style stock. Finest quality walnut. Easy to take-down for oiling and cleaning. Receiver dovetail grooved for tip-off mounts and top mounts. Positive safety. Removable bolt, automatic side ejection, self-cocking action. Open sights. Shoots .22 caliber short, long or long rifle cartridges, greased or waxed, regular or high-velocity loads, without adjustment. Overall length 41″; weight about 5¾ pounds depending on density of wood.

The Model 80DL was the Model 80C rifle with target sights, instead of the open sights of the Model 80C, and sling swivels.

The 1960 catalog described new changes to the Models 80C and 80DL as follows:

> Barrel: 22″ round tapered blued steel barrel with crowned muzzle made of Special Analysis Ordnance Steel. Gold-plated trigger, new streamlined black trigger guard and flat breech bolt handle. Streamlined receiver. New positive safety and new striker knob. Stock: One-piece Bishop-style stock with Monte Carlo comb made of finest quality walnut with special finish to withstand all kinds of weather and hard usage. Pistol grip with grip cap. Fluted comb. Equipped with Marlin's exclusive Micro-Groove® rifling for super-accuracy. Overall length 41″; weight about 5½ pounds depending on density of wood.

The Model 81DL description and specifications were the same, except for the addition of a peep rear sight and hooded front sight, and sling swivels.

The suggested retail prices of the Model 80C and 80DL were as follows:

Year	80C	80DL
1941	$10.80	$12.00
1942–1944	WW II – No production	
1945	12.45	13.85
1946–1947	18.25	20.05
1948	21.05	22.90
1949	22.30	24.15
1950	24.55	26.55
1951–1953	24.95	26.95
1954–1955	25.60	27.60
1956	27.60	30.60
1957–1959	29.95	32.95
1960	33.60	36.60

Second variation of Model 80C rifle.

Third variation of Model 80C rifle.

First variation of Model 80DL rifle.

Second variation of Model 80DL rifle.

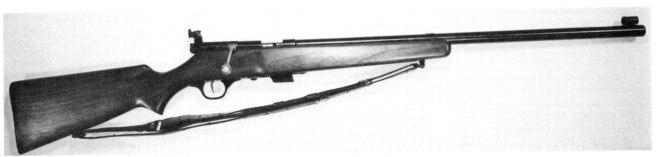

Experimental heavy-barrel Model 80 with Lyman target sights and sling.

Year	80C	80DL
1961	33.95	36.95
1962	34.95	38.95
1963	35.95	39.95
1964	36.95	39.95
1965	38.95	
1966–1967	39.95	
1968	42.95	
1969–1971	44.95	

Models 81C and 81DL, Tubular Magazine, Caliber .22 Rifles (81C, 1941–1971; 81DL, 1941–1964). The Models 81C and 81DL are tubular magazine repeating bolt action rifles, the same as the previous Models 81, 81DL, 81B, and 81BE. The DL model is a deluxe model that has target-type sights, instead of the usual open sights found on all Marlin standard models. The DL model also has sling swivels.

When introduced in 1941, the stocks of the Models 81C and 81DL had an enlarged forearm that resulted in a pronounced ridge along the sides of the stock. Post-WW II production did not have stocks with that feature.

The 1957 catalog description of the Model 81C rifle was as follows:

> Bolt action 25-shot tubular magazine .22 caliber repeating rifle. 22-inch round tapered blued steel barrel, crowned muzzle. Special new finish on bolt and receiver. Bishop style stock. Finest quality walnut. Easy to take-down. Receiver dovetail grooved for tip-off mounts and top mounts. Positive safety. Removable bolt, automatic side ejection, self-cocking action. Open sights. Shoots .22 caliber short, long or long rifle cartridges, greased or waxed, regular or high-speed loads, without adjustment. Overall length 41″; weight about 6 pounds depending on density of wood.

The 1960 catalog added information about the new features added that year as follows:

> An outstanding .22 caliber repeater for all types of small game and for target-plinking. For the great group of .22

First variation of Model 81C rifle.

Marlin 81 C bolt action rifle cal .22 S, L or LR
Scope 300

Second variation of Model 81C rifle.

caliber rifle shooters who prefer the bolt action type to other types they will find this rifle a reliable and accurate performer. It is excellent for all types of small game hunting. A bolt action .22 caliber repeater with full tubular magazine. Holds 25-short, 20-long or 18-long rifle .22 caliber cartridges, regular or high-velocity loads, greased or waxed, without adjustment. New positive, convenient safety. New striker knob. Easy to take-down for cleaning and oiling. Barrel: 22″ round tapered blued steel barrel and crowned muzzle made of Special Analysis Ordnance Steel. Special features: Automatic side ejection. Self-cocking action. Removable bolt for easy cleaning. Quick release trigger. Receiver dovetail grooved for low top mount scopes. Gold-plated trigger. New streamlined black trigger guard. Flat breech bolt handle. Receiver streamlined. New striker knob. Stock: One-piece Bishop-style stock with Monte Carlo comb of finest walnut with special finish to withstand all kinds of weather and hard usage. Pistol grip with grip cap. Custom-type hard rubber buttplate with white liner-cushion. Fluted comb. Exclusive feature: Has Marlin's exclusive Micro-Groove rifling for less bullet distortion; reduced gas leakage and 20% to 25% greater accuracy-performance. Length and weight: Overall length 41″; weight about 6 pounds depending on density of wood.

The suggested retail prices of the Models 81C and 81DL were as follows:

Year	81C	81DL
1941	$13.85	$15.15
1942–1944	WW II – No production	
1945	16.00	17.50
1946–1947	23.70	25.55
1948	25.15	26.95
1949	27.15	28.90

Year	81C	81DL
1950–1954	28.95	30.95
1955	29.65	31.65
1956	31.65	34.65
1957–1959	33.95	36.95
1960–1961	37.65	40.65
1962	38.95	42.95
1963–1964	39.95	43.95
1965	42.95	
1966	43.95	
1967	44.95	
1968–1971	46.95	

Models 101SB and 80SB, Smooth-Bore, Caliber .22 Shotguns (1940–1941). During 1940 and 1941, Marlin manufactured and sold two caliber .22 smooth-bore shotguns. Model 101SB was a single-shot, and Model 80SB was a clip magazine repeater.

The catalogs described the single-shot model as follows:

Marlin's new Model 101SB smooth bore .22 with same smart design and general specifications as the Model 101. Special recess choke, shotgun front sight. 24 inch round barrel. Overall length 40½ inches; weight 5 pounds.

The catalog description of the repeater read like this:

Marlin's new Model 80SB smooth bore gun, .22 repeater—for indoor and miniature skeet shooting. This new smooth bore was of the same general design and specifications of the Model 80C. Special recess choke and shotgun front sight. 24 inch round barrel.

Its fast, repeating action adds immensely to the enjoyment of the popular new shooting games.

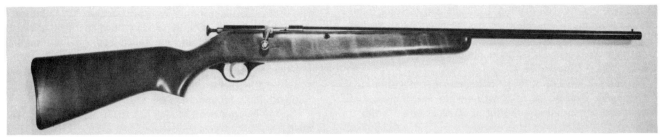

Model 100SB (Smooth Bore).

The barrel of these smooth-bore .22s was not dovetailed for a front or rear sight. The front sight was the usual brass bead shotgun type.

Both the Model 101SB and 80SB smooth-bore guns are very scarce and seldom encountered by collectors. They were listed in catalogs and price lists only during 1940 and 1941. The prices listed were as follows:

Year	Model 101SB	Model 80SB
1940	$8.03	$12.28
1941	9.50	14.60

Model 101, "Crown Prince," Single-Shot, Bolt Action, Caliber .22 Rifle (1959). The Crown Prince rifle was a special deluxe version of the Model 101 rifle previously discussed. It had all the same features, and it was boxed in a carrying-case-like cardboard box. It came equipped with a Marlin Micro-Vue 4-power telescope. Packed with the rifle were a wildlife game map, a tube of Marlin Rustopper, a Marlin target and game

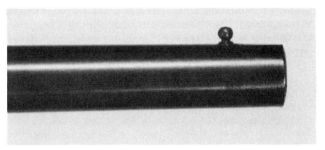

Front sight on Model 100SB barrel.

Roll-stamp on barrel of Model 100SB.

Model 101 "Crown Prince" rifle.

record book, a "Marlin Sighting-In Guide and Manual," and 50 assorted targets. The telescope was mounted and zeroed-in at the factory.

In 1959, the only year of its manufacture, the price of the Crown Prince rifle was $39.95.

A total of 7,166 Crown Prince rifles were manufactured.

Original Crown Prince rifles with the box and contents are rare. I have only examined one during 20 years with Marlin.

Model 122, Single-Shot, Caliber .22 Rifle (1961–1965). The Model 122 was first announced in the 1961 catalog as the Model 122 "Auto-Safe" rifle. The catalog also stated: "Price to be announced." The 1962 catalog listed the Model 122 as being "NEW" and as the "Marlin 122 Junior Target Model." It was described as follows:

> Caliber .22 short, long or long rifle. Single shot, 22-inch Micro-Groove® rifled barrel. Precision open rear sight, ramp front sight; drilled and tapped for receiver sights. Lyman 57-ES, Redfield 22-RW, Williams 5D-122 will fit the 122. Finest quality Monte Carlo style stock. Marlin "Auto-Safe" patented feed system. Receiver grooved for scope mounts. Gold plated trigger. Swivels and leather strap. Overall length 40 inches. Weight about 5 pounds.

The Model 122 was very similar to the Model 101, except that the 122 safety was different. The "Auto-Safe" feature of the 122 was a positive safety that automatically went on when the bolt handle was lifted and could not go off until the gun was fully locked. The safety then had to be put off manually before the gun could be fired. (The Model 59 single-barrel .410 shotgun had this same feature.)

The trigger and "Auto-Safe" feature of the Model 122 were covered by Tom Robinson's patent number 2,976,637, dated March 28, 1961. The feed throat mechanism of the Model 122

and Model 101 single-shot rifles was covered by Mr. Robinson's patent number 2,963,810, dated December 13, 1960. This special feed throat did not damage bullets and avoided fumbling in loading. All that was necessary was to drop the cartridge into the feed throat, and then close the bolt. The cartridge would then be pushed into the chamber. The same system is also used in the Model 15Y.

The total number of Model 122 rifles manufactured was 5,648.

The retail prices of the Model 122 were:

Year	Price
1962	$24.95
1963	18.75
1964	24.95
1965	26.95

Model 980, Clip Magazine, Bolt Action, Caliber .22 Winchester Magnum Rim Fire Rifle (1962–1970). The Model 980 rifle was Marlin's first bolt action rifle chambered for the powerful caliber .22 Winchester Magnum Rim Fire (WMRF) cartridge. It was styled very much like the Model 80 rifle. It had an 8-shot magazine, 24-in. Micro-Groove barrel, Monte Carlo walnut stock, gold-plated trigger, grooved receiver for tip-off telescope mounts, grip cap, and butt plate with white spacers. It measured 43 inches overall and weighed 6 pounds.

The magnum cartridge of the Model 980 gave extra range and more hard-hitting power over the regular .22 cartridges of Marlin's other .22s, and is found by many hunters ideal for chucks, foxes, turkeys, and other hard-to-stop small game. Please note that the .22 WMRF cartridge is *not* interchangeable with any other .22 cartridge, and no attempt to fire other types of .22 cartridges in the Model 980 should be made.

In 1962, the Model 980 did not have swivels and a sling or a

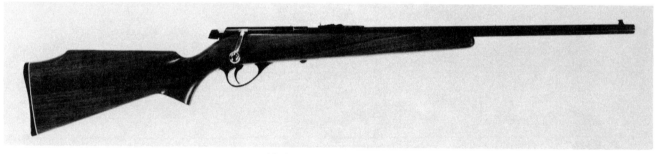

Model 122 "Auto-Safe" rifle.

Model 980 rifle.

hooded front sight that was screwed to the barrel. In 1969, the front sight was changed to a band type that did not have a hood. In 1970, the buttstock had embedded into the right side a 100th-year commemorative medallion. In 1971, the Model 980 was replaced by the Model 782.

The suggested retail prices of the Model 980 were as follows:

Year	Price
1962–1964	$39.95
1965	42.95
1966	43.95
1967	44.95
1968	46.95
1969	48.95
1970	49.95

A total of 33,643 Model 980 caliber .22 WMRF rifles were manufactured.

Model 780, Clip Magazine, Caliber .22 Rifle; Model 781, Tubular Magazine, Caliber .22 Rifle; Model 782, Clip Magazine, Caliber .22 WMRF Rifle; and Model 783, Tubular Magazine, Caliber .22 WMRF Rifle (1971–1988). In 1972, the Marlin line of .22 rifles was restyled and improved to make them equal to any other make of sporting rifle of their class on the market. The Models 780 and 781 were clip magazine rifles that were developed from the Model 80C and Model 980. The Model 781 and newly added Model 783 were tubular magazine rifles. The 781 was developed from the Model 81C. The 780 and 781 were conventional .22 short, long, and long-rifle rifles, whereas the Models 782 and 783 were chambered for the caliber .22 WMRF cartridge. The "700 Series" of new-look Marlin bolt actions was described in the catalog as follows:

Sleek and slick. That's the look of the all new 700 Series bolt action .22's. The new big game styled one-piece stocks feature handsome checking on grip and forearm. When it comes to high-score informal target shooting or small game, the 700's can't be beat. The sturdy, dependable new design bolt actions have the ruggedness to take the rough going of forest and field. Plenty of hard hitting power plus pin-point accuracy for informal target shooting. All of the benchmarks of traditional Marlin craftsmanship are here—like selected American walnut stocks carefully fitted to the smooth, positive actions.

The new Model 783 was described as an ideal rifle for chucks, foxes, turkeys, and other hard-to-stop small game. The extra power of the .22 WMRF gave greater range and improved results at the target.

It is important to note that the .22 WMRF is a larger and more powerful cartridge than any other .22 rimfire. *It is not interchangeable with any other cartridge.* It shoots a 40-grain, copper-jacketed hollow-point or fully metal jacketed bullet at 2,000 feet per second (compared with 1,145 feet per second for the standard .22 long rifle cartridge).

The Model 782 clip magazine rifle also used the .22 WMRF cartridge and only differed from the 783 by being a clip magazine model. The clip held 7 cartridges, and was convenient to load and unload.

The main changes in the 700 Series from the earlier 80C, 81C, and 980 rifles were the improved shape and style of the stock, which now had the same look and feel of a high-power bolt action rifle; impressed checkering on the pistol grip and bottom of the forearm; a new shape to the cocking piece; a fully shaped pistol grip, without a grip cap; and a graceful new trigger guard. The receiver top was now serrated to provide a nonglare surface. The Models 781 and 782 were equipped with swivels and slings until 1987, when the sling was dropped and only sling studs were furnished. The Models 780 and 781 were

Early Model 780 rifle.

Late Model 780 rifle.

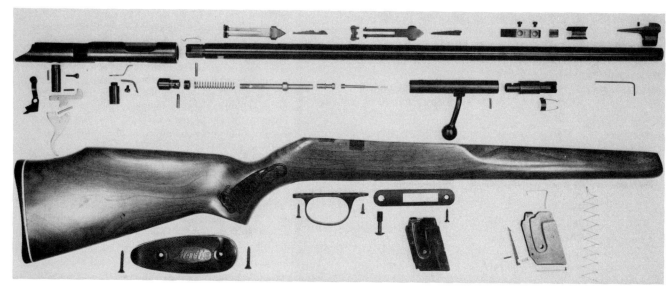

Parts of early Model 780 rifle.

Early Model 781.

Late Model 781.

the improved and newly styled models chambered for the .22 short, long, and long rifle cartridge. The 780 was the clip magazine model and the 781 was the tubular magazine model. These two rifles had all the new and stylish features of the 782 and 783 models, plus the advantage of using less expensive cartridges. The models 780 and 781 were described by Marlin as:

> The Popular Pair—These sleek, new all-around .22's are the perfect choice for young shooters and small game enthusiasts. For plenty of rapid-fire action, take your choice between the Marlin 781 with its big-capacity tubular magazine or the Marlin 780 Sporter with its 7-shot clip magazine. Both have new design receivers and both handle shorts, longs and long rifles safely and dependably. From the muzzle of their

Micro-Groove® barrels to the butts of their handsomely checkered stocks, Marlin craftsmanship is evident.

The suggested retail prices of the Models 780, 781, 782, and 783 were as follows:

Year	780	781	782	783
1971	$ 48.95	$49.95	$53.95	$54.95
1972	50.95	52.95	56.95	57.95
1973	53.95	55.95	58.95	59.95
1974	54.95	56.95	59.95	61.95
1975	59.95	61.95	65.95	67.95
1976	62.95	64.95	68.95	71.95
1977	65.95	69.95	72.95	74.95

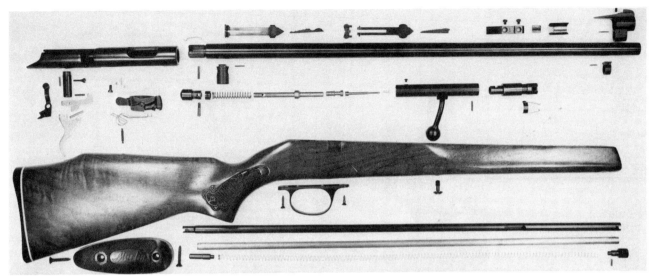

Parts of Model 781 rifle.

Early Model 782 rifle.

Late Model 782 rifle.

Late Model 782 rifle.

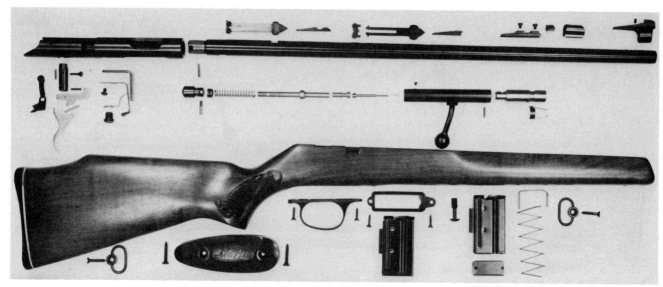

Parts of early-style Model 783 rifle.

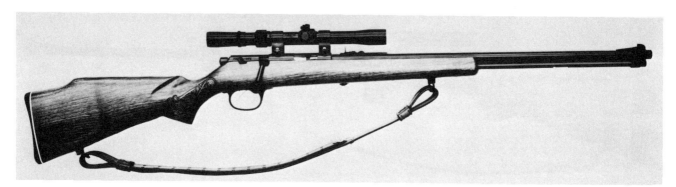

Early Model 783 rifle.

Late Model 783 rifle.

Year	780	781	782	783
1978	66.95	70.95	74.95	77.95
1979	73.95	76.95	81.00	84.95
1980	86.95	91.95	96.95	99.95
1981	105.95	110.95	117.95	122.95
1982	118.95	123.95	131.95	136.95
1983	119.95	124.95	133.95	138.95
1984	124.95	129.95	143.95	138.95
1985	134.95	140.95	148.95	153.95
1986	141.95	147.95	155.95	161.95
1987	152.95	159.95	168.95	174.95
1988	161.95	168.95	178.95	185.95

In 1988, the Models 780, 781, 782, and 783 were updated with new features that included a new safety. The model designations were changed to 880, 881, 882, and 883.

Model 880, Clip Magazine, Caliber .22 Rifle; Model 881, Tubular Magazine, Caliber .22 Rifle; Model 882, Clip Magazine, Caliber .22 WMRF Rifle; and Model 883, Tubular Magazine, Caliber .22 WMRF Rifle (1988 to date). In 1988, the Marlin caliber .22 bolt action 780 series of rifles was restyled and improved. The improvements and changes were listed as follows:

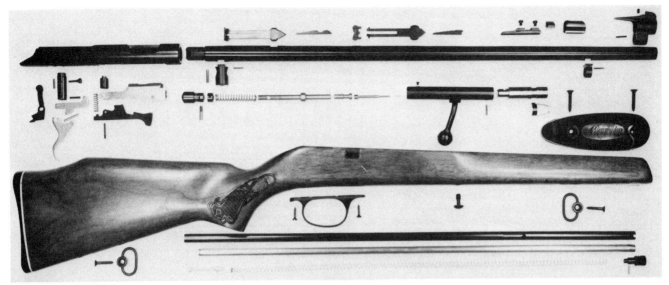

Parts of Model 783 rifle.

Model 880 rifle.

Model 881 rifle.

Model 882 rifle.

Model 883 rifle.

Glenfield Model 100G.

Glenfield Model 10.

1. New design "forward to fire" safety.
2. New shape to the strike knob.
3. New low profile pear shaped bolt handle.
4. Top of receiver now round on top without serrations.
5. Deeper telescope mounting dovetail on receiver.
6. Flush magazine plate.
7. 880 magazine is now the same as Marlin's .22 auto loading rifle magazine. It will handle only the .22 long rifle cartridge.
8. Sling swivel studs standard for all four models.
9. New design checkering.
10. Rubber rifle buttpad on all four models.
11. White line spacers no longer used.

The 880 and 881 have blued front bolts, whereas the 882 and 883 have bright front bolts.

Other than having the above-listed changes, the 880 series are made for the same purposes as were the Model 770 series — informal target shooting, plinking, and small game hunting. The new look they now have places them at the top of the list for quality and utility among all caliber .22 bolt action rifles in their price range.

Glenfield Bolt Action Caliber .22 Rifles

The original purpose of the use of the name Glenfield was to give mass-merchandisers and chain outlets their own brand names. The Glenfield models had less expensive cosmetics, but the quality of materials and workmanship was as high as that of the more expensive Marlin models. The Marlin models were reserved for the small shops and stores that traditionally handled the Marlin line. Now, mass-merchandisers no longer prefer to have their own brand name, but want the top-of-the-line items. Therefore, Marlin has dropped the use of the name *Glenfield*. Some of the later Glenfield models are now sold under a new Model number and under the Marlin name, without material changes to the Glenfield configuration.

Marlin marketed the following bolt action .22 rifles under the Glenfield name:

Glenfield Model 15.

Glenfiel Model 20.

Glenfield Model 25.

Years	Model	Type
1965	Model 100G	Single-shot rifle
1965	Model 80G	Clip magazine rifle
1965	Model 81G	Tubular magazine rifle
1966–1978	Model 10	Single-shot rifle
1966–1981	Model 20	Clip magazine rifle
1979–1982	Model 15	Single-shot rifle
1979–1982	Model 25	Clip magazine rifle

The Model 100G was the same rifle as the Marlin Model 101, except that it had a birch-wood stock and an old-style trigger guard. It did not have a Monte Carlo comb or a pistol grip cap and white line spacers. The cocking knob was of the earlier 101 type without a finger ring.

The Model 80G was the same rifle as the Marlin Model 80C, except that it did not have the Monte Carlo comb, pistol grip cap, white line spacers, streamlined trigger guard, and walnut stock of the Model 80C.

The Model 81G was the same rifle as the Marlin Model 81C, except that it too did not have the Marlin features mentioned above.

The Model 10 was the same as the Model 100G, above, and the Marlin Model 101. The only difference was the model number.

The Model 20 rifle was the same as the Model 80G. Only the model number was different.

The Model 15 rifle was the same as the Glenfield 10 and Marlin 101 except that it had a new cocking knob, safety mechanism, bolt, and ramp front sight. The stock had a Monte Carlo comb and the pistol grip was impressed-checked.

The Model 25 was the same as the Marlin Model 780, except that it had a birch-wood stock and an old-style trigger guard.

Promotion Models

When Marlin discontinued the use of the Glenfield name, some Glenfield models were converted to Marlin models. These few models were classified as promotion models to keep them from being confused with regular walnut-stocked Marlin models.

The model designation and year of introduction to the Marlin catalog were as follows:

Year	Model	Type
1983	Model 15	single-shot, caliber .22 rifle
1983 to date	Model 15Y	single-shot, caliber .22 rifle
1983 to date	Model 25	clip magazine, caliber .22 rifle
1983 to date	Model 25M	clip magazine, caliber .22 WMRF rifle
1987 to date	Model 25MB	clip magazine, caliber .22 WMRF rifle
1988 to date	Model 15YN	single-shot, caliber .22 rifle
1988 to date	Model 25N	clip magazine, caliber .22 rifle
1988 to date	Model 25MN	clip magazine, caliber .22 WMRF rifle

A brief description of each model follows:

Marlin Model 15, Single-Shot, Caliber .22 Rifle (1983). This model was available under the Marlin name during 1983; it was the same rifle as the Glenfield Model 15 rifle. It was discontinued in 1984 in favor of the Model 15Y rifle.

Marlin Model 15Y, Single-Shot, Caliber .22 Rifle (1983 to date). The Model 15Y rifle was the same as the Glenfield Model 15 and Marlin Model 15 rifles, except that it had a 16½-in. barrel, a shortened forearm, and a stock with a 12-in. length of pull. The 15Y was designed specifically with the youth in mind.

Marlin Model 25, Clip Magazine, Caliber .22 Rifle (1983 to date). The Model 25 rifle was the same rifle as the Glenfield Model 25 rifle, except without swivels. It had a black, instead of chrome, trigger.

Model 15 promotion model.

Model 15Y "Little Buckaroo" promotion model.

Model 25 promotion model.

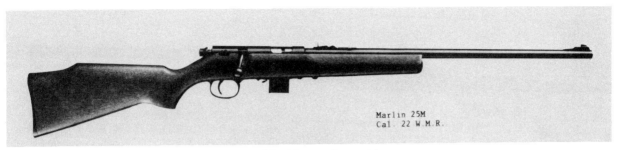

Model 25M promotion model.

Model 25MB "Midget Magnum" promotion model.

Marlin Model 25M, Clip Magazine, Caliber .22 WMRF Rifle (1983 to date). The Model 25M rifle is the Marlin Model 782 rifle without frills. It has a birch-wood stock, instead of walnut, a ramp front sight without a hood, and no white line spacer.

Marlin Model 25MB "Midget Magnum," Clip Magazine, Caliber .22 WMRF Rifle (1987 to date). A new addition to the promotion models in 1987, the Model 25MB is a Model 25 having a 16¼-in. barrel, instead of the 22-in. barrel of the Model 25. The forearm of the stock is also shortened, and it has an enlarged stock screw for quick takedown. Included with the Model 25MB is a 4X telescope, and the outfit is packaged in its own fully padded carrying case that has built-in flotation.

Marlin Model 15YN, Single-Shot, Caliber .22 Rifle; Marlin Model 25MN, Clip Magazine, Caliber .22 WMRF Rifle; and Marlin Model 25N, Clip Magazine, Caliber .22 Rifle (1988 to date). These three rifles are identical to the previous Models 15Y, 25, and 25M, except that they have the new forward-to-fire safety mechanism and other improvements of the 880 series.

Center-Fire Bolt Action Rifles

Models 322 and 422. The Marlin Model 322 bolt action rifle was introduced in 1954. It was in caliber .222. The 1954 catalog furnished the following information:

> Marlin is justifiably proud of its new Model 322 because it's the only center-fire rifle available today with the fabulously accurate Micro-Groove rifling. Built around the famous Sako miniature Mauser receiver, it's excellent for hunting woodchuck, crows, fox, coyote and other predators. The receiver is specially designed for the .222 cartridge. It is

Model 25MB taken down, with its individual carrying case.

equipped with a selected walnut stock, expertly hand-checkered at grip and forearm and has a full pistol grip with grip cap. It has a 24-inch medium weight barrel. The bolt is easily removed for cleaning and oiling. The Sako trigger is adjustable. The clip magazine holds three cartridges. The high comb is ideal for telescope use. The cocking piece safety locks both the striker and the bolt. The magazine catch is concealed. An indicator on the rear of the bolt automatically tells the fire position of the gun. A two position Sako peep sight (100 and 200 yards) is furnished. The receiver has integral Sako bases for low scope mounting. The stock was fitted with sling swivels and a hard rubber butt plate. The overall length was 42 inches and the rifle weighed 7⅛ lbs.

After numerous complaints about deterioration of accuracy from the Micro-Groove rifle barrel (after as few as 500 rounds), Marlin attempted to resolve the problem by fitting a 24-in. stainless steel barrel of featherweight configuration. The new rifle was identified as the Varmint King (Model 422) and, except for the new barrel and a new design of Monte Carlo

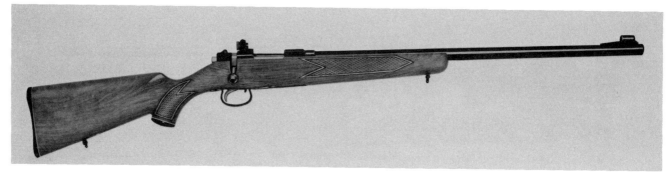

Model 322 rifle.

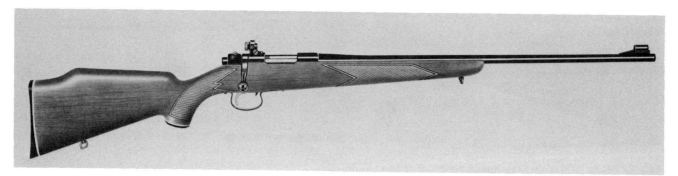

Model 422 rifle.

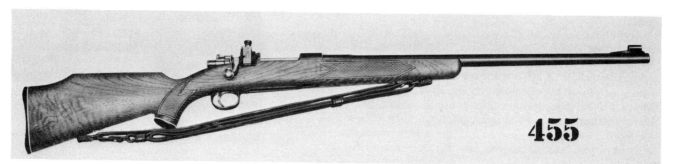

Model 455 rifle.

Bishop stock of Model 455 rifle.

stock that had a cheek piece, all other features remained the same.

Both the Model 322 and 422 rifles were neat little rifles that never had the few bugs in them worked out. Conventional rifling, more suited to high-velocity cartridges, more attention to the bedding of the metal parts into the stock, and a more classically designed and dimensioned stock would have made the rifles hard to beat. Both were somewhat before their time. If they had been available a few years later, when that style of rifle became more popular, they might still be around today.

Serial numbers of the 322 and 422 rifles were Sako numbers. Therefore, they are not consecutive, and are mixed between the Sako production and Marlin production, as well as with receivers and barrelled actions sold by Firearms International. Most of the Sako receivers used by Marlin were within the following ranges:

322	5077–31,300
422	3577–39,565

The suggested retail prices of the Models 322 and 422 were as follows:

Year	Model 322	Model 422
1954	$129.95	
1955–1956	130.95	
1956–1958	139.50	$139.95

A total of 5,859 Model 322 rifles were manufactured, and 354 Model 422 rifles were produced. Neither the Model 322 nor the Model 422 was listed in the 1959 catalog.

Marlin has no spare parts for these rifles and can make no repairs to them. (For a short time, Marlin could furnish barrels manufactured by George Wilson, North Branford, Conn. However, the Marlin supply of spare barrels was exhausted years ago.)

Model 455. The Model 455 rifle was introduced in 1955; however, deliveries did not start until 1956. It was described as a center-fire bolt action repeating rifle having a 5-shot magazine. It was first announced as available in caliber .30–06. However, in the 1956 catalog, the .270 and .308 cartridges were also listed. Starting in 1958, the only cartridge listed was the .30–06. None were produced in caliber .270.

The Model 455 rifle was built with the imported Fabrique National (FN) Belgian Mauser action and had an adjustable

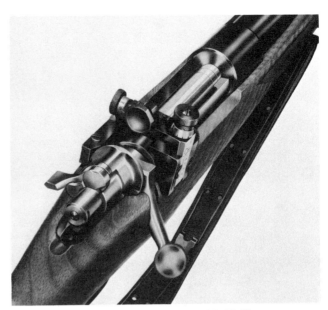
FN Mauser bolt action of Model 455 rifle.

Sako trigger mechanism. It had a Monte Carlo check-piece stock, designed and manufactured by Bishop (Bishop Gun Stock Company, Warsaw, Mo.). The stock was checkered and equipped with quick detachable sling swivels and a leather sling. The receiver was drilled and tapped for both telescope mounts and a receiver sight.

The stainless steel barrel was manufactured by Marlin. It was of medium weight and was equipped with a ramp front sight with detachable hood and a Lyman 48 rear sight. The FN Mauser safety was designed for use with low-mounted telescopes. The overall length was 42½ inches and the rifle weighted about 7¾ pounds, depending on the density of the wood. The suggested retail price was $149.95.

The first order for receivers to Firearms International Corporation, Washington, D.C., was for 500, specially serial-numbered from 1000 to 1500. The bolts were to be numbered to the receiver. The receivers were furnished polished but not blued.

Total production of the Model 455 rifle, by caliber and year, was as follows:

	1955	1956	1957	1958	1959	TOTAL
.30–06	1	91	386	195	406	1,079
.308	0	0	0	37	22	59
						1,138

Shotguns

GENERAL INFORMATION

The Marlin Fire Arms Company (1880 to 1915), The Marlin Firearms Corporation (1922 to 1925), and the present Marlin Firearms Company (1926 to 1933) successfully manufactured and sold pump action shotguns. Among the shotguns that were produced from 1898 to 1933 were both exposed hammer and hammerless types; 12-, 16-, and 20-gauge models; takedown and solid-frame models; and field, trap, brush, riot, and deluxe variations.

In addition to the differences between the models of pump shotguns manufactured, there were changes to the design of certain models, even while the model was in production.

The improved models had a suffix added to the model number to aid in ordering parts, or in correspondence with the company; this, of course, adds to the confusion of trying to understand the evolution of Marlin shotguns. Therefore, to put them into a logical and orderly sequence, the exposed hammer and hammerless models are discussed separately. Each variation within a model will be discussed briefly; however, some general information will be presented by model and will be listed in the numerical sequence of model numbers.

A total of 24 patents apply to the Marlin pump action shotguns. Of the total, 12 were inventions of Marlin's great inventor, L.L. Hepburn. Among his inventions were both the exposed hammer model and the hammerless model.

Most models of Marlin pump shotguns were manufactured in four grades, identified as Grades A, B, C, and D. There also were variations of some models such as Trap, Trap Special,

Field, Field Special, Brush, and Riot. The gauges were 12, 16, and 20. Barrel lengths varied from 25 inches to 32 inches, and some were matted on top. There were both takedown and solid-frame models; however, only two were of the solid-frame type. Buttstocks were either pistol grip or straight grip. All models had hard rubber butt plates, all were blued, and all, except the Grade D and some variations, had varnished walnut buttstocks and forearms.

Barrel markings indicated the Marlin name and patent dates. However, because of the interchangeability of takedown barrels between models, there are mixed combinations. From a study of a few hundred guns, it appears that Marlin and gun owners did mix barrels of one model with another.

The serial number of the receiver and that of the barrel are not the same, which also confirms that the two parts were not assembled and numbered together. The choke of the barrel is usually found beside the barrel serial number. *F* indicates full choke, *M* indicates modified choke, and *C* indicates cylinder bore (no choke at all).

Some of the pump action shotguns are not marked with the model number. To identify the specific model of these guns, both the features of the gun and the patent dates on the barrel must be used. To aid the collector, the features of the basic models and the patent dates that apply to each model (and which may be marked on the barrel) are tabulated in this section.

The models 1898, 16, 17, 19, 21, 24, 26, 28, 30, and 31, and their variations, were all manufactured by the original Marlin

TABLE 1

The various pump shotgun patents, the inventors, and the inventions were as follows:

Patent Number	Date	Inventor	Invention
400,679	Apr. 2, 1889	L.L. Hepburn	Magazine gun
525,739	Sept. 11, 1894	L.L. Hepburn	Magazine tube
528,905	Nov. 6, 1894	L.L. Hepburn	Magazine gun
560,032	May 12, 1896	L.L. Hepburn	Magazine firearm
561,226	June 2, 1896	L.L. Hepburn	Takedown mechanism
591,220	Oct. 5, 1897	L.L. Hepburn	Safety device
662,427	Nov. 27, 1900	L.L. Hepburn	Safety recoil device
755,660	Mar. 29, 1904	Melvin Hepburn	Takedown device
776,322	Nov. 29, 1904	L.L. Hepburn	Safety device
882,562	Mar. 24, 1908	L.L. Hepburn	Takedown device
888,329	May 19, 1908	Melvin Hepburn	Pump forearm
940,764	Nov. 23, 1909	J.H. Wheeler	Magazine cutoff
940,791	Nov. 23, 1909	H.W. DeJannatt	Magazine cutoff
943,828	Dec. 21, 1909	L.L. Hepburn	Hammerless shotgun
1,088,950	Mar. 3, 1914	J.H. Wheeler	Safety device
1,089,736	Mar. 10, 1914	J.H. Wheeler	Hammerless device
1,092,085	Mar. 31, 1914	J.H. Wheeler/F. Mauglier	Takedown magazine
1,099,621	June 9, 1914	A.C. Schildbach	Magazine cutoff
1,105,467	July 28, 1914	C.G. Swebilius/H.T.R. Hanitz	Hammerless mechanism
1,129,527	Feb. 23, 1915	C.G. Swebilius/H.T.R. Hanitz	Safety device
1,550,757	Aug. 25, 1925	C.G. Swebilius	Shotgun
1,550,758	Aug. 25, 1925	C.G. Swebilius	Shotgun
1,550,760	Aug. 25, 1925	C.G. Swebilius	Shotgun

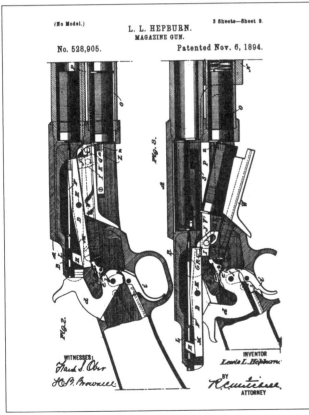

Mechanism of Model 1898 shotgun.

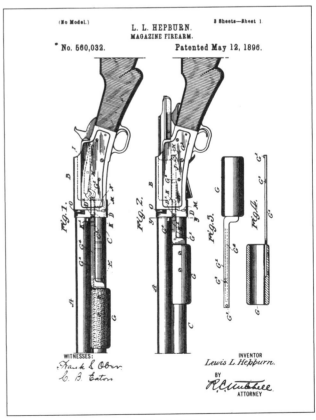

Basic patent of Model 1898 shotgun.

TABLE 2
Patent dates that may, or may not, be roll-stamped on the barrels of pump action shotguns, by model.

Patent Date	1898	16	17	19	19C	19G	19N	19S	21	24	24G	26	28	30	30G	31	42	43	44	49	49N	53	63
Apr. 2, 1889			X	X	X		X	X	X			X	X				X						X
Sept. 11, 1894			X	X								X											
Nov. 6, 1894	X	X	X	X	X		X	X	X			X	X				X						X
May 12, 1896	X	X		X	X	X	X	X	X	X		X				X	X	X					X
June 2, 1896	X	X		X		X	X	X	X	X		X				X	X	X					X
Oct. 5, 1897				X			X			X													
Nov. 27, 1900			X	X	X		X	X	X	X	X	X					X						X
Mar 29, 1904				X	X		X	X	X	X		X				X	X	X					X
Nov. 29, 1904			X	X	X		X	X	X	X	X	X					X						X
Aug. 7, 1906				X			X		X	X	X	X		X		X	X	X					
Mar. 24, 1908				X	X	X	X					X	X	X	X	X	X		X	X			
May 19, 1908				X	X	X	X	X				X		X	X	X	X	X	X	X			
Nov. 23, 1909						X			X				X	X	X	X	X		X	X	X		
Nov. 23, 1909																					X		
Dec. 21, 1909									X				X	X	X	X	X	X	X		X		
Mar. 3, 1914														X	X								
Mar. 10, 1914														X	X								
Mar. 31, 1914																X							X
June 9, 1914														X	X								X
July 28, 1914													X	X	X	X		X	X	X			
Feb. 23, 1915													X	X	X	X		X	X	X			
Aug. 25, 1925																X				X	X		
Aug. 25, 1925																X				X	X		
Aug. 25, 1925																X				X	X		
Pats. Pending						X										X				X	X		

Fire Arms Company. None of these models was manufactured by Marlin–Rockwell, The Marlin Firearms Corporation, or The Marlin Firearms Company of today.

The models 42, 43, and 44, and their variations, were manufactured by The Marlin Firearms Corporation until 1925, although some barrel markings may have the name of the earlier company. After 1925, these models were made by The Marlin Firearms Company, although the barrel markings may be of The Marlin Firearms Corporation.

The Models 53 and 63 were only manufactured after 1925 and by The Marlin Firearms Company, regardless of the barrel markings.

All of the various models can be broken down as to whether they had an exposed hammer or were hammerless. The exposed hammer models were 1898, 16, 17, 19, 21, 24, 26, 30, 42, and 49. The hammerless models were 28, 31, 43, 44, 53, and 63.

The gauge of each gun is marked on the left rear of the barrel. There were only three 20-gauge models, the Models 30-20, 31, and 44. There were two 16-gauge models, the models 16 and 30-16. All others were 12-gauge guns.

A number of the patents relate to the takedown mechanism, and the two basic systems used can help identify the model. The first system had a push-button release that allowed the magazine tube to be moved forward, and the second type had a latch-type mechanism for the same purpose. The button models were the Models 1898, 16, 19, 21, 49, and 53. The latch-type models were 24, 28, 30, 31, 42, 43, 44, and 63.

There were two types of forend assemblies. In the first type, the wooden pump handle was attached to the forend slide by two screws. The second type had the forend slide combined with a tube. The tube passed through the wooden part, and a forend cap nut held the parts together for a more rugged assembly that was less vulnerable to breakage. The models having the first type of forend were the models 1898, 16, 17, 19, 21, 26, and 49. The models having the second type of forend were 24, 28, 30, 31, 42, 43, 44, 53, and 63.

Another identifier of the model of an exposed hammer pump action shotgun is the method used to open the bolt when the action is closed and the firing mechanism is in either the cocked or half-cocked position.

The first pump action shotgun was the Model 1898. When it was first produced, it was necessary to push the firing pin forward with the thumb when one wanted to open the bolt to unload the chamber. After a new recoil safety device was added to this model, a serrated plunger on the right rear of the re-

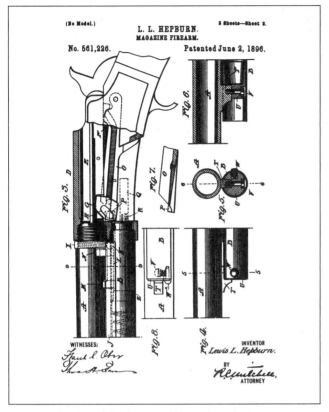

Patent drawing of the first type of magazine takedown system.

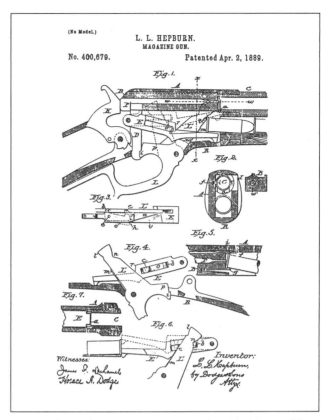

L.L. Hepburn rifle patent that also related to Model 17 and later exposed hammer pump action shotguns.

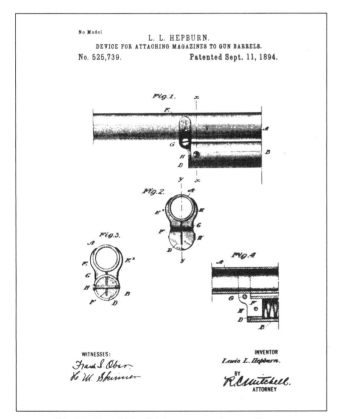

Models 17 and 26 solid-frame magazine attachment.

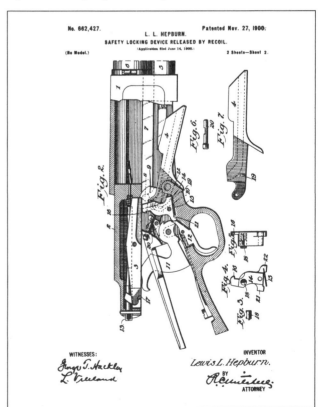

Patent that covered the first type of recoil safety device.

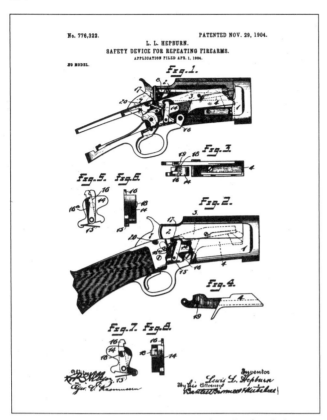

Patent illustration of the second type of recoil safety device.

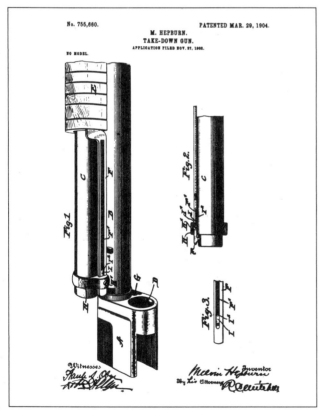

Illustration of the second type of magazine tube connection.

ceiver was pushed in, as well as the firing pin, thus allowing the forend to be pulled rearward to open the bolt and eject a loaded and unfired or misfired shell from the chamber.

The next patented system, which replaced the push-button method, had a serrated latch located at the bottom edge of the receiver, near the front part of the trigger guard. By pushing this piece, the recoil safety device was disengaged. Then, when the firing pin was pushed inward by the thumb, the bolt could be opened.

The exposed hammer models that had the first type of push button at the top of the right rear of the receiver were the Models 1898, 16, 17, 19, 21, and 26. The models that had the second type at the right bottom side of the receiver were the Models 24, 30, 42, and 49.

The hammerless models also had a system for opening the bolt when the gun was cocked. The first type was a serrated button on the top rear sloping surface of the receiver. The second type had a lever on the left bottom edge of the receiver, near the trigger. The hammerless models that had the push button on the top of the receiver were Models 28 and 31. The hammerless models that had the second type release were the Models 43, 44, 53, and 63.

The Marlin hangfire safety device, which required the manual operation of a button or lever to open the bolt of a cocked gun, was described by Marlin as follows:

THE HANG-FIRE SAFETY DEVICE

A "hang-fire" cartridge is a defective cartridge which delays ignition or explosion of the powder so that the cartridge is not instantly discharged when the firing pin has struck the primer. When a "hang-fire" occurs in fast shooting, the shooter may try, in his impatience, to eject the apparent misfire cartridge, and in guns not having the hang-fire safety device, the action might be part-way open at the time of the explosion.

Marlin repeating shotguns have an automatic safety lock to guard against hang-fire cartridges. It unlocks instantaneously and automatically every time the gun recoils from the explosion of a cartridge. It will operate perfectly when the trigger is held back and the gun fired by sliding the forearm forward and backward, as is often done in rapid shooting.

In case of a hang-fire, it is not possible to open the action of these guns by any involuntary or habitual action of the operating hand. It waits for the explosion, whether delayed one second or a couple of minutes.

To operate the gun when empty or to eject a misfired cartridge, you release the safety lock by pressing on the action release button and in the case of exposed hammer guns, you also push in on the firing pin with the thumb.

Marlin described the way it worked like this:

The slide carries the locking bolt and breech bolt forward by engagement of the slide with the cam cut in the locking bolt lug depending from the left forward side of the locking bolt. As the breech bolt goes into the battery position, the stud on the slide working against the cam surface in the locking bolt lug raises the front end of the locking bolt. Consequently, the rear end of the locking bolt drops into engagement with the locking surface on the frame. As the rear lower surface of the locking bolt comes into full engagement with the frame, it simultaneously contacts the forward

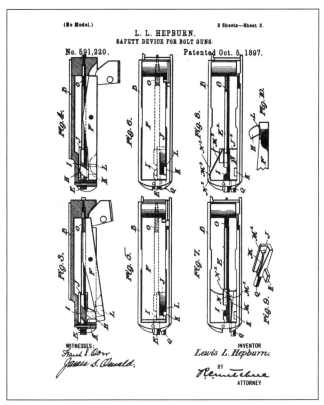

Patented firing pin safety mechanism that was not used; it was too fragile.

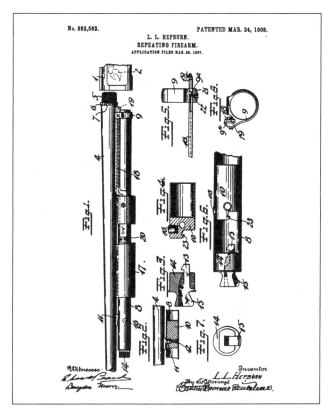

Illustration of patent covering the second type of magazine takedown system.

upper portion of the safety sear, which is an independent "trigger," releasing the safety sear from engagement with the independent notch on the hammer and allowing the hammer to drop into the full cock notch engagement with the standard trigger. Simultaneously the inertia block or recoil lock snaps into engagement with the hook surface on the rear right side of the locking bolt, positively retaining the locking bolt in the locked position. The inertia block latch continues to hold the tail of the locking bolt in the locked position until:

1. Gun recoil and inertia throw the block forward out of engagement or,
2. The manual release button is pressed with the same effect.

Additional safety is provided by the interlock of the firing pin and the upwardly extending horn on the locking bolt. The firing pin cannot be forced into the firing position by the hammer blow as long as the breech bolt is unlocked, that is, as long as the locking bolt is not rotated inside the breech bolt into locking engagement with the receiver. As the locking bolt rear drops into full engagement with the receiver, the horn on the top rear of the breech bolt disengages from the firing pin, permitting full forward firing pin motion. Also, when the locking bolt is in the locked position inside the breech bolt, the firing pin is normally held at the rear of its patch to travel by the firing pin retracting spring. In this position secondary interlock of the firing pin with the locking bolt horn prevents unlocking of the locking bolt. The firing pin must be held in the forward position by hand or by the hammer to clear this interlock and permit the locking bolt tail to ride into the breech bolt to the unlocked position.

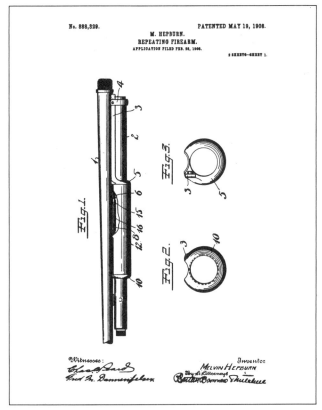

Patent illustration of second type of forearm mechanism.

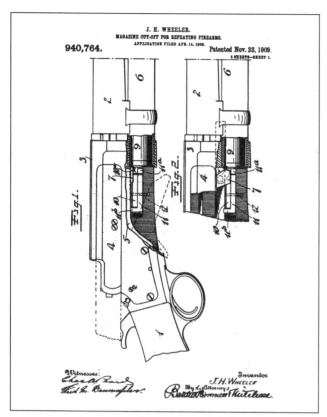

Patent illustration of improved shell stop.

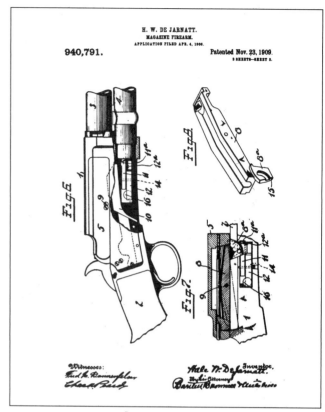

Illustration of second type of shell stop.

DANGER: It is necessary to caution all collectors and users of the old exposed hammer shotguns of two important matters.

1. Never put the hammer down on the firing pin with a shell in the chamber. If you do, the gun will fire if the hammer is struck even the slightest blow. The hammer should always be in the half-cocked postion.

2. If the gun is not in excellent repair, or if homemade parts have been substituted, it is possible for these old guns to break and cause personal injury. Correct locking of the breech bolt and locking bolt into the receiver is essential, and if parts are broken, jammed by dirt or rust, it is possible to fire these exposed hammer shotguns with the bolt not properly locked. In such a case, the bolt could be blown out of the receiver and into the shooter's face. (If I have alarmed you, I have accomplished my intent!)

The method of taking down the exposed hammer pump action shotguns did not change greatly during the 35 years of their production. The first procedure was described in catalogs as follows:

FIRST: To disconnect the action bar, move the forend and bar to the rear a slight fraction of an inch until the small notch on the inside of bar is opposite the action bar stop, then tip over the stop from the notch in the barrel to the notch in the action bar, when the handle, bar and bar-stop can be drawn forward clear of the frame.

SECOND: To disconnect the magazine, press in the catch (button) at the front end of the magazine tube with the left-hand thumb, at the same time drawing the magazine tube

straight forward until tube and follower are clear of the frame.

THIRD: To disconnect the barrel, the barrel can then be unscrewed by turning from left to right. *The thread on the barrel is left-handed.*

To put together the two assemblies, screw in the barrel, move the magazine back into place in the frame, then draw back the forearm until the action bar stop is opposite the notch in the barrel, then rotate the action-bar stop from the notch in the action bar to the notch in the barrel. The action bar connection is now complete and the gun can be operated in the usual manner.

With the introduction of the Model 24 and the Models 17G, 19G, 24G, 26G, and 30G, a new type of forearm mechanism was put into use. This new system had a magazine tube latch instead of a button. The new system did away with the forend slide stop, slide screw in the band, forearm screws and other small parts. To take down the new system, it was only necessary to press the latch at the front end of the magazine tube and then draw the tube forward. A button catch on the left side of the magazine held the tube in this forward position. The action bar and forearm could then be moved forward to allow the barrel to unscrew.

On the barrel of all Marlin takedown pump action shotguns is a lock nut that is threaded to the barrel. When it is properly adjusted to the frame and locked in place by a screw, it will ensure there is no play between the barrel and frame. The lock nut can be adjusted to take up any play as a result of wear.

The takedown system used by Marlin in all exposed hammer

and hammerless models allowed for interchangeability of barrels of different lengths and choke.

The standard guns had 30-in. full-choke barrels and were always shipped unless otherwise ordered. The 28- and 32-in. barrels were also shipped full choke unless ordered differently. The 26-in. barrels were shipped cylinder bore unless ordered with a different choke. On special order, Marlin would furnish 26-, 28-, 30-, or 32-in. barrels with cylinder bore, modified choke or full choke without extra charge. In some models the 32-in. barrel was furnished in Grade A only.

All Marlin barrels were interchangeable within the same model and it was not necessary to return the action part to have a barrel fitted.

Some models were available with a matted barrel. The cross lines of the matting cut down the reflections of light and heat radiation from the top surface of the barrel and aided the shooter in obtaining quick and accurate aim. When first introduced, matting on the barrel was at an additional charge. Later, matting was furnished without an extra charge.

Another barrel feature available on some models was a raised rib that was matted on top. It was available on the Model 28 Grades A, B, C, and Trap Special and on the Model 24 shotguns at an extra charge of $5.00.

The disassembly of the exposed hammer models is rather simple and explained in catalogs; however, the disassembly of the hammerless models was not explained. From a study of the hammerless mechanism, patent drawings, and experience, it is recommended that only those skilled in such work and having well-fitting screwdrivers and the necessary tools attempt to do so. It is really a job for the professional gunsmith!

The catalog procedure for removal of the breech mechanism of the exposed hammer guns was explained in this way:

Many people will appreciate a gun that can be taken apart by a man who is not an expert. Taking out one screw allows the entire breech mechanism to be removed from the frame in the Marlin Repeating Shotgun visible hammer models.

TO TAKE APART: With the action open take out the carrier screw, then holding the gun in the ordinary position, move the forearm forward slowly about an inch and the carrier will drop out through the opening in the bottom of the frame. The breech bolt containing the locking bolt can then be drawn out to the rear.

TO ASSEMBLE: Draw the forearm and action bar forward clear of the frame, disconnecting the action bar as when taking down; insert the breech bolt in its proper channel, sliding forward to its closed position. To close locking bolt press upward on its front end by inserting the fingers through the opening in the bottom of frame. Then connect action bar as after taking down. To put in carrier open the action half way; insert carrier through opening in bottom of frame, being sure that the groove or camway on left side of carrier passes on to the pin in locking bolt that operates it. Then supporting carrier so that it shall not slip off from this pin,

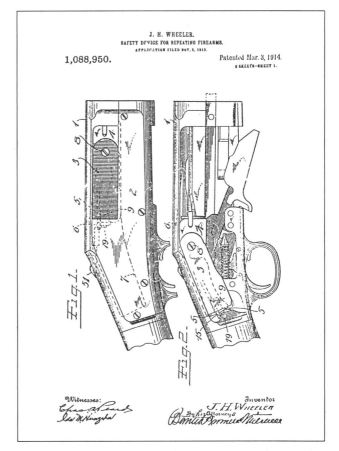

L.L. Hepburn's patent of the hammerless pump action shotguns that have the bolt release at the top rear of the receiver (#51) and safety in the front of the trigger guard (#33).

J.H. Wheeler's improved model of the second type of hammerless shotgun mechanism.

move carrier and breech bolt back slowly until the screw hole in carrier comes opposite the screw hole in frame, when the carrier screw can be replaced.

The operation of the exposed hammer gun was explained as follows:

> The breech mechanism consists of a large and strong breech bolt, a straight locking bolt lying inside of said breech bolt and pivoted near its center, so that its ends move through an arc of a vertical circle and each end travels about half an inch. When the action is open, the rear end of the locking bolt is up within the breech bolt, but when closed, this end drops down against a section of the frame, while the front end of the locking bolt engages the breech bolt near its front end and near the base of the shell in the chamber. This breech is simple (two pieces only), solid and very strong. The action is manipulated by sliding backward and foreward the forearm. This motion is short, very easy and smooth, free from noise, and the action bar connects directly with the locking bolt. The action can not be manipulated when the hammer is at half or full cock, and the gun can not be discharged until the action is locked. An extra sear in the lock prevents the hammer from falling until the action is locked, and the firing pin is held back by the locking bolt until the latter is in its place. The trigger may be held back and the gun discharged as rapidly as the left hand can operate.

The Models 17G, 19G, 24G, 26G, and 30G were improved versions of the Models 17, 19, 24, 26, and 30, and certain parts were not interchangeable between the two types.

The description and characteristics of the improved exposed hammer shotgun were described in 1906 as follows:

Our first model of repeating shotgun, with visible hammer, was brought out in 1898; we have had 17 years' experience with this form of gun and have put out over 150,000 of them. Every point that has shown by this practical experience a possibility of improvement has been refined, improved, perfected; and such features as the improved take-down construction, the shapely, comfortable forearm, the double extractors, and the improved automatic recoil safety lock, add greatly to the efficiency and value of the gun and the safety and convenience of the shooter.

Our aim has been to produce shotguns that should combine the elegance of outline, perfection of balance, ease of taking apart and quality of finish of the best double guns with the superiority in sighting and shooting of the single-barrel, and give 5 or 6 shots quickly instead of only two.

Our buttstocks and forearms are all of genuine American black walnut—not cheap wood stained in imitation of black walnut. The stock has all the style and shapeliness for which Marlin arms are famous. Buttplates are of hard rubber, extra quality, strongly crosslined on surface so they hold firmly on shoulder with no tendency to slip. Every metal part is of steel—the best quality obtainable for the purpose. There's not a piece of cheap material used anywhere in any Marlin gun, and the highest standard of workmanship is maintained.

Our barrels are of very high grade steel, with a big margin of extra strength, for our action is so simple and compact that we can put extra weight and strength into the barrel and use a very strong action, and still keep the weight of the gun just right. All barrels are proved in the rough by firing excessive charges. Each barrel is then tested for target by firing from 3 to 5 shots and counting the pellets. When the guns are assembled complete and have passed through a thorough shop inspection they go again to the proof house and the

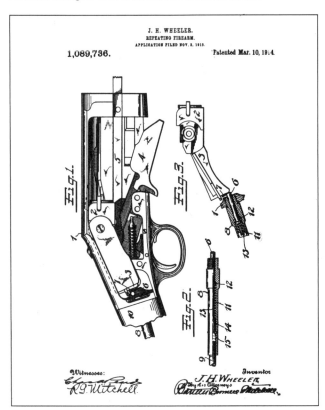

J.H. Wheeler's patent of a breech block buffer mechanism.

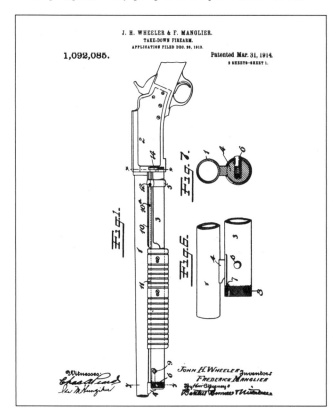

Third type of magazine tube takedown mechanism.

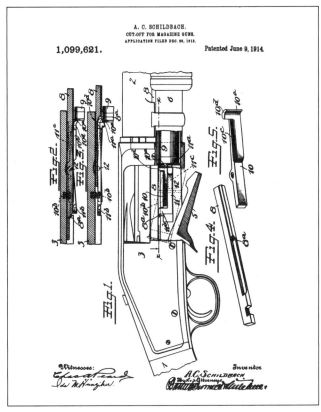

A.C. Schildbach's patent of a shell stop mechanism. Note that the safety button is now just forward of the trigger.

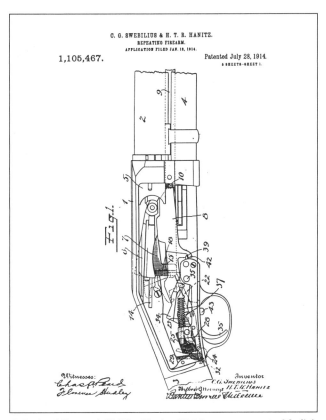

C.G. Swebilius and H.T.R. Hanitz 1914 improvements to Marlin's hammerless shotgun.

finished gun is proved with special heavy loads. Each gun is then fired 6 to 10 times with standard factory loaded shells, assorted, and if no fault can then be detected by the final inspection, they are ready for shipment.

Our solid top, side-ejecting construction acts both ways, protecting the head of the shooter from the exploding cartridge and the ejected shell, while at the same time protecting the action of the gun from rain, snow and all foreign substances.

The characteristics and operation of the hammerless guns were described in 1913, when the Model 28 shotgun was introduced, as follows:

> This new 12 gauge MARLIN shotgun is the finest repeating gun in the world. It has every up-to-date feature, perfected far beyond all previous standards, and exclusive advantages not obtainable in other guns:
>
> HAMMERLESS—Solid steel breech, inside as well as out—Solid top—Side Ejection—Matted Barrel—Press-Button Cartridge Release—Automatic Recoil Hang-Fire Safety Device—Double Extractors—Take-Down—Trigger and Hammer Safety.
>
> It is a fine appearing, beautifully balanced gun, without any objectionable humps or bumps; no holes on top for gas to blow out through and water to get in; and the solid steel breech permits a thoroughly symmetrical gun without sacrificing strength or safety at this important place. The action is thinner and neater, allowing a thin oval grip to be used. It is the safest breech loading shotgun ever built.

The action parts are entirely within the receiver with solid steel breech; the grip of buttstock is not cut away or weakened; the natural shape of the receiver allows fitting the most perfectly designed buttstock on any pump gun. Contrast this finely modeled comb and full pistol grip with the rounded grip and stubby comb of other hammerless models. The Marlin hammerless has better lines and more style than any other similar construction.

The barrel of Grade A Gun is our Special Rolled Steel, heavy at breech, tapering nicely toward muzzle; this clean, perfect tube with an even thickness of metal on all sides, gives uniform expansion and even distribution of the shot, secures extreme range and pattern; the single barrel shoots exactly where you hold, and is guaranteed to place more than 325 pellets in a 30 inch circle at 40 yards, using 1¼ ounces No. 8 chilled shot.

The barrel is handsomely matted on top for its entire length. The matted barrel prevents radiation of heat from top of barrel or reflection of the sunlight from interfering with your aim. This high-grade feature is not furnished on any other standard grade repeater.

The up-to-date designer of pump guns aims to have the receiver absolutely solid at the rear as well as on top, but no other hammerless gun has a solid steel gas-tight breech like this Marlin. Even a novice will realize that any defective shell which might be exploded in the gun could not blow back and break the buttstock or injure the shooter's hand in any way. We strongly urge you to take off the buttstock and compare the solid steel breech of the Marlin gun with the open breech of other hammerless guns.

An extra sear in the lock engages the hammer when action is opened, and hammer remains cocked on this sear until the action is closed and fully locked; with the final motion in locking the gun, the carrier raises front end of the sear, withdraws the rear end from notch in the hammer and allows hammer to cock on the trigger. This insures that, even if the trigger is held back, the hammer cannot possibly fall and discharge the cartridge until the action is closed and fully locked. The two-piece firing pin is another excellent safety device; the two pieces align only when gun is fully locked; at all other times, if rear firing pin were struck by hammer, the cartridge could not be discharged. This gun is also fitted with our automatic recoil hang-fire safety lock, giving full protection against hang-fire (defective) cartridges.

In carrying gun loaded and fully cocked, the hammer-and-trigger safety device located in the guard just in front of the trigger is drawn back so that it blocks the trigger and it is impossible to discharge the gun. To make this safety doubly effective, an extra spur is provided on the hammer with a square notch over which the safety block locks tightly when drawn back. Both of these locks are instantly released for firing by pressing forward the safety block with the finger as you throw the gun to your shoulder. No simpler, quicker or more effective device could possibly be designed.

OPERATION—The large stud at the rear end of link operates in a straight slot in the left side of frame. A stud at the rear end of the action bar connects with the front end of link; a corresponding stud on the link operates the carrier. Drawing back the action bar first depresses the front end of link and unlocks the gun by drawing down the locking bolt, then opens the action, ejects empty shell, cocks the hammer and allows a new cartridge to enter upon the carrier. The forward

motion raises carrier, inserts the new cartridge into the chamber, closes and locks action, leaving the gun ready to fire.

Buttstock is a fine quality of straight-grained American black walnut, thoroughly air seasoned and kiln dried, with darker color and finer grain than the sap wood used in some other guns. The stock is beautifully modeled, having a free, natural grip without cutting down the comb or otherwise reducing the perfect symmetry. It is not cut away inside for any operating parts, and is stronger than the buttstock of any other hammerless gun. No gas can enter the grip from the action. Buttplate is the highest quality hard rubber; a thinner buttplate of finer design is used than is possible with the cheaper composition buttplates.

The material throughout is of superior quality. Trigger is tool steel, hardened and tempered, not soft steel case-hardened. Coil springs are used. Breechbolt, firing pin and other important parts are Chrome Nickel Steel, the highest quality obtainable, specially heat treated, and nearly twice as strong as similar parts in other pump guns. All action parts are of high-grade steel, drop forged and machined to gauge. There is not a cheap piece of material in the entire gun.

The take-down construction, similar to the exposed hammer model, allows taking the gun apart for cleaning or packing in a few seconds' time. To take down, simply press latch at front end of magazine; draw forward magazine and action slide to clear the frame; unscrew barrel. When putting together, insert thumb through opening in bottom of frame and press on front end of link so action slide will connect. You can also have an interchangeable barrel portion complete, quickly changing your full choke gun into a field or brush

C.G. Swebilius and H.T.R. Hanitz 1915 changes to the hammerless shotguns.

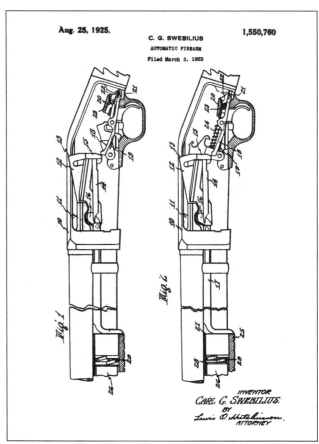

C.G. Swebilius patent of a hammerless shotgun.

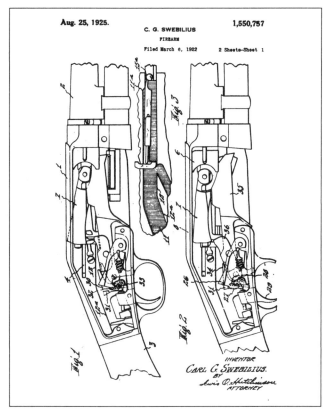

C.G. Swebilius patent of improvements made to the Marlin hammerless shotgun.

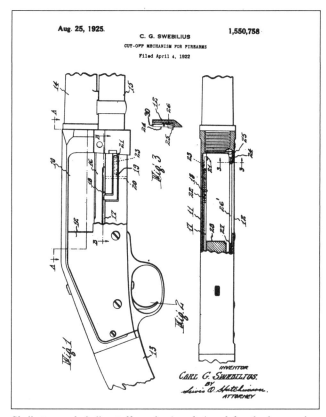

Shell stop and shell cutoff mechanism designed for the hammerless shotguns.

gun. The lock-nut on barrel is a moveable shoulder which takes up all wear and insures a firm, rigid union, no matter how long or hard the service. All Model 28 barrel portions interchange with one another; but barrel portions of Model 24 guns will not work in this gun.

To change loads quickly or remove loaded cartridges from magazine at end of the day's shooting, you simply press the cartridge release button on left side of receiver and the cartridges drop out into your hand. To remove a loaded cartridge from the chamber without firing, press in push-pin with thumb of right hand and operate action in usual manner.

This gun is loaded in the usual manner, inserting cartridges under carrier directly into magazine. As a single loader for trap shooting, just drop the cartridge into the action in front of breechbolt; then close the gun in the usual way.

The various grades of pump action shotguns were described by Marlin as follows:

"Grade A" This grade gun (the standard grade) has Special Rolled Steel barrel with a tensile strength of about 66,000 pounds per square inch. Frames are blued. Buttplates best quality of rubber.

"Grade B" This grade gun has "Special Smokeless Steel" barrel as on Grade "C" guns. The grip of the stock and forearm are both handsomely checked by hand.

"Grade C" This grade has "Special Smokeless Steel" barrel. It has a very high elastic limit and a tensile strength of about 100,000 pounds per square inch. Special care is given

to the boring and finishing of this grade. The stock and forearm are of selected fancy-figured walnut, and an extra fine finish is given to the wood. The stock and forearm are neatly checked by hand and the action is tastily relieved and ornamented with a good quality of hand engraving.

"Grade D" This grade gun has a high quality Damascus barrel, specially bored and finished. The stock and forend are of the finest imported "Circassian Walnut," finished by the London process of filling, giving a rich, dull surface that does not glisten or shine, and does not show scratches as plainly as the highly polished wood. The stock and forearm are checked with the finest possible handwork. The frame is elaborately engraved with a fine quality handwork. Screws and trigger are of tool steel, heavily gold plated. This is the finest repeating shotgun built.

The 32-in. barrel was only available in the Grade A gun.

Regular stocks for all grades were 13½ in. long, with 1⅝-in. drop at comb and 2½-in. drop at heel.

All magazines, except those of the Model 31–20 and Model 44A, held 5 shells; with one shell in the chamber, this totals 6 shots. Models 31–20 and 44A had short magazines that held only 4 shells; with one shell in the chamber, the shooter had 5 shots.

All full-choke barrels were guaranteed to target better than 325 pellets in a 30-in. circle at 40 yards, using 1¼ ounces of No. 8 chilled shot.

In addition to the various grades of shotguns available, both the exposed hammer and hammerless guns could be ordered with extra or special features, which were listed as follows:

TABLE 3

Special Feature	Price		
	1899	*1915*	*1917*
Checking on grip and forearm, Style A	$ 4.50	$ 4.00	$ 4.70
Changing length or drop of stock, to order	9.00	8.00	9.35
Selected walnut stock and forearm, not checked	9.50	8.50	—
Extra selected walnut stock and forearm, not checked, dull or polished	12.00	12.00	—
Checking on grip and forearm, Style B	6.35	6.00	7.00
Checking on grip and forearm Styles C, D, E, F, or G	9.75	10.00	11.65
Engraving, Grade No. 1	4.50	4.00	4.70
Engraving, Grade No. 2	9.00	8.00	9.35
Engraving, Grade No. 3	13.50	12.00	14.00
Engraving, Grade No. 5	22.50	20.00	23.40
Engraving, Grade No. 10	45.00	40.00	46.50
Engraving, Grade No. 15	67.50	60.00	70.00
Special smokeless steel barrel on Grade A gun	6.50	5.00	5.80
Best 4-blade Damascus barrel	18.00	—	—
Victoria canvas case, good quality, leather bound	1.40	1.50	—
Silver's recoil pad fitted	6.25	5.50	6.40
Nickel-plated trimmings	4.25	4.00	4.70
Swivels and sling strap (leather)	1.40	1.50	1.75
Solid matted rib barrel on Model 28, A, B, C and T.S.	—	5.00	5.75
Pistol grip stock on Model 28 Trap Gun only	—	—	5.75
Changing length or drop of stock on Model 28 Trap Gun or No. 24, No. 30, or No. 31 Field gun only, to order	—	—	3.00

TABLE 4

The characteristics of the various models of pump action shotguns were as follows:

	1898	*16*	*17*	*19*	*21*	*24*	*26*	*28*	*30*	*31*	*42*	*43*	*44*	*49*	*53*	*63*
Exposed Hammer	X	X	X	X	X	X	X		X		X			X		
Hammerless								X		X		X	X		X	X
12 Gauge	X		X	X	X	X	X	X			X	X		X	X	X
16 Gauge		X				X			X							
20 Gauge						X			X				X			
Takedown	X	X		X	X	X		X	X	X	X	X	X	X	X	X
Solid Frame			X				X									
Pistol Grip Stock	X	X		X		X		X	X	X	X	X	X	X	X	X
Straight Stock			X		X											
Early Forearm	X	X	X	X	X		X						X	X		
Late Forearm						X			X	X	X	X				X
Grooved Forearm	X	X	X	X	X	X	X	X	X	X	X	X	X	X	X	X
Hard Rubber Plate	X	X	X	X	X	X	X	X	X	X	X	X	X	X	X	X
Button Tube	X	X		X	X								X	X		
Latch Tube						X			X	X	X	X				X
Lock Screws																X
Bull's-Eye											X	X	X	X	X	X
M.F.A. Co.	X	X	X	X	X	X	X	X	X	X						X
M.F. Corp.											X	X	X			
M.F. Co.											X	X	X	X	X	X
Bolt Release: Button on Right Side	X	X	X	X	X		X									
Lever on Right Side						X		X		X				X		
Button on Top							X		X							
Lever on Left Side											X	X		X	X	X

Model 1898 shotgun of the first variation, which did not have a push-button bolt release.

EXPOSED HAMMER AND HAMMERLESS SHOTGUNS

Model 1898, Exposed Hammer, Shotgun, 12-Gauge, Takedown (1898–1905)

The first announcement of the Model 1898 exposed hammer shotgun indicated that it would be available June 1, 1898. It was described as being only in one style. No mention of its grade or special features was made. By 1899, however, there were Grades A, C, and D, and a Brush or Riot model. The first announcement indicated that this new gun had a lever attached to the barrel lock nut that had to be raised in the process of removing the barrel assembly. But no such device has been observed, except on an L.L. Hepburn prototype. It is assumed that by the time production was under way, the lever was found unnecessary.

This 12-gauge shotgun had a barrel made of "Special Rolled Steel." The frame and other parts were blued. The butt plate was hard rubber and the pistol grip stock and forearm were of walnut. The stock length was 13½ inches. The drop at the comb was 2¼ inches and at the heel, 2½ inches. The magazine held 5 shells and with one in the chamber, it held 6 shells. The forearm wood of the Grades A, B, and the Brush or Riot gun had circular grooves for added grip. The barrels and frame were serial-numbered, but in different series. The choke was marked on the barrel as previously mentioned. The Model 1898 Grades A, C, D, and Brush and Riot models all had the first-type button magazine tube release and also had the first-type bolt-opening plunger on the top rear of the frame.

The first variation of the Model 1898, which was manufactured in early 1898, did not have a grade designation and was called The Standard Gun. It is identified by the lack of the recoil safety device and the accompanying serrated button (pin) at the top rear of the frame, which was used to open the bolt.

The second variation (introduced in 1899) had the added feature of the recoil safety and bolt-unlocking button. It was in production until 1905 as follows:

Model 1898 Shotgun, Grade A (1899–1905). 12-gauge, 28-, 30-, or 32-in. barrels, 6 shots, weight, 7 to 7¼ pounds, full choke.

Model 1898 Shotgun, Grade A, Brush or Riot (1899–1902). 12-gauge, 26-in. barrel, 6 shots, weight, 6¾ pounds, cylinder bore.

Model 1898 Shotgun, Grade B (1899–1905). Identical to the Grade A gun, except it had a special smokeless steel barrel and handsomely hand-checked grip and forearm. It was 12-gauge, 26-, 28- or 30-in. barrels, 6 shot, weight, 6⅞ to 7⅛ pounds.

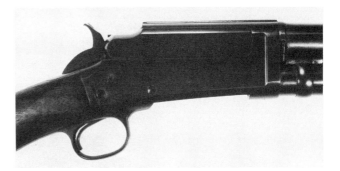

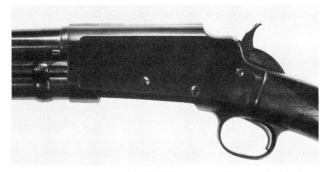

Top: *Right side of early Model 1898 shotgun.* Bottom: *Left side of Model 1898 shotgun.*

Roll-stamp on barrel of Model 1898 and Model 16 shotguns.

THIS gun is fitted with our patented automatic recoil-operated safety lock. This device prevents the gun from being opened by the left hand until after the cartridge has exploded. In case of a hang-fire the gun waits for the explosion, and cannot be operated by the left hand until the recoil of the cartridge unlocks the safety. The recoil safety is locked automatically every time the gun is opened and closed, and unlocked automatically every time a cartridge is exploded in the chamber. In case it is desired to open the gun without firing and with the hammer down, press in the small pin with checked end, at the right of the hammer. This is conveniently done with the thumb of the right hand. If it is desired to open the gun without firing and with the hammer cocked, press in check-head pin, as above, to unlock recoil safety, then press firing-pin forward with thumb of right hand.

Hang-tag instruction furnished with the second-variation Model 1898 shotguns.

Many people will appreciate a gun that can be taken apart by a man who is not an expert. *Taking out one screw allows the entire breech mechanism to be removed from the frame in the Marlin Repeating Shotgun.*

To Take Apart—With *the action open* take out the carrier screw E (see cut on page 78), then holding the gun in the ordinary position, move the forearm forward slowly about an inch and the carrier will drop out through the opening in the bottom of the frame. The breech bolt containing the locking bolt can then be drawn out to the rear.

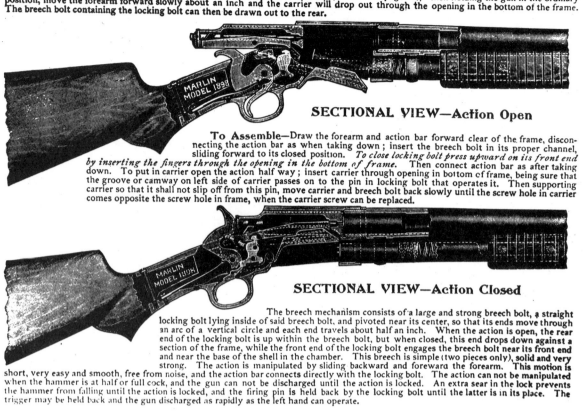

SECTIONAL VIEW—Action Open

To Assemble—Draw the forearm and action bar forward clear of the frame, disconnecting the action bar as when taking down; insert the breech bolt in its proper channel, sliding forward to its closed position. *To close locking bolt press upward on its front end by inserting the fingers through the opening in the bottom of frame.* Then connect action bar as after taking down. To put in carrier open the action half way; insert carrier through opening in bottom of frame, being sure that the groove or camway on left side of carrier passes on to the pin in locking bolt that operates it. Then supporting carrier so that it shall not slip off from this pin, move carrier and breech bolt back slowly until the screw hole in carrier comes opposite the screw hole in frame, when the carrier screw can be replaced.

SECTIONAL VIEW—Action Closed

The breech mechanism consists of a large and strong breech bolt, a straight locking bolt lying inside of said breech bolt, and pivoted near its center, so that its ends move through an arc of a vertical circle and each end travels about half an inch. When the action is open, the rear end of the locking bolt is up within the breech bolt, but when closed, this end drops down against a section of the frame, while the front end of the locking bolt engages the breech bolt near its front end and near the base of the shell in the chamber. This breech is simple (two pieces only), solid and very strong. The action is manipulated by sliding backward and forward the forearm. This motion is short, very easy and smooth, free from noise, and the action bar connects directly with the locking bolt. The action can not be manipulated when the hammer is at half or full cock, and the gun can not be discharged until the action is locked. An extra sear in the lock prevents the hammer from falling until the action is locked, and the firing pin is held back by the locking bolt until the latter is in its place. The trigger may be held back and the gun discharged as rapidly as the left hand can operate.

Catalog assembly and disassembly instructions for the Model 1898.

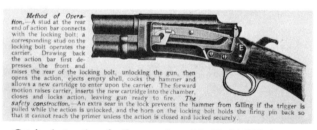

Method of Operation.—A stud at the rear end of action bar connects with the locking bolt; a corresponding stud on the locking bolt operates the carrier. Drawing back the action bar first depresses the front and raises the rear of the locking bolt, unlocking the gun, then opens the action, ejects empty shell, cocks the hammer and allows a new cartridge to enter upon the carrier. The forward motion raises carrier, inserts the new cartridge into the chamber, closes and locks action, leaving gun ready to fire. *The safety construction.*—An extra sear in the lock prevents the hammer from falling if the trigger is pulled while the action is unlocked, and the horn on the locking bolt holds the firing pin back so that it cannot reach the primer unless the action is closed and locked securely.

Catalog instructions for the operation of the Model 1898 shotgun.

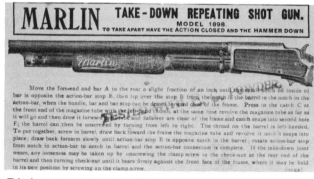

Takedown instructions for Marlin exposed hammer pump action shotgun.

Model 1898 Shotgun, Grade C (1899–1905). For the 26-in. barrel, weight was 6⅞ pounds; the 28-in. barrel weighed 7 pounds; the 30-in. barrel weighed 7⅛ pounds.

Model 1898 Shotgun, Grade D (1899–1905). The 26-in. Damascus barrel weighed 6⅞ pounds; for the 28-in. Damascus barrel, weight was 7 pounds; and for the 30-in. Damascus barrel, weight was 7⅛ pounds.

The catalog prices of the Model 1898 shotgun were as follows:

Grade	1898	1899	1900	1901	1902	1903	1904	1905
A	24.00	24.00	24.00	24.00	24.00	23.25	23.25	23.25
Brush or Riot	—	24.00	24.00	24.00	24.00	—	—	—
B	—	—	—	—	—	30.75	30.75	30.75
C	40.00	40.00	40.00	40.00	40.00	40.80	40.80	40.80
D	—	100.00	100.00	95.00	95.00	90.00	90.00	90.00

Barrels and frames are serial-numbered; however, the numbers for each are different. Barrels are marked *F, M,* and *C* to identify the choke.

Patent dates roll-stamped on the barrel are November 6, 1894; May 12, 1896; and June 2, 1896.

The lowest reported or observed serial number is 2618. The highest serial number reported or observed is 114,711. Records for the Model 1898 are on hand for serial numbers from 19,601 to 67,000.

Model 16, Exposed Hammer, Shotgun, 16-Gauge, Takedown (1903–1910)

This model is 16 gauge only and is chambered for the 2¾-in. shell. It is exactly like the Model 1898 shotgun, except that it is proportioned for the smaller 16-gauge shell. It was available in Grades A, B, C, and D. The full choke barrel would pattern 240 pellets or better, in a 30-in. circle at 40 yards when using one ounce of No. 7½ chilled shot.

It had a pistol grip walnut stock with a hard rubber butt plate. The takedown and bolt-opening mechanisms were of the first variations. Frames, barrels, and magazine tubes were blued. Both case-hardened and blued hammers were used. Weights for this model were the same as for the Model 1898 shotgun.

The catalog prices of the Model 16 were as follows:

Grade	1903	1904	1905	1906	1907	1908	1909	1910
A	25.00	25.00	25.00	25.00	25.00	23.25	23.25	23.25
B	32.75	32.75	32.75	32.75	32.75	30.75	32.00	32.00
C	44.50	44.50	44.50	44.50	44.50	40.80	43.00	43.00
D	95.00	95.00	95.00	95.00	95.00	90.00	95.00	95.00

Barrels and frames are serial-numbered; however, the numbers for each are different. The choke of the barrel was identified next to the barrel serial number by the letter *F, M,* or *C.*

All guns of this model are not marked on the top tang with the model number. The barrel is marked *16 GA.* just forward of the frame. The patent dates marked on the barrel are the same as those for the Model 1898 and include those of November 6, 1894; May 12, 1896 to June 2, 1896.

The lowest serial number recorded or observed for this model is 59,531. The highest recorded or observed is 142,847.

Marlin 1907 ad for the Model 16 shotgun.

Marlin announcement of Model 16 shotgun.

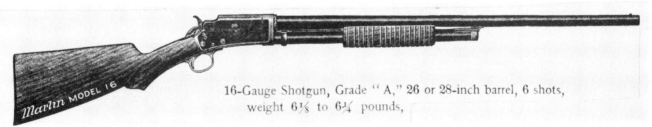

Marlin Model 16 shotgun.

Marlin's 1905 ad for the Model 17 shotgun.

Model 16 serial numbers and those of the Model 1898 shotgun are in the same series.

The Model 16 shotgun was the first 16-gauge gun Marlin manufactured. It was superseded in 1911 by both a 16-gauge Field gun that did not have a model number, and the Model 30-16 gun.

Model 17, Exposed Hammer, 12-Gauge, Solid-Frame Shotgun (1906-1908)

Marlin advertised the Model 17 as "the best low priced repeating shotgun in the world." It claimed that by making the gun with a solid frame and a straight-grip stock, a number of parts were eliminated, resulting in a stronger, simpler, and less costly gun.

The Model 17 was made as a standard Grade A gun, as a Brush Gun, and as a Riot Gun. The standard Grade A had a 30- or 32-in. full-choke barrel that would handle either 2¾- or 2⅝-in. shells and would pattern better than 325 pellets in a 30-in. circle at 40 yards, using 1¼ ounces of No. 8 chilled shot. (The Model 1898 and Model 16 listed 7½ chilled shot.)

The Model 17 Brush Gun has a 26-in. cylinder bore barrel that was designed for bird shooting in close cover. Modified and full-choke barrels were also available for this model on special order.

The Model 17 Riot Gun had a 20-in. cylinder bore barrel that was designed especially for buckshot. It was recommended for use by guards of all kinds, watchmen, express messengers, banks, and households as protection against burglars, thieves, and robbers.

The bolt-opening system of this model was of the first variation. The magazine tube front end was covered by L.L. Hepburn's patent number 525,739, dated September 11, 1894, for a device to attach magazines to gun barrels.

Other than its being a solid-frame, straight-stock shotgun, there was nothing that made this model materially different from the previous models. However, improved models of the Model 17 were made. For example, when a newly designed recoil safety mechanism was patented and put into Model 17 production, the model designation changed to Model 17G. The G series gun had a bolt-opening mechanism wherein the opening device was located on the lower edge of the receiver at the front of the trigger guard. There also were some Model 17S-marked guns, about which little is known. The patent dates on this model are April 2, 1889; September 11, 1894; November 6, 1894; November 27, 1900; November 29, 1904.

There were no Grade B, C, or D variations of the Model 17 shotguns produced.

Weight given for the Grade A was 7½ pounds for a 30- or 32-in. barrel. The brush gun, with a 26-in. barrel, weighed 7 pounds. The 20-in.-barreled riot gun weighed 6⅞ pounds.

The retail price for this model was listed as follows:

Grade	1906	1907	1908
A	$21.00	$21.00	$21.00
Brush	21.00	21.00	21.00
Riot	21.00	21.00	21.00

The low and high serial numbers reported or observed for this model are as follows:

Model	Low	High
Model 17	49,197	142,146
Model 17S	A1,513	A4,659
Model 17G	A17,570	A23,297
	119,861	149,385

The Model 17 was replaced by the solid-frame Model 26 shotgun that was listed as available from 1909 to 1916.

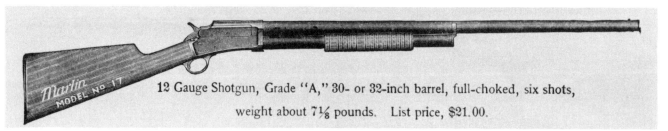

12 Gauge Shotgun, Grade "A," 30- or 32-inch barrel, full-choked, six shots, weight about 7¼ pounds. List price, $21.00.

Marlin Model 17 solid-frame shotgun.

MARLIN, MODEL No. 17, BRUSH GUN

This is a light, short, open bored gun, designed for bird shooting in cover. It can be used with smokeless or black powder and any size of shot, including buck shot. The regular stock gun will be cylinder bored, and this boring will always be sent unless otherwise ordered. Modified and full-choked barrels made to order at same price.

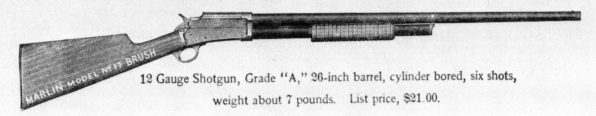

12 Gauge Shotgun, Grade "A," 26-inch barrel, cylinder bored, six shots, weight about 7 pounds. List price, $21.00.

Marlin Model 17 Brush Gun.

MARLIN, MODEL No. 17, RIOT GUN

This is an extra short and light gun, open bored, for buck shot especially. It is a most deadly arm for guards of all kinds, watchmen, express messengers, and is kept handy in many banks and households as a protection against burglars, thieves and robbers. In this service it is much more effective than a rifle or a dozen revolvers.

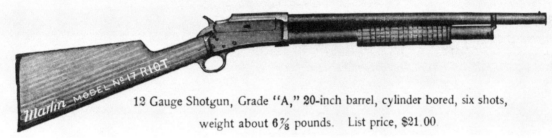

12 Gauge Shotgun, Grade "A," 20-inch barrel, cylinder bored, six shots, weight about 6⅞ pounds. List price, $21.00

Marlin Model 17 Riot Gun.

Marlin Model 17 shotgun.

Right side of Model 17 solid-frame shotgun.

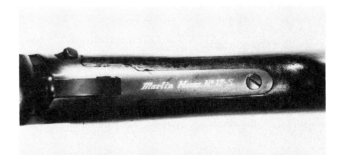

Roll-stamp on top tang of Model 17S shotgun.

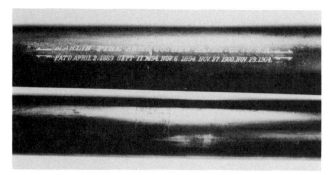

Barrel roll-stamp of Model 17 shotgun.

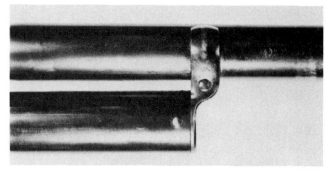

Solid-frame magazine tube of Model 17 and 26 shotguns.

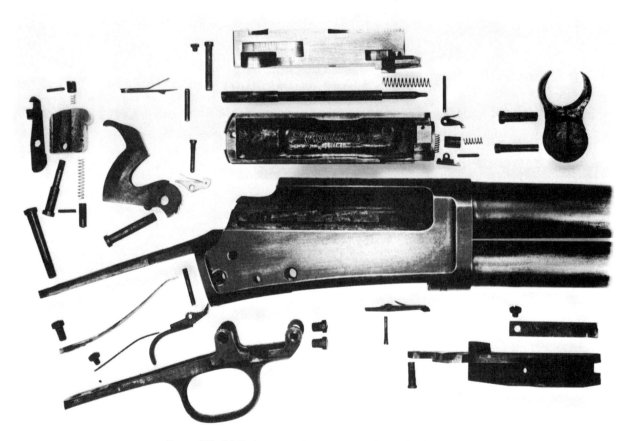

Parts of Model 17 shotgun in their positions relative to each other.

Wood and metal finish were the standard varnish and blue of the previous (and most later) models.

Model 19, Exposed Hammer, 12-Gauge, Takedown, Shotgun, (1906–1907)

This model was the main effort of the Marlin company during this period. The Model 16 in 16 gauge and the Model 17 solid-frame guns were also available, but the Model 19 had the advantage of being takedown and 12-gauge, which were the predominant choices of the sportsman in a pump action shotgun.

The Model 19 was produced in grades A, B, C, and D. Their weights, performance, and characteristics were the same as the shotguns previously described. Variations of the Model 19 included the Models 19S, 19N, and 19G. Differences in the variations included lock screws for the forearm screws, a lug on the locking bolt that prevented the action slide from being disconnected when the bolt was closed quickly, and, in the 19G, the second-variation forend and magazine tube.

Examination of barrel markings on the Model 19 indicate that they were inconsistent even within one variation. Some of the patent dates noted were as follows:

Model 19: Apr. 2, 1889; Sept. 11, 1894; Nov. 6, 1894; May 12, 1896; June 2, 1896; Nov. 27, 1900; Mar. 29, 1904; Nov. 29, 1904.

Model 19G: May 12, 1896; June 2, 1896; Oct. 5, 1897;

Nov. 27, 1900; Mar. 29, 1904; Nov. 29, 1904; Aug. 7, 1906; Mar. 24, 1908; May 19, 1908.

Model 19S: Apr. 2, 1889; Nov. 6, 1894; May 12, 1896; June 2, 1896; Oct. 5, 1897; Nov. 27, 1900; Mar. 29, 1904; Nov. 29, 1904; Aug. 7, 1906; Mar. 24, 1908; May 19, 1908.

The top tang of the Model 19 was roll-stamped with the model number. Frames and barrels were serial-numbered, but not with the same number.

The catalog retail prices of the Model 19 were listed as follows:

Grade	1906	1907
A	$23.25	$23.25
B	30.75	30.75
C	40.80	40.80
D	90.00	90.00

The low and high serial numbers recorded and observed for the Model 19 have been as follows:

Model	Low	High
Model 19D	814	94,939
Model 19S	A397	A26,775
Model 19S	66,039	149,947
Model 19G	A12,027	A30,297
Model 19N	241	10,019

Marlin ad for the Model 19, 12-gauge, exposed hammer, pump action shotgun.

Model 21, Exposed Hammer, 12-Gauge, Trap Model, Takedown, Shotgun (1907–1908)

This model, like the Model 17 gun, had a straight stock. Otherwise it was like the Model 19 shotgun. It was available in the regular A, B, C, and D grades and had the early button magazine release and the bolt-opening button on the right rear

Right side of special-order Model 19 shotgun that has all the features of a Grade D gun, plus special-order gold inlays and ornamentation not observed on any other exposed hammer Marlin shotgun. (JO)

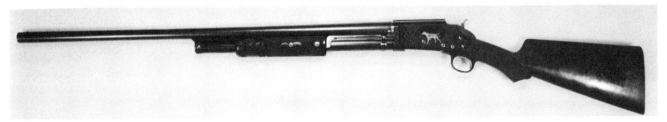

Left side of Model 19 shotgun of D grade with No. 15 engraving and inlay work. (JO)

Left: *Right side of special-order deluxe Model 19 shotgun.* Right: *Left side of same special Model 19 shotgun.*

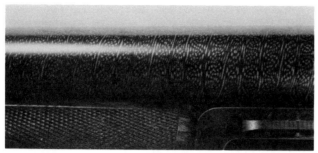

Typical pattern of damascus barrels furnished on Marlin Grade D shotguns.

Especially ornate checking of deluxe Grade D shotgun.

Parts of second-type recoil safety mechanism used in Marlin pump action shotguns.

Roll-stamp on top tang of Model 19 shotgun.

Barrel roll-stamp on barrel of Model 19 shotgun.

Marlin's pump action slide lock that was used on early takedown shotguns.

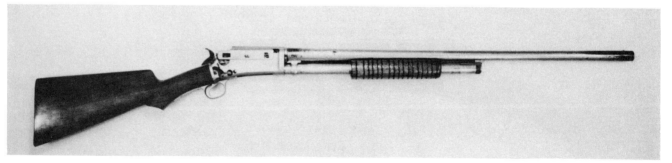

Sectionalized prototype of Model 21 shotgun.

of the frame. It was available during the same period as the Models 17 and 19. The only features in this model not already available on Models 17 and 19 were the combined features of a straight-grip stock and a takedown barrel.

The 1907 catalog called it a Trap Model and described the Model 21 as follows:

> This model is similar to the Model 24, except for the straight grip feature and the earlier form of take-down construction. These differences allow us to save something in the cost of construction, therefore we offer the Model 21 at a lower price, while maintaining exactly the same quality of material and workmanship throughout.
>
> The new straight grip stock is comfortable, shapely, well-made, adding much to the fine balance, neat and pleasing proportions of the gun. It comes up to the shoulder with that quick, easy swing that makes you sure of your game; it gives you the confidence that means good scores.

The 1908 catalog had the same information in it as the 1907 catalog.

The Model 21 was marked on the top tang with the model number, and frames and barrels were serial-numbered. The configuration and features of this model were those of previous models, but it had a straight stock. The patent dates on the barrel were from April 2, 1889 to November 29, 1904.

The Model 21 was the first pump shotgun that Marlin introduced and identified as a Trap Model. The early interest displayed in this gun resulted in the introduction of two new models that were better suited than the Model 21 for use at the traps. Interestingly, the next Trap Gun did not have a numerical model number, but was just called "Trap Model."

The Model 21 Trap Model was catalog-priced as follows:

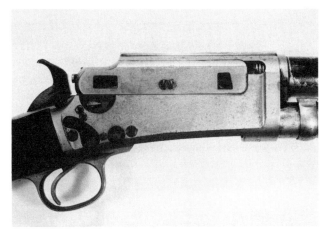

Top: *Right side of sectionalized prototype shotgun with the bolt-release button close to the hammer.* Bottom: *Left side of same.*

Model 21 Grade A 12 Ga

Marlin Take-Down Repeating Shot Guns
at
$14.50

Regular Wholesale Price, $17.53

Description—Take Down—Straight Grip—Special Rolled Steel Barrel—Rubber
Butt Plate—Smokeless or Black Powder
12 Ga—26 in., 28 in., 30 in., 32 in. barrels Full choke—Modified choke—Cylinder
Bore

QUALITY:--
THE BEST MADE!

Marlin announcement of special low price of $14.50 for the Model 21 shotgun.

GRADE "C." This grade gun has our "Special Smokeless Steel" barrel, the finest quality we can buy, and made specially for us for this use. It has a very high elastic limit and a tensile strength of about 100,000 pounds to the square inch. Special care is given to the boring and finishing of this grade. The stock and forearm are of selected fancy-figured walnut, and an extra fine finish is given to the wood. The stock and forearm are neatly checked by hand, as shown in cut, and the action is tastily relieved and ornamented with a good quality of hand engraving. See illustration.

Model No. 21, Grade "C," 12-Gauge, Take-Down, 26, 28 or 30-inch barrel, 6 shots, weight 6⅞ to 7⅛ lbs., ... Price, $38.50

GRADE "D." This grade gun has a high quality Damascus barrel, specially bored and finished. The stock and foreend are of the finest imported "Circassian Walnut," finished by the London process of filling, giving a rich, dull surface that does not glisten nor shine, and does not show scratches as plainly as the highly polished wood. The stock and forearm are checked with the finest possible hand work. The frame is elaborately engraved with fine quality hand work. Screws and trigger are of tool steel, heavily gold plated. This is the finest repeating shotgun built.

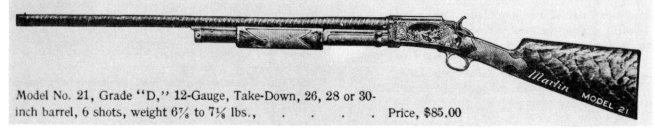

Model No. 21, Grade "D," 12-Gauge, Take-Down, 26, 28 or 30-inch barrel, 6 shots, weight 6⅞ to 7⅛ lbs., ... Price, $85.00

Catalog illustrations and description of the special-order Grades C and D Model 21 shotguns.

Grade	1907	1908
A	$22.25	$22.25
B	29.00	29.00
C	38.50	38.50
D	85.00	85.00

The lowest serial number recorded or observed for the Model 21 was 96,623; the highest, 147,413.

Model 24, 12-Gauge, Takedown, Pistol Grip Shotgun (1908–1917)

This model was the first of many of Marlin's exposed hammer shotguns that received improvements during its production. Added to the Model 24 were a new, improved forearm latch, new forearm, and new recoil safety mechanism. The improvements changed the designation from 24 to 24G; in addition, in 1913 the designation Marlin Field Gun and Marlin Trap Gun were added to the variations of the Model 24 when they too were updated with the new features.

The longest-lived of the exposed hammer models, the Model 24 was first identified as such in the 1908 catalog. It was con-tinuously listed in catalogs, or price lists, until 1917. However, probably no new manufacture was done after 1915 and those guns sold after that date were likely to have been in inventory or assembled from parts on hand.

The Model 24 was produced in pistol grip grades A, B, C, and D. The barrel was matted on top for its entire length. The pistol grip stock was of black walnut handsomely shaped and finished, 13½ inches in length, with 2-in. drop at comb and a 2½-in. drop at heel. All previous standard stocks had a drop of 1⅝ inches at the comb. A 32-in. barrel in addition to the usual 26-, 28-, and 30-in. barrels was available in the grades A, B, and C. Otherwise the features of the Model 24 were the same as previously described models and grades.

Marlin felt strongly about the quality of the new improvements in its pump shotgun and expressed it as follows:

The Model 24 Marlin 12 gauge repeating shotgun with visible hammer is a quick-handling, hard-hitting, long-range gun, especially adapted for trap shooting and for ducks, geese, foxes, etc.

It has the simplicity and strength of mechanism, the safety lock, double extractors and other up-to-date features of the Model 19 which it succeeds, with important improvements for the greater safety, comfort and convenience of the shooter.

The characteristic Marlin solid top is always a protection between your head and the cartridge and keeps gases from blowing back into your face and eyes.

The side ejection of shells, the quick operation of the simplest mechanism ever used in any repeating gun and the superior shooting qualities of the Marlin single barrel allow you to make doubles as readily as with any two-barrel gun, with four other shots instantly available.

The closed-in breechbolt is not only a feature of strength and beauty, but also keeps out all the rain, snow and sleet of good wild-fowling weather, the drifting sand of the goose-pit, the rushes, twigs, leaves and dirt that clog up other repeaters. It will not freeze up in cold wet weather like an open-top gun. The solid matted rib on frame and the matted barrel are great aids in quick shooting.

In the action, the Model 24 has one-third less parts than any other make of repeating shotgun, and the working parts engage directly with one another without intervening links or other complications. There's plenty of extra strength in every part and not a weak spot in the entire gun.

The improved automatic recoil block hooks on to the locking bolt when closing the action and holds the gun firmly locked until after the explosion of the cartridge, when it is instantly and automatically released by the recoil.

It prevents the possibility of opening the action just as the cartridge is exploding, and removes all danger from hang-

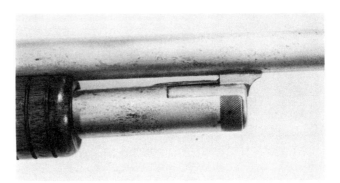

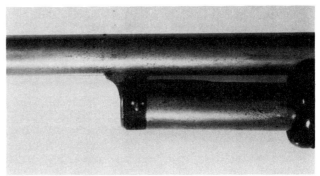

Top: *Right side of the second-variation button magazine release.* Bottom: *Left side of same magazine release.*

Catalog illustration and description of the 12-gauge Field guns.

Catalog illustration and description of the 16-gauge Field guns.

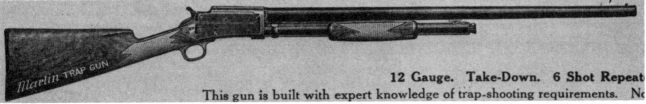

Catalog illustration of Marlin's 12-gauge Trap Gun.

Marlin sales brochure illustration of the Marlin Trap Gun.

fires, for no matter how long it may take the cartridge to explode after the primer is struck by the firing pin the gun remains tightly locked until after the explosion.

To operate the gun when empty or to eject a defective cartridge, hold back the recoil hook extension at front end of trigger guard with right forefinger (which throws off the recoil lock), and operate in the regular manner.

The Model 24 Trap and Field Guns, as previously mentioned, were straight-stock guns and were like the earlier Trap and Field Guns that did not have model numbers. Both the Standard and Special variations were listed under the Model 24 as follows:

Model	1913	1914–15	1916	1917
Standard Marlin Trap Gun	$35.00	$35.00	$38.00	$45.00
Special Marlin Trap Gun	37.50	37.50	—	—
Standard Marlin Field Gun	30.00	30.00	32.00	38.40
Special Marlin Field Gun	32.50	—	—	—

The A, B, C, and D grades were priced as follows:

Grade	1908–1910	1911–1915	1916	1917
A	$23.25	$21.60	$24.00	$28.80
B	30.75	33.25	33.20	39.90
C	40.80	43.25	43.25	51.90
D	90.00	95.00	95.00	114.00

PRESS LATCH at front end of magazine and draw tube forward. Draw forward action bar to clear frame. Unscrew barrel. That's all there is to taking down the

New Model 24 *Marlin* Repeating Shotgun

12 Gauge
Take-Down
6 Shots
7¼ lbs.

You can take it down anywhere in 10 seconds, even with cold fingers.

The **steel-lined, metal-capped forearm,** double extractors and automatic recoil hangfire safety device are other special features of this new model. It has also the *Marlin* solid-top side ejecting construction, with the close in breech-bolt that keeps out rain, snow, dirt, leaves, twigs and sand.

The *Marlin* Firearms Co.
30 WILLOW STREET   NEW HAVEN, CONN.

Marlin 1908 ad for the Model 24 shotgun.

The low and high serial numbers of the Model 24 recorded or observed have been the following:

Model	Low	High
24	100,229	149,664
24	A211	A32,848
24G	A20,101	A32,674

The top tang was marked *Model No. 24,* and frames and barrels were serial-numbered. The grades A, B, C, and D stocks were pistol grip, and the field and trap models had straight stocks.

Marlin Trap Gun, 12-Gauge, Exposed Hammer, Takedown, Shotgun (1909–1912). This gun was unique because it did not have a numerical designation and was listed as The Marlin Trap Gun until it became the Model 24 Trap Gun in 1913. It was listed in 1909 as The New Marlin Trap Gun. It was a 12-gauge takedown with a straight stock and was available in two styles. The Standard model had a regular straight-grip buttstock and 30-in. full-choke barrel, and weighed 7¼ pounds. The second variation, called the Special Marlin Trap Gun, was a custom-made-to-order gun the same as the Standard model except that the straight-grip buttstock was made to special order.

Interchangeable barrels were also available in 26-, 28-, 30-, or 32-in. length in full choke, modified choke, or cylinder bore, as desired.

The catalog description of the Marlin Trap Gun in 1909 was as follows:

The essential requirement of a good trap gun is one accurate, hard-shooting barrel. In the Marlin Trap Gun the barrel is Special Smokeless Steel—nearly twice as hard and strong as the rolled steel barrel used in other trap guns—specially built and bored for trap loads. It is guaranteed to make the extremely close, hard-hitting, ideal trap gun pattern—more than 325 pellets of No. 8 chilled shot in a 30 inch circle at 40 yards. The even distribution of metal on all sides of the barrel gives a uniform, even distribution of the shot; the extra quality material and special heavy breech secure the extreme range and smashing power; the single barrel shoots exactly where you hold.

The best amateur score ever made was made with a Marlin at the Missouri State Shoot, June 12th–13th, 1909—342 targets straight—the world's amateur record.

The trap gun has the Marlin solid top, side ejector and closed-in breech. It can't freeze up with rain, snow or sleet; rain can't run into the action and swell the shells in the magazine. Dirt, leaves, twigs and sand are also excluded from the action. The closed-in breechbolt protects the gun and the shooter, gives a symmetrical breech and helps quick sighting and good shooting.

The trap gun has every feature of strength and convenience of our famous Model 24, including the double extractors that pull any shell. The operating parts are few in number and very strong—they are finely adjusted and highly polished, giving the quickest, smoothest-working repeating mechanism used in any gun. The quick repeat shots allow doubles and trebles at the trap and great sport with birds and ducks.

An unusual and important feature is the special gas channel in the breechbolt, which prevents gas from a defective primer blowing back through the action. Two other safety devices doubly guard against premature explosion, and the automatic recoil safety lock positively prevents opening the action while a hang-fire cartridge is exploding.

The take-down construction similar to the Model 24, allows taking the gun apart for cleaning or packing in a few seconds' time. You can also have an interchangeable barrel portion complete, quickly changing your trap gun into a field or brush gun.

The buttstock shows a radical change from standard Marlin models. Short stocks, quickly brought to the shoulder, are better for field work, but the steady holding over the trap favors the use of the longer, straighter stock with a consequent better grip and firm pressure against the shoulder—better sighting and shooting, maximum range and smashing power with minimum kick from the recoil.

Buttstock and forearm are made of imported Circassian walnut and have the very rich, dull London oil finish as used on the most expensive guns made. The grip of stock and forearm are finely checked by hand. Buttstocks are all hand made and beautifully modeled; have comfortable oval straight grip, rounding bottle comb and a large, broad butt which balances the gun perfectly and further minimizes the effect of the recoil by covering more of the shooter's shoulder.

The specifications of the Trap Gun were listed in 1909 as follows:

THE NEW MARLIN TRAP GUN is a 12 gauge, take-down, 6 shot repeater, built with expert knowledge of trap-shooting requirements. No expense is spared to make this gun the best handling, best shooting, most efficient trap gun in the world. It is handsome, harmonious and distinctive, yet the excessive, expensive ornamentation has been eliminated, allowing the gun to be sold with Smokeless Steel barrel at the moderate price of $38.00. The shapely stock, the fine checking on grip and forearm and the clean simplicity of the single barrel construction allows this gun to swing precisely on the target.

The barrel is Special Smokeless Steel, with a tensile strength of over 100,000 pounds to the square inch. Handles 2¾ or 2⅝ inch shells, black or smokeless powders. Guaranteed to pattern more than 325 pellets in a 30 inch circle at 40 yards, using 1¼ ounces No. 8 chilled shot. Frames are the finest quality of gun frame steel, cut from the solid drop forging. Frames and breechbolts have blued finish. The mechanism is extremely simple, having one third less parts than any other repeating gun. Action parts are consequently larger, and being made of drop-forged steel are doubly strong for the purpose. They are highly polished to insure the smoothest possible operation.

Buttstocks and forearms are Circassian Walnut, with London oil finish and fine hand checking. Regular buttstocks are 14 inches long, with 1¾ inch drop at comb and 1¹³⁄₁₆ inch drop at heel. Buttstocks are hand made and beautifully modeled; buttplates are hard rubber and extra large, giving a heavier and more convenient stock for trap work. Trap gun with straight grip stock, any desired length or drop, at an additional charge of $3.50. Trap gun with pistol grip stock, any desired length or drop, to order, at an additional charge of $5.60.

Standard Marlin Trap Gun: 12 gauge, take-down, 6 shots, regular buttstock, 30 inch full choke barrel, weight about 7¾ pounds, $38.00.

Special Marlin Trap Gun: Same as above, but with special dimensions of buttstock, straight grip, made to order, $41.50.

Extra interchangeable barrel portion complete, $19.25.

The trap gun or barrel portion can be furnished with 26, 28, 30 or 32 inch barrel, full choke, modified choke or cylinder bore, as desired.

In 1911, Marlin started to mat the top of barrels to reduce glare. The announcement stated this:

1909 ad for the Model 24.

1910 ad for the Model 24.

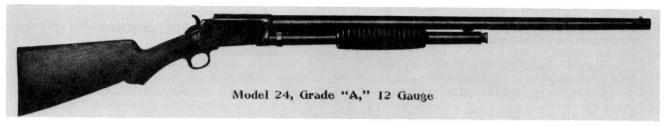

Model 24, Grade "A," 12 Gauge

Model 24 shotgun.

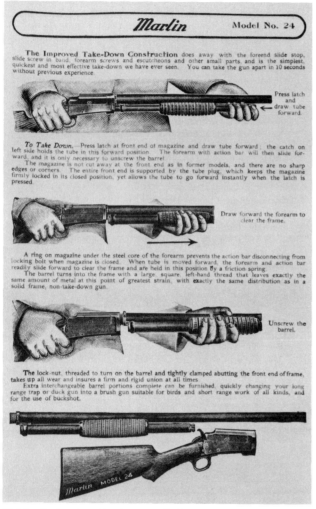

Catalog instructions for the new takedown system of the Model 24 shotgun.

As will be noted from the description of our respective models, we now regularly furnish all our Grade B, Grade C, Grade D and Trap Model shotguns with matted barrel.

In bright sunlight in some positions the reflection of light from the highly polished surface of ordinary gun barrels produces a blurred effect so that the front sight is not clearly defined and accordingly the shot is often lost. Again when a gun is fired many times in rapid succession (as in trap shooting) and the barrel becomes heated, the radiation of heat along the top of the barrel produces a similar blurred effect. The matted barrel overcomes all this.

The matting is in effect a series of cross lines, giving a dull streak which cannot reflect any light, does not show heat radiation, and which always shows clearly and instantly the position of the front sight. This helps quick, accurate aim, with correspondingly better scores. The properly matted barrel is one of the refinements in gun selection that indicate the experienced and discriminating shooter. It supplements fine build and balance and superb shooting ability; it makes for maximum efficiency; it adds greatly to the value of any good gun.

The matted-barrel trap gun was listed in the 1911 catalog at a price slightly reduced from 1909, as follows:

Standard Marlin Trap Gun: 12 gauge, take-down, 6 shots, regular buttstock, 30 inch full choke matted barrel, weight about 7¾ pounds, $35.00.

Special Marlin Trap Gun: Same as above, but with special dimensions of buttstock, straight grip, made to order, $37.50.

Extra interchangeable barrel portion can be furnished with 26, 28, 30 or 32 inch barrel, full choke, modified choke or cylinder bore, as desired.

Model 26, 12-Gauge, Solid-Frame, Exposed Hammer, Grade A, Brush, and Riot Guns (1909–1916)

The Model 26 gun has the mechanical improvements of the Model 24 gun except that it is a solid-frame model and has the

Sectionalized prototype of the Model 24 shotgun. Note that this model has the latch type of magazine release, the forearm of the second type, and the bolt release low on the right side of the receiver.

early forearm of the Model 17 solid-frame gun. Like the Model 17, it was made in Grade A, Brush, and Riot variations.

The characteristics of these three types were listed as follows:

26A, 12-gauge, 30 or 32 inch barrels, full choked, 6 shots, weight about 7⅛ pounds.

26A Brush Gun, 12 gauge, 26 inch barrel, cylinder bored, 6 shots weight about 7 pounds.

26A Riot Gun, 12 gauge, 20 inch barrel, cylinder bored, weight about 6⅞ pounds.

The catalog description of these models included much of the Model 17 verbiage, as follows:

Marlin Model No. 26A: This gun is very similar to the Marlin Model No. 24, Grade "A," except that it has a solid frame instead of the take-down construction, and has straight grip stock. The change allows of considerable economy in manufacturing, so that we can offer the gun at a much lower price than any good repeating shotgun has ever been regularly sold. The omission of the take-down feature saves a number of pieces, making the gun extremely clean, simple and light. The gun has two independent and positive extractors, also the improved automatic safety lock that waits for the cartridge to go off, and is operated automatically by the recoil. It is entirely satisfactory and will work with light or heavy loads. The best of material is used in every part, the workmanship and finish are of the finest quality and several important improvements, in details of operating parts, make it the easiest, most reliable and best working gun in the market, to date. Barrels are bored specially for smokeless powder as well as black, and chambered so that 2¾ inch or 2⅝ inch shells may be used. Stocks measure, length 13½ inches, drop at comb 2 inches, drop at heel 2½ inches. The full-choked barrels are guaranteed to target better than 325 pellets in a 30 inch circle at 40 yards, using 1¼ ounces of No. 8 chilled shot.

Marlin Model No. 26, Riot Gun: This is an extra short and light gun, open bored, for buck shot especially. It is a most deadly arm for guards of all kinds, watchmen, express messengers, and is kept handy in many banks and households as a protection against burglars, thieves and robbers. It gives 6 shots at one loading, and, as each cartridge contains 9 buck shot, it is much more effective in this service than a rifle or a dozen revolvers.

Marlin Model No. 26, Brush Gun: This is a light, short, open-bored gun, designed for bird shooting in cover. It can be used with smokeless or black powder and any size of shot, including buck shot. It is a quick-handling, well-balanced, fine-shooting model—the best possible brush gun at a very moderate price. The regular stock gun will be cylinder bored, and this boring will always be sent unless otherwise ordered. Modified and full-choked barrels made to order at same price.

The barrels and frame were serial-numbered, although not alike. The top tang was roll-stamped *Marlin Model 26*. The walnut wood parts were varnished and the forearm was grooved. Metal parts were blued. The Riot and Brush variations are extremely scarce and seldom found today.

The low and high serial numbers reported or observed have been:

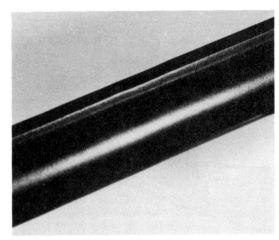

Solid rib available on some models as standard and for others on special order.

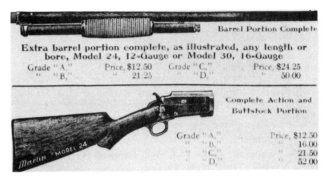

Catalog page illustrating the barrel parts that were available for take-down shotguns.

Roll-stamp on top tang of Marlin Model 24 shotgun.

Model	Low	High
Model 26	110,078	139,853
Model 26G	A5,236	A19,277

The catalog-listed retail prices for the Model 26 shotgun were as follows:

Variation	1909	1911–1915	1916
A	$21.00	$19.50	$21.50
Brush	21.00	19.50	21.50
Riot	21.00	19.50	21.50

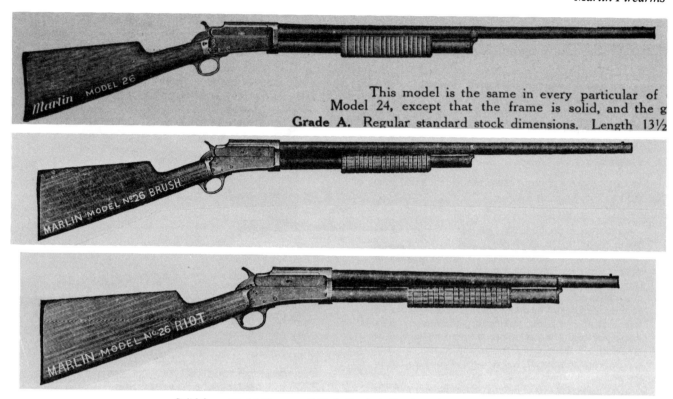

This model is the same in every particular of
Model 24, except that the frame is solid, and the g
Grade A. Regular standard stock dimensions. Length 13½

Solid-frame Model 26 was available in Grade A, Brush, and Riot models.

Marlin Field Gun, 12- or 16-Gauge, Exposed Hammer, Takedown, Shotgun (1911–1912). This gun was also unique because Marlin cataloged it separately and did not give it a number until 1913, when it was added to the list of variations of the Model 24.

Marlin described field shooting in the following statement:

> In field shooting you do not need the long barrel or the full choke which are so necessary in a gun for ducks, geese or other long range work that requires a close, hard-shooting gun. You can't use the long stock which is so desirable in a trap gun where the deliberate method of holding allows you to put the gun to your shoulder before the target is thrown. What you need is a gun that you can carry conveniently, ready for instant use, and the most satisfactory gun for this purpose is one built with a short, light-weight barrel, a short stock and a well balanced construction that will swing quickly and smoothly to the shoulder. These are the qualities which we have incorporated in our field guns, both 12 and 16 gauges.

The Field Gun was available in Standard and Special versions in both 12 gauge and 16 gauge. The Standard 12-gauge Field Gun was listed as having takedown, 6 shots, a regular straight-grip buttstock, a 25-in. modified choke barrel, and a weight of about 7¼ pounds.

The Special 12-gauge Field Gun was listed the same as the Standard gun but with special dimensions of the straight-grip buttstock made to order.

The Standard 16-gauge Field Gun was the same as the 12-gauge gun except that it weighed only 6¾ pounds because

of the smaller dimensions of the 16-gauge frame and barrel. Likewise, the 16-gauge Special model was the same except for weight.

The catalog specifications for the Field Guns were:

> Barrel is 25 inches long, made of Special Rolled Steel, with tensile strength of over 66,000 pounds to the square inch. Handles 2¾ inch and shorter shells, black or smokeless powders. Magazine holds 5 cartridges. Frame and breechbolt have blue finish. Buttstock and forearm are Circassian Walnut with London oil finish and fine hand checking as illustrated. Buttstocks are hand made and beautifully modeled, with hard rubber buttplate. Regular buttstocks have straight grip and are 13½ inches long with 1⅞ inches drop at comb and 2 inches drop at heel. Field Gun with straight grip stock, any desired length or drop, at an additional charge of $2.50.

The barrel portions of the Model 24 shotgun are interchangeable with the 12-gauge Field Gun, and the barrel portions of the Model 30 shotgun are interchangeable with the 16-gauge Field Gun.

The retail prices for the Field Gun were as follows:

Model	1911	1912
Standard 12-gauge Field Gun	$30.00	$30.00
Special 12-gauge Field Gun	32.50	32.50
Standard 16-gauge Field Gun	30.00	30.00
Special 16-gauge Field Gun	32.50	32.50

The 1911 catalog included the following explanation of the superiority of this gun for field shooting:

THE NEW MARLIN FIELD GUN

Our Models 24, 26 and 30 with their respective grades, lengths of barrel and styles of boring, comprise such an extensive line of repeating shotguns that almost any shooter should be able to select from them a gun perfectly adapted to his personal requirements.

However, with the superiority of the repeating gun construction so thoroughly established and appreciated, there is an increasing demand for repeating guns especially built for the individual branches of shooting. To meet the demand for a gun built expressly for trap shooting, we designed the Marlin Trap Gun, incorporating those features of special value for trap work.

Now, for the man who wants a gun especially designed for field shooting, we have brought out our special Field Model guns in 12 and 16 gauges. These guns complete the most extensive and most desirable line of repeating shotguns in the entire world.

In field shooting you do not need the long barrel or the full choke which are so necessary in a gun for ducks, geese or other long range work that requires a close, hard-shooting gun. You can't use the long stock which is so desirable in a trap gun where the deliberate method of holding allows you to put the gun to your shoulder before the target is thrown. What you need is a gun that you can carry conveniently, ready for instant use, and the most satisfactory gun for this purpose is one built with a short, light-weight barrel, a short stock and a well balanced construction that will swing quickly and smoothly to the shoulder. These qualities are the ones which we have incorporated in our new field guns, both 12 and 16 gauges.

The Marlin Field Gun is a high grade repeating shotgun, built extra light but extra strong—a light, short, superbly balanced gun that handles fast and has no equal for field shooting.

The barrel is Special Rolled Steel, 25 inches long—long enough for quick, accurate sighting, and far quicker in the handling than any gun with longer barrel. The barrel is modified choke, specially bored for this work. Buttstock and forearm are fancy figured Circassian walnut, specially selected for light weight, with the rich, dull London oil finish that does not show marks and scratches like the highly polished wood, and with a special grade of fine hand checking. Buttstock has straight grip and is 13½ inches long; 1⅞ inches drop at comb; 2 inches drop at heel; rubber buttplate.

Take-Down: The gun takes down quickly and conveniently for cleaning and carrying, and packs in a space 25 inches long. The take-down in both 12 and 16 gauges is the same system as that used in our Model 24 shotgun.

The Field Gun has blued frame, double extractors, automatic recoil safety lock and all the other up-to-date features of our Models 24 and 30. The 12 gauge Field Gun weighs about 7¼ lbs., the 16 gauge gun weighs about 6¾ lbs. Having every advantage of single barrel, single trigger, 6 shots at one loading if desired, it is the best Field Gun in the world.

Model 28, 12-Gauge, Hammerless, Takedown, Pump Action Shotgun (1913–1923)

The Model 28 shotgun was Marlin's first hammerless pump shotgun. It was introduced in 1913 and was described in the catalog for that year as follows:

This Model 28, 12 gauge Marlin shotgun is the finest repeating gun in the world. It has every up-to-date feature,

perfected far beyond all previous standards, and exclusive advantages not obtainable in other guns. It is hammerless and has a solid steel breech, inside as well as out, solid top, side ejection, matted barrel, press-button cartridge release, automatic recoil hang-fire safety device, double extractors, take-down and trigger and hammer safety.

It is a fine appearing beautifully balanced gun, without any objectionable humps or bumps; no holes on top for gas to blow out through and water to get in; and the solid steel breech permits a thoroughly symmetrical gun without sacrificing strength or safety at this important place. The action is thinner and neater, allowing a thin oval grip to be used. It is the safest breech loading shotgun ever built.

The action parts are entirely within the receiver with solid steel breech; the grip of buttstock is not cut away or weakened; the natural shape of the receiver allows fitting the most perfectly designed buttstock on any pump gun. Contrast this finely modeled comb and full pistol grip with the rounded grip and stubby comb of other hammerless models. The Marlin hammerless has better lines and more style than any other similar construction.

The barrel of Grade A Gun is our Special Rolled Steel heavy at breech, tapering nicely toward muzzle; this clean, perfect tube with an even thickness of metal on all sides, gives uniform expansion and even distribution of the shot, secures extreme range and pattern; the single barrel shoots exactly where you hold, and is guaranteed to place more than 325 pellets in a 30 inch circle at 40 yards, using 1¼ ounces of No. 8 chilled shot.

The barrel is handsomely matted on top for its entire length. The matted barrel prevents radiation of heat from top of barrel or reflection of the sunlight from interfering with your aim. This high-grade feature is not furnished on any other standard grade repeater.

The up-to-date designer of pump guns aims to have the receiver absolutely solid at the rear as well as on top, but no other hammerless gun has a solid steel gas-tight breech like this Marlin. Even a novice will realize that any defective shell which might be exploded in the gun could not blow back and break the buttstock or injure the shooter's hand in any way. We strongly urge you to take off the buttstock and compare the solid steel breech of the Marlin gun with the open breech of other hammerless guns.

1914 Marlin ad for the hammerless Model 28T and Model 28TS trap shotguns.

1915 Marlin ad for 12-, 16-, and 20-gauge hammerless shotguns.

An extra sear in the lock engages the hammer when action is opened, and hammer remains cocked on this sear until the action is closed and fully locked; with the final motion in locking the gun, the carrier raises front end of the sear, with-draws the rear end from notch in the hammer and allows hammer to cock on the trigger. This insures that, even if the trigger is held back, the hammer cannot possibly fall and discharge the cartridge until the action is closed and fully locked. The two-piece firing pin is another excellent safety device; the two pieces align only when gun is fully locked; at all other times, if rear firing pin were struck by hammer, the cartridge could not be discharged. This gun is also fitted with our automatic recoil hang-fire safety lock, giving full protection against hang-fire (defective) cartridges.

In carrying gun loaded and fully cocked, the hammer-and-trigger safety device located in the guard just in front of the trigger is drawn back so that it blocks the trigger and it is impossible to discharge the gun. To make this safety doubly effective, an extra spur is provided on the hammer with a square notch over which the safety block locks tightly when drawn back. Both of these locks are instantly released for firing by pressing forward the safety block with the finger as you throw the gun to your shoulder. No simpler, quicker or more effective device could possibly be designed.

The Model 28 was produced in six variations that included Grades A, B, C, and D as well as a Trap Grade and a Trap Special Grade. Although it is somewhat repetitious to describe these, since they have much in common with the same grades of other exposed hammer guns, there are a few subtle differences that should be included here. For example, there were options of rolled steel barrels or special smokeless steel barrels, and matted barrels or matted solid rib barrels. Also, the D grade no longer was listed as having a Damascus barrel. Instead, it could be ordered with either a rolled steel or a smokeless steel barrel.

The catalog information about the six variations of this new hammerless gun read as follows:

> Standard guns have 30 or 32 inch full choke barrel, but on special order guns with 26, 28, 30 or 32 inch barrel, full choke, modified choke or cylinder bore, can be furnished at the same price. Barrels are chambered for 2¾ or 2⅝ inch shells; specially bored for both black and smokeless powders; fully proved with excessive loads. All full choke barrels are guaranteed to pattern more than 325 pellets in a 30 inch circle at 40 yards, using 1¼ ounces of No. 8 chilled shot. The 30 inch full choke barrel is sent unless otherwise ordered.
>
> No. 28A, Grade "A" 12 gauge, take-down, 30 or 32 inch full choke matted barrel, 6 shots, weight about 8 pounds, price . . . $22.60. (Solid matted ribbed Rolled Steel barrel instead of plain matted barrel at an advance of $5.00, net. Special Smokeless Steel matted barrel instead of Rolled Steel barrel at an advance of $5.00, net.)
>
> Barrels are of Special Rolled Steel, tensile strength over 66,000 pounds to the square inch; and handsomely matted on top for entire length, which prevents any reflection of light and aids quick, clear sighting. This high-grade and exclusive feature has never before been furnished on standard grade repeating guns. Buttstocks are of fine, straight-grained American black walnut, handsomely shaped and finished, with pistol grip; regular buttstocks are 13½ inches long, drop at comb, 1⅝ inches; drop at heel, 2½ inches. Hard rubber buttplates.
>
> No. 28B, Grade "B," 12 gauge, take-down, 30 or 32 inch full choke matted barrel, 6 shots, weight about 8 pounds, price . . . $35.00. (Solid matted ribbed Rolled Steel barrel instead of plain matted barrel at an advance of $5.00 net.)
>
> This grade gun is built for the man who wants every advan-

Model 28 Grade A hammerless shotgun.

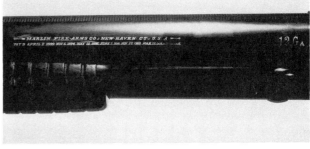

Typical Model 28 roll-stamp on the matted barrel.

Top: *Right side of Model 28 shotgun.* Bottom: *Left side of same shotgun.*

Matted barrel and top of Marlin hammerless shotguns.

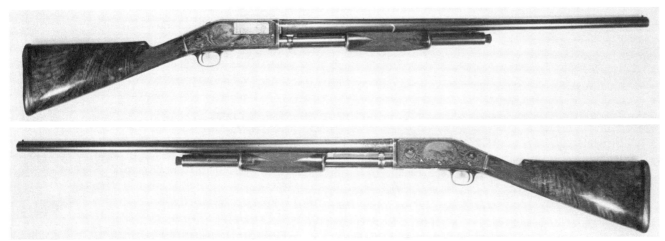

Top: *Grade D Model 28 Trap shotgun with a straight stock, solid rib barrel, and engraving and gold inlay work done by George Ulrich.* (JO) Bottom: *Left side of same shotgun.*

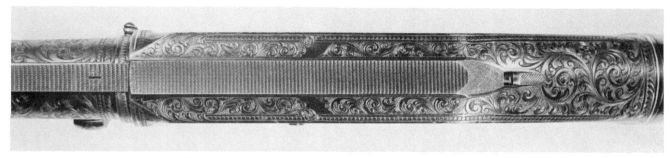

Typical George Ulrich engraving on top of Grade D Model 28 shotgun.

Right side of Model 28 Trap gun engraved by George Ulrich.

Left side of Model 28T shotgun that has all the extra features available at the time of manufacture.

tage of material and workmanship without expensive ornamentation. Barrels are of Special Smokeless Steel as in Grade "C", having tensile strength of about 100,000 pounds to the square inch, and handsomely matted on top for entire length. Buttstocks are a very nice quality of American black walnut (not as fancy figured as on Grade "C"), the stock and forearm both handsomely checked by hand, and specially finished. Regular stocks have pistol grip and are 18½ inches long, drop at comb, 1⅝ inches; drop at heel, 2½ inches; hard rubber buttplate.

No. 28C, Grade "C," 12 gauge, take-down, 30 or 32 inch full choke, matted barrel, 6 shots, weight about 8 pounds, price . . . $50.00. (Solid matted ribbed Rolled Steel barrel instead of plain matted barrel at an advance of $5.00 net.)

This grade gun has our Special Smokeless Steel barrel, the finest quality we can buy, having a very high elastic limit and a tensile strength of about 100,000 pounds to the square inch. Top of barrel is handsomely matted for its entire length. Special care is given to the boring and finishing of this grade. The stock and forearm are of selected, fancy-figured walnut and an extra fine finish is given to the wood. The stock and forearm are neatly checked by hand, as shown in cut, and the action is tastlly relieved and ornamented with a good quality of hand engraving. Regular buttstocks have pistol grip and are 13½ inches long, 1⅝ inches drop at comb, 2½ inches drop at heel; with hard rubber buttplate. This grade will be made to order, without extra charge, with buttstock having

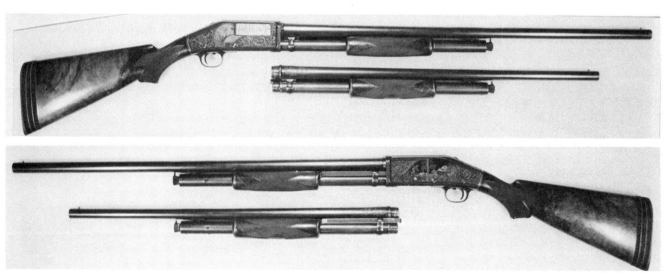

Top: *Model 28 pistol grip stocked Grade D hammerless shotgun that has an extra set of barrels. The engraving and inlay work was done by George Ulrich not long before his leaving Marlin and going to work for Winchester.* (JO) Bottom: *Left side of same shotgun.*

straight grip or pistol grip, lengths from 13 to 14½ inches, drops at comb, 1¼ to 1¾ inches; at heel, 2¼ to 3¼ inches.

No. 28D, Grade "D", 12 gauge, 30 or 32 inch full choke, matted barrel, 6 shots, weight about 8 pounds, price . . . $100.00. (Solid matted ribbed Rolled Steel barrel instead of plain matted barrel without extra charge.)

This is the finest repeating shotgun built. It has our Special Smokeless Steel barrel (the finest shotgun barrel ever made), specially bored and finished, and matted on top for its entire length. If preferred, the solid matted ribbed barrel (Rolled Steel) will be furnished at the same price. The stock and forearm are of the finest imported "Circassian Walnut," finished by the London process of filling, giving a rich, dull surface that does not glisten or shine and does not show scratches as plainly as the highly polished wood. The stock and forearm are checked with the finest possible hand work. The frame is elaborately engraved with fine quality hand work. Screws and trigger are of tool steel, heavily gold plated. Regular buttstocks have pistol grip, and are 13½ inches long, 1⅝ inches drop at comb, 2½ inches drop at heel; with hard rubber buttplate. This grade will be made to order, without extra charge, with buttstock having straight grip or pistol grip, length from 13 to 14½ inches, drops at comb, 1¼ to 1¾ inches; at heel, 2¼ to 3¼ inches.

No. 28T, "Trap Grade," 12 gauge, take-down, matted ribbed barrel, 6 shots, weight about 8 pounds, price . . . $43.00. (Special Smokeless Steel matted barrel instead of ribbed barrel will be furnished at same price.)

Specially designed for trap shooting. Has Special Rolled Steel barrel with raised rib, matted on top for its entire length and unequaled in shooting ability. (If preferred, the regular Special Smokeless Steel matted barrel will be furnished at same price.) Buttstock and forearm are imported "Circassian Walnut," finely modeled, with London oil finish and fine

hand checking. Regular buttstocks have straight grip; they are 14 inches long, with 1⅝ inches drop at comb, 2 inches drop at heel, and have a large, broad butt with hard rubber buttplate. Action parts are highly polished to insure smooth operation. This grade will be furnished with straight grip or pistol grip stock to order, without extra charge, having length from 13 to 14½ inches, drops at comb, 1¼ to 1¾ inches; at heel, 2 to 3¼ inches.

No. 28TS, "Trap Special Grade," 12 gauge, take-down, matted barrel, 6 shots, weight about 8 pounds, price . . . $26.00. (Solid matted ribbed Rolled Steel barrel instead of plain matted barrel at an advance of $5.00 net. Special Smokeless Steel matted barrel instead of plain matted barrel at an advance of $5.00 net.)

The Trap Special Grade is designed to provide at moderate cost a gun specially suited to the requirements of the average trap shooter. The barrel is of Special Rolled Steel, handsomely matted on top for its entire length, which prevents any reflection of light or heat waves from top of barrel, that might interfere with a quick, clear sight. The buttstock and forearm are of fine, straight-grained American black walnut, nicely checked on the grip and forearm, which aids in holding and sighting as well as in the rapid manipulation of action. Regular straight grip buttstock is 14 inches long, with 1⅝ inches drop at comb, and 2 inches drop at heel, with the large, broad butt which covers more of your shoulder and keeps the shock of the recoil down to a minimum. Hard rubber buttplate.

Top: *Right side of engraved Model 28 shotgun that was also engraved by George Ulrich with a pattern very similar to both the other Model 28 illustrated here and some Winchester shotguns he did after leaving Marlin.* Bottom: *Left side of same shotgun.*

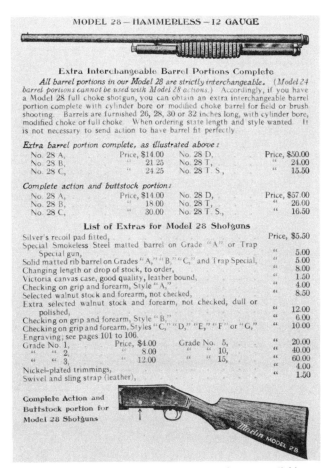

Catalog page of Model 28 barrels and extra features available.

Stocks would be made to order, in straight or pistol grip, with dimensions other than those listed for an advance of $8.00 net.

It should be noted that the Model 28 Trap Special is an economy model and not a special-order gun like the Model 24TS.

The catalog list prices for the Model 28 shotguns, by grade, were as follows:

Grade	1913–1915	1916	1917	1922	1923
A	$22.60	$25.75	$30.70	$50.00	$45.00
B	35.00	37.60	45.10	—	—
C	50.00	57.00	68.40	—	—
D	100.00	109.50	129.00	—	—
T	43.00	49.50	59.40	—	—
TS	26.00	29.50	35.40	—	—

The Model 28 shotgun had the first hammerless type of bolt-opening button, located on the back slope of the top of the frame. The magazine takedown system was the same as the second variation used on the exposed hammer Model 24. It had the latch type of device at the front end of the magazine tube. The safety was located inside the trigger guard and in front of the trigger. To facilitate unloading the magazine tube, a button was provided on the left side of the frame. Pushing in the button rotated the cartridge stop away from the head of shells in the magazine, allowing them to be removed out the bottom of the frame.

Extras for the Model 28 shotgun (also the same for the Model 31 16-gauge hammerless gun) were listed in the catalog as follows:

Silver's recoil pad fitted . . . .$ 5.50
Special Smokeless Steel matted barrel on Grade "A"
   Trap Special or Field Grade 5.00
Solid matted rib barrel on Mod. 28, grades A, B, C,
   and T.S. 5.00
Changing length or drop of stock, to order 8.00
Victoria canvas case, good quality, leather bound 1.50
Checking on grip and forearm, Style A 4.00
Selected walnut stock and forearm, not checked 8.50
Extra selected walnut stock and forearm, not
   checked, dull or polished 12.00
Checking on grip and forearm, Style B 6.00
Checking on grip and forearm, Styles C, D, E, F,
   or G 10.00

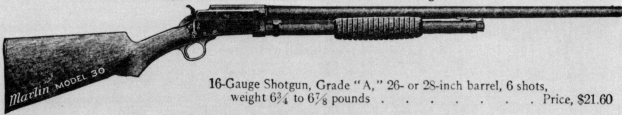

The Model 30 is not a 12-gauge gun with a 16-gauge barrel fitted, but is properly proportioned in every part, finely balanced, very quick and easy in operation, and it is **the only light weight 16-gauge repeating shotgun in the market.** It is fully as effective in all ordinary forms of bird and small game shooting as any 12-gauge gun, and, by reducing the weight of gun and shells carried, it adds greatly to the enjoyment of the day's sport.

GRADE "A." This gun has a Special Rolled Steel Barrel with a tensile strength of about 66,000 pounds to the square inch. The frames are blued and the buttplates are of the best quality rubber.

Regular buttstocks are 13½ inches long, with 2 inches drop at comb, and 2½ inches drop at heel. For special length or drop, see table of extras on page 80.

The full choked barrels are guaranteed to target better than 240 pellets in a 30-inch circle at 35 yards. The charge used in making the pattern is one ounce No. 7½ chilled shot. These barrels are specially bored for smokeless or black powders and are proved with excessive loads.

The capacity of the magazine is 5 shells, and with one in the chamber gives 6 shots.

16-Gauge Shotgun, Grade "A," 26- or 28-inch barrel, 6 shots,
   weight 6¾ to 6⅞ pounds . . . . Price, $21.60

GRADE "B." This gun has a "Special Smokeless Steel" barrel, which has a very high elastic limit and a tensile strength of about 100,000 pounds to the square inch. Barrel is matted on top for its entire length. Special attention is given to the boring and finishing of this grade. The action is reliable, simple and easy to operate. The grip of the stock and foreend are both handsomely checked by hand, which not only aids in holding and sighting, but assists in the rapid manipulation of the action.

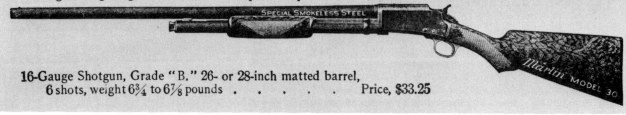

16-Gauge Shotgun, Grade "B." 26- or 28-inch matted barrel,
   6 shots, weight 6¾ to 6⅞ pounds . . . . . Price, $33.25

Catalog page that describes and illustrates the Model 30 shotgun.

Prototype of Model 30 shotgun.

Engraving:

Grade No. 1 . . . . Price, $ 4.00   Grade No. 5 . . . . . 20.00
Grade No. 2 . . . .   ”   8.00   Grade No. 10 . . . . 40.00
Grade No. 3 . . . .   ”   12.00   Grade No. 15 . . . . 60.00
Nickel-plated trimmings 4.00
Swivel and sling strap (leather) 1.50

Extra-barrel prices for the Model 28 were the following:

28A	$14.00
28B	21.25
28C	25.00
28D	50.00
28T	24.00
28TS	15.50

Complete action and buttstock could be ordered for the Model 28 for the following prices:

28A	$14.00
28B	18.00
28C	32.00
28D	60.00
28T	26.00
28TS	16.50

The patent dates roll-stamped on the left side of the Model 28 barrels were May 12, 1896; June 2, 1896; March 29, 1904; August 7, 1906; March 24, 1908; May 19, 1908; November 23, 1909; December 21, 1909.

The lowest serial number recorded or observed for the Model 28 is 2772; the highest, 15,413.

It is interesting to note that the Models 28 and 31 hammerless guns have a slotted screw that holds the guard plate covering the locking bolt, whereas the Models 43, 44, and 63 do not have this screw. Instead, a lug on the back of the guard is riveted to the flat plate of the guard.

Model 30 (Model 30–16), 16-Gauge, Exposed Hammer, Takedown, Pump Action Shotgun (1911–1917)

The first 16-gauge pump action shotgun was the previously discussed Model 16. The Model 30 was similar, except that it had the improved takedown system and the bolt-opening device of the second type.

The Model 30 was not a 12-gauge gun with a 16-gauge barrel. It was a gun that was proportioned for the smaller 16-gauge shell and was finely balanced, easy to operate, and

the only exposed hammer 16-gauge pump action shotgun on the market when introduced in 1911. It was an ideal gun for birds and small game and its reduced weight lightened the burden of the sportsman in the field.

The Model 30–16 was available in A, B, C, and D grades, as follows:

No. 30 "A", 16 Gauge: This gun has a Special Rolled Steel Barrel with a tensile strength of about 66,000 pounds to the square inch. Barrel is handsomely matted on top for its entire length. The frames are blued and the buttplates are of the best quality rubber. Regular buttstocks are 13½ inches long, with 2 inches drop at comb, and 2½ inches drop at heel. The full choked barrels are guaranteed to target better than 240 pellets in a 30 inch circle at 35 yards. The charge used in

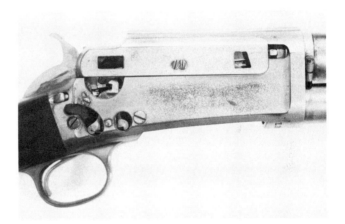

Top: *Sectionalized prototype of Model 30 shotgun. Note that the bolt release is low, like that of the Model 24.* Bottom: *Left side of same.*

Top: *Right side of unusual Model 30 shotgun that has an extra-wide band at front of receiver.* Bottom: *Left side of same receiver.*

making the pattern is one ounce No. 7½ chilled shot. These barrels are specially bored for smokeless or black powders and are proved with excessive loads. The capacity of the magazine is 5 shells, and with one in the chamber, gives 6 shots.

No. 30 "B": This gun has a "Special Smokeless Steel" barrel, which has a very high elastic limit and tensile strength of about 100,000 pounds to the square inch. Barrel is matted on top for its entire length. Special attention is given to the boring and finishing of this grade. The action is reliable, simple and easy to operate. The grip of the stock and forend are both handsomely checked by hand, which not only aids in holding and sighting, but assists in the rapid manipulation of the action.

No. 30 "C": This grade gun has the same quality of barrel as is used in the grade "B". Barrel is matted on top for its entire length which helps quick sighting and rapid accurate shooting. The stock and forearm are of a selected quality of fancy figured walnut, and an extra fine finish is given to the wood. The stock and forearm are neatly checked by hand, and the action is tastily relieved and ornamented with a good quality of hand engraving.

No. 30 "D": This grade gun has a high quality Damascus or "Special Smokeless Steel" barrel, specially bored and finished and matted on top for its entire length. The stock and forend are of the finest imported "Circassian Walnut", finished by the London process of filling, which gives a rich, dull surface that does not show scratches as plainly as the highly polished wood. The checking on the stock and forend is the very finest hand work. The frame is elaborately engraved with finest quality hand work. The screws and trigger are of tool steel, heavily gold plated. This is the finest repeating shotgun built in this size.

The Model 30-16 shotgun was furnished with 26- or 28-in. full-choke barrels that were matted full length. Depending on barrel length, the Model 30-16 weighed from 6¾ to 6⅞ pounds. All grades had a 6-shot capacity.

In 1913, after the Model 30-16 had become established in the marketplace, Marlin added to this model designation the Marlin 16-Gauge Field Gun that previously did not have a model number.

The Model 30-16 Field Gun was described as being similar to the 12-gauge field gun but made smaller, neater, and trimmer to the perfect standards of the Model 30 shotgun.

The Model 30-16 Field Gun was available as a Standard model and as a Special model. The Standard model was identical to the Model 30-16, except for a straight stock, 25-in. modified-choke barrel, 6¾-pound weight, and checking on the forearm and straight grip. The Special model was identical except that special dimensions of the buttstock and straight grip were made to order.

The Model 30-16 Field Gun specifications were:

> Barrel is 25 inches long, made of Special Rolled Steel, with the tensile strength of over 66,000 pounds to the square inch. Handles 2¾ or 2⅝ inch shells, black or smokeless powders, magazine holds 5 shells. Frame and breech bolt have blued finish.
>
> Buttstock and forearm are Circassian walnut with London oil finish and fine hand checking. Buttstocks are hand made and beautifully modeled, with hard rubber buttplate. Regular buttstocks have straight grip and are 13½ inches long with 1⅞ inches drop at comb and 2 inches drop at heel. Barrels are interchangeable.

The catalog list prices for the Model 30-16 gauge gun were as follows:

Grade	1911–1915	1916	1917
A	$21.60	$24.00	$ 28.80
B	33.25	33.25	39.90
C	43.25	43.25	51.90
D	95.00	95.00	114.00
	1913–1914	*1915–1916*	*1917*
Standard Field	$30.00	$30.00	$ 38.20
Special Field	32.50		

The low and high serial numbers recorded or observed for the Model No. 30-16 have been as follows:

Model	Low	High
30-16	A1987	A54,141
30G-16	3314	148,325

Serial numbers were marked on the frame and barrel. However, they were not the same number.

Model 30 (Model 30-20), 20-Gauge, Exposed Hammer, Takedown, Pump Action Shotgun (1915-1917)

The first 20-gauge exposed hammer pump shotgun Marlin manufactured was the Model 30. Already on the market with a

16-gauge Model 30 gun, Marlin reduced the size of the Model 30-16 to make this fine 20-gauge gun. Catalog literature contained the following information about Marlin's new 20-gauge offering:

> This is the only 20-gauge repeater with visible hammer. Many shooters will not use a hammerless—they insist on having the outside hammer, which tells them instantly, day or night, whether the gun is cocked or not cocked; safe or not safe, without depending on hidden safety devices and indicators that might be overlooked. With this gun you can cock the hammer or let it down instantly and noiselessly; the absence of extra parts makes the lock extremely simple and quick; the half-cock notch provides a splendid "safety" in carrying the gun loaded.
>
> The chief advantage sought in a twenty bore is reduced weight. To lighten the hunter's burden in his firearm and in his ammunition is to bestow on him a blessing. In these days of improved, condensed and powerful powders, a modern sixteen is more deadly than a twelve gauge of earlier days. The lightest gun and the lightest load that will do the work are the hall-marks of the up-to-date sportsman.
>
> For the average shooter, as an all-around gun, we recommend the Model 24, Model 26, or Model 28, 12 gauge repeater with 30 inch full-choke barrel. For trap shooting and duck shooting the 12 gauge is the standard size, and the right gun to use.
>
> The 20 gauge with good loads will shoot as far and as hard as the 12, but, spreading a smaller quantity of shot over an equal area, they have not the same close, effective, killing pattern at long ranges. Good scores at fairly long ranges are frequently reported with 20 gauge guns, but they are not to be expected as a regular performance.
>
> But for quail or "Bob White," partridge, woodcock, prairie chickens, rabbits, squirrels and all upland game at ranges from 20 to 35 or 40 yards, the average shooter will find that these 20 gauge Marlin repeaters do the work as well as a 12 gauge, and are much more comfortable and convenient to carry throughout a long day's tramp.
>
> Model 30 repeating shotgun are made in 16 and 20 gauges. They are very similar in design and construction to the Model 24, 12 gauge guns, but each part is made a little smaller, a little lighter and a little trimmer. The 16 gauge is perfectly proportioned for 16 gauge loads, and is materially lighter in weight than the 12 gauge; the 20 gauge is built even smaller and lighter, in perfect proportion and weight for the 20 gauge loads.
>
> The guns are all take-down, having the same simple take-down system as Model 24. The barrels are all specially bored and targeted for black or smokeless powders, and every gun is proved and tested by firing with excessive loads. The barrels are all chambered for 2¾ inch shells. The 20 gauge handles 2¾ inch as well as the ordinary 2½ inch shells. All barrels are tested at target by firing several shots and counting the pellets.

The Model 30-20 was available in Grade A, and on special order in Grades B, C, and D. The A grade had a 25-in. full-choke rolled steel matted barrel; however, on special order, guns with 25- or 28-in. barrels in full choke, modified choke, or cylinder bore would be made up at the same price. Grades B, C, and D had 25- or 28-in. Special Smokeless Steel barrels.

For more descriptive information about the A, B, C, and D grades, please refer to the Model 30-16 section.

The Model 30-20 shotguns were pistol grip only. The measurements were the classic 13½ inches in length with a 2-in. drop at comb and 2⁹⁄₁₆- in. drop at heel. Grade A, B, and C buttstocks could be furnished on special order with any reasonable dimension at $8.00 extra. All Grade D buttstocks were made to special order within reasonable limits at no extra charge.

Patent dates marked on Model 30 shotgun barrels were from August 7, 1906 to February 23, 1915.

Catalog prices listed for the Model 30-20 were as follows:

Grade	1915	1916	1917
A	$21.60	$24.00	$ 28.80
B	33:25	33.25	39.90
C	43.25	43.25	51.90
D	95.00	95.00	114.00

The low and high serial numbers recorded or observed are:

Model	Low	High
30-20	1257	148,385
30G-20	3243	35,173

All barrel portions for Model 30 20-gauge guns were strictly interchangeable. An interchangeable barrel portion with cylinder bore or modified-choke barrel would fit perfectly without

Roll-stamp on top tang of Model 30 shotgun.

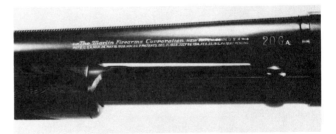

Barrel roll-stamp on Model 30-20 shotgun.

Roll-stamp on top tang of Model 30G shotgun.

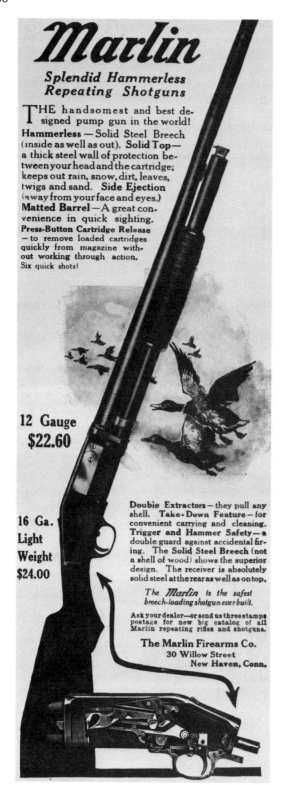

1914 Marlin ad for the 16-gauge hammerless Model 31 shotgun.

the latch-type magazine lock and the bolt-release mechanism that had a lever at the right bottom of the frame near the trigger guard.

Model 31 (Model 31–16), 16-Gauge, Hammerless, Takedown, Pump Action Shotgun (1914–1917)

The Model No. 31 shotgun, which was produced in both 16 and 20 gauge, was the hammerless version of the exposed hammer Model 30 shotguns, which were also manufactured in 16 and 20 gauge.

Marlin stated the following about the Model 31–16:

> The Model 31, 16 gauge Marlin hammerless repeater is the "happy medium" between the standard 12 gauge and the light, small bore "20." For snipe, quail, partridge, woodcock, squirrels, rabbits, etc., this light, hard-shooting 16 gauge Marlin has all the penetration and power of the 12 gauge without the weight. It throws a reasonably heavy charge of shot, and it handles faster with greater precision, in all the more difficult forms of bird shooting.
>
> The gun is chambered and built to handle all standard 16 gauge loads, black or smokeless, in 2¾ as well as 2⁹/₁₆ inch shells, permitting fairly heavy loads for duck and trap shooting when desired.
>
> Like the "20," the Model 31, 16 gauge is very similar in design to our well-known Model 28, 12 gauge gun, but is smaller neater and trimmer throughout, perfectly proportioned for 16 gauge loads. It has all the latest and best features: The solid-top receiver, a thick steel wall of protection between your head and the cartridge that also keeps out rain, snow, dirt, leaves, twigs and sand. Side ejection—away from your face and eyes. Matted barrel—the barrel handsomely matted on top for its entire length, a great convenience in quick sighting, costs extra on any other standard grade pump gun. Press button cartridge release—to change loads quickly or to remove loaded cartridges from magazine at end of the day without working through the action. Double extractors—they pull any shell. Six quick shots.—Take-Down feature—for convenient carrying and cleaning. Trigger and hammer safety—a double guard against accidental firing while carrying gun loaded—can be instantly released with the finger as you bring the gun to your shoulder. Solid steel breech—the receiver is absolutely solid steel at the rear as well as on top, making it the safest breech-loading gun built.

When introduced in 1914, the Model 31–16 was regularly available in Grade A and Field Grade models. The B, C, and D grades would be furnished only on special order.

The specifications for the Grade A gun were as follows:

> Grade "A" has Special Rolled Steel barrel, an extra strong and tough quality, with a tensile strength of over 66,000 pounds to the square inch. Breech bolt, firing pin and other important parts are of Chrome Nickel Steel, specially heat treated, with an elastic limit of over 100,000 pounds to the square inch—nearly twice as strong as similar parts in other guns. Trigger is of tool steel; coil springs are used. Buttstocks and forearms are fine straight-grained black walnut, handsomely shaped and finished. Buttstock measures 13½ inches in length; 1⅝ inches at drop at comb; 2½ inches drop at

sending the gun back to the factory. Barrel portions were furnished with 25- or 28-in. barrel, full choke, modified choke, or cylinder bore.

The Model 30–20 had the 1915 improvements that included

heel. Genuine rubber buttplate. Any other dimensions, $8.00 extra.

Regular guns have 28 inch full choke barrel only. On special order, guns with 26 or 28 inch barrel, and with choice of full choke, modified choke or cylinder bore, will be made up at the same price.

In addition to the Grade A gun, Grades B, C, D and Field could be made on special order. The B, C and D grades are described sufficiently elsewhere, and are not repeated here. The Field grade gun is like the Model 30-16 Field Gun, except that the 30-16 is an exposed hammer gun. The 31-16 Field Gun had a straight-grip stock that measured 13½ inches in length, with a 1¾-in. drop at comb and a 2⁵/₃₂-in. drop at heel. The Field Gun had a 25-in. modified-choke Special Rolled Steel matted barrel. The Grade A barrel was also Special Rolled Steel and matted full length. Likewise, the B, C, and D barrels were matted, but they were of Special Smokeless Steel. All Model 31-16 barrels were interchangeable, and other lengths and choke options were available.

The patent dates marked on Model 31-16 barrels may include dates from August 7, 1906 to March 10, 1914 and patents pending. The patent pending patents were finalized in 1914 and 1915 and are found marked on some barrels.

As with all other models, the serial number is stamped into the frame and barrel.

The catalog list prices for the Model 31-16 were as follows:

Insert sheet supplement to January 1913 catalog that illustrates and describes the new Model 31 16-gauge shotgun.

Grade	1914–1915	1916	1917
A	$ 24.00	$ 27.75	$ 33.30
B	38.00	40.85	48.90
C	55.00	59.10	70.90
D	110.00	118.25	141.90
Field	35.00	39.25	44.10

The lowest serial number recorded or observed for this model is 291; the highest serial number is 4282.

No. 31 D, 20 gauge, 25 or 28 inch Matted Barrel, $110.00. The finest repeating shot gun built. Has our Special Smokeless Steel matted barrel (the finest shotgun barrel ever made), specially bored and finished, and matted on top for its entire length. Buttstock and foreend are of the finest imported "Circassian Walnut," finished by the London process of filling, giving a rich, dull surface that does not glisten or shine and does not show scratches like the highly polished wood. Buttstock and forearm are checked with finest possible hand work. Frame is elaborately engraved with fine quality hand work. Screws and trigger are of tool steel heavily gold plated. Regular buttstock dimensions as in Grade A. This grade made to order without extra charge with straight or pistol grip buttstock, any reasonable length or drop.

No. 31 Field Grade, 20 gauge, 25 or 28 inch Matted Barrel, $35.00. Specially designed for field shooting. Has Special Rolled Steel matted barrel. Buttstock and forearm are imported "Circassian Walnut," finely modeled, with London oil finish and fine hand checking. Regular buttstocks have straight grip; they are 13½ inches long with 1¾ inch drop at comb and 2¼ inches drop at heel. This grade will be furnished with straight or pistol grip stock to order, any reasonable length or drop, at $2.50 extra. The 25-inch **modified choke** barrel is standard in Field Grade, but on special orders guns with 25 or 28 inch barrel, full choke, modified choke or cylinder bore, will be made up at the same price.

Catalog page that illustrates and describes the Model 31 D and Field grade guns.

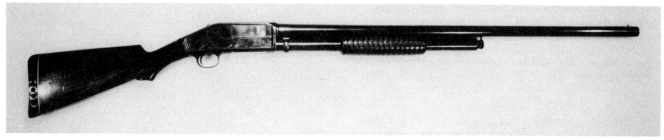

Model 31 shotgun.

The Model 31-16 has the bolt-opening button on the top rear sloping surface of the receiver and the latch type of magazine catch. The safety is inside the trigger guard.

Model 31, (Model 31-20) 20-Gauge, Hammerless, Takedown, Pump Action Shotgun (1911-1923)

The Model 31-20 was manufactured in Grades A, B, C, D, and Field. The features of the gun were cataloged as follows:

The 8 pound 12 gauge is a splendid all-around gun for upland game as well as ducks, geese, foxes, trap shooting and all long-range shooting.

But for woodcock, snipe, "Bob White" or quail, for grouse, partridge or prairie chicken, rabbits and squirrels, the neat little, sweet little 20 gauge handles faster and with wonderful precision—has ample range and power—and will delight the true sportsman by its clean simplicity and surprising efficiency as a game-getter.

Carrying two or three pounds less weight all day long keeps you brighter and quicker—adds zest to the sport—and you finish fresher at the end. There's a saving in cost of ammunition.

Not a featherweight—we could have made it lighter, but extreme light weight means excessive kick from the recoil. It is just a shade under the 6 pound limit which shooting-men advocate in a 20 gauge. Plenty of metal in the nicely tapered barrel makes a well-balanced construction throughout, and the gun points with the precision of a rifle.

You will like the handsomely matted barrel—it prevents heat radiation or reflection of sunlight from interfering with your aim, helps in quick sighting and adds to the fine appearance. This high-grade feature is not furnished on any other standard grade pump gun.

The Marlin is not handicapped like other guns. It is chambered and built to handle 2¾ inch shells as well as the ordinary 2½ inch shells, allowing good stiff loads for duck and trap shooting when desired.

The specifications for the Model 31-20 A, B, C, D, and Field grade guns were as follows:

The 20 gauge in design and construction is like our 12 and 16 gauge hammerless guns, and has all the latest and best features: the solid top receiver; side ejection; matted barrel— the barrel handsomely matted on top for its entire length, a great convenience in quick sighting; press-button cartridge release—to change loads quickly or to remove loaded cartridges from magazine at end of the day without working through the action; double extractors; short, neat forearm; short magazine; 5 quick shots; full pistol grip—shaped to fit

your hand; take-down feature—for convenient carrying and cleaning; trigger-and-hammer safety; automatic recoil safety device—against hang-fire (defective) cartridges. Solid steel breech—the receiver is absolutely solid steel at the rear as well as on top, making it the safest breech-loading gun built.

The standard gun in grades A, B, C and D has 25 inch full choke barrel only, and weighs about 5⅞ pounds. On special orders, guns with 25 or 28 inch barrel, and with choice of full choke, modified choke or cylinder bore will be made up at the same price. All 20 gauge full choke barrels are guaranteed to pattern more than 210 pellets in a 30 inch circle at 35 yards using ⅞ ounce of No. 7½ chilled shot.

Made to use all standard 20 gauge loads, black or smokeless, in 2½ or 2¾ inch shells. Barrels are our Special Rolled Steel, an extra strong and tough quality, having a tensile strength of over 66,000 pounds to the square inch. Breech bolt, firing pin and other important parts are of Chrome Nickel Steel; coil springs are used. There is not a cheap piece of material in the entire gun, and workmanship is of highest quality. Buttstocks and forearms are fine straight-grained black walnut, handsomely shaped and finished. Buttstock is 13½ inches long; 1¹³⁄₁₆ inches drop at comb; 2¹¹⁄₁₆ inches drop at heel; full pistol grip. Genuine rubber buttplate. Any other dimensions made to order, $8.00 extra.

The standard Grade A gun handles as well and shoots as well as the most expensive gun we make. It is tested with the same loads and covered by the same guarantee. But many gun lovers will want the added charm of engraving, fancy figured wood, fine checking, etc. We furnish the following special grades:

No. 31B, 20 gauge 25 or 28 inch matted barrel: For the man who wants every advantage in material and workmanship, without expensive ornamentation. Barrel is Special Smokeless Steel, as in Grade C, handsomely matted on top for entire length. Buttstock and forearm are of very nice quality American black walnut, handsomely checked and specially finished. Standard dimensions of buttstock as in Grade A; any special dimensions to order, $8.00 extra.

No. 31C, 20 gauge, 25 or 28 inch matted barrel: A very handsome gun. Has our Special Smokeless Steel matted barrel, the finest quality we can buy, with a tensile strength of about 100,000 pounds to the square inch, specially bored and finished. Buttstock and forearm are of selected, fancy figured walnut with an extra fine finish, neatly checked by hand. The action is tastily relieved and ornamented with fine hand engraving. Regular buttstock dimensions as in Grade A. Made to order without extra charge with straight or pistol grip buttstock, any reasonable length or drop.

No. 31D, 20 gauge, 25 or 28 inch matted barrel: The finest repeating shotgun built. Has our Special Smokeless Steel matted barrel (the finest shotgun barrel ever made), specially bored and finished, and matted on top for its entire length.

Buttstock and forend are of the finest imported "Circassian Walnut," finished by the London process of filling, giving a rich, dull surface that does not glisten or shine and does not show scratches like the highly polished wood. Buttstock and forearm are checked with finest possible hand work. Frame is elaborately engraved with fine quality hand work. Screws and trigger are of tool steel heavily gold plated. Regular buttstock dimensions as in Grade A. This grade made to order without extra charge with straight or pistol grip buttstock, any reasonable length or drop.

No. 31 Field Grade, 20 gauge, 25 or 28 inch matted barrel: Specially designed for field shooting. Has Special Rolled Steel matted barrel. Buttstock and forearm are imported "Circassian Walnut", finely modeled, with London oil finish and fine hand checking. Regular buttstocks have straight grip; they are 13½ inches long with 1¾ inch drop at comb and 2¼ inches drop at heel. This grade will be furnished with straight or pistol grip stock to order, any reasonable length or drop, at $2.50 extra. The 25 in modified choke barrel is standard in Field Grade, but on special orders, guns with 25 or 28 inch barrel, full choke, modified choke or cylinder bore, will be made up at the same price.

All Model 31, 20 gauge barrel positions interchange with one another—but the barrel portion of a 20 gauge cannot be used on the action of a 12 or 16 gauge, or vice versa, and the barrel portion of a hammer gun cannot be used on the stock and action of a hammerless gun.

If the sportsman wanted a heavier gun or one for longer-range shooting, Marlin would furnish a 28-in. barrel for the same price as the 25-in. barrel.

The Model 31-20 had a short magazine and held only 5 shells, but it had the same takedown system, safety, and bolt opening system as did the Model 31-16 gun. To take the gun down, all that was necessary was to press the latch at the front end of the magazine tube, draw the magazine and forearm forward, and unscrew the barrel. (All takedown pump action shotgun barrels had a left-hand thread.) To take up play between the barrel and frame, the lock nut could be readjusted by loosening its screw and then turning the lock until the play was removed. It sometimes took a few trials to adjust it correctly.

The catalog prices of the various grades of the Model 31-20 were as follows:

Grade	1914-1915	1916	1917	1922	1923
A	$ 24.00	$ 27.75	$ 33.30	$50.00	$50.00
B	38.00	40.85	48.90		
C	55.00	59.10	70.90		
D	110.00	118.25	141.90		
Field	35.00	39.25	47.10		

The lowest serial number recorded or observed for the Model 31-20 is 149; the highest, 4569.

Barrel and serial number markings are the same for this model as for the Model 31-16, except that the barrels are marked *20GA,* instead of *16GA.*

Model 42/42A, 12-Gauge, Exposed Hammer, Takedown, Pump Action Shotgun (1922-1933)

In 1922, the newly formed Marlin Firearms Corporation published its first catalog. In the catalog, there was listed the Model 31, 20-gauge hammerless shotgun, the Model 28, 12-gauge hammerless shotgun, and the Model 42, exposed hammer 12-gauge shotgun.

In a second 1922 printing of the Corporation's catalog, the Model 28 and Model 31 shotguns were no longer listed and the Model 43A, 43T, and 44A were added to the line of shotguns shown in the catalog, and the Model 42 was now listed in this catalog as the Model 42A. (It appears to me that the addition of the suffix *A* to the Model 42, and the listing of the Model 43A and Model 44A as such, indicated that the new company wanted the *A* suffix to identify a standard grade gun, since there was no longer an offering of Grades B, C, or D, or extra features of any kind that had been available from the former company.)

The Model 42A was the same gun as the Model 24G shotgun, except it had the Marlin Firearms Corporation roll-stamp on the barrel, and patent dates of March 24, 1908; May 19, 1908; November 23, 1909 (two patents); and patents pending.

The new corporation continued the pre-WW I company's description and specifications of the exposed hammer 12-gauge shotgun, as follows:

Model No. 42A Shotgun, 12 gauge, take-down, 30 or 32 inch full choke, 28 inch modified choke, or 26 inch cylinder bore matted barrel; Weight about 7½ pounds; 6 shots. Visible hammer; special Marlin steel barrel, barrel handsomely matted, facilitates quick sighting; chambered to handle both 2¾ and 2⅝ inch shells; black walnut pistol grip buttstock and action slide handle; length of buttstock, 13½ inches; drop at comb, 2 inches; drop at heel, 2½ inches; hard rubber buttplate. The improved automatic recoil block hooks on to

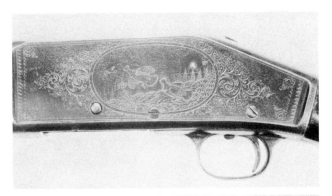

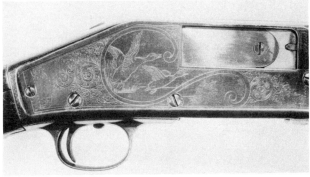

Top: *George Ulrich-engraved Model 31 shotgun. Note the similarity to the pattern of engraving of the deluxe gun illustrated in the Model 28 section.* Bottom: *Right side of the same Model 31 shotgun.*

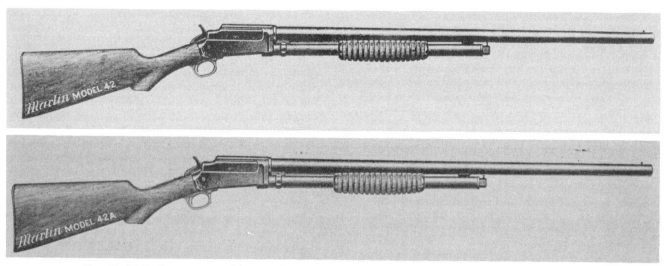

Top: *Model 42, 12-gauge, exposed hammer shotgun.* Bottom: *Model 42A, 12-gauge, exposed hammer shotgun.*

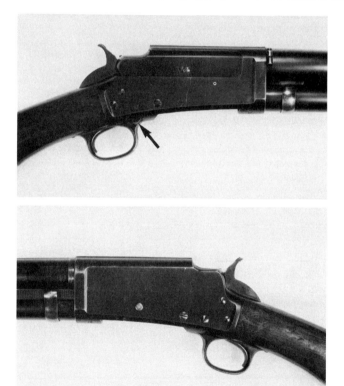

Top: *Right side of Model 42 receiver. Arrow indicates the new type of bolt release of this model.* Bottom: *Left side of same Model 42.*

Roll-stamp on top tang of Model 42 shotgun.

the locking bolt when closing the action and holds the gun firmly locked until after the explosion of the cartridge, when it is instantly and automatically released by the recoil. To operate the gun when empty or to eject a defective cartridge, hold back the recoil hook extension at front end of trigger guard with right forefinger (which throws off the recoil lock), and operate in the regular manner.

The Model No. 42A shotgun should have a bull's-eye embedded in the bottom edge of the buttstock. This bull's-eye was a Marlin trademark started in 1922.

The catalog retail prices of the Model 42 and Model 42A were:

Model	1922	1923–1925	1926–1931	1932–1933
42	$44.50			
42A	38.00	$40.50	$42.20	$40.00

The low and high serial numbers recorded or observed are:

Model	Low	High
Model 42	1036	33,731
Model 42A	4852	64,259

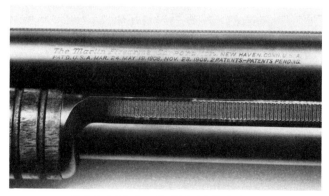

Roll-stamp on barrel of Model 42 shotgun.

The Model 42A was continued in production by the new Marlin Firearms Company after The Marlin Firearms Corporation failed in 1924; however, the barrel markings could still be marked *Corporation*. It was discontinued in 1934.

The receiver and barrel are serial-numbered although not alike. The receiver is also marked on the bottom, in front of the trigger guard, with the Model number.

Model 43A, 12-Gauge, Hammerless, Takedown, Pump Action Shotgun (1922–1930)

This shotgun was a new version of the old Model 28 shotgun. It had all the features and specifications of the older hammerless guns, with the addition of a new bolt-opening device that had an action release button on the left bottom of the frame instead of on top of the receiver.

The Marlin Firearms Corporation description of this new model shotgun was as follows:

The up-to-date designer of pump guns aims to have the receiver absolutely solid at the rear as well as on top, but no other hammerless gun has a solid steel gas-tight breech like this Marlin. We strongly urge you to take off the buttstock and compare the solid steel breech of the Marlin gun with the open breech of other hammerless guns.

In carrying gun loaded and fully cocked, the hammer-and-trigger safety device located in the guard just in front of the trigger is drawn back so that it blocks the trigger and it is impossible to discharge the gun.

Buttstock is a fine quality of straight-grained American black walnut, thoroughly air seasoned and kiln dried, with darker color and finer grain than the sap wood used in some other guns. The stock is beautifully modeled, having a free, natural grip without cutting down the comb or otherwise reducing the perfect symmetry. It is not cut away inside for

1925 ad for the Marlin Model 43A hammerless shotgun.

any operating parts, and is stronger than the buttstock of any other hammerless gun. No gas can enter the grip from the action. Buttplate is of the highest quality hard rubber; a thinner buttplate of finer design is used than is possible with the cheaper composition buttplates.

The take-down construction allows taking the gun apart for cleaning or packing in a few seconds time. To take down, simply press latch at front end of magazine; draw forward magazine and action slide to clear the frame; unscrew barrel. The lock-nut on barrel is a movable shoulder which takes up all wear and insures a firm, rigid union, no matter how long or hard the service.

To change loads quickly: to remove loaded cartridges from magazine, simply press the cartridge release button on left side of receiver and the cartridges drop out into your hand. To remove loaded cartridge from the chamber without firing, or to operate the gun when empty, press up on action release button at left of trigger and operate in usual manner.

This gun is loaded in the usual manner, inserting cartridges under carrier directly into magazine. As a single loader for trap shooting, just drop the cartridge into the action in front of the breechbolt; then close the gun in the usual way.

The Model No. 43A shotgun (succeeding Model No. 28) is

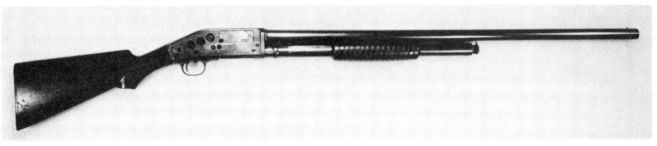

Sectionalized prototype of Model 43 shotgun.

Left: *Right side of sectionalized prototype of the Model 43 shotgun.* Right: *Left side of same shotgun.*

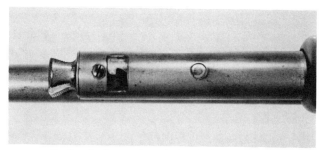

Sectionalized magazine tube latch of the third type.

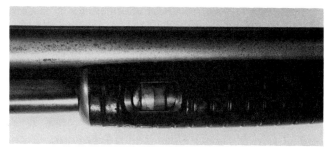

Cutaway forearm showing buffer spring that functions on recoil.

Model 43, pump action, hammerless, 12-gauge shotgun.

Left side of Model 43 shotgun. Arrows indicate (left to right) shell release, safety, and bolt release.

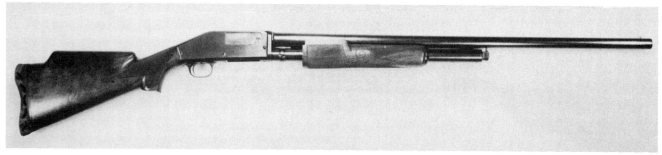

Model 43 shotgun with extended forearm and Monte Carlo stock for trap shooting.

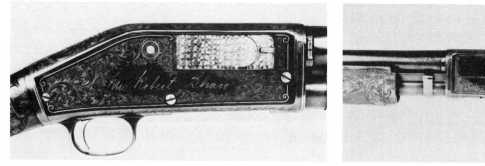

Left: *Right side of custom-engraved Model 43 shotgun done in the Ulrich style with gold-inlaid borders.* Right: *Left side of same shotgun.* (From the collection of Lewis B. Yearout and Leyton Yearout)

a 12 gauge, take-down, hammerless, shotgun with a 30 or 32 inch full choke, 28 inch modified choke or 26 inch cylinder bore barrel; weight about 8 pounds; 6 shots; special Marlin steel barrel; barrel handsomely matted, facilitates quick sighting; chambered to handle both 2¾ and 2⅝ inch shells; black walnut pistol grip buttstock and action slide handle; length of buttstock, 13½ inches; drop at comb, 1⅝ inches; drop at heel, 2½ inches; hard rubber buttplate; a fine looking, fine handling gun, for hunting ducks, geese, foxes, and for trap shooting. It will shoot further and make more long-distance kills than 12 gauge guns of other makes.

In addition to the Model 43A Standard Grade gun, the late 1922 catalog listed a Model 43T Trap Grade gun, made to order only. It was not described. The 1923 catalog listed a Model 43T Standard Trap Grade 12-gauge shotgun and a Model 43TS Trap Special Grade 12-gauge shotgun.

The Model 43T was takedown and hammerless, with a 30- or 32-in. full-choke matted barrel, 6 shots, a straight grip buttstock and forearm of imported Circassian walnut, a dull London oil finish, fine hand checking, and a fitted recoil pad. Stock length was 14 inches with a 1⅝-in. drop at comb and 2-in. drop at heel.

The Model 43TS shotgun was identical to the Model 43T gun except that the stock could be furnished in either straight or pistol grip and in any length or drop of buttstock. This model was made to order only.

From 1926 to 1929, extension slide handles for the Models 43T and 43TS could be furnished at an additional charge. Interchangeable barrel assemblies could be furnished for all Marlin takedown repeating shotguns.

The Model 43A, Model 43T, and Model 43TS were manufactured by both The Marlin Firearms Corporation (1922-1924) and The Marlin Firearms Company (1925-1930).

The success at the traps is attested to by the following report

Top: *Right side of Model 43 shotgun.* Bottom: *Left side of same gun.*

of the performance of some leading trap shooters using Marlin trap model shotguns:

Shooting a Marlin Model 43A shotgun as usual — Mark Arie broke 528 successive targets at the 1925 Grand American Handicap Trapshooting Tournament — a new World's Record long run.

During the entire week of shooting, with more than 700 of the country's best shots competing, no other record approached this.

In the Class AA Championship — the classic event of the whole tournament, for shooters rated 97% and better —

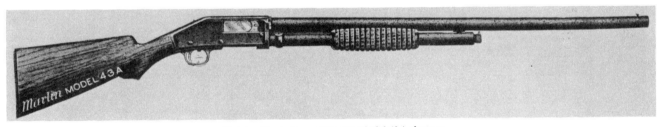

Catalog illustration of Marlin Model 43A shotgun.

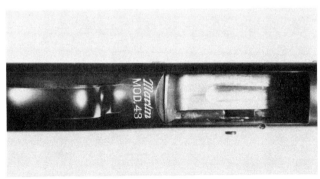

Model marking on bottom of Model 43 receiver.

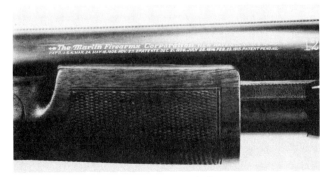

Roll-stamp on Model 43 shotgun.

Marlin Model 43 shotgun used by Mark Arie in winning the Olympic medals shown here.

Mr. Arie was the winner, with his Marlin making a perfect score, 200 X 200.

Shooting a Marlin Model 43 shotgun as usual, Homer Clark won the other premier class event, the Professional Championship. Score: 199 X 200.

O.N. Ford, one of the Directors of the Amateur Trapshooting Association, who lives at Portland, Oregon, has also made some wonderful scores with his Marlin shotgun this year. On three occasions he has broken 99 X 100, consisting of fifty singles at sixteen yards, twelve pair of doubles at sixteen yards and twenty-six singles at twenty-two yards. Mr. Ford made the remarkable score of 71 X 72 double targets shot at during these mixed programs.

Frames were serial-numbered and marked with the model number. Barrels were marked with the gauge, but may not be serial-numbered.

The barrel roll-stamp should be of the latest type, which included the Marlin Firearms Corporation name and patent dates of May 19, 1908; November 23, 1909 (two patents); December 21, 1909; July 28, 1915; February 23, 1915; and patents pending. The stock should have the Marlin bull's-eye trademark.

The catalog list prices for this model were as follows:

Model	1922	1923–1925	1926–1928	1929–1930
43A	$45.00	$48.00	$49.85	$49.80
43T	75.00	75.00	75.00	75.00
43TS	100.00	100.00	100.00	100.00

The lowest and highest serial numbers recorded or observed were 537 and 17,411, respectively.

The Model 43A shotgun was one of the guns given free during the 1930–1931 period upon the purchase of four $25.00 shares of Marlin preferred stock, payable in one sum or in monthly payments. The Model 43A was no longer available as a free gun upon introduction of the Model 63 shotgun in October 1931.

Model 44A and Model 44S, 20-Gauge, Hammerless, Takedown, Pump Action Shotguns (1922–1933)

The first catalog published by The Marlin Firearms Corporation in 1922 did not list a Model 44 20-gauge shotgun. It did, though, list the Model 31 20-gauge gun. A second printing of the 1922 catalog did not list the Model 31 20-gauge gun but did include a 20-gauge hammerless gun identified as the Model 44A shotgun. This second 1922 catalog also stated that the Model 44A had succeeded the Model 31.

This change in model designations of the 20-gauge hammerless shotgun was parallel to the similar change of the 12-gauge Model 28 into the Model 43A. It appears that the new Marlin

Marlin brochure describes the new 20-gauge Model 44 hammerless shotgun.

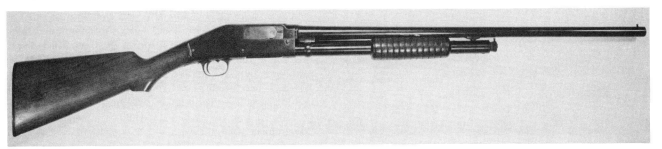

Marlin Model 44 shotgun.

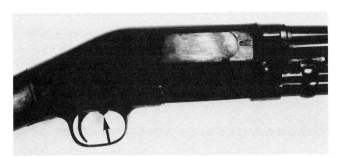 

Left: *Right side of Model 44. The arrow indicates the safety.* Right: *Left side of Model 44. The arrow indicates the location of the bolt release.*

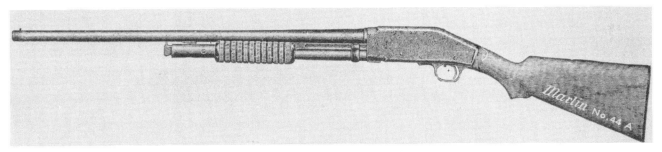

Catalog illustration of the Model 44A shotgun.

Firearms Corporation intended to have its own model designations, each of which incorporated the latest improvements developed by the former owners.

The Model 44A had the latest bolt-opening mechanism located near the trigger at the bottom left side of the receiver, instead of the button on top, as was on the Model 31 gun. It also had the second-variation magazine takedown latch and the short 4-shell magazine of the Model 31, making the gun a 5-shot repeater when one shell was also in the chamber.

The specifications and description of this well-made, well-balanced, and beautiful gun were as follows:

> New Model No. 44A shotgun, 20 gauge, take-down, hammerless, 25 or 28 inch full choke, 25 inch modified choke, or 25 inch cylinder bore matted barrel; weight about 5⅞ pounds; 5 shots; special Marlin steel barrel; barrel handsomely matted, facilitates quick sighting; chambered to handle both 2½ and 2¾ inch shells; specially bored for black, semi-smokeless and smokeless powders; black walnut pistol grip buttstock and action slide handle; length of buttstock, 13½ inches; drop at comb, 1¹³⁄₁₆ inches; drop at heel, 2¹¹⁄₁₆ inches; hard rubber buttplate.

It is generally estimated that 90% of upland game is

Model marking on bottom of Model 44.

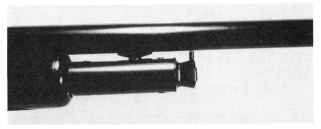

Typical front end of 20-gauge Model 44 magazine tube showing the added spacer and latch support because of the small diameter of the 20-gauge barrel.

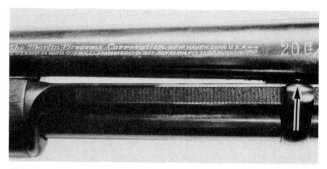

The Marlin Firearms Corporation roll-stamp on the barrel of a Model 44 20-gauge shotgun. The arrow indicates the third type of slide latch.

bagged at short ranges—well within a 35 or 40 yard limit. And at these ranges the Marlin "20", which comes up faster and points quicker, will bring down the game as cleanly and surely as the larger bores, if properly held. And the light, short, quick gun and light-weight loads eliminate the fatigue occasioned by carrying a heavy gun and heavy shells in an all-day tramp through the fields and brush or over the snipe bogs. This beautiful, light-weight repeater will greatly increase your enjoyment of the sport of shooting—it is a perfect gun for snipe, quail, partridge, woodcock, squirrels, rabbits, etc. Thousands of shooters are using this gun with the new powerful loads in 2¾ inch shells in preference to all others.

In 1923, a Model 44S Special Grade shotgun was added to the catalog. It was described as 20-gauge, takedown, and hammerless, with 25- or 28-in. full choke, 25-in. modified choke, or 25-in. cylinder bore, matted barrels, 5 shots, a straight or pistol grip buttstock and forearm of imported Circassian walnut, dull London oil finish, and fine hand checking on grip and forearm. Interchangeable barrel assemblies were available in 1925 for the Model 44S at $40.00. The Model 44S was discontinued in 1929.

The Model 44A and Model 44S were produced by both The Marlin Firearms Corporation and the later Marlin Firearms Company. The bull's-eye trademark should be located in the bottom edge of the buttstock on these models.

The Marlin Firearms Corporation name and patent dates of May 19, 1908; November 23, 1909 (two patents); December 21, 1909; July 28, 1914; February 23, 1915; and patents pending were marked on the barrel. Also, *20GA.* was marked on the barrel just forward of the barrel lock nut.

The bottom of the receiver was marked with the serial number and *MOD. 44.*

The catalog list prices of the Model 44 were as follows:

Model	1922	1923–1925	1926–1928	1929–1932	1933
44A	$45.00	$48.00	$49.80	$49.80	$48.00
44S		80.00	80.00	80.00 (1929)	

Typical breech mechanism parts of the Marlin hammerless shotgun. These are for a Model 44.

Side plate and internal receiver parts of the Model 44 shotgun.

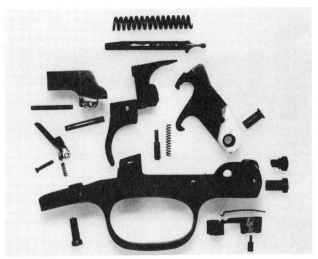

Trigger mechanism parts of the Model 44 hammerless shotgun. The large part to the left of the trigger is shown, reversed to the way it is normally assembled.

The lowest serial number recorded or observed for this model is 480; the highest, 7925.

The Model 44A shotgun was one of the guns given free during 1930 and 1931 to purchasers of four $25.00 shares of Marlin preferred stock. The stock paid a 7% annual dividend. By including the price of the gun given free, it amounted to a return of about 14% on the $100.00 investment.

Model 49, 12-Gauge, Exposed Hammer, Takedown, Pump Action Shotgun (1928–1930)

The Model 49 shotgun had features of the Model 42 shotgun and the Model 24 shotgun, as well as its own. The frame parts were like the Model 42 gun that had the bolt-release lever by the trigger on the right side of the frame. However, the barrel and magazine assembly were of the earlier Model 24 shotgun. The new and different features of this shotgun that are not found on other models are a smooth forearm; simple diamond pattern checking on grip and forearm; and, instead of the raised rib down the top of the frame, a short raised hump at the front end of the frame. The top tang is marked *Marlin Model No. 49* and the serial number is located behind the trigger guard on the lower tang. The stock and forearm of this model are walnut. The stock has a pistol grip and horizontally serrated hard rubber butt plate.

The interesting fact about the Model 49 shotgun is that it was not a catalog item and was made especially as an economy model that was to be given free to purchasers of four $25.00 shares of Marlin stock.

Other models that were also given free in Frank Kenna's money-raising program were the Model .410 lever action shotgun, Model 42A, 43A, 44A, and 63 pump action shotguns, the Model 39 caliber .22 lever action rifle, and the Model 37, 38 and 47 caliber .22 pump action rifles. By 1931, at least 2,629 sportsmen had purchased stock and accepted one of these Marlin firearms free. The total number of those choosing the Model 49 is not known, but based upon the few reported and the fact some of the other later models were also given free, it does not appear that many were assembled with the already replaced old-style barrel and magazine assembly.

The barrel of the Model 49 is marked: *The Marlin Firearms Corporation, New Haven, Conn. PAT'D. U.S.A. MAR. 24, MAY 19, 1908, NOV. 23, 1909, 2 Patents—Patents Pending.* The barrel is also stamped *12GA.* in the usual place, just forward of the receiver. The barrels were not serial-numbered, but do have the *JM* proofmark.

Low and high serial numbers recorded or observed have been the following:

Model	Low	High
Model 49	A776	A2103
	537	81,256
Model 49A	33	3063

Model 49 exposed hammer 12-gauge shotgun.

Roll-stamp on top tang of Model 49 shotgun.

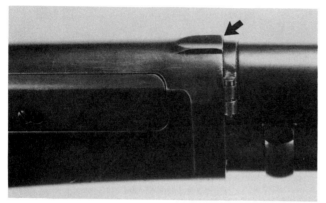

Typical Model 49 receiver. The arrow indicates the short hump on the top front of the receiver. This feature is found on only the Model 49.

Model 53, 12-Gauge, Hammerless, Takedown, Pump Action Shotgun (1929–1931)

This shotgun was a combination of old and new. The takedown barrel and pistol grip stock were of the standard type. Barrels were available in 30- or 32-in. full choke, 28-in. modified choke, or 26-in. cylinder. The receiver mechanism was of the first hammerless type that had the bolt-release button on the top rear of the receiver, and the magazine was of the first type, which had a button catch mechanism. Otherwise the Model 53 was similar to the earlier Model 43.

The Model 53 was chambered to handle both 2¾- and 2⅝-in. shells. The stock and forearm were of black walnut and the stock length was 13½ inches, with a drop at the comb of 1⅝ inches and 2½ inches at the heel. It had a hard rubber butt plate. The gun weighed 7¼ pounds and held 6 shots.

Although Marlin stated that the Model 53 had all the up-to-date features and the perfect balance and superior shooting

qualities for which Marlin guns were famous, the Model 53 was short-lived.

It is my opinion that the Model 53 shotgun served the purpose of using up the earlier receivers and magazine tube assemblies that were left over and on hand when the improved 12-gauge Model 43 shotgun, which replaced the Model 28 shotgun, was introduced.

The Model 53 was cataloged at $42.50 retail during the period of 1929 to 1931. It was manufactured by The Marlin Firearms Company; however, barrels may be marked *Marlin Firearms Corporation*. Buttstocks should have the bull's-eye trademark. Barrels, besides being marked as 12 gauge, should have the *JM* proofmark. The top of the receiver is matted.

Model 63, 12-Gauge, Hammerless, Takedown, Pump Action Shotgun (1931–1933)

The Model 63, 63T, and 63TS shotguns were introduced in 1931. These three new models replaced the older hammerless Models 43A, 43T, and 43TS, and, until the Model 120 shotgun was introduced in 1971, were the last of a long line of pump shotguns manufactured by Marlin.

During 1931, the Model 63 had an *A* suffix added to its Model designation; however, no mechanical or cosmetic changes were made.

The Models 63A, 63T, and 63TS had improvements made to them that Marlin felt would increase sales and bolster a market that had declined during the Great Depression. The 1930 announcement of this new version of the Marlin hammerless gun read as follows:

TO BE READY FOR DELIVERY OCTOBER 1ST

The new Marlin Model 63 12 Gauge Hammerless Repeating Shotgun is the result of carefully worked out ideas and improvements.

Marlin always made the best shooting shotgun barrel on the market and we set out to determine what would be necessary to make the most reliable action.

We have planned a new firing pin that is almost unbreakable.

A change in the style of the cartridge cut off which controls the feeding of the shells from the magazine insures accurate and positive feeding.

A different method of unlocking the hang fire safety to open the action without firing.

All the important screws will be locked in—they cannot work loose.

The result is a gun that is mechanically strong, simple and

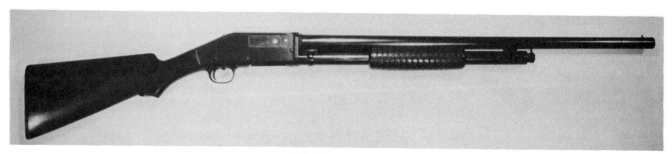

Model 53 shotgun.

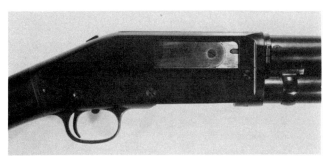

Right side of Model 53 shotgun showing that it had features of the earlier Model 43 shotgun.

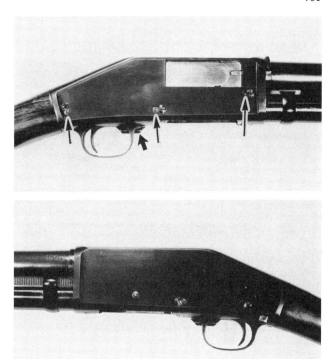

Top: *Model 63 shotgun receiver. The arrows indicate the location of this new gun's manual safety and the added lock screws.* Bottom: *Left side of Model 63 shotgun.*

wear-resisting. It handles fast, shoots even and close, hits hard and kills cleanly at long ranges.

It will be made with the following length and style of barrels; 30 and 32 inch Full Choke, 28 inch Modified Choke, 26 inch Cylinder Bore.

6 Shots – Price – $49.80

The Model 63 was also listed as a special stock bonus. If the sportsman purchased four $25.00 shares of Marlin preferred stock, he could have a Model 63 shotgun free. (Until the Model 63 was available, the Model 43 was furnished.)

The 1931 Marlin catalog described the Model 63A as follows:

> New Model No. 63A Shotgun, 12 gauge, take-down, hammerless, 30 or 32 inch full choke, 28 inch modified choke, or 26 inch cylinder bore matted barrel; weight about 8 pounds; 6 shots; special Marlin steel barrel; barrel handsomely matted, facilitates quick sighting; chambered to handle both 2¾ and 2⅝ inch shells; black walnut pistol grip buttstock and action slide handle; length of buttstock, 13½ inches; drop at comb 1⅝ inches; drop at heel, 2⅕ inches; hard rubber buttplate.
>
> This gun has every modern feature of safety and convenience, including; Take-down – easy to carry and clean; matted barrel – this feature alone costs several dollars extra on other makes of guns; press-button cartridge release – to remove loaded shells without firing; automatic recoil safety

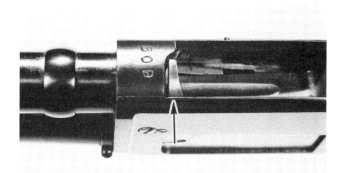

Bottom of Model 63 receiver. The arrows indicate the shell stop that is typical of only this model.

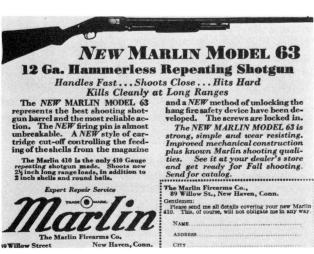

1930 ad for the new Model 63 12-gauge hammerless shot-gun.

Model 63 model marking on bottom of receiver.

Marlin
MODEL 1898·19·19G·19N·19S·17·21·26·49

Number		Price	Number		Price
1M	Barrel, Model 17 or Model 26	$13.75	28M	Locking Bolt	3.30
1MM	Barrel, Grade "A" Take Down	15.40		(Model 98 Cannot Supply Old Style)	
2M	Barrel Lock Nut	1.98	28M1	Locking Bolt Catch	.44
3M	Barrel Lock Nut Screw	.22	28M2	Locking Bolt Catch Spring	.33
4M	Breech Bolt	4.95	29M	Locking Bolt Pin	.33
	(Model 98 Cannot Supply)		29M1	Locking Bolt Pin Screw	.22
4M1	Breech Bolt Spur	1.32	30M	Mainspring	.88
4M2	Breech Bolt Spur Screw	.33	31M	Mainspring Screw	.22
4M3	Breech Bolt Spur Spring	.33	32M	Magazine Tube	3.30
5M	Buttstock, Grade "A"	4.95	33M	Magazine Tube Bank	2.20
6M	Buttplate	1.87	34M	Magazine Tube Catch	.44
7M	Buttplate Screws (2) each	.22	35M	Magazine Tube Catch P.n	.22
8M	Carrier	3.85	36M	Magazine Tube Catch Spring	.22
9M	Carrier Cartridge Stop	.99	37M	Magazine Tube Follower	1.10
10M	Carrier Cartridge Stop Screw	.22	38M	Magazine Tube Spring	.88
11M	Carrier Screw	.33	39M	Magazine Tube Plug	1.65
12M	Cartridge Stop in Frame,		40M	Magazine Tube Plug Screw	.22
	Model 1898 only	.88	40M1	Magazine Tube Support	
13M	Cartridge Stop in Frame Screw,			Model 17-26	2.20
	Model 1898 only	.33	40M2	Magazine Tube Support Screw	
13M1	Cartridge Stop in Frame	.88		Model 17-26	.22
13M2	Cartridge Stop in Frame Screw	.33	40M3	Magazine Tube Supporting	
13M3	Cartridge Stop in Frame Spring	.33		Binding Screw M. 17-26	.33
13M4	Cartridge Stop in Frame Spring		41M	Receiver (Cannot Supply)	
	Rivet	.22	42M	Sear	1.10
14M	Extractor (right side)	.88	43M	Sear Screw	.33
	(Model 98 Cannot Supply)		44M	Sear Spring	.22
15M	Extractor (right side) Pin	.22	45M	Sight, Front	.44
15M1	Extractor (right side) Spring	.22	46M	Tang Screw	.33
16M	Extractor (left side)	.88	47M	Trigger	1.10
16M1	Extractor (left side) Pin	.22	48M	Trigger Pin	.22
16M2	Extractor (left side) Spring	.22	49M	Trigger Plate or Guard	3.85
17M	Ejector	.88	50M	Trigger Plate Screws (2) each	.33
18M	Foreend, Grade "A"	2.50	51M	Trigger Spring	.33
19M	Foreend Screws (2) each	.33	52M	Trigger Spring Screw	.22
19M1	Foreend Screw Escutcheons (2)		53M	Recoil Safety Block (Old Style)	
	each	.33		Model 1898	1.98
20M	Foreend Slide	2.64	54M	Recoil Block	1.98
	(Model 19-G Cannot Supply)		55M	Recoil Safety Block Screw	.33
21M	Foreend Slide Screw in Band	.22	56M	Recoil Safety Block Spring	.33
22M	Foreend Slide Stop	1.54	57M	Recoil Safety Hook	.66
23M	Firing Pin	1.10	58M	Recoil Safety Hook Spring	.33
24M	Firing Pin Pin	.22	59M	Recoil Safety Push Pin	.44
25M	Firing Pin Spring	.33	60M	Recoil Safety Push Pin Screw	.22
26M	Hammer	1.76	61M	Recoil Safety Catch	.55
27M	Hammer Screw	.33	62M	Recoil Safety Catch Spring	.33
			63M	Recoil Safety Catch Pin	.22

Marlin parts catalog page of the component parts of the Models 1898, 19, 19G, 19N, 19S, 17, 21, 26, and 49. Parts for these models are no longer available and Marlin can no longer make repairs to them.

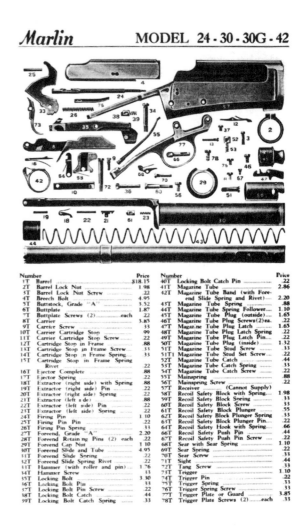

Marlin
MODEL 24·30·30G·42

Number		Price	Number		Price
1T	Barrel	$18.15	40T	Locking Bolt Catch Pin	.22
2T	Barrel Lock Nut	1.98	41T	Magazine Tube	2.86
3T	Barrel Lock Nut Screw	.22	42T	Magazine Tube Band (with Fore-	
4T	Breech Bolt	4.95		end Slide Spring and Rivet)	2.20
5T	Buttstock, Grade "A"	3.52	43T	Magazine Tube Spring	.88
6T	Buttplate	1.87	44T	Magazine Tube Spring Follower	1.10
7T	Buttplate Screws (2) each	.22	45T	Magazine Tube Plug (outside)	1.65
8T	Carrier	3.85	46T	Magazine Tube Plug Screws (2) ea.	.22
9T	Carrier Screw	.33	47T	Magazine Tube Plug Latch	1.65
10T	Carrier Cartridge Stop	.99	48T	Magazine Tube Plug Latch Spring	.22
11T	Carrier Cartridge Stop Screw	.22	49T	Magazine Tube Plug Latch Pin	.22
12T	Cartridge Stop in Frame	.88	50T	Magazine Tube Plug (inside)	1.32
13T	Cartridge Stop in Frame Screw	.33	51T	Magazine Tube Stud Screw	.33
14T	Cartridge Stop in Frame Spring	.33	51T1	Magazine Tube Stud Set Screw	.22
15T	Cartridge Stop in Frame Spring		52T	Magazine Tube Catch	.44
	Rivet	.22	53T	Magazine Tube Catch Spring	.33
16T	Ejector Complete	.88	54T	Magazine Tube Catch Screw	.22
17T	Ejector Spring	.22	55T	Mainspring	.88
18T	Extractor (right side) with Spring	.88	56T	Mainspring Screw	.22
19T	Extractor (right side) Pin	.22	57T	Receiver (Cannot Supply)	
20T	Extractor (right side) Spring	.22	58T	Recoil Safety Block with Spring	1.98
21T	Extractor (left side)	.88	59T	Recoil Safety Block Spring	.33
22T	Extractor (left side) Pin	.22	60T	Recoil Safety Block Screw	.33
23T	Extractor (left side) Spring	.22	61T	Recoil Safety Block Plunger	.55
24T	Firing Pin	1.10	62T	Recoil Safety Block Plunger Spring	.33
25T	Firing Pin Pin	.22	63T	Recoil Safety Block Plunger Pin	.22
26T	Firing Pin Spring	.33	64T	Recoil Safety Hook with Spring	.66
27T	Foreend, Grade "A"	2.20	66T	Recoil Safety Push Pin	.44
28T	Foreend Retaining Pins (2) each	.22	67T	Recoil Safety Push Pin Screw	.22
29T	Foreend Cap Nut	1.10	68T	Sear with Sear Spring	1.10
40T	Foreend Slide and Tube	4.95	69T	Sear Spring	.22
41T	Foreend Slide Spring	.22	70T	Sear Screw	.33
42T	Foreend Slide Spring Rivet	.22	71T	Sight	.44
33T	Hammer (with roller and pin)	1.76	72T	Tang Screw	.33
44T	Hammer Screw	.33	73T	Trigger	1.10
35T	Locking Bolt	3.30	74T	Trigger Pin	.22
46T	Locking Bolt Pin	.33	75T	Trigger Spring	.33
47T	Locking Bolt Pin Screw	.22	76T	Trigger Spring Screw	.33
38T	Locking Bolt Catch	.44	77T	Trigger Plate or Guard	3.85
39T	Locking Bolt Catch Spring	.33	78T	Trigger Plate Screws (2) each	.33

Parts catalog page illustrating the component parts of the Models 24, 30, 30G, and 42. Marlin can no longer furnish parts or make repairs to these obsolete shotguns.

hang-fire device—for protection against defective ammunition; double extractors—no shell can stick in the Marlin chamber; trigger and hammer safety—conveniently located for quick release. It is hammerless, with solid steel breech—not a shell of wood. A fine looking, fine handling gun, for hunting ducks, geese, foxes and for trap shooting. It will shoot further and make more long-distance kills than 12 gauge guns of the other makes.

The Model 63 barrel is roll-stamped *Marlin Fire-Arms Co., New Haven CT U.S.A.*; an arrow precedes and follows the roll-stamp. Also marked on the barrel is the following patent information: *PAT'D April 2, 1889. Nov. 6, 1894. May 12, 1896. June 2, 1896. Nov. 27, 1900. Mar. 29, 1904. Nov. 29, 1904.*

The safety of the Model 63 is different from that of the Model 43 by being in the front part of the trigger guard. The bolt-opening latch is like that of the Model 43 and is at the left rear of the trigger guard. In front of the trigger guard is

marked *MOD. 63.* Another feature different from the earlier Model 43 is that most external screws have lock screws. The magazine is of the latch type.

The Model 63T Standard Trap Grade shotgun was listed as 12-gauge, takedown, and hammerless, with a 30- or 32-in. full-choke matted barrel, 6 shots, a straight-grip buttstock and forearm of imported Circassian walnut with dull London oil finish, fine hand checking, and a fitted recoil pad. The buttstock was of standard dimensions only (length 14 inches overall, 1⅝-in. drop at comb, 2-in. drop at heel.)

The Model 63TS Trap Special Grade shotgun was made to order only. It was available with either a pistol grip or a straight stock, with any length or drop of buttstock desired. Otherwise, it was identical to the Model 63T shotgun.

Extension slide handles for the Models 63T and 63TS could be fitted, instead of the regular forearm, at an additional charge of $18.00.

MODEL 28 · 31 · *Marlin*

Number		Price
1N	Barrel, Spec. Rolled Steel, matted	$18.15
2N	Barrel Lock Nut	1.98
3N	Barrel Lock Nut Screw	.22
4N	Breech Block	4.13
5N	Buttstock, Grade "A"	4.95
6N	Buttstock Bolt	.55
7N	Buttstock Bolt Washers, each style	.22
8N	Buttplate	1.87
9N	Buttplate Screws (2) ....each	.22
10N	Carrier	3.85
11N	Carrier Screw	.33
12N	Cartridge Cut-Off	.88
13N	Cartridge Cut-Off Screw	.33
14N	Cartridge Release	.88
15N	Cartridge Release Button	.44
16N	Ejector Complete	.88
17N	Ejector Spring Only	.22
17NN	Ejector Retaining Screw	.33
18N	Extractor (left side)	.88
19N	Extractor (left side) Spring	.22
20N	Extractor (left side) Pin	.22
21N	Extractor (right side)	.88
22N	Extractor (right side) Spring	.22
23N	Extractor (right side) Pin	.22
24N	Firing Pin (front)	.55
25N	Firing Pin (front) Spring	.22
27N	Firing Pin (rear) (Cannot Supply)	
28N	Firing Pin (rear) Spring	.33
29N	Firing Pin (rear) Pin	.22
30N	Foreend, Grade "A"	2.20
31N	Foreend Cap Nut	1.10
32N	Foreend Slide and Tube	4.95
33N	Foreend Slide Spring	.22
34N	Foreend Slide Spring Rivet	.55
35N	Guard Plate	1.65
36N	Guard Plate Screw	.17
37N	Hammer	1.76
38N	Hammer Screw	.33
39N	Hammer Spring (spiral)	.33
40N	Hammer Spring Rod	.66
41N	Link	2.20
42N	Locking Bolt	2.48
	(Model 31, 20 ga. Cannot Supply)	
43N	Magazine Tube	2.86
44N	Magazine Tube Band (with Foreend Slide Spring and Rivet)	2.20
45N	Magazine Tube Spring	.88
46N	Magazine Tube Spring Follower	1.10
47N	Magazine Tube Plug (inside)	1.32

Number		Price
48N	Magazine Tube Plug (outside)	1.65
49N	Magazine Tube Plug Screws (2) each	.22
50N	Magazine Tube Plug Latch	1.65
51N	Magazine Tube Plug Latch Spring	.22
52N	Magazine Tube Plug Latch Pin	.22
53N	Magazine Tube Stud Screw	.33
54N	Magazine Tube Stud Set Screw	.22
55N	Magazine Tube Catch	.44
56N	Magazine Tube Catch Spring	.33
57N	Magazine Tube Catch Screw	.22
58N	Receiver with Sideplate (Cannot Supply)	
59N	Safety Latch with Spring (Cannot Supply)	
60N	Safety Latch Pivot Pin	.22
61N	Safety Latch Stop Pin	.22
62N	Safety Latch Spring	.22
63N	Safety Push Pin	.22
64N	Safety Push Pin Screw	.22
65N	Safety Unlocking Block	1.10
66N	Safety Push Pin Spring	.22
67N	Sear	1.10
68N	Sear Spring	.22
69N	Sear Screw	.33
70N	Sight	.44
71N	Sideplate (Cannot Supply)	
72N	Sideplate Screw (front)	.33
73N	Sideplate Screw (rear)	.33
74N	Trigger	1.10
75N	Trigger Spring	.33
76N	Trigger Spring Screw	.33
77N	Trigger Pin	.22
78N	Trigger Plate (Cannot Supply)	
79N	Trigger Plate Screw (left side front)	.33
80N	Trigger Plate Screw (left side, rear, and right side front and rear)	.33
81N	Trigger and Hammer Safety	1.32
82N	Trigger Safety Spring	.55
83N	Trigger Safety Spring Screw	.33
84N	Carrier Cartridge Lifter	.88
85N	Carrier Cartridge Lifter Spring	.22
86N	Carrier Cartridge Lifter Pin	.22
87N	Safety Slide	.88
88N	Safety Slide Pin	.22
89N	Safety Latch only	.88
90N	Safety Latch Pivot Pin	.22
91N	Safety Latch Spring (spiral)	.22
92N	Safety Latch Spring Rod	.22
93N	Safety Recoil Block	1.10
94N	Safety Recoil Block Pin	.22

Page from Marlin parts catalog for the Models 28 and 31 hammerless shotguns. Marlin cannot make repairs or furnish parts for these long-discontinued models.

Marlin MODEL 43 · 44 · 53 · 63

Number		Price
1P	Barrel, Spec. Rolled Steel, Matted	$18.15
2P	Barrel Lock Nut	1.98
3P	Barrel Lock Nut Screw	.22
4P	Breech Block	4.13
5P	Buttstock, Grade "A"	4.95
6P	Buttstock Bolt	.55
7P	Buttstock Bolt Washers, each style	.22
8P	Buttplate	1.87
9P	Buttplate Screws (2) ....each	.22
10P	Carrier	3.85
11P	Carrier Screw	.22
12P	Cartridge Cut-Off Style 1	.88
13P	Cartridge Cut-Off Pin Style 1	.22
14P	Cartridge Cut-Off Spring	.22
15P	Cartridge Cut-Off Style 2	.88
16P	Cartridge Cut-Off Screw Style 2	.22
17P	Cartridge Cut-Off Spring Style 2	.22
18P	Cartridge Cut-Off Rivet Style 2	.22
19P	Cartridge Cut-Off Style 3	.88
20P	Cartridge Cut-Off Screw Style 3	.22
21P	Cartridge Cut-Off Model 63	.88
22P	Cartridge Release Style 1	.22
23P	Cartridge Release Spring Style 1-2-3	.22
24P	Cartridge Release Spring Rivet Style 1-2-3	.22
25P	Cartridge Release New Style	.88
26P	Cartridge Release Button	.22
27P	Ejector Complete	.88
28P	Ejector Spring only	.22
29P	Ejector Retaining Screw	.22
30P	Extractor (left side)	.88
31P	Extractor (left side) Spring	.22
32P	Extractor (left side) Pin	.22
33P	Extractor (right side)	.88
34P	Extractor (right side) Spring	.22
35P	Extractor (right side) Pin	.22
36P	Firing Pin (front)	.55
37P	Firing Pin (front) Spring	.22
38P	Firing Pin (rear)	1.10
39P	Firing Pin (rear) Spring	.33
40P	Firing Pin (rear) Pin	.22
41P	Firing Pin (front) Model 63	.55
42P	Firing Pin (rear) Model 63	1.10
43P	Foreend, Grade "A"	2.20
44P	Foreend Cap Nut	1.10
44PP	Foreend Slide and Tube	4.95
45P	Foreend Slide Spring	.22
46P	Foreend Slide Spring Rivet	.22
47P	Guard Plate	1.65
48P	Hammer	1.76
49P	Hammer Pin	.22
50P	Hammer Model 63	1.76
51P	Hammer Spring (spiral)	.33

Number		Price
52P	Hammer Spring Rod	.66
53P	Link	2.20
54P	Locking Bolt	2.48
55P	Magazine Tube	2.86
56P	Magazine Tube Band, with Foreend Slide Spring and Rivet	2.20
57P	Magazine Tube Spring	.88
58P	Magazine Tube Spring Follower	1.10
59P	Magazine Tube Plug (inside)	1.32
60P	Magazine Tube Plug (outside)	1.65
61P	Magazine Tube Plug Screws (2) each	.22
62P	Magazine Tube Plug Latch	1.65
63P	Magazine Tube Plug Latch Spring	.22
64P	Magazine Tube Plug Latch Pin	.22
65P	Magazine Tube Stud Screw	.22
66P	Magazine Tube Stud Set Screw	.22
67P	Magazine Tube Catch	.44
69P	Magazine Tube Catch Screw	.22
70P	Receiver with Sideplate	18.15
71P	Recoil Block	1.10
72P	Recoil Latch	.44
73P	Recoil Latch Spring	.22
74P	Recoil Block (Model 63 only)	1.10
75P	Recoil Block Pin (Model 63 only)	.22
76P	Recoil Block Spring (Mod. 63 only)	.22
77P	Safety Lock ng Latch	1.65
78P	Safety Locking Latch Plunger	.22
79P	Safety Locking Latch Spring	.22
80P	Safety Locking Latch Pin	.22
81P	Safety Unlocking Latch	1.32
82P	Safety Unlocking Latch Spring	.22
83P	Sear	1.10
84P	Sear Plunger	.22
85P	Sear Spring	.22
85PP	Sear Trip and Rivet	.44
86P	Sight	.44
87P	Sideplate	3.58
88P	Sideplate Screw (front)	.22
89P	Sideplate Screw (rear)	.22
90P	Trigger	1.10
91P	Trigger Pin	.22
92P	Trigger Plate	3.74
93P	Trigger Plate Screw (left side front)	.22
94P	Trigger Plate Screw (left side rear; and right side front and rear)	.22
95P	Trigger Safety	1.32
96P	Trigger Safety Spring	.22
97P	Trigger Safety Spring Pin	.22
98P	Trigger Safety (Model 63 only)	1.32
99P	Trigger Safety Spring (Model 63 only)	.22

Component parts of Marlin Models 43, 44, 53, and 63 that are no longer available. Also, Marlin does not make any repairs to these old shotguns.

The retail prices of the Models 63A, 63T, and 63TS were as follows:

Model	1931–1932	4/1932	7/1932–1933
63A	$49.80	$48.00	$48.00
63T	75.00	75.00	80.00
63TS	100.00	100.00	106.00

OTHER PUMP ACTION SHOTGUNS

Marlin Premier Mark I, II, and IV Pump Shotguns

In 1959, the Model 90 over-under shotgun was being phased out; however, it was Marlin's desire to keep a quality shotgun in the line. Opportunely, the French-manufactured LaSalle (Manufrance) 12-gauge pump action shotgun was offered to Marlin at a price, and with a delivery schedule, that Marlin could accept. The guns were purchased without barrels through the importer, Firearms International. Marlin manufactured the barrels and put the Marlin name on them. Marlin called this shotgun the Marlin Premier Shotgun.

Three grades of guns were imported. The Mark I was described as follows:

> The ideal choice for sportsmen who want a custom-built shotgun at an attractive price. Superbly finished French Dordogne Walnut. Seven barrels interchange without tools. Here is a six-pound light weight shotgun with ruggedness, faultless balance, and an action that is smooth as melted ice.

The Mark II Premier shotgun was described the same as the Mark I with an added comment about its graceful hand engraving and fine 16-lines-to-the-inch hand-checked stock. The Mark IV (there was no Mark III) Premier shotgun was blessed

Marlin Mark I pump shotgun.

Marlin Mark II pump shotgun.

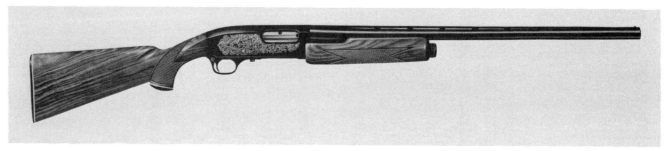

Marlin Mark IV pump shotgun.

with all of the superlatives of the other two grades with an added statement about the rich custom hand engraving on both sides of the receiver, and the fact that the interchangeable ventilated rib barrels were standard equipment. The checkering was 22 lines to the inch and the grip had a cap.

The seven barrels available were:

Ventilated rib: Full choke 30"; modified choke 28"; improved cylinder or skeet 26"; $49.95

Plain barrel: Full choke 30"; modified choke 28"; improved cylinder or skeet 26"; $29.95

Slug barrel: For rifled slugs 28"; $19.95

The one disadvantage to this gun was its light weight of 6 pounds. It was chambered for 2¾-in. shells, and 2¾-in. magnums could be used (with the penalty of the shooter being badly hammered).

The stock dimensions were as follows: length of pull, 14 inches; drop at comb, 1⅝ inches; drop at heel, 2¼ inches; pitch down, 1⅞ inches.

The suggested retail price for the Mark I was $89.95; for the Mark II, $99.95; and for the Mark IV, $159.95.

Total sales of the Marlin Premier pump action shotguns for the years 1960 through 1963 were as follows:

Model	Type	Number Sold
Mark I	12/30 Full	1,965
	12/28 Full	1,365
	12/28 Modified	3,530
	12/16 Improved Cylinder	789
	12/28 Slug	1
	Total	7,650
Mark II	12/30 Full	993
	12/28 Full	582
	12/28 Modified	3,105
	12/26 Improved Cylinder	346
	12/30 Ventilated Rib	1
	Total	5,027
Mark IV	12/30 Full	366
	12/28 Full	1
	12/28 Modified	477
	12/26 Improved Cylinder	220
	Total	1,064
	Grand Total	13,741

At the same time Marlin was importing this line of shotguns and putting its own barrels on them, at least one other U.S. company was doing likewise. This company marked the barrels with a Montgomery Ward brand name.

Marlin makes no repairs to these guns and has no spare parts for them. The spare barrels that were left on hand were sold as scrap to Numrich Arms Company, West Hurley, N.Y. It is believed at this writing that some plain barrels are still available from Numrich.

Model 120 12-Gauge Shotgun

The Model 120 was styled to look like the Winchester Model 12 shotgun. Unfortunately, it was featured as an "all-steel and walnut" shotgun at a time when other manufacturers were filling the sportsman's need for lightweight shotguns that could be easily carried in the field all day long. The waterfowl image that the weight and construction of the 120 conjured in the mind also worked against the gun's being well received. In addition, the usual new gun production problems resulted in an unfair and negative early evaluation that took a year to reverse. Once the bugs were shaken out, the gun proved itself. Many thousands are still being enjoyed where an all-steel gun is preferred.

Although short-lived, the Model 120 shotgun was the finest shotgun Marlin ever manufactured. The variations of the basic 120 were as follows:

Years Manufactured	Model
1971–1985	Model 120 Magnum
1973–1975	Model 120 Trap
1974–1975	Model 120 40-in. MXR Magnum
1974–1984	Model 120 Slug Gun
1978	Model 120 Field
1978–1984	Model 120 Deluxe
1979–1984	Model 778 Glenfield and Marlin

From 1971 to 1979, the Models 120 and 778 were serial-numbered with an *A* prefix to the number. From 1980 on, they were serial-numbered with an eight-digit number without an alphabetical prefix.

Model 120 Magnum 12-Gauge Shotgun (1971–1985). The Marlin catalog described this gun as follows:

This great new Marlin 120 Magnum pump action shotgun is winning wide acclaim among hunters everywhere. De-

signed to fill the need for a solid, reliable, all-steel pump gun, the new Model 120 is everything you'd expect in a Marlin and more. No compromises. No shortcuts. No substitute materials. And it's made entirely in the U.S.A.

Its clean, flowing, classic lines project the inherent elegance of this fine shotgun. It's an inspired design—created by devotees of the pump who are dedicated to true old-fashioned craftsmanship—sure to find a place of honor in every owner's gun rack.

Marlin pioneered pump action guns and today many of them are valuable collector's items. It took years of design study, and a thorough evaluation of the famous designs of John Browning, T.C. Johnson, and others, for Marlin to perfect this great new pump gun. No doubt about it, the New Marlin 120 pump will become the classic standard by which others will be judged.

• All-steel action. No compromise here. The entire receiver is made from a solid block of high tensile steel—and all parts, both operating and non-operating, are made from tough steel alloys.

• New design, exclusive slide lock release lets you open the action to remove unfired shells even with gloved hands.

• All-steel floating ventilated rib, serrated on top, provides "straight plane" sighting and reduces mirage. Front and middle sights aid barrel and target alignment.

• Handsomely engine turned bolt, shell carrier and bolt slide add elegance to a great design.

• Double action bars provide smoothest possible operation with no binding or twisting.

• Matte finish, grooved receiver top eliminates glare, aids natural gun pointing and sighting.

• Big safety button—serrated and located where it belongs, in front of the trigger—easily operates the cross bolt safety that positively blocks the trigger. And it's reversible for right or left hand operation.

• Deluxe recoil pad with smooth exterior for dirt fouling prevention and tear resistance.

• Choice of three barrels—carefully choked the painstaking Marlin way assures even patterns at all ranges. Select the length and choke of your choice. Buy extra barrels anytime—they're completely interchangeable.

• Big 5-shot magazine capacity (4 with 3″ shells); 3-shot plug furnished.

• Stainless steel, non-jamming shell follower.

• All-steel trigger guard—a vulnerable area requiring the solid strength only steel can provide.

• Like all Marlins, the new 120 Magnum has a genuine American walnut stock and fore-end. The trim buttstock design is made to fit American shooters with its full dimensions. Semi-beavertail fore-end is full and fits a full range of hands. Both stock and fore-end are checkered with a handsome pattern and feature our Mar-Shield finish.

• Designed and made entirely in the U.S.A.

Model 120 Magnum shotgun.

Specifications

Gauge: 12 gauge; handles 2¾" or 3" Magnum or Regular shells interchangeably.

Choke: Full, Modified or Improved Cylinder.

Capacity: 5-shot tubular magazine (4-shot with 3" shells); 3-shot plug furnished.

Action: Pump; all steel action; engine turned bolt, shell carrier and bolt slide; double action bars; exclusive, easy-to-use slide lock release; stainless steel shell follower; big cross-bolt safety; deeply blued metal surfaces.

Stock: Two-piece genuine American walnut with fluted comb and full pistol grip; semi-beavertail fore-end. Grip cap, recoil pad; white butt and pistol grip spacers; checkering on pistol grip and fore-end; tough Mar-Shield™ finish.

Stock Dimensions: Length of pull 14", including recoil pad; 1½" drop at comb; 2⅜" drop at heel.

Barrel: Choice of 30" Full, 28" Modified or 26" Improved Cylinder, with steel ventilated rib. Front and middle bead sights.

Overall Length: 50½" (with 30" barrel).

Weight: About 7¾ pounds.

The steel rib of the Model 120 shotgun was invented by George R. Snyder (patent number 3,727,319, dated April 17, 1973).

By year, the suggested retail prices of the Model 120 Magnum shotgun were as follows:

Year	Price
1971	$150.00
	(to be available summer of 1971)
1972	150.00
1973	154.95
1974	158.95
1975	169.95
1976	183.95
1977	194.95

The production of the Model 120 Magnum shotgun was as follows:

Model	Total
120 — 30 inch	27,646
120 — 28 inch	12,089
120 — 26 inch	1,932
120 — 40 inch/38 inch	6,984
	48,651

In 1974, extra barrels were available as follows:

1. 26-in. improved cylinder with vent rib
2. 28-in. modified choke with vent rib
3. 30-in. full choke with vent rib (standard)
4. 40-in. MVR full choke without rib
5. 26-in. slug barrel

In 1978, a 38-in. barrel without rib was added to the barrel list and in 1979, a 20-in. slug barrel replaced the 26-in. slug barrel. Also in 1978, an aluminum trigger housing replaced the steel one.

Model 120 Trap Gun (1973–1975). The consumer reaction to the Model 120 Magnum shotgun was to request the gun be made in a trap model. As a result of a general feeling that it might pay to explore that small segment of the shotgun market, Marlin developed a trap variation of the Model 120.

The 120 Trap Gun was the same gun as the 120 Magnum except for having a hand-cut checkered Monte Carlo buttstock and forearm. The stock dimensions were 14¼ in. length of pull, 1¼ in. drop at comb, and 1¾ in. drop at heel; the drop at the Monte Carlo was 1¼ inches. The trap model was available with either a 30-in. full choke or a 30-in. modified trap choke. Both barrels had steel floating ventilated ribs. A total of 298 Model 120 Trap Guns were made.

Model 120 40-in. MXR Magnum Shotgun (1974–1975). The 120 MXR shotgun was the 120 Magnum gun with a 40-in., full choke, plain barrel without rib. Marlin stated:

> A Marlin exclusive. You have to shoot with this barrel to believe it. Not only does it reach out for the long ones, but it shoots quieter and balances surprisingly well. The added radius is a big advantage for extra long range shooting.

A number of the 40-in. MXR shotguns were sold, and the 40-in. barrel was available as an extra barrel to owners of the regular 120 Magnum shotgun. But cutting 40-in. barrels did not make use of the full length of the bars supplied by steel mills, and wasted steel was the result. To remedy this, Marlin reduced the barrel length to 38 inches, thereby making use of the full length of the bar. The 38-in. barrel was also available as a separate spare barrel.

The long barrel ("Long Tom") concept has been around for over 200 years and it probably had some logic in early days. However, with the quality and performance of shotshells now

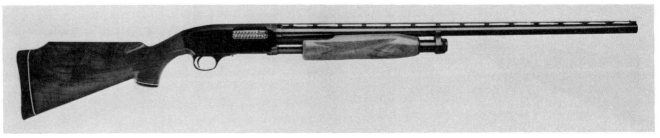

Model 120 Trap shotgun.

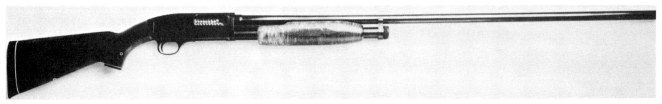

Model 120 40-in. MXR.

Model 120 Slug Gun.

manufactured in the U.S., the long barrel theory is no longer valid. After about 30 inches, the length of the barrel does not contribute to velocity and energy. Also, a barrel having a certain choke restriction results in an average performance. Marlin's full choke barrels give an average of 70% patterns in a 30-in. circle at 40 yards, regardless of the length of the barrel.

The suggested retail price of the Model 120 40-in. MXR shotgun was as follows:

Year	Price
1974	$158.95
1975	169.95

A total of 6,984 Model 120 40-in. MXR shotguns were manufactured.

Model 120 Slug Gun (1974–1984). Although a Model 120 Slug barrel was offered in 1973 to convert the Model 120 shotgun to an accurate deer gun in seconds, Marlin did not offer the sportsman the Model 120 Slug Gun, fitted with a 20-in. slug barrel, until 1974. The new shotgun had a 20-in. barrel equipped with an open rear sight and ramp front sight fitted with a brass bead. The rear sight base was drilled and tapped for scope mounting. The choke of the barrel was improved cylinder, which was recommended as the best choice of choke for slugs. In 1975, the slug barrel had a ramp front sight with a hood.

The 1976, 1977, and 1978 catalogs did not illustrate and describe a Model 120 Slug Gun, but the available optional barrels listed for the 120 included a 26-in. slug barrel.

In 1979, the Model 120 Slug Gun was reinstated in the catalog with a name change to Marlin Deluxe 120 Slug Gun. It had a 20-in. slug barrel but otherwise was no different from the earlier 26-in. barrel model.

In an attempt to breathe new life into the Model 120 shotgun, the Deluxe 120 Magnum and the Deluxe Slug Gun that Marlin introduced in 1983 had hand-cut checkering on the

pistol grip and forearm. In 1984, the prefix *Deluxe* was dropped from the model designation of the Model 120s; however, no change was made in either model. In 1982, Marlin advertised that the barrels of the Model 120s had burnished bores and honed chokes. The Model 120 Slug Gun was discontinued in 1985.

The Slug Gun's suggested retail price was as follows, year by year.

Year	Price
1974	$158.95
1975	169.50
1976–78	not listed
1979	217.95
1980	252.95
1981	297.95
1982	351.95
1983	351.95
1984	351.95

A total of 1,546 Model 120 Slug Guns were manufactured.

Model 120 Field Grade, 12-Gauge Shotgun (1978). To try to meet the demand of the sportsman for a shotgun designed more for field rather than waterfowl shooting, Marlin offered the Magnum gun as a Deluxe Model 120 and added a 120 Field Grade to the line. The 120 Field Grade was exactly like the Deluxe gun, except that the barrel was 28 inches long, without a rib, and choked modified. It weighed 7¾ pounds. The suggested retail price was $184.95.

By purchasing a 30-in. full-choke spare barrel, the sportsman could have a combination of the Deluxe gun and the Field Grade gun.

Only 1,083 Model 120 Field Grade guns were manufactured.

Model 120 Deluxe Grade, 12-Gauge Shotgun (1978–1982). When the Field Grade Model 120 was added to the 120 family,

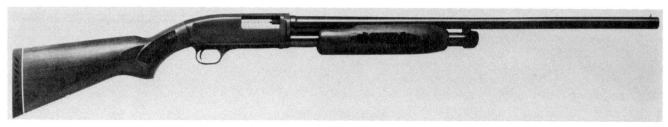

Model 120 Field Grade.

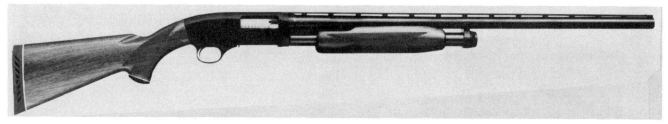

Model 120 Deluxe.

Model 778 shotgun, first variation.

the 120 Magnum gun was renamed the Deluxe Model 120. Nothing about the gun changed. The distinctive features of the previous Model 120 Magnum were retained. Barrel options also remained the same. The new model was listed as full choke with options of 6 barrels, as previously listed. In 1978, the weight of this model was listed as 8 pounds. In 1981, the weight was listed as 8¼ pounds. In 1982, the Deluxe Model 120 shotgun was offered with hand-cut checkering on the forearm and on the pistol grip. The prefix Deluxe was dropped in 1983. The Model 120 was discontinued in 1985.

The suggested retail prices of the Deluxe Model 120 shotgun were as follows:

Year	Price
1978	$199.95
1979	217.95
1980	252.95
1981	297.95
	(hand-cut checkering)
1982	351.95
	(hand-cut checkering)

From production records, the number of Deluxe Model 120 shotguns manufactured was as follows:

Year	Total
1978	2,956
1979	693
1980	1,930
1981	2,478
1982	2,623
Total	10,680

Model 778 Glenfield Pump Action, 12-Gauge Shotgun (1979–1984). In 1979, Marlin introduced into its shotgun line a Glenfield model of the 120 shotgun. It offered the sportsman an economically priced shotgun having all the features of the Model 120, except for the type of wood used in the buttstock and forearm. All Marlin models, traditionally, have had walnut stocks and forearms, whereas the Glenfield line of guns produced by Marlin have traditionally had walnut-stained hardwood (birch).

The Model 778 was shipped with a 28-in. modified choke barrel; however, all of the Model 120 barrel options were also available. The barrels were all interchangeable and could be purchased from the Marlin parts department as follows:

1. 26-in. improved cylinder with or without vent rib
2. 28-in. modified choke with or without vent rib
3. 30-in. full choke with or without vent rib
4. 40-in. MXR, full choke without rib
5. 20-in. slug barrel (improved cylinder) with front and rear sights and Wide-Scan hood. Drilled and tapped for scope mount.

Model 778 shotgun, second variation.

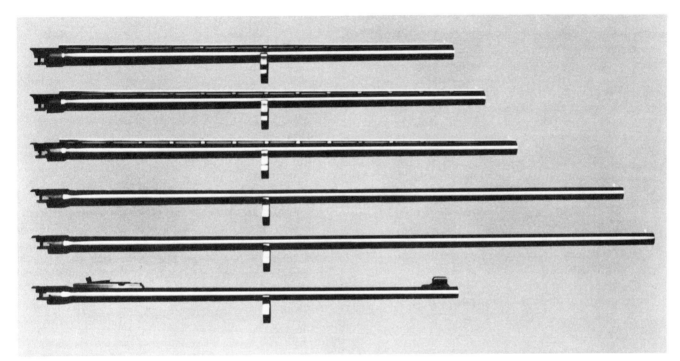

Extra barrels available for the Model 120 and 778 shotguns. From top to bottom: 26-in. improved cylinder choke, with ventilated rib; 28-in. modified choke, with ventilated rib; 30-in. full choke, with ventilated rib; 38-in. full choke, plain barrel; 40-in. full choke, plain barrel; 26-in. slug barrel, with rifle sights.

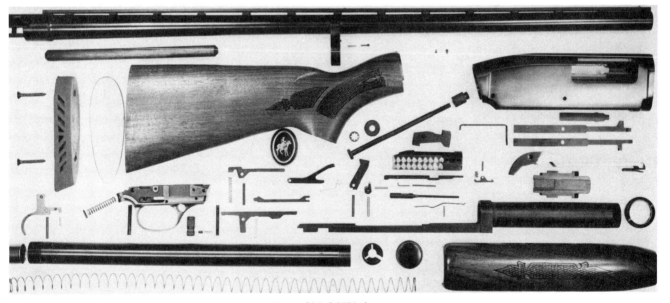

Parts of Model 120 shotgun.

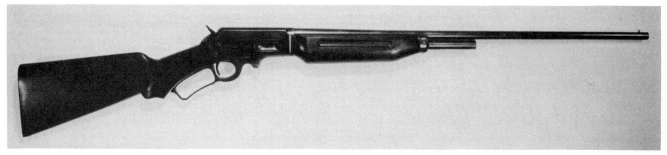

Marlin Model 410 shotgun.

In 1978, an aluminum trigger housing replaced the steel one.

From 1979 to 1981, the pistol grip of the Model 778 had an impressed checking design on the pistol grip and finger grooves in the forearm. In 1982, the checking of the grip was eliminated. In 1983, Marlin discontinued the use of the name *Glenfield* and integrated those models into the Marlin family of guns. However, there were no changes other than the name *Glenfield* being dropped from the model designation.

By year, the suggested retail price of the Model 778 was as follows:

Year	Price
1979	$150.00
1980	194.95
1981	216.95
1982	242.95
1983	244.95

The production of the Model 778 was as follows:

Close-up of Model 410 receiver.

Model	Total
778 – 30 full, plain	3,426
778 – 30 full, vent. rib	11,000
778 – 28 mod., plain	5,061
778 – 28 mod., vent. rib	13,664
778 – 26 I.C., plain	52
778 – 26 I.C., vent. rib	500
778 – 38 full, plain	731
778 – 40 full, plain	507
Total	34,941

MARLIN .410 LEVER ACTION SHOTGUN

In 1929, Marlin introduced a novel and different type of lever action firearm. It was chambered for the .410 shotgun shell. It held five 2- or 2½-in. shells in the magazine and one in the chamber, making it a 6-shot gun at only 6 pounds. Marlin described this gun as follows:

A light weight, nicely balanced repeater, using the scatter load and the round ball. A gun that will take the place of both your shotgun and rifle for many purposes. For the boy not old enough to handle a heavy gauge and a pleasant companion for your wife or daughter. Effective for brush and field shooting and at the gun club for skeet. An ideal gun on the farm for shooting pests and other small animals and with the round ball for deer at short ranges. Carefully made with Marlin accuracy.

The Model 410 buttstock and receiver mechanism were basically the same as those of the Model 93 rifle. The traditional square bolt, side ejection, solid top, and lever mechanism were like the Model 93. The smooth-bore barrel, forearm, and magazine tube were different, and the loading port in the receiver was lengthened to allow the .410 shell to be loaded into

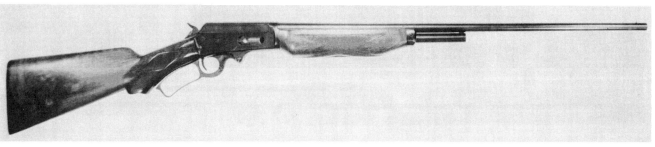

Deluxe Model 410.

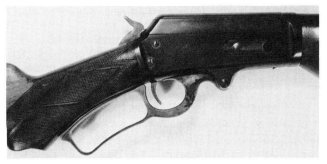

Close-up of Deluxe Model 410 showing checked grip and large loading port.

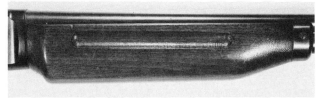

Standard 410 forearm.

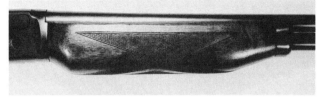

Deluxe Model 410 forearm.

the magazine. The forearm was more hand-filling than the rifle type. It also had finger grooves along each side.

The stock was of black walnut and had the regular S-shaped pistol grip. The butt plate was the rifle type of hard rubber. The length of the butt from the center of the trigger to the center of the butt plate was 13½ inches. The drop at the comb was 1½ inches and the drop at the heel was 2⅝ inches. The overall length was 44½ inches.

The Model 410 was available with either a 22- or 26-in. barrel.

Although not found in catalogs or price lists, a deluxe model of the 410 was produced. These guns have nicely checked forearms and pistol grips. A double diamond pattern of about 18 lines to the inch was used. The forearms were shaped exactly like the plain model's, but they did not have finger grooves.

In addition to some other models, Marlin offered the Model 410 as a free gun with the purchase of four shares of Marlin preferred stock at $25.00 per share.

The gun was cataloged from 1929 to 1932. It was not listed in the April 1932 Marlin price list.

Serial numbers of the Model 410 were in two series. One series had the letter *U* as a prefix. The other series had no prefix. Serial numbers of 184 of this model have been recorded. They were as follows:

	Low	High
U prefix	U535	U2174
No prefix	54	8435

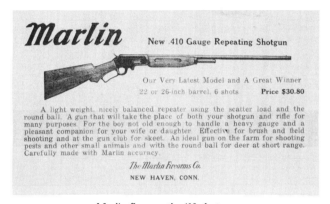

Marlin flyer on the 410 shotgun.

Top tang marking on the Model 410 shotgun.

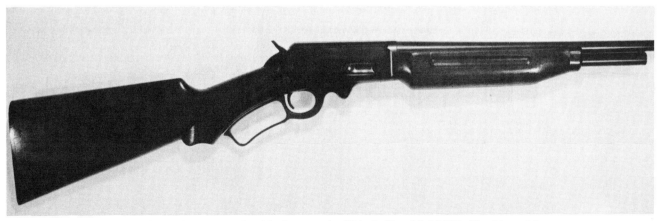

Except for the finger-grooved and fat forearm, the 410 looks like a Model 1893 rifle without sights.

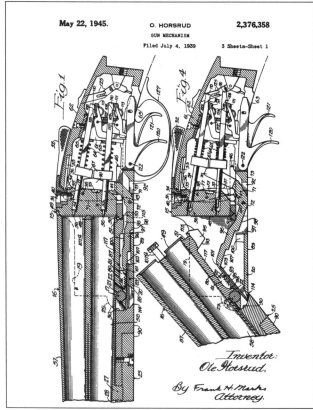

From 1929 to 1932, the list price of the Model 410 remained at $30.80.

It is speculated that this model was serial-numbered in a separate series and that about 10,000 were produced. The 22-in. barrel model is very scarce. The deluxe model is rare.

MODEL 90 OVER–UNDER SHOTGUN

In 1936, Sears, Roebuck and Company requested that Marlin make an over–under shotgun to be sold by Sears. The gun was invented by Ole Horsrud of Fox Grove, Ill. His patent number 2,376,358, dated May 22, 1945, was filed on July 4, 1939 and was assigned to the Sears Company. Marlin agreed, as long as Marlin could also make and sell the gun to Marlin customers with the Marlin name on the gun. However, the Marlin name was not to be marked on those guns delivered to Sears. Instead, the Sears guns were to be marked *Ranger* (before WW II) or *J.C. Higgins* (after WW II), Sears trade names. A decimal code, which indicated to Sears the model and manufacturer, was also marked on the gun. The Sears designation for Marlin was the prefix *103*. The numbers to the right of the decimal identified the specific model. The code used was as follows:

Code	Model
103.5	.22 Long Rifle & .410
103.7	16 Gauge

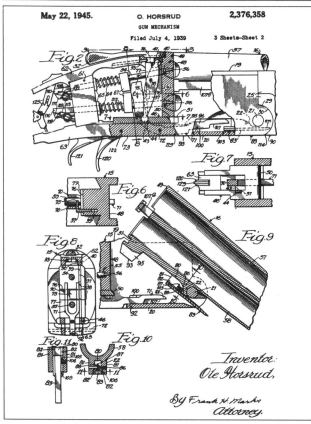

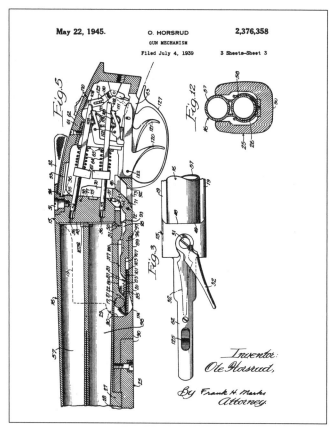

Ole Horsrud patent drawings of his 1945 patent assigned to Sears, Roebuck for the shotgun Marlin made for Sears (marked Ranger*) and as the Marlin Model 90.*

Parts List for Marlin Model 90 Shotgun

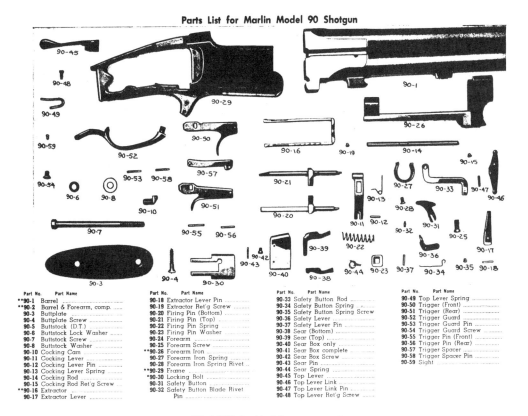

Part No.	Part Name	Part No.	Part Name	Part No.	Part Name	Part No.	Part Name
**90-1	Barrel	90-18	Extractor Lever Pin	90-33	Safety Button Rod	90-49	Top Lever Spring
**90-2	Barrel & Forearm, comp.	90-19	Extractor Ret'g Screw	90-34	Safety Button Spring	90-50	Trigger (Front)
90-3	Buttplate	90-20	Firing Pin (Bottom)	90-35	Safety Button Spring Screw	90-51	Trigger (Rear)
90-4	Buttplate Screw	90-21	Firing Pin (Top)	90-36	Safety Lever	90-52	Trigger Guard
90-5	Buttstock (D.T.)	90-22	Firing Pin Spring	90-37	Safety Lever Pin	90-53	Trigger Guard Pin
90-6	Buttstock Lock Washer	90-23	Firing Pin Washer	90-38	Sear (Bottom)	90-54	Trigger Guard Screw
90-7	Buttstock Screw	90-24	Forearm	90-39	Sear (Top)	90-55	Trigger Pin (Front)
90-8	Buttstock Washer	90-25	Forearm Screw	90-40	Sear Box only	90-56	Trigger Pin (Rear)
90-10	Cocking Cam	**90-26	Forearm Iron	90-41	Sear Box complete	90-57	Trigger Spacer
90-11	Cocking Lever	90-27	Forearm Iron Spring	90-42	Sear Box Screw	90-58	Trigger Spacer Pin
90-12	Cocking Lever Pin	90-28	Forearm Iron Spring Rivet	90-43	Sear Pin	90-59	Sight
90-13	Cocking Lever Spring	**90-29	Frame	90-44	Sear Spring		
90-14	Cocking Rod	*90-30	Locking Bolt	90-45	Top Lever		
90-15	Cocking Rod Ret'g Screw	90-31	Safety Button	90-46	Top Lever Link		
**90-16	Extractor	90-32	Safety Button Blade Rivet	90-47	Top Lever Link Pin		
90-17	Extractor Lever		Pin	90-48	Top Lever Ret'g Screw		

Model 90 double-trigger gun parts.

Parts List for Marlin Model 90 ST
Non-Selective Single Trigger Parts

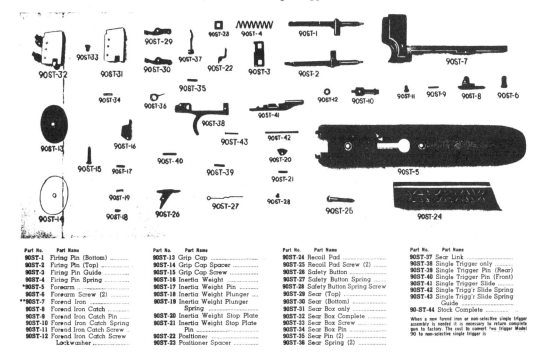

Part No.	Part Name	Part No.	Part Name	Part No.	Part Name	Part No.	Part Name
90ST-1	Firing Pin (Bottom)	90ST-13	Grip Cap	90ST-24	Recoil Pad	90ST-37	Sear Link
90ST-2	Firing Pin (Top)	90ST-14	Grip Cap Spacer	90ST-25	Recoil Pad Screw (2)	90ST-38	Single Trigger only
90ST-3	Firing Pin Guide	90ST-15	Grip Cap Screw	90ST-26	Safety Button	90ST-39	Single Trigger Pin (Rear)
90ST-4	Firing Pin Spring	90ST-16	Inertia Weight	90ST-27	Safety Button Spring	90ST-40	Single Trigger Pin (Front)
*90ST-5	Forearm	90ST-17	Inertia Weight Pin	90ST-28	Safety Button Spring Screw	90ST-41	Single Trigger Slide
90ST-6	Forearm Screw (2)	90ST-18	Inertia Weight Plunger	90ST-29	Sear (Top)	90ST-42	Single Trigg'r Slide Spring
**90ST-7	Forend Iron	90ST-19	Inertia Weight Plunger	90ST-30	Sear (Bottom)	90ST-43	Single Trigg'r Slide Spring
90ST-8	Forend Iron Catch		Spring	90ST-31	Sear Box only		Guide
90ST-9	Forend Iron Catch Pin	90ST-20	Inertia Weight Stop Plate	90ST-32	Sear Box Complete	90-ST-44	Stock Complete
90ST-10	Forend Iron Catch Spring	90ST-21	Inertia Weight Stop Plate	90ST-33	Sear Box Screw		When a new forend iron or non-selective single trigger
90ST-11	Forend Iron Catch Screw		Pin	90ST-34	Sear Box Pin		assembly is needed it is necessary to return complete gun to factory. The cost to convert two trigger Model
90ST-12	Forend Iron Catch Screw	90ST-22	Positioner	90ST-35	Sear Pin (2)		90 to non-selective single trigger is
	Lockwasher	90ST-23	Positioner Spacer	90ST-36	Sear Spring (2)		

Model 90 single-trigger gun parts that are different from double-trigger gun parts.

Code	Model
103.10	.22 Long Rifle & .410
103.11	16 Gauge
103.16	16 Gauge
103.350	12 Gauge
103.360	16 Gauge
103.370	20 Gauge
103.223	12 Gauge
103.2236	16 Gauge
103.2237	20 Gauge

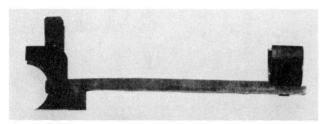
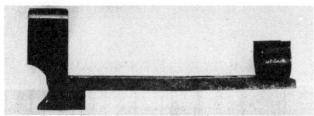

Top: *Early forearm iron of first variation with spring clip.* Middle: *Second variation of forearm iron with spring clip.* Bottom: *Third variation, with a latch mechanism.*

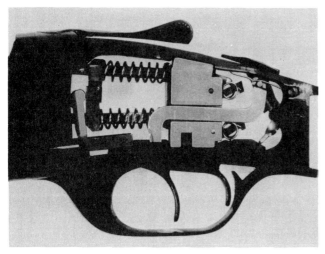

Internal mechanism of Model 90 double-trigger gun.

In 1945, Sears requested that the name of Marlin be added to the markings on the gun.

In 1937, the Model 90 was described as a 12-gauge over–under shotgun with two triggers. Barrel lengths were 26 inches or 30 inches. The 26-in. barrels were bored modified choke and improved cylinder. The 30-in. barrels were full choke and modified choke. The more open choke was in the bottom barrel.

Also in 1937, the Model 90 became available in 16 gauge and 20 gauge. This new offering had a lighter frame than the 12-gauge model. The 16- and 20-gauge guns were available with either 26-in. or 28-in. barrels.

In 1939, a smaller-framed .410-bore gun was offered. It had a 26-in. barrel and 3-in. chambers. In addition to this conventional small-bore over–under shotgun, a combination gun in the following rifle–shotgun combinations was also available: .22 long rifle/.410, .22 Hornet/.410, and .218 Bee/.410. (A very few .30–30 20-gauge guns were experimented with, but production was never started.)

The very early Model 90s had a forearm iron that did not extend to the top edge of the side of the frame. The second type did. Spring tension held both the first- and second-variation forearms to the barrel. Until about 1950, the barrels had ribs on the sides that closed the open space between the two barrels. After this time, the barrels were open and had a spacer block between the barrels at the muzzle.

When introduced, the Model 90 had a hard rubber butt plate as standard, but a recoil pad could be special-ordered.

In addition to the 12, 16, 20, .410 bore, and combination guns, 1939 was the year for another innovation. On special order (not subject to cancellation), a custom-built skeet gun could be purchased. Called the Skeetking, it was described as follows:

Marlin's "Skeetking" has been designed to give results hitherto unattainable for skeet, as well as for upland game. This shotgun is the highest quality throughout, with special atten-

Top: *Model 90 single-trigger gun mechanism.* Bottom: *Model 90 double-trigger gun mechanism with disassembly tool in place.*

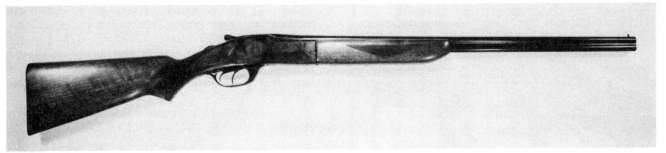

Model 90 in .410 bore.

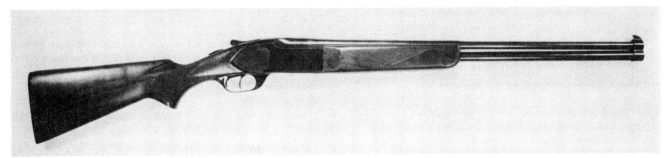

Model 90 rifle–shotgun combination gun.

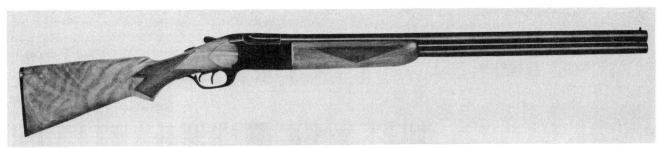

Second-variation double-trigger Model 90 shotgun.

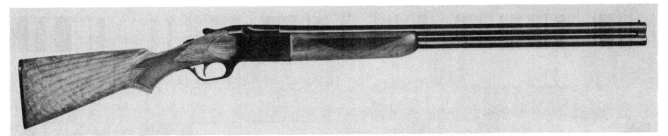

First variation of Model 90 single-trigger gun.

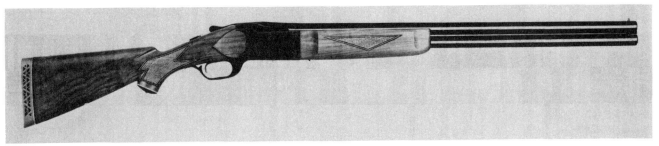

Second variation of Model 90 single-trigger gun.

Prototype engraving of Model 90 Skeetking shotgun.

tion to boring, fit, finish and balance. Made to order for delivery within four to six weeks.

The specifications were listed as follows:

12, 16, and 20 gauge and .410 bore barrels, 26″ long — with option of 28″ in all but .410 bore. Full pistol grip, half pistol or straight grip optional. Matted top barrel, ivory bead front sight. Hand filling, semi-beaver tail forearm, buttstock made to any reasonable specification. Recoil pad, hard rubber buttplate optional on 12, 16 and 20 gauge. .410 bore hard rubber buttplate, recoil pad optional. Automatic safety, independent safety optional. Cocks on opening, direct line locking, single sighting plane for faster, more accurate pointing. Straight line recoil. 12, 16, and 20 gauge chambered for 2¾ inch shells, .410 bore for 3-inch.

Skeetking guns made for inventory had the following specifications: 26-in. barrels; 14-in. buttstock; drop at comb, 1⅝ inches; at heel, 2¼ inches.

The frame and forearm iron were handsomely hand-engraved. The stock and forearm were of specially selected fancy figured American black walnut with a hand-rubbed finish.

The weights of the Skeetking and the Model 90 were listed as follows:

	Skeetking	*DT/ST*
12 gauge	7¼ to 7½ lbs	7½
16 & 20 gauge	6¼ to 6½ lbs	6¼
.410 bore	5¾ to 6 lbs	5¾

The Skeetking was only available during 1939 and 1940. It was priced at $69.50. Each Skeetking shotgun was proof tested with a special excessive load. It was then patterned and the chokes were adjusted for the best target-breaking spread at 20 and 30 yards.

In small print, the 1939 literature stated the .410-bore gun would not be ready until about September 1.

When introduced, the Model 90 was not checkered. In 1945, checking was added to the forearm and pistol grip. Also in 1945, Sears requested the Marlin name be added to the gun. This same year, Sears and Marlin had a discussion about who owned the tools and fixtures that were used in the production of the Model 90. It was agreed they belonged to Marlin and that Sears' monetary contribution was only to help pay for some of the start-up costs.

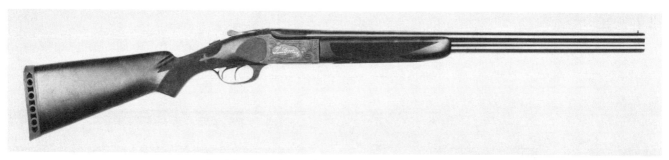

Special presentation Model 90 that was made for Tom Mix.

Left: *Right side of Tom Mix presentation shotgun.* Right: *Left side of same shotgun.*

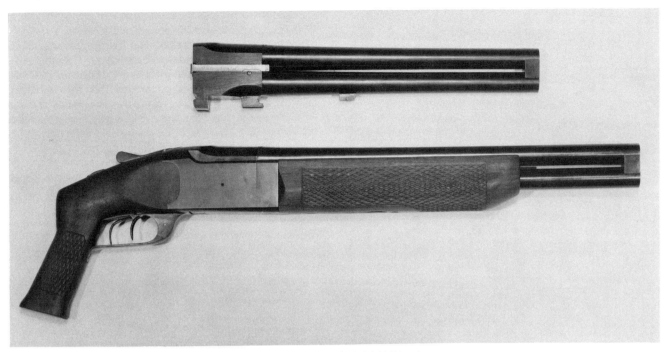

Experimental prototype of Model 90 Riot shotgun.

In 1951, the forearm had a change made to its attachment system. A new type of latch was added that required a lever to be moved for removal of the forearm. Previously, it had been held on by a spring clip, which did not secure the forearm adequately.

An early undated illustration of the standard Marlin Model 90 shows a stamped design of flying ducks in an oval on the receiver. A 1939 price list illustration shows a pointing dog in an oval. Subsequent illustrations do not show these features.

Marlin gun designer Robert L. Jenkinson obtained patent number 2,487,971, dated November 15, 1949, for a trigger-locking means for the two-trigger Model 90 shotgun. It was assigned to The Marlin Firearms Company, but was not added to the gun.

In 1954, a single-trigger version of the Model 90 was added to the line. It was a nonselective device that fired the lower barrel first. There was an inertia weight built into the system, which prevented the shooter from inadvertently doubling. The recoil of the first shot caused the inertia block to move to the rear and under a shoulder built into the inner back surface of the frame, thus preventing an involuntary pull of the trigger from firing the gun during recoil. The photographs shown here, with their captions, illustrate and describe this mechanism. For years the Model 90 was described as the only over-under shotgun made in America. The double-trigger model was discontinued in 1957. The single-trigger model was manufactured into 1959, but sales of inventory continued until 1963.

Two Model 90s having 28-in. 28-gauge barrels were made in 1953. From 1952 to 1957, 10,934 Model 90DT guns were sold and from 1953 to 1963, 8,919 Model 90ST guns were sold. It is estimated that at least 15,000 Model 90s were manufactured prior to 1941. The totals, by year, gauge, and barrel length were as follows:

Gauge/Barrel Length	90DT (1937–1942)	90DT (1952–1957)	90ST (1953–1963)
12/30		1,850	2,965
12/28		2,475	1,324
12/16		466	734
16/28		1,398	1,060
16/26		931	1,039
20/28		1,021	710
20/26		530	359
12/28 J.C. Higgins		895	
16/28 J.C. Higgins		927	
20/28 J.C. Higgins		441	
	15,000 est.	10,934	8,191

Wet-grinding Model 90 frames.

Old-time Marlin employee, the late George Rohr, inletting the frame of the Model 90 to the stock.

Before discontinuing the manufacture of the Model 90 in 1960, two new areas were explored. The first was the possibility of an aluminum frame. No aluminum-framed guns were made, but strength tests were conducted on receivers. The other project explored was a riot-type, short-barreled, pistol grip Model 90 for use by law enforcement agencies. The project was also dropped, as the law enforcement market was one Marlin had no experience in, and the restrictive laws with regard to manufacture of such guns were not compatible with the Marlin manufacturing and marketing operations.

The choke of Model 90 barrels is not marked on the barrel for easy identification. However, it was standard practice to choke the barrels to the following system:

	12		*16*		*20*		*.410*	
	O	*U*	*O*	*U*	*O*	*U*	*O*	*U*
30-in.	F	M						
28-in.	F	M	F	M	F	M		
26-in.	M	IC	M	IC	M	IC	F	F

O—Over barrel
U—Under barrel
F—Full choke
M—Modified choke
IC—Improved cylinder choke

Information in Marlin catalogs and price lists with reference to the Model 90 shotgun in .410 bore was as follows:

1939	.410 ready for delivery Aug. 1, 1939
1940	.410 available in custom-made Skeetking
1945	.410 listed with double trigger
1946	.410 listed with double trigger
1947	Not listed in catalog
1948	Not listed in catalog
1949	.410 listed in both DT & ST

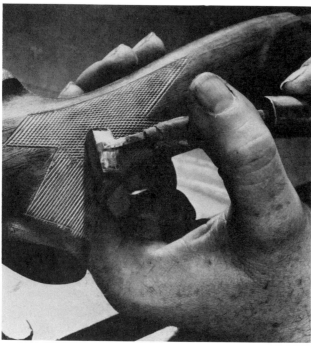

Checkering the Model 90 stock.

Robert Stack, world champion skeet shooter and movie star, holding his Model 90 shotgun during a visit to the old Marlin plant in New Haven, Conn.

1950	.410 listed in DT only
1951	Not listed in catalog
1952	.410 listed in price list — DT only
1953	Not listed in catalog or price list
1954–1960	Not listed

The number of combination rifle–shotgun Model 90s manufactured is estimated to be no more than 500. They were listed in the 1940 catalog. The .218 Bee and .22 Hornet combinations were available built to order only.

Choke and bore diameters had manufacturing tolerances. However, measurements of the choke and bore of Model 90 barrels will generally agree with the following chart:

Choke	*12 Ga.*	*16 Ga.*	*20 Ga.*
Full	.693–.697	.627–.631	.583–.587
Modified	.708–.714	.637–.643	.593–.600
Improved Cylinder	.721–.724	.654–.657	.607–.610
Bore	.729 + .004	.662 + .004	.615 + .004

Marlin can no longer furnish parts for the Model 90 shotgun and can no longer make repairs to these guns. Gun owners and gunsmiths are cautioned to be sure the safety features work correctly on any gun they use or work on. To do otherwise can cause damage to the gun, or personal injury.

The receiver of the Model 90 shotgun is of malleable iron. It will not blue by the usual bluing methods, but instead turns a dirty brown or plum color. In fact, Marlin did not blue the Model 90 during regular production. Instead, the parts were shipped to a commercial finishing plant, which could routinely process the parts with an acceptable blue-black finish. The barrels and ribs are soft-soldered and must not be blued by the current caustic-type bluing method used by most gunsmiths today. To do so will result in the barrels coming apart or being damaged.

Retail prices for the Model 90 were as follows:

Year	*90DT*	*90ST*	*Skeetking*
1936	$38.40		
1937	39.90		
1939	39.90		$69.50
1940	40.27		70.13
1940 (Nov.)	44.36	$48.83	70.13
1941	45.25	49.75	
1941 (Nov.)	51.55	56.70	
1945	52.75	58.00	
1946	76.15	Not Available	
1948	75.70	Not Available	
1949	82.45	Not Available	
1950	89.95	Not Listed	
1953	94.45	123.95	
1955	94.45	123.95	
1956	100.80	124.80	
1957		139.95	
1958		139.95	
1959		139.95	

1960 Model 90 not listed

Curtis, Cowe and Lard selective and Romberg and Peterson nonselective single triggers were evaluated. The Romberg nonselective trigger was the one finally adopted by Marlin and the only one produced.

Elmer E. Miller of Millersburg, Pa., modified some Marlin single- and double-trigger Model 90 shotguns by installing his design of single trigger. Mr. Miller also fitted his single triggers to L.C. Smith, Parker, and other makes of two-barrel guns. His son Howard is still carrying on this very special business for those who prefer the single trigger, as I do.

In appreciation for allowing Marlin to use his name with the 1937 Tom Mix Special .22 rifle, Marlin presented Tom Mix with an engraved and gold-inlaid 20-gauge Model 90 over-under shotgun. The receiver barrel trigger guard and forearm iron are tastefully engraved with oak leaf and scroll work that surround a cowboy hat, six-shooter, gun belt and holster, lariat, bucking horse, cowboy on a horse, and a standing cowboy watching the action. Inlaid in gold on the right side of the receiver is the signature of Tom Mix. The serial number of this gun, which is a one-of-a-kind engraved Model 90, is 1390. It is now in a privately owned collection of high-art Marlin firearms.

The metal ornamentation on the Tom Mix Model 90 shotgun was done by Charles Preiss and Dan Cavanaugh of Lehman Brothers, New Haven, Conn. The Lehman company is still in business and specializes in stationery engraving.

L.C. SMITH SIDE-BY-SIDE SHOTGUN

In early 1939, G. F. Gilles, president of the Hunter Arms Company in Fulton, N.Y., manufacturer of the L.C. Smith shotgun, was trying to sell the company. In 1941, The Marlin Firearms Company considered purchasing this company, but after careful study and investigation of the working conditions, leadership, and sales potential, decided to wait until the directors of the company submitted a fair proposal. The proposal was not forthcoming and the start of WW II eliminated any further consideration of a change in ownership.

During WW II, the Hunter Arms Company made a number of parts for the Navy 20-mm Oerlikon gun. It also continued manufacture of the L.C. Smith shotgun. Some went to the

L.C. Smith Gun Company plant, Fulton, N.Y.

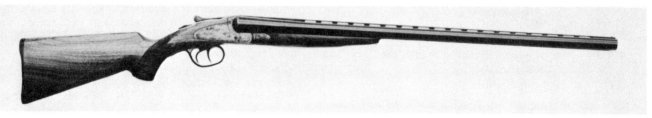

Field Grade L.C. Smith shotgun as manufactured by Marlin from 1968 to 1971.

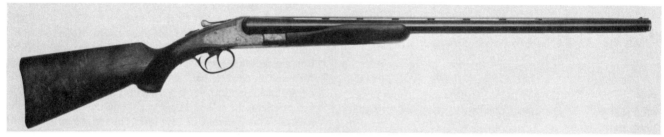

Deluxe Field Grade L.C. Smith, one of 182 manufactured by Marlin in 1971–72.

Army Air Force; however, from 1940 to 1944 a total of 22, 378 L.C. Smiths were sold.

The old Hunter Arms Company records reflect that the U.S. Navy, at the end of the war, had a claim against it for $167,000 for unfinished contracts, and tools and machinery paid for by the government.

The increased public interest in pump and automatic shotguns over the double-barrel shotgun, pressure from the government to pay the money owed, and weak management caused the Hunter Company to go into bankruptcy.

At the time of filing the Hunter Arms Company bankruptcy papers, the outstanding capital stock of 1,500 shares was distributed as follows: Stephen J. Gilles, 1,029 shares; Gertrude Gilles, 90; Mary Gilles, 50; Stephen Gilles, Jr., 50; James Cosgrove, 25; First National Bank of St. Johnsbury, Vt., 108; G.K. Simons, Jr., 36; Harland Simonds, 50; John Monihan, 10; and Joseph Murphy, 2.

The U.S. District Court judged the corporation bankrupt on April 25, 1945.

A plan of reorganization was immediately set up by the court, which provided that a new corporation of 1,000 shares of stock would be organized and the trustees would take bids on or before October 5, 1945 and sell the stock to the highest bidder. Under this new plan, the new corporation would pay all taxes, wage claims, and $52,000 in settlement of the Navy claim against the debtors of $167,000. The new corporation would also have to agree to complete manufacture of all guns on order and to repair all guns received for repair for which payment had been made. It also provided that all general creditor claims would be settled on the basis of 26 cents on the dollar, in cash, and that the new corporation would furnish additional capital in the amount of $75,000 to reestablish and resume operation in the present plant in Fulton, N.Y.

Liabilities of the Hunter Arms Company were listed as $311,000. Assets of the bankrupt company, totaling $214,761, were listed as

land — $10,000
buildings and fixed machinery — $105,501
machines and tools — $40,505
small tools, jigs, and dies — $4,100
raw materials — $3,079
finished guns — $2,200
guns and parts in progress — $17,715
office furniture and fixtures — $6,661
trade name and good will — $25,000
for a grand total of $214,761

The highest bid received by the deadline of October 5, 1945 was from The Marlin Firearms Company. It was for $80 per share, plus the agreed-to matters outlined above.

The following news release was published on November 20, 1945:

MARLIN FIREARMS BUYS ASSETS OF HUNTER ARMS

ALBANY, N.Y. — Nov. 20 — (Special) — Marlin Firearms Company of New Haven, Conn., today received confirmation of its purchase of the assets of the Hunter Arms Company, Inc., Fulton, N.Y., and will immediately reopen the Hunter plant as the L.C. Smith Gun Company for production of the L.C. Smith side-by-side shotguns.

The deal was completed here before Federal Judge Stephen W. Brennan in United States Court in Albany. Closed since last April 25, Hunter has been in process or reorganization under Chapter 10 of the Bankruptcy Act and was represented in court by Judge Maurice B. Conley of Fulton, trustee, and Leonard H. Amdursky, attorney for the trustee. Roger Kenna, vice-president, and Edward J. Brennan, counsel, represented Marlin. Under reorganization plans announced by Frank Kenna, Marlin president, the Hunter plant will be put into immediate operation, concentrating on the L.C. Smith guns, "to meet the present pressing demand for sporting weapons throughout the country." Repair work on guns sent

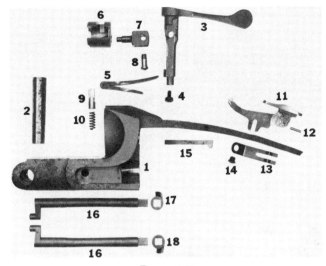

Frame parts.

1. Frame
2. Hinge Pin
3. Top lever
4. Top lever screw
5. Top lever spring
6. Bolt
7. Coupler
8. Coupler screw
9. Trip
10. Trip spring
11. Safety
12. Safety pin
13. Safety spring
14. Safety spring screw
15. Safety push rod
16. Cocking rod (2)
17. Lifter, right
18. Lifter, left

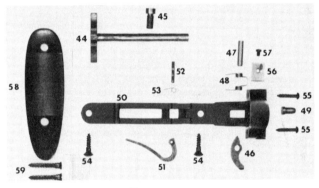

Trigger parts.

32. Trigger plate screw, top
33. Trigger plate
34. Trigger plate screw, front
35. Trigger plate screw, rear
36. Trigger, front
37. Trigger, rear
38. Trigger pin
39. Trigger spring
40. Safety link
41. Safety link pin
42. Trigger guard
43. Trigger guard screw

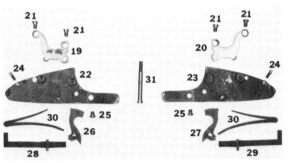

Lock plate parts.

19. Bridle, left
20. Bridle, right
21. Bridle screw (4)
22. Lock plate, left
23. Lock plate, right
24. Mainspring retaining screw (2)
25. Lock plate retaining screw (2)
26. Hammer, left, with pin
27. Hammer, right, with pin
28. Sear, left
29. Sear, right
30. Mainspring (2)
31. Lock plate connector screw

Forearm parts.

44. Extractor
45. Extractor screw
46. Extractor activator
47. Extractor activator pin
48. Extractor activator spring
49. Extractor activator bar
50. Forend iron
51. Forend spring
52. Forend spring pin
53. Forend spring retracting spring
54. Forend screw (2)
55. Rear forend screw (2)
56. Cocking plate
57. Cocking plate screw
58. Butt plate
59. Butt plate screw (2)

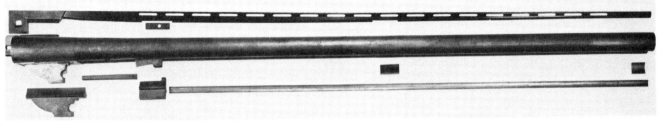

Barrel parts.

L.C. Smith Gun Company Ideal grade L.C. Smith shotgun.

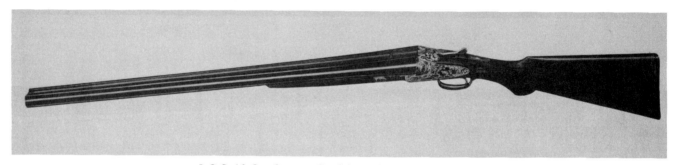

L.C. Smith Gun Company Specialty grade L.C. Smith shotgun.

to the factory during the period of receivership will be handled as speedily as possible, Mr. Kenna said, adding that if repairs cannot be made, owners will be so advised and in cases where money has been advanced, refunds will be made. Preliminary work has already been completed in the four-story brick Hunter building at Fulton, where new equipment will be installed, new production methods adopted and workers engaged in line with Marlin's extensive expansion program.

"This purchase represents part of the plan for increased production by the Marlin Firearms Company, which this year is celebrating its 75th anniversary in the sporting gun field," Mr. Kenna said. "Hunter has been producing three well-known shotguns, namely, the L.C. Smith, the Hunter and the Fulton. For the immediate future, we intend to concentrate chiefly on production of the L.C. Smith, which, as a side-by-side double-barreled shotgun, makes a perfect companion piece to our own Marlin over-and-under shotgun."

Under a plan of reorganization set up by Judge Conley as trustee, The Marlin Firearms Company, of which Frank Kenna is president, acquires 1,000 shares of stock of a new Corporation. This new Corporation will settle a claim pending from the United States Navy, and also, will settle the claims of all general creditors on a percentage basis. Marlin is contributing additional capital necessary to reestablish and resume operation at Fulton.

Hunter Arms Company achieved a wide reputation for some of the best guns ever manufactured for the use of sportsmen, and the manufacture of these famous guns will be continued by The Marlin Firearms Company.

On December 20, 1945, the following statement was released to New York City newspapers:

> Organization of the L.C. Smith Gun Company, Inc., of Fulton, N.Y., as a subsidiary of The Marlin Firearms Company, New Haven, Conn. with Roger Kenna as president, was announced in New York yesterday, December 19. Mr. Kenna continues as vice-president in charge of sales and advertising of the Marlin Company and will divide his time between the Marlin offices at New York (17 East 42nd Street) and New Haven, and the L.C. Smith plant at Fulton. Frank Kenna, president of The Marlin Firearms Company, is vice-president of the new Company.
>
> The new Corporation, incorporated in New York State, replaces the Hunter Arms Company, the assets of which Marlin recently purchased. The Fulton plant is now in operation, producing the L.C. ("Elsie") Smith side-by-side shotgun to complete the line of Marlin's shotguns and rifles. Former Hunter employees have returned to work in the plant, which was closed last April, and new employees are being added as rapidly as new equipment can be installed, Mr. Kenna said.

The Marlin Firearms Company did revitalize the production of the L.C. Smith shotgun, although the number of grades and options available were reduced. During the L.C. Smith Gun Company's short-lived production of the L.C. Smith from November 26, 1945 to January 17, 1949, a total of 58,083 were manufactured. During the preceding nine years of Hunter Arms Company operation, approximately the same number of guns was made. In fact, a careful review of the production figures for the period of 1918 to 1945 shows only two years with production over 13,000. (These figures also include Fulton and Hunter shotguns.) The L.C. Smith Gun Company manufactured 13,000 or more guns per year during three years of its four-year history. The first year of operation produced over 8,000 guns.

On January 16, 1949, after three years of full operation, the L.C. Smith Gun Company was hit with a catastrophe. As a result of a violent storm, a section of the first floor of the four-story factory collapsed into the 18-foot raceway that ran beneath the ground floor. Numerous pieces of equipment and about 14 milling machines were in the tangled pile. The other floors above were weakened by the collapse of support beams. All work was suspended until a complete evaluation of the damage could be made. Early estimates indicated that at least $75,000 in material damage was done.

On January 19, 1949, the *Oswego Valley News* reported the disaster as follows:

250 FORCED OUT OF WORK AS FULTON GUN CO. FLOOR COLLAPSES, LOSS $75,000

FULTON—A 30-foot-square section of flooring on the first floor of the L.C. Smith Gun Co. plant, N. Second and Eric Sts. collapsed with a roar shortly after 1 a.m. yesterday with beams, flooring, 14 milling machines and other equipment crashing into an 18-foot raceway running beneath the four-story plant.

Although company officials said they were unable at present to estimate damage, indications were that it would reach $75,000.

Supports Weakened

The collapse weakened supports for the second, third and fourth floors over the first floor area that broke thru and plant officials announced work would be suspended as a precautionary measure until surveys could determine measures necessary to strengthen the other floors.

Closing of the plant will temporarily put 250 employees out of work. Employees were notified by telephone and radio yesterday of the plant shutdown.

Officials said that had the collapse occurred during working hours, it might have resulted in a heavy loss of life.

Workmen were busy throughout the day removing heavy machinery on the second and third floors from the danger areas. Crews worked with blocks and tackle to move three lathe machines, each weighing two tons, from the second floor directly over the weakened first floor area.

The second floor over the collapsed section sagged considerably until the lathes were moved. It was reported approximately 12 tons of unfinished gun barrel stock stored on the fourth floor will be moved today.

John Victory, night watchman, was approximately 300 feet away on the first floor when the section collapsed. He notified company officials and work was begun to lessen further danger over weakened areas on other floors.

Engineers were reported enroute to Fulton from New Haven, Conn. and are expected to arrive Monday morning to make a complete survey on measures to be taken to repair the damage and to strengthen other areas of the building.

The gun company is one of the city's oldest manufacturing firms and has manufactured firearms of specific designs in many instances for several noted persons throughout the country.

L.C. Smith Gun Co. is a subsidiary of Marlin Firearms Co.

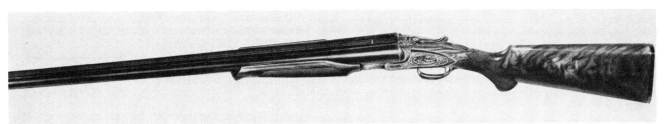

L.C. Smith Gun Company Crown grade L.C. Smith shotgun.

L.C. Smith Gun Company Premier Skeet grade L.C. Smith shotgun.

of New Haven, Conn. The Fulton plant, one of the oldest industries in the city, was operated for many years at the Hunter Arms Co.

The officials of the L.C. Smith Gun Company conducted an appraisal of the options available and decided upon a course that would furnish guns on hand and complete guns in process without major investment in reconstruction or in building a new factory. During this period, a study was also to be made with regard to a possible move of the L.C. Smith shotgun operation to the Marlin factory. The study of the feasibility of a relocation to New Haven would, of course, center on the question, "Can the L.C. Smith gun be manufactured in New Haven, at a profit?"

The study indicated that the loss of key supervisory personnel familiar with the many technicalities of making the Smith shotgun, and the already overloaded supervisory personnel at Marlin being assigned additional duties, would either cause Marlin production to suffer or show no gain in Smith production. In addition, part-by-part production of the Smith gun was more complex than any gun made by Marlin. Furthermore, the Smith gun, because of its construction, required a prolonged time span to carry components from early machining stages through to a completed gun. As a consequence, errors in manufacture could go undetected until many months after the mistake was made.

The L.C. Smith Company officials decided to stop production of the L.C. Smith shotgun and to close the Fulton operation, dispose of the property, and move the unfinished parts, tooling, fixtures, and machinery to New Haven, either for use in making Marlin firearms, or for storage in anticipation of making the Smith gun sometime in the future.

Frank Kenna, Jr., who became president of The Marlin Firearms Company upon the death of his older brother Roger in 1959, always appreciated fine guns and in particular the L.C. Smith shotgun. He felt that such a fine gun should not be stored away in cases and crates and never again see the light of day. The result of this deep feeling is best illustrated by the following news release dated January 2, 1967 (nearly 18 years to the day after the collapse of the old Fulton, N.Y. factory).

RETURN OF THE L.C. SMITH

Rumors about the return of the L.C. Smith have been flying for more than a year. Now they've come to roost right at The Marlin Firearms Co. The popular side-lock, side-by-side double gun really is making a comeback. The first of a very limited production of L.C. Smith field grade shotguns will be produced during 1967. There will be only a few made before the hunting season. And it will have to continue as a limited item. There's just too much handwork to do otherwise.

L.C. Smith came to Marlin through a direct purchase of the Company in 1945. Marlin management produced more than 60,000 guns at the old Fulton, N.Y. plant before rising costs forced the gun off the market in 1951. The Fulton plant was shut down. But somebody then was planning ahead. What could be salvaged was moved to Marlin's New Haven, Conn. plant. Tools, dies, sundry parts in various stages of manufacture—a partial production capability was put into storage.

"But the L.C. Smith is too good to let die," said Marlin president, Frank Kenna, Jr. "It's contrary to every principle of production economy, but we are finding ways to produce it without losing money."

Marlin engineers have been working more than two years to develop production techniques that do not compromise the quality that made the L.C. Smith famous. They started with the original design drawings and strict orders from President Kenna.

"It must be the L.C. Smith. It must close with an audible snap, have good case coloring and wood-to-metal fit. It must be made RIGHT."

That's a tall order at today's prices. But Marlin is one gunmaker with a dogged determination to build guns as they should be built. Traditional gun quality is the watchword with all Marlin models. Making the L.C. Smith just calls for more of the same.

As with any good double gun, the L.C. Smith is virtually handmade. Parts must be fitted together precisely. You can't scramble pieces of several guns and put them back any old way. There's no "mass production" here.

A side-lock gun is rare. It's harder to make than the common box-lock design. You can distinguish the side-lock by its sideplates fitted into the frame and extending back where they are inletted into the stock. These sideplates contain the entire firing mechanism, a separate plate for each barrel. A box-lock gun contains the lock mechanism inside the frame.

Most experts agree that the side-lock design is superior. It's stronger because less frame metal is removed. It's sleek and more attractive. But Marlin did find production economies. They had to or else forget the whole idea. Through the use of modern steels and production technology, the major problems were solved. The first of the new L.C. Smith shotguns will be copies of the original except for the addition of a ventilated rib. They will be side-lock, double trigger, standard extractor field grade guns just like Smith made—but 12 gauge only. They will have 28-inch barrels bored Modified and Full Choke but plans are to add Improved Cylinder and Modified in a 26 inch barrel.

What happens next will depend on the response and acceptance of this pilot model—and what is learned in final production stages.

Until they could be updated or replaced, some of the original fixtures were used by Marlin in making the Smith shotgun. Some of the original methods of fabrication also were used until new engineering and new technology could be introduced. Many parts of the gun were made from forgings or very expensive investment castings of the highest grade alloy steels. The only deviation from previously made Smiths was the aluminum ventilated rib (Poly-Choke).

A total of 1,959 L.C. Smith shotguns were manufactured by Marlin during this training and exploratory period, and it was concluded that a gun could be produced equal in quality to the earlier L.C. Smiths and at a reasonable profit; the double-barrel enthusiast, however, wanted the more expensive and difficult-to-manufacture features of a steel rib, single trigger, beavertail forend, automatic ejectors, and options in gauge, barrel length, choke, and engraving.

In consideration of the desires of sportsmen, and the increased competition from the European and oriental imports, it was wisely decided to once again box up the tools and retire from the production of the L.C. Smith shotgun.

PRODUCTION DATA

Date	Name	Gun	Total
1946–1950	L.C. Smith Gun Company	Double-Barrel	57,928
1946–1950	L.C. Smith Gun Company	Single-Barrel	155
1968–1971	The Marlin Firearms Company	Double-Barrel	1,959

Total L.C. Smith Shotguns Manufactured by the
L.C. SMITH GUN COMPANY
(Subsidiary of The Marlin Firearms Company)

	Dec. 21, 1945 to Jan. 19, 1948	May 27, 1946 to June 19, 1950	
	From serial number 202,968 to serial number 206,909	From serial number FWS 1 to serial number FWS 56,800	
Double-Barrel			Total
Grade			
Field	1,176	52,135	53,311
Ideal	121	3,829	3,950
Premier Skeet	—	507	507
Specialty	32	76	108
Crown	9	39	48
Deluxe	3	—	3
Skeet Special	1	—	1
Single-Barrel			
Grade			
Specialty	—	1	1
Olympic	4	150	154
Total			58,083

Total L.C. Smith Shotguns Shipped by
THE MARLIN FIREARMS COMPANY
1968–1971

Serial Number	Type	Total
56,801 to 59,152	Field Grade	1,777
100,000 to 100,188	Deluxe Field Grade	182
Total		1,959

Recapitulation of L.C. Smith Gun Company serial numbers by years (1944–1950).

From	To	Year	Total
202,960	204,084	1944	1,124
204,085	205,423	1945	1,338
FWS 1	8,595	1946	8,594
8,596	25,661	1947	17,065
25,662	41,825	1948	16,163
41,826	55,608	1949	13,728
55,609	56,800	1950	1,191

Recapitulation of Marlin Firearms Company L.C. Smith shotguns manufactured and shipped, by year.

Field Grade

1969	479
1970	631
1971	295
1972	168
1973	196
1974	9
Total	1,777

Deluxe Field Grade

1971	138
1972	44
Total	182

Collectors and dealers are always interested in the original sale price of valuable firearms. The L.C. Smith shotgun connoisseur can better appreciate his possession if he has a reasonable understanding of the original cost of the shotgun. Also, the changes in economic conditions that affect the marketplace can be noted. A recap of both L.C. Smith, Syracuse, N.Y., and Hunter Arms Company retail prices is shown here. I attempted to maintain a five-year interval; however, this varied somewhat due to the limited records available.

L.C. SMITH — SYRACUSE
BAKER

THREE-BARREL 1881–1885		DOUBLE-BARREL 1881–1884	
Quality 5	$200	Quality F	$200
4	150	E	150
3	125	D	100
2	100	C	80
1	75	B	55–60
		A	40–50

L.C. SMITH GUNS

NEW L.C. SMITH HAMMERLESS 1883–1888		NEW L.C. SMITH HAMMER 1883–1888	
Quality 7	$450	Quality AA	$300
6	300	A	200
5	200	B	150
4	150	C	125
3	100	D	95
2	80	E	70
		F	55

HUNTER ARMS COMPANY

HAMMERLESS	1892	1898	1901	1907	1912
A–3	POA	$740	$740	$740	$587
A–2	POA	390	390	390	325
A–1	POA	175	—	—	—
PIGEON	POA	150	140	140	110
MONOGRAM	$300	375	365	365	281
5	200	225	215	215	168
4	150	175	165	165	127
3	100	125	115	115	90
2	80	105	95	95	75
1	POA	75	75	75	60
0	—	47	60	60	48
00	—	—	50	50	32
HAMMER					
AA	$300	$300	$300	$300	—
A	200	200	200	200	—
B	150	150	150	150	—
C	125	125	125	125	—
D	95	95	95	95	—
E	70	70	70	70	—
F	55	55	55	25	$21

POA — Price on application

GRADE	1913	1919	1924	1931	1936	1941	1950
Deluxe	$1000	$1150	$1032	$1126	$1196	$1530	—
Premier	562	675	688	753	832	846	—
Monogram	281	397	408	468	525	639	—
Crown	157	244	221	243	292	315	$515
Eagle	115	180	150	176	—	—	—
Specialty	69	105	108	104	118	149	230
Trap	55	86	85	85	95	—	—
Skeet	—	—	—	61	65	100	251
Ideal	37	67	66	66	74	102	138
Field	25	54	57	50	57	80	99
One Barrel	—	138	138	135	146	154	159
Hammer	18	42	36	34	—	—	—
Fulton	—	42	35	29	30	41	—
Fulton Special	—	46	40	34	—	—	—

Marlin no longer makes repairs on or furnishes parts for L.C. Smith shotguns that were manufactured in Fulton, N.Y., by either the Hunter Arms Company or the L.C. Smith Gun Company. The few parts remaining for the L.C. Smith shotgun manufactured by Marlin between 1969 and 1974 are not sold as spare parts to individuals. They are for factory repair only. Correspondence with regard to these Marlin-made L.C. Smiths should be directed to the Marlin Gun Service Division, 100 Kenna Drive, North Haven, Conn. 06473.

No specific information is available for L.C. Smith shotguns manufactured by Lyman Cornelius Smith in Syracuse, N.Y., or the Baker shotguns that were manufactured by Mr. Smith.

BOLT ACTION SHOTGUNS

In 1956, Marlin introduced a bolt action repeating shotgun that is still in production. The original designs of the trigger mechanism, receiver and bolt, and the magazine were invented and patented by W.F. Roper and Frederick J. Wright. The patents were assigned by the inventors to Savage Arms Corporation, Utica, N.Y. The patent numbers were 2,765,558; 2,765,562; and 2,765,563; all dated October 9, 1956. The double extractor used in this gun was invented by Marlin's director of research and development, Tom Robinson; his patent number was 2,465,553. The patent also applied to the Model 336 rifles.

On August 2, 1957, Marlin acquired the rights from the Savage Arms Corporation to use, royalty-free, the Roper inventions under the Marlin name for the sum of $500.00.

The variations of the bolt action repeating shotgun that Marlin manufactured were as follows:

Year	Model	Gauge
1954–1964	Model 55 Hunter	12 and 20 gauge
1961–1966	Model 55 Hunter	16 gauge
1962–1988	Model 55 Goose Gun	12 gauge
1963–1965	Model 55 Swamp Gun	12 gauge
1961–1965	Model 55G (Glenfield)	12, 16, and 20 gauge
1966–1973	Glenfield Model 50	12 and 20 gauge
1973–1979	Model 55 Slug Gun	12 gauge
1976–1985	Model 5510	10 gauge

The variations of the bolt action single-shot shotguns were as follows:

Year	Model	Caliber
1959–1965	Model 59	.410
1960–1964	Model 60G (Glenfield)	.410
1962	Model 61G (Glenfield)	.410

Model 55 Hunter 12-Gauge Bolt Action Shotgun (1954–1964)

Although the rights to produce the gun patented by the Savage Arms Corporation had not been sealed until 1957, Marlin started production of the Model 55 Hunter shotgun in 1954. This model was first available in 12 gauge. In 1956, a 20-gauge version was added. The 12-gauge gun had a 28-in. full choke barrel, and the 20-gauge gun had a 26-in. barrel, also full choke. Also added to the line in 1956 was a 12-gauge model having an adjustable choke. The 1956 catalog described the Model 55 Hunter bolt action shotgun as follows:

Model 55 Hunter 12-gauge shotgun.

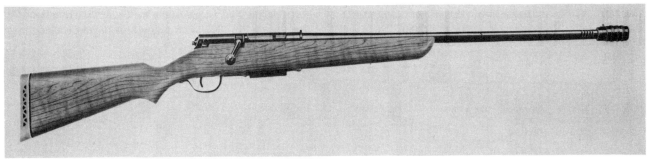

Model 55 Hunter 12-gauge shotgun fitted with Marlin's Micro-Choke.

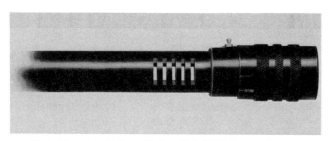

Vented barrel and Micro-Choke of Model 55 Hunter shotgun.

Model 55–Hunter shotgun is a bolt action repeater bored full choke in 12- or 20-gauge, 12-gauge 28″ barrel, 20-gauge 26″ barrel. Clip magazine holds 2 shots. Chambered for 2¾″ shells only. Available with three position choke device in 12-gauge only. It's the only shotgun offered currently with factory drilling and tapping for the Lyman 40 SM receiver peep sight. Peep sight ideal for hunters using shotgun slugs for big game and deer. Positive Sear Lock Safety. Patented Marlin double extractors for positive extraction and ejection. Barrel, receiver and all action parts made of high quality alloy and carbon steel carefully heat treated. High grade recoil pad on 12-gauge at no additional cost. One take-down screw for quick and easy disassembly. Improved recoil absorbing system. Visible indicator at rear of breech bolt tells when gun is cocked. Smartly fashioned walnut stock of finest quality with oil finish. Action taken down 35¾″; overall length 49″. Pull 14″, drop at comb about 1⅝″, drop at heel about 2½″. Weight about 7¼ lbs. in 12-gauge; 6½ lbs. in 20-gauge depending on density of wood.

The muzzle end of the 12-gauge gun with adjustable choke also had vent slots on both sides of the barrel. The new Micro-Choke's operation was as follows:

> Marlin's new Micro Choke is offered only with the Model 55-Hunter Shotgun in 12-gauge. New choke has 16 different settings from full choke through modified choke to improved cylinder. Eight marks on the Micro Choke sleeve allow 8 adjustments of choke between modified and full. Since two complete turns of the choke sleeve are used to move from full choke to improved cylinder, 8 more adjustments of choking are possible between modified and improved cylinder, thus giving better control of patterns for all distances, whether it's a close shot at a rabbit or a long shot at duck or geese.
>
> Micrometer markings on adjusting sleeve give finer choke settings than other adjustable chokes permit. Ventilated slots on muzzle end of gun improves patterns and reduces recoil by permitting radial gas escape before shot leaves muzzle.

In 1961, Marlin added the 16-gauge shell to the Model 55 Hunter shotgun. It remained available until 1966. The barrel

of the 16-gauge model was 28 inches. The gun weighed approximately 7¼ pounds.

The Model 55 Hunter 12-gauge gun was made for use with 2¾-in. shells. It was not designed for 3-in. shells. The same is true for the 20-gauge gun.

In 1958, a recoil pad was added to the 12-gauge model. In 1961, the barrel slots were eliminated from the 12-gauge barrels that were fitted with an adjustable choke.

In 1965, the Hunter models were no longer listed in the catalog.

The suggested retail prices of the Model 55 Hunter shotguns were as follows:

Year	12-gauge	12-gauge w/choke	16-gauge	20-gauge
1954	$32.80			
1955	32.80			
1956	34.80	$38.80		
1957–1959	35.95	39.95		$31.95
1960	35.95	39.95	$35.95	33.95
1961	38.95	43.95	38.95	38.95
1962	39.95	41.95	39.95	39.95
1963	39.95	44.95	39.95	39.95
1964	39.95	44.95		

The production of the Model 55 Hunter bolt action shotgun was 61,973 for 12-gauge; for 12-gauge with choke, the total production was 30,855. There were 3,079 16-gauges made, and 18,286 20-gauges.

Model 55 Goose Gun (1962 to date)

In 1962, Marlin introduced another 12-gauge bolt action shotgun. This one had a barrel 36 inches long. It was choked full. The new model was identified as the Model 55 Goose Gun and, with only minor changes, is still in production.

The 1962 catalog described the Model 55 Goose Gun as follows:

> Marlin "Goose Gun"—Shoots 12-gauge 3-inch Magnums and regular 2¾ inch shells! Extra long 36 inch full choke barrel for long-range shots at high-flying geese and ducks. Good for deer, fox, coyotes, too!
>
> Specifications: 3 shots; approx. wt. 7¼ lbs.; 57-in. overall length; patented extractors; drilled, tapped for deer slug receiver sights; swivels, carrying strap; gold-plated trigger; 2 clips; recoil pad.

In 1964, a sling was added to the Goose Gun to make carrying it easier. In 1980, Marlin introduced a new buckle sling, a

Model 55 Goose Gun.

white line butt spacer, a burnished bore, and an elevated rear sight. The stock was changed from American walnut to walnut-finished hardwood in 1982. In 1983, the white line spacer was dropped. In 1988, the sling and swivels were dropped and the stock was equipped with QD studs instead.

Some sportsmen purchase the Model 55 Goose Gun because of a long-standing opinion that a long barrel will shoot farther and harder than a short barrel. The fact is, however, that a 28-in. full choke barrel will pattern as well as a 36-in. full choke barrel. The advantage of the Goose Gun's 36-in. barrel is in the smooth swing of a long barrel and the added length to the sight radius. Otherwise, it gives an average of 70% patterns in a 30-in. circle at 40 yards.

The suggested retail prices of the Model 55 Goose Gun were as follows:

Year	Model 55 Goose Gun
1962–1963	$48.95 w/o sling
1964–1967	49.95
1968–1970	54.95
1971	62.95
1972–1974	69.95
1975	74.95
1976	81.95
1977	86.95
1978	88.95
1979	96.95
1980	115.95
1981	144.95
1982	159.95
1983–1984	160.95
1985	171.95

Year	Model 55 Goose Gun
1986	180.95
1987	194.95
1988	213.95

From 1962 to 1982, 172,745 Model 55 Goose Guns were manufactured.

Model 55 Swamp Gun (1963–1965)

To fill the needs of sportsmen wanting a short-barreled shotgun, Marlin introduced in 1963 a gun suited for use in heavy cover and for upland game. It was fitted with the Marlin Micro-Choke. It was described as follows:

> Marlin "Swamp Gun." New short, fast-handling shotgun at a modest price. Marlin Micro-Choke. 20½ inch barrel for hunting upland game, deer in heavy cover! Shoots 3 inch Magnum or regular 12 gauge shells.
>
> Specifications: 3 fast shots; 2 clips; approx. wt. 6½ lbs.; 41½ in. overall length; patented extractors; drilled, tapped for deer slug receiver sights; swivels, strap; gold-plated trigger recoil pad.

The Swamp gun's suggested retail price was, by year, as follows:

Year	Price
1963–1964	$46.95
1965	49.95

A total of 1,493 Swamp guns were manufactured.

Model 55 Swamp Gun.

Model 55G.

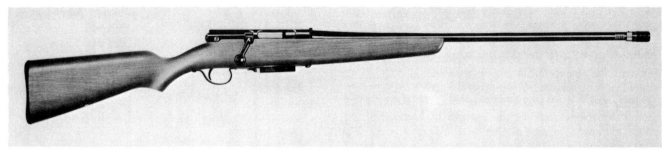

Model 55G with choke.

Model 55G (Glenfield) Bolt Action Shotgun (1961–1965)

The low-priced line of firearms made by Marlin for the mass-merchandisers and quantity buyers were identified as Glenfield models. This name was first used by the Glenfield Products Division of Marlin that handled all sales to chain outlets. In due time, the Glenfield Division was phased out and the name thereafter was used to identify certain less expensive models. The Model 55G shotgun was one of the first guns to be identified as a Glenfield. It was described as follows:

> Deluxe shotgun features at a low price. Outstanding field performance. Choice of 12, 16 or 20 gauge. 12 gauge also with Micro-Choke. 3 steady shots. 12 and 16 gauge have full choke 28″ barrels, 20 gauge has full choke 26″ barrel.

The 55G had a 2-shot clip magazine; one in the chamber gave it a 3-shot capacity. It handled 2¾ inch shells in 12, 16 and 20 gauges; the 12-gauge gun weighed about 7¼ pounds and the 20 gauge weighed about 6½ pounds, depending on the density of the wood. The 55G 12- and 16-gauge guns were 49 inches long and the 20-gauge gun was 47 inches long. The safety of the 55G was of the positive sear lock type and there was a visible indicator at the rear of the breech bolt that showed when the gun was choked.

By removal of one screw, the barrel and receiver could be removed from the stock. The receiver was drilled and tapped for the Lyman 40SM receiver sight. The stock was of one piece of finest-quality selected hardwood (birch). The length of pull was 14 inches; the drop at the comb was 1⅝ inches, with a 2½-in. drop at the heel. The 12-gauge model was available with the Marlin Micro-Choke.

The 55G had a hard rubber butt plate until 1965, when the 12-gauge model was fitted with a rubber recoil pad.

The suggested retail price of the Model 55G was as follows:

Year	12-, 16-, and 20-gauge	12-gauge w/choke
1961	$39.95	$36.95
1962–1968	41.95	38.95
1964	42.95	38.95
1965	46.95	39.95

The production of the Model 55G was as follows:

Model	12-gauge	16-gauge	20-gauge	12-gauge w/choke
55G	12,351	3,901	4,762	4,814

Model 50 Glenfield, 12- and 20-gauge, Shotguns (1966–1973)

In 1966, the Model 55G became the Model 50 Glenfield. The change in designation was made because the gun was now capable of handling 3-in. shells in both the 12- and 20-gauge models. Otherwise, the Model 50 was the same as the earlier Model 55G. The Model 50 was not manufactured in a 16-gauge model. Only in 1966 was it available with the Marlin Micro-Choke device fitted to the muzzle.

The Model 50 Glenfield was described by Marlin as follows:

> Model 50 Shotgun, bored full choke. Great 3-shot bolt action shotgun for all upland game, waterfowl and deer shooting. 12 gauge and 20 gauge available. Chambered for 3-inch Magnum shells (also uses standard 2¾ inch shells). 12 gauge guns have recoil pad. Walnut finish American hardwood stock. Barrel length: 12 gauge, 28 inches; 20 gauge, 26 inches.

The Model 50's suggested retail prices were as follows:

Glenfield 50 bolt action shotgun, 12 & 20 ga.

Model 50 Glenfield.

Year	12- or 20-gauge	12-gauge w/choke
1966	$41.95	$48.95
1967	41.95	
1968	41.95	
1969	48.95	
1970–1971	49.95	
1972–1973	52.95	
1979	89.95 (12 gauge only)	

Although discontinued in 1973, the Model 50 Glenfield was reinstated in 1979 for only that year.

The production of the Model 50 was as follows:

Model	12-gauge	20-gauge
50 Glenfield	89,883	8,723

Model 55 Slug Gun (1973–1979)

The Model 55 Slug Gun was another bolt action shotgun based on the Model 55 Hunter gun. Marlin described it thus:

> The new Model 55S is a perfect heavy cover deer gun. Its short 24 inch barrel gets into action fast. It comes with iron sights — rear sight is adjustable — and is drilled and tapped for scope mounting. Chambered for 2¾ and 3 inch shells, the 55S is also equipped with swivels, a handy leather carrying strap and a quality recoil pad. 2-shot clip magazine. About 7 pounds. Overall length 45 inches.

The model was discontinued in 1979. By year, the suggested retail price was as follows:

Year	Price
1973	$73.95
1974	74.95
1975	79.95
1976	86.95
1977	92.95
1978	94.95
1979	103.95

There were 4,221 Model 55 Slug guns manufactured from 1973 to 1979.

Model 5510, 10-gauge, Bolt Action Shotgun (1976–1985)

An oversize Model 55 shotgun was designed in 1976 to handle the 3½-in. 10-gauge magnum shotshell. By single loading, it would also fire the regular 3-in. shell. Called the Super Goose Gun, the Model 5510 would handle shells with two full ounces of No. 2 shot. The barrel was 34 inches long and choked full. The gun weighed 10½ pounds. It had an extra-thick ventilated recoil pad and was 55½ inches in overall length. The stock was American walnut, until 1983 when the stock was changed to walnut-finished hardwood (birch). The sling swivels were of the quick detachable (QD) type, and a leather sling was included. The trigger was gold-plated until 1983. From then on it was blued. At this same time, the white line spacer was eliminated.

The suggested retail prices of the Model 5510 Super Goose Gun were as follows:

Year	Price
1976	$149.95
1977	159.95

Model 55 Slug Gun.

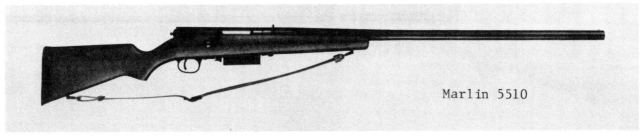

Model 5510 10-gauge shotgun.

Year	Price
1978	163.95
1979	177.90
1980	206.95
1981	238.95
1982–1983	263.95
1984	263.95
1985	281.95

Total production of the Marlin Model 5510 Super Goose Gun was 21,825.

SINGLE-SHOT SHOTGUNS

Model 59, Single-Shot, Bolt Action, .410 Shotgun (1959–1965)

The Model 59 single-shot shotgun was an ideal beginner's or youngster's shotgun. It was identified in the 1959 price list as the Model 59, "Olympic," .410 Gauge. However, in none of the catalogs from 1959 through 1965 was the Model 59 identified as Olympic. (I imagine that Marlin felt the name *Olympic* could be construed as being connected somehow to the Olympic Games, and thereby be misleading. Therefore, it was not used again in catalogs or later price lists.)

The Model 59 was chambered for use with either 2½- or 3-in. shells. It had an automatic safety (patent number 2,976,637, dated March 28, 1961) that was also used in the Model 122 single-shot .22 rifle. The safety could not be put off until the bolt was closed and fully cocked. Thus, the user had to put the safety into the fire position before a shot could be fired. Each time the bolt was operated, the safety automatically went to the on safe position. The stock had a pistol grip and was walnut. The barrel was 24 inches long and blued. The

choke was bored full and the barrel had a bead front sight. In the 1960 catalog, the overall length was listed as 41 inches. In the 1962 catalog, the overall length was 43¾ inches. The 1961 catalog listed the length of pull as 14 inches, or 12 inches for junior shooters. The shotgun weighed about 5 pounds, depending upon the density of the wood. The butt plate was hard rubber with white line spacer. The 1962 catalog illustrated the Model 59 without the white spacer and with a pistol grip cap. The 1963 catalog illustrated white line spacers with both the butt plate and the pistol grip cap.

The suggested retail prices of the Model 59 were as follows:

Year	Price
1959	$23.95 (Olympic)
1960–1961	26.95
1962	28.95
1963–1965	29.95

A total of 48,447 Model 59 shotguns were manufactured.

Model 60G (Glenfield) Bolt Action, Single-Shot, .410 Gauge Shotgun (1960–1964)

The Model 60 shotgun was identical to the Model 59 shotgun except that it had a chrome-plated trigger instead of gold-plated, and a stock made of walnut-finished hardwood (birch) instead of walnut.

The Model 60G was another ideal shotgun for youngsters and adults to use in learning to handle a shotgun. This model also had the automatic safety.

The 1960 catalog stated that a 12-in. trigger pull model was available for junior shooters, but no other reference has been located and production records do not reflect two types of Model 60 shotguns as being manufactured.

Model 59, .410-gauge shotgun.

Model 59, second variation.

Model 60, .410 gauge shotgun.

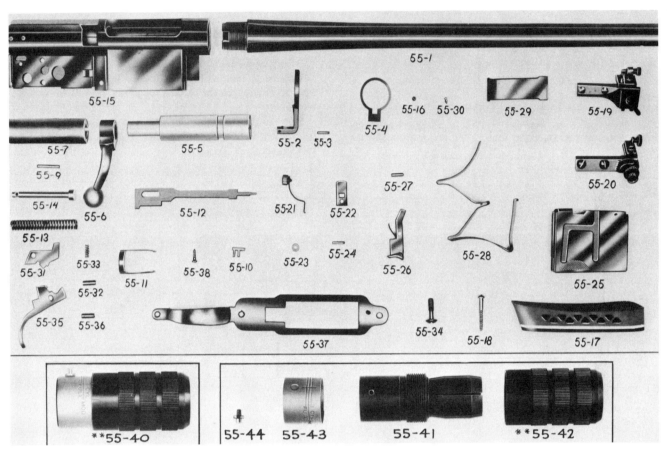

Parts of Marlin's bolt action repeating shotgun.

The full-choke Model 59 and Model 60G were bored to give 70% patterns into a 24-in. circle at 25 yards.

The suggested retail price of the Model 60G from 1960 to 1964 was $24.95.

A total of 18,603 of the Model 60G were manufactured.

Model 61G (Glenfield) Bolt Action, Single-Shot, .410 Gauge Shotgun (1962)

The Model 61G shotgun was identical to the Model 60G shotgun. It was listed for only one year, 1962. It was described and priced the same as the Model 60G. It was listed for a suggested retail price of $24.95, and records indicate that only 2,129 were manufactured.

9MM SHOTGUN

In some countries in Europe, hunting of small game and small birds is done with the 9-mm rimfire shot cartridge. Guns and ammunition are available in Europe chambered for the 9-mm shot cartridge, but in the U.S. only expensive imports are available. The Guilo-Fiocchi ammunition company of Italy approached Marlin in 1962 about Marlin making a gun chambered for the 9-mm shot cartridge, which it thought would help U.S. sales of its ammunition. In response to this idea, Marlin modified a few of the Model 122 single-shot caliber .22 rifles to 9-mm smooth bore. They were extensively tested, and patterns of all guns manufactured gave an average of 82 No. 9 pellets (out of 180 average No. 9 pellets per shotshell) in an 18-in. circle at 15 yards.

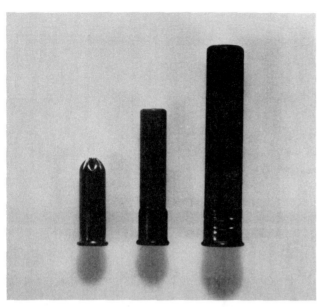

Left: *Metal-case 9-mm shotshell by Fiocchi.* Middle: *Paper-body 9-mm shotshell by RWS.* Right: *Short (2½") .410 bore shotshell for comparison.*

The modifications to the Model 122 included a lengthened square end to the receiver (for the lengthened bolt throw of the 9-mm shotshell); enlargement of the bolt face and firing pin; a 24-in. barrel; a .296-in. inside diameter; a cylinder bore; reduction of the Monte Carlo comb by ¼ inch; and a spring-loaded plunger to keep the bolt from sliding forward when the muzzle was depressed.

In 1963, the 9-mm rimfire shotshell was expensive. The German RWS shotshell cost $7.00 per hundred. It had a paper body with a gilded metal head. The Italian Fiocchi cost $8.50 a hundred; the entire case was metal. Marlin did not want to make a firearm dependent upon imported foreign ammunition. Therefore, the Federal Cartridge Company and Sears, Roebuck and Company were approached with the thought of a joint project—Federal to make the ammunition, Marlin to make the guns, and Sears to sell them.

After due consideration by all parties, the potential sales did not appear to support the cost of development of the ammunition by Federal, or the tooling for production of the new gun by Marlin.

Some of the fewer than 20 Marlin 9mm shotguns assembled have reached the collector's market. They are scarce and lots of fun to shoot.

Pump Action Rifles

GENERAL CHARACTERISTICS

From 1906 to 1932, Marlin manufactured a number of different pump action rifles (also frequently called trombone or slide action rifles). Rimfire and center-fire, and exposed hammer and hammerless were among the various models. The exposed hammer caliber .22 guns were the result of the inventive L.L. Hepburn. The hammerless models were the work of Carl "Gus" Swebilius and T.R. Hanitz. The pump action center-fire Model 27 was the work of J.H. Wheeler, G.A. Beck, and Melvin Hepburn.

The exposed hammer pump action Marlin caliber .22 rifles were as follows:

Model	Caliber	Years
18	.22 short or long rifle	1906–1908
20	.22 short, long, or long rifle	1907–1911
20A/20AS	.22 short, long, or long rifle	1911–1922
25/25S	.22 CB caps or shorts	1909–1910
29/29N	.22 short, long, or long rifle	1912–1917
37	.22 short, long, or long rifle	1923–1931
47	.22 short, long, or long rifle	1930–1931

The hammerless caliber .22 pump action rifles were the following two models:

Model	Caliber	Years
32	.22 short, long, or long rifle	1915
38	.22 short, long, or long rifle	1921–1930

The following models were exposed hammer center-fire pump action rifles:

Model	Caliber	Years
27	.25–20, .32–20	1909–1911
27S	.25RF, .25–20, .32–20	1913–1932

It was Marlin's usual practice to roll-stamp the barrel of each model manufactured with the date of the patents that applied to that model. In the case of the pump action rifles, some dates are for basic patents and other dates are for specific patents relating to that model only. The patents marked on the barrel of the Marlin pump action rifles were the following:

Pump Action Rifle Patents

Number	Date	Subject	Patentee	18	20	20A	20S	25	27	27S	29	29N	32	37	38	47
400,679	Apr. 2, 1889	Model 1889 rifle	L.L. Hepburn	X				X			X					
434,062	Aug. 12, 1890	Model 1891 rifle	L.L. Hepburn	X	X	X	X	X	X	X	X					
469,819	Mar. 1, 1892	Magazine tube	J.M. Marlin	X	X	X	X	X	X	X	X					
584,177	Jun. 8, 1897	Model 1897 T.D.	L.L. Hepburn	X	X	X	X		X	X						
776,243	Nov. 29, 1904	Pump action rifle	L.L. Hepburn		X	X	X	X	X	X	X					
882,563	Mar. 24, 1908	Pump action rifle	L.L. Hepburn								X			X		X
883,020	Mar. 24, 1908	Pump action rifle	L.L. Hepburn								X			X		X
997,642	Jul. 1, 1911	Model 27 rifle	*						X	X						
1,090,351	Mar. 17, 1914	Hammerless rifle	**										X		X	
1,110,827	Sept. 15, 1914	Hammerless rifle	**										X		X	
1,146,536	Jul. 13, 1915	Hammerless rifle	**										X		X	
1,147,659	Jul. 20, 1915	Hammerless rifle	**										X			

* J.H. Wheeler, G.A. Beck, and Melvin Hepburn
** C.G. Swebilius and H.T.B. Hanitz

It should be noted that the first pump action rifle was the Model 18, and that the mechanism of this rifle did not include Mr. Hepburn's innovations of 1904 or 1908. The 1904 invention was introduced with the Model 20. It was also used in the Model 25 and 29 rifles. L.L. Hepburn's 1908 patents were used in the late Model 20s, although the roll-stamp was not changed to reflect the improvement.

Serial numbers, high and low, for each of the pump action rifles observed or reported are as follows:

Model	Low	High
18	1581	18,246
20	29	29,134
20A	1303	15,928
20S	5808	A942
25	148	11,201
27	149	7889
27S	57	61,412
29	160	16,558
29N	214	3918
32	194	5957
37	490	12,455
38	782	10,938
	A-206	A-11,887
	D-393	D-1739
47	1247	5101

The serial number of most of the pump action rifles is found stamped into the metal on the left side of either the top or lower tang, underneath the wood stock. To see the number, the stock must be removed. However, the system was not uniform or consistent. For example, most Models 27, 37, and 38 have the serial number conspicuously marked on the bottom of the frame or tang.

The roll-stamp on the barrel of some models was not changed to reflect the incorporation in 1926 of the new Marlin Firearms Company as the manufacturer. Most examples examined of the Models 20, 27, 37, and 38 manufactured by The Marlin Firearms Corporation and The Marlin Firearms Company have the Marlin Firearms Corporation name roll-stamped on the barrel. Either the new company did not feel it important enough to invest in expensive new stamps, or there was a supply of already marked barrels on hand to last for some years. Even the Model 39 was not an exception to this. It too had the wrong company name on the barrel up until the Model 39A was introduced in 1938.

It is my guess that the lean years from 1926 to 1932 and the great cost of revitalizing a failed company prompted Frank Kenna and his new company to save money by using the old corporation stamps.

The characteristics of the basic models of the Marlin pump action rifles were as follows:

FEATURE		MODEL NUMBER								
		18	20	25	27	29	32	37	38	47
Exposed Hammer		X	X	X	X	X		X		X
Hammerless							X		X	
Caliber:	.22 short	X								
	CB cap & .22 short			X						
	.22 long rifle	X								
	.22 short, long, & long rifle		X				X	X	X	X
	.25–20, .32–20				X					
	.25 Rimfire				X					

FEATURE		18	20	25	27	29	32	37	38	47
Barrels:	Octagon	X	X		X		X		X	
	Round	X		X	X	X		X	X	X
	20-in.	X								
	22½-in.		X							
	23 in.			X		X				X
	24 in.				X			X	X	X
Takedown:	Stock	X		X						
	Receiver		X		X	X	X	X	X	X
Magazine:	Button								X	X
	Latch	X	X	X	X	X	X	X	X	
	½	X	X	X	X	X	X		X	
	⅔									X
	Full		X			X	X	X		
Rear Sight:	Fixed	X		X						
	Model 20		X							
	Swebilius						X		X	
	Rocky Mountain				X	X		X	X	X
Receiver:	Blued	X	X	X	X	X	X	X	X	
	Case Colored									X
Stock:	Pistol Grip				X		X		X	
	Straight	X	X	X		X		X		X
Butt Plate:	Steel (Blued)	X	X	X	X	X				X
	Hard Rubber						X	X	X	
Weight:	Octagon	3 lb., 11 oz.			5¾ lb.		5½ lb.		5½ lb.	
	Round	3 lb., 10 oz.		4 lb. 2 oz.	5¾ lb.	4¼ lb.			5½ lb.	
Length (in inches)		36	38¾	39½	42¼	39½	40	40	40	

DESCRIPTIONS OF PUMP ACTION RIFLES

Model 18

The Model 18 rifle was described by Marlin as follows:

> The Marlin Baby Featherweight Repeater is chambered to take both the .22 short and the .22 long rifle cartridges, but the rifles as sent out, will handle only the .22 short through the magazine and carrier. If the purchaser chooses to use the .22 long rifle cartridge, he can send to his dealer or to the factory and get an extra carrier for the .22 long rifle cartridge only, which will interchange with the carrier for shorts, in his rifle. These carriers may be interchanged at will, without tools, and in a moment's time. While the rifle with short carrier will not work any other length of cartridge through the action, and the rifle with long rifle carrier will not repeat with the short cartridge, all of these rifles can be used, single shot with the various short, long and long rifle cartridges, black or smokeless, including the hunting cartridges with mushroom bullet. The Model 18 will shoot these cartridges as accurately as any rifle made with equal length of barrel.

The breech mechanism of the Model 18 was simple. The locking bolt pivoted down in such a manner that it was against a part of the frame as soon as the action was closed. The action could be opened only when the firing pin was forward. To clean the inside of Marlin's exposed hammer pump action rifles, all that was necessary was to take off the side plate by unscrewing a thumbscrew. The internal parts were then exposed for removal and cleaning.

The roll-stamp on the Model 18 barrel read:

> Marlin Firearms Co., New-Haven CT USA. Pat'd April 2, 1889, Aug. 12, 1890, March 1, 1892, Nov. 29, 1904.

The Model 18 top tang was marked *Marlin No. 18*.

The Model 18 action was operated by moving the pump handle backward and forward about 1⅜ inches. The rifle with octagon barrel weighed 3 pounds, 11 ounces. With a round barrel, it weighed only 3 pounds, 10 ounces. It held 14 short cartridges in the magazine. Only 20-in. barrels were available. Rifles were blued. A case-colored frame was an extra. The standard butt plate was blued steel.

Prices for the Model 18 were as follows:

	1906	1907	1908
Model 18, round barrel	$12.50	$11.50	$11.50
Model 18, octagon barrel	13.00	12.00	12.00
Extra carrier	2.00	2.00	2.00
Extra for swivels and sling		1.50	1.50
See Extra section for other extras.			

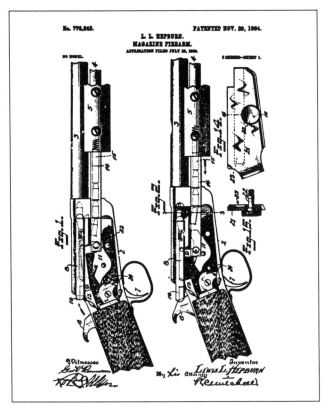

Patent drawing that illustrates the internal mechanism of Model 18, and later, slide action .22 rifles.

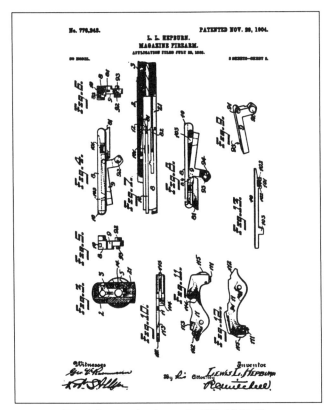

Patent drawing showing parts of Model 18 rifle.

1906 ad for the Model 18 rifle.

2—Breech Bolt.   6—Carrier.   13—Ejector.   25—Hammer.
29—Handle Slide.   30—Locking Bolt.

Catalog illustration of Model 18 rifle internal mechanism.

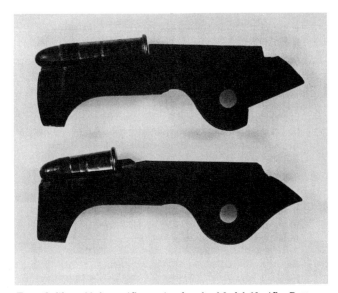

Top: *Caliber .22 long rifle carrier for the Model 18 rifle.* Bottom: *Caliber .22 short carrier for the Model 18 rifle.*

Pistol grips, half-octagon barrels, and other than blued steel butt plates could not be furnished. The overall length was 36 inches; with buttstock removed, 26¼ inches. The length of the buttstock from trigger to middle of butt plate was 13 inches; drop at comb, 1⅜ inches; drop at heel, 2½ inches.

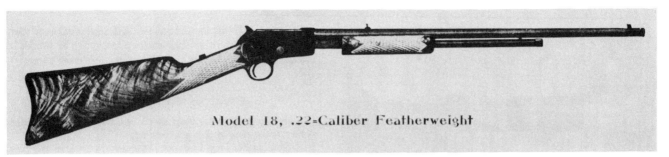

Catalog illustration of Model 18 rifle with special-order wood and checking.

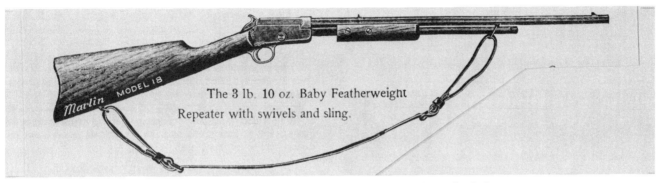

Catalog illustration of Model 18 rifle with special-order sling and swivels.

MODEL 18·25·25S

Number		Price
1I	Barrel, Round	$ 8.25
2I	Breech Bolt	3.30
3I	Buttstock	2.48
4I	Buttplate	1.65
5I	Buttplate Screws (2) ....each	.22
6I	Carrier	3.30
7I	Carrier Friction Spring	.44
8I	Carrier Pin	.22
9I	Carrier Stop Pin	.22
10I	Cartridge Cut-Off	.99
10I1	Cartridge Cut-Off Screw	.22
10I2	Cartridge Guard Base	.77
10I3	Cartridge Guard Base Screw	.22
10I4	Cartridge Guard Leaf	.88
10I5	Cartridge Guard Leaf Spring	.33
10I6	Cartridge Guard Leaf Spring Rivet	.22
10I7	Cartridge Guard Hinge Pin	.22
11I	Cartridge Guide Spring	.22
12I	Cartridge Guide Spring Screw	.22
13I	Ejector Base	1.32
14I	Ejector Wing	.22
15I	Ejector Screws (2) ....each	.22
16I	Ejector Pin	.22
17I	Ejector Spring	.33
18I	Extractor	.66
19I	Extractor Screw	.22
20I	Firing Pin Model 18	1.21
21I	Firing Pin Spring Model 18	.33
22I	Firing Pin Plunger	1.21
22I1	Firing Pin Spring Model 25	.33
23I	Firing Pin, Model 25-S	1.21
23I1	Firing Pin Plunger, Model 25-S	.44
23I2	Firing Pin Plunger Spring, Model 25-S	.33
23I3	Firing Pin Plunger, Model 25-S	.22
24I1	Forearm Screws (2) ....each	.33
24I2	Forearm Screw Escutcheons (2) ea.	.33

Number		Price
24I	Forearm	2.00
25I	Hammer	1.32
26I	Hammer Roller	.44
27I	Hammer Roller Pin	.22
28I	Hammer Screw	.44
29I	Handle Slide	1.65
30I	Locking Bolt	1.65
31I	Locking Bolt Plunger	.44
	(Cannot Supply Model 25)	
32I	Locking Bolt Plunger Spring	.33
33I	Locking Bolt Plunger Pin	.22
34I	Mainspring	.66
35I	Mainspring Screw	.22
36I	Magazine Tube (inside)	
	(Cannot Supply)	
37I	Magazine Tube (outside)	2.31
38I	Magazine Spring	.44
39I	Magazine Plug (inside)	.55
40I	Magazine Plug (outside)	.55
42I	Magazine Latch	.66
43I	Magazine Latch Pin	.22
44I1	Magazine Latch Spring	.33
44I	Magazine Follower	.66
45I	Magazine Follower Pin	.22
46I	Magazine Tube Stud	.55
47I	Magazine Tube Stud Screw	.22
48I	Receiver	
	(Cannot Supply)	
49I	Sideplate	
	(Cannot Supply)	
50I	Sideplate Screw	.44
51I	Sideplate Screw Collar	.22
52I	Tang Thumbscrew	.44
53I	Trigger	.99
54I	Trigger Pin	.22
55I	Trigger Spring	.44
56I	Trigger Spring Screw	.22

BE SURE TO GIVE MODEL AND PART NUMBER WHEN ORDERING.
MINIMUM CHARGE FOR ANY PART ORDER 30 CENTS.

Marlin parts list for the Models 18, 25, and 25S. Note the three different firing pins.

Right side of Model 18 takedown caliber .22 rifle.

Marlin **Model 18 Baby Featherweight Repeater.**
.22 Caliber, Take-Down.

Twenty years ago the standard of weight for a rifle was 12 or 15 lbs. Progress has rapidly and constantly been toward lighter weights. Will you be a leader, or more or less behind the times?

If you buy a watch, a bicycle, a wagon or an automobile, you don't look for the heaviest you can get for your money, but the lightest that will do the business. It takes better material, finer workmanship, simpler designs, less pieces, and it costs more to make the lighter weights. Quality counts.

Our Model 18 Baby Repeater, weighing but 3 lbs., 10 oz., is 1½ lbs. lighter than any other repeater. It has all of the accuracy and effectiveness of the larger, heavier guns, but weighs one-third less than any other repeating gun in the world. If you want extra weight of steel to carry around, you can buy it at any hardware store for two or three cents a pound. Don't pay gun prices for useless weight.

Rifle with 20-inch round barrel, weight about 3 lbs. 10 oz. Price $12.50 Catalog List.

Rifle with 20-inch octagon barrel, weight about 3 lbs. 10 oz. Price $13.00 Catalog List.

The *Marlin* Model 18, .22 Caliber Baby Repeating Rifle will hereafter be made Take-Down by using a thumb screw for a tang screw; simply unscrew the thumb screw a few turns, when it can be lifted out and the buttstock slipped off as above.
Length over all .... 36 inches. Length taken down (with buttstock removed) ...... 26½ inches.

Our Model 18 is an entirely new construction from muzzle to buttplate, with the simplest, quickest and easiest working action ever devised. The operating parts engage directly with one another, without intervening links or other connections to complicate and weaken the construction. There are no weak features, no parts liable to get out of order. Made of the very best material throughout, every ounce of needless weight has been eliminated, yet leaving a good margin of extra strength in every part.

Marlin flyer about the Model 18 rifle.

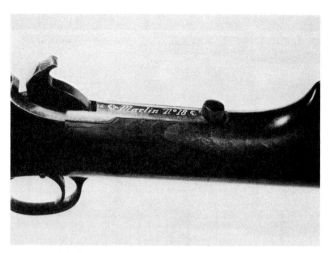

Model 18 top tang and head of takedown screw.

Model 18 rifle taken down.

1907 ad for the new Marlin Model 18 Baby Featherweight Repeater.

Model 20

The Model 20 was the first of five different models of take-down pump action rifles that Marlin produced. The Model 20 was introduced to dealers in 1906 with the following letter:

MARLIN, Model No. 20, Repeating Rifle
Advance Specifications, January, 1907.

A take-down .22 caliber using short, long and long-rifle cartridges without adjustment or change of any kind.

Barrel 22 inches long, made for the present in octagon only from best quality special gun barrel steel thoroughly welded and planished in the bar, free from seams and hard spots, carefully straightened; rifled with the Ballard system of rifling and guaranteed to shoot at least equal to anything of the same caliber, length and weight, up to 200 yards.

Minimum jobbing price..............................$ 9.25
Minimum retail & minimum printed price 11.00

We expect to have electrotypes of this rifle ready to supply the trade about January 15th. Printed matter giving full description and illustration will be ready in February and advertising will begin in March.

We expect to commence shipping the arms to dealers in March. We advise all dealers to place their orders early and to buy liberally as the quantity will be limited especially for the first six months, and the demand will be far greater than the supply.

Yours respectfully,
THE MARLIN FIREARMS CO.

The 1907 catalog described the Model 20 as follows:

The Model 20 is a take-down .22 caliber repeater with the popular trombone action, using in the same rifle without any alteration or adjustment the short, long and long-rifle cartridges, black and smokeless, as used in the Models 1892 and 1897.

The Barrel is 22½ inches long, octagon, made from the best quality special gun-barrel steel, thoroughly welded and planished in the bar, free from seams and hard spots, carefully straightened, and is bored, rifled, chambered and finished on the Ballard system and guaranteed to shoot at least equal to anything of the same caliber, length and weight up to 200 yards.

The arm is fitted regularly with ivory bead front sight and a new and improved adjustable rear sight, with a flat top that does not obstruct the view for quick shooting, and with a vertical white line to assist the eye in getting the range quickly.

The frame is drilled and tapped on top, and the tang is also drilled and tapped, so that the Marlin receiver sight or a tang peep sight may be used if desired.

The rifle has a tubular magazine, as used in our Models 1892, 1897, and No. 18, and handles at one loading 15 short, 12 long or 11 long-rifle cartridges. The feeding of the cartridges from magazine to chamber is controlled by the pressure of the handle slide on the cartridge cutoff. The cartridges may be loaded into the magazine all of one kind or mixed indiscriminately, and the gun will handle them perfectly.

In design, the action is extremely simple. The working parts engage directly with one another without links or other complications; there is no loss of power; the gun is extremely quick and easy of operation and without a single weak feature.

The frame is made of the best quality special gun-frame

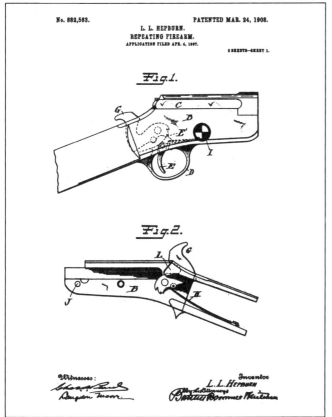

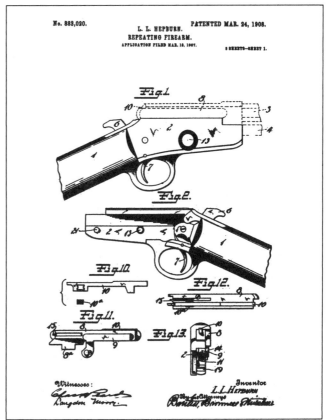

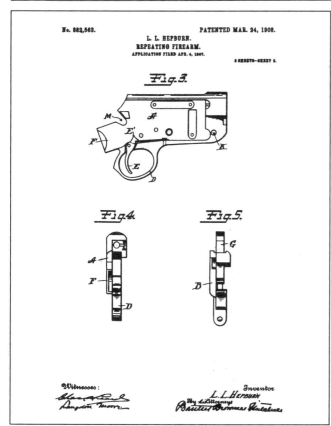

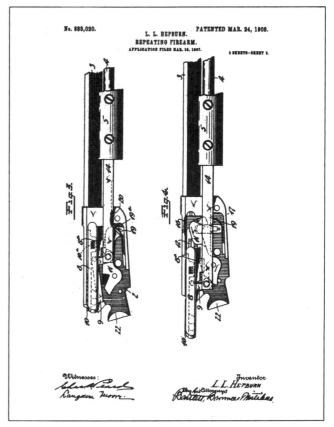

Patent drawings of Model 20 and later pump action exposed hammer .22 rifles.

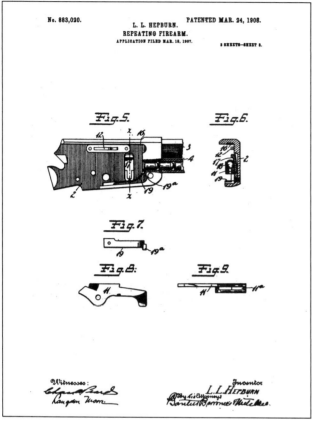

steel thoroughly welded, free from seams or hard spots, and has blued finish.

The small working parts of the action are made from best quality crucible steel, contact points hardened to prevent wear.

Flat springs in action made of best quality Jessop's spring steel imported from England.

Magazine spring, best quality music spring wire.

Buttstock and forearm black walnut, air seasoned for not less than two years, in our sheds, and afterward slowly kiln-dried before working, so that the wood will not warp or shrink after the gun is made up. The wood is especially well finished, as is every part of the rifle. There is not a piece of cheap material in it, and the workmanship is in every way of the highest quality.

The Model 20 action is operated on the trombone principle; has solid top, side ejector and regular closed-in Marlin frame. This makes for greater comfort and convenience and better service. The solid top does not catch rain or snow; keeps a wall of metal between your head and the cartridge; prevents powder and gases from blowing back into your face. The side ejector throws the shell away from you, not into your face and eyes; you do not get the habit of closing your eyes at each discharge; and as the ejected shell never crosses the line of sight, you do not lose your bead on the game or target, and can make repeat shots instantly.

The Take-Down principle, similar to Marlin Model 1897, provides for wear, both laterally and vertically, so that the take-down joint can never become loose or shaky, no matter how long it may be used or how much it may be worn.

Every action part is accessible for inspection and cleaning

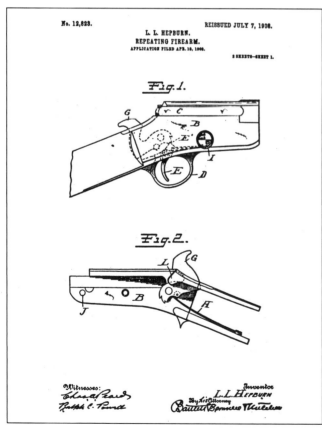

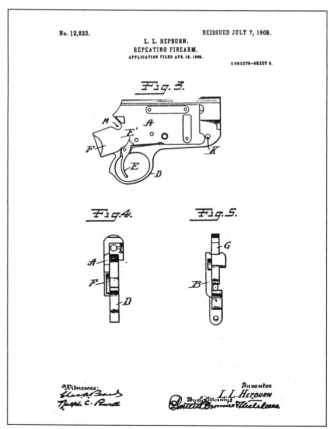

Patent drawings of Model 20 and later pump action exposed hammer .22 rifles.

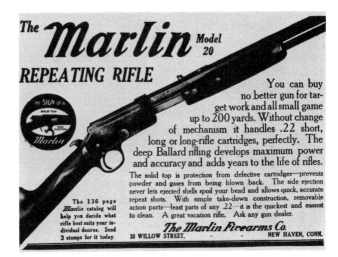

Top: *Model 20A with a full-length magazine of the button-release type.* Bottom: *Octagon-barrel Model 20 that has a steel butt plate and half magazine of the latch type.*

Model 20 rear sight.

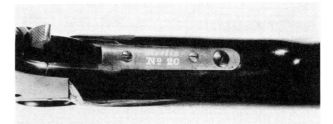

Model designation of first-variation Model 20 rifle.

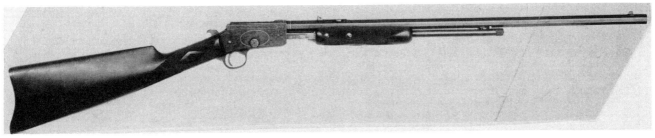

Deluxe engraved and gold-inlaid Model 20 rifle.

Top: *Right side of one of the two finest pump action .22 rifles produced by Marlin. Gold and platinum inlays, pristine engraving with No. F-checked deluxe wood are exceptionally rare. (RP)* Bottom: *Left side of same rifle.*

Second variation of Model 20 rifle receiver. The arrow indicates the short bolt lock.

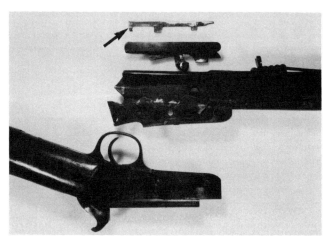

Third variation of Model 20 receiver. The arrow indicates the third type of firing pin.

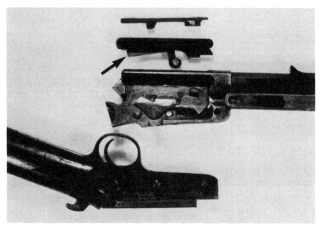

First variation of Model 20 rifle. Arrow indicates the long bolt lock.

without tools, and the barrel may be cleaned by inserting the wiping rod at the breech and drawing it entirely through the barrel, using a wiping rag twice as large as in any barrel where it is necessary to clean from the muzzle, doubling up the rag in the chamber. This is important to all shooters of .22 caliber ammunition, and especially to the gallery men who appreciate the saving in time and labor, the better results secured and the longer life of the barrel.

To take down the rifle with the action closed, cock the hammer and unscrew the thumbscrew, move the buttstock portion to the right and the barrel portion to the left. The parts are all locked in place when the gun is taken down so that they cannot drop out accidentally, but all of the parts may be removed in an instant, without tools.

To remove the action parts: With the gun taken down press forward the firing pin to release the locking bolt; raise the rear end of the locking bolt and draw back the forearm as far as it will go; draw forward the magazine tube as in loading — this allows a side play to the forearm; disconnect the forearm and handle slide from the locking bolt and draw them forward. The breech bolt and parts contained in same can then be taken out sideways and the carrier lifted out, giving access to everything. If desired, the locking bolt and firing pin may be removed from the breech bolt.

To re-assemble the action replace the carrier on its stud; replace the firing pin and locking bolt in the breech bolt; lay the breech bolt and contained parts in the frame at its rearmost position and then slide the breech bolt forward about half way, being sure that the firing pin on top of the rear end of the breech bolt engages in the groove on the under side of the top of the frame. With the breech bolt half open connect the handle slide with its stud on the locking bolt. Close the magazine. Then close and lock the action, pushing forward the forearm with the left hand, pressing breech bolt and handle slide against the frame with the thumb of right hand to guide breech bolt and insure that the slide will ride on the cartridge cutoff.

To put together the two portions of the frame, have the

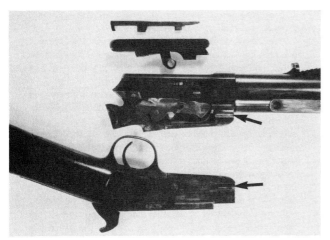

Fourth variation of Model 20 receiver. The arrow indicates the key and slot that replaced the pin and hole of the earlier receivers.

action closed and the hammer cocked; bring them together so that the tapered dowel pin in the front end of the right side enters its tapered recess and beveled tenons at the rear engage properly; then screw down the thumbscrew until tight.

Octagon barrels 22½ inches long were standard. Half-octagon or round barrels were not made for this model. The Model 20 had an ivory bead front sight and the new flat-top rear sight that had an adjusting screw for elevation, rather than the usual stepped elevator. The frames of this model were blued. Butt plates were blued steel. The overall length was 38¾ inches; the length when taken down was 25½ inches. The length of the buttstock was 13¼ inches and the drops at the comb and heel were 1⁹⁄₁₆ inches and 2¾ inches, respectively. For extras, please see the section on extras.

The roll-stamp on barrels of the Model 20 read either *Marlin Firearms Co. New Haven CT USA, Pat'd Aug 12, 1893. Mar. 1, 92. June 8, 97. Nov. 29. 1904* in two lines or

*The Marlin Firearms Corporation
New Haven, Conn. U.S.A. Patented*

Also marked on the top left flat of the octagon barrel, just forward of the receiver, was *22S–L&L–R.*

The top of the receiver was drilled and tapped for the Marlin–Hepburn receiver sight and the top tang was drilled and tapped for a tang sight.

Model 20S. The Model 20S was identical to the Model 20 with the exception of a shorter length locking bolt, the shape of the rear end of the firing pin, and the extractor. The shorter locking bolt allowed for greater strength to the receiver by adding more metal to the lug inside the receiver against which the thrust of a fired cartridge impinged.

Model 20A. The Model 20A was an extension of all the features of the Models 20 and 20S. The most important difference was the shape and spring action of the firing pin.

The Model 20 and 20S firing pins had a small coil spring entrapped in the forward part of the pin. This spring held the firing pin to the rear.

The Model 20A firing pin did not have the small spring in its

Marlin parts catalog list of parts for the Models 20, 20A, 20S, 29, 37, and 47 caliber .22 rifles.

front end, but rather a spring and plunger in the bolt that pushed against the front edge of a projection on the bottom of the rear end of the firing pin, thus forcing the firing pin to the rear.

There are three different bolts, two different extractors, two different locking bolts, three different firing pins, and two different receivers in the variations of the Model 20.

The prices of Model 20 rifles were as follows:

Year Made	Regular Magazine	Full Magazine
1911	$11.50	
1913	11.50	
1914	11.50	$11.50
1915	12.50	12.50
1916	14.00	14.00
1917	16.80	16.80
Jan. 1922		23.50
June 1922		19.50

Model 25

The Model 25 was a short-lived slide action .22 rifle that was introduced in 1909. It was chambered for .22 caliber conical bullet (CB) caps or .22 short cartridges.

This model was advertised as a takedown rifle. However, the takedown method was removal of the stock from the receiver, the same as for the earlier Model 18 rifle.

The Marlin catalog description of the Model 25 was as follows:

The Model 25 is a .22 caliber repeater using both .22 short cartridges and .22 C.B. caps without change in adjustment. In general construction it is similar to the well known Marlin Model 20. It has the same fine quality of material and workmanship; the popular quick-working trombone action; the safety, comfort and convenience of the solid-top, side-ejecting construction; and the Ballard accuracy which makes Marlin arms the most accurate of all repeaters.

The solid top does not catch rain or snow, keeps a wall of metal between your head and the cartridge; keeps the action clean; prevents powder and gasses from blowing back in your face.

The side ejection throws the shells away from you, not into your face and eyes; never interferes with your aim for the next shot; you can hold your aim and make repeat shots instantly.

This construction promotes rapid, accurate firing—the great pleasure and real test of a repeater.

The take-down feature of this gun is accomplished without the addition of a single part. Simply unscrew and remove the tang thumb-screw; the buttstock can then be slipped off and the gun will pack in a space 29¼ inches long.

In the action, the working parts are extremely simple, and very strong, engaging directly with one another without intervening links or complications; the special cartridge guide and cartridge guard insure perfect feeding of cartridges from the magazine into the chamber. The removable sideplate construction allows instant removal of all operating parts for cleaning, without using tools, and further allows the wiping rod to be inserted at one end and drawn entirely through the barrel—the only proper way to clean a .22 rifle. The locking bolt and firing pin are so adjusted that it is impossible for the cartridge to be exploded by the firing pin until the cartridge is in the chamber and the action fully closed and locked. The action can be opened only when the firing pin is forward.

To Clean—Take off side-plate after unscrewing thumb-screw; draw forward outside magazine tube as in loading magazine; lift rear end of handle—slide off connecting pin, and pull slide and fore-end forward out of the way; cock the hammer, press forward the firing pin, raise rear end of locking bolt; breech bolt and carrier can then be lifted out.

The barrel is round, 23 inches long, made from the best quality gun-barrel steel, bored, rifled, chambered and fin-

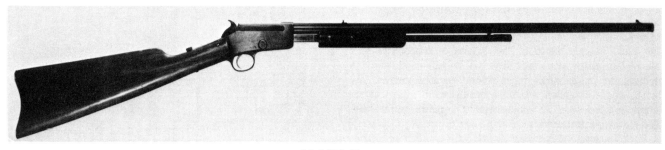

Model 25 rifle.

MODEL No. 25—.22 CALIBER RIM FIRE—.22 SHORT OR C. B. CAPS

Here is a gun that you can shoot around the house—in the attic or cellar or out in the yard—a gun that you can "blaze away" with, without regard to the cost of ammunition, and still a gun that will quickly bring down any small game, including foxes, and is accurate and effective up to 50 yards—150 feet.

It's a thorough repeating rifle in every way—guaranteed in accuracy and reliability—up to the **Marlin** standard in every respect. It handles the .22 short cartridges, black, semi-smokeless and smokeless, regular and mushroom; also the .22 C. B. caps, black, semi-smokeless and smokeless, of all makes as illustrated. The ammunition is the cheapest made, yet it is uniformly accurate and reliable in this rifle, and by obtaining the Model 25 **Marlin** repeater, you can enjoy greater pleasure at less expense for ammunition, than with any other gun ever made.

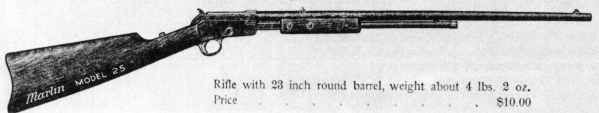

Rifle with 23 inch round barrel, weight about 4 lbs. 2 oz.
Price $10.00

Catalog illustration and description of the Model 25 rifle.

Loading Tube, allows instant refilling of magazine and doubles the efficiency of the rifle for gallery work, etc., Price, 60c.

Loading tube, with section cut away to show position of cartridges in tube.

Catalog illustration of loading tube designed for use with the Model 25 rifle.

ished on the Ballard system, and guaranteed an extremely accurate shooter.

The deep rifling does not foul as quickly and outlasts by many years the ordinary shallow rifling used in .22 caliber rifles of other makes.

Buttstock and forearm are made of black walnut, thoroughly air seasoned, carefully kiln dried and especially well made up. There is not a cheap piece of material in the entire gun, and the workmanship is in every way of the highest quality.

The gun is regularly loaded by drawing out the outer magazine tube and inserting the cartridges singly directly into the inner magazine tube.

But for the convenience of clubs, gallerymen and those who shoot at target, the loading hole is shaped to permit the use of a loading tube as illustrated.

A lip on the end of the tube engages a notch in the magazine tube; no "knack" is required to reload the magazine instantly; one rifle does the work of two.

The Model 25 Marlin repeater is a gun every man, woman and boy who shoots can buy and enjoy. It sells at a price all can afford, and quickly pays for itself in the reduced cost of ammunition.

Here is a gun that you can shoot around the house—in the attic or cellar or out in the yard—a gun that you can "blaze away" with, without regard to the cost of ammunition, and still a gun that will quickly bring down any small game, including foxes, and is accurate and effective up to 50 yards—150 feet.

It's a thorough repeating rifle in every way—guaranteed in accuracy and reliability—up to the Marlin standard in every respect. It handles the .22 short cartridges, black, semi-smokeless and smokeless, regular and mushroom; also the .22 C.B. caps, black, semi-smokeless and smokeless, of all makes as illustrated. The ammunition is the cheapest made, yet it is uniformly accurate and reliable in this rifle, and by obtaining the Model 25 Marlin repeater, you can enjoy greater pleasure at less expense for ammunition, than with any other gun ever made.

Extras such as selected wood, checking, etc., can be furnished. Pistol grip cannot be furnished.

The Model 25 had a long locking bolt and a firing pin like the Model 20 rifle. A variation of the Model 25 was the Model 25S. The *S* version had a firing pin like the third type used in the Model 20A rifle and, likewise, had a plunger and spring in the bolt that held the firing pin toward the rear of the bolt. The main disadvantage to the Model 25 was that, like the Model 18, it only chambered the petite short and CB cap cartridges, whereas the popular Model 20 handled short, long, and long-rifle cartridges interchangeably, without adjustment, through the magazine.

The Model 25 had a 23-in. round barrel. It held 15 .22 short cartridges or 18 CB caps. It had an open-notch rear sight that

Typical model designation on top tang of Model 25 rifle.

was not adjustable for elevation and a bead front sight. The frame was blued. The buttstock was of black walnut. The stock was 13¼ inches long, and had a drop at comb of 1⁹⁄₁₆ inches and a drop at the heel of 2¾ inches. The butt plate was blued steel. The overall length was 39½ inches. With the butt-stock removed, it was 29¼ inches long. Pistol grip stock and octagon barrels were not available.

Advertised along with the Model 25 was a loading tube to assist in loading the magazine for gallery use. The tube was different from the one advertised for use with the Model 1891 side-loading rifle and was described as follows:

> The gun is regularly loaded by drawing out the outer tube and inserting the cartridges singly directly into the inner magazine tube. But for the convenience of clubs, gallerymen and those who shoot at targets, the loading hole is shaped to permit the use of a loading tube. A lip on the end of the tube engages a notch in the magazine tube; no "knack" is required to reload the magazine instantly, one rifle does the work of two.

The barrel of the Model 25 was roll-stamped in two lines:

Marlin Firearms Co. NEW-HAVEN CT. U.S.A.
PAT'D APRIL 2, 1889. AUG 12, 1890 MAR 1, 1892. NOV 29, 1904.

The barrel was also stamped on the left side, forward of the receiver *22 SHORT & C.B. CAPS,* and the top tang was stamped *Marlin, No. 25.*

The Model 25 takedown, slide action caliber .22 rifle was only available for two years, 1909 and 1910. The price was $10.00 to the consumer and $8.50 to the dealer. The extra features available for the Model 25 are included in the Extra section elsewhere in this book.

Model 27

The Model 27 rifle was first introduced in an ad on the inside back cover of the 1909 catalog. At that time it was available with only an octagon barrel in .25–20 and .32–20

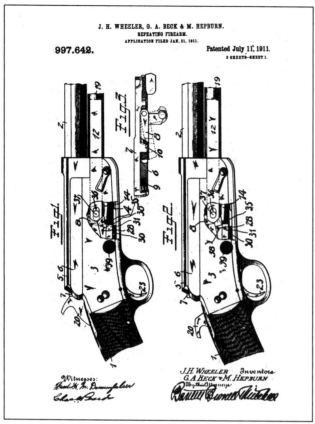

calibers. In 1913, round and octagon barrel variations were added that were chambered for the .25 rimfire cartridge. In 1910, a mechanism was added to this gun that permitted the gun to be opened while a cartridge was in the chamber. Instead of letting the hammer down on the firing pin to open the bolt, the user could push forward a button that was located on the right side of the receiver. This improved model was called the Model 27S. It was described in the 1911 catalog as follows:

This new Model 27 Marlin is the only repeater made in .25–20 and .32–20 calibers with the desirable trombone or "pump" action. Other popular and valuable features are the solid top frame, side ejector, Take-Down construction, the Special Smokeless Steel barrel, Rocky Mountain rear and Ivory Bead front sights. It handles the new high velocity smokeless cartridges as well as the regular black and low pressure loads. It is a gun of power and range for game and target shooting, yet safe to use in settled districts, and thoroughly covers all game smaller than deer up to 300 yards.

SPECIFICATIONS: Rifles are all Take-Down. All have Special Smokeless Steel barrel, 24 inches long, only. Blued frame; blued steel rifle buttplate. Black walnut stock and forend. Rocky Mountain (adjustable) rear sight and Ivory Bead front sight. Rifle measures 42¼ inches over all; 28½ inches taken down. Buttstock is 13½ inches long with 1⁹⁄₁₆ inches drop at comb and 2¾ inches at heel. Magazine holds 6 shots, giving with one in the chamber 7 shots at one loading. Pistol grip stock or round barrel cannot be furnished.

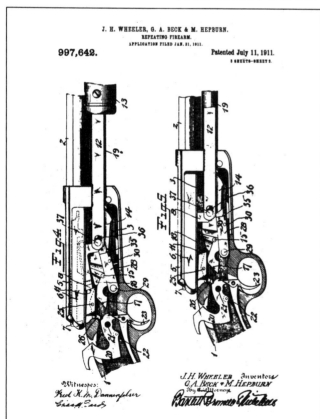

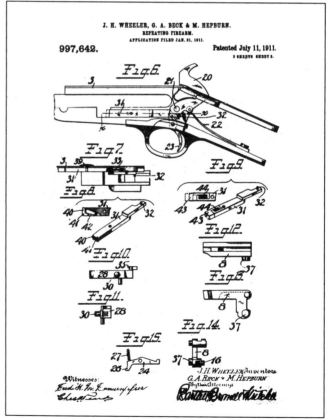

Patent drawings of Model 27 center-fire, pump action rifle.

(FORM S. 7095 C)

January, 1910 Supplement to *Marlin* Price List of July 1' 1909

New Model 27 *Marlin* Repeater

.25-20 or .32-20 Caliber, 5¾ pounds, 7 Shots. Trombone Action.

	Cost to You	Sell to Consumer
Model 27, .25-20 rifle, 24-inch octagon barrel,	$12.50	$15.00
Model 27, .32-20 rifle, 24-inch octagon barrel,	12.50	15.00

Terms, 2% discount for cash with order. F. O. B. New Haven. See regular price list.

☾ **Rifles are all Take-Downs.** All have **Special Smokeless Steel** barrel, 24 inches long, only. Blued frame; blued steel rifle buttplate. Black walnut stock and foreend. Rocky Mountain rear sight and **Ivory Bead** front sight. Seven shots at one loading. Pistol grip stock or round barrel cannot be furnished. Shoot black powder cartridges, low-pressure smokeless and high velocity smokeless cartridges.

Remember, the trombone action and Special Smokeless Steel barrel cannot be obtained in any other rifle of these calibers at any price; the take-down feature and Ivory Bead sight are never furnished in other .25-20 and .32-20 repeating rifles except at an additional charge; the modern Marlin solid top and side ejector cannot be duplicated in any other make of .25-20 or .32-20 rifle. Order to-day for prompt delivery.

The Marlin Firearms Co. . . . . . New Haven, Conn., U. S. A.

1910 catalog information about the Model 27 rifle.

.25 RIM-FIRE

Now ready! Here's the only repeating rifle made for the popular .25 rim-fire cartridge

Marlin MODEL 27

The New .25 Rim Fire *Marlin* Repeater

Take-Down, 8 Shots, Trombone Action

	Cost to You	Sell to Consumer
Model 27. .25 rim-fire rifle, 24-inch round Special Rolled Steel barrel,	$11.10	$13.15
Model 27. .25 rim-fire rifle, 24-inch octagon Special Smokeless Steel barrel,	12.50	15.00

Terms, 2% discount for cash with order. F. O. B. New Haven. See regular price list.

SPECIFICATIONS: **Rifles are all Take-Downs.**
Round barrels are of Special Rolled Steel, meeting perfectly all requirements of the .25 rim-fire cartridges.
Octagon barrels are of Special Smokeless Steel (as used in our high power rifles), giving a greater margin of extra strength and wear. All barrels are 24 inches long; no other length or style furnished.

Rifles have blued frame; blued steel rifle buttplate; black walnut stock and foreend; Rocky Mountain rear sight and **ivory bead** front sight. Eight shots at one loading. Pistol grip stock cannot be furnished.

The guns that sell easiest are small bore rifles using cheap ammunition that can safely be shot around home. That's why you can sell this superb new Marlin repeater! It uses the well-known .25 rim-fire

cartridge which is so powerful that it is used successfully on deer; so accurate it is extensively used in target work; not too powerful for settled districts; and extremely popular because extremely cheap!

This new rifle is our well-known Model 27 repeater adapted to the .25 rim-fire cartridge. It has the quick, smooth working "pump" action, and the modern **solid-top and side-ejector** for rapid, accurate firing, increased safety and convenience. It has **take-down** construction; action parts removable without tools; it's easy to keep clean.

It's a mighty fine rifle for rabbits, woodchucks, muskrats, crows, hawks, foxes and geese—for the large class of small game that requires something more powerful than the .22 long-rifle.

It's a rifle that you can sell!

Order a sample today—and write us for a quantity of circulars, or for catalogs or electrotypes.

Makers of Marlin Repeating Rifles and Shotguns, Ideal Reloading Tools, Etc. *The Marlin Firearms Co.* New Haven, Connecticut, U. S. A.

1913 introduction of the Model 27 rifle in caliber .25 rimfire.

Other extras, such as selected wood, checking, engraving, etc., can be furnished.

Remember, the trombone action and Special Smokeless Steel barrel cannot be obtained in any other rifle of these calibers at any price; the Take-Down feature and ivory bead sight are never furnished in other .25–20 and .32–20 repeat-

ing rifles except at an additional charge; the modern Marlin solid top and side ejector cannot be duplicated in any other make of .25–20 or .32–20 rifle.

The "Pump" Action in this excellent new gun is admirably adapted to .25–20 and .32–20 loads. It handles quickly and smoothly, and makes an attractive, finely balanced repeating

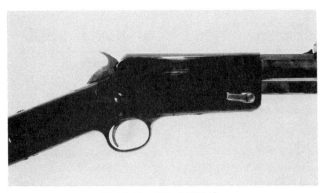

Right side of Model 27 rifle.

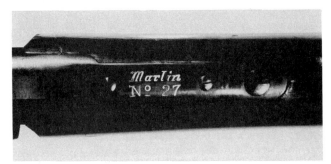

Top tang marking of Model 27 rifle.

Internal parts of Model 27 rifle.

rifle. The Special Smokeless Steel Barrel, the same extra quality material as in our big game rifles, is especially adapted to stand the pressure and resist the wear of high velocity smokeless loads with metal jacketed bullets.

The Solid Top and Side Ejector indicate the modern gun construction; they keep a protecting wall of metal at all times between your head and the cartridge; keep out rain, dirt and all foreign matter; throw the empty shells away from you, not into your face and eyes; promote rapid, accurate firing, the real test of a repeater.

The Model 27 is built extra strong throughout on account of the high velocity smokeless loads. The receiver and action parts are all cut from the solid steel drop forgings; the buttstock, forearm and all other parts are of first quality material throughout. Note the shapely stock and special rifle buttplate. This gun is guaranteed free from imperfection in material and workmanship. The deep, clean-cut Ballard rifling develops the full range and power, and insures the greatest possible accuracy and a long life for the gun.

The Ivory Bead Front Sight and Rocky Mountain adjustable rear sight are equally adapted to hunting or target work and are the best set of sights ever regularly furnished on a gun of this power. Ivory Bead sights cost extra on other .25–20 and .32–20 rifles.

The Take-Down Construction is invaluable for convenient carrying and cleaning.

Safety features: In operating the gun the hammer cocks into the sear notch until the action is fully closed and locked when the locking of the locking bolt releases the sear and lets the hammer down on the trigger in the full cock notch. You can hold back the trigger and shoot gun as fast as you can operate the action and yet the gun is always fully closed and locked before cartridge is exploded.

When the action is closed and locked ready for firing, two safety features prevent any accidental opening of the gun as the hammer falls. A spur on the firing pin rides on top of the solid portion of locking bolt until the hammer falls; the hammer pushes it forward far enough to allow the opening of the action.

Another special safety lock in the action, externally indicated by the finger button on right side of receiver, is so arranged that whenever the hammer is cocked the safety block is tightly locked in place and the action cannot possibly be opened until the hammer falls or until the shooter presses in on the firing pin to release the firing pin lock, at the same time drawing back the finger button to release this safety block.

These parts are entirely automatic in regular operation, the locks being released by the fall of the hammer, and accord-

Model 27 rifle that has had added to it a bolt-release button on the right side of the receiver.

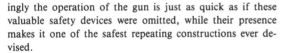

Top: *Right side of second variation Model 27 rifle identified as the Model 27S.* Bottom: *Left side of Model 27S receiver.*

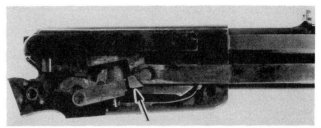

Top: *Internal parts of Model 27S receiver. The arrow indicates the slide lock of the second variation.* Bottom: *Internal parts of right half of receiver.*

Typical tang marking of Model 27S.

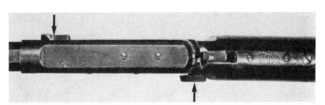

Top view of Model 27 rifle. The arrows indicate the takedown thumbscrew and takedown lever.

ingly the operation of the gun is just as quick as if these valuable safety devices were omitted, while their presence makes it one of the safest repeating constructions ever devised.

It is necessary to use the finger button only when you wish to extract a loaded shell from the chamber without firing; for of course at all other times the hammer can be dropped on the firing pin and the gun is then operated without any reference whatever to the finger button.

To Take Down the Rifle. With the action closed, cock the hammer and unscrew the thumb lever screw on right side of frame and thumbscrew on left side; move the buttstock portion to the right and the barrel portion to the left. The parts are all locked in place when the gun is taken down so that they can not drop out accidentally, but all of the parts may be removed in an instant without tools.

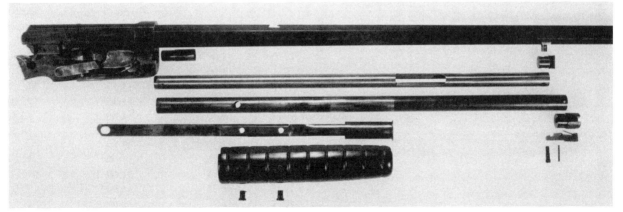

Magazine and forearm parts of the Model 27 rifle.

Left half of the receiver and bolt parts of the Model 27S rifle.

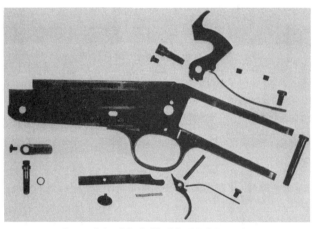

Parts of the right half of the Model 27 rifle.

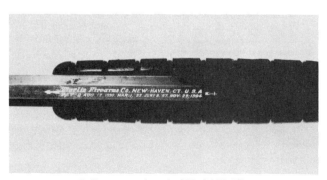

Roll-stamp on barrel of Model 27 rifle.

To Remove the Action Parts. While pressing in on the firing pin (which releases the locking bolt), draw back the forearm as far as it will go; draw forward the magazine tube as in loading—this allows side play to the forearm; disconnect the forearm and handle slide from the locking bolt and draw them forward. The breech bolt and parts contained in same can then be taken out sideways, the safety block can be lifted off its stud and the carrier lifted out, giving access to everything. If desired, the locking bolt and firing pin may be removed from the breechbolt.

To Reassemble the Action. Replace the carrier on its stud; replace the safety block on its stud; replace the firing pin and locking bolt in the breechbolt; lay breechbolt and contained parts in the frame at its rearmost position. Close the magazine. Draw back the forearm, using special care to see that the lower edge of the handle slide rides on top of the safety block, connect handle slide with its stud on the locking bolt. Then close and lock the action, pushing forward the forearm with the left hand, pressing breechbolt and handle slide against the frame with the thumb of right hand to guide breechbolt and insure that the slide will ride on the cartridge cutoff.

To Put Together the Two Portions of Frame. Have the action closed and the hammer cocked; bring them together so that the thumb lever screw in the front end of the right side enters its recess and beveled tenons at the rear engage properly; then screw down the thumb lever screw on right side and the thumb nut on left side until tight.

The Model 27 was of the same basic design as Marlin's other two-piece receiver rifles that included the Models 20, 29, 37, and 47, except that it was larger to accept the larger center-fire cartridges for which it was designed. The two-piece receiver system was strengthened in this model by having both a thumb nut on the left side of the receiver and a thumb lever screw on the right front side of the receiver.

Although the basic patents that cover the Model 27 were J.M. Marlin and L.L. Hepburn inventions, the improved safety block button feature was the invention of J.H. Wheeler, G.A. Beck, and L.L. Hepburn's son, Melvin Hepburn.

The Model 27 rifle was the longest-lived trombone action rifle that Marlin manufactured. It was in production nine years before WW I and for 12 years after that war. By year and model, the retail price to the sportsman was as follows:

| | | 25 Rimfire | |
.25–20; .32–20		Round barrel	Octagon barrel
1909	$16.00		
1910	15.00		
1911	15.00		
1913	15.00	July $13.15	$15.00
1914	15.00	13.15	15.00
1915	16.50	14.60	16.50
1916	18.60	16.50	18.60
1917	22.30	19.80	
1922 (Jan)	32.75	31.00	
1922 (Jun)	32.75	31.00	
1923	32.75	31.00	
1924	32.75	31.00	
1925	32.75	31.00	

.25–20; .32–20

1926	33.30
1927	33.30
1928	33.30
1929	28.50
1930	28.50
1931	28.50
1932	28.50

The barrel of the Model 27 is roll-stamped:

Marlin Firearms Co. NEW-HAVEN.CT U.S.A.
PAT'D AUG 12.1890. MAR 1. '92.JUNE 8. '97.NOV.29.1904

The top tang is marked *Marlin, No. 27-S.*

The caliber is stamped on top of the barrel just forward of the receiver.

The top of the receiver is drilled and tapped for the Marlin receiver sight and the top tang is drilled and tapped for a tang sight. There were two variations of the forend slide. The later one had an extension that went all the way through the wooden forend.

At the end of WW I, when the Marlin-Rockwell Corporation was finishing its government contracts, it attempted to return to the sporting arms business that had been terminated at the start of the war. A few of the regular Marlin models were roll-stamped with the Marlin-Rockwell name; others had the Marlin-Rockwell name on the barrel, as well as a new model designation. One example is the Model 27, a few of which have been observed marked with the Marlin-Rockwell name, and is identified as Model 40 on the top tang.

MODEL 27 - 27S

Number		Price	Number		Price
1L	Barrel, Octagon	$11.00	38L	Mainspring	.66
1LL	Barrel, Round .25 R. F. only	8.58	39L	Mainspring Screw	.22
2L	Breech Bolt	3.30	40L	Magazine Tube (inside)	2.48
3L	Breech Bolt Complete (with fir.ng		41L	Magazine Tube (outside)	2.48
	pin and extractor)	4.62	42L	Magazine Spring	.44
4L	Buttstock	3.96	43L	Magazine Plug (inside)	.55
5L	Buttplate	1.65	44L	Magazine Plug (outside)	.55
6L	Buttplate Screws (2) ea.	.22	45L	Magazine Latch (with spring)	.66
7L	Carrier	3.30	46L	Magazine Latch Spring	.33
8L	Carrier Pivot Pin	.22	47L	Magazine Latch P n	.22
9L	Cartridge Cut-Off	.99	48L	Magazine Follower	.66
10L	Cartridge Cut-Off Screw	.22	49L	Magazine Follower Pin	.22
11L	Dummy Screws (4) ea.	.22	50L	Magazine Tube Stud	.22
12L	Ejector Base	1.32	51L	Magazine Tube Stud Screw	.22
13L	Ejector Base Screws (2) ea.	.22	52L	Magazine Tube Complete	6.60
14L	Ejector Wing	.66	53L	Receiver (left side)	6.88
15L	Ejector Pin	.22	54L	Receiver (right side)	6.88
16L	Ejector Spring	.33	55L	Safety Block	1.10
17L	Ejector Complete	2.20	56L	Safety Block Plunger	.33
18L	Extractor	.66	58L	Safety Block Plunger Spring	.33
19L	Extractor Screw	.22	59L	Safety Block Plunger Pin	.22
20L	Firing Pin (Center-Fire)	1.32	60L	Safety Block Stud	.44
20LL	Firing Pin (Rim-Fire)	1.32	61L	Safety Latch	.77
21L	Firing Pin Plunger	.44	62L	Safety Latch Spring	.33
22L	Firing Pin Plunger Spring	.33	63L	Safety Latch Button	.44
23L	Firing Pin Plunger Pin	.22	64L	Sear	.66
24L	Foreend (wood)	2.50	65L	Sear Spring	.22
25L	Foreend Screws, (short or long) ea.	.33	66L	Sear Screw	.22
26L	Foreend Screws Escutcheons (2) ea.	.33	67L	Tang Screw	.33
27L	Foreend Slide (action bar) new style	2.20	68L	Thumb Lever Complete	1.10
27LL	Foreend Sl de, old style (without		69L	Thumb Lever Screw	.66
	forearm extension)	1.65	70L	Thumb Lever Screw Collar	.22
28L	Hammer (with roller and pin)	1.32	71L	Thumb Lever Retaining Screw	.22
29L	Hammer Roller	.44	73L	Thumb Nut (left side)	.44
30L	Hammer Roller Pin	.22	74L	Thumb Nut Plungers (2) each	.22
31L	Hammer Stud	.33	75L	Thumb Nut Plunger Springs (2) ea.	.22
32L	Hammer Stud Retaining Screw	.22	76L	Trigger	.99
33L	Locking Bolt	1.65	77L	Trigger Pin	.22
34L	Locking Bolt Plunger	.44	78L	Trigger Spring	.44
35L	Locking Bolt Plunger Spring	.33	79L	Trigger Spring Screw	.22
36L	Locking Bolt Plunger Screw	.22			

SIGHTS

80L	Front Sight (Ivory Bead)	1.10	82L	Rear Sight (Flat Top Rocky Mt.)	1.76
81L	Front Sight (Silver Bead)	1.10	81L	Rear Sight Elevator	.44

Note—When ordering parts state whether rifle is marked on upper tang "Model 27" or "Model 27-S." When ordering foreend or foreend slide, state whether or not old foreend slide has extension on front end.

Marlin parts catalog listing of Model 27 rifle parts.

Model 29

The Model 29 was introduced in 1913. It was, with only two exceptions, the same as the Model 20 rifle. In fact, the 1913 parts list for the Model 20 rifle has a footnote stating that the Model 29 parts are priced the same as for the Model 20, and that the only difference between the two are the 23-in. round barrel and the smooth wood forearm of the Model 29 versus the 24-in. octagon barrel and grooved forearm of the Model 20.

The Model 29, I feel sure, was a way for Marlin to add another Model to the line by making only two basic changes to the Model 20. The Marlin catalog stated this about the Model 29:

MODEL No. 29—Here's an up-to-date .22 caliber repeater that handles without change or adjustment the .22 short, .22 long and .22 long-rifle cartridges, black, semi-smokeless and smokeless, of all makes and styles, yet sells at the surprisingly low price of $8.50.

The Model 29 is similar in general construction to the well-known Marlin Model 20. It is a take-down, convenient to clean quickly and thoroughly and can be packed in a small space. It has the popular trombone action, quick and easy in operation. The modern solid top, side ejection and closed-in breech insure greatest safety, comfort and convenience.

It has a barrel long enough for all requirements; it shoots all .22 short, long and long-rifle cartridges, including the hunting cartridges with mushroom bullets; it is a thoroughly accurate and efficient arm for rabbits, squirrels, hawks, crows, foxes, and all small game, and for target work. Guaranteed in accuracy and reliability.

SPECIFICATIONS: All Model 29 rifles are take-down; all have trombone action and handle 15 .22 short, 12 .22 long or 11 .22 long-rifle cartridges at one loading without change or adjustment. Made with 23 inch round barrel only; no other length or style furnished. Buttstock is 13¼ inches long with 1⁹⁄₁₆ inches drop at comb and 2¾ inches drop at heel. Blued frame; blued rifle buttplate; black walnut buttstock and forend; metal bead front sight and flat top rear sight. Rifle measures 39½ inches over all; 26½ inches taken down. Fully guaranteed. Pistol grip stock or rubber buttplate cannot be furnished.

The Solid Top and Side Ejector indicate the modern gun construction; they keep a protecting wall of metal at all times between your head and the cartridge; keep out rain, dirt, and all foreign matter; throw the empty shells away from you, not into your face and eyes; promote rapid, accurate firing, the real test of a repeater.

It is not surprising that it actually handles the three cartridges satisfactorily. Just as we originated the solid-top,

(Form S7113C-Canada)

January, 1912 Supplement to *Marlin* Price List of July 1, 1911

The New Model 29 *Marlin* is an up-to-date repeater that handles without change or adjustment the .22 short, .22 long and .22 long rifle cartridges of all makes and styles, yet retails at the surprisingly low price of $8.50.

The Model 29 is similar in general construction to the well-known Marlin Model 20. **It is a take-down,** convenient to clean quickly and thoroughly and can be packed in a small space. **It has the popular trombone action,** quick and easy in operation. **The modern solid top, side ejection and closed-in breech** insure greatest safety, comfort and convenience.

It has a **barrel long enough for all requirements;** it shoots **all .22 short, long and long-rifle cartridges,** including the hunting cartridges with mushroom bullets; it is a thoroughly accurate and efficient arm for rabbits, squirrels, hawks, crows, foxes and all small game, and for target work. **Guaranteed in accuracy and reliability.**

Model 29 Rifle, .22 calibre, take-down, 23 inch round barrel, weight about 4 1-4 pounds. Price, - - - - - - - $7.00

Cost to You
$7.00

Terms 2% discount for cash with order. F. O. B. New Haven. See regular price list.

SPECIFICATIONS: All Model 29 rifles are take-down; all have trombone action and handle 15 .22 short, 12 .22 long or 11 .22 long-rifle cartridges at one loading without change or adjustment. **Made with 23-inch round barrel only;** no other length or style furnished. Buttstock is 13¼ inches long with 1⅛ inches drop at comb and 2¾ inches drop at heel. Blued frame; blued rifle buttplate; black walnut buttstock and foreend; metal bead front sight and flat top rear sight. Rifle measures 39½ inches over all; 26½ inches taken down. Fully guaranteed. Order to-day for prompt delivery.

The Marlin Firearms Co. - - New Haven, Conn., U. S. A.

1912 catalog insert illustrating and describing the Model 29 rifle.

1913 catalog information about the Model 29 rifle.

side-ejecting construction which is acknowledged superior and is being copied by the other gun makers, so also we were the first to bring out a .22 repeater using the three cartridges. For over 20 years we have made .22 repeaters guaranteed to handle the three cartridges without change in adjustment; this insures its entire reliability.

Accuracy. Like our other .22 repeaters, the Model 29 has the deep, clean-cut rifling as used in our famous old Ballard target rifles; they are extremely accurate and of course retain their accuracy for years after rifles with ordinary shallow rifling are worn out.

The Model 29 has a sensible, visible hammer that can be cocked or uncocked at will, and its position is always clear, day or night, without the complications of a concealed hammer gun. It's simpler, safer, and better.

The material and workmanship are first-class throughout; there is not a piece of cheap material in the entire gun. It gives the greatest gun value that has ever been produced at this moderate price.

The Model 29 Marlin repeater is a gun every man, woman and boy who shoots can afford to buy and enjoy.

To take down: Cock the hammer; unscrew thumbscrew on right side as far as it will go; move buttstock portion to right and barrel part to left.

To remove and replace action parts, follow same instructions as for Model 20.

The action parts cannot fall out accidentally, but can be instantly removed with the fingers when you are cleaning the gun. You can clean the barrel conveniently by inserting wiping rod and rag at breech and drawing entirely through the barrel; you can look through barrel and be sure it is clean before applying rust preventive.

The Marlin is the easiest of all .22's to keep clean—and frequent and thorough cleaning helps the accuracy and adds to the life of any rifle.

The roll-stamp on the barrel of the Model 29 was the same as for the Models 18 and 25:

Marlin Firearms Co.NEW-HAVEN.CT. U.S.A.
PAT'D APRIL 2.1889. AUG 12.1890.MAR.1892.NOV.29 1904

The left side of the barrel, just forward of the receiver, was stamped *22 S–L & L–R*.

Although the Model 29 does not appear in any of my price lists or catalogs after 1917, some Model 29s have been observed with the Marlin Firearms Corporation roll-stamp that includes only the two 1908 patent dates, as do the Models 37 and 47. One may wonder if the Corporation-marked rifles are the Model 29N, for which no written data has been located.

A Marlin Firearms Corporation parts list of repair parts that combines the Model 20 and Model 29 lists the Model 29 23-in. barrel as the only part different from the Model 20 parts. This confirms the opinion that the purpose of the Model 29 was to make available to the sportsman a rifle the same as the Model 20, but with a round barrel, thereby preserving the image of the Model 20 rifle with its octagon barrel. A comparison of the prices for both follows.

Year	Model 29 (Dealer)	Model 20 (Regular Magazine)
1912	$7.00	$11.50
1913	8.50	11.50
1914	9.25	11.50
1915	9.25	12.50
1916	11.80	14.00
1917	14.15	16.80

Model 32

C.G. "Gus" Swebilius and H.T.R. Hanitz invented and obtained a patent for a hammerless pump action rifle that was the forerunner of the Model 32 and Model 38 rifles.

Patent number 1,090,351, dated March 17, 1914, covers the first experimental hammerless rifle. Close examination of the

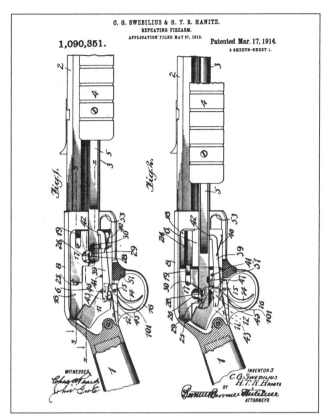

Patent drawing of Marlin's experimental hammerless .22 that was not put into production.

model gun and patent drawings show that the intention was to make it a takedown model similar to the earlier exposed hammer pump action rifles Marlin had produced. But improvements in the method of takedown and the bolt mechanism resulted in a different system being put into production.

Patent numbers 1,110,837, dated September 15, 1914; 1,146,536, dated July 13, 1915; and 1,147,659, dated July 20, 1915, which were issued to C.G. Swebilius and H.T.R. Hanitz and assigned to Marlin, cover the new mechanism, identified as the Model 32.

The Model 32 was Marlin's first production hammerless caliber .22 trombone action rifle. It was introduced in 1915; because of the change of the Marlin company from a sporting arms company to a maker of machine guns and arms for the military during WW I, the Model 32 was short-lived. It was

Prototype of Marlin's first hammerless .22.

Internal parts of experimental .22 rifle, some of which carried over to the Models 32 and 38.

not listed in Marlin Arms Corporation or Marlin–Rockwell price lists of 1916 and 1917. When reintroduced after the war by Marlin–Rockwell and The Marlin Firearms Corporation, this model was identified as the Model 38.

The 1915 catalog describes the Model 32 as "the 'thoroughbred' among .22 pump-action repeaters."

The rifle was hammerless and takedown, with a pistol grip

stock, one-half magazine, 24-in. octagon barrel, and ivory bead front sight. A rear sight adjustable for windage and elevation was designed by C.G. Swebilius, and the rifle had Ballard rifling.

The takedown feature was instantaneous and described thus:

> No other rifle has such a simple and effective take-down. Simply draw back take-down latch button; tip forward barrel portion; and then disconnect the barrel and receiver parts. The most effective take-down ever invented.

The safety button on this model, and on the Model 38, was just forward of the takedown latch. As a result, the takedown latch could be confused with a safety, such as the type of safety located on the top tang, which is used on some shotguns. To solve the problem, C.G. Swebilius designed a latch mechanism that had to be pressed down before the takedown slide could be moved rearward, thereby eliminating the possibility of inadvertently having the rifle separate into two pieces. (See Model 38 description for more information.)

The specifications for the Model 32 were cataloged as follows:

> Rifles are take-down, with trombone action and solid-top, side ejecting safety construction. They handle .22 short, .22 long and .22 long-rifle cartridges without change or adjustment. Made with 24 octagon barrel only; no other length or style furnished. Blued frame; black walnut buttstock and

Patent drawing of Model 32 hammerless, pump action .22 rifle.

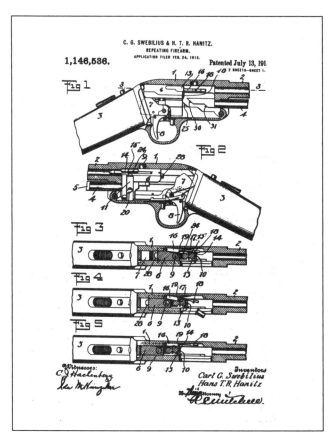

Patent drawing of the Model 32 ejector mechanism.

forend; ivory bead front sight and a special new flat top, adjustable wind-gauge rear sight. Buttstock is 13½ inches long, with 1⁷⁄₁₆ inches drop at comb, and 3 inches drop at heel; with a comfortable full pistol grip and genuine hard rubber buttplate.

Rifle measures 40 inches over all; 27¾ inches taken down. Regular 16-inch magazine holds 15 short, 12 long or 10 long-rifle cartridges. Full magazine (24 inches) holds 25 short, 20 long, or 18 long-rifle cartridges.

(Full magazine was available on special order at the same price as the standard model.)

It should be noted that the special rear sight introduced with this model was also used on some of the Model 38 rifles. However, both the Model 32 rifle and the Swebilius rear sight used on it are very scarce.

To take down the Model 32, all that was necessary was to grasp the barrel section in the left hand and, while holding the grip section with the right hand, pull back the latch button. The barrel section could then be tipped forward and disconnected from the stock and lower receiver section.

To remove the bolt mechanism, while the two parts are separated, one had to pull the forearm to the rear as far as it would go. The breech block would then be clear of the frame and could be removed.

To reassemble the gun, it was necessary to place the assembled breech block into the rear of the frame and push it forward to the closed position, hook the two receiver parts together at the front of the guard by engaging the hook onto the pin, and bring the butt part into place. The latch would then snap into place. The latch and its engaging surface in the top of the rear end of the receiver were tapered to allow for wear; this assured that the two parts of the receiver would not shoot loose.

When the Model 32 is cocked, the bolt is locked closed and cannot be opened until the gun is fired. However, to open the

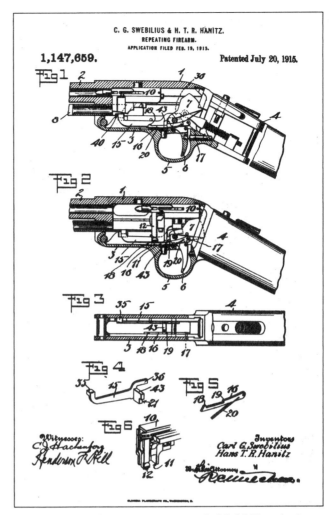

Patent drawing of 1915 improvements to the Model 32 mechanism.

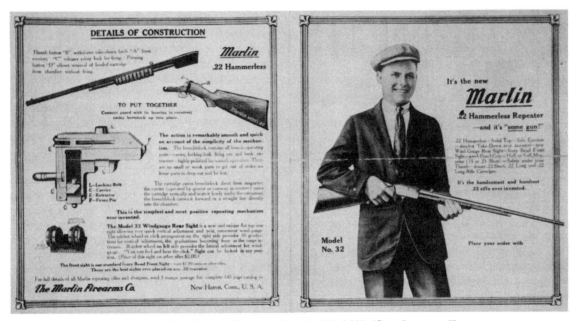

Marlin's advertising brochure advertising the Model 32 rifle as "some gun!"

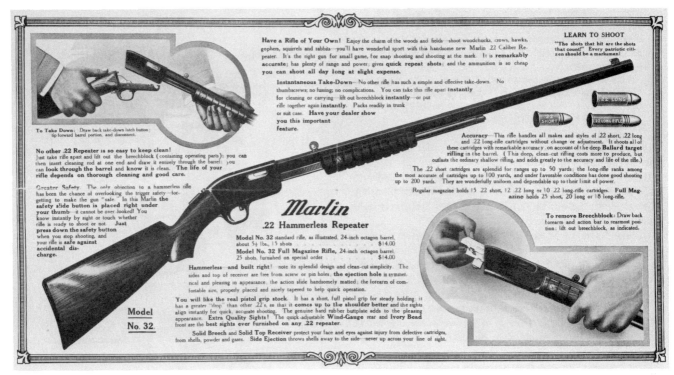

Illustration and description of Model 32 rifle.

Model 32 rear sight.

bolt without dropping the hammer or firing the gun, one can open the action by pressing in the sear release, which is located just forward of the trigger. The action lock is then released; the action can be opened and the cartridge in the chamber ejected without firing.

The safety on the Model 32 is a button that, when on safe, projects above the top of the tang. To put the safety of the rifle into the fire position, the button can be depressed by the thumb. To reactivate the safety, the safety slide that is located behind the trigger guard can be pressed up by a finger grasping the grip of the stock.

Marlin claimed the solid-top frame and side ejection protected the shooter from defective ammunition and ejected

shells and also prevented rain or snow, dirt, sand, and so on from getting into the gun. This was also Marlin's claim for the other pump action rifles that had exposed hammers and receivers not completely closed in at their rear end.

The Model 32 is marked *Marlin MOD. 32* on the bottom of the receiver, forward of the trigger guard. The serial number is stamped on the side of the upper tang of some Model 32s, and below the model marking on the bottom of the receiver on others.

Both Marlin Firearms Company and Marlin Firearms Corporation barrel markings have been observed on this model.

The lowest serial number reported is 194 and the highest observed is 5957.

The Marlin parts catalog combined the Model 32 and Model 38 in one list and, except for showing extractor pins and a round ejector spring for the Model 38 and extractor screws and a flat ejector spring for the Model 32, all parts are alike. (See Model 38 section for parts list; see Extras section for extra features that could be ordered.)

Model 36. If a rifle can be called "cute," the Model 36 single-shot caliber .22 pump action rifle is just that. It is made on the Model 18 receiver with the same type of detachable side-plate mechanism. The Model 36 does not have a tubular magazine; however, there is a dummy tube on which the forearm slides. When the forearm is pumped, the bolt lock is raised and the bolt is allowed to move rearward, extracting and ejecting the fired cartridge case. When loading, it was necessary only to drop the cartridge into the open breech and then pump the forearm forward. A spring-loaded loading tray positioned the cartridge so that it would feed into the chamber, because the

Marlin–Rockwell-marked Model 36 single-shot rifle.

Inside parts of Model 36 single-shot pump action caliber .22 rifle.

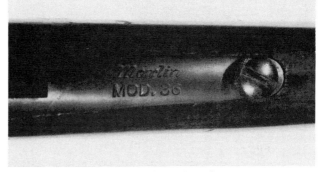

Top tang of Model 36 rifle.

opening was too small to allow the fingers to easily place a cartridge into the chamber.

Although it eliminated the extra cost of the usual magazine and carrier loading system of pump action rifles, the change did not reduce the price enough for the rifle to compete in the marketplace against the trend toward single-shot bolt action and drop-lever rifles.

Like the Model 18, the Model 36 had a knurled and headed stock screw that allowed removal of the stock.

To open the bolt with a cartridge in the chamber, it was necessary to push the firing pin forward.

It is believed that only prototypes and models of this rifle were made. No advertisements or production information have been located.

Model 37

The first Marlin exposed hammer pump action rifle that handled .22 short, .22 long, and .22 long-rifle cartridges interchangeably was the Model 20. Next came the Model 29. The Model 20 stayed in the catalog into 1922. The Model 29 was alive into 1917. In 1922, The Marlin Firearms Corporation introduced a rifle, nearly identical to these earlier two rifles, called the Model 37.

This new model designation did not include any changes to the characteristics of the earlier models. It just gave The Marlin Firearms Corporation a chance to bring out a new model under its own name.

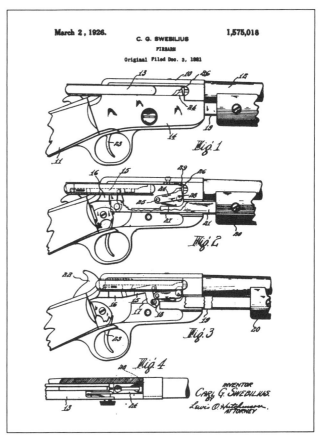

Patent drawing of Gus Swebilius's patent for the Model 36 single-shot .22 rifle.

The New Improved Marlin Model No. 37

Everybody needs a .22 Repeater—the universal rifle—for rabbits, squirrels, hawks, crows, foxes and all small game and target requirements.

Marlin Model 37—The tremendously popular .22 Caliber Slide Action Repeating Rifle with Visible Hammer.

Compare this rifle point by point with any other .22 with visible hammer and note its many superior features.

Marlin
Model No. 37

.22 Caliber Repeating Rifle, 24-inch Round Barrel, Genuine Ivory Bead Front and Flat Top Rocky Mountain Rear Sights, uses .22 Short, .22 Long and .22 Long-Rifle Cartridges.   Retail Price $21.75.

Solid-Top, Closed-In Receiver—the modern construction, which affords the shooter the greatest safety. Side-Ejection—ejected shells are thrown away from you—not rearward and across the line of sight. With the Marlin side-ejection construction you get quick sighting and fast shooting.

Take-Down construction—easy to clean and convenient to carry. The take-down system provides for wear; it cannot become loose or shaky, no matter how long it may be used. The barrel, full length, 24-inch round, has the deep, clean-cut Ballard rifling, which gives the greatest accuracy as well as extremely long life to the barrel.

Ivory Bead Front and Flat Top Rocky Mountain Rear Sights—the Ivory Bead Sight costs extra on other makes of .22 rifles. Barrel and Receiver have blued finish. Genuine Hard Rubber Buttplate.
A perfectly proportioned, finely balanced gun, made of the very best of materials, and guaranteed for Accuracy and Reliability. The choice of shooters who prefer the slide action, visible hammer type, .22 caliber rifle.

1923 circular announcing the "New Improved Marlin Model No. 37."

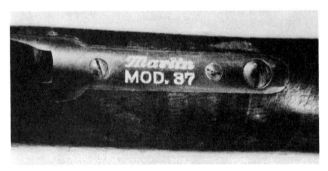

Top tang and model roll-stamp of the Model 37.

The Model 37 had a 24-in. round barrel and was chambered for use with the caliber .22 short, long, and long-rifle cartridges. It had a full-length magazine and was of the exposed hammer, pump action type, the same as the Model 20 rifle. The butt plate was hard rubber and had the Marlin name embossed in an oval pattern. The front sight had a genuine ivory bead and the rear sight was of the flat-top, V-notch, Rocky Mountain type. The barrel and action had a blued finish. The straight stock and forearm were walnut. The rifling was of the Ballard type, which gave great accuracy as well as long life.

For illustrations about parts and the operation of the Model 37 rifle, refer to the Model 20 section; except for using the late Model 20 type of firing pin and locking bolt, there are few differences between the two models.

Both the latch and button type of magazines have been observed on this model. In fact, the rifle illustrated in the Marlin ad reproduced here has the new button-type magazine.

Like the Models 18, 20, 25, 29, 32, 37, and some 38s, the serial number is stamped on the left side of the tang, under the wood. To read the number, it is necessary to remove the stock.

The upper tang of the Model 37 is stamped on top, in two lines, *Marlin Mod. 37.* The barrel is roll-stamped *Marlin Firearms Corporation. NEW-HAVEN CONN. U.S.A. PAT'D USA MAR 24, 1908. 2 PATENTS.* The left side of the barrel is marked *22 S–L & L–R.*

The low and high serial numbers reported or observed for this model, and the retail prices listed in price lists and catalogs, are as follows:

Model		Low		High	
37		490		12,455	
1923	$21.75	1927	$22.00	1931	$22.00
1924	21.75	1928	22.00	1932	22.00
1925	21.75	1929	22.00		
1926	22.00	1930	22.00		

Model 38

The hammerless Model 38 rifle is a post-WW I version of the Model 32 rifle. It is in caliber .22 rimfire and handles without adjustment all .22 short, long and long-rifle cartridges. The magazine holds 15 short, 12 long or 10 long-rifle cartridges. The solid-top, side-ejection closed-in frame has a trombone (slide) action that is ideal for quick and accurate shots. The length of the Model 38 is 40 inches, and when taken down is 27¾ inches long. The length of the buttstock is 13½

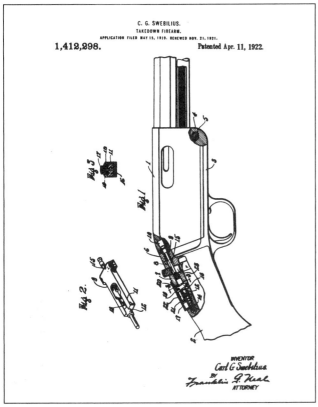

Patent drawing of takedown mechanism of Model 38 rifle.

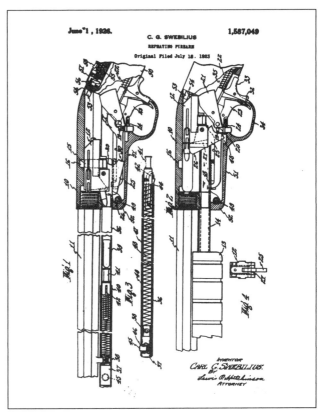

Patent drawing of button-type magazine tube and experimental safety and takedown latch.

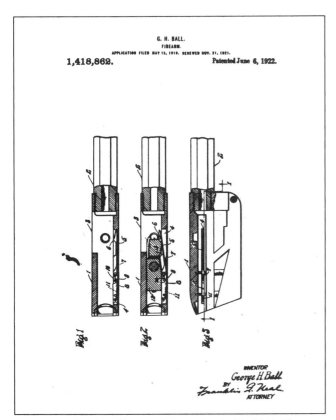

Patent drawing of improved ejector for the Model 38 rifle.

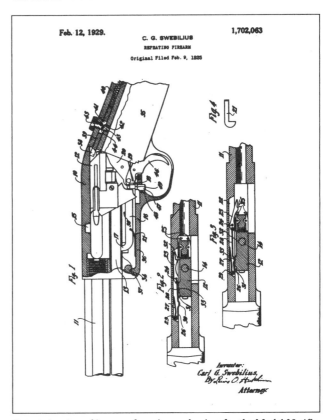

Patent drawing of improved carrier mechanism for the Model 38 rifle.

The Marlin Firearms Corporation 1922 ad for the Model 38 and 39 rifles.

inches. The drop at the comb is 1⁷/₁₆ inches and at the heel it is 3 inches.

It has a black walnut pistol grip buttstock and a grooved forearm. The barrel and receiver have the usual excellent Marlin blued finish. The butt plate is hard rubber and has embossed into it the Marlin name. The front sight is an ivory bead and the rear is a Rocky Mountain flat-top, V-notch adjustable sight.

The same patents for the Model 32 rifle apply to the Model 38 rifle. However, changes to the receiver, lock, ejector, magazine tube, and carrier resulted in additional patents for this model.

The additional patents of C.G. Swebilius that were incorporated into the model were the following:

Patent Number	Date	Invention
1,412,298	Apr. 1, 1922	Takedown mechanism
1,418,862	June 6, 1922	Ejector mechanism
1,587,049	June 1, 1926	Magazine tube
1,702,063	Feb. 12, 1929	Carrier mechanism

Two features in the 1926 patent that were not used were a new design of safety that was fitted into the rear of the trigger guard, blocking rearward movement of the trigger, and a latch behind the takedown button that prevented accidental unlocking of the two receiver parts.

It is of special importance to the Marlin collector to know that the magazine tube patented in patent number 1,587,049, dated June 1, 1926 (original filed July 18, 1923) is for the button type of release. Before this time, the magazine tubes had a latch that was squeezed to unlock the outer magazine tube.

Marlin brochure about the Model 38 rifle.

Marlin–Rockwell-marked Model 38 rifle with a Model 32 Swebilius rear sight installed.

Marlin Firearms Corporation Model 38 rifle with a 24-in. octagon barrel.

Model 38 rifle with a full-length magazine and Lyman tang sight.

First variation of roll-stamp on octagon barrel of Model 38 rifle.

Second variation of roll-stamp on round barrel of Model 38 rifle. Note the addition of two more patent dates.

Typical model marking and serial number of the Model 38.

Left: *Silver bead front sight.* Right: *Ivory bead front sight.*

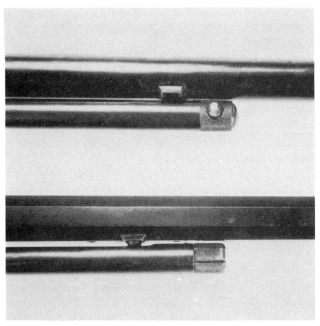

Top: *Button-type magazine tube introduced in Model 38 rifle.* Bottom: *Earlier latch-type magazine.*

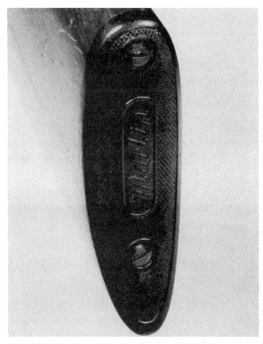

Typical hard rubber butt plate used on the Model 32 and 38 rifles.

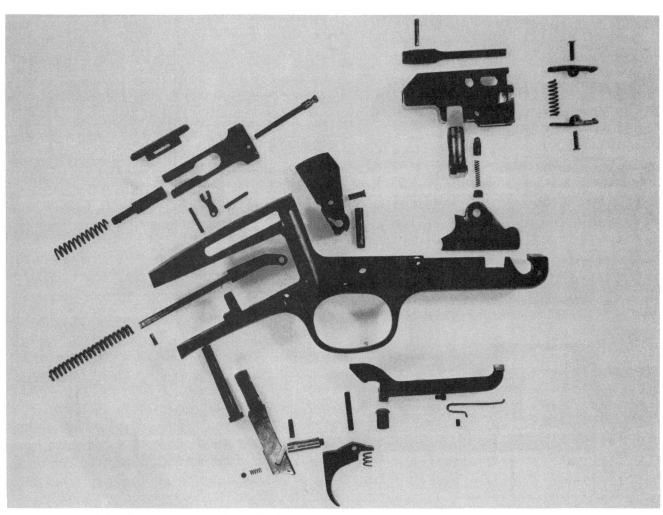

Bolt and receiver parts of the Model 38 rifle. Note that the bolt has the second type of carrier for this model.

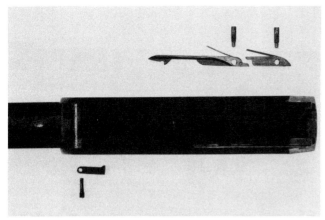

Ejector parts of Model 38 rifle.

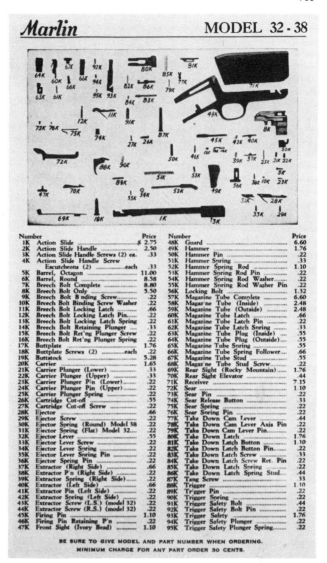

Marlin   MODEL 32 - 38

Number		Price	Number		Price
1K	Action Slide	$ 2.75	48K	Guard	6.60
2K	Action Slide Handle	2.50	49K	Hammer	1.76
3K	Action Slide Handle Screws (2) ea.	.33	50K	Hammer Pin	.22
4K	Action Slide Handle Screw		51K	Hammer Spring	.33
	Escutcheons (2)	each .33	52K	Hammer Spring Rod	1.10
5K	Barrel, Octagon	11.00	53K	Hammer Spring Rod Pin	.22
6K	Barrel, Round	8.58	54K	Hammer Spring Rod Washer	.22
7K	Breech Bolt Complete	8.80	55K	Hammer Spring Rod Washer Pin	.22
8K	Breech Bolt Only	5.50	56K	Locking Bolt	1.32
9K	Breech Bolt Binding Screw	.22	57K	Magazine Tube Complete	6.60
10K	Breech Bolt Binding Screw Washer	.22	58K	Magazine Tube (Inside)	2.48
11K	Breech Bolt Locking Latch	.66	59K	Magazine Tube (Outside)	2.48
12K	Breech Bolt Locking Latch Pin	.22	60K	Magazine Tube Latch	.66
13K	Breech Bolt Locking Latch Spring	.22	61K	Magazine Tube Latch Pin	.22
14K	Breech Bolt Retaining Plunger	.33	62K	Magazine Tube Latch Spring	.33
15K	Breech Bolt Ret'ng Plunger Screw	.22	63K	Magazine Tube Plug (Inside)	.55
16K	Breech Bolt Ret'ng Plunger Spring	.22	64K	Magazine Tube Plug (Outside)	.55
17K	Buttplate	1.76	65K	Magazine Tube Spring	.55
18K	Buttplate Screws (2)	each .22	66K	Magazine Tube Spring Follower	.66
19K	Buttstock	5.28	67K	Magazine Tube Stud	.55
20K	Carrier	1.65	68K	Magazine Tube Stud Screw	.22
21K	Carrier Plunger (Lower)	.33	69K	Rear Sight (Rocky Mountain)	1.76
22K	Carrier Plunger (Upper)	.33	70K	Rear Sight Elevator	.44
23K	Carrier Plunger Pin (Lower)	.22	71K	Receiver	7.15
24K	Carrier Plunger Pin (Upper)	.22	72K	Sear	1.10
25K	Carrier Plunger Spring	.22	73K	Sear Pin	.22
26K	Cartridge Cut-off	.55	74K	Sear Release Button	.33
27K	Cartridge Cut-off Screw	.22	75K	Sear Spring	.22
28K	Ejector	.66	76K	Sear Spring Pin	.22
29K	Ejector Screw	.22	77K	Take Down Cam Lever	.44
30K	Ejector Spring (Round) Model 38	.22	78K	Take Down Cam Lever Axis Pin	.44
31K	Ejector Spring (Flat) Model 32	.22	79K	Take Down Cam Lever Pin	.22
32K	Ejector Lever	.55	80K	Take Down Latch	1.76
33K	Ejector Lever Screw	.22	81K	Take Down Latch Button	1.10
34K	Ejector Lever Spring	.22	82K	Take Down Latch Button Pin	.22
35K	Ejector Lever Spring Pin	.22	83K	Take Down Latch Screw	.33
36K	Ejector Spring Pin	.22	84K	Take Down Latch Screw Ret. Pin	.22
37K	Extractor (Right Side)	.66	85K	Take Down Latch Spring	.22
38K	Extractor Pin (Right Side)	.22	86K	Take Down Latch Spring Stud	.44
39K	Extractor Spring (Right Side)	.22	87K	Tang Screw	.33
40K	Extractor (Left Side)	.66	88K	Trigger	1.10
41K	Extractor Pin (Left Side)	.22	89K	Trigger Pin	.22
42K	Extractor Spring (Left Side)	.22	90K	Trigger Spring	.22
43K	Extractor Screw (L.S.) (model 32)	.22	91K	Trigger Safety Bolt	.44
44K	Extractor Screw (R.S.) (model 32)	.22	92K	Trigger Safety Bolt Pin	.22
45K	Firing Pin	1.10	93K	Trigger Safety	1.76
46K	Firing Pin Retaining Pin	.22	94K	Trigger Safety Plunger	.22
47K	Front Sight (Ivory Bead)	1.10	95K	Trigger Safety Plunger Spring	.22

BE SURE TO GIVE MODEL AND PART NUMBER WHEN ORDERING.
MINIMUM CHARGE FOR ANY PART ORDER 30 CENTS.

Marlin parts catalog list of Model 32 and 38 parts.

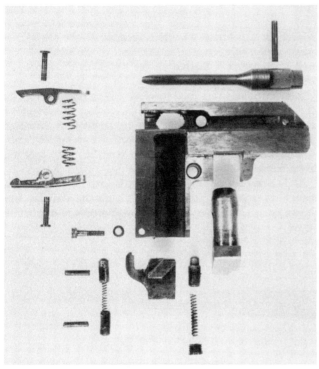

Bolt parts of Model 38 rifle.

As explained in other parts of this book, the Marlin–Rockwell Corporation did intend to return to the manufacture of sporting firearms after the wrap-up of its war production at the end of WW I. Evidence to support this can be found in a very few prewar production models that Marlin–Rockwell roll-stamped with its name and to which it gave a new model designation. One example is Model 27S marked as Model 40. Another is a single-shot pump action .22 marked Model 36. There are also Model 38 rifles marked *Marlin–Rockwell*. Therefore, it appears to me that the change from Model 32 to Model 38 was originally a decision of the Marlin–Rockwell people, rather than The Marlin Firearms Corporation organization. Interestingly, this Model 38 is serial number 1315 and it has the Model 32 adjustable rear sight.

The low and high serial numbers of the Model 38 reported or observed have been as follows:

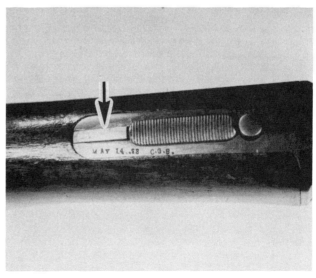

Arrow points to patented, but not used, safety latch for the takedown button.

Arrow indicates patented, but not used, safety for the Model 38 rifle.

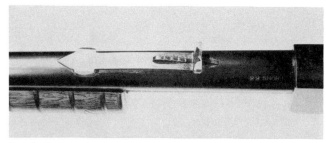

Standard rear sight of the Model 38 rifle. Note the .22 SHORT caliber marking on this 21½-in. round-barrel, serial number 920 rifle that has the Marlin Firearms Corporation name and 1922 patent date.

Model	Low	High
38	782	10,938
	A206	A11,389
	D272	D1,739

The prices for the Model 38 as shown in Marlin price lists were as follows:

Year	Octagon	Round
1922 (Jan.)	$26.50	
1922 (June)	21.50	$23.50
1923	26.00	24.75
1924	26.00	24.75
1925	26.00	24.75
1926	26.30	25.80
1927	26.30	25.80
1928	26.30	25.80
1929	30.00	22.80

A special tang receiver sight was manufactured by the Lyman Gunsight Company for the Model 38 rifle. It is illustrated in the Sight section of this book. The sight is rarer than the rifle.

Model 40. The Model 40 rifle is identical to the Model 27S pump action rifle, except that the name of the Marlin-Rockwell Corporation is marked on the barrel, and it is marked *Marlin/MOD. 40,* instead of *Marlin/No. 27S,* on the top tang.

It is speculated that the Model 40 was another attempt by the Marlin-Rockwell Corporation to change the image of models that had been in production by the previous company, and to give them a new identity as sporting arms models, since Marlin-Rockwell was attempting to reestablish the sporting arms business abandoned before WW I.

Only a rare few of the Model 40 variation of the Model 27S have been examined. No production figures are available. But it can be assumed that only a few were produced marked as

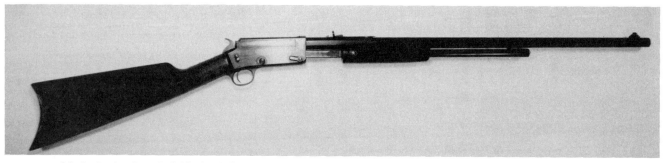

Marlin-Rockwell-marked rifle that is the same as the Model 27 rifle, except it is marked Marlin/MOD. 40 *on the top tang.*

Top tang marking of Model 40 rifle, serial number 17,196.

Marlin-Rockwell roll-stamp marking on Model 40 barrel. The patent dates are the same as on the early Model 27.

Marlin's free rifle and shotgun offer of 1931 that includes the Model 47.

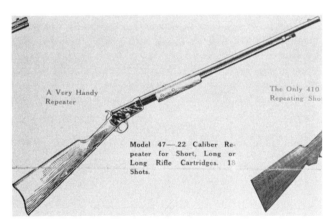

Blown-up section of Model 47 illustration in stock offer.

Internal parts of the Model 47 rifle.

Model 40, since the succeeding Marlin Firearms Corporation and The Marlin Firearms Company both advertised and sold this gun as the Model 27S.

Model 47

The Model 47 slide action, exposed hammer, caliber .22 takedown rifle was an exception to the rule. This was mainly because cosmetically, it did not fit the usual pattern of slide action .22s Marlin had been manufacturing for many years.

The exterior differences in this model from the others are the case-colored frame and checkered buttstock and forearm. Otherwise, it looks like the Model 20 rifle.

The internal mechanism has the same type of firing pin, locking bolt, and receiver as the Model 20A, although it does have a 23-in. round barrel and new type of magazine.

To operate the magazine of the Model 47 rifle, the inner tube is unlocked and withdrawn until a loading port is exposed in the outer tube into which the cartridges are then loaded. The inner tube is then pushed to the rear and locked in place by rotating the tube until a projecting pin is locked into the bayonet-type locking notch in the outer tube.

The smooth forearm and grip of the straight stock are checked in a diamond pattern. The case-colored receiver was case-hardened using a method different from the usual Marlin

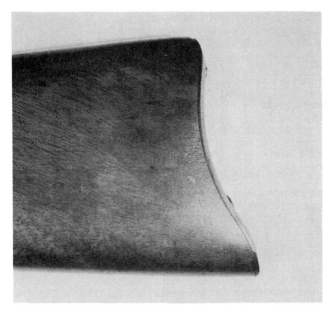

Typical steel butt plate of the Models 18, 20, 25, 29, and 47 rifles.

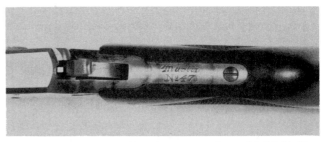

Model designation stamped into the top tang of some Model 47 rifles.

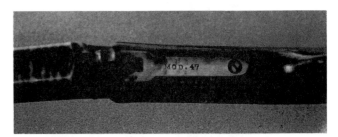

Top tang marking as found on some Model 47 rifles.

"packed in bone and charred leather" technique. The new method was to dip the parts while red-hot into molten cyanide, thereby making the skin of the pieces harder and adding varied colors to the surface. The cyanide method of casing metal does not duplicate the colors of the earlier method used by Marlin. However, the method used on the Model 47 receiver and bolt was to lower the pieces into the cyanide and then stop a number of times, giving the pieces the tiger stripes that are found on only the Marlin Model 47 rifle.

The checked wood and unique case-coloring of the receiver and bolt of the Model 47 made this rifle different from any other Marlin slide action rifle. But the most interesting fact about the rifle is that it was not a catalog-featured rifle. Instead, it was one of the rifles offered free with the purchase of four shares of Marlin preferred stock for $100.00.

The Model 47 was listed as an 18-shot repeater that handled .22 short, long, and long-rifle cartridges interchangeably.

The top tang was marked either *Marlin No. 47* or *MOD. 47.* The round barrel was roll-stamped the same as the Model 37 rifle with *The Marlin Firearms Corporation. NEW-HAVEN CONN. USA PAT'D USA MAR.24.1908.2 PATENTS* in two lines. The barrel was also marked *22 S.L&L.R.*

A Model 47 has been inspected that has all the previously mentioned characteristics along with added engraving. The decorative engraving is on both sides of the receiver and appears to have been done after case hardening. It is my opinion that this engraving was not done by Marlin.

The lowest serial number noted for this model is 1247; the highest, 5101.

SECTION III

Expanded Glossary

Expanded Glossary

Advertising

Marlin has always used the accepted advertising techniques to reach the sportsman of America. An annual product catalog that illustrated the many different models of firearms and other items Marlin manufactured or sold was the foremost method used; however, ads in national publications such as *Recreation, Country Gentleman, Field and Stream, Forest and Stream, Arms and the Man, The American Rifleman, Sports Afield, Outdoor Life, Hunting and Fishing,* and many others were used to keep the Marlin name in front of sportsmen everywhere. The ads usually featured one or more models, pointing out the important features of Marlin firearms and their superiority. Also mentioned in ads was that, upon receipt of postage, a catalog would be mailed free. (Catalogs for

1897 ad for Marlin repeating rifles.

1900 ad for Marlin big game rifles.

1905 ad selling Marlin's solid-top receiver.

470

1906 ad recommending that a Marlin rifle be selected where wet and cold prevail in the Klondike.

1909 ad for Marlin repeating shotgun.

1909 ad for Marlin .22 repeating rifles.

1930s picture of Marlin's New Haven plant advertising Marlin guns.

the last 30 years have been mailed to requesters, free and postpaid.)

Marlin has also used billboards and spot radio pitches to keep the name Marlin in front of the public. The old Willow Street, New Haven, plant had the Marlin name strategically placed on the water tank where it could be seen for miles and from heavily trafficked roads. The Marlin name and horse and rider logo are also in view at the present North Haven, Conn., plant, both on the side of the building and on the bright blue water tank. Since the plant is bounded by the Interstate 91 fence, hundreds of thousands of people see Marlin's modern plant and name annually.

Marlin also advertises by attending the annual Shooting, Hunting, Outdoor Trade Show (SHOT Show) and the National Rifle Association (NRA) annual meeting and display show. Booths manned by company officials and sales representatives give the public a chance to talk one-on-one with the folks who know the products.

Decals, jacket patches, posters, counter pads, counter displays, and contests have all been used by Marlin to advertise its product line; however, it is my opinion that the best method to inform the potential customer about Marlin firearms is still the catalog and early response to inquiries from the public.

Throughout this book, there are many ads illustrated that relate to specific models. Here are a few of the old classics and a few of the later type that illustrate and describe many of the models of Marlin firearms that were available to the sportsman.

Display stand furnished during the 1950s to dealers for use on counters or in display windows.

Counter display showing the parts and pieces of the Model 336. This was furnished through Marlin distributors to their retail outlets.

Pre-1897 Sports Afield *ad offering free Marlin rifles to sportsmen for subscriptions they send in.*

American Arms Company

A November 2, 1901 article in the *Army and Navy Journal* indicated that Marlin purchased the machinery of The American Arms Company, Boston, Mass. Numerous references state that the American Arms Company made Smith carbines at Chicopee Falls, Mass., during the Civil War and that from 1866 to 1893 the offices were located at 103 Milk St., Boston, Mass. These references also indicate that the company moved to Milwaukee, Wis., in 1897 and continued to manufacture shotguns until 1904 or later. From these various references it can be seen that Marlin did not purchase the company. The acquisition was of machine tools and equipment that were needed to expand the sporting arms business initiated in 1901 by Mahlon H. Marlin and J. Howard Marlin upon the death of their father, J.M. Marlin, in 1901.

American Cartridge and Ammunition Company

The June 1904 issue of *The National Sportsman* magazine indicated that The Marlin Fire Arms Company acquired The American Cartridge and Ammunition Company of Hartford. The article stated:

> The American Cartridge and Ammunition Co. was organized in Hartford on August 15, 1901. It has a large plant on Pearl St. and was capitalized at $100,000. The officers of the company are President C.F.A. Eddy, V.P. J.A. Wiley and Sec/Tres. Henry Farnum.

Ammunition

Frequently the collector asks: "What cartridge can I use in my old Marlin?" or "Where can I find ammunition for my old Marlin?"

With regard to the first question, all owners of old rifles, pistols, and shotguns must first establish if their gun is safe to use and if the ammunition planned to use in it is suitable for the gun. Next, no one should try to use cartridges for which the gun was not designed. Most old Marlins and all modern Marlins are marked on the barrel with the caliber of the gun.

However, there have been mistakes made in such markings, so a doublecheck should be made.

Every gun owner must recognize that any gun can be blown up, causing injury or death. Overloaded or incorrectly loaded ammunition, obstructions in the bore, incorrect ammunition, broken parts, or damaged guns could be the reason for such unfortunate happenings.

Many gun buffs want to handload cartridges for their old Marlins, and the old Marlin catalogs are full of information about loading ammunition. But this writer does not recommend any of the old Marlins manufactured before 1948 be kept in service by handloading cartridges for them. The main reasons for this position are that too frequently the wrong kind of powder, or too much powder, other errors in handloading, or guns not in serviceable condition frequently cause loss of eyes, bodily injury, or death. Why take a chance? If you're not sure, see a qualified gunsmith for advice.

In answer to the second question, owners of old Marlin firearms must recognize that many of the old cartridges for which their guns were made are now obsolete and no longer on the market. Or, if they are, they are hard to find and very expensive. The main thing to remember is not to experiment and try to use a cartridge just because it can be loaded into the gun. Damage to the gun, injury, or death could result.

None of the old Marlin single-shot derringers, and single-action and double-action revolvers should be used. They were not manufactured for use with today's ammunition and, at best, are dangerous to the user. It is better to be safe than sorry.

To better understand the names of cartridges, it is necessary to know the meaning of the numerical designations given to cartridges. Without getting too far afield from the purpose of this book, a few explanations are necessary to help the collector know the nomenclature of cartridges.

1. Early designations frequently included the name of the inventor of the cartridge, or the make of firearm for which it was designed.
   Examples: .40-65 Ballard, .40-90 Ballard, .40-90 Sharps, .44 Henry, .32 Short Colt, .45-70 Govt., .32-40 Marlin, .45-70 Marlin.
2. The diameter of the bullet, or the diameter of the bore, in 100ths of an inch, was usually the first designator.
   Examples: .22, .30, .32, .38, .40, .44, .45.
3. The black powder charge was also included along with the bullet size in the designation of a cartridge, and was the second designator.
   Examples: .30-30, .32-40, .38-40, .38-55, .45-70, .45-90.
4. The weight of the bullet (in grains) was often the third designation of a cartridge.
   Examples: .45-70-230, .45-70-350, .38-55-250 paper patched, .40-65-330 Ballard Everlasting.
5. The manufacturer of the ammunition, or the name of the company designing the cartridge, was frequently included as part of the official name of a cartridge.
   Examples: .32-20 Winchester (.32 WCF, .32-20 WCF), .38-40 WCF, .32-40 Marlin, .35 Remington, .33 Winchester.
6. The type of bullet is frequently listed by the manufacturer to identify the purpose for which the bullet was designed.
   Examples: .32 HPS (High Power Special) metal cased, soft point; .32-20 Marlin Smokeless, metal clad, soft point; .38-40 Marlin Smokeless, soft point HV (High Velocity), paper patch, grooved or greased.
7. The kind of powder is also included in some ammunition listings to help identify the cartridge.

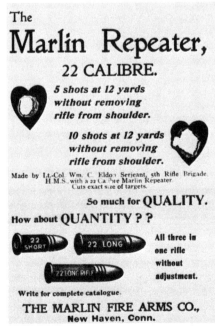

Marlin 1896 ad for Model 1892 caliber .22 rifle.

Marlin 1900 ad for the Model 1894 caliber .25-20 repeating rifles.

Marlin ad about the .32-40 Ballard & Marlin cartridge.

Marlin extolling the advantage of using the .32–40 Ballard & Marlin cartridge.

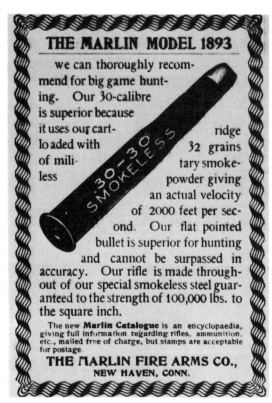

Marlin 1897 ad selling the Model 1893 cartridge and .30–30 cartridge.

Marlin ad stating that the .38–55 cartridge is conceded to be the most accurate and greatest game killer ever used in a repeater.

Examples: Black, Smokeless, Semismokeless, "Lesmok."

8. Suffix abbreviations were frequently part of the name of the cartridge.
Examples: .44–40 WCF = .44–40 Winchester Center-Fire; .45 ACP = .45 Automatic Colt Pistol; .32 HPS = .32 High Power Special.

9. Popular names were late additions to the name of cartridges, especially after the numerical caliber designation became cluttered because of the many different cartridges using the same basic bullet diameter (the common reference to identifying a cartridge).
Examples: .22 Hornet, .218 Bee, .219 Zipper, .22 Jet, and others.

10. When a cartridge is no longer with its box or container, the headstamp found on center-fire cartridges frequently can be used to identify it.
Examples: W.R.A. CO. .25–20 WCF, W.R.A. CO. .32 WCF, REM-UMC .38–40 Win, UMC .44–40 H.V., WESTERN .44–40.

11. Rimfire cartridges are not marked on the head with caliber designations. If marked at all, it is usually with a mark or initial that identifies only the manufacturer.
Examples: H (Winchester), P (Peters), U (Remington).

Few companies can go through years of manufacturing a product without some controversy or argument with another company in the same industry, and Marlin was not an exception. Winchester sued Marlin over what it thought was an infringement of its takedown patent and Marlin did the same to Savage for what Marlin thought was an infringement of the L.L. Hepburn Model 1897 takedown patent. However, the only argument Marlin had with a brother company that was publicly aired was Marlin's complaint that Winchester changed the primer size of cartridges that had been used by Marlin gun owners for many years. The Marlin position is outlined in the following circular addressed "To Whom it May Concern" and dated January 1887:

Page from Marlin 1887 catalog illustrating cartridges for Ballard rifles.

Rimfire and center-fire cartridges for which some Ballard rifles were chambered.

THE MARLIN FIRE ARMS COMPANY

New Haven, Conn., January 10th, 1887

To Whom It May Concern:

Some weeks ago we wrote to our customers advising them not to sell Winchester ammunition for 32, 38, and 40 caliber Marlin rifles for the reason that the cartridges made by the Winchester Repeating Arms Co.

in these sizes, were not properly constructed. Under date of December 10th, 1886, the Winchester Co. issued a printed circular to the public, making some remarks to which we deem a reply necessary.

To begin at the beginning: The first Marlin Rifles which we made were 45 calibre and intended to take the United States Government regulation cartridge. We were soon satisfied that the large primer used in the Government cartridge was not the proper one for a Magazine Rifle, and we induced both the U.M.C. and the Winchester Companies

Illustration in early Marlin catalog depicting cartridges used in the Model 1891, 1892, and 1894 rifles.

to furnish ammunition for our Rifles using small primers. These 45 calibre cartridges are still made in that manner (See page 63 of the Winchester Catalogue, dated October, 1886).

Shortly after this, we brought out the 40–60, an entirely new size, ammunition for which was made by both Companies, also with a small primer at our request and from our gauges. Some time after that, we called on the Winchester Co. with a model and gauge for the 38–55 cartridge; after examining the model cartridge and having noticed that it was made with a small primer and flat pointed ball, one of the officers of the Winchester Co., who was present, remarked that we were evidently intending to use this cartridge for a magazine gun. We affirmed that this was our intention and a further remark was made by this officer saying, that this was the proper way to get up a cartridge for that purpose. We introduce this incident to show that the Winchester Co. fully understood the point at issue. The 38–55 cartridge as well as the 32–40, which latter we brought out at the same time, were also made just like the 40–60 and 45–70 had been, with a small primer.

1. .32 Short, Colt, center-fire; 2. .32 Long, Colt, center-fire; 3. .32 Short, S&W, center-fire; 4. .32 Long, S&W, center-fire; 5. .32 Short, rimfire; 6. .32 Long, rimfire.

These cartridges are so advertised in their Catalogue of November, 1885, page 66. A significant fact in this connection is that the 40–60 Winchester cartridge (which was made to compete with our 40–60) was then and is now made with a small primer. We claim that ammunition for Repeating Rifles, where the cartridges follow each other consecutively in a tube, should in all cases, have SMALL primers to insure perfect safety, as when large primers are used, there is more or less liability, if the weapon be severely jolted, to an explosion of one or more cartridges in the magazine, because the bullet of one cartridge abuts against the primer of the next. If small primers are used, the apex of the bullet will not touch the primer but come against the solid head of the shell, thus insuring perfect safety in that respect. We guarantee the Marlin Rifle to be PERFECTLY SAFE, and therefore insist on small primers as the only proper ones.

In the matter of the Army Trials to which their circular refers and in which they claim that the Board tested large primers with entirely satisfactory results, the Report of the Board shows that an exhaustive test was made on this point and that large primer cartridges twice exploded in the magazine, thus proving that our objections to ammunition so made are well taken.

Some months ago we began to get complaints of miss-fires. These complaints continued to come in from all parts of the country, parties usually claiming that the cause must be some defect in the Arm. We investigated and found in each case, ammunition of the Winchester make had been used, and then for the first time we discovered that they had altered the cartridges 32–40, 38–55, and 40–60, and substituted large primers; we also found that the primer pockets had been made nearly $1/32$ of an inch too deep, so that the first blow sent the primer deeper into the pocket and it required another blow to explode it. We were much annoyed, had been put to considerable expense, and as a large amount of the Winchester make of Marlin cartridges were on the market distributed all over the country, it would have been serious for us to allow the matter to go any further. We called twice on the Winchester Co. to have the matter remedied, but received no satisfaction, and when we found, on the issue of their Catalogue of October, 1886, that they did not intend to accede to our request to go back to the original style of Marlin cartridges, which had been made from models and gauges furnished by us, we concluded the only way to protect ourselves and prevent our Arms being condemned and driven out of the market by faulty ammunition, was to take the same course that the Winchester Co. claim they had to take with regard to their own Arms, and guarantee our Rifles only when used with ammunition properly constructed.

We do not question the ability of the Winchester Co. to make good ammunition, as we have had abundant proof that they can do so, but what we claim is, that this particular ammunition is not properly made for the purpose it is intended for. We are not makers of ammunition and it is for our interest that any and all makes of cartridges can be used in our Arms. If the Winchester Co. will see fit to go back to first principles, we shall take pleasure in advising the use of their cartridges for Marlin Rifles equally with those of other manufacturers.

One other point: In the Winchester circular a fling is made at the quality of our Arms. The best comment to be offered upon this matter, is, that, with the prices of our Rifles about 20 per cent. higher than the Winchester, the sale during 1886 had INCREASED 35 PER CENT. over any previous year, and we have never been obliged to meet their prices to do all the trade our facilities would permit.

We do not like controversies and regret the necessity of this circular; but we desire to have the matter put in its true light and to keep our goods properly and favorably before the public.

Respectfully yours,
THE MARLIN FIRE ARMS CO.

During later years the primer problem disappeared and Marlin enjoyed a good relationship with Winchester and all other U.S. ammunition manufacturers.

For many years Marlin sold ammunition, reloading components, and reloading tools and accessories and, although no specific details or records have survived time that furnish details about Marlin manufacturing them, there are examples of boxed Everlasting cartridge shells, bullets of various sizes and weights, and shells that are marked *Manufactured by J.M. Marlin* or *The Marlin Fire Arms Co.*

1. .25–20 Marlin; 2. .32–20 Marlin; 3. .38–40 Marlin; 4. .44–40 Marlin.

Marlin also devoted many pages to descriptions and capabilities of various cartridges, reloading implements, and loading tools. The loading tools were either its own Ballard tools or the many types and kinds manufactured by The Ideal Manufacturing Company. In fact, Marlin must have been one of Ideal's best customers because in 1910 Marlin acquired that company.

Some of the many items Marlin cataloged were as follows, in this excerpt from the 1882 catalog:

Reloading tools for grooved bullets, per set $5.00
Bullet mould for grooved bullets 2.00
Bullet mould for patched bullets 1.50
Swage, made with great care 5.00

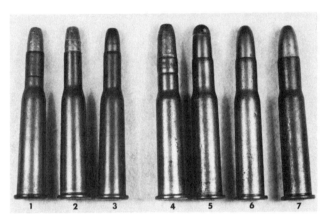

1. .25–36 Marlin Short Range; 2. .25–36 Marlin Soft Point; 3. .25–36 Marlin F.M. Patch; 4. .30–30 Short Range; 5. .30–30 Soft Point; 6. .32 Winchester Special (32 HPS); 7. .32 Winchester Open Point Expanding.

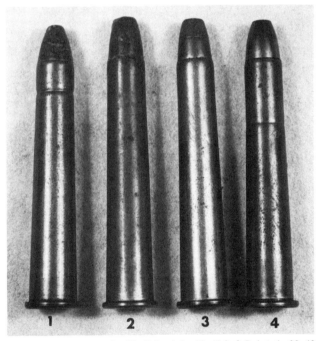

1. .32–40 Short Range; 2. .32–40 Lead; 3. .32–40 Soft Point; 4. .32–40 High Power.

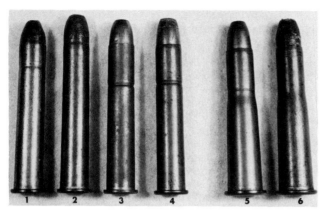

1. .38-55 Short Range; 2. .38-55 Lead; 3. .38-55 F.M. Patch; 4. .38-55 Smokeless; 5. .38-56 Soft Point; 6. .38-56 Lead.

1. .40-60 Marlin; 2. .40-65 WCF; 3. .40-82 WCF; 4. .40-70 WCF.

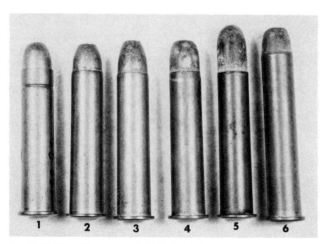

1. .45-70 Short Range; 2. .45-85 Ballard; 3. .45-85 Marlin; 4. .45-70 Marlin; 5. .45-70 Govt.; 6. .45-90.

Ball seater, nickeled	1.50
De- and Re-capper	1.40
Wad cutter	.40
Scoop for measuring powder	.15
Hawksley's Creedmoor Flask, 12 oz., 60-150 grams	3.50
Wilkinson's Shell loader	3.00
Loading Tube, 24 inches long	.50
Primer, per thousand	2.00
Wads, per thousand	.30
Lubricating disks, per thousand	.60
Farrow's Lubricating Material, per box	.25
Cut paper patches, per thousand	.50
Patch, paper, per quire	.75

The Marlin 1896 catalog described the Marlin Everlasting center-fire shells that were available from 1882 until 1905 as follows:

These [shells] are made of heavy metal, specially prepared, and are much stronger and more durable than the ordinary solid head shell. There is no necessity of reducing after firing. They are cheaper in the long run than ordinary shells, as each one will last for years, if properly used and thoroughly cleaned after firing, so that they will not corrode. The only practical shells for single shot target use.

They were available as follows:

Caliber	Price
.32-40	5¢ each
.38-50	8¢ each
.38-55	6¢ each
.40-63	7¢ each
.40-65	9¢ each
.40-70	7¢ each
.40-85	8¢ each
.40-90	11¢ each
.44-75	10¢ each
.44-100	12¢ each

Marlin and Ballard Bullets
Price per 1,000

Caliber	Grooved	Patched
.32-165	$ 7.25	$10.00
.32-185	7.75	9.75
.38-255	9.50	11.00
.38-330	11.00	11.50
.40-285	9.50	11.00
.40-330	11.00	11.50
.40-370	–	12.50
.40-260	9.00	–
.44-405	–	15.00
.45-420	–	15.00
.45-550	–	20.00

Until 1915, Marlin sold ammunition of the calibers for which it manufactured firearms. Catalog descriptions of the cartridges up to that time read as follows:

For the Models 1891, 1892, 1897, 39, and pump action 22s chambered for caliber .22 cartridges:

.22 SHORT: Loaded with three grains of black powder and a solid lead bullet 30 grains in weight. This is an extremely accurate cartridge for short ranges, and as now made gives very uniform results. It is the cartridge for gallery use and ordinary shooting where range and power are not desired. The penetration, as measured by dry pine boards ¾ inch thick, placed 20 feet from the muzzle of the rifle, is 4½ boards.

.22 SHORT MUSHROOM: Loaded with three grains of black powder and a hollow point bullet 27 grains in weight. As the bullet mushrooms on impact, the penetration is less, being but 3½ boards under the same conditions as previously described. This cartridge is designed for hunting at short range. The velocity of this bullet, owing to the slight reduction in weight, should be a trifle greater than that of the solid bullet, while the trajectory should also be a trifle flatter.

.22 SHORT SMOKELESS: Loaded with smokeless powder and a solid lead bullet 30 grains in weight. The velocity of this bullet is greater than with the black powder cartridge and the bullet holds up a trifle higher. This cartridge is accurate and clean to use. The penetration is five boards placed as above described.

.22 SHORT SMOKELESS MUSHROOM: Loaded with smokeless powder and a hollow-pointed bullet 27 grains in weight. This is another special hunting cartridge. The penetration is 3½ boards under the conditions above described, the penetration being less, owing to the mushrooming of the bullet.

.22 LONG: Loaded with five grains of black powder and a solid lead bullet 30 grains in weight. The penetration as measured above is 4½ boards. This cartridge has the same bullet as the short cartridge, with a greater charge of powder, giving the flatter trajectory with a little higher velocity. While it is not superior to the .22 short in accuracy and range, it is a better hunting cartridge at short distances.

.22 LONG MUSHROOM: Loaded with five grains of black powder and a hollow-pointed bullet 27 grains in weight. Naturally this cartridge would show a trifle higher velocity and flatter trajectory owing to the lighter bullet, but the difference is not appreciable except with very careful measurement. It is a good hunting cartridge.

.22 LONG SMOKELESS: Loaded with smokeless powder and solid lead bullet 30 grains in weight.

.22 LONG SMOKELESS MUSHROOM. Loaded with smokeless powder and hollow-pointed bullet 27 grains in weight.

.22 LONG SHOT: Loaded with black powder and No. 12 shot; gives a fair pattern up to 40 feet.

.22 LONG-RIFLE: Loaded with five grains of special black powder and a solid lead bullet 40 grains in weight. This cartridge has exactly the same shell as the .22-long, the bullet being 10 grains heavier and consequently projecting from the shell a little further, making a longer cartridge over all. As the shell is not crimped heavily on the bullet, this tends to produce greater accuracy. Owing to the heavier bullet, the velocity is not as great as that of the .22-long, while the trajectory is higher; but the penetration is much greater, the effective range is triple that of the long cartridge and the accuracy of this cartridge is almost phenomenal. The penetration of this bullet as measured by the ¾ inch dry pine boards, placed 20 feet from the muzzle of the rifle, is 7½ boards. The trajectory figures are as follows:

Shooting at 100 yards —

The height of the bullet at 25 yards is 3.47 inches.

Box of .45 caliber 405-grain grooved bullets manufactured by The Marlin Fire Arms Company.

Box of .32 caliber 185-grain patched bullets manufactured by Winchester for Marlin rifles.

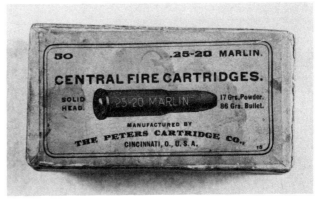

Box of .25–20 Marlin cartridges manufactured by The Peters Cartridge Company.

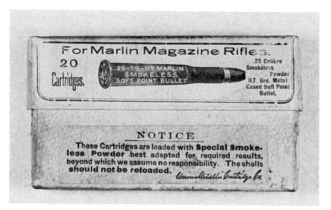

Box of .25–36–117 Marlin cartridges manufactured by Winchester for Marlin magazine rifles.

The height of the bullet at 50 yards is 4.44 inches.
The height of the bullet at 75 yards is 3.56 inches.
Shooting at 200 yards —
The height of the bullet at 50 yards is 14.79 inches.
The height of the bullet at 100 yards is 20.73 inches.
The height of the bullet at 150 yards is 16.07 inches.

.22 LONG-RIFLE MUSHROOM: Loaded with black powder and 35 grain hollow-pointed lead bullet.

.22 LONG-RIFLE SMOKELESS: This cartridge is the same as the regular Long-Rifle cartridge, except that it is loaded with Smokeless Powder. This was made to meet the great demand for a cartridge of this kind.

.22 LONG-RIFLE SMOKELESS MUSHROOM: Loaded with Smokeless Powder and 35 grain hollow-pointed lead bullet.

The .32 caliber rimfire and center-fire cartridges for the Model 1892 rifle were described as follows:

RIM-FIRE

.32 SHORT R.F.: This cartridge is loaded with nine grains of black powder and a lead bullet 82 grains in weight. It is accurate for 50 to 75 yards. The penetration, measured by ¾ inch dry pine boards, placed 20 feet from the muzzle of the rifle, is 6½ boards.

.32 LONG R.F.: This cartridge is loaded with 13 grains of black powder and a lead bullet 90 grains in weight. It is more powerful than the short cartridge, giving accurate results up to 100 yards. The penetration as measured above is 9½ boards.

.32 LONG-RIFLE R.F.: This is one of the new inside lubricated cartridges. It is loaded with 13 grains of black powder and a lead bullet 83 grains in weight. The penetration is nine boards arranged as above described. This cartridge is made especially for our rifle, and not only gives good results, but is clean and convenient to use.

CENTER-FIRE

.32 SHORT C.F.: This cartridge is also called the .32 short Colt. It is loaded with nine grains of black powder and a lead bullet 80 grains in weight.

.32 LONG C.F.: This cartridge is also called the .32 long Colt. It is loaded with 12 grains of black powder and a lead bullet 90 grains in weight.

In ordering the long center-fire cartridges, if of Winchester make, always specify Colt. What they call .32 long center-fire is not the original and standard .32 long, but a special longer cartridge. It will not fit this rifle.

.32 LONG-RIFLE C.F.: This is one of the new inside lubricated cartridges. It is loaded with 13 grains of black powder and a lead bullet 81 grains in weight.

In changing from outside to inside lubrication, there has been quite a transformation of the cartridges. Outside lubricated bullets are sometimes called heel bullets. They have two diameters, as the base is made smaller to fit in the shell, while the forward part is the size of the barrel bore, or the outside diameter of the shell. The projecting part of the bullet gives the bearing on the rifle. As made with inside lubrication, the shells are lengthened so as to inclose more of the bullet, which now has grooves to hold the lubrication. The bullets have a deep cavity at the base and are made of pure lead so that they will expand and take the rifling, since the bullet before firing will not fill the barrel bore. The length of the entire cartridge is the same as that of the outside lubricated cartridge, for the shell in the new cartridge is the same length as the shell and bearing part of the bullet in the old cartridge; consequently the new cartridge will chamber correctly in any rifle made for the original cartridge.

SMOKELESS POWDER: The Center-Fire cartridges are also loaded with smokeless powder.

The Model 27 and Model 1894, .25–20 rifles, handle all of the .25–20 Marlin cartridges, black, low pressure smokeless and high velocity smokeless. Marlin originated the .25–20 cartridge and was the first manufacturer to bring out a .25 caliber repeater, which was the Model 1894, to use the .25–20

Box of .32–40–165 cartridges for Marlin and Ballard rifles.

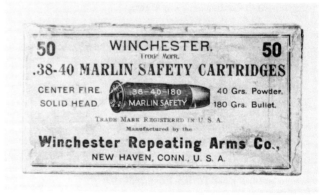

Box of .38–40–180 Marlin cartridges manufactured by Winchester.

Box of .36–56–255 cartridges manufactured for Marlin's Model 1895 rifle.

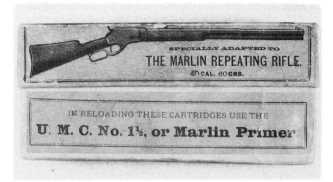

Box of .40–60 cartridges manufactured by Union Metallic Cartridge Company for the Marlin Repeating Rifle.

cartridge. The cartridge known as ".25-20 Winchester" varied somewhat from the .25-20 Marlin and Marlin suggested to get the proper cartridges to order Marlin's .25-20 cartridges. This is a very efficient and accurate cartridge at moderate ranges.

The factory cartridge is loaded with 17 grains of black powder and a bullet 86 grains in weight, the composition of which is one part tin to 60 parts lead.

The velocity of this bullet is 1547 feet per second; the penetration, as measured by dry pine boards, ⅞ inch in thickness, placed 20 feet from the muzzle of the rifle, is nine boards.

There is also the smokeless cartridge which has the same bullet and gives an increase in velocity, with a somewhat flatter trajectory. For hunting purposes many shooters prefer the 75 grain factory bullets, with which a higher velocity and flatter trajectory can be obtained, as owing to the shorter bullet the powder charge is increased when the bullet is seated with the regular tool, making the length over all the same as that of the cartridge with 86 grain bullet.

The .25-20 Marlin High Velocity cartridge is even more powerful. This has an 86 grain soft-point bullet, having an average velocity of over 1700 feet, and a penetration of 10 ⅞ inch boards.

.32-20 CARTRIDGES

The Model 27 and Model 1894 .32-20 Rifles use the .32-20 cartridge. This is a very accurate cartridge up to 200 yards. Beyond this distance it is less accurate, as the range is too great for the light load. Good results are obtained at longer ranges under favorable conditions. The factory cartridge is loaded with 20 grains of black powder and a bullet of pure lead, 100 grains in weight. The .32 W.C.F. cartridge, which is also suitable for this rifle, has a bullet 115 grains in weight.

The velocity of the bullet is 1234 feet per second. The penetration, as measured by dry pine boards one inch in thickness, placed 20 feet from the muzzle of the rifle, is six and one-quarter boards. The trajectory figures are as follows:

When shooting at 100 yards,
   The height of the bullet at 25 yards is 2.32 inches.
   The height of the bullet at 50 yards is 2.91 inches.
   The height of the bullet at 75 yards is 2.46 inches.
When shooting at 200 yards,
   The height of the bullet at 50 yards is 9.69 inches.
   The height of the bullet at 100 yards is 13.85 inches.
   The height of the bullet at 150 yards is 10.78 inches.

THE .32-20 SMOKELESS CARTRIDGE can be furnished with the 100 grain metal-cased bullet or with the 100 grain mushroom bullet (metal-patched with soft lead point). The velocity of the bullet in the smokeless cartridge is 1364 feet per second. The trajectory of the bullet is a little flatter than that obtained with the black powder cartridge. The full metal-cased bullet will penetrate eleven boards as above described. The cartridge with mushroom bullet is preferable for hunting purposes, because this bullet upon impact will spread, tearing a larger hole and using to a greater degree the energy of the bullet.

The .32-20 black and smokeless loads with hollow-point lead bullet have just been brought out. The hollow-point bullet mushrooms large, making an excellent hunting cartridge.

THE .32-20 MARLIN HIGH VELOCITY CARTRIDGE has a 115 grain soft point bullet, having an average velocity of about 1640 feet and a penetration of seven ⅞ inch boards.

   Shooting at 100 yards—Height at 50 yards, 2.09 inches.
   Shooting at 200 yards—Height at 100 yards, 10.70 inches.

THE MODEL 1894 .38-40 RIFLE uses the .38-40 cartridge. This cartridge is quite accurate up to 200 yards, but beyond this range will not give very accurate results. It is used at longer ranges, but is not to be compared with many other cartridges at such distances. The factory cartridge is loaded with 40 grains of black powder and a pure lead bullet 180 grains in weight. The velocity of this bullet is 1200 feet per second. The penetration, as measured by dry pine boards one

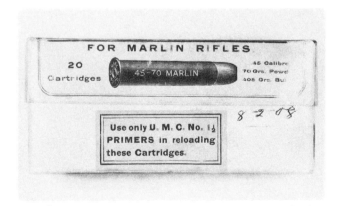

Box of .45–70–405 cartridges manufactured by Union Metallic Cartridge Company for Marlin rifles.

inch in thickness, placed 20 feet from the muzzle of the rifle, is seven and one-half boards. The trajectory is as follows:

When shooting at 100 yards:

The height of the bullet at 25 yards is 2.19 inches.

The height of the bullet at 50 yards is 2.71 inches.

The height of the bullet at 75 yards is 2.29 inches.

When shooting at 200 yards:

The height of the bullet at 50 yards is 9.46 inches.

The height of the bullet at 100 yards is 13.69 inches.

The height of the bullet at 150 yards is 10.58 inches.

The .38–40 SMOKELESS can be furnished with the 180 grain full metal-cased bullet, or the 180 grain mushroom bullet (metal patched with soft lead point). The velocity of the bullet in the smokeless cartridge is 1335 feet per second. The trajectory of the bullet is a little flatter than that obtained with the black powder cartridge.

The full metal-cased bullet will penetrate fourteen boards placed as usual.

The cartridge with mushroom bullet is preferable for hunting purposes, because this bullet upon impact will spread, tearing a larger hole and using to a greater degree the energy of the bullet.

The .38–40 black and smokeless loads with hollow point lead bullet have just been brought out. The hollow point bullet mushrooms large, making an excellent hunting cartridge.

THE .38–40 MARLIN HIGH VELOCITY CARTRIDGE has a 180 grain soft point bullet, having an average velocity of about 1776 feet, and a penetration of 10 ⅞ inch boards.

Shooting at 100 yards—Height at 50 yards, 1.80 inches.

Shooting at 200 yards—Height at 100 yards, 9.46 inches.

The .38–40 shell was made by sizing down the .44–40 shell.

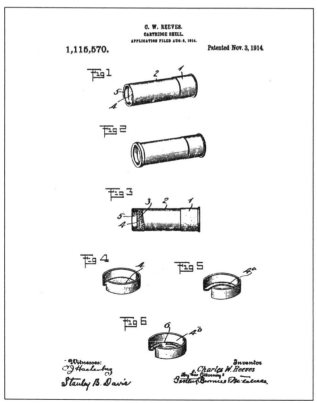

C.W. Reeves patent number 1,115,570 for a cartridge shell. The patent was assigned to Marlin. No information is available about why it was assigned to Marlin or what Marlin did with it.

The result was called ".38 Caliber," whereas this is really a .40 caliber.

THE MODEL 1894 .44–40 RIFLE uses the .44–40 or .44 W.C.F. cartridge. This cartridge has been very popular in its day, and up to very recently as many rifles were sold for this cartridge as for all others put together. It is a fairly accurate cartridge for 200 yards, but it does not compare in accuracy with the more powerful cartridges at this and longer ranges; nevertheless, it has a light recoil and is fairly effective in hunting. Its popularity is due, further, to the fact that the ammunition can be procured in any quarter of the globe. This cartridge is loaded by the factory with 40 grains of black powder and a pure lead bullet 217 grains in weight.

The velocity of this bullet is 1190 feet per second. Its penetration, as measured by dry pine boards, one inch in thickness, placed 20 feet from the muzzle of the rifle, is eight and one-half boards. The trajectory figures are as follows:

When shooting at 100 yards:

The height of the bullet at 25 yards is 2.56 inches.

The height of the bullet at 50 yards is 3.16 inches.

The height of the bullet at 75 yards is 2.73 inches.

When shooting at 200 yards:

The height of the bullet at 50 yards is 10.71 inches.

The height of the bullet at 100 yards is 15.32 inches.

The height of the bullet at 150 yards is 11.95 inches.

The .44–40 SMOKELESS CARTRIDGES can be furnished with the 200 grain full metal-cased bullet, or with the metal-patched bullet, soft point.

The velocity of the bullet in the smokeless cartridge is 1235 feet per second. The full metal-cased bullet will penetrate seventeen boards as usually placed.

The .44–40 black and smokeless loads with hollow point lead bullet have just been brought out. The hollow point bullet mushrooms large, making an excellent hunting cartridge.

THE .44–40 MARLIN HIGH VELOCITY CARTRIDGE has a 200 grain soft point bullet, having an average velocity of about 1570 feet, and a penetration of 10 ⅞ inch boards.

Shooting at 100 yards—Height at 50 yards, 2.32 inches.

Shooting at 200 yards—Height at 100 yards, 12.12 inches.

The Model 1893 was chambered for the following cartridges:

.25–36–117 MARLIN: Loaded with a high power smokeless powder and a metal-patched bullet with soft lead point, 117 grains in weight. The velocity of the bullet is about 2000 feet per second. The penetration as measured in dry pine boards ⅞ inch in thickness, placed 20 feet from muzzle of the rifle, is eleven and one-half boards, but extreme penetration is not sought, because the bullet is made with a soft lead point to mushroom.

This is an exceedingly accurate cartridge and does fine work at a considerable range. It is an especially valuable cartridge in hunting, owing to the fact that with its high velocity and flat trajectory the necessity of making great calculations at the longer ranges is removed. For instance, with its high velocity it traverses 600 yards in a second, and it can be readily observed that it is not necessary to hold far ahead of running game in order to bring it down, even if the game is at a considerable distance. Naturally the flat trajectory is a great assistance in case there should be an error in estimating distance for an error of 100 yards is not likely to prove very disastrous with this cartridge, while a much greater error can be made without missing the game.

For game up to and including deer this rifle is perfection. It is an extremely fine rifle for shooting geese, wild ducks, etc., at long ranges.

The .25-36 Marlin cartridges can also be furnished with full metal-case bullets.

The .25-36 Short Range, loaded with Smokeless Powder, has a lead bullet 86 grains in weight. This gives extremely accurate results up to 100 yards, and is a very pleasant cartridge to shoot.

.30-30 MARLIN: Uses the factory cartridges and also many special loads which can easily be prepared, furnishing a very extensive range in ammunition, as the one rifle will serve for a short-range light hunting arm, will do good work at medium ranges, and with a full power cartridge is a powerful hunting arm for the largest game. The factory cartridges are the following:

The .30-30-160 Smokeless—This cartridge is loaded with a high power smokeless powder and a bullet 160 grains in weight, full metal-cased. This cartridge is one of great power. The velocity of the bullet is 2020 feet per second. Its penetration as measured by dry pine boards ⅞ inch in thickness, placed 20 feet from the muzzle of the rifle, is 42 boards.

We claim that this cartridge with our type of bullet gives the most accurate results. It is also the best full metal-cased bullet for hunting purposes, as the flat point makes it more destructive on game, in case the full metal-cased bullet should be used for this purpose, although naturally the hunter would use a soft-pointed bullet. A bullet with a sharper point will penetrate more wood, but we are not looking for penetration only in a hunting cartridge; we seek sufficient penetration to have the bullet reach resistance or a vital part. We therefore claim that we have here developed the best cartridge for hunting purposes, in case the metal-patched bullet should be used. We have already stated that we believe it superior for target work.

The .30-30-170 Smokeless metal-patched bullet with soft point—this cartridge is exactly the same as the preceding with the exception of the bullet. This is the cartridge to use for hunting, as the bullet will penetrate a sufficient distance to bring down the game, and owing to its spreading, tears a larger hole, and so is more destructive. It will penetrate eleven boards as above described.

The .30-30 Short Range—Loaded with smokeless powder and a 117 grain lead bullet. This cartridge does admirable work at short ranges, being at its best up to 100 yards.

.30-30 Miniature—Loaded with smokeless powder and metal-cased bullet weighing 100 grains, giving accurate results up to 100 yards.

.32 SPECIAL H.P.S. CARTRIDGE: The .32 Special high power smokeless cartridge is much more powerful than the .30-30, having a larger diameter bullet and a higher velocity. It also has a great advantage in using a comparatively slow twist to the rifling of one turn in 16 inches. This reduces the pressure of the smokeless load and makes the use of black powder and lead bullets as satisfactory and convenient as in a regular black powder rifle.

The regular cartridge uses the 165 grain full metal-cased or soft-nosed bullet, and a high power smokeless powder, giving a muzzle velocity of 2112 feet per second, and a penetration, with full metal-patched bullet, of 45 ⅞ inch pine boards.

.32-40 CARTRIDGE: The .32-40 Repeater uses the well-known .32-40 Ballard & Marlin cartridge. This cartridge and its companion, the .38-55, were originated by this company for use in the Ballard rifle. They have been used for years in many different rifles and always with the most gratifying results, so that they have retained, if not increased, their

1. Headstamp of 444 Marlin made from .30-06 case. 2. Headstamp of 444 Marlin with .44 Magnum headstamp. 3. Headstamp of production 444 Marlin cartridge. 4. Headstamp of dummy 444 Marlin cartridge. 5. Headstamp of blackened 444 Marlin dummy.

popularity, although there have been many new cartridges brought out since these were first developed. No better all-around cartridges have ever been produced. They are still the standard for fine target work, while for hunting they are very extensively used because of their great power and accuracy. For deer and similar game they are very popular.

This rifle uses the following cartridges:

The regular factory cartridge is loaded with 40 grains of F.G. black powder and a bullet 165 grains in weight, 1 part of tin to 40 parts of lead. The velocity of this bullet is 1450 feet per second; the penetration, as measured by dry pine boards ⅞ inch in thickness, placed 20 feet from the muzzle of the rifle, is 8½ boards.

.32-40 CARTRIDGE: We recommend it without qualification for ranges from 100 to 400 yards. This cartridge will group its shots in a 6 inch circle at 200 yards with the greatest regularity, while under special conditions it has made much more creditable performances.

The .32-40 Short-Range cartridge is loaded with 13 grains of black powder and a bullet 98 grains in weight, 1 part tin to 20 parts of lead. This cartridge is designed for short-range work only. It fires extremely accurate results up to 100 yards, with fair results at somewhat greater ranges.

The .32-40 Marlin Miniature is loaded with smokeless powder and a 100 grain full metal-cased ball, giving a velocity of 1750 feet per second.

The .32-40 smokeless cartridge, with a full metal-cased bullet, 165 grains in weight, gives a velocity to the bullet of 1505 feet per second. The trajectory is flatter than that of the black powder cartridge, while the penetration, as measured by ⅞ inch boards placed as usual, is 20 boards.

The .32-40 smokeless cartridge with mushroom bullet has a bullet 165 grains in weight, metal-patched, with soft point. This cartridge is particularly designed for hunting purposes.

.32-40 Smokeless, Low Pressure, with lead bullet, gives excellent results to those who choose not to use black powder in the black powder barrel.

.32-40 MARLIN HIGH POWER SMOKELESS: The regular .32-40 Ballard & Marlin cartridge is now loaded with high power smokeless powder, giving a velocity of 2065 feet per second with a 165 grain jacketed bullet (either hard or soft nose) as against 1450 feet per second velocity with the regular black powder or low power smokeless load.

The penetration with metal-cased bullets is 38 pine boards ⅞ inch in thickness, and with soft nose bullets is 10 pine boards ⅞ inch in thickness, these boards being placed as usual.

This cartridge is suitable for use in all Marlin Rifles, Model 1893, having "Special Smokeless Steel" barrels. It is not recommended, and in our judgement it is unsafe, to use in old style rifles having soft steel barrels and actions made

Caliber Information for Marlin Rifles

CALIBER	Bullet Weight (Grains)	Muzzle Velocity (Ft./Sec.)	Muzzle Energy (Ft. Lbs.)	Traj. 50	Traj. 100	Traj. 150	Traj. 200	Max. Effective Range (yds.)	Rabbit	Squirrel	Crow	Woodchuck	Prairie Dog	Raccoon	Possum	Fox	Coyote	Javelina	Boar	Deer	Black Bear	Caribou	Moose	Elk
22 L.R. (Standard)	40	1150	117	+3.6	⊕	–	–	100	•	•	•	•	•	•	•	•								
22 L.R. (High Vel.)	40	1255	140	+4.0	⊕	–	–	125	•	•	•	•	•	•	•	•	•							
22 Win. Mag. Rim Fire	40	1910	324	+1.7	⊕	–	–	125								•	•							
357 Magnum	110	1385	470	NA	NA	–	–	75								•	•	•						
	125	2094	1225	NA	NA	–	–																	
	158	1757	1090	NA	NA	–	–																	
44 Rem. Mag.	240	1760	1650	–	⊕	-6.1	-18.1	100									•	•	•	•	•			
30/30 Win.	150	2390	1902	+.5	⊕	-2.7	-8.2	175									•	•	•	•	•	•		
	170	2200	1827	+.6	⊕	-3.0	-8.9																	
35 Rem.	150	2300	1762	+.6	⊕	-3.0	-9.2	175										•	•	•	•	•		
	200	2020	1812	+.9	⊕	-4.1	-12.1																	
45/70 Govt.	405	1330	1590	–	⊕	-8.7	-24.6	200										•	•	•	•	•		
375 Win.	200	2200	2150	+.6	⊕	-3.2	-9.5	200										•	•	•	•	•		
	250	1900	2005	+.9	⊕	-4.2	-12.0																	
444 Marlin	240	2350	2942	+.6	⊕	-3.2	-9.9	200										•	•	•	•	•	•	•
	265	2120	2644	+.7	⊕	-3.6	-10.8																	

*Inches above (+) or below (–) line of sight

Caliber information for some Marlin rifles.

of inferior materials, designed for black powder cartridges only.

The accuracy of this cartridge is surpising, considering its high velocity. We have had no difficulty in keeping 10 shots in a 2 inch circle at 100 yards, or in a 4 inch circle at 200 yards, using an ordinary Marlin hunting repeater. The rifling is one turn in 16 inches, exactly the same as used for many years in fine Ballard target rifles and in Marlin repeaters since 1881, but the "Special Smokeless Steel" has a tensile strength of from 100,000 to 130,000 pounds to the square inch as against an ultimate strength of about 50,000 pounds for the ordinary steel. The ordinary low priced steel is comparatively soft and the bore will quickly wear if hard jacketed bullets are used, but the "Special Smokeless Sneel" is hard, and jacketed bullets may be used for a long time and show no signs of wearing. This is the first straight taper shell to be put on the market loaded for high velocity, and we regard it as far superior to any bottle-necked shell made. For antelope, mountain sheep or goats, deer, moose, caribou, elk, bear or similar game, we recommend the .32–40 Marlin, using high power smokeless loads. The regular black powder loads can be used where less power is desired.

.38–55 CARTRIDGES: The .38–55 Rifle uses the .38–55 Ballard & Marlin cartridge.

This cartridge is loaded with 48 grains of F.G. black powder and a 255 grain bullet, one part tin and 40 of lead.

The .38–55 cartridge is extremely accurate, and with its companion, the .32–40, can be excelled by none up to 500 yards.

The cartridge as first made contained nearly 55 grains of powder, hence the name; but these were the thin folded head shells. When the solid head shells were made the walls of the shells were thickened and more stock left in the head, but the outside dimensions had to remain the same. Although the powder space was reduced, nevertheless the name could not be changed without causing confusion.

The velocity of this bullet is 1316 feet per second; the penetration, as measured by dry pine boards ⅞ inch in thickness, placed 20 feet from the muzzle of the rifle, is 9½ boards.

The .38–55 Short-Range cartridge is loaded with 20 grains of black powder and a bullet 155 grains in weight, one part tin to 20 parts of lead.

This cartridge is designed for short-range work only. It gives very accurate results up to 100 yards, with fair results at somewhat greater ranges.

The .38–55 smokeless cartridge is loaded with smokeless powder and a full metal-cased bullet 255 grains in weight, and gives a high velocity. The trajectory is flatter than that of the black powder cartridge, while the penetration, measured by ⅞ inch boards as above placed, is 14 boards.

The .38–55 smokeless cartridge with mushroom bullet has a bullet 255 grains in weight, metal-patched, with soft point. This cartridge is particularly designed for hunting purposes.

The smokeless shells have a groove to prevent the bullet from being crushed down on the powder.

.38–55 HIGH POWER SMOKELESS: The regular .38–55 Ballard & Marlin cartridge is now loaded with High Power Smokeless Powder, giving a velocity of 1700 feet per second with a 255 grain jacketed bullet (either hard or soft nose) as against 1316 feet per second velocity with the regular black powder or low power smokeless load.

Penetration with metal-cased bullets is 36 ⅞ inch pine boards and with soft nose bullets is 12 ⅞ inch pine boards.

This cartridge is suitable for use in all Marlin Rifles, Model 1893, having "Special Smokeless Steel" barrels. It is not recommended, and in our judgement it is unsafe, to use in old-style rifles having soft steel barrels and actions made of inferior materials, designed for black powder cartridges only.

The accuracy of this cartridge is surprising, considering its high velocity. We have had no difficulty in keeping 10 shots in a 2 inch circle at 100 yards or in a 4 inch circle at 200 yards, using an ordinary Marlin hunting repeater. The rifling is one turn in 20 inches, exactly the same as used for many years in fine Ballard target rifles and in Marlin repeaters since 1881, but the "Special Smokeless Steel" has a tensile strength of from 100,000 to 130,000 pounds to the square inch as against an ultimate strength of about 50,000 pounds for the ordinary steel. The ordinary low priced steel is comparatively soft and the bore will quickly wear if hard jacketed bullets are used, but the "Special Smokeless Steel" is hard and jacketed bullets may be used for a long time and show no signs of wearing. For antelope, mountain sheep or goats, deer, moose, caribou, elk, bear, or similar game, we recommend the .38–55 Marlin, using high power smokeless loads. The regular black powder loads can be used where less powder is desired.

The MARLIN MODEL 1895 REPEATING RIFLE is the same system as the Model 1893, and made of the same extra quality material, but larger and heavier throughout. It uses big bore, powerful cartridges, with large, heavy bullets and heavy powder charges, that give enormous shocking and smashing power, tear a big hole and quickly bring down any big game in North America.

.38–55: This cartridge is loaded with 56 grains of black powder and a bullet 255 grains in weight, one part tin to 20 parts lead.

The black powder cartridges can also be procured with full metal-cased bullet or metal-patched bullet with soft point.

The velocity of this bullet is 1360 feet per second. The penetration, as measured by dry pine boards, one inch in thickness, placed 20 feet from the muzzle of the rifle, is 10¾ boards.

Smokeless Cartridges — .38–55 Smokeless. Loaded with smokeless powder and a 255 grain bullet, full metal-cased. The velocity of this bullet is 1500 feet per second. The penetration as measured by dry pine boards, one inch in thickness, placed 20 feet from the muzzle of the rifle, is 15 boards.

.38–56 Smokeless, Soft Point. This cartridge is exactly like the preceding, except that the bullet, instead of being full metal-cased, is metal-patched, with a soft lead point.

THE .45–70 MARLIN: Loaded with 70 grains of black powder and a 405 grain flat-pointed bullet, one part tin to 16 parts of lead. The velocity of this bullet is 1361 feet per second. The penetration as measured by dry pine boards ⅞ inch in thickness, placed 20 feet from the muzzle of the rifle, is 15 boards.

THE .45–70–405 U.S. GOVERNMENT: This cartridge is practically the same as the preceding, with the exception of the bullet, which has a round point. The figures given for the preceding cartridge will apply equally well to this.

THE .45–70–500 U.S. GOVERNMENT: Loaded with 70 grains of black powder and a round-pointed bullet 500 grains in weight, one part tin to 16 parts lead.

METAL-CASED BULLETS: On special order any of the above black powder cartridges may be obtained with full metal-cased bullet or the metal-patched bullet with soft lead point.

SMOKELESS CARTRIDGES: These three cartridges are loaded by the factory with smokeless powder and the full metal-cased bullet or metal-patched bullet with soft lead point.

.45-70 HIGH VELOCITY: This is one of the new cartridges recently brought out. It is loaded with high power smokeless powder and a soft point bullet 300 grains in weight. This cartridge gives a velocity of about 1888 feet per second and the bullet penetrates 13 ⅞ inch boards.

.45-85 MARLIN: Loaded with 85 grains of black powder and a bullet 285 grains in weight, one part tin to 16 parts lead. Owing to the heavy charge of powder, with the proportionately light bullet, this bullet has a velocity of 1450 feet per second.

.45-70-330 GOULD EXPRESS: Loaded with 70 grains of black powder, and a 330 grain bullet with hollow point. This bullet has a velocity of 1380 feet per second. Owing to its mushrooming the penetration as usually measured is but 10 boards.

.45-70-350: Loaded with 70 grains of black powder and a bullet 350 grains in weight, one part tin to 16 parts lead. The velocity of this bullet is 1344 feet per second. The penetration as usually measured, is 13 boards. This bullet is exactly the same as the preceding, except that it is a solid bullet.

.45 GOVERNMENT SHORT-RANGE SMOKELESS: Loaded with 12 grains of DuPont "Sharpshooter" smokeless powder and a lead bullet 200 grains in weight. An excellent cartridge for armory or short-range work.

The Model 1895 was also chambered for the caliber .33 cartridge. Marlin described it as follows:

The .33 caliber cartridge is one of the most powerful of all modern high power smokeless cartridges. It throws the heavy 200 grain bullet with the extremely high velocity of over 2050 feet per second. Its trajectory is so flat that, shooting at 100 yards range, the bullet rises only 1.21 inches at 50 yards; at ordinary hunting ranges readjustment of sights is seldom necessary—no time is lost—you get in effective shots instantly. The full jacketed bullet has penetrated 47 ⅞ inch pine boards; the soft point bullet, mushrooming large, penetrates 13 boards. This heavy bullet, deep penetration and tremendous shocking and killing power, will quickly bring down moose, bear, deer and all other American big game.

MODERN CARTRIDGE CHARACTERISTICS OF MARLIN FIREARMS

	Bullet* Weight	Muzzle** Velocity	Muzzle*** Energy	Sight-in at (yds)	Zero at (yds)
.22 LR	40	1285	147	16.5	75
.22 Win. Mag.	40	2000	385	25	160
.22 Hornet	46	2690	740	25	155
.218 Bee	46	2760	778	—	—
.219 Zipper	56	3110	1200	—	—
.222 Remington	50	3200	1140	30	180
.256	60	2800	1040	30	150
.30 Carbine	110	1980	955	20	150
.30–30	150	2410	1930	22	200
.30–30	170	2220	1860	20	180
.30–06	150	2970	2930	25	225
.30–06	180	2700	2910	20	215
.308	180	2610	2720	20	215
.32 Special	170	2250	1911	—	—
.35 Remington	200	2100	1950	15	175
.356 Win.	200	2460	2688	—	—
.357 Mag.	158	1235	535	—	—
.375 Mag.	200	2200	2150	—	—
.38 Spec.	125	945	248	—	—
9-mm Luger	115	1225	383	—	—
.41 Mag.	210	1300	788	—	—
.44 Spec.	200	900	380	—	—
.44 Mag.	240	1750	1630	15	150
.45 ACP	230	810	335	—	—
.45 Colt	225	920	423	—	—
.444	240	2400	3070	25	178
.45–70	405	1320	1570	10	100

*Weight in grains
**Feet per second
***Foot-pounds

These data are taken from ammunition manufacturers' catalogs.

Left: *Obverse of 1888 Melbourne, Australia, award.* Right: *Reverse of same.*

Left: *Obverse of 1899 World's Columbian Exposition award.* Right: *Reverse of same.*

Awards

The predecessor companies to the present Marlin company won numerous awards for excellence at international and national exhibitions and World's Fairs. Unfortunately, complete details have not survived the many corporate changes that the various Marlin organizations went through.

The first major award known is the Highest Award of Merit, which Marlin received at the Centennial International Exhibition, held in Melboupne, Australia, in 1888.

The next award about which a little more is known is the Highest Award, attained at the World's Columbian Exposition, Chicago, Ill., in 1893. The judges' citation for the award read as follows:

> For: Strength, simplicity and ease of dismounting and assembling; accurate and fine barrels; elaborate decorations, finish and very good ornamentation; REMARKABLE SUPERIORITY IN SAFETY, ESPECIALLY FOR THE SIDE EJECTING. A large and complete assortment of repeating rifles shown.

The report of the Exposition's committee on awards noted the following about the Marlin exhibit:

> The exhibit of the Marlin Firearms Company of New Haven, Connecticut, consisted of a fine collection of repeating rifles, of two different styles of mechanism, both designed to be used either for military or sporting purposes. In general appearance, these guns resemble the well-known original Winchester, but differ therefrom in their operating mechanism, in which the reciprocating breech bolt is operated by direct connection with an arm of the lever, and is locked fast when closed by vertically moving the bolt or block, which, in turn, is operated by another arm of the same lever. The carrier which lifts the cartridge from the magazine to the chamber is operated by this same lever, and thus a single solid lever directly operates all the parts, the mechanism as a whole exhibiting great ingenuity. Another feature of this arm (Model 1889) is that the receiver or frame has the opening on its side instead of on the top, by which rain, dust, etc., is less liable to get into the operating mechanism.

> The later (Model 1892) gun differs from the former in the means of locking the breech piece closed, it being accomplished by the front end of the lever, which engages as a brace against a lug on the underside of the reciprocating breech piece when closed, and also in the means for operating the cartridge carrier.

> The smaller of these guns was shown with the side plate of the frame removable by loosening a thumbnut, by which the mechanism is rendered accessible for cleaning, oiling, etc. Their barrels are also made detachable, which enables the guns to be conveniently packed in a truck or case.

> These arms are well made of good material, and are largely used for hunting and sporting purposes, and to some extent, as a military arm.

An article about the Marlin exhibit was written by Emerson Hough, a correspondent for the old *Forest and Stream* magazine. (Later, Mr. Hough achieved fame as the author of *The Covered Wagon, Fifty-four Forty or Fight, The Passing of the Frontier,* and other stories of the West.) The report by this knowledgeable outdoor writer was as follows:

THE MARLIN EXHIBIT

"I claim for our exhibit," said Mr. Marlin, secretary of the company, "that it is probably the largest collection of repeating rifles ever gotten together. We have in one case 160 repeating rifles, and not one is a duplicate of any other. They run from the 15 inch carbine up to the military arm, single shot or repeater, and we think the aggregation is as handsome a one as any ever seen."

Mr. Marlin's pride is certainly a justifiable one, and his company can not have too much credit for the trouble and expense it must have undergone to put this display in place. It is a display remarkable for its variety and brilliancy of ornamentation. There are rifles with walnut stocks, and rifles with white birdseye maple stocks, and rifles with stocks as handsomely checkered by the finisher as any costly English arm. There are rifles whose engraving must have cost a little fortune, and the engraving shows the character of many different artists. There are blue and gold rifles, and silver and blue, and gold and silver, and all silver, antique silver, all gold, all blue, or all nickel and white, and all the combinations of these, both with the walnut and the odd-looking light birdseye stocks. The whole is hardly less than bewildering, and it shows how careful is the trade to please the fancy of every individual shooter of this and of other countries.

"It is hardly correct to say that these are special guns," said Mr. Marlin, "for we make many such fancy patterns for actual trade. Most of the gold and silver mounted, highly engraved guns, and also most of those with the white stocks, go to the Mexican and Spanish trade. We sell a great many in South America."

About as handsome as any of these arms are a pair of .22s,

all white nickel plate, barrel and all, with gold trimmings. Still another handsome thing is the lockplate of one rifle, which holds an etching of the old fence on the Yale campus. Yet another similar piece shows Osborne Hall, of Yale, on the place where the fence once was.

The Marlins show a single-shot which they think will be better than the old Ballard. It is not yet quite ready for the market. They also have a model '93, in .32–40 and .38–55, the only repeater using these shells. They also have a full line of Marlin revolvers and pistols in their cases. We might stop here for a showing of American energy and thoroughness, but there is one thing more. We hear much of catalogues, of course, but who has heard of an American gun catalogue in the Chinese language? The Marlin exhibit here contains one, all in Chinese, as used by their agents in selling the Marlin goods in China. It strikes me America can take care of herself pretty well.

E. Hough

Another award that Marlin received, but for which no information is available, is the Gold Medal of Highest Grade at Atlanta, Ga., in 1895.

Marlin acquired the L.C. Smith shotgun and the Hunter Arms Company in a court foreclosure in 1945. The L.C. Smith shotgun won the gold medal at the 1905 Lewis and Clark Centennial Exposition held in Portland, Ore. Although Marlin did not receive any award, Marlin did participate in a firearms industry display in the Connecticut pavilion during the 1964 New York World's Fair. The New England firearms industry, including High Standard, Smith & Wesson, Colt, Winchester, and Marlin companies, furnished guns for the display.

The contemporary Marlin firearms displayed were the following:

Model	Serial Number
39M	T2196
62/.256	3231
336T/.44 magnum	Z47,177
989M2	NSN
L.C. Smith Crown	526,150
90 shotgun	K873

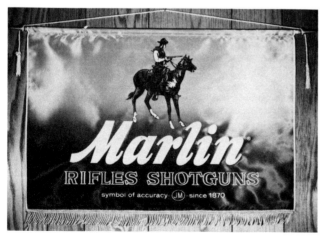

First Marlin banner.

The old Marlin guns were as follows:

Model	Serial Number
OK S/S pistol	16,586
DA revolver	12,032
38, .22 rifle	A5938
1881 lever action rifle	1
28 shotgun	7658
30G shotgun	5382
43 shotgun	15,998

The following two high-art Marlin rifles were lent to the exhibit by Harry Sefried, a well-known Connecticut collector and gun authority.

Model	Feature	Serial Number
1891	caliber .32	85,681
1893	with gold inlay	136,489

Banners

Most firearms manufacturers have at some time distributed banners to advertise their wares. Marlin was not an exception.

The first Marlin banner was 30 inches wide by 20 inches high. It was a brilliant orange color blended to a deep maroon. The Marlin horse and rider logo was centrally located at the top. Across the bottom in large white stylized letters was *Marlin—Rifles and Shotguns*. A wood dowel and gold cord were used for hanging. The bottom had gold fringe. This banner was available from 1960 to 1965.

The second type of banner distributed by Marlin was white with a multicolored large horse and rider logo centrally located. The name *Marlin* was across the top with *Rifles and Shotguns* in smaller letters. This banner was also hung from a gold cord and had gold fringe across the bottom edge. It was 20 inches wide and 28 inches deep. It was available from 1966 to 1969.

The third Marlin banner was the same as the second except that it had centrally located on it the Marlin 100th-anniversary medallion and *One Hundred Years of American Gunmaking* printed across the bottom. It was also hung and fringed like the first two types. It was available only during 1970.

Marlin has not distributed any banners for advertising purposes since 1970.

Bargain Sheets

Periodically, Marlin published a special "Dealers' Bargain Sheet." The foreword to these lists stated:

We offer below a list of goods which have accumulated in our stock, most of them being styles of goods that we do not carry regularly, and which we have on our hands from our inability to furnish them within a specified time.

Many were made specially for exhibitions and have been used for no other purpose, and are made and finished throughout with special care.

We are offering them at from 15 to 30 percent reduction

Second type of Marlin banner.

Third type of Marlin banner.

from the regular prices for the same, and in some cases, at a still larger reduction in price. All orders received are subject to stock on hand. NONE of these goods will be sent on approval or exchanged. Please order by number.

The earliest of these bargain sheets is dated June 1907. It is believed that two were printed each year in 1908 and 1909, although copies for these two years have not been inspected. The following numbered sheets have been examined: June 1907; No. 6, September 1910; No. 7, September 1911; No. 8, October 1911; No. 9, September 1912; No. 10, October 1912; No. 11, October 1913; No. 14, August 1914; No. 15, 1915; and No. 16, October 1915.

Some of the more interesting features listed by Marlin in these dealers' bargain sheets were the following: matted barrel; shotgun butt; takedown lever flush; RB (rubber butt plate); engraved No. 40, "Monarch of the Glen;" Lyman sights; Stevens telescopes; Marble sight; Marlin combination sight; extra special wood; bird's-eye maple stocks and forearms; checked trigger; gold plating; silver plating; swivels and sling strap fitted; London finish; gold nameplate, special design checking; Silver's recoil pad; pebble engraving; oil finish; and no rear sight slot.

Many of the one-of-a-kind guns described in these bargain sheets were repeated in following lists. This indicates to me, that even at the bargain price, sportsmen did not have a lot of money to spend on fancy guns. The price also increased or

decreased, depending on the market value. Some of the most interesting of the many variations, with the dealer price, were as follows:

1910 Model 18, .22, octagon, selected stock and forearm, finely checked, with swivels and sling strap fitted, $11.00.

1914 Model 18, Featherweight .22 caliber Repeater, 20 inch octagon, 3 pounds 10 ounces, selected stock and forearm, finely checked, $11.45.

1910 Model 20, .22 caliber, selected straight grip and forearm, finely checked, nickel plated buttplate, $12.50.

1910 Model 20, .22, 23-inch, octagon, extra selected stock and forearm, "F" checked, engraved and inlaid with gold, $35.00.

1911 Model 20, .22, 23-inch, octagon, extra selected stock and forearm, "F" checked, extra finished, engraved No. 2, $19.50.

1912 Model 20, .22 caliber, 23-inch, octagon, extra selected, "F" checked, stock and forearm, extra finish, engraved No. 10, $59.75.

1912 Model 20, .22 caliber, 24-inch, octagon, extra selected stock and forearm, "F" checked, engraved No. 10, $57.75.

1913 Model 20, .22, 23-inch octagon, selected stock and forearm, finely checked, engraving No. 1, $21.85.

1914 Model 20, .22, 24-inch octagon, full nickel plated, $12.00.

1911 Model 25, .22, 23-inch, round, Lyman combination rear sight, slot blank, ivory bead front sight fitted, $7.70.

1912 Model 27, .25-20, 24-inch, octagon, extra selected stock and forearm, "F" checked, extra finish, engraving No. 10, $61.25.

1907 '89, .44-40, 24-inch, octagon, selected and checked P.G., engraved No. 10, gold plated trimmings, blued screws, $35.00.

1914 1889 Musket, .44-40, 30-inch, $10.20.

1910 Model 1892, .22, 24-inch, half octagon, half magazine, selected and finely checked straight grip stock and forearm, full nickel plated, $15.00.

1907 '93, .25-36, 26-inch, ½ octagon, take-down, extra selected and checked P.G. special design checking, shotgun butt, engraved No. 18, figures inlaid in gold on receiver, matted barrel, $65.00.

1910 Model 1893, .25-36, 26-inch, half octagon, half magazine, take-down, cam lever flush, extra selected pistol grip stock and forearm, special checking No. 5 (4), R.B., engraved 5 (4), $42.50.

1911 Model 1893, .25-36, 24-inch, half octagon, half magazine, take-down, extra selected pistol grip stock and forearm, finely checked, extra finish, shotgun butt, rubber buttplate, engraved No. 5 (4), $61.00.

1911 Model 1893, .30-30, 18-inch, half octagon, half magazine, take-down, extra selected straight grip stock and forearm, "F" checked, extra finish, shotgun butt, rubber buttplate, London finish, $27.30.

1907 '93, .30-30, 18-inch, half octagon, half magazine, extra selected, fine "B" checked P.G. shotgun butt; take-down, cam lever flush, special lightweight, engraved No. 15, London finish, $55.00.

1912 Model 1893, .30-30, 20-inch, Special Light Weight, short magazine, take-down, selected straight grip stock and forearm, finely checked, rubber buttplate, engraved No. 1, Ivory Bead front sight fitted, $25.00.

1910 Model 1893, Carbine, .30-30, 20-inch, half magazine, R.B., swivels and sling fitted, Ivory Bead front sight No. 26 fitted, $11.00.

1907 '93, Carbine, .30-30, 20-inch barrel, U.S. Coat of Arms inlaid on receiver in gold, $35.00.

1910 Model 1893, .30-30, 20-inch, half octagon, short magazine, take-down, cam lever flush, selected, finely checked, straight grip stock and forearm, R.B. engraved No. 1, extra light weight, Ivory Bead front sight, $25.00.

1907 '93, .30-30, 24-inch, half octagon, half magazine, take-down, cam lever flush, selected and checked P.G., shotgun butt, birdseye maple, engraved No. 3, matted barrel, $25.00.

1910 Model 1893, .30-30, 24-inch, octagon, take-down, cam lever flush, extra selected, pistol grip stock and forearm, special checking 5 (4), R.B., engraved No. 15, matted barrel, gold plated hammer, trigger, and screws, Ivory Bead front sight fitted, $70.00.

1910 Model 1893, .30-30, 24-inch, octagon, take-down, extra selected pistol grip stock and forearm, No. 5 (4) checked,

extra finish, shotgun butt, rubber buttplate, engraved No. 10, matted barrel, gold plated hammer and screws, Ivory Bead front sight fitted, $60.00.

1911 Model 1893, .30-30, 26-inch, half octagon, half magazine, take-down, extra selected pistol grip stock and forearm, extra (G) checked and extra finish, shotgun butt, rubber buttplate, engraved No. 5 (2), blued receiver, gold plated screws, $45.00.

1912 Model 1893, .30-30, 24-inch, octagon, take-down, extra selected, No. 5 (4) checked, pistol grip stock and forearm, rubber buttplate, engraved No. 15, matted barrel, gold plated hammer, trigger, screws, Ivory Bead front sight, $72.50.

1910 Model 1893, .32 Special H.P.S., 26-inch octagon, take-down, extra selected pistol grip stock and forearm, No. 5 (3) checked, extra finish, engraved No. 5 (3), $43.50.

1910 Model 1893, .32-40, 20-inch, half octagon, short magazine, shotgun butt, rubber buttplate, $11.00.

1910 Model 1893, .32-40, 20-inch, half octagon, half magazine, take-down, pistol grip, checked, shotgun butt, rubber buttplate, Lyman combination rear sight with cup disk, Sheard's gold bead front sight, $17.50.

1914 Model 1892, .32-40, 26-inch, octagon, half magazine, Stevens telescope No. 700 fitted, $22.80.

1910 Model 1893, .32-40, 26-inch, half octagon, half magazine, take-down, cam lever flush, extra selected pistol grip stock and forearm, finely checked, large rubber buttplate, special carved, engraved No. 40, Tiger Hunt, $125.00.

1911 Model 1893, .38-55, 20-inch, half octagon, half magazine, pistol grip, checked, shotgun butt, rubber buttplate, combination receiver sight fitted, no rear slot in barrel, $18.60.

1911 Model 1893, .38-55, 24-inch, half octagon, half magazine, selected pistol grip stock and forearm, (Birdseye Maple), finely checked shotgun butt, rubber buttplate, engraved No. 5 (2), $37.20.

1910 Model 1893, .32-40, 24-inch, half octagon, half magazine, take-down, cam lever flush, extra selected pistol grip stock and forearm "G" checked, R.B. engraved No. 5 (2), blued receiver, gold plated screws, $36.50.

1910 Model 1893, .38-55, 24-inch, half octagon, half magazine, selected finely checked pistol grip stock and forearm (Birdseye Maple), R.B. engraved No. 5 (2), blued receiver, gold plated screws, $32.00.

1911 Model 1893, .38-55, 24-inch, half octagon, half magazine, take-down, extra selected pistol grip stock and forearm, "D" checked, extra finish, shotgun butt, rubber buttplate, engraved No. 5 (3), Ivory Bead front sight fitted, $48.50.

1907 '93, .38-55, 26-inch, half octagon, half magazine, take-down, extra selected and checked, P.G., special design checking, shotgun butt, engraved No. 40, $100.00.

1907 '93, .38-55, 26-inch, half octagon, half magazine, take-down, cam lever flush, extra selected checked P.G., special design checking, large shotgun butt, engraved No. 15, gold nameplate in end of P.G., $60.00.

1910 Model 1893, .38-55, 26-inch, half octagon, half magazine, take-down, extra selected, "C" checked, pistol grip stock and forearm, R.B. engraved No. 18, (Monarch of the Glen), $69.00.

1910 Model 1893, .38–55, 26-inch, half magazine, extra selected pistol grip stock and fore-end, "C" checked, R.B., engraved No. 5 (4), Lyman No. 1 sight fitted, no rear sight slot in barrel, $35.00.

1912 Model 1893, .38–55, 26-inch, half octagon, half magazine, take-down, extra selected pistol grip stock and forearm, "C" checked, extra finish, rubber buttplate, engraved No. 15, inlaid gold and platinum, $61.25.

1915 Model 1893, Carbine, .38–55, 20-inch round barrel, no sling ring, with Lyman Receiver sight and Jack Sight fitted, $12.25.

1910 Model 1893, Grade B, .38–55, 26-inch, octagon, selected pistol grip stock and forearm, finely checked, $16.50.

1910 Model 1893, Grade B, .32–40 Carbine, 20-inch, swivels and sling fitted, $9.25.

1911 Model 1893, Grade B, .38–55, Carbine, 20-inch, half magazine, shotgun butt, rubber buttplate, $8.25.

1911 Model 1893, Grade B, .38–55, 26-inch, octagon, half magazine, shotgun butt, rubber buttplate, $10.80.

1913 Model 1893, Grade B, rifle, .38–55, 15-inch round, $10.20.

1914 Model 1894, .25–20, 24-inch, octagon, take-down, selected pistol grip stock and forearm, finely checked; engraved No. 2, nickel plated buttplate, Ivory Bead front sight fitted, cam lever flush, $30.00.

1910 Model 1894, .32–20, 24-inch, half octagon, half magazine, take-down, selected pistol grip stock and fore-end, finely checked, oil finish, full nickel plated, $22.50.

1910 Model 1894, .32–20, 24-inch, half octagon, half magazine, take-down, cam lever flush, extra selected "C" checked, pistol grip stock and fore-end, R.B., engraved No. 3, blued receiver, nickel plated hammer, trigger, lever and forearm tip, Ivory Bead front sight fitted, $20.00.

1911 Model 1894, .32–20, 24-inch, octagon, extra selected pistol grip stock and forearm, Birdseye Maple, "C" checked, extra finish, shotgun butt, rubber buttplate, engraved No. 3, $40.95.

1913 Model 1894, .32–20, 24-inch, half octagon, half magazine, take-down, selected pistol grip stock and forearm, finely checked, nickel trimmed, oil finish, $22.80.

1907 '94, .38–40, 24-inch, half octagon, half magazine, take-down, cam lever flush, extra selected, fine "B" checked P.G., large shotgun butt, engraved No. 3, blued receiver and gold plated screws, $28.00.

1907 '94, Carbine, .44–40, 20-inch, selected stock and forearm, American Flag engraved and inlaid in gold and platinum on receiver, $25.00.

1910 Model 1894, .44–40, 24-inch, round, smooth bore, half magazine, take-down, selected straight grip stock and forearm, finely checked, oil finish, checked trigger, Slot blank and Ivory front sight fitted, $16.00.

1910 Model 1894, .38–40, 24-inch, half octagon, half magazine, take-down, cam lever flush, extra selected pistol grip stock and forearm, beautifully checked in special grape leaf design, R.B. engraved No. 5 (2), $35.00.

1910 Model 1894, .38–40, Carbine, 15-inch, R.B., Lyman sights Nos. 1, 12 and Ivory Bead front fitted, $10.00.

1911 Model 1894, .38–40, 24-inch, half octagon, take-down, extra selected pistol grip stock and forearm, leaf design checked, extra finish, shotgun butt, rubber buttplate, engraved No. 5 (2), $67.65.

1911 Model 1894, .44–40, 22-inch, round, short magazine, selected straight grip stock and forearm, finely "F" checked, London finish, combination receiver sight, slot blank and Ivory Bead front sight fitted, $27.70.

1913 Model 1894, Carbine, .44–40, 20-inch, no sling ring, $8.50.

1914 1894 Musket, .44–40, 30-inch, $10.20.

1913 Model 1894, .44–40, 22-inch round, short magazine, take-down, selected straight grip stock and forearm, finely checked, dull filled London oil finish, Lyman No. 1 Peep rear sight, slot blank, and Ivory Bead sight fitted, $21.60.

1914 10 Model 1894 Carbines, .44–40, 15-inch barrel, overrun from large lot made for Mounted Police of Chile, with their inscription on top of frame in small letters, $10.00.

1915 Model 1895, .40–65, 26-inch, half octagon barrel, take-down, selected pistol grip stock and forearm, finely checked, engraved No. 3, $28.50.

1915 Model 1895, .40–65, 26-inch, half octagon barrel, half magazine, pistol grip stock and forearm, checked, London finish, Lyman peep sight, Leaf and Jack sight fitted, $17.00.

1910 Model 1895, .45–90, 26-inch, half octagon, half magazine, take-down, selected pistol grip stock and forearm, "B" checked, R.B., pebble engraved (No. 10), $40.00.

1907 '97, .22, 24-inch, half octagon, half magazine, full nickel plated, $13.00.

1907 '97, .22, 24-inch octagon, selected and checked P.G., engraved No. 1, blued receiver, gold plated screws, $21.00.

1907 '97, .22, 24-inch, half octagon, half magazine, extra selected, "D" checked P.G., engraved No. 5 (2), gold plated trimmings, $30.00.

1910 Model 1897, .22, 24-inch, half octagon, half magazine, extra selected pistol grip stock and forearm, "F" checked, engraved No. 2, full gold plated, $36.50.

1910 Model 1897, .22, 24-inch, half octagon, half magazine, extra selected pistol grip stock and forearm, "F" checked, engraved No. 5, Squirrel and Rabbits as centerpieces, $38.50.

1911 Model 1897, .22, 24-inch, half octagon, half magazine, extra selected pistol grip stock and forearm, "F" checked, engraved No. 5, $57.50.

1911 Model 1897, .22, 24-inch, half octagon, half magazine, extra select pistol grip stock and forearm, "F" checked, extra finish, engraved No. 3, full gold plated, $56.30.

1912 Model 1897, .22, 24-inch, half octagon, extra selected, "F" checked, pistol grip stock and forearm, extra finish, engraved No. 3, $33.00.

1912 Model 1897, .22, 24-inch, half octagon, half magazine, extra selected, "F" checked, pistol grip stock and forearm, extra finish, engraved No. 3, full gold plated, $56.30.

1912 Model 1897, .22, 24-inch, half octagon, half magazine, extra selected, "F" checked, pistol grip stock and forearm, extra finish, engraving No. 3, $33.00.

1912 Model 1897, .22, 24-inch, half octagon, extra selected, "F" checked pistol grip stock and forearm, extra finish, engraved No. 3, $33.00.

1915 Model 1897 Rifle, .22, 24-inch round barrel, pistol grip stock and forearm, checked, Special Smokeless Steel barrel, Marble Adjustable Rear sight with special base, Lyman Leaf sight and Sheard Gold Bead front sight fitted, $17.00.

1915 Model 1897 Rifle, .22, 24-inch octagon barrel, with Stevens No. 700 telescope fitted, $22.80.

1907 '97, .22, 26-inch, half octagon, half magazine, P.G., nickel plated trimmings, $14.50.

1907 16 gauge, 28-inch Special Smokeless Steel, Special engraving on receiver and extra fine carving on stock and forearm, which are of an extra selected quality of American Walnut, $110.00.

1910 Special shotgun, 12-gauge, 30-inch, full choke, Damascus barrel, straight grip, Circassian walnut, stock and forearm carved, engraved and inlaid, gold plated screws, pins, etc. The finest Marlin repeating shotgun ever made, $150.00.

1911 Model 19 special gun, 30-inch Special Smokeless Steel barrel, extra selected stock and forearm, special design checking and carving, special design engraving, stock 13⅞ inches long, 1½ inches drop at comb, 1½ inches drop at heel, with Silver's recoil pad fitted, $167.75.

1910 Model 24, Grade "A", 12 gauge, 30-inch, full choke, special stock with Silver's recoil pad, 15¼x1¾x1½, $24.00.

1910 Model 24, Grade "B", 12 gauge, 32-inch, full choke, stock with Silver's recoil pad, 14x1¼x1⅜, $30.00.

1910 Model 24, Grade "C", 12 gauge, 30-inch, Silver's recoil pad, silver nameplate, stock 13¾x2x2½ inches, $40.00.

1911 Model 24, Grade "C", 12 gauge, 30-inch full choke, stock 14x2½x2, Silver's recoil pad fitted, nameplate in stock; barrel not matted, $48.00.

1915 Model 24 shotgun, 12 gauge, 30-inch full choke, Damascus barrel, extra selected straight grip stock and forearm, special design checking and carving, special engraving

and gold inlaying, gold plated trigger and screws, $100.00.

Barrels

Starting with the Marlin Ballard rifles and their great success on the range, as well as in the field, Marlin has always had an excellent reputation for finely made barrels. Starting in 1882, the Marlin catalog offered the following words about the quality of the Model 1881 barrel:

> The great reputation which the Ballard Rifle (manufactured by the Marlin Fire-Arms Co., late J.M. Marlin), has achieved as the leading rifle at the target, in the East, and as a hunting rifle on the mountains and plains of the West and on the Pacific Slope, insures the accuracy of the shooting, which we confidently assert is superior to that of any other repeating rifle in the world.

About the Ballard rifle, Marlin voiced in 1885 the following:

> The most important part of such a gun — the rifling in the barrel — is in the Ballard the best yet produced. It is done by the finest machinery, and particular care given to have it perfectly systematic, so that one gun will shoot just as well as another. We claim for the Ballard the greatest possible accuracy, and base this claim on the testimonials from well-known target experts, huntsmen and galleries.

In catalogs from 1896 to 1915, Marlin made this comment about accuracy:

> As the barrels now used in our rifles are exactly the same as the old Ballard Rifles in every respect, we regard this as sufficient recommendation of their shooting qualities and durability. The Ballard barrels have always been justly considered, even up to the present day, as the standard of accuracy. Our reputation will not suffer by comparison.

Until Micro-Groove rifling was introduced into the barrel-making process at Marlin, all barrels were made by the cut rifling method.

To make a gun barrel, the bar of steel must first have a hole

Shipment of steel being received at North Haven, Conn., plant.

Deep-hole barrel drilling machines at North Haven, Conn., plant.

Bank of sine-bar rifling machines at New Haven, Conn., plant.

Barrel-straightening operation during the 1920s.

drilled through its center. After the hole is drilled, it is then reamed to the required bore (land) diameter, after which it is rifled.

The machine used to rifle a barrel was called a sine bar machine. An angular bar could be adjusted so that as the cutter was pulled through the drilled and reamed hole, different twists of rifling for the different calibers to be manufactured could be cut. Rifling was a slow process, frequently taking 20 minutes or more to cut one barrel.

The shapes and lengths of the lever action rifle barrels varied. Full octagon, half octagon, and round were available in various lengths from 15 to 32 inches. On special order, most any reasonable length could be made to the customer's desire. However, most special-order work was discontinued when sporting arms production resumed after WW I.

Barrels could be ordered with a matted top to cut down glare or reflection while sighting. Barrels could also be special-ordered without the rear sight dovetail, or with the dovetail moved fore or aft from its normal location.

Examples have been noted of half-octagon barrels with the roll-stamp moved forward to the round part of the barrel, because the dovetail had been moved so far forward.

From the start of production of the Model 1893 rifle until about 1915, the steel from which barrels were manufactured was either special smokeless steel or a mild steel. The special smokeless steel barrels were marked *Special Smokeless Steel*. The mild steel barrels were for those models such as .22s that were manufactured for use with low-intensity cartridges; or, in the case of the Model 1893, for rifle barrels to be used with cartridges loaded with black powder. The Grade B mild steel barrels were marked *For Black Powder*. The "black powder only" Model 1893 was identified as the Model 1893B.

The special smokeless steel barrels were described by Marlin as follows:

In the barrel and action of these rifles we use our special smokeless steel, guaranteed to the regulation specifications of the United States Government, for steel used in the manufacture of the same parts of the Government rifle using the .30 caliber United States Government cartridge. In consequence, these rifles are perfectly adapted to the cartridges suitable for these rifles.

Grade B rifles were manufactured in calibers .32–40 and .38–55 only. Marlin used the following language to describe these rifles:

They are in every respect the same as the regular Model 1893, except the barrels are made of the highest obtainable grade of soft steel instead of our "Special Smokeless Steel," and the frames are blued instead of case hardened. These rifles are suitable for use with black powder ammunition and are made to meet the wants of the many shooters who don't care enough for the smokeless steel barrel to pay the extra price. We do not recommend this grade for High Power Smokeless ammunition.

B-grade barrels marked *For Black Powder* were not made for any other model except the Model 1893.

Special Smokeless Steel-marked barrels are found on only the Model 1893, Model 1895, and the Model 27 rifles.

Illustrations of full octagon, half-octagon, round, carbine, and shotgun barrels are included in the respective Model sections of this book and information about Micro-Groove rifling is fully covered in that section of this book.

Collectors frequently wonder why they find a few of the old

Barrel-straightening operation during the 1960s at the North Haven plant. (Tex Black, now retired, was the last of the old-time Marlin barrel straighteners. The process is now done by machine.)

Matted top flat of Special Smokeless Steel octagon barrel.

rifles with what appear to be caliber markings that are over-stamped, or that are a caliber that is different from the one listed for that serial number in the old records. The serial number records do not answer this question. Only the 1900 and 1901 catalogs allude to the possibility that Marlin, for a short period of time, may have rebored certain caliber barrels for use with a larger caliber cartridge.

The information about reboring is hidden within the catalog section called "When Barrels Will Interchange." It read as follows:

> In single shot rifles, it is quite a simple matter to make a change in cartridges, because this can be done by putting in a barrel which is correct for the cartridge desired. If the cartridges agree in head diameter the action will not have to be changed; if they do not, a slight change in the action is all that is required.
>
> But in a repeater, *in order to make a change in calibers, that is to re-bore the old barrel or put in a new barrel,* there are two points to be considered — first, the two cartridges must have the same head diameter, otherwise the head of the breech bolt with the extractor would not fit correctly; second, the old and new shells must be practically the same length over all, otherwise the action would not handle the new cartridge correctly.
>
> The following will show the changes which can be made in a Marlin Repeater:
>
> The .25–20 shell was made by necking down the .32–20 shell. Consequently these two cartridges have exactly the same head diameter and the length over all is the same. The action for these two cartridges is the same, the difference being in the barrels. *So a .25–20 barrel can be re-bored to a .32–20;* a .25–20 barrel can be fitted to a .32–20 rifle and a .32–20 barrel can be fitted to a .25–20 repeater. These are the only changes which can be made on this action. Our Take-

down we can furnish, if desired, with a .25–20 and a .32–20 barrel part so as to give the two rifles in one.

> The .38–40 shell was made by necking down the .44–40 shell, *consequently a .38–40 barrel can be re-bored to a .44–40,* a .38–40 barrel can be fitted to a .44–40 repeater, or a .44–40 barrel can be fitted to a .38–40 repeater. Likewise we can furnish a Take-Down repeater with two barrel parts, .38–40 and .44–40, giving the two rifles in one. These are the only changes which can be made on this action.
>
> The .25–36, .30–30, .32–40 and .38–55 all have exactly the same head diameter and all are practically the same length over all. The .25–36 shell was made by necking down the .32–40 shell. Consequently on an action adapted to one of these cartridges, a barrel for any of the other cartridges can be fitted with perfect results, *and likewise a barrel of smaller bore can be re-bored to one of larger caliber and then fitted.* We can also furnish one of the Model 1893 Take-Downs with four sets of barrel parts giving four rifles in one.
>
> All of the Model 1895 cartridges have exactly the same head diameter and while the cartridges are not all the same length, nevertheless the same action will handle all perfectly, so any Model 1895 rifle may have another barrel fitted to it *while the .38 and .40 caliber barrels may be re-bored to .45 caliber and then fitted, with perfect results.* We can also furnish Take-Down rifles in this model with as many sets of barrel parts as there are different sizes, giving a number of different rifles with but one action.

(Emphasis is the author's.)

It is speculated that reboring barrels was not a popular activity in the Marlin barrel department. Special handling and special operations would have been necessary that deviated from the regular production procedures used in making a barrel. It is no wonder that the texts of catalogs dated 1902 and later make no mention of rebored barrels.

Smooth-bore barrels were available on special order for the Models 1893, 1894, and 1895 from 1894 to 1904. The 1894 catalog described them as follows:

> Taxidermists desiring a smooth bore barrel as well as a rifle barrel can obtain a barrel to thus interchange. The price of smooth bore barrel is the same as that of a rifle barrel. Our action is especially adapted to such work, as it will allow the use of cartridges varying in length from the empty shell as a minimum up to the regular cartridge as a maximum. The price of an extra barrel portion complete is $15.00.

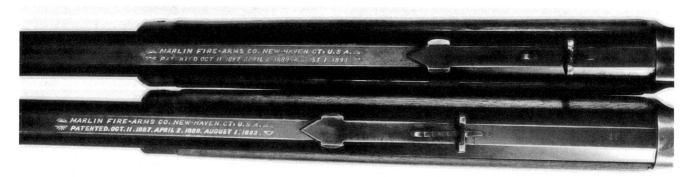

Shown are two Model 1894 barrels. The bottom barrel has the rear sight in the standard location; the top barrel has the sight located, by special order, farther to the rear.

Special Smokeless Steel *marking on an octagon barrel.*

For Black Powder *marking on a round barrel.*

Although available, according to the catalogs, for 10 years, smooth-bore Model 1893, 1894, and 1895 rifles are extremely scarce. Unfortunately, the old records that have survived for the period of 1883 to 1905–1906 do not reflect a barrel being bored smooth, except for those of the Model 1881 that are covered in that section of this book. Those that I have examined were drilled and reamed closer to the land diameter than to the groove diameter; therefore, it is my belief that the Marlin smooth-bore barrels were not a rifled barrel that had the rifling removed.

Pre-1915 catalogs explained the life and care of a Marlin firearm and barrel as follows:

We are often asked "What is the life of a barrel?" This question is very indefinite, and hardly admits of a definite answer. With the old black powder cartridges, thousands of shots have been fired in all the various calibers from .22 up to .50, and the barrel, as far as could be observed, continued to do work of the same quality. In fact, with such ammunition, presupposing proper care, frequent and thorough cleaning, we may say that the barrel will last almost indefinitely. In other words, the action of the bullet on the barrel is not perceptible enough to give this question any particular consideration, and with the superior steel which we are now using in Marlin Rifles, the barrel will wear even better than in former times. If a barrel is allowed to become foul or leaded, we then have another element, which has its influence.

In sporting rifles, the bullet of this type generally has a copper patch, nickel or tin plated. This bullet is hard enough to give all the penetration required, but at the same time not hard enough to wear the barrel rapidly like bullets of the type above mentioned. We have some of our rifles from which we have shot over 5000 rounds of ammunition, using our metal patched bullets, and the rifles today are showing accurate targets, although there must have been some wear. In general, we feel safe in saying, that no one will be disappointed in the wearing qualities of a Marlin barrel, even with our most powerful cartridges.

Firearms should always be thoroughly cleaned and well oiled before being laid aside for any length of time. This will not only keep the barrel and action in perfect order, but will further preserve the finish. After a day's shooting always clean out the barrel thoroughly until perfectly bright and then oil well inside and outside. The action should be occasionally cleaned and thoroughly lubricated.

Everybody realizes that a rifle or gun requires some consideration. Accidents will happen and serious situations may arise which will require the rifle to be treated with considerable roughness. We have, however, known of hunters and sportsmen who thoughtlessly make use of a rifle as a cane, crowbar or any one of the many implements which are occasionally in demand. Such usage will frequently result in the bending of the barrel, the filling of the muzzle with dirt, which will cause a barrel to swell when a cartridge is discharged and in general disarrange the efficiency of the rifle. Sometimes such a trifle as driving a sight in with too great force will spoil the bore of the barrel.

Never shoot a rifle or a weapon of any kind while there is an obstruction in the barrel, such as a bullet, piece of cloth, dirt, etc. If fired under these conditions, in almost every instance the air is compressed at the point of obstruction, giving a very high pressure at this point, causing the barrel to swell and forming a bulging ring, which destroys the accuracy of the barrel. We have seen a .22-caliber barrel, the metal of which was one inch in diameter, so badly swollen that the ring could be felt by passing the finger along the outside of the barrel, when the cartridge used was only the .22-short, with its three grains of black powder and 30-grain lead bullet. Sometimes the ring is perfect, extending entirely around the barrel, but often the obstruction is only partial and the swelling only a section of a ring. In small bores using high-pressure Military smokeless powders the pressure induced is sometimes great enough to cut the barrel entirely in two. This accident is an unfortunate one, as it often happens from no fault of the user. The results are characteristic and so different from any accident resulting from a flaw or seam in the barrel, however, that the cause is always known to an expert, for in no other way can a ring or powder-swell be produced.

During different periods of time since 1926, the diameter, contour, and length of barrels have changed. The length of the barrel has usually been standardized for a given model; however, there are exceptions, for example, the 39A Mountie. This model had a 24-in. barrel when introduced in 1953, but soon thereafter, the length was changed to 20 inches. Today it is only 18¼ inches. The outside contour, taper, and diameter of barrels have varied due to changes in the method of turning barrels. Early on, the taper of a round barrel was turned in a series of short tapers that were to blend into each other. With the introduction of more modern tracing lathes, the taper is now turned in one pass from muzzle to breech. This eliminates the mismatch of tapers and variation in diameters common with older techniques, as evidenced on the barrels of some Model 36 and 336 rifles.

From the early 1950s until 1969, Marlin manufactured some of the Sturm–Ruger Company's pistol and rifle barrels. These barrels were manufactured to Ruger specifications on the same machines that made Marlin barrels. After moving in 1969 to the new Marlin plant in North Haven, Conn., Marlin needed all of its barrel-making capacity for the increased sales being experienced at that time. Therefore, it was necessary for Marlin to curtail making barrels for Ruger. However, a close friendship with the Sturm–Ruger Company has continued to this day.

BARREL DRILLS   Dec. 10, 1915

Calibre	Model	Steel	Bore Diam.	Drill Diam.	Shank Tubes Outside Diam.	Inside Diam.
22	92, 97, 29, 20, 32	Soft	.217	.211	.208	.145
25 20 / 36	94, 93, & 27	Soft / Hard	.250	.244	.238	.178
30/30	93	Hard	.297	.2945	.281	.197
.32 R&CF	92	Soft	.302	.294	.286	.222
32/20	94 & 27	Soft	.305	.299	.289	.225
32/40	93	Hard	.313	.307	.297	.233
.33	95	Hard	.330	.324		
38 55 / 56	93 & 94	Hard / Hard	.370	.3645	.354	.274
38/40 65	94	Soft	.395	.387	.379	.299
40 70 82	95	Hard	.397	.3915	.381	.301
44/40 70	94	Soft	.418	.408	.402	.322
45 85 90	95	Hard	.449	.441	.433	.353
S.G. 12 Gage	S.G.	Hard	.728	.670		
12 Gage 12 Ga.	S.G.	Soft	.728	.700	.675	.550
Rib.BBL S.G.	S.G.	Soft	.728	.685		
16 Gage	S.G.	Soft	.665	.638	.615	.515
20 Ga.	S.G.	Soft	.615	.585	.560	Swaged Down from 16 GA. tube
12 Ga.	Mag. Tubes	Soft	.908	.900		
16 Ga.	Mag. Tubes	Soft	.850	.840		

TWIST OF RIFLING AS
MADE BY THE MARLIN FIREARMS CO.

.22 Rim Fire Ballard	One turn in 20 inches
.22 Rim Fire Magazine Rifle	One turn in 16 inches
.25 Rim Fire	One turn in 16 inches
.25–20 Marlin, Model 1894 and Model 27	One turn in 12 inches
.25–36 Marlin	One turn in 9 inches
.30–30 Marlin	One turn in 10 inches
.32 Ballard	One turn in 20 inches
.32 R. and C.F., Model '92, and .32–20 C.F., Model '94 and Model 27	One turn in 22 inches
.32–40 Ballard and M.H.P., and .32 Mar. H.P.	One turn in 16 inches
.33 Caliber, Model '95	One turn in 12 inches
.38–55 Ballard and M., and .38–56	One turn in 20 inches
.38–40 and .44–40, Model '94	One turn in 36 inches
.40 Calibers	One turn in 20 inches
.45–70 and .45–90 M	One turn in 20 inches

DIMENSION HEAD OF STEEL DUMMIES USED FOR BREECHING UP
The Marlin Fire Arms Co.

June 26, 1908

Model	Caliber	Thickness of Head	Diam. of Steel Dummy at Head
20	.22	.044	.275
92–97	.22	.044	.275
94	.25–20	.065	.408
93	.25–36	.063	.508
93	.30–30	.063	.508
92	.32 R.&C.	.054	.374
94	.32–20	.065	.410
93	.32–40	.063	.508
93	.32	.063	.508
93	.38–55	.063	.508
95	.38–56	.070	.594
94	.38–40	.065	.516
95	.40–65	.070	.594
95	.40–70–82	.070	.594
94	.44–40	.065	.516
95	.45–70–85	.070	.594
95	.45–90	.070	.594
Gauge	12	.072	.879
Gauge	16	.070	.825

The figures for thickness of the heads are the largest sizes to which we breech.

MODEL 1893
Regular

3/25/05

Length	Octagon HEAVY Diam. at		Round HEAVY Diam. at		½ Oct. HEAVY Diam. at	
	Front	Rear	Front	Rear	Front	Rear
32	.700	.825	.730	.875	.730	.825
30	.710	.825	.740	.875	.740	.825
28	.715	.825	.750	.875	.750	.825
26	.720	.825	.765	.875	.765	.825
24						
Standard	.730	.825	.770	.875	.770	.825
22	.740	.825	.780	.875	.780	.825
20	.750	.825	.790	.875	.790	.825
	LIGHT		LIGHT		LIGHT	
32	.580	.765	.645	.775	.645	.765
30	.590	.765	.635	.775	.635	.765
28	.600	.765	.630	.775	.630	.765
26	.605	.765	.640	.775	.640	.765
24						
Standard	.610	.765	.645	.775	.645	.765
22	.620	.765	.630	.775	.650	.765
20	.630	.765	.620	.775	.660	.765

MODEL 1894
Take Down   3/25/05

Length	Octagon HEAVY Diam. at		Round HEAVY Diam. at		½ Oct. HEAVY Diam. at	
	Front	Rear	Front	Rear	Front	Rear
32	.700	.825	.730	.875	.730	.825
30	.710	.825	.740	.875	.740	.825
28	.715	.825	.750	.875	.750	.825
26	.720	.825	.765	.875	.765	.825
24						
Standard	.730	.825	.770	.875	.770	.825
22	.740	.825	.780	.875	.780	.825
20	.750	.825	.790	.875	.790	.825
	LIGHT		*LIGHT*		*LIGHT*	
32	.580	.765	.645	.775	.645	.765
30	.590	.765	.635	.775	.635	.765
28	.600	.765	.630	.775	.630	.765
26	.605	.765	.640	.775	.640	.765
24						
Standard	.610	.765	.645	.775	.645	.765
22	.620	.765	.650	.775	.650	.765
20	.630	.765	.660	.775	.660	.765

MODEL 1895
Regular   3/25/05

Length	Octagon Diam. at		Round Diam. at		½ Oct. Diam. at	
	Front	Rear	Front	Rear	Front	Rear
32	.740	.910	.755	.935	.755	.910
30	.745	.910	.765	.935	.765	.910
28	.755	.910	.775	.935	.775	.910
26						
Standard	.780	.910	.790	.935	.790	.910
24	.790	.910	.795	.935	.795	.910
22	.800	.910	.815	.935	.815	.910
20	.815	.910	.830	.935	.830	.910
	Take Down					
32	.740	.910	.755	.935	.755	.910
30	.745	.910	.765	.935	.765	.910
28	.755	.910	.775	.935	.775	.910
26						
Standard	.780	.910	.790	.935	.790	.910
24	.790	.910	.795	.935	.795	.910
22	.800	.910	.815	.935	.815	.910
20	.815	.910	.830	.935	.830	.910

MARLIN CHAMBERS

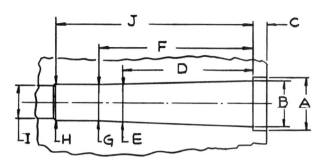

Cal./Ga.	A	B	C	D	E	F	G	H	I	J	Year
.25–20	.420	.354	.120	.800	.333	.900	.281	.278	.250	1.281	1909
.32–20	.420	.355	.120	.840	.344	.975	.330	.328	.305	1.300	1909
.38–40	.535	.469	.120	.853	.451	1.000	.421	.414	.395	1.300	1909
.44–40	.535	.472	.120	.825	.459	.958	.445	.439	.418	1.275	1909
.25–36	.533	.428	.120	1.317	.365	1.600	.289	.280	.250	2.095	1907
.32–40	.533	.427	.120	–	–	1.683	.348	.341	.313	2.042	1909
.32 Spec.	.533	.422	.120	1.305	.403	1.522	.347	.344	.313	2.008	1909
.38–55	.533	.422	.120	–	–	–	–	.395	.370	2.076	1909
.38–56	.617	.507	.176	1.178	.453	1.450	.411	.398	.370	2.100	1911
.40–60/65	.617	.507	.176	1.054	.457	1.395	.442	.416	.397	2.072	1911
.40–70/82	.617	.511	.176	1.528	.460	1.820	.435	.425	.397	2.340	1911
.45–70	.617	.508	.176	–	–	–	–	.476	.450	2.083	1911
.45–90	.617	.507	.176	–	–	1.900	.480	.476	.450	2.392	1911
20 Ga.	.700	–	39°	–	–	–	–	.684	.615	2¾	1917
16 Ga.	.751	–	39°	–	–	–	–	.729	.665	2²³/₃₂	1917
12 Ga.	.811	–	39°	–	–	–	–	.796	.725	2¾	1917

Shotgun body taper (double) = 2″ to 1′.

BORE DIMENSIONS

Feb. 25, 1909

Model	Caliber	Bore*	Width of Groove*	Width of Land*	Depth of Rifling*	No. of Grooves	Twist	Material
18, 20, 92, 97	22	.217	.090	.0463	.0015	5	16	S.S.
25	22	.217	.090	.0463	.0015	5	20	S.S.
18, 20, 92, 97	22	.217	.0691	.0461	.0015	6	16	S.S.
94	25/20	.250	.0785	.0520	.0020	6	12	S.S.
93	25/36	.250	.0785	.0520	.0020	6	9	H.S.
93	30/30	.297†	.0933	.0622	.0020	6	10	H.S.
92	32 R&C	.302	.0949	.0632	.0025	6	22	S.S.
94	32/20	.305	.0958	.0639	.0025	6	22	S.S.
93	32/40	.313	.0983	.0656	.0025	6	16	H.S.
93	38/55	.370	.1162	.0775	.0025	6	20	H.S.
95	38/56	.370	.1162	.0775	.0025	6	20	H.S.
94	38/40	.395	.1240	.0827	.0025	6	36	S.S.
95	40/60, 70, 82	.397	.1247	.0831	.0025	6	20	H.S.
94	44/40	.416	.1313	.0875	.0025	6	36	S.S.
95	45/70, 85, 90	.449	.1410	.0940	.0025	6	20	H.S.

*In inches
†Changed to .301 ± $^{.000}_{.001}$ 6/13/1923

CHARACTERISTICS OF MARLIN BARRELS

Date	Model	Caliber	Bore Diameter*	Groove Diameter*	Width of Groove*	No. of Grooves	Rate of Twist
Up to 1946	36	.30–30	.300	.308	.0933	6	1 in 10″
1946–1947	36	.30–30	.300	.308	.177	4	1 in 10″
1948 on	336	.30–30	.300	.308	.177	4	1 in 10″
Up to 1946	36	.32 Special	.313	.318	.0983	6	1 in 16″
1946–1947	36	.32 Special	.313	.318	.177	4	1 in 16″
1948 on	336	.32 Special	.313	.318	.177	4	1 in 16″
1950 on	336	.35 Remington	.349	.359	.110	7	1 in 16″
1932–1945	39A	.22 Rimfire	.218	.222	.069	6	1 in 16″
1945–1948	39A	.22 Rimfire	.215	.221	.075	5	1 in 16″
1948–1953	39A	.22 Rimfire	.217	.222	.069	6	1 in 16″
Up to 1950	80/81/88/100	.22 Rimfire	.215	.221	.075	5	1 in 16″
1950–1953	80/81/88/100	.22 Rimfire	.218	.222	.069	6	1 in 16″
Up to 1953	89	.22 Rimfire	.218	.222	.069	6	1 in 16″
1953 on	100/80/81 88/89/39A	.22 Rimfire	.219	.222	.014	16	1 in 16″
1954 on	322	.222 Remington	.221	.223	.015	16	1 in 14″
1955 on	336	.219 Zipper	.221	.223	.015	16	1 in 14″
1955 on	56	.22 Rimfire	.219	.222	.014	16	1 in 16″
1955–1958	455	.30–06; .308	.304	.308	.030	16	1 in 10″
1955 on	336	.30–30	.304	.308	.030	16	1 in 10″
1955 on	336	.32 Special	.318	.321	.035	16	1 in 16″
1955 on	336	.35 Remington	.354	.358	.040	16	1 in 16″
1958–1959	455	.30–06	.304	.308	.024	22	1 in 10″
1958 on	336	.30–30	.304	.308	.024	22	1 in 10″
1958–1959	422	.222 Remington	.221	.223	.022	16	1 in 14″
1957–1960	98	.22 Rimfire	.220	.223	.022	16	1 in 16″
1959 on	99/57/101	.22 Rimfire	.220	.223	.022	16	1 in 16″
1959 on	57 Magnum	.22 Rimfire	.221	.223	.020	20	1 in 16″
1934–1946	A1	.22 Rimfire	.215	.221	.075	5	1 in 16″
	99/57/101	.22 LR	.2195	.2235	.028	16	1 in 16″
	80/81	.22 LR	.2195	.2235	.028	16	1 in 16″
3–2–73	39	.22 LR	.2195	.2235	.028	16	1 in 16″
8–20–68	57M	.22 WMR	.2215	.2235	.020	20	1 in 16″
8–20–68	980	.22 WMR	.2215	.2235	.020	20	1 in 16″
	62	.256 WM	.2520	.2570	.022	22	1 in 14″
	62	.30 Carbine	.3010	.3085	.050	12	1 in 20″
	336	.30–30	.3025	.3080	.040	12	1 in 10″
	336	.35	.3520	.3575	.055	12	1 in 16″
	336	.44 Mag	.4230	.4315	.062	12	1 in 38″
8–20–68	444	444 Marlin	.424	.4330	.056	12	1 in 38″
1972	1895	.45–70	.4527	.4587	.060	8	1 in 20″
1973	1895	.45–70	.4527	.4587	.060	12	1 in 20″
9–1–78	1894	.357 Mag	.3515	.3577	.055	12	1 in 16″
2–23–87	1894	.41 Mag	.4047	.4107	.072	12	1 in 20″
2–23–87	336ER	.356 Win.	.3515	.3577	.0625	12	1 in 12″
2–28–87	9	9mm	.3495	.3567	.047	12	1 in 16″
2–23–87	45	.45 Auto	.4467	.4510	.079	12	1 in 18″
2–23–87	1894	.44 Mag	.4245	.4310	.062	12	1 in 38″
10–10–83	375	.375 Win.	.3695	.3767	.050	12	1 in 12″

*Bore diameter, groove diameter and width of groove are in inches.

Barrels Under 16 Inches

Because of the restriction in the U.S. against owning rifles having barrels shorter than 16 inches, the Marlin records have been reviewed to establish the serial numbers of those Marlin factory-manufactured firearms that originally had barrels shorter than 16 inches. Marlin barrel length is established by measuring from the face of the bolt to the muzzle, not from the front end of the receiver.

It has been previously mentioned that Marlin records, in every case, have not been complete. There are errors and omissions. Likewise, there are errors and omissions in the under-16-in. barrel list. For example, a New Zealand lady owns a 15-in. Model 1895, serial number 141,940, which is in the records as such, but was inadvertently left out of the list sent to the BATF (the U.S. Bureau of Alcohol, Tobacco and Firearms). Other 15-in.-barreled guns have been authenticated as "factory" that do not appear in the records. When a U.S. collector is aware of a short-barreled (under 16 inches) Marlin rifle that is not listed here, he should request an exemption from the BATF, so that he can legally own the gun and display it without fear of serious consequences. It has been my experience that the BATF has always been fair in handling this type of matter.

Before making a request, however, the owner of a Marlin rifle or carbine having a barrel under 16 inches should examine it carefully to determine if the serial number is one of those listed here, remembering, of course, that the old records only go to 1905–1906 and that short-barreled guns were produced much later.*

If your firearm has a barrel shorter than the law allows, to ensure it is original, measure through the bore from the muzzle to the face of the bolt. Commonly referred to as 15-in. barrels, they are actually 15¼ inches in length. The crown at the muz-

zle should be smooth and with a minimum of tool marks. If it's a carbine, the front sight should be the fixed-stud carbine type that is dovetailed and soft-soldered to the barrel. The area around the stud should be well finished and the union of the stud and barrel hardly noticeable (no gaps or space between the two); also, the muzzle diameter should be about .595 inch.

Included here are photos of a carbine barrel front sight stud showing how it is dovetailed into the barrel.

The records reflect the following breakdown of under 16-in. barrels:

1889 Carbine	325
1893 Carbine	83
1893B (Black Powder)	3
1894 Carbine	952
1894	45
1895 Carbine	8
Total	1,416

After my research was completed, I requested an exemption of the listed firearms from the restrictive federal regulations. The request and official exemption were as follows:

15-in. Carbine barrel.

Roll-stamp on 1893/94 carbine barrel.

Top view of carbine barrel front sight stud that has been removed from dovetail.

Side view of carbine barrel front sight stud.

*The list of serial numbers, not printed in the book, can be obtained by contacting the author.

100 KENNA DRIVE • NORTH HAVEN, CT. 06473
Telephone (203) 239-5621

Cable Address
"MARLIN NEW HAVEN"

The Marlin Firearms Co.

Makers of Fine Rifles and Shotguns Since 1870

April 1, 1980

Mr. G. Robert Dickerson, Director
Bureau of Alcohol, Tobacco and Firearms
Federal Building
1200 Pennsylvania Ave. N. W.
Washington, D. C. 20226

Dear Mr. Dickerson:

During the past year I have had conversations with personnel of your bureau with regard to old Marlin firearms having barrel lengths under 16 inches. It was my understanding that during these conversations that it was the desire of the BATF to classify these baby carbines as curios and relics, if it could be documented by factory records that the gun was, in fact, originally, manufactured having a barrel under 16 inches in length.

In the interest of the gun collector and your bureau, I have reviewed the old Marlin records and have extracted the serial numbers, model, caliber, barrel length, and the date of manufacture of all firearms which are listed in the old records of this company for the period 1883 to 1906 that have barrels shorter than 16 inches.

Therefore, by reason of the date of manufacture, value, design, and the fact that these firearms are collector's items and are not likely to be used in the commission of a crime, it is requested that the firearms listed by serial number in the attached 26 page enclosure be classified as curios and relics, so that collectors can acquire, hold and dispose of them under the provisions of Title 18, United States Code, Chapter 44, and Title 27, CFR, Part 178.

In making this request, it is recognized that these guns would still be classified as firearms as defined in Title 18, United States Code, Section 921 (a) (3).

Yours very truly,

William S. Brophy
Senior Technical Manager

WSB:mc
Enclosure
cc: Frank Kenna, President
E. Ernest Oberst, Legal Counsel

OVER A CENTURY OF AMERICAN GUNMAKING
MARLIN FIREARMS SINCE 1870

DEPARTMENT OF THE TREASURY
BUREAU OF ALCOHOL, TOBACCO AND FIREARMS
WASHINGTON, D.C. 20226

JUN 1 8 1981

REFER TO
T:T:F:CHB
7540

Mr. William S. Brophy
Senior Technical Manager
The Marlin Firearms Company
100 Kenna Drive
North Haven, Connecticut 06473

Dear Mr. Brophy:

This refers to your letter of April 1, 1980, in which you requested that a group of 1,418 original, factory documented Marlin Baby carbines, having barrels measuring less than 16 inches in length and identified by individual serial numbers, be considered for classification as curios or relics.

In our original reply dated November 5, 1980, we advised you that those carbines on your list, produced during 1899 through 1906, qualified as curios or relics as that term is defined in Title 27, Code of Federal Regulations (CFR), Part 178, Section 178.11, since they were manufactured at least 50 years prior to the current date. Further, those carbines produced in 1898 or earlier, were antique firearms as that term is defined in Section 921(a)(16) of the Gun Control Act of 1968. We also advised you that all of these firearms were still subject to the provisions of the National Firearms Act (NFA) and that we would consider removing them from the provisions of the NFA. We have now determined that due to their scarcity, value, design, and other characteristics, all of the firearms described on the attached list are collector's items and are not likely to be used as weapons; therefore, they are removed from the provisions of the NFA. Those firearms produced in or before 1898, are determined to be antique firearms which are not subject to any provisions of Title 18, United States Code (U.S.C.), Chapter 44. Those firearms produced between 1899 and 1906, are determined to be curios or relics as defined, thereby authorizing licensed collectors to acquire, hold, or dispose of them as curios or relics subject to the provisions of Title 18, U.S.C., Chapter 44, and the regulations in Title 27, CFR, Part 178; however, they are still firearms as that term is defined in Title 18, U.S.C., Section 921(a)(3).
We trust that the foregoing is of interest to you. Thank you for providing us with this information. If we can be of any further assistance, please do not hesitate to contact us.

Sincerely yours,

Assistant Director
(Technical and Scientific Services)

Belt Buckles and Paperweights

Buckles. Marlin has never authorized a commercial company to manufacture and sell a Marlin belt buckle. However, the company did authorize The Marlin Firearms Collectors Association, Ltd.—a nonprofit organization—to have manufactured and to sell two different variations of belt buckles.

The first type was a 2½-in.-diameter solid pewter buckle having *The Marlin Firearms Co. — Since 1870* in a circle around the Marlin "Danger Ahead" horse and rider logo.

The second type was a rectangular solid bronze buckle. It is 2 inches by 3 inches and accommodates belts up to 1¾ inches in width. This buckle also has the horse and rider logo centrally located over the Marlin Firearms Company name. The sculptor was the world-famous artist Joseph DiLorenzo.

A total of 827 of the first type were manufactured and sold by the association. A total of 500 of the second type were struck. A special run of 103 solid sterling silver buckles of the second type were also produced. They were sold only to Marlin employees and members of the association.

Paperweights. From the same die from which the second type of buckle was struck, 100 bronze paperweights were also made. The first 50 were ³⁄₁₆ inch thick. The second 50, through an error of the manufacturer, were made from material only ⅛ inch thick.

The design of both buckles, and the paperweight, were copyrighted by Marlin.

Bicycles

Frank Kenna, Sr., explored the bicycle business in 1937. He purchased bicycles from the Westfield Manufacturing Company. Westfield, Mass., with the Marlin name on them and then tried to sell them.

After selling only 303 by June 27, 1937, Mr. Kenna decided that he did not want to start manufacturing or marketing bicycles at that time. When the few left in inventory were sold, the department was closed. However, in September 1943, Frank Kenna again considered going into the bicycle business, but the war work and other commitments prevented serious steps being taken in that direction.

Bicycle Locks

Marlin manufactured, advertised, and sold the Merrill Automatic Bicycle Lock during the period of 1887 to 1891. It was described as follows:

> We desire to bring this lock to the attention of all Wheelmen. It is just as indispensable an adjunct to a bicycle as a wrench or oil can, and is in every respect far ahead of the chain which has been generally used for locking bicycles.
>
> It can be applied instantly and locks automatically, is neat, compact and cheap. This lock weighs only 2½ ounces, and is but four inches long, so that it may conveniently be carried in the book bag or in any clothes pocket. It is full nickel plated.
>
> The Merrill lock is composed of but five pieces, while an ordinary lock and chain has almost 35 pieces. It is evident from this that there is but very little chance to have it get out of order. Price, by mail, postpaid, $1.00. Can be had of any dealer in bicycles or bicycle sundries.

First type of Marlin belt buckle.

Second type of Marlin belt buckle.

Merrill's Bicycle Lock manufactured and sold by Marlin.

Marlin ad for Dr. F.W. Mann's classic book on ballistics and experiments he conducted.

Booklets

Marlin has at different times printed various types of booklets to advertise its firearms, as well as to educate and help the gun owner, dealer, or distributor. Some of the most worthwhile and successful were the following:

1. In 1936 Marlin published "How to Set up a Rifle Range and Shoot." The booklet contained 15 pages of information about safety, the indoor range, the outdoor range, good shooting habits, how to care for the Marlin rifle, sights and aiming, the gunsling strap, holding one's breath, trigger squeeze, shooting positions, and how to organize a Junior Rifle Club. Also included was an article called "Sound Advice" by the famous author and gun expert, Captain E.C. Crossman. The last two pages plugged the NRA Open Road National Rifle Match, which was held in conjunction with *The Open Road for Boys* magazine.

   Thousands of these booklets were distributed through advertisements and requests for catalog information. I remember working with junior shooters during the 1930s who had this booklet as one of their references. I feel sure it helped establish a good foundation for many a youngster.

2. Included with the Clipper King and Crown Prince rifles (1937–1938) was a "Straight Shooting" booklet. It described how to handle and care for firearms. It included information about "The Sportsmen's Code," the history of firearms, safety, how to handle a rifle, how to aim and fire a rifle, ranges, targets, and preventing rust. It had a dictionary of terms, and a list of Marlin's line of firearms. It was also mailed out in answer to inquiries and with catalogs.

3. Also packaged with Crown Prince and Clipper King rifles was a Marlin Target and Game booklet. The booklet contained information that the gun owner would find valuable for management of his gun when on the range and when in the field. There were also record pages designed for keeping accurate and perma-

1936 booklet about shooting and setting up a range.

"Straight Shooting" booklet of 1937.

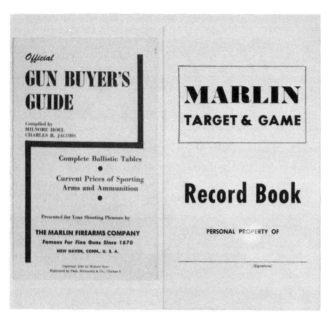

Left: *"Gun Buyer's Guide" of 1949*. Right: *"Target and Game Book" of 1937–1938*.

nent accounts of shooting activities. The booklet also covered information about sights, sighting in, trigger squeeze, aiming points, telescope sights, handling guns in the field, keeping from getting lost, and being an outdoor sleuth. This booklet was also distributed free upon request and in response to technical inquiries.

4. In 1949, Marlin had printed and distributed the "Gun Buyer's Guide," which was compiled by Milnore Hoel and Charles R. Jacobs. It included complete ballistic tables, and current prices of sporting arms and ammunition. It was used to answer questions about ammunition received in the mail. Due to the yearly changes in prices of ammunition and firearms it was short-lived, and too, it was not limited to Marlin firearms. In a sense it advertised firearms of the competition.

5. In 1956 Marlin distributed a booklet entitled "Pointers on Deer and Rabbit Hunting." The booklet was prepared by *Sports Afield* and included two previously printed *SA* articles. The K.M. Bradford article, "How to Get Your Deer," covered the ramifications of deer hunting with tips and tricks on how to be successful. "The ABC's of Rabbit Hunting," an article by Byron W. Dalrymple, included the same about hunting the wily rabbit. Like the other booklets, this one was also passed out free for the asking, at gun shops and at trade shows.

6. During the 1955–1956 period, Marlin made available to dealers a "Firearms Registry." It included pages for recording firearms sold and order forms to be submitted directly to Marlin with the various firearms wanted. (The order form also had a place for the dealer to specify the jobber to whom the order should be cleared, a departure from regular Marlin policy, which was for jobbers to do the selling at the dealer level.)

7. In 1957, Marlin mailed out and distributed at trade shows a booklet called "Meet Peter Progress and the Marlin Rifle." The booklet included a narrative discus-

sion by Peter Progress of the development of the rifle from Brown Bess musket to John Marlin's repeating rifles. His last-page statement is, "I've seen them all, and to me the Marlin rifles are the finest. Hope you're not having the same problem I am, picking the Marlin rifle I like best."

8. Marlin offered a booklet about the Ten Commandments of Safety and Safe Hunter Pledge, which was included in the box with the firearms for many years. Close to a million were distributed. There were two variations. The first had a brown cover and the second had a bright red cover. The text did not change.

9. In 1981, Marlin included in the box with each firearm a copy of a National Shooting Sports Foundation-prepared pamphlet entitled "The Ethical Hunter." At least one-half million of these pamphlets, which explain the views of a sportsman and his sport, were distributed. They covered the sportsman's philosophy, his preparation, his relationship to landowners, his companionship, his attitude toward wildlife, his responsibilities toward downed game, the unwritten laws, his use of the game he gets, his measure of real hunting success, his regard for the feelings of nonhunters, his conduct when hunting alone, his respect for the law and today's hunter, and the future of hunting. In summary, this pamphlet expresses the ingrained beliefs of The Marlin Firearms Company.

10. In 1975, Marlin developed and printed a brochure entitled "The History of Marlin Firearms." It includes a historical resumé, The Marlin Firearms Company of today, the predecessor companies, and their products. In thumbnail sketch form it gives the reader an idea of from where the company came, and of the various products along the line. It is still available today.

Brush Department

On March 24, 1937, Frank Kenna, Sr., financed John Morrison in starting a brush business at the cost of $1,500.00. Mr. Morrison had the expertise and the equipment, but not an established name. Mr. Kenna felt there was a possibility that clothes, shoe, and hair brushes might go hand-in-hand with the already established razor blade business he owned. Production of small quantities of some models were manufactured. However, by July 1937 all activities of the brush department had been stopped. As a result, Marlin-marked brushes are rare collector's items.

Rare Marlin hairbrush.

1900 hang-up calendar.

1901–1902 blotter calendar.

1902 hang-up calendar.

Calendars

Historically, firearm and ammunition companies have used calendars and posters to promote their products and to reach the consumer. Many of the companies used the finest artists of the day to illustrate their calendars with pictures of the outdoors and their product in use.

A few of the Marlin calendars have pictures similar to those on the cover of the annual catalog, and some have original artwork designed with a calendar in mind.

Marlin calendars are of two types. They are either an ink blotter or a small card to be hung in a convenient place. In some years, there were two types of calendars, one having a separate page for each month, which was torn off at the end of the month, or an ink blotter that had the whole year printed on it. Interestingly, the blotters cover from May of one year to April of the next year. The hang-up type usually had a printed reverse side, outlining the superior points of a Marlin firearm. The blotters, of course, had the usual fuzzy, absorbent texture that picked up excess ink without smearing it.

The calendars I have examined are as follows:

Year	Picture	Type	Size
1900	Hunter with two dogs on point	Hang-up	3½"x6¼"
May 1901– April 1902	Falling duck & animals	Blotter	3⅜"x6"
1902	Falling duck & animals	Hang-up	3½"x6¼"
1903	Antelope	Hang-up	3½"x6¼"

1903 hang-up calendar.

1903–1904 blotter calendar.

1904 hang-up calendar.

1905–1906 blotter calendar.

Year	Picture	Type	Size
May 1903– April 1904	Antelope	Blotter	3⅜″x6″
1904	Hunter in marsh	Hang-up	3½″x6¼″
May 1905– April 1906	Hunters & camp- fire (1905 catalog)	Blotter	3⅜″x6″

Any and all of the Marlin calendars are rare and bring a premium price in collectors' circles. None are known in the large wall size that is distributed by some other manufacturers.

Carbines, Standard and Baby

Standard Models. Designed for use by the rancher or sportsman who used a horse for transportation, the carbine could easily be carried in a scabbard attached to the saddle. The carbine was light, short, and always ready for use.

Carbines usually had a saddle ring attached to the left side of the receiver. By tying a latigo strap to the ring and then to the saddle, the carbine would not be lost when traversing rough terrain or dense foliage.

The first carbines Marlin manufactured were of the Model 1889, and until the 1930s they have had the same general characteristics of short round barrels; a band around the forearm; a band, forward of the front sight stud, that held the front end of the barrel and magazine in alignment; a leaf rear sight; a straight stock; and a steel butt plate. The length of Marlin carbine barrels was usually 15 or 20 inches for the Models 1889, 1893, and 1894, and 15 and 22 inches for the Model 1895.

All carbines had blued receivers, unless otherwise ordered. They were fitted with a sling ring mounted on the left side of the receiver as standard. However, if the gun was ordered with butt and forearm swivels for a sling strap, the ring was omitted, unless ordered to be retained.

The standard rear sight installed on all three models of carbines was a folding leaf sight. Marlin used this sight only on carbines. It had an open V-notch slide, adjustable to 900 yards when the leaf is up, and a fixed open notch when the leaf is down. The fixed notch is set for 100 yards.

The carbine front sight is a fixed stud, dovetailed and soldered to the barrel. The early type had a German silver blade pinned to the stud. Later carbines had a front sight stud with the blade as an integral part of the stud.

Baby Carbines. In 1905, Marlin introduced a Model 1894 baby carbine. The catalog stated: "We can furnish .38–40 and .44–40 carbines in special light weight, about 5½ pounds, with half magazines holding six cartridges, at the same price as regular Model 1894 Carbines."

The basic difference between the baby carbine and the regular carbine is the half magazine; otherwise the baby carbine is the same as the previously described carbine. However, the baby was not offered in the Models 1893 and 1895. Baby carbines cannot be identified as such from the old Marlin records.

Prices for standard carbines and baby carbines are as follows:

Model 1893 Carbine .32–40 or .38–55
With 15″ round barrel, 5 shots, 6¼ lbs.	$12.95
With 20″ round barrel, 7 shots, 6¾ lbs.	12.95

Model 1894 Carbine .25–20, .32–20, .38–40, or .44–40
With 15″ round barrel, 9 shots, 5¾ lbs.	12.00
With 20″ round barrel, 12 shots, 6 lbs.	12.00

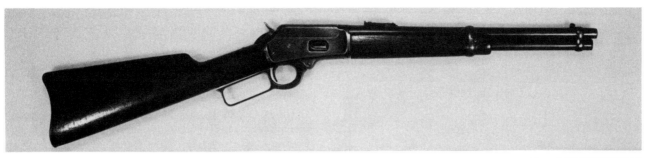

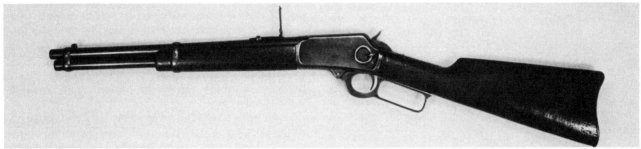

Top: *Model 1894 Carbine with a 15-in. barrel. This is representative of all Marlin carbines.* Bottom: *Left side of same carbine, showing the saddle ring and carbine leaf sight typical of Marlin carbines.*

Model 1894 Baby Carbine .38–40 or .44–40
    With 20″ round barrel, ½ magazine, 6
    shots, 5¼ lbs.   12.00
Model 1895 Carbine .38–56, .40–65, .40–70, .40–82, .45–70, .45–90
    With 15″ round barrel, 5 shots, 7 lbs.   16.50
    With 20″ round barrel, 8 shots, 7¾ lbs.   16.50

Carbines with 15-inch barrels

Model	Total
1889 Carbines	325
1893 Carbines	83
1893 B Carbines	3
1894 Carbines*	952
1895 Carbines	8

*There were also 45 Model 1894 rifles with 15-in. barrels that are not included here.

Carriage Department

In 1936, Frank Kenna, Sr., established a carriage department to manufacture baby carriages. Homer G. Sanborn, Jr., was designated manager.

Two styles of carriages were manufactured. The basic differences between them were the way the top folded down and the way the springs were attached to the body and axles.

Considered to be Eastern-style carriages, marketing of them was basically in New York City and done through stores such as Macy's, Bamburger's, and Gimbels.

After only a few thousand of the Marlin carriages were manufactured and sold, Mr. Kenna stopped production of the complete carriage and continued for a short period to make the metal parts for Mr. Rowe of Rowe Paint Company, who purchased the Carriage Department.

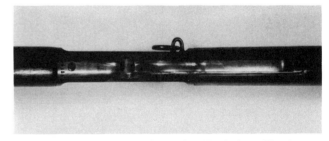

Ring and staple fitted to Marlin Model 1894 Carbine. The ring was standard unless the customer requested that it not be furnished.

Model 1894 Baby Carbine. Note the half magazine.

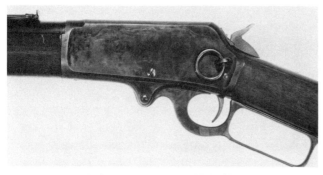

Saddle ring on Model 1893 Carbine.

CARBINE WITH SLING

Furnished in all calibers in Models 1893, 1894 and 1895; swivels and sling strap can also be furnished on any rifle of our make, for price of swivels and sling strap, see table of extras, page 25.

Catalog illustration of Model 1893 Carbine with factory swivels and sling.

At the time of disposing of the carriage business, it had a value of $10,000 in inventory and $6,000 in machines and tools.

Mr. Sanborn was transferred to the bicycle department.

Catalogs and Posters

Catalogs. One of the primary methods that have been used to present a company's product line to a prospective customer has been a product catalog. These annual catalogs usually described and illustrated the different models available, as well as any accessories or extra features that could be ordered. Marlin was not an exception and even to this day places a lot of importance on the catalog to fulfill a public relations and sales role.

The earliest Marlin catalog known is dated 1882 and has *Hartley & Graham, Agents, 19 Maiden Lane, New York* printed on the cover.

Later catalogs had Marlin's New Haven address on the cover along with space for the printing or stamping of the name and address of an agent or dealer. Some were printed with additional names, for example, the Montgomery Ward Company.

The format of catalogs over the years changed. Also the number of pages changed as more models were added and more extra information about ammunition and the reloading of ammunition was included.

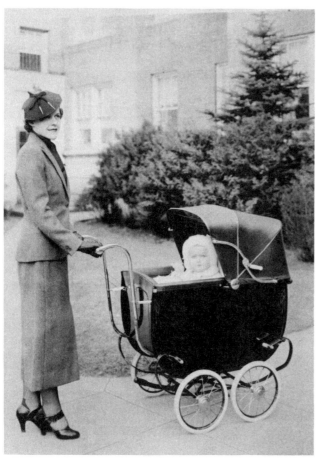

First style of Marlin baby carriage. (EG)

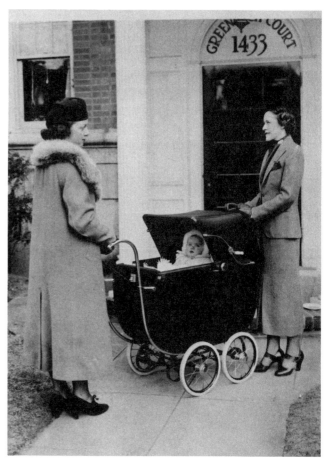

Second style of Marlin baby carriage. (EG)

1899 catalog cover.

1900 catalog cover.

The Marlin product catalogs are a primary source of information about Marlin's products. However, it must be recognized that the annual catalog is organized and put in draft form long before the year starts and frequently catalogs are printed with errors and omissions. Often, the intent of what is planned for the next year is printed in the catalog. Then, for some unknown reason, the product was not produced as described and illustrated in the catalog. A good example, although not the only one, is the announcement in the 1963 catalog that the Model 62 Levermatic rifle would be available in .357 magnum caliber. In fact, it was never produced in that caliber.

In spite of the above, catalogs can be used as a guide, and do offer a great store of information of importance to the collector and historian.

The most desirable catalogs, because of their rarity and value, are those that are pre-1917.

Frequently, Marlin reprinted catalogs and inserted a new price list to update them. It also distributed an insert sheet to be pasted into the catalog or price list to announce a new model or variation of a model during the year. Some examples were:

January 1910, supplement to July 1, 1909 (Model 27)
August 1912, supplement to July 1, 1911 (.33 caliber)
January 1912, supplement to July 1, 1911 (Model 29)
July 1913, supplement to January 1, 1913
(Model 27 in .25 RF)

Original Frederic Remington painting from which the horse and rider was copied for the 1900 catalog.

The following is a list of pre-1917 catalogs known. Please note, however, that a catalog is not listed for some years and that for other years two might be listed. If two are listed, the format and cover are different. If one is not listed, it is because one for that year has not been located.

MARLIN CATALOGS

Year	Pages	Cover	Size In Inches	
			Vertical	Horizontal
1882	23	Gray	7½	4½
1883	47	Brown	8⅝	5⅝
1885	48	Pink	9	5⅞
1886	48	Burnt Orange	9¼	5⅞
1887	56	Yellow	9¼	5⅞
1888	56	Green	9¼	5⅞
1891	39	Black	6⅛	9⅞
1892	39	Yellow	6⅛	9⅞
1893	43	Gray	6¼	9⅞
1894	51	Black	6¼	9⅞
1895	51	Gray/Green	6	9¾
1896	64	Plum	4⅜	6⅞
1897	192	Brown	4¼	7
1899	200	Blue	4⅜	7
1899	120	Hunter w/two dogs	8⅛	5¼
1900	120	Danger Ahead	8	5¼
1901	120	Indian	8	5¼
1902	120	Gentleman w/pipe	8	5¼
1903	128	Snowshoer	8	5¼
1905	128	Hunting camp at night (A great shot)	8	5¼
1906	136	Elk hunter behind large rock	8⅛	5¼
1906	136	Brown	8	5¼
1907	136	Canoers	8	5¼
1908	136	Ducks	8	5⅜
1909	136	Gray with three guns	7¾	5¼
1909	136	Quail shooting in England	7⅞	5⅜
1911	122	Three guns	7¾	5⅜
1913	128	One shotgun (butt to right, muzzle to upper left)	8	5⅜
1914	128	One shotgun (butt to left, muzzle to upper right)	7⅞	5¼
1915	136	Same as 1914	7⅞	5¼

Poster made from a John Scott copy of the Marlin 1900 catalog cover.

Counter card of John Scott's copy of the 1900 catalog.

1901 catalog cover.

1902 catalog cover.

1903 catalog cover.

1905 catalog cover.

The Marlin 1882, 1885, 1897, and 1915 catalogs have been reproduced. The Model 1882 and 1885 catalogs have had printed on page 2 of each one the logo of the All-Type Printing Company. The other two catalogs may or may not be identified as reproductions.

Catalogs for the following years have not been accurately identified or located: 1916, 1917, 1918, 1919, 1920, 1921, 1924, 1934, 1938, 1939, 1942, 1943, and 1944. Price lists for some of these years have been studied and it is possible some of the

missing catalogs were printed, except for those years Marlin was committed to war work.

Well-known artists of the period were commissioned to paint the outdoor scenes depicted on a few of the Marlin catalog covers. Some of the artists were Frederic Remington (1900 catalog); Everett Johnson (1901 and 1902 catalogs); Phillip R. Goodwin (1906 catalog); G. Muss. Arnolt (1908 catalog); and Rousseau (1909 catalog).

Marlin published a 96-page testimonial book entitled *Marlin*

Poster of 1906 catalog cover.

1907 catalog cover.

Poster of 1907 catalog cover.

1908 catalog cover.

Poster of 1908 catalog cover.

1909 catalog cover.

Experiences, which included extracts from letters sent into Marlin from all parts of the country by sportsmen stating their great admiration for Marlin shotguns and rifles. Some letters from overseas customers were also reproduced, for example, letters from Calcutta, India, and Otago, New Zealand.

There were two cover variations to *Marlin Experiences*. One had a picture of a hunter carrying a pack and massive antlers

Poster of 1909 catalog cover.

of a moose. The other had the name *Marlin* superimposed on a circular target.

Included on each page were interesting camp scenes and pictures of hunters with game. Also included were reproductions of targets and shooting skill.

The back cover of these two books had an ad for the Marlin Model 1898 shotgun. Only one reference to a date in the text has been noted. It was a reference to a 1902 newspaper article that was included in the New Zealand writer's letter. The Model 1898 shotgun was last listed in Marlin catalogs in 1905. Therefore the *Marlin Experiences* book was probably published during the period 1903–1904.

Posters. Like many other gun companies, Marlin had reproduced in poster size (15″x24″ and 17″x20″) lithographed copies of some of its catalog covers. Usually a hunting or outdoor scene, Marlin covers were well suited for poster use. When displayed in hardware stores, gun shops, and sporting goods stores they carried the message to the customer that Marlin rifles and shotguns were sold there.

The following list furnishes the catalog year, the cover picture, and whether poster is known to have been printed:

Year	Picture	Poster
1899	Hunter with dogs on point	?
1900	Remington's *Cowboy on a Horse*	No
1901	Indian holding rifle	No
1902	Man with shotgun and pipe	No
1903	Man on snowshoes with shotgun	?
1904	Unknown	?
1905	Two men at campfire	Yes
1906	Elk hunter behind rock	Yes
1907	Two hunters in birch bark canoe	Yes
1908	Ducks falling to the water	Yes
1909	Hunter with two dogs on point	Yes

Catalog covers from 1910 to 1915 had illustrations of Marlin shotguns and rifles on them. None are known to have been made into posters.

At least the 1900 and 1901 catalog covers were also printed as a small cardboard hang-up picture. They had a grommet in the top edge for hanging. Advertising was printed on the back side.

The Marlin Fire Arms company catalog of 1900 has a picture of a horse and rider on the cover that was painted by the noted Western artist Frederic Remington. Much conjecture has been bantered about with regard to the catalog cover, the original Remington painting, and the reproduction of the Remington cover commissioned by The Marlin Fire Arms Company.

The original Remington painting from which the catalog cover was copied has two men mounted on horses and dogs holding a bear at bay. The story has always been told by Marlin advertising personnel that John Marlin commissioned Frederic Remington to copy the central figure in his painting for use on a Marlin catalog. The story also goes that the copy Remington made for Marlin was lost in a fire. I have been unable to substantiate either of these stories with documents and can only contribute that it is very probable that Remington did make a copy for Marlin, as there are cases of his having painted copies of some of his other work.

In 1961, Marlin commissioned artist John Scott to make a copy of Remington's catalog cover. Mr. Scott's beautiful copy now hangs in an honored place in the lobby of The Marlin

Early 1950s catalog cover.

Late 1950s catalog cover.

Firearms Company. It is so well done that it takes careful examination to know it is not the original Remington.

In 1964 Marlin started to use the horse and rider figure as a logo. Marlin produced large 20″x30½″ colored posters of the John Scott 1961 picture. Because of the startled look of the cowboy and his horse, Marlin titled it "Danger Ahead."

There have been three printings of the "Danger Ahead" poster, as well as a special limited 1962 edition of the poster that was printed on cardboard and was made with an easel back for use as a counter display. The poster on cardboard is overprinted with advertising and the Marlin name (The counter type is very rare in today's collectors' market, since fewer than 250 were printed.)

Another special printing (fewer than 25 were made) is on a material having a very sandy surface, which gives a subdued oil-painting look. These pictures were mounted in a wood frame, with a half-round cross-section.

A few 8″x10″ sepia prints of "Danger Ahead" were printed by Marlin on a pebble-grained paper. They were used in a special advertising department mailing to announce the availability of the color poster. These too are scarce.

The large color posters sold for $2.00 each, postpaid. A total of about 4,000 were printed. The inventory of the last printing was depleted in 1982.

In 1986, Marlin produced a multicolor poster 18 inches by

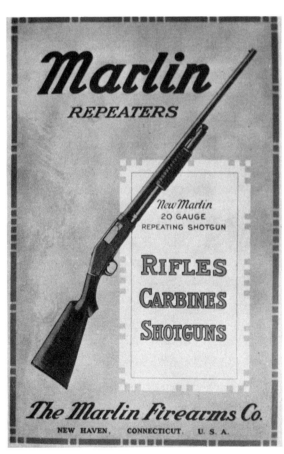

1914, 1915, and 1916 catalog cover.

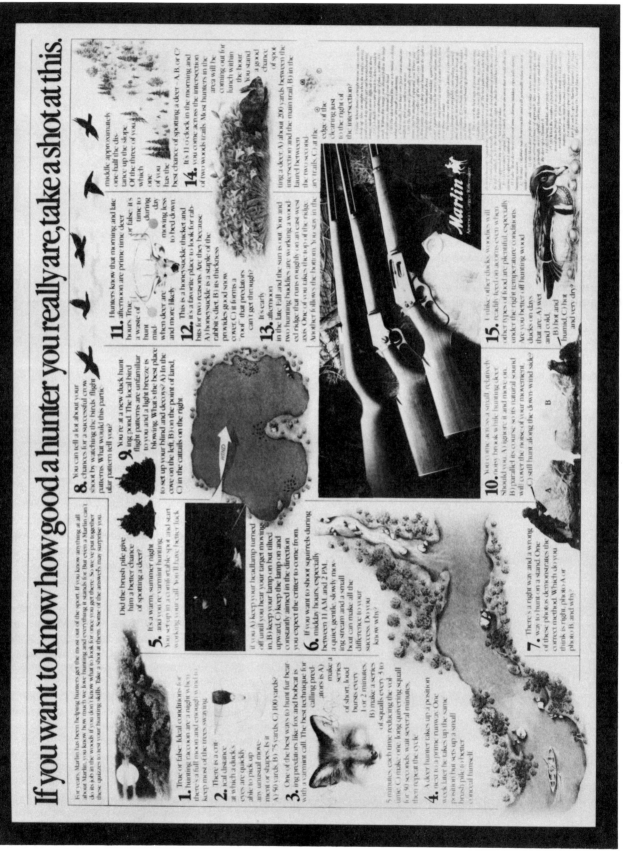

1986 multicolored poster that tests the knowledge of the sportsman.

24 inches that was a reproduction of the year's ads and was a quiz to test the sportsman in his outdoor and hunting knowledge. The title of the poster is "If you want to know how good a hunter you really are, take a shot at this."

Checking

Checkered (checked) stocks and forearms could be special-ordered for most Marlin rifles and shotguns from 1882 until 1915. Standard models, however, had unchecked wood.

Exceptions to the rule that standard models were not usually checked are the Ballard No. 6 Schuetzen; No. 6½ Rigby Off-Hand; No. 7 Long Range; and No. 6½ Pistol Grip Off-Hand. These models were regularly checked.

Checkering and engraving of the Model 1881 rifles were simple in form, but artistically done. The styles and patterns used did not vary much and in most examples, the checking was a standard coverage that did not become more elaborate with finer or greater engraving coverage.

In 1897, Marlin published a "Special High Grade" catalog that illustrated and described the various checking patterns that had been standardized. The grades were identified alphabetically from No. A to No. G. A special No. 10 was also listed that was recommended to be used with No. 10 engraving (grape leaf design). See the engraving section for more information.

The catalog indicated that the illustrations of checking only represented a few of the main styles. They could be varied when design changes in engraving and special ornamentation might be ordered by the sportsman. In other words, the customer could request a special design or a modification of the patterns listed for an additional charge.

The checkering patterns offered were as follows:

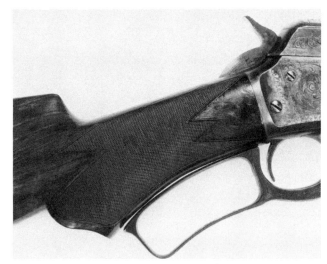

No. B checking on the pistol grip.

No. B checking on the forearm.

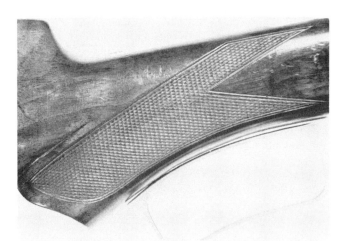

No. A checking on the pistol grip.

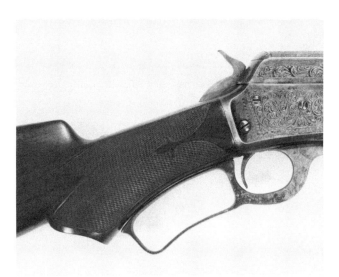

No. C checking on the pistol grip.

No. A checking on the forearm.

No. C checking on the forearm.

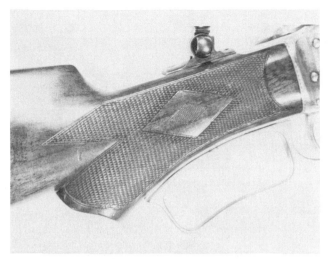

No. D checking on the pistol grip.

No. D checking on the forearm.

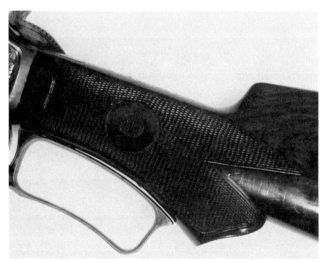

No. E checking on the pistol grip.

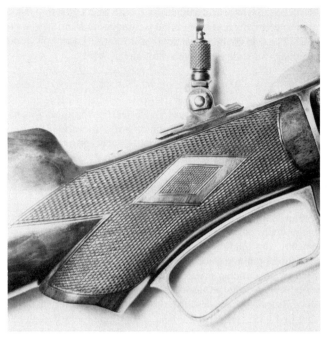

No. F checking on the pistol grip.

No. F checking on grip of rare Model 20 rifle.

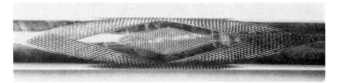

No. F checking on the forearm.

No. A   This is the checking used on plain pistol grip stocks and forearms. It consisted of a large diamond on the bottom of the forearm and simple coverage at the grip.

No. B   This checking is the regular style of fine checking used on selected walnut stocks and forearms. The forearm checking has double-pointed front and rear ends on both sides and grip coverage that has a double-pointed front end and single point toward the butt.

No. C   This checking was for extra selected pistol grip stocks and forearms. The rear end of the forearm checking and front part of the grip checking included stylized fleur-de-lis.

No. D   This checking pattern had double diamonds on each side of the forearm and grip, and the pattern on the front of the grip coverage and rear of the forearm was concave.

No. E   This pattern was the same as No. D, except that finely checked circles were used in place of the No. D diamonds.

No. F   This pattern is a combination of Nos. B and D. However, the diamond is much larger and on the bottom of the forearm rather than on the sides.

No. G   This style is like the No. B checking except that there is a smooth band that curves through the checking.

No. 10   This pattern of checking has special grape leaf figures that harmonize with the grape leaf design engraved on the receiver.

In 1899, Marlin listed for the first time four variations of the Grade No. 5 engraving. The illustration of the Grade No. 5 (3) and Grade No. 5 (4) show new checkering styles that are not identified by letter designation. They were ornate and were recommended for use with the high-art engraving patterns that had gold and platinum inlays and special game scenes.

With the introduction of the Model 1898 shotgun, special checking and engraving of the many pump action shotguns manufactured by Marlin could be special-ordered with the same style of engraving as that available for the rifles. The checking was listed as styles A, B, C, D, E, F, and G. Although called *style*, the patterns were the same as for the rifles.

To confuse matters, many shotgun models were listed by grade. There were Grades A, B, C, and D. The illustrations of these plain to extra-fancy guns do not show great differences in the checking patterns. The checked ones (Grades B, C, and D) have simple diamond patterns similar to B and C rifle designs. There are few examples extant that have special-order checking. Exceptions are illustrated in the Shotgun section.

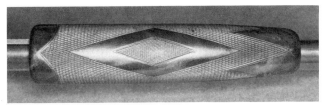

No. F checking on the forearm of rare Model 20 rifle.

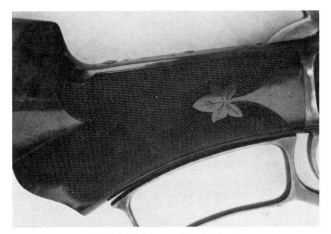

No. 10 checking on the pistol grip.

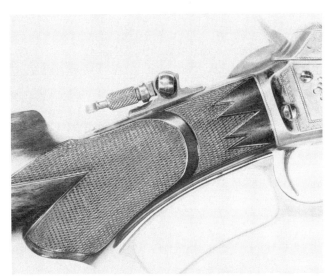

No. G checking on the pistol grip.

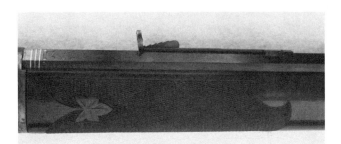

No. 10 checking on the forearm.

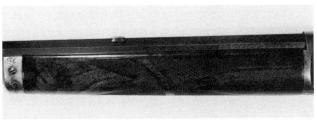

No. G checking on the forearm.

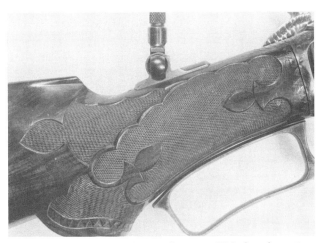

Special-order checking that does not fit any established catalog pattern and is found on only the most decorative of Marlin firearms.

Catalog illustration of No. A checking.

CHECKING ON SELECTED WALNUT STOCKS.

No. B. This cut illustrates our No. B checking, which is the regular style of fine checking used on our rifles with *selected walnut* stock and forearm (either straight or pistol grip stock). The stocks will be found fully illustrated on preceding pages.

SPECIAL CHECKING ON EXTRA SELECTED STOCKS.

The following are a few of the special checkings used on our extra selected stocks with special checking. These illustrations represent a few of the main styles which are varied from time to time, in view of the design of the engraving and special ornamentation which may be desired. The illustrations show only the forearm. It will be observed, however, from the preceding pages that the checking on the stock is exactly like that of the forearm.

No. C.

No. D.

No. E. In this style, circles filled with extra fine checking are substituted for the diamond of No. D. In other respects the checking is exactly like No. D.

No. F. This is a combination of Nos. B and D. The diamond, however, is much larger than in D and there is but one covering the whole front of the forearm instead of one small diamond on each side of the forearm.

No. G. In this style the band is continued unbroken around the forearm. It is our No. B checking with addition of band.

Our illustration of **No. 10** engraving shows a stock and forearm specially checked to accord with the grape-leaf design of the engraving.

Catalog page of special-order checking on selected walnut stocks.

Not all checking was to special order. Some Marlin models were checked as standard. For example, the Model 47 pump 22, Models 36ADL and 39 ADL, Model 90 shotgun, and Model 120 Trap gun all were checked.

The extra cost of special-order checkering varied from 1882 to 1915. In most cases, it is part of the extra cost of selected or extra selected wood. Prices fluctuated over the years. Charges probably related to the cost and availability of good wood and labor. Some of the extra charges were the following:

Rifles

Checking buttstock and forearms (1882–1885)	$ 5.00
Pistol grip, selected and checked (1885–1896)	15.00
Selected walnut stock and forearm finely checked (1886–1896)	10.00
Extra select English walnut stock and forearm, pistol grip finely checked and extra finely finished (1891–1915)	18.00
Selected straight-grip stock and forend, finely checked (1896–1915)	7.50
Selected pistol grip stock and forend, finely checked (1896–1915)	11.20
Special checking 5 (3) and 5 (4) (1907)	14.00

Shotguns

Checking Style A (1899)	4.50
Checking Style B	6.65
Checking Style C, D, E, F, & G	9.50

Cleaning and Preserving Equipment

Like many other firearms companies, Marlin sold or offered as an incentive to purchase a firearm cleaning and preserving material.

From 1896 to 1917, Marlin cataloged and sold a rust repellent packaged in a lead-foil tube. It was claimed to keep gun and rifle barrels perfectly bright, clean, and absolutely free from rust or pits. The preparation, it was stated, would retain its form in any climate and would not grow rancid, and it was the best preservative for fine tools and finished work. It was also said to make bicycle chains run easily. It sold for 15¢ for a 1½-ounce tube, 20¢ for a 3-ounce tube, and 60¢ for a one-pound can.

Marlin catalog page touting the merits of its rust repeller.

Marlin gun oil was also advertised from 1913 to 1915. It was "For Firearms Especially" and to be used for lubricating, cleaning, polishing, and preventing rust.

In 1952, Marlin offered a free cleaning kit, which was contained in a metal box. The contents included a bottle of sol-

Top: *Tag attached to Marlin shotgun telling about Marlin rust repeller.* Bottom: *Reverse of same tag advertising the rust repeller for use on bicycle chains.*

Catalog illustration of bottle of Marlin gun oil.

Marlin rifle cleaning kit — metal box and contents.

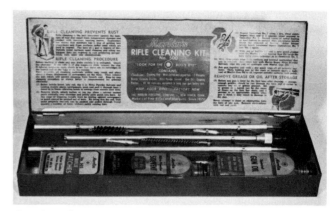

Open box of Marlin cleaning kit showing instructions inside the cover.

Marlin ad offering a free cleaning kit with the purchase of a Marlin Model 81 rifle.

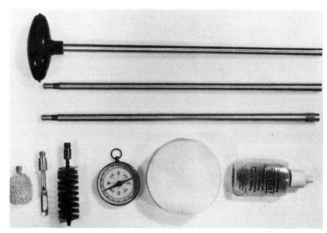

Shotgun cleaning kit packaged with Katz Model 50 shotguns. The compass was packaged with Katz caliber .22 rifles.

Tube of Rustopper™ and Rust Ban pads packaged with some Marlin Models during the 1952–1959 period.

vent, a bottle of gun oil, a package of patches, two cleaning brushes, and a caliber .22 cleaning rod. The kit was offered as a special gift with the purchase of a Marlin Model 81C or 81DL rifle. The offer ended in 1956.

Another rust preventive that Marlin packaged with the Clipper King and Crown Price rifles, as well as with some rifles sold through mass-merchandisers, was a Shell Oil Com-

pany product trade-named Rustopper.™ It was packaged in a yellow and red plastic tube that was filled with V.P.I.® Rust Preventive.

In 1959, Marlin packaged with firearms a box of 10 envelopes containing an oil-inpregnated parchment. The parchment paper was applied to metal and wood surfaces to dissolve harmful deposits and to clean and preserve at the same time.

One hundred thousand packages of "Rust Ban" pads were packaged with guns before the program was discontinued.

Copyrights, Logos, and Trademarks

From 1908 to 1955, Marlin used the slogan "The sign of a Marlin — solid top — side ejection." When used as a trademark on most printed matters of the period, it was enclosed in a red circle with a white eye shape in the center. In the oval white part were the receiver and open bolt of a Marlin lever action repeater. A fired cartridge case was superimposed on the receiver as if it were ejected from the gun.

In 1922, when the newly formed Marlin Firearms Corporation was formed, under the leadership of John Moran, a bull's-eye design became the new Marlin trademark. It not only was used on printed matter but also was inlaid into the bottom surface of the buttstock of each firearm.

A 1926 statement about the bull's-eye by The Marlin Firearms Company was as follows:

> Every single Marlin arm bears a "birthmark" which instantly identifies it. Customers in your store have but to glance at the butt of the gun to know it is a Marlin. The bull's-eye — symbol of accuracy — is the most fitting kind of trademark for Marlin, maker and breaker of World's target

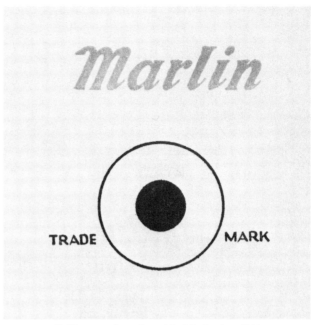

Bull's-eye trademark used by Marlin since 1922.

Buttstock with bull's-eye trademark.

Marlin logo used on butt plates.

Logo used in Marlin's catalogs during the period of 1908 to 1915.

JM proofmark used as a logo during 1960.

United States Patent and Trademark Office
Reg. No. 1,181,042
Registered Dec. 8, 1981

TRADEMARK
Principal Register

The Marlin Firearms Company (Connecticut corporation)
100 Kenna Dr.
North Haven, Conn. 06473

For: FIREARMS AND PARTS THEREOF, in CLASS 13 (U.S. Cl. 9).
First use Mar. 8, 1946; in commerce Mar. 8, 1946.
Owner of U.S. Reg. No. 55,158.

Ser. No. 237,813, filed Nov. 5, 1979.

B. C. WASHINGTON, Primary Examiner

1981 registered trademark name in script, as now used.

records. Inlaid in black and white on the butt of every Marlin arm, it makes not only a complete identification, but a beautiful accent of decoration.

You will realize what an enormously helpful thing this is, saving time and paving the way for a sale. Your years of selling experience will tell you that merchandise which can be immediately identified has selling value almost beyond price.

The bull's-eye trademark is still in use today, and except for a year or two during the Depression years in the 1930s, the bull's-eye has been installed in the stock of every Marlin model of rifle and shotgun. It has not been used on "brand name" or Marlin's Glenfield line of guns.

The location of the bull's-eye in the stock is usually 4 to 4½ inches forward of the toe of the stock.

Frequently, the bull's-eye is incorrectly thought to be the location where a lower sling swivel should be installed (lower swivels are usually about 3 inches from the toe of the stocks).

The name Marlin in this style of script, *Marlin*, is another Marlin trademark. It has been in use since March 8, 1946. Trademark registration numbers are U.S. Reg. No. 55,158 and No. 1,181,042.

This stylized Marlin name has been used on some butt plates, roll-stamps, and printed matter.

The list of other trademarks and copyrights include the following:

TRADEMARKS

Trademark	Date
Marlin (script)	August 7, 1906
M.F.A. Co.	September 4, 1906
Bull's-eye	1922–May 6, 1947
The Sign of a Marlin	1908–1936

Trademark	Date
Symbol of Accuracy	1960–1966
L.C. Smith	February 18, 1947
Hunter	February 18, 1947 (released)
Crown	March 18, 1947
Levermatic	November 22, 1955
Texan	August 2, 1955
Mountie	December 22, 1953
Micro-Groove	August 25, 1953
Crown Prince	February 17, 1959
Micro-Choke	November 3, 1959
Varmint King	November 3, 1959
Marauder	April 30, 1963
Glenfield	April 11, 1967
Marlin (Script)	December 8, 1981
Wide-Scan	1971
Veri-Fire	1971
Micro-Vue	1958
Mar-Shield	1970
Little Buckaroo	1983
Papoose	1986
The Alamo	June 12, 1984
PRIDE	October 23, 1984
MF Co.	

Marlin's copyrighted "Danger Ahead" picture, used since 1900.

1969 counter pad.

1970 counter pad.

Copyright (U.S.)	Date
Danger Ahead	1900
Roto Ballistic Guide	March 25, 1954
Sighting in Guide	December 15, 1955
Range Finder	January 17, 1956
Belt Buckle	May 24, 1982
Bull's-Eye	1922

From 1960 to 1966, Marlin used the *JM* proofmark as a trademark. The *JM* was in an oval, which had *Symbol of Accuracy* across the top, and *Since 1870* across the bottom.

Counter Pads

Marlin counter pads were distributed to sporting goods stores and gun shops for use on sales counters to protect both the counter (wood or glass) and the product the salesperson was showing. Made with a soft foam back, counter pads performed well. Early types had a soft felt-like surface that could not be cleaned easily and showed oil and dirt stains. The later types were made from a more dirt-resistant plastic material.

Marlin's first counter pad was a fawn color made from a felt-like material. It was 17 inches wide by 11 inches deep. It had the name *Marlin* and the horse and rider logo centrally located, and the edges were neatly scalloped. This first type of pad is scarce among today's Marlin collectors.

In 1970, Marlin introduced a 19½-in. by 11½-in. brown, wood-grained, plastic pad that had the 100th-anniversary medallion in gold, and the name *Marlin* in bright red. Of inferior quality, this pad did not wear well and the foam backing deteriorated quickly. Few have survived intact. They were distributed during 1970, Marlin's 100th-anniversary year.

The third type of counter pad was a brown felt-like material, as was the first, and had a quality foam backing. On the face were a facsimile of the Bill of Rights, Article II plaque and the Marlin horse and rider logo. It was 17½ inches by 10¾ inches and was available during the years 1971, 1972, and 1973. The soft absorbent surface of this pad did not stand up well under constant use. These pads are now scarce in their original condition.

The fourth type of pad was not much more durable than the second. The foam back of this one also crumbled easily. However, the white face, with its black bull's-eye and red Marlin name, held up well. It was the same size as the second type and was available during the years 1974, 1975, and 1976.

The fifth type of pad has been the most durable and best of all Marlin counter pads. Attractively decorated with Marlin history and old pictures, the tough oil- and dirt-resistant surface and soft foam backing make this one the most desired by shopkeepers. Two surfaces have been used. The first was mirror-like with a high shine. The second, and current one,

1971–1972 counter pad.

1974–1976 counter pad.

1978 to date counter pad.

18 inches by 12 inches with rounded corners, has a dull matte finish. It should be around a long time.

Covers

Some Marlin collectors do not collect firearms. Their interest, instead, lies in collecting paper—such as catalogs, posters, manuals, advertisements, and sales literature. Also high on the collector's list are original company envelopes, called "covers." Many of this group of collectors buy or trade these covers with the same interest and enthusiasm as that of the firearm collector.

Some firearms and ammunition manufacturers decorated their covers with attractive color illustrations, and frequently used both the back and front of the cover to display their messages. Marlin collectors are not that lucky. Only a few in

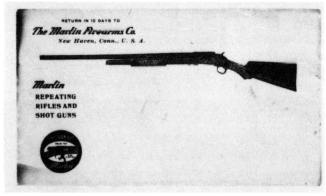

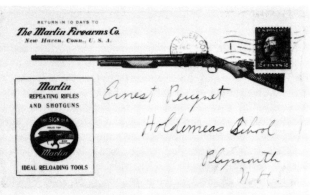

Marlin advertising covers dating from the 1880s to the 1930s.

color have been noted. Most early Marlin covers had illustrations of firearms on them. A rare one from the late 1880s period has the Ballard rifle, the Model 1881 rifle, the Model 1887 revolver, the Daley handcuffs, and Merrill's bicycle lock illustrated on the cover. Others have the Model 1881 rifle, pump action shotguns, Model 90 shotgun, and the Tom Mix Special rifle on the front. Those illustrated here are a few of those of interest to the collector.

Decals

Frequently companies do something, and in not too many years the details become forgotten, or no record of the details was kept. The first decal used by Marlin is one such thing. No one remembers when it was first used and no record of purchase can be found. However, an example is in the author's collection.

The first window-type decal was 8 inches high by 5 inches wide and had *Marlin* in red block letters across the top; *Rifles Shotguns* in black; the horse and rider logo in color centrally located; and at the bottom an oval with *JM* in the center, *Symbol of Accuracy* on the top, and *Since 1870* underneath. It was introduced around 1960.

A 5½-in.-square version of the above decal was introduced in 1963. It was available until 1973. (The last year of use of the Symbol of Accuracy logo in a catalog was 1963.)

A 6-in. round decal was introduced in 1970. It had printed on it *Marlin Firearms — Prefired — Presighted — Preferred;* the Marlin horse and rider logo was in color on the front (glass side); and the back side was silver with *100 Years of American Gunmaking — Marlin Firearms 1870–1970* in black letters.

A variation of the 1970 decal was nearly identical, with *Recommended Repair Station* on the glass side instead of *Prefired — Presighted — Preferred.*

In 1974 an oval 6⅞″x4½″ decal was introduced. It had *Marlin Firearms Since 1870,* the horse and rider, and *Made Now Like They Were Then* on the glass side, and *What Makes a Marlin Different . . . Solid Steel Forgings. Genuine American Black Walnut. Micro-Groove® Rifling. Side Ejection . . . Is What Makes a Marlin Better* on the back side.

Marlin advertising covers.

Left: *1960 decal.* Left center: *1963 decal.* Right center: *1970 decal.* Right: *1974 decal.* Bottom: *1984 decal.*

This oval decal was in use until 1974, when a new rectangular style was added.

The 1984 decal is two-sided and can be used on glass or on another solid surface. Both sides are a very bright red. It is 8¼ inches wide and 3¾ inches high with *Marlin — Rifles — Shotguns* and the horse and rider printed in silver. This decal is still in use today, except that the 1987 printing has *America's Largest Riflemaker* instead of the previous *Marlin — Rifles — Shotguns.*

A silver-colored decal with blue printing of the same type as the bright red one was distributed to recommended Marlin service centers. Instead of *Rifles — Shotguns* under the Marlin name, it had *Recommended Service Center.*

Duck Decoy Anchors and Body Weights

From 1915 to 1917, Marlin advertised decoy anchors and decoy body weights. Both were made of lead and were designed to be convenient to use and superior in construction.

The decoy anchor was described as follows:

> This convenient article is 5 inches long, weighs about 13 ounces, made of lead, can't rust, stows away on decoy's neck,

prevents tangling of lines, adjusts itself to any depth of water, unwinding just the required length of line, saves time, cold fingers, profanity, and is the finest little article ever devised for the convenience and comfort of the duck shooter. Price, $2.40 per dozen.

The decoy body weight sold for $1.50 a dozen. It was described in Marlin catalogs thus:

> The weight is oval and flat on top, so that it fits snugly against the body of the decoy. It is the only body weight which has the screw attached. The screw used as a sharp pointed brass screw with flattened and enlarged head, cast in the metal and so firmly embedded it cannot possibly work loose.

Neither of these two items has been inspected. Surely some have survived time, but are probably not marked with the Marlin name and have therefore gone unidentified.

DeGress Pistol Grips

On April 28, 1874, Francis DeGress of Bloomfield, N.J., was awarded patent number 150,229 for his "Improvement in Pistol-Handles."

These metal grips, manufactured by Mr. DeGress's system, were made for Marlin and other makes of pistols, and add considerably to the value of a pistol. The right-hand grip is

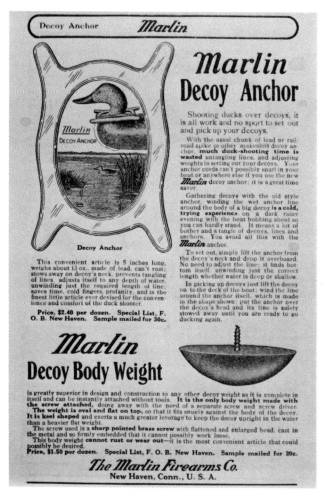

Illustration and description of Marlin's decoy anchor and decoy body weights.

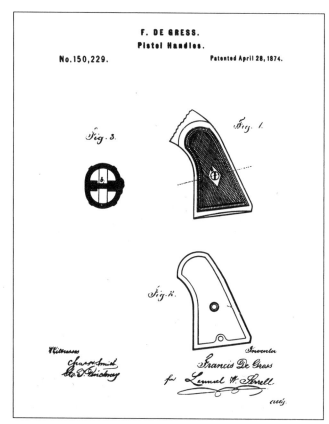

Francis DeGress patent illustration accompanying his April 28, 1874 patent for unique metal grips, which were produced for Marlin and other makes of handguns.

Top: *Marlin Standard revolver fitted with DeGress grips.* Bottom: *Left side of same revolver.*

embellished with a voluptuous, scantily clad lady. The left-hand grip has a grape leaf and scroll design. Around the screw hole on the left grip is the patent date: April 28, 1874.

The description of the process used to make these grips is best explained by quoting the procedure as outlined in the patent, as follows:

> I take a properly-prepared handle-piece that is accurate in all particulars, and make a copy thereof in gutta-percha, plaster, or other suitable material, and form therein an electro-type shell by the deposit of copper in any of the known modes. I provide a press-block of a piece of wood, metal or plaster, of shape corresponding to the inside or concave surface of the pattern-handle, and after pouring melted type or other metal into the inside of the electrotype shell, I press into the same the said press-block, so as to force out surplus metal, and give the required shape and thickness to the handle-piece, and at the same time form the holes required for the connecting screws or pins. Any fins or surplus metal are now dressed off, and the handle-piece is put into an acid to change the color of the copper to that of bronze, and the handle is ready for use, or the copper may be silver-plated or gilded in the usual manner.

The DeGress grips are frequently confused with the ornate and similar grips made by the famous Tiffany & Company jewelry house. They are not of the same quality as the Tiffany grips and do not add the same increase in value; however, the DeGress grips are desirable and a Marlin pistol fitted with them belongs in every serious Marlin pistol collector's collection. Examples of the DeGress grips have been observed fitted to Little Joker, Standard, and No. 32 Standard pistols.

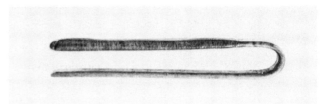

Leather-covered spring clip to hold down the ejector when using a cleaning rod.

Top: *Outside view of spring clip in place. Note that the leather-covered end prevented scratching of the receiver.* Bottom: *Inside view of spring clip designed to hold down the ejector during barrel cleaning.*

Ejector Tool

When cleaning the model 1897/97 caliber .22 rifles from the breech, users found that the ejector was always in the way of the cleaning rod. Likewise, the rod could damage the ejector if the rifle was being cleaned. To eliminate this problem, some users removed the two screws holding the ejector in place and removed the ejector from the receiver.

In 1923, J.M. Olinger, of Springfield, Ohio, submitted to the Marlin Corporation the idea of a leather-covered spring device that could be slipped over the rear edge of the left half of the receiver when the rifle was taken down. When cleaning the barrel from the breech, the device would then hold the ejector inward and out of the way of a cleaning rod.

Part of Marlin's response to Mr. Olinger's suggestion was as follows:

> As a matter of fact, our people here at the factory have made use of this identical device, but without the leather

covering, back as far as 1914; and we have also used a device in the shape of the breech bolt, but hollow, which is equally as good for the purpose.

Marlin's May 23, 1923 answer to J.M. Olinger goes on to relate that Marlin was now developing an equally efficient

device for the Model 39. It became the ejector hold-down rivet of today's 39s.

Engraving

The most-wanted data that Marlin collectors desire to know about their engraved firearms are: "is the engraving factory original?" and "who was the engraver?" Unfortunately, the few remaining factory records do not, with any regularity, indicate

Top: *Engraved 1st Model Marlin derringer pistol.* Bottom: *Plain unengraved 1st Model shown for comparison.*

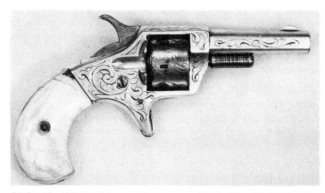

Right side of Little Joker revolver engraved in the New York style. The cylinder pin is a replacement.

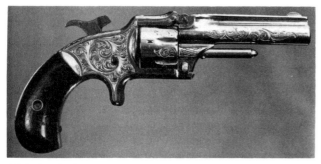

XXX Standard 1872 that is representative of the type of engraving found on Smith & Wesson, Colt, and Marlin revolvers of the period. This revolver is chambered for the .30 short.

Marlin Model 1887 revolver ornamented with engraving and silver plating, except for the cylinder latch, hammer, and trigger, which are case-colored, and the trigger guard, which is blued.

Another Model 1887 revolver engraved in the style typical of the Nimschke school, as done by various engravers of the New York and New England areas.

Typical engraving of the Model 1881 rifle period. Note the plain borders and minimal background work.

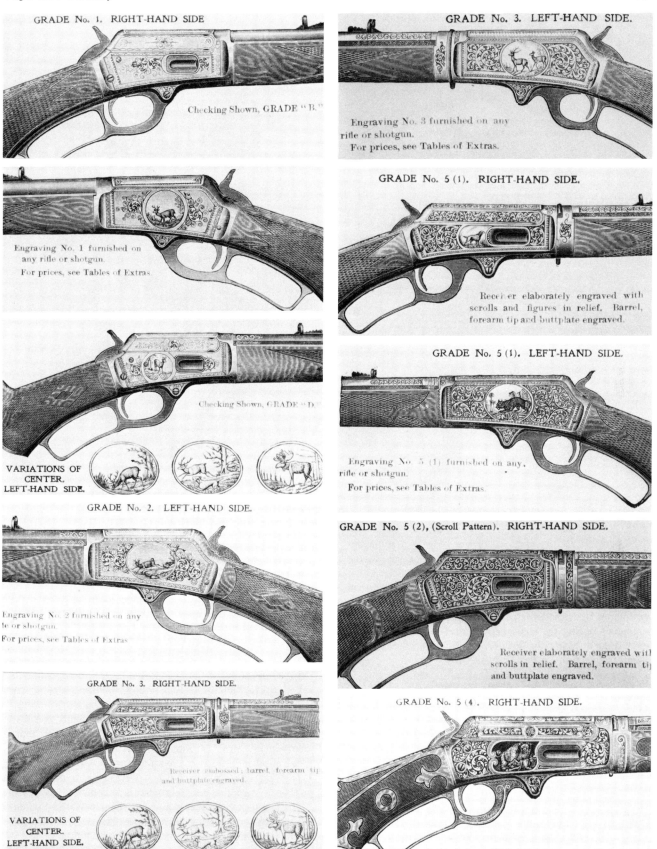

Grades of engraving available from Marlin.

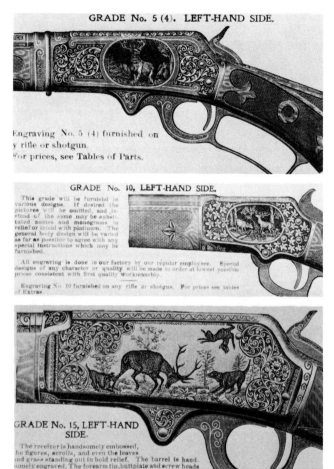

GRADE No. 5 (4). LEFT-HAND SIDE.

Engraving No. 5 (4) furnished on
y rifle or shotgun.
For prices, see Tables of Parts.

GRADE No. 10, LEFT-HAND SIDE.

This grade will be furnishd in
various designs. If desired the
pictures will be omitted, and instead of the same may be substituted names and monograms in
relief or inlaid with platinum. The
general body design will be varied
as far as possible to agree with any
special instructions which may be
furnished.

All engraving is done in our factory by our regular employees. Special
designs of any character or quality will be made to order at lowest possible
prices consistent with first quality workmanship.

Engraving No. 10 furnished on any rifle or shotgun. For prices see tables
of Extras.

GRADE No. 15, LEFT-HAND
SIDE.

The receiver is handsomely embossed,
he figures, scrolls, and even the leaves
ind grass standing out in bold relief. The barrel is hand-
omely engraved. The forearm tip, buttplate and screw heads
re all embossed with scrolls, while the above-mentioned
arts, as well as the hammer and lever, are inlaid with
croll lines of platinum and gold. The hammer and lever
re also slightly engraved.

Grades of engraving.

Conrad Friedrich Ulrich, 1844–1925. (Courtesy of R.L. [Larry] Wilson)

if the gun was factory engraved or not. Also, for some un-known reason, Marlin's engraved guns were not signed by the engraver.

Keeping in mind the above shortcomings, the collector can be reasonably assured, by studying extant examples and by researching signed engraved firearms manufactured by other companies during the same period, that the engraving was either done at Marlin or done for Marlin by an independent engraver of firearms and other items. Most engravers did work at home as well as for companies that contracted work out.

The two engravers who contributed the most toward early development of engraved firearms were L.D. Nimschke and Gustave Young.

L.D. (Louis Daniel) Nimschke was born July 1832 in Ger-many and immigrated to the U.S. about 1850. In addition to engraving Winchester, Colt, Manhattan, Merrimack, Smith & Wesson, Whitney, Sharps, Purdey, Scott and Son, Merwin Hulbert, and other makes of firearms, Mr. Nimschke engraved Ballard rifles for Merwin and Bray, the Brown Manufacturing Company, J.M. Marlin, and The Marlin Fire Arms Company.

L.D. Nimschke contributed to the establishment of the American style of engraving, which was an outgrowth of the Germanic mid-19th-century style. Some of Mr. Nimschke's

Ballards were engraved with a tight and close scroll. Others had more open and larger scrolls. Backgrounds had either beaded dots or nothing at all. L.D. Nimschke also used the very delicate scrolls of the British shotgun style, and less fre-quently the geometric Arabesque-style scroll.

A comparison of engraved American Standard Tool Com-pany revolvers, some Smith & Wesson engraved revolvers, and Marlin Standard Model revolvers shows a close similarity among the three of the scrollwork, borders, decorative cuts on the top and sides of barrels, back straps, and adornment of cylinders. In fact, illustrated in R.L. Wilson's classic work *L.D. Nimschke: Firearms Engraver* (published by John J. Malloy, Teaneck, N.J., 1965) is a .32 caliber Smith & Wesson revolver, engraved about 1875, serial number 87,669, that is nearly identical to J.M. Marlin's XXX Standard 1872 revolver, serial number 2565. If the Marlin pistol was not engraved by L.D. Nimschke, and the Smith & Wesson revolver was, it can at least be said that Mr. Nimschke was copied almost to the "T." I like to believe that many of the early Marlin Standard model revolvers, Ballards, and Model 1881s were, in fact, done by the hand of L.D. Nimschke, or under his guidance.

Gustave Young was Colt's master engraver. Under him, Con-rad Friedrich Ulrich, Jr., apprenticed and learned the engrav-

Top: *Model 1891 caliber .22 rifle engraved by Conrad Ulrich. Note the style of the scrolls and lack of background work. The scroll borders are also typical of the period.* Bottom: *Left side of same rifle.*

Top: *Marlin Model 1892 rifle engraved by Conrad Ulrich in the scroll pattern with a stippled background. Note that the scroll border is like that on the previous Model 1891 rifle.* Bottom: *Left side of same rifle.*

ing trade during the 1860s. Conrad's brothers, John and Herman, joined him at Colt and learned the art of engraving from Gustave Young and their brother Conrad. The three brothers left Colt and moved to New Haven about 1869. They did engraving primarily for Winchester, although they did some for other companies and individuals.

Among the guns Conrad F. Ulrich, Jr., engraved were Ballards for John Marlin; as a result of his fine work, he was hired to be the full-time master engraver for Marlin. Conrad F. Ulrich, Jr., did almost all of the engraved Marlins during the period of 1881 to 1910. Although not signed or otherwise identified, the work has been verified by experts who have studied Mr. Ulrich's work for Marlin as well as what he did after he left Marlin in 1910 and went to work for Winchester. After a lifetime of embellishing some of the finest high-art firearms, Conrad Ulrich, Jr., died on April 22, 1925.

The last of the Ulrich engravers was Alden George Ulrich, the son of Conrad F. Ulrich, Jr. "George," as Alden George Ulrich was always known, apprenticed under his father at Marlin, starting at age 17. From 1905 until 1919, he was employed by and engraved for Marlin. After his employment with Marlin ended at the close of WW I, he joined Winchester and engraved there until his death in 1949.

Enlarged section of engraving on Marlin Model 1892 rifle engraved by Conrad Ulrich. Note the stippled background and irregularity of the cuts made by the engraving chisel when being hammered. Like fingerprints, these minute tool marks are a clue to the artist's identity. Also note the irregularity of the beading in the background.

Enlargement of the animal scene typical of Marlin factory engraving. Note that there is a certain crudeness to the shape of the animals, trees, ground, and grass. The buck does not look to me like a North American deer. Something about his looks is wrong!

Top: *No. 1-engraved Model 1897 rifle.* Bottom: *Left side of same rifle.*

No. 3-engraved Model 1892. Note the Ulrich style border and fernlike scrolls.

No.-3 engraved Model 1897 rifle probably done by Alden George Ulrich.

Top: *No. 2-engraved Model 1897 rifle.* Bottom: *Left side of same rifle.*

As can be seen from the above discussion, the influence of L.D. Nimschke and Gustave Young, through Conrad F. and his son George Ulrich, resulted in Marlin firearms engraved during the period of 1881 to 1919 being equal to, or better than, those of many other companies. The work of the Ulrichs truly followed the style and quality of the two patriarchs of American engraving.

It is necessary for the collector to understand that during the period of manufacture of the Model 1881, Marlin did not identify the grade or quality of engraving available, as it did in later years. The style and patterns used were quite similar to many of the engraved Winchester Model 1876 rifles. A game scene in a circle, fine borders, and scrollwork, without a background, were usual. Initials, monograms, and names and dates are also found; however, precious metal inlays and carved

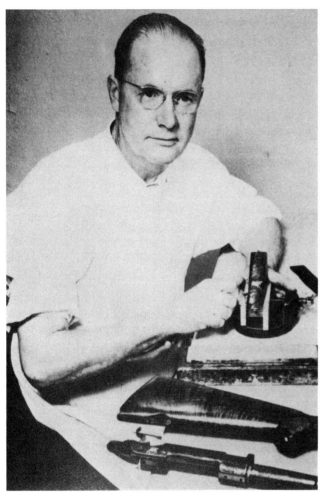

Alden George Ulrich, 1888–1949. (Courtesy of R.L. [Larry] Wilson)

No. 5-engraved Model 1897 rifle that was engraved by Conrad Ulrich in about 1908.

Special-order Model 1897 rifle engraved with a leaf and berry pattern. The receiver, hammer, and barrel have gold inlays. This rifle is one of very few gold-inlaid caliber .22 rifles.

Top: *Ulrich-engraved and gold-plated Model 1889 rifle of the No. 5 (1) style.* Bottom: *Left side of same rifle. Note the precious metal bands inlaid into the barrel.*

checking designs are unknown in the Model 1881, at least to me.

Factory-engraved Model 1888 rifles have been reported, but I have not examined one. I hope they exist—and what a rarity one would be, since only 4,814 of this model were produced.

Starting with the Model 1889, standard patterns were developed. To fix a price for engraving or special checking, the degree of coverage and extent of handwork would have to be agreed upon. Up to 1896, catalogs listed engraving available at $5.00 and up. In 1897, the price of engraving was listed by grade, but no illustrations of the grades were included. A footnote in the catalog added that if the customer were interested, he should send for a book of illustrations showing engraving, checking, and prices. In 1899, the product catalog included illustrations of the various standard-quality engraving and checking patterns that were available. This practice in catalogs continued until 1915, and until 1917 in price lists.

By studying the patterns shown in both the product catalogs and the 1897 "Special High Grade" catalog, the collector can establish which pattern of engraving and number of checking the firearm has.

In 1897, The Winchester Repeating Arms Company also brought out a catalog similar to Marlin's called "Highly Finished Arms." It too listed the engraving and checking styles

Gold-plated and engraved Model 1893 rifle of the Grade No. 10 style. Note the leaf and berry design and special-order monogram.

Top: *Ulrich No. 5-engraved Model 1893 rifle.* Bottom: *Left side of same rifle.*

Top: *Rarely encountered No. 2-engraved Model 1893 rifle that has special-ordered engraving on the hammer, lever, and barrel.* Bottom: *Left side of same rifle.*

Top: *Ulrich No. 10-engraved Model 1893 rifle with the added elegance of gold-inlaid borders around the game scenes, a gold circle on the bolt, and gold and platinum bands around the barrel.* Bottom: *Left side of same rifle.*

One of the finest examples of Conrad Ulrich's engraving and gold inlay work extant. This Grade No. 15 Model 1893 has both special-design engraving and game figures, and special-order gold inlay work on the bolt, hammer, barrel, lever, and trigger plate. The greyhound dog chasing a rabbit on the right side, and the two stags on the left are done in shaded flat gold inlay of unusual character. The special checking also adds a touch of elegance found on few Marlin rifles. Additional pictures of this rare rifle are found in the Model 1893 section.

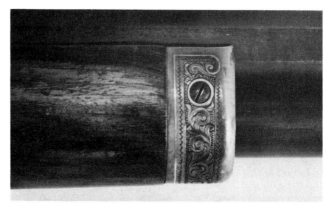

Special-order forearm tip that has gold inlays and No. 15 engraving.

Gold borders and engraved top tang of only the finest examples of engraved Marlin rifles.

Very few Marlin rifles have engraved game scenes on the trigger plate. This rare rifle has both a game head and gold inlay on the trigger plate.

Some of the higher-grade engraved rifles have engraved butt plates. This one also has gold inlay work.

Most model designations marked on the top tang of engraved Marlin's were roll-stamped. Only on the highest grades was the model hand-cut. This example is machine roll-stamped.

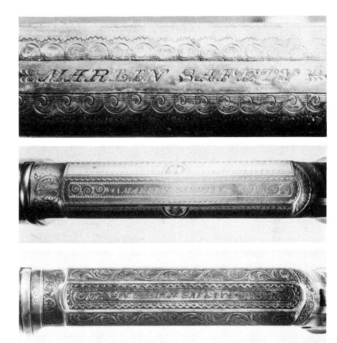

Top: *The* Marlin Safety *marking on the top of receivers was sometimes hand-cut over the usual roll-stamp. This example was reworked by the engraver.* Middle: *This example of the* Marlin Safety *marking was roll-stamped. Note the broken arrow at the left end.* Bottom: *Another example of roll-stamped top of receiver. Note that the same broken die of the above photo was also used on this gun.*

available, but the grading system was the opposite of Marlin's. Marlin's numbers, and alphabetical identifiers, went from the lowest grade (No. 1) to the highest (No. 15), whereas Winchester's highest grade was No. 1.

The Marlin patterns were established by Conrad Ulrich. The scrollwork, floral patterns, border designs, panel scenes, and quality of the work reflect L.D. Nimschke and Gustave Young's teachings and the influence they had on the Ulrich style and artistic renditions; owners of original factory-engraved Marlin rifles manufactured between 1881 and 1919 can say that they were engraved by an Ulrich—Conrad from 1881 to 1910, or his son George from 1905 to about 1917.

The Marlin engraving patterns established in 1897 were as follows:

No. 1 Receiver engraved with scroll engraving. Fancy borders were included and the left side had a game animal in a circle. Extra list, $5.00

No. 2 Receiver, barrel, forearm tip, and butt plate engraved with scroll engraving. Game animals were engraved on both sides in a decorative circle. A choice of the animal could be made. Moose, deer, elk, and others were available. The barrel engraving was just forward of the receiver and for about 1 to 1½ inches in length. Extra list, $10.00

No. 3 Receiver embossed; barrel, forearm tip, and buttplate engraved. Game scene usually on left side only. Engraving on the barrel extended forward to the rear sight. Both sides of the receiver were completely covered with engraving that had a stippled background. No. 1 and No. 2 engraving was without background work. Extra list, $15.00

No. 4 There was no No. 4 engraving listed in either the special catalog or in the product catalogs.

No. 5 Receiver elaborately engraved with scrolls and figures in relief. Barrel, forearm tip, and

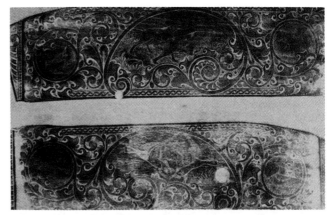

Ink impressions of a shotgun attributed to Alden George Ulrich that is shown in The Book of Winchester Engraving *by R.L. Wilson. It is interesting to note that the style of scrolls and game scenes closely follow the lines of the Model 28 Marlin shotgun illustrated here.*

Top: *Although grades and patterns of engraving were standardized, the engravers continually exercised their artistic right to not follow any rigid pattern. Scrolls, borders, and scenes were the choice of the engraver and seldom are two rifles of the same grade twins. This receiver bottom was done quite differently from others examined.* Middle: *Another takedown receiver of a similar grade as the one above but with an entirely different design.* Bottom: *A trigger plate of a solid-frame rifle is engraved much like those above, but again the engraver exercised his desire to not make "carbon copies," but rather to make each job a work of art.*

This Conrad Ulrich-engraved Marlin Model 19 shotgun is one of the finest high-art shotguns ever produced by Marlin. The finesse of the scroll work, gold inlaid borders, and raised gold dog figures are unsurpassed by any other single shotgun. The twist pattern of the fine damascus barrel, gold-plated screws, and superb wood add a touch of elegance to this gun found in very few Marlin firearms. A rare gun and fine example of the capability of Conrad Ulrich as an artist and engraver. (JO)

Top: *Alden George Ulrich-engraved Model 28 shotgun with gold-inlaid borders.* Bottom: *Left side of same shotgun.*

butt plate engraved. Animal scenes were available, as well as full scrollwork on both sides. The scrolls could be had with either a large scroll or small scroll, as preferred. Extra list, $25.00

Grade No. 5 (1) In 1900 the No. 5 styles were separated into Grades No. 5 (1); No. 5 (2); No. 5 (3); and No. 5 (4). The No. 5 (1) was the same as the original elaborately engraved type mentioned above.

Grade No. 5 (2) This was like the original No. 5, with scroll design.

Grade No. 5 (3) This Grade was new in 1900 and had oak leaf and acorn engraving, and included gold borders and inlays on the hammer, lever, bolt, receiver, and barrel.

Grade No. 5 (4) This Grade was also new in 1900 and had scroll engraving with a charging bear on the left side and the "Monarch of the Dell" elk on the left side. The figures were carved in relief and like Grade No. 5 (3) had gold bor-

Top: *Close-up of the detail work done by Conrad Ulrich on a Model 19 shotgun. Note the flying birds.* Bottom: *Close-up of the left side of the finest exposed hammer Marlin shotgun ever produced.*

Top: *Copy of a photograph in* The Book of Winchester Engraving *by R.L. Wilson, which is identified as a Marlin shotgun engraved by Alden George Ulrich and with checking and carving done by his father, Conrad Ulrich. This shotgun was for presentation to Czar Nicholas II of Russia (c. 1913). The Russian coat of arms in high relief was inlaid in gold on the right side of the receiver. It was also carved into the wood forearm. It is without a doubt the finest Marlin hammerless shotgun ever produced.* Bottom: *Illustration from the above-mentioned book of a rubbing of the Conrad F. Ulrich carving on the Czar Nicholas II shotgun.*

Right side of highly ornamented and gold-inlaid Model 1893 "Tiger Hunt" rifle.

ders and inlays on the receiver, hammer, lever, and barrel.

No. 10   This style of engraving included elaborately embossed figures of grape leaves with animal pictures in oval patterns on both sides. If desired, the purchaser could instead substitute names and monograms in relief or inlaid in platinum. The background was of the pearl type. The receiver, barrel, and forearm tip were inlaid with platinum lines. Extra list, $50.00

Grade No. 15   The receiver is handsomely embossed, with the figures, scrolls, and even the leaves and grass standing out in bold relief. The barrel is handsomely engraved. The forearm tip, butt plate and screw heads are all embossed with scrolls, as well as the hammer and lever being inlaid with scrolls of platinum and gold. The hammer and lever are also slightly engraved. If desired, a monogram or name would be engraved on the center of the breech bolt, and if requested, they could also be inlaid with platinum. Extra list, $66.00

Grade No. 40   This grade was the choice of the purchaser in

Left side of "Tiger Hunt" rifle showing the gold-inlaid figures and special-order work of this one-of-a-kind rifle.

Engraved and gold-inlaid Model 90 shotgun presented to cowboy movie star Tom Mix in 1937.

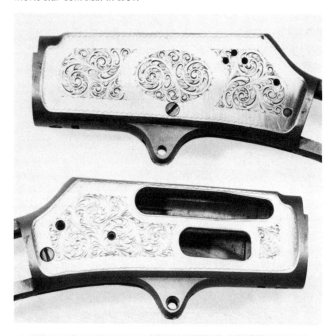

Top: *Prototype Model 336 receivers that were engraved in Spain in anticipation of a deluxe Model 336 that never materialized.* Bottom: *Another style of engraving that was done in West Germany for the deluxe Model that did not happen. Only five were ever assembled.*

Top: *Prototype Model 39A rifle that had a receiver engraved in Spain. Fewer than five rifles were assembled before the idea of a deluxe model was dropped.* Bottom: *Left side of same rifle.*

design style and inlays. It was a one-of-a-kind special-order gun of the highest quality.

Marlin stated in its literature that the effect of finely engraved work is often heightened by neat inlaying with platinum and gold. In all grades from No. 10 up, inlaying was included in the price. The work could also be added to other grades for a moderate expense, as, for instance, initials, insignia, and monograms.

Special designs were also available on request. Marlin engraved many rifles and shotguns with designs from photographs or pictures. These special-order guns do not fit any particular grade and are rare among Marlin high-art guns. Only a few have been examined and photographs of some are included in the various sections of this book covering specific models. A study of all sections should be made to fully appreciate the fine engraved Marlin rifles and shotguns that were produced.

Two Model 28 shotguns are shown in the pump shotgun section of this book that I feel may have been engraved and inlaid by George Ulrich just before he left Marlin. These guns are in the pattern and style of George Ulrich's work and very much like a Winchester shotgun illustrated on page 251 of R.L. Wilson's *Book of Winchester Engraving*. The scroll design, dog and bird game scene, and inlay work were done by George on the Winchester. The work on the Model 28s appears

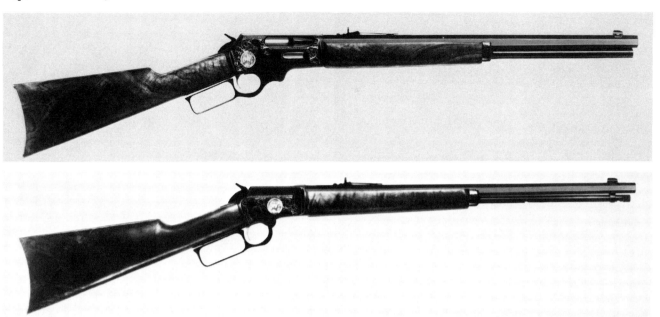

Top: *Marlin's 100th-year commemorative matched pair included this Kain-engraved Model 336.* Bottom: *Matching the engraved Model 336 was this octagon-barreled Model 39, the other gun in the commemorative pair. Only 1,000 pairs were produced.*

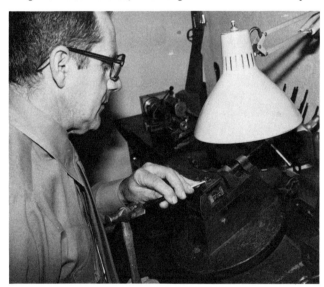

Robert Kain at his engraving bench. Mr. Kain and associates engraved the 2,000 rifles that made up the 100th-anniversary commemorative matched pair.

to be by the same hand. It was probably done between 1913 and 1917, when the Model 28 was in production.

Each engraver had a style and flair of his own. For more information about the history of American engraving and the early artists, a study should be made of the previously mentioned Nimschke and Winchester books and the *Book of Colt Engraving* by R.L. Wilson (Beinfeld Publishing, Inc., 1982), which includes additional information about early engravers and their work. Another book about American engravers is C. Roger Bleile's book, *American Engravers* (Beinfeld Publishing, Inc., 1980).

On special occasions Marlin has had one-of-a-kind engraved

Top: *A fine example of engraving and gold inlay work done on a Model 39A rifle by master engraver M. Courant. His unique style equals the work of the old masters. This rifle was commissioned by Jim Logiss, Marlin's West Coast sales representative, and was auctioned to the highest bidder at one of the MZURI Wildlife Foundation fund raisers. Jim is a trustee of this great organization that promotes wildlife conservation worldwide.* Bottom: *Left side of same rifle.*

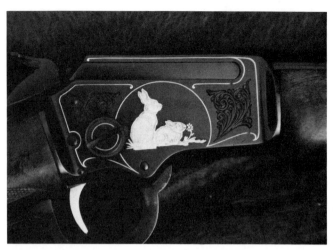 

Left: *Another M. Courant-engraved and gold-inlaid Model 39A rifle. Note the masterful way Mr. Courant has made use of blending different-colored gold to show detail and shading of the animal figures. This rifle was also commissioned by Jim Logiss and donated to raise funds for the MZURI Wildlife Foundation.* Right: *Left side of same rifle.*

Top: *Two-millionth Model 60 rifle, engraved by Robert C. Kain, that was presented to the NRA's National Firearms Museum.* Middle: *Three-millionth Model 336 rifle, engraved by Dan Goodwin, that was presented to the NRA's National Firearms Museum.* Bottom: *Two-millionth Model 39A that was engraved by Alvin A. White. This rifle was presented to the National Shooting Sports Foundation to be auctioned to raise funds for the NSSF expansion of its shooting education program in the nation's schools.*

pieces done. Examples of some of these are illustrated in the section covering presentation firearms. The ones most deserving of recognition are the Annie Oakley and the Tom Mix guns. The Annie Oakley was engraved by Conrad Ulrich. The Tom Mix shotgun was engraved and gold-inlaid by two employees of a stationery engraving company that did not do many jobs in steel (most of their work was done on copper plates used in printing).

The three-millionth Model 336 was engraved by Dan Goodwin, one of today's top engravers. He apprenticed at Colt and is now a free-lance engraver doing outstanding work. The rifle is now part of the NRA's National Firearms Museum collection.

The two-millionth Model 60 rifle was specially engraved by Robert C. Kain. (This rifle was also presented to the NRA's National Firearms Museum.) Mr. Kain also does free-lance work, as well as contract work for the arms industry. Among his credits are the Custer Memorial Battle of the Little Big Horn reproduction trapdoor Springfields for Harrington and Richardson; the Lyman Centennial Rifle, Special Issue for Lyman that was on the Ruger No. 1 rifle; and the one thousand cased Marlin Centennial Matched Pairs. The 1970 Marlin pair consisted of a Model 336 and Model 39 with matching serial numbers, octagon barrels, and engraved receivers. Robert Kain, with help, engraved the 2,000 receivers over a period of three years. One of the other engravers doing some of the work was Winston Churchill, who is now America's finest master engraver, bar none. The receivers of these Marlin matched-pair rifles are signed by either Kain or Churchill on the side of the receiver tang. The stock must be removed to see the mark. Robert Kain's work is marked with an *R* that has the symbol of a walking cane superimposed on it. Winston Churchill's work is signed with the initial *W*, with a *C* superimposed. Some sets will be found having one gun done by each of the two engravers. Other sets may have both guns engraved by only one of the two engravers. Those done by Winston Churchill have an added value because of the eminent place he occupies in the engraving world today.

One of the finest engraved Marlin rifles is the two-millionth Model 39A rifle that was superbly engraved and gold inlaid by Alvin A. White, the patriarch of modern American engraving. His relief-engraved horse and rider, squirrel, bust of John Marlin that is inlaid into the pistol grip, fine line gold borders, scroll engraving, and gold-inlaid scroll and leaf designs make this the finest Marlin-produced rifle in modern times. The rifle was presented by Marlin to the National Shooting Sports Foundation (NSSF) to be auctioned in order to raise funds for the expansion of NSSF's shooting education programs in the nation's schools.

The illustrations of some of the special one-of-a-kind engraved Marlins that are included here are representative of a new breed of fine engravers doing work equal to, or better than, the work of the Ulrich and others of years gone by. The artists, such as Winston Churchill, have prepared and educated themselves in basic art and animal figures to the degree that they now do work of "bank note" quality, including anatomically correct animals and scenes true to life. They also have the talent and desire to not do mass-produced engraving. Instead, their work is now done individually as a work of art. Marlin does not now have a custom shop doing special engraving or special-order features.

Expert and Fancy Shooters

Most of the arms and ammunition companies in the U.S. used public demonstrations of fancy shooting to publicize their products. Names such as Carver, Barker, Topperwein, Bogardus, Hill, Peret, Hillis, Razee, Miller, Annie Oakley, T.K. Lee, Olsen, Bartlett, O'Connell, Larson, and Capt. A.H. Hardy were famous for their demonstrated skill with handguns, shotguns, and rifles.

The only fancy shooter on the Marlin payroll was Colonel Larson. However, Annie Oakley, Captain A.H. Hardy, and Frank Miller all used Marlin firearms with great success and won worldwide recognition for their feats of endurance and markmanship.

Captain Hardy. Captain A.H. Hardy was a sales representative for The Peters Cartridge Company. At that time, Peters manufactured ammunition. Its chief competitors, Remington and

Captain A.H. Hardy demonstrating to cowboys the shooting of an Indian head profile while using a Marlin .22 repeater. Photo was dated January 16, 1922, and marked Office of the President of Marlin Firearms Corporation.

Captain Hardy hitting five targets thrown into the air while lying on his back, using a Marlin shotgun.

Winchester, manufactured both arms and ammunition. Therefore, in order not to publicize the competition's guns, Captain Hardy used Marlin rifles and shotguns during his years of fancy shooting.

Captain Hardy was raised in the West and began his early gun training just north of Columbus, Neb., his birthplace. He then settled in Hyannis, Neb., where he opened a saddle and leather shop. The cowboys gave him credit for being a crack shot, and he soon got "the bug" to see the Buffalo Bill Shows. He traveled 135 miles on one occasion in 1896 to see Annie Oakley and Johnny Baker shoot.

Captain Hardy started with Peters in 1904, and by 1907 he had established a record of hitting 994 out of 1,000 frozen apples thrown into the air. He continued to try for long-run endurance records, and in November 1907 he hit 5,152 wooden blocks without a miss at a 20-foot rise. Later, shooting four hours a day for four days, he hit 13,066 2¼-in. wooden balls without a miss.

A demonstration put on by Captain Hardy in 1928 at Camp Perry, Ohio, during the national rifle and pistol matches was described in *The American Rifleman* as follows:

Capt. Hardy opened his performance by shooting with a .38 revolver at a target at 300 yards. With a variable crosswind, the odds were strongly against him hitting the target. Yet the Captain actually scored four hits out of nine shots fired.

Captain Hardy then showed how two clay targets, one stationary and one swinging, could be hit simultaneously by using a revolver in each hand.

Many other interesting demonstrations followed, such as hitting small steel washers thrown into the air, using both .22 and .32-20 caliber rifles; bursting apples thrown into the air; shattering quartered bricks in the air with a .32-20; and hitting five targets thrown into the air simultaneously, using a Marlin repeating shotgun. One particularly difficult stunt Captain Hardy performed was ejecting a .22 cartridge from the Marlin slide-action repeating rifle, and then hitting this cartridge with the next shot before it reached the ground. A gallon can thrown about 20 feet into the air was hit five times before it reached the earth; a Marlin slide-action .22 caliber rifle was also used.

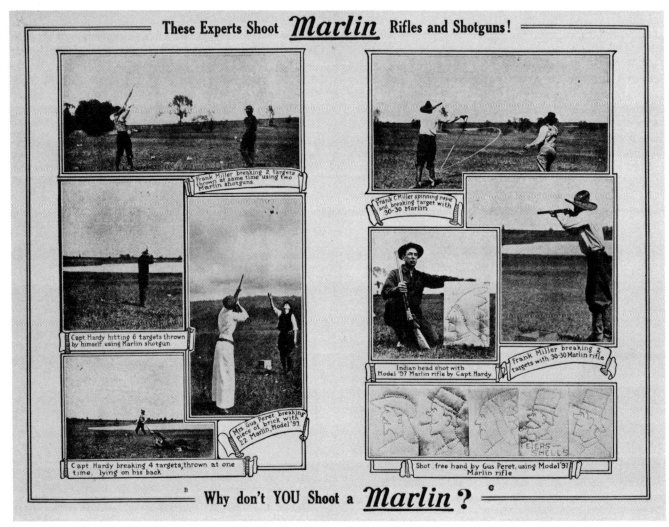

Page from Marlin catalog showing fancy shooting being done by Captain Hardy, Frank Miller, and Mr. & Mrs. Gus Peret, using Marlin firearms.

No demonstration of Captain Hardy's shooting would be complete without the trick in which he outlined the profile of an Indian on a sheet of tin, using a .22 caliber repeating rifle. The Indian's head, bedecked in feathers, was outlined faultlessly, and in an incredibly short time.

Captain Hardy used a caliber .22 lever action Marlin, a Marlin .32–20 slide-action, a Marlin .30–30 lever action, and a 12-gauge hammerless Marlin pump shotgun. Captain Hardy stated that back in the early days he and Mahlon H. Marlin were close personal friends. For this reason, he began using Marlin guns.

Captain Hardy wrote Marlin the following letter about the use of his Marlin shotgun in his exhibitions:

> Have just returned from Michigan where I have been giving daily exhibitions. Have used the new Marlin shotgun since July 4th and in no position or in any part of my exhibition has it given me the slightest trouble. You don't know how one feels to get a gun that is particularly adapted to his work. Here is a stunt that I have tried every other repeater out on and without success. I lie on my back and at a distance of 40 feet have an assistant throw four blue rock targets into the air and in this position break the four blue rock targets before they reach the ground. You can easily understand that the mechanism must be right to handle this "stunt" day after day without trouble, and your gun has done it.
>
> Capt. A.H. Hardy

In 1934, The Peters Cartridge Company was purchased by The Remington Arms Company, and Captain Hardy turned his interests to his earlier occupation in the leather business. He lived in Beverly Hills, Calif., and made classic leather holsters, belts, and cases, which are among today's collector's items.

Frank Miller and Annie Oakley. Frank C. Miller, expert shot of Irwin Brothers' Cheyenne Frontier Days Wild West Show, had the following to say in 1915 about his using Marlin guns in his exhibitions:

> Shooting for shows and large fairs is somewhat different from demonstration work; you can not explain to the spectators the shots that you expect to make. Your work must be fast and spectacular with plenty of action and yet simple enough for them to understand, as they cannot watch the shooter and target at the same time. Then again, the time is limited; therefore it is best to use guns that will stand by you, as on the move like we are it is impossible to carry a repair shop.
>
> Last season we showed in ten states and Canada at the leading state fairs and expositions, and I gave as high as 15 exhibitions a day, shooting under all conditions, rain, wind, night, in parades in the streets, and late last fall I used some of the same guns successfully on a hunting trip to Canada and Wyoming. From all this you can see what opinion I have of Marlin guns.

Annie Oakley also used Marlin rifles, along with other makes of guns, during her many years of demonstrating her shooting skills at Wild West shows and performances throughout the world. Annie's tricks included aerial targets with both rifle and shotgun, many of which were performed from horseback. She would also shoot coins from between the fingers of

1907 photo of Miss Annie Oakley shooting her Marlin Model 1897 rifle.

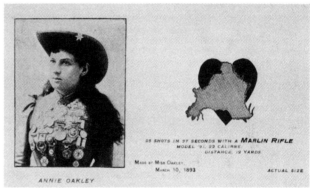

Advertising card used by Marlin to announce Annie Oakley's remarkable group of 25 shots fired in 27 seconds from her Marlin Model 1891 rifle.

her husband, Frank Butler, who also was an excellent marksman. In 1890, Annie and Frank joined Buffalo Bill's Wild West Show. During one such show, the famous Indian, Sitting Bull, was so amazed by her skill that he nicknamed her "Little Miss Sureshot."

One of Miss Oakley's favorite rifles was the Marlin Model 1891 side-loading caliber .22 lever action rifle. She used the rifle extensively and demonstrated her skill with it on March 10, 1893 at New York, when she shot into one jagged hole 25 shots in 27 seconds. The distance was 36 feet.

Another of her Marlin rifles was a Model 1889, which was presented to her by John Marlin. The gun is engraved and has the name *Annie Oakley* on the left side of the receiver. It is serial number 98,560. The records indicate it is caliber .32–20 with a 22-in. half octagon barrel. It was originally case-colored but later was nickel-plated by the owner, who had allowed it to rust while inadequately stored in humid Florida. The whereabouts of this rifle are now unknown. I examined it in the mid-1970s. At that time, it was all original except for the plating, and was in good condition.

An October 6, 1894 newspaper article reported the following:

The Marlin Firearms Co. of New Haven, Conn. have just made and delivered three rifles for Miss Annie Oakley. The rifles, which are beautiful weapons, are two .44's and one .38 caliber; and have been made expressly for Miss Oakley to use in "Miss Bora," the play she will star in in England this winter. She sails for the old country early in November.

In 1906, Marlin presented to Annie Oakley a gold-plated and engraved Model 1897 rifle. It is serial number 342,637.

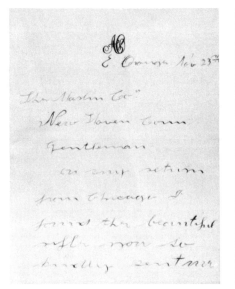
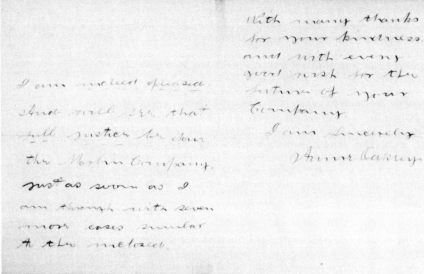

Annie Oakley's letter to Marlin thanking the company for the rifle it presented to her in 1906.

Model 1889 Marlin rifle, serial number 98,560, presented to Annie Oakley by Marlin.

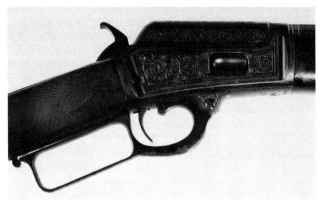

Right side of Annie Oakley Model 1889 rifle.

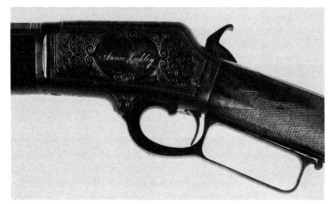

Left side of Annie Oakley Model 1889 rifle.

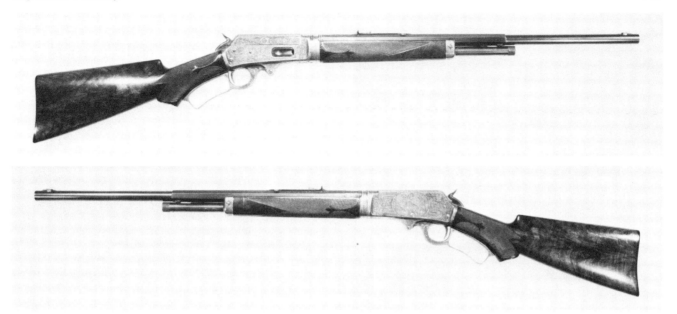

Top: *Model 1893 rifle presented to Annie Oakley.* Bottom: *Left side of same.*

Miss Oakley wrote J. Howard Marlin the following thank-you letter:

E. Orange, Nov. 23rd

The Marlin Co.
New Haven, Conn.

Gentlemen

On my return from Chicago I found the beautiful rifle you so kindly sent me. I am *indeed pleased* and will see that *full justice* be done the Marlin Company just as soon as I am through with seven more cases similar to the enclosed.

With many thanks for your kindness and with every good wish for the future of your company.

I am sincerely,
Annie Oakley

In 1917, Marlin presented Miss Oakley with another special rifle, a Model 1893, serial number 419,119. It has gold and platinum embellishments and special engraving. It is take-down, with a half octagon barrel. The caliber is .38–55.

A June 7, 1921 letter from the Marlin–Rockwell Corporation, Marlin Arms Division, to a Mr. L.J. Huber about this rifle was as follows:

New Haven, Conn.,
June 7, 1921.

Mr. L. J. Huber,
355 Ridge Ave.,
Spring City, Pa.

Dear Sir:—

We have your favor of June 6th giving us the number of the special model 1893 38-55 caliber Marlin rifle which you purchased in Phila-delphia a short time ago.

This is a rifle which we presented to Annie Oakley back in 1917, and we are somewhat disappointed that it has been now offered on the market for sale. Miss Oakley expressed a desire to have one of our 38-55 caliber rifles and we went to considerable extra bother in getting out a special fancy gun that we considered she would be proud to own and shoot.

The value at the time that it was made up was in the neighborhood of $150.00 but considering the advance that has been made in the market price of firearms during the past two or three years the present value would probably be somewhat in excess of this figure. You can consider that you have obtained a very beautiful rifle and an excep-tionally good shooter.

Under the present conditions we would not be in a position to furnish an extra 32-40 barrel part for the rifle with engraving or fore-arm to match the butt stock. The only thing that we could supply would be the plain forearm without checking and no engraving on the barrel, and our charge for a barrel part of this description would be $17.50.

There is a possibility that we will again take up the manufacture of the Marlin line in the near future and that guns will be on the market within the next four or five months. However, we do not think that we would be in a position to get out any special work for quite some time, although there is no doubt but what later on we could furnish a barrel part with the engraving and the checking to match the butt stock which you now have.

Yours very truly,
MARLIN ROCKWELL
CORPORATION
Marlin Arms Division
Fred Bradley

FEB-M

It has been estimated that Annie Oakley fired over two mil-lion shots. Her shooting spanned 58 years. In 1894, she and Frank settled in Nutley, N.J. In 1899–1900, they toured the U.S. A train accident on the return trip left Annie paralyzed. However, with her usual determination, she recovered and re-turned to shooting. She died November 3, 1926 at her home in Greenville, Ohio. She was 66 years old.

Mark Arie. Mark Arie, although not a trick or fancy shooter, was probably the greatest all-around trapshooter of his time.

Close-up of engraved and gold-inlaid Model 1893 Annie Oakley rifle.

The late Mark Arie, Trapshooting Hall of Famer, pointing his Marlin Model 43 shotgun, which is now displayed at the ATA Hall of Fame. (Courtesy of Trapshooting ATA Hall of Fame, Vandalia, Ohio)

Photo furnished by the Trapshooting Hall of Fame, Vandalia, Ohio, showing Mark Arie on left with his Marlin pump shotgun. Other shooters, from left to right, are E.F. Woodward, F.M. Troeh, S.W. Olney, and H.E. Woodward. Note that these four men are holding L.C. Smith double-barreled shotguns.

His accomplishments while using Marlin pump action shotguns were many, and are best described in the Amateur Trapshooting Association's Trapshooting Hall of Fame description at the time of his posthumous induction to the Hall of Fame. The citation reads as follows:

ATA HALL OF FAME
1970 Inductees
Installed August 25, 1970
MARK ARIE

Mark Arie, one of the most colorful and popular trapshooters in the sport's history, was considered to be one of the greatest handicap shots of all times. Born in 1883, Arie began his trapshooting career in 1905 when he entered his first tournament at Rantoul, Ill. and won top honors with 157x160. That year at the Grand, he hit 97 from 17 yards in the GAH, only two behind the winning 99.

Arie became the first Grand Doubles Champion in 1912 when he won the title with 89. A span of 22 years later, in 1934, he won his second Doubles crown. He was the first shooter to run 100 straight doubles from scratch when he broke the first 163 in a 200-bird race at the Great Western Handicap at the Denver (Colo.) Municipal TC on July 18, 1926.

Arie tied for the GAH title in 1917 with 98, only to lose the shootoff. He returned in 1923 to become the first maximum-yardage shooter (23 yards) ever to win the GAH, posting 96. Besides tieing for the GAH to 1917, Arie annexed the NACTC. He won the singles title again in 1928 and was High-Over-All leader at the Grand in 1912, 1913, 1917, 1918, 1923, 1924 and 1932. In 1932 he tied for the Jim Day Cup, symbolic of the All-Around Championship.

In 1919 he led the amateurs in singles with a .9780 mark on 2,920 targets, an amateur record at the time.

It was in 1920 that Arie added international fame to his list of accomplishments by winning the individual gold medal in the Olympics. He smashed 95x100 at Antwerp, Belgium. He was also a member of the U.S. group that won the team gold medal in the 1920 Olympics.

Arie decided to give it a try as an industry rep in 1921 but returned to the amateur ranks after one year. During the 1921 Grand, he tied for the rep championship.

Arie attended the Grand seven times as the Illinois State singles titlist and three of those times he won the Champion of Champions race (1917, 1926 and 1934). He was a member of the winning Illinois team at the Grand in 1926, 1934 and 1935.

At Iowa State in 1934, Arie was the second shooter to break 100 straight from 25 yards, turning in his perfect score from the then-maximum yardage. His all-around total at the shoot was 395x400, an ATA record at the time.

For the first four years of its existence—1927 through 1930—Arie was named to the All-America team. He also was placed on the squad in 1932 and 1934.

On Nov. 19, 1958, Mark Arie died at his farm near Champaign, Ill.

Marlin frequently used Mark Arie's performance and winning ways on the trap field in advertisements and flyers. He was presented with a Marlin pump shotgun, which had his signature engraved on the left side of the receiver. The gun is now proudly displayed in the ATA Hall of Fame, Vandallia, Ohio, where the Grand American Trapshooting Championships are held each year.

The late Colonel Larson, Marlin's trick and fancy exhibition shooter, who traveled far and wide to demonstrate Marlin firearms to young and old alike.

Colonel Larson. To tell the whole story of Colonel Larson and his long struggle to overcome a crippling illness would take a small volume. Therefore, to be brief, yet give Marlin's late friend and trick shooter his due, the following account about Colonel, which was printed in *Boy's Life* magazine and in Marlin advertising matter, is included here:

COLONEL LARSON, THE MARLIN MAN

What kind of man becomes World Champion Professional Rifleman?

What's behind the rifle? When you take good aim, as we did, you find a man with a story of almost-unbelievable courage, a man who used his head to help his body recover from a crippling illness, a man who finds time in a busy life to be a friend and teacher to youth, a lover of animals, devoted to his family, an ardent hobbyist.

Colonel (that's his real first name, he was not an army Colonel) Larson grew up in a small Wisconsin community. He was a boy who made his way by developing his talents in sports and hobbies and studying long and hard. He became ringmaster of his own little circus while still a schoolboy by training animals to do simple tricks and training himself in the ways of the whip, the boomerang and rodeo rope.

In high school, he became a star athlete with state honors in football, basketball, track and baseball. This continued until he reached Wisconsin State University on a scholarship and was outstanding in the four already-mentioned sports plus the decathlon. In his last year at State, All-American Larson was named to the All-star football team.

Then came the turning point in Colonel's life.

He was hired as a teacher after receiving his degree in chemistry and physics and starting work on a master's degree. By that time, too, he was married and the father of two. He thought he had it made.

While standing on a practice football field as the high school coach, Colonel felt a stiffness in his neck. He tried to ignore it, but days passed and it didn't go away. When the strapping six-footer finally saw a doctor it was almost too late. Colonel Larson had crippling polio. So severe was his condition that the local papers automatically reported his obituary.

It was probably his superb physique which saved him. Few people in those days survived such an attack. His family had been told that he would always remain a hopeless cripple and would have to be cared for like a baby.

But Colonel remembered his lessons. Develop what you have. His old muscles useless, he worked incessantly on new ones, secondary ones. He worked his hands and arms and managed to work rope tricks and master his Marlin .22. In two years he was able to walk and use his hands again.

Colonel Larson went on working and now leads an exciting, useful and inspiring life, raising his family, entertaining millions of people and holding his head proud and high.

Could this unidentified, handsome lady holding a Marlin Model 1891 side-loading rifle be Annie Oakley?

The six world rifle-shooting records won by Colonel Larson at the Professional Indoor Plain and Fancy Contest held at Rockerville, S.D., in 1960 were the following:

1. Splitting 125 playing cards, consecutively, at 52 feet.
2. Hitting 1,100 8-in. targets in 4½ hours without a miss.
3. Shooting 750 aspirin tablets at 30 feet—over the shoulder while sighting them through a mirror.
4. Leveling a gun and hitting 17 blocks of wood dead center in 18 seconds—each block measuring three inches square.
5. Scoring 3,600 consecutive hits in one day.
6. Discharging over 500,000 rounds through the same gun barrel—breaking the world's record of 250,000 previously made by Ad Topperwein of Texas.

In 1961, Colonel started to do exhibition shooting for Marlin. He had always used Marlin firearms, so it was easy for him to use them in his act. Most of his shows were put on with the youngster in mind. He always pitched safe gun handling. He dropped fast-draw and juggling routines, because he felt that to demonstrate acts that were not safe for the inexperienced or beginner did not represent Marlin's safe gun handling philosophy.

Colonel put on his demonstrations of fancy and trick shooting in stores, auditoriums, TV studios, and outdoors. He had his own bullet trap and system to protect the public, and never took a chance. His routine included twirling rope, throwing boomerangs, snuffing candles, splitting cards, and shooting aspirin tablets. His charm and charisma captured young and old alike, and by his dedication to Marlin he took the company name and products to hundreds of thousands of people throughout the country. I was privileged to call him my friend.

Extras

Until The Marlin Fire Arms Company was sold to a syndicate formed to manufacture tools of war, there were many extra features that could be special-ordered from the factory. Some were just a deviation from the standard model, such as a different length of barrel or magazine; a steel rather than a rubber butt plate, or vice versa; and a half octagon barrel rather than a round or full octagon barrel. Most extras added a touch of quality and elegance that not only increased the value

of the firearm but also made it a thing of beauty. For example, silver and gold plating and pearl or ivory grips did not make the early Marlin pistols any more practical, just more handsome. In fact, many of the high-art rifles that were produced from 1882 to 1915 were never used in the field, yet were treasured by their owners because of having been received as a gift, or presented to them as an award. Many have the name or initials of the receipient attractively engraved into the metal. Among the most desirable extra features to be found today are special engraving, silver and gold plating, extra-fancy wood, and special checking. The rarest of the special-order firearms are those few that have gold or gold and platinum inlays. Most frequently the inlays are only narrow gold borders around the game scene on the receiver, and bands around the barrel. Other, more elaborate work includes inlays in the hammer and lever. Some few and rare Marlin firearms have figures inlaid in gold. Examples of this type are illustrated in the engraving section of this book.

It should be noted that extras available to the gun purchaser were not consistent from year to year or model to model. Also, the catalog descriptions were not always consistent. But from the following tables the extra feature and its description can be arrived at if the approximate year of manufacture and model of the firearm are known.

Catalog comments about variations of the standard models for the period 1891 to 1900 were as follows:

Barrels can not be furnished longer than 32 inches.
Shotgun butt same price as rifle butt.
Half octagon barrels same price as octagon.
Half length magazine (7 shot) same price as full length magazine.
Short length magazine (5 shot) same price as full length magazine.
Model 1897 magazine 24 or 16 inches long (1900).
Rifle buttstock same price as rubber butt.
Model 1892 rifles have blued receivers.
Carbines have blued receivers.
Model 1888 and 1889 have blued receivers.
Model 1897 rifles have case hardened receivers.

The following two charts identify the extra features and their costs. The first chart covers the years 1882 through 1896. The second chart covers the years 1897 through 1915. Shotgun extras are covered in the shotgun section.

Rare bird's-eye maple buttstock that was one of the many special-order extras.

Rare cheek piece buttstock that was only available on special order and at an added cost.

Rifle with half-octagon barrel, pistol grip stock and forearm
of plain walnut, checked

LIST OF EXTRAS FOR RIFLES

	Price
Selected straight grip stock and foreend,	$4.00
" " " " " " finely checked,	6.75
" pistol " " " "	7.00
" " " " " finely checked,	10.15
Extra selected straight grip stock and foreend, extra checked, extra finish,	10.25
Extra selected pistol grip stock and foreend, extra checked, and extra finish,	13.50
Plain walnut pistol grip stock and foreend, checked,	3.40
Shortening or lengthening buttstock or changing drop,	6.75
Shortening buttstock not over ½ inch,	1.25
Swivels and sling strap (leather),	1.40
Nickel-plated trimmings,	1.70
Full nickel-plating,	2.70
Silver-plated trimmings,	2.70
Canvas cover, leather bound,	1.50

	Price
Special Smokeless Steel barrel instead of regular barrel, Models '92, '94, '97,	$2.50
Special light-weight (Model 1893 only),	5.75
Full silver-plating,	6.75
Gold-plated trimmings,	6.75
Full gold-plating,	16.00
Leaving off rear sight slot or changing its position,	.70
Matted barrels,	3.50
Engraving No. 1 (see pages 101 to 106),	3.60
" No. 2 (" 101 " 106),	7.20
" No. 3 (" 101 " 106),	10.80
" No. 5 (" 101 " 106),	18.00
" No. 10 (" 101 " 106),	36.00
" No. 15 (" 101 " 106),	54.00
Case-hardening receiver (Model 1892 rifle, 1894 carb., No. 20 and No. 29 rifles),	.70
Special checking [5 (3) and 5 (4)],	10.00
London dull finish,	2.50

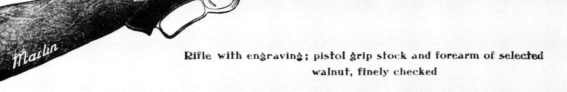

Rifle with engraving; pistol grip stock and forearm of selected
walnut, finely checked

Typical Marlin catalog listing of extras available for rifles.

We can furnish our Models 1893, 1894 and 1895 Take-Down rifles in all our accustomed styles, viz., with round, octagon or half-octagon barrel, any length up to 32 inches; full, half or short magazine; straight or pistol grip.

Interchangeable Barrels

Model 1893. All the calibers of this model, viz., the .25-36, .30-30, .32-40, .32 Special H. P. S. and .38-55 have exactly the same action, so they will interchange, and you can thus have, by purchasing extra barrel parts, as many as five Take-Down rifles on one action.

Model 1894. The .38-40 and .44-40 will interchange, as they have exactly the same action; so by purchasing an extra barrel part, you can have two Take-Down repeaters of these calibers with the one action.

Model 1895. All the regular rifles of this model, viz., the .38-56, .40-65, .40-70, .40-82, .45-70 and .45-90 have exactly the same action, and the .33 caliber and .45-70 light weight actions also interchange; so you can have, by purchasing extra barrel parts, as many as seven Take-Down rifles on one action.

When ordering extra barrel parts, return the rifle, to insure a perfect fit.

Models 1893, 1894 and 1895.

The extra price for Take-Down on any rifle,	**$ 3.50**
The price of an extra barrel part complete, standard length of barrel, 1893 B or 1894,	**12.00**
" " " " " " " with 26-inch Smokeless Steel barrel, 1893 or 1895,	**14.00**
" " " " " " " with 22-inch light weight barrel, 1895, .33 or .45-70 caliber,	**15.00**
" " " " " " " with plain checking on forearm, additional,	1.00
" " " " " " " with selected walnut forearm and "B" checking, additional,	4.00
" " " " " " " with extra selected walnut forearm and special checking, additional,	6.00
" " " " " **action and buttstock complete,** straight grip, except .33 and .45-70 light weight,	13.50
straight grip, .33 or .45-70 light weight,	15.00

Typical Marlin catalog listing of extra barrels and takedown feature that could be special-ordered.

EXTRAS 1882–1896

		1882	1883	1885	1886	1887	1888–1890	1891–1895	1896
1	Engraving	$5.00 and up	$5.00	$5.00	$5.00	$5.00	$5.00	$5.00	$5.00
2	Full nickel plating	5.00	5.00	5.00	5.00	4.00	4.00	4.00	4.00
3	Nickel-plated trimmings	3.00	3.00	3.00	3.00	2.50	2.50	2.50	2.50
4	Checking buttstock & forearm	5.00	5.00	5.00					
5	Shotgun butt w/rubber butt plate	2.00				1.00	1.00	2.00	
6	Double-set triggers	5.00	5.00	5.00		4.00	4.00		
7	Case hardening	1.50	1.00	1.00	1.00	1.00	1.00	1.00	
8	Swivels and Sling (fitting 50 cents extra)		1.50	1.50	1.50	1.50	1.50	1.50	
9	Pistol grip, plain wood (new in 1885)			5.00				5.00	
10	Pistol grip, selected and checked (new in 1885)			15.00	12.00	12.00	12.00	15.00	15.00
11	Gold-plated trimmings			10.00	10.00	8.00	8.00	10.00	10.00
12	Selected walnut stock and forearm, finely checked					8.00	8.00	10.00	10.00
13	Selected walnut stock		5.00	5.00				6.00	6.00
14	Nickel-plated trimmings (Ballard)			2.00					
15	Shortening or lengthening stock or changing drop					3.00	3.00	10.00	10.00
16	Leaving off rear sight slot or changing position					2.00	2.00	1.00	1.00
17	Blank piece to fill rear sight slot					.25	.25		
18	Pistol grip w/checking						4.00		5.00
19	Selected pistol grip stock and forearm							10.00	10.00
20	Extra-select English walnut stock and forearm, pistol grip, finely checked and extra-fine finish							18.00	20.00
21	Sling strap, webbing w/snap hook for carbine							.75	
22	Silver-plated trimmings							4.00	4.00
23	Full silver plating							9.00	9.00
24	Full gold plating							20.00	20.00
25	Matted barrels							5.00	5.00
26	Case-hardened receiver (Model 1891 rifle and Model 1894 carbine)								1.00
27	Selected straight-grip stock and forend								4.50
28	Selected straight-grip stock and forearm finely checked								7.50
29	Selected pistol grip stock and forend, finely checked.								11.20

EXTRAS 1882–1896 *(Continued)*

		1882	1883	1885	1886	1887	1888–1890	1891–1895	1896
30	Plain walnut pistol grip stock and forend, finely checked								4.00
31	Swivels and leather sling strap								1.20

EXTRAS 1897–1915

		1897–1899	1900–1902			1903–1909 All rifle models	1910–1915 All models
			1892, 1893, 1894	1895	1897		
1	Selected straight-grip stock and forend		$4.50	$5.20	$4.55	$4.55	$4.00
2	Selected straight-grip stock and forend finely checked		7.50	9.50	7.50	7.60	6.75
3	Selected pistol grip stock and forend	$7.50	7.50	9.50	7.50	7.60	7.00
4	Selected pistol grip stock and forend finely checked		11.20	13.00	11.15	11.30	10.15
5	Extra selected p.g. stock extra checked & extra finish	14.85	14.85	17.50	15.25	15.25	13.50
6	Extra selected straight stock extra checked & extra finish					12.00	10.25
7	Plain walnut p.g. stock and forend, checked		4.00	4.35	4.00	4.00	3.40
8	Shortening or lengthening buttstock or changing drop	7.50	7.50	7.50	7.50	7.70	6.75
9	Swivels and sling strap		1.20	1.20	1.25	1.40	1.40
10	Nickel-plating trimmings	2.00	2.00	2.30	2.00	2.00	1.70
11	Full nickel plating	3.00	3.00	3.50	3.10	3.10	2.70
12	Silver-plating trimmings	3.00	3.00	3.50	3.10	3.10	2.70
13	Canvas cover, leather-bound		1.40	1.40	1.40	1.40	1.50
14	Special lightweight (1893 only)					6.80	5.75
15	Full silver plating	6.75	6.75	7.80	6.85	7.25	6.75
16	Gold-plated trimmings		7.75	8.75	7.90	7.90	6.75
17	Full gold plating	15.20	15.20	17.35	15.75	17.00	16.00
18	Leaving off rear sight slot or changing its position	.75	.75	1.00	1.00	.80	.70
19	Matted barrel	3.75	3.75	4.35	4.00	4.00	3.50
20	Engraving No. 1	4.00	4.00	4.40	4.00	4.00	3.60
21	Engraving No. 2	8.00	8.00	8.80	8.40	8.00	7.20
22	Engraving No. 3	12.00	12.00	12.20	12.00	12.00	10.80
23	Engraving No. 5	20.00	20.00	22.00	21.00	20.00	18.00
24	Engraving No. 10	40.00	40.00	44.00	42.00	40.00	36.00
25	Engraving No. 15	63.00	63.00	66.00	63.00	60.00	54.00
26	Case-hardening receiver (1892, 1894 Carbine, 18, 20)	(1892) .75	(1892) .75			(1882) .75	.70
27	Special checking 5(3) & 5(4)			14.00	14.00	14.00	10.00
28	London dull finish			2.75	2.75	2.75	2.50
29	Extra for takedown	4.00					

Firearms Safety

The Marlin Firearms Company has always been a leader in the promotion of the safe use of firearms and the conservation of wildlife and the outdoors.

A good example of Marlin's promotion of safety with firearms is the many years of distributing a "Ten Commandments of Firearms Safety" booklet, and reproducing the 10 commandments in the Marlin annual product catalog. The Marlin 10 commandments were

1. Treat every gun with the respect due a loaded gun.
2. Guns carried into camp or home, or when otherwise not in use, must be unloaded and taken down or have actions open; guns always should be carried in cases.
3. Always be sure barrel and action are clear of obstructions, and that you have only ammunition of the proper size for the gun you are carrying. Remove oil and grease from chamber before firing.
4. Always carry your gun so that you can control the direction of the muzzle, even if you stumble; keep the safety on until you are ready to shoot.
5. Be sure of your target before you pull the trigger; know the identifying features of the game you intend to hunt.
6. Never point a gun at anything you do not want to shoot; avoid all horseplay while holding a gun.
7. Unattended guns should be unloaded; guns and ammunition should be stored separately beyond the reach of children and careless adults.
8. Never climb a tree or fence or jump a ditch with a loaded gun; never pull a gun toward you by the muzzle.
9. Never shoot a bullet at a flat, hard surface or the surface of water. When at target practice, be sure your back stop is adequate.
10. Respect farmers' property.

WARNING: All owners and users of Marlin exposed hammer lever action rifles, exposed hammer pump action shotguns, and exposed hammer pump action rifles are warned *never* to place the hammer in the forward position with the hammer resting on the firing pin when there is a cartridge, or shell, in the chamber, as a blow to the hammer when the hammer is in this position will cause the gun to fire.

This warning applies to all exposed hammer center-fire and caliber .22 lever action rifles which include Models 1881, 1888, 1889, 1891, 1892, 1893, 1894, 1895, 1897, 1936, 36, 336, 356, 375, 444, .45–70, and all variations of Models 39, 39A, and 39M. The warning also pertains to all the exposed hammer pump action shotguns, including Models 1898, 16, 17, 19, 21, 24, 26, 30, 42, and 49; and the exposed hammer pump action rifle Models 18, 20, 25, 27, 29, 37, and 47.

Failure to understand and comply with this warning could result in an injury to the user or a bystander.

Marlin also distributed, by packaging with each firearm, hundreds of thousands of copies of "Marlin Hunter's Pocket Guide." This guide included the National Shooting Sports Foundation version of the "Ten Commandments of Firearms Safety," and helpful information and hints for hunters about ethics, hunter–landowner relations, and conservation.

One of the most successful safety programs promoted by a firearms company has been "Marlin's Safety Pledge," promoted through news releases and back cover pages of the Marlin product catalog. Hundreds of thousands of sportsmen, young and old, have pledged the following:

> I pledge myself as a hunter to respect the environment which has made my sport possible.
> I pledge my support of state and national conservation programs and all hunter safety courses.
> I pledge to help protect my rights as an American to hunt and shoot by practicing the safe and proper use of firearms and obeying all game laws and safety rules.

By taking this pledge the sportsman committed himself to courteous, sportsmanlike conduct when using a firearm. By sending in 50¢ to help defray the cost of this nonprofit program, the sportsman received from Marlin an embroidered shoulder patch, a wallet card, a bumper sticker, and a Safety Pledge Certificate suitable for framing.

The pledge program has been in effect since 1975 and sportsmen are still encouraged to write Marlin and state they have taken the pledge. Over 10,000 have done so.

Another Marlin innovation is the Safety Minder, which was attached to every firearm Marlin has manufactured since 1974.

The Safety Minder (patent number 4,014,124) is a plastic piece that snaps into the trigger guard of a rifle or shotgun. Printed on the piece, in bold letters, is *IS IT LOADED?* One hundred Safety Minders are furnished free to dealers and hunter safety instructors who want to use them in stores and during classes. Additional quantities are $3 per hundred. Marlin feels that any effort, large or small, is worth making if it prevents even one tragic firearm accident.

During the period of 1976 to 1985, Marlin conducted an annual hunter safety essay contest. The contest was held in conjunction with state-sponsored hunter safety programs. It was divided into two classifications, junior (through grade 8) and seniors (grades 9–12).

To be eligible to participate, students had to be enrolled in, or have completed, a state hunter safety program. Each state participating had junior, senior, and instructor winners. The awards were personalized winner certificates and $50 L.L. Bean gift certificates. From the state winners in each category, a national junior and senior winner were selected. Each national winner was presented with a government savings bond and a Marlin model 39A rifle that had his or her name and achievement appropriately engraved on the receiver. The instructor of each national winner received a properly inscribed Marlin lever action .22 rifle with a plaque designating him or her the Marlin Hunter Safety Instructor of the Year.

Some of the essay topics have been the following:

"What can the hunter, as an individual, do to preserve the sport of hunting?"
"Is it enough to be a safe hunter?"
"Why should Americans preserve the sport of hunting?"
"What I should do to preserve the sport of hunting."
"What it means to be an ethical hunter."
"As a hunter, what sportsmanship means to me."

The winners of these special awards have been as follows:

Year	Name	Class	State	Instructor
1976	Mitch Boofer	Junior	AZ	David Cassells
	Kim Brodman	Senior	WI	Allen Kumm
1977	John R. Weir	Junior	OK	Gary Smeltzer
	Jerry Stramek	Senior	WA	James C. Kline
1978	Terry Lynn Comer	Junior	VA	Robert W. Inskeep
	James Dodson	Senior	MI	Jack W. Racklyeft
1979	Gilbert J. Debus	Junior	VT	Michael R. Narkewicz
	Joanne Luitich	Senior	NY	A. Burke Luitich
1980	Yurii Billiel	Junior	OH	Thomas Brennan
	Karen Lynn Pierce	Senior	OK	Robert Whitworth
1981	David A. Marr	Junior	FL	Dorothy E. Oak
	Scott N. Warner	Senior	PA	John G. Martin II
1982	Bobby Laux	Junior	MI	George Millenbach
	Jeff Kline	Senior	WA	James C. Kline
1983	Jason D. Cyper	Junior	NV	David Stickles
	Tim Rice	Senior	KA	Charles Rice
1984	Robert T. Biggs	Junior	KN	Brian B. Bullock
	Gary Rad	Senior	MI	Richard Murphy

Since 1970, Marlin has attached a comprehensive owners manual to each firearm it manufactures. This manual contains instructions for the safe use of the firearm, such as cautions and warnings that must be heeded. Also included is Marlin's "Guide to Gun Safety." An expansion of the original 10 commandments, Marlin's list includes the following:

1. Handle every gun as you would a cocked and loaded gun.
2. Keep the safety ON SAFE until you are ready to shoot.
3. Be sure of your target before you shoot.
4. Before target shooting, be sure you have an adequate back stop. Remember, all rifle ammunition is dangerous at ranges up to, and in excess of, a mile.
5. Never point a gun at anything you don't want to shoot.
6. Always wear protective glasses when shooting.
7. Wear hearing protectors when target shooting.
8. Do not use modified, damaged or dirty ammunition.
9. Use only ammunition of the correct caliber, size and bullet shape.
10. Cartridges that have been improperly handloaded can damage the gun and cause personal injury.
11. Avoid ricochets by never shooting at water, or any hard, flat surface.
12. Be sure no one is in path of ejecting shells.
13. Never climb or jump over an obstacle with a loaded gun.
14. Never pull a gun toward you by the muzzle.
15. Avoid alcoholic beverages before and during shooting.
16. Never use a gun that fails to function properly. Do not try to force a jammed action.
17. Be sure to keep the barrel and mechanism free of obstructions.
18. Before cleaning, be sure the chamber, action and magazine are completely unloaded.
19. Always unload a gun before storing, transporting, or leaving unattended.
20. Never enter a motor vehicle with a loaded gun.
21. Store guns and ammunition separately, beyond the reach of children.

Marlin now stamps into the metal of the barrel of every rifle the following warning:

WARNING: BEFORE USING GUN READ
OWNERS MANUAL FOR SAFE OPERATION

Marlin also recommends that every sportsman attend hunter safety courses and that people of all ages follow all the rules of safe gun handling and use.

Game Calendar

In 1975 Marlin made available to sporting goods stores and gun shops a game season calendar, which was used to show current and upcoming game season information. The vacuum-molded display showed a flying duck and pheasant at the top; at the bottom were places for the name of the game and open- and closed-season dates to be inserted. It came with preprinted

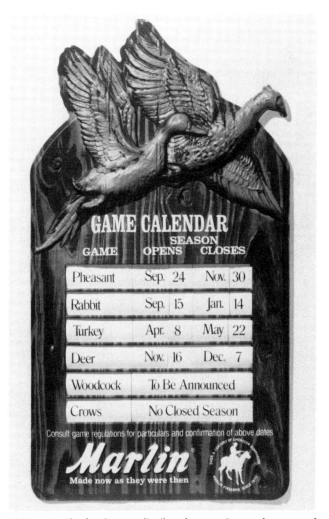

1975 game calendar that was distributed to sporting goods stores and gun shops.

inserts for all popular game and varmint species along with blank inserts to be filled in for species peculiar to a specific area.

Only 2,000 of these game calendars were distributed through jobbers.

Game Map

The Clipper King and Crown Prince rifles came with a special offer of targets, a target and game record book, a tube of

1958 packaging of Clipper King and Crown Prince rifles included a game map, targets, a "Target and Game Book," a 4X telescope, and a tube of Rustopper.

Rustopper, a 4X telescope, and a 23″x32½″ wildlife map. The map was of the U.S. and had superimposed on it illustrations of game animals and birds at the locations where they could be found and hunted. It was available as a paper poster and as a cardboard store display with a fold-up frame. It was an attractive wall piece. The paper poster could be purchased separately for $1.00 each. The cardboard type was sent to dealers and distributors free of charge. Many thousands of this great poster where packaged with guns, or sold separately. They are, today, a great addition to a den or youth's room. Educational and attractive, they are now scarce.

Game Recipe Books

During the 1954–1955 period, Marlin presented through the courtesy of *Sports Afield* magazine a booklet called "Famous Game Recipes" by Bill Wolf. The booklet stressed Marlin's traditional view that game should not be wasted and that it should be prepared skillfully and tastily for the family table. This little booklet was given away upon request.

The theme of the Marlin product catalogs from 1978 through 1980 was conservation of game, again emphasizing Marlin's view that it should not be wasted. Numerous "tried and true" recipes were included in the catalogs. In 1980, Marlin reproduced the catalog recipes into an attractive cookbook, which sold for $3.00 postpaid. It was printed on high-quality coated paper and included 16 full-color illustrations and original recipes. About 15,000 were printed and sold.

Gas Port

If, for some reason, the early Marlin lever action rifles had a cartridge failure that allowed gas to vent into the receiver, rather than be contained and exit out the muzzle, the gas could pass rearward toward the shooter's face. To prevent possible injury, the front end of the bolt was relieved at its top and bottom so that any escaping gas could go out the right side of the receiver. The amount of relief depended on the rifle model

1954–1955 game recipes book distributed free by Marlin.

1980 cookbook offered to sportsmen by Marlin for $3.00, postpaid; 15,000 were sold.

and cartridge size. These vents remained in use up to and including the Models 36 and 39 and into the Model 39A.

In 1979, a gas escape hole was added to the left side of the Model 39A/M receivers and to the left side of caliber .22 bolt action rifles. The purpose was the same as for the early Marlin lever action rifles.

General Information

BATF Classification of Marlin Firearms. Information of interest to the Marlin collector with regard to classification of short-barreled firearms can be found in the Department of the Treasury Bureau of Alcohol, Tobacco and Firearms (BATF) booklet, "Firearms, Curios, and Relics List" (1972-1986), ATFP 5300.11 (7-87), U.S. Government Printing Office 1987, (202) 966-7482. For a copy contact the BATF.

Catalogs, Parts Lists, and Owner's Manuals. Parts lists and owner's manuals are mailed at no charge upon request. However, manuals and parts lists for old discontinued models are not always available.

Owner's manuals are available for most models manufactured since 1975. However, because of changes frequently being made to various parts, giving the serial number of your firearm will help Marlin to determine what manual to send.

Cleaning Firearms. Frequently, sportsmen and collectors ask if they need to clean their firearms, and if so, how often.

The only answer to the first part of this question is YES! How often depends upon the kind of use the firearm is given, and the conditions of use. If the firearm is used in wet weather, or hot weather when a person perspires a lot, or in humid areas, cleaning the gun after use and then protecting it during storage is most important.

Light oiling of the bore for storage is necessary to preserve its accuracy. However, the oil must be removed before firing it again, as possible damage to the barrel could result.

The blued outside metal surfaces and inside parts also require cleaning and preserving. However, it is seldom necessary to completely disassemble a firearm for cleaning, unless used under extremely wet or snowy conditions.

A firearm must never be stored in a gun case or plastic bag. It is best to store a firearm in a dry and secure place, away from children, and preferably under lock and key, separate from ammunition. The moisture that is in the air gets trapped inside containers and will cause a firearm to rust.

The best source for cleaning equipment and firearm preservative material is the local gun shop. It usually has an assortment of items to choose from that will meet most requirements, and today's scientifically developed preservatives and lubricants are far superior to those of yesteryear.

Collectors who display their firearms have a problem different from those of the outdoor user of firearms. Theirs is mainly one of preservation during display and storage. For what feels like a hundred years, I have used RIG (Rust Inhibiting Grease) with great success. It is available at all good gun stores. A light coat will protect, and lasts a long time.

In the process of cleaning and oiling a firearm, there are two things to remember. First, if a firearm is taken from a warm

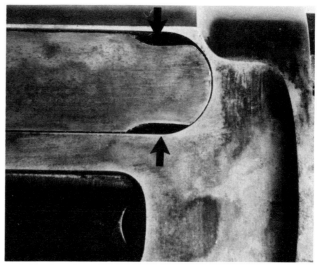

Arrows indicate the gas escape ports in pre-WW II square bolt lever action rifles.

area into the cold, any moisture may freeze. Also, oil or grease on the inside of the gun may congeal and result in the gun misfiring during cold weather. In fact, no oil on the inside of the bolt of a firearm is best when the weather is cold. Another problem with weather is that when it is cold outside and a cold firearm is taken inside where it is warm, condensation will form on the inside and outside of the gun, resulting in rust.

Condition. The National Rifle Association (NRA) has established, through its Firearms Collectors Committee and advice from both dealers and individual collectors, a set of standards that are recognized by everyone as being workable and understandable. Adhering to the following list of NRA condition standards, reprinted with the permission of the NRA, will eliminate misunderstandings during trades or sales, especially through the mail.

Factory New: All original parts; 100% original finish; in perfect condition in every respect, inside and out.

Excellent: All original parts; over 80% original finish; sharp lettering, numerals and design on metal and wood; unmarred wood; fine bore.

Fine: All original parts; over 30% original finish; sharp lettering, numerals and design on metal and wood; minor marks in wood; good bore.

Very Good: All original parts; none to 30% original finish; original metal surfaces smooth with all edges sharp; clear lettering, numerals and design on metal; wood slightly scratched or bruised; bore disregarded for collectors' firearms.

Good: Some minor replacement parts; metal smoothly rusted or lightly pitted in places, cleaned or reblued; principal lettering, numerals and design on metal legible; wood refinished, scratched, bruised or minor cracks repaired; in good working order.

Fair: Some major parts replaced; minor replacement parts may be required; metal rusted, may be lightly pitted all over, vigorously cleaned or reblued; rounded edges of metal and wood; principal lettering, numerals and design on metal partly obliterated; wood scratched, bruised, cracked or repaired where broken; in fair working order or can be easily repaired and placed in working order.

Poor: Major and minor parts replaced; major replacement parts required and extensive restoration needed; metal deeply pitted; principal lettering, numerals and design obliterated; wood badly scratched, bruised, cracked, or broken; mechanically inoperative; generally undesirable as a collector's firearm.

Handloading and Shooting Old Marlin Firearms. Some Marlin collectors and gun aficionados shoot their old firearms and are interested in handloading ammunition for the old guns. In fact, if they could not find or make ammunition to use in the gun, their interest would wane and some would turn to other makes and calibers with which to have their fun. Also, some Marlin collectors, as well as sportsmen, want to continue hunting with their old hunting gun. "If it was good enough for granddad then it must be good enough now" is their contention.

Marlin does not furnish handloading information for the old cartridges. Marlin also does not recommend that the obsolete pistols, rifles, and shotguns be kept in service, because there have been numerous accidents with old guns as a result of either mistakes made by the handloader or old guns in an unsafe condition being used. I agree with this position because Marlin has no knowledge of the condition of the gun, or its misuse or abuse. Marlin also has no way to test old guns for safety, or the parts to repair an old gun to make it safe. The same is generally true for the gun owner; he has no way to check the safety features of a gun, or to see if the metal of the gun has been weakened by age, misuse, or abuse.

An error in judgment can frequently be the cause of damage to a gun or injury to the user. Good examples of these problematic guns are the exposed hammer shotguns that sportsmen want to keep in service. Many of them are in poor condition and mechanically unsafe. It is my opinion that none of the pump action exposed hammer shotguns should be used, because, if internal parts are broken and safety features are not working, the gun can be fired unlocked. If this happens, it is possible for the bolt to be blown out of the gun.

If a person must use old and obsolete Marlin firearms, he should use care and caution and the standard references, and not guess or experiment. A few of the many references available are the following: *Cartridges of the World,* Frank C. Barnes (D.B.I. Books, Inc., Northfield, Ill.); *Handloading,* William C. Davis, Jr. (National Rifle Association of America, Washington, D.C.); *The Home Guide to Cartridge Conversions,* George C. Nonte, Jr. (Stackpole Books, Harrisburg, Pa.); *Lyman Cast Bullet Handbook* (Lyman Products Corp., Middlefield, Conn.); *Ken Waters' Pet Loads,* Ken Waters, (Wolfe Publishing Co. Inc., Prescott, Ariz.); *Speer Reloading Manual,* Speer (Omark Industries, Lewiston, Id.).

Marlin Firearms Characteristics. Frequently, the law enforcement crime laboratory firearm examiner needs to know the characteristics of a firearm to determine in what make and kind of a firearm a certain cartridge case was fired, or what signatures a firearm would leave on a cartridge that had functioned through its mechanism. To assist him in his identification, the following characteristics of modern Marlin firearms are listed:

Model	Firing Pin O'Clock Location	Shape	Extractor O'Clock Location	Ejector O'Clock Location
Autoloading .22s				
50	3 to 9	Bar		9
A1	6	Rec	3	9
88	12	Rd/Con	3	4
89	12	Rd/Con	3	3
98	12	Rd/Con	3	4
60/99 Marlin/Glenfield	6	Rec	3 & 9	8
49/40 Marlin/Glenfield	6	Rec	3 & 9	8
Bolt Action .22s				
80 Clip	12	Rd/Con	3 & 9	8
81 Tubular	12	Rd/Con	3 & 9	8
980 Clip (22 WMRF)	12	Rd/Con	3 & 9	8
780 Clip	12	Rd/Con	3 & 9	8
781 Tubular	12	Rd/Con	3 & 9	8
782 Clip (22 WMRF)	12	Rd/Con	3 & 9	8
783 Tubular (22 WMRF)	12	Rd/Con	3 & 9	8
880	11	Rec	3 & 9	8
881	11	Rec	3 & 9	8
882	11	Rec	3 & 9	8
883	11	Rec	3 & 9	8
25	11	Rec	3 & 9	8
25MB	11	Rec	3 & 9	8

Model	Firing Pin O'Clock Location	Firing Pin Shape	Extractor O'Clock Location	Ejector O'Clock Location
Bolt Action .22s cont'd.				
25M	11	Rec	3 & 9	8
100 Single-Shot	9	Rec	3	FP
101 Single-Shot	8:30	Rec	4:30	FP
15 Single-Shot	8:30	Rec	4:30	FP
122 Single-Shot	8:30	Rec	4:30	FP
10 Single-Shot/Glenfield	8:30	Rec	4:30	FP
Lever Action .22s				
56 Clip	12	Rec	3 & 9	8
57 Tubular	12	Rec	3 & 9	8
57 Tubular	12	Rec	3 & 9	8
39A, M Tubular	12	Rec/Con	3	9
Shotguns				
50 Glenfield	CF	Rd/Con	3 & 9	8 − 20, 16, 12 ga.
55 Marlin	CF	Rd/Con	3 & 9	8 − 20, 16, 12 ga.
120 Marlin	CF	Rd/Con	3 & 9:30	8 − 12 ga.
778 Glenfield	CF	Rd/Con	3 & 9:30	8 − 12 ga.
59, 60, 61, .410s	CF	Rd/Con	3	9 − .410
Center-fire Lever Actions				
336C, T, A	CF	Rd/Con	3	9
1894 − All	CF	Rd/Con	3	9
1895 .45−70	CF	Rd/Con	3	9
444	CF	Rd/Con	3	9
62	CF	Rd/Con	3 & 9	8

Note:

Rd = Round
Rec = Rectangle
Con = Convex
FP = Firing Pin
CF = Center-Fire

These data relate to the location of the firing pin, extractor, and ejector in the firearm when held in a normal shooting position with the muzzle forward and the butt to the rear.

Marlin Firearms Collectors Association. There is an active Marlin Collectors Association that mails out a periodical publication called *The Collector.* The group is about 350 dedicated collectors of various disciplines. Some collect only one type, such as lever actions of a certain model; others collect one of each model or only those that are factory engraved; and some collect only memorabilia, or "goodies," as they refer to them. A meeting is held each year in conjunction with one of the better gun shows. Nice Association awards are presented to the top displays, as well as show awards. A lot of trading also goes on. The address of the secretary–treasurer is:

Mr. Richard Paterson
407 Lincoln Building
44 Main Street
Champaign, IL 61820

Parts and Repairs. The Marlin Firearms Company is not capable of making repairs to the old antique firearms, or able to furnish any parts for them. There are no parts drawings or blueprints of the old parts and there is no known source for them. Also, Marlin does not have a custom shop that can make special barrels or variations of its catalog models on special order.

There are no parts or service available for the following discontinued models: Ballard rifles; pistols and revolvers; pump action rifles; pump action shotguns (prior to Model 120 & 778); L.C. Smith shotguns (prior to 1968); 1881; 1891; 1892/ 92; 1893/93; 1894/94, 1895/95; 1897/97; 1936/36; 50/50E; 56; 57; 57M; 59 shotgun; 60 shotgun; 61 shotgun; 62; 65; A1/A1E; 80C/80DL; 81C/81DL; 88/88E; 89/89E; 98/98E; 100; 122; 322; 422; 455; 980.

PRODUCTION YEARS BY MODEL

Model	Start	End
Ballard	1865	1880
1881	1881	1891
1888	1888	1889
1889	1889	1895
1891	1890	1897
1892	1895	1915
1893	1893	1934
1894	1894	1934
1895	1895	1914

Model	Start	End
1897	1896	1917
18	1906	1908
20	1907	1922
25	1909	1910
27	1909	1932
32, 29	1915	1915
38	1921	1930
39	1920	1937
37	1923	1931
47	1930	1931
50	1931	1935
65	1935	1937
80	1934	1971
A1	1936	1946
1936	1936	1937
100	1935	1959
81	1939	1971
39A	1938	1972
36	1937	1948
88	1948	1956
89	1948	1961
336	1948	1988
101	1941	1977
322	1954	1958
56	1955	1964
455	1956	1959
422	1956	1958
98	1957	1959
57	1959	1965
57M	1961	1969
99	1959	1978
122	1962	1965
980	1966	1971
62	1964	1969
989	1962	1965
989M2	1965	1978
444	1965	1970
49	1968	1978
99M1	1964	1978
40	1979	1979
990	1979	to date
995	1979	to date
70P	1986	to date
70HC	1986	to date
780	1971	1988
781	1971	1988
782	1971	1988
783	1971	1988
880	1988	to date
881	1988	to date
882	1988	to date
883	1988	to date
1898	1898	1905
16	1903	1910
17	1906	1908
19	1906	1907
21	1907	1908

Model	Start	End
24	1908	1917
Trap Gun	1909	1912
26	1909	1916
Field Gun	1911	1912
28	1913	1923
30	1911	1917
31 – 16 Gauge	1914	1917
31 – 20 Gauge	1911	1923
42	1922	1933
43	1922	1930
44	1922	1933
60	1923	1923
49	1928	1930
410	1929	1932
53	1929	1931
63	1931	1933
90	1936	1959
55	1954	1988
55GG	1962	1965
50	1966	1973
59	1959	1965
61G	1962	1962
60G	1960	1964
MK – I, II, IV	1960	1963
120	1971	1985
778	1979	1984
L.C. Smith	1968	1971

Requests for Factory Repair of Models in Production. Marlin states that if you want to return a gun for factory repair, follow these instructions:

1. Before shipping the gun, write to determine if parts and repair service are available.
2. Be absolutely certain the firearm is not loaded prior to mailing.
3. Pack the firearm carefully. Use ample cushioning material and a sturdy outer cardboard box. Do not ship in special container you want returned.
4. Remove accessories such as telescopes, scope mounts, gun cases, QD swivels, slings, and other items prior to shipping the firearm.
5. Attach a complete letter of information to the firearm. It should describe the model and serial number and a description of the damage or problem, and under what conditions the difficulty occurs. Also include your name and full address, not just a post office box number.
6. Clearly mark the outside of the box with your name and address.
7. If the firearm is not covered by warranty, Marlin will supply an estimate of the repair cost. Repairs will be made upon receipt of check or money order. If repairs are not possible, the gun will be returned.
8. Do not ship ammunition.
9. Ship your firearm by UPS or insured Parcel Post. Shipment must be prepaid and addressed to:

Marlin Gun Service
Attn: Repair Department
100 Kenna Drive
North Haven, CT 06473

10. There is a minimal service charge.

Requests for Historical Information. Unfortunately, Marlin records are not as complete as those of some other firearms companies. However, Marlin records for the period of 1883 to 1906 are quite good. Although information such as to whom a gun was shipped, or extra features such as engraving or special sights, is not listed. The records do list for the above period the model, caliber, barrel length, and date of shipment. Marlin will send a factory letter, at no charge, attesting to the limited data available.

For those basically interested in knowing when a firearm was manufactured, please see the section about serial numbers, as a breakdown by year is included there.

Retail Prices: Where possible, the new retail, or suggested retail, price of various models has been listed. However, it must be understood that suggested retail prices are only valid for a comparison between models and that they may, or may not, be the actual retail prices. A federal law precludes a manufacturer from establishing a retail price. The retailer is free to charge as little, or as much, as he feels his customers will pay. Manufacturers' suggested retail prices are only a guide, and are not generally followed closely by retail merchandisers.

Values. Values of Marlin firearms are explained below.

General. Collectors of both antique and modern Marlin firearms are cautioned against purchasing a pistol, rifle, or shotgun that is incomplete or needs a replacement part. Parts for the antique models and many of the modern models are nonexistent. Rarely can an original barrel, stock, or flat type of spring be found for the old ones, and Marlin cannot furnish drawings or parts, or make repairs to many of the discontinued later models. A collector is way ahead of the game if he will be choosy and only purchase complete representative models that do not need repair or parts.

The greatest sin of the new collector is to refinish and rework an old firearm. If he does, the collector's value of the gun will be diminished, if not gone completely.

Some restoration and replacement of parts can legitimately be done; however, care and caution must be exercised, otherwise the value of the item will be affected the wrong way.

A good, clean, complete gun in original used condition is of much greater value than one that has been shined up and refinished in an amateur way. The new collector would be wise to be patient and to save his money until he can afford a good representative item. One good gun is better than a dozen junkers.

Antique. The value of a firearm depends upon two things. The first is, of course, the rarity of the firearm, and the second is the condition of it. The combination of the two result in a market value. The market value can also be divided into two categories. The first is what a dealer, who will inventory the firearm and then sell it at a profit, will pay. The second is what

the firearm is worth to the collector (retail purchaser). Frequently, dealers and collectors are poles apart. Some dealers will dicker on the price and others will hold firm, usually knowing what the item is worth and that there is that one person who will pay his price because of exceptional rarity or super condition.

Serious collectors should study prices listed in sales catalogs, auction catalogs, magazine ads, and prices displayed at gun shows. They must then compare the price of the item they are interested in with what they and their family can afford. Purchases should be considered an investment and should have some potential for monetary growth. Reckless spending, just to own something, should be avoided. Each purchase should have a purpose and emotions should be held in check. (Sometimes this cannot be done at auctions.)

There is no single reference that lists current values. A value book or reference is no more than in print when it is outdated. Therefore the values listed can only be used as a guide. Also, the description of condition, by comparison with a factory-new firearm, can be in error because of the mental picture the reader develops, based on the writer's discourse. Unfortunately, sellers, both dealer and collector, frequently overrate the item they have for sale with regard to its originality and its condition. If purchases are through the mail, a 5-day return privilege should be agreed upon.

Two references that include values for the old Marlin rifles, pistols, and shotguns, are *Flayderman's Guide to Antique American Firearms, and Their Values* (DBI Books Inc., Northbrook, Ill. 60062, 1987) and *Blue Book of Gun Values,* S.P. Fjestad (Investment Rarities, Inc., Minneapolis, Minn. 55420).

Modern. The used-gun values of Marlin firearms manufactured since 1924 are dependent upon condition and scarcity. With few exceptions, the modern models were manufactured by the thousands. However, there are some that are considered collectible by a small group of Marlin collectors who collect only the modern variations. Two references that may be of help to those interested are *Modern Gun Values,* Jack Lewis (DBI Books, Inc., Northbrook, Ill. 60062, 1987) and *Gun Traders Guide,* Paul Wahl, (Stoeger Publishing Co., So. Hackensack, N.J., 1986).

Glenfield Products

There is some confusion about the name Glenfield and its relationship with The Marlin Firearms Company. A short explanation here should help settle once and for all the rumors and innuendos that have been quoted and misquoted for years.

The name Glenfield started when Roger Kenna in the 1950s formed the Glenfield Products Division, as a solely owned subsidiary of Marlin. The division was a paper organization that had an address the same as the Marlin office in New York City. The original purpose of the Glenfield operation was to handle all Marlin matters with mass-merchandisers, chain outlets, and brand-name models. By so doing, the two marketing fields, distributors versus the big outfits, could be evaluated, and concentration and cost of doing business could be determined better. For a few years, this system resulted in the impression that there were two different companies making fire-arms, when, in fact, they were both one.

The Glenfield Products Company was dissolved and a separate line of models was given the Glenfield name. At first, the only identifier of the economy models was a *G* suffix to the model number. Later, the Glenfield models had their own model numbers.

The practice of the large arms manufacturers having a separate name to identify the less expensive models, or models sold through mass-merchandisers, has been universal. For example, Remington has used Mohawk, Savage has used Springfield and Stevens, Winchester has used Ranger, and Mossberg has used New Haven.

Some sportsmen have been misled to believe that the economy models of a company were manufactured from inferior material, or that the firearm was a reject being sold as a "second." Nothing is further from the truth. For example, Marlin Glenfield models had the same mechanism as the Marlin models. Usually the only difference between the two was in the type of wood—birch versus walnut—and the sights fitted to the gun. Some of Marlin's best bargains were in the Glenfield line. For example, the Glenfield Model 30A was the best utility lever action center-fire carbine on the market. It was in direct competition with the Marlin 336 models.

For many years mass-merchandisers wanted their products to have a name exclusive to them, for example, Sears' use of Ranger- and J.C. Higgins-marked firearms. Montgomery Ward, Western Auto, Speigel Company, J.C. Penney, Cotter & Company, Coast to Coast Stores, and others wanted their own model numbers and special features. Some of this is still done; however, a recent switch of the large outlets is back toward selling "name" items. By so doing, they take advantage of the good name of the company manufacturing the product, and the millions of dollars spent in promoting that name.

As a result of the general switch away from having a different name for an economy line, Marlin discontinued the use of the Glenfield name in 1983. However, some of the model designations were continued as Marlin models. Two examples: the Model 60 and Model 30A.

From 1960 to 1983, the following Glenfield models were manufactured and marketed by Marlin:

Years	Model	Type
1960–1961	Model 60G	single-barrel .410 shotgun
1960–1965	Model 100G	caliber .22 single-shot rifle
1960–1965	Model 80G	caliber .22 bolt action rifle
1960–1965	Model 81G	caliber .22 bolt action rifle
1961–1965	Model 55G	bolt action shotgun
1962	Model 61G	single-barrel .410 shotgun
1962–1964	Model 989G	caliber .22 autoloading rifle
1963–1964	Model 60G	single-barrel .410 shotgun
1963–1965	Model 99G	caliber .22 semiautomatic rifle
1964–1965	Model 36G	caliber .30–30 lever action rifle
1966–1970	Model 30	caliber .30–30 lever action rifle
1966–1977	Model 20	caliber .22 clip magazine, bolt action rifle

Years	Model	Type
1966–1978	Model 10	caliber .22 single-shot rifle
1966–1979	Model 50	12-gauge bolt action shotgun
1966–1982	Model 60	caliber .22 semiautomatic rifle
1966–1982	Model 70	caliber .22 semiautomatic rifle
1971–1983	Model 30A	caliber .30–30 lever action rifle
1977–1981	Model 20	caliber .22 bolt action rifle
1979	Model 40	caliber .22 semiautomatic rifle
1979–1982	Model 15	caliber .22 single-shot rifle
1979–1980	Model 30GT	caliber .30–30 lever action rifle
1979–1982	Model 778	12-gauge pump action shotgun
1982	Model 25	caliber .22 bolt action rifle
1983	Model 30AS	caliber .30-30 lever action rifle

The disposition of the Glenfield models was as follows:

10 Glenfield, now discontinued
15 Glenfield became Marlin Model 15Y
20 Glenfield, now discontinued
25 Glenfield became Marlin Model 25, now discontinued
30 Glenfield became 30A Glenfield, now Marlin 30A
30GT Glenfield, discontinued after two years
36G became 30 Glenfield, now Marlin Model 30A
40 Glenfield, discontinued after one year
50 Glenfield, discontinued
55G became 50 Glenfield, now discontinued
60 Glenfield, now Marlin 60
60 Glenfield shotgun, discontinued
61 Glenfield, discontinued after one year
65 Glenfield, now discontinued
70 Glenfield, now Marlin 70
75C Glenfield, now Marlin 75C
80G, became 25 Glenfield, now Marlin 25
81G, discontinued
99G became 60 Glenfield, now Marlin 60
100G became 10 Glenfield, now Marlin 15
778 became Marlin 778, now discontinued
989G, became Marlin Model 995

Grip Cap

In 1950, in addition to adding a white line spacer to the buttstock, Marlin added a special pistol grip cap with a white line spacer to the Model 39A and Model 336.

The unique feature of this grip cap was explained in the catalog as follows:

> As long as materials are available, Model 39As and all High-Power Repeaters will be equipped with an attractive medallion on the pistol grip cap on which owner's initials—up to three letters—may be engraved. See instruction envelope tied to trigger guard for details.

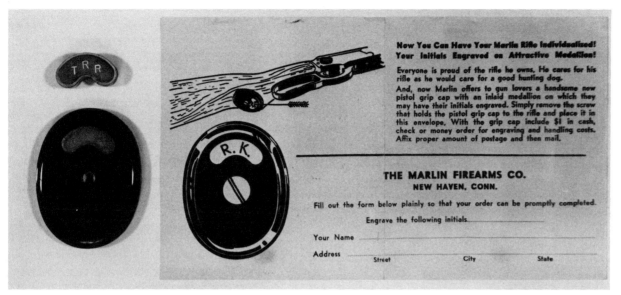

Pistol grip cap, engraved insert (TRR-Thomas R. Robinson, director of R&D and R.K.-Roger Kenna, president), and card attached to new Model 336 rifles.

This project started in February 1949, but finding the source for the plastic cap took a long time. Added delay also resulted from trying to find a vendor that could make the powdered metal (sintered) insert. After many quotations from at least four vendors for each part, General Electric and Seymour Products made the tooling and 50,000 pieces each at a total cost of $6,518.00, or 13.04 cents for each pistol grip cap. This price did not include the price of the screw, advertising, packing, or labor to install the cap, or the costs of engraving it and returning it to the owner.

Very few examples of Marlin lever action rifles of the 1950–1951 period are in the used gun market. The reason must be that the added personal touch of engraved initials in the grip cap has encouraged the sportsman to keep his own Marlin in the family and not to trade or sell it.

The individualized grip cap was only available during 1951 and 1952. In 1953, a grip cap was not mentioned in catalogs; however, the white line spacer added to the butt plate was retained and is still on some models to this day.

Gun Cases and Cartridge Belts

From 1899 to 1915, Marlin listed among the extras for its shotgun line a "Victoria" gun case. It was described as a canvas case of good quality, leather bound. It was priced from $1.40 to $1.50, depending on the year.

From 1906 to 1911, Marlin illustrated two new cases, which were in addition to the rifle case and Victoria case listed in the extras for rifles and shotguns. The catalog stated:

> We can furnish cases to fit the rifles and shotguns made by us, either in take-down style or full length. These cases are made of a good quality canvas, leather reinforced, and have a handle for carrying. They are lined with flannel and make a good serviceable case. Price of take-down case – $1.40; Price of full length case – $1.40.

The 1906 to 1911 catalogs also stated:

> We have in stock cases to fit any of our standard length rifles or guns; if case is wanted for a special gun, we can furnish it at the same price, but will be obliged to make up the case, which will require a few days' time.
>
> We can furnish leather cases of any length or style made. These cases are not carried in stock, and are made only to order. Price depending on quality of leather and style of finish, $5.00 and up.

The 1911 to 1915 catalogs, in addition to the previously mentioned takedown case, full-length case, Victoria case, and rifle case added a leg-o-mutton-style case for $5.00, and a takedown, straight-line-style case for $7.00. Both of these cases were all leather, flannel-lined, brass-trimmed, and with lock and key. These two leather cases, the previously described 1906 to 1911 cases, the canvas rifle case, and Victoria shotgun case also remained in the extra listings until 1915.

A word of caution to the gun collector and sportsman: *DO NOT STORE FIREARMS IN GUN CASES OR CLOSED CONTAINERS.* Condensation of moisture can take place in gun cases and containers if a firearm is not fully protected with a preservative. The best method is to lightly oil firearms and store them in a dry place where the air can circulate.

From 1889 to 1894, a Morocco case for Marlin double-

Early catalog illustration of a gun case and a cartridge belt available on order from Marlin.

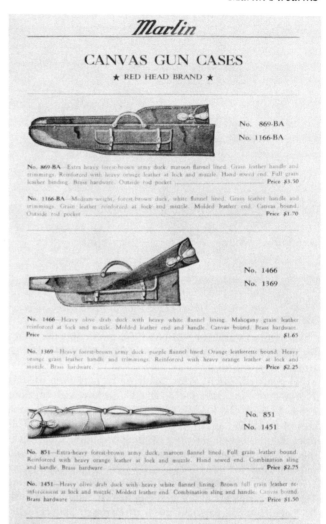

1911–1915 catalog information about gun cases and cartridge belts.

1934–1936 parts catalog page advertising gun cases that could be ordered from Marlin.

action revolvers was listed in catalogs. It was priced at $3.50 in 1889, and $3.75 in 1894.

With the introduction of the model 1897 lever action caliber .22 bicycle rifle, Marlin cataloged a takedown canvas case, leather bound, complete with straps, of proper form to fit securely within the diamond frame of a bicycle. It was priced at $1.75 in 1897 and, when last listed in 1915, was $1.50.

Marlin again listed gun cases for sale in its parts catalog

Southwick Gun, Oar, and Rod Rest.

during 1934 to 1936. The cases were manufactured by the makers of RED HEAD-brand hunting clothes. There were four styles of takedown cases and two styles of full-length cases. Prices ranged from $1.65 to a high $3.50 for the best extra-heavy army duck case, which had a leather handle and trimmings.

In the 1886 catalog, Marlin listed the Mills woven cartridge belt for $1.25. In 1887, the Mills belt was dropped, and a leather cartridge belt with loops was listed for $1.25. In 1888, Marlin listed both the Mills and leather cartridge belts at $1.25 each.

Gun, Oar, and Rod Rest

In the 1936 parts catalog, along with gun cases, recoil pads, Lyman and Marble sights, razor blades, slings, and swivels, Marlin advertised the "Southwick Gun, Oar and Rod Rest," which could be easily attached to or removed from the side of a boat. For the hunter, the rest would protect the gun from damage and make it readily available. For the fisherman, it kept the rod and reel high and dry and kept them from damage. For the boat user, the oars could be kept from dripping inside the boat by reversing the brackets.

Southwick rests made of enameled metal sold for $1.00 a set. Rubber-encased metal sets sold for $2.50.

Gun Rack

Marlin sold a wooden knockdown gun rack that would hold four firearms vertically. It had a small storage compartment at the bottom. Assembled, it was 7½ inches deep by 21 inches wide and 4 feet high. It was shipped with easy-to-follow instructions, and could be painted or stained to fit the individual's wish. It sold to dealers for $13.65 and had a suggested retail value of $19.95. About 1,000 were sold during the post-WW II period.

A wood and a metal gun rack were also made up for sales personnel and distributors to use when displaying Marlin firearms at trade and dealer shows. Neither was made in large quantities.

Hammer Spur

When some telescopes are low-mounted on the top of Marlin Models 336, 30, 30A, 39A, 39M, and Marlin's brand-named exposed hammer center-fire rifles, there is interference between the bottom of the telescope and the thumb on top of the hammer spur during the process of cocking the hammer, or when placing the hammer in the half-cock safe position.

To overcome some of this interference, Marlin initially lowered the height of the spur. Then in 1956, after the Williams Gun Sight Company developed an offset extension for the hammer, Marlin designed an offset extension and modified hammer that have been in use ever since. The extension can be installed for either left- or right-hand use. It is recommended that the extension be removed when a telescope is not being used.

There are five different variations of the Marlin device. Made from a black anodized aluminum extrusion, the first offering, in November 1956, was packaged in a small cardboard box. It sold for $2.95 and included an Allen wrench, which was used to tighten the set screw holding the spur to the hammer. This first type had the initials *JM* in an oval embossed into the flat on top. The embossing was filled with white paint.

By early 1958, the offset hammer spur was included with the gun at no additional cost. The second type was furnished with the brand name and Glenfield models; it was identical to the

Marlin knockdown gun rack sold to sportsmen.

Wooden gun rack used by dealers and salesmen.

Metal gun rack used at gun and trade shows.

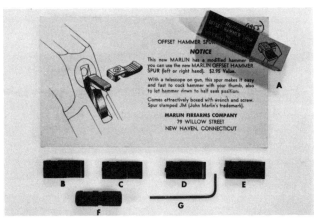

A. First type of packaging for Marlin offset hammer spur. B. Second type of hammer spur furnished with all brand-name lever actions. C. JM-marked first type of offset spur. D. Third type of spur with additional cross-hatching on finger piece. E. Fourth type of spur, which has serrations added to top part of spur. F. Round-type hammer spur furnished with center-fire lever action rifles after inclusion of cross-bolt safety. G. Allen wrench used to tighten or loosen binding screw.

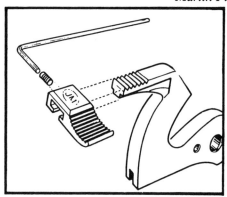

MARLIN OFF-SET HAMMER SPUR

For the Marlin Models Golden 39-A, Golden 39-A Mountie and all the high-power lever action Marlin 336's The Marlin Firearms Co. is manufacturing a modified hammer that takes a newly designed off-set hammer spur. With a low mounted scope on a rifle, the spur makes it easy and fast to cock the hammer with your thumb and to let the hammer down to half-cock position. Marlin's new removable off-set hammer spur may be used for right-handed and left-handed shooting. The spur comes individually packed with wrench and screw. The new spur will not fit the old type hammers.

Retail price of the Marlin off-set hammer spur is $2.95

Catalog illustration and text of offset hammer spur that originally sold for $2.95.

Packaging of new round type of offset hammer spur.

first except that it did not have *JM* embossed into the top surface. The third type of spur had added cross-hatch serrations on the finger piece, and the fourth type had additional serrations on the top surface that covered the spur of the hammer. The third and fourth types also were not marked with the *JM* of the first type.

A hammer spur and wrench are now furnished free with every lever action exposed hammer rifle Marlin manufactures. To ensure that the gun owner receives them, the pieces are packaged in an envelope with instructions for attachment; this is affixed to the inside flap of the carton in which the gun is packed. Marlin warns all users of exposed hammer lever action rifles equipped with a telescopic sight to use the offset hammer spur for ease of operation and safety, and to remove it if a telescope is not used.

When Marlin introduced the cross-bolt safety into the center-fire lever action models in 1982, a wider hammer was also introduced. The old offset hammer spur would not fit the new hammer; therefore, a new design of offset spur was developed. It is a close copy (with the manufacturer's permission) of the commercially available "Uncle Mike's" offset spur, which is cylindrical.

Marlin includes the new offset spur in the box in which each lever action rifle is packed. It too is enclosed in an envelope along with the Allen wrench used to install and remove the spur. The envelope is printed with instructions and glued to the carton.

Purchasers of Marlin rifles should insist that the dealer furnish them the owner's manual and offset hammer spur that

Marlin has included with the rifle to ensure safe use of the firearm. The purchaser should also understand the instructions furnished by Marlin and should follow the printed warnings, cautions, and rules for safe gun handling. If the purchaser did not receive the owner's manual or offset hammer spur, he should contact The Marlin Firearms Company, 100 Kenna Drive, North Haven, Conn. 06473 and request that he be furnished the missing items.

Handcuffs

During the years 1885 to 1888 and 1911 to 1915, Marlin manufactured and sold handcuffs that were patented by Robert H. Daley. His patent number 222,252 was issued December 2, 1879; however Marlin did not list the handcuffs in catalogs until 1885.

The Los Angeles, Calif., police and many other law enforce-

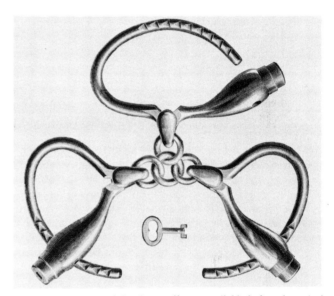

Catalog illustration of the three-cuff type available before the swivel was added between the two cuffs.

Top: *Swivel-type Daley handcuffs.* Center: *Unique key used to open Daley handcuffs.* Bottom: *First type of Daley handcuffs.*

R.H. Daley patent illustration of the handcuffs Marlin manufactured.

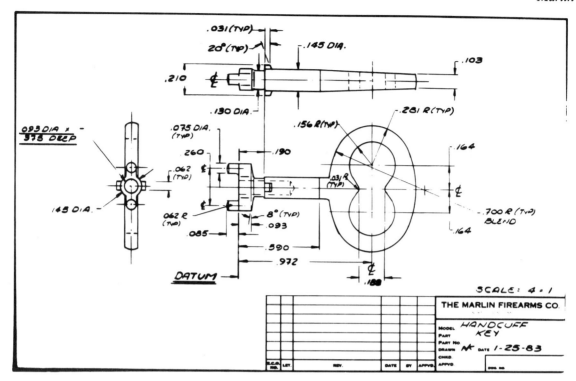

Drawing made by averaging the measurements taken from a number of Daley handcuff keys.

ment agencies purchased the Daley handcuffs. Known examples having the Canadian *C* and broad arrow are in handcuff collections, and reports received by Marlin as late as 1980 indicated that some of these cuffs were still in service at that time.

Three types of cuffs were available. The earliest had two cuffs connected by a link chain which could be used as a "come-along." The second type had a swivel between the cuffs. The third type had three cuffs, the third one being attached in the center of the connecting links of a regular pair.

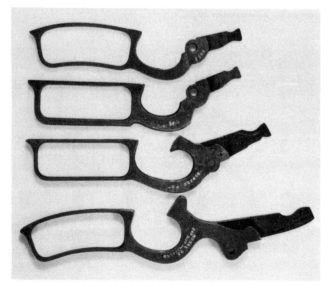

Levers for the Model 1891, 1892, 1894, and 1895 that were used by inspectors for comparison with production parts.

The Daley handcuffs with the swivel could also be ordered for 75¢ extra with a steel ring attached to the swivel through which a chain could be passed.

Marlin cataloged the Daley cuffs polished for $3.75, and nickel-plated for $4.45. Extra keys were 40¢ each.

Inspection

The full story of the inspection of Marlin firearms would require a book in itself. However, it is important to the sportsman and collector to know that every operation on every part is inspected at one time or another. Some operations are 100% inspected, others are inspected on a sample basis. Some inspections are done by the machine operator in addition to being done by a department inspector. In the J.M. Marlin and Ballard days, gauges required a judgment call by the inspector. He checked the part using a hole, thread, profile, or plug gauge. It was his judgment as to whether the part looked, felt, or fit right when he checked it with his gauge. Later techniques included "go" and "no go" gauges that eliminated the judgment call of the inspector or operator. The part either met the gauge requirements or was scrap. Today's methods use comparators, hardness testers, electronic gauges, lasers, micrometers, microscopic analysis, and functional testing that includes proof firing with a high pressure cartridge, function firing, targeting, and manual inspection for operation and cosmetic flaws.

The finished firearm was also checked by a final inspector. To show the extent of inspection conducted, two lists follow. They were used from 1926 to 1934, and show how many things were checked to ensure that the firearm was functional and safe.

RIFLE CODE

1. Doesn't feed
2. Doesn't eject
3. Doesn't extract
4. Stubs on bottom of chamber
5. Stubs on top of chamber
6. Stubs on left of chamber
7. Stubs on right of chamber
8. Misfires
9. Firing pin hits chamber
10. Cartridge's head catches on ejector slot
11. Inaccurate
12. Magazine spring broken
13. Locks hard on cartridge's head
14. Action works too hard
15. Firing pin broken
16. Does not stay locked
17. Long cartridge doesn't work up through action
18. Bolt doesn't line up with chamber
19. Doesn't breech up tight enough
20. Cartridges come one-half in action
21. Opens hard after shooting
22. Doesn't feed 1st cartridge
23. Takes down too hard
24. Tight action
25. Cartridges drop off bolt
26. Chamber rough
27. Lets in two cartridges
28. Hammer binds
29. Sears don't work

Shotgun and rifle head space gauges used to check the breach of firearms to ensure correct chambering.

30. Cartridge's head hangs on flipper
31. Cartridge's head hangs on flipper slot
32. Doesn't feed in well
33. Loose takedown
34. Cartridges jump out of action
35. Magazine pulls up too hard
36. Safety works too hard
37. Cartridges go up under extractors hard
38. Mainspring broken
39. Misfires holding back on slide
40. Doesn't eject quickly enough
41. Trigger creeps
42. Takedown doesn't hold
43. Action catches closing up
44. Cartridges hang on cutoff coming up
45. Ejects too hard
46. Cartridges don't come up on carrier well
47. Bolt doesn't push cartridge back in magazine

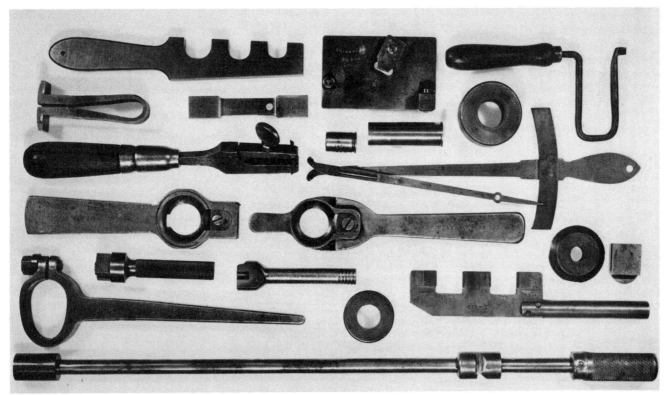

Various old Marlin tools and gauges used in the production and inspection of Marlin firearms.

48. Locking bolt plunger stuck
49. Cartridge guide broken
50. Magazine latch spring broken
51. Extractor cuts scratch shell
52. Long cartridges hang on magazine hole coming up

SHOTGUN CODE MODELS 42A, 43A, 44A

1. Buttstock cracked
2. Opens hard after shooting
3. Buttstock damaged
4. Cartridges come halfway in
5. Butt plate broken
6. Does not feed
7. Does not eject
8. Does not extract
9. Does not unlock
10. Does not unlock holding back
11. Does not unlock with heavy load
12. Does not unlock closing easily
13. Extractor cuts in barrel
14. Feeds out from under
15. Firing pin does not lock
16. Forearm loose
17. Front firing pin sticks
18. Firing pin broken
19. Forearm cracked
20. Hangs on cutoff
21. Handle slide thick
22. Lets in two cartridges
23. Lock nut over too far
24. Magazine shoots up
25. Misfires
26. Magazine loose on barrel stud
27. Stubs on right of chamber
28. Stubs on left of chamber
29. Stubs on bottom of chamber
30. Shells hang on receiver
31. Sear trips too early
32. Sear does not hold
33. Locking latch does not hold

34. Safety latch broken
35. Right action
36. Recoil does not hold
37. Sight shoots out
38. Extractor cuts in receiver
39. Hammer follows bolt
40. Hammer doesn't fall holding back on slide
41. Cartridge guide hangs on bolt
42. Latch sticks
43. Trigger creeps
44. Safety works too hard
45. Hangs on slide
46. Hangs on cutoff and release coming up on carrier
47. Hangs on magazine hole coming up on carrier
48. Latch does not hold closing easily
49. Slide does not stay up
50. Slide goes in link too hard
51. Opens hard with magazine full of cartridges
52. Magazine does not snap locked
53. Magazine does not line up with receiver
54. Tube stud screw missing
55. Tube band loose
56. Breeches up too tight
57. Breeches up too loose
58. Cartridges go under extractors hard
59. Cartridges do not get under extractors coming up
60. Slide shoots up

Today, a similar procedure is followed. In addition, Marlin attaches the owner's manual to the firearm and admonishes the dealer with printing on the packing box that the manual be furnished to the ultimate consumer. The box is also sealed, and inspected before sealing to ensure that the manual is enclosed.

Johnson Rifle

A short while after the Springfield Armory-designed M1 rifle (Garand) was adopted as the standard service rifle for the U.S. military forces, Melvin M. Johnson, Jr. (Captain, USMC Reserve) offered a new design of rifle that he claimed to be

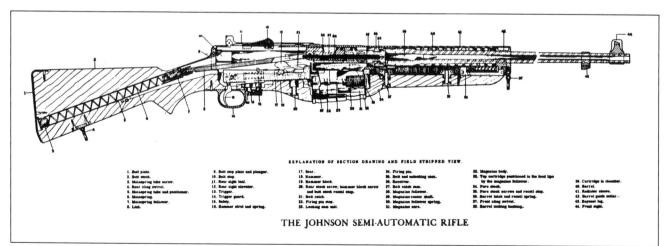

THE JOHNSON SEMI-AUTOMATIC RIFLE

Drawing of Johnson semiautomatic rifle showing the respective parts and pieces for which Marlin had design and prototype responsibilities.

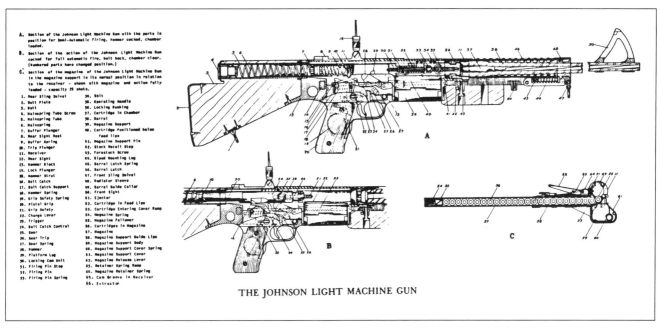

THE JOHNSON LIGHT MACHINE GUN

Johnson light machine gun, for which Marlin had early design and prototype responsibilities.

better than the new M1 rifle. There were many military and political charges and countercharges with regard to which was the superior rifle. The M1 won out, and proved itself during WW II and Korea as the finest infantry rifle ever.

Interesting to the Marlin collector is the fact that Melvin M. Johnson, Jr.'s semiautomatic rifle, caliber .30, Mark I and his light machine gun, caliber .30, Mark I had design help from Marlin engineers, and the first prototypes of both models were manufactured by Marlin.

Mr. Johnson described his recoil operated military rifle as follows:

> The rifle was invented and the first working model made during the summer of 1936. Patents were taken out the same year. The basic action is a short recoil rotary bolt system with 8 lugs and unlocking by the rearward movement of the slide-ably, mounted barrel. Unlocking is accomplished by cams on the bolt working in a cam chamber and channel in the top of the receiver.
>
> During the development of the rifle, a light machine gun operating on the same basic principle was also designed and patented.
>
> The rifle is 45½ inches long, and weighs approximately 9½ pounds. It is a rotary feed type with 11-shot capacity loaded from standard Model 1903 rifle 5-shot clips.

Melvin Johnson founded a company (Johnson Automatics) to market his guns. Some work was done by Universal Winding Company of Providence, R.I., and part by Johnson Automatics Manufacturing Company, which occupied space in the Winding company's buildings. A brochure published by Melvin Johnson that illustrates and describes the prototype rifle is dated October 1936 (last revision, January 26, 1938); and one for the prototype light machine gun is dated November 8, 1937 (last revision, January 27, 1938). Both state: "Manufactured for Johnson Automatics, Inc. by Marlin Firearms Co., New Haven, CT."

Johnson clip-magazine short-recoil rifle made by Marlin for R.H. Johnson.

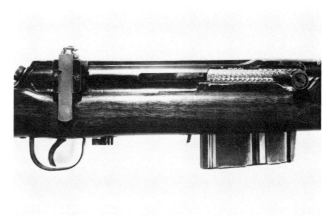

Receiver markings on Johnson semiautomatic rifle.

Another Johnson rifle manufactured by Marlin for Melvin Johnson is a caliber .30–06 semiautomatic, clip magazine, short-recoil-operated rifle that is illustrated here. There are few facts known about this rifle; it does not have the rotary magazine of Johnson's military model (Model 1941) that was used by the Netherlands and the U.S. Marine Corps, and it is checkered and stocked more like a sporting rifle. On the receiver of this well-made rifle is stamped:

JOHNSON SEMI-AUTOMATIC
CAL. .30
MARLIN FIREARMS CO.
NEW HAVEN. CONN.

Key Chain

Marlin has had made and distributed two different key chains as an advertising gimmick. The first is a real collector's item

Top: *Obverse of early Marlin key chain.* Bottom: *Reverse of above.*

1960 and 1966 screwdriver/key chains.

and is seldom found. It is a miniature of the receiver and buttstock of a hammer-type shotgun. On one side is *MARLIN REPEATERS, THE GUN FOR THE MAN WHO KNOWS.* On the other is *Marlin Firearms Co. NEW HAVEN, CONN.* The word *Firearms* being in one word and the slogan "The gun for the man who knows" place this item around 1905. Attached to the plated brass shotgun replica is a chain loop, and a folding latch that allows keys to be placed on or taken off the chain.

The second type of key chain given away by Marlin was the classic beaded chain and four-way circular pocket screwdriver that has been used, at one time or another, by most arms companies, as well as other companies wanting an inexpensive giveaway.

Marlin was not an exception and gave away two different variations of the screwdriver/key chain. Both variations were of highly polished steel. The first of this type of key chain was given away during 1960, the 90th anniversary of Marlin. On one side, in the center of the 1¼-in. round disk, was *90th YEAR* and a 39A rifle. *MARLIN-FIREARMS CO./Micro Groove Rifling* was stamped in a circle around the edge. The other side had *MARLIN GUNS SINCE 1870* and a Model 39A rifle embossed on it.

The second issue of the four-bladed screwdriver/key chain had *MARLIN 1870* on one side and the Marlin horse and rider logo on the other side. This second type was first ordered in 1966 and was reordered in 1967. A total of 250,112 were given away with catalogs and at NRA and trade shows.

Letter Opener

A brass-handled German silver letter opener was distributed as a gift to friends and business associates by Marlin. The period of time is unknown; however, the words "solid top-side ejection" and picture of an open bolt on the letter opener were used with the slogan "The sign of a Marlin" from 1908 until about 1915.

The letter openers were made in Soligen, Germany. The brass handle pieces were riveted to the blade. They are rare items seldom found today.

Lever Action Shotgun

In early 1956, a Levermatic center-fire rifle was on the drawing board, and a shotgun combining the new Levermatic mechanism with the magazine and barrel of the Model 55 bolt action shotgun was being considered. A prototype shotgun was

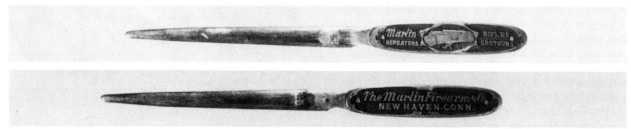

Top: *Obverse of Marlin letter opener.* Bottom: *Reverse of same.*

fabricated; however, no further efforts were made to produce this new shotgun, as it was considered to be too cumbersome and much too heavy. The project was dropped on April 9, 1957 after a great deal of research and development time and test effort went into the project.

Lighter

In the 1960s, Marlin gave away to customers and friends a cigarette lighter that was made in Japan and marked *Crown Design Reg'd*. The lighter body was a long oval, 2½"x ⅜", and was painted with red enamel. On one side was the name *Marlin,* the bull's-eye trademark, and *Fine Guns Since 1870.* On the other side was an illustration of a Marlin 39A. Of course, it was the old flint and wick type that didn't work well in the wind. How many were distributed is unknown. They are now scarce.

Lightweights

In 1897, Marlin added to its regular Model 1893 rifle and carbine models a "Special Light Weight Rifle." The catalog stated:

> We furnish rifles of this style with 18 and 20 inch barrels, short forearm, short magazine and special light weight barrel. The weight of such a rifle with 20 inch barrel in .30 caliber is 6½ pounds; in .38–55 caliber, 6¼ pounds. These rifles are very convenient inasmuch as they can be packed in the length of the barrel.

The catalog listed the prices for the Model 1893 as follows:

Extra for Special Lightweight $6.00
Extra for Take-down 4.00
Price of Special Light Weight Rifle, with stock
  of fine imported walnut, London oil finish, stock
  and forearm finely checked — with length of
  barrel up to 26 inches, Take-Down in .25–36 or
  .30–30 caliber, straight grip 36.60
With pistol grip 41.95
In .32–40 and .38–55 calibers, straight grip 34.50
With pistol grip stock 39.85

Marlin cigarette lighter given away during the 1960s to advertise the name of Marlin.

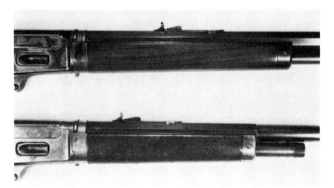

Lightweight forearm (bottom) *shown in comparison with standard forearm.*

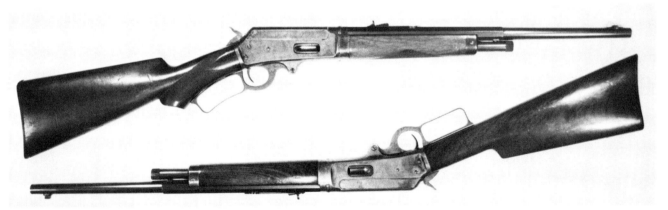

Pair of Model 1893 Lightweights. One has a pistol grip stock, and the other has a straight stock. Both are takedown. (JB)

Model 1895 Lightweight, serial number 148,384. (DS)

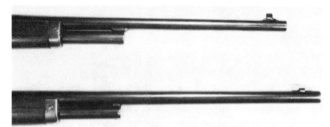

Lightweight Model 1895 (top) *shown in comparison with standard rifle.*

Top: *Standard Model 1895 saddle ring carbine.* Bottom: *Model 1895 Lightweight. Arrows point to narrower-than-standard receiver flanges of some lightweight Model 1895s.*

Rebated lever of Model 1895 Lightweight.

Left: *Rear end of bolt on standard Model 1895.* Right: *Bolt on lightweight Model 1895. The bolt has more metal removed than the standard model bolt.*

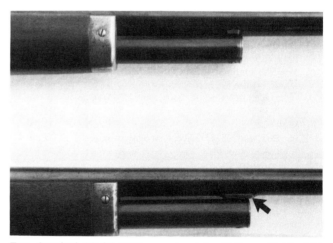

Top: *Standard Model 1896 magazine tube.* Bottom: *Lightweight Model 1895 magazine tube.*

The 1912 information about the special lightweight Model 1895 added the following information:

The powerful New Model 1895 .33 or .45–70 caliber; high power Marlin rifle; Special Light Weight; 24″ round, Special Smokeless Steel barrel; half magazine, shotgun rubber butt plate; 5 shots; weight about 7½ pounds for .33 caliber and 6⅞ pounds for .45–70.

August 1912 supplement to 1911 catalog, showing Model 1895 Special Lightweight.

Price of solid frame rifle $18.50
Price of take-down rifle 22.00

The illustrations included here of the Model 1893 and 1895 lightweight rifles show the characteristics of each. The Model 1895's light barrel, reduced front and rear receiver flanges, and lightened lever and bolt were its major changes. The shortened barrel, forearm, and magazine tube made the noticeable weight difference in the Model 1893 from the standard model. Both 1893 and 1895 models are scarce, with the 1895 model being especially so.

All lightweights have the regular rifle forearm tip and should not be confused with the regular carbine that has a band attaching the forearm to the barrel.

The Model 1893 lightweight forearms average about 6¹³⁄₁₆ inches long, whereas the standard rifle forearm is about 8⁷⁄₁₆ inches in length. The 1895 rifle forearm is 8⅜ inches long. The length of the lightweight model forearm is also 8⅜ inches.

Both the Model 1893 and Model 1895 lightweights have hard rubber butt plates.

The number of lightweight rifles produced can not be determined from the existing records. But the number observed in collections indicates to me that not many were manufactured.

Loading Tube

As an accessory to the Model 1891 caliber .22 side-loading rifle, Marlin listed in catalogs from 1892 to 1894 a loading tube that facilitated loading the magazine of the Model 1891 rifle and Colt .22 caliber repeating rifles.

The tube was 9¼ inches long, weighed 5 ounces, and held 10 cartridges. It was priced at 75¢.

The catalog description of the loading tube was the following:

This implement is a great convenience when it is desired to load a large number of cartridges into a .22 caliber Repeating rifle in a short space of time. It is especially recommended for gallery use. In filling the tube, it is not necessary to count the cartridges, as by means of a graduated slot in the side the exact number in the tube is plainly indicated.

The recommended procedure to operate the loading tube was as follows:

Lay the rifle down so that the loading hole shall be on top. Drop the cartridge, bullet first, into the tube at the plain end. Hold the tube in the left hand at a 30° angle to the bore of the

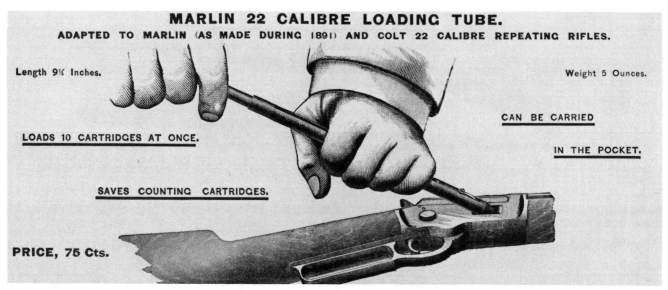

Catalog illustration of Marlin loading tube.

rifle, and press the bevel end down on the bevel of the side cover, causing the side cover to open. The tube should not be pressed against the front edge of the loading hole, but held back at least one-eighth of an inch from it. Hold the tube firmly and press the cartridges into the magazine with the rod. Before removing the implement, swing it to a position at right angles to the rifle, and push the head of the last cartridge into the receiver. These loaders are put up in a neat cardboard box. They can be sent by mail and are for sale by all dealers and by the Marlin Firearms Co., New Haven, Conn.

Magazine Tubes

The standard length of most of the early magazine tubes was the full length of the barrel. But short and half magazines could be special-ordered for some models at the same price as for a full-length magazine. A review of the catalog information about the different lengths of magazines available is as follows:

Catalog	Model	Magazine
1883	1881	All models can be furnished with half magazines holding 4 shots at same price
1885	1881	.32 and .38 calibers can be furnished with half magazine at same price as full length
1887	1881	Same
1888	1881	Same

Model 1881 with full-length magazine and octagon barrel.

Model 1881 with half magazine and octagon barrel.

Catalog	Model	Magazine
	1888	Explanation of how to hold cartridges in reserve by pushing in the spring cover over the loading hole very slightly
1891	1889	Half magazine same price as full, short magazine same price as full (short magazine flush with end of forearm tip)
	1891	Side load—two-thirds magazine standard—short magazine holds 10 cartridges (flush with forearm tip)
1892	1892	Half magazine holds 7 shots; short magazine holds 5 shots
	1891	Caliber .22 full length standard; caliber .32 full length standard
1893	1891	26- and 28-in. barrels can be furnished. Magazine will be only 24 inches long

Catalog	Model	Magazine
	1889	Half magazine same price as full
1894	1893 & 1894	Half magazine and short magazine same price as full length
1895	1893 & 1894	Same
1896	1893, 1894, & 1895	No extra charge for half or short magazine
1897	1892	Magazines are 24 inches long in all cases

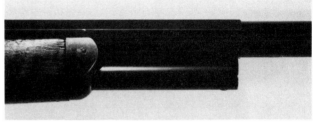

Model 1881 with half magazine and half-octagon, half-round barrel.

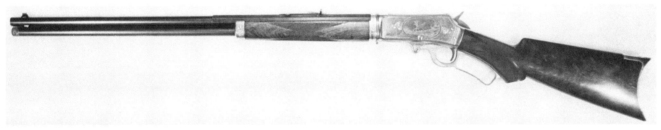

Model 1893 takedown rifle with half-octagon barrel and full-length magazine. (JO)

Model 1895 rifle with 32-in. full octagon barrel and 30 in. magazine (longest magazine available). (DS)

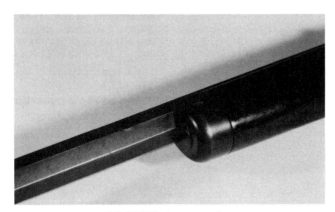

Model 1891 short magazine.

Model 1893 short magazine.

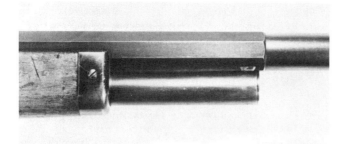

Solid-frame Model 1893 with half-octagon barrel and half magazine.

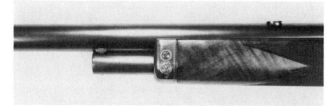

Solid-frame Model 1893 with round barrel and half magazine.

Model 1893 takedown rifle with short magazine.

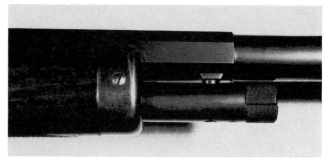

Takedown Model 1893 Lightweight with half-octagon barrel and short magazine.

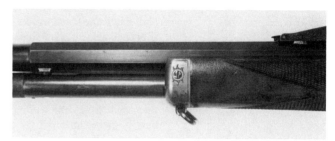

Takedown Model 1893 rifle with half magazine.

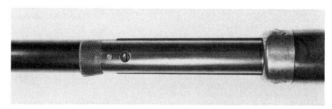

Bottom view of takedown magazine tube.

Catalog	Model	Magazine
	1894	Longest magazine is 30 inches. With short magazines reaching to end of forearm tip and half magazines projecting 3¼ inches beyond forearm tip, same price as full length magazine. Half magazine has 8 shots; short magazine, 6 shots
	1893	No extra charge for half or short magazines
	1895	Magazine will hold .38–56 — .40–65 — .45–70

	20-in.	7
	24-in.	9
	26-in.	9
	28-in.	10
	30-in.	10
	32-in.	10

Catalog	Model	Magazine
		.40–82 — .40–70 — .45–90 will hold one less. Half magazine will hold 5 of the shorter cartridges. Short magazines will hold 4 of the shorter cartridges and 3 of the longer cartridges. No extra charge for half or short magazines. Lightweights will have short magazines and short forearms
1899	1892 (.22)	Magazine capacity 25S–20L–18LR
		Half magazine capacity 16S–12L–10LR
	1892 (.32)	In all cases magazines are 24 inches long. Capacity is 17 short or 14 long, center- or rimfire
	1897	Full magazine holds 25S–20L–18LR. Half magazine holds 16S–12L–10LR. Bicycle rifle magazine 16 inches regardless of barrel length

Catalog	Model	Magazine	Catalog	Model	Magazine
	Shotgun	Shotgun magazines were standardized by model for length and capacity. See the particular shotgun model for magazine capacities			with short forearms and short magazines had the cartridge capacity reduced to 4 shots and the Model 1895 lightweight with its half magazine was reduced to 5 shots
	1894	Longest magazine made is 30 inches long. Half magazines that are 3¼ inches beyond the end of the forearm tip will hold 8 shots. Short magazines will hold 6 shots	1922	93 Carbine	Full-length magazine—7 shots
				93 Rifle	Full-length magazine—10 shots
1895–1915		No significant changes to magazines available or in capacity. However, when the baby carbine with its half magazine was introduced, it changed the carbine capacity to 6 shots. Also, the special lightweight Model 1893 rifles	1923	93 Rifle	Same as 1922
				93 Sporting Carbine	Two-thirds magazine—5 shots
			1933	410	Half magazine—6 shots
			1936	1936	Same as Model 93s
			1937	36 Carbine	Full-length magazine
				36 SC	Two-thirds magazine—6 shots

Right side view of Model 1893 solid-frame rifle with an octagon barrel and special-order two-thirds magazine.

Model 1892 half-octagon barrel and half magazine (latch type).

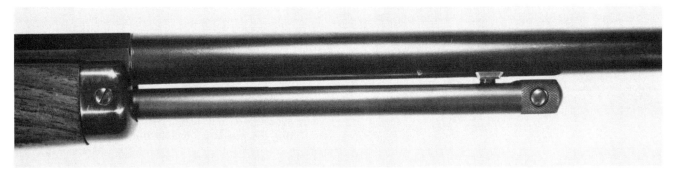

Model 1897 half-octagon barrel and half magazine (button type).

Typical magazine plug, magazine stud, and magazine tube stud screw of solid-frame tubular magazine.

Second (Osborne) type of bayonet catch magazine tube.

Typical forearm tip, tip tenon, and tip tenon screws.

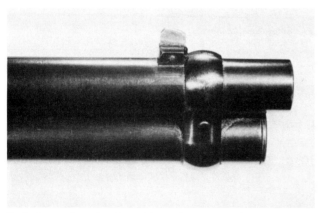

Typical magazine tube, front sight, and magazine tube front band of Marlin carbine.

Catalog	Model	Magazine
	36 Rifle	Two-thirds magazine—6 shots
1939–1947		Same
1948	336 Carbine	Same as for Model 36
	336 Sporting Carbine	Same as for Model 36
	336 Rifle	Same as for Model 36

Magazine tubes of the Marlin pump action rifles were as follows:

Model	Half	Two-thirds	Full Length
18	X		
20	X		X
25	X		
27	X		
29	X		X
32	X		X
37			X
38	X		
47		X	

After 1915, Marlin did not give the sportsman an option in the length of the magazine tube he could order. In most cases thereafter, a model had a specific magazine length and cartridge capacity with no other choices available.

The first type of magazine tube used on caliber .22 rifles was the latch type that had an outer and inner tube. To load the magazine, the latch was depressed and the outer tube was withdrawn to expose the loading port. Upon loading, the outer tube was returned to its locked position.

During the period of manufacture of the Model 37 slide action rifle (1923–1927) a button type of magazine tube was introduced for .22s. This method also had an outer tube that was withdrawn during the loading process. The only difference was that a button detent, instead of a latch piece, held the outer magazine tube in the open or closed position.

A new bayonet-type magazine catch was introduced with the Model 47 rifle. The inner magazine tube of this new magazine was withdrawn to load the gun. It was standard at Marlin for all tube-loading magazines, and was used as a replacement magazine for the Model 39 and 97 magazines of the button type, until a similar mechanism was patented in 1975 by William E. Osborne and Gerald Norman (number 3,883,976). This new mechanism required that the magazine tube plug be pushed down against spring tension before the inner tube could be rotated to unlock the bayonet catch, and then withdrawn. It is the standard, to this date, for all tubular-magazine .22 rifles.

Experimental magazine systems have been tried by Marlin for tubular-magazine firearms. For example, a magazine cut-off was designed to facilitate unloading; Marlin also experimented with a method to single-load a side-loading magazine; and a tube-loading magazine (like a .22 magazine wherein the inner tube is withdrawn to load) for center-fire rifles was tried. However, none of these mechanisms were found to be practical or reliable and were dropped in the prototype stage.

Marlin Estate

Mahlon H. Marlin lived at 911 Townsend Ave., New Haven, Conn., from 1913 until his death in 1949. His daughter, Janet Marlin, continued to live in the house until her death in 1969.

This beautiful Victorian home with its dormers, nooks, corners, and gingerbread was a landmark for years. It was the center of social and business gatherings for the Marlin family.

Upon the death of Janet Marlin, the city of New Haven acquired the house and property, intending to add the acreage to the adjoining city park property. The price paid was $150,000; half was paid by the U.S. Department of Housing and Urban Development, and the city and state paid 25 percent each. Unfortunately, soon after acquisition by the city, vandals burned the house down. All that remains today are the carriage house and the unkept grounds.

1913 newspaper photograph of the Victorian home of Mahlon H. Marlin. (The New Haven Colony Historical Society)

Marlin Loader

John M. and Mathew S. Browning of Ogden, Utah Territory, were awarded patent number 247,881, dated October 4, 1881. The patent was for a cartridge-loading implement that provided in a single tool all the appliances necessary for loading or reloading a cartridge. The steps included decapping, recapping, wadcutting, case mouth straightening, bullet casting, bullet seating, and crimping. Both single-vent and multiple-vent cases could be decapped with this tool.

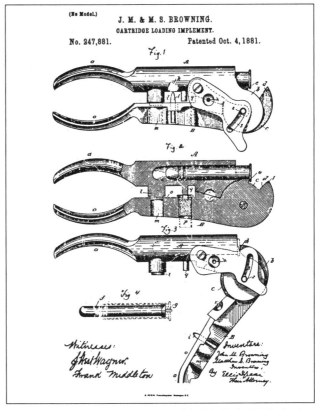

Patent drawing of Browning patent used by Marlin in Marlin loader.

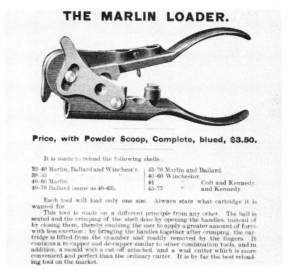

Catalog ad for Marlin loader.

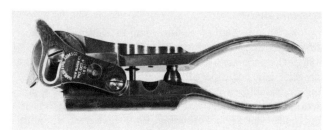

Marlin loader for the .32–40 cartridge. Marlin manufactured it for reloading cartridges for the Marlin Model 1881 and other makes of rifle.

Various matchbox covers advertising Marlin products. The razor blade cartoons were also used in advertisements in national publications.

1969 Marlin matchbox cover advertising the Model 336.

The patent rights were purchased from the Brownings by Marlin, and the new tool was first offered to the reloader in the 1883 catalog. When first advertised in national publications by Marlin's agents, Shoverling, Daly & Gales, New York, N.Y., it was described as:

> More convenient, more powerful, more compact than any other. The ball is seated and crimping is done by opening the handles instead of closing, giving the maximum of force, with minimum of exertion. Contains re- and de-capper, bullet mold and wad cutter. The workmanship is superior to that of any other tool in the market. Are now made .45–70 and .40–60, for Marlin and other magazine rifles. Will be made soon for all sizes of rifles. Price, with powder scoop, $4.00.

The first calibers available were .40–60; .45–70 Marlin and Ballard; .38 Winchester; .44 Winchester and Kennedy; and .45 Winchester and Kennedy. By 1886 the following cartridges had been added to the list: .32–40 Marlin, Ballard, and Winchester; .38–55 Marlin, Ballard, and Winchester; .40–70 Ballard (same as .40–63); .44 Winchester, Colt, and Kennedy; and .45–75 Winchester and Kennedy.

There have been slight variations in some of the tools examined. Non-Marlin-marked examples have been observed and are believed to be of original Browning manufacture. The known Browning-manufactured tools are marked *J. M. Browning, Ogden UT.* (Lewis Yearout has a .40–70 tool so marked in his collection.)

The Marlin loader was not listed in catalogs after 1887. The tool is well made and nicely finished, but restricted to one cartridge and only those of the large rifle type. Popularity of new, shorter, pistol-type cartridges resulted in Marlin adding the Ideal tong-type tools to its catalog in 1885. The Ideal tool was also less expensive, which must have added to its popularity over the Marlin loader.

The Marlin loading tools were serial-numbered and marked *MARLIN FIRE ARMS CO. NEW HAVEN, CT. PAT. OCT. 4 1881.* The caliber was also marked on the tool. Serial numbers as high as 7712 have been noted.

Match Covers

One man's treasure is another man's junk. Match covers can fall into both categories, depending on one's particular interests.

Marlin collectors, as well as matchbox collectors, have frequently asked about the variations and periods of time matchbox covers were used by Marlin as an advertising medium.

The Marlin razor blade division used various advertisements on match covers. Among them was a series in the 1940s of at least 10 different cartoons touting how good Marlin blades were, or would be if just given a try. At least two types of matchboxes advertised Marlin firearms. One featured the Model 39A and Micro-Groove rifling, and the other had the Marlin horse and rider logo. One razor blade match cover distributed in 1926 advertised 100 book matches free with one's name imprinted on them, upon receipt of a Marlin Blades boxtop and $1.00. This cover was blue and red with an illustration of a Marlin single- and double-edge blade on the back cover. The price was shown as 12 for 25¢. They were only trivia, but fun to add to a collection.

Micro-Groove Rifling

In 1950, Marlin studied and tested caliber .22 barrels manufactured by Remington Arms Company. Remington was using a new process about which Marlin had little knowledge. The process was called button rifling, which was known in Europe and to some degree here in the U.S. Remington had the first successful commercial application of the process.

Prior to WW II, the usual technique used to rifle gun barrels was to use a machine called a sine-bar machine. The cutter scraped the metal, rather than cutting it. Later, the hook cutter replaced the scrape cutter. Using either method was time-consuming. The scrape cutter method took about one hour to rifle a barrel, and the hook cutter method took about 10 to 15 minutes to rifle the same barrel.

Another system developed to perfection was the broach method. This system required a long pull-rod cutter with many cutting teeth that progressed from bore size to groove diameter. Usually a roughing broach was first pulled through the bore and was then followed by a finish broach, which sized all grooves to the required shape and diameter.

The button method of rifling barrels—exclusively used by Marlin since 1957—is done by pulling (some companies push) a preformed hardened tungsten-carbide swedge through the barrel. The advantages to using this method are uniformity in rifling shape, length of life of the tool, uniformity in bore and groove finish, dimensional uniformity, and reduced time to rifle a barrel. Whereas the original scrape cutter system (used in rifling Ballard barrels) took one hour to rifle a barrel, the button process takes 2 to 5 seconds.

When Marlin introduced the button method of rifling on July 29, 1953, Thomas R. Robinson, Jr., invented and applied for a patent for a new and advantageous type of rifling. His patent (number 3,100,358, dated August 13, 1963) for "Micro-Groove" rifling states the following as his claims:

> 1. A gun barrel provided with a plurality of helically disposed rifling grooves in the bore thereof with lands between the grooves, there being at least 5 of such grooves for every 1/10 inch of bore diameter, and the driving side of each of said lands being disposed substantially tangentially to a circle having a center at the bore axis and a radius equal to the radius of gyration of a cylindrical section of the bore.
>
> 2. A gun barrel provided with a plurality of helically disposed rifling grooves in the bore thereof with lands between the grooves, there being at least ten of such grooves, and the driving sides of each of said lands being disposed substantially tangentially to a circle having a center at the bore axis and a radius equal to the radius of gyration of a cylindrical section of the bore.

The Marlin 1954 catalog placed the following claim for Micro-Groove rifling into the hands of the public:

> Hunters and shooters the world over will be intensely interested in the Marlin Firearms Company's new and revolutionary type of rifle barrel that was perfected after several years of careful design and testing, because it has shown a net gain

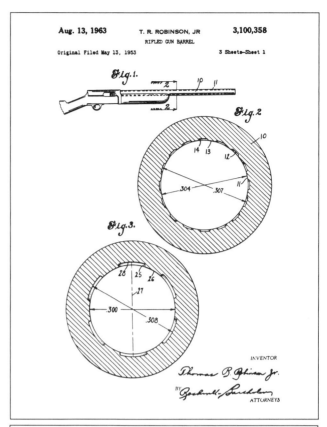

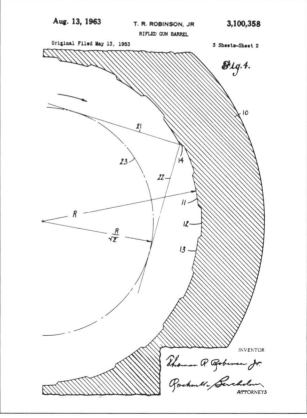

Illustrations of Thomas R. Robinson, Jr.'s patent number 3,100,358 for Micro-Groove rifling.

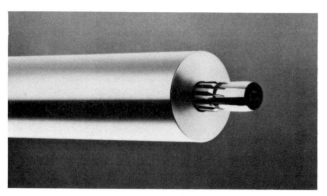

Tungsten-carbide button entering bore of barrel during the Micro-Groove process of rifling a Marlin gun barrel.

in accuracy-improvement of about 20% as compared to conventional barrels.

This new and novel type rifle barrel is now available in all Marlin .22's—Lever Actions, Bolt Actions, Semi-Automatic Actions, the new model 100 Single Shot, as well as the model 322 chambered for the .222 cartridge.

The Marlin "Micro-Groove" barrel is revolutionary both in its exceptional accuracy, generally high bullet velocities and low chamber pressure. It is also striking in the ease with which it may be cleaned and in durability. The unique design of the "Micro-Groove" barrel, with many more rifling lands than conventional barrels have, results in engraving on the bullet, made gently but firmly, giving a secure spinning grip for stabilization.

The relatively shallow grooves of the "Micro-Groove" barrel, coupled with a bore of greater than standard size, result in a bullet or bullet jacket not deeply grooved or distorted as is the case with conventional barrels in their action on bullets or bullet jackets.

The "Micro-Groove" barrel develops a light multiple grip on the bullet or bullet jacket, with more than adequate driving area in the lands to assure reliable bullet spinning. This is accomplished without objectionable finning or squeezing-out-of-shape the bullet fired, which occurs in other barrels to a marked degree.

Marlin's "Micro-Groove" barrel has been deliberately designed to produce the required rotation in the bullet with an absolute minimum of plastic deformation, that is, disturbance of the original cylindrical shape of the bullet. By use of a special land design, the barrel more effectively grasps the bullet than can be done with the standard rifle barrel. Gas leakage by bullet—between bullet and bore—is practically eliminated. Leading and other types of bore fouling are minimized by shape and surface condition of the bore.

By 1956, Micro-Groove rifling had been added to all Marlin firearms. That year's catalog stated the following:

After several years of careful design and testing, The Marlin Firearms Co. announced in July 1953, its research and development engineers had perfected a new and revolutionary type barrel called the Marlin "Micro-Groove" rifle barrel. Based on results of many general firing tests at 100 feet and more intensive firing at 100 yards, the new barrels showed a substantial net gain in accuracy improvement as compared to conventional barrels.

Micro-Groove barrel was first made available with the Marlin Model 89–C and, as production facilities were expanded, made available in all Marlin .22 caliber rim-fire rifles.

At the time Marlin announced the availability of its rifles with Micro-Groove barrels in .22 caliber rim-fire cartridges, it had already made pilot tests of Micro-Groove rifling in high-power cartridges. These tests were extremely encouraging, but not sufficiently comprehensive for any announcement. Exhaustive tests of Micro-Groove rifling with high velocity centerfire cartridges were continued through 1954. Results of these tests were highly dramatic and they were carefully assembled for public announcement.

The Marlin Model 322 was selected as the rifle to undergo endurance and accuracy tests with Micro-Groove rifling for two reasons. First, at the time of testing, it was Marlin's newest model; second, it fires a high velocity, centerfire cartridge. Thus Marlin engineers could efficiently test both the new model and the stamina of Micro-Groove rifling under high velocity, centerfire conditions simultaneously. The .222 caliber cartridge develops higher bullet velocity and is loaded

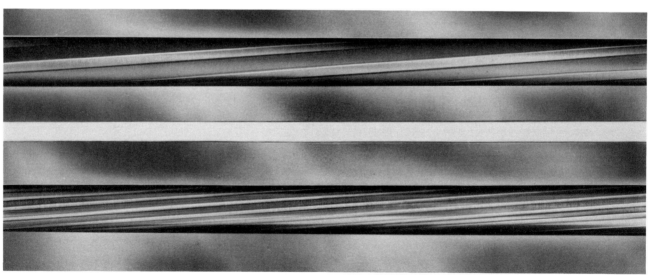

Top: *Conventionally rifled barrel.* Bottom: *Micro-Groove-rifled barrel.*

to higher pressure than most other cartridges for which current models are chambered. Results of the prolonged tests of the Marlin 322 with Micro-Groove barrel effectively proved the suitability of Micro-Groove rifling for centerfire cartridge shooting.

Early in 1956 The Marlin Firearms Co. announced to sportsmen through advertising space that all of its high-power rifles, in all calibers were being equipped with Micro-Groove rifling for extreme accuracy-performance.

The Micro-Groove barrel is revolutionary both in its exceptional accuracy, its generally high bullet velocities and its low chamber pressure.

Many industry people questioned Marlin's claim that Micro-Groove rifling resulted in a 20% increase in accuracy. Most asked "20% over what?"

Marlin's accuracy claim was based on tests conducted mostly with low-priced caliber .22 rifles not in the category of target rifles with match ammunition, but rather rifles used for plinking, informal target shooting, and hunting small game. The results were as claimed; in fact, Clarence Deem of Industry, Pa., on July 14, 1957, using his Model 322, tied the Varmint Rifle world record for 5 shots at 100 yards. (The .2268-in. group Mr. Deem shot was not .001 inch smaller than the previous record of .2273 inch, so Mr. Deem was made coholder of the world record.) Clarence Deem shot a standard Sako action Model 322 in .222 caliber. The rifle had the standard Marlin Micro-Groove barrel and a Unertl telescope. The rifle weighed 10½ pounds. His ammunition was handloaded.

Some Marlin gun owners complain that center-fire rifles having Micro-Groove rifling do not perform well with lead bullets or hot loads. In most cases this is true; however, tests conducted by firearms expert Ed Harris and published in *American Rifleman* magazine indicate that lead bullets can be successfully used in Micro-Groove barrels. Those interested should write Marlin for a copy of his article.

In simple terms, Micro-Groove rifling, in comparison with conventional four-groove rifling, is a large number of lands and grooves, with the grooves being rather shallow. Production of some Marlin center-fire barrels now have a modified form of Micro-Groove rifling, with the trend being to make the grooves deeper. There will be no change in caliber .22 Micro-Groove rifling, as the process is well developed and the product meets the demands of the Marlin owner. The name "Micro-Groove" was registered as a trademark on August 25, 1953.

Micro-Groove rifling characteristics are included in the section on barrels.

Money Clip

At the same time that Marlin had a tie bar with the bull's-eye trademark on it, Marlin gave out a money clip that also had the bull's-eye trademark affixed to it. The clip was 2″x1″, and had a fingernail file on one side and a knife blade on the other. The whole thing was of highly polished stainless steel. It was quite a neat item. The clip was packaged in a gray cloth bag inside a white cardboard box marked with the Robbins, Attleboro, Mass., maker's name. The highlight of this rare Marlin advertising item is that it was made in the U.S. See the necktie section for a photograph.

Left: *Bullets engraved by conventionally rifled barrel.* Right: *Bullets engraved by Micro-Groove-rifled barrel.*

Muskets

Model 1889 Musket. The Marlin 1893 catalog illustrated and described a Model 1889 Musket. The catalog stated:

> The system was now in use in the Chinese army. It is the lightest musket on the market, weighing but seven pounds, and yet is without doubt, the strongest and safest. This arm is arranged with a magazine stop, by means of which the magazine can be shut off, enabling one to use the gun as a single shot or repeater at will. The whole supply of fifteen cartridges can be thus held in reserve, and the gun used as a single breech-loader in the meantime. This cut-off is a sure one, cannot get out of order, and can be operated without moving the musket from the shoulder.

The barrel length was 30 inches, the gun weighed 7 pounds without bayonet, and it held 16 shots.

The catalog illustration of the Model 1889 Musket shows it with a sling loop at the forend and a hook in front of the lever for attaching the bottom end of the sling. The illustration also shows a cleaning rod fitted into the full-length stock beside the barrel, and both a triangular and a sword bayonet. However, a means of attaching the sword bayonet is not evident in the illustration. The triangular bayonet is the same as the one for the Winchester Model 1866 musket.

I do not remember having examined a Model 1889 Musket and wonder if any exist in the U.S. The records indicate that 64 were manufactured in caliber .44 and that 3 were made in caliber .38. Perhaps the few produced were all shipped to China. It seems unlikely, as the records reflect shipping dates from 1892 to 1895. However, the majority of them were dated October 18, 1893.

The Model 1889 Muskets listed in the records are as follows:

Serial Number	Caliber	Date
72476	*	8/1/1892
72477	44	2/6/1894
72478	*	2/27/1892

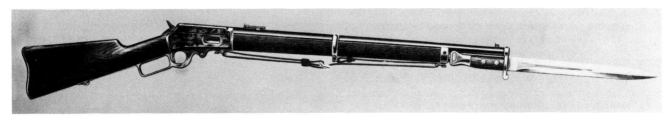

Model 1893 Musket with sling in the ready position.

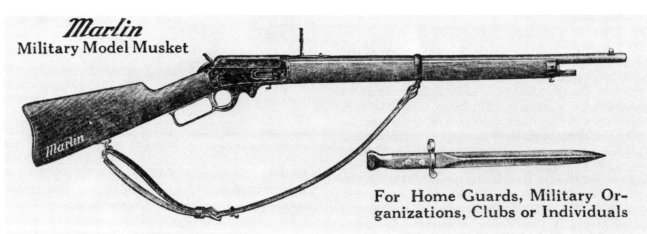

Marlin
Military Model Musket

For Home Guards, Military Organizations, Clubs or Individuals

The standard arm is .30-30 caliber; 24-inch round barrel, 7 shots (6 in the magazine and 1 in the chamber); weight complete with slingstrap and bayonet, 8½ pounds; with bayonet removed, 7½ pounds. Retail price, complete, $23.00.

Quantity Prices and Terms on Application

Bayonet is instantly affixed or removed. Pressing a spring-button releases the lock.

The military rear sight has crossbar slide, quickly adjustable for medium and long ranges; the leaf folds flat for short range, making it a flat top sight with "V" notch.

Sling strap snaps into position shown for carrying over shoulder; folds flat under magazine when not in use. It does not interfere with quick operation of gun, whether in closed or open position.

To load magazine: Press down loading spring cover with front of bullet and push cartridge forward into magazine. **Can be fired rapidly as a single-shot breech-loader:** Just drop the cartridge into receiver, ahead of breechbolt, when action is open; close breechbolt and the gun is loaded and cocked, ready for firing. **To hold the magazine in reserve**, while constantly shooting, just insert a new cartridge into the magazine as fast as one is chambered.

The solid-top receiver and side ejection keep out rain, snow or sleet, dirt, twigs, sand, etc.; throw the empty shells away from you. This action **will not freeze up** in cold, wet weather like a top-ejecting rifle.

Model 1893 Musket information in Marlin catalog that illustrates the sling in the carry position.

Serial Number	Caliber	Date	Serial Number	Caliber	Date
72479	*	8/1/1892	93156	44	10/18/1893
92818	44	6/6/1893	93157	44	10/18/1893
92819	44	6/6/1893	93158	44	10/18/1893
93141	44	10/18/1893	93159	44	10/18/1893
93142	44	10/18/1893	93160	44	10/18/1893
93143	44	10/18/1893	93161	44	10/18/1893
93144	44	10/18/1893	93162	44	3/16/1895
93145	44	10/18/1893	98823	44	8/16/1894
93146	44	10/18/1893	98824	44	10/18/1893
93147	44	10/18/1893	98825	44	10/18/1893
93148	44	10/18/1893	98826	44	9/1/1894
93149	44	10/18/1893	98827	44	10/18/1893
93150	44	10/18/1893	98828	44	10/18/1893
93151	44	10/18/1893	98829	44	10/18/1893
93152	44	10/18/1893	98830	44	10/18/1893
93153	44	10/18/1893	98831	44	10/18/1893
93154	44	10/18/1893	98833	44	3/22/1895
93155	44	10/18/1893	98834	44	10/18/1893

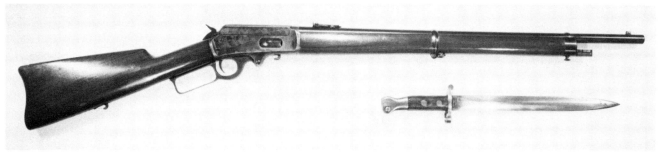

Model 1893 Musket and bayonet.

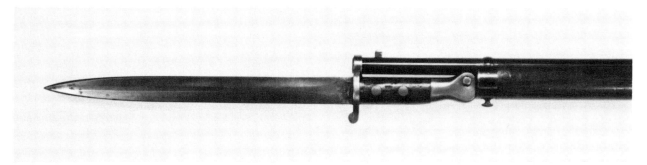

Muzzle end of 1893 Musket with bayonet attached.

Serial Number	Caliber	Date
98835	44	10/18/1893
98836	38	1/2/1895
98837	44	10/18/1893
98838	44	10/18/1893
98840	44	5/6/1894
98841	44	10/18/1893
98842	44	10/18/1893
98843	44	10/18/1893
98845	44	10/18/1893
98846	44	10/18/1893
98848	44	10/18/1893
98849	44	10/18/1893
98850	44	10/18/1893
98851	44	9/6/1895
98852	44	10/18/1893
98853	44	10/18/1893
98854	44	5/29/1895
98855	44	10/18/1893
98856	44	10/18/1893
98858	38	9/26/1895
98859	44	10/18/1893
98860	44	10/18/1893
98861	38	2/13/1894
98862	44	10/18/1893
98863	44	10/18/1893
98864	44	10/18/1893
98865	44	10/18/1893
98866	40**	5/29/1895

*Caliber not listed.
**Shown as caliber .40, which is assumed to be a clerical error.

ALL BARREL LENGTHS ARE LISTED AS 30 INCHES.

NUMBER MADE

By Year		By Caliber	
1892 – 3		.38–40 – 3	
1893 – 52		.44–40 – 64	
1894 – 5		Total – 67	
1895 – 7			
Total – 67			

Model 1893 Musket. The Model 1893 Musket was listed in Marlin catalogs from 1896 to as late as 1915; however, the records indicate that only a few of this model were manufactured. The catalog description was as follows:

Unique hand guard of rare Model 1893 Musket. (JB)

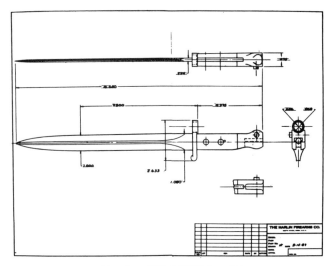

Drawing of Model 1893 bayonet.

This 30-30 Marlin Military Model Musket has every requisite of power, range, accuracy and construction for efficient military service; uses standard ammunition not excessively high in cost; and is at the same time, one of the most desirable big game hunting rifles ever invented.

It is a quick handling, powerful and accurate arm. The mechanism is extremely simple and very strong; it is especially adapted to stand the strain and resist the wear of high power smokeless cartridges with jacketed bullets.

The standard musket is 30-30 caliber; 30-inch round barrel, 7 shots (6 in magazine and 1 in the chamber); weight complete with sling strap and bayonet, 8½ pounds; with bayonet removed, 7½ pounds. Retail price, complete, $23.00.

Bayonet is instantly affixed or removed. Pressing a spring button releases the lock. The military rear sight has crossbar slide, quickly adjustable for medium and long ranges; the leaf folds flat for short range, making it a flat top sight with "V" notch. Sling strap snaps into position shown for carrying over the shoulder; folds flat under magazine when not in use. It does not interfere with quick operation of gun, whether in closed or open position.

Only 31 Marlin Model 1893 Muskets are listed in the records. Of the 31, 20 are listed for 1895. Two variations have been observed. The first is like the catalog illustration, having the long wood forearm, bayonet lug forearm cap, carbine rear sight, carbine buttstock, sling snap on the bottom of the stock, and L-shaped stud in the bottom of the trigger plate to which the sling is attached when not in the carry position. The other type noted has a wood hand guard covering the barrel from in front of the receiver to the barrel band. Hammers, levers, butt plates, and receivers were case-colored. Other parts were blued.

The bayonet furnished with the Model 1893 Musket is a knife bayonet manufactured by the British for use with their Lee-Enfield bolt action rifle. These bayonets do not have the Marlin name marked on them and still retain the British identifying marks. They are also bright and not blued.

Extremely rare, the Model 1893 Musket is a desirable item, seldom encountered.

The Model 1893 Muskets manufactured are as follows:

Serial Number	Caliber	Date
90433	.32–40	10/15/95
130842	.32–40	12/14/95
130879	.32–40	12/14/95
130900	.32–40	12/14/95
130992	.32–40	12/14/95
131011	.32–40	12/14/95
131012	.32–40	12/14/95
131015	.32–40	12/14/95
131017	.32–40	12/14/95
131019	.32–40	12/14/95
131022	.32–40	12/14/95
131024	.32–40	12/14/95
131031	.32–40	12/14/95
132560	.32–40	12/14/95
132561	.32–40	12/14/95
132562	.32–40	12/14/95
132563	.32–40	12/14/95
132564	.32–40	12/14/95
132565	.32–40	12/14/95
132566	.32–40	12/14/95
135359	.38–55	11/22/99
135360	.25	5/24/00
135361	.30–30	2/20/96
135362	.30–30	2/20/96
135364	.30–30	2/20/96
135365	.30–30	3/25/96
135622		
171936	.30–30	10/08/98
211441	.38–55	9/19/00
250535	.32–40	6/13/02
336301	.32–40	2/13/06

NUMBER MADE

By Caliber		By Year	
.25	1	1895	20
.30–30	5	1896	4
.32–40	22	1898	1
.38–55	2	1899	1
Unknown	1	1900	2
Total	31	1902	1
		1906	1
		Unknown	1
		Total	31

Model 1894 Musket. The 1894 Marlin catalog describes the Model 1894 Musket similarly to its description of the Model 1889 Musket. However, in addition to saying the muskets are "now in use by the Chinese," it says that the magazine cutoff is an option and that "if desired," the arm can be equipped with such a device. The 1894 Musket was also listed as being 15 shot, having a 30-in. barrel and weighing 7 pounds without bayonet. Both an angular bayonet and a sword bayonet were illustrated and special quotations would be made "upon application."

A total of 152 Model 1894 Muskets are listed in the available records. Of the 152 recorded or known to exist, a number of them are crudely stamped on top of the receiver *Bureau*

Catalog illustration of Model 1894 Musket.

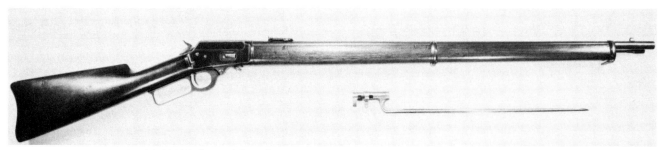

Model 1894 Musket, serial number 112,258, and triangular bayonet used with this model. (ES)

County. Some references state that those so marked were used at the Bureau County, Ill., prison. However, Bureau County was a farming community that never did have a prison. Its detention facility was no more than a small county lockup, only large enough to hold a couple of the local roughnecks waiting to appear before the county magistrate. It does appear, however, from the investigative work done by Marlin collectors Robert Wong and Richard Ellis, that Bureau County did purchase from Marlin about 80 of the Model 1894 Muskets, which were issued to deputized county residents felt to be able and ready to respond to an emergency in their community, or in response to a request from the county sheriff.

The Model 1894 Musket was different from the Model 1893 Musket by being blued and having a sling loop on the trigger plate, rather than a hook, as well as no catch on the bottom of the stock for the sling. The 1894 model also had no lug for a bayonet catch. The upper band instead had a sling loop. Also, this model had the Model 1889 Musket cleaning rod on the side of the forearm. The bayonet was of the military triangular type that locked to the barrel by means of a ring that locked behind the carbine-type front sight stud. It is identical to the Winchester Model 1866 Musket bayonet. (The sword bayonet in the catalog illustration could possibly be used with the Model 1893 Musket, but surely could not be used with either the Model 1889 or 1894 Muskets!)

The base for the lower sling loop was a hump that was nicely machined to integrate with the trigger plate. There was no sling loop on the lower band. Both upper and lower bands were especially made to accept the cleaning rod.

The triangular bayonet was bright, as was the knife bayonet of the Model 1893 Musket.

No Marlin musket has been observed that has the magazine cutoff alluded to in catalogs. (However, it is interesting to note that in the 1950s a prototype rifle having a magazine cutoff designed by Bob Jenkinson was studied for possible incorpora-

tion into the Model 336, but its unreliable performance resulted in the idea being dropped.)

Serial numbers of the Model 1894 Muskets listed in the records are as follows:

Serial Number	Caliber	Date
112209	.38	9/21/94
112210	.38	9/21/94
112211	.38	9/21/94
112212	.38	9/21/94
112213	.38	9/21/94**
112214	.38	9/21/94**

Muzzle end of 1894 Musket showing cleaning rod, carbine front sight stud, and special upper band. (ES)

Top view of Model 1894 Musket bayonet attached to muzzle of barrel. (ES)

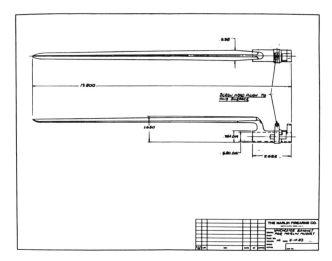

Drawing of bayonet used on Winchester 1894 and Marlin Model 1894 muskets.

Serial Number	Caliber	Date
112215	.38	9/21/94
112216	.38	9/21/94
112217	.38	9/21/94
112219	.38	9/21/94
112220	.38	9/21/94
112221	.38	5/29/95
112222	.38	9/21/94
112223	.38	9/21/94
112224	.38	9/21/94
112225	.38	9/21/94
112226	.38	9/21/94
112227	.38	9/21/94
112228	.38	9/21/94
112229	.38	9/21/94
112230	.38	6/22/06
112231	.38	9/21/94
112232	.38	9/21/94**
112233	.38	9/21/94
112234	.38	9/21/94
112235	.38	9/21/94
112236	.38	9/21/94
112237	.38	9/21/94
112238	.38	9/21/94
112239	.38	9/21/94
112240	.38	9/21/94
112241	.38	9/21/94
112242	.38	9/21/94**
112243	.38	9/21/94
112244	.38	9/08/02
112245	.38	9/21/94
112246	.38	9/21/94
112247	.38	9/21/94
112248	.38	9/21/94**
112249	.44	6/22/95
112250	.38	9/21/94
112251	.38	9/21/97
112252	.38	9/21/94

Serial Number	Caliber	Date
112253	.38	9/21/94
112254	.38	9/21/97
112255	.38	9/21/97
112256	.38	9/21/97
112257	.38	9/21/97
112258	.38	9/21/94**
112259	.38	9/21/94
112260	.38	9/21/94
112261	.38	9/21/94
112262	.38	9/21/94
112264	.38	9/21/94
112265	.38	9/21/94
112266	.38	9/21/94
112267	.38	9/21/94
112268	.38	9/21/94
112269	.38	9/21/94
112270	.38	9/21/94
112271	.38	9/21/94
112272	.38	9/21/94
112273	.38	9/21/94
112274	.38	9/21/94**
112275	.38	9/21/94
112276	.38	9/21/94
112277		**
112278	.44	6/11/95
112279	.38	9/21/94
112280	.38	9/21/94
112281	.38	9/21/94
112282	.38	9/21/94
112283	.38	9/21/94
112284	.38	9/21/94
112285	.38	9/21/94
112286	.38	9/21/94**
112287	.38	9/21/94
112288	.38	9/21/94
112289	.44	1/25/96
112290	.38	9/21/94
112291	.38	4/17/95
112292	.38	9/21/94
112293	.38	10/10/99
112294	.38	9/21/94
112295	.38	9/21/94
112296	.38	9/21/94

Bureau County marking on top of Model 1894 Musket. (ES)

CHARGER LOADING LEE-ENFIELD.

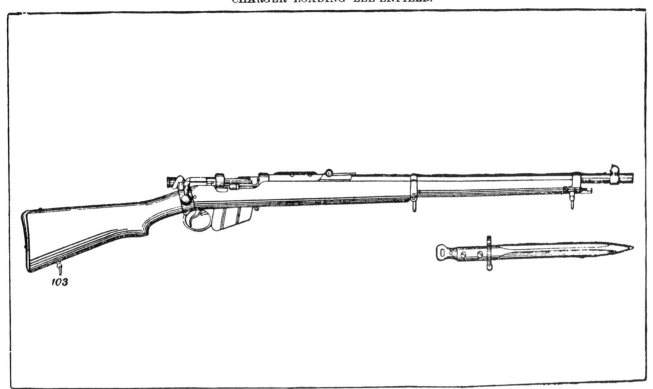

Drawing of British Lee-Enfield rifle, and the bayonet used with Marlin Model 1893 Musket.

Serial Number	Caliber	Date	Serial Number	Caliber	Date
112297	.38	9/21/94**	125454	.38	12/13/04
112298	.38	9/21/94	125459	.44	9/06/95
112299	.38	9/21/94	125463	.44	10/12/99
112300	.38	9/21/94	125466	.44	10/21/96
112301	.38	9/21/94	125470	.38	12/13/04
112302	.38	9/21/94	125471	.38	12/13/04
112303	.38	9/21/94	125472	.38	12/13/04
125434	.44	6/17/95	125474	.44	7/26/95
125435	.44	6/17/95	125475	.44	7/11/95
125436	.44	6/17/95	125476	.44	12/28/95
125437	.44	6/17/95	125477	.44	12/28/95
125438	.44	6/17/95	125478	.44	12/28/95
125439	.44	6/17/95	125479	.38	12/13/05
125440	.44	6/17/95	125480	.44	7/26/95
125441	.44	6/17/95	125481	.44	9/06/95
125442	.44	6/17/95	125482	.44	12/28/95
125443	.44	6/17/95	125483	.44	12/28/95
125444	.44	6/17/95	125486	.44	8/20/95
125445	.44	6/17/95	125489	.38	12/20/98
125446	.44	6/17/95	125492	.44	12/28/95
125447	.44	6/17/95	125493	.44	12/28/95
125448	.44	6/17/95	125494	.44	12/13/04
125449	.44	6/17/95	125496	.44	12/28/95
125450	.44	6/17/95	125497	.38	10/14/01
125451	.44	6/17/95	125498	.44	12/28/95
125452	.44	6/17/95	125499	.44	12/28/95
125453	.44	6/17/95	125500	.44	12/28/95

Serial Number	Caliber	Date
125487 *	.38	
332002	.44	9/16/05
332003	.44	9/16/05
332004	.44	9/16/05
332005	.44	9/16/05
332007	.44	9/16/05
332008	.44	9/16/05
332009	.44	9/16/05
332011	.44	9/16/05
332012	.44	9/16/05
332013	.44	9/16/05
332014	.44	9/16/05
332015	.44	9/16/05

*Not entered in records as Musket; however, known to be one.
**Reported to be Bureau County, Ill., muskets.

NUMBER MADE

By Year		By Caliber	
1894	85	.38–40	97
1895	41	.44–40	55
1896	2	Total:	152
1898	1		
1899	1		
1901	1		
1902	1		
1904	5		
1905	13		
1906	1		
Unknown	1		

Neckties

The Marlin Industrial Division had specially manufactured neckties, which were worn by Marlin sales and management personnel during business meetings, at symposiums, and at trade shows.

The first style was a wide, dark blue tie that had diagonal lines of the Marlin horse and rider logo embroidered on a round orange background.

The second tie was also a dark blue tie that had alternate diagonal rows of the Marlin logo and the American flag. This tie was given to personnel during the U.S. bicentennial year of 1976.

Left: *First style of Marlin necktie.* Right: *Second style of necktie.*

Left: *Fourth type of necktie.* Right: *Third type of necktie.* From top to bottom: MFCA Ltd. *tie tack, late Marlin tie bar, bull's-eye tie bar (scarce), horse and rider tie bar (rare), Micro-Groove bullet tie bar (rare), Micro-Groove bullet cufflinks (rare), money clip with bull's-eye, cigarette lighter.*

The third tie also had diagonal rows of the logo alternately with a narrow double stripe.

The fourth and latest tie was like the third, except that it had a wider stripe.

When Marlin ordered the fourth tie, The Marlin Firearms Collectors Association, Ltd., was offered an opportunity to purchase 100 ties for members of the association.

Necktie Bars

The first Marlin tie bar had the Marlin horse and rider logo on a short (1¼-in.) bar. The man on the horse was in low relief and cut out in profile. The tie bar was gold in color and very attractive. It was not manufactured in large quantities and is now scarce.

The second type of tie bar had a 1¾-in. bar with the circular black-and-white bull's-eye trademark mounted on it. The bar was gold in color and, like the first type, had an alligator clip on the back. This type is also very scarce, because only limited numbers were manufactured by the Robbins Company.

At the time of introduction of the Model 322 (Sako action) rifle, Marlin had the Robbins Company make a few sets of tie bars and cuff links. The unique feature of these sets is that actual caliber .222 bullets, with Micro-Groove rifling marks on them, were used in their fabrication. Plated in a gold-color finish and specially packaged, they are rare. I have seen only two sets in 17 years of looking—the company doesn't even have a set.

Sport–Style Associates, Inc., was authorized to make a tie bar having a facsimile of the Marlin Model 336C lever action rifle on it. The tie bars were manufactured in three different finishes: gold, silver, and bronze. Marlin purchased a limited number of the bronze-colored model for promotional use. The three types were commercially available from the manufacturer.

The last, and most recent, tie bar is one that is 2¼ inches long with a ¾-in. round, high-relief, bronze-color medallion of the Marlin horse and rider mounted on it. Made by the Anson jewelry people, it is attractive and frequently worn by those fortunate to have one. *Note:* When Marlin purchased these tie bars, the company authorized The Marlin Firearms Collectors Association, Ltd., to have made a tie tack/lapel pin, which was the medallion part of the tie bar with a clutch back. Also made to special order for the association members were a few novelty items such as money clips, pocket knives, belt buckles, blazer buttons, and cuff links. None were made in quantities over 20. They are now all in collections.

Newton Rifles

Charles Newton was a lawyer-turned-rifle manufacturer and cartridge designer. His rifle businesses were anything but successful. His ability as a lawyer must have been adequate to permit him to survive failure after failure of the companies he formed and headed.

Mr. Newton was determined to manufacture a bolt action rifle he felt superior to all others. He never quite got his companies into volume production and he was always trying to

Third style of Marlin tie with bull's-eye tie bar, and silver and bronze tie bars in the shape of the Model 336 rifle.

raise money by making promises of future delivery. His first company was the Newton Arms Company, Inc., Buffalo, N.Y., organized in 1914. His second firm was the Charles Newton Rifle Corporation, formed in 1919, also in Buffalo. In 1923, the Buffalo Newton Rifle Company replaced the previous company and a new model of rifle was designed. Also in 1923, the Buffalo Newton Company was moved to New Haven, Conn. In 1924, still in financial trouble, John H. Meeker, head of the group that had been financing Newton, foreclosed and took over the Buffalo Newton Rifle Company. Newton reacquired the company by legal action in January 1925. During the frustrating years of Charles Newton's rifle business, he was able to have Marlin make .256 Newton caliber barrels for the Model 1903 rifle. However, he could not persuade Marlin President Frank Kenna to make his bolt action rifle for him.

From 1925 to 1929, Charles Newton did make approximately 400 rifles in New Haven. The last were sold by means of a factory clearing-out sale. Some sold for as little as $35.

The following letter, postmarked March 28, 1929, was sent by Charles Newton to Frank Kenna trying again to convince him to manufacture Mr. Newton's newly designed straight pull "LeverBolt" rifle:

THE LEVERBOLT RIFLE

Caliber .30 U.S.G., Model 1906, .256 Newton, .280 Newton, .30 Newton and, .35 Newton.

The general appearance of the rifle is shown by the cuts.

As its name indicates, it combines the best features of both lever action and bolt action rifles and avoids the objectionable points of both types. It has—

ALL THE STRENGTH AND SIMPLICITY OF THE BOLT ACTION TYPE, therefore can, and does, use the most powerful of our modern cartridges, with their superior velocity, flatness of trajectory, range and killing power; and with these qualities are combined—

THE SPEED AND EASE OF OPERATION OF THE LEVER ACTION TYPE, thus giving the sportsman the benefit of the greater speed of fire of those rifles without being forced to use cartridges of inferior ballistic properties.

TO OPERATE, merely **draw straight back on the knob of the operating lever;** this unlocks the bolt and extracts and ejects the fired shell. Then **push straight forward,** and it feeds in the fresh cartridge and locks the bolt ready for firing.

THE BOLT, from the operating lever forward, is exactly like, and works exactly like, that of the Springfield and Mauser, it differing only in the the method by which it is turned. It is all in one piece, is round, has the same locking lugs at its front end, makes a full one quarter turn to lock and unlock, has an extractor of the same type and fastened on by the same type of extractor collar; so with all details of the bolt and its action the same, it has all their strength and extracting power. It is turned by—

Description of LeverBolt Rifle, Charles Newton's last effort in the high-power rifle business.

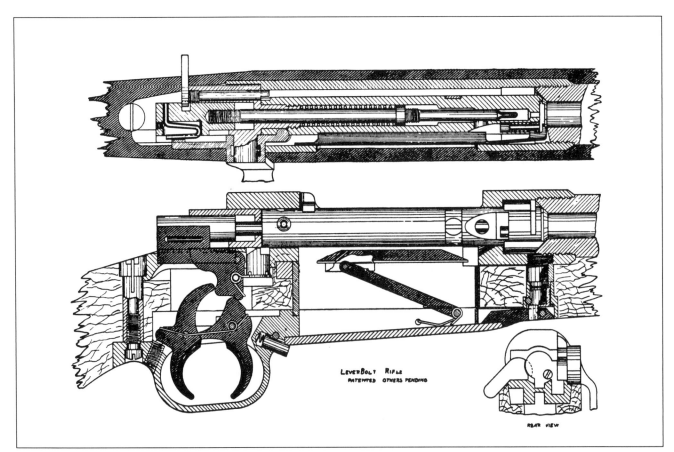

Sectionalized drawing of Newton's LeverBolt (straight pull) rifle.

BUFFALO NEWTON RIFLE CO.
Manufacturers of and Dealers In
HIGH-GRADE FIREARMS, AMMUNITION AND SUPPLIES
New Haven, Conn.

Frank Kenna, Esq.,
c/o Marlin Firearms Co.,
New Haven, Conn.

Dear sir: — Four years ago last spring I interviewed you on the subject of manufacturing, at the Marlin plant, the rifle designed by me and bearing my name. You referred the matter to your Marlin staff and four men came to my plant to look it over, Mr. Cahill, Mr. Scharf, Mr. Goodyear and Mr. Beck. They spent less than an hour and reported to you that it was not well to take it up for the following reasons:

Mr. Cahill stated that there was a very small demand for bolt action rifles, and Mr. Scharf stated that I had not sufficient tools and gages to manufacture the rifles without large and costly numbers being added thereto. I wish, at this time to comment upon both statements:

Mr. Cahill's statements were based upon the uniform and unanimous opinions of the entire trade, on that subject, and he was entirely sincere therein. But he would not allow me to place before him a statement of reasons why that opinion would not apply to my rifles. In this connection let me suggest that but a few years before I had started manufacturing them in Buffalo, N.Y., and had sold, during 1½ years, over 4,200 rifles for over $200,000.00 doing it all myself and without leaving my desk. Since that time the sales of bolt action rifles did not run 2,000 per year by all firms. Here is the reason:

A bolt action rifle was much slower and clumsier to operate than a lever or trombone action, therefore in order to induce people to buy them they must possess some property, not possessed by the lever action, and important enough to outweigh the clumsiness of the bolt action. None of the rifles with which the trade were familiar had such property, but those made by me did have, in that they used far more powerful and longer ranged cartridges. As a measure of this I am enclosing some pages torn from one of my catalogues, which please read and consider. But the trade knew nothing of these rifles, as I sold nearly all direct to the consumers. The firm was wrecked by war conditions in the spring of 1918. Thus the superior ballistics of the cartridges used by my rifle was responsible for their sales where other bolt action rifles would not sell.

The objection of the public to the bolt action was because of its slowness and clumsiness of operation, and the lever action Winchester, model 1895, took just as powerful cartridges as any bolt action except mine, so naturally there was not much demand for those. Now, by virtue of a newly invented action, the slowness and clumsiness of the bolt action has been done away with, and it works as fast and smoothly as any other rifle. I have the patents on that invention and wish to apply that system to my rifle, which will then displace all the bolt action rifles now in use and also prevent the sales of any more of the older models. This forms a second answer to Mr. Cahill's report.

Touching Mr. Scharf's report on the tools, he was sincere but misled by appearances. His active life had been spent in Marlin's and he knew their work like a book and viewed all gun manufacturing from the Marlin standpoint.

Now Marlin had made from fifteen to twenty different models of firearms, and the number of operations per model would average over three times as many as on my rifle, and I had but one model. The number of tools required varies almost as the number of operations to be performed. Therefore since the average of their models required three times the number of tools required by mine, their fifteen models would require 3x15 or 45 times as many tools as mine.

Mr. Scharf was accustomed to seeing a given quantity of tools at Marlin's, and when he saw only one forty fifth as many at my place they looked like nothing.

Now the only way to pass upon whether or not we have sufficient tools is to consider first the various parts to be made; then consider the various operations required to make each part; then consider the various tools and gages to perform each operation, and see if I have them all. Mr. Scharf has not done anything like this, but would be glad to do so if you wished; it would take him more than one but less than two days. We have built about 500 rifles since Mr. Scharf looked at the tools and we certainly had to have tools to do it with.

Now I wish to state that my rifles can be built in small quantities for $12.00 each and in lots of 1,000 each for $10.00 each.

I can sell 5,000 of them the first year and 10,000 per year thereafter.

The above statements are like the pleadings in a lawsuit; they are merely my claims, and mean nothing unless either admitted by the adversary or established by competent proof; What I ask for is an opportunity to meet you and submit that proof to you.

I will prove to you *by your Mr. Scharf* that he can build the rifles within the prices mentioned, and that I have the tools with which to do it except those made necessary by adopting the new action, and that those can be made for less than $1500.00; that by spending less than $5000.00 you can turn out 400 rifles which will sell for $16,000.00 to the jobber.

I can also prove to yourself that I can sell the rifles at the prices mentioned.

May I have the opportunity of meeting you again and talking over the matter with a view to getting the opportunity to submit the proofs? If I can convince you of those facts I wish to make a proposition that you build the rifles and I sell them, and the profits be divided, 50–50 or about 100% to each.

Yours truly,

Frank Kenna's response in 1929 is not known. But he must have decided he had nothing to lose if he agreed to make the Newton straight pull rifle on the condition that sufficient orders would be generated, along with deposits adequate to cover start-up costs. The following special notice by the Leverbolt Rifle Company in 1932 tells the story:

SPECIAL NOTICE

The LEVERBOLT rifle is the result of a combination of the expert knowledge and inventive ability of Charles Newton and other up-to-date inventors of firearms, who designed it, with the plant, equipment, manufacturing ability and experience of the Marlin Firearms Co., who will make them for us under contract.

Mr. Newton has long been known to riflemen, first as the designer of high power cartridges such as the Savage line of .22 High power, .250-3000 and .300 Savage; later of the .256 Newton, .30 Newton and .35 Newton cartridges, all of which have far longer range, higher velocity, flatter trajectory and greater killing power than any other cartridge made. He also designed the first model Newton rifle, made at Buffalo, N.Y. until war conditions forced that firm out of business; then he designed the Buffalo Newton model and started its manufacture at New Haven but failed because he lacked an organization of workmen, skilled in mass production methods, for his factory on account of which his rifles cost too much to build and the quality of the work left much to be desired. Now he has gone a step farther and designed the LEVERBOLT RIFLE, which has all the strength and simplicity of the bolt action type combined with the speed and ease of operation of the lever action, thus bringing within reach of the sportsmen that thirty year old dream of "a lever action rifle for the highest power cartridges."

Mr. Newton not having the financial ability to put this new rifle on the market, we have acquired all rights to it, also to the first model Newton and the Buffalo Newton. We have also retained Mr. Newton himself as a member of our organization, that our customers may

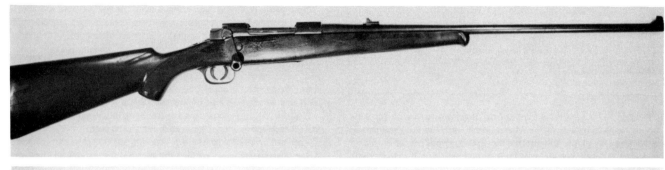

Top: *Photo of Newton's prototype LeverBolt rifle.* Bottom: *Same rifle shown with the bolt in its most rearward position.*

always have the benefit of his expert knowledge of rifles and cartridges.

The Marlin Firearms Co. needs no introduction to American sportsmen. Sixty years ago its Ballard single shot led the field of target rifles
at Creedmoor, Wimbledon, Dollymount and other great long range
matches, since which time it has been constantly growing and furnishing to the sportsmen firearms of many kinds and all of the best quality.
It has a large plant, ample equipment of all kinds, and an organization
of workmen most of whom have spent nearly their whole lives in its
service. Therefore, it is admirably equipped for building rifles and
building them right in every way.

We believe, as Mr. Newton has always believed, there will be a large
demand from American sportsmen for a rifle which will work as
rapidly and easily as the lever action, yet handle the most powerful
cartridges with all the strength and certainty of the bolt actions, which
are objectionable because they are so slow and clumsy to operate. On
the other hand, the Marlin Co. is very conservative and cannot see why
anyone should want a rifle more powerful than their .30-30, Model
1893. Once they are "shown" they are ready, willing and able to build
them for us to sell. You alone can "show" them.

If we are right your orders will come in promptly, work will be
started on the first lot of rifles as soon as orders for five hundred of
them are received, and the business will grow as big and as fast as the
demand of the American sportsmen for better rifles will make it. If the
Marlin Co. is right you will not order and the rifles will not be built.

But in ordering you do not want to take any chances as to the quality
of the rifles or of not having your rifle delivered. We have arranged to
assure you the quality will be right by having them manufactured by
one of the oldest and most experienced of our great arms factories. As
to your being sure of getting your rifles, since you do not yet know us
we have planned for your protection as follows:

Make out your order on the enclosed blank, first having carefully
read its terms and conditions. Make your check or money order for the
first payment of $25.00 per rifle payable directly to The New Haven
Bank, of whose standing your own banker can advise you, so that
bank alone can endorse and cash it. Send both order and check direct
to that bank, so it alone can handle them, and it will at once place the
money to your credit on its books and there it will stay until such time
as we have made the rifle, shipped it to you C.O.D. for the balance,

and presented to that bank the duly signed shipping receipt for it.
Then and not till then, will that bank turn your money over to us. If
the rifles are not made, due to not enough orders having been received,
that bank returns your money direct to you.

Thus, you have the full responsibility of that bank that you will
receive either your rifle or your money back, and that rifle, when
received, will be of the best quality one of our oldest and best factories
can produce.

So, for the first time in history, the question as to whether or not one
of our greatest arms factories shall bring out a new and better rifle is
put up directly to you, the individual sportsman. You determine
whether it shall or shall not be done. And it is not a big undertaking
for you. You do not have many tens of thousands of dollars worth of
tools to build for the work. All you have to do is to buy one rifle, at the
regular price. If you buy that rifle, the rifles will be built; if not they
will not be built. If they are built they will continue being built so long
as the sportsmen will buy them.

In case you would like the better ballistics of the Newton cartridges,
these rifles will be built to use them. If you prefer the .30 U.S.G.
cartridges, they will also be built to use that line. Just specify in your
order which you prefer and that you will get.

And remember there is no more difficulty in getting all the Newton
cartridges you want. They are made by the Western Cartridge Co., of
East Alton, Illinois, are regularly catalogued by them and carried by
jobbers who carry WESTERN goods. And as soon as these new rifles
come out they will be made by all the large factories and carried
everywhere that the .30 U.S.G. are carried, as the demand will cause
them to be carried. And they will be sold for exactly the same prices
per 100 as are the .30 U.S.G. sporting cartridges.

In case your verdict be in favor of better rifles, we are prepared to
follow these rifles with a full line of other firearms, all far better, both
ballistically and in mechanism, than any others of their types now
made. This covers rifles of .22 caliber rim fire, and of medium power;
also shotguns and pistols. If sportsmen actually want better firearms,
of any kind, and this is proven by the sale of these rifles, the others will
follow. If they do not, the others will not be built.

So it is now definitely up to you. An order now is a vote of "yes." A
failure to order now is a vote of "no" regardless of the reason for that
failure. It is a case of "thumbs up" or "thumbs down," and the thumbs

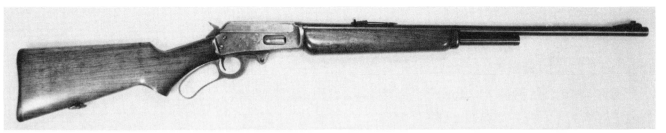

Marlin Model 1936 rifle, serial number B9,014, which has the Canadian broad arrow and C government ownership mark on barrel, receiver, and buttstock.

which will deliver that judgement are YOURS. The question of BETTER RIFLES is entirely in your hands. We have done what we could to make them available.

Trusting our efforts in that direction will meet your approval and support, we remain

> Yours Truly,
> LeverBolt Rifle Co.
> New Haven, Conn.

The fact that Newton's new rifle was never put into production by Marlin is proof that Frank Kenna was correct in his judgment.

Although Charles Newton's rifles were not successful, many of his cartridge developments were, and some still are popular. A few of Mr. Newton's ammunition inventions were the .22 Savage Hi Power; .250–3000 Savage; .256 Newton; .30 Newton; and .35 Newton. Charles Newton died in 1932, never a quitter and pressing on until his death.

Pacific Coast Militia Rangers

During the early part of WW II, when Canada was at war against the Japanese and Axis countries, various paramilitary organizations were formed to protect Canada's coasts from invasion. One such organization was the Pacific Coast Militia Rangers (PCMR), made up of rugged Canadians from all walks of life, most of whom were skilled in the outdoors.

When first organized, the PCMR men used their personal equipment, clothes, and firearms. In due time the Canadian government provided some arms, uniforms, and equipment. Many of the rifles were civilian-type hunting guns purchased for PCMR use. Included among the rifles were a number of Marlin lever action rifles. Examples examined were all Model 1936 rifles with a 24-in. barrel and pistol grip stock. The one photographed here is a Marlin Model 1936 and is serial number B9014. (The lower sling swivel was added at a later time.)

The identifying feature of these very scarce rifles is the Canadian government property mark of a broad arrow in a *C*, thus: ⬆ The mark was stamped into the top rear of the barrel, top front end of the receiver, and side of the buttstock. It is unknown if Canada purchased these rifles directly from the factory or if they were acquired from dealers and distributors having them in inventory.

Patches

Marlin has distributed a variety of different cloth patches to Marlin gun owners and sportsmen. Many get sewn to hunting

Arrows indicate the broad arrow and C government property marks on the PCMR rifle.

Buttstock of PCMR Model 1936 rifle that has the Canadian property mark.

or shooting jackets. Others become a part of a collection of the various patches made available by most of the firearms companies.

Marlin's first cloth patch was red with white (silver) edging and letters. It was shaped like a shield 4½ inches high by 4 inches wide. The letters read *Marlin Firearms Co.* with a telescoped rifle superimposed on two circles. At the bottom was *1870*.

The next type of patch was brought out in 1963. This patch is 5 inches in diameter and has a multicolor horse and rider

1. *First type of Marlin patch; 2–7. Second-style patch made in different colors and in two types of material; 8. 1972 patch with green border; 9. 1975 patch with red border; 10. Safe Hunter patch; and 11. Series of patches from 1980 to date. Background colors and borders are described in the text.*

with *Micro-Groove* and *Marlin 1870* in black letters. A total of 6 variations were produced. Three were of a felt-like material and two wcrc of a cloth matcrial. The color combinations were as follows:

Felt
> Blue felt with blue stitched border
> Yellow felt with green stitched border
> Green felt with green stitched border
> Gray felt with fawn stitched border

Cloth
> Gray cloth with fawn stitched border
> Orange cloth with maroon stitched border

These 5-inch-round patches were given out through 1971.

The 1972 patch was like the earlier round patch except that it was only 3 inches in diameter. Two types were manufactured. Both were quality white cloth patches with the horse and rider logo in seven colors and *Micro Groove* and *Marlin 1870* in black. The border of the first variation was green. Later production had a red border. This patch was in use through 1979.

In 1980, a new rectangular patch was introduced. It is 4 inches wide by 2 inches high. The various color combinations have been as follows:

	Cloth	Letters	Border
1	Yellow	Black	Red
2	Brown	Gold	Red
3	Red	Silver	Gold
4	Yellow	Red	Gold
5	Blue	Silver	Gold

Some unauthorized bootleg patches have been manufactured by unscrupulous people who copy the Marlin trademarked name and horse and rider logo. The original factory patches can be identified by the photos shown here.

Marlin has never authorized any baseball caps, patches, or any other item using the Marlin name and logo, except to the Marlin Employees Athletic Association and The Marlin Firearms Collectors Association Ltd. for their use on mutually authorized items. All other items are illegal and have no collector's value.

Another patch given out by Marlin is the 3-in. Safe Pledged Hunter patch, which is part of Marlin's safety with firearms program. This patch is orange in color with a gold border. The Marlin name and horse and rider logo are in black with *Safe Pledged Hunter* in silver. It is a striking reminder of a pledge that should be taken by all sportsmen.

Patents

Patents are awarded to an individual or individuals who have thought of, or worked out the details of, an invention for the first time. If done on company time, they are usually assigned to the company at the time of application for the patent. Some patents, however, are purchased by a company from the inventor, or use of the patent is agreed to by the inventor—usually for a fee or royalty.

Many of the patents used by the various Marlin companies were by independent inventors; others were by individuals on the payroll and thereby became the property of the company.

The purpose of a patent is to ensure protection to the inventor of a new idea so that others cannot make use of his invention or profit on another's new idea. A patent gives the inventor 17 years of exclusive use of the idea, unless he agrees to another person's making use of his invention.

There are many frivolous inventions that are new and unique, but impracticable or too expensive to use. Marlin's patents have been rather straightforward and were not obtained just to have an impressive file of patents. The important ones are listed here, and many are also illustrated or listed in various other sections of this book.

Patents used by the various Marlin companies have been as follows:

Patent Number	Patent Date	Inventor
2,627	Nov. 5, 1861	C.H. Ballard (Reissue)/Ballard
33,631	Nov. 5, 1861	C.H. Ballard/Ballard
41,166	Jan. 5, 1864	Merwin-Bray/Ballard
46,286	Feb. 7, 1865	H.F. Wheeler/1881
63,605	Apr. 9, 1867	C.H. Ballard/Ballard pistol
99,690	Feb. 8, 1870	J.M. Marlin/Pistol
101,637	Apr. 5, 1870	J.M. MarlinPistol
134,589	Jan. 7, 1873	A. Burgess/1881
140,516	July 1, 1873	J.M. Marlin/Pistol
159,592	Feb. 9, 1875	J.M. Marlin/Ballard
167,712	Sept. 14, 1875	E.A.F. Toepperwein/1881
210,091	Nov. 19, 1878	A. Burgess/1881
210,181	Nov. 26, 1878	A. Burgess/1881
210,182	Nov. 26, 1878	A. Burgess/1881
210,294	Nov. 26, 1878	A. Burgess/1881
210,295	Nov. 26, 1878	A. Burgess/1881
216,080	June 3, 1879	A. Burgess/1881
222,064	Nov. 25, 1879	J.M. Marlin/Exp. lever action
222,065	Nov. 25, 1879	J.M. Marlin/Exp. lever action

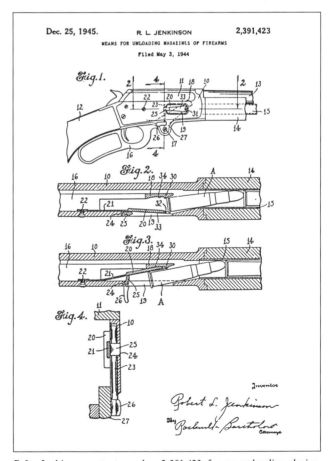

C.E. Ekdahl patent number 1,851,696 for Marlin A1 semiautomatic caliber .22 rifle.

R.L. Jenkinson patent number 2,391,423 for an unloading device, which was not used.

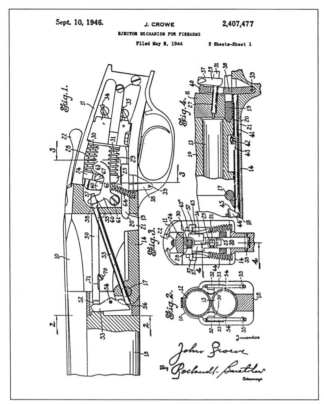

J. Crowe patent number 2,407,477 for a Model 90 ejector system, which was not used.

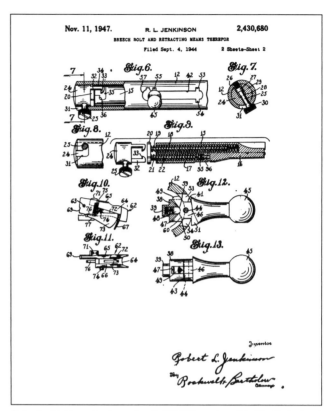

R.L. Jenkinson patent number 2,430,680, assigned to Marlin but not used.

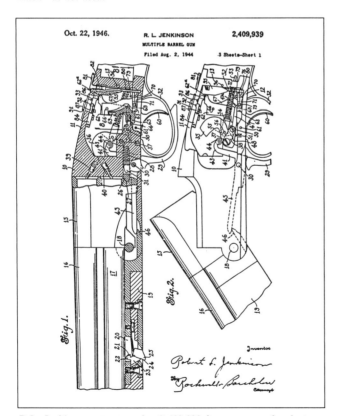

R.L. Jenkinson patent number 2,409,939 for an over–under shotgun, which was not manufactured.

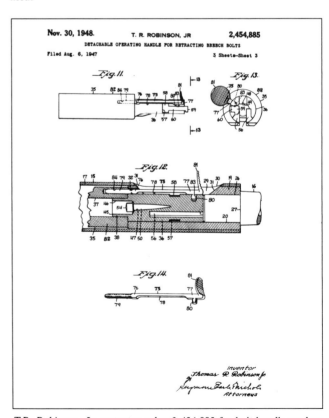

T.R. Robinson, Jr., patent number 2,454,885 for bolt handle used on Model 88 and 89 rifles.

Patent Number	Patent Date	Inventor
222,066	Nov. 25, 1879	J.M. Marlin/Pistol action
222,414	Dec. 9, 1879	J.M. Marlin/1881
9,461	Nov. 9, 1880	H.F. Wheeler (Reissue)/ 1881
234,309	Nov. 9, 1880	J.M. Marlin/1881
247,881	Oct. 4, 1881	J.M. Browning/Loading tool
250,825	Dec. 13, 1881	J.M. Marlin & A. Burgess
271,091	Jan. 23, 1883	J.M. Marlin
297,424	Apr. 22, 1884	J.M. Marlin
308,183	Nov. 18, 1884	J.M. Marlin/Pistol
315,645	Apr. 14, 1885	J.M. Marlin/Mag. tube
316,485	Apr. 28, 1885	D.H. Rice/Cal. .22 feed mechanism
316,554	Apr. 28, 1885	J.M. Marlin/Mag. tube
334,535	Jan. 19, 1886	J.M. Marlin/Cal. .22 feed mechanism
354,059	Dec. 7, 1886	L.L. Hepburn/Model 1888
366,794	July 19, 1887	D.H. Rice/Pistol—not used
367,535	Aug. 2, 1887	J.M. Marlin/Pistol
367,820	Aug. 9, 1887	J.M. Marlin/Pistol
367,821	Aug. 9, 1887	J.M. Marlin/Pistol
368,599	Aug. 23, 1887	J.M. Marlin/Pistol
371,455	Oct. 11, 1887	L.L. Hepburn/Model 1889
371,608	Oct. 18, 1887	J.M. Marlin/Pistol
385,009	June 26, 1888	D.H. Rice/Pistol

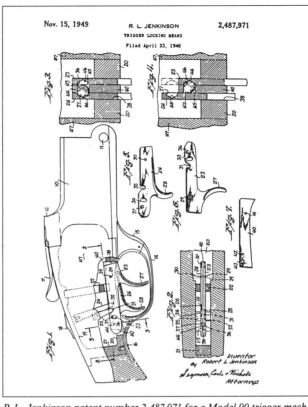

R.L. Jenkinson patent number 2,487,971 for a Model 90 trigger mechanism, which was not used.

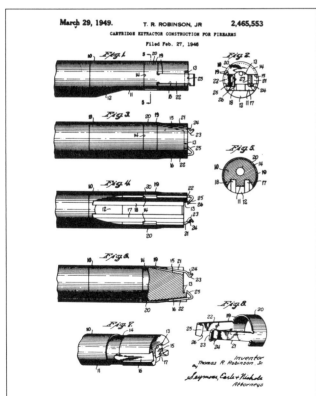

T.R. Robinson, Jr., patent number 2,465,553 for extractor, which was used on Marlin bolt action .22 rifles.

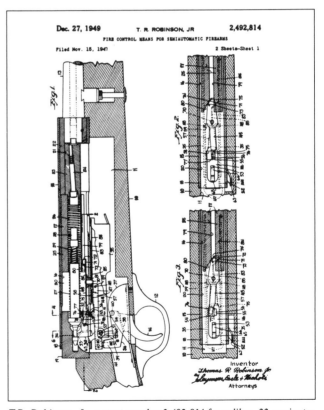

T.R. Robinson, Jr., patent number 2,492,814 for caliber .22 semiautomatic rifle.

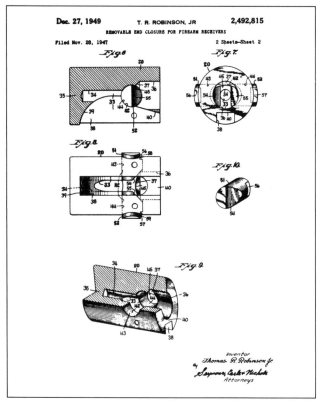

T.R. Robinson, Jr., patent number 2,492,815 for part of Model 88 and 89 receivers.

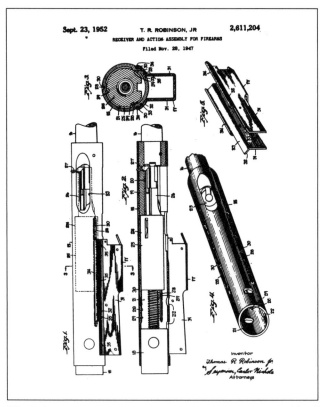

T.R. Robinson, Jr., patent number 2,611,204 for receiver assembly of semiautomatic rifle.

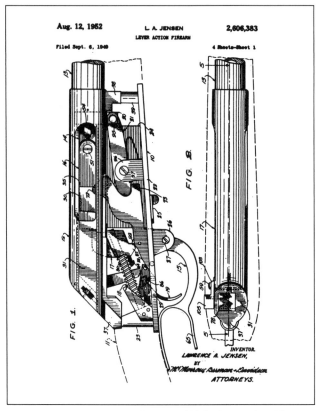

L.A. Jensen patent number 2,606,383 for lever action rifle.

Patent Number	Patent Date	Inventor
400,679	Apr. 2, 1889	L.L. Hepburn/1889
413,196	Oct. 22, 1889	J.M. Marlin/Mag. tube—cal. .22
413,197	Oct. 22, 1889	J.M. Marlin/Pistol
434,062	Aug. 12, 1890	L.L. Hepburn/1891
463,832	Nov. 24, 1891	L.L. Hepburn/Exp.
469,819	Mar. 1, 1892	J.M. Marlin/Mag. tube
502,489	Aug. 1, 1893	L.L. Hepburn/Model 1893
518,950	May 1, 1894	L.L. Hepburn/Rifle takedown
525,739	Sept. 11, 1894	L.L. Hepburn/Shotgun
528,905	Nov. 6, 1894	L.L. Hepburn/Shotgun
529,455	Nov. 20, 1894	J.M. Marlin/Rifle takedown
534,691	Feb. 26, 1895	L.L. Hepburn/Exp. takedown—cal .22
549,722	Nov. 12, 1895	L.L. Hepburn/Lever action shotgun
560,032	May 12, 1896	L.L. Hepburn/Pump shotgun
561,226	June 2, 1896	L.L. Hepburn/Takedown shotgun bbl.
584,177	June 8, 1897	L.L. Hepburn/1897 takedown
591,220	Oct. 5, 1897	L.L. Hepburn/Shotgun safety

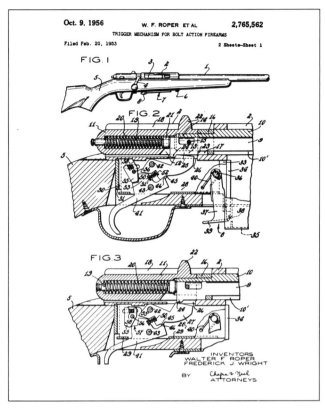

W.F. Roper patent number 2,765,562 for Marlin Model 50 and 55 shotguns.

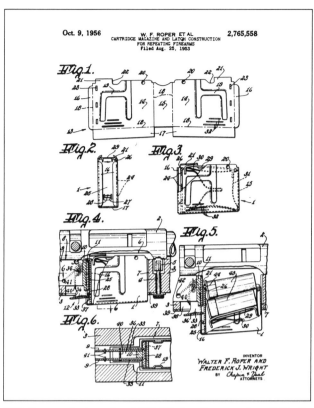

W.F. Roper patent number 2,765,558 for clip magazine of Marlin Model 50 and 55 shotguns.

Patent Number	Patent Date	Inventor
662,427	Nov. 27, 1900	L.L. Hepburn/Shotgun safety
732,075	June 30, 1903	L.L. Hepburn/Sight
755,660	Mar. 29, 1904	Melvin Hepburn/Takedown feature
776,243	Nov. 29, 1904	L.L. Hepburn/Model 20
776,322	Nov. 29, 1904	L.L. Hepburn/Shotgun safety
818,669	Apr. 24, 1906	H.W. DeJarnatt
882,562	Mar. 24, 1908	L.L. Hepburn/Shotgun takedown
882,563	Mar. 24, 1908	L.L. Hepburn/Model 20
883,020	Mar. 24, 1908	L.L. Hepburn/Model 20
888,329	May 19, 1908	Melvin Hepburn/Shotgun takedown
12,823	July 7, 1908	L.L. Hepburn (Reissue)/ Model 20
918,447	Apr. 13, 1908	L.L. Hepburn/ Semiautomatic
927,464	July 6, 1909	L.L. Hepburn/ Semiautomatic
940,764	Nov. 23, 1909	J.H. Wheeler/Shotgun cutoff
940,791	Nov. 23, 1909	H.W. DeJarnatt/Shotgun cutoff
943,828	Dec. 21, 1909	L.L. Hepburn/Shotgun

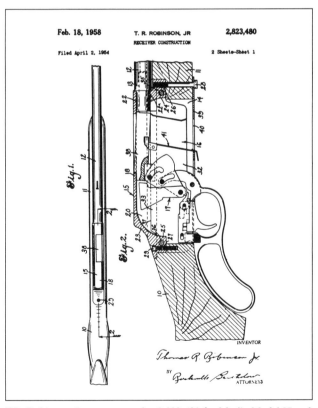

T.R. Robinson, Jr., patent number 2,823,480 for Marlin Model 57 and 62 rifle receivers.

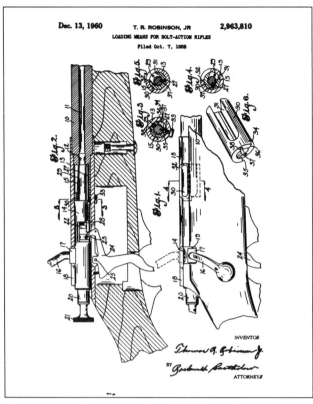

T.R. Robinson, Jr., patent number 2,963,810 for Marlin single-shot caliber .22 rifle.

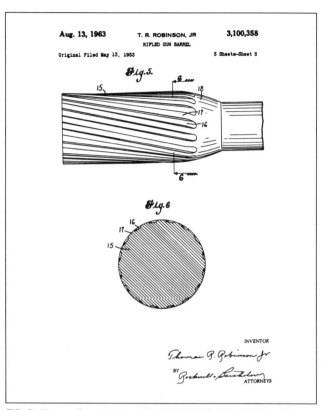

T.R. Robinson, Jr., patent number 3,100,358 for Marlin Micro-Groove rifling.

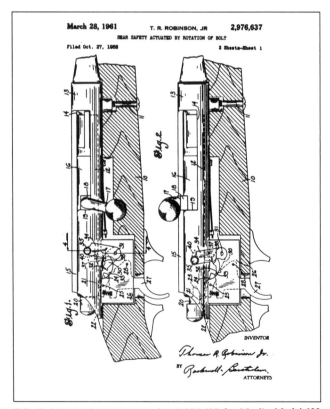

T.R. Robinson, Jr., patent number 2,976,637 for Marlin Model 122 single-shot rifle and Model 59 shotgun.

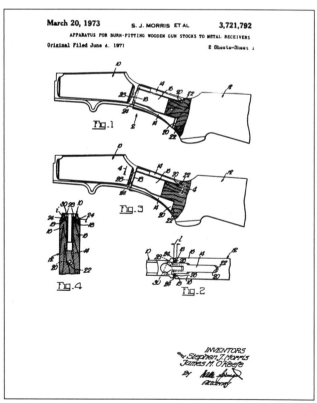

Marlin patent number 3,721,792 for apparatus for fitting stocks to receivers.

Patent Number	Patent Date	Inventor
997,642	July 11, 1911	J.H. Wheeler, G.A. Beck & Melvin Hepburn/Model 27
1,083,708	Jan. 6, 1914	C.G. Swebilius & H.T.R. Hanitz/Pump rifle
1,088,950	Mar. 3, 1914	J.H. Wheeler/Pump shotgun safety
1,089,736	Mar. 10, 1914	J.H. Wheeler/Pump safety
1,090,351	Mar. 17, 1914	C.G. Swebilius & H.T.R. Hanitz/Exp. .22 pump
1,092,085	Mar. 31, 1914	J.H. Wheeler & F. Manglier/Shotgun takedown
1,099,621	June 9, 1914	A.C. Schildbach/Shotgun cutoff
1,103,228	July 14, 1914	H.T.R. Hanitz & C.G. Swebilius/Pump center-fire rifle
1,105,467	July 28, 1914	C.G. Swebilius & H.T.R. Hanitz/Pump shotgun
1,110,837	Sept. 15, 1914	C.G. Swebilius & H.T.R. Hanitz/Model 38
1,115,570	Nov. 3, 1914	Charles W. Reeves/Shotshell
1,129,527	Feb. 23, 1915	C.G. Swebilius & H.T.R. Hanitz/Hammerless shotgun

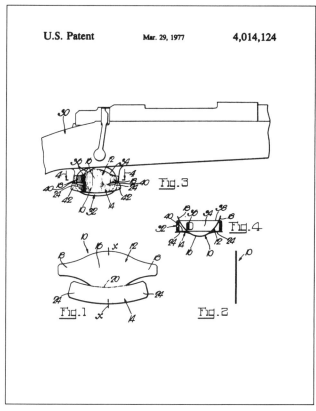

E.E. Oberst patent number 4,014,124 for Safety Minder.

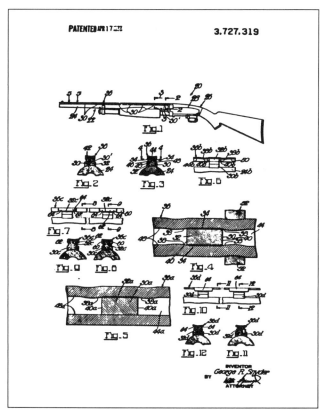

George R. Snyder patent number 3,727,319 for shotgun ventilated rib.

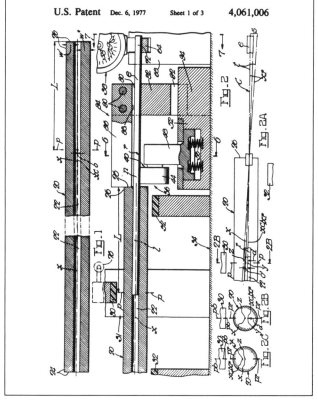

Arthur Burns patent number 4,061,006 for barrel-straightening device.

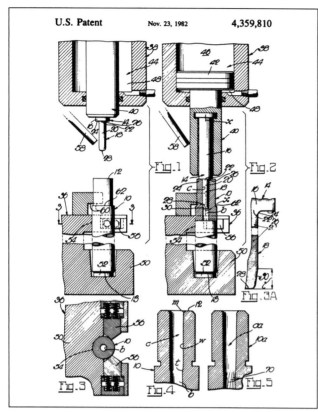

Marlin patent number 4,359,810 for method of chambering barrels.

Patent Number	Patent Date	Inventor
1,146,536	July 13, 1915	C.G. Swebilius & H.T.R. Hanitz/Model 38
1,147,659	July 20, 1915	C.G. Swebilius & H.T.R. Hanitz/Model 38
1,147,906	July 27, 1915	C.G. Swebilius & H.T.R. Hanitz/Pump center-fire rifle
1,149,795	Aug. 10, 1915	C.G. Swebilius & H.T.R. Hanitz/Pump center-fire rifle
1,150,791	Aug. 17, 1915	C.G. Swebilius & H.T.R. Hanitz/Sight
1,176,873	Mar. 28, 1916	C.G. Swebilius & H.T.R. Hanitz/Gas-operated rifle
1,335,487	Mar. 30, 1920	W.B. Darton/Marlin MG
1,337,327	Apr. 20, 1920	H.M. Rockwell/BAR gun mount
1,401,568	Dec. 27, 1921	C.G. Swebilius/Pump rifle
1,402,459	Jan. 3, 1922	C.G. Swebilius/Marlin MG
1,412,287	Apr. 11, 1922	Michael Kovaleff/Magazine for MG
1,412,298	Apr. 11, 1922	C.G. Swebilius/Model 38 safety
1,418,862	June 6, 1922	G.H. Ball/Model 38
1,422,237	July 11, 1922	C.G. Swebilius/Marlin MG
1,422,238	July 11, 1922	C.G. Swebilius/Marlin MG

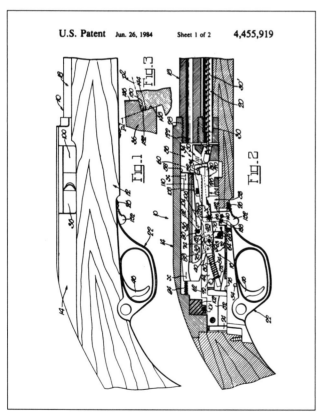

W.E. Osborne patent number 4,455,919 for bolt hold-open device.

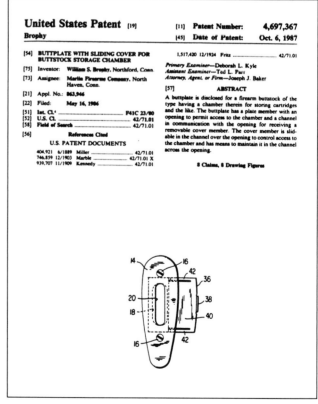

W.S. Brophy patent number 4,697,367 for a butt plate.

Patent Number	Patent Date	Inventor
1,444,890	Feb. 13, 1923	C.G. Swebilius/Marlin MG
1,450,653	Apr. 3, 1923	C.G. Swebilius/Browning MG
1,468,870	Sept. 25, 1923	H.M. Rockwell/Belt loading machine
1,483,987	Feb. 19, 1924	H.M. Rockwell/Turreting mount
1,496,324	June 3, 1924	H.M. Rockwell/Synchronizer for Marlin MG
1,504,584	Aug. 12, 1924	C.G. Swebilius/Marlin MG
1,521,730	Jan. 6, 1925	C.G. Swebilius/Automatic rifle
1,550,757	Aug. 25, 1925	C.G. Swebilius/Shotgun
1,550,758	Aug. 25, 1925	C.G. Swebilius/Shotgun
1,550,759	Aug. 25, 1925	C.G. Swebilius/Automatic rifle
1,550,760	Aug. 25, 1925	C.G. Swebilius/Shotgun
1,552,457	Sept. 8, 1925	C.G. Swebilius/Pump center-fire rifle
1,557,627	Oct. 20, 1925	C.G. Swebilius/Pump center-fire rifle
1,558,566	Oct. 27, 1925	H.M. Rockwell/Browning MG
1,565,756	Dec. 15, 1925	H.M. Rockwell/Browning MG
1,565,826	Dec. 15, 1925	C.G. Swebilius/BAR
1,571,975	Feb. 9, 1926	C.G. Swebilius/BAR
1,575,018	Mar. 2, 1926	C.G. Swebilius/Model 36 SS pump .22
1,575,019	Mar. 2, 1926	C.G. Swebilius/Shotgun
1,578,777	Mar. 30, 1926	C.G. Swebilius/Model 39 ejector
1,587,049	June 1, 1926	C.G. Swebilius/Model 38
1,601,514	Sept. 28, 1926	C.G. Swebilius/Bar
1,702,063	Feb. 12, 1929	C.G. Swebilius/Model 38
1,851,696	Mar. 29, 1932	C.E. Ekdahl/Semiautomatic .22
2,391,423	Dec. 25, 1945	R.L. Jenkinson/Unloading mechanism
2,407,477	Sept. 10, 1946	J. Crowe/Ejector/Model 90
2,409,939	Oct. 22, 1946	R.L. Jenkinson/Shotgun
2,454,885	Nov. 30, 1948	T.R. Robinson
2,465,553	Mar. 29, 1949	T.R. Robinson/Extractor
2,487,971	Nov. 15, 1949	R.L. Jenkinson/Trigger/Model 90
2,492,814	Dec. 22, 1949	T.R. Robinson
2,492,815	Dec. 27, 1949	T.R. Robinson
2,611,204	Sept. 23, 1952	T.R. Robinson
2,765,558	Oct. 9, 1956	W.F. Roper/55 Mag.
2,765,562	Oct. 9, 1956	W.F. Roper/55 Shotgun
2,823,480	Feb. 18, 1956	T.R. Robinson/Levermatic
2,963,810	Dec. 13, 1960	T.R. Robinson
2,976,637	Mar. 28, 1961	T.R. Robinson/Model 59 and 122 sear safety
3,100,358	Aug. 13, 1963	T.R. Robinson/Micro-Groove

Patent Number	Patent Date	Inventor
3,721,792	Mar. 20, 1973	S.J. Morris/Stock burring
3,727,319	Apr. 17, 1973	G.R. Snyder/Shotgun rib
3,755,912	Sept. 4, 1973	W.E. Osborne/Receiver sight
3,883,976	May 20, 1975	Gerald Norman & W.E. Osborne/Mag. tube catch
4,014,124	Mar. 29, 1977	E. Ernst Oberst/Safety minder
4,061,006	Dec. 6, 1977	Arthur H. Burns/Barrel straightener
4,359,810	Nov. 23, 1982	W.E. Osborne, A.H. Burns & James M. O'Keefe/Chamber
4,455,919	June 26, 1984	W.E. Osborne & Nicholas S. Ketre/Bolt hold-open
4,697,367	Oct. 6, 1987	W.S. Brophy/Butt plate

The following design patents were also issued to The Marlin Firearms Company:

Patent Number	Design
D 218,891	Forearm stock design
D 218,892	Buttstock design
D 218,893	Forearm stock design
D 218,894	Forearm stock design
D 218,895	Buttstock design
D 218,896	Buttstock design

Plaque

In 1971, as a companion to the Article II commemorative model rifles, Marlin made available to gun owners and gun shops an Article II Wall Plaque. The plaque was a compelling reminder of the precious, fundamental right to "keep and bear arms," guaranteed to all Americans by Article II of the United States Constitution. It was made from a molded material resembling wood grain, and made an attractive decoration for gun room, office, den, or store. Only 8,000 of these plaques were produced. They were 10"x13¼" and sold for $5.00 postpaid.

Playing Cards

Two different decks of playing cards were used by Marlin to advertise Marlin repeating rifles. One deck has a blue color on the back of the cards and the other has a pinkish-red color. The joker, ace of spades, and ace of hearts of both decks are the same. The joker has *Safest-Lightest-Strongest-Simplest* around a black circle, on which is imprinted *Marlin Repeating Rifles*. The ace of spades has a decorative spade in the middle with *The Marlin Fire Arms Co.* above it and *New Haven, Conn. U.S.A.* below it. The ace of hearts is most impressive. The central heart has a pattern of 25 bullet holes, which all touch to make one large hole. Around the heart target is printed:

1971 Marlin plaque that reminds us of the fundamental right to "keep and bear arms."

Design on back of first style of Marlin playing cards.

Four aces and Joker of Marlin playing cards. Note that the ace of hearts has Annie Oakley's spectacular 25-shot group shot from her Model 91 Marlin in 27 seconds at 12 yards.

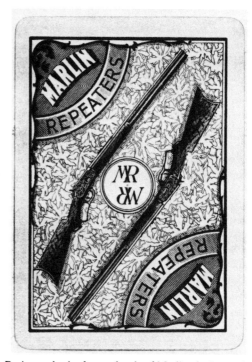

Design on back of second style of Marlin playing cards.

25 shots in 27 seconds with a Marlin rifle Model '91, .22 caliber, distance 12 yards. Made by Miss Annie Oakley at New York, March 10th, 1893, at an ace of hearts. Actual size.

The printed backs of the two decks of playing cards are different. One has an engraved Model 1893 with the action open diagonally across the card and *The Marlin Fire Arms Co., New Haven, Conn.* and *Repeating Rifles and Revolvers* divided above and below the rifle. The other deck of cards has *Marlin Repeaters* diagonally in two corners and two lever action rifles spaced around *MR* (for Marlin Repeaters) in a circle.

Powell, Wyo., 75th-anniversary commemorative rifle.

A very desirable addition to any Marlin collection, and adding a touch of class to a gun-show type of display, these playing cards are rare.

The Marlin Firearms Collectors Association, through The Marlin Firearms Company, has reproduced the first type of playing cards mentioned above in red and blue ink. To ensure they are not mistaken as original, they were dated 1988.

Powell, Wyoming, Diamond Jubilee

In 1984, The Marlin Firearms Company teamed up with the First National Bank of Powell, Wyo., to commemorate the city of Powell's 75th anniversary by offering a special rifle.

The press release announcing the availability of this special Marlin stated the following:

> The rifle, a 30/30 lever action, was produced in a limited edition of 500. It is being offered, along with a Limited Edition Gerber presentation knife, only to First National Bank depositors as payment "in lieu of interest" on selected certificates of deposit.
>
> The Commemorative rifle is a special version of the famous Marlin 336TS straight grip saddle carbine. Etching on both sides of the receiver is done in 22-karat gold plating, with inscriptions and motifs appropriate for Powell's Diamond Jubilee. Each rifle is also engraved with a special serial number, from PW 1 to PW 500, and "1 of 500" is roll-engraved on the barrel. A commemorative mint-struck bronze medallion is inlaid in the butt stock, and the trigger and special saddle ring are plated in 14-karat gold.
>
> The stock of each rifle is crafted from fancy American black walnut and oil finished by hand.

At this writing, a few of these limited edition Marlin rifles are still available. Interested persons should contact the First National Bank of Powell, P.O. Box 907, Powell, Wyo., 82435, for deposit and loan schedules, plus information on obtaining a carbine or Gerber knife. Although marked *1 of 500,* only 350 were produced.

Presentation Firearms

Companies in the firearms industry—in particular, Colt, Smith & Wesson, and Winchester—have presented to important people on special occasions guns having elaborate engraving, fancy wood or grips, and gold, silver, or platinum inlays. Marlin was not an exception, but Marlin did not make and give away exotic pieces such as those the other companies were

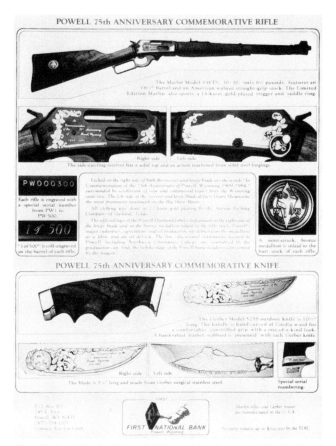

First National Bank of Powell, Wyo., ad for the special Marlin Model 336TS and Gerber hunting knife.

noted for. Marlin was much more conservative; thus, Marlin presentation guns are very rare.

The earliest identified presentation rifle is the Annie Oakley Model 1889, which is described elsewhere in this book. It and other Marlins were presented to Miss Oakley prior to WW I.

In 1923, a Model 44A pump action shotgun was presented to H.E. Winans, champion wing- and trapshooter, by John F. Moran, president of The Marlin Firearms Corporation. It has the name *H.E. Winans* inlaid in gold on the left side of the receiver. The quality of the wood and metal finish is superb.

A Marlin Model 44 was presented to Mark Arie, another champion trapshooter. (See the section on expert and fancy shooters.) The shotgun he was presented is now on display at the Trapshooters Hall of Fame, Vandalia, Ohio. It is also inscribed with his name.

Annie Oakley's Model 1889 rifle.

Annie Oakley.

Model 90 shotgun presented to Tom Mix, king of the movie cowboys in the 1930s.

H.E. Winans's Model 44A shotgun.

In 1937, Marlin presented Tom Mix, the cowboy movie star of the 1930s, with an engraved and gold-inlaid Model 90 shotgun. Marlin had used Tom Mix's name in the promotion of the Tom Mix Special caliber .22 rifle and wanted to show its appreciation by having this shotgun specially made for presentation to him. The engraving and gold inlay work were done by Charles Preiss and Dan Cavanaugh of the Lehman Brothers Company of New Haven, Conn. The Lehman company specialized in stationery engraving but, because of being close by the Marlin plant and friendly with the company, Lehman made an exception and did the Tom Mix, Mark Arie, King Farouk, Allan Shivers, and other jobs that did not require extensive ornamentation or heavy cutting of steel.

In May of 1947, Roger Kenna, president of Marlin, presented to Mexican President Miguel Aleman an Ideal Grade custom-made side-by-side 16-gauge L.C. Smith shotgun. The lock plates were engraved in an oak leaf design, and the president's name was engraved in gold on the trigger guard.

Upon receiving the gun in his suite in the Waldorf–Astoria Hotel in New York City, President Aleman told Mr. Kenna he would not trust the gun to be shipped home with other presents, but instead he would carry it with him throughout his tour to make certain nothing would happen to his beautiful new gun.

In March 1951, Roger Kenna presented to King Farouk of Egypt a Model 336 Sporting Carbine. On the left side of the receiver, it was gold-inlaid and engraved *To His Majesty, King Farouk*. The carbine was presented to Wendell Phillips, the leader of the expedition for the American Foundation for the Study of Man, which was uncovering many great archaeological discoveries in Egypt; Mr. Phillips presented the carbine to King Farouk at a later date. Also present at the presentation was Abdel Mequid Ramadan, press counselor of the Royal Egyptian Embassy in Washington, D.C.

King Farouk rifle.

The first production model of the Marlin Model 336 Texan was presented in June of 1952 to Texas Governor Allan Shivers. The governor accepted the carbine on behalf of the people of Texas. The left side of the receiver is engraved in silver with the governor's signature.

In October 1959, Marlin gave a deluxe Model 336C to John Bromfield, star of the show "U.S. Marshall." Two standard models were also presented for use in Bromfield's station wagon and by his deputies.

In 1960 Marlin presented to Ted Williams, the famous baseball player, a special Model 39A Mountie. The buttstock and forearm are checkered. A squirrel is carved into the stock and the right side of the receiver is gold-inlaid and engraved *TED WILLIAMS/THE 500 YEAR*. The rifle was presented in recognition of his having hit over 500 home runs.

In 1962, Marlin presented to Colonel Larson, the company's exhibition shooter, a Model 336 inscribed on the left side: *Presented to World's Champion Colonel Larson by The Marlin*

First 336 Texan, presented to Texas Governor Allan Shivers.

Model 336 presented to John Bromfield.

Ted Williams's Model 39A Mountie.

Colonel Larson's Model 336T.

Mickey Mantle holding his new Model 444, which was just presented to him by Marlin Activity Director Peter Grillo.

Colonel Larson's Model 39A Mountie.

Firearms Co. 1962. In 1963, Marlin presented to Colonel Larson a Model 39A Mountie on which was inscribed: *Presented to Colonel Larson on his 5,000th Exhibition, Marlin Firearms Co. January 17, 1963.* This rifle is checkered and has carved into the right side of the stock the Marlin horse and rider (Danger Ahead) logo.

In 1972, two Zane Grey Commemorative rifles were presented to two stalwart Americans. Zane Grey would have been proud, I'm sure.

One was given by Marlin to John Wayne, movie and television hero. Jim Devere, then a Marlin Firearms Company representative, made the presentation. The rifle occupies a featured position in the John Wayne gun collection.

The other Zane Grey Commemorative was presented to Senator Barry Goldwater (R–Ariz.) by the late Robert Wallack, Marlin's advertising agency vice president and friend of mine. In making the presentation, Mr. Wallack said,

> Zane Grey lived and wrote in Arizona for years and Mr. Goldwater, you are an outstanding sportsman and hunter, therefore, it is only fitting you have this rifle to add to your collection. On behalf of Marlin, we hope you will enjoy the rifle.

In 1979, Marlin commemorated the three-millionth Marlin center-fire lever action rifle by having made a special engraved and gold inlaid Model 336C. The rifle was engraved by Daniel Goodwin and the wood was done by Fred Wenig of Reinhart Fajen Company. The rifle was presented by Marlin President Frank Kenna to Harlon Carter, executive vice president of the National Rifle Association, for permanent display at the NRA Museum in Washington, D.C.

In 1983, Marlin presented a Model 1894M to Harlon Carter, in appreciation for the contribution he had made as executive vice president of the NRA to all sportsmen and gun owners in America. The rifle was hand-engraved and had select checkered wood. The bolt had *Harlon Carter Victory, 1983* inlaid in gold. Engraving and gold work was done by Robert Kain.

Also in 1983, Marlin presented to the NRA Museum, Washington, D.C., a unique version of the Model 60 semiautomatic .22 caliber rifle. The rifle commemorated the two-millionth Model 60. *Marlin Glenfield Model 60 No. 2,000,000* is inlaid in gold on the barrel. The receiver, barrel, front sight, and trigger guard are also engraved in a floral design. The work was done by Robert Kain. The rifle was presented to Warren Cassidy, executive director of NRA's Institute for Legislative Action, during ceremonies at NRA headquarters.

In 1984, Marlin made the two-millionth Model 39 rifle. To commemorate such a milestone, the rifle was engraved and gold inlaid by Alvin A. White. Fancy wood was especially fitted, finished, and checkered by Fred Wenig of the Reinhart Fajen Company. In the interest of firearms safety and educa-

Jim Devere of Marlin presenting Zane Grey rifle to John Wayne.

Marlin President Frank Kenna presenting Marlin center-fire lever action rifle, serial number 3,000,000, to the NRA.

Robert Wallack presenting Zane Grey rifle to U.S. Senator Barry Goldwater.

Marlin's senior technical manager, William S. Brophy, and Harlon Carter looking at the Model 1894M rifle Mr. Carter had just been presented.

Glenfield Model 60, serial number 2,000,000.

tion of the youth of America, this 2,000,000th Model 39 was given to the National Shooting Sports Foundation (NSSF), Riverside, Conn., to be auctioned at the annual Shooting, Hunting, Outdoor Trade Show (SHOT Show), which is held each year by the NSSF. The proceeds of the annual auction go toward the NSSF Education Program. The Marlin rifle added over $20,000 to the fund.

In 1987 Marlin again had commissioned a special rifle, which is also to be used as a fund-raiser for the NSSF Education Program. The rifle commemorates the 100th anniversary of *Sports Afield* magazine. It is engraved and gold inlaid by Alvin A. White and the wood, again, is the artistry of Fred Wenig of Fajen. It is serial numbered SA100. When auctioned, it should bring a pretty penny!

In the interest of promoting gun collecting and gun show displays, a number of Marlin rifles have been given to The Marlin Firearms Collectors Association, Ltd., as "Excellence in Display" awards. Some have been engraved with the place and date of the show, and some have had the winner's name engraved upon them. Otherwise, these awards were standard or commemorative models.

Many other Marlin rifles and shotguns were presented to dignitaries, sports figures, and friends of the company. However, no company records exist to identify them, or to describe any special features or special markings.

Private Brand Models

At the turn of the century it was not uncommon for hardware, mail-order, and sporting goods companies to have guns manufactured for them under a private brand name. Some of the early Marlin-manufactured models of its pump action exposed hammer shotguns were made for the following companies and were marked as follows:

1. *Rev-O-Noc*—Hibbard, Spencer and Bartlett and Company, Chicago.
2. *H.S.B. Co. Model A*—Hibbard, Spencer and Bartlett and Company, Chicago.
3. *Chicago*—Hibbard, Spencer and Bartlett and Company, Chicago.
4. *Marswell Model 1914*—Marshall Wells Company, Duluth, Minn.
5. *National Fire Arms Co.*—H.&D. Folsom Arms Company, New York City.

The following two memos from Marlin sales to the plant manager are quoted to show the special attention given to orders for these early brand name Marlin-manufactured guns. It should also be noted that the letters are dated in January 1915, not too long before the company was acquired by a syndicate that produced machine guns during WW I.

Jan. 8, 1915

Mr. Charles Scharf (Plant manager)

We have orders for 250 Marswells 20 gauge 25″ to be shipped as follows:
50 at once
200 on July 1st
This gun is to be made up in hammer style (like our model 30 20 gauge). They must be stamped the same as the 12 gauge Marswells that

Marking on Marlin shotgun sold to H & D Folsom that has the Folsom brand name, "National Fire Arms Co.," on it.

Bolt action .22 marked Mohawk *for Blish, Mize and Silliman Hardware Company, Atchison, Kan.*

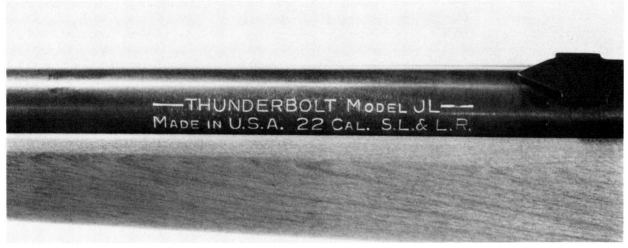

Caliber .22 single-shot rifle sold to Marky Bros., Detroit, under its exclusive brand name, "Thunderbolt Model JL."

Pre-WW II Sears Ranger-*marked Model 34 rifle.*

we have made for them before. They must be equipped with the latest style for-end tip, three screw holes and cup shaped tip.

We also have an order for 100 Marswells 12 gauge 30″ to be made up the same as before and to be ready for shipment on July 1st.

R.S. Robinson

January 20, 1915

Mr. Scharff.

We have received orders for 100 Chicago guns 20 gauge 25″ full choke. These are to have standard style receivers with raised square matted top. These are to be shipped as soon as completed. We have also received an order for 150 12 gauge 30″ to be made up with standard style receivers with raised square matted top, and 20 32″ the same. All to be ready for shipment by Aug. 1st.

We also have an order for 50 Rev-O-Noc 12 gauge 30″ standard style. The receiver to have raised square matted top. These are to be shipped as soon as completed.

R.S. Robinson

All of the above guns were standard models without any frills or special-order features. They sold competitively at a time in American gunmaking history when the pump gun was making inroads into side-by-side double gun popularity. Interestingly, the pump shotgun was an American development that had

little or no competition from imported European guns, as did double- and single-barrel shotguns.

The number of pre-WW I shotguns that Marlin marked with another's brand name is not known, but from the few examples reported it can be assumed they were not sold in large numbers. Most of the examples examined show a great amount of use, and, in many cases, abuse. Therefore, it is assumed they were inexpensive, compared with the Marlin line of shotguns, and sold to the working man as a tool, rather than to the connoisseur of fine firearms.

The practice of U.S. manufacturers producing private brand-named firearms for chain outlets and mass-merchandisers reached a peak during the 1960–1980 period. Since 1980, however, the trend has been away from that practice.

Since 1969, Marlin has embossed its name on all firearms it manufactured, regardless of for whom they were manufactured, or special model designation, or serial number series they were given at the request of the purchaser.

The following is a recapitulation of the private brand models Marlin has produced for the various mass-merchandisers and others. The totals shown are not complete and only reflect the period of 1952 to 1986.

Coast to Coast Stores, Minneapolis, Minn. The Coast to Coast Company has for many years featured Marlin-manufactured

Deer head carved in special Model 336 carbine produced for Spiegel & Company, Chicago, during 1963 and 1964.

firearms under its own name and model designation. The list is as follows:

C-C Model	Comparable Marlin Model	Total Made
40	99 tube magazine	2,109
42	989 clip magazine	27,529
SA 654 (Widgeon)	55/12 gauge (1955)	7,065
440	70	4,798
550	60	7,065
3030S	30AS	NA

Cotter & Company, Chicago, Ill. Marlin produced West Point brand rifles for Cotter and Company for many years. Their model designation and the comparable Marlin model and the years were as follows:

C&C Model	Marlin Model	Year	Total Made
33	336	1966–1970	7,289
10–40	10	1968–1970	5,101
60–50	60	1968–1970	2,991
75–45	75	1968–1970	9,877
601	60	1979–1982	12,219
701	70	1979–1982	7,290
GA-22	75C	1983 to date	NA

An exclusive limited edition caliber .22 Model GA22 rifle has been produced for the Cotter & Company's True Value Stores. It is identified as "West Point by Marlin" and was called the "Great American Game Series." The rifle was the same as the Glenfield Model 70C, except that it had a gold trigger, brass-colored medallion inlaid into the stock, and a 4X telescope packed with the rifle. The production of the GA22 has been as follows:

Year	Medallion	Production
1983	Squirrel	4,955
1984	Rabbit	3,000
1985	Woodchuck	4,550
1986/87	Fox	9,465
1988	Raccoon	NA

Ducks Unlimited (DU). Each year, firearms companies are selected by Ducks Unlimited to furnish special editions that have the DU medallion embedded into the stock; these models aid DU's fund-raising projects. In 1986, Marlin sold DU two models, as follows:

Model	Production	Medallion
781DU	99	DU
990DU	500	DU

From 1978 to 1986, the following private-brand medallions have been used: A—*1983 Cotter and Company,* B—*1984 Cotter and Company,* C—*1985 Cotter and Company,* D—*1986/87 Cotter and Company,* E—*1982 Woolco,* F—*1984 Powell, Wyoming,* G—*1986 Ducks Unlimited,* H—*1978 OTASCO,* I—*1979 OTASCO,* J—*1980 OTASCO,* K—*1981 OTASCO,* L—*1982 OTASCO,* M—*1983 OTASCO,* N—*1984 OTASCO,* O—*1985/86 OTASCO.*

Firestone Tire & Rubber Company. Firestone Models and comparable Marlin models were as follows:

FTR Model	Marlin Model
10P30	81
10P37	80
10P68	88
10P90	39A
10P64	336
10P253	56

Frank M Katz Inc., New York City. Models manufactured for the Katz company were as follows:

Katz Model	Marlin Model
F 1185	989 w/4X scope
F 1180	55 w/choke
F 71	80C w/4X scope
F 1143	55

Two other models manufactured for Katz by Marlin were the 50K (1969) (F 1287), which was the same as the Marlin 50/12 except for a warranty on the barrel, and a gun case and shotgun cleaning kit with rod, knife, and shell belt packed with the gun; and the 60K (1965-1969) (F 1282), which was the same as the Marlin Model 60 except for a warranty stamped on the barrel, and a gun case, set of 12 targets, .22 cleaning kit, and Model 200 telescope packed with the gun.

Mages & Company.

Mages Model	Marlin Model	Years Made
M 25 Coronet	55 w/o choke	1955-1956
M 25C Huntsman	55 w/choke	1955-1956

Marky Bros., Detroit, Mich. One thousand caliber .22 single-shot rifles, like the Marlin Model 101, were marked *Thunderbolt Model JL* for the Marky Company.

Montgomery Ward. Marlin manufactured brand name models for Montgomery Ward. The rifles were marked with the Ward's model designation and *Western Field*. The models and their equivalents were as follows:

Montgomery Ward Model	Marlin Model	Year
33	336	
40	101	
45	989M2	
50	60	
EMN-740A	336 w/recoil pad	1964-1965
EMN-174	55 w/choke	1957-1958
EMN-175A	55/12 ga.	1955-1958
EMN-176A	55/20 ga.	1956-1958
890	39A	
891	39M	
737	336C/.32 spec.	

OTASCO (Oklahoma Tire and Supply Company). Upon the occasion of OTASCO's 50th anniversary in 1969, OTASCO had Marlin produce two models to commemorate the event. The models chosen were the OTASCO Model 30 which was the caliber .30-30 Glenfield Model 30A marked *Golden 50* on the barrel, and the OTASCO Model 65, which was the Marlin Model 60 caliber .22 autoloader, having a brass outer magazine tube, and also so marked. A total of 1,900 of the Model 30 were manufactured for OTASCO from 1968 to 1970, and 7,576 of the Model 65 were made from 1971 to 1974.

Since 1978, Marlin has manufactured exclusively for OTASCO a special commemorative model firearm. The 3000 series models are like the Glenfield Model 30A and the 6000 series models are like the Model 60 Glenfield. Both models had brass commemorative medallions inlaid into the stocks, and some had special alphabetical prefixes to the serial number. The various models were as follows:

Year	Model	Serial Number Prefix	Medallion
1978	3030	OK	Diamond Jubilee
	6060	OT	Diamond Jubilee
1979	3079	OB	American Hunting Tradition
	6079	TK	American Hunting Tradition
1980	3080	TR	Trail Rider
	6080	RT	Trail Rider
1981	3081	OR	Alamo Commemorative
	6081	OZ	Alamo Commemorative
1982	3082	2T	U.S. Cavalry Commemorative
	6082	2R	U.S. Cavalry Commemorative
1983	3083	TL	Wagon Train
	6083	WR	Wagon Train
1984	3084	RL	Mountain Man
	6084	GO	Mountain Man
1985	3085	UR	Round Up
	6085	RU	Round Up
1986	6086	RU	Round Up
1987	3087	UU	Long Horn
	6087	RR	Long Horn

J.C. Penney Company. Marlin manufactured rifles marked *Formost* for the J.C. Penney Company. The Penney model numbers and equivalent Marlin models were:

J.C. Penney Model	Marlin Model
2035	20
2066	49
3040 (1971)	336 w/birch wood
6630	50/12 gauge, 28″ barrel
6660	60 w/gold safety button (1968-70)

Sears, Roebuck & Company. Sears used two systems to identify the manufacturer of its brand name models. The first was to assign each different manufacturer an identification number, and then to identify the specific model by a number following the manufacturer's number. For example, the model designation 103.1988 breaks down to 103. for Marlin, and 1988 for the Marlin Model 57.

The other system used by Sears did not include the manufacturer's code number, but used model numbers of Sears' own selection. For example, the Sears Model 41 was the Marlin Model 101, and the Sears Model 46 was the Marlin Model 56.

All Sears models prior to WW II were marked *Ranger*. Those made by Marlin after WW II were marked *J.C. Higgins* and had the Sears catalog number stamped into the barrel. The prefix 103. indicated the gun was manufactured by Marlin. Other models were identified as follows:

Model	Catalog Number	Marlin Model	Year	Total
34	Ranger	65		
36	Ranger	80		
	103.2	80		
	103.5	90 − .22/.410		
	103.7	90 − 16		
	103.10	90 − .22/.410		
	103.16	90 − 16		
	103.13	81		
	103.14	90 − .410		
	103.16	80		
	103.18	100		
	103.181	101		
	103.209	80	1948−1949	
	103.211	81	1948−1949	
	103.228	80DT	1955−1959	26,031
	103.229	81DT	1955−1959	56,966
45	103.237	336 − 35	1958−1964	11,585
45	103.238	336 − 30	1958−1964	35,734
	103.248	81	1950−1954	11,173
	103.252	80	1950−1954	12,755
42DLM	103.273	980	1961−1965	5,284
41DL	103.274	122	1961	9,643
41DL	103.275	122	1962−1964	15,461
	103.277	100	1963−1965	19,329
42	103.279	80	1963−1965	712
43	103.281	81	1962−1965	5,562
43	103.285	81	1965	
43	103.285	81	1965	
44DL	103.288	57	1963	1,952
44DLM	103.289	57M	1963−1964	
	103.310	90 − 20		
	103.350	90 − 12		
	103.360	90 − 16		
	103.370	90 − 20		
	103.450	336		
	103.451	336		
	103.500	12 gauge		
	103.700	16 gauge		
74	103.720	59	1960−1964	6,287
74	103.740	59	1960−1964	22,143
	103.1977			
43	103.1981			17,854
43DL	103.1982			20,487
	103.2751			
	103.2840			
43	103.2850	81		
46	103.2870	56	1963	5,065
41	103.19770	101	1959−1962	66,424
41	103.19771	101		
41DL	103.19780	101	1959−1960	7,085

Model	Catalog Number	Marlin Model	Year	Total
42	103.19790	80	1959–1960	24,763
42	103.19791	80		
42DL	103.19800	80	1959–1962	19,410
42DL	103.19801	80DL		17,854
43	103.19810	81	1959–1962	
43DL	103.19820	81	1959–1962	20,487
43DL	103.19821	81		
46DL	103.19840	56	1961–1962	5,232
44DL	103.19880	57	1959–1962	13,169
44DL	103.19881	57		
44DLM	103.19890	57M	1960–1962	7,377
	103.2235	90 – 12/28DT	1956–1957	
	103.2236	90 – 16/28DT	1956–1957	
	103.2237	90 – 20/28DT	1956–1957	
42DL	103.2800	80	1963–1965	3,950
42	103.2840	80	1965	
43	103.2850	81	1965	

Spiegel Company, Chicago, Ill. Marlin manufactured a special model of the Model 336 for the Spiegel Company. It is identified by a deer head that is carved into the right side of the buttstock. During 1963 and 1964, 4,264 of this scarce model were sold by Spiegel. Another Spiegel model was a 12-gauge shotgun called the Model 32C American Eagle. It was like the Marlin Model 50 bolt action shotgun, but with an adjustable choke. Without the choke, it was the Model 31. The Spiegel .22 autoloader, like the 60, had a carved insert in the stock.

The shotguns were as follows:

Spiegel Model	Years	Total
32C 12-gauge w/choke	1955–1961	6,136
32 12-gauge	1955–1961	2,008
32 16-gauge	1961	837
32 20-gauge	1961	840

United Merchandising (Big 5). Marlin manufactured for the Big 5 stores two models, as follows:

Big 5	Marlin Model
5	60
3000	30AS

Western Auto Supply Company. Western Auto models manufactured by Marlin were marked *Revelation*. The Western Auto model designations and comparable Marlin models were as follows:

Western Auto Model	Marlin Model	Year
105-2060	80C	1962–1965
110-2140	81	1961–1965
115-2270	57	1962–1965
116-2276	57M	1964–1965
120-2220	99	1960–1965
150-2225	49	
200-2550	336	1960–1965
200-2554	336/.44 mag.	
200-2280	39A	
200-2282	39A Mountie	
335-3725	59	1962–1965

Woolco (Woolworth Company) A one-time limited-edition rifle was produced for Woolco. Unfortunately, the model was ordered and delivery made at a time Woolco was going out of

1987 OTASCO medallion.

1988 Cotter and Company medallion.

1988 Coast to Coast medallion.

First type of Marlin proofmark.

Second type of Marlin proofmark, shown on Model 1889 barrel.

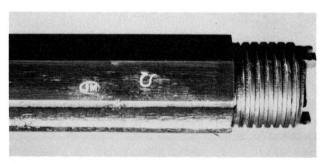

Second type of proofmark on octagon Special Smokeless Steel barrel.

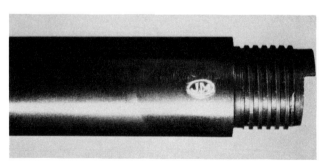

Late type of JM proofmark, as used in 1986.

business. However, the complete shipment was sold. It was truly a limited edition.

Year	Model	Production	Medallion
1982	75-20	8,605	Woolco Limited Edition

Proofmarks

To ensure that a barrel or finished firearm has the strength desired, and that the chamber has no imperfections, a proof (high-pressure) shell or cartridge is used during final inspection.

The inspector examines the ease of extraction of the fired proof cartridge case; he also examines the case for bulges and rings, and the primer for firing pin indent. The proof cartridges will disclose any defects in lockup of the bolt, defects in the chamber, or functional problems due to the chamber.

The proof cartridge or shotgun shell is always fired before function rounds, and in a steel box to protect the gunner. After the firearm is proofed, it has been the general practice to stamp the barrel with a proofmark. The mark first used by Marlin was the letter *M* in a circle. It was usually stamped on the bottom of the barrel, forward of the receiver. In later years (after the Model 1889), the mark used was the letters JM (John Marlin) in an oval. On June 16, 1986, a *JM* proofmark without the oval was authorized; however, it has not been used exclusively. Some rifles will have the *JM* in an oval and some will have just the *JM* mark.

Since 1986, Marlin no longer proof-tests those firearms hav-

British proofmarks on Model 1893.

British proofmarks on Model 1881.

ing a blow-back mechanism. Instead, it tests statistical samples on a scheduled basis.

Many foreign countries have very strict rules about the testing and proofing of firearms, with a requirement that any firearm sold in their country must pass their government's proof house tests. When passed, they place marks on the gun that identify the type of firearm and the tests conducted. Rather scarce in the U.S. and infrequently observed, they add to any collection. Most of those noted have British proofmarks; however, German ones have also been examined, and recent production guns shipped to France are proofed there.

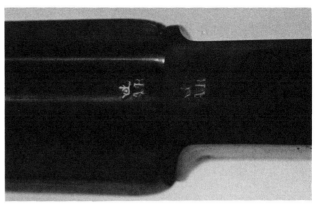

French proofmark on a Model 39A barrel and receiver.

Range Finder

The Marlin Range Finder was a 3″x6″ thin piece of plastic having a series of 6 holes from ½ inch to ⅛ inch in size. The large hole represented 100 yards, and the smallest one 600 yards.

The instructions printed on the range finder were as follows:

> The Marlin Range Finder works by measuring an angle. It must be held exactly 24 inches from your eye. Mark a spot on your rifle 24 inches from the eye in shooting position—or tie a string in the hole provided, knot it at 24 inches and hold the knot to your face.
>
> Each range hole measures a field of view of six feet at the distance marked—when the Range Finder is 24 inches from your eye. The accuracy of your estimate depends on your ability to judge a six foot object. A deer, about three feet at the shoulders, should fill half of the proper range hole—or all of the hole marked for twice the distance. Approximate height at shoulders of other animals is: deer 3, elk 5, antelope 3, moose 6, black bear 2½.

It was nothing more than a gimmick. The thing sold for $1.00; however, hundreds were given away.

British proofmark on Model 1892.

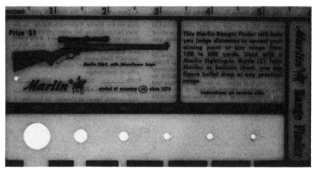

Marlin Range Finder.

Eugene G. Reising

In 1940 Eugene G. Reising, formerly an assistant to John Browning, developed a submachine gun that was manufactured until about 1945. His first model was called the Model 50 and was capable of either full automatic or semiautomatic fire. The second Model was the Model 55, which differed from the

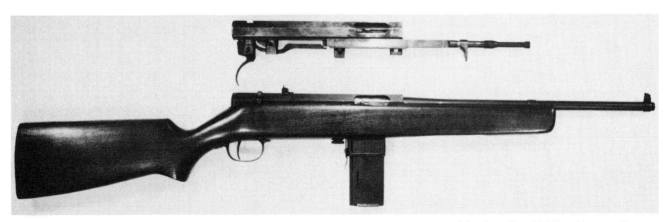

Prototype of Eugene G. Reising's semiautomatic rifle manufactured by Marlin. It was chambered for the caliber .30 M1 carbine cartridge.

Model 50 only in having a folding stock, no flash suppressor, and a shorter barrel. Both models were in caliber .45 ACP. A semiautomatic-only model, called the Model 60, was also manufactured by the Harrington & Richardson Arms Company, Worcester, Mass., the manufacturer of all three.

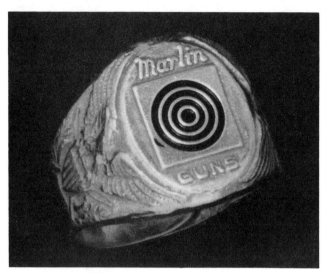

Photograph of Marlin finger ring.

BOYS!

Here is a Chance to Earn Some Extra Money Easy

BULL'S EYE RING

Thousands of boys have sent in 10 cents each for our simulated Gold Bull's Eye Ring. There are thousands of more boys who would want one of these but who have not heard about it. It really looks like an expensive ring as it is real smart and attractive and in fact could sell for 25 cents.

You could make money easy by selling them to your friends who would like them as a club insignia. You can even organize a Marlin Club in your vicinity and have every member wear one as a membership pass ring.

Here Is Our Offer To You — 66 2/3% Profit

We will sell these Rings to you in lots of 10 or more at 6 cents each. You can resell them for 10 cents each and make 4 cents. (That's 66 2/3% profit.) You could easily sell 25 or 50 and possibly 100. Look at the money you would make.

Free Rifle Book

We will give FREE one Rifle Book with each Ring ordered. This book tells "How to set up a Rifle Range and Shoot. It was written by National Rifle Association experts with articles by Captain Crossman, America's No. 1 gun authority.

ORDER NOW.

The supply of Rings is limited, so use the order blank on reverse side and get your order in the next mail. This offer is only good while the supply lasts.

The Marlin Firearms Co.

Marlin pitch to youngsters to earn some extra money.

In June 1944, Marlin discussed with Mr. Reising the possibility of manufacturing a semiautomatic rifle, similar to his Model 50 gun, under the Marlin name. The new gun was to be chambered for the caliber .30 M1 cartridge.

Two prototype guns were made by Marlin and extensively tested. However, objections by H&R that the basic design of Eugene Reising's Models 50, 55, and 60 belonged to them resulted in Marlin's dropping the project.

Ring

Prized among Marlin collectors and their families is the Marlin finger ring, which was used as a promotional item during the 1936–1940 period. Its simulated gold color, bull's-eye, and eagle on each side made it an eye-catching ring that would appeal to any young sportsman. Thousands of these rings were sent through the mail to young people taking advantage of Marlin's profit-making offer:

> We will sell these Rings to you in lots of 10 or more at 6 cents each. You can sell them for 10 cents each and make 4 cents. (That's 66⅔% profit.) You could easily sell 25 or 50 and possibly 100. Look at the money you would make.

Hundreds more were handed out to people visiting the Marlin booth at annual National Rifle Association meetings and exhibits during the 1950s.

Roll-Stamps

The Marlin company name was shown in the 1882 and 1883 catalogs with the word *firearm* hyphenated, thus: "The Marlin Fire-Arms Co." The 1885 catalog showed the name of the company without the hyphen between the two words. In 1905, the two words became one and the company name became "The Marlin Firearms Co." However, the roll-stamp on barrels did not keep pace with the advertising, catalog, and writing stationery changes to the name. The hyphenated "Fire-Arms"

Roll-stamp on Model 1881 barrel.

Roll-stamp on Model 1891 barrel, serial number 47,889.

Roll-stamp on Model 1897 and Model '97 rifles, serial-numbered 151,420 and 354,062.

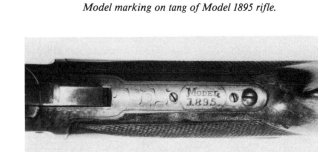

Model marking on tang of Model 1895 rifle.

Roll-stamp on Model 1893 rifle that has Firearms *as one word.*

Model marking on tang of engraved Model 1895 rifle.

Model marking on tang of Model 1891 rifle.

Marking on tang of engraved Model 1897 rifle.

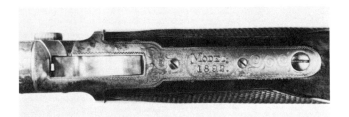

Model marking on tang of Model 1892 rifle, serial number 140,491.

Marking on tang of engraved Model '97 rifle.

Model marking on tang of Model '92 rifle, serial number 424,501.

Typical Marlin Safety *roll-stamp on top of a receiver. Both the* Marlin Safety *and tang model markings were roll-stamped on plain and some engraved models.*

Typical caliber marking on barrel of lever action .22 rifles.

Example of rarely encountered Marlin–Rockwell roll-stamp.

Marlin Firearms Corporation roll-stamp on the Model '93 carbine.

Models 29, 37, and 47 roll-stamp.

Model 20 roll-stamp.

continued in use for many years after it was dropped from use in the catalog. Additionally, it was still used on some models even after it was dropped from other roll-stamps.

The 1905 catalog had the two-word name (not hyphenated) and the 1906 catalog had the one-word firearm name. But many changes don't always happen on schedule or with enthusiasm. For example, a December 20, 1905-dated letter with the letterhead "The Marlin Firearms Co." has the salutation typed by the typist as "The Marlin Fire Arms Co."

If the roll-stamp on a barrel has the one-word name, it can be assumed that it was manufactured in 1906 or later. Some models will be found for the same period of time with both styles of name marked on them. But if *firearm* is found on the gun one word, it is a relatively late gun.

Another inconsistency is the use by The Marlin Firearms Company (1926) of the previous Marlin Firearms Corporation roll-stamps. Good examples are the Model 39 lever action .22, Model 65 bolt action .22, and Model 50 .22 autoloader. All are found with the *corporation* name on them, although manufactured by the *company* that followed. This was seen as late as the 1930s.

The use of the *Special Smokeless Steel* marking was a separate stamp until the Marlin Firearms Corporation name came into use. At that time, *Special Smokeless Steel,* when marked on the Model 93, was stamped just below the company name.

Another change noted in barrel roll-stamps is the hyphenated and nonhyphenated use of the city name, New Haven. It appears that during the 1905–1906 period, when the hyphenated Fire-Arms became Firearms, the hyphen in the name New Haven was also dropped.

Collectors are intrigued with the arrows and arrow-looking things that start and end barrel roll-stamps. Unfortunately, other than being a means to start taking the pressure of the round piece of steel that has engraved on it in reverse the name

The Marlin Firearms Corporation roll-stamp on a Model 38 with a round barrel.

The Marlin Firearms Corporation roll-stamp on an octagon-barreled Model 38 rifle.

The Marlin Firearms Corporation roll-stamp that was used on the Model 39 rifle and many other models, including some manufactured by The Marlin Firearms Company from 1926 into the 1930s.

Roll-stamp used on Model 322 Sako/Marlin caliber .222 rifle.

Model 50 roll-stamp.

Model A1 roll-stamp.

Early Model 39A roll-stamp.

Model 1936 roll-stamp.

Model 36ADL roll-stamp.

Model 80E roll-stamp.

Roll-stamp on Marlin's Model 39 carbine of the 1963–1967 period.

One of Marlin's roll-stamps on the 1970–1987 period.

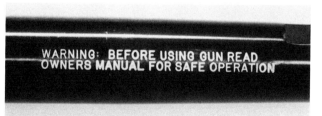

Roll-stamp added to all Marlin firearms in 1981.

to be embossed into the metal, they do not have any significant purpose. Decorative, and frequently different from model to model or between periods of time, the arrows take the brunt of the impact of the die pressing into the steel. They also add an artistic touch to the rather plain company name.

Early on, roll-stamps were hand-cut by engravers. Frequently the same engraver who engraved the deluxe models also engraved the dies used to mark the name of the company, caliber, patent dates, and model number on the gun. In later years, these dies have been manufactured by companies that specialize in such work. The decorative start and finish to the markings have also been eliminated. Today's roll-stamp is usu-

Roll-stamp on barrels of Royal Canadian Models manufactured in limited numbers for the Canadian market.

Royal Canadian flyer distributed in Canada by Marlin.

ally squared off on the ends, eliminating a need for the decorative arrows.

Additional roll-stamp information can be found in the separate model sections of this book.

Royal Canadian

In 1961, Marlin started a program to expand the Canadian market. The main thrust was to add a Canadian roll-stamp to certain models to which Canadians could identify.

The first choice was to mark the barrels *Royal Crown Canadian*. The second choice was to mark them *Royal Marlin Canadian*. Both of these suggested markings were rejected in favor of *Royal (Maple Leaf) Canadian*.

Nine models were selected for the Canadian program. The only differences between the Royal Canadian models and the standard Marlin line was that the Canadian models had the extra features of high-grade wood; swivels and slings; and Model 336 front sights of the dovetail type, rather than of the ramp type. Some models had Monte Carlo stocks. All had the Royal Canadian roll-stamp on the barrel.

The nine RC models were:

Model	Price	1962	1963	Total
336C/.30–30	$99.95	133	138	271
336C/.35 Rem	99.95	144	126	270
336T/.30–35	99.95	76	47	123
989	44.95	317	362	679
980	51.95	351	386	737
99C	49.95	126	154	280
57M	73.50	126	54	180
57	69.95	174	86	250
56	64.95	222	67	289
55	46.25		Unknown	

The Royal Canadian guns were sold to Canadian distributors and dealers. However, many are found in the U.S. In general, they are scarce.

The Royal Canadian program did not go well, mainly because the Canadian Government would not issue Marlin a trademark for the Royal Canadian name. They felt the name could be erroneously considered as having so-called royal approval; or falsely suggest a connection with the Royal Canadian Mounted Police, and possibly mislead the public that they were either used by the Mounties in their official duties, or that the organization had somehow endorsed the guns. The final result was that the program was discontinued due to the Canadian position with regard to the trademark issue. Those left in inventory were sold in the U.S.

Savage Rifle

The June 1895 catalog of the Savage Repeating Arms Company, Utica, N.Y., states inside the flyleaf that the guns illustrated in the catalog were manufactured for Savage by The Marlin Fire Arms Company.

Correspondence during 1968 between E.M. Savage, son of Savage Arms Company founder Arthur W. Savage, and Thomas R. Robinson, Jr., Marlin's director of research and

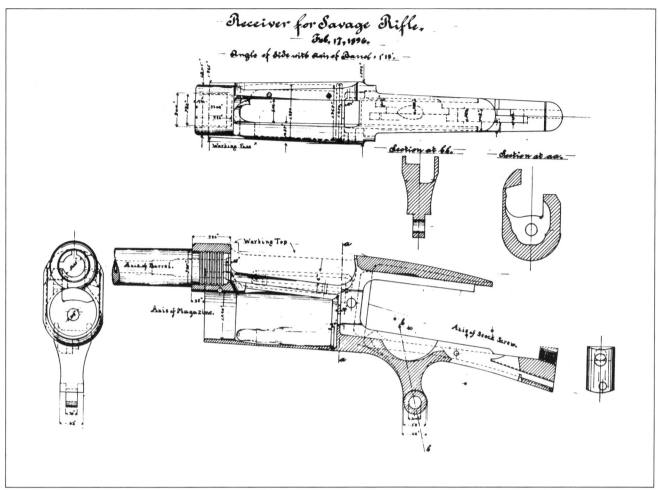

Receiver drawing from Marlin's files of Savage lever action rifle. Marlin manufactured for Savage the first run of the Model 1895 Savage rifle.

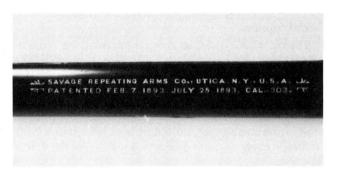

Roll-stamp on Savage rifle barrel manufactured by Marlin.

Bottom of Savage rifle barrel on which can be seen a partial impression of the Marlin JM proofmark.

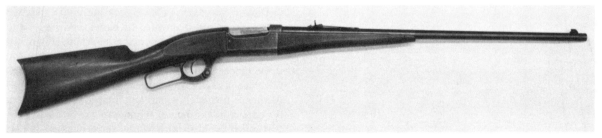

Model 1895 Savage rifle manufactured by The Marlin Fire Arms Company.

development, indicates that possibly the prototype of the Savage Model 1895 rifle was made by Colt, but that the tooling and gauges to make the rifle were produced by Marlin. The first 5,000 rifles were also manufactured by Marlin and have the *JM* proofmark on either the bottom area of the barrel or on the upper surface of the barrel, just forward of the receiver.

The 1896 sketch shown here is the only Marlin item remaining of Marlin's interesting contribution to the success of a competitor in the firearms industry. The Savage lever action rifle was still in production in 1987.

During the 1944–1945 period, Marlin manufactured some sporting rifle barrels for Savage. This helped Savage get back into the sporting rifle business after some years of dedicated war work.

It should also be noted here that in 1948 E.M. Savage, as head of the Savage Laboratories (gunsmiths), La Mesa, Calif., offered Marlin a razor blade dispensing magazine. Similar to the little 10-blade cardboard box, it had a metal spring insert that, when pushed or pulled, would dispense one blade from the package. The device was never adopted by Marlin.

Seconds

What does a company do with items it manufactures that, for some noncritical or cosmetic reason, do not meet the standards established by the company for the product?

Since the 1940s, The Marlin Firearms Company has not sold guns that did not pass the strict tests and examinations given each firearm. There are no "seconds." Each firearm must pass rigid tests, or it is returned by the inspectors to the assembly department for correction and retesting.

Prior to that time, however, Marlin did sell to employees guns that were rejected for cosmetic reasons, and on occasion special offers were made to persons making catalog inquiries. The following 1928-dated letter describes one such offer.

THE MARLIN FIREARMS CO.

Offices & Works
New Haven, Conn. U.S.A.

June 18, 1928.

Mr. N. J. Jones
So. Alton, Mass.

Dear Sir:

The Chance of a Lifetime

We have on hand a few Marlin Model 44A 20 gauge take down hammerless repeating shotguns, five shots. These are so called "Factory seconds." As a matter of fact, the marks or blemishes are on the

outside and would not be noticed by the casual observer. Unfortunately, however, in keeping with our standards, we cannot offer these shotguns to our distributors as firstclass guns.

We have only a few of them and rather than offer them in a job lot to sources other than our regular channels, we believe that it is only fair to offer them first to a few of our consumer friends who, as a result of catalog inquiries, we feel are interested in Marlin arms.

These guns carry the regular Marlin guarantee as to precision and satisfactory service and regularly retail for $49.80. We offer them prepaid to destination for $34.50. There is a saving here of over $15.00.

Model 44A is suitable for snipe, partridge, woodcock, squirrels, rabbits, etc. Weighs about 5½ pounds. It is not, however, a featherweight. It is well constructed, well balanced thruout and points with the precision of a rifle.

Send $5.00 with your letter; balance C.O.D. Try your gun 10 days, money back if you are not satisfied. An answer within a week is requested.

Very truly yours,
General Manager

TC:A

These guns, sold to employees or to customers on special occasions, were all stamped *SECOND*. This mark is usually found on the barrel just forward of the receiver.

When they were sold, these guns were not defective in strength or function. Only a few guns marked *SECOND* have been inspected, and in each case it was difficult to determine what might have been the reason for the classification. I thought the reason might be poor contouring, a hole out of round, or the incorrect location of the roll-stamp, but I was never sure. (One had the roll-stamp under the barrel band and another had the roll-stamp partially hidden by the forearm wood.)

Marlin guns marked *SECOND* are scarce.

Serial Numbers

The old Marlin serial number records are quite complete from 1883 to 1906 for the Models 1881, 1888, 1889, 1891, 1892, 1893, 1894, 1895, and 1897. However, they do not indicate to whom the gun was shipped, or all extra features. For example, checking and engraving are seldom listed. There are numerous duplicate and triplicate entries for one number and there are many serial numbers for which there is no information listed, although many of these numbers do exist and have been examined.

The records include serial numbers 4096 to 355,000 for the period of 1883 to 1906. However, it is known that serial numbers did go to over 450,000.

The old records, in general, show the model; the caliber; the barrel length and frequently the barrel type, i.e., round, octagon, and half octagon; the magazine length (full or half); the takedown feature, if the model had it; and the pistol grip stock, if the model had it. Also listed is a date. Because there is no reference in the records that identifies it as the date of manufacture or the date the gun was shipped, I arbitrarily consider the date to be the date of shipment.

Another problem with Marlin serial numbers is that a specific model does not have its own block of serial numbers. All

Typical Second *marking found on some early Marlin firearms.*

of the different models that were in production are mixed. As a result, two sequential numbers could be for two different models. Also the year of manufacture or shipment can not be accurately established by the serial number of the gun. Examples of this problem are as follows:

Model	Serial Number	Date
1891	80,270	10/31/1892
1891	80,272	3/13/1895
1891	80,277	4/21/1893
1894	150,021	6/5/1897
1897	150,022	6/4/1897
1892	157,386	12/27/1897
1893	157,387	10/15/1897

To assist in establishing the year of manufacture of lever action rifles manufactured during the 1883 to 1906 period, a review of serial numbers and dates has been done. By selecting an arbitrary serial number in the middle of the overlap of a year ending and of the next year starting, a range of serial numbers for each year was established.

By using the following list, the year for a serial number can be approximated within an accuracy of one year.

The total production figures are also only an approximation and include only lever action rifles.

Serial Numbers

Year	From	To	Production
1883	4001	6700	2,700
1884	6700	8850	2,150
1885	8850	11,300	2,450
1886	11,300	15,000	4,200
1887	15,000	17,800	2,800
1888	17,800	21,500	2,600
1889	21,500	30,000	8,500
1890	30,000	45,000	15,000
1891	45,000	63,250	18,250
1892	63,250	80,250	17,000
1893	80,250	95,750	15,500
1894	95,750	115,000	19,250
1895	115,000	133,000	18,000
1896	133,000	144,400	11,400
1897	144,400	161,200	16,800
1898	161,200	175,500	14,300
1899	175,500	196,000	20,500
1900	196,000	213,000	16,000
1901	213,000	233,300	20,300
1902	233,300	262,500	29,200
1903	262,500	287,300	24,800
1904	287,300	310,500	23,200
1905	310,500	329,000	18,500
1906	329,000	355,300	26,300

Marlin has no serial number records for the following models of Marlin rifles, pistols, and shotguns:

1. Ballard rifles
2. All models of single-shot pistols and revolvers
3. Model 1881 rifles serial-numbered lower than 4096
4. All models manufactured between 1906 and 1962
5. All pump action shotguns, except the Model 1898s numbered from 19,601 to 67,000
6. The Models 322, 422, and 455 bolt action rifles
7. The Model 90 shotgun
8. L.C. Smith, Hunter Special, and Fulton shotguns manufactured by the Hunter Arms Company, Fulton, N.Y.
9. Hopkins & Allen firearms of all models
10. Marlin–Rockwell machine guns and automatic rifles
11. Model 410 lever action shotgun
12. Models 1936 and 36 rifles
13. Mark I, II, and IV shotgun
14. All pump action .22 rifles
15. All bolt action .22 rifles manufactured prior to 1962

The nice thing about the Model 336 family of lever action rifles and carbines, and the Model 39A and 39M rifles, is that they are all serial-numbered in such a manner that the year of production is very easily established.

The year identifier, up to 1969, was an alphabetical prefix to the serial number. The sequence went as follows:

E	1948 (Start of Model 336)
F	1949 (Started chambering for the .35 Rem. cartridge Carrier rocker blued)
G	1950 (Has solid-type lever)
H	1951 (New type of trigger and sear in Model 336)
J	1952 (First Texan — 2/7/1952 — serrations on top)
K	1953 (Sandblasted receivers — no serrations on top)
L	1954
M	1955 (Starting on April 14, 1955, the last digits of the serial number were etched on the bottom of the bolt of the 336)
N	1956
P	1957
R	1957–1958
S	1958–1959
T	1960
U	1960 (August)–1961
V	1961 (August)–1962
W	1963
Y & Z	1964
AA	1965
AB	1966
AC	1967
AD	1968

Upon the passage of a new federal firearms law in 1968, all manufacturers of firearms in the U.S. were required to serial-number all firearms manufactured. Previously, .22 rifles and shotguns were not subject to serial-numbering, but Marlin's center-fire lever action rifles and the Model 39/39A .22s were always serial-numbered.

To comply with the law and to make the task of numbering hundreds of thousands of firearms each year easier, Marlin adopted a system of an eight-digit number, with the first two digits identifying the year of production.

From 1969 to 1972, the first two digits of the serial number were the last two digits of the year. For example: 1969 started with 69000000.

In 1973, the system was changed by having the first two digits subtracted from 100 to equal the year of manufacture. For example: 27000000 = 100 − 27 = 1973.

When serial numbers were located under the lever on the trigger plate, the number was also stamped into the side of the top tang. When the serial number was relocated to behind the hammer on the top tang, the duplicate number on the side was dropped.

Since 1968, both halves of the Model 39A and 39M lever action caliber .22 rifles have been serial-numbered. The left half has the number stamped on the inside. The right half has the number stamped behind the hammer on the top tang.

During the period of 1962 to 1968, firearms other than the lever action models were coded to indicate the year of manufacture. Usually stamped on the left side of the barrel, just forward of the receiver, the first letter of the code indicated the month, and the second indicated the year, as follows:

Jan.	A	July	G	1962	F
Feb.	B	Aug.	H	1963	G
Mar.	C	Sept.	I	1964	H
Apr.	D	Oct.	J	1965	I
May	E	Nov.	K	1966	J
June	F	Dec.	L	1967	K
				1968	L

Example: CH = March 1964

Since 1971, each family of Marlin firearms has been grouped into a block of serial numbers. Listed below are the blocks of serial numbers assigned to each model or model group for the years 1971 to 1988.

1971	*From*	*To*
39 Article II	71,000,001	71,050,000
336 Octagon	71,050,001	71,065,000
39D	71,065,001	71,135,000
336, 444, 1895	71,135,001	71,300,000
10, 101, 50, 55, 20, 25, 80, 81, 980	71,300,001	71,400,000
All 99 series	71,400,001	71,600,000

1973		
120 shotgun	Continue to	A30,000
336, 444, 1894	27,000,001	27,090,000
1895	Continue to	B30,000
39s	27,120,001	27,145,000
99s & 49s	27,145,001	27,370,000
	27,090,001	27,120,000
10, 101, 50, 55, 20, 25, 80, 81, 980	27,370,001	27,535,000

1974		
120 shotgun	Continue to	A30,000
336, 444, 1894	26,000,001	26,150,000
1895	Continue to	B30,000
39s	26,150,001	26,180,000

1974	*From*	*To*
99s & 49s	26,180,001	26,500,000
10, 101, 50, 55, 20, 25, 80, 81, 980	26,500,001	26,750,000

1975		
120 shotgun	Continue to	A50,000
336, 444, 1894	25,000,000	25,200,000
1895	Continue to	B40,000
39s	25,200,001	25,250,000
99s & 49s	25,250,001	25,600,000
10, 101, 50, 55, 20, 25, 80, 81, 980	25,600,001	25,750,000

1976		
120 shotgun	Continue to	A50,000
336, 444, 1894	24,000,000	24,200,000
1895	Continue to	B40,000
39s	24,200,001	24,250,000
99s & 49s	24,250,001	24,600,000
10, 101, 50, 55, 20, 25, 80, 81, 980	24,600,001	24,750,000

1977		
120 shotgun	Continue to	A100,000
336, 444, 1894, 1895	23,000,000	23,250,000
39s	23,250,001	23,280,000
99s & 49s	23,280,001	23,680,000
10, 101, 50, 55, 20, 25, 80, 81, 980	23,680,001	23,800,000

1978		
120 shotgun	Continue to	100,000
336, 444, 1894, 1895	22,000,000	22,250,000
39s	22,250,001	22,280,000
99s & 49s	22,280,001	22,680,000
10, 101, 50, 55, 20, 25, 80, 81, 980	22,680,001	22,800,000

1979		
120/778 shotguns	Continue to	100,000
336, 444, 1894, 1895	21,000,000	21,250,000
39s	21,250,001	21,280,000
99s & 49s	21,280,001	21,580,000
15, 20, 25, 780, 781, 782, 783, 50, 55	21,580,001	21,700,000

1980		
336, 444, 1894, 1895	20,000,001	20,285,000
39s	20,285,001	20,320,000
60s & 99s	20,320,001	20,690,000
15, 20, 25, 780, 781, 782, 783, 50, 55	20,690,001	20,815,000
120/778 shotguns	20,815,001	20,835,000

1981		
336, 444, 1894, 1895	19,000,001	19,230,000
39s	19,230,001	19,280,000
60s & 99s	19,280,001	19,680,000

1981	From	To
15, 20, 25, 780, 781, 782, 783, 50, 55	19,680,001	19,800,000
120/778 shotguns	19,800,001	19,825,000

1982		
336, 444, 1894, 1895	18,000,000	18,260,000
39s	18,260,001	18,300,000
60s & 99s	18,300,001	18,650,000
15, 20, 25, 780, 781, 782, 783, 50, 55	18,650,001	18,800,000
120/778 shotguns	18,800,001	18,825,000

1983		
336, 444, 1894, 1895	17,000,000*	17,260,000*
39s	17,260,001	17,300,000
60s & 99s	17,300,001	17,650,000
15, 20, 25, 780, 781, 782, 783, 50, 55	17,650,001	17,800,000
120/778 shotguns	17,800,001	17,825,000

1984		

1985		
336, 444, 1894, 1895	15,000,001	15,250,000
39s	15,250,001	15,300,000
60s & 99s	15,300,001	15,650,000
15, 20, 25, 780, 781, 782, 783, 50, 55	15,650,001	15,800,000
9mm	15,800,001	15,825,000

1986		
336, 444, 1894, 1895	14,000,001	14,250,000
39s	14,250,001	14,300,000
60s & 99s	14,300,001	14,650,000
15, 20, 25, 780, 781, 782, 783, 50, 55	14,650,001	14,800,000
9mm	000,001	050,000
45	45,000,001	45,050,000

1987		
336, 444, 1894, 1895	13,000,000	13,250,000
39s	13,250,001	13,300,000
60s & 99s	13,300,001	13,650,000
15, 20, 25, 780, 781, 782, 783, 25MB, 55	13,650,001	13,800,000
9mm	13,800,001	13,825,000
45	13,826,001	13,900,000

1988		
336, 444, 1894, 1895	12,000,000	12,250,000
39A & 39M	12,250,001	12,300,000
60s & 99s	12,300,001	12,650,000
15, 25, 780, 781, 782, 783, 25M, 25MB, 55	12,650,001	12,800,000
9mm	12,800,001	12,825,000
45	12,826,001	12,900,000
39TDS	TDS00,001	TDS03,500
336LTS	LTS00,001	LTS0,300
1894CL (.25-20)	CL320,001	CL32,300
1894CL (.32-20)	CL250,001	CL25,300

*Block 17,030,000 to 17,039,999 not used.

Shoehorn/Buttonhook

For three years, from 1915 through 1917, Marlin manufactured, advertised, and sold a shoehorn/buttonhook. It was claimed that it combined two awkward articles of everyday necessity into "one harmonious whole, making the handiest, most convenient shoehorn imaginable, and the most practical and satisfactory buttonhook ever designed."

Marlin advertising stated that the shoehorn/buttonhook was first made to be used as gifts for Marlin staff and friends. However, since Marlin already had the expensive forging dies and tools made, and Marlin's employees liked the items so well, it made sense to sell them. They were made from a forging, and were well polished and nickel-plated. They are about 11 inches long; Marlin claimed this length would ensure their never being lost, and the extra 5 inches would help the stout person to put on his shoes comfortably.

There are two variations of the shoehorn/buttonhook. One has the Marlin company name and address stamped in large letters into the back side of the shoehorn. The other type has

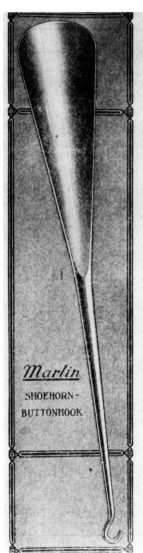

Marlin catalog ad for the shoehorn/buttonhook.

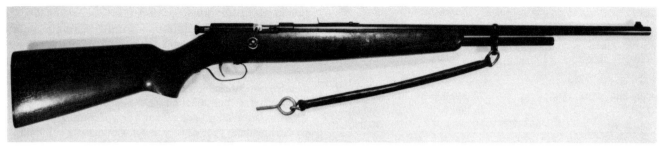

Marlin single-shot shooting gallery rifle that has a tube for fired cartridge cases to exit, and a connecting cable to affix the rifle to the counter of a shooting gallery. Except for the tube, the rifle is the same as the Model 65.

This photo shows the fired cartridge case tube that allows the fired case to fall to the front of the counter. Also shown is the special spanner wrench used to remove the disassembly screw.

Roll-stamp on gallery rifle that is like the one used on the Model 65 single-shot rifle.

First type of sighting-in guide, which was round.

the name stamped in much smaller letters into the round shaft, about midway down its length.

Shooting Gallery Rifle

Any rifle used in a shooting gallery, rightfully, can be called a gallery rifle. But the Marlin gallery rifle is unique in that it was specially designed for use in a shooting gallery.

The Marlin shooting gallery rifle was a standard Model 100, caliber .22 bolt action single-shot rifle having an unusual fired-cartridge-case ejection system. Instead of the usual system of the fired cartridge case being extracted from the chamber and then ejected from the gun, this rifle had a hollow tube extending from below the front end of the receiver to about 6 inches forward of the front end of the stock.

Upon extraction of the fired cartridge case from the chamber, the case would drop down into the long tube. When the rifle was tipped forward, the empty would then roll out of the tube and forward of the shooting gallery counter. That way, there would be no empties around the feet of the shooters or on top of the counter.

A band with an eye in it was attached around the barrel and tube. In use, the rifle was secured to the counter by a chain fastened to the eye on the band. Only 500 of these special rifles were assembled. Because they were single-shot, they were not popular among shooting gallery proprietors, who wanted repeaters so their customers would shoot more shots and pay more money. They are now scarce and are seldom identified correctly. Most owners think that the gun had some kind of a tubular magazine and that parts are missing, but it is a unique Marlin single-shot shooting gallery gun.

Sighting-In Guide

In 1956 Marlin introduced an aid for hunters and shooters who wanted to sight in their rifles accurately and quickly with minimum use of ammunition. Called the Marlin Sighting-In Guide, it was designed to take full advantage of the trajectory of the cartridge the sportsman was planning on using.

The guide gave instructions for firing to be done at a close range, which permitted sighting-in the rifle faster and easier. Most cartridges can be sighted-in at 20 to 30 yards because the bullet first crosses the line of sight at a close distance, and then continues above the line of sight until it again crosses the line of sight as it travels in its parabolic curve to the target.

A good example of the ballistic data included in the guide

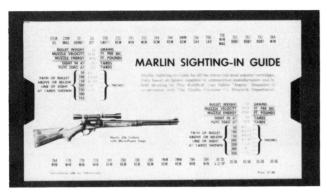

Second type of sighting-in guide, which was made of white plastic.

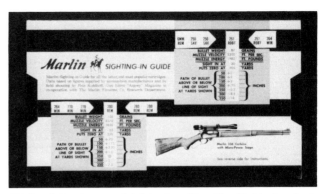

Third and fourth types of sighting-in guides. The third had a plastic sleeve and a cardboard insert, whereas the fourth type had both parts made of cardboard.

for cartridge ranging from the .22 to the belted magnums such as the .338 is best represented by the .30–30 Win. cartridge. The data for this cartridge with 150-grain bullet are shown in the guide as follows:

Bullet Weight 150 Grains
Muzzle Velocity 2410 Ft.Per.Sec.
Muzzle Energy 1930 Ft. Pounds
Sight In At 22 Yards
Puts Zero at 20 Yards

Path of bullet above or below line of sight at yards shown		
50	+ 1.25	
100	+ 2.50	
150	+ 2.0	Inches
200	⊕	
250	− 6.	
300	− 18.5	

The original data were gathered from ammunition manufacturers' catalogs; however, all data were confirmed through test firing by the late gun writer Peter Kuhlhoff.

There have been five variations of the Marlin Sighting-In Guide. The first, in 1959, was circular. By rotating the front disk to the caliber marked on the periphery, the sighting-in information could be read through a window in the front disk. In 1963, another type was made available. There are four variations of this second type, which were rectangular, either plastic or cardboard, and with a movable slide that could be pushed or pulled sideways to show the caliber data through a window cut into the outer sleeve.

Many thousands of these guides have been sold for $1.00 each. The last printing was in 1977 and the supply has been exhausted since 1979.

Sights

Frequently, Marlin collectors ask: "Are the sights on my old Marlin original to the gun, and were they manufactured by Marlin?" or, "Were the commercially marked sights on my Marlin installed by the factory and were they a special-order item available from the factory?"

The only reliable source for data about Marlin and Ballard sights is from Marlin catalogs and advertisements, because, unfortunately, the few Marlin records that have survived do not identify all special-order features. In fact, the type or make

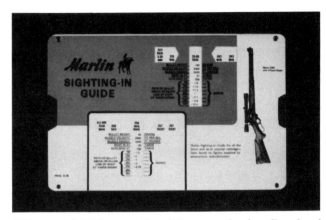

Fifth type of sighting-in guide, which was made of cardboard and riveted at the corners.

Marlin gallery peep sight.

Early Marlin vernier mid-range peep sight.

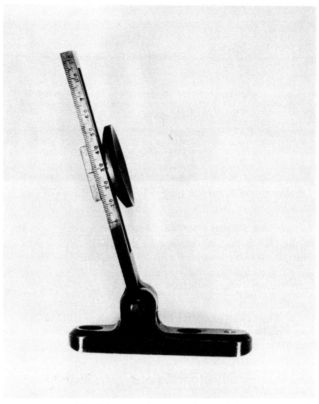

Marlin improved graduated peep sight.

Two variations of early vernier peep sights, one with thumb screw, the other with standard slotted hinge screw.

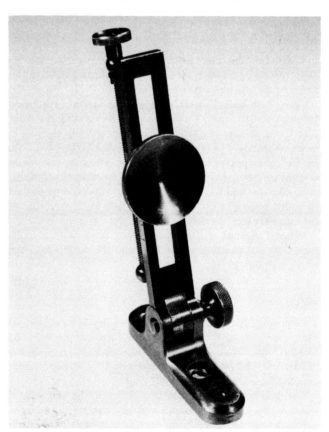

Marlin improved vernier midrange sight.

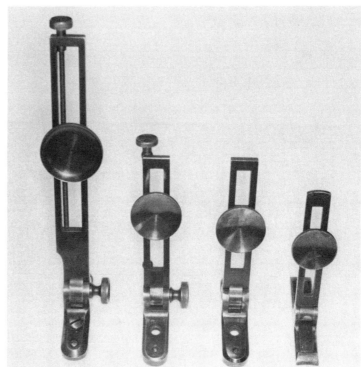

Tang peep sights shown for size comparison. Left to right: long-range, mid-range vernier, graduated peep, and gallery.

of sights on the gun was not recorded for the 350,000 serial numbers listed from 1883 to 1906.

When John Marlin first entered the rifle-making business he manufactured the Ballard single-shot hunting and target rifle. The sights for the hunting models were not fancy or complicated to make. The sight usually fitted at the factory was the Rocky Mountain open-type sight, which was adjusted by means of a step elevator for elevation and was moved in the barrel dovetail for lateral correction. Front sights were Rocky Mountain knife edge sights with a German silver blade. They, too, were fitted to the barrel by means of a dovetail. Target sights, however, were more complex and required considerable finesse to make. The rear sight was usually a tang sight with an aperture, the sight mounted on the top rear part of the receiver, behind the hammer. Four basic types were available. The first, and least expensive, was for shooting gallery rifles. The next had a graduated leaf for easy recording of sight settings for various distances. The last two were extensions of the second type, except that they had taller leaves. The aperture could be adjusted for greater shooting distances, and had the added feature of an adjusting screw that simplified the adjustment of the movable peep. Front sights for use with the target and long-range tang sights were also designed especially for precise shooting at targets, rather than game. The two types Marlin supplied were of the globe (hooded) type that had interchangeable inserts (bead, post, and aperture), which came with the sight. There was also available a spirit level front sight that had an adjusting screw built into the base, which allowed for lateral wind and zero adjustment. The spirit level was part of the dovetailed clip that held the insert into the globe. When one sighted the rifle, he could observe the bubble in the level and correct any cant in the rifle.

After the Ballard rifle was discontinued and Marlin was manufacturing mostly lever action rifles, the hunting sights

Marlin wind gauge front sight.

Marlin wind gauge front sight with spirit level.

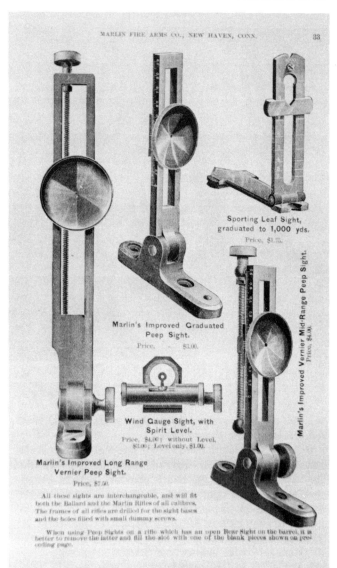

Pages from Marlin catalog showing sights available.

Rocky Mountain rear sight.

Elevators for Rocky Mountain rear sights.

Second-variation Rocky Mountain front sights.

Beach front sight.

Catalog illustration of Rocky Mountain rear sight.

Catalog illustration of Beach and Rocky Mountain front sights.

Model 1889 rifle tang screw holes.

Tang of Model 1893 rifle, showing dummy screws in two tang sight screw holes.

Tang of Model '97 rifle showing the location of the two tang screw holes found in the Model 1891, 1892, 1897, and 39 rifles.

Catalog illustration of second variation of Rocky Mountain knife edge front sight.

Catalog illustration of front and rear sights found on caliber .22 Model 1891 rifles.

Model 1891 rear sight.

Catalog illustration of Marlin's sporting leaf sight.

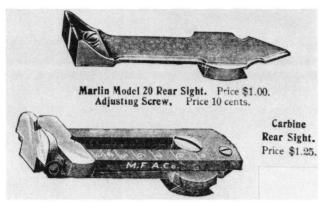

Catalog illustration of Marlin's Model 20 and carbine rear sights.

Rear sight for Model 20 rifle.

Unusual carbine rear sight, fitted to a Marlin rifle, that has range marks in meters.

did not change to any degree. On all models except the Model 1888, two drilled and tapped screw holes were in the top tang for attachment of tang sights until into the 1950s.

On special order, Marlin would leave out the dovetail for the rear sight. Marlin would also move the rear dovetail to any reasonable location the customer would want. In 1903, when the L.L. Hepburn receiver sight was introduced, the tops of receivers were drilled and tapped for the screwholes. In July 1945, both the 336 and 39 had receiver sight screw holes drilled and tapped into the left side of the receiver; the practice remains so today for all center-fire lever actions and the 39s.

Most commercial (non-Marlin) sights have the maker's name or patent dates marked on them. Marlin sights, except for the L.L. Hepburn and Gus Swebilius sights, are not marked in any manner that will identify them as Marlin. (Catalog illustrations are misleading, as they show sights having the name *Marlin* or *M.F.A.Co.* on them. The purpose of the illustrations is assumed to be to identify the sights as "factory," and not Lyman.)

Tang sights were installed on Marlin rifles by two screws. The Model 1893 and 1895 mounting was farther to the rear than for the Model 1894 and lever action .22s because it was necessary for the sight to be clear of the rear end of the bolt when the bolt was fully open. This necessity created a problem for some hunters who liked to hold the rifle with the thumb crossed over the top of the stock. Also, on heavy recoil rifles, the aperture of the tang sight was dangerously close to the face of one who "crawled" the stock, or had a slight build and long neck.

Sights on the Marlin carbine models were distinctly different from those on rifles. Why? I'm not sure, other than in the early use of Marlin firearms, a number of them were used by western horsemen and cowboys who carried them in saddle scabbards. Thus we find the low and small front sights and saddle rings on the side of the receiver. But why have a rear sight graduated to 900 yards just because it is to be carried on a horse?

There were two variations of the carbine front sight. One had a German silver blade pinned into a slot in the fixed stud. The other type had the blade part integral with the base. Both types had bases that were dovetailed to the barrel, then soft-soldered in place and carefully dressed down to the contour of the barrel, and then blued with the barrel. (Careful examination of the joint between the base and barrel will reveal the dovetail. Marlin did this so well that it is difficult to determine if a 20-in. carbine barrel has been clandestinely shortened to a scarce under-16-in. barrel.)

Another rear sight that is frequently confused with the carbine sight is the Marlin sporting leaf sight. The main difference between this sight and the carbine sight is that this one is graduated to 1,000 yards, whereas the carbine sight is graduated to 900 yards. To obtain the 1,000-yard setting on this sight, all that Marlin did was to put a notch in the very top of a slightly taller leaf.

It is unbelievable to me that any firearm manufacturer would think it practical to shoot at game at ranges of 600 to 1,000 yards, as 500 yards is stretching it for even the most skilled marksman, under the most favorable of conditions, and when using today's flat-shooting modern rifles and cartridges.

Top: *Carbine front sight of the second variation.* Bottom: *Carbine front sight of the first variation.*

Carbine front sight of the third variation.

The sighting notch of both the carbine and sporting leaf sight is a deep open V-notch on the vertical slide and a smaller V-notch on the part of the leaf that automatically stands up when the long leaf is laid flat.

The Marlin-manufactured sights for the pre WW I lever action rifles are illustrated in catalogs along with Lyman sights that were suitable for use with Marlin rifles. Many of the Lyman sights could be special-ordered by the sportsman who had a particular preference for a certain type. When ordered, they would be fitted at the factory.

The standard rear sight was the open Rocky Mountain buckhorn type. There were two lengths. The long one was for the 1889, 1893, 1894, and 1895 models, and the short one was for the Model 1891 and other small-caliber rifles.

There were also two types of folding leaf rear sights. The carbine type was graduated to 900 yards and the sporting leaf sight was graduated to 1,000 yards.

Front sights were of the Rocky Mountain knife edge type or the Beach combination type. The Beach had a tipping hood that had a pinhead post, or when folded down, a standing flattop post. On top of the hood of the early Beach sight was a

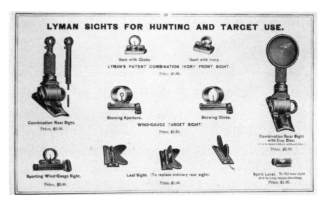

Lyman sights as cataloged by Marlin in 1894.

Arrows indicate holes in top of receivers (after 1903) that were used to install the L.L. Hepburn receiver sight.

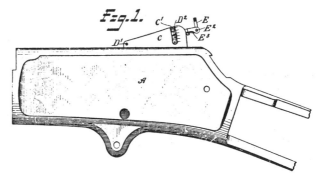

Patent illustration from L.L. Hepburn's patent number 732,075 dated June 30, 1903.

L.L. Hepburn's top-mounted receiver sight, with the peep in the up position.

Marlin Combination Receiver Sight

Has folding leaf and may be used as a peep or open sight. It is an all-round hunting and target sight, having all the advantages of a tang peep sight without its inconveniences. It gives greatest possible distance between front and rear sights without in any way interfering with grip of right hand. Allows free and unobstructed manipulation of hammer. No danger of injuring the shooter's eye by recoil or hasty throwing of rifle to the shoulder. Raised or lowered instantly—just press thumb forward on peep hole leaf.

Marlin Combination Receiver Sight.
Price $3.25; Drill, 30 cts.; Tap, 60 cts.

Catalog information about Marlin's folding leaf receiver rear sight.

small bead. I am not sure of its purpose. I can't imagine it being used for sighting.

The early knife edge front sight had a straight-sided and flattop blade. The late Rocky Mountain front sight had a knife edge blade, which was made of German silver, as was the earlier type, but the top of the blade was shaped into a bead. There were four different heights of these Rocky Mountain front sights. Each was for a certain caliber and model.

A list of some of the Marlin factory sights that were standard equipment is as follows:

Pre-WW II Rear Sights

Sight	*Models*
Gallery peep	Ballard
Improved graduated peep	Ballard & repeating
Improved vernier midrange	Ballard & repeating
Improved long-range vernier peep	Ballard
Rocky Mountain (buckhorn) (long)	Ballard & repeating 1888–1895
Rocky Mountain (buckhorn) (short)	1891 caliber .32 and later
Standing fixed notch	Ballard, 1891, 1892 cal. .22
Carbine (900 yards)	1889–1895
Model 20 w/adjusting screw	Model 20
Sporting leaf (1,000 yards)	1881, Ballards and later (to order)
L.L. Hepburn receiver sight	1893, 1894, 1895

Pre-WW II Front Sights

Rocky Mountain (knife edge)	Ballard & repeating
Beach combination	Ballard & repeating
Carbine German silver blade	1889–1895
Caliber .22 Front Sight	Ballard 1891, 1892, cal. .22

Post-WW II Rear Sights

Rocky Mountain w/o adjusting plate	39
Two-piece Rocky Mountain w/screw	A1E, 88E, 89E
Stepped notch	336 and others
Stamped & folded	Glenfield Models
Osborne folding leaf	Marlin models after 1974
Marlin receiver Sight	80 & 81DLs
Marlin receiver sight	50 & A1
Marlin receiver sight	88 & 89DLs
Lyman 40-SM	Bolt action shotguns
Lyman 16B folding leaf	336A (early)
Marble	Commemorative pair
Marble	Zane Grey
Marble	Century Limited
Receiver sight w/dovetail	.22 Autoloader
Lyman folding leaf	444

Post-WW II Front Sights

Dovetail front sight w/hood	80, 81 and other DLs
Dovetail ramp (flat on barrel)	39A & 336
Long ramp w/insert & hood	39A & 336
Short ramp w/insert & hood	39A & 336
Short ramp w/o hood	336
Short ramp w/Wide-Scan hood	39A, 336, 780, 781, 782, 783
Dovetail Lyman sights	444
Dovetail bead front sight	39ACL, 39A Art. II, 39M Art. II, 336 Zane Grey, 336 Octagon, 336M Octagon

Ballard Sights. Ballard hunting rifles usually had either conventional open rear and blade-type front sights or aperture tang sights and hooded globe front sights.

The Marlin open sights were of the Rocky Mountain type with a V-notch rear and a German silver knife edge front blade. Commercial variations and custom-made similar sights were also available. The full list is too long to be included here, but Marlin did favor Lyman sights of those suited for the Ballard, and rifles could be ordered with certain Lyman sights installed. Many of the sights are illustrated here.

The most interesting to the collector are the Ballard sights of the tang type, which Marlin manufactured. There were four basic types which could be ordered at the time the rifle was ordered, or purchased separately. They were the gallery peep

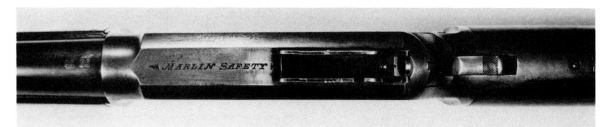

Note that the Marlin Safety *marking on this Model 1983 rifle is moved forward so that it is not covered when the receiver sight is fitted to the top of the receiver.*

sight, the Marlin graduated peep sight (spring and plunger in base), the improved graduated peep sight, the improved vernier midrange peep sight, and the improved long-range vernier peep sight. The improved sights had a flat spring, held in place by a screw, instead of the spring and plunger of the first type.

The front sights generally used with the above sights were either the globe sight or the wind gauge sight with or without the spirit level.

The rarest of sights for the Ballard are the cased sets that included the sight base, the sight leaf with aperture, knife blade front sight, wind gauge front sight with spirit level, extra rear aperture, extra front sight inserts, and the hinge screw. All the above were fitted into a leather-covered and plush-lined box. The box was gold-embossed *Ballard-Rifle.* The value of these fitted boxes, complete with contents, in today's collector's market is frequently more than many Ballard rifles. In excellent condition, they are rare.

Illustrated here and in the Ballard section are both the commercial and Marlin sights used with the Ballard rifle.

Marlin Combination Receiver Sight. L.L. Hepburn invented and patented (number 732,075, dated June 30, 1903) a combination rear sight. It was advertised as an all-around hunting and target sight because it had a folding leaf that had both a peep and open sight. It mounted on the top of the receiver.

Marlin claimed the following for this sight:

> It gives greatest possible distance between front and rear sights without in any way interfering with grip of hand. Allows free and unobstructed manipulation of hammer. No danger of injuring the shooter's eye by recoil or hasty throwing of rifle to the shoulder. Has folding leaf and may be used as a peep or open sight.

All rifles manufactured after August 1903 have two holes drilled and tapped in the receiver for mounting this sight to the rifle. It should be noted that those receivers factory drilled have the *Marlin Safety* marking on the top of the receiver moved forward, so that the sight does not cover it. Marlin would drill and tap an earlier untapped receiver if the rifle was returned to have the work done.

When rifles were ordered with a receiver sight installed, the regular rear sight was removed and the dovetail filled with a slot blank. If so ordered, the regular sight would be left on the gun.

When testing this sight, I found the peep and vertical adjustment quick and easy to use, but the open sight notch was found to be much too close to the eye for accurate use, and worthless.

The Marlin combination receiver sight was priced at $3.25. These sights are not uncommon, but loose ones—not installed on rifles—are very rarely encountered.

Swebilius Rear Sight. Patent number 1,150,791 was awarded to Marlin's C.G. Swebilius and H.T.R. Hanitz on August 17, 1915, for an open rear sight. The sight was a clever device that included adjustment for both windage and elevation. The sight mounted in the standard rear sight dovetail. It was advertised as standard for the Model 32 pump action .22 rifle. However, it

Marlin Model 32 wind gauge rear sight.

Model 32 Wind-gauge Rear Sight.
A new and unique flat top rear sight allowing very quick vertical adjustment and neat, convenient wind-gauge. The ratchet wheel or click arrangement on the right side provides 10 graduations for vertical adjustment, the graduations becoming finer as the range increases. The corresponding ratchet wheel on the left side provides the lateral adjustment for wind-gauge. "You can feel and hear the click." Price $2.00.

Catalog illustration and description of the Model 32 sight.

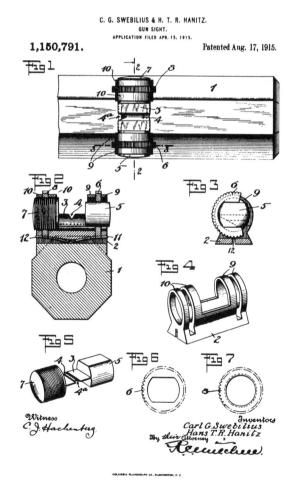

C.G. Swebilius patent drawing of Model 32 sight.

Lyman combination rear sight No. 1. Note that the No. 1 sight does not have the stem-locking device.

Lyman combination rear sight No. 1A. Note that this sight has a lock for the stem.

Lyman combination rear sights showing the different heights that were available for use on different models of Marlin rifles.

has been noted on other models. One "like-new" example on a rifle, marked *Marlin–Rockwell Corporation,* has been examined. In good condition, the sights are scarce, because the adjustment and adjustment locking system were prone to damage.

Marlin Post-WW II Receiver Sight. The special target sights furnished by Marlin for many of the bolt action and early semiautomatic series of rifles were described as follows:

Special Target Sights—The receiver on this rifle is drilled and tapped for the new Marlin Receiver Peep Sight. It can be quickly attached with the two screws furnished with it.

It has elevation and windage adjustments, both controlled by locking levers so that adjustments can be instantly made without special tools.

Two discs are supplied with each sight. The extra disc is screwed into the thumb nut on the left side. One disc has a small aperture for target shooting and one a larger aperture for hunting. You can remove the disc from the slide and sight through the hole, which gives you a very large aperture.

When fitting the receiver peep sight it is advisable to remove the factory rear sight. To do this simply remove the screw from it and lift the leaf off. This will leave the base in the barrel to act as a blank for the sight slot. If you ever want to use the sight again you can screw it back on and by not having disturbed the base it will always be properly lined up.

The front sight is constructed so that it can be fitted with a detachable hood. This hood snaps on right over the sight by fitting one side in the groove on the sight and pressing down.

Your dealer can supply the peep sight and hood or you can purchase them direct from the factory.

The price of the receiver peep sight complete is $2.00, and the hood only for front sight, 30 cents.

Lyman Sights. There is no end to the sights manufactured by the Lyman Gunsight Company that could be used on the many models of Marlin and Ballard rifles. Some of the types available from Marlin and fitted to rifles were the following:

Combination rear sight, with and without disk
Combination rear sight, with locking feature
Combination rear sight, with windage adjustment

Bottom of Lyman tang sight bases, showing the code markings that identify the Marlin model for which they were designed (H, E, JA, and M).

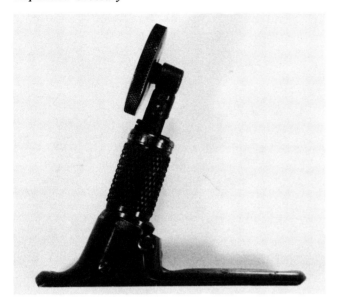

Lyman No. 15 wind gauge sight for Marlin center-fire rifles.

Lyman No. 47 wind gauge stem that, when fitted to No. 1, No. 1A, No. 2, or No. 2A sight, is called the Lyman No. 52A sight.

Lyman combination ivory front sight No. 5.

Lyman folding leaf sight No. 6.

Lyman wind gauge target front sight No. 7.

Lyman wind gauge sporting front sight No. 8.

Lyman target front sight No. 17.

Lyman ivory bead wind gauge front sight No. 18.

Lyman spirit level.

Marble Simplex rear sight.

Marble flexible rear sight.

Marble Duplex front sight.

Marble reversible front sight that is partially turned.

Leaf sight, to replace regular rear sight
Globe front sight, with ivory blade
Wind gauge target sight, with inserts
Sporting wind gauge sight
Spirit level, to fill rear sight dovetail slot
Ivory bead front sight

The most prolific Lyman sight found on Marlin rifles is the combination rear sight (tang sight), and fortunately the Lyman people had the wisdom to mark the bottom of the bases with an alphabetical code that identifies the model for which the sight was designed. The code was as follows:

B   Ballard, Models 1891 and 1892 (.32 caliber)
E   Models 1888, 1889, and 1894
H   Models 1891, 1892, 1897, and 39 (.22 caliber)
J   Model 1893, .32–40 and .38–55 black powder cartridge

JA	Model 1893 high-power smokeless cartridges (.25–36, .32 H.P.S., .30–30)
JM	Models 1895 and 25
M	Model 1881
K	Model 18
KM	Model 20

Many sportsmen preferred Lyman front sights over the standard Marlin blade-type Rocky Mountain front sights. Lyman could supply variations in bead size and type of front sight for most of Marlin's lever guns. Lyman's 1902 catalog included the following information of interest to Marlin collectors:

> The front sight, blank, spirit level and leaf sights should be driven into the barrel slot from the right-hand side. Do not drive them with great force if they fit too tightly. Use a file a little if necessary.

Extra "Light Weight" models of various makes and rifles with shorter barrels than standard, take special front sights. When ordering sights for such arms, particular attention and care should be given in advising us of the make, model, caliber, length of barrel, whether round, octagon or half octagon barrel, and stating "Extra Light Weight."

Many manufacturers of rifles use the "Standard" base and height of front sights for their rifles, hence we call our front sights for such rifles the "Standard."

Standard Lyman front sights will fit Marlin Model '81, '94, '95 and '93 when made in .32/40 and .38/55 only.

The Lyman front sights that were used on Marlin rifles were as follows:

No. 3   Ivory bead on sloping neck with dovetail base
No. 4   Blade on dovetailed base with well-protected ivory insert

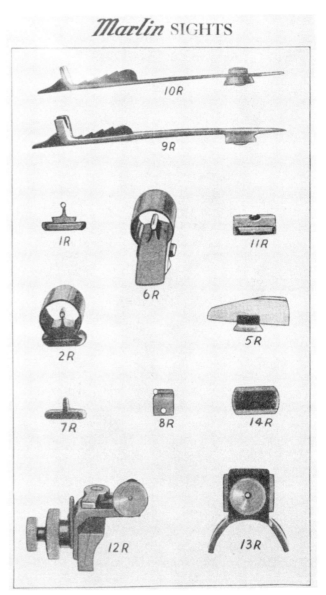

Marlin 1936 parts catalog page advertising Marble sights.

Marlin 1936 parts catalog page illustrating standard Marlin sights.

H. M. Pope tang sight with Marlin base.

Carver vernier peep sight with a base that will fit Marlin rifles.

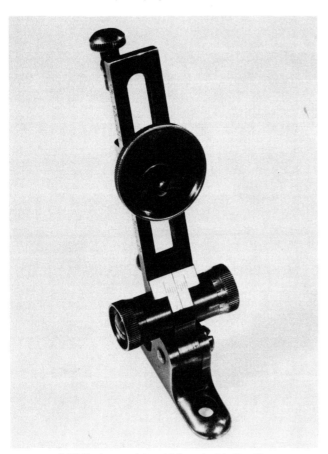

J. W. Soule tang sight with base for Marlin rifles.

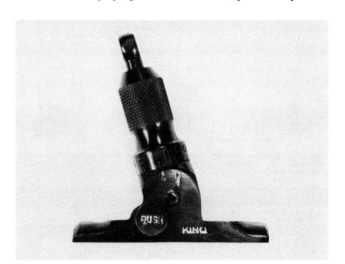

King autolocking tang sight. This sight was stamped M1 *for Marlin rifles.*

King triple bead front sight.

No. 5   Globe front sight similar to Beach front sight that has a pinhead bead within the globe and an ivory blade when the globe is tipped forward. Used for all-around shooting

No. 7   Hooded front sight with windage in the base and a reversible globe and aperture within the hood

No. 8   Sporting front sight like the No. 5 sight, except that it has an added windage adjustment in the base

No. 17   Hooded target-type front sight that has a reversible aperture and globe

No. 18   Windage front sight having the same height and bead as the No. 3 ivory bead sight

No. 20   Like the No. 3 sight, except the ivory bead is larger for quick shooting in poor light, or with the Jack at night

No. 28   Called the Semi-Jack front sight, this sight has an ivory bead between the size of the No. 3 bead and the No. 20 Jack bead

Lyman would furnish the Nos. 3, 4, 5, 20, 24, and 28 sights with copper beads, or with red ivory beads, instead of white ivory, at no extra charge.

To show interchangeability of sights, Lyman stated the following in its catalog:

> Lyman front sights Nos. 3, 4, 20 and 28, when made for the Marlin Model '97, will also fit the Marlin '91 and '92 in all calibers.
>
> Lyman front sight No. 5, when made for Winchester Model '90 rifle, will also fit Marlin '91, '92 and '97 rifles.
>
> "Standard" Lyman Leaf sight No. 6 will fit Marlin Model 1881, '93, '94 and '95 when made in .32/40, .38/55 and .32 H.P.S.
>
> Lyman Leaf sight No. 6 when made for the Winchester Model '90 rifle, will also fit Marlin Models '91, '92, '97 and the '93 in .25/36 and .30/30.

Marble Sights. Among the popular commercial sights manufactured for use on Marlin firearms were those made by the Marble Arms and Manufacturing Company.

The Marble Company started business in 1898 as the Marble Safety Axe Company. In April 1911, it became the Marble Arms & Manufacturing Company. In 1964, it became the Marble Arms Corporation, which it remains today.

The pre-WW II Marble sights most frequently encountered by the collector are tang sights and combination front sights. The tang sights were similar to Lyman's combination sight No. 1 and the front sights were unique to Marble. The best-grade tang sight was a flexible type that adjusted like a Lyman tang sight. The vertical stem was spring-loaded and tough to

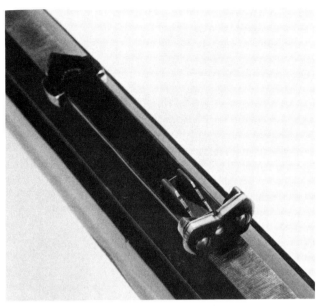

F. W. Freund open rear sight.

Lyman receiver sight fitted to Model 1893 rifle.

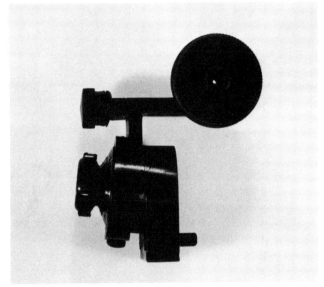

Vaver Dial micrometer rear sight for the Model 39 rifle.

Top view of King triple bead sight.

Tang peep sight by unknown maker for the Model 39 rifle.

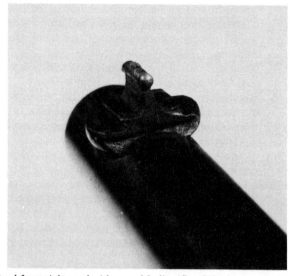

Bead front sight used with some Marlin rifles. It had a snap-on hood.

Clockwise from the left are shown the following front sights that are frequently found on Marlin rifles: Lyman early patent date (October 6, 1885); Lyman No. 3; Lyman hunting No. 4; Lyman No. 20; Marble redbead No. 5; Lyman No. 28MI; Lyman No. 28.

Side view of Marlin hooded bead front sight.

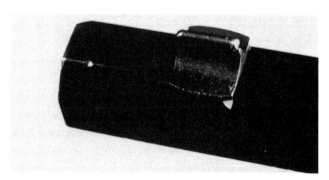

Typical Marlin bead front sight.

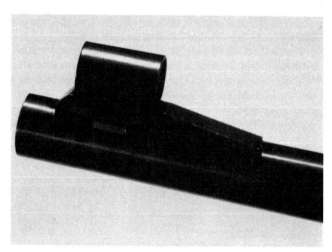

Marlin first-generation ramp front sight used on Model 39A and 336 rifles.

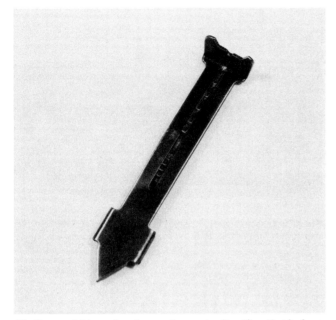

Marlin rear sight, used on lever action center-fire rifles, that had projecting ears on each side of the sighting notch.

Rear sight of Model 88DL rifle.

reassemble if ever taken apart. The cheaper Marble tang sight was called the Simplex rear sight; adjustment was made by sliding the peep up and down the vertical staff. Both types had screw-in peep apertures, available in different hole sizes.

In 1936, Marlin advertised Marble sights in its parts catalog, but those listed included only an assortment of open rear sights and sheared bead front sights.

Two early Marble front sights found fitted to old Marlin rifles are the Marble Duplex sight, which had two sizes of beads (one gold and the other ivory), one of which would fold down to expose the other; and a reversible sight, which had beads at both ends of a spring-loaded blade. The blade could be reversed fore and aft, allowing the use of either a metal bead or one of ivory.

It appears that Marlin only sold Marble sights in the 1930s, and there is no evidence located so far that establishes that rifles could be ordered from Marlin with Marble sights fitted.

The Marble tang sight model numbers and the Marlin rifles they could be used on were as follows:

Marlin rear peep sight used on some deluxe models.

Flexible Tang	Simplex Tang	Marlin Model
M1		1892 — .32
M2		1888, 1889, & 1894
M3	M3S	1891 — .22, 1892 — .22, 1897, 18, 25, 27, 29, 39
M4	M4S	1893 — .32-40, .38-55 with or without "For Black Powder"
M5	M5S	1893 — .25-36, .32 HPS, .30-30, .32-40 HPS, .38-55 HPS. Only for guns marked "Special Smokeless Steel"
M6		1895 — .38-56, .40-65, .40-70, .40-82, .45-70, .40-85, .45-90, .33 HP

Marlin extension rear peep sight used on some deluxe models.

Rear view of Marlin peep sight. The knurled knob on the extreme left is the extra aperture disk that was furnished with the sight.

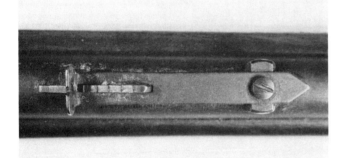

Marlin rear sight used on early bolt action and early autoloading rifles.

Early Marlin receiver peep sight used on some single-shot .22 rifles.

Model 39As sold to Sears, Roebuck at one time had the barrels drilled and tapped for the Weaver N telescope mount, as shown here.

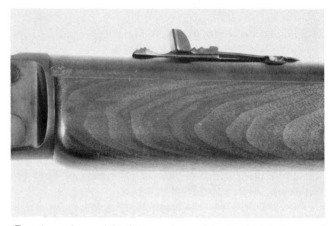

Experimental rear sight that was designed by Ewal Nichols, one of Marlin's gun designers.

Receiver sight used on the semiautomatic caliber .22 Model 99M1 and Model 989M2 rifles.

Flexible Tang	Simplex Tang	*Marlin Model*
M7		1881 — .40–60, .40–65, .45–70, .45–90
M8		20
		37
	M3S	38

Marble Arms Company rear and front sights were used on the 100th-anniversary Commemorative Pair, 39 Century Limited, Article IIs, and Zane Grey rifles. The front sight was Marble's contour sight No. 37W that is .375 inch high, .531 inch wide and has a .065-in. gold bead (¹/₁₆ in.). The rear sight for the center-fire rifles was Marble's sporting semibuckhorn long blade rear sight No. 67. The one used on the .22 rifles was the short blade No. 63 semibuckhorn sight.

Other Commercial Sights. Target shooters and hunters have very decided opinions of the type and quality of the sights they want on their firearms. In fact, there have been more different types and kinds of sights produced to try to satisfy the many wants of the firearm user than any other firearm component, piece, or part manufactured by all the American arms makers put together. Marksmen and target shooters were probably the most critical group with regard to sights. As a result of individual preference, many sights of other manufacturers, such as Winchester, Sharps, Remington, custom gunmakers, and custom sight makers are found on Marlin rifles, and in particular Ballard rifles. To illustrate this point, photos of J.W. Soule, H.M. Pope, and Carver's tang mounted peep sights, which fit the Marlin tang screw holes, are shown here. These sights represent the kind of sight that incorporates features felt to be essential to a sight by the maker as well as the user. Some of the types shown are rare and very valuable today.

The famous gunsmith, F.W. Freund of Cheyenne, Wyo., manufactured during the 1880s variations of sights he felt were an improvement over others. One that is quite rare is his open sight that is semibuckhorn but with an ivory outline.

It should be noted that the Freund sight fitted to a Marlin shown here is on a matted octagon barrel. That makes this rifle "two-for-two." Both the sight and factory-matted barrels are rare.

The King Gun Sight Company of Denver, Colo., also manufactured numerous sights for most all American-manufactured firearms. Two of interest to the Marlin fancier are the King Micrometer Auto Locking Peep Sight (tang) that had an easy

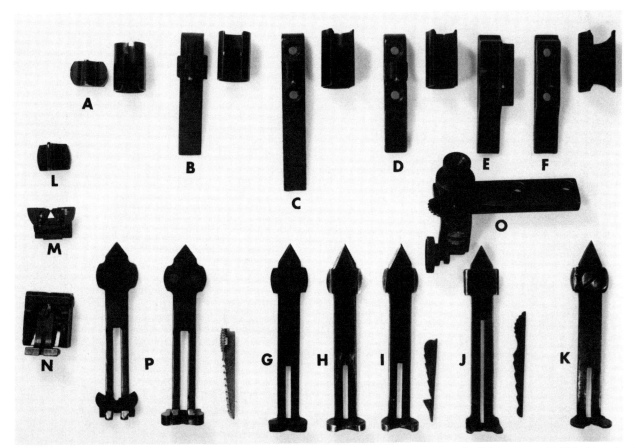

A. *Model 80 and 81 deluxe front sight;* B. *39A dovetail sight with hood;* C. *39A, 336A, and SC long ramp;* D. *336 short ramp;* E. *336 without hood;* F. *336 with Wide-Scan hood;* G. *Center-fire lever action Rocky Mountain sight;* H. *Rocky Mountain sight with elevation-adjusting plate;* I. *Rocky Mountain buckhorn rear sight;* J. *39A and 336 sight;* K. *Model A1, 50, 80, 81, and 65 sight;* L. *Model 444 front sight;* M. *Model 444 rear sight;* N. *Model 99M1 and 989M2 sight;* O. *Model 80, 81 deluxe rear sight;* P. *Osborne folding leaf rear sight shown with leaf up and down; also shown is elevator.*

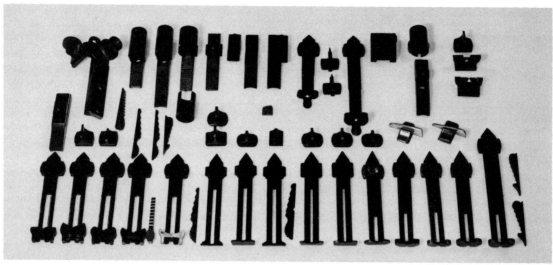

Various front and rear sights that were used or manufactured by Marlin.

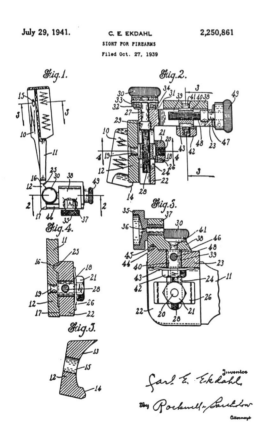

Marlin's C.E. Ekdahl patent illustration for an adjustable extension target rear sight that was never manufactured.

micrometer elevation adjustment built into the vertical staff and the King Triple Bead Front Sight. This front sight came in three different heights for use with different makes of rifles. The unique thing about this sight, however, is that each sight has three different beads. By tipping the front blade to the right or left, the user could choose an ivory, gold, or silver bead. They were made in different-sized beads, as well as different heights.

Sighting a Rifle. Pre-1915 catalogs furnished the following instructions for sighting rifles:

> Every Marlin rifle is shot at a target and the sights properly adjusted before it leaves our factory. Rifles as sent from the factory are generally sighted at from 50 to 65 yards, as this distance seems best to meet the general demand. You may sometimes have to adjust a trifle, as your ammunition may give a different velocity from that used at the factory. Rifles sighted correctly for one person, especially in the case of open sights, may not be so sighted for another, the difference being due not only to the eye, but also to the manner of taking sight, whether fine or coarse. We would recommend that the purchaser of a rifle sight it to his own eyes and to such range as he prefers as soon as convenient. It is generally advisable to sight the rifle at the shortest range for which it may be used, and then it is easy to adjust it for longer ranges by elevation of the rear sight. To test the rifle and adjust it for your eyes, never fasten the rifle in a vise. This is enough to make an accurate rifle shoot wildly. Rest the rifle on some solid object with, if convenient, a cushion of some soft material. We would recommend resting the rifle about six inches from the muzzle. Secure a steady rest for the body and arm, and when shooting press the butt to the shoulder firmly and with as near a uniform pressure as possible. Use the cartridge that you intend to use regularly for hunting or target purposes. First ascertain how the bullets go with respect to the mark. If the rifle shoots too high, this can be adjusted by lowering the slide in the rear sight; if too low, by raising the slide in the rear sight. It will be observed that we have provided an adjustment so that the proper range can be secured, leaving the elevator in its lowest position, and then the elevator can be used to provide the adjustment for longer ranges.

A higher front sight would cause a rifle to shoot lower, while a lower front sight would cause a rifle to shoot higher. In other words, the elevation of the rear sight, the lowering of the front sight, or the substitution of a lower front sight increases the range. The lowering of the rear sight, the raising of the front sight, or the substitution of a higher front sight reduces the range.

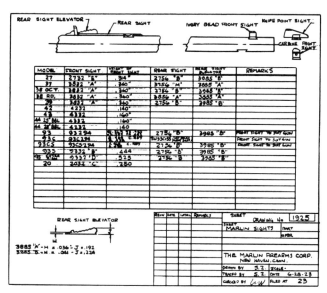

1925 drawing of Marlin front and rear sights.

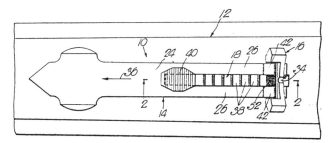

Osborne rear sight patent drawing.

For horizontal variation the adjustment is as follows:

If the rifle shoots to the right, move the front sight to the right, or move the rear barrel sight to the left. If the rifle shoots to the left, move the front sight to the left, or the rear barrel sight to the right. If the adjustment required should be so great as to cause the sight, if you attempt to adjust by one sight only, to appear any distance away from the center of the bore, do not try to adjust by one sight, but adjust with both. In this way a considerable distance may be taken up without bringing the sights apparently from the center of the bore. When you move the sights this should be done by a little rod of brass, say one-quarter of an inch in diameter. By striking the blow on the brass you do not dent the sights and you will not injure the barrel, whereas if you attempt to strike the blow directly on the sight, you are apt to injure the barrel, to say nothing of battering the sights. In case it is desired to drive out a barrel sight, as for instance, to substitute another, always drive out the sight from the left side to the right. In putting in sights always drive in from the right to the left.

Silencers

During the early 1900s, Hiram Percy Maxim designed and patented gun silencers. His efforts were directed toward both military and sporting arms and resulted in his forming the Maxim Silencer Company, Hartford, Conn. Later, the name

Remington Model 12 with Maxim Silencer.

PRICE LIST OF SILENCER ACCESSORIES.

Extra .22 cal. Coupling only	$1.00
" 25-20 " "	1.00
" 32-20 " "	1.00
" thread protecting caps, all calibres	.25
Bullet Stop Target Box	3.50
Threading barrels to receive Silencer	2.00
Sight Type Couplings, any rifle barrel	2.50
Clamp Type Couplings, any rifle barrel	2.50

Rifles with full length magazines must have magazine tube shortened to make room for Coupling. In ordering be sure and state MAKE, MODEL and CALIBRE of rifle to be fitted and whether barrel is ROUND or OCTAGON.

Savage Model 1909 with Maxim Silencer.

Marlin Model 1897 with Maxim Silencer.

Maxim Silencer Company ad for Marlin Model 1897 rifle fitted with a Maxim silencer.

Muzzle end of Model 1897 rifle barrel, showing threaded end to which a Maxim silencer could be fitted.

was changed to the Maxim Silent Firearms Company with a New York City office address and Hartford factory address.

The Maxim silencer devices were attached to the muzzle of a rifle or pistol, and would slow down the velocity and expansion of the gases exiting the muzzle. In so doing the report or "bang" of the gun's firing was reduced. It was also theorized that the device would reduce recoil, making the gun more pleasant to shoot, as well as reduce the noise that would startle game or be objectionable in populated areas.

The Maxim Silent Firearms Company sold not only their silencers, designed for different makes and calibers of firearms, but also firearms with the device attached to the muzzle.

There were three methods of attaching Maxim silencers to the muzzle. One factory method was to thread the front end of the barrel with an interrupted thread and to then attach the

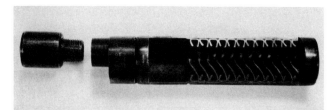

Maxim silencer, and the muzzle adapter that was one of the methods of fitting a silencer to the barrel of a rifle.

device onto the barrel by turning the device 90°. Another method was to install a coupling to the barrel, which would then accept the device. The third method was to thread the muzzle of the barrel and to then screw the silencer onto the threaded barrel.

Examples of Marlin caliber .22 rifles have been inspected that have all three types of muzzle alteration. No center-fire Marlins have been observed that have been altered for a silencer.

The Maxim Company furnished a knurled ring that would protect the thread on the muzzle when the device was removed. The company also furnished extra couplers so one device could be used on more than one gun.

In 1912, a Maxim silencer for a Marlin Model 1897 rifle cost $5.00; extra couplers were $1.00. Devices for center-fire rifles cost from $7.00 to $9.50 each, dependent upon caliber and barrel configuration.

Although the subject of silencers is interesting and most U.S. collectors would like to own an original Marlin with one attached, it must be remembered that the U.S. National Firearms Act of 1934 regulates the ownership of silencers. The law is clear and very restrictive. Active silencers are illegal, unless registered with the Treasury Department's Bureau of Alcohol, Tobacco and Firearms (BATF). Any collector would be foolish to make or own such an unregistered device. In fact, possession of an unregistered silencer in the U.S., even without a firearm to attach it to, is illegal.

Special Sales and Stock Offerings

Few companies can conduct their business without, on occasion, adding to their financial position by borrowing money, mortgaging property and assets, or selling their product at a reduced profit.

The Marlin people introduced some novel approaches to financing when the company needed cash to operate. One scheme used successfully in 1894 was to offer a Marlin rifle or pistol at a reduced price if the publisher would insert in his publication a 2-in. advertisement that was furnished along with a listing of the 36 various propositions available. Typical examples of the different propositions offered were as follows:

> Proposition No. 27: Model 1891 rifle with pistol grip stock, checked.
>
> If you will insert the annexed 2-inch advertisement to the value of $14.50 at your regular rates, and mail us a copy of the paper while advertisement is running, we will send you, on receipt of paper containing first insertion, our due bill, which, when accompanied by $10.00 in cash, will be accepted

in full payment for the rifle which is regularly priced at $24.50.

> Proposition No. 36: Marlin double action automatic ejecting revolver, 32 or 38 caliber, with fine selected pearl stocks, finely engraved, full silver with gold trimmings.
>
> Same as rifle above except 2-inch advertisement valued at $10.00 and $8.00 cash. Regular price of the revolver was $18.00.

Until 1909, this part-cash, part-advertising scheme went along without incident. But some newspapers took exception to the scheme. One trade paper wrote the following:

> The scheme, theirs is one in which the retailer loses, while the publisher does not gain, having paid full price for the goods and having lost some of the regard of local merchants handling those goods. The manufacturer is the only factor in the deal who wins. He gets his full price—cash in hand before he sends the goods—and after the publisher has paid transportation charges from the factory and donated a good-sized chunk of advertising space for a considerable period, he has paid more for the goods than a home merchant would have charged him.

The article went on to state that

> It is only fair to say that the Marlin Firearms Company has the reputation of protecting both jobbers and retailers in the marketing of its products. But whether the company has done everything within its power to shut off supplies of its goods from the price-slaughtering pirates we do not know.
>
> Certainly, however, the Marlin Company should either discontinue or radically change its present method of making newspaper advertising contracts. Both retailers and jobbers will doubtless make that point plain to the company.

In 1928, Frank Kenna, Sr., initiated a different and unusual sales program. The plan promoted direct sales to individuals. It is best described by the following letter response sent by the Club Plan Manager, 507–10 Malley Building, New Haven, Conn., to individuals requesting a Marlin catalog.

> ADDRESS ALL ANSWERS TO
> CLUB PLAN MANAGER 507–10 MALLEY BLDG.
> NEW HAVEN, CONNECTICUT
>
> February 13, 1928
>
> Here is a plan that will
> help you to get that gun.

All it costs, to find out about it, is a 2¢ stamp and enough of your time to answer the questions on the enclosed sheet, for if you really want a MARLIN gun and WILL DO YOUR PART, you may, like a lot of others we are interesting in this plan, soon be SHOOTING instead of WISHING.

The Club Plan is NEW—and it works. It is offered as a SAVING and a SERVICE to those who have no MARLIN dealer close at hand. If there is a MARLIN dealer near you, we would appreciate your giving us his name. He too can profit if he will cooperate in this Plan and we will write him in your behalf.

We want you to have that MARLIN gun and we are willing to go to the trouble of making it EASY for you to get it and this letter is the first step. It is YOUR NEXT MOVE and the mailing of the information asked for, will bring you, promptly, the details of a plan whereby you may be able to own one of the World's FINEST FIREARMS, on a basis that almost anybody can afford. You take no chances, for MARLINS are AS REPRESENTED. Behind every claim made for these fine guns, are resources and an organization that has treated shooters fairly, since 1870.

In the meantime, show the catalog to your friends; tell them that there is a deal going around, in which they might like to share. Get them to write to The Club Plan Manager, 507-10 Malley Building, New Haven, for full information — and don't forget to mail YOUR INQUIRY, TODAY.

Sincerely yours,

Club Plan Manager
507-10 Malley Bldg.
New Haven, Conn.

The results of this sales program are unknown, but it does show the innovative efforts by Marlin to promote sales during the early years of Frank Kenna, Sr.'s development of his newly formed and struggling gun company.

It is interesting to note that an address different from the Marlin Firearms address was used. (Was this intended to give the program a "CLUB" image, and that by purchasing through the plan the purchaser belonged to a select group?)

In 1930, Frank Kenna introduced another plan wherein a person could purchase four $25.00 shares of Marlin Firearms Company preferred stock for $100.00 and receive a free rifle or shotgun of his choice. The guns available were the Model 50 caliber .22 autoloader; the Model 39 lever action caliber .22 rifle; the Model 37, 38, and 47 caliber .22 pump repeating rifles; the Model .410 lever action shotgun; the Model 42A, 43A, 44A, and the new Model 63 12-gauge repeating shotguns. The stock paid a 7% annual dividend. By including the price of the gun given free it amounted to about a 14% return on the $100.00 investment. By the end of 1930, 1,269 sportsmen had purchased stock. The offer was again made in 1931 with about 1,000 more sportsmen accepting the offer.

In 1931, Marlin introduced a limited-time-only special trade-in offer. The flyer announcing the program was as follows:

Special introductory offer on a new Marlin rifle or shotgun good for a limited time only.

We will make you a liberal allowance on your old Rifle or Shotgun, regardless of make, in trade for a new MARLIN Rifle or Shotgun fresh from our stock.

Write and tell us what make of a gun you have and its condition, also what Model MARLIN you are interested in securing and we will let you know what offer we can make. Your gun does not even have to be in working order to get in on this, as our Repair Department will attend to any repairs.

We want more new MARLINS in use in this section so here's your chance to get one at a remarkable price.

If you do not have a gun to trade in we will make you a special advertising offer on any one of our guns in consideration that you do all you can to promote MARLIN interest.

Don't forget — "Good for a Limited Time Only" — so write, telephone or wire at once.

The Marlin Firearms Company
Trade-In Department
New Haven, Connecticut

Also in 1931, Marlin used another method of promoting the sale of the recently introduced Model 50 autoloading rifle. The promotion offered the person interested in a Model 50 the opportunity of getting one direct from the factory on a trial basis. The offer was that, if one's favorite dealer could not furnish a rifle, a card could be sent in with a $5.00 deposit along with a promise to pay, after a week's trial, the balance of $11.65. If the customer was not happy with the gun after the trial period, he could return it and his deposit would be refunded.

In 1932 Mr. Kenna introduced another "Sporting" proposition to the sportsman. The plan was described as a "Special Plan," which was charged to "Good Advertising."

The plan was outlined in a circular that went to a mailing list of Marlin owners and to people requesting catalogs. The presentation went like this:

A MARLIN GUN FREE!

All we need to know is, which of these fine guns will be yours? This is a sporting proposition. Read it carefully and be ready for the hunting season.

MARLIN is a BIG name. Its factory is one of the oldest. It achieved this GOOD NAME by hard, honest work in two ways, through FINE GUNS, maintaining their QUALITY, and through ADVERTISING. Since 1870, it has been telling MARLIN EXCELLENCE to the shooters' World. It has made MARLIN friends among a million owners. And the big family is still growing.

In addition to the regular yearly amount for advertising, MARLIN issues a special proposition DIRECT to Gun Owners and those who have long wished to own a MARLIN. This PLAN is a BIG SUCCESS as a friend maker for MARLIN, because for every gun distributed under this ORIGINAL PLAN, there follow many sales.

The PLAN is this: a certain number of MARLIN Guns are set aside for the operation of the PLAN. Their COST represents a sum of money which is charged to GOOD ADVERTISING.

This circular announces the setting aside of 600 guns for the 1932 Season offer: 100 of the 20 Gauge Shot Gun, Model No. 44A, 100 of the 12 Gauge Shot Gun, Model No. 63A, 100 of the Model 410-410 Gauge Repeating Shotguns, 100 of the NEW Automatic Loading .22 caliber Rifles, Model No. 50, and 200 of the celebrated Model No. 39, .22 caliber Rifles.

These 600 guns will be distributed absolutely free on this special PLAN to people in many communities; people whom we want to hear from upon receipt of this circular and to whom we will explain the EASIEST and MOST CONVENIENT PLAN of securing a gun, that has ever been offered. The PLAN provides a gun to those whom we select — and if you are interested enough to enquire about it, we want to hear from you.

This PLAN seeks the cooperation of gun lovers in the localities where they live. Pick out the Gun you would like to own — and WRITE US. In return, we will submit you the details of this PLAN; then it is up to you. You won't have to sell any guns. If your application is approved, you will get the gun and we will BOTH benefit from the arrangement, for it's a MARLIN WINNER for YOU and a good advertisement for MARLIN.

Upon the receipt of a communication from the interested sportsman, a letter was sent outlining the plan and the amount of deposit necessary to receive one of the "free" firearms along with a Marlin five-year note for the amount of the deposit. The letter was as follows:

Dear Sir:

This is our Special Plan, in answer to your letter:

You must know that we want more people to own MARLINS. Well, how should we go about it? . . . Advertise . . . ? Yes — but how? Direct to the people? Yes, that's it exactly.

So we adopted this plan to give away a good many guns. But we will only give them to responsible people who can make a deposit with us of the amount stated below, because we return the deposit to you in full. Thus you not only get the gun — but your money back! You are assured of the return of the deposit, because we give you a five-year note, like the one enclosed, signed by the Marlin Firearms Company.

Now you don't have to handle the full deposit — unless you want the gun quickly. You can join this plan and receive all its benefits with as little as a $10 deposit, paying the balance as you can. When the deposit is all made, we send you the gun and the signed note.

Marlin wants only SATISFIED Shooters. If you are not fully satisfied, you may return the gun and the note within ten days and we will return your full deposit. You have the Marlin catalog sent you sometime ago. You must realize that this is a wonderful offer; too good to pass up! More than 1500 sportsmen accepted a similiar offer — and this one is even better.

Fill out the application blank and attach your first deposit. This will hold the gun for you. If you cannot take it up, be sure to return the note so that we can set the gun aside for someone else. Fair enough isn't it?

You must act promptly — so please start today. It's a good plan and you *know* it. Obey that impulse now. Waiting to hear, we remain,

Cordially yours,
The Marlin Firearms Company

Frank Kenna, President

Deposit of $25 (returnable per promissory note) on Model 50.

The deposit for a Model 39 was $50. For a Model 50 it was $25. The Model 39 listed for $32.40 and the Model 50 was $17.85. In addition to the gun, a five-year note was sent for the full amount of the deposit.

There are no records available that indicate how many takers there were of this offer. However, with the great shortage of cash in the working man's pocket in 1932, it is my guess that not many could afford to accept what appeared to be a pretty good proposition.

In 1937, Frank Kenna introduced yet another scheme to advertise the Marlin name and to raise money. Instead of the usual banking and mortgage methods, his offer was to give a gun free to those who bought a five-year note from the company. The plan first went like this:

By buying one of our non-interest bearing promissory notes of $12.00 to $75.00, payable in five years, you can secure a rifle or shotgun or a combination of arms, free of cost, which is our consideration for your letting us have the use of the cash for five years without charge. At the end of that time your note is payable in full and in the meanwhile you will have the rifle or shotgun of your selection free of cost and have it from the very start. Just look through the list and pick your gun.

All the guns in the Marlin catalogue were available to be acquired in this manner.

This offer of non-interest-paying five-year notes was found to be illegal in the states of Missouri, Ohio, and Pennsylvania. As a result, in 1938 the notes already purchased and those to be sold were changed by adding a 2% annual interest rate.

The full extent of these programs is not known; however, it is felt that they did help Marlin through some economically tough times.

Early in 1943, Marlin introduced a contest. The purpose was to encourage sportsmen to send in suggestions that they felt would improve a Marlin firearm.

The contest, prizes, and rules were advertised in the leading outdoor magazines, as follows:

$1,000 For Your Ideas in the Big Marlin Gun Contest! Closes July 1, 1943. Jot down your ideas for improving any current model Marlin Gun. Follow the simple contest rules and send your entry in. If you wish you may suggest new features, not at present in the line. A free catalog is yours for the asking, to review the features of Marlin guns.
PRIZES — First prize is $500 in cash; second prize is $100; third is $50; fourteen additional prizes of $25 cash each. Seventeen prizes in all! (Marlin suggests the purchase of US Savings Bonds with the prize money).
JUDGING — Three famous gun editors — Bob Nichols of Field & Stream, Jack O'Connor of Outdoor Life, Maj. Chas. Askins of Sports Afield — will select the winning entries. All ideas for which prizes are given become the property of the Marlin Firearms Company and none will be returned. Prizes awarded for the seventeen ideas which are most valuable and practical, in the opinion of the judges. Duplicate prizes will be awarded in the event of a tie. Winners will be determined and prizes announced as soon as possible.
CONTEST RULES — The Marlin Gun Contest is open to all sportsmen and dealers in guns, with the exception of Marlin employees. Written suggestions must not exceed 300 words, the shorter the better. No limit to number of entries which may be submitted. Write name and address clearly on each suggestion. Mail entries to Dept. 7, the Marlin Firearms Co. 17 East 42nd St., New York City. Entries must be received on or before July 1, 1943.

In October 1943, Marlin announced the prizewinners and thanked the thousands of participants in the contest. It was mentioned that many of the ideas would later be embodied in Marlin sporting guns. Unfortunately, there are no records available now that list the suggestions. It is known, however, that the winning suggestion was for an interchangeable chamber that could be used to adapt a .22 for hunting or indoor shooting.

The prize winners were the following:

First Prize	Charles E. Hoffelt, Estelline, S.D.
Second Prize	Lt. G.R. Hunter, Quitman, Ga.
Third Prize	Pvt. Geo. E. Larsson
14 Additional Prizes	Paul St. Gardens, Coconut Grove, Fla.
	James E. Nogle, Jacksonville, Fla.
	Louis Belanger, Montreal, Canada
	Collier H. Kear, Richmond Hill, N.Y.

C.E. Reardon, Chicago, Ill.
F.E. Knowles, Taunton, Mass.
J.R. Haver, San Francisco, Calif.
Art Dyson, Fresno, Calif.
LT. Comdr. A.K. Espenas, Annapo-
    lis, Md.
Theaddius F. Allen, Zanesville, Ohio
Melvin Ruebush, Chicago, Ill.
Sylvester J. Lefebure, Milwaukee,
    Wis.
Paul McGowen, Roseburg, Ore.
Jack Mills, Wall Lake, Ind.

Typical star mark on tang, which indicated that the Marlin was "as near perfection as the finest of materials, equipment and skill can make it."

One can only wonder if Marlin did use any of the ideas submitted. It is known, though, that the first-prize suggestion was not used.

Although not designed to raise cash, another promotion program that helped sell firearms was conducted in the early 1950s. It was designed to assist the gun dealer and to encourage the retail purchaser to take advantage of the layaway method of making a purchase. Marlin furnished the dealer with pre-printed record books, buyer's payment record books, and tags that were to be attached to the firearm being held on layaway. Marlin did not establish the amount of first payment or length of time for full payment. Marlin only furnished the printed matter and motivation. The dealer did the rest.

In 1956, Marlin introduced another plan wherein the dealer could sell Marlin firearms on a pay-later plan. Each gun shipped that year had a tag attached to the gun, which included the following information:

Typical star-marked Model 93 to p tang.

> This gun can be yours for only a small down payment, ask your dealer for full details. Own it now . . . and pay-later on time. The Marlin Pay-Later Plan is the only one that insures your investment. Included automatically is insurance protection that makes all remaining payments for you in the event of your death or 90 day permanent total disability as described in a certificate which will be furnished you after your application for financing has been accepted by the Seaboard Finance Company. This valuable purchaser-protection is underwritten by one of America's largest Insurance Companies . . . Continental Assurance Company, Chicago, Illinois.

The promotions described served their purpose at the time. Each helped Marlin through lean years, or through periods of a depressed market. All of them attest to the excellent leadership of the company.

Star

During the first few years of production of firearms under the leadership of Frank Kenna, Sr., a star was stamped into the metal of each gun made.

When I first joined Marlin, in 1969, I heard various explanations for the star marked on some old Marlin guns. The most common was that the gun had been factory-refinished and the star was to identify that fact. Another explanation was that the gun was a factory second and was so identified by the star.

The fact is, however, that it is an inspector's mark placed on the gun. Literature published in 1926–1927 states that when a

Star marking on Model 39 rifle.

Marlin gun leaves the factory bearing the Marlin star stamped into the metal, it is "as near perfection as the finest of materials, equipment, and skill can make it."

The star was usually stamped on the top tang of lever action guns and behind the trigger guard of the pump shotguns.

Both Marlin Firearms Corporation-marked guns and Marlin Firearms Company-marked guns have been noted with the inspector's star stamped into the metal. Some of those noted are as follows:

Model	Serial Number
39	9992
39	10571
39	12959
39	S2600
39	S4888
39	S5329
39	S14100
39	S16135
43	14449
93	210

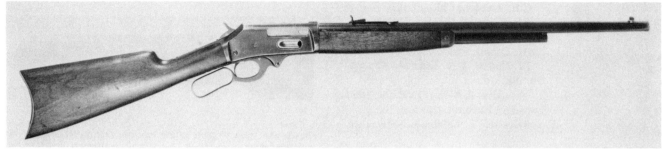

Stevens Model 425 lever action rifle.

Model	Serial Number
93	1739
93	9336
94	1041
94	1527

Stevens Model 425

The J. Stevens Arms and Tool Company, Chicopee Falls, Mass., introduced in 1911 a solid top, side-ejecting lever action rifle chambered for the Remington .25, .30, .32, and .35 cartridges. It was identified as the Model 425; however, a Model 430 that was checked was available, and a deluxe engraved

1962 Marlin flyer announcing availability of special stock carvings.

Model 435 could be ordered. The standard gun sold for $20.00. The checked stock and forearm model sold for $27.50 and the engraved gun sold for $38.00.

Stevens's catalogs described the Model 425 as having a 22-in. nickel steel barrel; blued receiver, barrel, and magazine; coil mainspring; walnut stock with checkered butt plate; walnut forearm with blued steel cap; German silver blade front sight and sporting rear; tang tapped for tang sight and receiver tapped for telescope sight; two-piece firing pin for safety and extreme ease of operation. The weight of the rifle was 7 pounds and the overall length was 41 inches. The magazine held 5 cartridges.

In direct competition with the Marlin lever action rifle, the Stevens Model 425 lever action rifle did not fare well in the marketplace. A number of things were against success. First was the solid position of Marlin and Winchester in the lever action market. Next came the poor performance record of the Stevens mechanism. As a result, the rifle was short-lived. Only about 1,000 were manufactured up to 1917.

Information about this rifle is included here only because its close resemblance to a Marlin has, in some circles, caused confusion. It is not a Marlin and was not manufactured by Marlin for the Stevens company.

Stock Carving

In 1962, Marlin introduced a stock-carving service. Having already set up a pantograph carving machine to carve the 90th-anniversary commemorative, 336 Deluxe Texan, and 39ADL stocks, it was a simple matter for Marlin to have brass masters made for other patterns of carving to be offered to Marlin owners.

This special work was not offered through the annual product catalog, but was advertised by Marlin's feature ads in shooting publications. The cost was $19.95 per stock.

There were nine design choices. A longhorn steer superimposed on the map of Texas (as on the 336 Deluxe Texan), and a squirrel (of the 39A and 39M 90th-anniversary commemorative, and 39ADL), as well as a mountain lion, rabbit with hound, moose, deer, grouse, duck, and bear with dogs, could be ordered.

Robert Kain (who also engraved 100th-anniversary commemorative rifles) did the design work.

The early offering was actual machine carving of the stock. Later, however, to reduce the cost and to expedite the process, a round "cookie," with the design compressed into it, was fitted into a circular recess routed into the wood stock.

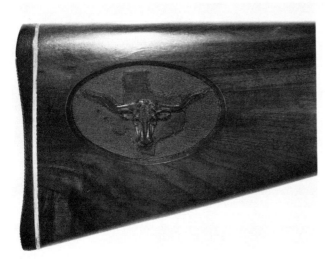

Longhorn steer machine-carved into the stock of Model 336 Deluxe Texan.

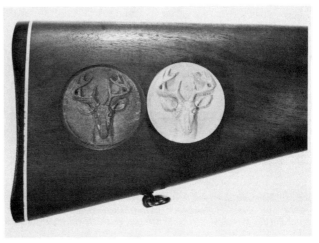

Pressed and glued-in deer head. Shown resting next to it on the stock is a "cookie" that was glued into the stock and then stained.

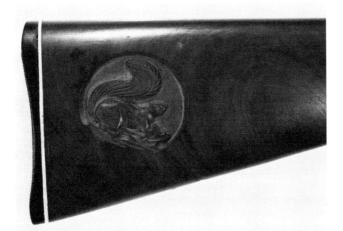

Machine-carved squirrel of the 90th-anniversary stocks and the Model 39ADL.

Carved squirrel offered in 1962 for $19.95.

Deer carved into 336 stock for the Spiegel Company, Chicago.

Glued-in carving of a rabbit done on special order for the Spiegel Company of Chicago.

Left to right: *Pistol grip rifle stock cut for steel rifle butt plate; pistol grip rifle stock cut for S-shaped butt plate; pistol grip rifle stock cut for hard rubber butt plate; rifle buttstock cut for pistol grip and steel rifle butt plate; Model 36 buttstock cut for hard rubber butt plate; straight-grip carbine stock cut for S-shaped butt plate; straight grip rifle stock cut for steel rifle butt plate; straight grip rifle buttstock cut for crescent butt plate.*

This special carving offer was short-lived, and examples of the early carved type are scarce.

A special run of the Model 336, which had a different deer head carved into the stock, was made for the Spiegel Company, Chicago. A total of 4,264 of this special offering were produced.

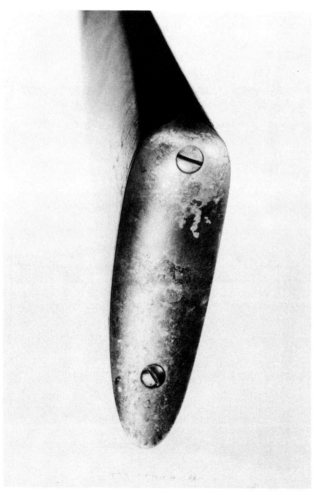

Steel Ballard and Model 1881 butt plate.

Stocks, Forearms, and Butt Plates

Stocks and Forearms. Pre-WW I Marlin buttstocks were of the rifle, carbine, or shotgun type and were either straight or pistol grip. However, the carbine stock has historically always been of the straight type. (Short-barreled straight-stocked rifles should not be confused with carbines, even though rifles have been observed that were factory fitted with a carbine-type buttstock.)

Upon special order, Marlin would furnish extra select and select wood, as well as checked, pistol grip, and straight stocks. Bird's-eye maple stocks could also be special ordered; however, the few examples of bird's-eye maple observed indicate that this type of wood was not the choice of many sportsmen. London dull finish and oil finish were also choices over the usual varnish that could be ordered. There were a very few Marlin repeating rifle stocks produced that were fitted with a Ballard-type Swiss butt plate. Examples of these stocks are shown elsewhere in this book.

Lightweight rifles had special short forearms. Please see the Lightweight section for more details.

Rifle and shotgun stocks could be special-ordered shorter or longer than the standard stock. The drop at the heel and comb could also be made to the desire of the sportsman. Please see the Extra section for more details. The 1917 Marlin–Rockwell Corporation's jobber's net price list was the last to include any of the extras; however, since the company was engrossed in making machine guns at that time, it is doubtful that any but sporting arms on hand and in inventory were being shipped.

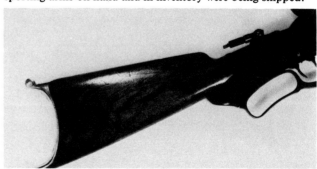

Special-order Swiss-type butt plate.

Ballard-type hard rubber butt plate.

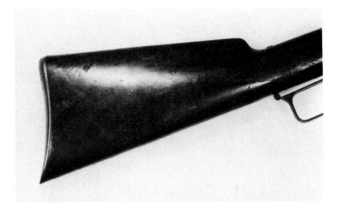

Model 1889 buttstock with Model 1881 steel butt plate.

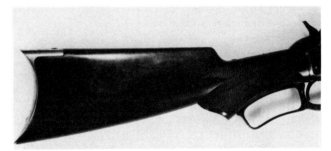

Pistol grip buttstock with classic Marlin steel rifle butt plate.

Straight stock with classic steel butt plate.

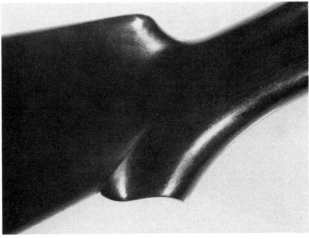

Classic S-shaped pistol grip used by Marlin into the 1930s.

After WW I, none of the previous extras could be ordered, and by 1935 the classic S-shaped pistol grip on Marlin stocks was just about eliminated. The new line of caliber .22 bolt action and semiautomatic rifles had finger grooves in the forearm and grips with flat bottoms. The Model 93 had lost its pistol grip and only straight stocks were available. When the new model 1936 was introduced, the pistol grip stock was back. However, it had a much fuller pistol grip that was flat on the bottom, and a fluted comb.

Nineteen thirty-nine was the year of new wood for the Model 39 rifle and a change in its name from Model 39 to Model 39A. The buttstock had a larger flat-bottomed pistol grip and new design of a long semibeavertail forearm. (In my opinion, the new style was not as classic or cosmetically correct as the old buttstock and forearm, but probably easier to machine-shape and -sand than the old style.) Up until the Model 1936 rifle was introduced, forearms had been slim and not much larger than the forearm tip or front end of the receiver. With the advent of new leadership in the company, after WW II, rather large, bulky, and ugly forearms developed.

The Marlin pump action shotguns, until they were discontinued in the 1930s, had conventional pistol grip or straight stocks with either a hard rubber butt plate or rubber recoil pad. The forearms were either grooved or smooth and checked. Also, some models had checked pistol grips.

The Marlin Firearms Corporation introduced in 1922 a bull's-eye trademark that was used in advertising matter, catalogs, and price lists. Also embedded into the bottom edge of buttstocks was a black dot centered on a circle of white that was made of plastic. Except for a few Depression years, the bull's-eye in the stock was used on all Marlin models. (It appears that the reason it was not used those few years was one of

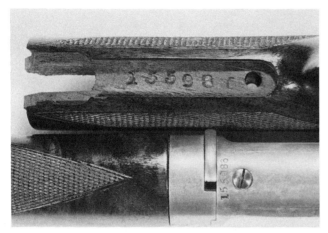

Marlin buttstocks were usually serial-numbered to the receiver. However, the practice was not consistent after 1922.

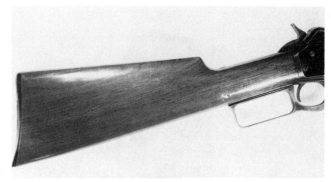

Straight-grip stock with a Marlin hard rubber butt plate.

The second-type hard rubber butt plate, which was optional at no extra charge for all lever action rifles, up to and including the Model 1897.

Typical crescent butt plate that superseded the first steel type.

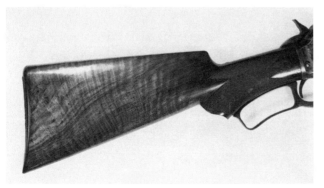

Pistol grip stock with a Marlin hard rubber butt plate.

economy, as at the same time a much less expensive butt plate was also used.)

Birch-wood stocks (Glenfield and brand-name models) did not have the bull's-eye, and even today, after Marlin dropped the Glenfield line and redesignated its models with Marlin model numbers, the practice of no dots in birch wood remains. However, the birch wood is given a walnut stain and is frequently thought to be walnut, whereas it is a walnut-colored hardwood having great strength and often a pleasing grain figure. The outside finish given the birch wood has always been the same as was given walnut, except that walnut is selectively stained by hand. Birch wood, however, is stained all over to give it a brown color.

Marlin used a varnish finish as the standard on all stocks and forearms until 1926. The varnish was applied by hand and then rubbed down between coats. The final polish was done by hand-rubbing the varnish with a fine pumice and water or rubbing oil.

Straight-grip stock that has a crescent butt plate.

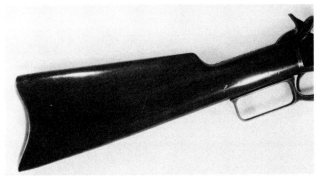

Typical S-shaped butt plate on straight-grip Model 1894 carbine.

Typical S-shaped steel butt plate.

Steel carbine butt plate.

Varnish was a superior finish that required lots of man hours to achieve. However, it scratched easily and was hard to repair.

Upon special order, a London oil finish was available. It was a dull oil finish that was done by hand-rubbing in many coats of boiled linseed oil. Sometimes a varnish base was applied to speed up the operation.

Upon organization of The Marlin Firearms Corporation after WW I, the stock-finishing methods used remained the same as before the war. But after this corporation failed and the new Marlin Firearms Company began production in 1926, other stock finishes were tried. During this period, both varnish and dipped linseed oil finishes were used. However, with the advent of the high-gloss stock finish used by some custom gun shops and manufacturers of expensive and flashy high-power rifles, the sportsman expected a wood finish with a high gloss. To meet this demand, Marlin continued with a hand-sprayed and -rubbed varnish semigloss finish until the company moved in 1969 to a new plant in North Haven, Conn. The move to the new plant allowed for the introduction of new technology and resulted in an industry breakthrough in stock finishing. Marlin's 1970 announcement of its new process and finish was as follows:

Typical Marlin Model 1893 carbine buttstock with a carbine buttplate.

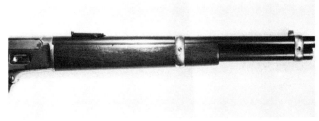

Early Model 1894 carbine forearm.

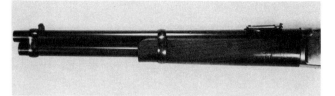

Late Model 93 carbine forearm.

Third type of hard rubber butt plate.

Shotgun butt plate of the first type. A later type was used that was identical, except that it did not have the name Marlin *impressed into the rear surface.*

Marlin became the first in the firearms industry to solve the problems of electrostatic spraying of wood finish with the inauguration of its new "Mar-Shield" process.

"Electrostatic spraying is a proven process in metal finishing and there have been many companies experimenting with this method but we are the first to solve the problems of clogging, drips, runs and unevenness, and loss of spray," said Steve Morris, Marlin's production control manager.

Wood finishing has always been a messy job. It formerly involved hand-spraying stocks in front of a curtain of water, or filters, to catch the spray that missed. The process was "mechanized" insofar as an overhead conveyor carried the stocks past the spray booth. But a lot of spray was lost.

Marlin's new electrostatic spray process overcomes these disadvantages. And many more pieces can be produced with the same number of craftsmen in a shorter period of time.

Gunstocks are first dipped into a saline solution so they will take an electrical charge. By using an alcohol base fluid for the dip, this solution completely evaporates leaving no effect on the wood.

Then the stocks are hung on an overhead conveyor that travels at five feet a minute.

This conveyor carries the stocks around a cylindrical spray booth where an electrical contact gives them a negative charge. The reciprocating automatic spray gun in the center

of the booth spews the Mar-Shield mist onto a whirling disc and charges it with 90,000 volts.

The stocks rotate as they revolve around this spray gun and the negative polarity of the wood attracts the positively charged Mar-Shield finish. Every out-of-the-way place is covered, even places that can't be reached directly by the spray. It wraps around the "negative pole" until coverage is complete. After the spray the stocks are hand scuffed and then given a second gloss coat of varnish.

When the stocks reach the end of the conveyor they are dry and the finish is "set" to protect them from the use they are likely to get in the field.

During 1970, the stock of each Marlin rifle manufactured (not Glenfields) had a 100th-year medallion embedded into the right-hand side of the stock. The $^{15}/_{16}$-in. hole for the medallion was recessed into the wood $^1/_{16}$ inch. An epoxy two-part compound was used to hold the medallion in place.

Unfortunately, over my objection, Marlin made available to owners of non-1970 rifles a kit that included a medallion, epoxy adhesive, and instructions for installation. Therefore, there are some rifle stocks that were not manufactured in 1970 that are sporting a commemorative medallion that is not original to the rifle.

The flat and thin butt plate used for only a short period on a few models.

Butt Plates. Ballard butt plates were of three types, which were Swiss pattern, hard rubber, and steel. The Swiss pattern was nickel-plated and had hooks that extended rearward. The steel type was curved, smooth, and nickel-plated, and had a pointed top part that fitted into the wood at the heel of the stock. The hard rubber butt plate was shaped like the steel one except that it was checked and had an elaborate *M.F.A. CO.* monogram embossed on its center.

The old classic rifle butt plate was case-hardened steel and had an extension that covered the top of the heel of the stock. One mounting screw went into the stock from the top of the extension and the other screw went into the butt end of the stock.

Stocks could be ordered with either the steel rifle butt plate or with a hard rubber butt plate at no extra charge. The early hard rubber type found on some deluxe guns was of the Ballard type with the fancy Marlin monogram centered between the two mounting screws. The next hard rubber butt plate had the Marlin *MFA CO. — MARLIN SAFETY* logo in a circle and centered on the checked and bordered back surface.

The third type of hard rubber butt plate was curved, checked like the previous one, and had the name *MARLIN* embossed vertically into the checked surface. This plate was used on the Models 32, 37, 38, 39, and others.

The fourth type of butt plate, although not manufactured of hard rubber, was one designed in 1944. It did not have a logo embossed on the surface and instead of being checked it had multiple horizontal grooves between the two mounting screws. Until 1946 this plate was made of Bakelite. Thereafter it was made of American Hard Rubber #30 Ace-Tuff. It was used on many different Marlin models and all brand-name models until 1960.

The fifth hard rubber type of butt plate was designed in

Hard rubber butt plate found on a few Model 39A rifles.

1948. It was checked all over except for the area around the top screw and above. It also had the Marlin name in script impressed vertically in an oval between the two screws. Glenfield and other brand-name models had the same butt plate, except that the center oval was plain and without the Marlin name. During 1988, the plain butt plate was dropped and all butt plates now have the name *Marlin* on them.

The following types of steel butt plates were used by Marlin:

1. A Ballard Swiss type that was made of nickel-plated steel and had prongs that extended rearward was the first type.

2. A Ballard, Model 1881, Model 1888, and Model 1889 steel butt plate that was smooth, case-hardened, and had a concave rear surface and a convex projection at the top front was the second type.

3. The classic steel butt plate that was used on all the center-fire lever action rifles was concave shaped and case-hardened and had an extension that covered the top of the heel of the stock. One mounting screw went into the stock through the top of the extension and another screw went into the butt end of the stock. This butt plate was made from a forging. It was usually serial-numbered to the rifle.

4. A crescent-shaped steel rifle butt plate was the fourth steel type used. It had about the same curvature as the previous one, but it did not have the top extension over the heel. It was

made from stamped steel, was either blued or case-colored, and was attached to the buttstock by means of two wood screws into the rear end of the butt.

5. The fifth type of steel butt plate was one used on carbines. It had the classic shape of many carbine butt plates of other manufacturers and also as used on carbines designed for the military. It was S-shaped and had a top extension that extended over the top of the heel of the stock. It was different from the classic rifle butt plate in that the top part was inletted into the wood and was flush with the top of the wood, whereas the rifle type was notched into the top of the stock. One retaining screw went in from the top and the other went into the butt end near the toe.

6. The sixth type of steel butt plate was S-shaped and was used on both rifles and carbines. It was manufactured from a steel stamping, like the previous type, and except for being recurved at both ends, the concave curve was about the same.

The recurved and rounded top and bottom of this butt plate eliminated the sharp points of the previous butt plate and the possibility of chipping the heel and toe if the gun was dropped on the butt end. This butt plate was strong and well-shaped to fit the shoulder, and did not have pointed ends that could catch on clothing when the gun was being shouldered quickly during use. It was made from a formed steel stamping and was either blued or case-colored.

Early hard rubber shotgun butt plates were of only one style; they had horizontal grooves and the name *Marlin*, in script, impressed across the bottom and below the lower screw. Later shotguns, such as the Model 90, L.C. Smith, Mark I and IV, Model 50, and Model 55, had the standard Marlin or Glenfield butt plate of the period.

Rubber shotgun recoil pads were used as standard equipment on the Model 55 Goose Gun, Model 120, and Model 55/10 shotguns. The Model 120 Trap Gun had a custom Pach-

Variations of Marlin butt plates.

Left to right: *Rubber butt plate used on Marlin Models 1895, 444, and 375; hard rubber butt plate used on the Model 1895, Model 336 Octagon, Model 1894 Sporter, Model 39A Octagon, Model 39M Octagon, and the Model 1894 Octagon; late fifth-type hard rubber butt plate introduced in 1948 and still in use today; butt plate used on brand-name and Glenfield models; brass butt plate used on 1970 commemorative pair, Model 39CL, Model 39A and 39M Article II rifles, and the Model 336 Zane Grey Commemorative.*

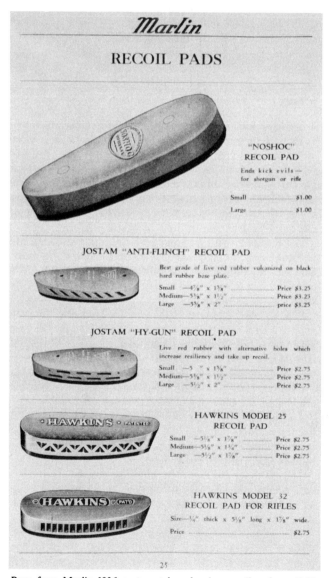

Page from Marlin 1936 parts catalog showing recoil pads available from the parts department.

meyer recoil pad peculiar to that model. The pad on the Model 120, Model 55, and Model 55/10 was of brown rubber without the Marlin name. A second variation had the Marlin name embossed vertically on a cross-hatched background.

In the late 1930s, when the Model 39 was phasing out and the Model 39A with its new design of buttstock was being added to the model, a new corrugated butt plate of light, unbreakable material was adopted. Used for only a short period of time, this butt plate will be found on some late (HS prefix) Model 39s and very early Model 39As. It has seven groups of four serrations, laid horizontally across the thin, flat, fiber-like black material. It was also used on some other models. A second variation is found that is slightly curved that is of similar material, but with 27 evenly spaced grooves. A third variation had the same type of grooves except that the material was ¼-in. thick Bakelite that was contoured thicker at the heel and toe than in the middle, and had up to 57 grooves. This type of plate was used on other rifle models and on the Model 90 over–under shotgun.

The Model 39A and 336 Centennial Pair produced in 1970 both had a curved butt plate made of cartridge brass. The same butt plate was also used on the Model 39 Century Limited, 39A and 39M Article II rifles, and the Zane Grey Century Commemorative rifle. Although this butt plate was not practical, it was decorative.

When the re-creation of the Model 1895 rifle was introduced in 1972, an old-design butt plate was also reintroduced. This new butt plate was like the traditional one used years before. It was curved, of hard rubber, and had the *M.F.A. CO− MARLIN SAFETY* logo. It was checked, but did not have a border on the outer edge as did the earlier type. This butt plate was also used on the Model 336 Octagon, Model 1894 Sporter, Model 39A Octagon, Model 39M Octagon, and Model 1894 Octagon.

Listed as an extra for shotguns in the early catalogs was a Silvers recoil pad that could be ordered for a few dollars extra at the time of ordering one of the many different models

Electrostatic spraying of the finish on Model 39CL buttstocks.

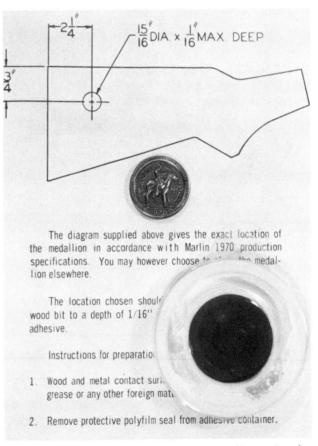

The diagram supplied above gives the exact location of the medallion in accordance with Marlin 1970 production specifications. You may however choose to the medallion elsewhere.

The location chosen shoul wood bit to a depth of 1/16" adhesive.

Instructions for preparatio

1. Wood and metal contact sur grease or any other foreign mat

2. Remove protective polyfilm seal from adhesive container.

1970 commemorative medallion, epoxy adhesive, and instructions furnished by Marlin for the use of owners of Marlin firearms not manufactured in 1970.

Left to right: *Recoil pad used on Models 50 and 55. Recoil pad used on Model 55–10. Recoil pad used on Model 120.*

Side view of Marlin carbine lower band with swivel.

Bottom view of Marlin carbine lower-band swivel.

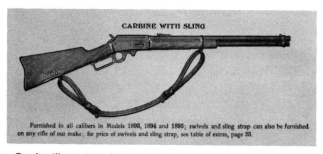

CARBINE WITH SLING

Furnished in all calibers in Models 1893, 1894 and 1895; swivels and sling strap can also be furnished on any rifle of our make; for price of swivels and sling strap, see table of extras, page 25.

Catalog illustration of Marlin carbine fitted with sling and swivels.

Carbine band with swivel removed.

Marlin manufactured. Marlin also listed for sale in the 1936 parts catalog Jostom and Hawkins recoil pads. In addition, there was listed a Hawkins Model 25 pad for rifles. These pads sold for from $1.00 to $2.75 each. In the catalog there was no mention of these pads being fitted to a stock by the factory. It is assumed they were listed primarily for the gunsmith to use in his work.

The Model 444 rifle, with its stiff recoil, had a ventilated recoil pad in 1965 when the model was introduced. This shotgun-type pad remained standard for the Model 444 until 1980, when Marlin introduced a rubber butt plate for the models 1895, 444, and 375. The rubber butt plate is red and has the Marlin horse and rider logo with cross-hatching embossed on the rear surface.

On February 17, 1950, a white plastic insert between the butt plate and the buttstock of the Model 336 was approved. Later, the same insert was approved for other models and also for use between grip caps and the stock. Ever since, the white line spacer has been traditional on most Marlin models. It was not used on Glenfield or brand-name models.

Swivels and Slings

Swivels. A question that the collector frequently has is, "Are the swivels on my Marlin rifle original equipment?" Sometimes referred to as sling loops, sling swivels have been an option available on special order ever since 1883, when swivels and a sling were listed for $1.50 (fitting them cost 50¢ more).

The practice of furnishing swivels only on special order changed. Some later models had them as standard equipment. Also swivels, bands with swivels attached, and forearm tips with swivels fitted were available from the Marlin parts department, as some still are today.

In the 1888 catalog, swivel and sling straps (leather) were first listed for the Model 1888, and in the 1889 catalog, the Models 1889 and 1891 were added. Also in the 1889 catalog a "Sling strap, webbing, with snap hook for carbine at 75¢" was listed.

Unfortunately, the old Marlin records do not indicate if swivels were fitted to the gun prior to its being shipped. The forearm swivel was never installed into the wood. It was, with only one exception, fitted to the forearm band of the carbine and to the forearm tip of the rifle. Marlin's lower swivel was inletted into the bottom edge of the buttstock about 3 inches from the toe of the stock.

The one exception, illustrated here, is a special order of about 50 Model 1936/36 rifles that had Winchester quick detachable (QD) sling swivels installed on them. Both the front and rear swivels were attached with two wood screws. Neither base was inletted into the wood, as would normally be done in installing this type of swivel. The swivels were furnished by the distributor.

Early carbines could be ordered without the usual saddle ring. They could also be ordered with sling swivels fitted. When swivels were fitted, the saddle ring was eliminated, unless it was specifically ordered to be retained.

Special-order sling swivels and slings were listed in price lists until 1917, but once the Marlin Arms Corporation was fully

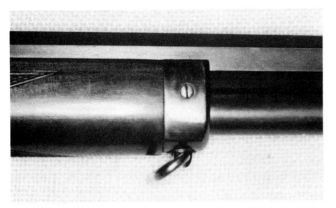

Side view of Model 1893 rifle forearm tip with swivel fitted by Marlin.

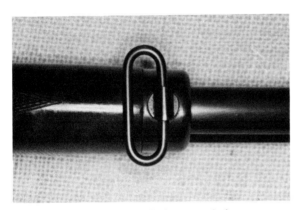

Bottom view of rifle forearm swivel.

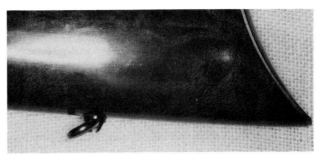

Side view of Model 1893 rifle butt swivel fitted by Marlin.

Bottom view of Marlin butt swivel.

committed to war work, there was no production of sporting arms. Only spare parts could be ordered.

The bull's-eye trademark found in the stock of many of the Marlin firearms manufactured since 1922, when the bull's-eye became Marlin's trademark, should not be misconstrued as the place to install the butt swivel. Butt swivels are normally about 3 inches from the toe of the stock, whereas the bull's-eye trademark is usually about 4 inches from the toe.

Slings. Other than the brief description found in catalogs, little is known about early Marlin slings. They were listed as leather, but the carbine sling in 1889 was described as being of webbing and with a snap hook.

Late Marlin slings have been described as the Whelen type (leather thong at one end), a military-type adjustable sling, and carrying straps. Shown here are a parts catalog page showing these two slings, and a photograph of other slings furnished since the 1930s.

It was common for a company like Marlin to purchase items such as slings from a manufacturer already in that business. In fact, many Marlin vendors would sell to others in the firearms business as well as to Marlin. However, today's slings are purchased from a manufacturer of leather products capable of making a sling to Marlin's specifications on a competitive basis. Today's slings also have the Marlin logo embossed on them. In 1988, Marlin discontinued furnishing slings with certain models. However, studs for QD swivels continue to be furnished for those models.

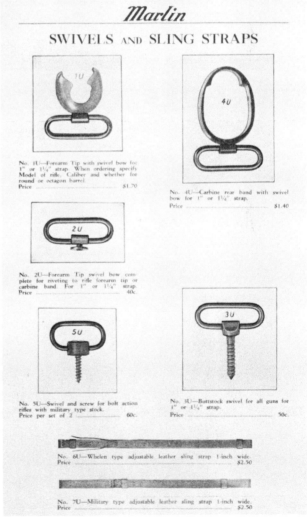

Marlin parts catalog page showing swivels and slings available in 1936.

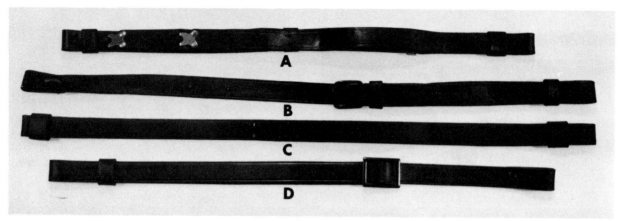

A. *Military-type sling;* B. *Whelen-type sling;* C. *sling used from 1960 to 1970.* D. *Sling introduced in 1980.*

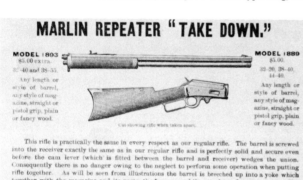

MARLIN REPEATER "TAKE DOWN."

MODEL 1893
$5.00 extra.
32-40 and 38-55.

Any length or
style of barrel,
any style of mag-
azine, straight or
pistol grip, plain
or fancy wood.

MODEL 1889
$5.00.
32-20, 38-40,
44-40.

Any length or
style of barrel,
any style of mag-
azine, straight or
pistol grip, plain
or fancy wood.

Cut showing rifle when taken apart.

This rifle is practically the same in every respect as our regular rifle. The barrel is screwed into the receiver exactly the same as in our regular rifle and is perfectly solid and secure even before the cam lever (which is fitted between the barrel and receiver) wedges the union. Consequently there is no danger owing to the neglect to perform some operation when putting rifle together. As will be seen from illustrations the barrel is breeched up into a yoke which together with the magazine and its parts, the forearm and the cam lever form one part. The magazine has a knurled plug with latch by means of which it is drawn out about one inch, in order to bring the follower back from the receiver and allow the barrel part to be turned around. The magazine is automatically held in position both when drawn out and when down as usual.

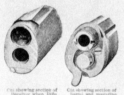

*Cut showing section of
Receiver when rifle
is taken apart.*

*Cut showing section of
barrel and magazine
when rifle is taken
apart.*

To take Rifle apart.—Draw out the magazine. Throw forward the lever to remove the breech bolt from the barrel. Loosen cam and unscrew.

To put Rifle together.—See that the magazine is drawn out and lever thrown down. Screw barrel into receiver. Tighten cam. Push down magazine.

INTERCHANGEABLE BARRELS.

Inasmuch as the action of the 38-40 is exactly like action of the 44-40, in case a person desires a rifle to use both of these cartridges, we can furnish an extra barrel part consisting of barrel, magazine, forearm, etc., and one may have a *rifle* using *both* of these cartridges at about one-half the expense of purchasing another rifle. Less trouble to carry than two rifles and just the same for practical use. The 32-40 and 38-55 rifles can also be furnished to interchange in the same manner.

Taxidermists desiring a smooth bore barrel as well as a rifled barrel can obtain a barrel to thus interchange. The price of a smooth bore barrel is the same as that of a rifled barrel. Our action is especially adapted to such work, as it will allow the use of cartridges varying in length from the empty shell as a minimum up to the regular cartridge as a maximum.

Marlin catalog instructions for takedown rifles.

Barrel section of takedown rifle.

Takedown Feature

Some Marlin shotguns and rifles had the extra feature of takedown—being able to separate the barrel and magazine from the receiver and stock. The method of takedown of most interest to the collector is the one for the lever action center-fire rifle. Next of interest is the takedown of the Model 1897 caliber .22 rifle; last are takedown shotguns.

The method of separating the barrel and stock sections of the Models 1893, 1894, and 1895 was invented and patented by L.L. Hepburn. Mr. Hepburn also invented and patented the takedown feature of the Model 1897. However, before the Model 1897 method of separating the rifle into two parts was standardized, Mr. Hepburn patented in 1895 a method to hold the barrel, magazine tube, and forearm into the receiver by means of a tapered lock screw. This method for takedown was not considered for production; only a prototype was fabricated.

William Mason, one of the Winchester Arms Company's top inventors, invented and patented a shotgun takedown system in 1892, and a rifle takedown system in 1893, which Winchester felt that Marlin had infringed upon when Marlin produced its center-fire rifle takedown based upon L.L. Hepburn's patent. Winchester took legal action, but did not prevail in court, and Marlin continued to make takedown center-fire rifles up until 1915.

In November 1894, John Marlin patented a takedown method much like L.L. Hepburn's patent of May 11, 1894. However, it too reached only the prototype stage.

The Hepburn center-fire takedown feature was an extra, which could be ordered for the models 1893, 1894, and 1895. It was described in catalogs as follows:

We can furnish our Models 1893, 1894, and 1895 Take-Down rifles in all our accustomed styles viz., with round, octagon or half-octagon barrel, any length up to 32 inches; full, half or short magazines; straight or pistol grip.

MODEL 1893: All the calibers of this model viz., the .25–36, .30–30, .32–40, .32 Special H.P.S. and .38–55 have exactly the same action, so they will interchange, and you can thus have, by purchasing extra barrel parts, as many as five takedown rifles in one action.

MODEL 1894: The .38–40 and .44–40 will interchange, as they have exactly the same action; so by purchasing an extra barrel part, you can have two take-down repeaters of these calibers with the one action.

MODEL 1895: All the regular rifles of this model, viz., the .38-56, .40-65, .40-70, .40-82, .45-70, and .45-90 have exactly the same action, and the .33 caliber and .45-70 light weight actions also interchange; so you can have, by purchasing extra barrel parts as many as seven take-down rifles on one action.

When ordering extra barrel parts, return the rifle, to insure a perfect fit.

The extra price for Take-Down on any rifle . . . . $ 3.50
The price of extra barrel part complete:
    Standard length of barrel, 1893B or 1894 . . . . 12.00
    With 26″ Smokeless barrel, 1893 and 1895 . . . . 14.00
    With 22″ lightweight barrel, 1895, .33 or .45-70 . . . 14.00
    With plain checking on forearm additional 1.00
    With selected walnut forearm and "B"
checking, add. 4.00
    With extra selected walnut forearm & special
checking 6.00
Action and buttstock complete:
    Straight grip, except .33 and .45-70 lightweight . . . 13.50
    Straight grip, .33 or .45-70 lightweight 15.00

Marlin catalogs went on to say:

> Strong as the regular rifle; no looseness; no danger of coming apart owing to accident or carelessness. No wear. No adjustments necessary. Can be placed in a "Victoria" case. As light and compact to carry as a shotgun.

The takedown systems used in Marlin shotguns will be covered in their respective sections.

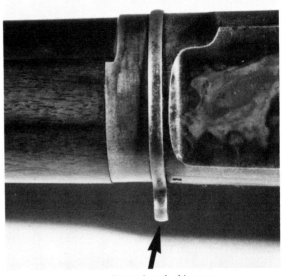

Arrow indicates long locking cam.

Arrow indicates medium-length locking cam.

Receiver sections of takedown rifle.

Arrow indicates short flush-type locking cam.

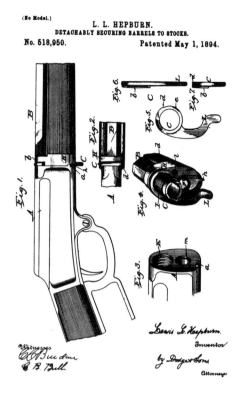

L.L. Hepburn-patented takedown.

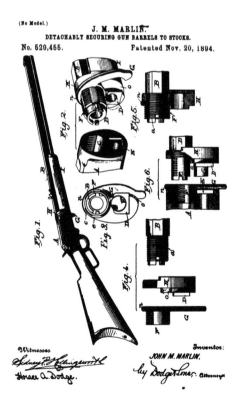

J.M. Marlin-patented takedown.

MARLIN TAKEDOWN PATENTS

518,950	May 1, 1894	L.L. Hepburn	1893, 1894, 1895
529,455	Nov. 20, 1894	J.M. Marlin	experimental center-fire takedown
534,691	Feb. 26, 1895	L.L. Hepburn	experimental caliber .22 takedown
561,226	June 2, 1896	L.L. Hepburn	shotgun safety
584,177		L.L. Hepburn	Model 1897 takedown
775,660	March 29, 1904	Melvin Hepburn	
882,562	March 24, 1908	L.L. Hepburn	shotgun takedown
888,329	May 19, 1908	Melvin Hepburn	shotgun takedown
1,092,085	March 31, 1914	J.H. Wheeler	shotgun takedown

WINCHESTER TAKEDOWN PATENTS

487,487	Dec. 6, 1892	W. Mason	shotgun takedown
498,983	June 6, 1893	W. Mason	Model 1894 takedown

In October 1903, The Marlin Fire Arms Company brought Suit in Equity No. 1137 against John J. Dinnan for infringement of L.L. Hepburn's patent number 584,177 dated June 8, 1897.

Mr. Hepburn's patent covered the takedown feature of Marlin's Model 1897 caliber .22 rifle; he had assigned the patent to Marlin at the time of his application.

The specifications of patent number 584,177 state that it relates to improvements in firearms and provides for inexpensive and effective means to disassemble the barrel and stock sections for ease of transportation and accessibility of the interior parts for cleaning or repair.

The rifle that Marlin claimed infringed patent number 584,177 was the Savage Model 1903 (later identified as the Model 1911). This Savage rifle was an unusual pump action caliber .22 rifle that had a clip magazine instead of the usual tubular magazine and disassembled into two parts, very similar to the Marlin Model 1897 rifle.

The Marlin complaint in Equity was heard in the Circuit Court of the United States, District of Connecticut in August 1904. Based on examination and cross-examination of witnesses for both the complainant and the defendant, the court did not find the defendant in violation of the L.L. Hepburn patent.

Savage continued to make the Model 1903 rifle and did not discontinue producing it until 1916, although it has been reported that 1,000 more were assembled in 1922.

Marlin's takedown lever action rifle, which was the basis for the complaint, is still in production today as the Models 39A and 39M.

The Models 18, 20, 25, 27, 29, 32, 38, and 47 were all takedown rifles. The 20, 27, 29, and 47 had receivers that sepa-

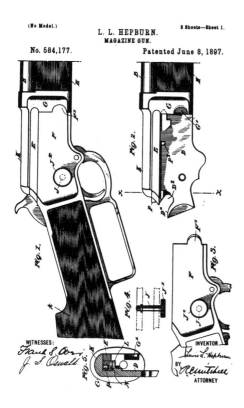

L.L. Hepburn Model 1897 takedown patent.

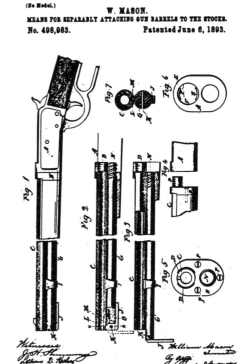

Winchester (W.E. Mason) takedown patent number 498,983.

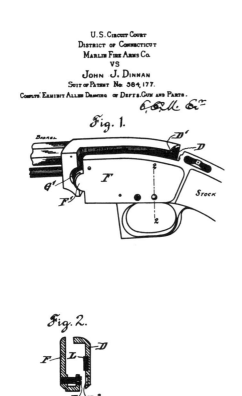

Savage (Model 1903) takedown system.

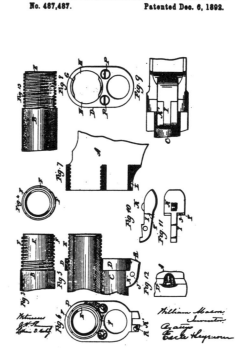

Winchester (W.E. Mason) takedown patent number 487,487.

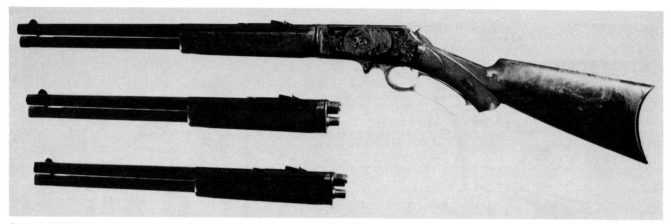

Rare Model 1893 three-barrel set. Not only is the rifle an extremely fine piece on its own, but the two extra barrels make it one of only three known three-barrel sets extant. (CF)

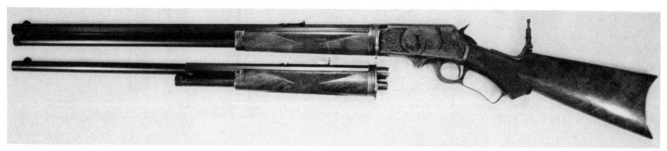

Scarce two-barrel set. Note that one barrel is full octagon with a full magazine, and the other is half octagon with a half magazine—a great pair for any type of big-game hunting. (JO)

rated. By loosening takedown screws and then separating the receiver laterally, one could separate the rifles into two pieces. The Models 32 and 38 had takedown latches that, when pulled to the rear, allowed the top and bottom sections of the receiver to separate. The Models 18 and 25 had buttstocks that could easily be removed.

The Marlin Model 18 pump action caliber .22 rifle was introduced in 1906. These rifles were similar to the other Marlin pump action .22 rifles except that they did not take down by separating the two halves of the receiver. Their takedown system was unique—to take down the Model 18 and Model 25, all one had to do was unscrew and remove the tang screw, which had a large knurled head, and then slide the stock off the receiver tangs. By so doing, one could pack the rifle into a space the length of the barrel and receiver. The Model 18 was discontinued in 1909, and the Model 25 was discontinued in 1910.

Target Rifle

In 1959, Marlin manufactured 10 special caliber .22 target rifles for use by the Marlin Junior Rifle Team, organized and coached by Charles E. Lyman III, who was at that time president of the Lyman Gun Sight Corporation.

Designated the Model 102, these rifles were unique to Marlin's product line in that the barrel and receiver were one piece and the bolt and loading system were a modification of the Model 101 single-shot rifle mechanism. A special lami-nated wood target-type stock was used and a special adjustable trigger mechanism was installed.

The metallic front and rear sights, telescope blocks, and Super-Targetspot telescopes were furnished to the team by the Lyman Company. The following are extracts from Mr. Lyman's report about the rifles and the accomplishments of the team.

As the Junior Team commenced its program of competing in registered small bore matches using the new rifle, it gradually became apparent that an increasing number of shooters at each match were becoming aware that a new and highly accurate target rifle was being used. At Camp Perry, Ohio during the National Matches one of the window displays in the Lyman exhibit contained two of the Marlin #102 rifles, one was equipped with the new Lyman #60 Micrometer Receiver Sight and the Lyman #77 Aperture Front Sight. The other was equipped with a Lyman Super-Targetspot Scope Sight. Between the two rifles was a photograph of the Junior Team together with placards describing the various features of the rifle. At the base of the window were the many trophies won by the Juniors with these rifles.

This display coupled with the most attractive shooting jackets worn by the children on the firing line attracted over what we believe was a majority of the many thousands of competitors and spectators at the matches to give the rifle a most careful looking-over. Some of the comments overheard were, "Laminated stock. Wonderful on a production rifle." "One piece barrel and action, clever manufacturing idea and should add much to the rifle's accuracy." "Micro-groove

In 1959, Marlin manufactured 10 of these special target rifles.

rifling, my Marlin hunting rifle is very accurate and I imagine that this type of rifling will be equally great on the target range." "Trigger pull, (this amazed them all), what a sweet trigger, and adjustable too. They sure have something." "Self centering cartridge loader, an excellent idea and should be especially good for gallery shooting where poor light at the firing point is the rule rather than the exception."

The general consensus of opinion amongst most all competitors and my own feelings as well, is that the Marlin #102 is capable of competing right along side of the Winchester Model 52 and the Remington 40X which over the past several years have been the main stay of the serious competitor shooter. The seven children who competed as the Marlin Junior Team shot much better scores with the Model #102 than they had in any previous time using either Winchester or Remington target rifles.

Although the young marksmen had a lot of success when shooting the Model 102 rifles, and Charley Lyman felt the rifle would be well received in the marketplace, the workload of developing other new products and refinements of the existing line of firearms prevented Marlin from giving this target rifle serious consideration, and the Junior Rifle Team was discontinued.

Marlin-sponsored Junior Rifle Team that used an experimental target rifle at the National Rifle Matches in 1959. The eight Middlefield, Conn., residents were as follows: Back row (left to right): *Frank Koba, Charles Lyman IV, James Austin, Wallace Lyman, John Kalinowski, and David Winter.* Front row: *Nancy Hancock and Charles Lyman III.*

Targets

Packaged with the Clipper King and Crown Prince rifles were paper targets. They were 6″x9″ and had silhouettes of animals with scoring rings superimposed on them, sighting-in bull's-eyes, and conventional 5-bull 50-foot targets. They were printed on buff-colored paper.

Similar targets were packaged with Sears, Roebuck's J.C. Higgins rifles, except that the set had 12 game and round bull's-eye targets marked *J.C. Higgins.*

Marlin also packaged with Katz Company models 6″x9″ tar-

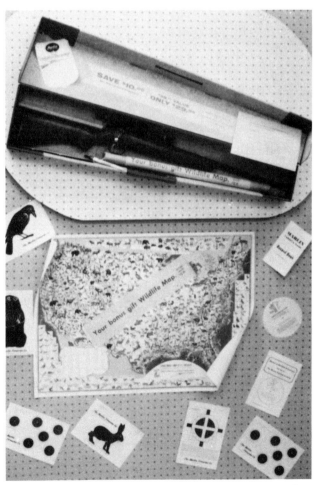

Marlin furnished targets with other promotional items. This photo shows those packaged with the Clipper King and Crown Prince rifles.

Typical target packaged with Marlin .22 rifles during the 1960s.

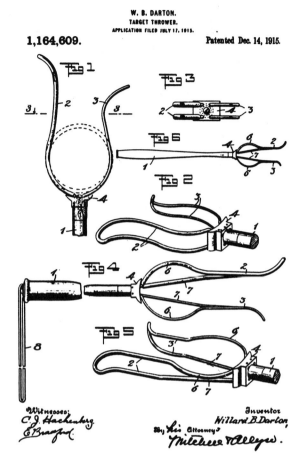

W.B. Darton patent for Marlin's target thrower.

gets, which were in pads and included crow, rabbit, squirrel, and woodchuck targets for use at 50 feet.

All of the above targets, except the J.C. Higgins, had the Marlin name and address printed on them. In 1960 alone, Marlin purchased 200,000 targets, which were given out free. They cost Marlin $2.10 per thousand.

Target Thrower

In 1915, Willard B. Darton of Portland, Me., filed an application for a patent on a target thrower. The patent for the device was awarded to Mr. Darton on December 14, 1915 (num-

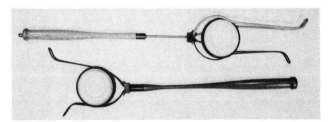

Top: *Breech-loading target thrower.* Bottom: *Muzzle-loading target thrower.*

ber 1,164,609) which he, in turn, assigned to The Marlin Firearms Company. At this same time, the acquisition of the Marlin Firearms Company by a syndicate organized as the Marlin Arms Corporation also took place. This change resulted in the new company being the manufacturer and seller of Willard Darton's target thrower.

The few examined specimens of these rare Marlin devices have the Marlin Arms Corporation name and the patent date stamped on the metal head. Two types are known. Both types are illustrated in the patent drawings, and specimens examined are identical in all respects to those shown in the patent. One type was advertised as the "muzzle loader," because the clay target was inserted into the front end. The other type was called the "breech loader," since the target was inserted into the handle end of the wire guide arms.

Attempts to throw clay birds from one of these devices convinced me that they were not flexible enough to make the clay bird fly fast enough or far enough to be equal to later types of throwers, which had spring action built into the handle. However, it was fun to use an old Marlin device, even though a sore shoulder resulted!

Marlin ads stated that the new hand trap weighed less than a pound and that it would throw targets from 20 to 80 yards or more, and so convenient it could be carried in a coat pocket.

W.B. Darton demonstrating his patented target thrower to Marlin employees.

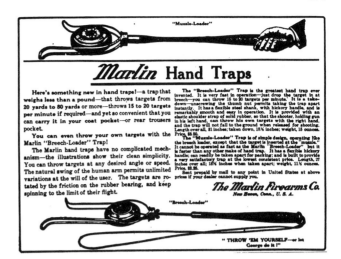

Marlin ad for the Darton Hand Trap (target thrower).

The ads went on to say that the Marlin hand traps have no complicated mechanism, and that the elastic shoulder cord attached to the handle allowed a person to throw his own targets without the hand trap dropping to the ground.

The breech loader was 31 inches long overall; taken down, 18½ inches; it weighed 15 ounces. It sold for $3.50. The muzzle loader was 27 inches overall and 18½ inches when taken apart. It weighed 11½ ounces. The price for this model was $2.25.

Telescopic Sights

Marlin rifles and telescopic sights have been connected since the introduction by John Marlin of the Ballard and Model 1881 rifles. Although telescopic sights don't make a gun–ammunition combination more accurate, telescopic sights do make the aiming of the firearm more accurate and easier for the shooter.

The Ballard rifle enjoyed a fine reputation—second to none—in the target rifle category, as did the Marlin Repeating Rifle among hunting guns. During the late 1800s and early 1900s, as could be expected, such telescope makers as Malcolm, Sidle, Stevens, L.L. Mogg, and Cataract Tool and Optical Company made telescopes and mounts ideal for use with Marlin firearms.

William Malcolm's 1887 Malcolm Telescope Catalog listed his telescopes for Marlin Model 1881 and 1888 rifles with the telescope mounted on the left side (this allowed the regular rifle sights to be used at the same time). His prices for Marlin rifles fitted with his scopes were as follows:

Marlin Rifles, Model 1881, 32, 38, 40, 45 caliber; 24 inch octagon barrel, 8 shot, 7¼ lbs, rifle ball; 28 inch octagon barrel, 8 shot, 7½ lbs., rifle ball; net.
Fitted with No. 1 Telescope, on side only $60.00
Fitted with No. 2 Telescope, on side only $45.00
Fitted with No. 3 Telescope, on side only $40.00
Fitted with No. 4 Telescope, on side only $31.00
Extra length and extra weight from the above will cost $1.00 for every pound, and $1.00 for every inch in length; set triggers will be $3.00 extra.
Marlin Repeating Rifle, model 1888; 32, 38, 44 caliber; 6½, 6¾, 7 lbs; 13, 14, 16 shot; 24, 26, 28 inch octagon barrels. (Prices same as for Model 1881 except No. 4 telescope is priced at $30.00)
Ballard Rifles
No. 2. Sporting Rifle 32 or 38 caliber, for fixed ammunition only, rim or central fire.
No. 1 Telescope on top of rifle $57.00
No. 2 Telescope on top of rifle $40.00
No. 3 Telescope on top of rifle $37.00
No. 4 Telescope on top of rifle $32.00
No. 5 Pacific Rifle, octagon barrel, double set trigger, extra heavy wrought frame; cleaning rod under barrel, using either everlasting shells or factory ammunition. As the name indicates, it is the favorite on the Pacific coast. It is the hunting rifle of the west for all kind of large game. 30 and 32 inch barrels; 38-55, 40-65, 40-85, 44, 45-70, 45-100.
Fitted No. 1 Telescope on top of barrel $63.00
Fitted No. 2 Telescope on top of barrel $50.00
Fitted No. 3 Telescope on top of barrel $40.00
Fitted No. 4 Telescope on top of barrel $38.00
Union Hill rifle, for off-hand target and rest shooting, set-trigger pistol grip, checkered grip, Swiss butt plate; 32-40, 38-55.

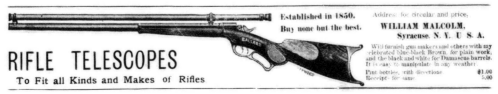

Malcolm ad for his telescope fitted to a Ballard rifle.

Fitted with No. 1 telescope $69.00
Fitted with No. 2 telescope $50.00
Fitted with No. 3 telescope $45.00
Fitted with No. 4 telescope $40.00
Any rifle not named in the above list will be furnished on application at as low a figure as possible. On all orders for Rifles and Telescopes, half cash must accompany the order.

Malcolm telescopes, like Sidle and others, were usually 30 to 40 inches long. However, 12- to 40-in. lengths could be ordered. The rear mount was adjustable for elevation and the front mount could be adjusted for windage.

The J. Stevens Arms and Tool Company of Chicopee Falls, Mass., took over the Cataract Tool and Optical Company, Buffalo, N.Y., in 1901. By 1902, Stevens had the machinery in

Full-length telescope fitted to Marlin Model 1881 rifle.

Front mount offset to the left of early type of rifle telescope.

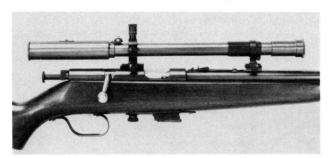

Marlin Model 80 rifle fitted with a 1937 Sears, Roebuck & Company Ranger 4 to 8 power telescope. The mounts were made by Marlin.

place and started a similar line of scopes for use in target shooting and hunting.

The 1908 Stevens telescope catalog listed the following information about telescopes for Marlin rifles:

The telescopes in this series were designed for the "Marlin" Rifle. The telescope slides and rests on springs. Top Mounting screwed to the barrel. Fine screw adjustment for both elevation and windage. The telescope is of the same grade as the "Winchester" and we commend it to those who favor the "Marlin" rifle. Diameter of tube, ¾ inch. The price of telescopes follows.
No. 700 — Power 4 Diameters — Length 19 inches — Price w/mounts, $13.00
No. 705 — Power 4 Diameters — Length 14 inches — Price w/mounts, $16.00
No. 710 — Power 6 Diameters — Length 16 inches — Price w/mounts, $17.00
No. 715 — Power 8 Diameters — Length 18 inches — Price w/mounts, $18.00
No. 720 — Power 12 Diameters — Length 22 inches — Price w/mounts, $19.00

During the 1906 to 1911 period, Marlin advertised in its catalog that rifles could be ordered with telescopes fitted to them. The 1909 catalog illustrated and described the Stevens telescope identically to the Stevens 1908 catalog quoted above. The model numbers and prices are also identical.

The Marlin collector should not be hasty in thinking that his Marlin mounted with a Stevens telescope is not "factory." It

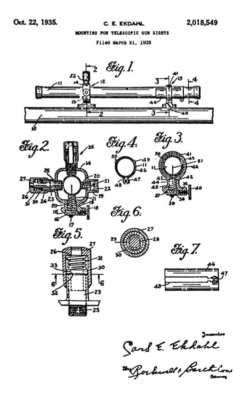

C.E. Ekdahl patent drawing of Marlin telescope and mount.

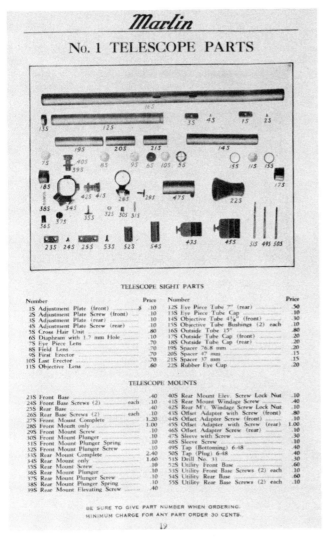

Catalog information for the No. 2 telescope.

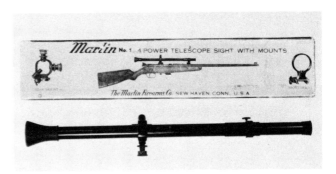

No. 1 telescope with original box.

Parts catalog page showing parts for the No. 1 telescope and mounts.

very likely could be. If well done, and still in good repair, telescopes add measurably to the value of a gun.

In November 1936, Sears, Roebuck brought to Marlin a telescope mount it wanted manufactured. Marlin engineer and gun designer (WW I and 1928 to 1936) Carl Ekdahl improved the Sears front mount sleeve idea and obtained a patent on it. Marlin paid Sears $1,000 for all rights, title, and interest in Sears telescope mounts; in addition to using the mount on Marlin telescopes, Marlin manufactured them for Sears.

Shown in the Sears fall 1937 catalog is a Sears Ranger 4 to 8 Power Scope with Thumb Screw Power Adjuster. The telescope shown has a brass tube and listed for $13.95 with mounts, $10.95 for only the scope, and $3.25 for the micrometer click mounts only.

Also illustrated on the same page is the Marlin No. 2 4X telescope with the same Marlin mounts as the Sears variable power telescope. The Marlin telescope was manufactured by the Wollensak Optical Company for Marlin and was a copy of the earlier telescope similar to the Stevens, Lyman, and Winchester telescopes that had micrometer adjustments. All of these scopes were mounted on the rifle by means of dovetail

Micrometer Click rear mount of No. 2 telescope.

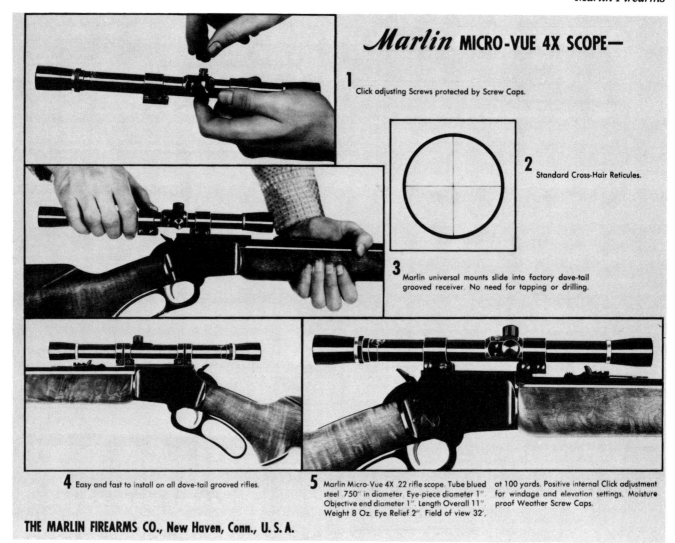

Marlin Micro-Vue 4X telescope.

bases that were attached to the rifle by screws. Easy removal of the telescope was accomplished by loosening two mount screws. Marlin literature described the telescope and mounts as follows:

1. High quality, ground and polished optical glass lenses which magnify target or game four times.

2. Objective lens diameter of ⅝" gives brilliant image.

3. Larger field of vision than many other scopes — approximately 30 ft. diameter at 100 yards.

4. No. 1 telescope has 3-point suspension rear mount and micrometer adjustment for windage and elevation.

5. No. 2 telescope has 4-point suspension rear mount with ¼ minute micrometer adjustment for elevation and windage. Each "click" is distinctly heard and felt and represents an adjustment of .0005 inch.

6. Front mount with spring plunger which prevents scope from rotating and permits scope to slide with recoil thus avoiding constant shock to which it would be subject to if held rigidly.

7. Sleeve — fits in the front mount and works with it in preventing scope from rotating and letting it slide forward

from recoil action. The forward lug acts as a stop so that scope can be quickly returned to its correct position should it slide forward from recoil.

8. Standard bases — case hardened, are regular equipment which fit on the top of the barrel or receiver.

9. Taps (6–48 plug and 6–48 bottoming) and No. 31 Drill furnished.

The No. 1 telescope was called the Marlin Precision 4 Power Rifle Telescope Sight. The No. 2 telescope was called the Marlin No. 2 Clearfield Rifle Telescope Sight.

The prices of these telescopes when introduced were as follows:

	No. 1	No. 2
Complete w/mounts & bases	5.75	7.35
Telescope only	5.50	5.50
Mounts only w/taps and drill	5.00	5.00
Offset bases	1.50	1.50

Marlin Micro-Power 4X telescope.

Micro-Vue telescope mounted on 39M rifle.

Available from Marlin were various heights of dovetail bases for use in installing these sights on many other makes of firearms. Included with each sight were instructions in the use of the sight and its installation, and a table giving the location of the bases, distance between the two, and the heights of bases required for Marlin and various other rifles.

The No. 1 telescope was introduced about 1936 and the No. 2 about 1937. They were discontinued when Marlin became fully dedicated to WW II war production in 1942, and were not reintroduced in 1946.

In 1958, Marlin introduced a Micro-Vue 4X telescope for use with caliber .22 rifles, and in 1959 introduced a Micro-Power 4X telescope for use with center-fire rifles. These were the first in a rather long list of various makes and styles of telescopes suitable for use on Marlin firearms. Both domestic-manufactured and imported scopes were marketed by Marlin. The peak year was 1970, when 11 different fixed- and variable-power scopes having the Marlin or Glenfield name were available.

During the 1970s Marlin was the largest user of telescopes in the world. None, however, were manufactured by Marlin. Marlin did not attach or mount the telescope to the rifle. If it did, the government's 11% excise tax on the rifle would also apply to the telescope and mount. To save the ultimate consumer this added expense, telescopes have been only packaged with the rifles and not fitted to them.

Marlin offered telescope–rifle combinations to distributors and mass-merchandisers on only certain models and in certain minimum quantity orders. However, the same telescopes and mounts have always been available to the sportsman through Marlin's gun service division.

From 1958 through 1967, Marlin used names to identify its telescopes. Micro-Vue identified the telescopes suited for caliber .22 rifles, and Micro-Power was the name for those designed for center-fire rifles (one exception was the M22–V4X–8X variable scope, listed in 1966).

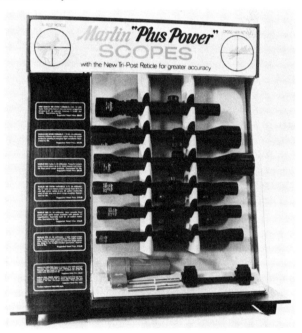

Telescope display case.

The 1966 and 1967 Micro-Vue 4X telescope had a sloping front sun shade. The 1969 M22–V4X–8X variable had a sloping front sun shade and gold-colored power-adjusting ring.

From 1968 to date, the Marlin system of identifying telescopes has been by a numerical model number. (An alphabetical suffix to the number was for internal control purposes, as it identified a different source than that for the original models.)

A recapitulation of the various telescopes, their characteristics, years of availability, and suggested retail price from 1958 to 1986 is as follows:

Model	Power	Field of View (feet)	Eye Relief (inches)	Exit Pupil (mm)	Objective Diameter (inches)	Body Tube Dia. (inches)	Weight (ounces)	From	To	Rifle	Price
Micro-Vue	4	30	2	2.5	13/16	3/4	7	1958	1967	.22	14.95
Micro-Power	2½	44	3–5	8.2	1 1/16	1	8	1959	1967	CF	44.95
Micro-Power	4	31	3–5	8.5	1 9/16	1	9	1959	1967	CF	49.95
Micro-Power	6	20	3–5	6.2	1 11/16	1	10	1959	1967	CF	59.95
Micro-Power	3–9	11½–32½	3–5	4–12	1 11/16	1	11	1964	1967	CF	79.95
M22-V	4–8				1 3/16	3/4		1966	1966	.22	16.95
200 G	4	16	2–3	1.5	31/32	3/4	7	1969	1983	.22	8.00
275	4	21	2	5.0	1	3/4	6½	1970	1971	.22	13.95
300	4	21	2	5.0	1	7/8	9	1968	1971	.22	13.95
300 B	4	23	3			7/8		1972	1977	.22	13.95
300 A	4	23.5	2.3	5.0	28mm	7/8	8			.22	13.95
400 G	4	28	3½	8	1½	1	9	1969	1976	CF	20.00
400 AG	4					1		1977	1984	CF	
425	4	28	3½	8	1½	1	9	1972	1976	CF	
500	3–7	12–28	3	2.85–6.5	20mm	7/8	9.5	1968	1977	.22	16.95
500 A	3–7	12–28	3	2.85–6.5	28mm	7/8	10	1978	1980	.22	16.95
600	3	30	3.6	13.3	40mm	1	11½	1968	1976	CF	32.95
700	5	18	3.6	8	40mm	1	12	1968	1971	CF	34.95
750	1.5	25	9–15		20mm	1		1973	1975	CF	
800	1.75–5	18–47	3–3¾	8–22	1 27/32	1	12⅓	1968	1976	CF	42.95
800 A	1.5–5	31–47	4	8–26.6	47mm	1	14			CF	
825	3–9	11-34	2–3¼		40mm	1	11	1974	1976	CF	
850	2–5	17½–50	33	4–10	1	1	11	1970	1971	CF	
900	3–9	12–35	3½	4.5–13.3	40mm	1	14	1968	1971	CF	39.95/44.95
900 A	3–9	14–35	3	4.4–13.3	47	1	14			CF	
High Power Mount								1970	1973	CF	
#10 Set								1968	1983	CF	10.00
#15 (fixed)								1973	1974	CF	
#29 Glenfield								1969	1969	CF	5.00

During the time the Sovereign Instrument Company of Dallas, Tex., manufactured the Micro-Power telescope for Marlin, there were six sighting-in targets packaged with the scope. The target was 24"x20½" and had inch squares around a center-aiming circle, which helped the shooter make adjustments to the telescope, thus bringing shot-group and aiming point into alignment.

This target and the Marlin Sighting-In Guide helped many sportsmen to become quickly proficient with their new telescope and Marlin rifle.

Since about 1980, the Marlin and Glenfield names have been dropped from telescopes and mounts. Instead, they are marked with the name of the manufacturer.

Since 1979, Marlin no longer listed telescopes separately in the annual product catalog. They were only sold through the parts catalog or in combination with rifles to distributors.

Telescope Mounts. When the Marlin Model 39A was first drilled and tapped for telescope, it was at the request of Sears,

Roebuck and Company. Sears wanted the rifle to accept the U.S.-manufactured Weaver telescope by use of the Weaver N-mount. Therefore, those Model 39s delivered to Sears had drilled and tapped holes in the left side of the barrel for the N-mount, a poor combination at best. Marlin decided two drilled and tapped holes in the top of the receiver to accommodate a telescope-dovetailed mounting rail was a better system. Thereafter, all Model 39s were drilled and tapped for a detachable telescope base. Until 1971, the base was made to accept only the small-diameter telescope with the usual tip-off scope rings. The mounting base with screws was furnished free and packed with each rifle. It was made of steel.

In 1972, Marlin developed a new mounting rail for the 39s that had a double dovetail. The narrower upper dovetail was the same as the previous mounting base. The wider lower dovetail was added to accept the larger high-power telescopes having 1-in. tubes and tip-off rings.

In 1956, Marlin first drilled and tapped the top of the 336 receivers to accept telescope mounts.

Marlin Veri-Fire sight collimator.

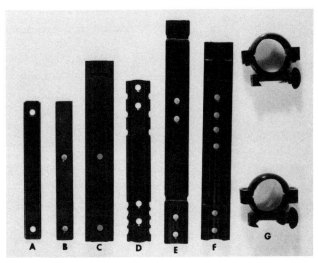

A. *Telescope adapter base for Model 57 and early Model 58 rifles;* B. *first type of Model 39 dovetail scope base;* C. *second type of Model 39 double dovetail sight base;* D. *Glenfield Model 30 telescope base;* E. *early Model 336 adapter base;* F. *set of #10 high power telescope mounts;* G. *rings for set #10.*

Marlin advised purchasers of the Micro-Power 2½X and 4X telescopes and Micro-Vue 4X telescopes that if their Model 336, 39A or 39M did not have the holes drilled and tapped on the top of the receiver, that they could return the gun to the factory and Marlin would do the work for a cost of $3.00 plus return postage.

Since 1968, Marlin has marketed sets of rings and bases for the Model 336 rifle. The first was identified as the High Power Mount Set #10. It was a close copy of the Weaver top mount and accepted 1-in. telescopes. Similar sets are still available today. A more cheaply made mount called the Glenfield #29 mount was available in 1969, and in 1973–1974 a two-piece fixed mount, #15, was also sold.

Other good telescope mounts have been and still are commercially available for the Model 336 family of lever action rifles, and because the Marlin levers are particularly suited to low scope mounting, any number of makes of telescopes and mounts can be successfully used by the sportsman.

Marlin Veri-Fire. Marlin marketed from 1971 through 1973 a device used by the sportsman or gun shop to put his shots "on the paper" in minutes. The use of the Veri-Fire saved time and ammunition in the sighting-in process, as well as realignment due to changes in game, range, bullet weights, or misalignment in the field. The device was packaged in a leatherette tote case and came with bore spuds for .30–30 and .22 calibers at a $25 suggested retail price. Spuds for other bore sizes were available at a suggested $3.00 each retail price. The Marlin device was bright red with a yellow case.

Telescope Display Cabinet. In 1970, Marlin offered a "Scope Special," which consisted of a mix of 10 quality Marlin scopes; one V70 Veri-Fire with .22 and .30 caliber spuds; one free V70 Veri-Fire with spuds; two sets of #10 telescope mounts; and one counter display cabinet.

The display included overhead illumination and storage space in the rear for an inventory of the telescopes displayed.

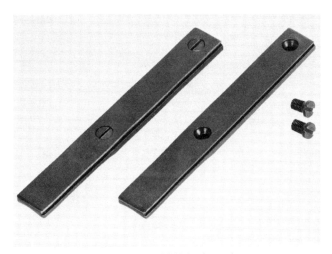

First type of Model 39A adapter base.

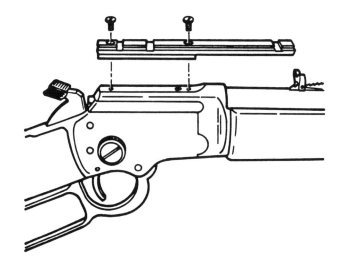

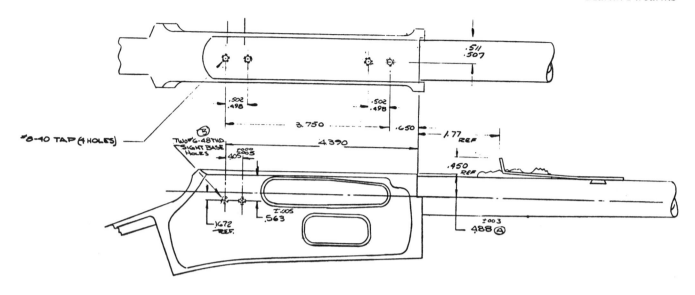

Receiver and telescope sight screw holes of Marlin center-fire lever action rifles and carbines.

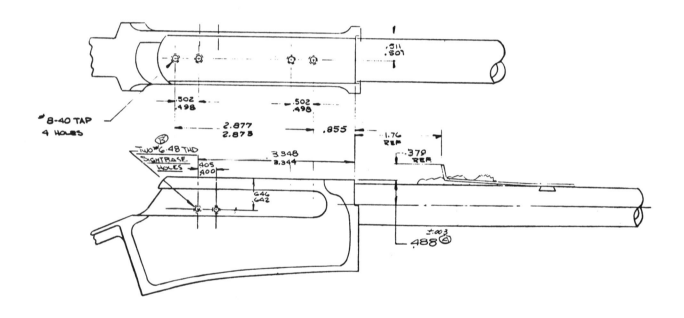

Receiver and telescope sight screw holes of new Model 1894 rifles and carbines.

Rare Marlin ad lithographed in multicolor on tin. Not an outdoor sign, it was to be hung in gun shops and sporting goods stores.

The total dealer cost was $199.59. The suggested retail price of the items was $302.44 for a 38% gross profit.

A total of 500 of these combinations of telescopes, mounts, Veri-Fires, and cabinets were sold.

Tin Sign

One of the scarcest advertising items distributed by Marlin was a tin sign. It was 27 inches wide and 6 inches high, and was printed in color. On the left half was printed *Marlin* (in script), *REPEATERS, Rifles and Shotguns*. The right half had a picture of the Marlin plant, after the fence, water tank, and Marlin–Rockwell buildings were built. The letters and picture are raised in half relief and attractively colored, and get the message across that a Marlin firearm is "The Gun for The Man Who Knows."

Toy Gun (Marlin Jr.)

In 1945, when Marlin was changing back to manufacturing sporting arms after years of manufacturing items in the support of the war, a toy gun was fabricated from surplus rough-turned and sanded, but not fully machined, stock blanks left over from the manufacture of stocks for the Army's M1 Carbine.

The barrel of this toy gun was a wood dowel painted black, which was inserted and glued to the front end of the stock. The front sight was a flat stamped piece of thin metal that was pressed into the barrel. The trigger was a star-shaped piece of wood that, when pulled, rotated and clicked a thin wood piece to simulate a gun firing. The sling was a machine gun web cartridge belt looped and riveted to two stamped and bent sling loops. A decal that read *Marlin Jr.* was stuck to the bottom of the stock.

These wooden toy guns sold in 1945 at wholesale for $2.00 each, and are today a rare Marlin collector's item. Records indicate that about 31,000 Marlin Junior toy rifles were sold.

United States Marine Corps Training Rifles

Full Automatic Caliber .22 Rifle. A one-of-a-kind full automatic caliber .22 rifle was manufactured by Marlin and demonstrated at Quantico, Va., during early August 1956 by Tom Robinson, Marlin's director of research and development, for possible use by the Marines. It was to simulate the Browning Automatic Rifle and was bipod-mounted. On August 30, 1956, Lt. General V.E. Megee sent Marlin the following comments

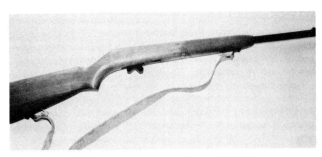

Marlin Jr. toy gun, manufactured in 1945.

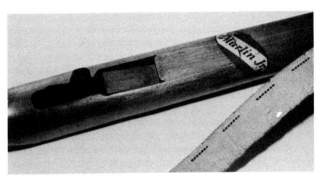

Trigger clicker, decal, and sling of Marlin Jr. toy gun.

with regard to possible use of the rifle for training by the Marine Corps:

DEPARTMENT OF THE NAVY
Headquarters United States Marine Corps
Washington 25, D.C.

In Reply Refer To
A04F-gld
Aug 30 1956

Mr. Thomas R. Robinson, Jr.
Director, Research and Development
Marlin Firearms Company
79 Willow Street
New Haven, Connecticut

Dear Mr. Robinson:

I wish to acknowledge your recent letter and to offer my sincere appreciation for your interest in demonstrating the Marlin .22 Caliber Full-automatic Rifle at Quantico on 8 August 1956. As a result of the demonstration firing, I am able to express our reaction to this weapon for possible Marine Corps use in training.

We have made the following evaluation of the Marlin Rifle for use as

Marlin semiautomatic rifle tested for possible use by the U.S. Marine Corps.

a training weapon for Marines who are required to be proficient with the Browning Automatic Rifle. The latter weapon, as you know, is the principal means of automatic rifle small arms fire in the Marine Division. Both the carbine and sub-machine gun have limited special application in the Marine Corps.

The accuracy and operation of the Marlin weapon during firing appeared to be excellent. However, when fired without the bipod, the rifle displayed the same climbing characteristics as other full-automatic weapons. While the use of such a training rifle would be economical from the standpoint of cost of ammunition expended, it appears doubtful that the weapon would offer any realistic advantage in the training of personnel who are required to fire the Browning Automatic Rifle. The recoil, operation, sights, weight and configuration of the Marlin weapon do not resemble that of the BAR. Further, even though the weapon could probably be modified to possess sights, weight and configuration similar to the BAR, the value obtained from training with a .22 caliber automatic weapon in a BAR role is considered to be *marginal when compared to the procurement cost of the number of such rifles which would be required by the Marine Corps.

*am open to conviction on this point

With regard to your inquiry about the possibility of furnishing Marlin .22 Caliber Semi-automatic Rifles for a test as a premarksmanship training weapon, your firm will be invited to submit a bid to furnish five such rifles for inclusion in the current test program at Quantico. The invitation to bid will be tendered by separate correspondence. We are at a loss to explain why the original invitation to bid was not received by Marlin since our records indicate that one was mailed from this Headquarters on 30 January 1956.

I appreciate the time and effort on your part in calling on me in Washington as well as your interest on behalf of the Marine Corps.

Sincerely yours,

V.E. Megee
Acting

Training Rifle MC–58. As mentioned in General Megee's letter, The Marlin Firearms Company was invited by the U.S. Marine Corps to submit five caliber .22 semiautomatic rifles having special characteristics, which were to be used for evaluation in the development of a training rifle. The new rifle would be used during early markmanship training of Marines, and was to simulate the M1 rifle.

The Marine Corps characteristics for the training rifle were as follows:

1. The rifle must possess a semi-automatic action which is in commercial production.
2. The rifle must be magazine fed with a magazine capacity of 10 rounds.

Close-up view of the prototype rifle submitted by Marlin for testing by the U.S. Marine Corps as a possible trainer for the M1 service rifle.

3. Commensurate with cost in production lots, it is desired that the rifle be stocked to simulate to the maximum extent possible the configuration and weight of the Rifle, U.S., Caliber .30, M1.
4. The stock must be equipped with sling swivels capable of mounting either the sling, gun, M1 (webbing) or the sling, leather, gun, M1907.
5. The sights must represent the same "sight picture" as the M1 rifle and must be adjustable for both elevation and windage. The correct sight picture for the M1 rifle is that an imaginary horizontal line passing through the center of the aperture just touches the top of the front sight blade and an imaginary vertical line passing through the center of the aperture divides the front sight blade in half with the bull's eye centered on and just touching the front sight blades. The protecting wings on the sides of the front sight blade are also visible.
6. It is desirable that the elevation and windage adjustments be similar to that of the M1 rifle as outlined in paragraph 1.c.
7. The rifle must be equipped with a positive, easily operable, manual safety. The rifle shall be provided with integral safety design features which will prevent dangerous malfunctions.
8. The rifle must operate with a minimum of malfunctions when exposed to the dust, mud, and inclement weather conditions under which any Marine Corps rifle range operates. It must be durable and rugged enough to withstand the hardest usage encountered in the marksmanship training program. Without cleaning, the rifle must be capable of firing 1000 rounds with a minimum of malfunctions.
9. The rifle must be capable of firing and functioning properly with *standard velocity* .22 long rifle ammunition of the type purchased by the Armed Forces.
10. The manufacturer must be able to insure a continued source for spare parts and replacement items.

The five rifles Marlin submitted embodied the Model 89 barrel, action, and magazine. The sights, stock, handguard, swivels, and so on were specially designed to give the appearance and feel of the M1 rifle. They were delivered to the Marines on December 4, 1956.

By May 1957, the Corps had tested and evaluated the rifles and found that in their present form they were not suitable for Marine Corps use. However, they believed the following deficiencies could be corrected:

1. Military stock assemble and front sight must be completely disassembled prior to removing barrel and receiver from stock proper.
2. Gas cylinder dummy loosens during firing.
3. *Extractors break at tip and fail to maintain original configuration during firing.
4. Front sight screws loosen during firing.
5. Sear pin loosens and falls out.
6. Weapon too heavy in weight.
7. Lacks a bolt holding open device.
8. Click springs lose tension.
9. Peep rack spring loses tension.
10. Windage knob assembly pin loosens during firing.
11. Sight base and windage slide lack windage graduations.

12. Elevation knob and windage slide lack elevation graduations.
13. Click system improperly calibrated.

*It is to be noted that approximately 70 percent of the malfunctions that occurred with the Marlin test items were failures to eject. The majority of these malfunctions were caused by the inability of the extractors on the Marlin test items to maintain their original configuration. The extractor, which is stamped from sheet steel, bends outward from the face of the bolt during repeated firing. When this occurs, the extractor does not maintain sufficient hold on the lip of the cartridge case. As a result, when the bolt travels to the rear, the empty cartridge case becomes loosened from the extractor and does not receive sufficient force from the ejector assembly to expel it from the receiver.

After the five rifles were returned to Marlin, the rifles were modified to eliminate the problems. By this time, Marlin had 694 man-hours in the two prototype R&D rifles and the five Marine rifles.

Upon completion of the second test conducted at Quantico, Va., the only problems with the rifles were that one rifle had a large chamber and proper bedding could not be maintained because the stock screw was too small, and the bolt handle became loose in the bolt. Failures to feed were attributed to certain magazines.

The rather complicated special rear sight designed by Marlin for this training rifle used some Lyman Gun Sight Company parts. Except for a couple of too-soft click springs, they were acceptable and worked well.

All of the rifles were made by hand and parts were not interchangeable. They were serial numbered No. 1 through 5.

After some adjustments were made and new barrels, firing pins, nylon washers, and windage springs were fitted, the guns were returned to Quantico for the third time.

On April 24, 1958, Marlin was invited to bid on 3,000 Rifle, Caliber .22 Long Rifle, United States Marine Corps Training, MC-58, complete with military leather sling and two extra magazines. Marlin's bid was not accepted and no contract for production was offered.

To my knowledge, the Marines did not adopt any of the training rifles submitted (by any of the manufacturers) that looked, felt, and operated like the standard M1 service rifle.

Interestingly, on September 8, 1958, the U.S. Marine Corps accepted from The Marlin Firearms Company the five Marlin training rifles that were on loan to the Corps. It has been reported that some of them were sold by the Corps and are now in the collecting world.

Vest

The Marlin 1913 and 1914 catalogs advertised a sportsman's vest. The claim made for this vest was as follows:

> Don't suffer on cold days! — don't load yourself down with heavy clothes to keep warm! You'll be as warm as toast in any weather if you wear the featherweight Marlin vest for outdoor sportsmen. This garment weighs a trifle over two pounds, is of special design, very dressy in appearance, as illustrated. The body of the vest, front and back, is English Corduroy, "tobacco brown" in color. Lined throughout with finest tanned Mocha leather, same color as corduroy. Sleeves made of Mocha leather alone, not covered by any other material, are extra large and full, allowing absolutely free use of arms, and have large corduroy cuffs, that fit snug at the wrists. . . . Absolutely wind proof, and warmer than 10 times

Catalog illustration of Marlin Sportsman's Vest.

its weight in woolen clothing . . . It is ideal for hunting, trap or duck shooting, motoring, or any outdoor cold weather sport. . . . Each vest is fully guaranteed as to wearing quality and general satisfaction. Stock sizes 36, 38, 40, 42 and 44. Price — $8.25 each.

Wagon

In late 1929, Frank Kenna added another sideline to his firearms business — the Auto Wagon. Whether this was to augment the firearms business in the hope it would develop and expand into a major part of the business, or if it was to add an item to his business that would keep his wood and metal fabrication operations busy, and help meet the payroll, is not known. However, it can be speculated that it was some of both.

Marlin brochure advertising the Auto Wagon.

Marlin watch fob.

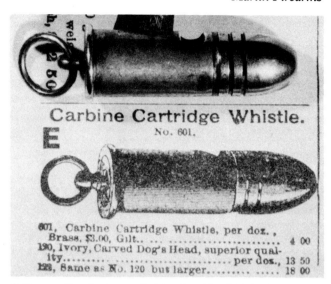

Bridgeport Gun Implement Carbine Cartridge Whistle that is neatly stamped Marlin Rept'g Rifle Is The Best, *shown with 1884 ad for the same whistle.*

Revitalizing a sick firearms company and making use of the extensive plant facilities he now owned, and making a profit, were surely justification enough to Mr. Kenna to venture into the children's wagon business.

The Marlin Auto Wagon was unique in that it could be used as a wagon with a solid bottom, or as an auto with the floor boards folded up to make a seat for the child so that it could be operated by foot pedals and steered by the folded back tongue.

The specifications for the Auto Wagon were as follows:

Size:	16"x38"
Body:	Floorboards and body selected North Carolina pine
Wheels:	10" heavy stamped steel discs with enclosed bearings
Tires:	1" corrugated rubber
Axles:	½" diameter, cold rolled steel
Pedals:	Rubber with steel bushings, adjustable
Tongue:	Never break type of heavy tubular steel, bent for ease of steering and convenience in hauling
Finish:	Body well painted throughout. Top, inside and out, bright red; bottom green. Wheels enameled bright red; metal parts green.
Weight:	40 pounds. Packed and shipped one to a carton
Assembly:	The assembly of the Auto Wagon is similar to that of an ordinary wagon with the addition of connecting up the pedals for which full instructions are provided with each Auto Wagon.

Manufacturer:	The Auto Wagon is built in the plant of The Marlin Firearms Co. with the same care and skill used by them in the successful production of Marlin guns for over 50 years. The best materials are used in the Auto Wagon's construction; it is built to stand hard use.

A December 24, 1931 invoice in the amount of $5.00 for one Marlin Auto Wagon (made out to Mr. Walter Pierson, Marlin's advertising manager, and most likely a Christmas present to a child in his family) is the only original paperwork remaining with regard to the Auto Wagon. No Auto Wagons have been examined by collectors of Marlin memorabilia.

Watch Fob

Another Marlin item for which knowledge has been lost with time is the Marlin watch fob. Examples are exceptionally rare. The 1¼-in.-diameter nonmagnetic pendant has scalloped edges. It has a duck hunter with his gun shouldered, and birds in hand walking through marsh grass embossed on it. The name Marlin is in blue enamel letters at the bottom. They were originally gold plated. It is believed that the watch fob was furnished along with a catalog for a nominal fee.

Whistle

As an advertising gimmick, Marlin gave away whistles that looked like a carbine cartridge. The body was like a center-fire cartridge case and the mouthpiece was shaped like a bullet. A ring was soldered to the center of a dummy primer. Marked on the body of the whistle was the patent date, November 29, 1881, and *MARLINS REP'G RIFLE IS THE BEST.* Also marked on the head of the case was BGI (Bridgeport Gun Implement Company) 601. An identical cartridge whistle was listed as a BGI catalog item in 1884 at $3.00 a dozen in brass, or $4.00 a dozen in gilt.

Bibliography

MAGAZINE ARTICLES

"1880 Marlin .45-70." *American Rifleman,* January 1953.

"A Fine .22 Hunting Rifle." *American Rifleman,* September 1952.

Adkins, G.S. "Improving the Looks and Functioning of Marlin's Model 39A." *Shooting Times,* January 1968.

"American Sporting Arms—1948: A Complete Survey." *Hunting & Fishing,* October 1948.

Anderson, Robert. "Hunt Small Game with a .22 R.F. Rifle." *Shooting Times,* October 1979.

Askins, Col. Charles, Ret. "Old Timer Revived." *Army Times,* January 2, 1972.

———. "Marlin's New 'Brush Buckling' .444 Magnum." *Gunsport,* February/March 1965.

———. "The New Marlin .45-70." *Guns,* December 1972.

———. "The Marlin Chronicles." *American Rifleman,* July 1987.

Atkins, Lee. "Reloading Winchester's 'Big Bore.'" *Guns,* August 1979.

Barach, Mike. "Reloading for Marlin's Brush-Busting .44!" *Guns,* February 1979.

Bennington, Bill. "The 1895 Marlin—79 Years Later." *Gunsport,* June 1974.

Blatt, Art. "Marlin 1895S." *Guns & Ammo,* March 1981.

———. "Model 336 Marlin .375 Winchester." *Guns & Ammo,* March 1980.

———. "Saddlegun or Sixgun—The .44 Magnum is Tops." *Guns & Ammo,* July 1977.

Brophy, Lt. Col. Bill. "Two Million Marlins." *American Rifleman,* January 1984.

———. "The Marlin Model 1881." *American Rifleman,* November 1981.

Brown, Pete. "The Old Lever Loaders." *Sports Afield,* n.d.

Bruce, Peter. "The Story Behind Marlin." *Guns & Hunting,* March 1968.

Burnside, Graham. "Marlin's .444 Starts Fire Under Cartridge Fans." *Shooting Times,* April 1965.

Byrd, Mark. ".44 Magnum Carbine from Marlin." *Guns & Hunting,* March 1963.

———. "Magnum Carbine from Marlin." *Guns & Hunting,* March 1965.

"Cal. .32 Cartridges." *American Rifleman,* July 1963.

Carmichel, Jim. "Rebirth of the .45/70." *Outdoor Life,* n.d.

Carpenter, Russ. "Marlin's Model 1894M." *American Hunter,* n.d.

Cary, Lucian. "The Ballard of J.M. Marlin." *True,* April 1949.

Chenery, Gus. "The Micro-Groove Story: A Reappraisal." *Gunsport,* November 1959.

Clark, Bob. "Marlin's 22 Mag." *Shooter's Journal,* February 1980.

Clede, Bill. "John Mahlon Marlin—the Practical Gunmaker." *Shooting Times,* March, April, May, 1963.

Colombano, Pietro. "John Mahlon Marlin un Perfezionista." *Aiana-ARMI,* n.d.

Crum, Gene B. "Writer Calls it the People's Rifle." *Gun Week,* December 17, 1976.

———. "*Gun Week* Visits Marlin Firearms." *Gun Week,* August 27, 1976.

David, Peter. "Marlin's 2,000,000th Glenfield Model 60." *Guns & Ammo,* July 1982.

Dean, Harry O. "Levermatic Marlin." *Shooting Times,* May 1967.

———. "How It's Made: the Marlin Model 336 Rifle." *Shooting Industry,* January 1968.

DeHaas, Frank. "Cast Bullets in the .444 Marlin." *Handloader,* January/February 1980.

Eades, Dick. "Improving With Age . . . Marlin's Lever-Action Rifles," *Shooting Times,* December 1981.

Elliot, Brook. "Loads for Marlin's .41 Magnum Carbine." *Handloader,* May/June 1986.

Fears, J. Wayne. "Marlin's Model 70P Papoose." *Shooting Times,* January 1987.

Ferber, Steve. "Confessions of a Duck Addict." Reprint. *Argosy,* n.d.

Fitser, Jim. "Marlin Glenfield 778 Shotgun." *Northeast Hunt'n & Fish'n,* January 1984.

Flanagan, Mike. "Little Sure Shot." Reprint from book *Out West. Women's World,* November 2, 1987.

Flores, Dan. "Get the Most From Your .22." *Guns & Ammo,* November 1975.

Forgett, Val III. "Proof House Marlin's Little Buckaroo .22." *Guns & Ammo,* June 1985.

Fulgham, Tom. "New Foundland Isle of The Bulls." *American Hunter,* June 1986.

Geer, Galen L. "Marlin 9MM Carbine." *Colorado Outdoor Journal,* Summer 1986.

Geering, Marcel. "Marlin 336CS in .35 Remington." *Schweizer Waffen-Magazine,* January/February 1985.

"Grade 'B' Marlin Rifle." *American Rifleman,* February 1971.

Grennell, Dean A. "The Marlin M1894C .357 Carbine." *Gun World,* August 1979.

———. "Reloading Marlin's 9MM Carbine." *Gun World,* n.d.

Grey, Zane. "Yes! Lever Action Rifles." *Sports Afield,* May 1935.

Grimm, Peter Ernst. "Selbstlade Karabiner Marlin 45." *Schweizer Waffen-Magazine,* October 1987.

———. "Selbstlade Karabiner Model 9." *Schweizer Waffen-Magazine,* March 1988.

Grotto, Dale. "Marlin's All-Time Great—the 1897." *Guns & Ammo,* June 1961.

Hacker, Rick. "Marlin 375." *Guns & Ammo,* 1981.

Hagel, Bob. "Marlin 1895 .45-70." *Handloader,* September/October 1972.

Harris, C.E. "Marlin: Where the Lever-Action Is Still King." *Outdoor Life Guns & Shooting Yearbook,* 1985.

Hatcher, J.S., Maj. Gen. "1947 Production Prospects." *American Rifleman,* January 1947.

Hecht, Theodore S. "The Marlin Model 122: The World's First Really Safe Rifle." *Guns/Game,* April 1962.

———. "To Build a Better Gun." *Guns & Ammo,* n.d.

Heiderich, Bob. "How to Tune Your Centerfire Lever-Action Rifle." *Shooting Times,* June 1977.

Heigel, Hans J. "Das Comeback der Kaliber .25-20 und .32-20 Win." *Schweizer Waffen-Magazine,* June 1988.

Helbig, Christian H. "The 444 Marlin and its Big Bore Brothers." *Gun Digest,* 1968.

Hetzler, Dave. "A Pair of Winners." *Guns & Ammo,* February 1979.

Hill, Ralph Nading. "Winston Churchill: Master Engraver." *Vermont Life,* 1979.

Hinman, Bob. "Marlin's New M120 12-Gauge Magnum." *Shooting Times,* October 1971.

Hughes, B.R. "Burning Powder." *.444 Gunsport,* April 1968.

Irwin, Tim. "A Reliable Rifle at a Reasonable Price." *American Hunter,* August 1979.

James, Garry. "The Terrific .45-70." *Guns & Ammo,* December 1978.

Jamison, Rick. "Marlin's Lever Action." *Shooting Times,* September 1984.

———. "Marlin's New Little Buckaroo .22." *Shooting Times,* July 1984.

———. "Handloading the 30-30." *Shooting Times,* October 1984.

———. "Combination Calibers," *Handgun,* 1987.

———. "Marlin's Unheralded .444." *Shooting Times,* April 1987.

———. "Help the .22 Magnum Make It." *Shooting Times,* November 1987.

Koller, Larry. "New Guns—Winchester—Marlin—Savage—Mossberg." *Guns & Hunting,* September 1960.

———. "The Winner and Still Champion." *Guns & Hunting,* May 1962.

———. "Marlin's M-1 Carbine." *Gun News,* January 1965.

———. "World's Most Powerful Lever-Action." *Guns & Hunting,* February 1965.

———. "A Lever Action .30." *Guns & Hunting,* September 1966.

———. "Return of the L.C. Smith." *Guns & Hunting,* February 1967.

Kuhloff, Peter. "Revolutionary New Barrel." *Argosy,* October 1953.

———. "20% More Accuracy—With the New Marlin Micro-Groove Rifling." *Argosy,* October 1953.

———. "America's Favorite Guns." *Argosy,* August 1961.

———. "Marlin—98 Years of Firearms History." *Sports Age,* December 1961.

Lachuk, John. "Lever Action Rimfire Rifle Roundup." *Guns & Ammo,* June 1979.

———. "Autoloading .22 Rimfire Rifles." *Guns & Ammo,* September 1979.

———. "Centerfire Scopes for Rimfire Rifles." *Guns & Ammo,* January 1980.

———. "The Affordable .22s." *Guns & Ammo,* January 1981.

Libourel, Jan. "Marlin's New 9MM: Fast, Fun & Accurate." *Guns & Ammo,* October 1985.

Logan, Herschel C. "J.M. Marlin's Handguns." *American Rifleman,* October 1958.

Lombard, Dave. "Marlin Model 1894." *Guns & Ammo,* June 1974.

Macewicz, J.J. "The Lever-Action Legacy of Marlin and Ulrich." *American Rifleman,* July 1975.

"Marlin Over-Under." *American Rifleman,* March 1940.

"Marlin Pump Shotgun." *American Rifleman,* June 1952.

"Marlin Shotgun." *American Rifleman,* January 1953.

"Marlin Lever Action .219." *American Rifleman,* October 1955.

"Marlin Levermatic .22 Repeater." *American Rifleman,* November 1955.

"Marlin .22." *American Rifleman,* January 1959.

"Marlin 57-M Rifle." *American Rifleman,* July 1960.

"Marlin Premier." *American Rifleman,* March 1961.

"Marlin Model 99-C." *American Rifleman,* July 1961.

"Marlin Goose Gun." *American Rifleman,* September 1962.

"Marlin Model 62." *American Rifleman,* December 1963.

"Marlin 44 Carbine." *American Rifleman,* May 1964.

"Marlin 989 M2 Carbine." *American Rifleman,* May 1965.

"Marlin 444 Rifle." *American Rifleman,* May 1966.

"Marlin M62 Carbine." *American Rifleman,* September 1966.

"Marlin .410 Shotgun." *American Rifleman,* December 1966.

"Marlin M1881 Rifle." *American Rifleman,* February 1968.

"Marlin Model 49." *American Rifleman,* June 1968.

"Marlin 39 Century Ltd. Carbine." *American Rifleman,* March 1970.

"Marlin M336 Zane Grey Rifle." *American Rifleman,* November 1971.

"Marlin Model 120 Magnum." *American Rifleman,* November 1972.

"Marlin Baby Repeater." *American Rifleman,* March 1973.

"Marlin Model 1894 Carbine." *American Rifleman,* December 1973.

"Marlin Set-Trigger." *American Rifleman,* July 1974.

"Marlin Model 70 Papoose Rifle." *Sporter Shooter,* July 1987.

"Marlin 9m/m Camp Carbine." *Guns Review,* December 1987.

"Marlin's New 12 Mag. Pump Gun." *Shooting Times,* February 1978.

"Marlin's New M1894 .357 Magnum Lever-Action Carbine." *Shooting Times,* November 1979.

Matthews, Paul A. "Big Bore for Brush Bucks." *Outdoor Life Hunting Annual,* n.d.

Matunas, Edward. "The .30-30 Winchester and .35 Remington." *Shooting Industry,* September 1985.

Metcalf, Dick. "Caliber Comparisons: Handgun/Rifle Matchups in .357 and .44 Magnum." *Shooting Times,* May 1982.

———. "The .41 Magnum . . . The Caliber that Gets no Respect." *Shooting Times,* March 1984.

———. "Marlin's New .41 Magnum Lever-Action Rifle." *Shooting Times,* January 1985.

———. "Marlin's Model 9 Camp Carbine." *Shooting Times,* December 1985.

Michaels, Jeff. "Marlin 780 Rimfire Rifle." *Guns & Ammo,* March

1979.

———. "Marlin's .444 Sporter." *Sporter's Journal,* September 1979.

Milek, Bob. "The Great Lever-Action Repeating Rifles." *Petersen's Hunting,* March 1981.

Miller, Al "Cast Bullets in Marlins Once More." *Handloader,* July/August 1982.

Minor, Elliott L. "The Short, Happy Gun Career of L.C. Smith." *American Rifleman,* April 1971.

"Model 45 Carbine." *American Rifleman,* June 1987.

M.M.K. "UDM '42." *Schweizer Waffen-Magazine,* March 1988.

Murray, Bob. "Useful Little Lever Guns." *Wyoming Outdoor Reporter,* August 31, 1979.

Nesbitt, Mike. "Marlin's New Lever Action." *Northwestern Sportsman,* June 1979.

———. "Pacing the .45–70." *Guns,* April 1981.

———. "Cast Loads for the Big Bores." *Guns,* May 1981.

———. "Marlin's M1894M—A Rifle for the Trail." *Gun Week,* December 23, 1983.

———. "Axton Bags a Bear: Then and Now." n.p., October/November 1985, December 1985/January 1986.

"New Marlin Brush Rifle." *American Rifleman,* November 1950.

"New Marlin Rifle." *American Rifleman,* May 1948.

"New Marlin Varmint Rifle." *American Rifleman,* September 1954.

"Ninety Years of Gun Making." Reprint. *Connecticut Industry,* n.d.

Nonte, George. "Marlin Goose Gun." *Shooting Times,* November 1962.

———. "Marlin's Model 62 .256 Mag." *Shooting Times,* January 1964.

———. "Marlin's New Brush Buster." *Shooting Times,* March 1965.

Norberg, Peter. "BusKrojaren (Marlin 444)." *Jakt & Vapen,* October 1986.

"Not for Bee or Zipper." *American Rifleman,* June 1952.

O'Connor, Dave. "Why I Prefer the 'Big, Fat, Slow' .444 on Game." *Gun Week,* July 4, 1980.

Olson, Ludwig, and M.E. Bussard. "Marlin Model 1895 Rifle." *American Rifleman,* October 1972.

Paddock, Bill. "Marlin Observes 90th Year." *The Sporting Goods Dealer,* May 1960.

Page, Warren. "The Lever Action Still Lives." *Field & Stream,* December 1948.

PeLardy, Joel. "Marlin 'Sporter' 444." *Chasse,* n.d.

Petrini, Frank B. "Marlin's Model 1894 Magnum Carbine." *Shooting Times,* April 1979.

———. "Marlin's Model 39A & 39M Lever-Action .22 Rim fires." *Shooting Times,* December 1979.

Perez DeLeon, Luis. "Marlin 444s." *ARMAS,* November 1983.

Peterson, Harold L. "A Man to Remember." *American Rifleman,* June 1960.

Randles, Slim. "Glenfield Model 778 Pump Shotgun." Reprint. *Hunting,* October 1978.

Rees, Clair. "Marlin Model 49DL." *Guns & Ammo,* January 1977.

———. "The Marlin Model 101 Rimfire." *Guns & Ammo,* February 1977.

———. "Marlin's Marvelous Model 39." *Guns & Ammo,* May 1979.

———. "Revival of the Venerable .45–70." *Shooting Times,* June 1979.

———. "Get a Jump on Jacks—Hunt with a .22 WMR Rifle." *Shooting Times,* August 1979.

———. "Plinker's Delight: The .22 Auto Rifle." *Shooting Times,* August 1980.

———. "Marlin's 1894 and 1894C Lever Carbines." *Shooting Times,* May 1981.

———. "A Superior Game-Getter: The .35 Remington." *Shooting Times,* July 1981.

Robb, Bob. "Marlin 1894M." *Petersen's Hunting,* December 1984.

———. "Marlin 336ER." *Petersen's Hunting,* July 1985.

Robbins, John. "Anticosti Whitetails." *American Hunter,* July 1987.

Robbins, Peggy. "Rediscovering Philip Goodwin." *Sporting Classics,* July/August 1983.

Robinson, John. "Marlin Papoose." *Australian Shooter's Journal,* July 1987.

Rockefeller, John. "Marlin's Four Forty Four." *Guns & Ammo,* May 1971.

———. "New Rimfire Magnums from Marlin." *Guns,* March 1985.

Rogoski, W.L. "Marlin Pump Guns." *The Gun Report,* December 1957.

Rue, Leonard Lee III. "Whitetail Deer Rifles." *Guns & Ammo,* November 1980.

"Scope on Lever Action." *American Rifleman,* October 1955.

Sell, Francis E. "Author Sold on Marlin Model 39 .22 Rifle." *Gun Week,* June 8, 1979.

Silva, Lee. "The Legend and the Gun." *Guns & Ammo,* December 1982.

Simpson, Layne. "Marlin's Magnificent Model 39," *Guns & Ammo,* 1985.

———. "Tight-Cover Deer Rifles and Loads." *Magnum Guns & Shooting,* 1986.

———. "Marlin's Handgun Cartridge Carbines." *Shooting Times,* August 1988.

Sivulla, Jatko. "Marlin 444SS Vipulykkoiner Metsas Tysluodiko." *Metsastys ja Kalastus* 75, July 1986.

Spangenberger, Paul. "1881 Marlin." *Guns & Ammo,* August 1988.

Stebbins, H.M. "Semi-Auto Hunting Rifles." *American Rifleman,* April 1953.

Steiner, Anton. "Marlin Super Goose Gun." *Schweizer Waffen-Magazine,* June 1985.

Sterett, Larry. "Marlin Model 1894 .357 Magnum." *Gun Digest,* 1982.

———. "Marlin 120 Trap." *Trap & Field,* October 1984.

Sundra, Jon R. "Your Best Bet in a .22 Lever Gun." *Shooting Times,* September 1972.

———. "The Marlin 336." *Shooting Times,* June 1975.

———. "Marlin's Big Bruiser—The .444." *Shooting Times,* December 1976.

———. "Uniquely American: The .30–30 Lever-Action Carbine." *Shooting Times,* October 1978.

———. "Bullshots." *Shooting Times,* January 1980.

———. "The 444: Marlin's Mauler." *Guns & Ammo,* September 1982.

Swiggett, Hal. "Two New Marlin Camp Guns: Plinking Partners." *The Complete Gun Annual,* 1987.

Terrell, Ron. "Varmintizing Marlin's .256 Magnum." *Guns & Hunting,* August 1985.

Thill, Mike. "Marlin .357 Carbine." *Guns,* March 1980.

Tishue, Jack R. "African Hunt." *Gunsport,* December 1973.

Torrance, Bill. "Marlin's Done It Again." *AWN,* July 1979.

Tremaine, Bob. "The Secret is the Grooving." *Shooting Times,* n.d.

———. "Marlin's .444 Brush Buster." *Guns,* March 1965.

Triggs, J.M. "Marlin Model 336." *American Rifleman,* January 1957.

Trzoniec, Stanley. "A History of SAKO Sporting Rifles." *Guns,* December 1985.

"Tubular Magazines." *American Rifleman,* July 1957.

Venturino, Mike. "Bear Guns." *Guns & Ammo,* June 1982.

———. "Marlin's Big 4." *Guns & Ammo,* February 1988.

Virgines, George E. "The Guns of Tom Mix." *Guns,* February 1970.

Wagner, J.V.K. "Single Shot Rifles." *American Rifleman,* January 1941.

Waters, Ken. "Classic Rifles—The Marlin Model 1897." *Rifle,* March/April 1986.

———. "Marlin Announces New .444 Rifle and Cartridge." *Shooting Times,* July 1964.

Wallack, Bob. "Used Gun Shop." *Guns & Hunting,* September 1966.

Wallack, L.R. "Marlin: A Tradition of Excellence." *The Complete Gun Annual,* n.d.

———. "Marlin's Model 39." *American Rifleman,* June 1978.

———. "Marlin's 336! The Other Lever-Action." American Rifleman,

July 1978.

———. "Call for New Look at State of Shotgun Slug Art." *Gun Week,* November 23, 1979.

———. "America's Largest Rifle Maker." *Gun Week,* 1980.

———. "Checking the Facts on the Claim." *Gun Week,* 1980.

———. "World's Fastest Selling Rifle." *Gun Week,* April 25, 1980.

———. "Testing the Accuracy of Slugs." *Gun Week,* August 8, 1980.

———. "What Choke For Steel Shot." *Gun Week,* December 12, 1980.

Weldon, D. "Marlin Hunter's Rimfires by the Millions!" *Gun Digest Hunting Annual,* 1986.

Wessel, T.E. "Marlin Model 39-A." *American Rifleman,* September 1960.

———. "Marlin Model 90ST Shotgun." *American Rifleman,* October 1961.

Williams, Mason. "Marlin's 9MM Carbine." *Law & Order,* October 1986.

Wootters, John. "New Punch for the 10-Gauge Magnum." *Guns & Ammo,* November 1976.

———. "The 45/70 Is Alive and Well in its Second Century." *Guns & Ammo,* November 1979.

———. "Reloading Rifle/Pistol Cartridges." *Guns & Ammo,* August 1980.

———. "The Lever Action." *Guns & Ammo,* February 1981.

———. "Is the .44 Magnum a Rifle Cartridge?" *Guns & Ammo,* June 1981.

———. "Those Amazing Anticosti Bucks." *Petersen's Hunting,* March 1988.

Zambone, Joe. "Behind Every Marlin Rifle There's a Computer." *Shooting Industry,"* May 1984.

———. "Marlin's Model 45 Carbine." *Guns,* August 1988.

Zutz, Don. "L.C. Smith—The Man and the Gun." *Guns.* January 1973.

———. "Updating the 44 Marlin." *Gun Digest,* 1977.

———. "The Gun Rack—'Carbine Calibers.'" *Fur-Fish-Game,* August 1980.

Zwirz, Bob. "Cutting Up With Marlin's .444." *Gun World,* n.d.

———. "Marlin's Model 120 Pump." *Gun World,* n.d.

———. "Marlin's New Model 995 .22 Rimfire." *Gun World,* n.d.

———. "Newest Lever Action," *Gun World,* n.d.

———. "The Marlin .444 Goes 'Western.'" *The Gun Illustrated,* 1965.

———. "The Rec of the Old '95.'" *Gun World,* August 1972.

———. "9MM: Nothing Campy Here." *Gun World,* December 1985.

———. "Partial to the Papoose!" *Gun World,* August 1987.

———. "The Triple Four Revisited." *Gun World,* June 1988.

———. "Update for the Golden 39." *Gun World,* August 1988.

BOOKS AND REPORTS

Alderman, Clifford L. *Annie Oakley and the World of her Time.* New York: Macmillan, 1979.

Barnes, Frank C. *Cartridges of the World.* 5th ed. Northfield, Ill.: D.B.I. Books, Inc., 1985.

Beriss, Dorothy. *Shooting Communicator.* n.p.: C.B.T. Corporation, 1974.

Bleile, Roger C. *American Engravers.* North Hollywood, Calif.: Beinfeld Publishing, Inc., 1980.

Brophy, William S. *L.C. Smith Shotguns.* Highland Park, N.J.: The Gun Room Press, 1983.

———. *Plans and Specifications of the L.C. Smith Shotgun.* Montezuma, Ia.: F. Brownell & Son, 1981.

Cary, A. Merwyn. *American Firearms Makers.* New York: Thomas Y. Crowell Co., 1953.

Chinn, Lt. Col. George M., USMC. *The Machine Gun.* Washington, D.C.: Superintendent of Documents, 1951.

Chinn, George Morgan, Jr., and Bayless Evans Hardin. *Encyclopedia of American Hand Arms.* Huntington, W.V.: n.p., 1942.

Crowell, Benedict, and Robert Forrest Wilson. *The Armies of Industry: Our Nation's Manufacture of Munitions for a World in Arms, 1917–1918.* New Haven: Yale University Press, 1921.

Farrow, Edward S. *American Small Arms.* New York: n.p., 1904.

Gardner, Robert, Col. *Small Arms Makers.* New York: Bonanza Books, 1963.

Gould, A.C. *Modern American Rifles.* Boston: n.p., 1892.

Grant, James J. *Single-Shot Rifles.* New York: Marrow & Co., 1947.

———. *More Single-Shot Rifles.* New York: Marrow & Co., 1959.

———. *Boys' Single-Shot Rifles.* New York: Marrow & Co., 1967.

———. *Still More Single-Shot Rifles.* Union City, Tenn.: Pioneer Press, 1979.

Graves, Charles. *Annie Oakley, the Shooting Star.* n.p.: Garrard Publishers, 1961.

Hardin, Albert N. *The American Bayonet: 1776–1964.* Philadelphia: Riling and Lentz, 1964.

Havighurst, Wallace. *Annie Oakley of the Wild West.* New York: Macmillan, 1954.

Jinks, Roy G. *History of Smith & Wesson.* North Hollywood, Calif.: n.p., 1977.

Johnson, M.M., Jr., and Charles T. Haven. *Automatic Weapons of the World.* New York: Morrow, 1941.

Latham, R.J. Wilkinson, *British Military Bayonets.* New York: n.p., 1969.

Meek, James B. *The Art of Engraving.* Montezuma, Ia.: F. Brownell & Son, 1973.

Miller, Warren H. *Rifles & Shotguns.* New York: n.p., 1917.

Nelson, Thomas B. *The World's Submachine Guns.* Cologne, Federal Republic of Germany: n.p., 1963.

Prudhomme, E.C. *Gun Engraving Review.* Shreveport, La.: n.p., 1961.

The Ranger. *Pacific Coast Militia Rangers.* Vancouver: Vancouver Barracks, n.d.

Reynolds, Maj. E.G.B. *The Lee–Enfield Rifle.* London, 1960.

Sayers, Isabelle. *Annie Oakley and the Buffalo Bill Wild West.* New York: Dover Publishers, 1981.

Sharpe, Philip B. *The Rifle in America.* New York: Funk & Wagnalls, 1953.

Smith, W.H.B. *The Book of Pistols & Revolvers.* Harrisburg, Pa.: Stackpole Books, 1962.

———. *The Book of Rifles.* Harrisburg, Pa.: Stackpole Books, 1963.

———. *Small Arms of the World.* 12th ed., rev. Edward Ezell. Harrisburg, Pa.: Stackpole Books, 1983.

Stockbridge, V.D. *Digest of Patents Relating to Breech-Loading and Magazine Small Arms: Except Revolvers.* Originally published in 1874. Washington, D.C.: N. Flayderman, 1963.

Suydam, Charles R. *U.S. Cartridges and their Handguns.* North Hollywood, Calif.: Beinfeld Publishing Co., 1977.

U.S. Congress. Special Committee, Seventy-Third Congress. *Investigating the Munitions Industry.* 13 vols. Washington, D.C.: U.S. Government Printing Office, 1934.

Van Rensselaer, Stephen. *American Firearms.* Watkins Glen, N.Y.: Century House, 1947.

Whelen, Maj. Townsend. *The American Rifle.* New York: n.p., 1918.

———. *Telescope Rifle Sights.* Harrisburg, Pa.: Stackpole & Sons, 1937.

———. *The Hunting Rifle.* Harrisburg, Pa.: Stackpole & Sons, 1940.

Wilson, Ellen. *Annie Oakley, Little Sure Shot.* New York: Bobbs-Merrill, 1982.

Wilson, R.L. *L.D. Nimschke: Firearms Engraver.* Teaneck, N.J.: John S. Malloy, 1965.

———. *The Book of Winchester Engraving.* Los Angeles: n.p., 1975.

Additional Sources

PERIODICALS

The American Rifleman
Arms and the Man
Forest and Stream
Gun Report
Man at Arms
Marlin Gunzette: Intermittent issues, 1950–1969
Military Collector and Historian: Winter 1984.

MISCELLANEOUS

Correspondence with numerous collectors and historians.
Dealer's lists and catalogs.
Patent files, U.S. Patent Office.
Various Marlin catalogs, 1882 to 1988, listed as follows:

MARLIN CATALOGS

1882	1903	1927	1948	1961	1975
1883	1905	1928	1949	1962	1976
1885	1906	1929	1950	1963	1977
1886	1907	1930	1951	1964	1978
1887	1908	1931	1952	1965	1979
1891	1909	1932	1953	1966	1980
1893	1911	1933	1954	1967	1981
1895	1913	1935	1955	1968	1982
1896	1914	1936	1956	1969	1983
1897	1915	1937	1957	1970	1984
1899	1922	1940	1958	1971	1985
1900	1922	1941	1958	1972	1986
1901	1923	1945	1958	1973	1987
1902	1925	1946	1959	1974	1988
	1926	1947	1960		

MARLIN DEALER AND DISTRIBUTOR PRICE LISTS

Dealers, June 1901
Net Trade, January 19, 1902
Net Trade, January 18, 1903
Dealers, March 1907
Dealers, June 1, 1907
Canada Dealers, August 20, 1908
Reselling Dealers, July 1, 1909
Reselling Dealers, July 1, 1911
Reselling Dealers, January 1, 1913
Canada Dealers, January 1, 1913
Dealers, January 1, 1914
Jobbers, January 1, 1914
Jobbers, November 1, 1915
Dealers, November 1, 1915
Jobbers, May 10, 1916
Jobbers, October 1, 1917
Jobbers, January 1922
Dealers, January 1, 1922
Article, July 1922
Dealers, February 1, 1923
Dealers, July 1, 1924
Dealers, January 1, 1925
Dealers, January 1, 1928
Dealers, March 15, 1929
Jobbers, March 1, 1931
Dealers, June 21, 1932
Jobbers, March 15, 1933
Dealers, January 20, 1939
Confidential, April 1, 1939
Jobbers, April 1, 1939
Distributors, 1940
Confidential, January 1, 1940

Dealers, January 1, 1940
Dealers, July 1, 1940
Confidential, November 20, 1940
Jobbers, November 20, 1940
Dealers, November 20, 1940
Export, July 9, 1940
Jobbers, November 24, 1941
Confidential, November 24, 1941
Dealers, May 26, 1941
Dealers, November 24, 1941
Jobbers, November 24, 1941
Jobbers, January 22, 1945
Confidential, September 23, 1946
Jobbers, February 1, 1948
Confidential, February 1, 1948
Dealers, January 15, 1949
Jobbers, January 15, 1949
Jobbers, September 18, 1950
Dealers, September 18, 1950
Jobbers, September 18, 1950
Dealers, December 15, 1950
Jobbers, January 2, 1953
Jobbers, November 1, 1955
Jobbers, March 1, 1956
Jobbers, January 15, 1957
Jobbers, February 1, 1958
Jobbers, January 1, 1959
Dealers, January 1, 1959
Jobbers, January 1, 1959
Distributors, January 15, 1960
Distributors, January 15, 1960
Distributors, January 15, 1961
Dealers, January 15, 1962
Distributors, January 15, 1963
Distributors, January 15, 1964
Distributors, January 1, 1965
Dealers, January 3, 1966
Distributors, January 3, 1966
Distributors, January 3, 1967
Distributors, January 2, 1968
Dealers, January 2, 1969
Distributors, January 2, 1969
Distributors, January 2, 1970
Distributors, January 2, 1970
Military Stores, February 1, 1971
Dealers, January 2, 1971
Distributors, January 2, 1971
Dealers, January 2, 1972
Distributors, January 2, 1972
Distributors, January 1, 1973

Distributors, January 1974
Distributors, January 1, 1975
Dealers, January 1, 1976
Distributors, January 1, 1976
Dealers, January 1, 1977
Distributors, January 1, 1977
Dealers, January 1, 1978
Distributors, January 1, 1978
Dealers, 1979
Revised Distributors, June 4, 1979
Distributors, 1979
Dealers, 1980
Revised Distributors, April 28, 1980
Distributors, 1980
Dealers, 1981
Distributors, 1981
Dealers, 1982
Distributors, 1982
Dealers, 1983
Distributors, 1983
Dealers, 1984
Distributors, 1984
Dealers, 1985
Distributors, 1985
Distributors, 1986
Dealers, 1986
Dealers, 1987
Distributors, 1987
Dealers, 1988
Distributors, 1988

MARLIN RETAIL PRICE LISTS

November 1, 1915	July 1932
May 10, 1916	June 1933
January 1922	August 1933
June 1, 1922	August 1936
February 1, 1923	November 1936
Rep. February 1, 1923	January 1, 1937
January 1, 1925	April 1, 1939
March 10, 1926	July 1, 1940
October 30, 1926	May 26, 1941
April 1927	January 22, 1945
September 1928	September 23, 1946
August 1929	September 18, 1950
March 1929	January 1, 1959
March 1, 1930	January 2, 1970
April 1931	January 1, 1973
January 1932	January 1, 1974
April 1932	January 1, 1975

Index